WileyPLUS Learning Space

Includes **ORION** ⭐ Adaptive Practice

An easy way to help your students **learn**, **collaborate**, and **grow**.

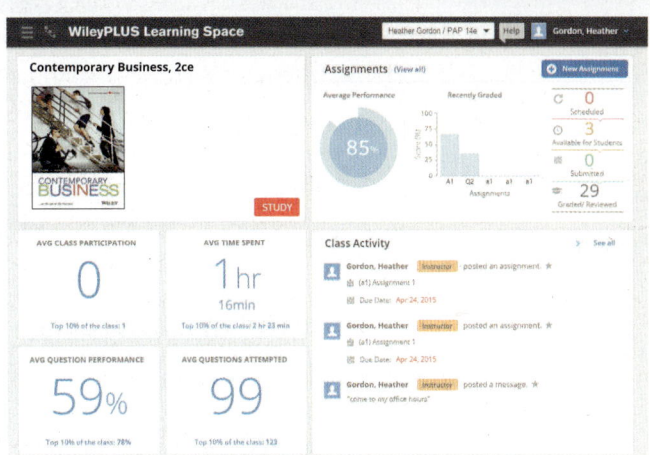

Diagnose Early
Educators assess the real-time proficiency of each student to inform teaching decisions. Students always know what they need to work on.

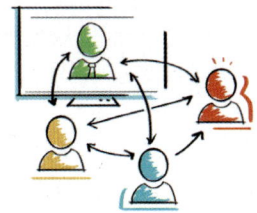

Facilitate Engagement
Educators can quickly organize learning activities, manage student collaboration, and customize their course. Students can collaborate and have meaningful discussions on concepts they are learning.

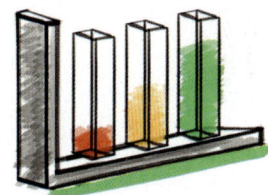

Measure Outcomes
With visual reports, it's easy for both educators and students to gauge problem areas and act on what's most important.

Instructor Benefits

- Assign activities and add your own materials
- Guide students through what's important in the interactive e-textbook by easily assigning specific content
- Set up and monitor collaborative learning groups
- Assess learner engagement
- Gain immediate insights to help inform teaching

Student Benefits

- Instantly know what you need to work on
- Create a personal study plan
- Assess progress along the way
- Participate in class discussions
- Remember what you have learned because you have made deeper connections to the content

www.wileypluslearningspace.com

WILEY

SECOND CANADIAN EDITION

CONTEMPORARY BUSINESS

| **LOUIS E. BOONE** | **MICHAEL H. KHAN** |
| *University of South Alabama* | *University of Toronto* |

| **DAVID L. KURTZ** | **BRAHM M. CANZER** |
| *University of Arkansas* | *John Abbott College* |

WILEY

Copyright © 2016 by John Wiley & Sons Canada, Ltd.

All rights reserved. No part of this work covered by the copyrights herein may be reproduced or used in any form or by any means—graphic, electronic, or mechanical—without the prior written permission of the publisher.

Any request for photocopying, recording, taping, or inclusion in information storage and retrieval systems of any part of this book shall be directed to the Canadian copyright licensing agency, Access Copyright. For an Access Copyright licence, visit www.accesscopyright.ca or call toll-free, 1-800-893-5777.

Beau's logo © Beau's All Natural Brewing Company.

Table 16.1: Standard & Poor's Financial Services LLC (S&P) does not guarantee the accuracy, completeness, timeliness or availability of any information, including ratings, and is not responsible for any errors or omissions (negligent or otherwise), regardless of the cause, or for the results obtained from the use of ratings. S&P gives no express or implied warranties, including, but not limited to, any warranties of merchantability or fitness for a particular purpose or use. S&P shall not be liable for any direct, indirect, incidental, exemplary, compensatory, punitive, special or consequential damages, costs, expenses, legal fees, or losses (including lost income or profits and opportunity costs) in connection with any use of ratings. S&P's ratings are statements of opinions and are not statements of fact or recommendations to purchase, hold or sell securities. They do not address the market value of securities or the suitability of securities for investment purposes, and should not be relied on as investment advice.

Care has been taken to trace ownership of copyright material contained in this text. The publishers will gladly receive any information that will enable them to rectify any erroneous reference or credit line in subsequent editions.

Care has been taken to ensure that the web links recommended in this text were active and accessible at the time of publication. However, the publisher acknowledges that web addresses are subject to change.

Library and Archives Canada Cataloguing in Publication

Boone, Louis E., author
    Contemporary business / Louis E. Boone, David L. Kurtz, Michael H. Khan, Brahm M. Canzer. — Second Canadian Edition.

Includes bibliographical references and index.
Issued in print and electronic formats.
ISBN 978-1-119-19433-0 (loose leaf).—ISBN 978-1-119-24506-3 (paperback).—ISBN 978-1-119-24038-9 (ebook)

    1. Management—Textbooks. 2. Business—Textbooks. I. Kurtz, David L., author II. Khan, Michael H., author III. Canzer, Brahm, author IV. Title.

HD31.B626 2015   658   C2015-906812-6
                                                        C2015-906813-4

Production Credits

V.P. & Director Market Solutions: Veronica Visentin
Executive Editor: Darren Lalonde
Senior Marketing Manager: Anita Osborne
Editorial Manager: Karen Staudinger
Developmental Editor: Gail Brown
Media Editor: Luisa Begani

Production and Media Specialist: Meaghan MacDonald
Assistant Editor: Ashley Patterson
Typesetting: SPi Global
Cover Design: Joanna Vieira
Cover Image: © Mel Yates/Getty

Printing and binding: Quad Graphics
Printed and bound in the United States.
1 2 3 4 5 QG 19 18 17 16 15

WILEY

90 Eglinton Avenue East, Suite 300
Toronto, Ontario, M4P 2Y3 Canada
Visit our website at: www.wiley.ca

PREFACE

Canadian college and university students have questions about business and the role businesspeople play. Some questions relate to their personal experiences, and others concern understanding issues we all face as Canadians living in an increasingly global society. Students want answers to these questions and more:

- What products are "made in Canada" and why can't we make more?
- Why do Canadian consumers pay more than Americans for many products and services?
- Why did BlackBerry lose its global leadership role in smartphone technology?
- Why are some countries wealthy and others not?
- Which Canadian businesses will provide job opportunities for me when I graduate?
- Should I start my own business?

Contemporary Business, Second Canadian Edition, is a comprehensive introductory textbook. Rooted in the basics of business, this textbook provides students with a foundation upon which to build a greater understanding of current business practices and issues that affect their lives.

Chapter 1 opens with a close-up look at the role of the Internet and social media in launching Drake's and Justin Bieber's career. The changes brought on by Internet and other technologies are illustrated throughout the textbook. As regular users of the Internet, students understand firsthand how the Internet has changed their behaviour—starting with communications and digital media. We use this familiarity to build an understanding of businesses that have been affected by the Internet, such as BlackBerry, discussed in Chapter 7. We also examine Canadian businesses that have succeeded in large part due to the marketing power of the Internet, such as StockTrak in Chapter 14.

Another theme throughout the textbook is globalization and the growing challenges facing Canadian businesses as they compete not only against American and Mexican firms in North America but against firms everywhere in the world. We look at changes in production of tangibles and intangibles, the use of automation, and outsourcing to lower-cost countries, such as China and India. Chapter 8 opens with a closer examination of the decline of the Canadian apparel industry and how some apparel companies have managed to succeed by focusing on niche markets.

Responsible Business

A current topic of major interest is the use of business ethics and corporate social responsibility (CSR). Chapter 2 is rich in content related to CSR. It opens with a look at Canada's world-renowned Cirque du Soleil and its model of global CSR. Throughout the textbook, and particularly in each chapter's *"Solving an Ethical Controversy"* feature, we focus on ethical issues and CSR. Similarly, each chapter's *"Going Green"* feature looks at green issues, including conservation, pollution, recycling, and reusing. The *"Hit & Miss"* feature shines a spotlight on companies, business leaders, and entrepreneurs.

Student-Focused

We present Canadian content that speaks directly to students about the world of business. Many examples included in this textbook were inspired by student peers. From companies such as Cirque du Soleil to lesser-known success stories across Canada, this textbook brings Canadian business and businesspeople face-to-face with students so that the roles played by businesspeople in our economy can be better understood, questioned, and debated. New to this edition is a running case featuring the Canadian company Beau's All Natural Brewing Company. The case is presented in six parts, corresponding to the six parts of the textbook, and is located following the last chapter of each part. Beau's takes students through the decision-making that resulted in the establishment of a successful family-run micro-brewery based in Vankleek Hill, in the Ottawa region. Instructors may choose to use some or all of the parts in sequence or as one longer case assignment. As well, the *"Career Kickstart"* feature provides useful tips and information for students who will embark on a business career. Students said they wanted to understand business beyond the simple concepts of profit as a goal or maximizing the provision of services for not-for profit organizations. We believe we have produced a textbook that meets these needs.

Contemporary Business, Second Canadian Edition, is written in a conversational style that has been thoroughly edited for plain language to ensure readability for all students, including students for whom English is their second language.

ACKNOWLEDGEMENTS

Contemporary Business, Second Canadian Edition, is the result of the efforts of many people who rightfully need acknowledgement. We would first like to thank our publishing team, beginning with our developmental editor, Gail Brown, for her suggestions on style and content throughout the writing effort. We thank Leanne Rancourt for an excellent job on the copy edit, Leslie Saffrey for her accurate proofreading, Hadi Ahmad for providing editorial insight, and Martin Eichler for his dedicated work as a research coordinator on the project.

We wish to thank the Wiley team on the business side of the project, beginning with Darren Lalonde, Veronica Visentin, and all of the marketing and sales representatives for their field knowledge and support of this book.

We thank the faculty members who contributed to the development of the textbook's resources and ancillaries, specifically Cheryl Dowell, Algonquin College (instructor's manual), Philip Eng, George Brown College (quizzes), Joyce Manu, George Brown College (test bank), and Wendy Tarrel, Nova Scotia Community College (quizzes and clicker questions), and a special thank you to Deanna Durnford for coordinating these ancillaries..

We especially want to thank our academic colleagues for their suggestions and constructive criticisms—both for the previous Canadian edition and this second Canadian edition. We know we could not have produced a textbook of this quality and calibre without their contributions.

Editorial Advisory Board

Colin Boyd, University of Saskatchewan
Dave Fleming, George Brown College
Radha Koilpillai, St. Mary's University
Hugh Laurence, University of Toronto, Scarborough
Margaret Mason, Fanshawe College
Valerie Miceli, Seneca College
Frank Saccucci, Grant MacEwan University
David Swanston, University of Toronto, Mississauga
Kent Walker, University of Windsor

Reviewers

Peggy Carter, Nova Scotia Community College
Scott Cawfield, York University
David Delcorde, University of Ottawa
Joyce Manu, George Brown College
Gordon McFarlane, Langara College
Donna McRae-Murphy, Eastern College
Peter Mombourquette, Mount Saint Vincent University
Paul Myers, St. Clair College
Hyacinth Randall, Seneca College
Andrea Rennie, Seneca College
Al Ruggero, Seneca College
Ronnalee Rylance, CDI College
Drew Smylie, Centennial College
Michael Wade, Seneca College
Claudia Zhang, Grant MacEwan University

Finally, we extend special thanks to the following group of University of Toronto students for their insightful and invaluable contributions to the text.

From the left: Mouri Khan, Martin Eichler, Zachary Bunting, Elliot Spicer, Daouii Abouchere. Absent: Pascal Elliott Chong

This book is lovingly dedicated to my growing family: my wife Carole; my son Matthew and his wife Leslie Grenier; and my daughter Sarah and her husband James Wiseman.

Brahm Canzer

This book is dedicated to my parents, for providing my foundation; my wife Asma, who encourages me in all of my endeavours; my children, Khadijah and Zakariyah, who can always bring a smile to my face; and finally, all of my friends, family, and students who have supported me throughout the years.

Michael Khan

ABOUT THE AUTHORS

Dave Kurtz

During Dave Kurtz's high school days, no one in Salisbury, Maryland, would have mistaken him for a scholar. In fact, he was a mediocre student, so bad that his father steered him toward higher education by finding him a succession of backbreaking summer jobs. Thankfully, most of them have been erased from his memory, but a few linger, including picking peaches, loading watermelons on trucks headed for market, and working as a pipefitter's helper. Unfortunately, these jobs had zero impact on his academic standing. Worse yet for Dave's ego, he was no better than average as a high school athlete in football and track.

But four years at Davis & Elkins College in Elkins, West Virginia, turned him around. Excellent instructors helped get Dave on a sound academic footing. His grade point average soared—enough to get him accepted by the graduate business school at the University of Arkansas, where he met Gene Boone. Gene and Dave became longtime co-authors; together they produced more than 50 books. In addition to writing, Dave and Gene were involved in several entrepreneurial ventures.

This long-term partnership ended with Gene's death in 2005. But, this book will always be Boone & Kurtz's *Contemporary Business*.

Today, Dave is back teaching at the University of Arkansas, after tours of duty in Ypsilanti, Michigan; Seattle, Washington; and Melbourne, Australia. He is the proud grandfather of six "perfect" kids and a sportsman with a golf handicap too high to mention. Dave, his wife, Diane, and four demanding canine companions (Daisy, Lucy, Molly, and Sally) live in Rogers, Arkansas. Dave holds a distinguished professorship at the Sam M. Walton College of Business in nearby Fayetteville, home of the Arkansas Razorbacks.

Michael Khan

Michael Khan is an Associate Professor, Teaching Stream at the Rotman School of Management at the University of Toronto. He teaches in both the MBA and Commerce programs and has won awards for excellence in teaching at both the graduate and undergraduate levels. His involvement in professional accounting training includes teaching for the Chartered Professional Accountants of Ontario. Michael is a Chartered Professional Accountant (CPA, CA) and holds an MBA from the Schulich School of Business, York University. He also has specialized professional designations in the field of Information Technology Audit and Governance (CISA—Certified Information Systems Auditor; CGEIT—Certified in the Governance of Enterprise Information Technology; and CITP—Certified Information Technology Professional). His professional experience includes internal and external audit, accounting, and consulting positions at Ernst & Young (EY), Deloitte, Rogers Communications, and George Weston Limited. In his spare time, he enjoys travelling and scuba diving.

Brahm Canzer

Brahm Canzer currently teaches business management courses to John Abbott College students in Montreal. He is also an adjunct lecturer at McGill University and Concordia University. During his teaching career, he has also taught undergraduate courses in a corporate learning program under the auspices of the University of Toronto. Brahm received his PhD (1995) and MBA (1976) from Concordia University in Montreal. His strong interest in the use of the Internet technology in education led him to be among the first pioneers to design and teach online MBA courses for Simon Fraser University. He is a contributing author to several business textbooks and author of *eBusiness: Strategic Thinking and Practice*. He has helped create a variety of web-based supplemental learning materials in academic and corporate learning settings. Brahm also provides consulting services to businesses seeking assistance as they explore web-based opportunities and solutions for improving their operations.

FEATURES OF THIS BOOK

Numbered "Learning Objectives" at the opening of each chapter guide student learning. These are repeated in the margin at the start of each major chapter section and appear again in the "Summary of Learning Objectives" at the end of the chapter.

WHAT IS BUSINESS?

What do you think of when you hear the word *business*? Do you think of big corporations like Rogers Communications or TD Bank? Or do you think about your local bakery or shoe store? Maybe you recall your first summer job. *Business* is a broad, all-inclusive term that can be applied to many kinds of enterprises. Businesses provide most of our employment opportunities and most of the products that we enjoy every day.

1 | THE CHANGING FACE OF BUSINESS

LEARNING OBJECTIVES

- **LO 1.1** Distinguish between business and not-for-profit organizations.
- **LO 1.2** Identify and describe the factors of production.
- **LO 1.3** Describe the private enterprise system.
- **LO 1.4** Identify the seven eras in the history of business.
- **LO 1.5** Explain how today's business workforce and the nature of work itself are changing.
- **LO 1.6** Identify the skills and attributes needed to lead businesses in the twenty-first century.
- **LO 1.7** Outline the characteristics that make a company admired.

SUMMARY OF LEARNING OBJECTIVES

LO 1.1 Distinguish between business and not-for-profit organizations.

Business consists of all profit-seeking activities that provide goods and services necessary to an economic system. Not-for-profit organizations are business-like establishments whose primary objectives involve social, political, governmental, educational, or similar functions instead of profits.

✓ **ASSESSMENT CHECK ANSWERS**

1.1.1 What activity lies at the heart of every business endeavour? At the heart of every business endeavour is an exchange between a buyer and a seller.

1.1.2 What are the primary objectives of a not-for-profit organization? Not-for-profit organizations place public service above profits, although they need to raise money to operate and achieve their social goals.

LO 1.2 Identify and describe the factors of production.

1.3.2 What is the most basic freedom under the private enterprise system? The most basic freedom is the right to private property.

1.3.3 What is an entrepreneur? An entrepreneur is a risk taker who is willing to start, own, and operate a business.

LO 1.4 Identify the seven eras in the history of business.

The seven historical eras are the colonial period, the Industrial Revolution, the age of industrial entrepreneurs, the production era, the marketing era, the relationship era, and the social era. In the colonial period, businesses were small and rural, emphasizing agricultural production. The Industrial Revolution brought factories and mass production to business. The age of industrial entrepreneurs built on the Industrial Revolution through an expansion in the number and size of firms. The production era focused on the growth of factory operations through assembly lines and other efficient internal processes. During and following the Great Depression, businesses concentrated on finding markets for their products through advertising and selling, giving

"Assessment Check" questions correspond to each of the numbered "Learning Objectives" and appear at the end of each major section in the chapter. "Assessment Check Answers" can be found in the "Summary of Learning Objectives" at the end of the chapter.

 ASSESSMENT CHECK

1.1.1 What activity lies at the heart of every business endeavour?

1.1.2 What are the primary objectives of a not-for-profit organization?

for families and h
bestsellers.[5] The L
more than 40 mill
men, women, and
support patients ar
Merchandisin
ness skills and exp
not-for-profit orga

Features of this book   xi

A vignette that looks "Inside Business" opens each chapter and is revisited at the end of the chapter in "Return to Inside Business." "Questions for Critical Thinking" help students apply concepts discussed in the chapter to this real business case.

"Solving an Ethical Controversy" feature boxes discuss an ethical issue in debate format. Students are presented with pro and con arguments and then a summary of the controversial subject.

"Career Kickstart" feature provides useful insight, tips, and information for students to succeed in their business careers.

Two "Hit & Miss" feature boxes in each chapter profile the successes and failures of a wide variety Canadian and international businesses. Students are asked to evaluate each case by answering "Questions for Critical Thinking."

HIT  & MISS

Beyoncé Thrills Fans and Surprises Marketers

Grammy Award–winning entertainer Beyoncé recently took the music industry—and marketing strategists—by storm. Without any advance warning, she released a new self-titled album by simply posting a trailer on her Instagram account with the caption "Surprise!" Beyoncé announced her latest release exclusively on iTunes. And in its first three days, consumers downloaded the album with its 14 songs and 17 videos more than 828,000 times.

Stunned by this approach, some executives believe that Beyoncé has changed music marketing forever. Others think her strategy worked because the singer's superstar brand allowed her to bypass traditional marketing channels. Some marketing experts have compared Beyoncé's album release to a form of relationship marketing. Beyoncé's surprise announcement about her new album catapulted its release to the top of iTune's all-time downloads list because she has a very loyal fan base with whom she has built a rock-solid relationship.

Questions for Critical Thinking

1. How will Beyoncé's move to bypass traditional marketing channels impact future projects?
2. What is the downside to Beyoncé's marketing strategy?

Sources: "Did Beyoncé's Album Just Prove Marketing Is Dead?" *CNBC*, December 17, 2013, accessed July 3, 2015, www.cnbc.com/id/101277017; Lyneka Little, "Target Doesn't Plan on Carrying New Beyoncé Album," *Wall Street Journal*, December 17, 2013, accessed July 3, 2015, http://blogs.wsj.com/speakeasy/2013/12/17/target-doesnt-plan-on-carrying-new-beyonce-album; Abigail Tracy, "Beyoncé Shows How Social Media Is Changing Marketing," *Inc.*, December 16, 2013, accessed July 3, 2015, www.inc.com/abigail-tracy/beyonce-shows-the-true-power-of-social-media.html; Lyneka Little, "Beyoncé Surprises Fans with Sudden Release of New 'Visual Album,'" *Wall Street Journal*, December 13, 2013, accessed July 3, 2015, http://blogs.wsj.com/speakeasy/2013/12/13/beyonce-surprises-fans-with-sudden-release-of-new-visual-album.

The growing importance and influence of environmental issues on contemporary business decisions is examined in the "Going Green" feature boxes.

GOING GREEN — DRILLING FOR NATURAL GAS—CLEAN ALTERNATIVES

Drilling for natural gas doesn't usually lead to images of an undisturbed landscape. In fact, studies by the government and by private environmental groups show that the main method for extracting natural gas from the earth—hydraulic fracturing—can result in contaminated water supplies. Hydraulic fracturing involves injecting millions of litres of water, sand, and chemicals deep into the ground to crack open the beds of shale that contain natural gas. Then, the gas can rise to the surface. Environmental scientists and the people who live near the drilling sites are concerned about two things: the amount of water being used and the possible contamination of their water supplies by the chemicals used in the process. These concerns have been voiced in many communities across Canada. In Quebec, the provincial government decided to go ahead with its planned natural gas development. The Quebec government's handling of the decision and how it dealt with public opinion led to much criticism.

But many energy companies *are* paying attention to these concerns—including those that drill for oil and natural gas. Environmental Technologies Ltd. makes a nontoxic alternative to the toxic chemicals. This firm says that its product kills bacteria just as effectively as the toxic chemicals. Ecosphere Technologies Inc. claims antibacterial chemicals aren't needed because its product can completely kill the bacteria at the surface before water is injected into the gas wells. Ecosphere also reduces water use and water waste by helping energy producers to reuse the water used in hydraulic fracturing. That means companies no longer need to pay to ship millions of litres of waste water to treatment plants or disposal sites.

None of these firms suggests that the drilling should stop. Instead, the firms are researching and developing greener technologies. New companies—and divisions or subsidiaries of the larger energy firms—are forming rapidly to take advantage of this business opportunity.

Questions for Critical Thinking

1. What type of production system is used by natural gas drilling companies? Explain your answer.
2. Do you predict that the firms that are investing in greener processes will ultimately be successful? Why or why not?

Sources: Marianne White, "Quebec Moved Too Fast on Shale Gas: Watchdog," *Montreal Gazette*, March 31, 2011, accessed April 14, 2011, http://www.montrealgazette.com/news/decision-canada/Quebec+moved+fast+shale+watchdog/4532660/story.html#ixzz1JW9Ku1zL; "Hydraulic Fracturing," EPA website, accessed April 29, 2010, www.epa.gov; "Sustainable Technology," Baker Hughes website, accessed April 29, 2010, www.bakerhughes.com/company/corporate-social-responsibility/sustainable-technology; Ben Casselman, "Firms See 'Green' in Natural-Gas Production," *The Wall Street Journal*, March 30, 2010, www.wsj.com/articles/SB10001424052748704091104575143771963721284; "EPA Launches Hydraulic Fracturing Study," *Environmental Leader*, March 19, 2010, www.environmentalleader.com/2010/03/19/epa-launches-hydraulic-fracturing-study.

BUSINESS TERMS YOU NEED TO KNOW

brand 13	creativity 21	nearshoring 19	relationship management 15
branding 13	critical thinking 20	not-for-profit organizations 5	social era 15
business 4	diversity 19	offshoring 19	strategic alliance 15
capital 7	entrepreneur 10	outsourcing 19	transaction management 14
capitalism 8	entrepreneurship 7	private enterprise system 8	vision 20
competition 8	factors of production 6	private property 9	
competitive differentiation 8	human resources 7	profits 4	

Key terms are bolded in the chapter and appear in the adjacent margin with their definitions. Key terms are also listed in "Business Terms You Need to Know" at the end of the chapter with page references.

The Entrepreneurship Alternative

entrepreneur a person who seeks a profitable opportunity and takes the necessary risks to set up and operate a business.

The entrepreneurial spirit beats at the heart of private enterprise. An **entrepreneur** is a risk taker in the private enterprise system. You hear about entrepreneurs all the time—two college students starting a software business in their dorm room, or a mom who invents a better baby carrier. Many times their success is modest, but once in a while the risk pays off in huge profits, as it did for Justin Bieber. People who can see marketplace opportunities are able to use their capital, time, and talents to pursue those opportunities for profit. The willingness of people to start new ventures leads to economic growth and keeps pressure on existing companies to continue to satisfy customers. If no one were willing to take economic risks, the private enterprise system wouldn't exist.

The entrepreneurial spirit leads to growth in the Canadian economy. Of all new businesses created in Canada, 99 percent are small businesses. Thousands of new businesses start each year. The Canadian economy depends on small businesses for their growth and strength. Statistics Canada data suggest that 5 percent of all businesses employ fewer than five employees, and 95 percent employ fewer than 50. The small-business sector creates 80 percent of all new jobs and generates 45 percent of Canada's economic output. Thus, Canada's small businesses are the majority of all Canadian businesses.[10]

End-of-Chapter Questions and Exercises

"Review Questions" encourage students to review their understanding of the chapter content.

REVIEW QUESTIONS

1. How does a business decide whether to trade with a foreign country? What are the key factors for participating in the information economy on a global basis?
2. Why are developing countries such as China and India becoming important international markets?
3. What is the difference between absolute advantage and comparative advantage? Give an example of each.
4. Can a nation have a favourable balance of trade and an unfavourable balance of payments? Why or why not?
5. Identify several potential barriers to communication when a company attempts to do business in another country. How might these be overcome?
6. Identify and describe briefly the three dimensions of the legal environment for global business.
7. What are the major nontariff restrictions affecting international business? Describe the difference between tariff and nontariff restrictions.
8. What is NAFTA? How does it work?
9. How has the EU helped trade among European businesses?
10. What are the key choices a company must make before reaching the final decision to go global?

PROJECTS AND TEAMWORK APPLICATIONS

1. In 1997, Britain transferred Hong Kong to China. China agreed to grant Hong Kong a high degree of autonomy as a capitalist economy for 50 years. Do you think this agreement is holding up? Why or why not? Consider China's economy, population, infrastructure, and other factors in your answer.
2. The huge growth of online business has introduced new legal concerns for international business. Patents, brand names, copyrights, and trademarks are difficult to monitor because the Internet has no boundaries. What steps can businesses take to protect their trademarks and brands online? Come up with at least five suggestions. Compare your list with your classmates' lists.
3. The WTO monitors GATT agreements, mediates disputes, and continues the effort to reduce trade barriers all over world. But many are concerned that the WTO's focus on lowering trade barriers encourages businesses to keep costs down by using methods that may lead to pollution and human rights abuses. Others argue that human rights should not be linked to international business. Do you think environmental and human rights issues should be linked to trade? Why or why not?
4. Describe briefly the EU and its goals. What are the pros and cons of the EU? Do you think the European alliance will hold up over the next 20 years? Why or why not?
5. Find the most recent edition of "The Fortune Global 500." It is usually published in Fortune magazine in late July or early August. You can also go to Fortune's online version at http://fortune.com/global500. Use the Global 500 to answer the following questions.
   a. On what is the Global 500 ranking based (e.g., profits, number of employees, revenues)?
   b. List the home countries of the world's 10 largest corporations.
   c. For the following industry classifications, identify the top-ranked company, its Global 500 ranking, and country: food and drug stores; industrial and farm equipment; petroleum refining; utilities: gas and electric; telecommunications; pharmaceuticals.

WEB ASSIGNMENTS

1. **WTO.** Visit the website of the World Trade Organization (www.wto.org). Research two current trade disputes. Which countries and products are involved? Do the two disputes have anything in common? What steps does the WTO follow to resolve trade disputes between member countries?
2. **EU.** Europa.eu is the Web portal for the European Union. Go to the http://europa.eu/index_en.htm and answer the following questions:
   a. What steps must a country take to become a member of the EU?
   b. How many EU members have adopted the euro? Which countries will be adopting the euro over the next few years?
   c. What is the combined GDP of EU members? Which EU member has the largest GDP? Which has the smallest GDP?
3. **Nestlé.** Nestlé is one of the world's largest global corporations. Visit the firm's website (www.nestle.com). Where is the company headquartered? What are some of its best-known brands? Are these brands sold in specific countries, or are they sold worldwide? List three or four issues Nestlé faces as a global corporation.

Note: Internet Web addresses change frequently. If you do not find the exact sites listed, you may need to access the organization's or company's home page and search from there or use a search engine such as Bing or Google.

"Projects and Teamwork Applications" encourage active learning and give students the chance to work in groups. Projects can be used either in or out of the classroom.

"Web Assignments" ask students to research chapter topics using resources on the Internet.

"Launching Your . . . Career" at the end of each part of the book explores resources and opportunities available for careers in contemporary business including: Global Business and Economics, Entrepreneurial Pursuits, Marketing, Management, Technology and Information, and Finance.

1 LAUNCHING YOUR . . .

GLOBAL BUSINESS AND ECONOMICS CAREER

In Part 1, "Business in a Global Environment," you have learned about the role of contemporary business in today's society. You also learned about the major forces that shape contemporary business. The part includes four chapters that discuss the changing face of business, business ethics and social responsibility, economic challenges facing contemporary business, and competing in world markets. Business has always been an exciting career field. You can choose to start your own company, work at a local business, or take a position with a multinational corporation. Today's business opportunities are very attractive. Businesses are expanding to compete in a global economy—and they need loyal and talented people to help them reach their goals. Professional and business service jobs are found in some of the fastest-growing industries in the North American economy. These jobs are projected to grow by more than 23 percent over a decade.[1] Now is the time to learn about several career options that can lead you to your dream job. Each part in this text includes a profile of some of the many opportunities available in business. Here are a few opportunities related to Chapters 1 through 4.

> **PART 1: CASE STUDY** Beau's All Natural Brewing Company
> **Building a Craft Brewery in a Competitive Canadian Industry**
>
>
>
> **Meet Co-Founders Steve and Tim Beauchesne**
>
> Steve Beauchesne was familiar with the "hows and whys" of running a business. He grew up working at his father's leather finishing plant in the small farming community of Vankleek Hill, about an hour drive south of Ottawa. The plant finished leather for use in the fashion industry, which was rapidly moving offshore to places like China and India. Business was in a gradual decline. Although Steve was never particularly enamoured with the business, his time spent at the plant was a worthwhile education on how things get done. In his words, "I learned how to work with people, how people should be treated and I gained the confidence to run things." After studying business at Ryerson University in Toronto, he found himself working for a provincial government agency researching and writing business plans. At the same time he was devel-
>
> creative tastes once spices, herbs, and other flavourings like fruit were introduced to the brew.
>
> The concept is a familiar one found in other industries where customers seek out variety, especially food and beverages. And because of new technology that allows for smaller but economical production operations, craft brewers can start up small and gradually expanded as sales grow. Many craft brewers are also built around a pub or restaurant where beer is normally sold and then look to expand sales through other restaurants, pubs, and venues such as golf courses.
>
> Today, about 10 million Canadians drink over $5 billion worth of beer annually. Total beer consumption in Canada amounts to more than 2 billion litres, averaging 64 litres per capita. It is greatest in Newfoundland (79 litres), followed by Quebec (73 litres) and Alberta (69 litres) with the remaining provinces close to the national average. There are two large-scale brewers: Anheuser-Busch InBev, headquartered in Belgium, is the

A running "Case Study" featuring Beau's All Natural Brewing Company is presented in the last chapter of each of the six parts of the textbook. The case study takes students through the decision making of a real Canadian company and provides further insight into the world of contemporary business.

Appendices

Additional Cases related to the concepts presented in the book are provided in Appendix A. Each case profiles a different company and asks students to apply what they have learned in answering Critical Thinking Questions about the case.

Other appendices at the end of the book include Appendix B Business Law, Appendix C Insurance and Risk Management, Appendix D Personal Financial Planning, and Appendix E Developing a Business Plan. Two additional appendices—Appendix F Video Cases, based on Wiley Business Video Series and Appendix G Careers in Contemporary Business—are available online at www.wiley.com/go/boonecanada.

SUPPLEMENTS

WileyPLUS Learning Space

WileyPLUS Learning Space

Learning experts have shown greater gains in outcomes and improved retention when students are able to read, interact with, discuss, and write about course content. Research also shows that when students collaborate with each other, they make deeper connections to the content. Typically, when students work together, they also feel part of a community. This sense of community helps them grow in areas beyond topics in the course—they are able to develop skills like critical thinking and teamwork that can be applied down the road in future careers and life.

WileyPLUS Learning Space will transform any course into a vibrant, collaborative, learning community. This exciting online platform invites students to experience learning activities, work through self-assessment, ask questions and share insights. As they interact with the course content, their peers, and their instructor, *WileyPLUS Learning Space* creates a personalized study guide for each student.

Through a flexible course design, you can quickly organize learning activities, manage student collaboration, and customize your course—having full control over content as well as the amount of interactivity between students.

WileyPLUS Learning Space lets you:

- Assign activities and add your own materials
- Guide your students through what's important in the interactive e-textbook by easily assigning specific content
- Set up and monitor group learning
- Assess student engagement
- Gain immediate insights to help inform teaching

Defining a clear path to action, the visual reports in *WileyPLUS Learning Space* help both you and your students gauge problem areas and act on what's most important.

With the visual reports, you can:

- See exactly where your students are struggling and intervene as needed
- Help students see what they don't know to better prepare for exams
- Give students insight into their strengths and weaknesses to succeed in the course

Integrated with *WileyPLUS Learning Space* is ORION. Based on cognitive science, ORION is a personalized, adaptive learning experience that helps students build proficiency on topics while using their study time most effectively.

Resources

Contemporary Business, Second Canadian Edition, is accompanied by a suite of instructor and student resources and ancillaries designed to facilitate teaching and learning.

Resources can be found within the *Contemporary Business*, Second Canadian Edition, *WileyPLUS Learning Space* course. Selected resources are available on the textbook's companion website, www.wiley.com/go/boonecanada. Consistent with the first edition of *Contemporary Business*, the instructor resources are designed to propel the instructor into the classroom with all the materials needed to engage students and help them understand concepts.

For Instructors

CBC Videos. Two sets of CBC Videos are available for *Contemporary Business*, Second Canadian Edition—short clips with discussion questions to generate interest and initiate discussion into relevant business topics and longer video cases with discussion questions that take an in-depth look at key subjects of interest to students, such as entrepreneurship and sustainability.

Test Bank. The Test Bank contains a variety of question types—matching, essay/short answer, multiple choice, and true/false. The Test Bank is available in a Word® document format, as well as a Computerized Test Bank. Instructors can generate multiple test versions, rearrange question order, or customize tests for specific content.

Instructor's Manual. This Instructor's Manual is designed to help instructors maximize student learning and encourage critical thinking. It presents a lecture outline for each section and objective in each chapter, and includes answers to review questions and suggested responses to the Project and Teamwork Applications in the textbook. The instructor's manual also includes collaborative learning exercises.

PowerPoint® Presentations. PowerPoint® Presentations are provided for each chapter and include an outline of key points (with accompanying lecture notes), learning objectives, key terms, and figures and tables from the textbook.

Clicker Questions. This resource offers questions about key chapter concepts and can be used with a variety of personal response (or "clicker") systems.

Wiley Contemporary Business Weekly Updates Site, http://contemporarybusinessupdates.ca. This weekly update site provides highlights of the very latest in business news and current affairs. Each week's update includes links to relevant business news articles and video clips, with discussion questions to help guide an understanding of the news item and to encourage classroom analysis and discussion. Instructors who wish to receive email alerts with each week's highlights can subscribe directly on the website. New to the Weekly Updates are Video Case Exercises that correspond to the six parts of the textbook.

For Students

Free Study Guide. The *Study Guide to Accompany Contemporary Business*, Second Canadian Edition, is available free to students and provides a solid review of the concepts covered in the textbook and in a contemporary business course. The study guide includes a variety of question material and application exercises and is available in *WileyPLUS Learning Space*.

Practice Quizzes. This resource allows students to test their knowledge and understanding of key chapter content. Practices quizzes are available in *WileyPLUS Learning Space*.

Video Summaries. This resource is an author-presented summary and overview of the key concepts and learning objectives in each chapter.

BRIEF CONTENTS

PART 1 Business in a Global Environment 1
- **Chapter 1** The Changing Face of Business 2
- **Chapter 2** Business Ethics and Social Responsibility 28
- **Chapter 3** Economic Challenges Facing Contemporary Business 58
- **Chapter 4** Competing in World Markets 88

PART 2 Starting and Growing Your Business 121
- **Chapter 5** Forms of Business Ownership and Organization 122
- **Chapter 6** Starting Your Own Business: The Entrepreneurship Alternative 152

PART 3 Management: Empowering People to Achieve Business Goals 177
- **Chapter 7** Management, Leadership, and the Internal Organization 178
- **Chapter 8** Human Resource Management: From Recruitment to Labour Relations 208
- **Chapter 9** Top Performance through Empowerment, Teamwork, and Communication 234
- **Chapter 10** Production and Operations Management 258

PART 4 Marketing Management 289
- **Chapter 11** Customer-Driven Marketing 290
- **Chapter 12** Product and Distribution Strategies 320
- **Chapter 13** Promotion and Pricing Strategies 352

PART 5 Managing Technology and Information 387
- **Chapter 14** Using Technology to Manage Information 388

PART 6 Managing Financial Resources 413
- **Chapter 15** Understanding Accounting and Financial Statements 414
- **Chapter 16** The Financial System 444
- **Chapter 17** Financial Management 470

Appendix A Additional Cases 497
Appendix B Business Law 533
Appendix C Insurance and Risk Management 543
Appendix D Personal Financial Planning 553
Appendix E Developing a Business Plan 563

CONTENTS

Preface v
About the Authors viii
Features of this Book x
Supplements xv

PART 1 Business in a Global Environment — 1

Chapter 1 The Changing Face of Business — 2

Inside Business
Canadian Entertainers Are Cultivating Global Audiences Online

Hit & Miss
Live Nation Connects Superstar Artists and Fans

Career Kickstart
Social Networking

Hit & Miss
Twitter's Dorsey: 140 Characters at a Time

Going Green
Internet Billionaire's Goal: Help China Breathe Easier

Solving an Ethical Controversy
Securities Oversight?

What Is Business? — 4
Not-for-Profit Organizations 5

Factors of Production — 6

The Private Enterprise System — 8
Basic Rights in the Private Enterprise System 8, The Entrepreneurship Alternative 10

Seven Eras in the History of Business — 12
The Colonial Period 12, The Industrial Revolution 12, The Age of Industrial Entrepreneurs 12, The Production Era 13, The Marketing Era 13, The Relationship Era 14, The Social Era 15

Today's Business Workforce — 17
Changes in the Workforce 18

The Twenty-First-Century Manager — 20
Importance of Vision 20, The Importance of Critical Thinking and Creativity 20, Ability to Lead Change 21

What Makes a Company Admired? — 22

What's Ahead — 23
Return to Inside Business 23, Summary of Learning Objectives 24, Business Terms You Need to Know 25, Review Questions 26, Projects and Teamwork Applications 26, Web Assignments 27

Chapter 2 — Business Ethics and Social Responsibility — 28

Inside Business
Cirque du Soleil: A Class Act in Social Responsibility

Career Kickstart
How to Avoid Ethical Issues at Work

Going Green
Starbucks Introduces a New Store-Design Strategy

Solving an Ethical Controversy
To What Extent Should a CEO Be Held Responsible?

Hit & Miss
Pacific Biodiesel Recycles Oil from French Fries to Fuel

Hit & Miss
Balancing Life and Work with a Cup of Tea

Concern for Ethical and Societal Issues — 30

The Contemporary Ethical Environment — 31
Sarbanes-Oxley and Bill 198 **33**, Individuals Make a Difference **33**, Development of Individual Ethics **34**, On-the-Job Ethical Dilemmas **34**

How Organizations Shape Ethical Conduct — 37
Ethical Awareness **37**, Ethical Education **38**, Ethical Action **39**, Ethical Leadership **39**

Acting Responsibly to Satisfy Society — 40
Responsibilities to the General Public **42**, Responsibilities to Customers **47**, Responsibilities to Employees **49**

Responsibilities to Investors and the Financial Community — 53

What's Ahead — 54
Return to Inside Business **54**, Summary of Learning Objectives **55**, Business Terms You Need to Know **56**, Review Questions **56**, Projects and Teamwork Applications **57**, Web Assignments **57**

Chapter 3 — Economic Challenges Facing Contemporary Business — 58

Inside Business
Vancouver's 2010 Olympic Village: Seemed Like a Great Idea at the Time

Hit & Miss
Five Guys Burgers and Fries: A Simple Recipe for Success

Solving an Ethical Controversy
Should Alternative Energy Development Be Relied on to Create New Jobs?

Hit & Miss
Vancity Provides a "Microcredit Toolkit" to Local Not-for-Profit Organizations

Going Green
Tax Credits for an Energy Star

Career Kickstart
Tips for International Travel

Microeconomics: The Forces of Demand and Supply — 60
Factors Driving Demand **61**, Factors Driving Supply **63**, How Demand and Supply Interact **64**

Macroeconomics: Issues for the Entire Economy — 66
Capitalism: The Private Enterprise System **67**, Planned Economies: Socialism and Communism **69**, Mixed Market Economies **70**

Evaluating Economic Performance — 71
Flattening the Business Cycle **71**, Productivity and the Nation's Gross Domestic Product **73**, Price Level Changes **74**

Managing the Economy's Performance — 78
Monetary Policy **78**, Fiscal Policy **78**

Global Economic Challenges of the Twenty-First Century — 80

What's Ahead — 82
Return to Inside Business **82**, Summary of Learning Objectives **83**, Business Terms You Need to Know **84**, Review Questions **85**, Projects and Teamwork Applications **85**, Web Assignments **86**

Chapter 4 — Competing in World Markets — 88

Inside Business
PotashCorp: Genesis for Economic Development

Hit & Miss
The Tiny Nano—A Potential Hit for Tata Motors

Why Nations Trade — 90
International Sources of Factors of Production **90**, Size of the International Marketplace **91**, Absolute and Comparative Advantage **92**

Measuring Trade between Nations — 93
Major Canadian Exports and Imports **93**, Exchange Rates **95**

xx Contents

Sidebar

Solving an Ethical Controversy
Delivering Alberta Oil through the Keystone XL Pipeline versus by Rail

Going Green
IBM Helps Keep Water Flowing

Hit & Miss
Ford Motor Company: Engineered and Made in Mexico

Hit & Miss
Apple Brings Manufacturing Work Back Home

Barriers to International Trade — 96
Social and Cultural Differences 96, Economic Differences 97, Political and Legal Differences 99, Types of Trade Restrictions 102

Reducing Barriers to International Trade — 104
Organizations Promoting International Trade 104, International Economic Communities 105

Going Global — 107
Levels of Involvement 108, From Multinational Corporation to Global Business 111

Developing a Strategy for International Business — 112
Global Business Strategies 112, Multidomestic Business Strategies 112

What's Ahead — 113
Return to Inside Business 113, Summary of Learning Objectives 113, Business Terms You Need to Know 115, Review Questions 116, Projects and Teamwork Applications 116, Web Assignments 116

Part 1: Case Study Beau's All Natural Brewing Company: Building a Craft Brewery in a Competitive Canadian Industry — 117

Part 1: Launching Your Global Business and Economics Career — 118

PART 2 Starting and Growing Your Business — 121

Chapter 5 Forms of Business Ownership and Organization — 122

Sidebar

Inside Business
Pi Athlete Management Inc.: Advising Athletes about Their Careers and More

Going Green
Green Mama: Small Business with a Big Message

Career Kickstart
How to Use Social Networking in Your Job Search

Hit & Miss
CBC's *Dragons' Den* Highlights Entrepreneurial Thinking and Investing

Hit & Miss
One Small Franchise Produces One Big Idea

Solving an Ethical Controversy
Do Some CEOs Earn Too Much?

Most Businesses Are Small Businesses — 124
What Is a Small Business? 124, Typical Small-Business Ventures 125

Contributions of Small Business to the Economy — 127
Creating New Jobs 127, Creating New Industries 127, Innovation 128

Why Small Businesses Fail — 129
Management Shortcomings 129, Inadequate Financing 130, Government Regulation 131

The Business Plan: A Foundation for Success — 131

Assistance for Small Businesses — 132
Business Development Bank of Canada 133, Financial Assistance 133, Business Incubators 133, Private Investors 133, Small-Business Opportunities for Women 134

Franchising — 135
The Franchising Sector 135, Franchising Agreements 136, Benefits and Problems of Franchising 136

Forms of Private Business Ownership — 138
Sole Proprietorships 138, Partnerships 139, Corporations 140
Not-for-Profit Corporations 140

Public and Collective Ownership of Business — 140
Public (Government) Ownership 141, Collective (Cooperative) Ownership 141

Organizing a Corporation — 142
Where and How Businesses Incorporate 142, Corporate Management 143

When Businesses Join Forces — 145
Mergers and Acquisitions (M&A) 145, Joint Ventures: Specialized Partnerships 145

What's Ahead — 146
Return to Inside Business 147, Summary of Learning Objectives 147, Business Terms You Need to Know 149, Review Questions 150, Projects and Teamwork Applications 150, Web Assignments 150

Chapter 6 — Starting Your Own Business: The Entrepreneurship Alternative — 152

Inside Business
Sharing Economy Sparks Start-Ups

Career Kickstart
Communicating by Email, Text Message, or Social Networking Updates: You Don't Have to Be All Thumbs

Hit & Miss
Fruits & Passion for Lifestyle Products

Hit & Miss
Businesses Based at Home Are Booming

Solving an Ethical Controversy
Entrepreneurs and Ethics: It's Good Business

Going Green
Holy Crap: Corin and Brian Mullins Sure Know How to Pick a Name for Their Organic Cereals

What Is an Entrepreneur? — 154
Categories of Entrepreneurs 155

Reasons to Choose Entrepreneurship as a Career Path — 156
Being Your Own Boss 156, Financial Success 158, Job Security 158, Quality of Life 158

The Environment for Entrepreneurs — 159
Globalization 159, Education 160, Information Technology 160, Demographic and Economic Trends 161

Characteristics of Entrepreneurs — 162
Vision 162, High Energy Level 163, Need to Achieve 163, Self-Confidence and Optimism 163, Tolerance for Failure 163, Creativity 164, Tolerance for Ambiguity 165, Internal Locus of Control 165

Starting a New Venture — 165
Selecting a Business Idea 165, Creating a Business Plan 167, Finding Financing 168, Government Support for New Ventures 169

Intrapreneurship — 169

What's Ahead — 170
Return to Inside Business 170, Summary of Learning Objectives 170, Business Terms You Need to Know 172, Review Questions 172, Projects and Teamwork Applications 172, Web Assignments 173

Part 2 : Case Study Beau's All Natural Brewing Company Getting Started: Choosing a Location, Building the Plant, and Hiring Employees — 174

Part 2: Launching Your Entrepreneurial Career — 175

PART 3 Management: Empowering People to Achieve Business Goals — 177

Chapter 7 — Management, Leadership, and the Internal Organization — 178

Inside Business
Can John S. Chen Save BlackBerry?

What Is Management? — 180
The Management Hierarchy 180, Skills Needed for Managerial Success 182, Managerial Functions 182

Sidebar

Solving an Ethical Controversy
Google Stands Alone: When Ethics and Business Don't Mix

Going Green
Johnson & Johnson: Caring for the World

Hit & Miss
Hands-Off Approach Works for Buffett

Hit & Miss
GM's First Female CEO Faces Challenges and Opportunities

Hit & Miss
WestJet Airlines: Most Admired Corporate Culture in Canada

Career Kickstart
Managing a Multigenerational Workforce

Setting a Vision and Ethical Standards for the Firm	183
Importance of Planning	185
Types of Planning 185, Planning at Different Organizational Levels 187	
The Strategic Planning Process	187
Defining the Organization's Mission 188, Assessing Your Competitive Position 188, Setting Objectives for the Organization 190, Creating Strategies for Competitive Differentiation 190, Implementing the Strategy 190, Monitoring and Adapting Strategic Plans 190	
Managers as Decision Makers	191
Programmed and Nonprogrammed Decisions 191, How Managers Make Decisions 192	
Managers as Leaders	193
Leadership Styles 194, Which Leadership Style Is Best? 195	
Corporate Culture	195
Organizational Structures	196
Departmentalization 198, Delegating Work Assignments 198, Span of Management 200, Centralization and Decentralization 200, Types of Organization Structures 200	
What's Ahead	202
Return to Inside Business 202, Summary of Learning Objectives 203, Business Terms You Need to Know 205, Review Questions 205, Projects and Teamwork Applications 206, Web Assignments 206	

Chapter 8

Inside Business
Canadian Apparel Manufacturing: Seeking Solutions in a Global Marketplace

Hit & Miss
Accenture's Mobile Recruitment Strategy

Career Kickstart
How to Ask for a Raise

Hit & Miss
AOL Employees Don't Exit Voluntarily

Solving an Ethical Controversy
Monitoring Employees' Social Media Activities

Going Green
Labour Unions and Green Construction

Human Resource Management: From Recruitment to Labour Relations	**208**
Human Resources: The People Behind The People	210
Recruitment and Selection	211
Finding Qualified Candidates 211, Selecting and Hiring Employees 211	
Orientation, Training, and Evaluation	213
Training Programs 213, Performance Appraisals 214	
Compensation	215
Employee Benefits 216, Flexible Benefits 217, Flexible Work 217	
Employee Separation	218
Voluntary and Involuntary Turnover 218, Downsizing 218, Outsourcing 220	
Motivating Employees	220
Maslow's Hierarchy of Needs Theory 221, Herzberg's Two-Factor Model of Motivation 222, Expectancy Theory and Equity Theory 223, Goal-Setting Theory and Management by Objectives 224, Job Design and Motivation 224, Managers' Attitudes and Motivation 225	
Labour–Management Relations	225
Development of Labour Unions 225, Labour Relations Board 226, The Collective Bargaining Process 226, Settling Labour–Management Disputes 226, Competitive Tactics of Unions and Management 227, The Future of Labour Unions 228	

Contents   xxiii

What's Ahead   229
Return to Inside Business 229, Summary of Learning Objectives 229,
Business Terms You Need to Know 231, Review Questions 231, Projects and
Teamwork Applications 232, Web Assignments 232

Chapter 9 — Top Performance Through Empowerment, Teamwork, and Communication   234

Inside Business
Pam Cooley and CarShareHFX

Solving an Ethical Controversy
Employee Empowerment: Yes or No?

Hit & Miss
Team Diversity at Ernst & Young

Career Kickstart
Tune Up Your Listening Skills

Hit & Miss
Henry Mintzberg: Observing What Managers Do

Going Green
Clorox Comes Clean—Naturally

Empowering Employees   236
Sharing Information and Decision-Making Authority 236, Linking Rewards
to Company Performance 236

Teams   238

Team Characteristics   240
Team Size 240, Team Level and Team Diversity 240, Stages of Team Development 242

Team Cohesiveness and Norms   242

Team Conflict   243

The Importance Of Effective Communication   244
The Process of Communication 244

Basic Forms of Communication   246
Oral Communication 246, Written Communication 247, Formal Communication 248,
Informal Communication 249, Nonverbal Communication 249

External Communication and Crisis Management   251

What's Ahead   253
Return to Inside Business 253, Summary of Learning Objectives 254,
Business Terms You Need to Know 256, Review Questions 256, Projects and
Teamwork Applications 256, Web Assignments 257

Chapter 10 — Production and Operations Management   258

Inside Business
Building a 3D Future at GE

Going Green
Drilling For Natural Gas—Clean Alternatives

Hit & Miss
Mexico Becomes a Major Hub for Auto Manufacturing

Hit & Miss
Harley-Davidson Turns Lean

Career Kickstart
Making the Most of Business Meetings

The Strategic Importance of Production   260
Mass Production 261, Flexible Production 262, Customer-Driven Production 262

Production Processes   262

Technology and the Production Process   263
Green Manufacturing Processes 263, Robots 264, Computer-Aided Design
and Manufacturing 265, Flexible Manufacturing Systems 265, Computer-Integrated
Manufacturing 266

The Location Decision   266

The Job of Production Managers   269
Planning the Production Process 269, Selecting the Facility Layout 269,
Carrying Out the Production Plan 271

Solving an Ethical Controversy
Multivitamins Produced in China: Are Stricter Quality Controls Necessary?

Controlling the Production Process — 275
Production Planning 275, Routing 276, Scheduling 276, Dispatching 277, Follow-Up 277

Importance of Quality — 278
Quality Control 278, ISO Standards 279

What's Ahead — 280
Return to Inside Business 280, Summary of Learning Objectives 281, Business Terms You Need to Know 282, Review Questions 283, Projects and Teamwork Applications 283, Web Assignments 284

Part 3: Case Study Beau's All Natural Brewing Company: Managing the Pains of Early Growth — 284

Part 3: Launching Your Management Career — 286

PART 4 Marketing Management — 289

Chapter 11 Customer-Driven Marketing — 290

Inside Business
Handmade Items: Etsy.com Has Them All

Hit & Miss
Beyoncé Thrills Fans and Surprises Marketers

Going Green
Häagen-Dazs Focuses on Honey Bee Research

Solving an Ethical Controversy
When Free Credit Reports Aren't Free

Hit & Miss
Disney XD TV: Marketing to Boys

Career Kickstart
Calming the Angry Customer

What Is Marketing? — 292
How Marketing Creates Utility 293

Evolution of the Marketing Concept — 294
Emergence of the Marketing Concept 295

Not-for-Profit and Nontraditional Marketing — 295
Not-for-Profit Marketing 296, Nontraditional Marketing 296

Developing a Marketing Strategy — 299
Selecting a Target Market 299, Developing a Marketing Mix for International Markets 301

Marketing Research — 302
Obtaining Marketing Research Data 302, Applying Marketing Research Data 303, Data Mining 304

Market Segmentation — 304
How Market Segmentation Works 305, Segmenting Consumer Markets 305, Segmenting Business Markets 310

Consumer Behaviour — 311
Determinants of Consumer Behaviour 311, Determinants of Business Buying Behaviour 311, Steps in the Consumer Behaviour Process 311

Relationship Marketing — 312
Benefits of Relationship Marketing 313, Tools for Nurturing Customer Relationships 314, One-on-One Marketing 315

What's Ahead — 315
Return to Inside Business 315, Summary of Learning Objectives 316, Business Terms You Need to Know 318, Review Questions 318, Projects and Teamwork Applications 319, Web Assignments 319

Contents   xxv

Chapter 12 — Product and Distribution Strategies — 320

Inside Business
Montreal's Fitness City Complex: Bringing Fitness Businesses Together Under One Roof

Hit & Miss
Canadian Tire: Changing with the Times

Going Green
Sunchips Introduces Greener Packaging

Hit & Miss
Gourmet Chips & Sauces Targets a Niche Market

Solving an Ethical Controversy
Teens at the Mall: Good or Bad for Business?

Career Kickstart
Effective Use of Social Media for Your Small Business

Product Strategy — 322
Classifying Goods and Services 322, Marketing Strategy Implications 324

Product Life Cycle — 325
Stages of the Product Life Cycle 325, Marketing Strategy Implications of the Product Life Cycle 326, Stages in New-Product Development 328

Product Identification — 329
Selecting an Effective Brand Name 330, Brand Categories 330, Brand Loyalty and Brand Equity 331, Packages and Labels 332

Distribution Strategy — 334
Distribution Channels 334

Wholesaling — 336
Manufacturer-Owned Wholesaling Intermediaries 337, Independent Wholesaling Intermediaries 337, Retailer-Owned Cooperatives and Buying Offices 337

Retailing — 338
Nonstore Retailers 338, Store Retailers 339, How Retailers Compete 340

Distribution Channel Decisions and Logistics — 343
Selecting Distribution Channels 344, Selecting Distribution Intensity 345, Logistics and Physical Distribution 345

What's Ahead — 347
Return to Inside Business 347, Summary of Learning Objectives 348, Business Terms You Need to Know 350, Review Questions 350, Projects and Teamwork Applications 350, Web Assignments 351

Chapter 13 — Promotion and Pricing Strategies — 352

Inside Business
WorkSafeBC: Promoting Safety to Young Workers

Hit & Miss
NBA Says Yes to Floor Ads

Going Green
How Much Would You Pay for a Plastic Shopping Bag?

Career Kickstart
How to Negotiate in a Difficult Economy

Solving an Ethical Controversy
Free E-books: Good or Bad for Business?

Hit & Miss
A Bis Gourmet—Quality Fast Food At Competitive Prices

Integrated Marketing Communications — 354
The Promotional Mix 355, Objectives of Promotional Strategy 356, Promotional Planning 357

Advertising — 358
Types of Advertising 358, Advertising and the Product Life Cycle 359, Advertising Media 359

Sales Promotion — 364
Consumer-Oriented Promotions 364, Trade-Oriented Promotions 366, Personal Selling 367

Pushing and Pulling Strategies — 371

Pricing Objectives in the Marketing Mix — 372
Profitability Objectives 372, Volume Objectives 372, Pricing to Meet Competition 373, Prestige Objectives 373

Pricing Strategies — 374
Price Determination in Practice 374, Breakeven Analysis 375, Alternative Pricing Strategies 376

Consumer Perceptions of Prices — 378
Price–Quality Relationships 378, Odd Pricing 378

Contents

What's Ahead — 379

Return to Inside Business 379, Summary of Learning Objectives 379, Business Terms You Need to Know 381, Review Questions 381, Projects and Teamwork Applications 382, Web Assignments 382

Part 4: Case Study Beau's All Natural Brewing Company: Building Brand Awareness — 383

Part 4: Launching Your Marketing Career — 384

PART 5 — Managing Technology and Information — 387

Chapter 14 — Using Technology to Manage Information — 388

Data, Information, and Information Systems — 390

Components and Types of Information Systems — 391
Databases 392, Types of Information Systems 393

Computer Hardware and Software — 394
Types of Computer Hardware 394, Computer Software 396

Computer Networks — 398
Local Area Networks and Wide Area Networks 398, Wireless Local Networks 398, Intranets 399, Virtual Private Networks 400, VoIP 400

Security and Ethical Issues Affecting Information Systems — 400
Cybercrime 400, Computer Viruses, Worms, Trojan Horses, and Spyware 401, Information Systems and Ethics 403

Disaster Recovery and Backup — 404

Information System Trends — 404
The Distributed Workforce 404, Application Service Providers 405, On-Demand, Cloud, and Grid Computing 405

What's Ahead — 406
Return to Inside Business 406, Summary of Learning Objectives 407, Business Terms You Need to Know 409, Review Questions 409, Projects and Teamwork Applications 409, Web Assignments 410

Part 5: Case Study Beau's All Natural Brewing Company: Using Technology to Manage Communications and Information — 410

Part 5: Launching Your Information Technology Career — 412

Sidebar (Chapter 14)
- **Inside Business**: Stock-Trak: Learning about the Stock Market through Simulation
- **Hit & Miss**: Business Intelligence Software Helps with Information Overload
- **Career Kickstart**: Courteous Communications via Mobile Devices
- **Going Green**: Can Cloud Computing Also Be "Green" Computing?
- **Solving an Ethical Controversy**: Should Employers Monitor Employees' Internet Use?
- **Hit & Miss**: Cisco Systems Tackles Cloud Security

PART 6 — Managing Financial Resources — 413

Chapter 15 — Understanding Accounting and Financial Statements — 414

Users of Accounting Information — 416
Business Activities Involving Accounting 417

Sidebar (Chapter 15)
- **Inside Business**: Cooking the Books

Sidebar (left column)

Hit & Miss
Forensic Accountants: Fraud Busters

Career Kickstart
Tips for Complying with the Corruption of Foreign Public Officials Act

Going Green
Deloitte Educates Itself—and Others—on Sustainability

Solving an Ethical Controversy
Should Whistle-Blowers Be Rewarded?

Hit & Miss
Accounting: Hong Kong Meets China

Accounting Professionals	418
Public Accountants 418, Management Accountants 418, Government and Not-for-Profit Accountants 419	
The Foundation of the Accounting System	420
The Accounting Cycle	422
The Accounting Equation 422, The Impact of Computers and the Internet on the Accounting Process 424	
Financial Statements	425
The Balance Sheet 426, The Income Statement 427, Statement of Changes in Equity 429, The Statement of Cash Flows 429	
Financial Ratio Analysis	432
Liquidity Ratios 433, Activity Ratios 433, Profitability Ratios 434, Leverage Ratios 435	
Budgeting	435
International Accounting	437
Exchange Rates 438	
What's Ahead	438
Return to Inside Business 438, Summary of Learning Objectives 439, Business Terms You Need to Know 441, Review Questions 441, Projects and Teamwork Applications 441, Web Assignments 442	

Chapter 16

Sidebar (left column)

Inside Business
Canada Weathers the Credit Crisis

Going Green
Td Bank: "As Green as Our Logo"

Hit & Miss
A Major Spinoff for Citigroup

Hit & Miss
How News Lifts—or Sinks—Shares around the World

Career Kickstart
What to Do When Your Credit Gets Pulled

Solving an Ethical Controversy
Can the Securities Market Regulate Itself?

The Financial System	**444**
Understanding the Financial System	446
Types of Securities	448
Money Market Instruments 448, Bonds 448, Shares 450	
Financial Markets	451
Understanding Stock Markets	453
The Toronto Stock Exchange 453, Foreign Stock Markets 453, ECNs and the Future of Stock Markets 455, Investor Participation in the Stock Markets 455	
Financial Institutions	455
Commercial Banks 455, Credit Unions 458, Nondepository Financial Institutions 459, Mutual Funds 459	
The Role of the Bank of Canada	460
Monetary Policy 460	
Regulation of the Financial System	461
Bank Regulation 461, Government Regulation of the Financial Markets 462, Industry Self-Regulation 462	
The Financial System: A Global Perspective	463

What's Ahead — 465

Return to Inside Business 465, Summary of Learning Objectives 465, Business Terms You Need to Know 468, Review Questions 468, Projects and Teamwork Applications 468, Web Assignments 469

Chapter 17 — Financial Management — 470

Inside Business
The Wooing of Ratiopharm

Hit & Miss
Apptio Calculates the Cost of Information Technology

Career Kickstart
Tips for Managing Assets

Solving an Ethical Controversy
Executive Pay: Should Shareholders Decide the Salaries of CEOs?

Going Green
A Knight In Shining Capitalism

Hit & Miss
Harvest Partners Grows Its Investments

The Role of the Financial Manager — 472

Financial Planning — 474

Managing Assets — 476
Short-Term Assets 476, Capital Investment Analysis 478, Managing International Assets 478

Sources of Funds and Capital Structure — 479
Leverage and Capital Structure Decisions 479, Mixing Short-Term and Long-Term Funds 481, Dividend Policy 482

Short-Term Funding Options — 483
Trade Credit 483, Short-Term Loans 483, Commercial Paper 484

Sources of Long-Term Financing — 484
Public Sale of Shares and Bonds 485, Private Placements 485, Venture Capitalists 486, Private Equity Funds 486, Hedge Funds 488

Mergers, Acquisitions, Buyouts, and Divestitures — 488

What's Ahead — 489
Return to Inside Business 490, Summary of Learning Objectives 490, Business Terms You Need to Know 492, Review Questions 492, Projects and Teamwork Applications 493, Web Assignments 493

Part 6: Case Study Beau's All Natural Brewing Company: Financial Growth — 494

Part 6: Launching Your Accounting or Finance Career — 495

Appendix A	Additional Cases	497
Appendix B	Business Law	533
Appendix C	Insurance and Risk Management	543
Appendix D	Personal Financial Planning	553
Appendix E	Developing a Business Plan	563
Glossary		571
Notes		581
Name Index		605
Subject Index		611

© Ariel Skelley/Getty Images

PART 1

BUSINESS IN A GLOBAL ENVIRONMENT

Chapter 1 The Changing Face of Business

Chapter 2 Business Ethics and Social Responsibility

Chapter 3 Economic Challenges Facing Contemporary Business

Chapter 4 Competing in World Markets

1 | THE CHANGING FACE OF BUSINESS

LEARNING OBJECTIVES

LO 1.1 Distinguish between business and not-for-profit organizations.

LO 1.2 Identify and describe the factors of production.

LO 1.3 Describe the private enterprise system.

LO 1.4 Identify the seven eras in the history of business.

LO 1.5 Explain how today's business workforce and the nature of work itself are changing.

LO 1.6 Identify the skills and attributes needed to lead businesses in the twenty-first century.

LO 1.7 Outline the characteristics that make a company admired.

INSIDE BUSINESS

Canadian Entertainers Are Cultivating Global Audiences Online

Since its commercial debut in the mid-1990s, the Internet has evolved into an integral communications tool for the entertainment industry. Artists and audiences can easily experience two-way communication through software tools designed to create a sense of familiarity and relationship. Besides websites where samples of music can be tested out with audiences, artists can ask for feedback and create a dialogue through YouTube, Facebook, Twitter, and other social media. The Internet has democratized the industry by allowing any artist to develop a relationship with audiences online. Bypassing the traditional barriers to entry has meant many artists have been discovered who perhaps might have followed a different path to success if the Internet were not available to them.

Aubrey Drake Graham is better known to his fans by his stage name—Drake. The Toronto native was a child actor on the television series *Degrassi: The Next Generation,* but he always loved music. He released a mixtape that eventually found its way into rap-star Lil Wayne's hands, who became Drake's mentor. Drake signed with Lil Wayne's record label, Young Money Entertainment, in 2009, but it was his 2004 YouTube postings that provided him with a tool to develop his music career. By the age of 25 he had made over $25 million as a rapper—far more than the $40,000 annual salary he earned starring on *Degrassi*! Like many in his industry, Drake regularly uses social media to connect with fans and keep them up to date on his career.

Similarly, Justin Bieber, whose public image some might think of as "good boy turned bad boy turning good boy again," has made good use of the Internet as a means to interact with his fans. Love him or hate him, no one can deny that his rise to fame was meteoric. In 2007 he had a modest fan base who watched him on YouTube. Eventually these "Mom-produced" videos came to the attention of talent agent Scooter Braun, who became Bieber's agent and introduced him to the many industry insiders who would make his dream of a music career a reality.

It is an understatement to say that YouTube and social media led to Bieber's discovery and career development. Social media have made it easier for talented young artists such as Bieber and Drake to get recognized and have their chance at stardom. Agents like Scooter Braun use the Internet regularly to search for new talent. Online popularity and an online fan base can be early signs of likely success.

The Internet also plays a major role in linking the various players in the music industry. A close connection with fans is made easier by posting personal comments, articles, interviews, television shows, music videos, and other content. Such posts help to build "buzz," which is critical to drawing the attention of agents like Scooter Braun.

The Internet has become a showplace for musical entertainment and a disruptor of the old ways of doing business. As a result, the Internet has dramatically drawn advertising dollars away from traditional media such as radio, television, and magazines. These traditional media depend on large audiences to justify their high advertising costs. Social media sites succeed by providing content to much smaller niche markets. For example, when viewers want to see Drake or Justin Bieber perform, they can log on to their dedicated YouTube channels, which are also available on mobile devices. And, unlike television or radio, YouTube allows customers to not only listen to songs but also purchase the songs through sites such as Apple's iTunes store or subscribe to Apple Music.

Today, the Internet delivers samples of an artist's work to fans. It also delivers related content to help develop a relationship with fans and provides a direct channel for customers to purchase products. The Internet's promotional power speaks to the new world of music and entertainment today.[1]

CHAPTER 1 OVERVIEW

Business is the nation's engine for growth. A growing economy is an economy that produces more goods and services but uses fewer resources over time. Growing economies are important because they yield more income for business owners, their employees, and shareholders. A country depends on the wealth its businesses generate, from large enterprises like BlackBerry to startups like Justin Bieber, and from venerable firms like Bell Canada Enterprises to powerhouses like the Royal Bank of Canada. These companies and many others share a creative approach to meeting society's needs and wants while generating the wealth we enjoy.

Businesses solve our transportation problems by marketing cars, tires, gasoline, and airline tickets. They bring food to our tables by growing, harvesting, processing, packaging, and shipping everything from spring water to cake mix and frozen shrimp. Restaurants buy, prepare, and serve food, and some even deliver. Construction companies build our schools, homes, and hospitals, while real estate firms bring property buyers and sellers together. Clothing manufacturers design, create, import, and deliver our jeans, sports shoes, work uniforms, and party wear. Hundreds of firms work at entertaining us during our leisure hours. They create, produce, and distribute films, television shows, video games, books, and music downloads.

To succeed, business firms must know what their customers want, and they must supply it quickly and efficiently. The products that firms produce often reflect changes in consumer tastes, such as the growing preference for sports drinks and vitamin-fortified water. But firms can also *lead* by promoting technology and other changes. Firms have the resources, the know-how, and the financial incentive to bring about real innovations, such as smartphones, new cancer treatments, and alternative energy sources like wind power. Thus, when businesses succeed, everybody wins.

You'll see throughout this book that businesses require physical inputs such as auto parts, chemicals, sugar, thread, and electricity. They also need the accumulated knowledge and experience of their managers and employees. Businesses also rely heavily on their own ability to change with the times and with the marketplace. Flexibility is a key to long-term success—and to growth.

Business is a leading force in our economy—and *Contemporary Business* is right there with it. This book explores the strategies that allow companies to grow and compete in today's interactive marketplace. This book also explores the skills you will need to turn ideas into action for your own success in business. This chapter sets the stage for the entire text by defining what business is and describing its role in society. The chapter's discussion illustrates how the private enterprise system encourages competition and innovation while preserving business ethics.

WHAT IS BUSINESS?

LO 1.1 Distinguish between business and not-for-profit organizations.

What do you think of when you hear the word *business*? Do you think of big corporations like Rogers Communications or TD Bank? Or do you think about your local bakery or shoe store? Maybe you recall your first summer job. *Business* is a broad, all-inclusive term that can be applied to many kinds of enterprises. Businesses provide most of our employment opportunities and most of the products that we enjoy every day.

Business consists of all profit-seeking activities and enterprises that provide goods and services necessary to an economic system. Some businesses produce tangible goods, such as automobiles, breakfast cereals, and digital music players; others provide services, such as insurance, hair styling, and entertainment, ranging from theme parks and sports events to concerts.

Business drives the economic pulse of a nation. It provides the means for improving a nation's standard of living. At the heart of every business is an exchange between a buyer and a seller. A buyer has a need for a good or service and trades money with a seller to receive that product or service. The seller hopes to gain a profit—a main indicator of business success and what continuously improves society's standard of living.

Profits are rewards for businesspeople who take the risks involved in blending people, technology, and information to create and market want-satisfying goods and services. In contrast,

---

business all profit-seeking activities and enterprises that provide goods and services necessary to an economic system.

profits rewards for businesspeople who take the risks involved in offering goods and services to customers.

accountants only think of profits as the difference between a firm's revenues and the expenses it incurs in generating these revenues. More generally, however, profits serve as incentives for people to start companies, expand them, and provide consistently high-quality competitive goods and services. Profits are also a primary source of funds needed to expand operations.

The quest for profits is a central focus of business: without profits, a company could not survive or grow. But businesspeople also recognize their social and ethical responsibilities. To succeed in the long run, companies must deal responsibly with employees, customers, suppliers, competitors, government, and the general public.

Not-for-Profit Organizations

What is a common feature of Simon Fraser University's athletic department, the Canadian Society for the Prevention of Cruelty to Animals, the Canadian Red Cross, and your local library? They are all **not-for-profit organizations**, business-like establishments that have primary goals other than returning profits to their owners. These organizations play important roles in society by placing public service above profits. It is important to understand that these organizations need to raise money to operate and to achieve their social goals. Not-for-profit organizations operate in both the private and public sectors. Private sector not-for-profits include museums, libraries, trade associations, and charitable and religious organizations. Government agencies, political parties, and labour unions are not-for-profit organizations that are part of the public sector.

A business survives because of the exchange between buyer and seller. In this hair salon, the exchange occurs between the customer and the stylist.

not-for-profit organizations organizations whose primary aims are public service, not returning a profit to their owners.

Not-for-profit organizations form a large part of the Canadian economy. The not-for-profit field is an industry just like any other industry: Revenues are raised and employees earn incomes by providing services. Canada has more than 160,000 registered not-for-profit organizations in categories ranging from arts and culture to science and technology. Most are local organizations that provide sports and recreational activities. Not-for-profits receive funding from both government sources and private sources, including donations. These organizations are commonly exempt from federal, provincial, and local taxes. Not-for-profits raise more than $112 billion in revenues each year and employ more than 2 million people. Approximately one-third of these jobs are in hospitals, universities, and colleges. About half of all revenue comes from government grants, mostly provincial. These organizations also receive more than $8 billion in donations from individuals and require more than 2 billion volunteer hours, the equivalent of more than 1 million full-time jobs.[2]

Managers of not-for-profit organizations focus on goals other than making profits, but they face many of the same challenges as executives of for-profit businesses. Without funding, organizations cannot do research, obtain raw materials, or provide services. Toronto's Hospital for Sick Children (SickKids) is one of the world's top healthcare institutions for children. It is Canada's leading centre dedicated to children's health and succeeds by uniting patient care, research, and education. SickKids was founded in 1875 and is affiliated with the University of Toronto. It is one of Canada's most research-intensive hospitals: Its more than 600 staff researchers operate within a $140 million budget.[3]

Other not-for-profits organize their resources to respond to emergencies. For example, the Red Cross and Doctors Without Borders (also known as Médecins Sans Frontières, or MSF) acted quickly when the earthquake in Nepal in 2015 left hundreds of thousands of people homeless. Relief agencies around the world worked hard to supply enough tents and tarpaulins for immediate shelter. These agencies then turned their attention to constructing more permanent living spaces.[4]

Some not-for-profits sell merchandise or set up profit-making side businesses to sell goods and services that people are willing and able to pay for. For example, college bookstores sell products with the school logo—everything from sweatshirts to coffee mugs. SickKids supports learning for families and healthcare providers by selling parenting books, many of which are Canadian

The Red Cross organizes its efforts to respond to natural disasters around the world, such as setting up medical clinics in the aftermath of the earthquake in Nepal.

✓ ASSESSMENT CHECK

1.1.1 What activity lies at the heart of every business endeavour?

1.1.2 What are the primary objectives of a not-for-profit organization?

bestsellers.[5] The Livestrong Foundation, formerly the Lance Armstrong Foundation, has sold more than 40 million yellow Livestrong wristbands. It also sells sports gear and accessories for men, women, and children. All funds raised through these sales are used to fight cancer and support patients and their families.[6]

Merchandising programs and fundraising campaigns need managers who have effective business skills and experience. As a result, many of the concepts discussed in this book apply both to not-for-profit organizations and to for-profit firms.

LO 1.2 Identify and describe the factors of production.

FACTORS OF PRODUCTION

An economic system requires certain inputs for successful operation. Economists use the term **factors of production** to refer to the four basic inputs: natural resources, capital, human resources, and entrepreneurship. **Table 1.1** identifies each of these inputs and gives examples of the types of payment received by firms and individuals who supply them.

Natural resources include all production inputs that are useful in their natural states. Examples are agricultural land, building sites, forests, water, and mineral deposits. Calgary-based Encana Corporation is a leading Canadian developer of natural gas supply in North America. Toronto-based Barrick Gold Corporation is the global gold industry leader. Its 25 operating mines

factors of production four basic inputs for effective economic operation: natural resources, capital, human resources, and entrepreneurship.

natural resources all production inputs that are useful in their natural states, including agricultural land, building sites, forests, and mineral deposits.

Table 1.1 Factors of Production and Their Factor Payments

FACTOR OF PRODUCTION	CORRESPONDING FACTOR PAYMENT
Natural resources	Rent for land leased for operations
Capital	Interest for money used to acquire capital items
Human resources	Wages for employees
Entrepreneurship	Profit for starting and managing operations

and projects are located on five continents and include African Barrick Gold. Mining companies generally pay landowners for the right to extract minerals. Farmers expand their operations by paying rent for the right to grow more crops on a neighbour's land. Natural resources are the basic inputs required in any economic system and are the genesis of wealth creation. Places in the world with valuable natural resources have an economic advantage in developing more wealth, whereas those without natural resources will have to acquire them.

Capital, another key resource, includes technology, tools, information, and physical facilities. *Technology* refers to such machinery and equipment as computers and software, telecommunications, and inventions designed to improve production. Information, which is frequently improved by technological innovations, is another critical factor. Both managers and employees require accurate, timely information to effectively perform their assigned tasks. Technology plays an important role in the success of many businesses. Technology can lead to a new product, such as hybrid cars that run on a combination of gasoline and electricity. In recent years, most major car companies have introduced hybrid versions of their bestselling models.

Technology often helps a company improve its own products. Netflix, once famous for its subscription-based DVD-by-mail service, now offers on-demand Internet streaming media and original content streaming over their TV service. Netflix has exclusive rights to streaming movies and original TV shows like *Orange Is the New Black* and pays for the rights to distribute content produced by others to its subscribers. Like YouTube, Netflix is a company disrupting the old business method of distributing digital entertainment.[7]

Technology can also help a company operate more smoothly by tracking deliveries, providing more efficient communication, analyzing data, or training employees. Canada Post cut costs by expanding the electronic side of its business. Customers can now track their own registered mail online.

To remain competitive, a firm needs to continually acquire, maintain, and upgrade its capital. All these activities need money. A company's funds may come from the owner's investments, profits that are turned back into the business, or loans from others. Money is used to build factories; purchase raw materials and component parts; and to hire, train, and pay employees. People and firms that supply (lend) capital receive factor payments in the form of interest.

Human resources represent another important input in every economic system. Human resources include anyone who works, from the chief executive officer (CEO) of a huge corporation to a self-employed editor. Their input includes both physical labour and intellectual effort. Companies rely on their employees' ideas, innovation, and physical effort. Some companies ask for employee ideas through traditional means, such as through staff meetings and by setting up an online "suggestion box." Others encourage creative thinking during company-sponsored events, such as hiking or rafting trips, or during social gatherings. Effective, well-trained human resources can provide firms with a significant competitive edge. Competitors cannot easily match another company's talented, motivated employees in the same way they can buy the same computer system or purchase the same grade of natural resources.

Hiring and keeping the right people matters. Competent, effective human resources can be a company's best asset. Providing perks to those employees to keep them is often in a company's best interest.

Entrepreneurship is the willingness to take risks to create and operate a business. An entrepreneur is someone who sees an opportunity to make a profit and creates a plan to earn those profits and achieve success. Montreal-based Beyond the Rack is a private online shopping club for women and men. Authentic designer merchandise is offered at deeply discounted sale prices to members through limited-time events. Each event starts at a specific time and typically lasts only 48 hours. After each event ends, the merchandise is no longer available. Members are notified by email in advance of each event that matches their preferences. Beyond the Rack's customer base has grown to more than 2.5 million members, and it is recognized as an industry leader in the emerging field of online marketing.[8]

Canadian businesses operate within an economic system called the *private enterprise system*. The next section looks at the private enterprise system, including competition, private property, and the entrepreneurship alternative.

capital production inputs consisting of technology, tools, information, and physical facilities.

human resources production inputs consisting of anyone who works, including both the physical labour and the intellectual inputs contributed by workers.

entrepreneurship the willingness to take risks to create and operate a business.

ASSESSMENT CHECK

1.2.1 Identify the four basic inputs to an economic system.

1.2.2 List four types of capital.

LO 1.3 Describe the private enterprise system.

THE PRIVATE ENTERPRISE SYSTEM

No business operates completely freely and on its own. All businesses operate within a larger economic system of rules and constraints that directs how goods and services are produced, distributed, and consumed. The type of economic system used in a society also affects the patterns of resource use. Some economic systems enforce strict controls on business ownership, profits, and resources whereas others, like Canada's, offer more freedoms to individuals.

In Canada, businesses function within the **private enterprise system**, an economic system that rewards firms for their ability to identify and serve the needs and demands of customers. The private enterprise system minimizes government interference in business activity. Businesses that are skillful at satisfying customers are able to gain access to the necessary factors of production and earn profits. Success primarily depends on the businesspeople involved.

Another name for the private enterprise system is **capitalism**. Adam Smith, often called the father of capitalism, first described the concept of capitalism in his book *The Wealth of Nations*, published in 1776. Smith believed that an economy is best regulated by the "invisible hand" of **competition**, which is the battle among businesses for consumer acceptance. Smith thought that competition among firms would lead to consumers receiving the best possible products and prices because less efficient producers would gradually be driven from the marketplace.

The idea of the "invisible hand" is a basic principle of the private enterprise system. In Canada, competition shapes much of economic life. To compete successfully, each firm must find a basis for its **competitive differentiation**, the unique combination of organizational abilities, products, and approaches that sets one company apart from its competitors in the minds of customers. Businesses in a private enterprise system must keep up with changing marketplace conditions. Firms that fail to adjust to shifts in consumer preferences and firms that ignore their competitors risk failure. Live Nation Entertainment connects millions of concert-goers with their favourite artists at venues worldwide; see the "Hit & Miss" feature for keys to the company's success.

Our discussion in this book focuses on the tools and methods that twenty-first-century businesses apply to compete and differentiate their goods and services. We also discuss many of the ways that market changes will affect business and the private enterprise system in the future.

private enterprise system an economic system that rewards firms for their ability to identify and serve the needs and demands of customers.

capitalism an economic system that rewards firms for their ability to perceive and serve the needs and demands of consumers; also called the private enterprise system.

competition the battle among businesses for consumer acceptance.

competitive differentiation the unique combination of organizational abilities, products, and approaches that sets one company apart from its competitors in the minds of customers.

Basic Rights in the Private Enterprise System

For capitalism to operate effectively, the citizens of a private enterprise economy must have certain rights. As shown in **Figure 1.1**, these include the rights to private property, profits, freedom of choice, and competition.

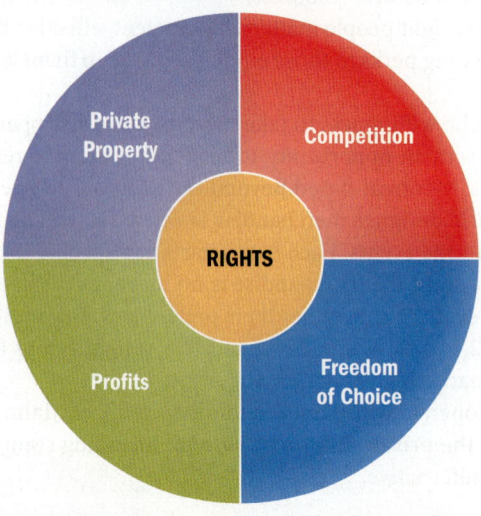

FIGURE 1.1 Basic Rights within a Private Enterprise System

HIT & MISS

Live Nation Connects Superstar Artists and Fans

Chances are, the last concert you attended may have been produced by Live Nation Entertainment of Beverly Hills, California. Michael Rapino, a Canadian-born music mogul, has guided the firm since he became CEO and president in 2005 and is credited with its rapid growth and diversification of services. The largest producer of live music concerts worldwide, Live Nation sells millions of tickets each year for events that range from folk to electronic dance music and that feature entertainers from new artists to music legends. A few years ago, Live Nation merged with ticket-selling giant Ticketmaster Entertainment to create Live Nation Entertainment.

Over 250 million fans access various entertainment platforms each year, attending more than 180,000 events in 47 countries. While more than 65 percent of the company's revenues come from its concert segment, other distinct business units include venue operations, ticketing services, and artist management and services. In an interview, Michael Rapino talked about the 2015 deal Live Nation made with Vice to "launch a full 24-hour, live, choice music channel with original programming and ongoing concerts. We think it's going to find a sweet spot with consumers who are looking for some high-quality, editorial original program and access to that magical live moment."

If you've ever thought about a career as a concert promoter, consider the "accidental trajectory" of then–college student Jodi Goodman. After urging a failing jazz club owner in Boston to allow her to book a few rock music events, Goodman not only turned the club around, but word soon got out about her knack for managing both artists and fans. It was not long before other venues sought her talent, and her career took her to San Francisco. Jodi Goodman is now president of Live Nation Entertainment for Northern California. With skill and market expertise, Goodman continues to bring artists and fans together in one of the top music markets in the country.

Concert revenues continue to rise and the future looks bright. Some of this success can be attributed to the Boston college kid who read the local music market by bringing some good old rock 'n' roll to a jazz club on the brink of closure, and creative thinkers like Michael Rapino.

Questions for Critical Thinking

1. Ticketmaster, now part of Live Nation Entertainment, responded to the threat of the secondary ticket resale market (by firms like Craigslist and StubHub) by launching its own ticket marketplace. How will Ticketmaster's marketplace impact secondary market competitors?

2. Live Nation anticipates double-digit growth in the number of concert-goers worldwide over the next several years. What factors could contribute to such a healthy increase in attendance?

Sources: Katie Richards, "Live Nation CEO Michael Rapino Discusses Why Rock Stars Are the Greatest Marketers in the World," *Adweek*, March 18, 2015, accessed March 20, 2015, www.adweek.com/news/advertising-branding/live-nation-ceo-michael-rapino-discusses-why-rock-stars-are-best-marketers-world-163430; Tim Adams, "Shane Smith: 'I Want to Build the Next CNN with Vice—It's within My Grasp,'" *The Guardian*, March 24, 2013, accessed Marc 20, 2015, www.theguardian.com/media/2013/mar/23/shane-smith-vice-interview;; Live Nation, 2013 *Annual Report*, accessed January 9, 2014, http://livenation.com; "Live Nation's New Groove: Electronic Dance Music and Scalped Tickets," *Bloomberg Businessweek*, August 9, 2013, accessed January 9, 2014, www.bloomberg.com/bw/articles/2013-08-09/live-nation-jumps-on-electronic-dance-music-scalped-tickets; Glenn Peoples, "Live Nation Revenue Hits a Record $2.26 Billion in Third Quarter," *Billboard Biz*, November 5, 2013, accessed January 9, 2014, www.billboard.com/biz/articles/news/touring/5778225/live-nation-revenue-hits-a-record-226-billion-in-third-quarter; Christine Ryan, "Hot 20: The Music Woman, Jodi Goodman," *7x7 Magazine*, October 14, 2013, accessed January 9, 2014, www.7x7.com/music-nightlife/hot-20-music-woman-jodi-goodman; Ina Fried, "Live Nation Aims to Unify Ticketmaster, Ticket Resale Businesses," *All Things Digital*, February 12, 2013, accessed January 9, 2014, http://allthingsd.com/20130212/live-nation-aims-to-unify-ticketmaster-ticket-resale-businesses.

The right to **private property** is the most basic freedom in the private enterprise system. Every participant has the right to own, use, buy, sell, and hand down most forms of property, including land, buildings, machinery, equipment, patents on inventions, individual possessions, and intangible properties.

The private enterprise system also guarantees business owners the right to all after-tax profits they earn through their activities. Although a business is not assured of earning a profit, its owner is legally and ethically entitled to any income it makes that is greater than its costs.

Freedom of choice means that a private enterprise system relies on citizens to choose their own employment, purchases, and investments. They can change jobs, discuss and agree on wages, join labour unions, and choose among many different brands of goods and services. People living in the capitalist nations of North America, Europe, and other parts of the world are so conditioned to having this freedom of choice that they sometimes forget how important it is. A private enterprise economy maximizes individual wealth by providing options. Other economic systems

private property the most basic freedom under the private enterprise system; the right to own, use, buy, sell, and hand down land, buildings, machinery, equipment, patents, individual possessions, and various intangible kinds of property.

sometimes limit the freedom of choice to accomplish government goals, such as by increasing industrial production of certain items or by military strength.

The private enterprise system also allows fair competition by allowing the public to set the rules for competitive activity. For this reason, the Canadian government has passed laws to prohibit excessively aggressive competitive practices designed to remove the competition. The Canadian government has established ground rules that make the following illegal: price discrimination, fraud in financial markets, and deceptive advertising and packaging. For example, in recent years, the Canadian Radio-television and Telecommunications Commission (CRTC) issued a decision that increased the costs charged to small Internet service providers (ISPs) that buy access to the larger ISP networks of Bell and Bell Aliant, mainly in Ontario and Quebec. The CRTC allowed the larger ISPs to control network traffic, especially high-volume traffic, to the smaller ISPs. The CRTC also began charging "usage-based billing." The smaller ISPs, who sold popular unlimited packages before, were forced to introduce limits, charge more for bandwidth, and change their infrastructure strategy. These changes ended their competitive advantage over the bigger ISPs, which typically charge more for high-volume users. After much complaining from the smaller ISP customers, a compromise pricing model was introduced. The new pricing model limits usage but still allows the smaller ISPs to offer unlimited usage packages to those customers that demanded them.[9]

The Entrepreneurship Alternative

entrepreneur a person who seeks a profitable opportunity and takes the necessary risks to set up and operate a business.

The entrepreneurial spirit beats at the heart of private enterprise. An **entrepreneur** is a risk taker in the private enterprise system. You hear about entrepreneurs all the time—two college students starting a software business in their dorm room, or a mom who invents a better baby carrier. Many times their success is modest, but once in a while the risk pays off in huge profits, as it did for Justin Bieber. People who can see marketplace opportunities are able to use their capital, time, and talents to pursue those opportunities for profit. The willingness of people to start new ventures leads to economic growth and keeps pressure on existing companies to continue to satisfy customers. If no one were willing to take economic risks, the private enterprise system wouldn't exist.

The entrepreneurial spirit leads to growth in the Canadian economy. Of all new businesses created in Canada, 99 percent are small businesses. Thousands of new businesses start each year. The Canadian economy depends on small businesses for their growth and strength. Statistics Canada data suggest that 5 percent of all businesses employ fewer than five employees, and 95 percent employ fewer than 50. The small-business sector creates 80 percent of all new jobs and generates 45 percent of Canada's economic output. Thus, Canada's small businesses are the majority of all Canadian businesses.[10]

So where are the jobs in Canada? **Figure 1.2** shows that the most employment is in the retail trade, followed by accommodation and food services. Notice that small businesses are major employers in these and other segments.[11]

Entrepreneurship creates jobs and sells products. Entrepreneurship also leads to innovation. In contrast to more established firms, startup companies tend to innovate in fields of technology that are new and have few competitors. Because small companies are more flexible than large companies, they can change their products and processes more quickly than larger corporations. Entrepreneurs often find new ways to use natural resources, technology, and other factors of production. Often they find these new ways because they have to—they may not have enough money to build an expensive prototype or launch a nationwide ad campaign. Sometimes, an entrepreneur may innovate by simply tweaking an existing idea or technology. For example, Quebec-based ExoPC introduced the Ciara Vibe tablet to the North American market after selling earlier versions in Europe and Asia. Software engineer Jean-Baptiste Martinoli adapted Microsoft's Windows 7 operating system to make it able to function with a touch screen and perform like a PC or tablet. By making the screen larger and adding some additional features, he created another competitor for Apple's iPad. By collaborating with Microsoft, this small business created a niche for itself in a global marketplace.[12]

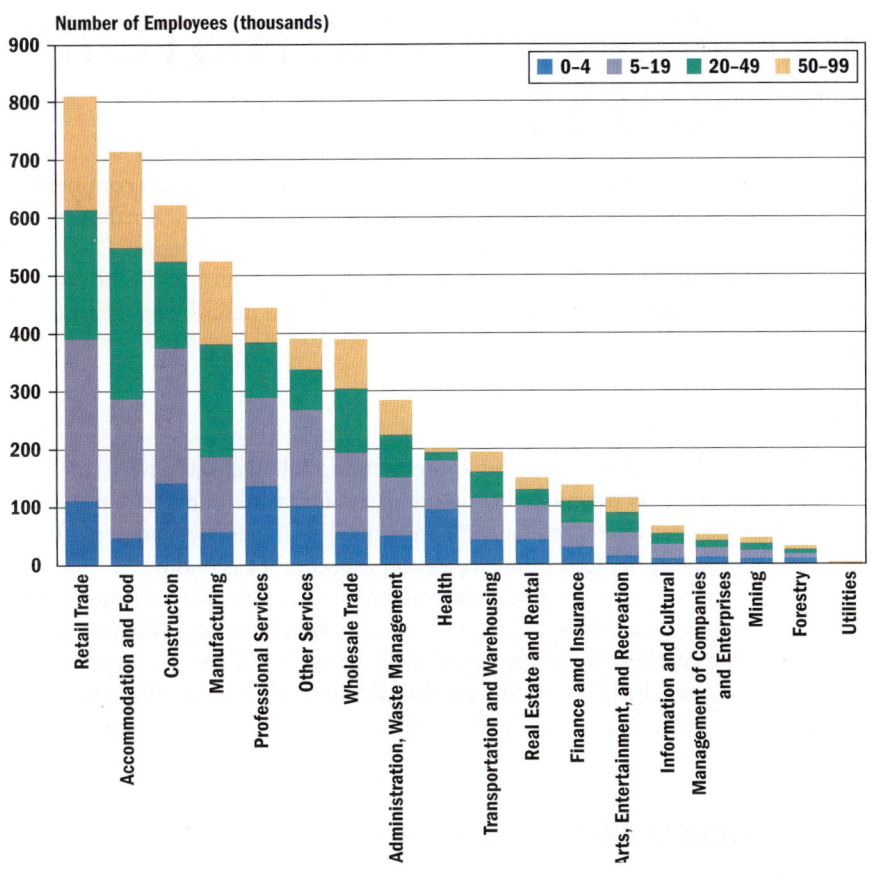

FIGURE 1.2 Number of Private Sector Employees by Industry and Size of Business Enterprise, 2011

Source: From Industry Canada, "Key Small Business Statistics, July 2012," Figure 7, p. 20. Statistics Canada, *Survey of Employment, Payrolls and Hours* (SEPH), April 2012, and calculations by Industry Canada. Industry data are classified in accordance with the North American Industry Classification System (NAICS). Reprinted with the permission of the Minister of Industry, 2015.

ASSESSMENT CHECK

1.3.1 What is an alternative term for the private enterprise system?

1.3.2 What is the most basic freedom under the private enterprise system?

1.3.3 What is an entrepreneur?

Entrepreneurship is also important to existing companies. More and more, large firms are realizing the value of entrepreneurial thinking among their employees. These companies hope to benefit from enhanced flexibility, improved innovation, and new market opportunities. Apple also reaches out to its customers by inviting entrepreneurs of all kinds to develop applications for the iPhone. If the new apps are successful, then Apple profits from those efforts. Already, the iPhone has more than a million different applications, including some developed by Apple. Together, all the apps have been downloaded billions of times.[13] Introduction of the Apple Watch and other wearable technologies is expected to generate a new wave of opportunities for app developers.

As the next section explains, entrepreneurs have played a vital role in the history of Canadian business. They have helped create new industries, developed successful new business methods, and improved Canadian standing in global competition.

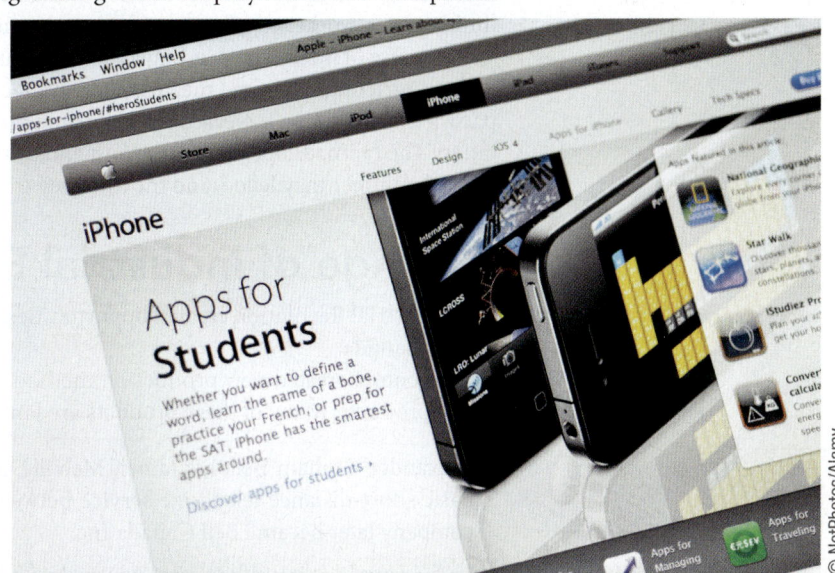

Apple invites entrepreneurs of all kinds to develop applications for the iPhone. If the new apps are successful, then Apple profits from those efforts.

LO 1.4 Identify the seven eras in the history of business.

SEVEN ERAS IN THE HISTORY OF BUSINESS

In the 400 or so years since the first Europeans settled on the North American continent, amazing changes have occurred in the size, focus, and goals of Canadian businesses. North American business history is divided into seven distinct time periods: (1) the colonial period, (2) the Industrial Revolution, (3) the age of industrial entrepreneurs, (4) the production era, (5) the marketing era, (6) the relationship era, and (7) the social era. The next sections describe how events in each of these time periods have influenced business practices.

The Colonial Period

Colonial society featured rural and agricultural production. Colonial towns were small compared with European cities, and they functioned as marketplaces for farmers and craftspeople. The economic focus of North America centred on rural areas because success depended on the output of farms. The success or failure of crops influenced every aspect of the economy.

Colonists depended on Europe for manufactured items and for financial help for their infant industries. Surprising to some, even after the American Revolutionary War (1775–1783), the United States maintained close economic ties with England. The Canadian experience is more understandable. In Canada, British investors continued to provide much of the money needed for developing the North American business system. This financial influence continued well into the nineteenth century.

The Industrial Revolution

The Industrial Revolution began in England around 1750. It changed how businesses operated. Instead of a focus on independent, skilled workers who specialized in building products one by one, businesses moved to a factory system that mass produced items by using numerous semi-skilled workers. The factories made profit from the savings created by large-scale production and by increasing their use of machines. As businesses grew, they could often purchase raw materials more cheaply in larger lots. Production was also improved by specialization of labour, such as by limiting each worker to a few specific tasks in the production process.

Because of these events in England, Canadian businesses also began a time of rapid industrialization. Agriculture became mechanized, and factories set up in cities. During the mid-1800s, the pace of the revolution increased as newly built railroad systems provided fast, economical transportation. The railroads opened up the West and transported people and the agricultural products they grew, the timber they felled, and the furs they trapped to markets back east and on to Europe.

The Age of Industrial Entrepreneurs

The Industrial Revolution created opportunities, and those opportunities increased entrepreneurship in Canada.

Inventors created new production methods and a virtually endless number of commercially useful products. Many of these products are famous today:

- Alexander Graham Bell, his father, Melville, and friend Reverend Thomas Henderson started basic short-distance telephone service between office buildings and warehouses in 1877. The company later became Bell Canada Inc.
- In the United States, Eli Whitney introduced the idea of interchangeable parts, which later led the way to mass production on a previously impossible scale.

The entrepreneurial spirit of this golden age in business advanced the Canadian business system and increased the overall standard of living for Canadians. That market transformation, in turn, created new demand for manufactured goods.

The Production Era

Demand for manufactured goods continued to increase in the 1920s. Businesses focused even more attention on the activities needed to produce those goods. Work became more specialized, and huge, labour-intensive factories were common in North America. Henry Ford started using assembly lines, which later became commonplace in major industries. Business owners turned over their responsibilities to a new group of managers who had been trained in operating companies. These new managers were able to produce even more goods by using quicker methods.

During the production era, business focused their attention on internal processes instead of external influences. Marketing was rare and was used only to distribute a business's products. Little attention was paid to what the consumer wanted or needed. Instead, businesses decided what products were available to purchase. If you wanted to buy a Ford Model T automobile, your colour choice was black—the only colour the company made.

The Marketing Era

The Great Depression of the early 1930s changed Canadian businesses yet again. When most people's incomes dropped, businesses could no longer count on selling everything they produced. Managers began to pay more attention to the markets for their goods and services, and sales and advertising became important activities. During this period, selling often meant the same as marketing.

After World War II, demand increased for all kinds of consumer goods. After nearly five years without new automobiles, appliances, and other items, consumers were buying again. At the same time, competition was also increasing. Businesses soon began to think of marketing as more than just selling; managers thought about a process of deciding what consumers wanted and needed first, and then designing products to meet those needs. In short, they developed a **consumer orientation**.

Businesses began to analyze consumer desires before beginning any production. Consumer choices skyrocketed. Automobiles were sold in a wide variety of colours and styles, and car buyers could choose their favourite colour. Companies also learned how important it was for their goods and services to stand out from those of competitors. **Branding** is the process of creating in consumer's minds an identity for a good, service, or company. Branding is an important marketing tool in contemporary business. A **brand** can be a name, term, sign, symbol, design, or some combination that identifies the products of one firm and shows how they differ from competitors' offerings.

The Home Depot, the world's largest home improvement specialty retailer, operates more than 2,200 retail stores in the United States, Canada, Mexico, and China. It also exports products around the world. Its carefully guarded brand name stands for excellent customer service, an entrepreneurial spirit, and the desire to give back to the communities where it operates. The company sells thousands of products, including RIDGID tools, Behr paint, LG appliances, and Toro lawn equipment, as well as many of its own sub-brands.[14]

Alexander Graham Bell opening a long distance phone line from New York to Chicago in 1892. In 1877, Alexander Graham Bell assigned 75 percent of the Canadian telephone patents rights to his father, Melville Bell. He and his friend Reverend Thomas Henderson then began leasing out pairs of wooden hand telephones for use on private lines. These lines were constructed by their clients between close locations, such as between a store and warehouse.

consumer orientation a business philosophy that focuses first on consumers' unmet wants and needs, and then designs products to meet those needs.

branding the process of creating in consumers' minds an identity for a good, service, or company; a major marketing tool in contemporary business.

brand a name, term, sign, symbol, design, or some combination that identifies the products of one firm and shows how they differ from competitors' offerings.

The marketing era has had a huge impact on the way business is conducted today. Even the smallest business owners recognize the importance of understanding what customers want and the reasons they buy.

The Relationship Era

In the twenty-first century, a major change is taking place in the ways companies relate with their customers. Since the Industrial Revolution, most businesses have concentrated on building and promoting products in the hope that enough customers will buy the products to cover costs and earn acceptable profits. This approach is called **transaction management**.

In contrast, in the **relationship era** businesses are taking a different, longer-term approach to how they relate with customers. Firms now look for ways to actively promote customer loyalty by carefully managing every interaction. These firms earn huge paybacks for their efforts. A company that keeps its customers over the long term reduces its advertising and sales costs. Because customer spending tends to increase over time, the firm's revenues also grow. Companies with long-term customers often find they no longer need to offer price discounts to attract new business. Instead, they find that many new customers are referred by their loyal customers.

Business owners gain several advantages when they develop ongoing relationships with customers. Serving existing customers is less costly than trying to attract new customers. Thus, businesses that develop long-term customer relationships can reduce their overall costs. Long-term relationships with customers mean that businesses can improve their understanding of what customers want and prefer from the company. As a result, these businesses increase their chances of holding on to real advantages through competitive differentiation.

The relationship era is an age of connections—between businesses and customers, employers and employees, technology and manufacturing, and even between separate companies. More and more, the world economy is interconnected as businesses expand beyond their national boundaries. In this new environment, techniques for managing networks of people, businesses, information, and technology are critically important to contemporary business success. As you begin your

transaction management building and promoting products in the hope that enough customers will buy them to cover costs and earn profits.

relationship era the business era where firms seek to actively promote customer loyalty by carefully managing every interaction.

CAREER KICKSTART
Social Networking

Most young people hear a lot of career advice. One reliably good tip is to build a network of personal contacts in your chosen field. Online social networks make this task especially easy—but the Internet's informality can make it tricky to network in a professional way. Here are suggestions for presenting yourself in a positive light on sites like Facebook, LinkedIn, Twitter, and others.

1. Know the purpose of the networking site you choose. Most people consider Facebook more social, while LinkedIn purposely maintains a more professional look and feel.

2. Remember that potential employers, mentors, and other professionals will check your Facebook page to learn about you, despite the site's mostly fun-oriented profile. Look objectively at what they'll see there.

3. Review and edit your posted photos to make sure they present the image of yourself you want others to see.

4. Resist the impulse to share. Keep your posts brief and neither overly detailed nor overly personal. People you hope to tap for potential job leads don't need to know what you ate for breakfast. Limit the information about your family, too.

5. To network with someone you haven't met, first find someone you have in common and ask that person to make an online introduction.

6. Contribute to the community. "Help the people around you and you help yourself," advises one author. Posting interesting information about your area of professional expertise is one way to both help the community and build relationships.

7. Avoid posting any information or opinions about your current or past employers.

8. Always remember that everything you post is as public as the newspaper's front page. Edit yourself, and check your privacy settings.

Sources: Lauren Simonds, "Business, Etiquette and Social Media," *Time*, August 13, 2013, accessed January 9, 2014, http://business.time.com/2013/08/13/business-etiquette-and-social-media; C. G. Lynch, "Facebook Etiquette: Five Dos and Don'ts," *PC World*, November 22, 2008, accessed January 9, 2014, www.pcworld.com/article/154374/facebook_etiquette.html; Susan M. Heathfield, "10 Reasons Social Media Should Rock Your World," About.com, accessed January 9, 2014, http://humanresources.about.com.

own career, you will soon see the importance of relationships, including your online presence. See the "Career Kickstart" feature for suggestions on presenting yourself in a positive way through social networking.

The Social Era

The **social era** of business can be described as a new approach to the way businesses and individuals interact, connect, communicate, share, and exchange information with each other in virtual communities and networks around the world.

The social era, based on the premise that organizations create value through connections with groups or networks of people with similar goals and interests, offers businesses immense opportunities, particularly through the use of technology and **relationship management**—the collection of activities that build and maintain ongoing, mutually beneficial ties with customers and other parties.

Social media tools and technologies come in various shapes and sizes. They include blogs, podcasts, and microblogs (such as Twitter); social and professional networks (such as Facebook and LinkedIn); picture-sharing platforms (such as Instagram and Tumblr); and content communities (such as YouTube), to name a few.[15]

As consumers continue to log fewer hours on computers and more time on mobile devices, companies have implemented mobile strategies using real-time data and location-based technology. Businesses use mobile social media applications to engage in marketing research, communications, sales promotions, loyalty programs, and other processes. In the social era, businesses tailor specific promotions to specific users in specific locations at specific times to build customer loyalty and long-term relationships. For example, Facebook offers free Wi-Fi to users in exchange for checking in at selected retailers, hotels, and restaurants.[16]

Businesses are also finding that they must form partnerships with other organizations to take full advantage of opportunities—often using social media tools and technologies for communications. One form of partnership between organizations is a **strategic alliance**, which creates a competitive advantage for the businesses involved.

Ebusiness has created a new type of strategic alliance. A firm whose entire business is conducted online, such as Amazon or Overstock.com, may team up with traditional retailers who have expertise in distribution and in buying the right amount of the right merchandise. Overstock.com is an online-only retailer for bargain hunters looking for discount prices on brand-name consumer goods, including clothing, appliances, electronics, and sporting goods. Overstock.com partners with manufacturers and distributors that gain a new outlet for reducing their inventory; in return, Overstock.com sells more than 2 million different products on its website. Overstock.com earned revenues of more than $800 million in one recent year and received several top customer service awards.[17]

Another way to build relationships is to have your business address some of the issues that your customers care about using social media. For example, environmental concerns now influence consumers' choices on everything from yogurt to clothing to cars and light bulbs; many observers say the question about "going green" is no longer whether a company should, but how. The need to develop environmentally friendly products and processes is a major new force in business today. Companies in every industry are researching how to save energy, cut emissions and pollution, reduce waste, and of course save money and increase profits. Endura Energy is an Ontario-based developer of large-scale rooftop solar energy systems. This company works with building owners to capture value from unused roof space and to promote green energy. Using the Ontario government's Feed-in Tariff Program, Endura Energy is building a 100-kilowatt rooftop solar power system in Richmond Hill, just north of Toronto. This system will generate approximately 110,000 kilowatt hours of clean energy each year, equivalent to reducing approximately 85 tonnes of carbon emissions annually. The owners of the building do not need to contribute financially, which will make it easier to develop more rooftop systems that will contribute to the electric grid. Endura uses Facebook and other social media tools to reach out to businesses and consumers interested in building greener solutions.[18]

Energy is among the biggest costs for most firms. Traditional carbon-based fuels like coal are responsible for most of the additional carbon dioxide in the atmosphere. Ford Motor Company is upgrading lighting fixtures in its manufacturing facilities. The old, inefficient equipment will be replaced with fluorescent lighting that saves energy and money. The new lighting will include

social era the business era in which firms seek ways to connect and interact with customers using technology.

relationship management the collection of activities that build and maintain ongoing, mutually beneficial ties with customers and other parties.

strategic alliance a partnership formed to create a competitive advantage for the businesses involved; in international business, the business strategy of one company partnering with another company in the country where it wants to do business.

HIT & MISS

Twitter's Dorsey: 140 Characters at a Time

At age 13, Jack Dorsey was fascinated with dispatch routing. While a student in college, he began to create software related to dispatch logistics, which is still used by taxi companies today.

Dorsey has always been interested in business. In San Francisco, he started Odeo, a podcasting company that quickly became extinct when iTunes surfaced. This setback didn't stop Dorsey from trying again, though. Twitter began as an interoffice microblogging platform created by Odeo programmers. When a small earthquake shook San Francisco, word of the quake spread quickly via Twitter—and a new company was born.

Square, Dorsey's most recent business venture, allows credit card payments to be made to individuals and businesses by attaching a small device to a smartphone or tablet.

Dorsey is guided by three principles—simplicity, constraint, and craftsmanship—which are still very much part of Twitter's culture today. Dorsey serves as Twitter's executive chair, Square's CEO, and recently joined Disney's board of directors.

Questions for Critical Thinking

1. How can businesses apply Dorsey's three guiding principles to create a strategic vision?
2. What lessons can be learned from Jack Dorsey about perseverance, technology, and starting a business?

Sources: Anthony Ha, "Dorsey Joins Disney's Board of Directors," *TechCrunch*, December 23, 2013, accessed January 12, 2014, http://techcrunch.com/2013/12/23/jack-dorsey-joins-disney; Kit Eaton, "The Twitter IPO Player's Club," *Fast Company*, accessed January 12, 2014, www.fastcompany.com/tag/ipo-players-club; Nicholas Carlson, "The Real History of Twitter," *Business Insider*, April 13, 2011, accessed January 12, 2014, www.businessinsider.com/how-twitter-was-founded-2011-4; Brandon Griggs, "Twitter's Jack Dorsey Eyes New York Mayor's Job," CNN.com, March 18, 2013, accessed January 12, 2014, www.cnn.com/2013/03/18/tech/social-media/dorsey-twitter-nyc; Noah Robischon, "Square Brings Credit Card Swiping to Mobile Masses," *Fast Company*, accessed January 12, 2014, www.fastcompany.com/1643271/square-brings-credit-card-swiping-mobile-masses-starting-today; Mitch Wagner, "Twitter CEO Jack Dorsey Talks About Its Business Model," *InformationWeek*, June 4, 2008, accessed January 12, 2014, www.informationweek.com/desktop/twitter-ceo-jack-dorsey-talks-about-its-business-model/d/d-id/1068539.

---

motion detectors to reduce energy use during periods of low activity.[19] Clean solar energy is becoming more common and may soon be easier to set up and more widely available. Endura Energy is currently developing more than 5 megawatts of projects covering more than 93,000 square metres of roof space across 20 separate sites. The Ontario government's Feed-in Tariff Program guarantees the purchase of electricity produced at set rates. Thus, we will likely see more projects built on available rooftops.[20]

Companies in every industry are researching how to save energy, cut emissions, reduce waste, and save company money. Clean solar energy is one option that is becoming more common and may soon be easier to set up and more widely available.

GOING GREEN

INTERNET BILLIONAIRE'S GOAL: HELP CHINA BREATHE EASIER

Less than two decades ago, Jack Ma founded Alibaba Group in his Hangzhou apartment. Alibaba Group includes an online payment system, Alipay, and two ecommerce sites, Tmall and Taobao. The company has been described as the Chinese version of eBay, Amazon, and PayPal combined. Its most recent sales exceed the combined sales of eBay and Amazon.

The *Financial Times* recently named Ma its Person of the Year, referring to him as the "godfather of China's scrappy entrepreneurial spirit." Ma, in his late forties, commands a cult-like following among the younger Chinese generation and is the face of China's new age of entrepreneurs.

At a speech given upon his retirement as Alibaba's CEO, Ma reminded the audience that business cannot prosper when it continues to be ruined by overdevelopment, which includes China's hazardous levels of pollution.

Alluding to China's increased economic prosperity and rising middle class, Ma points out that the dreams of the Chinese people may fade away if they cannot see the sun. He has committed 0.3 percent of Alibaba's annual profits to help preserve the environment. As a self-made Internet billionaire, Ma's next business plan involves making China's air a little easier to breathe.

Questions for Critical Thinking

1. How can Ma enlist other business owners to get involved in his environmental causes?

2. What are some of the issues that can arise in a country experiencing substantial economic prosperity among segments of its population?

Sources: Jamil Anderlini, "Person of the Year: Jack Ma," *Financial Times*, December 12, 2013, accessed January 9, 2014, www.ft.com/cms/s/2/308e46a8-6189-11e3-916e-00144feabdc0.html#axzz3ZYLESUcn; Steven Millward, "'Godfather of China's Scrappy Entrepreneurial Spirit': Alibaba's Jack Ma Is FT's Person of the Year," *Techinasia*, December 13, 2013, accessed January 9, 2014, www.techinasia.com/alibaba-founder-jack-ma-ft-person-of-year-2013; Bryan Walsh, "From Gold to Green," *Time*, June 10, 2013, accessed January 9, 2014, http://content.time.com/time/magazine/article/0,9171,2144568,00.html; William Brent, "With Jack Ma Out, Who Is the Next Global Chinese CEO?" *Forbes*, May 6, 2013, accessed January 9, 2014, www.forbes.com/sites/williambrent/2013/05/06/with-jack-ma-out-who-is-the-next-global-chinese-ceo.

Some "green" initiatives can be costly for firms. General Electric, though, has found a hit in its Ecomagination line of environmentally friendly products. For General Electric, thinking "green" satisfies not only consumers' environmental concerns but also shareholders' concerns about saving money and earning profits. "We've sold out in eco-certified products for [a year in advance]," says Bob Corcoran, the company's vice-president for corporate citizenship. The company's energy-saving wind turbines are backordered for two years. GE believes it is doing what its shareholders expect it to do. "No good business can call itself a good corporate citizen if it fritters away shareholder money," Corcoran says.[21] The "Going Green" feature provides an example of how entrepreneurial success can translate into a better environment.

In each new era in business history, managers have had to re-examine their tools and techniques. Tomorrow's managers will need creativity and vision to stay on top of rapidly changing technology and to manage complex relationships in the global business world of the fast-paced twenty-first century. As green operations become more cost effective, and as consumers and shareholders demand more responsive management, few firms will want to be left behind.

ASSESSMENT CHECK

1.4.1 What was the Industrial Revolution?

1.4.2 During which era was the idea of branding developed?

1.4.2 What is the difference between transaction management and relationship management?

TODAY'S BUSINESS WORKFORCE

LO 1.5 Explain how today's business workforce and the nature of work itself are changing.

A skilled and knowledgeable workforce is an essential resource for keeping pace with the rapid rate of change in today's business world. Employers need reliable workers who are dedicated to promoting strong ties with customers and partners. Employers need to build workforces that are capable of efficient, high-quality production, which is needed to compete in global markets. Smart business leaders also realize that the brainpower of employees plays a vital role in a firm staying on top of new technologies and innovations. In short, a first-class workforce can be the foundation of a firm's competitive differentiation, providing important advantages over competing businesses.

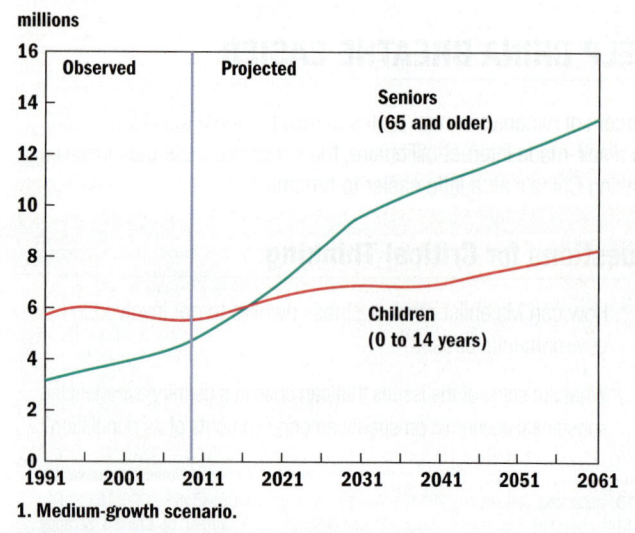

FIGURE 1.3 Population Projections, Children and Seniors

Source: Statistics Canada, CANSIM tables 051-001 and 052-005.

FIGURE 1.4 Top 10 Birthplaces of Immigrants Who Landed in Canada from 2001 to 2006

Source: Statistics Canada, 2006 Census of Population.

diversity the blending of individuals of different genders, ethnic backgrounds, cultures, religions, ages, and physical and mental abilities to enhance a firm's chances of success.

Changes in the Workforce

Companies face several trends that challenge their skills for managing and developing human resources. These challenges include the aging population and a shrinking labour pool, the growing diversity of the workforce, the changing nature of work, the need for flexibility and mobility, and the need to work with others to innovate.

The Aging Population and a Shrinking Labour Pool

As people retire from the workforce, they take their experience and expertise with them. As **Figure 1.3** shows, the Canadian population as a whole is aging. Today, though, many of those from the baby boom generation, the huge number of people born between 1946 and 1964, are still hitting the peaks of their careers. At the same time, members of so-called Generation X (born from 1965 to 1981) and Generation Y (born from 1982 to 2005) are building their careers. As a result, employers are finding more people from different generations together in the workforce than ever before. This broad age diversity brings management challenges, such as the need to accept a variety of work–life styles, the changing expectations of work, and varying levels of technological expertise. Still, despite the wide range of ages in the workforce today, some economists predict the Canadian labour pool could soon fall short as the baby boomers retire.

Technology has intensified the hiring challenge by requiring workers to have ever-more advanced skills. Although the number of college-educated workers has increased, the demand for these workers is still greater than the supply. Because of these changes, companies are increasingly seeking—and finding—talent at the extreme ends of the working-age spectrum. Teenagers are entering the workforce sooner, and some seniors are working longer—or seeking new careers after retiring from their primary careers. Many older workers work part time or flexible hours. Meanwhile, for those older employees who do retire, employers must look after a variety of retirement planning and disability programs, retraining, and insurance benefits.

Increasingly Diverse Workforce

The Canadian workforce is growing more diverse, in age and in other ways, too. Two-thirds of Canada's population growth is due to international immigration, particularly from Asia. As illustrated in **Figure 1.4**, Chinese immigration is closely followed by immigration from India and other Asian countries.

Diversity is the blending of individuals of different genders, ethnic backgrounds, cultures, religions, ages, and physical and mental abilities. Having a diverse workplace can enhance a firm's chances of success. Some firms that recently made the top 10 in a list of "Top 50 Companies for Diversity" were also leaders and innovators in their industries, including Johnson & Johnson (number one on the list), AT&T, the accounting firm Ernst & Young, Marriott International, The Coca-Cola Company, and IBM.[22] Several studies have shown that diverse employee teams and workforces tend to perform tasks more effectively. They also develop better solutions to business problems than homogeneous employee groups. This result is due in part to the varied perspectives and experiences that promote innovation and creativity in multicultural teams.

Practical managers also know that attention to diversity issues can help them avoid damaging legal battles. Losing a discrimination lawsuit can be very costly; yet, in a recent survey, a majority of executives from racial and cultural minorities said they had seen discrimination in work assignments.[23]

Outsourcing and the Changing Nature of Work

The Canadian workforce is changing, but so is the nature of work. Manufacturing once accounted for most of Canada's annual output, but most Canadian employment has now shifted to services, such as financial management and communications. Because of this change, firms must now rely on well-trained service workers who have knowledge, technical skills, the ability to communicate and deal with people, and a talent for creative thinking. The Internet offers another business tool for increasing employment flexibility. **Outsourcing** is the use of outside vendors to produce goods or fulfill services and functions that were previously handled in-house or in-country. In the best situation, outsourcing can reduce costs and allow a firm to concentrate on what it does best, while also accessing expertise it may not have. But outsourcing also creates its own challenges, such as differences in language or culture.

Offshoring is the relocation of business processes to lower-cost locations overseas. Offshoring can involve both production and services. In recent years, China has emerged as a prime location for production offshoring, whereas India has become the key player in offshoring services. Some companies are now structured so that entire divisions or functions are developed and staffed overseas—the jobs were never in Canada to start with. Another trend in some industries is **nearshoring**, outsourcing production or services to nations near a firm's home base.

outsourcing using outside vendors to produce goods or fulfill services and functions that were previously handled in-house or in-country.

offshoring the relocation of business processes to lower-cost locations overseas.

nearshoring the outsourcing of production or services to locations near a firm's home base.

Flexibility and Mobility

Younger workers are looking for an experience different from the "work comes first" lifestyle of the baby boom generation. Workers of all ages are exploring different work arrangements, such as telecommuting from remote locations and sharing jobs among two or more employees. Employers are also hiring more temporary and part-time employees, some of whom are less interested in climbing the corporate ladder and more interested in using and developing their skills. The cubicle-filled office will likely never disappear, but technology has made certain tasks easier. For example, employees can take part in productive networking and virtual teams because technology allows people to work from where they choose yet easily share knowledge, a sense of purpose or mission, and a free flow of ideas across any geographical distance or time zone.

Managers of such spread-out workforces need to work hard to build and earn the trust of their staff. Managers aim to retain valued employees and ensure that all members are acting ethically and contributing their share without the day-to-day supervision of a conventional workplace. These managers and their employees need to be flexible and sensitive to change, while work, technology, and the relationships between them continue to evolve.

Innovation through Collaboration

Some observers also see a trend toward more collaborative work in the future, as opposed to individuals working alone. Businesses that use teamwork hope to build a creative setting where all members contribute their knowledge and skills to solve problems or seize opportunities.

The old relationship between employers and employees was simple: Workers arrived at a certain hour, worked at their jobs, and went home every day at the same time. Companies rarely laid off workers, and employees rarely left for a job at another firm. But all that—and more—has changed. Employees are no longer likely to remain with a single company throughout their entire careers. Employees do not expect lifetime loyalty from the companies they work for, and they do not expect to give that loyalty to any company either. Instead, today's employees build their own careers however and wherever they can. These changes mean that many firms now recognize the value of partnering with employees to encourage creative thinking and problem solving and to reward risk taking and innovation.

✓ ASSESSMENT CHECK

1.5.1 Define *outsourcing*, *offshoring*, and *nearshoring*.

1.5.2 Describe the importance of collaboration and employee partnership.

THE TWENTY-FIRST-CENTURY MANAGER

LO 1.6 Identify the skills and attributes needed to lead businesses in the twenty-first century.

Today's companies look for managers who are intelligent, highly motivated people who can create and sustain a vision of how an organization can succeed. The twenty-first-century manager must apply critical thinking skills and creativity to business challenges and lead change.

Importance of Vision

vision the ability to perceive marketplace needs and what an organization must do to satisfy them.

To thrive in the twenty-first century, businesspeople need **vision**, the ability to perceive marketplace needs and what an organization must do to satisfy them. Canadian James Cameron is the Oscar-winning writer and director of such blockbuster sci-fi films as *The Terminator*, *Aliens*, *The Abyss*, and the most successful film of all time, *Avatar*. Cameron has an uncanny ability to know what audiences want and how to produce it. After he exceeded the budget for *Titanic*, Cameron persuaded his financial backers to continue funding the project. To show his confidence that *Titanic* would succeed, he offered to give up his fees for writing the screenplay and directing in exchange for receiving a percentage of box office sales. His financial backers recognized his motivation to complete the film, and their funding of the film proved to be a good decision. *Titanic* earned more than $25 million the first weekend of its release and went on to replace George Lucas's *Star Wars* as the biggest money-making film in history. Cameron's futuristic 3D creation *Avatar* broke through that milestone and won 11 Oscars.[24]

Film director, writer, and inventor James Cameron knows how to entertain audiences.

The Importance of Critical Thinking and Creativity

critical thinking the ability to analyze and assess information to pinpoint problems or opportunities.

Critical thinking and creativity are essential characteristics of workers in the twenty-first century. Today's businesspeople need to look at a wide variety of situations, draw connections between dissimilar information, and develop future-oriented solutions. This need applies to top executives, mid-level managers, and entry-level workers.

Critical thinking is the ability to analyze and assess information to pinpoint problems or opportunities. The critical thinking process includes activities such as determining the authenticity, accuracy, and worth of information, knowledge, and arguments. It involves looking beneath

- In a group, brainstorm by listing ideas as they come to mind. Don't criticize other people's ideas, but build on them. Wait until later to evaluate and organize the ideas.
- Think about how to make familiar concepts unfamiliar. A glue that doesn't stick very well? That's the basis for 3M's popular Post-it® notes.
- Plan ways to rearrange your thinking by asking simple questions, such as "What features can we leave out?" or by imagining what it feels like to be the customer.
- Cultivate curiosity, openness, risk, and energy as you meet people and encounter new situations. View these encounters as opportunities to learn.
- Treat failures as additional opportunities to learn.
- Get regular physical exercise. When you work out, your brain releases endorphins, and these chemicals stimulate creative thinking.
- Pay attention to your dreams and daydreams. You might find that you already know the answer to a problem.

Figure 1.5 Exercises and Guidelines to Promote Creative Thinking

the surface for deeper meaning and connections that can help identify critical issues and solutions. Without critical thinking, a firm may encounter serious problems.

Creativity is the capacity to develop novel solutions to perceived organizational problems. Most people think of creativity in terms of writers, artists, musicians, and inventors, but that definition is very limited. In business, creativity refers to being able to see better and different ways of doing business. A computer engineer who solves a glitch in a software program is performing a creative act, as is a shipping clerk who finds a way to speed up the delivery of the company's overnight packages. Sometimes a crisis calls for creative leadership. For example, Captain Chesley Sullenberger famously guided US Airways Flight 1549 to a safe landing in New York's Hudson River. In doing so, he had already made immediate and critical decisions when both his plane's engines quit after hitting birds upon takeoff. Sullenberger's quick thinking and years of training saved the lives of his passengers and crew members and the people on the ground. "Losing thrust on both engines, at low speed, at a low altitude, over one of the most densely populated areas on the planet. Yes, I knew it was a very challenging situation," he said. As the plane lost altitude, Sullenberger ruled out returning to LaGuardia Airport or attempting to land at a nearby New Jersey airport. Instead, he opted to splash down in the river, close to a ferry terminal. "I needed to touch down with the wings exactly level . . . the nose slightly up . . . [and] just above our minimum flying speed, but not below it." He accomplished those seemingly impossible feats and saved all 155 people on board.[25]

creativity the capacity to develop novel solutions to perceived organizational problems.

Some practice and mental exercise can cultivate your own ability to think creatively. See **Figure 1.5** for some exercises and guidelines to improve your creativity.

Creativity and critical thinking must do more than generate new ideas. They must lead to action. In addition to creating an environment in which employees can nurture ideas, managers must give employees opportunities to take risks and try new solutions.

Ability to Lead Change

Today's business leaders must guide their employees and organizations through the changes brought about by technology, marketplace demands, and global competition. Managers must be skilled at recognizing employee strengths and motivating people to move toward common goals as members of a team. Throughout this book, real-world examples show how companies have initiated major change initiatives. Most, if not all of these companies, have been led by managers who are comfortable with making the tough decisions that are needed in today's fluctuating conditions.

Factors that require organizational change can come from both external and internal sources; successful managers must be aware of both types of factors. External forces might include feedback from customers, developments in the international marketplace, economic trends, and new technologies. Internal factors might arise from new company goals, emerging employee needs, labour union demands, or production problems.

✓ **ASSESSMENT CHECK**

1.6.1 Why is vision an important managerial quality?

1.6.2 What is the difference between creativity and critical thinking?

LO 1.7 Outline the characteristics that make a company admired.

WHAT MAKES A COMPANY ADMIRED?

Who is your hero? Is it someone who has achieved great feats in sports, government, entertainment, or business? Why do you admire this person? Does he or she run a company, earn a lot of money, or give back to the community and society? Every year, business magazines and organizations publish lists of companies that they consider to be "most admired." Companies, like individuals, may be admired for many reasons. Some of these reasons might include solid profits,

---

SOLVING AN ETHICAL CONTROVERSY

Securities Oversight?

In Canada and the United States, the laws surrounding buying and selling securities, such as stocks and bonds, require full disclosure of information to discourage fraud. Enforcement is typically by authorities and the businesspeople who earn their living persuading investors to undertake risks with their money. This arrangement has worked well enough that extreme cases of abuse of trust are very rare. However, when they do happen they can be extreme.

A whopping $65 billion securities fraud came to light during the economic downturn that began in 2008. The investment company run by Bernard Madoff turned out to be the biggest Ponzi scheme of all time. Madoff used new investors' funds to pay off the older investors. The investment profits that Madoff claimed were only an illusion. Independent investigator Harry Markopolos told U.S. Congress he had been warning the Securities and Exchange Commission (SEC) about Madoff's activities for years. "I gift-wrapped and delivered the largest Ponzi scheme in history to them and somehow they couldn't be bothered to conduct a thorough and proper investigation because they were too busy on matters of higher priority," Markopolos testified. Thousands of individual and institutional investors faced financial ruin as Madoff's scheme evaporated.

If the SEC was not doing its job, does it bear part of the blame for investors' losses?

PRO

1. A $65 billion fraud could flourish only under a flawed regulatory system. "Our current fragmented regulatory system can allow bad actors to engage in misconduct outside the view and reach of some regulators," said an officer of the securities industry's watchdog organization. "It is undeniable that . . . the system failed to protect investors."

2. "The SEC is . . . captive to the industry it regulates, and it is afraid of bringing big cases against the largest, most powerful firms," said Markopolos. "Clearly the SEC was afraid of Mr. Madoff."

CON

1. The SEC's director of enforcement told a Senate committee, "We don't turn a blind eye to fraud. If we see it and we suspect it, we pursue it. We don't want fraudsters out there."

2. The director also said the SEC doesn't have enough resources to pursue all the tipoffs of potential fraud that come before it: "If we had more resources, we could clearly do more." Other regulators blamed lack of coordination among government agencies for the lapses in oversight that allowed Madoff to operate.

Summary

Madoff pled guilty to charges of felony securities fraud and was sentenced to 150 years in prison. The SEC is conducting an internal investigation to learn why it failed to act on the information that Markopolos and others had provided over the years.

Sources: Jenny Anderson and Zachery Kouwe, "SEC Enforcers Focus on Avoiding Madoff Repeat," *New York Times*, February 8, 2010, www.nytimes.com/2010/02/09/business/09sec.html; U.S. Securities and Exchange Commission, "The Investor's Advocate: How the SEC Protects Investors, Maintains Market Integrity, and Facilitates Capital Formation," accessed February 13, 2009, www.sec.gov/about/whatwedo.shtml; Linda Sandler, "Madoff Said Only Brother Could Do Audit, Witness Tells Congress," *Bloomberg News*, February 5, 2009, www.bloomberg.com/apps/news?pid=newsarchive&sid=aLCQkClE6JHI; Allan Chernoff, "Madoff Whistleblower Blasts SEC," CNNMoney, February 4, 2009, http://money.cnn.com/2009/02/04/news/newsmakers/madoff_whistleblower; Diana B. Henriques, "Witness on Madoff Tells of Fear for Safety," *New York Times*, February 3, 2009, www.nytimes.com/2009/02/04/business/04madoff.html; Julian Cummings, "Madoff: SEC Defends Its Role," *CNNMoney*, January 28, 2009, http://money.cnn.com/2009/01/27/news/economy/madoff_senate/?postversion=2009012809; Liz Moyer, "How Regulators Missed Madoff," *Forbes*, January 27, 2009, www.forbes.com/2009/01/27/bernard-madoff-sec-business-wall-street_0127_regulators.html.

stable growth, a safe and challenging work environment, high-quality goods and services, and business ethics and social responsibility. *Business ethics* refers to the standards of conduct and moral values involved in decisions made in the work environment. *Social responsibility* is a management philosophy that includes contributing resources to the community, preserving the natural environment, and developing or participating in not-for-profit programs designed to promote the well-being of the general public. We explore these topics more deeply in Chapter 2. You'll also find business ethics and social responsibility examples throughout this book. For businesses to behave ethically and responsibly, their employees need strong moral guidance. The "Solving an Ethical Controversy" feature debates the responsibility of watchdogs—the people and organizations that monitor companies—when they fail to perform their duties.

As you read this text, you'll be able to make up your mind about why companies should—or should not—be admired. *Fortune* publishes two lists of most-admired companies each year, one for U.S.-based firms and one for the world. The list is compiled from surveys and other research conducted by the Hay Group, a global human resources and organizational consulting firm. Criteria for making the list include innovation, people management, use of corporate assets, social responsibility, quality of management, and quality of products and services.[26] *Fortune* ranked Apple as the number-one most-admired company in 2014. Their complete "Top Ten" list can be found online.

✓ ASSESSMENT CHECK

1.7.1 Define *business ethics* and *social responsibility*.

1.7.2 Identify three criteria used to judge whether a company might be considered admirable.

WHAT'S AHEAD

As business speeds along in the twenty-first century, new technologies, population shifts, and shrinking global barriers will alter the world at a frantic pace. Businesspeople trigger many of these changes by creating new opportunities for individuals who are prepared to take action. Studying contemporary business will help you prepare for the future.

Throughout this book, you'll be exposed to the real-life stories of many businesspeople. You'll learn about a range of business careers and the daily decisions, tasks, and challenges that businesspeople face. By the end of the course, you'll understand how marketing, production, accounting, finance, and management work together to provide competitive advantages for firms. This knowledge can help you become a more capable employee and enhance your career potential.

Now that this chapter has introduced some basic terms and issues in the business world of the twenty-first century, Chapter 2 takes a detailed look at the ethical and social responsibility issues facing contemporary business. Chapter 3 deals with economic challenges, and Chapter 4 focuses on the difficulties and opportunities faced by firms competing in world markets.

RETURN TO INSIDE BUSINESS

Canadian Entertainers Are Cultivating Global Audiences Online

The Internet has changed the way many artists like Drake and Justin Bieber communicate and develop their relationships with their fan base using social media. Drake and Justin Bieber use a variety of tools such as blogs, tweets, and videos to develop and maintain their relationship with fans.

QUESTIONS FOR CRITICAL THINKING

1. How would you improve Drake's or Justin Bieber's web presence?
2. What is another type of business that could use the Internet to improve communications between participants?

SUMMARY OF LEARNING OBJECTIVES

LO 1.1 Distinguish between business and not-for-profit organizations.

Business consists of all profit-seeking activities that provide goods and services necessary to an economic system. Not-for-profit organizations are business-like establishments whose primary objectives involve social, political, governmental, educational, or similar functions instead of profits.

✓ ASSESSMENT CHECK ANSWERS

1.1.1 What activity lies at the heart of every business endeavour? At the heart of every business endeavour is an exchange between a buyer and a seller.

1.1.2 What are the primary objectives of a not-for-profit organization? Not-for-profit organizations place public service above profits, although they need to raise money to operate and achieve their social goals.

LO 1.2 Identify and describe the factors of production.

The factors of production have four basic inputs: natural resources, capital, human resources, and entrepreneurship. Natural resources include all productive inputs that are useful in their natural states. Capital includes technology, tools, information, and physical facilities. Human resources include anyone who works for the firm. Entrepreneurship is the willingness to take risks to create and operate a business.

✓ ASSESSMENT CHECK ANSWERS

1.2.1 Identify the four basic inputs to an economic system. The four basic inputs are natural resources, capital, human resources, and entrepreneurship.

1.2.2 List four types of capital. Four types of capital are technology, tools, information, and physical facilities.

LO 1.3 Describe the private enterprise system.

The private enterprise system is an economic system that rewards firms for being able to perceive and serve the needs and demands of consumers. Competition in the private enterprise system means success for firms that satisfy consumer demands. Citizens in a private enterprise economy enjoy rights to private property, profits, freedom of choice, and competition. Entrepreneurship drives economic growth.

✓ ASSESSMENT CHECK ANSWERS

1.3.1 What is an alternative term for the private enterprise system? *Capitalism* is an alternative term for private enterprise system.

1.3.2 What is the most basic freedom under the private enterprise system? The most basic freedom is the right to private property.

1.3.3 What is an entrepreneur? An entrepreneur is a risk taker who is willing to start, own, and operate a business.

LO 1.4 Identify the seven eras in the history of business.

The seven historical eras are the colonial period, the Industrial Revolution, the age of industrial entrepreneurs, the production era, the marketing era, the relationship era, and the social era. In the colonial period, businesses were small and rural, emphasizing agricultural production. The Industrial Revolution brought factories and mass production to business. The age of industrial entrepreneurs built on the Industrial Revolution through an expansion in the number and size of firms. The production era focused on the growth of factory operations through assembly lines and other efficient internal processes. During and following the Great Depression, businesses concentrated on finding markets for their products through advertising and selling, giving rise to the marketing era. In the relationship era, businesspeople focus on developing and sustaining long-term relationships with customers and other businesses. The social era of business can be described as a new approach to the way businesses and individuals interact, connect, communicate, share, and exchange information with each other in virtual communities and networks around the world. Technology promotes innovation and communication, while alliances create a competitive advantage through partnerships. Concern for the environment also helps build strong relationships with customers.

✓ ASSESSMENT CHECK ANSWERS

1.4.1 What was the Industrial Revolution? The Industrial Revolution began around 1750 in England. It moved business operations from an emphasis on independent, skilled workers to a factory system that mass-produced items.

1.4.2 During which era was the idea of branding developed? The idea of branding began in the marketing era.

1.4.3 What is the difference between transaction management and relationship management? Transaction management focuses on building, promoting, and selling enough products to cover costs and earn profits. Relationship management is the collection of activities that build and maintain ongoing ties with customers and other parties.

LO 1.5 Explain how today's business workforce and the nature of work itself are changing.

The workforce is changing in several significant ways: (1) It is aging and the labour pool is shrinking and (2) it is becoming increasingly diverse. The nature of work has shifted toward services and a focus on information. More firms now rely on outsourcing, offshoring, and nearshoring to produce goods or to fulfill services and functions that were previously handled in-house or in-country. Today's workplaces are also becoming increasingly flexible, allowing employees to work from different locations and through different relationships. Companies promote innovation through teamwork and collaboration.

✓ ASSESSMENT CHECK ANSWERS

1.5.1 Define *outsourcing*, *offshoring*, and *nearshoring*. Outsourcing involves using outside vendors to produce goods or to fulfill services and functions that were once handled in-house. Offshoring is the relocation of business processes to lower-cost locations overseas. Nearshoring is the outsourcing of production or services to nations near a firm's home base.

1.5.2 Describe the importance of collaboration and employee partnership. Businesses are increasingly focusing on collaboration, rather than on individuals working alone. No longer do employees just put in their time at a job they hold their entire career. The new employer–employee partnership encourages teamwork, creative thinking, problem solving, and innovation. Managers are trained to listen to and respect employees.

LO 1.6 Identify the skills and attributes needed to lead businesses in the twenty-first century.

Today's managers need vision, which is the ability to perceive both marketplace needs and the way their firm can satisfy those needs. Critical thinking skills and creativity allow managers to pinpoint problems and opportunities and plan novel solutions. Finally, managers are dealing with rapid change, and they need skills to help lead their organizations through shifts in external and internal conditions.

✓ ASSESSMENT CHECK ANSWERS

1.6.1 Why is vision an important managerial quality? Managerial vision allows a firm to innovate and adapt to meet changes in the marketplace.

1.6.2 What is the difference between creativity and critical thinking? Critical thinking is the ability to analyze and assess information to pinpoint problems or opportunities. Creativity is the capacity to develop novel solutions to perceived organizational problems.

LO 1.7 Outline the characteristics that make a company admired.

A company is usually admired for its solid profits, stable growth, a safe and challenging work environment, high-quality goods and services, and business ethics and social responsibility.

✓ ASSESSMENT CHECK ANSWERS

1.7.1 Define *business ethics* and *social responsibility*. Business ethics refers to the standards of conduct and moral values involved in decisions made in the work environment. Social responsibility is a management philosophy that includes contributing resources to the community, preserving the natural environment, and developing or participating in not-for-profit programs designed to promote the well-being of the general public.

1.7.2 Identify three criteria used to judge whether a company might be considered admirable. Criteria in judging whether companies are admirable include the following: solid profits, stable growth, a safe and challenging work environment, high-quality goods and services, and business ethics and social responsibility.

BUSINESS TERMS YOU NEED TO KNOW

brand 13	creativity 21	nearshoring 19	relationship management 15
branding 13	critical thinking 20	not-for-profit organizations 5	social era 15
business 4	diversity 18	offshoring 19	strategic alliance 15
capital 7	entrepreneur 10	outsourcing 19	transaction management 14
capitalism 8	entrepreneurship 7	private enterprise system 8	vision 20
competition 8	factors of production 6	private property 9	
competitive differentiation 8	human resources 7	profits 4	
consumer orientation 13	natural resources 6	relationship era 14	

REVIEW QUESTIONS

1. Why is business so important to a country's economy?
2. In what ways are not-for-profit organizations a substantial part of the Canadian economy? What challenges do not-for-profits face?
3. Identify and describe the four basic inputs that make up the factors of production. Give an example of each factor of production that an auto manufacturer might use.
4. What is a private enterprise system? What four rights are critical to the operation of capitalism? Why would capitalism function poorly in a society that does not ensure these rights for its citizens?
5. In what ways is entrepreneurship vital to the private enterprise system?
6. Identify the seven eras of business in North America. How were businesses changed during each era?
7. Describe the focus of the most recent era of business. How is this era different from previous eras?
8. Define *partnership* and *strategic alliance*. How might a motorcycle dealer and a local radio station benefit from an alliance?
9. Identify the major changes in the workforce that will affect the way managers build a world-class workforce in the twenty-first century. Why is brainpower so important?
10. Identify four qualities required by the "new" managers of the twenty-first century. Why are these qualities important in a competitive business environment?

PROJECTS AND TEAMWORK APPLICATIONS

1. The entrepreneurial spirit fuels growth in the Canadian economy. Choose a company that interests you—one you have worked for or dealt with as a customer—and read about the company in the library or visit its website. Learn what you can about the company's early history: Who founded it and why? Is the founder still with the organization? Do you think the founder's original vision is still embraced by the company? If not, how has the vision changed?

2. Brands distinguish one company's goods or services from its competitors. Each company you purchase from hopes that you will become loyal to its brand. Some well-known brands are Tim Hortons, Burger King, Coca-Cola, Hilton, and Old Navy. Choose a type of good or service you use regularly and identify the major brands associated with it. Are you loyal to a particular brand? Why or why not?

3. More and more businesses are forming strategic alliances to become more competitive. Sometimes, businesses pair up with not-for-profit organizations in a relationship that is beneficial to both. Choose a company whose goods or services interest you, such as Lululemon Athletica, Timberland, FedEx, General Mills, or Canadian Tire. On your own or with a classmate, research the firm on the Internet to learn about its alliances with not-for-profit organizations. Describe one of the alliances, including the goals and benefits to both parties. Create a presentation for your class.

4. This chapter describes how the nature of the workforce is changing: the population is aging, the labour pool is shrinking, the workforce is becoming more diverse, the nature of work is changing, the workplace is becoming more flexible and mobile, and employers are promoting innovation and collaboration among their employees. Form teams of two to three students. Select a company and research how that company is responding to changes in the workforce. When you have completed your research, be prepared to present it to your class. Choose one of the following companies or select your own: BCE, TELUS, 3M, Marriott, or Dell.

5. Many successful companies today use technology to help them improve their relationship management. Suppose a major grocery store chain's management team has asked you to assess its use of technology for this purpose. On your own or with a classmate, visit one or two local grocery stores and explore their corporate websites. Note the ways in which firms in this industry already use technology to connect with their customers. List at least three new ways these firms can use technology to connect with their customers, or list three improvements to their existing methods. Present your findings to the class as if you were presenting to the management team.

WEB ASSIGNMENTS

1. **Using search engines.** Gathering information is one of the most popular applications of the Internet. Using two of the major search engines, such as Google and Bing, search the Internet for information pertaining to brand and relationship management. Sort through your results—you're likely to gets thousands of "hits"—and identify the three most useful. What did you learn from this experience regarding the use of a search engine?

    www.google.ca
    www.bing.com

2. **Companies and not-for-profits.** In addition to companies, virtually all not-for-profit organizations have websites. Four websites are listed below, two for companies (Alcoa and Sony) and two for not-for-profits (the Humane Society of Canada and the National Audubon Society). What is the purpose of each website? What type of information is available? How are the sites similar? How are they different?

    www.alcoa.com
    www.sony.com
    www.humanesociety.com
    www.audubon.org

3. **Characteristics of the Canadian workforce.** Visit the website listed below. It is the home page for the *Canada Year Book*. Published annually by Statistics Canada, the *Canada Year Book* is a good source of basic demographic and economic data. Use the relevant data tables to prepare a brief profile of the Canadian workforce (gender, age, educational level, etc.). How is this profile expected to change over the next 10 to 20 years?

    www.statcan.gc.ca/pub/11-402-x/index-eng.htm

Note: Internet Web addresses change frequently. If you don't find the exact sites listed, you may need to access the organization's home page and search from there or use a search engine such as Bing or Google.

2 | BUSINESS ETHICS AND SOCIAL RESPONSIBILITY

LEARNING OBJECTIVES

LO 2.1 Explain the concepts of business ethics and social responsibility.

LO 2.2 Describe the factors that influence business ethics.

LO 2.3 Discuss how organizations shape ethical behaviour.

LO 2.4 Describe how businesses can act responsibly to satisfy society.

LO 2.5 Explain the ethical responsibilities of businesses to investors and the financial community.

INSIDE BUSINESS

Cirque du Soleil: A Class Act in Social Responsibility

Have you ever attended a Cirque du Soleil (Cirque) performance? If you have, you've seen creativity, ingenuity, and perseverance throughout the show from beginning to end. Maybe you saw "O" at the Bellagio, where performers dive into and out of a 5.7-million-litre pool. Or perhaps "Michael Jackson, the Immortal World Tour." Cirque puts on a great show and is a hard act for its imitators to follow.

How creative can a company like Cirque be, in terms of social responsibility? Cirque prides itself on impressing audiences. But what can it do to impress the wider community?

Cirque's founder, Guy Laliberté, has an idea. He is convinced that the company can become a leader in promoting social responsibility. Then, a trickle-down effect will inspire other companies to follow suit. Cirque has decided to publicize its efforts. It hopes to encourage other companies to be more socially responsible. Cirque also wants to keep its stakeholders aware of its plans.

Cirque's work on global citizenship affects the community, the environment, the workplace, its business partners, and its suppliers.

Cirque du Monde (one of Cirque's social action programs) can be found in nearly 80 communities in 20 countries. The company spends, on average, 1 percent of its earnings on cultural and social action programs. Laliberté set up the One Drop Foundation, which works with Oxfam and others to provide sanitation and access to water in countries where there is a need. Project Haiti began after an earthquake devastated the country in 2010 and continued until 2013. It involved 135,000 participants and had a $2.8-million budget. Cirque du Monde also helps at-risk youth regain their self-confidence. These youth are invited to attend personal development programs presented by circus instructors and social workers.

Cirque has also been a major innovator in the area of environmental responsibility. The rate of global warming has been increasing, especially over the past two decades, which were the hottest in more than 400 years. Cirque has started many projects to reduce its carbon footprint and protect the environment. Yannick Spierkel, Cirque's tour general manager, believes Cirque can "influence the lives and buying habits of employees and even set up awareness campaigns with clients." At home, Cirque chose to build its Montreal headquarters on a recovered landfill. Recently, Cirque was able to reduce its headquarters' water consumption by 20 percent, or 8.4 million litres (equivalent to the water in 168 swimming pools). Cirque reduced water use by installing rainwater collection basins in the parking lot and on the building's seventh floor and by replacing plumbing fixtures with low-flow models. When Cirque goes on tour, Green Committees look at how the group can continue to operate in an environmentally responsible manner in the cities it visits. For example, in Las Vegas, the staff of "Mystère" has been given the task of going completely paperless by rethinking all of their work habits.

Cirque is well aware that its responsibility to the community begins with its own staff right at its international headquarters. Marie Trottier, director of property services, says, "Working for a company that promotes and facilitates environmental initiatives and provides the means to make a difference has certainly influenced me personally." For example, Cirque takes pride in ensuring its staff is well taken care of. Cirque has no dress code, so staff can come to work wearing whatever feels comfortable. This physical comfort suits the workplace's sense of creativity. Staff can watch the performers practise and thus see the result of their efforts behind the scenes. "Wherever you go, you can feel creativity, you can smell it, you can touch it, because that is what we are about," says Murielle Cantin, senior vice-president of creative content. Staff can relax on couches or have lunch from a low-cost cafeteria that serves vegetables grown in in-house gardens.

Companies can indirectly have a large impact on their community and the environment through their suppliers. Cirque takes an extra step to ensure that its relationships with business partners also include an attitude of social responsibility. Cirque is part of Business for Social Responsibility (BSR). This global network of more than 250 companies seeks to develop and maintain sustainable business strategies and solutions. As a result, Cirque has reduced its deliveries to tour destinations by approximately 40 percent. It also groups its inbound shipments to warehouses to reduce transportation-related emissions. A tool has also been developed to help buyers select more environmentally friendly materials. Formal training sessions ensure that buyers are trained on how to purchase supplies in an environmentally responsible manner.

Cirque is trying to create a ripple effect with its business partners by making social responsibility a requirement when selecting future business partners. It has also built a social responsibility clause into all of its partnership agreements. This clause applies to employee relations, working conditions, ethical sourcing, environmental protection, and social and cultural actions in the community. Éric Choquette, Cirque's merchandising director, explains: "The objective is to keep the bottom line in mind while making increasingly responsible choices."[1]

CHAPTER 2 OVERVIEW

Cirque du Soleil's efforts to create sustainable operations are not unique in the world of business. Many companies are concerned about the environment and the societies in which they do business. This concern may lead to action, such as growing more slowly than they might have or reducing short-term profits for longer, sustainable benefits. Cirque du Soleil changed its own operations to help the environment while still maintaining a reasonable profit.

Most organizations strive to combine ethical behaviour with profitable operation. Some have had difficulties overcoming major ethical errors in recent years. Ethical failures in many large and well-known firms have led to lawsuits, indictments, and judgments against firms. We have all seen news reports of executives receiving millions of dollars in pay while their companies struggle to operate. This kind of news has damaged the image of the chief executive officer (CEO)—and of business in general.

Sometimes, though, bad news leads to good news. As a result of such bad news stories, both the government and companies have made changes. Businesses have renewed their efforts to behave in an ethical manner to show their responsibility to society, to consumers, and to the environment. In 2010, Industry Canada began a new voluntary standard on social responsibility known as ISO 26000. It focuses on seven principles: accountability, transparency, ethical behaviour, stakeholder interests, rule of law, international norms of behaviour, and human rights. This new standard has led to more firms paying attention to creating clearer standards and procedures for ethical behaviour. Companies now understand the enormous impact of setting a good example instead of a bad one. Today, you are likely to hear about the goodwill produced by such companies as CIBC, TELUS, and Tim Hortons. These companies create goodwill when they give back to their communities by funding youth camping programs and recycling or energy-conservation programs, or by paying fair prices to suppliers.[2]

As we discussed in Chapter 1, the basic aim of business is to serve customers at a profit. Most companies try to do more than that. Most companies want to give back to customers, society, and the environment. Sometimes, though, they face difficult questions. When does a company's self-interest work against society's and customers' well-being? Does the goal of seeking profits always work against having high principles of what is right and wrong? Many businesses of all sizes answer no.

LO 2.1 Explain the concepts of business ethics and social responsibility.

CONCERN FOR ETHICAL AND SOCIETAL ISSUES

business ethics standards of conduct and moral values regarding right and wrong actions in the business environment.

An organization that wants to do well over the long term should consider its **business ethics**. Business ethics refers to the standards of conduct and moral values that lead to our actions and decisions in the business environment. Businesses also must consider a wide range of social issues, including how a decision will affect the environment, employees, and customers. These issues are at the heart of *corporate social responsibility (CSR)*. CSR's primary objective is to enhance society's well-being through philosophies, policies, procedures, and actions. In other words, businesses must find a balance between doing what is right and doing what is profitable.

Maclean's has partnered with Sustainalytics to create a list showcasing the top 50 Canadian companies demonstrating exceptional corporate social responsibility. Tim Hortons, for example, requires its Canadian millwork suppliers to use only wood certified by the Forest Stewardship Council in its Canadian restaurants. Through the expansion of their recycling and waste-diversion programs, the company is also currently diverting 80 percent of its waste from landfills. Bank of Montreal (BMO), who also made the list, enacted a board diversity policy that requires at least one-third of the bank's independent board of directors to be women. Furthermore BMO provides funds for a financial literacy program with the goal of educating 45,000 students in personal finance.[3]

In business, as in life, deciding what is right or wrong is not always an easy choice. Firms have many responsibilities—to customers, to employees, to investors, and to society as a whole. Trying to serve the different needs of these groups can lead to conflicts. The ethical values of executives and individual employees at all levels can influence a business's decisions and actions. In your own career, you will encounter many situations where you will need to weigh right and wrong before making a decision or taking action. We begin our discussion of business ethics by focusing on individual ethics.

The concept of right and wrong can be complex. It is certainly not "black and white." Business ethics are also shaped by the ethical climate within an organization or even within a country. For example, an acceptable age to start working may be 16 in a developed country but could be 10 in a developing country. Ethics also goes beyond what is legal and what is not legal. Codes of conduct and ethical standards play important roles in businesses that support and applaud doing the right thing. This chapter shows how a firm can create a framework to encourage—and even demand—high standards of ethical behaviour and social responsibility from its employees. The chapter also considers the complex questions of what business owes to society and how society's forces shape the actions of businesses. Finally, this chapter examines the influence of business ethics and social responsibility on global businesses.

This boy from Bangladesh is working to help earn money for his family. Is this ethical?

ASSESSMENT CHECK

2.1.1 To whom do businesses have responsibilities?

2.1.2 If a firm is meeting all its responsibilities to others, why do ethical conflicts arise?

LO 2.2 Describe the factors that influence business ethics.

THE CONTEMPORARY ETHICAL ENVIRONMENT

Business ethics is in the spotlight now as never before. Companies realize that they need to work harder to earn the public's trust. Many companies have taken on the challenge as if their survival depends on it. This movement toward corporate social responsibility should benefit everyone—consumers, the environment, and the companies themselves.

Most business owners and managers have built and maintained successful companies without breaking the rules. One example of a firm with a long-term commitment to ethical practice is Johnson & Johnson, the giant multinational manufacturer of healthcare products. It is the most admired pharmaceutical maker and the nineteenth most-admired company in the world, according to *Fortune*. Johnson & Johnson has worked with the same basic code of ethics, its well-known credo, for more than 50 years (see **Figure 2.1**).[4]

Many business schools include programs on ethics and social responsibility in their course curriculum. MBA students from the University of Ottawa's Telfer School of Management are now required to swear an ethics-related oath upon graduation (see **Figure 2.2**).

Many companies are aware of how ethical standards can translate into concern for the environment and society at large. According to Shelley Broader, president and CEO of Walmart Canada, the company has grouped its social responsibility priorities into four broad categories:

1. Environmental sustainability
2. People
3. Ethical sourcing
4. Community giving and investment

FIGURE 2.1 Johnson & Johnson Credo

> **Our Credo**
>
> We believe our first responsibility is to the doctors, nurses and patients, to mothers and fathers and all others who use our products and services. In meeting their needs everything we do must be of high quality. We must constantly strive to reduce our costs in order to maintain reasonable prices. Customers' orders must be serviced promptly and accurately. Our suppliers and distributors must have an opportunity to make a fair profit.
>
> We are responsible to our employees, the men and women who work with us throughout the world. Everyone must be considered as an individual. We must respect their dignity and recognize their merit. They must have a sense of security in their jobs. Compensation must be fair and adequate, and working conditions clean, orderly and safe. We must be mindful of ways to help our employees fulfill their family responsibilities. Employees must feel free to make suggestions and complaints. There must be equal opportunity for employment, development and advancement for those qualified. We must provide competent management, and their actions must be just and ethical.
>
> We are responsible to the communities in which we live and work and to the world community as well. We must be good citizens—support good works and charities and bear our fair share of taxes. We must encourage civic improvements and better health and education. We must maintain in good order the property we are privileged to use, protecting the environment and natural resources.
>
> Our final responsibility is to our stockholders. Business must make a sound profit. We must experiment with new ideas. Research must be carried on, innovative programs developed and mistakes paid for. New equipment must be purchased, new facilities provided and new products launched. Reserves must be created to provide for adverse times. When we operate according to these principles, the stockholders should realize a fair return.

Source: Johnson & Johnson, "Our Company: Our Credo," accessed August 11, 2014, http://www.jnj.com. © Johnson & Johnson.

FIGURE 2.2 Telfer School of Management MBA Oath

> *As a manager my actions will affect the wellbeing of all stakeholders; accordingly, I will strive to create and sustain value over the long term while maintaining a commitment to social, ethical and global values.*
>
> *I will be responsible to all stakeholders, and this will include employees, shareholders, customers, the community in which I operate, and all those that may be affected by my actions.*
>
> *I will act with integrity and respect in all my dealings, making transparency paramount and demanding the same in return.*

Source: Excerpted from Telfer School of Management, "Taking the Oath," http://sites.telfer.uottawa.ca/mbaoath/taking-the-oath/.

Walmart Canada has started selling fresh produce. The company has developed an efficient, cost-effective, and more sustainable process by sourcing produce locally, where possible. Local sourcing means lower transportation costs and reduced transportation-related emissions. Local sourcing also supports local suppliers, addressing many concerns raised that shopping at Walmart leads to lost Canadian jobs.[5]

Walmart also surveyed its suppliers about their sustainability practices. This survey was a first step in developing a "sustainability index" to help its customers measure the impact of Walmart products on the environment and on society. In 2013 Walmart topped the list of companies using solar energy. CSR is important for Walmart because of the ongoing controversy about some of its business practices.[6]

Not all companies set and meet high ethical standards, but the ethical climate is improving despite the recent recession. A recent study found that 41 percent of employees surveyed "witnessed misconduct on the job" in 2013, down from a record high of 55 percent in 2007. However, fewer employees said they reported misconduct when they saw it, down to 63 percent in 2013 from 65 percent in 2011. About 25 percent of employees said the recent recession had a negative impact on their company's ethical culture.[7]

Sarbanes-Oxley and Bill 198

In the United States, the **Sarbanes-Oxley Act of 2002** established new rules and regulations for securities trading and accounting practices. Companies are now required to publish their code of ethics, if they have one, and inform the public of any changes made to it. The law may actually motivate even more firms to develop written codes and guidelines for ethical business behaviour. The provisions of this act apply to Canadian companies who trade on any American stock exchange. Similar legislation has been enacted in Canada, known as Bill 198 of 2003, which has come to be referred to as "C-SOX," or the Canadian version of Sarbanes-Oxley.

Today's ethical environment for business also includes new corporate officers who are appointed to deter wrongdoing and ensure that ethical standards are met. Ethics compliance officers are responsible for conducting employee training programs that help spot potential fraud and abuse, investigating sexual harassment and discrimination charges, and monitoring potential conflicts of interest. Practising corporate social responsibility is more than just monitoring behaviour. Many companies now adopt a three-pronged approach to ethics and social responsibility:

1. Engaging in traditional corporate philanthropy, such as giving to worthy causes
2. Anticipating and managing risks
3. Identifying opportunities to create value by doing the right thing[8]

Walmart Canada has started sourcing produce locally, such as these Quebec-grown radishes on sale in its Laval store, to increase efficiency, lower costs, and reduce greenhouse gas emissions.

Sarbanes-Oxley Act of 2002 U.S. federal legislation designed to deter and punish corporate and accounting fraud and corruption. It is also designed to protect the interests of workers and shareholders by requiring enhanced financial disclosures, criminal penalties for CEOs and CFOs who defraud investors, and safeguards for whistle-blowers. The act also established a new regulatory body for public accounting firms.

Individuals Make a Difference

In today's business environment, individuals can make the difference in ethical expectations and behaviour. Executives, managers, and employees show their personal ethical principles—or lack of ethical principles. In turn, their behaviour can affect the expectations and actions of those who work for them and with them.

What is the current state of individual business ethics in Canada? Ethical behaviour can be difficult to track or define in all situations. The evidence suggests that some individuals act unethically or illegally on the job. Their behaviour includes putting their own interests ahead of the organization, lying to employees, misreporting hours worked, Internet abuse, and safety violations.[9]

Technology may have expanded the range and impact of unethical behaviour. For example, anyone who has computer access to data may be able to steal or manipulate the data or shut down the system, even from a remote location. Recently, Target alerted customers that a data breach compromised 40 million credit card numbers. This data breach led to both the CIO and CEO losing their jobs. The cost of dealing with a data breach can be up to $5.4 million per incident.[10] Although some people might not be concerned about these breaches, they can affect how investors, customers, and the general public view a firm. It can be difficult to rebuild trust. The company may also lose some long-term customers.

Nearly every employee at every level faces ethical questions at some time. Some people explain questionable behaviour by saying, "Everybody's doing it." Others act unethically because they feel pressured in their jobs or because they need to meet performance goals. Yet others avoid unethical acts because these acts don't fit with their personal values and morals. We all use different methods to make our ethical choices. The next section focuses on how we develop our personal ethics and morals.

Development of Individual Ethics

An individual's moral and ethical development is the result of many factors. Experiences shape our responses to different situations. Our family, educational, cultural, and religious backgrounds also play a role, as does the environment within the firm. We also have different styles of deciding ethical dilemmas, no matter what our stage of moral development.

This textbook can help you understand and prepare for the ethical dilemmas you may face in your career. Let's take a closer look at the factors that can help you solve ethical questions on the job.

CAREER KICKSTART

How to Avoid Ethical Issues at Work

Creating a Good Ethical Foundation

You might be surprised to discover how easy it is to make an ethical slip at work. If you've mastered the fundamentals of business etiquette, however, you'll have a good ethical foundation for making good decisions in tough situations. Here are some guidelines:

- Stay focused on your business purpose. If you develop a close personal relationship with a client or supplier, you may risk a conflict of interest.

- Don't abuse privileges. It's tempting to use sick days or personal days for mini-vacations, but if your company distinguishes between these breaks, you should too.

- Live your values. Few people are brought up to be untrustworthy. Even if no one knows about it, an unethical choice that betrays your personal values weakens your self-respect and reduces your contribution to the workplace.

- Don't depend on excuses. If you're constantly making excuses for your behaviour, what does that say about your behaviour?

- Monitor your digital reputation. Never post anything online you wouldn't want to see on the news tomorrow.

- Don't steal. Using your work computer for personal tasks like shopping and social networking is just as much theft of company resources as is taking home office supplies.

- Treat others as you would be treated. This rule never fails to point the way to ethical behaviour and decisions you can be proud of.

Sources: Pamela Eyring, "Modern Etiquette: Minding Your Manners in the Workplace," Reuters, accessed January 17, 2014, www.reuters.com; Susan M. Healthfield, "Did You Bring Your Ethics to Work Today?" About.com, accessed January 17, 2014, http://humanresources.about.com; Lydia Ramsey, "The Top Twelve Business Etiquette Tips for Social Media," Business Know How, accessed January 17, 2014, www.businessknowhow.com.

On-the-Job Ethical Dilemmas

In the fast-paced world of business, you will sometimes be asked to consider the ethics of your decisions. These decisions can affect not just your own future but also the futures of your coworkers, your company, and its customers. As we already mentioned, deciding what is right and wrong can be difficult in many business situations. The decision is especially tricky when the needs and concerns of two or more parties conflict. In the recent past, some CEOs (or their companies) who were accused of wrongdoing simply claimed that they had no idea crimes were being committed. Today's top executives make a greater effort to be aware of all activities taking place in their firms.

For example, many clothing retailers donate unworn, unsold garments to charities such as clothing banks. A graduate student discovered that the H&M store on New York's 34th Street was destroying unsold clothing. She tried to speak to store officials and then tried to speak to someone at the company's headquarters in Sweden. Her requests for information and her offer to put H&M in contact with aid organizations went unanswered. She then contacted the *New York Times*. The newspaper published a story about how H&M—among other retailers—was damaging unsold garments before discarding them. The damage was intended to make the clothing unsalable by street vendors or other black-market sellers. The New York City Clothing Bank, founded by the city's mayor during the 1980s, accepts unsold garments and slightly defaces them—not to destroy them, but to protect retailers by negating the garments' street value. When the story was published, H&M promised to stop destroying unsold clothing and instead donate the garments to charity. A company spokesperson in New York declared, "It will not happen again. We are committed 100 percent to make sure this practice is not happening anywhere else, as it is not our standard practice."[11]

On a global level, businesses sometimes refuse to purchase goods or services from a particular country because of civil rights abuses by that country's government. Some of the world's largest and most prestigious jewellers, including Cartier and Tiffany & Co., announced they would not purchase rubies and other gems from Myanmar (formerly Burma). Their boycott is the result of that government's civil rights violations and the severe measures it has taken against protests by students and monks. The United States and the European Union have also agreed to ban the import of gems from Myanmar.[12]

Solving ethical dilemmas is not easy. Often, each possible decision can lead to both good and bad outcomes that must be considered. The ethical issues that face manufacturers who have unsold merchandise are one example of many different types of ethical situations in the workplace. **Figure 2.3** identifies four of the most common ethical challenges that businesspeople face: conflict of interest, honesty and integrity, loyalty versus truth, and whistle-blowing.

FIGURE 2.3 Common Business Ethical Challenges

Conflict of Interest

A **conflict of interest** occurs when a businessperson is faced with a situation where an action that benefits one person or group has the potential to harm another. Conflicts of interest may pose ethical challenges when they involve the businessperson's own interests and the interests of a person or party to whom the businessperson has a duty. For example, lawyers, business consultants, and advertising agencies face a conflict of interest if they represent two competing companies: A strategy that might benefit one client might harm the other client. Similarly, a real estate agent would face an ethical conflict by representing both the buyer and seller in a transaction. Handling the situation responsibly is possible, but is also difficult. A conflict may also exist between someone's personal interests and the interests of an organization or its customers. An offer of gifts or bribes for special treatment can lead to a situation where the buyer may benefit personally, but the company may not.

A conflict of interest may also occur when one person holds two or more similar jobs in two different workplaces. Conflicts of interest can be handled ethically by (1) avoiding them and (2) disclosing them. Some companies have policies against taking on clients who are competitors of existing clients. Most businesses and government agencies have written policies that either prevent employees from accepting gifts or specify a maximum gift value. A member of a board of directors or a committee member might abstain from voting when he or she has a personal interest in the decision. In other situations, people state their potential conflict of interest so that others can decide whether to use another source instead.

conflict of interest a situation in which an employee must choose between a business's welfare and personal gain.

Honesty and Integrity

Employers highly value honesty and integrity. An employee who is honest can be relied on to tell the truth. An employee with **integrity** goes beyond truthfulness. Having integrity means behaving according to one's deeply felt ethical principles in business situations. It includes doing what you say you will do and accepting responsibility for your mistakes. Behaving with honesty and integrity inspires trust. As a result, integrity can help to build long-term relationships with customers, employers, suppliers, and the public. Employees, in turn, want their managers and the company as a whole to treat them honestly and with integrity.

Unfortunately, violations of honesty and integrity are common. Some people misrepresent their academic standing and previous work experience on their résumés or job applications. An ADP survey revealed that one in five Canadians has lied on his or her résumé. Although it may be tempting to

integrity behaving according to one's deeply felt ethical principles in business situations.

Employers and employees value honesty and integrity, but what should happen when employees misuse their Internet privileges for personal purposes?

lie on a résumé in a competitive job market, it shows a lack of honesty and integrity—and eventually the lies will catch up with you. Recently, it was learned that an Osgoode Hall law student, Quami Frederick, had purchased a fake undergraduate degree to gain admission to law school. She also submitted an Osgoode Hall transcript with inflated grades to obtain an articling position at the Bay Street law firm Wildeboer Dellelce, LLP. Frederick now faces a disciplinary hearing that will likely result in her expulsion from Osgoode Hall. The law firm has withdrawn its offer.[13]

Some employees steal from their employers by taking home supplies or products without permission or by carrying out personal business when they are being paid to work. For example, Internet misuse during the workday is increasing. Employees use the Internet during work hours for personal email, shopping, gaming, and visiting bulletin boards and blogs or social networking sites such as Facebook and YouTube. The use of laptops, cellphones, and other wireless devices makes this misconduct easier to hide.[14] The frequency of such activity varies widely. Employers may feel more strongly about taking strong measures on some activities than on others. Most people will agree that Internet misuse is a problem. Some employers have resorted to electronic monitoring and surveillance. These employers have another reason to monitor their employees: complying with the laws regarding the privacy and security of client information.

Loyalty versus Truth

Businesspeople expect their employees to be loyal and to act in the best interests of the company. But when the truth about a company is not favourable, an ethical conflict can arise. Individual employees may need to decide between loyalty to the company and truthfulness in business relationships. People resolve such dilemmas in various ways. Some place the highest value on loyalty, even at the expense of truth. Others avoid volunteering negative information but answer truthfully when asked a direct question. People may emphasize truthfulness and actively disclose negative information, especially when the cost of silence is high, such as when operating a malfunctioning aircraft or selling tainted food.

Whistle-Blowing

When an employee encounters unethical or illegal actions at work, that employee must decide what action to take. This person may conclude that the only solution is to "blow the whistle." **Whistle-blowing** is usually an employee's disclosure to company officials, government authorities, or the media of illegal, immoral, or unethical practices.

For example, in May 2014, Robert Buckingham, a University of Saskatchewan dean, was fired and escorted by police from university grounds after alerting the public to planned university budget cuts (in an initiative known as TransformUS) and expressing his opposition to the cuts. Buckingham indicated that the former university president Ilene Busch-Vishniac "expected her senior leaders to not 'publicly disagree with the process or findings of TransformUS'; she added that if we did our 'tenure would be short.'" In a matter of days the University of Saskatchewan reconsidered its decision to fire Mr. Buckingham and strip him of his tenure. His tenure was reinstated, but he was not allowed to return to his former role of dean. Hundreds of angry students, staff, and alumni staged a protest demanding that the school's administration be held accountable. Brett Fairbairn resigned from his position as provost, and Ilene Busch-Vishniac was fired from her position as president.[15]

Whistle-blowing disclosure to company officials, government authorities, or the media of illegal, immoral, or unethical practices committed by an organization.

Although no specific law protects whistle-blowers in Canada, many Canadian companies, such as Air Canada, have policies to protect whistle-blowers. In 2004, Bill C-25, the Public Servants Disclosure Protection Act, was introduced. This bill was intended to protect people who expose problems in the government's bureaucracy. The government said this act will help ensure "transparency, accountability, financial responsibility and ethical conduct."[16]

Despite these protections, whistle-blowing has its risks. Zues Yaghi from Edmonton blew the whistle on casino video slot machines. He said the machines could be made to pay on demand. Yaghi claimed that the computer program had a "back door" that would allow players to collect jackpots after making a few clicks. Yaghi was sued by the company for $10 million, and a warrant was issued to search Yaghi's home. A few days later, a gag order was issued to prevent him from saying how a player could make the slots pay out. The company offered him $50,000 to remain quiet about the issue, but Yaghi asked for more money.[17]

Obviously, whistle-blowing and other ethical issues are rare in firms that have strong organizational climates of ethical behaviour. The next section examines how a business can develop an environment that discourages unethical behaviour among individuals.

ASSESSMENT CHECK

2.2.1 What is the role of a firm's ethics compliance officer?

2.2.2 What factors influence the ethical environment of a business?

HOW ORGANIZATIONS SHAPE ETHICAL CONDUCT

LO 2.3 Discuss how organizations shape ethical behaviour.

No individual makes decisions in a vacuum. Most organizations have established standards of conduct that strongly influence the choices employees make. Most ethical lapses in business reflect the values in the firms' corporate cultures.

As shown in **Figure 2.4**, a corporate culture that supports business ethics develops on four levels:

1. Ethical awareness
2. Ethical education
3. Ethical action
4. Ethical leadership

If any of these four factors is missing, the ethical climate in an organization will weaken.

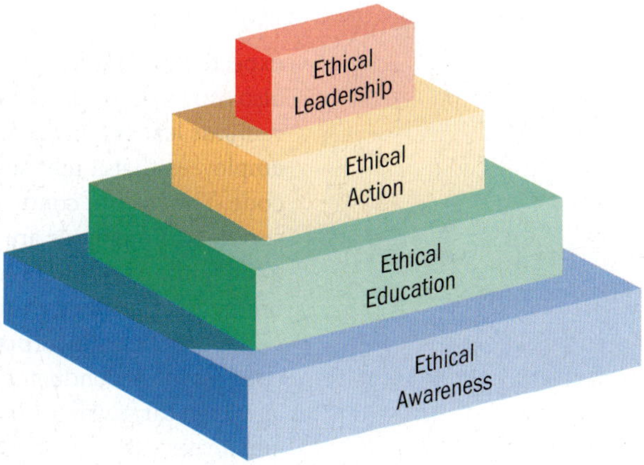

Ethical Awareness

The foundation of an ethical climate is ethical awareness. As we have already seen, ethical dilemmas occur frequently in the workplace. Employees need help in identifying ethical problems when they occur. They also need guidance about how the firm expects them to respond.

One way for a firm to provide this support is to develop a **code of conduct**. This formal statement defines how the organization expects its employees to resolve ethical questions. Johnson & Johnson's credo, presented in **Figure 2.1**, is such a code. At the most basic level, a code of conduct may simply be the ground rules for acceptable behaviour, such as the laws and regulations that employees must obey. Other companies use their codes of conduct to identify key corporate values and provide frameworks that guide employees as they resolve moral and ethical dilemmas.

Air Canada is headquartered in Montreal, Quebec, and has offices around the world. Its code of conduct defines the company's values and helps employees to put these values into practice. The code of conduct emphasizes "honesty and integrity" and treating employees with fairness, dignity, and respect. The code applies to "all directors, officers and employees." Portions of the policy even include retirees who have travel pass privileges. All employees at every level are

FIGURE 2.4 Structure of an Ethical Environment

code of conduct a formal statement that defines how an organization expects its employees to resolve ethical issues.

Air Canada requires all of its directors, officers, and employees, and even some of its retirees, to sign a code of conduct to promote ethical behaviour.

expected to treat fellow employees, suppliers, and customers with dignity and respect. They are also expected to comply with environmental, health, and safety regulations. The code of conduct reminds leaders that their language and behaviour must not even seem to put pressure on their employees that might suggest they should perform a task differently from the standards in the code. The code of conduct also outlines how to report violations to a supervisor or the corporate secretary. Employees are promised confidentiality and non-retaliation for problems reported in good faith. Air Canada requires all employees to sign this code of conduct, which is also posted on the Air Canada website.[18]

Other firms incorporate similar codes in their policy manuals or mission statements; some issue a code of conduct or statement of values in the form of a small card that employees and managers can carry with them. For example, Harley-Davidson has developed a brief code of ethics that employees can apply both at work and in their personal lives. It reads: "Tell the truth, keep your promises, be fair, respect the individual and encourage intellectual curiosity."

Ethical Education

A code of conduct can provide an overall framework, but it does not have a solution for every ethical situation. Some ethical questions have black-and-white answers, but others do not. Businesses must provide the tools employees need to evaluate the options and arrive at suitable decisions.

Many firms have started their own ethics training programs. Other firms have hired organizations such as The Skald Group, based in Hamilton, Ontario, which provides outsourced ethics programs to businesses.[19] Other organizations, such as SAI Global, host employee-reporting services that offer an anonymous hotline and an ethics case management system. SAI Global also helps companies to develop ethics codes and customizes ethics training to each company's needs, including specialized online, interactive training systems.[20]

Many have debated whether ethics can be taught. Ethics training is helpful, though, because employees can practise applying ethical values to sample situations before they face real-world situations. Similar strategies are used in many business schools, where case studies and practical scenarios work best. Walter Pavlo is a convicted white-collar criminal and a former employee at the telecommunications firm MCI. Pavlo once worked with other MCI staff to hide $6 million in offshore accounts. He now speaks at colleges and universities about his experiences, both in the firm and in prison, to warn students of the consequences of cheating.

Ethical Action

Codes of conduct and ethics training help employees recognize and reason through ethical problems. In addition, firms must provide structures and approaches that allow decisions to be turned into ethical actions. Texas Instruments gives its employees a reference card to help them make ethical decisions on the job. The card is the size of a standard business card and lists the following guidelines:

- Is the action legal?
- Does it comply with our values?
- If you do it, will you feel bad?
- How will it look in the newspaper?
- If you know it's wrong, don't do it!
- If you're not sure, ask.
- Keep asking until you get an answer.

Businesses often set goals for the whole business and for individual departments and employees. These goals can affect ethical behaviour. For example, a firm's managers may set unrealistic goals for employee performance. These goals may lead to an increase in cheating, lying, and other misdeeds as employees attempt to protect themselves. In today's Internet economy, a high value is often placed on speed. But valuing speed can lead to a climate where ethical behaviour is challenged. Ethical decisions often require careful and quiet thought, which can be a challenging task in today's fast-paced business world.

Some companies encourage ethical action. These companies provide support for employees facing dilemmas. One common tool is an employee hotline, which is a telephone number that employees can call anonymously for advice or to report unethical behaviour they have seen. As already mentioned, some firms have ethics compliance officers who guide employees through difficult ethical issues.

Ethical Leadership

Executives must not just talk about ethical behaviour—they also need to show it in their actions. Employees need to be personally committed to the company's core values, and they must be willing to base their actions on those values. The recent recession exposed executive-level misdeeds that damaged or even destroyed entire organizations; some people lost their life savings. After hearing of these misdeeds, two students at the Harvard Business School interviewed corporate leaders they regarded as being highly moral. The students concluded that these "ethical mavericks" follow a moral code with three simple characteristics:

1. Use clear, explicit language rather than euphemisms for corrupt behaviour.
2. Encourage behaviour that generates and fosters ethical values.
3. Practise moral absolutism, insisting on doing right even if it proves financially costly.[21]

However, ethical leadership should also go one step further. Each employee at every level should be charged with the responsibility to be an ethical leader. Everyone should be aware of problems and be willing to defend the organization's standards.

Unfortunately, not all organizations can build a solid framework of business ethics. Because the damage from ethical misconduct can powerfully affect a firm's **stakeholders**—customers,

stakeholders customers, investors, employees, and the public who are affected by or have an interest in a company.

ASSESSMENT CHECK

2.3.1 For an employee, when does loyalty conflict with truth?

2.3.2 How does ethical leadership contribute to ethical standards throughout a company?

investors, employees, and the public—businesses are pressured to act in acceptable ways. But when businesses fail, the law must step in to enforce good business practices. Many of the laws that affect specific industries or individuals are described in other chapters in this book. For example, legislation affecting international business operations is discussed in Chapter 4; laws designed to assist small businesses are examined in Chapter 5; laws related to labour unions are described in Chapter 8; legislation related to banking and the securities markets is discussed in Chapters 16 and 17; and finally, for an examination of the legal and governmental forces designed to safeguard society's interests when businesses fail at self-regulation, see Appendix B, "Business Law."

LO 2.4 Describe how businesses can act responsibly to satisfy society.

ACTING RESPONSIBLY TO SATISFY SOCIETY

social responsibility a business's consideration of society's well-being and consumer satisfaction in addition to profits.

A second major issue affecting business is the question of social responsibility. In a general sense, **social responsibility** is management's acceptance of its obligation, when evaluating firm performance, to consider profit to be of equal value to other qualitative indicators, such as employee satisfaction, consumer satisfaction, and societal well-being. Businesses may exercise social responsibility for many reasons: because such behaviour is required by law, because it enhances the company's image, or because management believes it is the ethical course of action. The "Going Green" feature discusses Starbucks's efforts to introduce environmentally sound practices.

Going Green: STARBUCKS INTRODUCES A NEW STORE-DESIGN STRATEGY

In June 2009, the coffee-selling giant Starbucks announced that the company will design new stores and renovate existing stores worldwide with two goals in mind: to reflect the character of the neighbourhood and to reduce the company's environmental impact.

The project is part of Starbucks's efforts to reposition itself. Arthur Rubinfeld, chief creative officer for Starbucks and president of Global Innovation and Evolution Fresh Retail, said, "We recognize the importance of continuously evolving with our customers' interests, lifestyles and values in order to stay relevant over the long term."

The company will make each store unique by employing local artisans and local materials, including recycled and reclaimed items. It has also committed to conserving water and energy, recycling where possible, and using "green" construction methods. Among its goals are the following:

- To use renewable resources for 50 percent of the energy used in its stores
- To make its stores 25 percent more energy efficient to reduce greenhouse gas emissions
- To meet U.S. Green Building Code LEED (Leadership in Energy and Environmental Design) certification standards for all its new stores
- To implement a 100 percent reusable or recyclable cup supply
- To have recycling in stores where it controls waste collection

The company has already met some of these goals. For instance, it reduces its prices by 10 cents for customers who bring in their own travel cup. This reduced the amount of paper the company sends to landfills by 1.4 million pounds in 2013. The company is also replacing incandescent light bulbs with LED bulbs to save energy and expense. Signage will be installed in new and renovated stores to explain their "green" and sustainable features and construction methods.

This new strategy is shaping Starbucks stores in more than 40 countries, including Hong Kong, Saudi Arabia, Spain, and Argentina.

Questions for Critical Thinking

1. How do Starbucks's new plans for its stores reflect its sense of social responsibility?
2. How has Starbucks involved its customers in these efforts?

Sources: Starbucks, "Starbucks Reinvents the Store Experience to Speak to the Heart and Soul of Local Communities," June 25, 2009, accessed January 31, 2012, http://news.starbucks.com; "Make a Difference," Starbucks, accessed January 31, 2012, www.starbucks.com/thebigpicture; Brian Clark Howard, "5 Major Companies Innovate by Going Green," *Daily Green*, November 18, 2009, accessed August 11, 2014, www.thedailygreen.com; Sharon van Schagen, "Starbucks Brews Global Green-Building Plan, Renovates Seattle Shop," *Grist*, June 30, 2009, accessed August 11, 2014, www.thedailygreen.com.

A business is often judged by its interactions with the community. To demonstrate their social responsibility, many corporations highlight their charitable contributions and community service in their annual reports and on their websites. PricewaterhouseCoopers Canada (PwC) has a "Team Volunteering" program that regularly sets up teams to work with charities throughout Canada in daylong projects. Upon request, PwC will send up to 50 PwC employees to volunteer for a day for registered Canadian charities. All PwC employees are also given a paid day off to volunteer for a local charity.[22]

The Tim Horton Children's Foundation was established in 1974. It provides camp environments for children from disadvantaged homes. Each year, one day is set aside as Camp Day, when every Tim Hortons store in Canada and the United States donates the value of all that day's coffee sales to the Tim Horton Children's Foundation. In 2013, Camp Day raised more than $11.8 million to fund community outreach programs.[23]

Some firms measure social performance by conducting **social audits**, which are formal procedures that identify and evaluate all company activities related to social issues, such as conservation, employment practices, environmental protection, and philanthropy. The social audit tells management how well the company is performing in these areas. After seeing this information, management may decide to revise its current programs or develop new ones.

Outside groups may do their own evaluations of businesses. Various environmental, religious, and public-interest groups have created standards of corporate performance. Reports on many of these evaluations are available to the general public. The Canadian Business for Social Responsibility (CBSR) organization offers CSR assessments that examine the internal activities of a company and compares them to industry CSR best practices. The CBSR also offers advisory services to assist firms in creating a companywide CSR strategy.

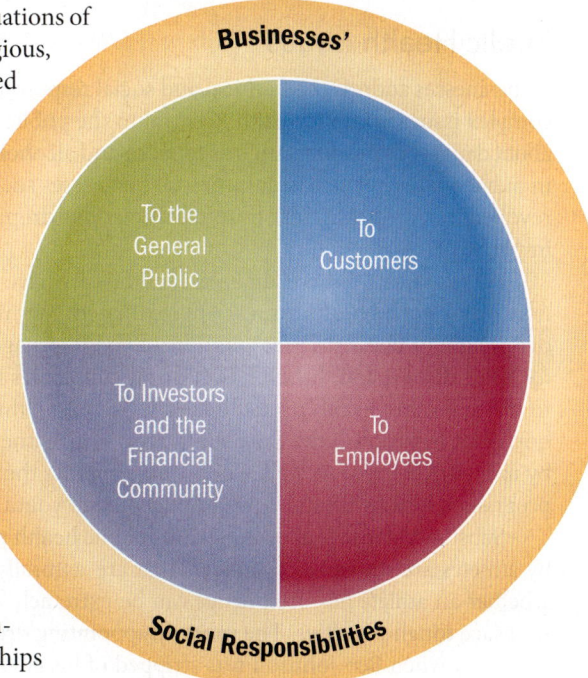

As **Figure 2.5** shows, businesses' social responsibilities can be segmented by their relationships to the general public, customers, employees, investors, and other members of the financial community. Many of these relationships extend beyond national borders.

Tim Hortons Camp Day highlights the company's commitment to the community and social responsibility.

social audits formal procedures that identify and evaluate all company activities related to social issues, such as conservation, employment practices, environmental protection, and philanthropy.

FIGURE 2.5 Businesses' Social Responsibilities

Steve Ruark/AP Images for Boys & Girls Clubs of America/The Canadian Press

To do its part to aid the general public, Coca-Cola supports programs such as the Boys & Girls Clubs of America's Triple Play program, a healthy lifestyles program whose goal is to promote health and wellness among youth and their families.

Responsibilities to the General Public

The responsibilities of business to the general public include dealing with public health issues, protecting the environment, and developing the quality of the workforce. Many argue that businesses also have responsibilities to support charitable and social causes and organizations that work toward the greater public good. In other words, businesses should give back to the communities in which they earn profits. Such efforts are called *corporate philanthropy*.

Public Health Issues

As businesses address their ethical and social responsibilities to the general public, one of the most complex issues is public health. Central to the public health debate is what businesses should do about dangerous products such as tobacco and alcohol. Many cities have banned smoking not only in public places but also in commercial businesses such as restaurants. A 10-year study in Toronto revealed that cardiovascular hospital admissions dropped by 39 percent after smoking was banned in public places.[24]

Rates of heart disease, diabetes, and obesity have been increasing. These three conditions are now major public health issues. Approximately 1.6 million Canadian children (or 26 percent) are overweight or obese.[25] Three-quarters of obese teenagers will become obese adults who are at risk for heart disease and diabetes. Soft drink companies have been highly criticized for contributing to this and other health related issues. In response, the Coca-Cola Foundation provided a $3 million grant to establish the Coca-Cola Troops for Fitness, a fitness program with classes instructed by military veterans. As well, Coca-Cola supports the Boys & Girls Clubs of America's Triple Play program, a healthy lifestyles program geared to youth and their families.[26]

Substance abuse is another serious public health problem worldwide. Many of the drugs used by athletes are similar to chemicals that are naturally present in the body. As a result, knowing whether an athlete has used drugs can be extremely difficult. Professional players who fail drug tests face tough penalties. The most disappointing drug use scandal involving a Canadian athlete was likely when Ben Johnson was stripped of his gold medal for the 100-metre sprint at the 1988 Olympics for having used the anabolic steroid stanozolol.[27]

SOLVING AN ETHICAL CONTROVERSY

To What Extent Should a CEO Be Held Responsible?

In September 2015, Volkswagen was accused of installing software in its vehicles that would "trick" emissions tests. This software would recognize that an emissions test was being performed and put the vehicle in a mode to temporarily reduce the emissions for the duration of the test. After the test was completed, the emissions would return to as high as 40 times the legal limit. Engineers later admitted to installing this software for as far back as seven years in as many as 11 million cars. The scandal led to Volkswagen shares dropping by 40 percent and expected costs of over 39 billion euros in fines and recalls. CEO Martin Winterkorn resigned shortly after the scandal started.

Should CEOs be replaced for scandals such as the one at Volkswagen in 2015?

PRO

1. Holding the CEO responsible demonstrates to the public that the head of the company is willing to accept responsibility for the actions of all of the company's employees.
2. Current and prospective customers may renew their trust in the company if they feel that someone at a high level is held accountable and that significant measures have been taken to "repair" the problem.

CON

1. Holding the CEO responsible punishes the CEO for something he or she may not have been aware of, as the problem may not have made its way all the way up the corporate ladder.
2. Replacing the CEO creates a clear admission of guilt, which could cause irreparable damage to the company and its brand.

Summary

While in this case the CEO voluntarily stepped down from his position, a company forcing the replacement of a CEO would draw further attention to the situation and portray an admission of guilt. In the case of Volkswagen, several jobs were put at risk since one in seven jobs in Germany are linked to the auto sector, as is 14 percent of the country's GDP. On the other hand, not holding the CEO responsible could have been perceived as the company as a whole not taking responsibility for the impact of its employees' actions.

Sources: *CBC News*, "Volkswagen Flouting Emissions Rules for 7 Years: Report," October 5, 2015, www.cbc.ca/news/business/volkswagen-flouting-emissions-rules-for-7-years-report-1.3257254; *CTV News*, "Costs from Emissions Scandal Piling up for Volkswagen," October 6, 2015, www.ctvnews.ca/autos/costs-from-emissions-scandal-piling-up-for-volkswagen-1.2596840; Kritika Sethi, "Volkswagen Diesel Scandal: Engineers Reportedly Admit to Installing Software," *Car and Bike*, October 5, 2015, http://auto.ndtv.com/news/volkswagen-diesel-scandal-engineers-reportedly-admit-to-installing-software-1226257; Thomson Reuters, "Volkswagen CEO Matthias Mueller Warns of 'Massive' Cost Cutting," *CBC News*, October 6, 2015, www.cbc.ca/news/business/volkswagen-ceo-matthias-mueller-warns-of-massive-cost-cutting-1.3258438; Bronte Lord, "3 Things You Need to Know about the Volkswagen Scandal," *CNN Money*, http://money.cnn.com/video/news/2015/09/22/volkswagen-emissions-cheating-scandal-explained.cnnmoney?iid=EL; Kalyeena Makortoff, "What You Need to Know about the Volkswagen Scandal," *CNBC*, September 22, 2015, www.cnbc.com/2015/09/22/what-you-need-to-know-about-the-volkswagen-scandal.html; "Volkswagen Hit by Cheating Allegations," *CNN Money*, http://money.cnn.com/video/news/2015/09/21/volkswagen-cheating-allegations.cnnmoney.

Protecting the Environment

Businesses consume huge amounts of energy, which increases the use of fossil fuels such as coal and oil for energy production. This activity introduces carbon dioxide and sulphur into Earth's atmosphere. Meanwhile, the sulphur from fossil fuels combines with water vapour in the air to form sulphuric acid. The acid rain that results can travel across continents, killing fish and trees and polluting groundwater. Although acid rain has been tracked for many decades, companies are still being identified and punished for their violations. Mount Polley Mining Corporation currently faces fines of up to $1 million for mistakes leading to the breach of a dam in British Columbia that resulted in the release of 4.5 million cubic metres of metals-laden fine sand that contaminated several lakes, creeks, and rivers in the Cariboo region. This dumping took place on the same day that Ottawa promised to improve environmental monitoring of the Canadian oil sands.[28] In another example of environmental violation, automaker Volkswagen admitted to installing software that would "trick" emissions tests in some of its diesel vehicles. While the company faces potentially billions of dollars in fines and lawsuits, the more immediate fallout from the scandal was the suspension of senior managers and the resignation of its CEO (see "Solving an Ethical Controversy").

Recycling can help companies do their part to protect the environment. Best Buy stores will take your old TVs, DVD players, computers, cellphones, and other electronic devices to avoid having them end up in landfills.

Canadian Tire demonstrates its commitment to preserving the environment through its "Take Back the Light" program. Consumers can take their old CFLs and fluorescent tube light bulbs to Canadian Tire for safe disposal.[30]

Other production and manufacturing methods leave behind large quantities of waste materials. These materials can further pollute the environment and fill already bulging landfills. Some products are difficult to reuse or recycle, particularly electronics that contain toxins such as lead and mercury. Few manufacturers are equipped to deal with recycled materials; some refurbish products and sell them abroad—where they are less likely to be recycled. Hewlett-Packard, however, is making its scanners with a combination of new and recycled plastics. Lead, mercury, and cadmium will soon be banned from new equipment manufactured in Europe. As stricter laws on electronics recycling are passed, many manufacturers and retailers are offering take-back, mail-in, and trade-in programs for discarded electronic equipment. For example, many Best Buy stores now accept televisions, DVD players, computer monitors, cellphones, and other electronic devices. The stores charge a small fee for televisions 81 centimetres and under, CRTs (cathode ray tubes, which are now obsolete), monitors, and laptops, but will give customers a gift card in an equal amount.[29]

For many managers, minimizing pollution and other environmental damage caused by their products or their operating processes is an important economic, legal, and social issue. When General Motors unveiled the Chevrolet Volt, the new car instantly became more popular than conventional hybrids that use a combination of electricity and gasoline. The Volt is entirely electric. After its battery runs down, a gasoline engine powers an onboard generator that recharges the battery. In 2014, Elon Musk, CEO of Tesla Motors, announced that "Tesla will not initiate patent lawsuits against anyone who, in good faith, wants to use our technology." Tesla Motors wants to accelerate the advent of sustainable technology. By sharing their technology with the world in an open-source fashion, the economy can move toward more environmentally friendly modes of transportation that use renewable energy sources. BMW has also entered the mix of electric car manufacturers. The BMW i3 was created as an emissions-free car for city driving that is designed in an environmentally sustainable manner.[31]

Despite difficulties, companies find they can be environmentally friendly and profitable too. Another solution to the problems of pollutants is **recycling**—reprocessing used materials for reuse. Recycling can sometimes provide much of the raw material that manufacturers need, thereby conserving the world's natural resources and reducing the amount of waste sent to landfills.

According to Statistics Canada, the diversion of discarded electronic items away from landfill sites has increased by 115 percent in two years.[32] Manufacturers and federal agencies are struggling to devise a workable system to further manage the problem of electronic waste. In some provinces, consumers pay a surcharge on certain electronics purchases, such as computers, monitors, fax machines, and televisions. In Ontario, this surcharge is part of the Waste Electrical and Electronic Equipment (WEEE) Program.[33] In the meantime, Best Buy, Staples, and other retailers accept all

recycling reprocessing used materials for reuse.

HIT & MISS

Pacific Biodiesel Recycles Oil from French Fries to Fuel

In 1980, Robert King founded King Diesel on the island of Maui in Hawaii. The company used conventional diesel fuel to run the generators at the Central Maui Landfill. In 1995, King became concerned about the large amounts of used cooking oil being dumped. He contacted Daryl Reece at the University of Idaho. Reece helped develop a process that successfully converted used restaurant oils into biodiesel fuel. Together, King and Reece founded Pacific Biodiesel. This company uses biodiesel to run the generators at the landfill in one of America's first commercially viable, community-based biodiesel plants. Today, Pacific Biodiesel and its associated companies produce and sell biodiesel fuel. They also design, build, and support biodiesel plants throughout the United States.

Biodiesel fuel is biodegradable and nontoxic and can be used in any diesel engine. This fuel is produced from renewable resources such as used cooking oil and soybean oil. If not converted to fuel, these oils would be dumped in landfills or down drains. Biodiesel significantly reduces many pollutants and reduces dependence on foreign oil.

On Maui, restaurants pay haulers to take their used cooking oil to the landfill. The haulers pay the county of Oahu for the right to dump garbage at waste facilities. Pacific Biodiesel's facility at the landfill is rent free. The haulers' fees cover most of the county's payment to Pacific Biodiesel for processing the waste. Shipping this waste off the island would be much more expensive, while recycling the oil prolongs the useful life of the landfills and guarantees a local source of energy. On Maui alone, Pacific Biodiesel recycles about 757,000 litres of oil and grease each year.

King says, "We definitely took a leap of faith, but . . . we wanted to do more . . . something to contribute to society . . . [I]t is important to do . . . something that brings you happiness—because the feeling you get by 'doing the right thing' never disappears."

Canadian Pacific and Natural Resources Canada have recently partnered in a pilot project to test the effectiveness of biodiesel in Canada's cold weather regions. So far, these tests have indicated that biodiesel could work effectively despite Canada's colder climate.

Questions for Critical Thinking

1. How might Pacific Biodiesel spread the message that recycling is not only good for the environment, but also good business? How might it reach out to other industries?
2. How does Pacific Biodiesel fulfill its responsibilities to the general public?
3. Would Canadian Pacific likely be as successful as Pacific Biodiesel in making a public impact, given that a U.S. competitor has already established the technology?

Sources: Pacific Biodiesel, accessed February 2010, http://biodiesel.com/; U.S. Environmental Protection Agency, "Food to Fuel: Pacific Biodiesel, Inc.," accessed February 2010, http://www.epa.gov/; Deidre Tegarden, "Pacific Biodiesel," Maui Weekly, November 26, 2009; Canadian Pacific, "Cold Weather Biofuel Testing," accessed March 2, 2012, http://www.cpr.ca/en/in-your-community/environment/Pages/cold-weather-biodiesel-testing.aspx.

---

gadgets for recycling, no matter where they were purchased. Manufacturers Hewlett-Packard and Dell have agreed not to send waste materials overseas. The "Hit & Miss" feature describes a company that puts a creative twist on recycling: Pacific Biodiesel turns used restaurant oil and grease into clean, biodegradable biodiesel fuel.

Many consumers like to support environmentally conscious businesses. To target these customers, companies often use **green marketing**, a marketing strategy that promotes environmentally safe products and production methods. But a business cannot simply claim that its goods or services are environmentally friendly. The Competition Bureau has guidelines for environmental claims. For example, a firm must be able to prove that any environmental claim can be supported by reliable scientific evidence. In addition, as shown in **Table 2.1**, the Competition Bureau states how various environmental terms can be used in advertising and marketing.[34]

Many firms focus on other environmental issues, such as finding renewable sources of clean energy and developing **sustainable** agriculture. Vinod Khosla, founder of Sun Microsystems, is working with a group of high-powered entrepreneurs and investors in the Silicon Valley. They hope to develop a new generation of energy.[35] They're not alone. Many entrepreneurs, large energy firms, and small engineering companies are developing solar energy, geothermal energy, biodiesel, and wind power. As we saw in the "Hit & Miss" feature, Pacific Biodiesel started with one plant and now has branches across the United States. Canadian Pacific is likely to match Pacific Biodiesel's growth in Canada, especially with the support of the Canadian government which has spent nearly $5 billion on the ecoENERGY Innovation Initiative that encourages Canadians and Canadian companies to use and develop cleaner technologies.[36]

green marketing a marketing strategy that promotes environmentally safe products and production methods.

sustainable the capacity to endure in ecology.

Table 2.1 Competition Bureau's Guidelines for Environmental Claims in Green Marketing

IF A COMPANY SAYS A PRODUCT IS...	THE PRODUCT OR PACKAGE MUST...
Degradable	be photodegradable or biodegradable within a given period of time under normal disposal conditions for that type of product or package.
Compostable	biodegrade, generating a relatively homogeneous and stable humus-like substance.
Recyclable	be able to be processed and returned to use in the form of raw materials or products.
Refillable	to be refillable with the same or similar product.

Source: Competition Bureau, *Environmental Claims: A Guide for Industry and Advisors*, June 2008, accessed August 12, 2014, http://www.competitionbureau.gc.ca/eic/site/cb-bc.nsf/eng/02701.html#s10_2.

As another example, the Tim Hortons Coffee Partnership works with the Hanns R. Neumann Stiftung Foundation to contribute to the sustainability of the coffee sector in Guatemala, Colombia, Brazil, Honduras, and El Salvador by working with both the private sector (primarily coffee roasters) and the public sector (donors).[37]

Developing the Quality of the Workforce

In the past, a nation's wealth was often based on its money, production equipment, and natural resources. But a country's true wealth is in its people. An educated, skilled workforce provides the know-how needed to develop new technology, improve productivity, and compete in the global marketplace. To remain competitive, Canadian businesses must take more responsibility for enhancing the quality of its workforce, including encouraging diversity of all kinds.

In developed economies like Canada, many new jobs require a university or college education. Demand is high for workers with advanced skills. That means the difference between the highest-paid and lowest-paid workers is increasing. Education plays an important role in earnings, despite success stories of those who dropped out of college or high school to start a business. Workers with education beyond an undergraduate degree earn an average of $1,200 a week, whereas those with some high school but no diploma earn about $750. Businesses must encourage students to stay in school, continue their education, and sharpen their skills. Tim Hortons provides 220 post-secondary scholarships each year to students who "believe in giving back to the community (through volunteer work)." These scholarships are valued at $1,000 each and are awarded to students in Canada and the United States.[38]

Organizations also face responsibilities for helping women, members of various cultural groups, and those who are physically challenged to contribute fully to the economy. Failure to do so is not only a waste of more than half the nation's workforce, but may be harmful to a firm's public image. Some socially responsible firms also encourage diversity in their business suppliers. COSTI Immigrant Services, based in Toronto, has set up programs to assist immigrant women move into strong roles in the workforce, helping them overcome economic challenges and cultural barriers. COSTI has been helping new immigrants for over 50 years.[39]

The Coca-Cola Company is committed to developing employee diversity. It strives to create an inclusive atmosphere, offers diversity training for employees and managers, and encourages regular dialogue among colleagues, suppliers, customers, and stakeholders. "By building an inclusive workplace environment, The Coca-Cola Company seeks to leverage its worldwide team, which is rich in diverse people, talent, and ideas" according to the company's website.[40] For any global organization to function competitively, diversity is vital.

Corporate Philanthropy

As noted in Chapter 1, not-for-profit organizations play an important role in society by serving the public good. They provide the human resources that enhance the quality of life in communities around the world. To fulfill this mission, many not-for-profit organizations rely on financial donations from the business community. Firms donate billions of dollars each year to not-for-profit organizations. This **corporate philanthropy** includes cash contributions, donations of equipment and products, and supporting the volunteer efforts of company employees. Recipients include cultural organizations, adopt-a-school programs, community development agencies, and housing and job training programs.

Corporate philanthropy can have many positive benefits beyond the "feel-good" rewards of giving. Corporate philanthropy can lead to higher employee morale, enhanced company image, and improved customer relationships. Each year, CIBC and other Canadian companies sponsor the CIBC Run for the Cure, Canada's largest single-day, volunteer-led fundraising event specifically for breast cancer research, education, and awareness. This event not only raises funds for an important cause, but also increases the corporate profiles of CIBC and the other corporate sponsors.[41]

Companies often want to tie their marketing efforts to their charitable giving. For example, many firms contribute to the Olympics; they then create advertising that features the company's sponsorship. This type of advertising is known as *cause-related marketing*. In a recent survey, nearly nine out of ten young people said they believed companies had a duty to support social causes. Nearly seven in eight said they would switch brands to reward a company that supported social causes. Consumers will often pay more for a product if they know the proceeds are going to a good cause. KitchenAid Canada started a "Cook for the Cure" campaign, where it donates $75 of the $470 selling price of its pink line of stand mixers and $50 for every "Cook for the Cure" party to the Canadian Breast Cancer Foundation.[42]

corporate philanthropy an organization's contribution to the communities where it earns profits.

CIBC has taken the lead in the CIBC Run for the Cure, which encourages many other businesses to also participate.

Another form of corporate philanthropy is volunteerism. Thousands of businesses encourage their employees to contribute their time to such projects as Habitat for Humanity, the Red Cross, and the Humane Society. These programs make tangible contributions to the well-being of other citizens while also creating public support and goodwill for the companies and their employees. Sometimes the volunteer work takes place when employees are off the job. Other times firms allow their employees to volunteer during regular working hours. Volunteers with special skills are always needed. After the earthquake in Haiti in 2010, the pilots' union at UPS volunteered to transport supplies and personnel as part of the relief effort.[43]

Responsibilities to Customers

Businesspeople share a social and ethical responsibility to treat their customers fairly and to act in a way that does not cause harm. **Consumerism** is the public demand that a business consider the wants and needs of its customers when making decisions. Consumerism has gained wide acceptance. It is based on the belief that consumers have certain rights. In 1962, U.S. President John F. Kennedy

Consumerism public demand that a business consider the wants and needs of its customers when making decisions.

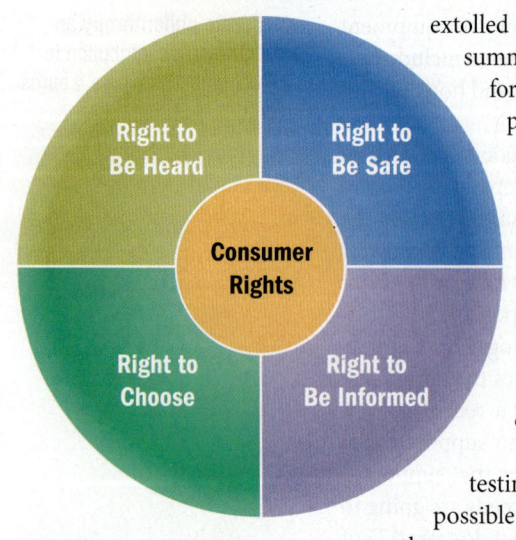

FIGURE 2.6 Commonly Referred-to Consumer Rights

product liability the responsibility of manufacturers for injuries and damages caused by their products.

extolled four basic consumer rights, later called the Consumer Bill of Rights. **Figure 2.6** summarizes these consumer rights. The Consumers' Association of Canada (CAC) was formed in 1947. It helps educate and inform consumers on issues related to buying products and services. It also helps people solve consumer problems by working with government and industry.[44]

The Right to Be Safe

Today's businesspeople have moral and legal obligations to ensure their products are safe to use. Consumers should know that the products they purchase will not cause injuries in normal use. **Product liability** refers to the responsibility of manufacturers for injuries and damages caused by their products. Items that lead to injuries, either directly or indirectly, can have lasting consequences for their manufacturers.

Many companies test their products thoroughly to avoid safety problems. Still, testing cannot check for every possible problem. Companies must try to think of all possible problems and warn consumers of any potential dangers. When a product poses a threat to customer safety, a responsible manufacturer responds quickly. The manufacturer can either correct the problem or recall the dangerous product. We often take for granted that our food supply is safe. But contamination can leak in, causing illness or even death. Maple Leaf Foods had a listeria outbreak at one of its Toronto plants. The company recalled 220 packaged meats in August 2008. Maple Leaf had direct costs of more than $20 million, which did not include the loss of future customer goodwill. At least 42 cases of listeriosis were confirmed, and at least 15 deaths were blamed on the outbreak, resulting in a class action lawsuit settlement of between $25 million and $27 million.[45]

The Right to Be Informed

Consumers should be able to get enough education and product information to make responsible buying decisions. Companies can easily forget the consumer's right to be fully informed while they are busy promoting and selling their goods and services. The Competition Act contains provisions against false or misleading representations and deceptive marketing as well as rules and regulations that lead to advertising truthfulness. These rules keep businesses from making unproven claims about how its products perform or why its products are superior. The act also requires businesses to avoid misleading consumers. Businesses that don't follow these rules may face questions from the Competition Bureau and consumer protection organizations. Persons who are guilty can face criminal penalties of up to 14 years in prison and fines, or both. On a civil level, if a person is found to be liable the fine could be up to $1 million or $15 million for corporations. For instance, Rogers Communications Inc. aired ads that claimed its new discount text-and-talk service Chatr had fewer dropped calls than its competitors. In 2010, the Competition Bureau started an investigation against Rogers resulting in a $500,000 fine, significantly less than the $10 million the Competition Bureau was seeking. The Competition Bureau said that Rogers's claims were misleading according to the Competition Act. "We take misleading advertising very seriously," says Melanie Aitken, commissioner of competition. "Consumers deserve accurate information when making purchasing decisions and need to have confidence they are not being misled by false advertising campaigns." Rogers also aired ads that claimed it had Canada's most reliable network. Competitor TELUS took Rogers to court, and Rogers pulled the ads.[46]

Health Canada supports the Food and Drugs Act. This act defines the standards for safety and advertising to be followed by makers of drugs, cosmetics, and therapeutic devices. The act also requires that all ingredients be listed on product labels so consumers are fully informed.[47]

A business's responsibility to maintain the consumer's right to be informed goes beyond avoiding advertising that misleads. All communications with customers—from salespeople's comments to warranties and invoices—must be checked so that they clearly and accurately inform customers. The labels of most packaged goods, personal computers, and other products include toll-free customer service telephone numbers so that consumers can get answers to their questions.

The Right to Choose

Consumers should have the right to choose the goods and services they need and the goods they want to purchase. Socially responsible firms try to preserve this right, even if it means they need to reduce their own sales and profits. Brand-name drug makers have taken a defensive stand in an issue being discussed by provincial governments, insurance companies, consumer groups, unions, and major employers such as General Motors. These groups want to force down the rising price of prescription drugs. They believe that the government should ensure that consumers have the right and the opportunity to buy cheaper generic brands of drugs. In 2011, however, Ontario enacted regulations stopping pharmacies such as Shoppers Drug Mart and Rexall from selling their lower-priced generic alternatives to brand-name drugs. The reason? Experts claimed these savings were unlikely to be passed on to consumers.[48]

The Right to Be Heard

Consumers should be able to express their valid complaints to the appropriate people. Many companies expend much effort to ensure that consumers' complaints receive a full hearing. The auction website eBay assists buyers and sellers who believe they were unfairly treated in transactions that occur through the site. It uses a 200-employee team to work with eBay users and law enforcement agencies to fight against fraud. The company has strict guidelines for buyers and sellers. It also has rules about leaving feedback about a buyer or seller. For example, sellers must only sell items that are included on a list of acceptable goods for sale. They cannot offer such items as alcohol, pornography, drugs, counterfeit currency, or artifacts from cave formations or graves. The protection of copyright is also an important part of eBay's policy.[49]

Responsibilities to Employees

Companies that can attract skilled and knowledgeable employees are better able to meet the challenges of competing globally. In return, businesses have wide-ranging responsibilities to their employees, both here and abroad. These responsibilities include workplace safety, quality-of-life issues, ensuring equal opportunity on the job, avoiding age discrimination, and preventing sexual harassment and sexism.

Workplace Safety

The safety and health of workers on the job is an important business responsibility. The Canadian Centre for Occupational Health and Safety (CCOHS) promotes workplace health and safety. Workers' compensation programs are managed mostly at the provincial level by organizations such as the Workplace Safety and Insurance Board in Ontario, the Workers' Compensation Board of Nova Scotia, and the Workers' Compensation Board of Alberta. These organizations are responsible for setting workplace safety and health standards. These standards range from broad guidelines on storing hazardous materials to specific standards for worker safety in industries such as construction, manufacturing, and mining. These organizations track and investigate workplace accidents and pay claims to employees who are injured on the job.

According to a 2010 research study, 1 in every 53 employed workers each year is injured and receives workers' compensation.[50] Many people die every year in Canada as a result of work-related injuries. Most of these fatalities occur because of unsafe equipment, inadequate safety training, and dangerous work that is illegal or inappropriate for youth. Provincial workers' compensation boards, labour ministries, and the CCOHS are working to educate employers and young workers about safety, health, and a positive work environment.

Workplace safety is an important business responsibility. Workers are required to wear safety equipment, such as hard hats, goggles, and reflective wear, when in potentially dangerous areas.

Quality-of-Life Issues

Balancing work and family is becoming harder for many employees. They work long hours then go home to face childcare tasks, caring for their elderly parents, and solving other family crises. A *sandwich generation* of households has arisen. This term refers to people caring for two generations—their children and their aging parents. The population is growing older, and more and more Canadians provide some type of care to a relative or friend aged 50 or older. At the same time, most mothers spend more time working outside the home. That means they have fewer hours to spend with their family.

The employees who juggle work with life's other demands aren't just working mothers. Childless couples, single people, and men all say they are frustrated with having to balance work with family and personal needs. Some employers are trying to help their employees find a work–life balance. They do this by offering flexible work schedules so that parents can do their jobs *and* meet the needs of their children (or aging parents). Each year, the editors of *Canada's Top 100 Employers* organize a competition called Canada's Top Family-Friendly Employers. Employers who make the top 100 have made a big commitment to help their employees balance work and family commitments. Some of the employers who made this list in 2014 were the University of Toronto, Manitoba Hydro, and CIBC.[51]

Increasingly, women are starting their own businesses so they can set their own hours and goals. The "Hit & Miss" feature describes one woman who started her own business so she could provide her ailing son with the care he needed.

Some companies have come up with truly innovative ways to deal with work schedules, including paid time off for vacation or illness. At some of its locations, IBM has done away with vacation time altogether—instead, the focus is on results. Employees have an informal agreement with their supervisors about when they will be out of the office. This time away is based on their ability to complete their work on schedule. The number of days they take off is not tracked; instead,

fair trade a market-based approach of paying higher prices to producers for goods exported from developing countries to developed countries in an effort to promote sustainability and to ensure the people in developing countries receive better trading conditions.

HIT & MISS

Balancing Life and Work with a Cup of Tea

In 2000, Zhena Muzyka, a 25-year-old single mother, had an infant son who needed kidney surgery. Muzyka had no health insurance and only a few dollars in the bank. As a young girl, she had watched her Rom (gypsy) grandmother tend a huge garden and blend teas. Muzyka had always been interested in herbal medicine, so she borrowed money from her parents and her brother and started Zhena's Gypsy Tea. She started selling tea from a cart in a friend's antique store. At first, she worked with her son, Sage, in a baby carrier at her side. When her teas became popular—and Sage outgrew the carrier—she knew she had reached a turning point.

Muzyka searched for new sources and started blending her own loose-leaf teas. She added essential oils for their medicinal value. She learned that none of the teas she was buying was organic or **fair trade**. She made the change to fair trade teas after learning that infant mortality rates among tea pickers on non-fair trade farms can reach 70 percent. Fair trade tea workers have guaranteed healthcare, clean water, education, and maternity leave and childcare.

As Zhena's Gypsy Tea has grown and diversified, Muzyka has searched for new ways to put her values into practice. Her Pink Tea for Women's Health is a partner of the Breast Cancer Research Foundation. The company now uses corn silk for its teabags. It buys wind credits, even though it lowers profits. Muzyka says, "[Zhena's Gypsy Tea] is the most 'worth it' thing I've ever done. Knowing that we're sincerely making a difference for people and helping them out of poverty—while providing a delicious cup of tea for consumers here—is pretty satisfying."

And Sage? After three operations, he had a clean bill of health in 2007.

Questions for Critical Thinking

1. How did Zhena Muzyka translate her life experiences into her company's ethics culture?
2. Do you have an idea for starting your own business? If so, brainstorm some ideas for balancing your life and values with your work.
3. What key provincial or federal legislation would you need to be aware of, especially if your business was to grow and employ a significant number of staff members?

Sources: Zhena's Gypsy Tea, www.zhenas.com, accessed February 2010; Eve Gumpel, "Gypsy Tea Steeped in Health and Fun," *Women Entrepreneur.com,* January 24, 2010, www.womenentrepreneur.com; "Oh, That's So Yesterday: A California Tea Company Gets a Brand Makeover," *Inc.,* December 2009/January 2010.

vacation time is considered open ended. But the catch is, the work needs to be done. With some surprises, the firm found that employees put in just as many hours, if not more hours, under the new program. According to an IBM representative, "there is no policing, and employees are empowered to take vacation when they want."[52]

Ensuring Equal Opportunity on the Job

Businesspeople face many challenges when managing an increasingly diverse workforce in the twenty-first century. Technological advances are expanding the ways people with physical disabilities can contribute in the workplace. Businesses also need to find ways to responsibly recruit and manage older workers and workers with varying lifestyles. In 1982, Lotus Development (later Lotus Software) was the first major company to offer full benefits to its employees' partners, regardless of sexual orientation. This means that the company offers such benefits as health insurance to its employees' unmarried domestic partners if it also offers the same benefits to its employees' married spouses. Companies that now offer these gender-neutral benefits include Avon Products, Costco Wholesale, Disney, General Mills, and Mattel. Companies such as WestJet and BlackBerry advertise that their hiring practices do not discriminate in terms of sexual orientation, colour, race, religion, and so on.[53]

The Canadian Charter of Rights and Freedoms is an all-encompassing act that addresses **discrimination** in Canada. Section 15 states "Every individual is equal before and under the law and has the right to the equal protection and equal benefit of the law without discrimination and, in particular, without discrimination based on race, national or ethnic origin, colour, religion, sex, age, or mental or physical disability." **Table 2.2** describes other specific types of equal opportunity employee protections.[54]

discrimination biased treatment toward a job candidate or employee.

Table 2.2 Protections Designed to Ensure Equal Opportunity

FOCUS	LAW	KEY PROVISIONS
Equal rights	Canadian Charter of Rights and Freedoms, 1982	Every individual is equal before and under the law and has the right to the equal protection and equal benefit of the law without discrimination and, in particular, without discrimination based on race, national or ethnic origin, colour, religion, sex, age, or mental or physical disability.
Physical and mental disabilities	Canadian Human Rights Act and provincial human rights codes	Forbids age discrimination in employment—with exceptions in some cases regarding mandatory retirement and bona fide occupational requirements. Requires employers to make reasonable accommodations for employees with new or pre-existing mental or physical disabilities.
Equal pay for equal work	Provincial employment standards acts	Ensures equal pay for equal work when work is substantially the same, requires the same effort, and is performed under the same working conditions at the same establishment.
Physical and mental disabilities	Canadian Disability Vocational Rehabilitation Program and provincial vocational rehabilitation acts	Provides work and personal adjustment training and support for people with disabilities who seek gainful employment.
Pregnancy and parental leave	Provincial labour ministries	Employers cannot penalize employees for taking pregnancy or parental leave. Employees who take such leaves have the right to earn credit toward their length of service. They typically must be returned to their job after their pregnancy or parental leave is over.
Family medical leave	Provincial labour ministries	Allows an employee to take up to 8 weeks of unpaid leave in a 26-week period to care for a seriously ill family member.
Reservists	Provincial labour ministries	Employees who are reservists and deployed on an operation are to be granted unpaid leave without benefits. While on leave, their seniority and length of service will accumulate.

Employment Equity Act (EEA) an act created (1) to increase job opportunities for women and members of minority groups and (2) to help end discrimination based on race, colour, religion, disability, gender, or national origin.

The **Employment Equity Act (EEA)** was created for two reasons: to increase job opportunities for women and members of minority groups and to help end discrimination in any personnel action that is based on race, colour, religion, disability, gender, or national origin. To enforce fair-employment laws, this act is overseen by the Canadian Human Rights Commission, which investigates charges of discrimination and harassment. The EEA can also help employers set up programs to increase job opportunities for women, members of minority groups, people with disabilities, and people in other protected categories.

Age Discrimination

The average age of Canadian workers is steadily rising. In a few years, more than half the workforce will be aged 40 or older. Some employers find it less expensive to hire and retain younger workers. These younger employees generally have lower medical bills and typically receive lower salaries and benefits packages. But many older workers have training and skills that younger workers lack. The Canadian Human Rights Act (CHRA) prohibits age discrimination except in very specific cases.

In 2008, Kim Ouwroulis, aged 44, was an exotic dancer at the New Locomotion club in Mississauga, Ontario. She filed a complaint with the Ontario Human Rights Commission, claiming she was fired because of her age. These types of cases require the employer to prove that "sex appeal is the essence of the job," says Denise Reaume, a University of Toronto professor who specializes in discrimination law. "This is tricky because sexual response is as variable as human beings are."[55]

Legal issues aside, employers should consider not only the experience that older workers bring to the workplace but also their enthusiasm. "Job satisfaction is especially high among those 65 and over because most people working at that age are not forced to still work, due to financial reasons, but choose to do so because they like their jobs," says the leader of a recent study. Nearly 75 percent of people over age 65 who were interviewed said they were very happy with their jobs.[56]

In all cases, employers need to plan ahead for the aging of the workforce. Such planning includes finding ways to retain accumulated business wisdom, preparing for the demand for health services, and being ready for growth in the industries that serve older adults. The number of people aged 55 to 64 has increased by almost 30 percent in the past few years. It is expected that the retirement of the baby boomers will lead to an $11,500 per capita loss of productivity.[57] These numbers show a coming shift in the workforce and in the goods and services needed.

Employers are responsible for avoiding age discrimination in the workplace. As the average age of workers rises, employers will benefit from the older generation's knowledge.

Sexual Harassment and Sexism

Every employer has a responsibility to ensure that all workers are treated fairly and are safe from sexual harassment. **Sexual harassment** refers to unwelcome and inappropriate actions of a sexual nature. It is a form of sex discrimination that violates the CHRA, which gives both men and women the right to file lawsuits for intentional sexual harassment. Thousands of sexual harassment complaints are filed each year, and many complaints are filed by men. Thousands of other cases are either handled internally by companies or never reported.

The workplace has two types of sexual harassment. The first type occurs when an employee is pressured to go along with unwelcome advances and requests for sexual favours in return for job security, promotions, and raises. The second type results from a hostile work environment, where an employee feels hassled or degraded because of unwelcome flirting, lewd comments, or obscene jokes. The courts have ruled that allowing sexually oriented materials in the workplace can create a hostile atmosphere that interferes with an employee's ability to work. Employers are also legally responsible to protect employees from sexual harassment by customers and clients. The Canadian Human Rights Commission's website helps employers and employees by listing the criteria for identifying sexual harassment and how it should be handled in the workplace.

Firms should prevent sexual harassment for ethical and legal reasons. But did you know that sexual harassment can also be costly? The cost in settlements or fines can be huge. It makes good business sense for firms to prevent this kind of behaviour. Many firms have set up policies and employee education programs aimed at preventing such problems. An effective harassment prevention program should include the following:

- A specific policy statement prohibiting sexual harassment
- A complaint procedure for employees to follow
- A work atmosphere that encourages sexually harassed staffers to come forward
- A commitment to investigate and resolve complaints quickly and to take disciplinary action against harassers

These components need to be supported by top management; otherwise, sexual harassment is difficult to get rid of.

Sexual harassment is often part of the broader problem of **sexism**—discrimination against members of either sex, but usually against women. One important sexism issue is equal pay for equal work.

On average, a Canadian woman earns 74 percent of what a man earns.[58] The difference can't be explained by differences in education, occupation, work hours, or other factors. The only explanation seems to be being female.[59] In some extreme cases, differences in pay and advancement can lead to sex discrimination suits. These suits, like sexual harassment suits, can be costly and time consuming to settle. As in all business practices, it is better to act legally and ethically in the first place.

RESPONSIBILITIES TO INVESTORS AND THE FINANCIAL COMMUNITY

A fundamental goal of any business is to make a profit for its shareholders. But investors and the financial community also demand that businesses behave ethically and legally. When firms fail in this responsibility, thousands of investors and consumers can suffer.

Provincial regulators such as the Ontario Securities Commission and the Alberta Securities Commission are primarily responsible for protecting investors from financial misdeeds. These provincial regulators investigate suspicions of unethical or illegal behaviour by publicly traded

---

Sexual harassment unwelcome and inappropriate actions of a sexual nature.

sexism discrimination against members of either sex, but usually against women.

✓ ASSESSMENT CHECK

2.4.1 What is meant by social responsibility, and why do firms pay attention to it?

2.4.2 What is green marketing?

2.4.3 What are the four main consumer rights?

LO 2.5 Explain the ethical responsibilities of businesses to investors and the financial community.

ASSESSMENT CHECK

2.5.1 Why do firms need to do more than just earn a profit?

2.5.2 What is the role of the provincial securities regulators?

firms. They look into accusations that a business is using faulty accounting practices to inaccurately report its financial resources and profits to investors. Recall that legislation such as Bill 198 in Canada and the Sarbanes-Oxley Act of 2002 in the United States protect investors from unethical accounting practices. In 2009, Garth Drabinsky and Myron Gottlieb were found guilty of preparing fraudulent accounting information at Toronto-based Livent Inc. They defrauded investors of approximately $500 million. Livent was well known as the producer of *The Phantom of the Opera*, Toronto's longest-running musical.[60] Chapter 16 discusses securities trading practices further.

WHAT'S AHEAD

The decisions and actions of businesspeople are often influenced by outside forces, such as the legal environment and society's expectations about business responsibility. Firms are also affected by the economic environment where they operate. The next chapter discusses the broad economic issues that influence businesses around the world. Our discussion will focus on how certain factors—supply and demand, unemployment, inflation, and government monetary policies—pose both challenges and opportunities when firms seek to compete in the global marketplace.

RETURN TO INSIDE BUSINESS

Cirque du Soleil: A Class Act in Social Responsibility

Businesses in today's corporate environment try to operate in a socially responsible manner. Companies like the Cirque du Soleil have taken significant measures to both operate in a socially responsible manner and publicize their efforts.

QUESTIONS FOR CRITICAL THINKING

1. Do you feel that corporate social responsibility has a significant impact on Cirque du Soleil's success, or is it just a "nice to have"?

2. Does a firm need to publicize its corporate social responsibility efforts? Or does company-sponsored publicity make it appear that these efforts are undertaken solely to generate revenues through positive public relations?

SUMMARY OF LEARNING OBJECTIVES

LO 2.1 Explain the concepts of business ethics and social responsibility.

Business ethics are the standards of conduct and moral values that businesspeople rely on to guide their actions and decisions in the workplace. Businesspeople must consider a wide range of social issues when making decisions. Social responsibility is management's acceptance of the obligation to put an equal value on profit, consumer satisfaction, and societal well-being when evaluating the firm's performance.

✓ ASSESSMENT CHECK ANSWERS

2.1.1 To whom do businesses have responsibilities? Businesses have responsibilities to customers, employees, investors, and society.

2.1.2 If a firm is meeting all its responsibilities to others, why do ethical conflicts arise? Ethical conflicts arise because businesses must balance doing what is right and doing what is profitable.

LO 2.2 Describe the factors that influence business ethics.

Many factors shape individual ethics, including personal experience, peer pressure, and organizational culture. Individual ethics are also influenced by family, cultural, and religious standards. The culture of the workplace can also be a factor.

✓ ASSESSMENT CHECK ANSWERS

2.2.1 What is the role of a firm's ethics compliance officer? Ethics compliance officers must discourage wrongdoing and ensure that ethical standards are met.

2.2.2 What factors influence the ethical environment of a business? Individual ethics and technology influence the ethical environment of a business.

LO 2.3 Discuss how organizations shape ethical behaviour.

Conflicts of interest occur when an action that benefits one person may harm another person. For example, a businessperson's own interests may conflict with the interests of a customer. Honesty and integrity are valued qualities that lead to trust, but a person's immediate self-interest may lead to actions that go against these principles. Loyalty to an employer sometimes conflicts with being truthful. When misconduct occurs in the workplace, some employees may think about being whistle-blowers, but the personal costs may be high. Employees are strongly influenced by the standards of conduct already set up and supported in their workplace. Businesses can help shape ethical behaviour by using codes of conduct that define what they expect from employees. Organizations can also use this training to develop employees' ethics awareness and reasoning. Employers can promote ethical action by providing decision-making tools, supporting goals that are consistent with ethical behaviour, and by setting up advice hotlines. Executives must also provide ethical leadership by showing ethical behaviour in all their decisions and actions.

✓ ASSESSMENT CHECK ANSWERS

2.3.1 For an employee, when does loyalty conflict with truth? Truth conflicts with loyalty when the truth about a company or a situation is unfavourable.

2.3.2 How does ethical leadership contribute to ethical standards throughout a company? When leaders and managers behave ethically, employees are more likely to commit to the company's core values.

LO 2.4 Describe how businesses can act responsibly to satisfy society.

Today's businesses are expected to weigh two things: their qualitative impact on consumers and society and their quantitative economic contributions in terms of sales, employment levels, and profits. Social responsibility can be measured by charitable contributions and compliance with labour laws and consumer protection laws. Some businesses choose to conduct social audits. Public-interest groups also create standards for measuring companies' performance. A business's responsibilities to the general public include protecting public health and the environment and developing the quality of the workforce. Some also argue that businesses have a social responsibility to support charitable and social causes in the communities where they earn profits. Businesses must also treat customers fairly and protect consumers. Businesses do this by upholding consumers' rights to be safe, to be informed, to choose, and to be heard. Businesses have wide-ranging responsibilities to their employees. They need to ensure that the workplace is safe, address quality-of-life issues, ensure equal opportunity, and prevent sexual harassment and other forms of discrimination.

✓ ASSESSMENT CHECK ANSWERS

2.4.1 What is meant by social responsibility, and why do firms pay attention to it? Social responsibility is management's responsibility to consider profit, consumer satisfaction, and society's well-being as having equal value when evaluating the firm's performance. Businesses pay attention to it for many reasons: because it is required by law, because it enhances the company's image, and because it is the right thing to do.

2.4.2 What is green marketing? Green marketing is a marketing strategy that promotes environmentally safe products and production methods.

2.4.3 What are the four main consumer rights? The four main consumer rights are the rights to be safe, to be informed, to choose, and to be heard.

LO 2.5 Explain the ethical responsibilities of businesses to investors and the financial community.

Investors and the financial community demand that businesses behave ethically and legally in their handling of financial transactions. Businesses must be honest in reporting their profits and financial performance to avoid misleading investors. Provincial securities regulators investigate suspicions that publicly traded firms have engaged in unethical or illegal financial behaviour.

✓ ASSESSMENT CHECK ANSWERS

2.5.1 Why do firms need to do more than just earn a profit?
Firms need to do more than just earn a profit for two reasons: because the law requires them to behave in a legal and ethical manner and because investors and shareholders demand such behaviour.

2.5.2 What is the role of the provincial securities regulators?
Among other functions, provincial securities regulators investigate suspicions of unethical or illegal behaviour by publicly traded firms.

BUSINESS TERMS YOU NEED TO KNOW

business ethics 30
code of conduct 37
conflict of interest 35
consumerism 47
corporate philanthropy 47
discrimination 51
Employment Equity Act (EEA) 52

fair trade 50
green marketing 45
integrity 35
product liability 48
recycling 44
Sarbanes-Oxley Act of 2002 33
sexism 53

sexual harassment 53
social audits 41
social responsibility 40
stakeholders 39
sustainable 45
whistle-blowing 36

REVIEW QUESTIONS

1. What do the terms *business ethics* and *social responsibility* mean? Why are they important components of a firm's overall philosophy in conducting business?

2. How do individuals make a difference in a firm's commitment to ethics? Describe the three stages an individual goes through when developing ethical standards.

3. Identify the ethical dilemmas in each of the following situations (a situation might involve more than one dilemma):
   a. Due to the breakup with a client, an advertising agency finds itself working with rival companies.
   b. A newly hired employee learns that the office manager plays computer games on company time.
   c. A drug manufacturer offers a doctor an expensive gift to encourage the doctor to prescribe a new brand-name drug.
   d. An employee is told to destroy documents that show a firm's role in spreading pollution.
   e. A company spokesperson agrees to a media conference that puts a positive spin on the firm's use of underpaid labour.

4. Describe how ethical leadership helps to develop each of the other ethical standards.

5. How do firms demonstrate their social responsibility?

6. What are the four major areas where businesses have responsibilities to the general public? How can meeting these responsibilities lead to a competitive advantage?

7. Describe the four basic rights that consumerism tries to protect. How has consumerism improved the contemporary business environment? What challenges has consumerism created for businesses?

8. What five major responsibilities do companies have to their employees? What changes in society are affecting these responsibilities?

9. Which equal opportunity laws or acts protect the following workers?
   a. An employee who must care for an elderly parent.
   b. A Canadian Armed Forces member who is returning from deployment overseas.
   c. A job applicant who is HIV positive.
   d. A person who is over 40 years old.
   e. A woman who has been sexually harassed on the job.
   f. A woman who has a family history of breast cancer.

10. How does a company show its responsibility to investors and to the financial community?

PROJECTS AND TEAMWORK APPLICATIONS

1. Write your own personal code of ethics. Create standards for your behaviour at school, in personal relationships, and on the job. Assess how well you meet your own standards. Revise your code of ethics, if necessary.

2. On your own or with a classmate, visit the website of one of the following firms, or choose another that interests you. Use what you can learn about the company from the website to construct a chart or figure that shows examples of the firm's ethical awareness, ethical education, ethical actions, and ethical leadership. Present your findings to the class.

   a. Tim Hortons
   b. National Hockey League (NHL), or any major professional sports league
   c. TELUS Mobility
   d. RBC Financial Group
   e. BlackBerry
   f. RONA
   g. IKEA

3. Using the company you studied for question 2 (or another company), conduct a social audit. Do your findings match the firm's culture of ethics? If not, what are the differences and why did they occur?

4. On your own or with a classmate, go online, flip through a magazine, or surf television channels to identify a firm that uses green marketing. If you see a commercial on television, go to the firm's website to learn more about the product or process advertised. Does the firm make claims that comply with the Competition Bureau's guidelines? Present your findings in class.

5. As a consumer, you expect the companies you do business with will have a certain level of responsibility toward you. Describe a situation when you felt that a company did not recognize your rights as a consumer. How did you handle the situation? How did the company handle it? What was the final outcome?

WEB ASSIGNMENTS

1. **Ethical standards.** Go to the website listed below. It summarizes the ethical standards for all TELUS employees. Read the material and write a brief report that compares TELUS's ethical standards to the discussion on corporate ethics in this chapter. In addition, consider how TELUS's ethical standards are integrated into the firm's overall efforts at global citizenship.

   http://about.telus.com/community/english/investor_relations/corporate_governance

2. **Starting a career.** Each year, *Canada's Top 100 Employers* rates the best companies to work for. Visit the *Canada's Top 100 Employers* website and review the most recent list. What criteria did *Canada's Top 100 Employers* use when building this list? What role does ethics and social responsibility play?

   www.canadastop100.com/national

3. **Social responsibility.** Footwear manufacturer La Canadienne is one of the few companies in its industry that still manufactures products in Canada. Go to the website listed below to learn more about the firm's commitment to Canadian manufacturing. Prepare a report that relates this commitment to the firm's other core values.

   www.lacanadienneshoes.com

Note: Internet addresses change frequently. If you don't find the exact sites listed, you may need to access the organization's home page and search from there or use a search engine such as Bing or Google.

3 ECONOMIC CHALLENGES FACING CONTEMPORARY BUSINESS

LEARNING OBJECTIVES

LO 3.1 Discuss microeconomics and the forces of demand and supply.

LO 3.2 Describe macroeconomics and the three major types of economic systems.

LO 3.3 Explain how productivity, price level changes, and employment levels affect economic performance.

LO 3.4 Discuss how monetary policy and fiscal policy are used to manage an economy's performance.

LO 3.5 Describe the major global economic challenges of the twenty-first century.

INSIDE BUSINESS

Vancouver's 2010 Olympic Village: Seemed Like a Great Idea at the Time

The idea was simple—build condominium apartments to house athletes during the Vancouver 2010 Olympic Games and then sell the apartments and make a profit. And it had seemed like a good idea to most people in business and government. The public–private apartment development with Millennium Development Corporation was part of an environmentally positive effort to reclaim polluted land in Vancouver's False Creek area.

But timing is everything. Sometimes real estate markets are hot and prices are high, and sometimes they're not. The expected buyers didn't step forward. Everyone accepted that the market forces of supply and demand were at work in Vancouver's real estate market. One year later, only 30 units had been sold. The Olympic Village went into receivership. The appointed receiver, Ernst and Young, looked at how to sell units in the overpriced complex. Its study suggested cutting prices on 230 of the 1,100 units and renting 127 units. This plan would increase occupancy to 70 percent of the complex. It would also help to kick-start more interest in buying. According to some analysts, the City of Vancouver might be forced to pay lenders $50 million to $150 million if the $500-million loan repayment by project developer Millennium is reduced by any losses from the project.

Real estate is usually a sure route to lower-cost housing for Canadians—in the long run. Most homeowners can expect to pay more than renters for the first 7 to 10 years of a mortgage. Then, the financial benefit shifts from the renter to the homeowner. This pattern is generally true because rents continue to rise but the cost of owning rises at a slower pace. This effect is mostly because the price of the real estate is fixed at the time of sale, whereas rents may go up or down depending on the demand and supply for rental property.

Many people think that buying real estate is a "no brainer" and that they can't really lose when they make mortgage payments instead of paying rent. After all, what do you have after paying rent year after year? But it is different for homeowners. After homeowners pay down a mortgage loan for a few years, they are closer to full ownership of their real estate investment.

But is that always true? Many people do not understand how supply and demand work in the real estate and rentals markets. Sometimes it's clearly better to buy than to rent. But sometimes during a short period of only a few years it can make little financial difference. And sometimes renting is the best financial choice. According to some analysts, we might now be in a longer than usual period of poor performance for real estate, when buying is financially equivalent to renting.

Think about today's market forces: The demand for real estate is highly linked to changes in population. After all, the more population grows in an area, and the more incomes increase, the greater is the demand for a place to live. Many factors affect the demand for home ownership, such as homeowners' ages and their number of children. We also need to think about whether people plan to stay around for a long time or if they are only moving in for a short time before moving on again. When it's time to move, it's a lot easier to hand the keys of a rental over to the landlord than to have to sell a property.

The amount of real estate available for sale is the supply side of this equation. If there is not enough housing for the people who need it, prices will rise; but if people are moving away the market will have difficulty keeping prices stable.

Maybe the greatest influence on whether to buy real estate is the expectation of profit. One way people can better decide whether to buy or rent is to compare the total cost of renting for, say, a 10-year period, to the costs of owning the same property. Predicting rents over a 10-year period is difficult, and predicting changes to the value of the property, interest rates on the mortgage loans, and local taxes is even more of a challenge.

From 1992 to 2002, Vancouver real estate prices were virtually flat, showing very little upward movement. The trend broke in 2003. Prices have continued to grow higher until now. Some people think that prices might have increased too much. Others think that prices might flatten out for a long period, as they did from 1992 to 2002. Some fear prices might take a sudden drop. The only certain thing is that prices, high or low, will affect the relative business success of the Olympic condominium properties.[1]

CHAPTER 3 OVERVIEW

When we look at the exchanges that companies and societies make as a whole, we are focusing on the *economic systems* in different nations. These systems show the combination of a nation's policies and how it divides its resources among its citizens. Countries divide up their scarce resources in different ways.

Economics studies the choices people and governments make when dividing up their scarce resources. Economics affects each of us because everyone is involved in producing, distributing, or consuming goods and services. Your life is affected by economics every day. When you decide what product to buy, what services to use, or what activities to fit into your day you are making economic choices. An important part of economics is understanding how the activities of one industry affect the activities of other industries, and how these activities fit into the overall picture of a country.

The choices you make may have international effects. For example, if you want to buy a new car, you might visit several dealers on the same street—Ford, Chrysler, Honda, Hyundai, and General Motors. You might decide to buy a car from Toyota, a Japanese firm, but your car might have been made in Canada using parts from all over the world. Firms sometimes advertise the Canadian origin of their products in hopes that consumers will buy their products to support the Canadian economy. But many products are made of parts imported from several nations.

Businesses and not-for-profit organizations also make economic decisions when they choose how to use human and natural resources; how to invest in equipment, machinery, and buildings; and how to form partnerships with other firms. **Microeconomics** is the study of small economic units, such as individual consumers, families, and businesses.

The study of a country's overall economic issues is called **macroeconomics** (*macro* means "large"). Macroeconomics studies how an economy uses its resources and how government policies affect standards of living. For example, using ethanol in place of gasoline or biodiesel instead of diesel fuel has macroeconomic outcomes. It affects the Canadian economy and suppliers around the world. Macroeconomics studies not just the economic policies of individual nations but how those individual policies affect the overall world economy. Much business takes place around the world, so a law in one country can easily affect a transaction in another country. Macroeconomic issues have broad effects. They also help shape the decisions made by individuals, families, and businesses every day.

This chapter introduces economic theory and the economic challenges facing individuals, businesses, and governments in the global marketplace. We begin by discussing the microeconomic concepts of supply and demand and their effect on the prices for goods and services. Next we explain the various types of economic systems and the tools for comparing and evaluating their performance. Then we look at how governments try to manage economies to create stable business environments. The final section looks at some of the driving economic forces currently affecting people's lives.

economics the social science that studies the choices people and governments make when dividing up their scarce resources.

microeconomics the study of small economic units such as individual consumers, families, and businesses.

macroeconomics the study of a nation's overall economic issues, such as how an economy maintains and divides up resources and how a government's policies affect its citizens' standards of living.

LO 3.1 Discuss microeconomics and the forces of demand and supply.

MICROECONOMICS: THE FORCES OF DEMAND AND SUPPLY

Think about your own economic activities. You shop for groceries, subscribe to a cellphone service, pay tuition, and fill your car's tank with gas. Now think about your family's economic activities. When you were growing up your parents might have owned a home or rented an apartment; you might have taken a family vacation; your parents may have shopped at discount clubs or local stores. These decisions about spending money relate to the study of microeconomics. The choices about where to spend money help to set both the prices of goods and services and the amounts sold. Information about these activities is important to companies because staying in business and growing means they need to sell enough products priced high enough to cover costs and earn profits.

The same information is also important to consumers who need to decide what to buy and where to buy it. Consumers' decisions are usually based on the prices and the supply of the goods and services they need.

At the heart of every business is an exchange between a buyer and a seller. The buyer needs or wants a good or service—such as a hamburger or a haircut—and is willing to pay a seller for that good or service. The seller needs the exchange to earn a profit and stay in business. The exchange process involves both demand and supply. **Demand** is the willingness and ability of buyers to purchase goods and services at different prices. The other side of the exchange is **supply**, the amount of goods and services for sale at different prices. When you understand the factors that lead to demand and supply, and how demand and supply work together, you then know more about the many actions and decisions made by individuals, businesses, and government. This section takes a closer look at these ideas.

demand the willingness and ability of buyers to purchase goods and services.

supply the willingness and ability of sellers to provide goods and services.

You shop for groceries, subscribe to a cellphone service, pay tuition, and fill your car's tank with gas. These decisions about spending money relate to the study of microeconomics. The choices about where to spend money also help to set the prices of goods and the amounts sold.

Factors Driving Demand

For most of us, economics is a balance between what we want and what we can pay. Each person must choose how much money to save and how much to spend. We must also decide what to buy from all the goods and services available. Suppose you want to buy a smartphone. You have to choose one smartphone from many brands and models. You also have to decide where to go to buy your smartphone. After shopping around, you might decide you don't want a smartphone after all. You might decide to purchase something else or to save your money.

Demand is driven by many factors that affect how people decide to spend their money. Demand can be driven by price or by what consumers like best. It may also be driven by outside conditions or by larger economic events. During the 2008–2010 recession, 2009 sales in the video game industry—including portable players and consoles, software, and associated items—dropped 8 percent from the previous year. Nevertheless, the past several years were the strongest years for video game sales.[2]

Demand can also increase the number of certain types of websites and services. For example, major Canadian satellite and cable distributors, such as Rogers and Bell, are increasing the number of "on demand" programs that customers can view. Also, after many popular television programs have aired, they can be viewed from their television websites, such as Citytv.com. In the American television market, the popularity of Google's YouTube has led to networks NBC and Fox teaming up to launch an advertising-supported online video site. The site, called Hulu.com, offers full-length movies and television shows. It also hosts programming from NBC and Fox and shows from Sony and MGM Studios (Disney joined later).[3] Hulu is not yet available in Canada, but the service will likely be channelled through Canadian providers or replicated by a Canadian source someday.

In general, when the price of a good or service goes up, people buy smaller amounts. In other words, as price rises the quantity demanded declines. At lower prices, consumers are generally willing to buy more of a good. A **demand curve** is a graph showing the amount of a product that buyers will purchase at different prices. Demand curves typically slope downward because lower and lower prices attract larger and larger purchases.

Gasoline prices are a classic example of how demand curves work. The left side of **Figure 3.1** shows a possible demand curve for the total amount of gasoline that people will purchase at different prices. The prices shown may not be the actual prices in your location today, but they still show how the demand curve works. When gasoline is priced at $1.39 per litre, drivers may fill up their tanks once or twice a week. At $1.69 per litre, many drivers start reducing the gas they use. They may combine errands or carpool. The quantity of gasoline demanded at $1.69 per litre is lower than the amount demanded at $1.39 per litre. The opposite happens when gas prices drop to $1.09 per litre. More gasoline is sold at $1.09 per litre than at $1.39 per litre because people choose to run more errands or to take more weekend trips. However, as noted earlier, other factors may lead to consumers paying higher prices. They may have already made vacation plans and do not want to cancel them or they may need to drive to work every day.

Economists make it clear that changes in the quantity demanded at various prices are different from changes (shifts) in overall demand. A change in quantity demanded, such as the change that occurs at different gasoline prices, is simply movement along one demand curve. A change in

Demand is driven by consumer tastes and preferences and by economic conditions. Consumers tend to fill up their gas tanks more frequently when the per-litre price is low.

demand curve a graph of the amount of a product that buyers will purchase at different prices.

A. Demand Curve for Gasoline and Change in Quantity Demanded

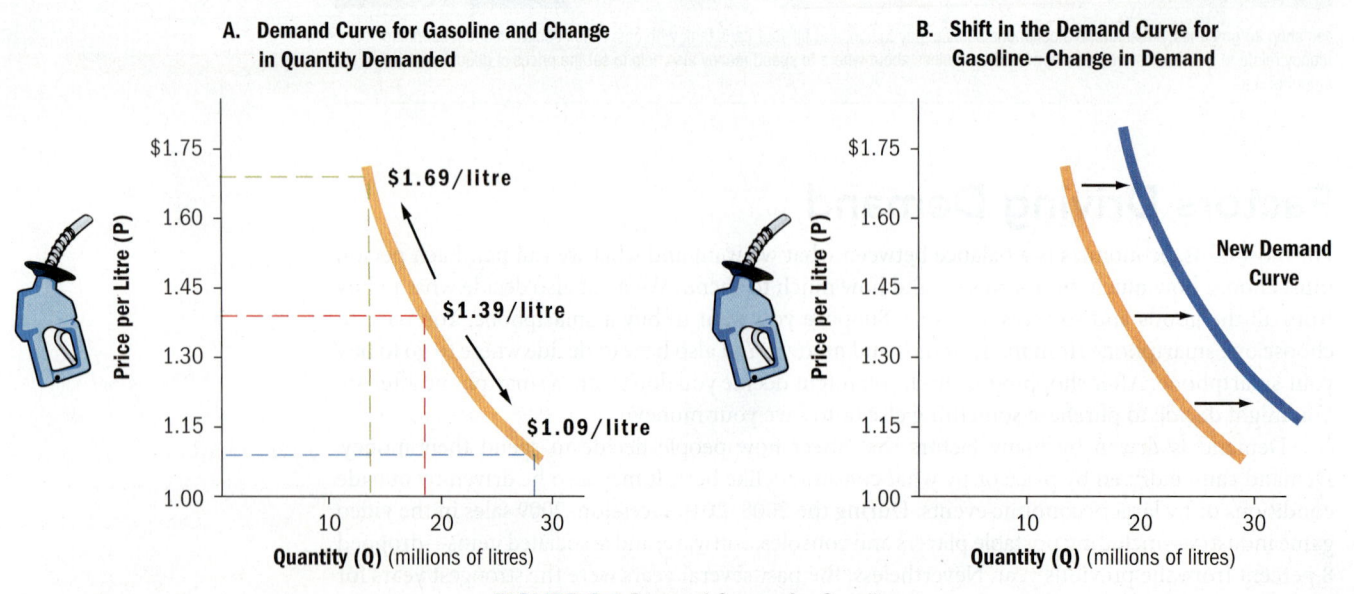

B. Shift in the Demand Curve for Gasoline—Change in Demand

FIGURE 3.1 Demand Curves for Gasoline

Table 3.1 Expected Shifts in Demand Curves

	DEMAND CURVE SHIFTS	
FACTOR	TO THE RIGHT *IF*:	TO THE LEFT *IF*:
Customer preferences	Increase	Decrease
Number of buyers	Increase	Decrease
Buyers' incomes	Increase	Decrease
Prices of substitute goods	Increase	Decrease
Prices of complementary goods	Decrease	Increase
Future expectations become more	Optimistic	Pessimistic

overall demand is different. This kind of change results in a shift to an entirely new demand curve. Businesses are always trying to predict both kinds of demand, and making the wrong decision can lead to problems. For example, gasoline is made from crude oil, which means many factors come into play. One major impact is the growing investment in and development of alternative fuels, such as biodiesel, wind, and solar power. If these alternative fuels are developed and readily available, then demand for oil may (shift) decrease. Another issue is the Canadian economy. When a downturn occurs, the demand decreases for oil and other goods. But changes in energy sources can have the opposite effect. For example, political unrest in oil-rich nations like Nigeria or extreme weather that closes refineries can increase the demand for the oil that is available.[4]

Figure 3.1 shows how the increased demand for gasoline worldwide has created a new demand curve. The new demand curve shifts to the right of the old demand curve. This shift means that overall demand has increased at every price. A demand curve can also shift to the left. This shift means the demand for a good or service has decreased. However, the demand curve still has the same shape.

Although a change in price leads to movement along a demand curve, many factors can combine to change the overall demand for a product. The shape and position of the demand curve show the demand for a product. Demand is affected by customer preferences and incomes, the prices of substitute and complementary items, the number of buyers in a market, and the strength of the buyers' outlook for the future. Changes in any of these factors lead to a new demand curve.

Changes in household income also change demand. When consumers have more money to spend, firms can sell more products at every price. This means the demand curve has shifted to the right. When income drops, nearly everyone has a tougher time, and the demand curve shifts to the left. For example, higher-end Canadian retailers, such as Holt Renfrew, experienced a decrease in demand for their luxury goods because consumers thought twice about buying designer handbags, shoes, and clothing. Meanwhile, discount retailers, such as Walmart, increased their sales, so their demand curves shifted to the right.[5] **Table 3.1** describes how a demand curve is likely to respond to each of these changes.

For a business to succeed, its managers must carefully watch the factors that may affect demand for the goods and services it hopes to sell. Costco sets up free sampling stations in its stores so customers can try small portions of foods prepared onsite. These sampling stations encourage customers to buy something in the department where they are sampling and maintain demand.

Factors Driving Supply

Economic factors also affect supply, which is the willingness and ability of firms to provide goods and services at different prices. Consumers must decide how to spend their money, and businesses must decide what products to sell and how to sell them.

Sellers would like to charge higher prices for their products. A **supply curve** shows the relationship between different prices and the amount of goods that sellers will offer for sale at those prices, regardless of demand. Movement along the supply curve is the opposite of movement along the demand curve: As price rises, the quantity that sellers are willing to supply also rises. At lower and

supply curve a graph that shows the relationship between different prices and the amount of goods that sellers will offer for sale regardless of demand.

lower prices, the quantity supplied decreases. In **Figure 3.2**, a supply curve for gasoline shows that increasing prices for gasoline should bring increasing supplies to market.

Businesses need certain inputs to operate effectively. As discussed in Chapter 1, these *factors of production* include natural resources, capital, human resources, and entrepreneurship. Natural resources include land, building sites, forests, and mineral deposits. Capital refers to resources such as technology, tools, information, physical facilities, and financial capabilities. Human resources include employees' physical labour and intellectual inputs. Entrepreneurship is the willingness to take risks to create and operate a business. Factors of production play a central role in the overall supply of goods and services.

A change in the cost or availability of any inputs can shift the entire supply curve by either increasing or decreasing the amount available at every price. For example, suppose the cost of land increases. A firm might not be able to purchase land to build a more efficient manufacturing plant, which would have lowered production levels and shifted the supply curve to the left. But if the company can find a way to speed up the production process, then it can make more products with less labour. The change in production can reduce the overall cost of the finished products, which shifts the supply curve to the right.

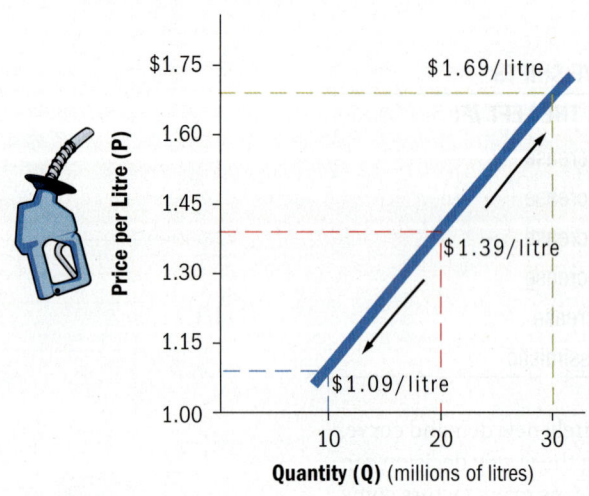

FIGURE 3.2 Supply Curve for Gasoline

Table 3.2 shows how changes in four factors can affect the supply curve. Forces of nature can also affect the supply curve. During a record-breaking freeze in 2010, much of Florida's fruit crop was severely damaged. Because the oranges and lemons could not be harvested and shipped, the supply dropped.[6]

The agriculture industry has often had similar shifts in the supply curve. As consumers increase their demand for locally grown produce, farmers are trying to supply more produce. For example, farmers in colder regions are making the growing season longer by using heated greenhouses to grow vegetables and fruits normally available only during the summer. Winter farming—some of it organic—can help rural economies by creating new jobs that bring new income to an area. A Vancouver company, Spud.ca, is an online grocery retailer. It is trying to meet the increased demand for locally grown organic produce. More than 50 percent of Spud's products are sourced locally. In an average grocery store or natural foods store, only 15 to 20 percent of the items are locally sourced. The company's website has a "meet our local suppliers" link. It lets customers view photos of the owners, read about them, and click through to their websites. Spud.ca is also a founding member of Eat Local, a not-for-profit organization that promotes buying locally by organizing public markets.[7]

Table 3.2 Expected Shifts in Supply Curves

	SUPPLY CURVE SHIFTS	
FACTOR	**TO THE RIGHT *IF*:**	**TO THE LEFT *IF*:**
Costs of inputs	Decrease	Increase
Costs of technologies	Decrease	Increase
Taxes	Decrease	Increase
Number of suppliers	Increase	Decrease

How Demand and Supply Interact

Separate shifts in demand and supply can affect prices and the availability of products. In the real world, changes do not take turns affecting first demand and then supply. Several factors often change at the same time—and they keep changing. Sometimes changes in more than one factor can lead to conflicting pressures on prices and quantities. Other times, the final upward or downward direction of prices and quantities depends on the factor that has changed the most. Most of our examples show how demand and supply affect products, but demand and supply can also affect employment.

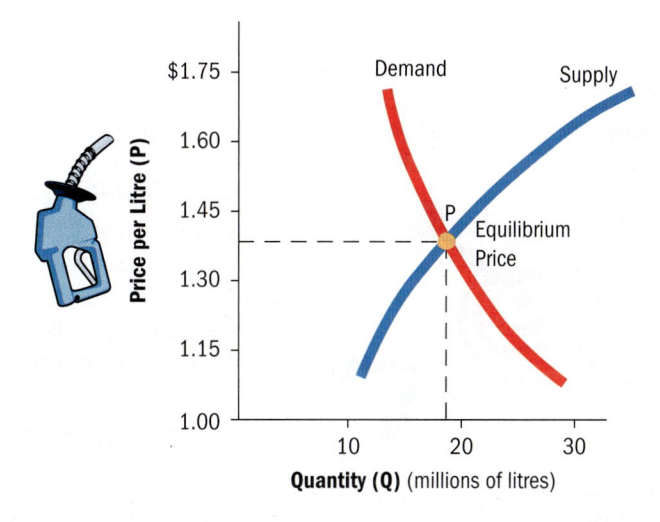

FIGURE 3.3 Law of Supply and Demand

Figure 3.3 shows the interaction of both supply and demand curves for gasoline on a single graph. Notice that the two curves intersect at P. The law of supply and demand states that prices (P) are set by the intersection of the supply and demand curves. The point where the two curves meet identifies the **equilibrium price**, the current market price for an item.

If the actual market price differs from the equilibrium price, buyers and sellers tend to make choices that restore the equilibrium level. However, over time the equilibrium price can change dramatically, as it has for many commodities like oil and gold. The price of gold hit a record high in December 2009, but gold prices dropped when the U.S. Federal Reserve raised interest rates and the U.S. dollar gained strength against the euro. Economists say that investors always seem to return to gold as a safe haven when they worry about other ways to store their wealth. If investors believe the stock market will be heading lower, they may move some wealth into gold. Consumers who want to buy jewellery will usually continue to do so, but they may buy more or fewer pieces depending on the price of gold.[8] Each of these reasons cause the equilibrium price to change. **Figure 3.4** shows the equilibrium price of gold over the last 10 years. Each point on the graph indicates a point of equilibrium between the forces of supply and demand at that moment. Gold buyers and sellers seemed to have found an equilibrium at about $500 per ounce from 2002 to 2006, but since then the price has continued an upward trend to increasingly higher record-breaking levels in 2011 before falling back in recent years.[9]

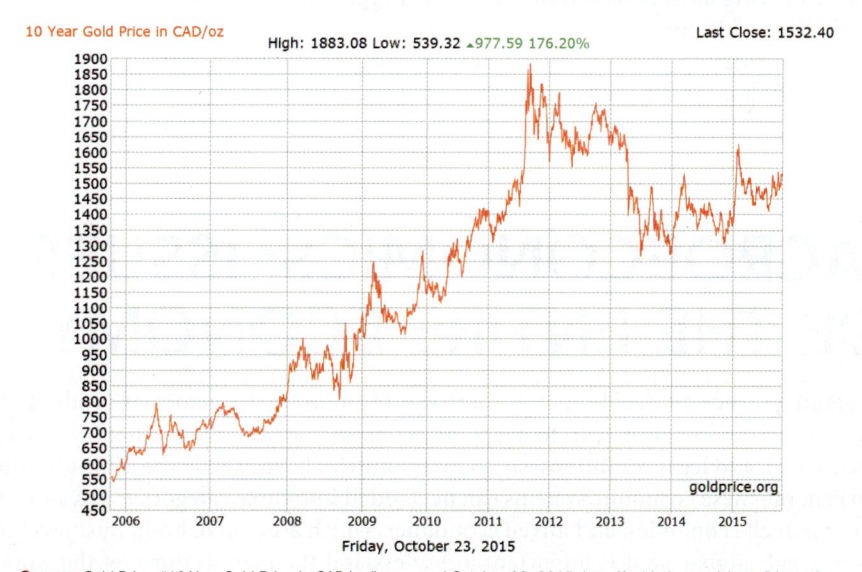

equilibrium price the current market price for an item.

Source: Gold Price, "10 Year Gold Price in CAD/oz," accessed October 23, 2015, http://goldprice.org/charts/history/gold_10_year_o_cad.png. Reprinted with permission.

FIGURE 3.4 Price of Gold over the Past 10 Years

HIT & MISS

Five Guys Burgers and Fries: A Simple Recipe for Success

Jerry Murrell's two oldest sons told him they were not going to college. Murrell wanted to keep the boys close to home and at work. He and his wife, Janie, used the money they had saved for their tuition to open a hamburger take-out shop. Five Guys and a Burger (named for Murrell's five sons) soon grew to 570 franchises in the United States and Canada. All the sons joined the company, and the family still owns and runs it today.

Murrell knew it would be hard to compete with the fast-food chains. He decided Five Guys would need to focus on the food. All the restaurants have the same simple red-and-white-tile décor. The meat for the burgers—80 percent lean—is always fresh, never frozen, burgers are made to order, and diners can choose from 17 toppings. To make the buns tastier, they are toasted on a grill, not in a bun toaster. The Murrells buy potatoes from northern Idaho, where they grow more slowly. The fries are cut from these potatoes and then cooked in peanut oil. Five Guys insists on buying the highest-quality ingredients. That means its food prices change depending on what the company pays its suppliers.

The family tried some dishes that didn't sell, such as serving coffee and a chicken sandwich. Aside from a few hot dogs, they have stayed with the original burger-and-fries formula that first brought them success.

The food-industry research firm Technomic named Five Guys the fastest-growing chain for a recent year. That same year, the company took in an estimated $570 million—up 50 percent from the previous year. "We figure our best salesman is our customer," Murrell says. "Treat that person right, he'll walk out the door and sell for you."

Questions for Critical Thinking

1. Why do you think Five Guys and a Burger prospered during the 2008–2010 recession?
2. How might supply and demand lead to the price the company pays its suppliers?

Sources: Five Guys Burgers and Fries, accessed April 10, 2010, www.fiveguys.com; Liz Welch, "How I Did It: Jerry Murrell, Five Guys Burgers and Fries," *Inc.*, April 1, 2010, accessed May 14, 2015, www.inc.com/magazine/20100401/jerry-murrell-five-guys-burgers-and-fries.html; "Business Opening: Five Guys Burgers and Fries," *Green Bay Press Gazette*, March 25, 2010, www.greenbaypressgazette.com; Ashley Miller, "Five Guys Named Fastest Growing Chain Restaurant," *Examiner*, March 30, 2010, accessed May 14, 2015, www.examiner.com/article/five-guys-named-fastest-growing-chain-restaurant; Roger Yu, "Fast-Growing Five Guys Burger Chain Sticks to Basic, Fresh Food," *USA Today*, June 8, 2009, accessed May 14, 2015, http://usatoday30.usatoday.com/money/companies/management/entre/2009-06-07-fast-food-hamburger-franchise_N.htm.

ASSESSMENT CHECK

3.1.1 Define *microeconomics*.

3.1.2 Explain demand and supply curves.

3.1.3 How do factors of production affect the overall supply of goods and services?

Sometimes, suppliers react to market changes by reducing prices. For many years, fast-food chains such as McDonald's and Wendy's attracted customers by offering everyday value menus and coupons. The 2008–2010 recession and the resulting economic downturn meant people were eating at home more and going out less. As a result, the fast-food chains saw a drop in their profits. Economic recovery takes time. Competition among the chains, which was already strong, could grow even stronger, depending on how long the economic recovery takes.[10] One fast-food chain that did well during the recession is the Five Guys Burgers and Fries chain. Read about this chain in the "Hit & Miss" feature.

As noted earlier, the forces of demand and supply can be affected by many different factors. One important variable is the larger economic situation. The next section explains how macroeconomics and economic systems influence market forces and, ultimately, affect demand, supply, and prices.

LO 3.2 Describe macroeconomics and the three major types of economic systems.

MACROECONOMICS: ISSUES FOR THE ENTIRE ECONOMY

Every country needs to decide how to best use the four basic factors of production. Each nation's policies and choices help to shape its economic system. Every country has different political, social, and legal conditions, so no two countries have exactly the same economic system. In general, these economic systems can be divided into three categories: private enterprise systems, planned economies, and mixed economies, which are a bit of both. Business is becoming increasingly global, so it is important to understand the main features of the world's economic systems.

Capitalism: The Private Enterprise System

Most industrialized nations operate economies that are based on the *private enterprise system*, also known as *capitalism* or a *market economy*. A private enterprise system is based on competition and rewards businesses for meeting the needs and demands of consumers. Government tends to prefer a hands-off position when it comes to controlling business ownership, profits, and resource allocations. Instead, competition manages economic life by creating opportunities and challenges that businesspeople must deal with to succeed.

The relative competitiveness of an industry is important for every firm to think about. Relative competitiveness affects the cost of doing business and how easy it is to do business in that industry. Four basic types of competition take shape in a private enterprise system: pure competition, monopolistic competition, oligopoly, and monopoly. **Table 3.3** shows the main differences among these types of competition.

Pure competition is a market structure, such as the structure of small-scale agriculture or fishing. Large numbers of buyers and sellers exchange similar products, and no single participant has a large influence on price. Instead, prices are set by the forces of supply and demand. Firms can easily enter or leave a purely competitive market because no single company controls the market. In pure competition, buyers see little difference between the goods and services offered by competitors.

pure competition a market structure where large numbers of buyers and sellers exchange similar products and no single participant has a large influence on price.

Fishing is a good example of pure competition. Clams gathered by one person are similar to those gathered by others, so the price for clams rises and falls with changes in supply and demand. When a poisonous "red tide" of algae infests the clam beds, the supply of fresh clams drops and the price increases.

Fishing and agriculture are good examples of pure competition. The wheat grown and sold by one farmer in Manitoba is about the same as the wheat sold by others. Rainfall and temperatures can affect crop growth, and the price for wheat rises or falls depending on the law of supply and demand. The same idea applies to the shellfish industry that gathers clams and mussels off the east and west coasts. The "red tide" of algae sometimes means part of the season's supply of shellfish can't be eaten just when summer tourists want fresh shellfish. The rising demand and short supply can mean rapid price increases.

Monopolistic competition is a market structure similar to the structure for retailing: Large numbers of buyers and sellers exchange distinct and differentiated (dissimilar) products, so each participant has some control over price. The sellers can show that their products are different from

monopolistic competition a market structure where large numbers of buyers and sellers exchange distinct and differentiated (dissimilar) products so each participant has some control over price.

Table 3.3 Types of Competition

CHARACTERISTICS	TYPES OF COMPETITION			
	PURE COMPETITION	**MONOPOLISTIC COMPETITION**	**OLIGOPOLY**	**MONOPOLY**
Number of competitors	Many	Few to many	Few	No direct competition
Ease of entry into industry by new firms	Easy	Somewhat difficult	Difficult	Regulated by government
Similarity of goods or services offered by competing firms	Similar	Different	Similar or different	No directly competing products
Control over price by individual firms	None	Some	Some	Considerable in a pure monopoly; little in a regulated monopoly
Examples	Small-scale farmer in Ontario	Local fitness centre	Telecommunications companies like Bell and Rogers	Rawlings Sporting Goods, exclusive supplier of major-league baseballs

competing offerings because of price, quality, or other features. In an industry that features monopolistic competition, a firm can begin or stop selling a good or service relatively easily. The success of one seller often attracts new competitors. Individual firms also have some control over how their goods and services are priced.

One example of monopolistic competition is the market for pet food. Consumers can choose from private-label products (store brands such as Loblaw's President's Choice Nutrition First Pet Foods) and brand-name products, such as Purina, in bags, boxes, and cans. Producers of pet food and the stores that sell it have wide range when setting prices. Consumers can choose the store or brand with the lowest prices, or sellers can convince consumers that a more expensive offering (for example, the Fromm brand) is worth more because it offers better nutrition, more convenience, or other benefits.

An **oligopoly** is a market situation where few sellers compete and high startup costs act as barriers to keep out new competitors. In some oligopolistic industries, such as the paper and steel industries, competitors offer similar products. In others, such as the aircraft and automobile industries, competitors sell different models and features. The huge investment needed to enter an oligopoly market tends to discourage new competitors. The limited number of sellers also increases the control these firms exercise over price. Competing products in an oligopoly usually sell for very similar prices because any major price competition can reduce profits for all firms in the industry. That means a price decrease by one firm in an oligopoly will usually mean its competitors will lower their prices. But prices can vary from one market to another, just as they can vary from one country to another.

The final type of market structure is a **monopoly**, where a single seller controls trade in a good or service and buyers can find no close substitutes. A pure monopoly occurs when a firm has unique features so important to competition in its industry that these features act as barriers to prevent entry by would-be competitors. There are a number of companies once thought to dominate their respective markets, but disruptive technology—a new technology that unexpectedly replaces an existing one—has changed that. PayPal's ecommerce payment system, Google's search engine, Facebook's social networking platform, and Apple's iTunes no longer dominate their respective markets as they once did.[11]

Many firms create short-term monopolies when research breakthroughs allow them to receive exclusive patents on new products. In the pharmaceuticals industry, big drug companies such as Merck and Pfizer invest billions of dollars in research and development. When the research leads to successful new drugs, the companies can benefit from their patents: They can set prices without fear of competitors undercutting them. After the patent expires, generic substitutes enter the market, and prices decrease.

Because a monopoly market lacks the benefits of competition, many governments control monopolies. The Canadian government issues patents for new applications and limits the life of patents. The Canadian government also makes most pure monopolies illegal by passing antitrust legislation such as the Competition Act. The government applies these laws against monopoly behaviour and by not allowing some large companies to merge, such as our banks. In other cases, the government allows some monopolies to be in business in exchange for controlling their activities.

A **regulated monopoly** is a firm that is granted exclusive rights in a specific market by a local, provincial, or federal government. Pricing decisions—mainly rate increase requests—are subject to control by regulatory authorities, such as the Ontario Energy Board that sets electricity and natural gas rates.

During the 1980s and 1990s, the U.S. government tried to avoid regulated monopolies and instead preferred deregulation. Regulated monopolies that have been deregulated include

oligopoly a market situation where relatively few sellers compete and high startup costs act as barriers to keep out new competitors.

monopoly a market situation where a single seller controls trade in a good or service and buyers can find no close substitutes.

Google Play has disrupted the monopoly Apple's iTunes once enjoyed because of the licensing popularity of the Android operating system on mobile devices.

regulated monopoly a firm that is granted exclusive rights in a specific market by a local, provincial, or federal government.

long-distance and local telephone services, cable television services, cellphone services, and electric utilities. The idea is to improve customer service and to reduce consumer prices by increasing competition. This trend has not been followed as much in Canada, which partly explains the different prices paid for products and services in each country. To illustrate the differences, the Canadian Radio-television and Telecommunications Commission (CRTC) recently set rules for video-on-demand providers. These rules require that no less than 5 percent of English-language feature films are Canadian, no less than 8 percent of French-language films are Canadian, and no less than 20 percent of all programming (other than feature films) is Canadian. In another licence condition, video-on-demand services must contribute 5 percent of their gross annual revenues to a Canadian program production fund. These requirements and their related expenses are passed along in the form of higher rates charged to Canadian customers.[12]

Planned Economies: Socialism and Communism

A **planned economy** is an economic system where business ownership, profits, and resource allocation are shaped by a plan to meet government goals, not goals set by individual firms. Two forms of planned economies are communism and socialism.

Socialism is an economic system where the government owns and operates the major industries, such as energy or communications. Socialists believe that major industries are too important to a society to be left in private hands. They also believe that government-owned businesses can serve the public's interest better than private firms. Socialism allows private ownership in industries considered less important to social welfare, such as retail shops, restaurants, and some manufacturing facilities. Scandinavian countries such as Denmark, Sweden, and Finland have many socialist features in their societies, as do some African nations and India.

The writings of Karl Marx in the mid-1800s formed the basis of communist theory. Marx believed that private enterprise economies created unfair conditions. He believed these conditions led to workers being taken advantage of because business owners controlled most of society's resources *and* reaped most of the economy's rewards. Instead, Marx suggested an economic system called **communism**, where all property would be shared equally by the people in a community under the direction of a strong central government. Marx believed that getting rid of private ownership of property and businesses would mean a classless society that would be good for everyone. Each individual would contribute to the nation's overall economic success, and resources would be divided up depending on each person's needs. Under communism, the central government owns the means of production, and the people work for state-owned enterprises. The government decides what people can buy because it controls what is produced in the nation's factories and farms.

Several nations adopted communist-like economic systems during the early twentieth century. These nations wanted to correct abuses they believed existed in their previous systems. In practice, though, these new economic systems usually gave people less freedom of choice in terms of their jobs and purchases, and the governments might be best described as totalitarian socialism. These nations often made mistakes in dividing up resources to compete in the growing global marketplace. Government-owned monopolies often suffer from inefficiency.

Consider the former Soviet Union, where large government bureaucracies controlled nearly every aspect of daily life. Shortages happened all the time because producers had little or no incentive to satisfy their customers. The quality of goods and services also suffered for the same reason. When Mikhail Gorbachev became the last president of the Soviet Union he tried to improve the quality of Soviet-made products. But the Soviet Union faced severe financial problems. It was shut out of trading in the global marketplace and got caught up in a costly arms race with the United States. Eventually, these events led to the collapse of Soviet communism and the breakup of the Soviet Union.

Today, communist-like systems exist in just a few countries, such as North Korea. Even the People's Republic of China now has a more market-oriented economy. Its national government has given local government and individual plant managers more say in business decisions, and some private businesses are now allowed in China. Households also have more control over agriculture, in contrast to the collective farms where many people once worked. Today, Chinese workers make products for export to other countries. Western products such as McDonald's restaurants and Coca-Cola are also now part of Chinese consumers' lives.

planned economy an economic system where business ownership profits and resource allocation are shaped by a plan to meet government goals, not goals set by individual firms.

socialism an economic system where the government owns and operates the major industries, such as communications.

communism an economic system where all property is shared equally by the people in a community under the direction of a strong central government.

Mixed Market Economies

mixed market economy an economic system that draws from both private enterprise economies and planned economies to different degrees.

Private enterprise systems and planned economies use opposite approaches to operating economies. In reality, though, many countries operate a **mixed market economy**, an economic system that draws from both types of economies to different degrees. Some nations are generally considered to have a private enterprise economy. In these countries, government-owned firms frequently operate beside private enterprises. In Canada, healthcare, education, and electricity generation are run by the government.

France has blended socialist and free enterprise policies for hundreds of years. The nation's energy production, public transportation, and defence industries are run as nationalized industries and are controlled by the government. Meanwhile, a market economy operates in other industries. Over the past two decades, the French government has loosened its hold on state-owned companies, inviting both competition and private investment into industries that once operated as government monopolies.

privatization the conversion of government owned and operated companies to privately held businesses.

The percentages of private and public enterprise can vary widely in mixed economies, and the mix changes. Dozens of countries have converted government owned and operated companies into privately held businesses. This trend is known as **privatization**. Even Canada has seen discussions of privatizing everything from public transportation to roads, schools, and hospitals.

Governments may privatize state-owned enterprises so they can raise funds and improve their economies. The objective is to cut costs and run the operation more efficiently. For most of its history, Air Canada was a federal government–owned airline. In 1989, the airline became fully privatized. In 2000, the firm acquired Canadian Airlines International and became the world's tenth-largest international air carrier. Air Canada now has an extensive global network. It flies to the United States, Europe, the Middle East, Asia, Australia, the Caribbean, Mexico, and South America.[13]

Table 3.4 compares the alternative economic systems by ownership and management of enterprises, rights to profits, employee rights, and worker incentives.

✓ ASSESSMENT CHECK

3.2.1 What is the difference between pure competition and monopolistic competition?

3.2.2 Which economic system is the Canadian economy based on?

3.2.3 What is privatization?

Table 3.4 Comparison of Alternative Economic Systems

SYSTEM FEATURES	CAPITALISM (PRIVATE ENTERPRISE)	COMMUNISM (PLANNED ECONOMIES)	SOCIALISM (PLANNED ECONOMIES)	MIXED ECONOMY
Ownership of enterprises	Businesses are owned privately, often by large numbers of people. Very little government ownership means that production is in private hands.	Government owns the means of production with few exceptions, such as small plots of land.	Government owns basic industries, but private owners operate some small enterprises.	A strong private sector works with public enterprises.
Management of enterprises	Enterprises are managed by owners or their representatives with very little government involvement.	Centralized management controls all state enterprises in line with three- to five-year plans. Planning now is being decentralized.	Much government planning is involved in socialist nations. State enterprises are managed directly by government bureaucrats.	Management of the private sector resembles the management under capitalism. Professionals may also manage state enterprises.
Rights to profits	Entrepreneurs and investors are allowed to receive all profits (minus taxes) that their firms earn.	Profits are not allowed under communism.	Only the private sector of a socialist economy generates profits.	Entrepreneurs and investors are allowed to receive private sector profits, although they often must pay high taxes. State enterprises are also expected to produce returns.

continued

Table 3.4 Comparison of Alternative Economic Systems (*continued*)

SYSTEM FEATURES	CAPITALISM (PRIVATE ENTERPRISE)	PLANNED ECONOMIES		
		COMMUNISM	SOCIALISM	MIXED ECONOMY
Rights of employees	Employees have the rights to choose their own occupation and to join a labour union. These rights have long been recognized.	Employee rights are limited in exchange for promised protection against unemployment.	Workers may choose their occupations and join labour unions, but the government influences many people's career decisions.	Workers may choose their own jobs and may join a labour union. Unions often become quite strong.
Worker incentives	Large incentives motivate people to perform at their highest levels.	Incentives are emerging in communist countries.	Incentives usually are limited in state enterprises but are used to motivate workers in the private sector.	Capitalist-style incentives operate in the private sector. More limited incentives influence public sector activities.

EVALUATING ECONOMIC PERFORMANCE

> **LO 3.3** Explain how productivity, price level changes, and employment levels affect economic performance.

Ideally, an economic system should provide two important benefits for its citizens: a stable business environment and sustained growth. In a stable business environment, the overall supply of needed goods and services matches the overall demand for these items. There are no wild ups or downs in price or availability to make economic decisions difficult. Consumers and businesses have access to supplies of desired products at affordable prices and also have money to buy the items they demand.

Growth is another important economic goal. An ideal economy is always changing because it is always expanding the amount of goods and services it produces from the nation's resources. Growth leads to expanded job opportunities, improved wages, and a rising standard of living.

Flattening the Business Cycle

At any given moment, a nation's economy is understood to be in one of several stages of a business cycle: prosperity, recession, depression, and recovery. Each of these stages reflects business conditions, such as the rate of growth and unemployment levels. Canada has not had a true economic depression since the 1930s; however, for those that suffered through the 2008–2010 recession it probably felt like a major depression. Most economists believe that effective economic policies should prevent future depressions. Thus, economists expect recessions to lead to a time of economic recovery without any catastrophic widespread depression. Governments can increase their spending and lower taxes so consumers can increase their spending to help stimulate economic activity during a slowdown. Sometimes major projects that are mainly financed by governments, like developing alternative energy, are given a boost in funding. The "Solving an Ethical Controversy" feature looks at whether developing alternative sources of energy will create new jobs to stimulate the economy.

Both business decisions and consumer buying patterns differ at each stage of the business cycle. In times of prosperity, unemployment is low, consumers are confident about the future and make more purchases, and businesses expand. Businesses hire more employees, invest in new technology, and purchase new technology to take advantage of new opportunities.

SOLVING AN **ETHICAL** CONTROVERSY

Should Alternative Energy Development Be Relied on to Create New Jobs?

Someday, we will run out of fossil fuels such as oil and coal. We need to look at developing more alternative energy sources: solar, wind, ethanol, biodiesel, geothermal, and nuclear power. Developing alternative energy could create thousands of new jobs, help revive the economy, and slow down global warming.

Some people are critical of alternative energy development. They say the cost of government subsidies to make these businesses competitive is too high and does not make good economic sense. For example, in Ontario the cost of the energy produced is estimated at 13.5 cents per kilowatt hour (kWh) for wind farms and 44.5 cents per kWh for solar power. But the cost of a natural gas generator is only 7.5 cents per kWh. Critics also estimate the Government of Ontario would need to pay a subsidy of more than $200,000 per job to make these business projects viable for their owners.

In the United States, a study paid for by American renewable energy corporations is urging Congress to pass a federal standard of 25 percent reliance on alternative energy by 2025. Supporters claim that a national renewable electricity standard (RES) of 25 percent would create hundreds of thousands of jobs in renewable energy fields. China is now the world's leading manufacturer of wind turbines, ahead of Denmark, Germany, Spain, and the United States. Don Furman of Iberdrola Renewables says, "Without a strong RES, the U.S. wind industry will see no net job growth, and will likely lose jobs to overseas competitors."

Should we develop alternative energy sources to help economic recovery and create jobs?

PRO
1. Investing in clean, alternative sources of energy could create new "green" jobs for North Americans. Some energy sources—for example, wind and solar power—are renewable and sustainable.
2. Clean, renewable energy will help end North America's dependence on foreign oil. Fossil fuels cause environmental destruction, and their prices are not stable.

CON
1. Fossil fuels will last for many more years. Continual advances could make these fuels a more energy-efficient, less expensive choice.
2. Alternative energy sources are still in early development. More time and more costly research are needed before alternative energy is less expensive and practical on a national scale.

Summary

Canada and the United States are not alone in developing "green" energy sources. Several European countries along the North Sea have joined to create an environmentally clean "supergrid." These countries will receive their energy from green sources in Scotland, Germany, and Norway through energy-efficient undersea cables. Canada enjoys the financial benefits of having huge reserves of oil and natural gas. Some provinces, such as Quebec and Newfoundland and Labrador, produce surplus hydro-electricity that they export to the U.S. market.

Sources: Terrance Corcoran, "Ontario Burns up More Green Cash," *National Post,* February 25, 2011, p. FP11; American Wind Energy Association, "Stronger National Renewable Electricity Standard Needed for Significant Clean Energy Job Stability and Growth, Study Finds," BusinessWire, February 4, 2010, www.businesswire.com/news/home/20100204006052/en/Stronger-National-Renewable-Electricity-Standard-Needed-Significant#.VVVIOPIVhHw; "Can Alternative Energy Effectively Replace Fossil Fuels?" ProCon, accessed February 4, 2010, http://alternativeenergy.procon.org; Keith Bradsher, "China Leading Global Race to Make Clean Energy," *New York Times,* January 30, 2010, accessed February 4, 2010, www.nytimes.com/2010/01/31/business/energy-environment/31renew.html?_r=0; "Renewable Energy 'Supergrid' Coming to Europe," *Energy Economy,* December 31, 2009, www.alternative-energy-news.info.

---

recession a cycle of economic contraction that lasts for six months or longer.

A **recession** is a cycle of economic contraction that lasts for six months or longer. During a recession, consumers often wait before making major purchases. They also shift what they buy, preferring basic, practical products at low prices. Businesses do something similar. They slow production, decide to wait before expanding, reduce their stock, and often reduce the number of employees. During recessions, consumers may worry about being laid off and using up their savings. Many consumers become more careful in how they spend money. Some wait before making luxury purchases and taking vacations. Others start to shop at lower-priced retailers, such as Costco and Walmart. Some people sell their cars, jewellery, and shares to help pay their bills.

Sometimes, an economic slowdown continues in a downward spiral over a long period of time. When that happens, the economy falls into depression. Many Canadians have heard stories about their great-grandparents who lived through the Great Depression of the 1930s. During this time, food and other basic products were hard to find, and many people were out of work.

In the recovery stage of the business cycle, the economy comes out of the recession and consumers start spending again. Businesses often still need part-time and other temporary workers during the early stages of a recovery. Unemployment begins to decline as business activity starts up again and firms seek more workers to meet growing production demands. Slowly, the concerns of recession begin to disappear, and consumers start spending again: eating out at restaurants, booking vacations, and purchasing new cars.

During a recession, consumers may shift what they buy, preferring to buy basic, practical products at low prices. Consumers may worry about being laid off and using up their savings. Many consumers become more careful in how they spend money. Some people sell their cars, jewellery, and shares to help pay the bills.

Productivity and the Nation's Gross Domestic Product

Every economy focuses on **productivity**, the relationship between the goods and services produced and the inputs needed to produce them. In general, as productivity rises, an economy's growth increases and its citizens' wealth increases. In a recession, productivity stalls and may decline.

Productivity describes the relationship between the number of units produced and the number of human and other production inputs needed to produce them. Productivity is a ratio of output to input. When a steady amount of inputs creates an increased number of outputs, productivity has increased.

Total productivity looks at all inputs needed to produce a specific amount of outputs. It can be written as an equation:

$$\text{Total Productivity} = \frac{\text{Output (goods or services produced)}}{\text{Input (human/natural resources, capital)}}$$

Many productivity ratios focus on only one input in the equation: labour productivity or output per labour-hour. An increase in labour productivity means that the same amount of work produces more goods and services than before. Many gains in Canadian productivity are because of technology. In recent years, Canada's economy has done well because of technology and productivity. Productivity can also be increased by outsourcing work to lower-cost employees. For example, many businesses have shifted their manufacturing to countries such as China and India, where labour is cheaper. The Internet makes it easy to provide services from anywhere in the world. Overseas workers can use the Internet to provide customer service, accounting, engineering design, and even legal processing. We will discuss this globalization of business activity more in the next chapter.

Productivity is a widely recognized measure of a company's efficiency. In turn, the total productivity of a nation's businesses has become a measure of its economic strength and standard of living. Economists call this measure the country's **gross domestic product (GDP)**. GDP is the total of all goods and services produced within a country, so the greater a nation's productivity, the greater will be its GDP. **Figure 3.5** lists the top 10 countries by their GDP at purchasing power

productivity the relationship between the number of units produced and the number of human and other production inputs needed to produce them.

gross domestic product (GDP) the sum of all goods and services produced within a country during a specific time period, such as a year.

Country	GDP
United States	$15.94
China	$12.6
India	$4.8
Japan	$4.7
Germany	$3.2
Russia	$2.55
Brazil	$2.39
United Kingdom	$2.37
France	$2.29

FIGURE 3.5 Nations with Highest Gross Domestic Products (measured in trillions of U.S. dollars using PPP)

Source: Central Intelligence Agency, *World Factbook*, accessed January 24, 2014, www.cia.gov.

parity (PPP) exchange rates. The PPP method uses the total value of all goods and services produced in the country valued at equivalent prices in the United States. This is the measure most economists prefer when looking at per capita welfare and when comparing living conditions or use of resources across countries. The GDP per capita output of a country is the total national output divided by the number of citizens. GDP per capita is better than GDP for measuring the average wealth of any individual citizen of a country. As Figure 3.5 shows, the United States is the world's largest economy as measured by GDP. The differences between the countries are interesting, especially when you look at each country's GDP per capita. With a population approximately four times greater than the United States, China's GDP per capita of $9,800 is substantially lower than that of the United States at $52,800. Furthermore, Canada's $1.5-trillion economy and 35 million population means that Canada's GDP per capita of $43,100 is similar to that of the United States, United Kingdom, France, Germany, and many other countries with advanced economies of various sizes and populations.[14]

Price Level Changes

inflation rising prices caused by a combination of excess consumer demand and higher costs of raw materials, component parts, human resources, and other factors of production.

core inflation rate the inflation rate after energy prices and food prices are removed.

hyperinflation an economic situation marked by soaring prices.

The general level of prices is another important indicator, or measure, of an economy's stability. For the last 100 years, economic decision makers have focused on **inflation**, rising prices caused by a combination of excess consumer demand and higher costs of raw materials, component parts, human resources, and other factors of production. The **core inflation rate** is the inflation rate of an economy after energy prices and food prices are removed. This measure is often an accurate estimate of the inflation rate that consumers, businesses, and other organizations can expect in the near future.

Excess consumer demand creates *demand-pull inflation*. Increases in the costs of factors of production create *cost-push inflation*. North America's most severe inflationary period of the last half of the twentieth century peaked in 1980, when general price levels increased almost 14 percent in one year. An economy may experience **hyperinflation**, an economic situation marked by soaring prices. Hyperinflation has occurred in South America and in the countries that once formed the Soviet Union.

Inflation devalues money because the constant price increases mean that people can purchase fewer goods and services with a given amount of money. It is bad news for many people: those whose earnings do not keep up with inflation, those who live on fixed incomes, and those who have investments that pay a fixed rate of interest. Inflation can be good news for people whose income is rising and those with debts at a fixed rate of interest. A homeowner with a fixed-rate mortgage during inflationary times is paying off that debt with money that is worth less and less each year. Over the past decade, inflation and a strong stock market increased the number of North American millionaires to more than 7.8 million.[15] But inflation also means being a millionaire does not mean the same as it once did. To live like a 1960s millionaire, you need almost $7 million today.

When increased productivity keeps prices steady, it can have a major positive impact on an economy. In a low-inflation environment, businesses can make long-range plans without worrying about sudden inflationary shocks. Low interest rates encourage firms to invest in research and development and in capital improvements. Both are likely to produce productivity gains. Consumers can purchase growing stocks of goods and services with the same amount of money. Low interest rates encourage people to make major purchases, such as new homes and cars. But some people have concerns. The changing cost of oil—which is used to produce many goods—is a continuing issue. Businesses need to raise prices to cover their costs. Also, smaller firms have gone out of business or have been merged with larger companies. Thus, the amount of competition has been reduced and the purchasing power of the larger corporations has increased. Business owners continue to keep an eye on signs of inflation.

The opposite situation—**deflation**—occurs when prices keep falling. In Japan, deflation has been a reality for several years. Shoppers pay less for many products, ranging from groceries to homes. Lower prices may sound like good news to consumers, but this situation can weaken the economy. The housing industry and auto makers need to keep prices strong to support all the businesses that depend on them. Think about it for a moment. Would you want to buy a house today if you thought the price would be lower in a year? As global oil prices dropped dramatically in 2014, Alberta's oil-dependent economy slowed down as well. The consequences were a drop in real estate prices and new home construction. Oil workers who lost their jobs at the same time rushed to sell homes they could no longer afford to own.

Increased productivity keeps prices steady. It can also have a major positive impact on the economy. Low interest rates encourage firms to invest in capital improvements—such as building a new company headquarters or expanding its existing space. These improvements are likely to lead to productivity gains.

deflation the opposite of inflation, occurs when prices continue to fall.

Measuring Price Level Changes

The Canadian government tracks price changes with the **Consumer Price Index (CPI)**. The CPI measures the monthly average change in the prices of goods and services. Statistics Canada calculates the CPI each month using the prices of a "market basket," a mix of the goods and services commonly purchased. **Figure 3.6** shows the categories in the CPI market basket. Each month price checkers visit thousands of stores, service businesses, rental units, and doctors' offices all over Canada to price the items in the CPI market basket. The prices they collect are used to create the CPI. Thus, the CPI provides a running measurement of changes in consumer prices.

Consumer Price Index (CPI) a measurement of the monthly average change in prices of goods and services.

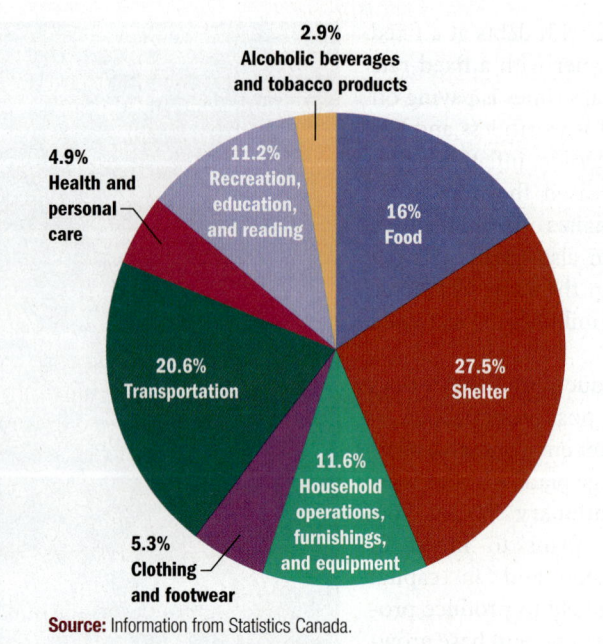

FIGURE 3.6 Contents of the CPI Market Basket

- 2.9% Alcoholic beverages and tobacco products
- 11.2% Recreation, education, and reading
- 4.9% Health and personal care
- 16% Food
- 27.5% Shelter
- 11.6% Household operations, furnishings, and equipment
- 5.3% Clothing and footwear
- 20.6% Transportation

Source: Information from Statistics Canada.

HIT & MISS

Vancity Provides a "Microcredit Toolkit" to Local Not-for-Profit Organizations

Individual economic progress can often be helped by small loans to people who can use the money to purchase the equipment or training they need. Many new immigrants want to start a small business or add to their incomes by starting a microbusiness. But they can face difficulty when trying to borrow money because they may lack collateral (to back up the loan), personal credit history (to show they have paid back previous loans), and full-time employment.

Vancity wants to change this. It provides a Microcredit Toolkit to local not-for-profit organizations that help new immigrants through a partnership with MOSAIC, a Vancouver not-for-profit organization that works with new immigrants and refugees. The toolkit helps new immigrant entrepreneurs get better access to financial services. Vancity is Canada's largest credit union. It has 400,000 members and $14.5 billion of assets to manage. Vancity views the MOSAIC arrangement as a socially responsible way to serve people who would face great difficulty in getting a loan, even a small one, without this help. The average loan to a MOSAIC client is $3,200, and more than 98 percent of the loans have been repaid. Many loans are used to pay for retraining programs and for help to obtain Canadian certification.

MOSAIC was the first to use the kit. The organization received a $167,000 grant from Vancity to develop its Peer Lending Program and to translate the toolkit into other languages. "We are excited about being the first non-profit to use the Toolkit. Every day we see people who could benefit from this program. People who are highly motivated with skills and talents, but who don't qualify for support from a traditional financial institution," says Sherman Chan of MOSAIC. "By removing those barriers we can help our clients achieve financial independence."

For example, Dharmasena (Sena) Yakadawela has 13 years of legal experience and had been a judge in Sri Lanka. After he couldn't find work in his profession, he took a job at a 24-hour convenience store. But Sena met with MOSAIC and learned about Vancity's Back to Work microloan program. It helps skilled immigrants such as Sena by loaning funds to retrain in Canada. Sena's microloan helped him to go to the University of British Columbia. There he studied for his Certificate of Immigration Consultants. After graduation, a second loan allowed him to write the exam with the Canadian Society of Immigration Consultants and pay the membership registration fees. Soon afterward, Sena started his own business. He now helps overseas healthcare professionals obtain Canadian work permits.

Peer Lending is Vancity's unique credit arrangement. A small group of borrowers guarantee loans for each other instead of using collateral. The program looks at commitment and ability, not financial assets. Vancity is the only financial institution in Canada to offer a program like this. The Peer Lending loans range from $1,000 to $5,000.

Since the Peer Lending Program was introduced seven years ago, it has helped about 700 people. More than half have generated $500 to $1,000 additional income per month, and 10 percent now have enough skills to leave the program to take new jobs or grow their small businesses.

Questions for Critical Thinking

1. How does this program benefit the borrower, lender, and society in general?
2. Why do you think that the payback rate on microloans is so high?

Sources: Vancity, "All Great Businesses Start with a Little Help: Microloans Fund Big Dreams," accessed February 3, 2011, www.vancity.com/MyCommunity/NotForProfit/Microloans; Microfinance, accessed February 3, 2011, www.microfinance.ca.

Employment Levels

People need money to buy the goods and services produced in an economy. Most consumers earn that money by working, so the number of people who are working is an important measure of how well the economy is doing. In general, employment has increased over the past few years, but there have been some decreases. The services-producing sector has seen some increases, but manufacturing hasn't had much change.[16] The "Hit & Miss" feature discusses how immigrants to Canada can receive small loans to help get started in their new country.

Economists use a nation's **unemployment rate** as an indicator, or measure, of its economic health. The unemployment rate is usually shown as a percentage of the total workforce actively seeking work but currently unemployed. The total labour force includes all people who are willing and available to work at the going market wage. It includes people who currently have jobs and those who are seeking work. Statistics Canada tracks unemployment rates and measures so-called discouraged workers. These individuals want to work but have given up looking for jobs for various reasons. Unemployment can be grouped into the four categories shown in **Figure 3.7**: frictional, seasonal, cyclical, and structural.

Frictional unemployment describes the joblessness of people in the workforce who are temporarily not working but are looking for jobs. These potential workers include new graduates, people who have left jobs for any reason and are looking for work, and former workers who have decided to return to work. **Seasonal unemployment** is the joblessness of people in a seasonal industry. Construction workers, farm labourers, fishing boat operators, and landscape employees may have times of seasonal unemployment when weather conditions keep them from working.

Cyclical unemployment describes the joblessness of people who are out of work because of a cyclical contraction in the economy. During periods of economic expansion, overall employment is likely to rise, but when growth slows and a recession begins, more people are unemployed. Even workers who have good job skills may face temporary unemployment. Workers in high-tech industries, air travel, and manufacturing have all faced unemployment during economic contractions.

Structural unemployment describes the joblessness of people who are unemployed for long periods of time. These people often have little hope of finding a job. Some of these workers don't have the skills needed for available jobs or their skills are no longer in demand. For example, technology has increased the need for people with computer-related skills, but technology has also led to structural unemployment for manual labourers and workers who are injured and cannot return to work.

---

unemployment rate the percentage of the total workforce actively seeking work but currently unemployed.

frictional unemployment the joblessness of people in the workforce who are temporarily not working but are looking for jobs.

seasonal unemployment the joblessness of workers in a seasonal industry.

cyclical unemployment the joblessness of people who are out of work because of a cyclical contraction in the economy.

structural unemployment the joblessness of people who remain unemployed for long periods of time, often with little hope of finding a job.

✓ ASSESSMENT CHECK

3.3.1 Describe the four stages of the business cycle.

3.3.2 What do economists use to measure the health of an economy?

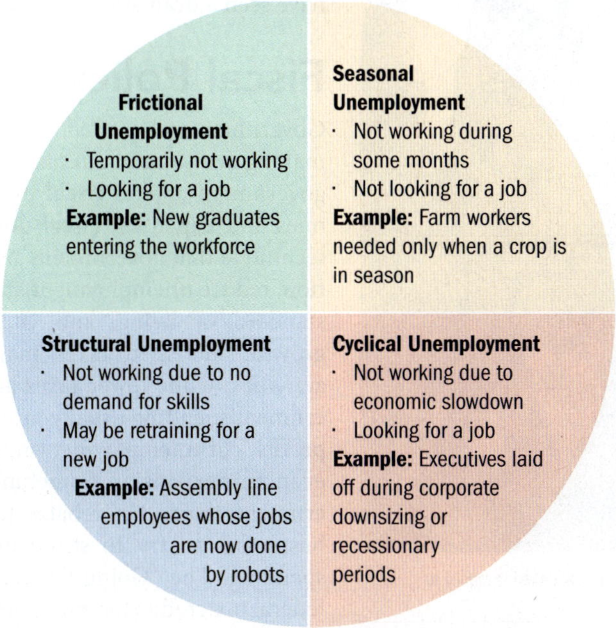

Frictional Unemployment
- Temporarily not working
- Looking for a job

Example: New graduates entering the workforce

Seasonal Unemployment
- Not working during some months
- Not looking for a job

Example: Farm workers needed only when a crop is in season

Structural Unemployment
- Not working due to no demand for skills
- May be retraining for a new job

Example: Assembly line employees whose jobs are now done by robots

Cyclical Unemployment
- Not working due to economic slowdown
- Looking for a job

Example: Executives laid off during corporate downsizing or recessionary periods

FIGURE 3.7 Four Types of Unemployment

LO 3.4 Discuss how monetary policy and fiscal policy are used to manage an economy's performance.

monetary policy a government plan to increase or decrease the money supply and to change banking requirements and interest rates to affect bankers' willingness to make loans.

expansionary monetary policy a plan to increase the money supply to try to decrease the cost of borrowing. Lower interest rates encourage businesses to make new investments, which leads to employment and economic growth.

restrictive monetary policy a plan to reduce the money supply to control rising prices, overexpansion, and concerns about overly rapid economic growth.

fiscal policy a plan of government spending and taxation decisions designed to control inflation, reduce unemployment, improve the general welfare of citizens, and encourage economic growth.

MANAGING THE ECONOMY'S PERFORMANCE

Government can use two policies—monetary policy and fiscal policy—to fight unemployment, increase business and consumer spending, and reduce the length and severity of economic recessions. For example, the Bank of Canada can increase or decrease interest rates, and the federal government can cut taxes, offer tax rebates, or propose other changes.

Monetary Policy

A common way for a government to affect economic activity is to use a policy. A **monetary policy** is a government plan to increase or decrease the money supply and to change banking requirements and interest rates to affect spending by changing bankers' willingness to make loans.

An **expansionary monetary policy** increases the money supply to try to decrease the cost of borrowing. Lower interest rates encourage businesses to make new investments, which leads to employment and economic growth. By contrast, a **restrictive monetary policy** reduces the money supply to control rising prices, overexpansion, and concerns about overly rapid economic growth.

The Bank of Canada governor, Stephen S. Poloz, is responsible for the country's monetary policy. He works independently of the current government. In the United States, the Federal Reserve System ("the Fed") is responsible for American monetary policy. It is headed by a chair and a board of governors, all of whom are nominated by the U.S. president. The current chair, Janet Yellen, is the first woman to hold the position and is also chair of the Federal Open Market Committee, the Fed's main agency for monetary policymaking. Just as Canadian banks function alongside the Bank of Canada, all American banks must be members of the Fed.

The Bank of Canada uses various tools to control the economy. By changing the required percentage of chequing and savings accounts that banks must deposit with the Bank of Canada, the governor can expand or shrink the funds available to lend. The Bank of Canada also lends money to Canadian banks. The banks then make loans at higher interest rates to businesses and individuals. When the Bank of Canada changes the interest rates charged to commercial banks, it affects the interest rates charged to borrowers. Changing the interest rates affects borrowers' willingness to borrow. To deal with the economic decline caused by the 2008–2010 recession, interest rates have been reduced to historic lows, making the cost of borrowed money less costly. However, those dependent on interest income have seen a dramatic drop as a result.

The Bank of Canada uses various tools to control the economy. The Bank of Canada lends money to Canadian banks. The banks then make loans to businesses and individuals.

Fiscal Policy

Governments also affect economic activities by making decisions about taxes and spending. The government applies **fiscal policy** through revenues and expenses. Fiscal policy is the second technique that governments use to control inflation, reduce unemployment, improve the general standard of living, and encourage economic growth. Increased taxes may limit economic activities, while lower taxes and increased government spending usually increase spending and profits, cut unemployment rates, and encourage economic expansion. Sometimes the federal government issues tax rebates to individuals and businesses to try to stimulate investment and spending. The "Going Green" feature discusses federal tax credits for energy-efficient products.

GOING GREEN: TAX CREDITS FOR AN ENERGY STAR

For the past several decades, the Government of Canada has promoted its EnerGuide labelling program. This program supports energy conservation by helping consumers understand the heavy energy consumed by washing machines, dryers, stoves, refrigerators, computers, and air conditioners. Energy conservation helps reduce air pollution caused by energy-producing technologies such as coal- and gas-driven power plants. Energy conservation also helps reduce the need to build more production facilities, which are typically a government responsibility.

Energy is needed to drive the economy. If our economy is to grow, then governments must find the funds needed to develop more energy. A better way to control the costs of supplying energy is to reduce the demand for energy. Governments often use both "the carrot" and "the stick" to do so. Higher prices are "the stick" that helps reduce energy use. Energy use also drops when consumers learn about how much energy they use, often when they purchase new appliances. Tax incentives are "the carrot" that helps consumers make better and more energy-efficient choices. Recently, the government has offered tax credits to people who buy hybrid gas-electric vehicles, vehicles that use alternative fuels, and plug-in electric vehicles.

Canada's Energy Efficiency Act was passed in 1992. This act sets the minimum energy-efficiency standards for some energy-consuming products, including appliances imported to Canada and those traded between provinces and territories. The ENERGY STAR program was introduced in 1992. This program encourages Canadians to save energy and reduce pollution. The ENERGY STAR symbol goes one step further and identifies the specific models that meet or exceed the highest levels of energy efficiency.

In many communities, when you replace certain appliances with qualified appliances you receive a rebate and lower your utility bills. Your local government may help you choose from among boilers, central or room air conditioners, washing machines, dishwashers, freezers, oil and gas furnaces, heat pumps (air source and geothermal), refrigerators, and water heaters. Whether your community takes part depends on climate, geography, and other factors.

Certain kinds of home improvements can receive tax credits, including the replacement of furnaces, windows, hot-water tanks, and insulation. To get an idea of the scale of incentives, visit Natural Resources Canada's Office of Energy Efficiency website.

Questions for Critical Thinking

1. How does paying rebates and granting tax credits stimulate the economy?
2. Which would you prefer to receive—an income tax credit or a rebate? Why?

Source: Natural Resources Canada's Office of Energy Efficiency, accessed March 21, 2015, http://oee.nrcan.gc.ca.

International Fiscal Policy

Canada and other nations in the industrial world are trying to help developing nations improve their economies. Many African countries have large debts. One idea is to forgive the debts of some of these countries to help their economies grow. But not all fiscal experts agree. Some say that any debt forgiveness should also have certain conditions so that these countries can build their own fiscal policies. Countries need to lower their tax rates, avoid devaluing their currencies, plan for new business startups, and reduce trade barriers. They also need to allow citizens to own property and should encourage home ownership. In addition, they must improve agriculture, education, and healthcare so their citizens can begin to set and reach financial goals. The World Bank offers low-interest loans and interest-free credit and grants to developing countries. The World Bank has been involved in helping Haiti recover from the catastrophic earthquake of 2010.[17]

The Federal Budget

Each year, the federal government presents a **budget** to Parliament for approval. The budget is a plan for how the government will raise and spend money during a specific period of time, often the coming year. The federal budget includes numerous spending categories, ranging from defence to interest payments on the national debt. The decisions about what to include in the budget have a direct effect on the economy. During a recession, the federal government may increase spending on highway repairs to improve transportation and increase employment in the construction

budget an organization's plan for how it will raise and spend money during a specific period of time.

budget deficit a situation where the government spends more than it raises through taxes.

national debt the money owed by a government to individuals, businesses, and government agencies who purchase Treasury bills, Treasury notes, and Treasury bonds.

budget surplus the excess funding when a government spends less than it raises through taxes and fees.

balanced budget a situation where total revenues raised by taxes and fees equal the total proposed government spending for the year.

✓ ASSESSMENT CHECK

3.4.1 What is the difference between an expansionary monetary policy and a restrictive monetary policy?

3.4.2 What are the three primary sources of government funds?

3.4.3 Does a balanced budget erase the government debt?

industry. During prosperity, the government may fund scientific research on new medical treatments or alternative fuels.

The main sources of government funds to pay for the annual budget are taxes, fees, and borrowing. The overall total of these funds and how these funds are combined can have major effects on the economic well-being of the nation. Governments can raise money by setting taxes on sales, income, and other sources. But increasing taxes means that people and businesses have less money to spend. Raising taxes might reduce inflation, but overly high taxes can slow economic growth. Governments often try to balance taxes so that people can receive the services they need without slowing economic growth.

Taxes don't always bring in enough funds to cover every government spending project. When the government spends more than it raises through taxes, it creates a **budget deficit**. To cover the deficit, the government borrows money by selling Treasury bills, Treasury notes, and Treasury bonds to investors. This borrowing makes up the **national debt**. If the government takes in more money than it spends, it has a **budget surplus**. In a **balanced budget**, total revenues raised by taxes equal the total proposed spending for the year.

Balancing the budget—or even having a budget surplus—does not erase the national debt. Canadian politicians are always discussing how quickly the nation should use revenues to reduce its debt and how much debt is a concern for the economic well-being of the country. We can think about the national debt on a personal level. Most families want to wipe out debt—from credit cards, automobile purchases, and postsecondary education. But the decision is more complex for the federal government. When the government raises money by selling Treasury bills, it makes safe investments available to investors worldwide. If foreign investors cannot buy Treasury notes from Canada, they might turn to other countries. Then the money flowing into Canada is reduced. The government uses part of the funds it borrows to invest in public infrastructure, such as highways, hospitals, and hydro-electric dams. As long as debt is used to increase productivity and economic growth, we can consider it worthwhile. Concerns are raised when little perceived value is provided by spending done with borrowed funds that will eventually need to be repaid along with interest costs. Canada has approximately 35 million people. Our national debt is about $620 billion. That works out to about $18,000 per person. The United States has approximately 318 million citizens and a national debt of $18 trillion. Thus, each American's share of debt is about $56,000.[18]

LO 3.5 Describe the major global economic challenges of the twenty-first century.

GLOBAL ECONOMIC CHALLENGES OF THE TWENTY-FIRST CENTURY

Businesses face many important economic challenges in the twenty-first century. The economies of countries around the world are becoming more interconnected. Governments and businesses must now compete and will need to meet several challenges to stay competitive in the global market. **Table 3.5** shows five key global economic challenges: (1) international terrorism, (2) the shift to a global information economy, (3) the aging of the world's population, (4) the growth of China and India, and (5) efforts to enhance the competitiveness of every country's workforce.

Today, we have a global economy. No country is an economic island. An ever-increasing stream of goods and services crosses national borders. More and more businesses are becoming true multinational firms by operating manufacturing plants and other facilities around the world. Global trade and investments continue to grow, so events in one nation can set off effects around the world. The "Career Kickstart" feature offers some tips for international travel.

Table 3.5 Global Economic Challenges

CHALLENGE	FACTS AND EXAMPLES
International terrorism	• Many nations assist in locating and holding known terrorists. • Most nations cooperate by changing their banking laws to cut off funds to terrorist organizations. • Many countries are concerned about the safety of mass transit systems after bombings in Moscow and elsewhere.
Shift to a global information economy	• Half of all North American workers hold jobs in information technology or in industries that intensively use information technology goods and services. • The software industry in India employs more than 2.3 million people. • The number of Internet users in Asia and Western Europe has more than doubled in five years.
Aging of the world's population	• The median age of Canadians is 39-plus. By 2030, the median could reach 44. More than 25 percent of people will be 65 or older—nearly double today's number.[a] This aging population will increase demands for healthcare, retirement benefits, and other support services. Governments will need to deal with extra budget pressures. • As the baby boomers begin to retire, businesses around the world will need to replace their workplace skills.
Growth of India and China straining commodity prices	• China and India combined make up more than one-third of the world's population. China's economic growth has been in the industrial sector, and India has focused on services. Both countries now consume more oil and other commodities. Their increasing use means higher demand, which can increase prices.
Enhancing competitiveness of every country's workforce	• Leaner organizations (those with fewer supervisors) need employees who have the skills to control, combine, and supervise work operations.

[a] Statistics Canada, "Canada's Population Estimates: Age and Sex," *The Daily*, July 9, 2009, accessed February 8, 2011, www.statcan.gc.ca/daily-quotidien/091127/dq091127b-eng.htm.

World trade has its risks, but Canadian firms can profit from expanding around the world. Canada is home to only a small portion of the world's 7 billion people. Canadian companies that want to grow need to look toward the world market.[19] Canadian businesses can also benefit from the lower labour costs in other parts of the world. Some businesses are successful at importing goods and services from foreign firms. But it is important for Canadian firms to track the foreign firms that supply their products. Canadian firms recently had to recall thousands of toys made by Chinese manufacturers that contained lead paint, which can be harmful to children. The Associated Press did some research and found that some Chinese manufacturers had used cadmium in place of lead in children's jewellery sold in North America. Cadmium is known to cause cancer. Like lead, cadmium impairs brain development in young children. Federal government agencies warned Asian firms not to use other toxic substances in place of lead. They also began looking into products sold in North America that might contain cadmium or other toxic heavy metals. However, many products we buy are now being made by businesses that operate far away. We need to be careful when looking for lower-priced *and* quality-made products from other places in the world.[20]

✓ ASSESSMENT CHECK

3.5.1 Why is no country an economic island today?

3.5.2 Describe two ways in which global expansion can benefit a Canadian firm.

CAREER KICKSTART

Tips for International Travel

Good manners and good communication have always been important in business. Both are even more important as global business increases. If your work takes you to a foreign country—or even to an international videoconference—you need to understand the manners and etiquette of the country you are visiting, either actually or virtually. These useful tips for international business travel are based on suggestions by Dana Persia of DP Image Consulting.

Before Leaving

1. Research the business etiquette and customs of the country you will visit. Travel guides have lots of tips. Also, look on the Internet. The Foreign Affairs, Trade and Development Canada website is very helpful.

2. If you don't know the country's language, learn a few important phrases. Your hosts will thank you for your effort, even if you can't say the words exactly right.

3. Research what you should wear in the country you are visiting. The standards for women are stricter in many countries. In general, try to fit in as best you can.

Getting There

1. If you can, arrange your flight so you arrive early. You will need to get used to the time-zone change, especially before an important conference or meeting.

2. Get enough sleep before you travel to help reduce the effects of jet lag.

3. Drink water before, during, and after your flight to help with jet lag. Avoid alcohol and caffeine. Both are dehydrating and make the effects of jet lag worse.

When You Arrive

Remember the research you did. Remind yourself that other cultures look differently at gender roles, especially for women. Think about when and where to talk about business. Knowing the etiquette about business cards, alcohol, and gifts is also important. What is accepted in one country may be unacceptable somewhere else!

Sources: DP Image Consulting, accessed February 4, 2010, www.dpimageconsulting.com; International Business Etiquette and Manners, accessed February 4, 2010, www.cyborlink.com; U.S. Department of State, accessed February 4, 2010, www.state.gov; Phillip Khan-Panni, "20 Tips on International Business Etiquette," *Eacademy,* June 12, 2009, www.eacademy.com; Foreign Affairs, Trade and Development Canada, accessed February 8, 2011, www.international.gc.ca/international/index.aspx?lang=eng.

WHAT'S AHEAD

Global competition is a key factor in today's economy. In Chapter 4 we focus on the global dimensions of business. We cover basic concepts of doing business internationally and look at how nations can ready themselves to benefit from the global economy. Then we describe the specific ways that individual businesses expand beyond their national borders to compete successfully in the global marketplace.

RETURN TO INSIDE BUSINESS

Vancouver's 2010 Olympic Village: Seemed like a Great Idea at the Time

Vancouver was trying to get people and businesses to move to the former Olympic Village. The early response from people and businesses seemed positive. As more buyers and renters moved into the empty condominium units, several businesses opened, including a bank, grocery stores, and drugstores. The people who moved there like their new community. It seems to be changing into a neighbourhood instead of being just a collection of buildings. Vancouver's real estate market seems to be dealing with the higher supply of property contributed by the Olympic Village conversion to condominiums. Overall, prices have changed very little.

QUESTIONS FOR CRITICAL THINKING

1. How do you expect condominium prices to change over the next 10 years?
2. What primary factors will affect these price changes the most?

SUMMARY OF LEARNING OBJECTIVES

LO 3.1 Discuss microeconomics and the forces of demand and supply.

Microeconomics is the study of economic behaviour among individual consumers, families, and businesses. Together, their overall behaviour in the marketplace leads to the quantity of goods and services that are demanded and supplied at different prices.

Demand is the willingness and ability of buyers to purchase goods and services at different prices. Several factors drive demand for a good or service: customer preferences, the number of buyers and their incomes, the prices of substitute goods, the prices of complementary goods, and consumer expectations about the future. Supply is the willingness and ability of businesses to offer products for sale at different prices. Supply depends on the cost of inputs and technology resources, taxes, and the number of suppliers in the market.

✓ ASSESSMENT CHECK ANSWERS

3.1.1 Define *microeconomics*. Microeconomics is the study of economic behaviour among individual consumers, families, and businesses. Together, their overall behaviour in the marketplace leads to the quantity of goods and services that are demanded and supplied at different prices.

3.1.2 Explain demand and supply curves. A demand curve is a graph showing the amount of a product that buyers will purchase at different prices. A supply curve shows the relationship between different prices and the amount of goods that sellers will offer for sale at those prices, regardless of demand.

3.1.3 How do factors of production affect the overall supply of goods and services? A change in the cost or availability of any of the factors of production can shift the entire supply curve by either increasing or decreasing the amount available at every price.

LO 3.2 Describe macroeconomics and the three major types of economic systems.

Macroeconomics is the study of the broader economic picture. It looks at how an economic system maintains and divides up its resources. Macroeconomics focuses on how a government's monetary and fiscal policies affect the overall operation of an economic system.

The major economic systems are private enterprise systems, planned economies (such as communism or socialism), and mixed economies. In a private enterprise system, individuals and private businesses pursue their own interests without too much governmental restriction. Four basic types of competition take shape in a private enterprise system: pure competition, monopolistic competition, oligopoly, and monopoly. Pure competition is a market structure, such as the structure of small-scale agriculture. Large numbers of buyers and sellers exchange similar products, and no single participant has a large influence on price. Monopolistic competition is a market structure similar to the structure for retailing: Large numbers of buyers and sellers exchange distinct and differentiated (dissimilar) products, so each participant has some control over price. Oligopolies are market situations such as the steel and airline industries, where just a few sellers compete. High startup costs form barriers to keep out new competitors. In a monopoly, one seller controls trade in a good or service, and buyers can find no close substitutes.

In a planned economy, the government has stronger control over business ownership, profits, and the resources needed to accomplish governmental and societal goals, not goals set by individual firms. Socialism is one type of planned economic system where the government owns and operates the major industries. Communism is a planned economic system without private property. Under communism, goods are owned in common, and factors of production and production decisions are controlled by the state. A mixed market economy blends government ownership and private enterprise, drawing from both planned and private enterprise economies.

✓ ASSESSMENT CHECK ANSWERS

3.2.1 What is the difference between pure competition and monopolistic competition? Pure competition is a market structure where large numbers of buyers and sellers exchange similar products. Monopolistic competition is a market structure where large numbers of buyers and sellers exchange differentiated products.

3.2.2 Which economic system is the Canadian economy based on? The Canadian economy is based on the private enterprise system.

3.2.3 What is privatization? Privatization is the conversion of government owned and operated agencies to privately held businesses.

LO 3.3 Explain how productivity, price level changes, and employment levels affect economic performance.

As productivity rises, an economy's growth increases and its citizens' wealth increases. In a recession, productivity stalls and may decline. Changes in general price levels—inflation or deflation—are important indicators of an economy's general stability. The Canadian government measures price level changes by using the Consumer Price Index. A nation's unemployment rate is an indicator of both overall stability and growth. The unemployment rate shows, as a percentage of the total labour force, the number of people actively seeking employment who are unable to find jobs.

✓ ASSESSMENT CHECK ANSWERS

3.3.1 Describe the four stages of the business cycle. The four stages are prosperity, recession, depression, and recovery. During prosperity, unemployment is usually low and there is strong consumer confidence. In a recession, consumers may wait before making major purchases, may worry about being laid off, and may use up their savings. A depression occurs when an economic slowdown continues in a downward spiral over a long period of time. During recovery, consumers start spending again. Business activity increases, and more people have jobs.

3.3.2 What do economists use to measure the health of an economy? To measure the health of an economy, economists use gross domestic product (GDP), the general level of prices, the core inflation rate, the Consumer Price Index, and the unemployment rate.

LO 3.4 Discuss how monetary policy and fiscal policy are used to manage an economy's performance.

Monetary policy is a government's plan to control the size of the nation's money supply. Increasing or decreasing the overall money supply can affect interest rates, which also affects borrowing and investment decisions. By changing the size of the money supply, a government can encourage growth or control inflation.

Fiscal policy involves decisions about government revenues and expenditures. Changes in government spending affect economic growth and employment levels in the private sector. A government must also raise money, through taxes or borrowing, to finance its spending. The taxes paid by individuals and businesses are funds that would have been spent on goods and services. Thus, any taxation changes also affect the overall economy.

✓ ASSESSMENT CHECK ANSWERS

3.4.1 What is the difference between an expansionary monetary policy and a restrictive monetary policy? An expansionary monetary policy increases the money supply to try to decrease the cost of borrowing. A restrictive monetary policy reduces the money supply to control rising prices, overexpansion, and concerns about overly rapid economic growth.

3.4.2 What are the three primary sources of government funds? The Canadian government acquires funds through taxes, fees, and borrowing.

3.4.3 Does a balanced budget erase the government debt? No, a balanced budget does not erase a government's debt. In a balanced budget, total revenues raised by taxes equal the total proposed spending for the year.

LO 3.5 Describe the major global economic challenges of the twenty-first century.

Businesses face five key global economic challenges in the twenty-first century: (1) international terrorism, (2) the shift to a global information economy, (3) the aging of the world's population, (4) the growth of India and China, and (5) efforts to enhance the competitiveness of every country's workforce.

✓ ASSESSMENT CHECK ANSWERS

3.5.1 Why is no country an economic island today? No business or country is an economic island because many goods and services travel across national borders. Many companies are now becoming multinational firms.

3.5.2 Describe two ways in which global expansion can benefit a Canadian firm. A firm can benefit from global expansion by attracting more customers and by using less expensive labour and production to produce goods and services.

BUSINESS TERMS YOU NEED TO KNOW

balanced budget 80
budget 79
budget deficit 80
budget surplus 80
communism 69
Consumer Price Index (CPI) 75
core inflation rate 74
cyclical unemployment 77
deflation 75

demand 61
demand curve 62
economics 60
equilibrium price 65
expansionary monetary policy 78
fiscal policy 78
frictional unemployment 77
gross domestic product (GDP) 73
hyperinflation 74

inflation 74
macroeconomics 60
microeconomics 60
mixed market economy 70
monetary policy 78
monopolistic competition 67
monopoly 68
national debt 80
oligopoly 68

planned economy 69
privatization 70
productivity 73
pure competition 67
recession 72

regulated monopoly 68
restrictive monetary policy 78
seasonal unemployment 77
socialism 69
structural unemployment 77

supply 61
supply curve 63
unemployment rate 77

REVIEW QUESTIONS

1. How does microeconomics affect business? How does macroeconomics affect business? Why is it important for businesspeople to understand the basics of microeconomics and macroeconomics?

2. Draw supply and demand graphs that estimate what will happen to demand, supply, and the equilibrium price of coffee if these events occur:
   a. Widely reported medical studies suggest that coffee drinkers are less likely to develop certain diseases.
   b. The cost of manufacturing paper cups increases.
   c. The government sets a new tax on takeout beverages.
   d. The biggest coffee chain leaves the area.

3. Describe the four different types of competition in the private enterprise system. Which type of competition is most likely for the following businesses?
   a. a large drugstore chain
   b. a small yoga studio
   c. a steel mill
   d. a large farm whose major crop is corn
   e. Microsoft

4. Distinguish between the two types of planned economies. What factors keep them from working in today's environment?

5. What are the four stages of the business cycle? What stage do you believe the Canadian economy is in now? Why?

6. What is gross domestic product? What is its relationship to productivity?

7. What are the effects of inflation on an economy? What are the effects of deflation? How does the Consumer Price Index work?

8. What does a nation's unemployment rate show? Describe what type of unemployment is most likely for each of the following:
   a. a discharged Armed Forces veteran
   b. a bus driver who has been laid off because of cuts in the city transit budget
   c. a worker who was injured on the job and must start a new career
   d. a lifeguard
   e. a dental hygienist who has quit one job and is looking for another

9. Explain the difference between monetary policy and fiscal policy. How does the government raise funds to cover the costs of its annual budget?

10. What is the difference between the budget deficit and the national debt? What are the benefits of paying down the national debt? What are the negative effects?

PROJECTS AND TEAMWORK APPLICATIONS

1. Describe a situation when you had to make an economic choice to try to balance your wants with limited means. What factors helped you reach your decision?

2. Choose one of the following products. Describe the factors that might affect its supply and demand.
   a. UGG boots
   b. a Kindle
   c. miles by MasterCard credit card
   d. a newly created brand-name drug
   e. a bicycling tour in Europe

3. Go online to research one of the following government departments or agencies. Read about its responsibilities, its budget, and the like. Make the case for privatizing it.
   a. Veterans Affairs Canada
   b. Statistics Canada
   c. Library and Archives Canada
   d. Transport Canada
   e. Canadian Radio-television and Telecommunications Commission

4. Some businesses always experience seasonal unemployment. But more and more, owners of these businesses are trying to increase demand—and employment—during the off season. Choose a classmate to be your business partner. Together, select one of the following businesses. Create a plan for increasing business and keeping employees for a season when your business does not usually operate.

   a. a children's summer camp
   b. a ski lodge
   c. an inn located near a beach resort
   d. a house-painting service
   e. a greenhouse

5. On your own or with a classmate, go online to research the economy of one of the following countries. Learn about the type of economy the country has, its major industries, and its competitive issues. (Note which industries or services are privatized and which are government owned.) Take notes on unemployment rates, monetary policies, and fiscal policies. Present your findings to the class.

   a. China
   b. New Zealand
   c. India
   d. Sweden
   e. Mexico
   f. United States
   g. Brazil

WEB ASSIGNMENTS

1. **Credit card regulations.** Several federal regulations were passed governing credit cards. Visit the website listed here. After reviewing these rules, prepare a brief report highlighting the most significant changes.

   www.fcac-acfc.gc.ca/Eng/forIndustry/publications/lawsReg/Pages/CodeofCo-Codedeco.aspx

2. **Unemployment.** Statistics Canada compiles and publishes data on Canada's unemployment rate which is then available for research and analysis by other research organizations. Go to the Trading Economics website (www.tradingeconomics.com/canada/unemployment-rate). Read through the most recent reports and answer the following questions:

   a. What is the current unemployment rate in Canada? How does it compare with the rates of other developed countries?
   b. Which province has the highest unemployment rate? Which province has the lowest unemployment rate?
   c. What is the so-called underemployment rate?

3. **Gross domestic product.** Visit the Statistics Canada website, www.statcan.gc.ca/tables-tableaux/sum-som/l01/ind01/l3_3764_3012-eng.htm?hili_gdps04. Access the most recent statistics on Canadian GDP. Prepare a brief report. What is the current GDP? What is the difference between real and nominal GDP? What individual components make up GDP?

Note: Internet Web addresses change frequently. If you don't find the exact sites listed, you may need to access the organization's home page and search from there or use a search engine such as Bing or Google.

4 | COMPETING IN WORLD MARKETS

LEARNING OBJECTIVES

LO 4.1 Explain the primary reasons why nations trade.

LO 4.2 Describe how trade is measured between nations.

LO 4.3 Identify the major barriers to international trade.

LO 4.4 Explain how international trade organizations and economic communities reduce barriers to international trade.

LO 4.5 Compare the different levels of involvement used by businesses when entering global markets.

LO 4.6 Distinguish between a global business strategy and a multidomestic business strategy.

INSIDE BUSINESS

PotashCorp: Genesis for Economic Development

Where does wealth come from? How did Canada become the complex economic society it is today? Why do some countries have wealth while others seem to always be living in poverty? What roles do Canadian businesses play in the challenge to generate and distribute wealth in our country and around the world? We need to understand these questions, concepts, and our framework for how business and economic development work. Let's take a closer look at just one international Canadian business.

PotashCorp of Saskatoon, Saskatchewan, is one of many businesses that generate wealth by producing commodities for Canadian and international customers. Commodities are basic products like oil, natural gas, gold, silver, forest products, and many other resources that businesses need to make the products they sell.

Sometimes a commodity is used directly in production. For example, natural gas is burned in kilns to dry fresh-cut lumber when making building materials like 2 × 4 wall studs. But commodities can also be ingredients in a recipe for producing an important product—fertilizer.

PotashCorp is the world's largest producer of fertilizer. It has about 20 percent of the entire global capacity and annual sales of about $6.5 billion. Fertilizer replaces the nutrients in the soil that are absorbed by crops. In simple terms, the key recipe ingredients of fertilizer—potash, phosphate, and nitrogen—are put back in the soil so that the soil can continue to produce higher-yield crops. Potash and phosphate are mined, and nitrogen is extracted from the air. This simple but important product has allowed PotashCorp to grow into a $50 billion giant. It has global operations and part ownership in businesses in China, Chile, Israel, and Jordan.

The demand for fertilizer is directly related to two factors: the demand for agricultural products and the ability of the growers to pay. The growing demand for agricultural products is clearly associated with population growth. For example, the populations of India and China together make up more than one-third of the world's population. As these countries grow economically richer, they are more able to afford the cost of fertilizers to better feed their growing populations.

Let's think about what happened during the global financial crises that occurred between 2008 and 2010. Around the world, demand dropped for all commodities, particularly in India and China. As a result, sales and prices of commodities, including fertilizers, also dropped. Mining of the ingredients decreased, and some mines were closed until prices and demand became profitable again.

At the same time, PotashCorp's shares dropped from $233 per share on June 20, 2008, down to $67 per share on December 5, 2008. By January 2011, demand and prices had recovered to increase the share value to $170, which meant the business could be profitable again.

China has the world's largest population, estimated to be more than 1.3 billion people. China is also the world's largest user of fertilizer, using 28 percent of all available fertilizer. China's own potash production is limited. Historically, 75 percent of potash used in China is imported. As incomes have grown in China, Chinese agribusinesses have increased their use of fertilizers to meet the growing demand for more food, and for meat products in particular. India, with an estimated 1.2 billion people, is the second-largest consumer of fertilizer. It takes up about 13 percent of the world demand for fertilizer. Brazil has an estimated population of 200 million people. It imports 90 percent of the potash it needs, and uses 7 percent of the world's fertilizer. North America has an estimated population of about 340 million people; it needs about 14 percent of the world's fertilizer. North American demand has been more stable than in these other markets. Demand for fertilizer has increased by 85 percent in China, India, Southeast Asia, and Brazil over the past 20 years. These figures closely match food production trends during that time.

Some countries are rich in highly valued commodities. These countries have an immediate source of wealth on which they can build more economic activity. The countries that are not rich in these commodities must look for other strategies or face the economic consequences. Canada has an economic advantage over other countries because of our rich natural resources. Canadians benefit from the sale of commodities to customers in other countries, wherever they may be in the world.[1]

CHAPTER 4 OVERVIEW

Take a moment and think about how many products you used today that came from outside Canada. Did you drink Brazilian coffee with your breakfast? Are your clothes manufactured in China? Did you drive to class in a German or Japanese car fuelled by gasoline refined from Venezuelan crude oil? Or did you watch a movie on a television set assembled in Mexico for a Japanese company such as Sony? A fellow student in Germany may be wearing Zara jeans, using a BlackBerry smartphone, and drinking Pepsi.

Canadian and foreign companies know the importance of international trade to their future success. Economic interdependence is increasing throughout the world as companies look for new markets for their goods and services and the most cost-effective locations to set up factories. Businesses cannot rely only on sales in their home country. Today, Canadian mining, manufacturing, agricultural, and service firms need foreign sales. Other countries are sources of new markets and profit opportunities. Foreign companies also look to Canada when they need new markets.

Thousands of products cross national borders every day. The automobiles that Canadian manufacturers sell in the United States are **exports**, domestically produced goods and services sold in markets in other countries. **Imports** are foreign-made products purchased by domestic consumers. Together, Canadian exports and imports make up about 30 percent of Canadian gross domestic product (GDP). Canada is the world's tenth-largest exporter. Canada's exports and imports are worth about $525 billion each.[2]

Sometimes goods are bought and sold across national boundaries. Companies that do business with other countries need to work with new social and cultural practices, different economic and political environments, and legal restrictions. Before entering world markets, companies must take the business plans they use in their home market and change them to work with the markets in other countries.

This chapter looks at the world of international business. We will see how large and small companies deal with globalization. First, we look at why nations trade, the importance of the global marketplace, the features of the global marketplace, and how nations measure international trade. Then we look at barriers to international trade as a result of cultural and environmental differences. To reduce these barriers, countries turn to organizations that promote global business. Finally, we look at the strategies firms use for entering foreign markets and how they create international business strategies.

exports domestically produced goods and services sold in other countries.

imports foreign goods and services purchased by domestic customers.

LO 4.1 Explain the primary reasons why nations trade.

WHY NATIONS TRADE

When their home markets mature and sales slow, companies in every industry know the importance of expanding business to other countries. TD Ameritrade is Toronto Dominion Bank's online brokerage business in the United States. It was set up when TD Bank acquired Ameritrade in 2006. Lululemon Athletica is based in Vancouver, British Columbia, but operates stores in the United States. Bombardier sells jet aircraft to companies around the world. These are only a few of the thousands of Canadian companies selling their products in other countries. These firms take advantage of large populations, healthy resources, and rising standards of living abroad that increase foreign interest in their goods and services. Likewise, the Canadian market's high purchasing power attracts thousands of foreign companies to its shores.

International trade is vital to a nation and its businesses. Trading with other countries increases economic growth in two ways: by providing a new market for products and by providing access to needed resources. Companies can expand their markets, seek growth opportunities in other nations, and make their production and distribution systems more efficient. They can also reduce their dependence on the economies of their home nations.

International Sources of Factors of Production

Business decisions to operate abroad depend on the basic factors of production in the other country: the availability, price, and quality of labour, natural resources, capital, and entrepreneurship. Indian colleges and universities produce thousands of highly qualified computer scientists and engineers each year. To take advantage of this talent, many global computer software and hardware firms have set up operations in India. Many other companies outsource their information technology and customer service jobs to Indian companies.

Trading with other countries also allows a company to spread risk, because different nations may be at different stages of the business cycle or in different phases of development. If demand falls in one country, the company may find strong demand in other nations. In India and China, sales of automobiles for personal use are just getting started. For many years, companies such as General Motors, Kellogg, and IKEA have used international sales to balance lower sales at home.

Size of the International Marketplace

We have discussed that companies choose international trade because of the benefits to human and natural resources, entrepreneurship, and capital. Companies are also attracted to international business because of the size of the global marketplace. The world's population is approximately 7.2 billion now, but only one in six people live in a well-developed country. The portion of the world's population living in less-developed countries will increase in the coming years because more-developed nations have lower birthrates. But the global birthrate is slowing overall. Today's average woman has half as many children as the average woman had 35 years ago.[3]

When firms in developing nations increase their global business, they also increase their ability to reach new groups of customers. Firms that are looking for new revenue are usually attracted to giant markets such as China and India. China has a population of about 1.3 billion, and India's population is 1.2 billion. But people alone do not create a market. Consumer demand also needs purchasing power. **Table 4.1** shows that population size does not guarantee economic prosperity. Of the 10 countries with the highest population, only one country also has a GDP on the top 10 list—the United States. Note also that countries with smaller populations can create great wealth for their citizens, as measured by GDP per capita. Where does Canada rank? With a population of 35 million people, Canada places 36th from the top of the population rankings but 12th with $51,958 per capita real GDP.

People in developing nations have lower per capita incomes than people in the highly developed economies of North America and Western Europe. Despite having lower incomes, the huge populations in developing countries represent profitable markets for some companies. The higher-income group may only be a small percentage of the entire country's population, but their numbers still represent important and growing markets.

Table 4.1 The World's Top 10 Nations

	BASED ON POPULATION			BASED ON WEALTH	
Rank	COUNTRY	POPULATION (IN MILLIONS)	Rank	COUNTRY	PER CAPITA GDP (IN REAL U.S. DOLLARS)
1	China	1,349	1	Luxembourg	$110,697
2	India	1,221	2	Norway	$100,818
3	United States	317	3	Qatar	$93,714
4	Indonesia	251	4	Macau SAR, China	$91,376
5	Brazil	201	5	Switzerland	$84,815
6	Pakistan	193	6	Australia	$67,458
7	Nigeria	175	7	Sweden	$60,430
8	Bangladesh	164	8	Denmark	$59,831
9	Russia	142	9	Singapore	$55,182
10	Japan	127	10	United States	$53,042
36	Canada	38	12	Canada	$51,958

Sources: CIA, *World Factbook*, accessed January 6, 2014, www.cia.gov; World Bank, "GDP per Capita (Current US$)," accessed March 25, 2015 http://data.worldbank.org.

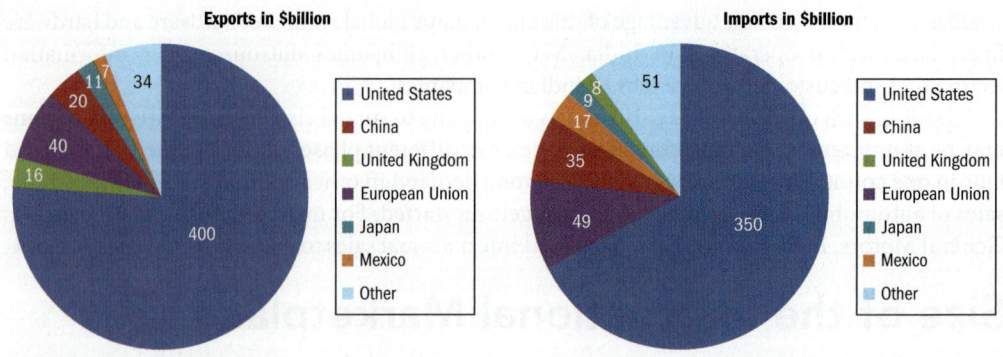

FIGURE 4.1 Canada's Top International Trade Partners

Exports in $billion

- United States: 400
- China: 16
- United Kingdom: 40
- European Union: 20
- Japan: 11
- Mexico: 7
- Other: 34

Imports in $billion

- United States: 350
- China: 49
- United Kingdom: 35
- European Union: 17
- Japan: 9
- Mexico: 8
- Other: 51

Source: Data from Statistics Canada, "Imports, Exports and Trade Balance of Goods on a Balance-of-Payments Basis, by Country or Country Grouping," accessed March 25, 2015, www.statcan.gc.ca/tables-tableaux/sum-som/l01/cst01/gblec02a-eng.htm.

Many developing countries have typically posted high growth rates in their annual GDP. Until the 2008–2010 economic slowdown, U.S. and Canadian GDP rates grew at an annual rate of about 4 percent. By contrast, GDP growth in less-developed countries was much greater—China's GDP growth rate, recently slowing, had exceeded double digits for most of the last decade, and India's averaged 7.5 percent over the last decade.[4] These countries represent opportunities for global businesses, even though their per capita incomes are lower than in more-developed countries. Many North American firms are setting up operations in these and other developing countries. They want to benefit from local sales as a result of expanding economies and rising standards of living. For example, Walmart has opened dozens of new stores in developing countries from China to Brazil. As the largest retail firm in the world, Walmart employs 2.2 million workers (called "associates") in 11,000 stores worldwide. Walmart International is currently the fastest-growing segment of Walmart's business, with more than 6,400 stores and 900,000 employees in 27 countries as far-ranging as Lesotho and Swaziland in Africa. More than 90 percent of Walmart's overseas stores operate under a local banner.[5]

Canada's trade is overwhelmingly tied to the United States, and U.S. trade is tied to Canada. Both countries are similar in their social and cultural values. That means that when a business finds a market in one country, it will most likely find buyers in the other country, too. Almost all of Canada's population is spread along the American border. The closeness of the two countries makes it easier to transport goods and to communicate, and that helps develop cross-border trade.

Figure 4.1 shows Canada's top trade partners. Notice the amount of trade Canada has with the United States. Much of our trade with the United States is resource based. The demand for Canada's energy supplies of oil, natural gas, and hydro-electricity will continue to grow as the United States continues to need safe, secure, and reliable sources of energy.

Absolute and Comparative Advantage

Few countries can produce all the goods and services they need. For centuries, trading has helped countries meet the demand for goods and services. A country can focus on producing what it does best. It can then export the extra output and buy foreign products that it doesn't have or cannot produce efficiently. The foreign sales of a product depend on whether the country has an absolute advantage or a comparative advantage.

A country has an *absolute advantage* in making a product when it has a monopoly on making that product or when it can produce the product at a lower cost than any other country. China has had an absolute advantage in silk production for centuries. Silk is woven from fibres from silkworm cocoons

Saffron is possibly the world's most expensive spice. This pricey spice is extracted from crocus flowers. The plants grow well in Spain but not in most other countries. Spain has a near absolute advantage in saffron production.

and is a prized raw material in high-quality clothing. European demand for silk led to the famous Silk Road, an 8,000-kilometre link between Rome and the ancient Chinese capital city of Xian.

Today, absolute advantages are rare. Some countries almost have absolute advantages in some products. For example, climate differences can give some nations or regions an advantage in growing certain plants, such as the plant that produces saffron. Saffron may be the world's most expensive spice, costing around $4,650 per kilogram. Saffron is the stigma of a flowering plant in the crocus family that is native to the Mediterranean, Asia Minor, and India. Today, saffron is grown mainly in Spain, where the plant thrives in the Spanish soil and climate. Attempts to grow saffron in other parts of the world have generally been unsuccessful.[6]

A nation can develop a *comparative advantage* when it can supply its products more efficiently and at a lower price than it can supply other goods, compared with the outputs of other countries. For example, China profits from its comparative advantage in producing textiles. A nation can also develop a comparative advantage in skilled human resources by ensuring that its people are well educated. India, for example, has a comparative advantage in software development because of its highly educated workforce and low wage scale. Several companies have moved part or all of their software development to India.

IBM wanted to increase its longstanding advantage in research and innovation as global competition increased. The company took the unusual step of forming six global research collaborations with companies, universities, and governments in Saudi Arabia, China, Switzerland, Ireland, Taiwan, and India. IBM hopes to sign at least four more international partnerships. Working with these countries breaks the tradition of doing research in secret. "The world is our lab now," says IBM's director of research.[7]

ASSESSMENT CHECK

4.1.1 Why do nations trade?

4.1.2 What are some measures of the size of the international marketplace?

4.1.3 How does a nation acquire a comparative advantage?

MEASURING TRADE BETWEEN NATIONS

LO 4.2 Describe how trade is measured between nations.

International trade provides competitive advantages to both the countries and the individual companies involved. But how do we measure global business activity? We need to look at two ideas: the balance of trade and the balance of payments. These two ideas can help us understand what the trade inflows and outflows mean for a country. Another important factor is the currency exchange rates for the trading countries.

A nation's **balance of trade** is the difference between its exports and imports. When a country exports more than it imports, it has a positive balance of trade, called a *trade surplus*. When a country imports more than it exports, it produces a negative balance of trade, called a *trade deficit*. Canada tends to maintain a balance between exports and imports by running a trade surplus with the United States and a trade deficit with other trading partners, particularly China.[8] The United States has run a trade deficit every year since 1976. The United States is one of the world's top exporters, but it has an even greater demand for foreign-made goods, which creates a trade deficit.

A nation's balance of trade plays a central role in shaping its **balance of payments**—the overall flow of money into or out of a country. The balance of payments is also affected by overseas loans and borrowing, international investments, profits from international investments, and foreign aid payments. To calculate a nation's balance of payments, subtract the monetary outflows from the monetary inflows. A positive balance of payments, or a *balance-of-payments surplus*, means more money has moved into a country than out of it. A negative balance of payments, or a *balance-of-payments deficit*, means more money has gone out of the country than entered it.

balance of trade the difference between a nation's exports and imports.

balance of payments the overall money flows into and out of a country.

Major Canadian Exports and Imports

The global economy has grown to more than $74 trillion of total GDP. Canada's economy represents about $1.8 trillion, and the U.S. economy represents about $16.7 trillion. Trade is an important reason why global GDP has grown and keeps growing.[9]

Table 4.2 Major Canadian Imports and Exports in 2014

	EXPORTS $ BILLIONS 2014	RANK	IMPORTS $ BILLIONS 2014	RANK
Totals from All Categories	529		524	
Farm, fishing, and intermediate food products	31	7	15	10
Energy products	129	1	44	7
Metal ores and nonmetallic minerals	18	11	11	11
Metal and nonmetallic mineral products	58	4	46	5
Basic and industrial chemical, plastic, and rubber products	36	6	45	6
Forestry products and building and packaging materials	37	5	23	8
Industrial machinery, equipment, and parts	29	8	51	4
Electronic and electrical equipment and parts	24	9	59	3
Motor vehicles and parts	75	2	90	2
Aircraft and other transportation equipment and parts	22	10	17	9
Consumer goods	59	3	106	1
Special transactions trade	2	12	7	13
Other balance of payments adjustments	9	13	10	12

Source: Data from Statistics Canada, "Exports of Goods on a Balance-of-Payments Basis, by Product," accessed March 26, 2015, www.statcan.gc.ca/tables-tableaux/sum-som/l01/cst01/gblec04-eng.htm; "Imports of Goods on a Balance-of-Payments Basis, by Product," accessed March 26, 2015, www.statcan.gc.ca/tables-tableaux/sum-som/l01/cst01/gblec05-eng.htm.

Table 4.2 shows the ranking of the major categories of Canadian merchandise exports and imports. Canada's top merchandise exports in 2014 were energy products ($129 billion), motor vehicles and parts ($75 billion), and consumer goods ($59 billion). Energy product exports increased 38 percent from 2010 to 2014 after doubling from 2000 to 2010. This growth reflects both increased export quantities and the dramatic increase in market prices for oil. Prices peaked in 2014 at about $150 per barrel before falling back to the $50 range in early 2015. The average price of oil in 2000 was about $27 per barrel, and it was about $71 in 2010.[10] Canadian manufacturing export sales increased as the 2008–2010 recession gave way to economic recovery and increasing exports of Canadian motor vehicle products and consumer goods.

On the import side, Canada's top imports were consumer goods ($106 billion), motor vehicles and parts ($90 billion), and electronic and electrical equipment and parts ($58 billion). These increases grew as the 2008–2010 recession gave way to economic recovery and Canadians returned to normal spending on the imported goods we enjoy.

In 2014, Canada exported over $84 billion of services and imported over $106 billion worth. Services include travel and tourism as well as consulting and business services. The service sector employs thousands of Canadian workers who are often working in conjunction with international companies.[11]

The United States leads the world in the international trade of goods and services. It has combined exports and imports of about $4.9 trillion. The goods exchanged by U.S. exporters and importers range from machinery and vehicles to crude oil and chemicals.

Although the United States imports more goods than it exports, the opposite is true for services. U.S. exporters sell more than $600 billion in services annually. Much of that money comes from travel and tourism—money spent by foreign nationals visiting the United States.[12]

U.S. annual imports are nearing $2.7 trillion, making the United States the world's leading importer. Like Canadians, Americans demand foreign-made goods for everything from clothing to consumer electronics. These preferences create huge trade deficits with the two nations that export the most consumer goods to North America—China and Japan.

Exchange Rates

An **exchange rate** is the value of one country's currency in terms of the currencies of other countries. We need to learn how foreign exchange works because we live in a global community. The value of currency is an important economic measure for every country. Each currency's exchange rate is usually stated in terms of another currency. For example, about 12 Mexican pesos are needed to purchase one Canadian dollar. A Canadian dollar can also be exchanged for approximately $0.85 in the United States at the time of writing this textbook. The euro is the currency used in most European Union (EU) member countries, and like any currency the euro has had ups and downs in value. European consumers and businesses use the euro to pay bills by cheque, credit card, or bank transfer. Euro coins and notes are also used in many EU member countries.

Many factors can affect foreign exchange rates: economic and political conditions, actions by the central bank, balance-of-payments position, and speculation over future currency values. Currency values fluctuate, or "float," depending on the supply and demand for each currency in the world market. In this system of *floating exchange rates*, currency traders create a market for the world's currencies based on each country's trade and the likelihood of investments. The idea is that exchange rates can go up and down freely as supply and demand change. But exchange rates do not float in total freedom. National governments often step in to change their exchange rates.

Nations can affect exchange rates in other ways. They may form currency blocs by linking their exchange rates to each other. Many governments practise protectionist policies that try to protect their economies against trade imbalances. For example, nations sometimes take actions to devalue their currencies as a way to increase exports and encourage foreign investment. **Devaluation** is a reduction in a currency's value in terms of other currencies or in terms of a fixed standard. Brazil recently devalued its currency, making investing in Brazil less costly than investing in other countries. After the devaluation, foreign investment in Brazil increased. Pillsbury bought Brazil's Brisco, a company that makes *pao de queijo*, a cheese bread formed into rolls and served with morning coffee. Other foreign companies invested in Brazil's construction, tourism, banking, communications, and other industries.

For an individual business, the impact of currency devaluation depends on where the business buys its materials and where it sells its products. Usually, business transactions use the currency of the country where the transactions take place. When business takes place in Japan, the transactions will likely be in yen. In the United Kingdom, transactions are in pounds. Many EU countries now use the euro, so fewer currencies are used in Europe. Today, the EU member countries that use the euro include Austria, Belgium, Cyprus, Estonia, Finland, France, Germany, Greece, Ireland, Italy, Latvia, Luxembourg, Malta, the Netherlands, Portugal, Slovakia, Slovenia, and Spain. Other currencies include the British pound, the Australian dollar, the Indian rupee, the Brazilian real, the Mexican peso, the Taiwanese dollar, and the South African rand.

Exchange rate changes can quickly create—or destroy—a competitive advantage. They are important factors when investors decide whether to invest in other countries. In Europe, a declining Canadian or American dollar means that the price of euros go up, so European companies are pressured to lower their prices to keep foreign customers who generally pay for goods in U.S. dollars. When the value of the Canadian dollar falls, European vacations are more costly for Canadian tourists because their dollars are worth less in terms of the euro.

Currencies that easily convert into other currencies are called *hard currencies*. Examples of hard currencies are the euro, the U.S. dollar, and

exchange rate the value of one country's currency in terms of the currencies of other countries.

devaluation a reduction in a currency's value in terms of other currencies or in terms of a fixed standard.

Because we live in a global community, we need to understand how currency exchange rates work. Many factors affect foreign exchange rates.

ASSESSMENT CHECK

4.2.1 Compare balance of trade and balance of payments.

4.2.2 Explain the function of an exchange rate.

4.2.3 What happens when a currency is devalued?

the Japanese yen. The Russian ruble and many central European currencies are soft currencies because they cannot be converted as easily. Exporters that trade with these countries sometimes prefer to barter, or accept payment not in cash but in goods, such as oil, timber, or other commodities. They then resell these goods in exchange for payment in hard currencies.

The foreign currency market is the largest financial market in the world. Its daily volume is more than US$5.3 trillion.[13] This amount is about 10 times the size of all the world's stock markets combined. The foreign exchange market is the most liquid and most efficient financial market in the world.

LO 4.3 Identify the major barriers to international trade.

BARRIERS TO INTERNATIONAL TRADE

All businesses face barriers, whether they sell only to local customers or trade in international markets. International companies must follow a variety of laws and deal with multiple exchange currencies. They may also need to change their products to suit different tastes in other countries. Kraft recently won nearly a quarter of China's $1.6 billion cookie market by making its Oreo cookies less sweet to suit local tastes. The company also launched new products such as Oreo Wafer Sticks, Wafer Rolls, Soft Cakes, and Strawberry Cremes.[14]

Companies that do international business face social and cultural differences, economic barriers, and legal and political barriers. Some of the barriers are shown in **Figure 4.2**. Some of these barriers are easy to deal with, but other barriers require a company to make major changes in its business strategy. To be successful in global markets, companies and their managers need to understand not only how these barriers affect international trade but also how to overcome these barriers.

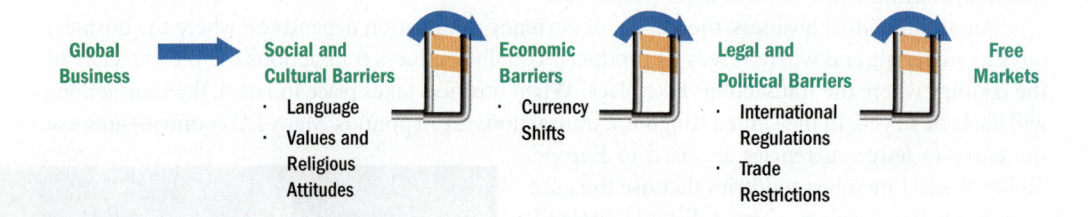

FIGURE 4.2 Barriers to International Trade

Global Business → Social and Cultural Barriers
- Language
- Values and Religious Attitudes

Economic Barriers
- Currency Shifts

Legal and Political Barriers
- International Regulations
- Trade Restrictions

Free Markets

Social and Cultural Differences

The social and cultural differences among nations range from language and customs to educational background and religious holidays. Understanding and respecting these differences are important for international business success. Businesspeople who understand the host country's cultures, languages, social values, and religious attitudes and practices are prepared for the marketplace and the negotiating table. Businesspeople can win customers and meet their business goals by being sensitive to local views, to how people like to be addressed, and to suitable ways of dressing, using body language, and being on time.

English is the second most-widely spoken language in the world, followed by Hindustani, Spanish, Russian, and Arabic. Only Mandarin Chinese is more common than English. In other countries, some students whose first language is not English take eight years of English language classes in elementary and high school. Understanding a business colleague's primary language can make the difference between closing an international business transaction and losing the sale. Company workers in foreign markets not only must choose the correct and suitable words, but also need to translate words correctly so they say what they want to say. Some firms rename their products or rewrite slogans for foreign markets.

Some communication barriers involve more than just bad translations. Companies may make mistakes by presenting messages using unsuitable media, overlooking local customs and regulations, or ignoring differences in taste. One executive recently lost a deal in China because he gave the prospective client a set of four antique clocks wrapped in white paper. But the number four and the Chinese word for *clock* sound like the word *death*. And white is the traditional colour for funerals.[15]

Cultural sensitivity is especially important in cyberspace. Website developers need to remember that website visitors come from anywhere in the world. Some icons that seem friendly to Canadian Internet users may shock people from other countries. For example, a person making a high-five hand signal would be insulting people in Greece, and making a circle with the thumb and index finger in Brazil is not appropriate, nor is using a thumbs-up sign in Egypt or showing a two-fingered peace sign with the back of the hand facing out in Great Britain.

Gift-giving traditions use the language of symbolism. For example, in Latin America knives and scissors are not suitable gifts because they represent the severing of friendship. Flowers are generally acceptable, but Mexicans use yellow flowers in their Day of the Dead activities, so yellow flowers are linked to death.

Values and Religious Attitudes

Today's world is shrinking in many ways, but people in different countries do not always share the same values or religious feelings. Major differences can exist between people—even those living in the same country.

North American society places a higher value on business efficiency and lower unemployment than European society. But in Europe, employee benefits are more valued. In Canada, vacation time is decided on by each provincial government. For example, in Ontario the Employment Standards Act states that employees earn two weeks' vacation after working for a 12-month vacation entitlement period. In contrast, the EU gives employees a minimum paid vacation of four weeks per year, but most Europeans get five or six weeks. When a Canadian company opens a factory in an EU country, it can hire local employees only if it offers vacation time as set by that nation's business practices.

North American culture values national unity and accepts regional differences. Canada and the United States are seen as separate national markets that have independent economies. European countries that are part of the 27-member EU are trying to create a similar marketplace, but many people don't like the idea of being European citizens first and British, Danish, or Dutch citizens second. British consumers differ from Italian consumers in important ways. Canadian companies that don't understand these differences and that don't change their activities to suit the other country will face problems with being accepted.

Religion plays an important role in every society. Businesspeople must also learn to be sensitive to the major religions in countries where they operate. International businesspeople need to understand religious cycles and the timing of major holidays. Their knowledge can help prevent embarrassing moments when booking meetings, trade shows, conferences, and events such as the opening of a new factory. People who do business in Saudi Arabia need to remember Islam's month-long observance of Ramadan, when work ends at noon. Friday is the Muslim Sabbath, so the Saudi workweek runs from Saturday through Thursday. Also, Muslims don't drink alcohol and think of pork as being unclean. That means gifts of pigskin or liquor would not be welcomed.

Economic Differences

North American businesses usually do well in densely populated countries such as China and India. There, the local consumers eagerly buy Western products. Although selling products there is tempting for Canadian firms, managers must think about the economic factors of doing business in China or India: the country's size, its per capita income, and its stage of economic development. These economic factors are important to think about when deciding whether a country is right for an international business venture. For example, Tata Motors, the largest automobile company in India, is thinking about selling cars to Western auto buyers, even as it works on selling its low-cost Nano car in its home market. The "Hit & Miss" feature discusses the Nano's evolution.

HIT & MISS

The Tiny Nano—A Potential Hit for Tata Motors

The Tata Nano is a tiny car that sells for $2,500 in India. When the Tata Nano arrived in North America it wasn't on the road—it was on display at the Cooper–Hewitt Smithsonian Design Museum in New York as "the world's most affordable car [and] a design achievement," said a museum director.

The Nano is a safe and sturdy vehicle, but more importantly it is a major step in changing transportation for millions of Indian families that can't afford the high price of most cars. Tata built "the people's car" by using existing parts and a simple design to keep costs down.

"My particular fascination about the Nano is what I refer to as the 'Nano effect' on the rest of the world's vehicle industry," said one research director. He thinks that people everywhere will ask, "If Indians can buy a four-door car for $2,500, why can't I?"

Maybe they soon can. Tata is a $63-billion Indian company. It backed the Nano during legal issues over the land needed for a factory, which delayed production for two years. The recent recession also meant Tata had its first financial losses in seven years, occurring about the same time as the company faced heavy debts after having bought the money-losing Jaguar and Land Rover brands from Ford.

Tata's strategic plan is still to achieve international standing by solving the transportation problems of low-income car markets in the developing world. Tata will sell the Nano in Nigeria next, and it has already passed Europe's crash-safety test. In just a few years, you may see slightly higher-priced Nanos on the streets of Europe and even in North America.

Questions for Critical Thinking

1. Do you think Tata's goal of making transportation affordable in developing countries is realistic? Why or why not?
2. Can you think of any disadvantages for low-income markets if thousands of cars suddenly show up on the road?

Sources: Phil Patton, "A Tata Nano Takes Manhattan," *New York Times*, February 11, 2010, accessed May 28, 2015, www.nytimes.com/2010/02/14/automobiles/14NANO.html; April K, Gupta and Haiyan Wang, "Tata Nano: Not Just a Car but also a Platform," *Businessweek*, January 20, 2010, accessed May 28, 2015, www.bloomberg.com/bw/stories/2010-01-29/tata-nano-not-just-a-car-but-also-a-platformbusinessweek-business-news-stock-market-and-financial-advice; Madhur Singh, "India's Top Automaker, Tata Motors, Hits a Rough Patch," *Time*, February 24, 2009, accessed May 28, 2015, http://content.time.com/time/world/article/0,8599,1881404,00.html.

Infrastructure

infrastructure the basic systems of a country's communication, transportation, and energy facilities.

Businesses that compete in world markets need to think about the host country's economic measures, including its **infrastructure**. Infrastructure refers to the basic systems of communication (telecommunications, television, radio, and print media), transportation (roads and highways, railroads, and airports), and energy facilities (power plants and gas and electric utilities). The Internet and technology use can also be considered part of infrastructure.

India's industrialization is growing. A recent forecast estimates that India will soon have 30 million air passengers each year. India's civil aviation minister says that means India will soon need at least 400 new airports. The Indian aviation industry is growing at nearly 20 percent a year, so 3,000 new planes will also be needed. It will take about one year to complete the bidding process for contractors to work on building a new airport in the capital city of Mumbai. "Our job is not over by creating infrastructure for aviation industry to grow," said the minister. "We need safe and secure aviation. Indian aviation will not grow at the cost of safety and security." Part of India's new air travel security is a CT scanner that inspects luggage at India's biggest new airport in New Delhi, which was built in only three years.[16]

Financial systems provide a type of infrastructure for businesses. In Canada, buyers have widespread access to cheques, credit cards, debit cards, and the electronic systems needed to process these payments. In many African countries, like Ethiopia, local businesses do not accept credit cards. Visitors to Ethiopia's capital city, Addis Ababa, are warned to bring plenty of cash and traveller's cheques with them.

Currency Conversion and Shifts

Countries share many similarities in their infrastructure. But businesses that cross national borders face a basic economic difference: national currencies. Foreign currency fluctuations, or ups and downs, may mean more problems for global businesses. As explained earlier in the chapter, the values of the world's major currencies rise and fall in relation to each other. Rapid and unexpected currency shifts can make it difficult to price items in the local currency. Shifts in exchange rates can also affect business decisions. A devalued currency may make a nation less desirable as a country to export to because of reduced demand in that country. But devaluation can also make the nation desirable as an investment opportunity. Investments there will be a bargain in terms of the buying power of the investor's currency.

Political and Legal Differences

We have discussed how social, cultural, and economic differences can build barriers to international trade. Legal and political differences can also act as barriers. To compete in today's world marketplace, managers in international businesses need to be familiar with the legislation that affects their industries. Some countries have general trade restrictions. Others have detailed rules that state how foreign companies can operate.

Political Climate

In any international business investment, an important factor is the stability of the political situation. The political structures of many nations promote stability similar to the political stability in Canada. Other nations have very different political structures that change frequently. This is the situation in Indonesia, the Congo, and Thailand. Nations often pass laws to protect their own interests, sometimes at the expense of foreign businesses. See the "Solving an Ethical Controversy" feature for a look at the environmental issues involved in energy trade between Canada and the United States.

SOLVING AN **ETHICAL** CONTROVERSY

Delivering Alberta Oil through the Keystone XL Pipeline versus by Rail

The Keystone XL Pipeline proposal from Calgary-based TransCanada Corporation would connect Alberta oil production fields with the American pipeline grid that transports oil south to refineries on the Gulf of Mexico. There are two areas of debate that have surrounded the proposal to build the pipeline: There is the positive economic value of the project, but there is also the negative environmental impact.

PRO

1. The pipeline would provide thousands of jobs as it is built and would be a safer and cheaper way to transport oil to refineries.
2. Producing more oil would result in lower fuel prices and lower inflation in general.
3. North American consumers would reduce dependency on Middle Eastern sources of oil.

CON

1. Increased Alberta oil production would be environmentally damaging to Alberta as well as cause more pollution by users burning more fossil fuels.
2. Making more oil products available at lower prices would delay development of alternative, more ecologically friendly energy technologies.
3. Potential spills from the pipeline would be devastating to local ecosystems and may even threaten sources of drinking water.

Summary

Higher-priced oil may speed up the adoption of more ecofriendly alternative energy sources, but it will impede economic development, especially for those countries that can least afford it. Energy is a requisite for economic development. Without it, little happens in the way of manufacturing and transportation of goods and people.

Further complicating this debate is the use of rail to transport oil because pipeline is unavailable. Rail is considered more dangerous and risky than pipeline, and recent events like the tragic derailment in Lac-Mégantic, Quebec, in 2013 have driven public debate over rail safety.

Approximately 90 billion barrels of oil are consumed each day. About 4.5 billion barrels of Middle East oil enter through the Gulf coast every day. Alberta oil is an alternative supply that would keep revenues within North America.

Sources: Geoffrey Morgan, "A 'Pure Fabrication': TransCanada CEO Fuels War of Words over Obama's Keystone Comments," *Financial Post*, November 19, 2014, accessed March 29, 2015, http://business.financialpost.com; Mark Silva, "Obama's Keystone Options Shrink as State Downplays Impact," January 21, 2014, Bloomberg, accessed March 29, 2015, www.bloomberg.com/news; CNNMoney, "Goldman Sachs CEO on the Benefits of Low Oil," March 2, 2015, accessed March 29, 2015, http://money.cnn.com/video/investing/2015/02/24/lloyd-blankfein-goldman-sachs-oil.cnnmoney; "Are Low Oil Prices Good or Bad for the Economy?" *Fortune*, January 19, 2015, accessed March 29, 2015, http://for.tn/1BcnAhx; Nathan Vanderrklippe, "With Pipelines under Attack, Railways Lead Race to Move Oil," *The Globe and Mail*, January 12, 2013, accessed March 29, 2015, www.theglobeandmail.com.

The political structures have had huge impacts in Russia, Turkey, the former Yugoslavia, Hong Kong, and several central European countries, including the Czech Republic and Poland. Such political changes almost always bring changes in the legal environment. Hong Kong is considered to be part of China. Thus, political developments have led to changes in Hong Kong's legal and cultural environments. Since the collapse of the Soviet Union, Russia has struggled to develop a new market structure and political processes.

Legal Environment

When doing business internationally, managers must be familiar with three dimensions of the legal environment: Canadian law, international regulations, and the laws of the countries in which they plan to trade. Some laws protect the rights of foreign companies to compete in Canada. Others spell out the actions allowed for Canadian companies doing business in foreign countries.

Canada's Corruption of Foreign Public Officials Act (CFPOA) and the U.S. Foreign Corrupt Practices Act (FCPA) make it illegal for companies to bribe foreign officials, political candidates, or government representatives. These acts set out the fines and jail time for managers who are aware of illegal payoffs.

The Russian national flag flies atop Bank Rossii, Russia's central bank, in Moscow, Russia. Since the collapse of the Soviet Union, the political and economic structures in Russia have undergone huge changes and the country has struggled to develop a new market structure.

Until recently, many countries, including France and Germany, accepted the practice of bribing foreign officials in countries where such practices were customary—and even allowed tax deductions for these expenses. Canada, the United States, the United Kingdom, France, Germany, and 35 other countries have signed the Organisation for Economic Co-operation and Development's Anti-Bribery Convention. Many police forces do not actively enforce this law, but this agreement makes offering or paying bribes a criminal offence. It also ends the tax deduction for bribes.[17] Regardless of global business strategies, companies need to be aware of cultural and business customs in the countries in which they do business and of whether certain behaviours are accepted or possibly illegal.

Corruption continues to be an international problem from which no country is immune, as illustrated by the European-based FIFA soccer bribery scandal which emerged in 2015. The commonness of bribing and the international rules against bribery create difficulties for Canadian businesspeople who want to do business in foreign countries: Chinese pay *huilu*, and Russians rely on *vzyatka*, while in the Middle East palms are greased with *baksheesh*. **Figure 4.3** compares 179 countries on measures of supposed corruption. This Corruption Perceptions Index is computed by Transparency International, a Berlin-based organization that rates the degree of corruption observed by businesspeople and the general public.

The growth of online business has introduced new elements to the legal situation of international businesses. Patents, brand names, trademarks, copyrights, and other intellectual property are difficult to keep watch over, given the availability of information on the Internet. Some countries have laws to protect information obtained by electronic contacts. Malaysia has stiff fines and long jail terms for people convicted of illegally accessing computers and using the information that passes through them.

International Regulations

To make international commerce more standard, Canada and many other countries have treaties and signed agreements that describe the expected conduct of international business and protect some of its activities. Canada has entered into many *friendship, commerce, and navigation treaties*

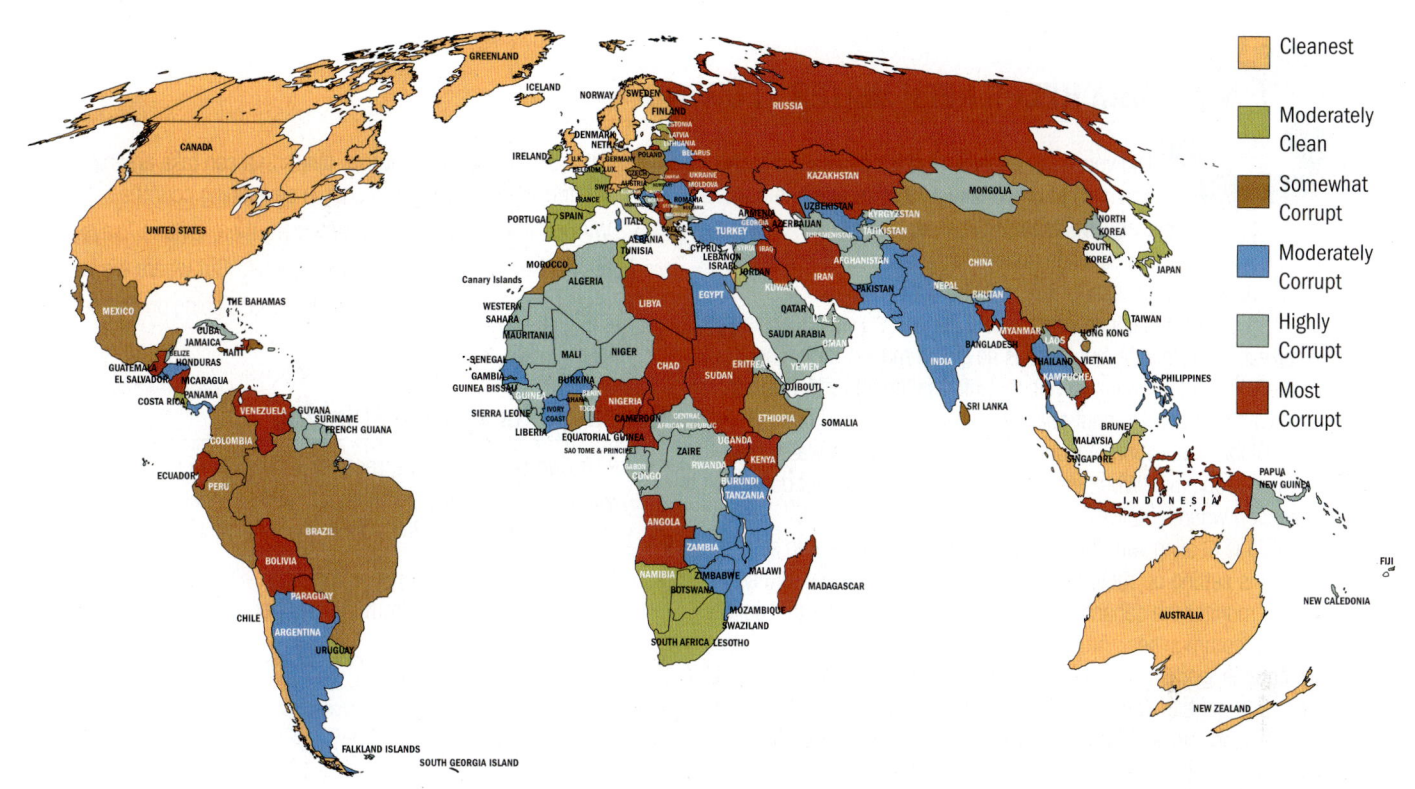

Source: Data from Transparency International, "Annual Corruption Perceptions Index," accessed January 6, 2014, www.transparency.org.

FIGURE 4.3 Corruption in Business and Government

with other nations. These treaties describe many aspects of international business relations, including the right to conduct business in the treaty partner's home market. Other international business agreements involve product standards, patents, trademarks, tax policies, export controls, international air travel, and international communications. One area has no international regulations—the use and protection of water supplies. IBM is stepping in to help provide the international community with water management methods and tools, as we see in the "Going Green" feature.

After China was granted full trade relations with the United States, China agreed to lower its trade barriers, including subsidies that hold down the prices of food exports, restrictions on where foreign law firms can open offices, and taxes charged on imported goods. In exchange for China's promise to halve these taxes, called *tariffs*, the United States granted Chinese businesses access to U.S. markets equal to the access enjoyed by most other countries.

Many rules affect the actions of managers that do business in international markets. Worldwide producers and marketers must keep required minimum levels of quality in all countries where they operate. They must also comply with numerous local regulations. In Britain, advertisers cannot encourage children to engage in unhealthy behaviour such as overeating or skipping regular meals and having candy and snack foods instead. Malaysia's Censorship Board outlaws nudity and swearing on TV. Germany and France let publishers set the prices that retailers charge for books.

Italian clothing manufacturers have long enjoyed high status for their fabrics and workmanship. However, they believed they were being victimized by a lax labelling system when international clothing designers bought less-expensive fabric in China or Bulgaria, had the garments cut in countries with lower labour costs, then sent them to Italy for final sewing. There, they tacked on the prestigious "Made in Italy" label and charged a high price for the goods. The Italian manufacturers pushed for a law requiring that two of the four stages of clothing production must take place in Italy to earn the "Made in Italy" label.[18]

Going Green: IBM Helps Keep Water Flowing

Did you know it takes 42 litres of water to make one slice of bread, and 133 litres to make a single cup of coffee? Water is one of our greatest resources, but it is under much stress. One in five people worldwide lack access to safe drinking water.

IBM is taking major steps to protect the world's supply of water. Water exists worldwide, but there is no global market for it. There is also very little international or national information about how to conserve water. "Water is about quantity, quality, space, and time," says IBM's Global Innovation Outlook report on the world's water management problems. "Whether you have a big problem or not depends entirely on where you live."

IBM is dealing with the future of water management in several ways. It is setting up meters and sensors that use special IBM software to monitor the capacity and quality of water systems that serve nations, communities, organizations, and individual homes. The company is working to ensure that treated drinking water doesn't come into contact with waste from thousands of kilometres of old underground pipes. IBM's acoustic technology helps to find the worst leaks so they can be repaired right away. IBM is also collecting information on pollution, marine life, and waves for commercial fishers. It is also working to improve filters that can take arsenic and salt from drinking water at a low cost in developing countries.

"We're not going to create water where there is none," says the vice-president of IBM's Big Green Innovations. "But where we know water is under stress, we need to monitor what's going on and better manage it."

Questions for Critical Thinking

1. *Fast Company* magazine recently voted IBM eighteenth in the world in innovation because of IBM's water management efforts. What makes IBM particularly suitable for this award?

2. IBM is an information services company. What can other socially responsible firms learn from IBM's water management efforts?

Sources: IBM, "Advanced Water Management," accessed March 23, 2010, www-304.ibm.com/easyaccess/fileserve?contentid=182044; IBM "Smarter Water Management," accessed March 23, 2010, www.ibm.com/smarterplanet/ca/en/water_management/ideas; Chuck Salter, "#18. IBM," *Fast Company*, February 17, 2010, www.fastcompany.com; Mary Tripsas, "Everybody in the Pool of Green Innovation," *New York Times*, October 31, 2009, accessed March 23, 2010, www.nytimes.com/2009/11/01/business/01proto.html.

Types of Trade Restrictions

Trade restrictions such as taxes on imports and complicated administrative procedures create additional barriers to international business. They may limit the products and services available to consumers and can increase the costs of foreign-made products. Trade restrictions are also used to protect citizens' security, health, and jobs. A government may limit exports of strategic goods to unfriendly countries and ban imports of farm products that have been contaminated by insecticide to protect people's health. Imports are also restricted to protect domestic jobs in the importing country.

Other restrictions are used to promote trade with certain countries. Still other restrictions protect countries from unfair competition. Trade restrictions may be used for different political reasons, but most are in the form of tariffs. Governments also impose some nontariff barriers, also called *administrative barriers*. These barriers include quotas, embargoes, and exchange controls.

Tariffs

tariffs taxes imposed on imported goods.

Taxes, surcharges, and duties on foreign products are referred to as **tariffs**. Governments assess two types of tariffs—revenue tariffs and protective tariffs. Both tariffs make imports more expensive for domestic buyers. Revenue tariffs generate income for the government. For example, Canadian leisure travellers who have been outside Canada for 24 to 48 hours can bring back only up to $200 worth of goods free of duty and tax, and after 48 hours or more, $800 worth of goods. Any amounts greater are charged revenue tariffs.[19]

A protective tariff has one purpose: to raise the retail price of imported products to match or top the prices of similar products made in the home country. In other words, protective tariffs try to limit imports and give local competitors an equal chance to succeed.

Tariffs are a disadvantage to companies that want to export to the countries that have the tariffs. Governments do not always agree on the reasons behind protective tariffs. As a result, tariffs do not always have the desired effect. Canada, like most countries, has a tariff on foreign competitors selling products in Canada at prices lower than Canadian manufacturers charge.

Nontariff Barriers

Nontariff trade barriers are also called administrative trade barriers. These barriers restrict imports without using the strict rules that tariffs use. Nontariff trade barriers may be in the form of quotas on imports, restrictive standards for imports, and export subsidies. Many countries have recently reduced their tariffs or removed them entirely. These countries can use nontariff barriers to control the flow of imported products.

Quotas limit the amounts of particular products that countries can import during specified time periods. Limits may be set as quantities, such as the number of cars or bushels of wheat. Limits can also be set as values, such as dollars' worth of cigarettes.

Quotas help prevent **dumping**. In one form of dumping, a company sells products in other countries at prices below the cost of production. In another form of dumping, a company exports a large quantity of a product at a lower price than the same product in the home market. This action drives down the price of the domestic product. Dumping benefits domestic consumers in the importing market, but it hurts domestic producers. Dumping is also a way for companies to gain quick entry to foreign markets.

An **embargo** is more severe than a quota. An embargo is a total ban on importing a specified product. It can also be a complete stop to trading with a particular country. Many countries, including Canada, have longstanding trade embargoes with North Korea and Iran. Embargo durations can vary depending on changes in foreign policy.

Another form of administrative trade restriction is **exchange control**. A central bank or government agency applies the exchange controls, which affect both exporters and importers. Firms that gain foreign currencies by exporting must sell those currencies to the central bank or another agency. Importers must buy foreign currencies to pay for their purchases from the same agency. The exchange control authority then assigns, expands, or restricts foreign exchange, depending on the national policy.

quota a limit set on the amounts of particular products that can be imported.

dumping selling products in other countries at prices below production costs or below typical prices in the home market to capture market share from domestic competitors.

embargo a total ban on importing specific products or a total stop to trading with a particular country.

exchange control a restriction on importing certain products or a restriction against certain companies to reduce trade and the spending of foreign currency.

✓ ASSESSMENT CHECK

4.3.1 How can values and attitudes form a barrier to trade, and how can these barriers be overcome?

4.3.2 What is a tariff? What is its purpose?

4.3.3 Why is dumping a problem for companies marketing goods internationally?

International trade restrictions include *quotas*, or limits, on the amount of a product, such as wheat, that can be imported into a country.

LO 4.4 Explain how international trade organizations and economic communities reduce barriers to international trade.

REDUCING BARRIERS TO INTERNATIONAL TRADE

Although tariffs and administrative barriers restrict trade, the world is generally moving toward free trade. Several types of organizations ease barriers to international trade, such as groups that monitor trade policies and practices and institutions that offer monetary assistance. The multinational economic community, like the European Union, is made up of multiple federations designed to ease trade barriers. This section looks at the roles these organizations play.

Organizations Promoting International Trade

The **General Agreement on Tariffs and Trade (GATT)** is an international trade accord. Since GATT began more than 60 years ago, it has sponsored a series of negotiations, called rounds, that have greatly reduced worldwide tariffs and other barriers. Major industrialized nations founded the multinational organization in 1947. GATT's aim is to work toward reducing tariffs and relaxing import quotas. The last set of completed negotiations—the Uruguay Round—cut average tariffs by one-third, or by more than $700 billion; reduced farm subsidies; and improved protection for copyright and patent holders. Also, international trading rules now apply to various service industries. Finally, the new agreement established the **World Trade Organization (WTO)** to succeed GATT. This organization includes representatives from 157 countries.

World Trade Organization

Since 1995, the WTO has monitored GATT agreements among its member nations. It has also mediated disputes and continues GATT's aim to reduce trade barriers throughout the world. Unlike the provisions in GATT, the WTO's decisions are final and must be followed by all parties involved in disputes.

The WTO has had its fair share of controversy in recent years. Much disagreement has come from WTO decisions that affect working conditions and the environment in member nations. Many are concerned that the WTO's focus on lowering trade barriers encourages businesses to keep costs down by using methods that may increase both pollution and human rights abuses. Some find it troubling that the organization's member nations must agree on policies. The problem is that developing countries do not want to lose their low-cost advantage by agreeing to stricter labour and environmental policies. Other critics say that if wealthy firms such as fast-food chains, entertainment companies, and Internet retailers can freely enter foreign markets, they may mean the end of smaller foreign businesses that serve the unique tastes and practices of other countries' cultures.

Trade unions in developed nations complain about the WTO's support of free trade. They say free trade makes it easier to export manufacturing jobs to low-wage countries. For example, Canadian textile manufacturing has just about disappeared, and U.S. glassmaking is in a long decline that began in the 1990s, aided by increased imports and bigger profits to be made overseas.[20] In recent years, more new auto plants are being built in Mexico as Canadian and American plants are closed or reduced in size.

The most recent round of WTO talks was called the Doha Round, after the city in Qatar where it began. After several years of heated discussions and negotiations that fell apart, the eight leading industrial nations recommitted themselves to successfully concluding the talks. The discussion included ways to improve global agricultural trade and trade among developing countries. The leaders worked to reduce domestic price supports, eliminate export subsidies, and improve market access for goods. Such changes can help farmers in developing countries compete in the global marketplace.[21]

World Bank

Soon after the end of World War II, industrialized nations formed an organization to lend money to less-developed and developing countries. The **World Bank** primarily funds projects that build or expand nations' infrastructure. These projects include transportation, education, and medical systems and facilities. The World Bank and other development banks provide the largest source of

---

General Agreement on Tariffs and Trade (GATT) an international trade accord that has greatly reduced worldwide tariffs and other trade barriers.

World Trade Organization (WTO) a 157-member international institution that monitors GATT agreements and mediates international trade disputes.

World Bank an organization established by industrialized nations to lend money to less-developed countries.

advice and assistance to developing nations. In exchange for granting loans, the World Bank often sets requirements that are meant to help build the economies of borrower nations.

Some say the World Bank makes loans with conditions that ultimately hurt the borrower nations. When developing nations need to balance government budgets, they are sometimes forced to cut vital social programs. Critics also say that the World Bank should consider the impact of its loans on the environment and working conditions.

International Monetary Fund

The **International Monetary Fund (IMF)** was established a year after the World Bank. It was created to promote trade through financial cooperation and, in the process, eliminate barriers. The IMF makes short-term loans to member nations that cannot meet their expenses. It operates as a lender of last resort for troubled nations. In exchange for these emergency loans, IMF lenders frequently require the borrowing nations to address the problems that led to the crises. These steps may include limiting imports or devaluing currencies. Since it began, the IMF has worked to prevent financial crises by warning the international business community when countries face difficulty meeting their financial obligations. Often, the IMF lends to countries to keep them from defaulting on prior debts. These loans also help to prevent an economic crisis in one country from spreading to other countries.

Some countries owe more money than they can ever hope to repay. The debt payments make it impossible for their governments to deliver desperately needed services to their citizens. After a devastating earthquake in Haiti, the G7 countries (the world's most industrialized nations, including the United States, Canada, and France) promised to cancel any remaining debt owed to them by Haiti. The World Bank not only decided to financially support Haiti but also chose to drop the payments on Haiti's debt for five years. It was also looking for a way to cancel the remaining debt.[22]

International Monetary Fund (IMF) an organization created to promote trade, eliminate barriers, and make short-term loans to member nations that are unable to meet their budgets.

International Economic Communities

International economic communities reduce trade barriers and promote working together to create regions that share economic benefits. In the simplest approach, countries may establish a *free-trade area* where they trade freely among themselves without tariffs or trade restrictions. Each country maintains its own tariffs for trade outside this area. A *customs union* sets up a free-trade area and specifies a tariff structure for members' trade with nonmember nations. In a *common market*, or economic union, members go beyond a customs union and try to bring all of their trade rules into agreement.

One example of a free-trade area is the **North American Free Trade Agreement (NAFTA)** agreed to by the United States, Canada, and Mexico. In 2015, Canada, the United States, and Mexico signed on to the Trans-Pacific Partnership (TPP), a growing list of Pacific Rim countries (Japan, Malaysia, Vietnam, Australia, New Zealand, Peru, Singapore, Brunei, and Chile) working towards reducing trade restrictions. The TPP is seen by many observers as a means to counter the tremendous trading power of China in the region. Other examples of regional trading blocs include the Mercosur customs union (joining Brazil, Argentina, Paraguay, and Uruguay) and the 10-country Association of Southeast Asian Nations (ASEAN).

North American Free Trade Agreement (NAFTA) an agreement among the United States, Canada, and Mexico to break down tariffs and trade restrictions.

NAFTA

NAFTA became effective in 1994. It created the world's largest free-trade zone with the United States, Canada, and Mexico. North America has a combined population of more than 471 million and a total GDP of more than $20 trillion. North America is one of the world's most attractive markets. The United States is the single-largest market, and it controls much of North America's business. Although fewer than 1 person in 20 lives in the United States, the nation's more than $16 trillion GDP represents about one-fifth of total world output.[23]

Canada is far less densely populated but has reached a similar level of economic standing. Canada's economy has been growing at a faster rate than the U.S. economy

NAFTA permits free trade for the United States, Canada, and Mexico. The amount of goods and services traded is healthy for the economy, both in Canada and in the United States.

HIT & MISS

Ford Motor Company: Engineered and Made in Mexico

Three of Ford Motor Company's 77 worldwide factories are located in Mexico, a country once viewed by carmakers as an assembly-only manufacturing destination. Ford's Mexico unit has tripled its engineering staff and produced 40 patents in less than three years, which may be one reason why the number of engineering students enrolled in Mexican universities has doubled.

Mexico's appeal to U.S. and foreign carmakers alike has to do with its proximity to the largest auto market in the world, lower wages, and the growing demand for cars in other parts of Latin and South America. In addition, labour costs for engineers in Mexico are 40 percent of what they are for their U.S. counterparts.

As Mexico continues to transform into a world-class manufacturing destination, foreign carmakers have also taken notice and poured over $12 billion of investments into the country over the last few years. With less than a decade of experience, as Ford's engineers gain momentum, look for quality Ford cars not only to be made but also designed by engineers in Mexico.

Questions for Critical Thinking

1. Considering Mexico's history of drug violence, what challenges do you see for the auto industry in Mexico?

2. How can foreign auto companies ensure there are skilled job candidates available to work in Mexican manufacturing facilities?

Sources: Ford Motor Company, "List of Operations Worldwide," accessed January 6, 2014, http://corporate.ford.com; Brendan Case, "Mexico's Surprising Engineering Strength," *Bloomberg Businessweek*, November 27, 2013, accessed January 6, 2014, www.bloomberg.com/bw/articles/2013-11-27/mexicos-surprising-engineering-strength; "Mexico's Car Industry: Steaming Hot," *The Economist*, November 15, 2013, accessed January 6, 2014, www.economist.com/blogs/schumpeter/2013/11/mexico-s-car-industry; Andrés Martinez, "Mexico: The Stranger Next Door," *Bloomberg Businessweek*, May 1, 2013, accessed January 6, 2014, www.bloomberg.com/bw/articles/2013-05-01/mexico-the-stranger-next-door.

---

in recent years. More than two-thirds of Canada's GDP is generated in the services sector. That makes sense because three of every four Canadian workers work in service occupations. Canada's per capita GDP places it among the top nations in terms of its spending power. Canada's economy is fuelled by trade with the United States, and its home markets are strong. The United States and Canada are each other's biggest trading partners. About 75 percent of Canada's exports and about 50 percent of its imports involve the United States.[24] U.S. business is also attracted to Canada's human resources. For example, all major U.S. automakers have large production facilities in Canada.

Mexico is moving from being a developing nation to gaining industrial nation status because of NAFTA (see the "Hit & Miss" feature). Mexico's trade with the United States and Canada has tripled since the signing of NAFTA. But 15 percent of the country's 119 million people live below the poverty line, and Mexico's per capita income is about a third of the per capita income in the United States. Mexico's border with the United States is busy with a stream of traffic moving goods from Mexican factories into the United States. The United States is Mexico's largest trading partner, receiving about 78 percent of Mexico's total exports and supplying almost 50 percent of Mexico's imports.[25]

The United States, Canada, and Mexico removed all trade barriers and investment restrictions over a 15-year period. NAFTA opened more doors for free trade. The agreement also eased rules about services, such as banking, and set up standard legal requirements for protecting intellectual property. The three nations can now trade with one another without tariffs or other trade barriers. It is also easier to ship goods across the partners' borders, since standardized customs and labelling regulations create economic efficiencies. They also help to make importing and exporting easier. Trade among the partners has increased and is now more than double what it was before NAFTA took effect.

CAFTA-DR

Central America–Dominican Republic Free Trade Agreement (CAFTA-DR) an agreement among the united states, costa rica, the dominican republic, el salvador, guatemala, honduras, and nicaragua to reduce tariffs and trade restrictions.

The **Central America–Dominican Republic Free Trade Agreement (CAFTA-DR)** created a free-trade area among the United States, Costa Rica, the Dominican Republic (the DR of the title), El Salvador, Guatemala, Honduras, and Nicaragua. The agreement ends most tariffs on nearly $56 billion in products traded between the United States and its Latin American neighbours.[26] Agricultural producers such as corn, soybean, and dairy farmers stand to gain under the relaxed trade rules. U.S. sugar producers fought against CAFTA-DR's passage. They had been supported

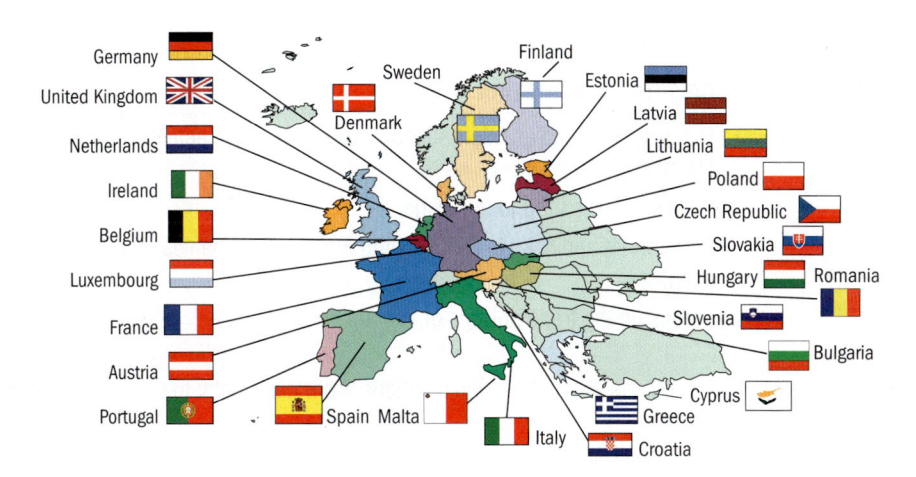

Figure 4.4 The 28 Nations of the European Union

by subsidies that kept their prices higher than in the rest of the world. Labour unions complained that the agreement would lower labour standards and export millions more jobs to lower-wage countries. Overall, CAFTA-DR's effects should be positive and have increased both exports and imports, much as NAFTA did.

European Union

The best-known example of a common market is the **European Union (EU)**. The EU combines 28 countries, nearly 506 million people, and a total GDP of roughly $16 trillion to form a huge common market representing 20 percent of the world's GDP.[27] **Figure 4.4** illustrates the 28 member states. Thirteen countries are the latest EU members—Croatia, Cyprus, Malta, Estonia, Latvia, Lithuania, Hungary, Poland, the Czech Republic, Slovakia, Slovenia, Bulgaria, and Romania. The Treaty of Lisbon took effect in 2009. Its goal is to make the union governance more efficient.

The EU's goals are to promote economic and social progress, to introduce European citizenship as a complement to national citizenship, and to give the EU a major role in international affairs. To achieve its goal of a borderless Europe, the EU is first removing barriers to free trade among its members. This highly complex process involves standardizing business regulations and requirements, standardizing import duties and taxes, and getting rid of customs checks so that companies can transport goods from England to Italy or Poland as easily as goods can be moved from St. John's to Vancouver.

Bringing standards and laws together can contribute to economic growth. But NAFTA had scared people in Canada and the United States who weren't sure about free trade with Mexico. Some people in Western Europe feel the same. They are worried that opening trade with such countries as Poland, Hungary, and the Czech Republic will cause jobs to flow to those lower-wage economies.

The EU also introduced the euro to replace currencies such as the French franc and Italian lira. For the 18 member nations that have adopted the euro, potential benefits include eliminating the economic costs of currency exchange and simplifying price comparisons. Businesses and their customers now make cheque and credit card transactions in euros and use euro notes and coins in making cash purchases.

European Union (EU) a 28-nation european economic alliance.

ASSESSMENT CHECK

4.4.1 What international trade organization succeeded GATT, and what is its goal?

4.4.2 Compare and contrast the goals of the World Bank and the International Monetary Fund.

4.4.3 What are the goals of the European Union, and how do these goals promote international trade?

GOING GLOBAL

Expanding into overseas markets can increase profits and marketing opportunities. It can also make a firm's business operations more complex. Before deciding to go global, a company must make many key decisions, such as the following:

- Which foreign market(s) to enter
- The costs of entering a new market
- The best way to organize the overseas operations

LO 4.5 Compare the different levels of involvement used by businesses when entering global markets.

Table 4.3 International Trade Research Resources on the Internet

WEBSITE AND ADDRESS	GENERAL DESCRIPTION
Foreign Affairs, Trade and Development Canada www.international.gc.ca	Gateway to Canadian international trade and foreign activities involving businesses.
Bloomberg—www.bloomberg.com	Business news around the world.
Europages www.europages.com	Directory of and links to Europe's top 500,000 companies in 33 European countries.
World Trade Organization www.wto.org	Details on the trade policies of various governments.
CIA World Factbook www.cia.gov/library/publications/resources/the-world-factbook/index.html	Basic facts about the world's nations, from geography to economic conditions.
STAT-USA www.usa.gov/Topics/Reference-Shelf/Data.shtml	Extensive trade and economic data, information about trends, daily intelligence reports, and background data (access requires paid subscription to the service).
The Canadian Trade Commissioner Service www.tradecommissioner.gc.ca/eng/home.jsp	Valuable information that will help companies prepare an export plan and develop a market entry strategy. Canada's trade commissioners, located in more than 160 cities worldwide, can help implement strategies and provide advice on how to take advantage of international business opportunities.
Canadian Trade Data Online www.ic.gc.ca/eic/site/tdo-dcd.nsf/eng/Home	Customized reports can be generated on Canada and U.S. trade in goods with over 200 countries.
Canada's Gateways www.canadasgateways.gc.ca/index2.html	Information on Canada's *National Policy Framework for Strategic Gateways and Trade Corridors*, which supports strategies to strengthen Canada's position in international commerce. Here you will find links to Canada's three main gateway and corridor initiatives and information on foreign trade zones.

These issues have more or less importance depending on the level of involvement a company chooses. Education and employee training in the host country are much more important for an electronics manufacturer building an Asian factory than for a firm that plans to export Canadian-made products.

Before deciding which markets to enter, companies usually take time to do research. This research focuses on local demand for the firm's products, availability of needed resources, and ability of the local workforce to make world-class, quality products. Other factors are existing and potential competition, tariff rates, currency stability, and investment barriers. Government and other sources can help with this research. A good starting place is the CIA's *World Factbook*. It contains country-by-country information on geography, population, government, economy, and infrastructure.

Foreign Affairs, Trade and Development Canada and the U.S. Department of Commerce have counsellors who work at district offices. These counsellors offer a full range of international business advice, including computerized market data and names of business and government contacts in dozens of countries. As **Table 4.3** shows, the Internet provides access to many resources for international trade information.

Levels of Involvement

After a firm has completed its research and has decided to do business overseas, it can choose one or more strategies:

- Exporting or importing
- Entering into contract-based agreements such as franchising, licensing, and subcontracting deals
- Choosing direct investment in the foreign market through acquisitions, joint ventures, or by setting up an overseas division

The company's risk increases with the level of its global involvement. But its overall control of all aspects of producing and selling its goods or services also increases.

Importers and Exporters

An *importer* is a firm that brings in goods produced abroad to sell at home. *Exporters* are companies that produce or purchase goods at home and sell them in other countries. An importing or exporting strategy provides the most basic level of international involvement and the least risk and control.

Exports are often handled by export trading companies. These firms search out competitively priced local merchandise, and then resell these items abroad at prices high enough to cover expenses and earn profits. Suppose a retail chain such as Pier 1 Imports wants to purchase West African products to sell in its stores. It may contact an export trading company that deals in a country such as Ghana. The local firm monitors the quality of goods, packs the order for overseas shipment, arranges transportation, and completes customs paperwork and other steps to move the product from Ghana to Canada.

Exporting can be one of two types: indirect or direct. A company uses *indirect exporting* when it makes a product, such as an electronic component, that becomes part of another product sold in foreign markets. The second method is *direct exporting*. This type of exporting occurs when a company tries to sell its products in markets outside its own country. Direct exporting is often the first step for companies entering foreign markets. It is also the most common form of international business. Firms that succeed at direct exporting may then move on to other strategies.

Export trading companies are one way to reach foreign markets. Two other methods are to use export management companies or offset agreements. An export management company can give an exporting firm advice and expertise. These international specialists help the exporter complete paperwork, make contacts with local buyers, and comply with local laws for labelling, product safety, and performance testing. The exporting firm retains more control than it would if it used an export trading company.

An *offset agreement* matches a major international firm with a smaller business. The smaller firm basically becomes a subcontractor to the larger firm. For example, Bombardier might contract with a small American supplier of electrical cables used to manufacture aircraft made in Canada and exported to the United States. Both firms benefit from the agreement, and the smaller firm can often gain international experience.

Countertrade

International trade often involves payments made in the form of local products, not currency. This system of international bartering agreements is called **countertrade**.

A common reason for using international barter is poor access to the needed foreign currency. To complete an international sales agreement, the seller may agree to accept part or all of the purchase cost in merchandise instead of in currency. The seller may try to find a buyer for the bartered goods before the transaction is completed. To make this task easier, several international buyers and sellers sometimes join together in a single agreement.

Countertrade is sometimes a firm's only way to enter a certain market. Many developing countries simply cannot get enough credit or financial help to afford the imports that their people want. Countries that have heavy debt also use countertrade. Russian buyers sometimes find their currency is less acceptable to foreign traders than the stronger currencies of the United States, Great Britain, Japan, and EU countries. Thus, Russian buyers may trade local products, ranging from crude oil to diamonds to vodka. These products become the payments when the foreign companies selling goods do not want to receive Russian rubles. Other countries, such as China, may restrict imports. For those countries, countertrade may be the only practical way to get government approval to import needed products.

countertrade a barter agreement whereby trade between two or more nations involves payment made in the form of local products instead of currency.

Contract-Based Agreements

After a company gains some experience in international sales, it may decide to enter into contract-based agreements with local parties. These agreements can include franchising, foreign licensing, and subcontracting.

Franchising Franchising is common among Canadian and U.S. companies. Franchising can also work well for companies that want to expand into international markets. A **franchise** is a contract-based agreement in which a wholesaler or retailer (the franchisee) can sell the

franchise a contract-based agreement in which a franchisee can produce or sell the franchisor's products under that company's brand name if the franchisee agrees to the operating terms and requirements.

franchisor's products under that company's brand name if the franchisee agrees to the operating terms and requirements. The franchisor also helps the franchisee with marketing, management, and business services. Franchises are common in the leading fast-food brands, such as Tim Hortons and McDonald's. In 1995, Tim Hortons merged with Wendy's International, Inc., which helped Tim Hortons gain entry into the United States. Tim Hortons can be found in Michigan, Maine, Connecticut, Ohio, West Virginia, Kentucky, Pennsylvania, Rhode Island, Massachusetts, and New York. Tim Hortons's Canadian operation is 95 percent franchise owned and operated. In 2014, Tim Hortons agreed to be acquired by 3G Capital, the investment firm that owns Burger King. At the time of the merger Tim Hortons had more than 3,000 restaurants across Canada and more than 600 locations in the United States. Burger King had over 13,667 restaurants in over 100 countries. The combined company is the third-largest fast-food restaurant in the world, generating over $22 billion in sales.[28] Franchising is described in detail in Chapter 5.

foreign licensing agreement an international agreement in which one firm allows another firm to produce or sell its product or use its trademark, patent, or manufacturing processes in a specific geographical area in return for royalties or other compensation.

Foreign Licensing In a **foreign licensing agreement**, one firm allows another firm to produce or sell its product or use its trademark, patent, or manufacturing processes in a specific geographical area. In return, the firm receives a royalty or other compensation.

Licensing can be good for a small manufacturer that wants to launch a well-known product overseas. The small manufacturer gets a proven product from another market, and just a little or no investment is needed to start operating. Licensing can also allow a company entry into a market that would otherwise be closed to imports because of government restrictions. Sometimes a licensing agreement can ensure product freshness by allowing manufacturing to take place in the local market. For example, Morinaga, a Japanese food manufacturer, holds licences to produce Lipton teas, Kraft cheeses, and Sunkist fruit drinks and desserts in Japan.[29]

subcontracting an agreement that involves hiring other companies to produce, distribute, or sell goods or services; in international subcontracting, local companies in a specific country or geographical region are hired to produce, distribute, or sell goods or services.

Subcontracting The third type of contract-based agreement is **subcontracting**. This agreement involves hiring local companies to produce, distribute, or sell goods or services. Subcontracting allows a foreign firm to use the subcontractor's expertise in local culture, contacts, and regulations. Subcontracting works equally well for mail-order companies. They can hire local businesses to fill the orders and serve customers. Manufacturers use subcontracting to save money on import duties and labour costs. Businesses choose to subcontract to market products that are best sold by locals in a given country.

The key downside of subcontracting is that companies cannot always control their subcontractors' business practices. Several major companies have been embarrassed by reports that their subcontractors used child labour to manufacture clothing.

Offshoring

Offshoring is not generally considered to be a way of starting business internationally. *Offshoring* is the moving of business processes to a lower-cost location overseas. It has become a widespread practice. China is the preferred location for production offshoring, and India is the preferred location for services offshoring. Many business leaders support offshoring. They believe that global firms must keep their costs as low as possible to stay competitive. The apparent link between jobs sent overseas and jobs lost at home has led to much debate about offshoring.

Offshoring shows no signs of slowing down, but it is changing, mostly for manufacturers. Mexico, India, and Vietnam are now the countries with the lowest manufacturing costs. According to one consultant, during 2005–2006 there was a surge in companies moving manufacturing to China. At the time, China offered competitive advantages, such as more infrastructure, over other low-cost countries. However, by 2007–2008, with the increasing costs of transportation and materials, that began to change. If companies are setting up factories abroad to sell to foreign markets, offshoring may make some sense. But it doesn't make sense to make heavy or bulky products abroad and then ship them to North American markets. The time needed to move the goods is also a factor. Offshoring to a few low-cost locations may be an international firm's lowest-risk strategy. For example, if India's currency, the rupee, strengthens, North American manufacturers can move some production away from India and if transportation costs start to climb, they can shift more production closer to home, in Mexico.[30]

International Direct Investment

The highest level of control is investing directly in another country's production and marketing. Over time, a firm may become successful at doing business in other countries through exporting

HIT & MISS

Apple Brings Manufacturing Work Back Home

As recently as a decade ago, you could purchase an Apple product made in the USA. Apple, along with numerous other companies, took pride in their "Made in USA" status. But in recent years, Apple and other companies chose a lower-cost labour structure in overseas countries. But that strategy seems to be slowly changing, with a small but gradual boomerang back to the United States—mainly from China. It's called reshoring, and Apple is part of the trend to bring manufacturing back to the United States.

Recently, the company created 2,000 engineering, manufacturing, and construction jobs in a facility in Arizona, where components for its products will be produced. In addition, Apple is producing its redesigned Mac Pro computer in Austin, Texas. The benefits of this move back home include quicker response to production problems and increased quality control.

Significant wage increases in China over the past decade and concerns over protecting intellectual property overseas are two reasons that helped prompt the move. In addition, geographically close-knit design and production teams leave less room for error in the manufacturing process.

For Apple, bringing jobs home is certainly a positive way to help the U.S. economy. With reshoring—and reuniting design and production in one country—Apple will need to change the slogan on some of its products back to "Made in USA."

Questions for Critical Thinking

1. Are there certain types of products, companies, or industries in which reshoring makes the most sense?
2. Is your decision to purchase a product ever influenced by where it was produced? If so, explain.

Sources: Clare Goldsberry, "As 'Made in USA' Gains in Popularity, Companies Reshore Manufacturing," *Plastics Today*, January 3, 2014, accessed January 6, 2014, www.plasticstoday.com/articles/%E2%80%9Cmade-usa%E2%80%9D-gains-popularity-companies-reshore-manufacturing; Juliette Garside, "Apple Creates 2,000 Jobs Shifting Production Back to US," *The Guardian*, November 5, 2013, accessed January 6, 2014, www.theguardian.com/technology/2013/nov/05/apple-creates-us-jobs-renewable-energy; Joel Johnson, "'Made in America,' or How Re-Shoring Can Transform the Global Procurement Landscape," *Spend Matters*, October 22, 2013, accessed January 6, 2014, http://spendmatters.com/2013/10/22/made-america-reshoring-can-transform-global-procurement-landscape.

---

and contract-based agreements. Its managers may then decide to start manufacturing in those countries, open branch offices, or buy ownership in local companies. Apple is involved in the trend of reshoring, or bringing jobs back to the United States, mainly from China. See the "Hit & Miss" feature for more.

In an *acquisition*, a company purchases another firm in the host country. An acquisition means that a mostly domestic business operation can quickly become an international company. For example, the big U.S. retailer Target paid $1.8 billion to Hudson's Bay Company to acquire Canadian retailer Zellers. Target gained a quick entry to 133 prime locations in the Canadian market. However, the planned expansion into Canada failed, and Target closed its Canadian operations in 2015, losing an estimated $6 billion.[31]

In a **joint venture**, a company shares risks, costs, profits, and management responsibilities with one or more host-country companies. By setting up an *overseas division*, a company can do much of its business overseas. This strategy differs from a multinational company's strategy. A firm with overseas divisions stays primarily a domestic organization with international operations. Matsushita established Panasonic Automotive Systems Asia Pacific to develop and sell new technology products in India, Thailand, Indonesia, Malaysia, the Philippines, and Vietnam.

From Multinational Corporation to Global Business

A **multinational corporation (MNC)** is an organization with many foreign operations. Many U.S. multinationals, including Nike and Walmart, have expanded their overseas operations. They believe that domestic markets are peaking, and foreign markets offer greater potential for sales and profit. Other MNCs are making large investments in developing countries, partly because these countries provide low-cost labour compared with the wages in North America and Western Europe. In addition, many MNCs are locating high-tech facilities in countries that have large numbers of technical school graduates.

---

joint venture a partnership between companies for a specific activity.

multinational corporation (MNC) a firm with many operations and marketing activities outside its home country.

✓ ASSESSMENT CHECK

4.5.1 Name three possible strategies for beginning overseas operations.

4.5.2 What is countertrade?

4.5.3 Compare and contrast licensing and subcontracting.

4.5.4 Describe joint ventures.

LO 4.6 Distinguish between a global business strategy and a multidomestic business strategy.

DEVELOPING A STRATEGY FOR INTERNATIONAL BUSINESS

Managers need to develop a framework from which to conduct international business. But managers must first evaluate their corporate objectives, organizational strengths and weaknesses, and strategies for product development and marketing. They can choose to combine these elements in either a global strategy or a multidomestic strategy.

Global Business Strategies

global business strategy the offering of a standardized worldwide product and the selling of it in basically the same way throughout a firm's domestic and foreign markets.

In a **global business strategy** (or a *standardization strategy*), a firm sells the same product in basically the same way all over the world. Many companies simply change their domestic business strategies by translating promotional brochures and instructions into the languages of the host nations.

A global marketing perspective can be suitable for some goods and services and for market segments that are common to many nations. The approach works for products with nearly universal appeal, for luxury items such as jewellery, and for commodities such as chemicals and metals. Alcoa, for example, is the world's largest producer of aluminum for use in aerospace and automotive building and construction, consumer electronics, packaging, and commercial transportation. In many applications, aluminum's strength and light weight mean there are no good substitutes for it. The company forecasts a long-term increase in global demand, especially in China, India, Russia, the Middle East, and Latin America. It also sees itself as committed to a global strategy that blends sustainability with profitability. That means it will "build financial success, environmental excellence, and social responsibility through partnerships in order to deliver net long-term benefits to our shareowners, employees, customers, suppliers, and the communities in which we operate."[32]

Multidomestic Business Strategies

multidomestic business strategy a plan to develop and market products to serve different needs and tastes in separate national markets.

In a **multidomestic business strategy** (or an *adaptation strategy*), the firm treats each national market in a different way. It develops products and marketing strategies that appeal to the customs, tastes, and buying habits of specific national markets. Some companies do not change their strategy

Internet users in Western Europe were slow initially to order products online, but now make online purchases for such items as railroad tickets.

for different markets. These companies don't pay attention to the global nature of the Internet, which can cause problems for potential customers. For example, European consumers were slow to order products online. But Internet use in Western Europe has had huge growth. All types of companies have seen increases in the number of website visitors and in their Internet revenues.

✓ **ASSESSMENT CHECK**

4.6.1 What is a global business strategy? What are its advantages?

4.6.2 What is a multidomestic business strategy? What are its advantages?

WHAT'S AHEAD

The examples in this chapter show that both large and small businesses rely on world trade, not just major corporations. Chapter 5 looks at the special advantages and challenges facing small-business owners. A critical decision facing any new business is choosing the most suitable form of business ownership. Chapter 5 also looks at the major ownership structures—sole proprietorship, partnership, and corporation—and measures the pros and cons of each. The chapter closes by discussing recent trends affecting business ownership, such as the growing impact of franchising and business consolidations through mergers and acquisitions.

RETURN TO INSIDE BUSINESS

PotashCorp: Genesis for Economic Development

PotashCorp is a good example of a resource business that has a comparative advantage. Canadian mines are very profitable operating at today's commodity prices. The firm can expand globally by using its expertise at other mines around the world. As mentioned earlier, potash is a commodity, which means the product is the same whether it comes from this mine or that mine. That means PotashCorp can sell potash throughout its distribution network. International mining firms sometimes merge or acquire other firms to grow the business and increase profits. PotashCorp was the object of a takeover bid by Australian mining giant BHP Billiton, which also operates in Saskatchewan. The Saskatchewan government refused the sale with the argument that it was not in the best interests of the company and people of Saskatchewan.

QUESTIONS FOR CRITICAL THINKING

1. What are the upsides and downsides to a company that sells a commodity in competitive international markets?
2. Is PotashCorp an MNC or a global business?

SUMMARY OF LEARNING OBJECTIVES

LO 4.1 Explain the primary reasons why nations trade.

The world's economies are becoming increasingly global. That means Canadian and other foreign businesses have opportunities to expand into new markets for their goods and services. Doing business globally provides new sources of materials and labour. Trading with other countries reduces a company's dependence on economic conditions in its home market. Countries that encourage international trade usually have higher levels of economic activity, employment, and wages than countries that restrict international trade.

Nations usually benefit if they specialize in producing certain goods or services. A country has an absolute advantage if it holds a monopoly or if it produces a good or service at a lower cost than other nations. It has a comparative advantage if it can supply one product more efficiently or at a lower cost than it can produce other products.

✓ **ASSESSMENT CHECK ANSWERS**

4.1.1 **Why do nations trade?** Nations trade because trading increases economic growth. Trade provides a new market for products and access to needed resources. Trading makes production and distribution systems more efficient and reduces dependence on the economy of the domestic market.

4.1.2 **What are some measures of the size of the international marketplace?** Developing countries have lower per capita incomes than the developed nations in North America and Western Europe, but developing nations have populations that are large and growing. China's population is about 1.3 billion and India's is roughly 1.2 billion.

4.1.3 **How does a nation acquire a comparative advantage?** A nation has a comparative advantage when it can supply a product more efficiently and at a lower price than it can supply other goods, compared with the outputs of other countries.

LO 4.2 Describe how trade is measured between nations.

Countries measure their level of international trade by comparing exports and imports. They then calculate whether they have a trade surplus or a trade deficit. The balance of trade is the difference between a country's exports and its imports. The term *balance of payments* refers to the overall flow of money into or out of a country. It includes overseas loans and borrowing, international investments, and profits from such investments. An exchange rate is the value of one country's currency in terms of the currency of another country. Currency values fluctuate, or "float," depending on the supply and demand for each currency in the world market. When the value of the Canadian dollar falls compared with other currencies, the cost paid by foreign businesses and households for Canadian products declines, and demand for exports may rise. An increase in the value of the dollar raises the prices of Canadian products sold abroad, but it reduces the prices of foreign products sold in Canada.

✓ ASSESSMENT CHECK ANSWERS

4.2.1 Compare balance of trade and balance of payments. Balance of trade is the difference between exports and imports; balance of payments is the overall flow of money into or out of a country.

4.2.2 Explain the function of an exchange rate. A nation's exchange rate is the rate at which its currency can be exchanged for the currencies of other nations. An exchange rate makes it easier for countries with different currencies to trade with each another.

4.2.3 What happens when a currency is devalued? Devaluation is a reduction in a currency's value in terms of other currencies or in terms of a fixed standard.

LO 4.3 Identify the major barriers to international trade.

Businesses face several barriers in the global marketplace. Companies that operate in other countries need to be sensitive to social and cultural differences, such as languages, values, and religions. Economic differences include standard-of-living variations and levels of infrastructure development. Legal and political barriers are difficult to judge. Each country sets its own laws for business practices. Trade restrictions such as tariffs and administrative barriers are also barriers to international business.

✓ ASSESSMENT CHECK ANSWERS

4.3.1 How can values and attitudes form a barrier to trade, and how can these barriers be overcome? Marked differences in values and attitudes, such as religious attitudes, can form barriers between traditionally capitalist countries and countries adopting new capitalist systems. Many of these barriers can be overcome by learning about the values and attitudes in other cultures and by respecting such differences.

4.3.2 What is a tariff? What is its purpose? A tariff is a surcharge or duty charged on foreign products. Its purpose is to protect domestic producers of those items.

4.3.3 Why is dumping a problem for companies marketing goods internationally? Dumping is selling products in other countries at prices below production costs or below typical prices in the home market. Dumping decreases the cost of products in the market where they are dumped. Thus, dumping hurts the domestic producers of those products.

LO 4.4 Explain how international trade organizations and economic communities reduce barriers to international trade.

Many international organizations try to promote international trade by reducing trade barriers among nations. Some of these organizations are the World Trade Organization, the World Bank, and the International Monetary Fund. Multinational economic communities create partnerships to remove barriers to the flow of goods, capital, and people across the borders of its member countries. Three economic agreements are the North American Free Trade Agreement, CAFTA-DR, and the European Union.

✓ ASSESSMENT CHECK ANSWERS

4.4.1 What international trade organization succeeded GATT, and what is its goal? The World Trade Organization (WTO) succeeded GATT. Its goals are to monitor GATT agreements, mediate disputes, and continue GATT's aim to reduce trade barriers throughout the world.

4.4.2 Compare and contrast the goals of the World Bank and the International Monetary Fund. The World Bank funds projects that build or expand nations' infrastructure. These projects include transportation, education, and medical systems and facilities. The International Monetary Fund makes short-term loans to member nations that cannot meet their expenses. The fund operates as a lender of last resort for troubled nations.

4.4.3 What are the goals of the European Union, and how do these goals promote international trade? The European Union's goals are to promote economic and social progress, to introduce European citizenship as a complement to national citizenship, and to give the EU a major role in international affairs. Bringing standards and laws together can contribute to international trade and economic growth.

LO 4.5 Compare the different levels of involvement used by businesses when entering global markets.

The first level of involvement in international business is exporting and importing. This strategy involves the lowest degree of both risk and control. Companies may use export trading companies or management companies to help distribute their products. Other options are contract-based agreements, such as franchising, foreign licensing, and subcontracting. Franchising and licensing are especially suitable for services. Companies may also use local subcontractors to produce goods for local sales. The highest level of control is investing directly in another country's production and marketing, known as international direct investment. This strategy also has the greatest risk. Firms make direct investments by acquiring foreign companies or facilities, forming joint ventures with local firms, or setting up their own overseas divisions.

✓ ASSESSMENT CHECK ANSWERS

4.5.1 Name three possible strategies for beginning overseas operations. Three strategies are exporting or importing; using contract-based agreements such as franchising, licensing, or subcontracting; and making direct investments in foreign markets through acquisition, joint venture, or setting up an overseas division.

4.5.2 What is countertrade? Countertrade is an agreement to make payments in the form of local products, not in currency.

4.5.3 Compare and contrast licensing and subcontracting. In a foreign licensing agreement, one firm allows another firm to produce or sell its product or use its trademark, patent, or manufacturing process in a specific geographical area. In return, the firm receives royalty payments or other compensation. In international subcontracting, a firm hires local companies in other countries to produce, distribute, or sell its goods and services.

4.5.4 Describe joint ventures. In a joint venture, a company shares risks, costs, profits, and management responsibilities with one or more host-country companies.

LO 4.6 Distinguish between a global business strategy and a multidomestic business strategy.

A company that adopts a global strategy (or a standardization strategy) develops a single, standardized product and marketing strategy for worldwide sales. The firm sells the same product in basically the same way in all countries where it operates. Under a multidomestic strategy (or an adaptation strategy), the firm treats each foreign market in a different way. It develops products and marketing strategies that appeal to the customs, tastes, and buying habits of specific nations.

✓ ASSESSMENT CHECK ANSWERS

4.6.1 What is a global business strategy? What are its advantages? A global business strategy is a standardized competitive strategy. The firm sells the same product in basically the same way all over the world. This strategy works well for goods and services that are common to many nations. The firm can market the products to many countries without making many changes.

4.6.2 What is a multidomestic business strategy? What are its advantages? In a multidomestic business strategy, the firm treats each foreign market in a different way. The firm tries to appeal to the customs, tastes, and buying habits of specific national markets. This strategy allows the firm to change its marketing appeals to suit individual cultures or areas.

BUSINESS TERMS YOU NEED TO KNOW

balance of payments 93

balance of trade 93

Central America–Dominican Republic Free Trade Agreement (CAFTA-DR) 106

countertrade 109

devaluation 95

dumping 103

embargo 103

European Union (EU) 107

exchange control 103

exchange rate 95

exports 90

foreign licensing agreement 110

franchise 109

General Agreement on Tariffs and Trade (GATT) 104

global business strategy 112

imports 90

infrastructure 98

International Monetary Fund (IMF) 105

joint venture 111

multidomestic business strategy 112

multinational corporation (MNC) 111

North American Free Trade Agreement (NAFTA) 105

quota 103

subcontracting 110

tariffs 102

World Bank 104

World Trade Organization (WTO) 104

REVIEW QUESTIONS

1. How does a business decide whether to trade with a foreign country? What are the key factors for participating in the information economy on a global basis?
2. Why are developing countries such as China and India becoming important international markets?
3. What is the difference between absolute advantage and comparative advantage? Give an example of each.
4. Can a nation have a favourable balance of trade and an unfavourable balance of payments? Why or why not?
5. Identify several potential barriers to communication when a company attempts to do business in another country. How might these be overcome?
6. Identify and describe briefly the three dimensions of the legal environment for global business.
7. What are the major nontariff restrictions affecting international business? Describe the difference between tariff and nontariff restrictions.
8. What is NAFTA? How does it work?
9. How has the EU helped trade among European businesses?
10. What are the key choices a company must make before reaching the final decision to go global?

PROJECTS AND TEAMWORK APPLICATIONS

1. In 1997, Britain transferred Hong Kong to China. China agreed to grant Hong Kong a high degree of autonomy as a capitalist economy for 50 years. Do you think this agreement is holding up? Why or why not? Consider China's economy, population, infrastructure, and other factors in your answer.
2. The huge growth of online business has introduced new legal concerns for international business. Patents, brand names, copyrights, and trademarks are difficult to monitor because the Internet has no boundaries. What steps can businesses take to protect their trademarks and brands online? Come up with at least five suggestions. Compare your list with your classmates' lists.
3. The WTO monitors GATT agreements, mediates disputes, and continues the effort to reduce trade barriers all over world. But many are concerned that the WTO's focus on lowering trade barriers encourages businesses to keep costs down by using methods that may lead to pollution and human rights abuses. Others argue that human rights should not be linked to international business. Do you think environmental and human rights issues should be linked to trade? Why or why not?
4. Describe briefly the EU and its goals. What are the pros and cons of the EU? Do you think the European alliance will hold up over the next 20 years? Why or why not?
5. Find the most recent edition of "The *Fortune* Global 500." It is usually published in *Fortune* magazine in late July or early August. You can also go to *Fortune's* online version at http://fortune.com/global500. Use the Global 500 to answer the following questions.
   a. On what is the Global 500 ranking based (e.g., profits, number of employees, revenues)?
   b. List the home countries of the world's 10 largest corporations.
   c. For the following industry classifications, identify the top-ranked company, its Global 500 ranking, and country: food and drug stores; industrial and farm equipment; petroleum refining; utilities: gas and electric; telecommunications; pharmaceuticals.

WEB ASSIGNMENTS

1. **WTO.** Visit the website of the World Trade Organization (www.wto.org). Research two current trade disputes. Which countries and products are involved? Do the two disputes have anything in common? What steps does the WTO follow to resolve trade disputes between member countries?
2. **EU.** Europa.eu is the Web portal for the European Union. Go to the http://europa.eu/index_en.htm and answer the following questions:
   a. What steps must a country take to become a member of the EU?
   b. How many EU members have adopted the euro? Which countries will be adopting the euro over the next few years?
   c. What is the combined GDP of EU members? Which EU member has the largest GDP? Which has the smallest GDP?
3. **Nestlé.** Nestlé is one of the world's largest global corporations. Visit the firm's website (www.nestle.com). Where is the company headquartered? What are some of its best-known brands? Are these brands sold in specific countries, or are they sold worldwide? List three or four issues Nestlé faces as a global corporation.

Note: Internet Web addresses change frequently. If you do not find the exact sites listed, you may need to access the organization's or company's home page and search from there or use a search engine such as Bing or Google.

PART 1: CASE STUDY Beau's All Natural Brewing Company
Building a Craft Brewery in a Competitive Canadian Industry

Meet Co-Founders Steve and Tim Beauchesne

Steve Beauchesne was familiar with the "hows and whys" of running a business. He grew up working at his father's leather finishing plant in the small farming community of Vankleek Hill, about an hour drive south of Ottawa. The plant finished leather for use in the fashion industry, which was rapidly moving offshore to places like China and India. Business was in a gradual decline. Although Steve was never particularly enamoured with the business, his time spent at the plant was a worthwhile education on how things get done. In his words, "I learned how to work with people, how people should be treated and I gained the confidence to run things." After studying business at Ryerson University in Toronto, he found himself working for a provincial government agency researching and writing business plans. At the same time he was developing a musical career in a band and promoting his record label. Life was good.

Meanwhile, back in Vankleek Hill, Tim Beauchesne had just said goodbye to his last customer. Like most small-business owners, he had planned to sell his business and cash out what would be his retirement funds when the time came. Tim had invested 20 years in the business but was still at least 10 years away from retirement. If his retirement was going to be what he had envisioned, an alternative course of action would be needed. Like many small-business owners, he had no debts and could have sold the land and building the plant stood on but was open to the idea of starting another business, if Steve was interested.

On a visit to Toronto, father and son talked about the possibilities and what course of action to take. Obviously the choice, if there was to be one, would have to resonate with Steve and be motivating enough for him to want to take over full management responsibilities one day and leave the secure government career path he was presently pursuing. The discussions eventually came around to starting a microbrewery—something Steve and Tim were equally passionate about. Steve was an amateur brewer and considered himself knowledgeable about small-batch production, but both men recognized that larger-scale production and distribution would require careful research and consideration before jumping in with Tim's current pool of retirement funds.

The Canadian Craft Brewing Industry

The craft beer industry is growing in Canada, as it is elsewhere in the world. Long-established beer giants are facing competition from much smaller craft beer producers. Also referred to as microbrewers, craft brewers are known for their unique beer products that provide something "different" for beer drinkers looking for more variety in beer tastes. The basic recipe of barley, hops, and yeast can result in very unusual and creative tastes once spices, herbs, and other flavourings like fruit were introduced to the brew.

The concept is a familiar one found in other industries where customers seek out variety, especially food and beverages. And because of new technology that allows for smaller but economical production operations, craft brewers can start up small and gradually expanded as sales grow. Many craft brewers are also built around a pub or restaurant where beer is normally sold and then look to expand sales through other restaurants, pubs, and venues such as golf courses.

Today, about 10 million Canadians drink over $5 billion worth of beer annually. Total beer consumption in Canada amounts to more than 2 billion litres, averaging 64 litres per capita. It is greatest in Newfoundland (79 litres), followed by Quebec (73 litres) and Alberta (69 litres) with the remaining provinces close to the national average. There are two large-scale brewers: Anheuser-Busch InBev, headquartered in Belgium, is the largest brewing company in the world and has a 41 percent share of the Canadian market. U.S.-based Molson Coors, the world's seventh-largest brewer, is in second place in Canada with a 33 percent share. The remainder is divided among more than 200 breweries, mostly craft brewers defined as producing less than 2 million barrels (117 litres = 1 barrel) annually and whose ownership by a large brewer is no greater than 25 percent. Together, more than 9,000 people work directly in the industry. From large cities to small towns, local entrepreneurs are considering the opportunities and risks that come with starting up a craft brewery.

Steve Reflects on His Decision

In 2004, Tim Beauchesne and his son Steve began exploring the idea of becoming craft brewers. Two years later they opened Beau's All Natural Brewing Company in the refurbished leather finishing plant with a loan and Tim's capital totalling $300,000. Upon reflection, Steve said, "I just couldn't say no to the idea of doing something I had only dreamed about. I loved everything about the idea—the product, running my own business. I knew in my gut that people would love our beer if we offered them something different than 'same old standard beer' the big breweries were pumping out." In their first year of operation Beau's produced and sold 30,000 litres of beer, and eight years later were selling 3.5 million litres—a 100-fold increase.

Questions for Critical Thinking

1. What were the specific factors of production Steve and Tim Beauchesne needed to start the brewery?
2. How has Beau's contributed to the local and national economies?
3. Given the risks and barriers to entry at the time, would you have started Beau's? Explain your reasoning.

1 LAUNCHING YOUR...

GLOBAL BUSINESS AND ECONOMICS CAREER

In Part 1, "Business in a Global Environment," you have learned about the role of contemporary business in today's society. You also learned about the major forces that shape contemporary business. The part includes four chapters that discuss the changing face of business, business ethics and social responsibility, economic challenges facing contemporary business, and competing in world markets. Business has always been an exciting career field. You can choose to start your own company, work at a local business, or take a position with a multinational corporation. Today's business opportunities are very attractive. Businesses are expanding to compete in a global economy—and they need loyal and talented people to help them reach their goals. Professional and business service jobs are found in some of the fastest-growing industries in the North American economy. These jobs are projected to grow by more than 23 percent over a decade.[1] Now is the time to learn about several career options that can lead you to your dream job. Each part in this text includes a profile of some of the many opportunities available in business. Here are a few opportunities related to Chapters 1 through 4.

If you're good at numbers and are interested in how societies and companies work, then you may be suited to a career as an *economist*. Economists study how resources are divided up, research information by collecting and studying data, watch economic trends, and develop forecasts. Economists study the cost of energy, foreign trade and exchange between countries, the effect of taxes, and employment levels—both from a national or global viewpoint and from the viewpoint of individual businesses. Some economists work for corporations to help them run more efficiently. Others work for consulting firms to offer their special knowledge, or for government agencies to oversee economic decision making. Usually economists need advanced degrees to work in top-level positions. Economists usually earn more than $80,000 per year.[2]

Are you interested in global business? Many companies search the world for the best employees, supplies, and markets. You could work in Canada for a foreign-based firm such as Nokia or Toyota. Or you could work in Australia, Asia, Europe, or Latin America for a Canadian-based firm such as Royal Bank of Canada. You could also use computer networks to work with overseas co-workers to develop new products for a firm such as General Electric. Today's technology and telecommunications mean that distance is no longer a barrier to doing business. Global business careers can be found in all the areas you will read about in this text—business ownership, management, marketing, technology, and finance.

Global business leaders are not born, they're made. So how can you start on that career path? Businesses consider three areas when hiring employees for overseas assignments:

- *Competence*—technical knowledge, language skills, leadership ability, experience, and past performance
- *Adaptability*—interest in overseas work, communication skills and other personal skills, empathy for other cultures, and appreciation for varied management styles and work environments
- *Personal characteristics*—education, experience, and social compatibility with the host country[3]

Solid experience in your field or company is the most needed skill. Firms want employees who are skilled in their business and are loyal to the firm. Only the best are hired to represent the firm overseas. People who obtain their master's of business administration (MBA) degree are doing well financially; in a recent year, the average salary for MBA graduates a few years out of school was $126,000.[4] Companies don't usually want to send new graduates overseas immediately. Instead, they invest in training to make sure employees are suited to the new assignment.

The second-highest skill that companies look for is two-fold: knowledge of and interest in other languages and cultures. Businesspeople need to be able to work smoothly in another society, so they are selected for their abilities with other languages and cultures. China is a business hotspot, so some people have become fluent in Mandarin Chinese to increase their career prospects. Some school systems offer Chinese language classes in addition to the standard offerings of French, German, and Spanish.

Finally, employees are assessed on their personal characteristics. After all, firms want to be certain that employees will fit well in their new country. A person's talent is still the most important factor when assigning work, but executives with cross-cultural skills are in high demand.[5]

CAREER ASSESSMENT EXERCISES IN ECONOMICS AND GLOBAL BUSINESS

1. The Canadian economy has had many ups and downs. As a result, economists are often in the news. The head of the Bank of Canada, Stephen Poloz, manages the country's general financial condition. To learn about the role economists play in a federal government agency, research Poloz's background and qualifications. Assess how he is performing at the Bank of Canada. Now make a list of your own skills. Are there areas where your skills match his? What do you need to change?

2. To see the effect of the global economy in your community, visit a major retailer. List the countries that make the products on the shelves. Compare your list with your classmates' lists. See who found the most countries and what goods those countries made. Go online to research the career opportunities at the retailer's website.

3. To learn more about other countries, go online and research a country you are interested in. The following sources may be useful:

   - *The World Factbook*, published by the Central Intelligence Agency, www.cia.gov/library/publications/the-world-factbook. This publication is updated yearly. It contains much information about countries—geography and climate, population statistics, cultural and political information, transportation and communications methods, and economic data.

   - *Bloomberg Businessweek*, www.bloomberg.com/businessweek. This site provides business news from around the world and information on global companies.

   - Online news sites Yahoo! News and Google News, http://news.yahoo.com and http://news.google.com. Both of these online news sites have links to global business news.

   Write a one-page summary of the information you found. List the abilities and skills you would need to function well as a businessperson in that country. Focus on the areas of competence, adaptability, and personal characteristics. Now formulate a plan to gain those skills.

PART 2
STARTING AND GROWING YOUR BUSINESS

Chapter 5 Forms of Business Ownership and Organization

Chapter 6 Starting Your Own Business: The Entrepreneurship Alternative

5 | FORMS OF BUSINESS OWNERSHIP AND ORGANIZATION

LEARNING OBJECTIVES

LO 5.1 Describe the characteristics of a small business.

LO 5.2 Discuss the contributions of small businesses to the economy.

LO 5.3 Discuss why small businesses fail.

LO 5.4 Describe the features of an effective business plan.

LO 5.5 Identify the assistance available to small businesses.

LO 5.6 Explain franchising.

LO 5.7 Outline the forms of private business ownership.

LO 5.8 Describe public and collective business ownership.

LO 5.9 Discuss the organizational structure of corporations.

LO 5.10 Describe mergers, acquisitions, and joint ventures.

INSIDE BUSINESS

Pi Athlete Management Inc.: Advising Athletes about Their Careers and More

Young athletes and their families face many challenges. Take a moment and imagine their complex world of information and decision making. Most successful athletes are very young when they first realize they have talent in a sport. These athletes and their families need to figure out how to encourage further athletic development and plan for higher education. The smart players know the value of education and think about what they can do if a sports career doesn't work out. Coaches and trainers remind them that injuries have ended many sports careers and will continue to do so—just ask Sidney Crosby how injuries have affected his career. At some point, aging brings all athletic careers to an end. Professional athletes often retire in their early thirties—if they can stay healthy and active. Hockey players Gordie Howe and Chris Chelios played into their forties, but their long careers are a rarity.

Some athletes want to work at a career in sports while getting a college or university education. These athletes need to look for scholarship programs, especially programs affiliated with the National Collegiate Athletic Association (NCAA) in the United States. Some amateur athletes succeed and become professional athletes. These athletes will face contract negotiations, relocation costs, and many financial, tax, and legal issues. Amateur athletes cannot be represented directly by agents. Usually their families act as the go-between, dealing with the agents and consulting firms until the athlete becomes a professional.

During their careers, athletes use their public recognition to make extra money through endorsements and speaking engagements. Some athletes develop products such as games, books, and equipment. Sports personalities often earn more money through their activities off the field than on. For example, Tiger Woods has earned more than $100 million through tournament winnings but more than $1 billion when you include his earnings from product endorsements, especially his profitable relationship with Nike.

So where do athletes find a team of consultants to help manage their careers and advise them along the way? Pi Athlete Management Inc. of Montreal offers a full set of services under one roof.

The firm has a team of consultants to advise athletes and their families when making decisions related to education, athletic training, media relations, marketing and endorsements, and financial planning. Pi Athlete Management provides services and develops trusting relationships with athletes and their families—and hopes to share in their professional success. Receiving fees for services helps to pay the bills, but the big money is earned when a sports professional starts earning big salaries, bonuses, and revenues from endorsements. Agents who manage this part of the business activity usually earn money on a commission. The average player's salary is high: in basketball, $5.15 million; in baseball, $3.3 million; in hockey, $2.4 million; and in football, $1.9 million. It is easy to understand why athletes, their families, and their agents are all attracted to the dream of a professional sports career.

For example, 22-year-old Marc Bourgeois, from Granby, Quebec, signed as a free agent with the Arizona Diamondbacks in 2011. He played for the University of Southern Mississippi, and then was drafted by the Minnesota Twins in 2009. His friend and former teammate from Granby, Michael Carbone, suffered a back injury that ended his dream of a sports career. But today, Michael Carbone is an agent (working with Pi Athlete Management), and Marc Bourgeois receives public relations help from the firm's PR expert and co-founder, Daniel Smajovits.

The formal structure of the business requires a contract with the consultants and agents that provide services on behalf of Pi Athletic Management. According to Marty Bindman, one of the founding partners of Pi Athlete Management, "every member of our team, with the exception of the founding partners, can be considered as an independent contractor. They operate under our brand as affiliates and receive our support. In exchange, they are paid a referral fee and we cover their expenses. Daniel Smajovits and I are involved in all meetings with clients and potential clients. Client contracts are entered into with Pi. Michael Carbone is affiliated with us in just such a capacity. He is heading up our baseball initiative. He recently graduated with an MBA in sports management under an NCAA baseball scholarship. His career was cut short by a back injury. Marc Bourgeois came to us through Michael. He was not happy with his previous representation and asked us to take over after signing with the Diamondbacks organization."

As more athletes and their families share their stories with others who need management services, word-of-mouth will help build the enterprise.[1]

CHAPTER 5 OVERVIEW

PART 2 Starting and Growing Your Business

Do you want to work for a big company or a small one? Do you plan to start your own business? If you want to start your own company, you're not alone. Every day, more North Americans are starting a new business than those who are getting married or having a baby. Before you enter the business world—as an employee or an owner—you need to know a few things: the industry the company operates in and the size and framework of the firm. For example, Pi Athlete Management Inc. is a small company that has many associates. These associates and the founders bring to the firm their knowledge and past work experience with professional sports management.

Several factors affect how a business is organized, including how easily it can be set up, its access to financing, its tolerance of financial risk, its strengths and weaknesses, and the strengths and weaknesses of competing firms.

This chapter begins by focusing on small-business ownership, including the advantages and disadvantages of small-business ventures, the contributions of small businesses to the economy, and the reasons small businesses fail. The chapter examines the services provided by the Business Development Bank of Canada (BDC), the role of women and members of minority groups in small business, and alternatives for small businesses, such as franchising.

The chapter then discusses the forms of private business ownership—sole proprietorships, partnerships, and corporations. In addition, we discuss the features of not-for-profit organizations. Public and collective ownership are also examined. The chapter concludes with an explanation of structures and operations typical of larger companies, and a review of the major types of business alliances.

LO 5.1 Describe the characteristics of a small business.

MOST BUSINESSES ARE SMALL BUSINESSES

When we hear the term *business*, many of us think of big corporations, such as Bell Canada Enterprises, Royal Bank of Canada, or Rogers Communications. But most businesses are small businesses. In fact, more than 98 percent of all Canadian businesses, just over 1.1 million, employ fewer than 100 people. Small businesses employ people other than the owner, but Canada also has 2.7 million self-employed individuals. Setting up a self-employed business is not the same as running a business that employs other people. Interestingly, Statistics Canada reports that the numbers of self-employed people have been quite steady for the past decade.[2]

What Is a Small Business?

small business an independent business with fewer than 100 employees and revenues less than $2 million that is not dominant in its market.

How can you tell a small business from a large one? The definition varies depending on the source, but Industry Canada defines a **small business** as an "independent business having fewer than 100 employees, not dominant in its market and revenues not more than $2 million."[3]

Natura Foods Inc. is a Quebec-based manufacturer of tofu, almond, rice, and soy milk beverages. It sells products under the brand name Natur-a. The company is making products that meet North Americans's growing demand for natural and healthy foods and beverages. Today, this industry is valued at more than $4 billion in revenue, 10 times what it was 15 years ago. When the company was acquired in 1988, its revenue was only about $400,000. That made it a small business by Industry Canada's definition. Today, Natura's revenue is more than $30 million annually. The firm is both a small business and a mid-sized business. Its revenue places it above the cut-off revenue for small businesses, but its 20 employees fall within the definition for a small company. Many businesses fall into this sort of hybrid definition: When trying to classify the business, one requirement conflicts with another requirement. Whether a company is small or medium sized does not really matter unless the firm is applying for work, grants, or loans. Then, a means test is used to decide which firms qualify.[4]

Government agencies offer benefits to help small businesses compete with larger firms. Thus, small-business owners will want to know whether their companies meet the standards for being a small business. If a company qualifies, it may be able to receive government loans or take part in government programs that encourage purchasing goods and services from smaller suppliers. Some companies that receive such assistance might one day expand to other areas of the country and eventually become a larger business.

Typical Small-Business Ventures

Small businesses have always competed against each other and against some of the world's largest organizations. John Stanton created a retail concept for runners and walkers like himself in 1981, when sports retailing didn't try to meet the needs of such small markets like they do today. North America has 100 Running Room retail stores that employ more than 1,200 people. The Edmonton-based firm continues to grow, profiting from the popularity of walking and running. John Stanton uses the firm's website to build on personal relationships with loyal followers who support healthier living and giving back to the communities where they live. That formula seems to have been successful for Stanton, and The Running Room has been voted one of Canada's 50 Best Managed companies.[5]

In the past 15 years, many small businesses have closed because larger firms have bought out the small independent businesses and replaced them with larger operations. For example, we have fewer independent bookstores and hardware stores because bigger chains such as Indigo or Home Depot have increased the size and number of their stores. Some businesses are not very likely to be gobbled up by bigger firms, such as businesses that sell personalized services, rely on certain locations, and keep their overhead costs low.

Small firms have created an important space for themselves: They provide busy consumers with customized services that range from pet sitting to personal shopping. These businesses meet the needs of individual customers in a way that big firms often can't. About 25 percent of all business establishments produce goods; the remainder provide services. Small firms make up 98 percent of goods-producing businesses and 98 percent of all service-producing businesses.[6] **Table 5.1** provides a breakdown of the number of small, medium, and large employer businesses by sector. The majority of small businesses are concentrated in four industries—wholesale trade and retail; construction; professional, scientific and technical services; and other services.

Small business also plays a major role in agriculture. Canada has 68 million hectares of farmland. Most of this land is owned by large corporate farms, but most of Canada's 327,000 farms are owned by individual farmers or their families. The family farm is a classic example of a small-business operation. It is independently owned and operated, and it employs a limited number of people, including family members.[7]

Many small businesses are **home-based businesses**—firms that operate out of the business owner's residence. People often choose to operate home-based firms to have more control over both their business and their personal time. People who run home-based businesses can be morning people or night people, but they can usually choose to work when it suits them best. A home-based business is easier to run because of access to the Internet and communications devices such as smartphone technology. People who run home-based businesses don't need to worry about overhead costs such as leasing office or warehouse space. The downside is isolation and less visibility to customers—except, of course, if customers visit online. Those customers don't care where your office is located.

Many small businesses become more competitive because of the Internet. But the Internet doesn't guarantee success—there are so many websites that a small firm needs to find ways to make its online presence effective. Setting up a website is generally less expensive than opening a retail store. A website can also reach a wider range of customers.

North American business history has many stories of great inventors who started their companies in barns, garages, warehouses, and attics. For example, Steve Jobs and Steve Wozniak, who founded Apple Computer, Inc., used a family garage to transform their technical idea into a commercial reality. The impact of today's entrepreneurs, including home-based businesses, is discussed in more depth in Chapter 6.

John Stanton has built The Running Room into one of Canada's 50 Best Managed Companies.

home-based businesses firms operated from the residence of the business owner.

ASSESSMENT CHECK

5.1.1 How does Industry Canada define *small business*?

5.1.2 In what industries do small businesses play a significant role?

Table 5.1 Employer Businesses by Firm Size (Number of Employees) in Industrial Sector, December 2012

INDUSTRIAL SECTOR (RANKED BY NUMBER OF EMPLOYER BUSINESSES)	Total	1–4	5–9	10–19	20–49	50–99	SMALL (1–99)	100–199	200–499	MEDIUM (100–499)	LARGE (500+)
Wholesale Trade and Retail	208,489	81,481	57,859	37,535	20,646	6,749	204,270	3,140	1,012	4,152	67
Construction	128,021	77,811	26,013	13,336	7,588	2,094	126,842	807	286	1,093	86
Professional, Scientific and Technical Services	127,612	96,547	15,134	8,347	5,022	1,475	126,525	688	327	1,015	72
Other Services	115,655	76,052	23,577	10,297	4,273	931	115,130	345	146	491	34
Finance, Insurance, Real Estate and Leasing	97,664	59,854	15,283	9,955	9,708	1,619	96,419	620	406	1,026	219
Health Care and Social Assistance	90,078	51,008	18,125	11,443	5,967	1,988	88,531	1,056	432	1,488	59
Accommodation and Food Services	76,105	20,560	18,143	17,035	14,385	4,661	74,784	1,004	259	1,263	58
Management of Companies and Enterprises and Other Support Services*	64,814	35,192	12,525	7,452	5,155	2,143	62,467	1,255	736	1,991	356
Transportation and Warehousing	52,532	34,821	7,242	4,615	3,617	1,252	51,547	509	364	873	112
Manufacturing	51,613	17,478	10,427	8,556	8,001	3,638	48,100	2,113	1,115	3,228	285
Agriculture	39,328	28,296	6,236	2,896	1,425	328	39,181	115	28	143	4
Information, Culture and Recreation	32,493	16,057	5,894	4,423	3,742	1,284	31,400	670	285	955	138
Forestry, Fishing and Hunting	13,365	9,400	2,001	976	639	217	13,233	85	27	112	20
Mining, Quarrying, and Oil and Gas Extraction	9,771	5,621	1,312	1,165	858	418	9,374	212	127	339	58
Total	1,107,540	610,178	219,771	138,031	91,026	28,797	1,087,803	12,619	5,550	18,169	1,568

*Includes management of companies and enterprises; administrative support, waste management and remediation services.

Source: Industry Canada, "Small Business Research and Statistics: Key Small Business Statistics—August 2013, How Many Businesses Are There in Canada?" Table 3 www.ic.gc.ca/eic/site/061.nsf/eng/02804.html, accessed April 4, 2015. Reprinted with the permission of the Minister of Industry, 2015.

CONTRIBUTIONS OF SMALL BUSINESS TO THE ECONOMY

LO 5.2 Discuss the contributions of small businesses to the economy.

Small businesses are important to the Canadian economy. Together, they generate more than 30 percent of the nation's gross domestic product (GDP).[8] Only 10.4 percent of small and medium-sized businesses export. Nonetheless, they are responsible for $150 billion, or about 41 percent, of Canada's total value of exports.[9]

Creating New Jobs

Small businesses make significant contributions to the Canadian economy and to society as a whole. One major contribution is the number of new jobs that small businesses create each year. The number of new jobs varies from year to year, but in many years more than half of all new jobs are created by companies with fewer than 100 employees. According to Statistics Canada, small businesses created 77.7 percent of all private jobs from 2002 to 2012, which on average works out to a little over 100,000 jobs each year. Over the same 10-year period, medium-sized and large businesses created 12.5 percent and 9.8 percent, respectively, representing approximately 17,000 and 11,800 new jobs each year.[10]

Small businesses also help the economy by hiring people who have difficulty finding jobs at larger firms. Some of these employees are people returning to the workforce after a period of not working, people who receive social assistance, and workers with various challenges.

You might never want to start your own company, but you will probably work for a small business at some point in your career, especially in your first few jobs. Small firms often hire the youngest workers.

Creating New Industries

Small firms give businesspeople the opportunity and outlet for developing new ideas. Sometimes these new ideas become entirely new industries. Many of today's largest and most successful firms, such as Whole Foods, Google, and Amazon, began as small businesses. Facebook co-founders Mark Zuckerberg, Dustin Moskovitz, Chris Hughes, and Eduardo Saverin launched their new business from their college dorm room. In five years, Facebook had more than 300 million users. It had successfully positioned itself as a leader in the new industry of social networking.[11]

New industries are sometimes created when small businesses shift their focus to provide needed services to a larger corporate community. Corporate downsizing creates a demand for activities previously handled by in-house employees. These support businesses may become an industry themselves. For example, the need for wireless communication devices and services to support businesses has led to a huge number of small businesses trying to meet this demand.

New industries can be created when small businesses shift their focus to meet consumer interests and preferences. For example, many North Americans are too busy working to shop for the things they need. New businesses have been created to meet this demand by offering customized services. The Trunk Club is an online shopping service that uses Web

New industries can be created when small businesses shift their focus to meet consumer interests and preferences. One such company is Trunk Club, which combines expert advice from a personal stylist with the convenience of shopping online.

GOING GREEN

GREEN MAMA: SMALL BUSINESS WITH A BIG MESSAGE

The Green Mama isn't a mythical figure. She's a consultant, writer, and environmentalist who believes the world can be made more sustainable, one mom at a time. Manda Aufochs Gillespie had been living and promoting an environmentally conscious lifestyle for several years when she was featured in a *Chicago Tribune* article. Suddenly, Gillespie became a guru for like-minded parents who also wanted to improve the health and lives of their families while reducing their impact on the planet. Since then she has launched a website, www.thegreenmama.com. She also hosts a weekly playgroup/seminar for parents, the Green Mama Café; writes a blog; consults for daycare businesses and educational institutions; gives workshops; appears on television; and provides everyday advice to consumers. She's also a mom.

The website is the centre of Gillespie's green universe. "The site is for people who are trying to be green parents in any major city," she explains. "It's a tool for living." Visitors to the site can get shopping tips for the best cloth diapers, learn how to clean their floors with white vinegar (instead of commercial cleaners), become informed about buying local produce, and learn about everything from the effectiveness of hand sanitizers to the cost of organic produce. No question is too simple for Gillespie. She also suggests how to save money—and reduce waste—such as by re-gifting gently used children's clothing to another child instead of buying new clothing for a birthday gift.

How does her philosophy become a business? It's not just the $5 that each mom pays for one of Gillespie's workshops at the Green Mama Café, or her consulting fees. Marketing experts say that these moms represent some 20 million North American consumers who are now demanding green goods and services. It's not just cloth diapers and natural floor cleaners. These consumers now look carefully at every item they put in their reusable shopping bags. If they have to pay a bit more for those products, they will—because they are usually saving money somewhere else. "It turns out that what saves money also saves resources and what is better for the environment can also make parenting easier, if you have the right mindset," says one mom who goes to Gillespie's Green Mama seminars. These green moms have nearly $210 billion in purchasing power—and manufacturers, media, and service providers are paying attention.

Questions for Critical Thinking

1. Manda Gillespie owns one of many small businesses that are creating a whole new industry: green goods and services for parents. What factors will contribute to the success of these businesses? What risks do these businesses face?

2. As a consumer, do you purchase any green goods or services? Why or why not? Have these goods and services been offered by small or large companies?

Sources: Green Mama, accessed April 2, 2010, www.thegreenmama.com; Jessica Levco, "The Green Mama Speaks," *Chicago Magazine*, May 2009, www.chicagomag.com/Chicago-Magazine/May-2009/The-Green-Mama-Speaks; Robyn Monaghan, "Green Mamas Unite," *Chicago Parent*, March 20, 2009, www.chicagoparent.com/magazines/chicago-parent/2009-april/green-mamas-unite.

---

cams to meet with men who are too busy to shop for clothes. The company interviews customers to learn about their clothing needs, and then selects new clothing and sends it directly to the customer.[12]

New industries can also be created when both the business world and consumers see a need for change. For example, environmental responsibility has changed how we do things—from recycling and reusing goods to reducing the amount of energy we use. These changes have led to a new industry of green goods and services. Small companies provide many of these goods and services. The "Going Green" feature describes one small-business owner who uses her passion and talent to provide environmentally responsible services.

Innovation

Small businesses are good at innovation—developing new and improved goods and services. Innovation is often the entire reason for starting a new business. For example, 58.1 percent of small and medium-sized businesses in the manufacturing sector innovated within the three years from 2009–2011, and other industries also show high levels of innovation coming from small and medium-sized businesses: in knowledge-based industries, 50.0 percent innovated; professional, scientific, and technical services, 43.5 percent; and wholesale and retail trade, 41.1 percent.[13] In a

CAREER KICKSTART

How to Use Social Networking in Your Job Search

Online social networking is likely part of your everyday life. But you can also use this technology to look for a job. During one recent year, networking sites such as LinkedIn registered 1 million new users each month. Worried you'll get lost when so many other people are also using social networking? Use a few simple tips to stand out from the millions of others who have discovered the benefits of social networking.

- *Research a network before jumping in.* Some networks, such as Facebook, are mainly for connecting with friends. Others, such as LinkedIn, are stronger networks when looking for work. Twitter attracts both types of users. To decide what is right for you—and to make the most of a social network—learn about it before you log on to look for work.

- *Complete your online profile.* Help prospective employers by filling out your online profile, and update your bio as often as you can. Provide a link to your own blog or webpage. Don't try to be perfect—if you know your weaknesses or if you made a mistake in a previous job, describe how you've improved or learned from your mistakes.

- *Share information.* Be willing to share information about companies or career opportunities with other job seekers. You can help an online employer find the right person—even if it's not you.

- *Search for people.* First, look for companies that interest you. Next, talk to your friends, family members, classmates, alumni—anyone who might know someone at those companies. A specific job might not be available now, but a personal connection can help you when that job does open up.

- *Respect privacy.* You want to provide only certain information about yourself online, so respect the privacy of potential employers and colleagues. Read about the privacy settings of a social networking site and abide by them.

Sources: DeLynn Senna, "Recruiters Reveal Pet Peeves about Job Seekers," *Yahoo! Hot Jobs*, accessed April 2, 2010, http://hotjobs.yahoo.com; Alex Williams, "Mind Your BlackBerry or Mind Your Manners," *New York Times*, June 21, 2009; David LaGesse, "Turning Social Networking into a Job Offer," *U.S. News & World Report*, May 2009, pp. 44–45.

---

typical year, small firms develop twice as many product innovations per employee as larger firms. Small firms also produce 13 times more patents per employee than larger firms.[14]

During the twentieth century, small businesses developed several major innovations: the airplane, the personal computer, soft contact lenses, and the zipper. In the twenty-first century, small businesses are developing innovations that involve social networking, security, and green energy industries. The "Career Kickstart" feature offers tips for using online social networking successfully.

✓ **ASSESSMENT CHECK**

5.2.1 What are the three key ways that small businesses contribute to the economy?

5.2.2 How are new industries formed?

WHY SMALL BUSINESSES FAIL

LO 5.3 Discuss why small businesses fail.

Small businesses play a huge role in the Canadian economy. One of the reasons they are so successful is the same reason they fail—the willingness to take a risk. The most common difficulties for a small firm are management inexperience, inadequate financing, and the challenge of meeting government regulations. About 96 percent of small businesses that enter the marketplace are in business for one full year, 85 percent are in business for three years, and 70 percent are in business for five years.[15] Let's see why this happens.

Management Shortcomings

One of the most common causes of small-business failure is management inexperience. For example, managers may not have the right people skills, may not have much knowledge of finance, may not be able to track inventory or sales, may be poor at judging their competition, or may simply not have enough time to do everything that needs to be done. Large firms are often big enough that they can hire specialists in marketing and finance, but the owner of a small business often has to take on all the firm's roles at the same time.

Trying to do all the business functions can lead to bad decisions that can end in the firm's failure. Krispy Kreme was once a small business that expanded too fast because its management made poor decisions. The company's near failure had nothing to do with its doughnuts. Instead, as the company grew bigger, so did its debt. Some blamed management misconduct. At the same time, consumers began to turn their attention away from doughnuts and toward more healthful snacks and breakfast foods. Krispy Kreme is now recovering. It has new management and is operating on a smaller scale.[16]

Owners of small businesses can increase their chances of success by learning the principles of business, knowing the industry they operate in, developing good interpersonal skills, understanding their own limitations, hiring motivated employees, and asking for professional advice on finance, regulations, and other legal matters.[17]

Inadequate Financing

Money is the foundation of any business. Every business—large or small—needs some financing to operate, thrive, and grow. Another big problem of small businesses is inadequate financing. First-time business owners often assume that their firms will make enough money from their initial sales to finance continuing operations. But building a business takes time. Products need to be developed, employees need to be hired, a website needs to be constructed, distribution needs to be planned, and office or retail space may need to be rented or purchased. Most small businesses—even those with minimal startup costs—sometimes don't turn a profit for months or even years.[18]

We have all heard about people starting firms with just a few hundred dollars borrowed from a friend or with a cash advance from a credit card. But most small businesses get their startup money from commercial banks and other financial institutions. This type of financing includes credit lines and loans for nonresidential mortgages, vehicles, specialized equipment, and leases.[19]

Credit cards have high interest rates. Still, they are an important source of financing for small businesses. The heaviest users of credit cards for business financing are firms with fewer than 10 employees. Inadequate financing can make management shortcomings worse by making it more difficult for small businesses to attract and keep talented people. Typically, a big company can offer a better benefits package and a higher salary.

Successful small companies need to be creative to operate with less money to spend on employees, marketing, inventory, and other business costs. Asafumi Yamashita started his business with $500. He used the money to buy specialty vegetable seeds from Japan. In his own greenhouse, he planted Japanese spinach, radishes, and other special produce. Yamashita had become friends with the head chef at a Japanese restaurant in Paris. The chef told Yamashita that these vegetables were nearly impossible to buy locally. Within a year of planting those first seeds, Yamashita was supplying several top restaurants in Paris. Others heard about Yamashita's high-quality vegetables, and he now supplies his vegetables to only the most exclusive restaurants. Yamashita has limited

Asafumi Yamashita started his business with $500. He used the money to buy specialty vegetable seeds from Japan. Within a year, Yamashita was supplying several top restaurants in Paris. Yamashita has limited his number of customers and has no employees. This means he needs less financing and maintains control over all the vegetables he grows.

his number of customers and has no employees. This means he needs less financing and maintains control over all the vegetables that leave his garden.[20]

Government Regulation

Small-business owners say that meeting the terms of government regulations is one of their biggest challenges. Some firms close because of how difficult it is to deal with government regulations. Small businesses spend billions of dollars on paperwork each year. A large company has an easier time dealing with all the government forms and reports. Larger firms can often hire or contract specialists to deal with specific regulations, such as employment law and workplace safety requirements. But small businesses often have difficulty paying the costs of government paperwork because they have fewer staff and smaller budgets. Statistics Canada is doing research to help reduce the problem. In a recent year, small and medium-sized businesses in five sectors spent $1.17 billion filling out forms to meet 11 key government information requirements, such as filing income tax forms and paying federal and provincial sales taxes.[21]

Taxes are another big expense for a small business. All employers pay provincial and federal income taxes. They must also pay taxes for workers' compensation insurance, pension payments, and unemployment benefits. Although large companies have the same expenses, most have more resources to pay their taxes. The government has created tax incentives to help small businesses. These incentives include the Small Business Investor Tax Credit, which returns a 30 percent tax credit to an investor to a maximum $75,000 credit.[22]

ASSESSMENT CHECK

5.3.1 What percentage of small businesses are still operating five years after starting?

5.3.2 What are the three main causes of small-business failure?

LO 5.4 Describe the features of an effective business plan.

THE BUSINESS PLAN: A FOUNDATION FOR SUCCESS

Large or small, every business needs a plan to succeed. We sometimes hear about firms that started with an idea scribbled on a restaurant napkin or sketched out on graph paper in a dorm room. But a business idea must have a solid plan to become reality. A **business plan** is a formal document that details a company's goals, the methods it will use to achieve those goals, and the standards it will use to measure its achievements. Firms often need a business plan to obtain financing. The business plan also creates a framework for the organization.

Business plans give the organization a sense of purpose. They identify the firm's mission and goals. Business plans create measurable standards and outline a strategy for reaching company objectives. A typical business plan includes the following sections:

- An *executive summary* that briefly answers the who, what, where, when, why, and how questions for the business
- An *introduction* that includes a general statement of the concept, purpose, and objectives of the business
- Separate *financial* and *marketing sections* that describe the firm's target market, marketing plan, and detailed financial forecasts of the need for funds and when the firm is expected to break even—the level of sales where revenues equal costs
- *Résumés of principals*—these are especially important in plans written to obtain financing.

An effective business plan uses the five sections above, contains the company's mission, and addresses the following issues:

- *The company's mission and the vision of its founders.* Look at the home page of any firm's website and you will find its mission. At the website for TOMS Shoes, visitors learn that "TOMS Shoes was founded on a simple premise: With every pair you purchase, TOMS will give a pair of new shoes to a child in need. One for one. Using the purchasing power of individuals to benefit the greater good is what we're all about."[23] This simple statement says why the company was founded and what it intends to achieve.

business plan a formal document that details a company's goals, methods, and standards.

Firms often need a business plan to obtain financing. Business plans identify the firm's mission and goals. They create measurable standards and outline a strategy for reaching company objectives. The business plan also creates a framework for the organization.

- *An outline of why the company is unique.* Why start a business that's just like hundreds of others? An effective business plan describes why the firm and its products differ from the rest of the pack. TOMS Shoes illustrates a unique business model with its "one-for-one" donation program.
- *The customers.* A business plan identifies who the firm's customers will be and how the firm will serve their needs.
- *The competition.* A business plan addresses its existing and potential competitors. It then suggests a strategy for creating better or unique offerings. A firm can study the competition to learn valuable information about what works and what doesn't work.
- *Financial evaluation of the industry and market conditions.* This knowledge helps develop a reasonable financial forecast and budget.
- *Assessment of the risks.* Every business undertaking involves risks. A solid business plan acknowledges these risks and outlines a strategy for dealing with them.[24]

One firm may want to change an entire industry, while another firm wants to improve the lives of children by giving them shoes. Both firms need a business plan to be a success. For more information on how to write a business plan, see Appendix E, "Developing a Business Plan," at the back of the textbook.

✓ ASSESSMENT CHECK

5.4.1 What are the five main sections of a business plan?

5.4.2 Why is an effective business plan important to the success of a firm?

LO 5.5 Identify the assistance available to small businesses.

ASSISTANCE FOR SMALL BUSINESSES

Financing is an important part of setting up a small business. After writing a business plan, the business owner needs to look for loans and other types of financing. Government agencies and private investors often provide the needed funds. Many people want to start a business, which means government agencies can provide funds only to some firms. A strong business plan justifying the use of funds and growth potential can help persuade lenders.

Business Development Bank of Canada

The **Business Development Bank of Canada (BDC)** is a government agency that assists, counsels, and protects the interests of small businesses in Canada. BDC was created by an act of Parliament in 1944. It operates across Canada through offices and resource centres that provide long-term financial assistance and management counselling. The BDC also provides training, technical assistance, and education to help small businesses prepare for doing business in foreign markets. Statistics show that most small-business failures happen because of poor management. For this reason, the BDC works to improve the management skills of small-business owners and managers. The BDC offers individual counselling, courses, conferences, workshops, and a wide range of publications. BDC's management courses cover all the functions, duties, and roles of managers. Instructors may be teachers from local colleges or universities. They may also be management consultants, bankers, lawyers, and accountants. Fees for these courses are low. The most popular course is a general survey of eight to ten areas of business management. Businesspeople can then focus on one or more of these areas, depending on their strengths and weaknesses. The BDC sometimes offers one-day conferences. These conferences are aimed at keeping owner-managers up to date on new management developments, tax laws, and the other helpful information.[25]

The Small Business Administration (SBA) is the main government agency that helps small U.S. firms. The SBA is the advocate, or supporter, for small businesses within the U.S. federal government. Many small-business resources are available at the websites of both organizations.

Business Development Bank of Canada (BDC) a governmental agency that assists, counsels, and protects the interests of small businesses in Canada.

Financial Assistance

Most small businesses borrow money directly from Canada's financial institutions. These banks, trust companies, and credit unions actively believe in lending money to small businesses. The Canada Small Business Financing Program (CSBFP) is typical of federal and provincial government assistance. When a bank loans money to a small business and is not paid back, the government will guarantee payment for as much as 85 percent of the loan. Some small businesses cannot borrow from traditional lending institutions because they don't have a financial history. These small businesses may be funded by the BDC or other organizations that may want to help higher-risk firms.

The CSBFP tries to increase the number of loans for establishing, expanding, modernizing, and improving small businesses. It does this by encouraging financial institutions to make their financing available to small businesses. By sharing the risks with financial institutions, the program may help businesses obtain loans of up to $500,000. The loans can cover 90 percent of the costs to purchase or improve land or property, to purchase leasehold improvements or improve leased property, or to purchase new equipment or improve used equipment. Eligible small businesses must be operating for profit in Canada and must have annual gross revenues less than $5 million.[26]

Business Incubators

Some community agencies want to encourage business development. These agencies use a concept called a **business incubator** to provide low-cost, shared business facilities to small startup companies. A typical incubator might section off space in an abandoned plant and rent it to various small firms. Tenants often share clerical staff, computers, and other business services. The goal is for new businesses to be ready to move out and operate on their own after a few months or years.

The Canadian Association of Business Incubation (CABI) is a national association of member organizations. CABI supports the growth of new and early-stage businesses. According to CABI and Statistics Canada research, Canada has at least 83 operating business incubators that generate more than $45 million in funds. Their almost 900 client firms raised more than $93 million in revenue and created full- and part-time jobs for more than 13,000 people. Incubation firms make a positive impact. After one year, 2,958 client companies had generated revenues.[27]

business incubator a local program designed to provide low-cost, shared business facilities to small startup companies.

Private Investors

A small business may start with cash from a personal savings account or a loan from a family member. But small-business owners need larger sums of money to continue operating and to grow. They may want to continue receiving funds from private investors. **Venture capital** is money

venture capital money invested in a business by another business or a group of individuals in return for an ownership share.

HIT & MISS

CBC's *Dragons' Den* Highlights Entrepreneurial Thinking and Investing

The CBC's popular reality show *Dragons' Den* is the Canadian version of a show that is seen around the world. The format is the same in every country. Entrepreneurs present their ideas for a new business to a panel of venture capitalists with whom they hope to make a deal. The idea is to partner with one or more panel members to improve the chances the business will be developed successfully.

The show succeeds partly because of the entertainment value: the viewers at home act as armchair-panelists. The show is also educational. Viewers watch the "dragons" review the presentations. They quickly learn about business valuation, patents, and the managerial mindset that venture capital partners like to see.

Many viewers are probably thinking about starting a business of their own. The biggest lesson that all viewers learn is the role of expertise and knowledge to move the business to the "next level." The entrepreneurs that make deals with the dragons are usually business owners who have been successful but need help to grow the business. They now need the dragons' expertise and business connections as much as they need their investment funds. Having the dragons on their side can help take their business to a higher level.

Questions for Critical Thinking

1. Why is *Dragons' Den* successful in Canada and around the world?
2. How would the show differ in other countries?

Sources: CBC, *Dragons' Den*, accessed March 18, 2012, www.cbc.ca/dragonsden; "Dragons' Den" *Financial Post*, accessed March 18, 2012, http://business.financialpost.com/tag/dragons-den; "Business Titans Jim Treliving and W. Brett Wilson Jump at FROGBOX Offering," *Marketwire*, January 27, 2011, accessed March 18, 2012, www.marketwire.com/press-release/business-titans-jim-treliving-and-w-brett-wilson-jump-at-frogbox-offering-1386326.htm; "Dragons' Den & Venture Capital," *Financial Blogger*, February 13, 2012, accessed March 18, 2012, www.thefinancialblogger.com/dragons-den-venture-capital.

Arlene Dickinson started working at Venture Communications in 1988. She took full ownership of the marketing firm 10 years later. Her success in marketing and communications led her to the panel of *Dragons' Den*, the CBC's popular business show. On the show, entrepreneurs compete for funding and partnership with the panel members. Dickinson is also in demand as an author and speaker at events that highlight her entrepreneurial ability and success.

invested in the small business by another business or a group of individuals in return for an ownership share. Venture capital (VC) can give the small business the funding it needs to succeed. Even when the economy is slow, venture capitalists are looking for companies to invest in. Canada's Venture Capital and Private Equity Association reports that Canadian VC investment in 2014 increased to $1.9 billion. The story is similar in the United States. There, the U.S. National Venture Capital Association reported that venture capitalists had invested more than $7 billion in small startup firms despite a slow economy. These investors preferred funding small-business owners who had a previous success or who were proposing new ways to commercialize products such as solar energy, low-emission cars, and new medications. These investors have high requirements for a solid business plan. They also expect small-business owners to run lean operations.[28] The "Hit & Miss" feature discusses the popular show *Dragons' Den*, which features venture capitalists, such as Arlene Dickinson,[29] listening to pitches from small-business owners.

Small-Business Opportunities for Women

The number of women-owned firms in Canada has increased over the past few decades. Today, nearly half of all small and medium-sized enterprises (SMEs) in Canada have at least one female owner. Women also hold majority ownership in 18 percent of SMEs. Women-owned firms also contribute significantly to employment. About one-third of all self-employed people in Canada are women.

Women, like men, start their own companies for many different reasons. Some have a unique business idea that they want to bring to life. Others decide to form their own company when they lose their job or become frustrated with the working conditions in large companies. Many women start their own companies in hopes of finding a better balance between family and work.

The presence of women in business ownership means more than just more jobs. Majority women-owned SMEs produce annual commercial revenues of more than $72 billion, representing approximately 8 percent of all revenues from Canada's SMEs. Women are present across all sectors of the Canadian economy, although most work in service industries. Today, 80 percent of majority women-owned SMEs operate in the services sector, compared with 59 percent of SMEs owned by men.[30]

ASSESSMENT CHECK

5.5.1 What are the various ways the BDC helps small businesses?

5.5.2 What are business incubators?

5.5.3 Why are small businesses good opportunities for women?

FRANCHISING

LO 5.6 Explain franchising.

Franchising combines large and small businesses into a single entity. It is also a major factor in the growth of small businesses. **Franchising** is a contract-based business arrangement between a manufacturer or another supplier and a dealer, such as a restaurant operator or a retailer. The contract spells out how the dealer will market the supplier's product. Franchises can involve both goods and services, such as food and wait staff.

Starting a small, independent company can be risky, time-consuming work, but franchising can reduce the amount of time and effort needed to grow. The parent company has already developed and tested the concept, and the brand is often already familiar to customers.

franchising a contract-based business arrangement between a manufacturer or other supplier and a dealer, such as a restaurant operator or retailer.

The Franchising Sector

Canada has the second-largest franchise industry in the world, after the United States. Canadians are as familiar with American franchise businesses in Canada, such as McDonald's, as they are with Canadian franchises, such as Tim Hortons.

The franchise industry has more than $100 billion in sales each year. Approximately one out of five consumer dollars is spent on goods and services at a franchise business. Canada has approximately 76,000 individual franchise businesses operating under 900 different brand names. These franchises employ more than 1 million people. One out of every 14 working Canadians is employed by a franchise.

The average franchise fee is $23,000, and the average franchisee investment is $160,000. Of all the franchises opened in Canada within the last five years, 86 percent are under the same ownership and 97 percent are still in business. Ontario leads the rest of Canada in franchising: 56 percent of Canadian franchises are based in Ontario, mostly in the Greater Toronto Area, and 65 percent of all Canadian franchise outlets (that is, the number of individual locations of all franchises combined) are in Ontario. The hospitality industry is the largest franchised sector, making up almost 40 percent of all Canadian franchised brand names. The franchise industry is active in more than 30 business, service, and retail sectors.[31]

Franchised businesses are also a huge part of the U.S. economy. There, franchises account for nearly 50 percent of all retail sales. The International Franchise Association reports that franchising is responsible for about 825,000 businesses, 18 million jobs, and more than $2 trillion in sales. A new franchise is opened every eight minutes every business day.[32]

Franchising overseas is also a growing trend for businesses who aim to expand into foreign markets. You can go almost anywhere in the world and find a McDonald's burger. Other international franchises are also becoming more common. The 2014 merger between Burger King and Tim Hortons was driven by the desire to accelerate growth of Tim Hortons in the United States and globally. Restaurant Brands International Inc., the parent company of Tim Hortons and Burger King, plans to follow Burger King's strategy of opening large numbers of outlets in a specific geographic area to better compete against U.S. giant Dunkin' Donuts. In France, Burger King is accelerating franchise openings with guidance from local consultants that are more familiar

International franchises are becoming more common. Baskin-Robbins has nearly 7,300 stores in more than 50 countries, including Australia, Canada, China, Japan, Vietnam, Russia, and the United Arab Emirates.

franchisee the individual or business firm purchasing a franchise.

franchisor the firm whose products are sold to customers by the franchisee.

with the best locations. To do so, large investments need to be made by 3G Capital, the Brazilian investment firm that financed the merger.[33]

Franchising Agreements

A franchising agreement is a contract between the franchisee and the franchisor. The individual or business firm that buys the franchise is called the **franchisee**. This business owner agrees to sell the franchisor's goods or services under certain terms. The **franchisor** is the firm whose products are sold by the franchisee. For example, Tim Hortons Inc. is a franchisor, while your local Tim Hortons restaurant owner is a franchisee.

Franchise agreements can be complex. They involve an initial purchase fee plus agreed-on startup costs. Because the franchisee represents the franchisor's brand, the franchisor can require the franchisee to purchase certain ingredients or equipment, use standard pricing, and market the business in a certain way. McDonald's is one of the more expensive franchises—total startup costs can be more than $1 million. In contrast, the total startup cost for a SUBWAY franchise in Canada ranges from $108,000 to $234,000 including the franchise fee of $15,000.[34] Because of the costs, businesspeople often work together to purchase a more expensive franchise.

Benefits and Problems of Franchising

Like other businesses, franchising has its upsides and downsides. The upsides for the franchisor include being able to expand a business, which might not be possible without the franchise. A franchised business can move into new locations, including overseas, at less cost than a traditional business. In other countries, franchises employ local workers and businesspeople who know what consumers like. A good franchisor can manage a much larger and more complex business—with fewer direct employees—than a traditional business. Most franchisees pay attention to how their franchises are managed because they have a stake in the company as business owners. If the business is run efficiently, the franchisor will probably make more money on the investment than if the firm were run entirely as a company-owned chain of retail shops, restaurants, or service providers.

A successful franchisor has financial strength and can usually bargain for better deals on ingredients, supplies, and even real estate. This strength is also a benefit for the franchisees if the savings are passed on to them.[35]

Franchising can be the quickest way to become a business owner. Some people say that it's also the least risky way to own a business. Franchisees benefit from having a business name that people know, such as McDonald's, Tim Hortons, SUBWAY, Pizza Hut, or Super 8 motels. Having a familiar name usually means a loyal following of customers. The franchisor has already set up a management system, and it has already shown that it can be successful. Franchisors provide support to franchisees, including financing, assistance in obtaining a location, business training, supplies, and marketing tools.[36]

Franchisees say they like the idea of franchising because it combines the freedom of business ownership with the support of a large company. Like other small-business owners, franchisees want to make their own business decisions and decide on their own work hours. They also want to have more control over the amount of money they make, instead of taking what they might earn in a salaried job. In an economic slowdown, franchisees might be former executives who have been laid off. These highly trained and motivated businesspeople are looking for a way to restart their careers.[37] Sometimes the ideas or successes of individual franchisees can be good for the entire company. That's what happened with SUBWAY, as described in the "Hit & Miss" feature.

Franchising also has its downsides—for both franchisors and franchisees. If franchisees fail, their failure reflects on the franchisor's brand and the bottom line. The same is true for the franchisee: A firm that is mismanaged at the top level, by the franchisor, can be bad for the franchisees who are running the individual locations. When a firm decides to offer franchise opportunities, it may lose money for several years. Of course, by

Tim Hortons is one of Canada's most popular and successful franchises.

HIT & MISS

One Small Franchise Produces One Big Idea

SUBWAY has enjoyed top franchise rankings consistently for more than a decade. SUBWAY has more than 30,000 sandwich restaurants in over 100 countries, including 21,000 franchisees. The firm is set to become the single largest fast-food chain in the world. But SUBWAY is made up of many small businesses—franchises. Sometimes, a small idea by one franchisee can change the entire organization.

Stuart Frankel is a SUBWAY franchisee, and his idea was simple: On weekends, he wanted to charge a special price of $5 for a footlong SUBWAY sandwich. This special price was about $1 less per sandwich than the regular price. It took some time for Frankel and two other Florida SUBWAY franchisees to convince the corporate franchisor that the idea was a good one. The economy was slow, food costs were increasing, and SUBWAY shops were almost empty because people were eating at home to save money. Frankel's employees stood around at their stations, and sandwich sales decreased. But after some time, Frankel got the OK from corporate headquarters. From there, a chain reaction began.

"I like round numbers," said Frankel about the $5 price. SUBWAY customers liked the number, too. When the special pricing was announced, customers returned for the $5 sandwiches. Sales increased by double digits. Employees made sandwiches as fast as they could. SUBWAY's corporate marketing team pushed the $5 promotion nationwide. When the initial four-week promotion was up, marketing executives extended it to seven weeks. When that time was up, they extended it indefinitely but with a limited number of sandwich variations.

Something else happened. Demand for the $5 footlongs was so great that franchise owners began to run out of certain ingredients. They couldn't get enough bread, turkey, ham, or tuna. One franchisee recalls being in a panic. "The whole thing took on a life of its own," said Jeff Moody, CEO of SUBWAY's advertising.

With one motion, Stuart Frankel had a great idea for consumers who wanted to eat out and get a good deal at the same time. "There are only a few times when a chain has been able to scramble up the whole industry, and this is one of them," notes restaurant consultant Jeffrey T. Davis. "It's huge." Sometimes a small idea is really big.

Questions for Critical Thinking

1. Why was Stuart Frankel's idea successful with consumers? Would it have been as successful during a different economic time? Why or why not?

2. A franchise company is only as good as its franchisees. And a franchisee's success is based in part on the decisions and support of corporate leadership. If the $5 footlong promotion had failed, how would that failure have affected Frankel's franchise business? How might it have affected SUBWAY?

Sources: Subway Restaurants, "Subway FAQs," accessed April 8, 2015, www.subway.com/ContactUs/CustServFAQs.aspx; "Subway Brand Ranked Number One Provider of Healthy Options in Zagat Survey," accessed April 2, 2010, www.subway.com; "Subway Restaurants Again Named #1 Worldwide Franchise Opportunity for 2009," accessed April 2, 2010, www.subway.com; Matthew Boyle, "The Accidental Hero," *Businessweek*, November 10, 2009, accessed April 2, 2010, www.bloomberg.com/bw/magazine/content/09_46/b4155058815908.htm.

offering franchise opportunities, the franchisor—often the founder of what was once a small business—loses control over every aspect of the business. Not having control can make it difficult to select the right franchisees to carry out the company's mission.[38]

The franchisee has many cash expenses: the initial investment, franchise fees, supplies, maintenance, leases, and so on. The most expensive franchises are usually franchises that involve hotels and resorts. These franchises can cost millions of dollars.[39] It is not unusual for groups of businesspeople to purchase a franchise (or several franchise locations) together.[40] The franchisees' payments to the franchisor can add to the difficulty of keeping the business going until the owner begins to earn a profit. Choosing a low-cost startup may be a good alternative. But it's important for potential franchisees to check carefully how much profit they can make after they pay their expenses.

Franchises are closely linked to their brand, so franchisors and franchisees must work together to maintain standards of quality in their goods and services. If customers are unhappy with their experience at one franchise location, they might not stop at another location several kilometres away, even if the second location is owned and operated by someone else. This is especially true where food is involved. The discovery of bad meat or produce at one franchise restaurant can cause panic to spread throughout the entire chain of restaurants. A potential franchisee is smart to thoroughly research the financial performance and reputation of the franchisor. This research can be done using resources such as other franchisees, the Better Business Bureau, Industry Canada, the U.S. Federal Trade Commission, and the Canadian Franchise Association (CFA). The CFA is a trade association representing franchisors. CFA members agree to a review before they are accepted as members. They also agree to follow the association's code of ethics.

Some franchisees have found the franchising agreement to be too confining. As the saying goes, you can't add a tuna salad sandwich to the menu at McDonald's no matter how many stores you own. The agreements are usually strict, which helps to maintain the brand's good standing. Some franchise companies control promotional activities, select the site location, and might even get involved in hiring decisions. These activities may seem overly controlling to some franchisees, especially those who want more independence and freedom.

Controls can also cost franchisees more than they feel is fair. Recently, the National Franchise Association, a group that represents more than 80 percent of Burger King's U.S. franchisees, sued Burger King because Burger King forced its franchisees to offer consumers a $1 double cheeseburger, which supported the company's promotional efforts. While the $1 burger offering may seem like a great way to attract and serve hungry consumers, Burger King franchisees said the promotion has cost them a loss of at least 10 cents per burger. In other words, it costs most franchises $1.10 to make and serve a double cheeseburger, but the franchisor told them they must charge $1.[41]

ASSESSMENT CHECK

5.6.1 What is the difference between a franchisor and a franchisee?

5.6.2 How does franchising benefit both parties?

5.6.3 What are the potential downsides of franchising for both parties?

LO 5.7 Outline the forms of private business ownership.

FORMS OF PRIVATE BUSINESS OWNERSHIP

No matter how big or small, most businesses are organized as one of three legal structures: sole proprietorship, partnership, or corporation. Each legal structure offers unique advantages and disadvantages. In addition to the three main legal structures, there is the option of creating and running a not-for-profit organization.

Sole Proprietorships

The most common, oldest, and simplest form of business ownership is the **sole proprietorship**. In a sole proprietorship, the sole proprietor's status as an individual is not legally separate from his or her status as a business owner. Although sole proprietorships are common in many industries, they are found mostly among small businesses such as repair shops, small retail stores, and service providers such as plumbers, hairstylists, and photographers.

sole proprietorship a business ownership structure in which the sole proprietor's status as an individual is not legally separate from his or her status as a business owner.

Sole proprietorships have some unique advantages. Because sole proprietorships have a single owner, they are easy to form *and* dissolve. A sole proprietorship gives the owner the most management flexibility. The owner also has the right to all profits after paying business-related bills and taxes. A highly motivated owner of a sole proprietorship directly receives all the benefits of his or her hard work.

It is easy to enter and exit a sole proprietorship because there are very few legal requirements. The owner registers the business or trade name to make sure that another firm does not use the same name. Next, the owner pays for any necessary licences. Local governments require certain licences for businesses, such as restaurants, motels or hotels, and retail stores. Some occupational licences require that business owners have specific insurance, such as liability coverage.

Sole proprietorships are also easy to dissolve. This factor is particularly important to temporary or seasonal businesses that set up for a limited period of time. It's also helpful if the owner needs or wants to close the business for any reason—for example, to relocate or to accept a full-time position with a larger firm.

Management flexibility is another advantage of a sole proprietorship. The owner can make decisions without reporting to a manager, take quick action, and keep trade secrets. A sole proprietorship always bears the individuality, or style, of its owner, whether it's a certain way of cutting hair or how a store window is decorated.

The greatest disadvantage of the sole proprietorship is the owner's personal financial liability for the business's debts. Also, the business must operate with financial resources that are limited to the owner's personal funds and to money that he or she can borrow. Such financing limitations can keep the business from expanding.

Another disadvantage is that the owner must handle a wide range of management and operational tasks. He or she may not have skills in every area, which may keep the firm from growth or may even cause the firm damage. Sole proprietors may also face a higher chance of being audited by the Canada Revenue Agency. Finally, a sole proprietorship usually lacks long-term continuity because a change in personal circumstances or finances can terminate the business on short notice.

Partnerships

Another option for organizing a business is to form a partnership. A **partnership** is an association of two or more persons who operate a business as co-owners by voluntary legal agreement. Many small businesses begin as partnerships between co-founders.

partnership an association of two or more persons who operate a business as co-owners by voluntary legal agreement.

Partnerships are easy to form. The partners need to register the business name and obtain any necessary licences. Having a partner usually means greater financial capability and someone to share in the tasks and decision making. It's even better if one partner has a particular skill, such as design, while the other is good at finance.

Most partnerships have the downside of being exposed to unlimited financial liability. Each partner bears full responsibility for the debts of the firm, and each is legally liable for the actions of the other partners. If the firm fails and has debt, every partner is responsible for those debts; it doesn't matter if the debts are the fault of only one partner. If one partner defaults, the others are responsible for the firm's debts, even if they have to use their personal funds. To avoid these problems, many firms set up a limited-liability partnership. This type of partnership limits the liability of partners to the value of their interests in the company.

Breaking up a partnership is more complicated than dissolving a sole proprietorship. The partner who wants to leave cannot just withdraw his or her portion of the funds from the bank. Instead, the partner who wants out may need to find a new partner to buy his or her interest in the firm. The death of a partner also threatens the business. A new partnership must be formed, and the estate of the deceased can take a share of the firm's value. To ease the possible financial difficulties of this situation, business planners suggest life insurance coverage for each partner, combined with a buy-sell agreement. The insurance proceeds can be used to repay the deceased partner's heirs. That way, the surviving partners can retain control of the business.

Businesses that are based on partnerships also risk having personal conflicts. Partners need to choose each other carefully; best friends sometimes don't make the best partners. Good partners work hard and try to plan for the future.

Corporations

corporation a legal organization with assets and liabilities separate from the assets and liabilities of its owners.

A **corporation** is a legal organization that has assets and liabilities separate from the assets and liabilities of its owners. A corporation can be a large or small business—it can be Air Canada or a local auto repair shop.

Corporate ownership offers many advantages. Because a corporation is a separate legal entity, its shareholders have only limited financial risk. If the firm fails, the shareholders lose only the money they invested. The same goes for the firm's managers and executives. Because they are not the sole proprietors or partners in the business, their personal savings are not at risk if the company closes or goes bankrupt. This protection also extends to legal risk. Class action lawsuits against automakers, drug manufacturers, and food producers are filed against the companies, not the owners of those companies.[42]

Corporations offer other advantages. They can gain access to more funding because they can offer direct outside investments such as sales of shares. A large corporation can legally raise internal funds for projects by transferring money from one part of the corporation to another.

One major disadvantage for a corporation is the double taxation of corporate earnings. A corporation pays federal and provincial income taxes on its profits, but its owners (the shareholders) also pay personal taxes on dividends, the distributions of profits they receive from the corporation.

Not-for-Profit Corporations

not-for-profit corporations organizations whose goals do not include pursuing a profit.

The same business concepts that apply to commercial companies also apply to **not-for-profit corporations**—organizations whose goals do not include pursuing a profit. Canada has about 160,000 not-for-profits, including charitable groups, social-welfare organizations, government agencies, and religious congregations. Not-for-profit corporations also include museums, libraries, hospitals, conservation groups, and private schools.

Governments have separate legal provisions for organizational structures and operations of not-for-profit corporations. These organizations do not issue shares because they do not pay dividends to owners, and their ownership rarely changes. They are also exempt from paying income taxes. However, they must meet very strict guidelines to keep their not-for-profit status.

Montreal's Sun Youth Organization was founded in 1954 by a small group of kids tired of the few sports and recreational activities in the St. Lawrence Boulevard/Boulevard Saint Laurent area (now Le Plateau). The entrepreneurial kids created a handwritten newspaper called the *Clark Street Sun*. They sold the newspaper door to door to raise funds to pay for the sports activities. The children themselves organized most of the activities. Finally, they were able to purchase equipment and uniforms for the increasing number of children involved. As these early groups of children grew older, Sun Youth became the social services organization known to and supported by Montrealers of every language and ethnic background. Today, the organization works with schools, police officers, firefighters, medical professionals, corporations, and volunteers to deal with referrals from more than 170 social service agencies from the Greater Montreal area.[43]

✓ ASSESSMENT CHECK

5.7.1 What are the key differences between sole proprietorships and partnerships?

5.7.2 What is a corporation?

5.7.3 What is the main characteristic of a not-for-profit corporation?

LO 5.8 Describe public and collective business ownership.

PUBLIC AND COLLECTIVE OWNERSHIP OF BUSINESS

Most businesses in Canada are owned by the private sector, but some firms are owned and operated by local, provincial, or federal governments. For example, Manitoba Hydro, New Brunswick Power, and many other electricity utility companies are owned entirely or partially by governments.[44]

MEC (formerly Mountain Equipment Co-op) is a collectively owned retailer that sells outdoor gear and clothing.

In another type of ownership structure, groups of customers can collectively own a company. At the end of the year, after paying suppliers, employees, and operating costs, the co-op returns any remaining funds to members as patronage shares. In another collective ownership structure, smaller firms can group together to own a larger organization. Both types of collective ownership structures are called *cooperatives*.

Public (Government) Ownership

One alternative to private ownership is some form of *public ownership*. In public ownership, a government unit or agency owns and operates an organization. In Canada, local governments often own the city's bus companies, parking structures, and water systems. For example, the Toronto Transit Commission operates the network of buses, subways, and streetcars that serve the city of Toronto. People who support public ownership believe that services can be provided to more people when profits are turned back to the company to provide more services. However, some people disagree. These people say the supporters' belief has no proof. There is evidence to support parts of both sides of the argument.

Sometimes public ownership results when private investors are unwilling to invest in a high-risk project—or when operating an important service is simply unprofitable. VIA Rail Canada operates the national passenger rail service for the Government of Canada. VIA was established as an independent Crown corporation in 1977. It provides public transportation by operating trains that serve 450 communities across the country. Each year, VIA carries more than 4 million customers on a fleet of 400 passenger cars.[45]

Collective (Cooperative) Ownership

Collective ownership sets up an organization called a *cooperative* (or *co-op*). The owners work together to operate all or part of the activities in their firm or industry. Currently, about 100 million people are employed by cooperatives around the world.[46] Cooperatives allow small businesses to pool their resources for purchases, marketing, equipment, and distribution. Discount savings can be split among members, and cooperatives often share equipment and expertise. During difficult economic times, members of a cooperative find a variety of ways to support each other.

ASSESSMENT CHECK

5.8.1 What is public ownership?

5.8.2 What is collective ownership? Where are cooperatives typically found, and what benefits do they provide small businesses?

LO 5.9 Discuss the organizational structure of corporations.

Canada has more than 8,400 co-ops. These co-ops employ more than 152,000 people: More than 87,000 work in nonfinancial cooperatives and more than 32,000 work in the agricultural sector. Canada has 5.9 million cooperative members, which means that four of every ten Canadians are members of a cooperative. At least seven co-ops are listed in the top 500 companies in Canada. Several financial cooperatives, such as Vancouver's Vancity Credit Union network, have been rated among the best places to work in Canada.[47]

ORGANIZING A CORPORATION

A corporation is a legal structure. It also requires a more complex organizational structure than a sole proprietorship or a partnership. This complexity explains why we often think of a corporation as a large entity, even though it does not have to be a big company.

Where and How Businesses Incorporate

Businesses owners who want to incorporate must decide where to locate their headquarters. They must also follow the correct procedure for filling out the legal document that sets up the corporation.

Where to Incorporate

The business decision of where to incorporate—and establish headquarters—may be based on a number of factors. Most businesses want to be near their customers. Other factors are real estate prices, public transportation, and communications networks. Access to a good source of employees is another reason for choosing a location. Online businesses such as Amazon.ca and eBay don't need to worry about being located near their customers, but they should think about the local source of employees.

Most small and medium-sized businesses are incorporated in the provinces where they operate, but a Canadian firm can actually incorporate in any province it chooses. The founders of large corporations or the founders of corporations that do business nationwide often compare the benefits, such as tax incentives, of different locations. Some provinces are considered to be more "business friendly" than others. For example, Alberta has one of the lowest taxes for incorporated businesses in Canada.

The Corporate Charter

A corporation is like an artificial person created by law, with most of the legal rights of a real person. These rights include the rights to start and operate a business, to buy or sell property, to borrow money, to sue or be sued, and to enter into binding contracts.

Incorporation of a business can be done at the federal or provincial level. Legally, if you incorporate provincially your corporation has the right to carry on business only in the province where your business is incorporated. This rule is not a problem for restaurants and other businesses that have a fixed location, but it might be a problem for others. Federally incorporated businesses are permitted to operate everywhere in Canada.

Each province has a specific process for incorporating a business. For example, the individual or individuals who create the corporation must select a name that is different from the names used by other businesses. **Figure 5.1** lists the 10 elements that are typically required for chartering a corporation.

- Name and Address of the Corporation
- Corporate Objectives
- Type and Amount of Stock to Issue
- Expected Life of the Corporation
- Financial Capital at the Time of Incorporation
- Provisions for Transferring Shares of Stock among Owners
- Provisions for Regulating Internal Corporate Affairs
- Address of the Business Office Registered with the Province
- Names and Addresses of the Initial Board of Directors
- Names and Addresses of the Incorporators

FIGURE 5.1 Traditional Articles of Incorporation

The information in the articles of incorporation forms the basis on which a government grants a *corporate charter*. This charter is the legal document that formally establishes a corporation. After securing the charter, the owners prepare the company's bylaws, which set out the rules for operation.

Corporate Management

Every corporation, large or small, has levels of management and ownership. **Figure 5.2** illustrates the typical levels—although a smaller firm might not have all five levels. These levels range from shareholders down to supervisory management.

Stock Ownership and Shareholder Rights

At the top of Figure 5.2 are **shareholders**. They buy shares of stock in the corporation, which makes them part owners. Some companies, such as many family businesses, are owned by only a few shareholders and the shares are generally unavailable to outsiders. In such a firm, known as a *closed* or *closely held corporation*, the shareholders also control and manage all of the company's activities.

shareholders owners of a corporation as a result of their purchase of shares in the corporation.

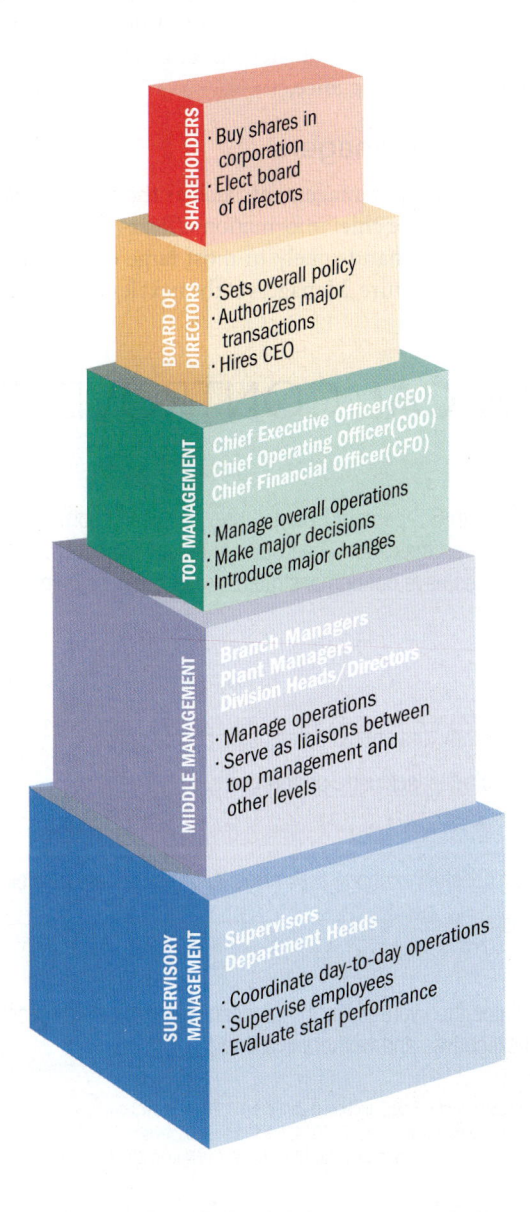

FIGURE 5.2 Levels of Management in a Corporation

SHAREHOLDERS
- Buy shares in corporation
- Elect board of directors

BOARD OF DIRECTORS
- Sets overall policy
- Authorizes major transactions
- Hires CEO

TOP MANAGEMENT
Chief Executive Officer (CEO)
Chief Operating Officer (COO)
Chief Financial Officer (CFO)
- Manage overall operations
- Make major decisions
- Introduce major changes

MIDDLE MANAGEMENT
Branch Managers
Plant Managers
Division Heads/Directors
- Manage operations
- Serve as liaisons between top management and other levels

SUPERVISORY MANAGEMENT
Supervisors
Department Heads
- Coordinate day-to-day operations
- Supervise employees
- Evaluate staff performance

An open corporation, also called a *publicly held corporation*, is different. It sells shares to the general public, which sets up a diversified ownership. This type of ownership often leads to a broader range of operations than in a closed corporation. Publicly held corporations usually hold annual shareholders' meetings. During these meetings, managers report on corporate activities, and shareholders vote on decisions that require their approval, including elections of officers.

The shareholders' role in the corporation depends on the class of shares they own. Shares are usually either common shares or preferred shares. Although owners of **preferred shares** have limited voting rights, they receive dividends before the holders of common shares. If the corporation is dissolved, the owners of preferred shares also have first claims on assets once all debtors are repaid. Owners of **common shares** have voting rights but only residual claims on the firm's assets. That means they are the last to receive any income distributions. Because one share is typically worth only one vote, small shareholders generally have little influence over corporate management actions.

preferred shares shares that give owners limited voting rights and the right to receive dividends or assets before owners of common shares.

common shares shares that give owners voting rights but only residual claims to the firm's assets and income distributions.

Board of Directors

board of directors the governing body of a corporation.

Shareholders elect a **board of directors**—the governing body of a corporation. The board sets overall policy, authorizes the corporation's major transactions, and hires the chief executive officer (CEO). Most boards include both inside directors (corporate executives) and outside directors—people who are not employed by the organization. Sometimes the corporation's top executive also chairs the board. Generally, outside directors are also shareholders, so they have a financial stake in the company's performance.

Corporate Officers and Managers

The CEO and other members of top management, such as the chief operating officer (COO), the chief financial officer (CFO), and the chief information officer (CIO), make most major corporate decisions. Top executives get paid handsomely in most large organizations, as discussed in the "Solving an Ethical Controversy" feature. Managers at the next level down, the middle management,

---

SOLVING AN **ETHICAL** CONTROVERSY

Do Some CEOs Earn Too Much?

Median CEO pay reached $9.7 million in North America recently, up 6.5 percent from the previous year. Enormous pay packages are meant to reward stellar company performance, but this has not always been the case. Some CEOs in recent years have been paid large amounts of money as part of their compensation packages, yet their companies have not demonstrated strong business gains.

Is executive pay excessive?

PRO
1. CEO compensation should reflect the overall state of the company and should be adjusted accordingly.
2. CEOs do not merit high rewards when their company demonstrates lacklustre performance.

CON
1. CEOs must take huge personal and professional risks to successfully manage their firms, and they should be well rewarded.
2. High pay ensures that firms attract and keep talented CEOs.

Summary
CEO salaries have continued to skyrocket to more than 300 times the average North American worker's pay in recent years. Should there be a formula or set of rules to control the growing gap between executives and workers in a firm?

Sources: Daily Viewpoint, "GMI Ratings' 2013 CEO Pay Survey Reveals CEO Pay Is Still on the Rise," accessed January 17, 2014, www3.gmiratings.com/home; Rob Silverblatt, "New Report Condemns Trends in CEO Compensation," *U.S. News and World Report*, accessed January 17, 2014, http://money.usnews.com/money/personal-finance/mutual-funds/articles/2013/09/03/new-report-condemns-trends-in-ceo-compensation; Christina Rexrode, "Median CEO Pay Rises to $9.7 million in 2012," *USA Today*, accessed January 17, 2014, www.usatoday.com/story/money/business/2013/05/26/ceo-pay-rises-in-2012/2350545.

handle the ongoing operational functions of the company. At the bottom tier of management, supervisory personnel coordinate day-to-day operations, assign tasks to employees, and evaluate job performance.

Today's CEOs and CFOs work under stricter regulations than in the past. They must verify in writing the accuracy of their firm's financial statements. The process for nominating candidates for the board has also become more complex. In short, more checks and balances are in place for the governance of corporations.

ASSESSMENT CHECK

5.9.1 What are the two key elements of the incorporation process?

5.9.2 Identify the five main levels of corporate ownership and management.

LO 5.10 Describe mergers, acquisitions, and joint ventures.

WHEN BUSINESSES JOIN FORCES

Today's business environment includes many complex relationships among businesses and not-for-profit organizations. Two firms may team up to develop a product or to co-market products. One company may buy another company. Large corporations may split into smaller units. The list of alliances can be as varied as the organizations themselves, but the major trends in corporate ownership are mergers and acquisitions (M&A) and joint ventures.

Mergers and Acquisitions (M&A)

The terms *merger* and *acquisition* are often used interchangeably, but their meanings are different. In a **merger**, two or more firms combine to form one company. In an **acquisition**, one firm purchases the other. This purchase means that the buyer acquires the firm's property and assets *and* takes on the firm's debt. Acquisitions also occur when one firm buys a division or a subsidiary from another firm. A recent study looked at mergers and acquisitions in the global mining sector. The study suggests Canadian firms are major players in this sector. Canadian firms were involved in 36 percent of the almost 3,000 deals that represented more than $113 billion in value.[48]

Mergers can be classified as vertical, horizontal, or conglomerate. A **vertical merger** combines firms operating at different levels in the production and marketing process. For example, the combination of a manufacturer and a large retailer is a vertical merger. A vertical merger pursues one of two main goals: (1) to ensure adequate flows of raw materials and supplies needed for a firm's products, or (2) to increase distribution. Microsoft is well known for acquiring small firms that have developed products with strong market potential, such as Teleo, a provider of voice over Internet protocol (VoIP) software and services that can be used to make phone calls via the Internet.

A **horizontal merger** joins firms in the same industry. Firms use a horizontal merger to diversify, to increase their customer base, to cut costs, or to expand product lines. This type of merger is popular in the auto industry. India-based Tata Motors bought the Jaguar and Land Rover brands from Ford Motor Corp., and Volkswagen owns Audi and Porsche.

A **conglomerate merger** combines unrelated firms. The most common reasons for a conglomerate merger are to diversify, to increase sales, or to spend a cash surplus to avoid a takeover attempt. Conglomerate mergers may join firms in totally unrelated industries. General Electric is well known for its conglomerate mergers, including its ownership of healthcare services and household appliances. Experts debate whether conglomerate mergers are a good idea. Those in favour of such mergers say that a company can use its management expertise to succeed in a variety of industries. But the obvious downside is that a huge conglomerate can spread its resources too thin to be successful in any one market.

Joint Ventures: Specialized Partnerships

A **joint venture** is a partnership between companies for a specific activity. Sometimes a company enters into a joint venture with a local firm to share the operation's costs, risks, management, and profits. This type of joint venture is common when a firm wants to start a business in a foreign market. A joint venture can also help companies solve a common problem.

merger an agreement in which two or more firms combine to form one company.

acquisition an agreement in which one firm purchases another.

vertical merger a merger that combines firms operating at different levels in the production and marketing process.

horizontal merger a merger that joins firms in the same industry for the purpose of diversification, increasing customer bases, cutting costs, or expanding product lines.

conglomerate merger a merger that combines unrelated firms usually with the goal of diversification, increasing sales, or spending a cash surplus to avoid a takeover attempt.

joint venture a partnership between companies for a specific activity.

Joint ventures between for-profit firms and not-for-profit organizations provide great benefits for both parties. Becel has been the title sponsor for the Heart and Stroke Foundation's Ride for Heart for over 20 years, helping to raise funds supporting research and education on heart disease and stroke.

Joint ventures between for-profit firms and not-for-profit organizations are becoming common. These partnerships provide benefits for both parties. Not-for-profit organizations receive the funding, marketing exposure, and sometimes the staff they might not have on their own. The CIBC, New Balance, East Side Mario's, The Running Room, Canpar, and Revlon are some of the Canadian businesses that have partnered with the Canadian Breast Cancer Foundation's Run for the Cure. The annual event raised $25 million in 2014 across the country.[49]

Joint ventures between not-for-profits and for-profit firms are often good for businesses, too. Firms that partner with environmental groups can cut costs, save energy, and reduce waste. For example, McDonald's partnered with the Environmental Defense Fund. McDonald's was then successful in phasing out harmful packaging, converting much of its cooking oil to biodiesel, getting rid of more than 136 million kilograms of packaging, and reducing restaurant waste by more than 30 percent.[50]

✓ ASSESSMENT CHECK

5.10.1 Distinguish between a merger and an acquisition.

5.10.2 What are the different kinds of mergers?

5.10.3 What is a joint venture?

WHAT'S AHEAD

The next chapter focuses on the driving forces that lead to new businesses: entrepreneurs. It examines the differences between a small-business owner and an entrepreneur. It also identifies the personality traits common to most entrepreneurs. The chapter also describes the process of launching a new venture, including identifying opportunities, locating financing, and turning good ideas into successful businesses. Finally, the chapter explores a method for infusing the entrepreneurial spirit into established businesses—intrapreneurship.

RETURN TO INSIDE BUSINESS

Pi Athlete Management Inc.: Advising Athletes about Their Careers and More

According to Daniel Smajovits of Pi Athlete Management, the firm avoids "hustling" athletes. Instead, it relies on word-of-mouth referrals to attract new clients.

"Our short game is to represent professional athletes. The athletes come to us via word-of-mouth and through athletes whom we currently represent. We are not actively trying to poach other athletes from their agents for two reasons: (1) We are trying to eliminate the sleaze factor in this industry. I do not want to be the guy in the hotel lobby passing out business cards to currently represented players. (2) We do not want to take on more than we can handle. If an athlete comes to us, we will see what we can do for him: While it might sound nice to say that we represent 20 professional athletes, if I can't be there equally for each guy, then it's all smoke and mirrors. If we know that an athlete is unhappy with his current representation, we would love to speak with him as we know we can do better by him, but it's not something we actively pursue.

"Additionally, for our professional athletes, one unique selling point about us is that we can take care of all their off-field needs in house. We're working with one lawyer and one CA/CPA, both with a tremendous amount of experience and a vast international network, so all their legal, financial, and tax work can be handled by us. My background in marketing and PR is vital to provide media training, to seek out marketing opportunities, and [to] coordinate media appearances."

QUESTIONS FOR CRITICAL THINKING

1. What other professional consulting services would be helpful for Pi Athlete Management to offer to athletes?
2. What else can Pi Athlete Management do to increase its network of consultants and athletes?

SUMMARY OF LEARNING OBJECTIVES

LO 5.1 Describe the characteristics of a small business.

A small business is an independently owned business that has fewer than 100 employees and revenues less than $2 million. A small business is not usually the leading business in its field. It meets industry-specific size standards for income or number of employees. A business is classified as large when its number of employees or revenue exceeds these standards.

✓ ASSESSMENT CHECK ANSWERS

5.1.1 How does Industry Canada define *small business*? Industry Canada defines a small business as an independent business that has fewer than 100 employees and revenues not more than $2 million.

5.1.2 In what industries do small businesses play a significant role? Small businesses provide many jobs in construction, agriculture, wholesale trade, services, and retail trade.

LO 5.2 Discuss the contributions of small businesses to the economy.

Small businesses create new jobs and new industries. They often hire people who have difficulty finding jobs at larger firms. Small firms give businesspeople the opportunity and outlet for developing new ideas. Sometimes these new ideas become entirely new industries. Small businesses also develop new and improved goods and services.

✓ ASSESSMENT CHECK ANSWERS

5.2.1 What are the three key ways that small businesses contribute to the economy? Small businesses create new jobs, create new industries, and provide innovation.

5.2.2 How are new industries formed? New industries are formed when small businesses shift their focus to meet consumer interests and preferences. Innovation and new technology can play a significant role. In addition, new industries can be created when both the business world and consumers see a need for change.

LO 5.3 Discuss why small businesses fail.

About 96 percent of small businesses that enter the marketplace are in business for one full year, 85 percent are in business for three years, and 70 percent are in business for five years. Failure is often attributed to management inexperience, inadequate financing, and difficulty meeting government regulations.

✓ ASSESSMENT CHECK ANSWERS

5.3.1 What percentage of small businesses are still operating five years after starting? About 70 percent are in business after five years.

5.3.2 What are the three main causes of small-business failure? The three main causes of small-business failure are management inexperience, inadequate financing, and difficulty meeting government regulations.

LO 5.4 Describe the features of an effective business plan.

A complete business plan contains an executive summary, an introduction, financial and marketing sections, and résumés of the business principals. An effective business plan uses these five sections and includes the company's mission, an outline of what makes the company unique, identification of customers and competitors, financial evaluation of the industry and market, and an assessment of the risks.

✓ ASSESSMENT CHECK ANSWERS

5.4.1 What are the five main sections of a business plan? The five sections of a business plan are the executive summary, introduction, financial section, marketing section, and résumés of the principals.

5.4.2 Why is an effective business plan important to the success of a firm? The business plan puts in writing all the reasons the firm can be successful. It contains the company's mission and addresses many issues, including the vision of its founders and why the company is unique. It is the document that is needed to obtain financing. The business plan also creates a framework for the organization.

LO 5.5 Identify the assistance available to small businesses.

The Business Development Bank of Canada (BDC) is a government agency that assists, counsels, and protects the interests of small businesses in Canada. The BDC was created by an act of Parliament in 1944. It operates across Canada through offices and resource centres that provide long-term financial assistance and management counselling. The BDC also provides training, technical assistance, and education to help small businesses prepare for doing business in foreign markets. Statistics show that most failures in small businesses happen because of poor management. For this reason, the BDC works to improve the management skills of small-business owners and managers.

✓ ASSESSMENT CHECK ANSWERS

5.5.1 What are the various ways the BDC helps small businesses? The BDC provides long-term financial assistance and management counselling. It also provides business information, advice, and training to owners of small businesses.

5.5.2 What are business incubators? Business incubators are programs that community agencies set up to help small businesses get started. Their services can include low-cost rental space, shared clerical staff, and shared office equipment, such as computers.

5.5.3 Why are small businesses good opportunities for women? Women feel they can achieve more as small-business owners and can balance family and work more easily if they own their own firms.

LO 5.6 Explain franchising.

A franchisor is a large firm that allows a small-business owner (a franchisee) to market and sell the larger firm's products under its brand name in return for a fee. The franchisor's opportunities include the possibilities of expansion and greater profits. The franchisee's benefits include name recognition, quick startup, support from the franchisor, and the freedom of small-business ownership.

✓ ASSESSMENT CHECK ANSWERS

5.6.1 What is the difference between a franchisor and a franchisee? A franchisor permits a small-business owner (the franchisee) to market and sell the franchisor's products under its brand name in return for a fee.

5.6.2 How does franchising benefit both parties? Benefits to the franchisor include opportunities for expansion and greater profits. Benefits to the franchisee include name recognition, quick startup, support from the franchisor, and the freedom of small-business ownership.

LO 5.7 Outline the forms of private business ownership.

The three legal forms of business ownership are sole proprietorships, partnerships, and corporations. A sole proprietorship is owned and operated by one person. Sole proprietorships are easy to set up and offer great operating flexibility, but the owner is personally liable for all of the firm's debts and legal responsibilities. In a partnership, two or more individuals share responsibility for owning and running the business. Partnerships are relatively easy to set up, but they do not protect either partner from liability. A corporation is a separate legal entity from its owners. Investors receive shares of stock in the firm, and owners have no legal and financial liability beyond their individual investments. The legal structure of a not-for-profit corporation requires that its goals do not include earning a profit.

✓ ASSESSMENT CHECK ANSWERS

5.7.1 What are the key differences between sole proprietorships and partnerships? Sole proprietorships have more management flexibility and are easier to dissolve than partnerships. Partnerships require shared workload and decision making, whereas sole proprietorships are entirely the responsibility of one business owner.

5.7.2 What is a corporation? A corporation is a legal organization that has assets and liabilities separate from the assets and liabilities of its owners. A corporation can be a large or small business.

5.7.3 What is the main characteristic of a not-for-profit corporation? A not-for-profit corporation is an organization whose goals do not include pursuing a profit. Governments have separate legal provisions for organizational structures and operations of not-for-profit corporations. They are also exempt from paying income taxes.

LO 5.8 Describe public and collective business ownership.

In public ownership, a government unit or agency owns and operates an organization. Collective ownership sets up an organization called a cooperative. The owners join forces to operate all or part of the activities in their firm or industry.

✓ ASSESSMENT CHECK ANSWERS

5.8.1 What is public ownership? Public ownership occurs when a unit or agency of government owns and operates an organization.

5.8.2 What is collective ownership? Where are cooperatives typically found, and what benefits do they provide small businesses? Collective ownership sets up an organization called a *cooperative* (or *co-op*). The owners work together to operate all or part of the activities in their firm or industry. Cooperatives are frequently found among agricultural businesses. They can also occur in retail. Cooperatives allow small firms to pool their resources, share equipment and expertise, and help each other through difficult times.

LO 5.9 Discuss the organizational structure of corporations.

Shareholders are the owners of a corporation. In return for their financial investments, they receive shares of stock in the company. Shareholders elect a board of directors, who sets overall policy. The board hires the chief executive officer (CEO), who then hires the managers.

✓ ASSESSMENT CHECK ANSWERS

5.9.1 What are the two key elements of the incorporation process? The two key elements are where to incorporate and the corporate charter.

5.9.2 Identify the five main levels of corporate ownership and management. The five levels are the shareholders, the board of directors, top management, middle management, and supervisory management.

LO 5.10 Describe mergers, acquisitions, and joint ventures.

In a merger, two or more firms combine to form one company. A vertical merger combines firms operating at different levels in the production and marketing process. A horizontal merger joins firms in the same industry. A conglomerate merger combines unrelated firms. An acquisition occurs when one firm purchases another. A joint venture is a partnership between companies for a specific activity.

✓ ASSESSMENT CHECK ANSWERS

5.10.1 Distinguish between a merger and an acquisition. In a merger, two or more firms combine to form one company. In an acquisition, one firm purchases another company. The buyer acquires the firm's property and assets *and* takes on the firm's debt. Acquisitions also occur when one firm buys a division or a subsidiary from another firm.

5.10.2 What are the different kinds of mergers? Mergers can be classified as vertical, horizontal, or conglomerate. A vertical merger combines firms operating at different levels in the production and marketing process. A horizontal merger joins firms in the same industry. A conglomerate merger combines unrelated firms.

5.10.3 What is a joint venture? A joint venture is a partnership between organizations formed for a specific activity.

BUSINESS TERMS YOU NEED TO KNOW

acquisition 145	common shares 144	home-based businesses 125	preferred shares 144
board of directors 144	conglomerate merger 145	horizontal merger 145	shareholders 143
Business Development Bank of Canada (BDC) 133	corporation 140	joint venture 145	small business 124
	franchisee 136	merger 145	sole proprietorship 138
business incubator 133	franchising 135	not-for-profit corporations 140	venture capital 133
business plan 131	franchisor 136	partnership 139	vertical merger 145

REVIEW QUESTIONS

1. Describe how a small business might use innovation to create new jobs.
2. Why do so many small businesses fail before they reach their fifth year?
3. What are the benefits of developing and writing an effective business plan?
4. What is the Business Development Bank of Canada? How does it assist small companies, financially and in other ways?
5. Describe how local governments and business incubators help small firms to set up and grow.
6. Why are so many small-business owners attracted to franchising? When would it be better to start an entirely new business instead of purchasing a franchise?
7. What are the upsides and downsides of the traditional corporate structure?
8. Cooperatives appear frequently in agriculture. Describe another industry where collective ownership would work well, and explain why.
9. In a sole proprietorship and in partnerships, the owners and the managers are the same people. How are ownership and management separated in corporations?
10. How can a joint venture between a commercial firm and a not-for-profit organization help both parties achieve their goals?

PROJECTS AND TEAMWORK APPLICATIONS

1. Research a large firm to learn more about its beginnings as a small business. Who founded the company? Does the firm still produce its original product or service, or does it provide a new product or service?
2. Go to the Canadian Franchise Association website, www.cfa.ca, to research franchises. Choose a franchise that interests you and look up its startup requirements. Would you run a franchise in a partnership with someone you know? Why or why not? Present your findings in class.
3. Think of an idea for a small business. Research the industry and the major competition online. Draft a business plan. Will your firm be a sole proprietorship or a partnership? Include this decision in your business plan.
4. Identify an organization that is owned by a unit or agency of government, such as VIA Rail or BC Hydro. Imagine that you have been hired by as a consultant. You must decide whether the organization should remain publicly owned. Research its successes and failures. Write a memo to explain your conclusion.
5. Identify a business and a not-for-profit organization that could form a joint venture that would be good for both parties. Write a proposal or create an advertisement for the event or activity that the organizations could present.

WEB ASSIGNMENTS

1. **Small-business successes.** Visit the website www.inc.com/31-stories-of-small-business-success/index.html. Scroll through the success stories and choose one that interests you. Read the feature and prepare a brief report answering these questions:
   a. What does the firm do?
   b. Where did the idea come from?
   c. What expertise does the owner have?
   d. How did the business begin?
   e. Who are its competitors?
2. **Business Development Bank of Canada (BDC).** Go to the BDC's website at www.bdc.ca. Click on Articles and Tools and have a look at the articles. Identify one article that you believe provides the most useful information for a small-business owner. Write a summary of the article's highlights.

Note: Internet Web addresses change frequently. If you do not find the exact sites listed, you may need to access the organization's or company's home page and search from there.

6 | STARTING YOUR OWN BUSINESS: THE ENTREPRENEURSHIP ALTERNATIVE

LEARNING OBJECTIVES

LO 6.1 Describe what is an entrepreneur and the different types of entrepreneurs.

LO 6.2 Explain why people choose to become entrepreneurs.

LO 6.3 Discuss factors that support and expand opportunities for entrepreneurs.

LO 6.4 Identify the traits of successful entrepreneurs.

LO 6.5 Summarize the process of starting a new venture.

LO 6.6 Explain intrapreneurship.

INSIDE BUSINESS

Sharing Economy Sparks Start-Ups

Find a need and fill it is the age-old way to start a new business venture. New business opportunities are rapidly emerging in what is referred to as the "sharing economy" and technologies like smartphone apps are providing individual entrepreneurs the opportunity to participate like never before. Individuals are sharing their cars, apartments, clothes, tools, sports equipment—the list continues to grow daily. The business models that bring participants together usually include direct money payment and can include services as well. For example, the ride sharing service Uber allows anyone with a car to offer rides for a fee. Needless to say, Uber is facing complaints of unfair competition from the taxi industry across Canada, as Uber drivers do not pay the same licensing and other fees required of registered taxis.

Perhaps a shared transportation solution is at hand with FlightCar. For most travellers, parking at the airport is the easiest, although not the least expensive, option. If you head to a typical large airport, you will see parking lots filled with private cars. Upon closer inspection, you will also see lots filled with rental cars waiting for customers. What if the owners of these parked cars could be connected with travellers who want to rent cars? In this way, cars would not sit idle while travelers are away and there would be no need for large fleets of rental cars to own and maintain. In exchange for allowing FlightCar to rent their car to a traveller, the car owner is paid a small fee and is provided with free parking—hopefully the car is actually being rented by a fellow traveler. The rental charges are lower than what a traditional car rental firm would charge.

Airbnb is probably the best-known sharing business. Started a little more than five years ago, this firm offers a web-based service linking travellers who want to rent rooms with individuals who have space in their homes or apartments to rent. Airbnb charges owners 3 percent of the nightly room charge and renters 10 percent.

The company prescreens individuals to ensure guests and owners have a good experience and even suggests that individuals check each other's information on social media sites such as Facebook. For the room owners, it is a good deal because they can make some money from their unused rooms; for the travellers, they can stay in private homes for a fraction of the cost of a hotel room. More than 9 million people have used Airbnb's services, with more than a half a million listings worldwide.

Peer-to-peer sharing is part of a fast-growing trend toward renting and not owning. *Forbes* estimates that this new "share economy" will be greater than $3.5 billion and grow at over 25 percent per year. What is fuelling this trend? For one thing, it is the access to information via the Internet, which provides search engines, mobile devices, and social media pages and profiles. There is also the idea that spending money for little-used goods may not make much sense. So, the next time you drive by airport parking, open your closet, or store holiday decorations in an unused room, think about the items you own that could be shared with others—for a fee. You might be able to make a few dollars by renting these items out or, like FlightCar, Uber, and Airbnb founders, maybe make millions, by starting a company to help others do the same.[1]

CHAPTER 6 OVERVIEW

You think you want to start and run your own company. Like the founders of Uber, Airbnb, and other start-ups you have a great idea for a new business and you dream of fame and fortune. If you are entrepreneurial, you're not alone. More than ever, people like you, your classmates, and your friends are choosing to be entrepreneurs.

How do you become an entrepreneur? Experts advise people who want to be entrepreneurs to learn as much as possible about business. Take courses and complete academic programs such as the one you are currently taking. Try to gain practical experience by working part-time or full-time. Shoshana Finn learned about the fashion business while she was growing up. Both her grandfather and father ran successful garment manufacturing businesses. You can also learn about the upsides and downsides of entrepreneurship by reading newspaper and magazine articles and biographies of successful entrepreneurs. You will learn how entrepreneurs handle the challenges of starting their businesses. Need advice on how to launch and grow a new venture? Turn to magazines such as *Entrepreneur*, *Forbes*, *Fast Company*, *Success*, and *Inc.* You can also get assistance from entrepreneurship associations, such as the Canadian Federation of Independent Business (CFIB). Anyone who wants to be an entrepreneur should visit the websites listed in **Figure 6.1**.

Canada Business	www.canadabusiness.ca
Business Development Bank	www.bdc.ca
Entrepreneur.com	www.entrepreneur.com
Canadian Chamber of Commerce	www.chamber.ca
U.S. Chamber of Commerce	www.uschamber.com
Kauffman Foundation	www.kauffman.org
U.S. Small Business Administration	www.sba.gov
The Wall Street Journal Small Business	http://www.wsj.com/public/page/small-business.html

FIGURE 6.1 Internet Resources for Entrepreneurs

In this chapter, we focus on how to enter the world of entrepreneurship. This chapter describes the activities of entrepreneurs, the different kinds of entrepreneurs, and the reason more and more people are choosing to be entrepreneurs. We will discuss the business environment where entrepreneurs work, the characteristics that help entrepreneurs succeed, and how they start new ventures. The chapter ends with a discussion of how large companies try to keep the entrepreneurial spirit alive and well.

LO 6.1 Describe what is an entrepreneur and the different types of entrepreneurs.

WHAT IS AN ENTREPRENEUR?

entrepreneur a person who seeks a profitable opportunity and takes the necessary risks to set up and operate a business.

An **entrepreneur** is a risk taker in the private enterprise system, a person who seeks a profitable opportunity and takes the necessary risks to set up and operate a business. Think about Vancouver's Jim Pattison, founder of the Jim Pattison Group. He started by purchasing a car dealership in 1961. Today, he is head of a private Canadian corporation with over 39,000 employees worldwide and 2014 revenues of about $8.4 billion. The company works in the automotive, media, packaging, food sales and distribution, magazine distribution, entertainment, export, and financial industries. Today, the Jim Pattison Group is Canada's second-largest private company.[2]

Entrepreneurs differ from many small-business owners. Many small-business owners share the same drive, creative energy, and desire to succeed. But entrepreneurs are different because one of their major goals is expansion and growth. (Many small-business owners want to keep their businesses small.) Jim Pattison wasn't happy having just one successful business, so he purchased

Chapter 6 Starting Your Own Business: The Entrepreneurship Alternative 155

Vancouver's Jim Pattison is founder of the Jim Pattison Group. In 1961, he purchased a car dealership. Today, he is head of Canada's second-largest private corporation.

and developed others. Entrepreneurs combine their ideas and drive with money, employees, and other resources to create a business that meets a need.

Entrepreneurs also differ from managers. Managers are employees who direct others to reach an organization's goals. Owners of some small startup firms work as owner-managers to carry out their plans for their businesses and to make up for human resource limitations at their new companies. Entrepreneurs may also perform a managerial role, but their main responsibility is to use the resources of their organizations—employees, money, equipment, and facilities—to accomplish their goals.

Studies have identified certain personality traits and behaviours common to entrepreneurs that differ from the traits and behaviours needed for managerial success. One of these traits is the willingness to take on the risks of starting a new venture. Some take that risk because they need to—they've left or lost their previous jobs or just need a way to make money. Others, like Jim Pattison, want a challenge or a different quality of life. Entrepreneurial characteristics are examined in detail later in this chapter.

Categories of Entrepreneurs

Entrepreneurs use their talents in different situations. These differences can be classified into three categories: classic entrepreneurs, serial entrepreneurs, and social entrepreneurs.

Classic entrepreneurs see business opportunities and set aside resources to gain access to those markets. Andrew Henle of TronSports.ca is a classic entrepreneur. As an avid amateur hockey player in Montreal-area leagues, he saw a niche in the sports equipment and accessories market and built an online storefront. The site caters mostly to teams and serious athletes looking for high caliber equipment such as hockey skates, sticks, protective padding, and other equipment at competitive prices and regular promotional deals.

A classic entrepreneur starts a new company by seeing a business opportunity and setting aside resources to gain access to a new market. **Serial entrepreneurs** are different. They start one business, run it, and then start and run more businesses, one after another. Elon Musk, the founder of such businesses as PayPal, Tesla Motors, Solar City, and SpaceX, is a serial entrepreneur. Jessica Herrin is also a serial entrepreneur. When Herrin graduated from college with an economics degree, she joined a software startup firm where she got hooked on the idea of "unlimited potential." At age 24, Herrin co-founded WeddingChannel.com in Los Angeles, which grew within a few

classic entrepreneur a person who sees a business opportunity and sets aside resources to gain access to that market.

serial entrepreneur a person who starts one business, runs it, and then starts and runs more businesses, one after another.

social entrepreneur a person who sees societal problems and uses business principles to develop new solutions.

✓ ASSESSMENT CHECK

6.1.1 What tools do entrepreneurs use to create a new business?

6.1.2 How do entrepreneurs differ from managers?

6.1.3 What do classic entrepreneurs and social entrepreneurs have in common?

6.1.4 Is a social entrepreneur simply a philanthropist who gives to good causes to help others?

years to 100 employees and $21 million in revenues. When her firm was purchased by The Knot, Herrin went on to start Stella & Dot, a high-quality fashion jewellery business sold by more than 14,000 independent representatives at parties and online. Stella & Dot now has $200 million in revenues, and the jewellery has been featured in the business and fashion press—and perhaps more important, on celebrities.[3]

Some entrepreneurs focus on solving society's challenges through their businesses. **Social entrepreneurs** see a societal problem and use business principles to develop new solutions. Social entrepreneurs develop new solutions that help humanity. More than 50 years ago, a group of seven Indian women gathered one afternoon to roll out dough to make traditional crackers. They saw an opportunity to make and market these crackers for a wider audience. They set up a women's cooperative that was based on this idea. They called their business Lijjat Papad and hoped to empower Indian women entrepreneurs. Since then, the cooperative's president, Jyoti Naik, has led the cooperative to become one of India's most successful business ventures. The company now produces a wide variety of bakery products, spices, and flour. It has 62 branches across India. The cooperative brand is one of the most popular and trusted in India. It is viewed as the best-run small-village cooperative in the nation.[4]

LO 6.2 Explain why people choose to become entrepreneurs.

REASONS TO CHOOSE ENTREPRENEURSHIP AS A CAREER PATH

If you want to run your own business, you have lots of company. During one recent year, about 10,000 new businesses were created each month in Canada. The United States has more people and created more businesses—there, 543,000 new businesses were created each month. In both countries, new businesses in services and the construction industry had the highest rates of activity.[5]

In the past few decades, more people have shown interest in entrepreneurial careers. They may have been encouraged in part by publicity around the successes of entrepreneurs such as Mark Zuckerberg. He launched the global social-networking website Facebook while he was a student at Harvard University.

As shown in **Figure 6.2**, people become entrepreneurs for one or more of four major reasons: a desire to be their own boss, a desire to succeed financially, a desire to attain job security, and a desire to improve their quality of life. Each of these reasons is described in more detail in the following sections.

Being Your Own Boss

One of the biggest reasons for becoming an entrepreneur is the chance to be your own boss. Entrepreneurs have the freedom to make all the decisions. In Montreal's West Island area, Carmine Petrillo has made Monster Gym an inviting community-oriented gym for people who are serious and not-so-serious about exercise. When gym clients need to decide whether to renew their memberships or join another club, they often consider the condition of the exercise equipment. For gym owners, deciding when to upgrade to new equipment is an expensive decision: a single exercise machine can cost thousands of dollars. Monster Gym clients are lucky. Carmine has made such decisions on his own since opening his doors in 1994. He is good at looking ahead to keep meeting the needs of his suburban clientele. After all, they have grown used to having the latest and best exercise equipment. Carmine's decision to upgrade equipment often and regularly has helped grow the client base to 4,500 people.[6]

FIGURE 6.2 Why People Become Entrepreneurs

Desire to Be One's Own Boss
Desire to Succeed Financially
Desire for Job Security
Desire for an Improved Quality of Life

Carmine Petrillo created Monster Gym, an inviting community-oriented gym for people who are serious and not-so-serious about exercise. For many people, the main reason for being an entrepreneur is to control when, where, and how they work.

CAREER KICKSTART

Communicating by Email, Text Message, or Social Networking Updates: You Don't Have to Be All Thumbs

Most entrepreneurs use email, texting, social networking updates, and other electronic communications to reach their customers, suppliers, distributors, employees, and others. That communication often takes place on the run; when you are your own boss, you are busy taking care of many tasks. You may think of yourself as being fast with the cellphone or smartphone keyboard, and maybe you can send off an email in no time. Still, it might be a good idea to review a few etiquette tips to make sure your messages sound professional.

- Don't write in all caps. Using all capital letters makes the message look frantic, or as if you are yelling.

- On the subject line, do *not* write "Important—Please Read." That kind of message is likely to end up in a "delete" box, unread. Also, try to avoid sending any kind of "forwarded" messages—for the same reason. Instead, use a short but descriptive subject line so the person you are emailing knows what the message is about. An example is "Review of Tuesday's Meeting."

- Avoid slang expressions and shorthand, such as "LOL," "ru," and "L8." Also don't use smiley or sad-face icons.

- Be friendly but not too familiar. Never include jokes in a business email or text message.

- Be brief. A short message is more helpful than a long message. If you need to say more, then end the email by saying you will follow up with a phone call.

- Remember that your computer and your phone are like a tape recorder. Messages can be saved and stored. You do *not* want to make an unprofessional comment that could cause problems later. Never add personal messages to professional messages. Avoid complaints or criticisms that could hurt your company's image or the reputation of others.

Sources: Mark Grossman, "Email Etiquette Is Important," Grossman Law Group, accessed March 16, 2010, www.ecomputerlaw.com; "Business Email Etiquette: What You Should Know BEFORE You Hit Send," accessed March 16, 2010, www.evancarmichael.com/Women-Entrepreneurs; Karl Stolley and Allen Brizee, "Email Etiquette," *Purdue Owl*, accessed March 16, 2010 http://owl.english.purdue.edu; Nina Kaufman, "Making it Legal," *Entrepreneur*, accessed March 16, 2010, http://legal.entrepreneur.com.

Being your own boss usually means having to make all the important decisions. It also means engaging in most—if not all—of the communication related to your business, including dealing with customers, suppliers, distributors, retailers, and others. The "Career Kickstart" feature offers tips for professional-style communication—even if you're on the run and using your thumbs.

In 1987, Cora Tsouflidou opened her first restaurant in Montreal. She offered a big-breakfast menu of crepes, omelettes, fruits, and cereals. Her recipe of high-quality, healthier food was a hit with customers. Today, the family-run company has 130 Chez Cora franchise locations across Canada. Family members actively manage the firm and enjoy their financial success.[7]

Financial Success

Entrepreneurs create wealth. Many start their ventures with the specific goal of becoming rich—or at least financially successful. Entrepreneurs often believe they have an idea for a better product. They want to be the first to bring it to market—and to receive the financial rewards as a result. Entrepreneurs believe they won't achieve their greatest success by working for someone else—and they're generally right. Of course, the downside is that when they fail, they become unemployed.

Job Security

The demand for skilled employees remains high in many industries. But working for a company, even a *Fortune* 500 firm, is no guarantee of job security. In fact, over the past 10 years, large companies have looked for efficiencies by downsizing and getting rid of more jobs than they created. As a result, more and more workers—both first-time job seekers and laid-off long-term employees—are deciding to create their own job security by starting their own businesses. Having your own business doesn't guarantee job security, but research has found that most newly created jobs come from small businesses. Many of those new jobs are in new companies.[8]

Economies are changing overseas. Workers there are discovering the benefits of entrepreneurship compared with being employed by big firms. In China, entire industries are government-owned, such as banking, steel, and telecommunications. Many young Chinese businesspeople are starting their own small firms. China has nearly 500 million people under the age of 30. Their role models are Bill Gates and Michael Dell, reports an entrepreneurship professor at the Europe International Business School in Shanghai.[9]

Quality of Life

Entrepreneurship is a good career option for people who want to improve their quality of life. Starting a business means independence and some freedom to decide when, where, and how to work. A **lifestyle entrepreneur** is a person who starts a business for two reasons: to gain flexibility in work hours and to gain control over his or her life. It does *not* mean working fewer hours or easier work. Generally it is the opposite—people who start their own businesses often work longer and harder than ever before, at least in the beginning. But they enjoy being successful, both materially and in the way they live their lives.

Zhena Muzyka, a single mom, needed a job that gave her flexibility and earning power. Her young son, "needed operations [for kidney disease], and the insurance wasn't going to cover them. I had to come up with a job where I could have him with me because he had special needs," Muzyka explains. So she combined her interest in herbal medicine with fair-trade practices. That's how she started her firm, Gypsy Tea. Today, Muzyka's son is healthy, and Gypsy Tea is a multimillion-dollar firm. It produces flavoured teas grown on fair-trade farms in Peru, India, and other countries. Workers at these farms receive health care, clean water, maternity leave, child care, and other benefits. New products have been added to the Gypsy Tea line, including candles and beads. "It's the most 'worth-it' thing I've ever done," says Muzyka of Gypsy Tea.[10] Another group of entrepreneurs also found a way to make their business fit their lifestyle and their creative interest in home fragrance products. Read about Fruits & Passion co-owners Jean Hurteau; his wife, France Menard; and brother, Guy Hurteau, in the "Hit & Miss" feature.

lifestyle entrepreneur a person who starts a business to reduce work hours and create a more relaxed lifestyle.

✓ ASSESSMENT CHECK

6.2.1 What are the four main reasons people choose to become entrepreneurs?

6.2.2 What factors affect the entrepreneur's job security?

HIT & MISS

Fruits & Passion for Lifestyle Products

Fruits & Passion is a popular beauty, body, and lifestyle products retailer. This business is the result of a great success story in a very competitive global marketplace. The firm creates unique fragrances for oils, candles, other personal care products. It uses ingredients gathered from around the world to make its products and then wraps them in attractive packaging.

Fruits & Passion was started in 1991 by Jean Hurteau; his wife, France Menard; and his brother, Guy Hurteau. The threesome believed that the "lifestyle market" for personal luxuries was beginning to grow, and they wanted to be part of it. Stores like The Body Shop were leading the way in the personal care market. But the partners sensed that people's desire for personal lifestyle quality would also lead to demand for other products for the home. For example, small decorative candles could enhance a room's quality if the design and fragrance were just right. Little things could make a big difference in their kitchens, bathrooms, and bedrooms.

Before long, the firm was selling its creative products through a dozen Canadian retail stores, which they still own and operate today. But, to truly realize the potential sales, the company needed a large retail distribution network to provide products to customers in more markets.

Currently, the firm sells its products through 175 Fruits & Passion retailers—93 are in Canada—and through more than 2,000 independent retailers around the world. Fruits & Passion franchise retailers can be found in England, Taiwan, China, Morocco, Mexico, France, the United States, and Canada. The company's website helps people to learn about the variety of products it sells and is set up for online sales.

Questions for Critical Thinking

1. Why do these products sell so well around the world?

2. What entrepreneurial characteristics do you think were needed to make this business a success?

Sources: Fruits and Passion, accessed April 8, 2015, www.fruits-passion.ca.

THE ENVIRONMENT FOR ENTREPRENEURS

LO 6.3 Discuss factors that support and expand opportunities for entrepreneurs.

Are you ready to start your own company? Do some research about the environment where you want to do business. You'll need to think about several important overall factors. First is the economy—whether it is stalled or booming, you may find opportunities. Think about where you want to locate your business.

The general attitude toward entrepreneurs in North America is positive. In addition to favourable public attitudes and more financing options, four additional factors also support and expand opportunities for entrepreneurs: globalization, education, information technology, and demographic and economic trends (see **Figure 6.3**). Each of these factors is discussed in the following sections.

Globalization

The rapid globalization of business has created many opportunities for entrepreneurs. Entrepreneurs market their products abroad and hire international talent. Most of the fastest-growing small Canadian companies have international sales—usually to the United States. For example, despite being based in Montreal, TronSports.ca sells hockey and other sports equipment to Americans through its dedicated U.S. site Besthockey.com.[11]

Entrepreneurship is growing around the world. The role of entrepreneurs is growing in most industrialized countries, in newly industrialized countries, and in the emerging free-market countries in central and eastern Europe. However, the level of entrepreneurship varies. Worldwide,

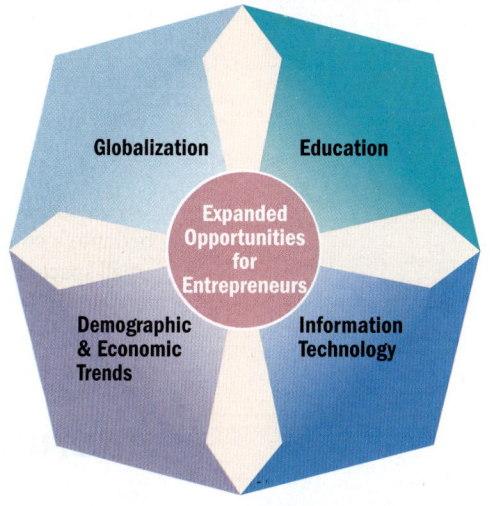

FIGURE 6.3 Factors Supporting and Expanding Opportunities for Entrepreneurs

more than 9 percent of adults are starting or managing a new business. Thailand leads in the number of adults engaged in entrepreneurial activity (27 percent), followed by Peru (26 percent), Colombia (23 percent), Venezuela (20 percent), Dominican Republic (17 percent), and China (16 percent).[12]

India has experienced a big increase in the number of female entrepreneurs. Shahnaz Husain knew the effects that chemical-based beauty care products can have on consumers—and on the environment. In 1971, she opened India's first professional herbal salon on the balcony of her house in Delhi. She now runs a respected beauty care empire called Ayurvedic. Husain's Ayurvedic products contain natural ingredients, ranging from vegetables to diamond dust. "The ancient Indian system of Ayurveda is the oldest and most organized system of herbal healing in the world. I was convinced that it could offer ideal answers to cosmetic care," explains Husain. "I entered highly competitive international markets, without commercial advertising or fancy packaging." Ayurvedic supplies its products to high-end stores in London, Paris, and Milan, and in shops located in Spain and Japan.[13]

Education

In the past 20 years, more educational opportunities have been offered for would-be entrepreneurs. Today, students at many colleges and universities can take a major in entrepreneurship. Dozens of other colleges and universities offer an emphasis in entrepreneurship, and hundreds more offer one or two courses in how to start a business.

Many schools offer opportunities to intern with a startup or to work toward launching a company. Most large universities in Canada, such as Simon Fraser University's Beedie School of Business, host entrepreneurial centres for research and development of new business. The school recently hosted an event that included two expert judges from the CBC program *Dragons' Den*, Jim Treliving and Bruce Croxon.[14]

In addition to schools, many other organizations have opened in recent years to teach entrepreneurship to young people. The Kauffman Center for Entrepreneurial Leadership offers training programs for learners from kindergarten through community college. The centre's Entreprep summer program is taught in cooperation with local colleges and universities. This summer program teaches high-school juniors how to start and manage a company. Students in Free Enterprise (SIFE) is a worldwide not-for-profit organization. College students work with faculty advisors to teach grade-school and high-school students and others the value of private enterprise and entrepreneurship.[15] The Association of Collegiate Entrepreneurs has chapters on many school campuses in Canada and the United States.

You don't have to major in business to become an entrepreneur, but students who major in entrepreneurship or take entrepreneurship courses are three times more likely to start their own business or to help someone else to start a business.[16] You don't have to wait for graduation to launch your first startup, and your business idea doesn't have to change the world. Record numbers of college students are launching their own businesses—while still in school. When Ryan Dickerson was a junior living in a small dorm room at university, he figured out how to turn his bed into a couch during the day. It was a good idea that gave him the furniture he needed for the small space. He designed a special bolster pillow that was the same length as his bed. During the day, this pillow became the "back" of the couch. He called his invention the Rylaxer. The pillows were first made locally and sold on campus. Dickerson immediately drew up a business plan for selling them nationwide.[17]

Information Technology

The explosion in information technology (IT) has been one of the biggest advances for entrepreneurs. Computer and communications technologies have merged, and their costs have dropped. Low-cost technology has given entrepreneurs the tools they need to help them compete with large companies. Information technology helps entrepreneurs to work quickly and efficiently and to provide immediate and helpful customer service. Information technology also increases sales and gives businesses a professional image. In fact, technology has made it possible for a dorm-room

HIT & MISS

Businesses Based at Home Are Booming

The idea itself makes perfect sense: you've been laid off from your full-time job, or you've recently moved to a new area, or you just had a baby. Working from home seems like the ideal solution. But until a few years ago, home-based businesses were not really considered to be real businesses by many in the business community. Most people viewed home-based work as no more challenging—or successful—than stuffing envelopes. All that has changed. Today, more than 6.6 million home-based businesses contribute at least half of their owners' household income. *Homepreneurs* are estimated to employ about one in every 10 private-sector workers—and their businesses are competitive. Technology has made all this possible.

Some homepreneurs run businesses that are entirely based on technology, such as Web development. Stephen Labuda is president of Agency3. He is a former programmer for Deutsche Bank, a large international banking firm. Labuda built websites on the side for several years. Then he quit his job and made Agency3 his full-time, home-based career. The firm's revenues are in the millions, and Labuda has about half a dozen employees. Labuda loves working from home. "I'm not intending to go rent office space," he notes.

Other homepreneurs rely on technology to reach customers, fulfill orders, ship goods, and provide other services. When Michael and Mary Ferrari retired, they realized they needed to supplement their savings—and they didn't want to stop working. So they formed UnusualThreads.com, a company that sells fashions worn by celebrities. The couple still only works the site part-time, but they earn enough money to add to their savings and can take time off to travel. Another homepreneur is Marco Barberini, who launched OvernightPetTags.com several years ago. He now grosses more than $8,000 a month. Barberini discovered how to manufacture and ship pet-identification tags cheaper than his competition. Barberini echoes the advice of every successful homepreneur. "Most people give up too quickly," he says. "Just make sure that [your product] is going to be something that's in demand, and do it."

Questions for Critical Thinking

1. Could any of these home-based businesses succeed without the heavy use of information technology? Why or why not?

2. Outline your own idea for a home-based business that relies on technology.

Sources: Steven Berglas, "Wake-up Call for Newly Hatched Entrepreneurs," *Forbes*, February 6, 2010, www.forbes.com/2010/02/06/baby-boomer-risk-entrepreneur-human-resources-berglas.html; Carol Tice, "Homepreneur Winners Keep Growing Despite Downturn," *Entrepreneur*, February 1, 2010, www.entrepreneur.com/article/218626; John Tozzi, "The Rise of the Homepreneur," *Businessweek*, October 23, 2009 accessed January 8, 2010, www.businessweek.com/smallbiz/content/oct2009/sb20091023_263258.htm.

---

innovator like Ryan Dickerson to compete with a much larger firm. Technology has also assisted in the huge increase of *homepreneurs*—entrepreneurs who run home-based businesses. These successful ventures are described in the "Hit & Miss" feature.

Social networking has also changed the business environment for entrepreneurs. According to a recent study, more than 90 percent of successful companies now use at least one social media tool. Many entrepreneurs have included the use of sites such as Twitter, LinkedIn, and Facebook in their business strategy. They believe that social media will help them reach more customers and grow faster. Social media will give these entrepreneurs a competitive edge. Eric Mattson, a researcher for *Inc.* magazine, believes that social networking is more useful to small firms run by entrepreneurs than to larger firms because "in smaller organizations, there is more room for innovation because it requires [fewer] processes to adopt."[18]

Demographic and Economic Trends

Who else is starting a business? Two groups are most likely to start their own businesses: immigrants to North America and people between the ages of 55 and 64.[19] As baby boomers continue to age and control a large share of North American wealth, the trend is expected to continue. Older entrepreneurs will also have access to their retirement funds and home equity for financing. Many boomers plan to work after retiring from their traditional jobs or careers. Some just want to keep working; others want to add to their income and savings.

As mentioned earlier, more college and university students are becoming entrepreneurs. Ted Livingston, the founder and chief executive officer (CEO) of Waterloo-based Kik Interactive Inc.,

ASSESSMENT CHECK

6.3.1 To what extent is entrepreneurship possible in different countries, and what opportunities does globalization create for today's entrepreneurs?

6.3.2 Identify the educational factors that help expand current opportunities for entrepreneurs.

6.3.3 Describe current demographic trends that suggest new goods and services for entrepreneurial businesses.

studied mechatronics engineering at the University of Waterloo between 2005 and 2009. He founded Kik (then called Unsynced) while in the VeloCity residence in the winter term of 2009. VeloCity is a student residence–based startup incubator that was set up in September 2008 at the University of Waterloo. VeloCity is a community that educates and connects talented, like-minded students with each other and with the surrounding startup community for support and mentorship. At age 23, Livingston showed his appreciation by donating $1 million to VeloCity.[20]

Demographic trends can create opportunities for entrepreneurs. For example, the aging of the population, the growth of ethnic groups, and two-income families can lead to new markets for products and services. Services designed for older consumers, foods that cater to ethnic preferences, and convenience products for busy parents all have an opportunity for success. As the economy rises and falls, entrepreneurs who are flexible and can adapt quickly have the best chance for success. When consumers are less willing to spend money, certain businesses do well. For example, a shoe-repair shop will likely see an increase in business. The Play It Again chain of North American stores sells used sports equipment. This retail chain's business will also likely increase. Skates and protective hockey gear are often used for only one or two seasons before a child has outgrown them. The slightly used equipment will be a great bargain for another family looking to outfit the next Sidney Crosby in their family.[21]

CHARACTERISTICS OF ENTREPRENEURS

LO 6.4 Identify the traits of successful entrepreneurs.

People who start a business of their own are true innovators. They aren't satisfied with things the way they are but want to achieve certain goals on their own terms. Successful entrepreneurs often have parents who were entrepreneurs—or who had dreams of starting their own business. Most entrepreneurs share some specific personality traits. Researchers have studied successful entrepreneurs and report that they are more likely to be curious, passionate, self-motivated, honest, courageous, and flexible. The eight traits shown in **Figure 6.4** are especially important for people who want to succeed as entrepreneurs.

Entrepreneurial Personality

- Vision
- High Energy Level
- Need to Achieve
- Self-Confidence and Optimism
- Tolerance for Failure
- Creativity
- Tolerance for Ambiguity
- Internal Locus of Control

FIGURE 6.4 Characteristics of Entrepreneurs

Vision

Entrepreneurs generally begin with a *vision*—an overall idea for how to make their business idea a success. Then they follow this vision with energy and excitement. Bill Gates and Paul Allen launched Microsoft with the vision of a computer on every desk and in every home, all running Microsoft software. Their vision helped Microsoft become the world's largest marketer of computer software. It guided the company and provided clear direction for employees. This kind of direction was especially helpful as Microsoft grew, adapted, and prospered during huge technological changes.

It can be said that every invention, from the light bulb to the cellphone, started with someone having a vision—viewing the world in a slightly different way. Some inventions have been created out of need or because of a mistake. True entrepreneurs can turn these situations into opportunities. In the healthcare field, penicillin was created by accident. Products with narrower markets have also found success. Jodi Pliszka has an autoimmune disorder that causes baldness. She's an athlete who spent years searching for a product that would keep her head cool and dry under helmets and during exercise. She couldn't find anything, but instead of giving up, she invented what she needed. The result is called HeadlineIt, a thin, lightweight disposable liner worn under helmets, wigs, and hats. Within a few years, Pliszka received a design patent for her product, and sales hit the $1 million mark. Pliszka was first a clinical therapist and an author. Now she is also a successful entrepreneur.[22]

High Energy Level

Entrepreneurs work long and hard to make their visions a reality. Many entrepreneurs work full-time at their regular day jobs and spend weeknights and weekends launching their startups. Many entrepreneurs work alone or with a very small staff. That means that the entrepreneurs themselves do most—if not all—of the work needed to get the business going. This work includes tasks related to the startup's design, marketing, sales, and finances. Most entrepreneurs spend at least 70 hours a week on their new business. This time can affect their other job (if they have one) and their personal life—at least in the beginning.[23] Thus, entrepreneurs need a high level of energy if they want to succeed.

Need to Achieve

Entrepreneurs work hard because they want to do well. Their strong desire to compete helps them to enjoy the challenge of reaching difficult goals. It also promotes a commitment to personal success. A poll by About.com showed Oprah Winfrey as the most admired entrepreneur among adults. She is the first African-American woman to become a billionaire. Winfrey has built an empire that includes television, magazines, and radio. Her own words best illustrate her strong drive: "I don't think of myself as a poor, deprived ghetto girl who made good. I think of myself as somebody who from an early age knew I was responsible for myself, and had to make good."[24] But when teens were polled by Junior Achievement, they picked Apple founder Steven Jobs as their most admired entrepreneur. Teens said that Jobs "made a difference in/improved people's lives or made the world a better place."[25] Both of these entrepreneurs have achieved very high goals.

Self-Confidence and Optimism

Entrepreneurs believe that they can succeed, and their self-confidence and excitement leads to optimism in others. Their optimism can seem like fearlessness in the face of difficult odds. They see opportunities where others see danger. Ishita Khanna founded her not-for-profit organization, Ecosphere, in one of the harshest living areas on the planet, the Spiti valley in Tibet. But this valley is also one of the most beautiful—and searched for—locations for eco-travellers. Khanna believed that if small entrepreneurial businesses in Tibet—especially those run by women—could be linked, they would have more power. She knew it wouldn't be easy. "Spiti's geographical isolation and poor communication infrastructure has been one of the major hurdles," Khanna now admits. But Khanna didn't give up, and Ecosphere recently received the Green Livelihoods Achievement Award from The Sierra Club. "There are numerous doubts that plague one before one takes the plunge," Khanna says. "But if you are passionate about what you want to do, that is half the battle won already."[26]

Tolerance for Failure

Entrepreneurs often succeed because of their strong will and because they continue to try again and again when others would give up. They also view setbacks and failures as learning experiences. They are not easily discouraged or disappointed when things don't go as planned. Bobbi Brown has built a big name in the cosmetics industry. Estée Lauder bought her company, and Brown stayed on in an active role. The brand faced some setbacks after its acquisition. Sales decreased, but Brown never gave up. She met with the CEO, who said the problem was that the cosmetics were not setting themselves apart from the competition. Brown tried to understand the criticism, learned from the setback, and decided to change the culture of the company. She made the advertising photographs more editorial, and approached the cosmetics business as if it were a magazine. The company's numbers improved and today the Bobbi Brown empire is valued at over a billion dollars.[27]

Entrepreneurs often succeed simply because they won't give up. When sales of Bobbi Brown's cosmetics line slowed, she moved the company to a new location and updated its advertising. In the process, she successfully made her company stand out from the competition.

SOLVING AN ETHICAL CONTROVERSY

Entrepreneurs and Ethics: It's Good Business

When you're starting a new business, it's easy to get caught up in the excitement: a fresh start, a new idea, visions of fame and fortune. It might seem harmless to present an overly optimistic sales picture or to be a bit vague about where and how your product will be produced. After all, once your invention hits the stores, sales will skyrocket and everyone will forgive what you said before. But experts in every industry warn against unclear communication and decision making. Your business could fall flat, and failure may come in the form of a damaged image or legal problems. You might be someone who can tolerate some failures, but a wise entrepreneur knows how to prevent other failures—such as a failure of ethics.

Should every new business have a formal code of ethics?

PRO

1. A code of ethics "embodies the ethical commitments of your organization," writes business author Chris MacDonald. "It tells the world who you are, what you stand for, and what to expect when conducting business with you." It also shows leadership.

2. A code of ethics is a necessity in today's business environment. Without it, when a difficult incident or event happens, a small firm may be exposed to "greater risk from regulatory and prosecutorial authorities," observes Michael Connor, publisher of *Business Ethics*.

CON

1. Not every entrepreneurial enterprise, particularly those run by one person, needs a formal code of ethics. A person's word or a handshake is just as effective. The important thing is to convey honesty and integrity about the way your firm will do business.

2. There are too many stories in the media about businesspeople who have failed to make ethical decisions—and not enough stories about the many entrepreneurs who conduct business every day in an ethical manner. A code of ethics will not make a bad person good; nor will lack of a code turn a good person bad.

Summary

Some people argue that writing a formal code of ethics takes too much time; others recommend outsourcing the task to a consultant or another third party. However, the overwhelming majority of business experts advise taking the time and effort to develop a code of ethics. If a company has more than one employee, then all employees should be required to become familiar with the code. As an entrepreneur, you will face many challenges and probably a few failures; but none should be a failure of ethics.

Sources: "Business Ethics," Small Business Administration, accessed March 16, 2010, www.sba.gov; Carter McNamara, "Complete Guide to Ethics Management," *Management Help*, accessed March 16, 2010, www.managementhelp.org; Chris MacDonald, "Considerations for Writing a Code of Ethics," *Streetwise Small Business Book of Lists*, accessed March 16, 2010, www.ethicsweb.ca/codes/writing-a-code-of-ethics.htm; Josh Spiro, "How To Write a Code of Ethics for Business," *Inc.*, February 24, 2010, www.inc.com/guides/how-to-write-a-code-of-ethics.html; Don Knauss, "The Role of Business Ethics in Relationships with Customers," *Forbes*, January 19, 2010, www.forbes.com/2010/01/19/knauss-clorox-ethics-leadership-citizenship-ethics.html.

When things go well, it's easy to take personal credit. But when poor business decisions result in failure, it's more difficult. Truly successful entrepreneurs are willing to take responsibility for their mistakes. That is why an important part of launching any new business is establishing a code of ethics, as discussed in the "Solving an Ethical Controversy" feature.

Creativity

Entrepreneurs think of new ideas for goods and services. They also devise new ways to overcome difficult problems and situations. When we look at the top entrepreneurs in the world, we can see that creativity is a common trait. *Inc.* magazine presents an annual list of the 500 top small businesses, most of which were started by entrepreneurs. The word *solution* is one of the most common words in the names of these companies.

Some entrepreneurs find creative solutions to problems; others find creative ways to complete a task or provide a service. Still others create entirely new products. Aaron Patzer started Mint.com because he and his friends and family were frustrated with Intuit's Quicken products. He believed that he could develop a more user-friendly personal-finance software—and he did. Two years later, Patzer sold his website to Intuit for $170 million.[28]

Tolerance for Ambiguity

Entrepreneurs take in stride the uncertainties of launching a business. Dealing with unexpected events is normal for most entrepreneurs. Tolerance for ambiguity is different from the love of risk taking that many people relate to entrepreneurship. Successful entrepreneurship is not at all like gambling. Entrepreneurs look for strategies that they believe have a good chance of success. When a strategy isn't working, they quickly make changes. An important way entrepreneurs manage ambiguity is by staying close to customers so that they can change their offerings to match customer desires. One such entrepreneur is Kevin Mitnick. In the mid-1990s, Mitnick was arrested by the FBI for computer hacking, after which he served five years in prison. When he was released, Mitnick could have hidden his identity and started a new life—or gone on to further crimes. Instead, Mitnick went legitimate, opening his own computer security consulting company. He maintains a solid relationship with the businesses whose systems he once might have compromised. "The lifestyle of an entrepreneur is not so different from that of a hacker," quips Mitnick. "The only thing lacking is the sneakiness, the seduction of adventure." His firm, Mitnick Security Company, is earning more than $750,000 a year.[29]

Internal Locus of Control

Entrepreneurs have an internal locus of control. That means they believe that they control their own future. You won't find entrepreneurs blaming others or outside events for their successes or failures—they own it all.

Ralph Braun was diagnosed with a degenerative illness when he was 6 years old. By the time he was 14, he was in a wheelchair. Braun attended college but for only one year. He had to drop out because he couldn't get around the large campus in his wheelchair. So he decided to design his own transportation. Within about four months, he had built his first scooter. Then he got a job at a local automotive supply factory. There, he was able to get around easily on his scooter. People noticed and told him about friends or family members who needed a scooter like that. He started building them to order. Braun then began to focus on the van he was driving. He redesigned the interior to include a wheelchair/scooter lift that is now standard on buses and other mass transit. Again, he received requests to convert the vans of other wheelchair-bound drivers. Eventually Braun quit his factory job to focus on his business full-time. BraunAbility is now a $200 million empire. When he began building scooters, Braun recalls, "everyone told me it wasn't going to work. But when it comes to commonsense engineering, I'm very blessed. I think it is a [natural] ability." Braun is clearly in charge of his fate.[30]

✓ ASSESSMENT CHECK

6.4.1 What do we mean when we talk about an entrepreneur's vision?

6.4.2 Why is it important for an entrepreneur to have a high energy level and a strong need for achievement?

6.4.3 How do entrepreneurs generally feel about the possibility of failure?

STARTING A NEW VENTURE

LO 6.5 Summarize the process of starting a new venture.

Entrepreneurs can start a business in many different ways. This section discusses how to choose an idea for a new venture and how to turn a good idea into a working business.

Selecting a Business Idea

When choosing an idea for your business, remember the two most important things: (1) find something you love to do and are good at doing and (2) find an idea that meets a need in the marketplace. People willingly work hard doing something they love, and the experience will bring personal fulfillment. The old sayings "Do what makes you happy" and "Be true to yourself" are the best guidelines for deciding on a business idea.

Success also depends on customers. Would-be entrepreneurs need to be sure that the idea they choose will interest customers in the marketplace. The most successful entrepreneurs tend to work in industries where lots of change is taking place. These are usually the same industries where customers have difficulty deciding on their exact needs. In these industries,

Corin and Brian Mullins are the founders of Hapi Foods Group. Their company uses organic ingredients to make two artisan cereals, Holy Crap and Skinny B. The mom-and-pop startup business is located in Sechelt, on the Sunshine Coast of British Columbia. This startup is doing well in the very competitive breakfast cereal market. Read their story in the "Going Green" feature.

entrepreneurs can make use of their strengths, such as creativity, hard work, and tolerance of ambiguity. They can use these strengths to build customer relationships. But outstanding entrepreneurial success happens in every industry. Maybe you want to build a business based on your grandmother's cookie recipes, or maybe you have a better idea for tax-preparation software. Whatever your idea is, you are more likely to succeed if you ask yourself the right questions from the beginning.

Consider the guidelines in **Figure 6.5** as you think about your business ideas.

Many entrepreneurs invent new products or new ways of doing things. The inventor–entrepreneur needs to protect the rights to his or her invention by obtaining a patent. In Canada, the Patent Office is part of the Canadian Intellectual Property Office (CIPO), an agency of Industry Canada. The U.S. Patent and Trademark Office provides information about this process from an American perspective.

- List your interests and abilities. Include your values and beliefs, your goals and dreams, things you like and dislike doing, and your job experiences.
- Make another list of the types of businesses that match your interests and abilities.
- Read newspapers and business and consumer magazines. Learn about demographic and economic trends that discuss future needs for products that no one yet offers.
- Carefully evaluate existing goods and services. Look for ways to improve them.
- Decide on a business that matches what you want and offers profit potential.
- Do marketing research to decide whether your business idea will attract enough customers to earn a profit.
- Learn as much as you can about the industry in which your new venture will operate, your product or service, and your competitors. Read surveys that project growth in different industries.

FIGURE 6.5 Guidelines for Selecting a Business Idea

Buying an Existing Business

Some entrepreneurs prefer to buy established businesses instead of taking on the risks of starting new businesses. Buying an existing business brings many advantages: employees are already in place to serve regular customers and to deal with familiar suppliers, the good or service is already known in the marketplace, and the necessary permits and licences have already been obtained. It is easier to get financing for an existing business than for most startups. Some sellers may even help the buyers by providing financing and by offering to stay on as consultants. Most people want to buy a healthy business so that they can build on its success. But an experienced entrepreneur might buy a struggling business with the idea of turning it around. Entrepreneurs who are thinking about buying a business can use many resources, ranging from information provided by government agencies to websites listing actual companies for sale.

Buying a franchise is similar to buying an established business. Both are a less risky way to begin a business than starting an entirely new firm. But franchising (which was discussed in detail in Chapter 5) involves risks. It is a good idea to do thorough research before making any decision to start a new business.

GOING GREEN

HOLY CRAP: CORIN AND BRIAN MULLINS SURE KNOW HOW TO PICK A NAME FOR THEIR ORGANIC CEREALS

They named their cereals "Holy Crap" and "Skinny B." Everyone remembered these names when the couple appeared on the CBC's *Dragons' Den*. But the brand name was only one of several smart business decisions made by the Mullins. Their product is a good choice for customers who want a good-tasting organic cereal that (to be polite) helps with digestion and moving things along on the inside. Holy Crap has no genetically modified organisms (GMOs). It is made from all-natural ingredients: organic chia, hulled hemp hearts, organic buckwheat, organic cranberries, organic raisins, organic apple bits, and organic cinnamon.

The recipe is perfect for physically active young adults who want foods that fit with their lifestyle and taste good. Customers post "taste-imonials" on the company's website. Their comments show how much they believe in the products. For example, Will Kelsay is a professional XTERRA triathlete from Boulder, Colorado. His profile is titled "Holy Crap Cereal Is Rocket Fuel for Triathletes." It shows photos of Will in competition and bylines like "Will loves Holy Crap and the benefits of its super food ingredients." Will describes his belief in the product this way:

"The key ingredient of Holy Crap is chia, or Salvia Hispanica L. This oil seed crop is considered a perfect food because it's one of the few vegetarian sources of complete protein. The Aztecs valued it more highly than gold. Holy Crap cereal is a chia based wheat free, gluten free, lactose free breakfast cereal. The Tarahumara Indians in Copper Canyon, Mexico, the greatest long distance runners on the planet, have had a long history of using this slow burning rocket fuel for both athletes and warriors alike. The main cereal ingredient is Chia or Salvia Hispanica L., which typically contains 20% protein, 34% oil, and 25% dietary fiber. Salvia Hispanica L. contains the highest Omega-3 nutrient source found in nature with perfectly balanced Omega 3, 6, 9 profiles and ratios. The next most abundant ingredient is hulled hemp hearts, which are low in carbohydrates, contain more protein than milk, meat or eggs and are suitable for those unable to digest gluten, sugar, milk, nuts and meat." This kind of comment helps promote the cereals to serious athletes and to not-so-serious athletes that want to be like serious athletes—at least in what they eat.

The company has a warm relationship with its customers. It continues to do well because of brand name recognition. The company has retail distribution across North America at health food stores, specialty grocery stores, and through online shopping from their website.

Questions for Critical Thinking

1. Will the brand name help or hurt the company as it tries to grow further?

2. What are some other products that the company should consider developing and what names would you give them?

Sources: Holy Crap, accessed April 8, 2015, http://holycrap.ca; Julie Greco, "Is Holy Crap Cereal Milking the Hype?" *St. Catharines Standard*, November 26, 2010, accessed April 13, 2012, www.stcatharinesstandard.ca/ArticleDisplay.aspx?e=2862817; Allison Cross, "Sales Explode for Cereal with Cheeky Name," *Toronto Star*, November 23, 2010, accessed April 13, 2012, www.thestar.com/living/article/895792--sales-explode-for-cereal-with-cheeky-name; Remy Scalza, "Holy Crap: Local Cereal with Funny Name Goes Global," December 27, 2011, accessed April 13, 2012, www.insidevancouver.ca/2011/12/27/holy-crap-local-cereal-goes-global.

Creating a Business Plan

In the past, many entrepreneurs launched their businesses without writing formal business plans. Planning is an important part of managing in contemporary business. But entrepreneurs often go after opportunities as they arise and then they change course when they need to. Flexibility seems to be the key to business startups, especially in rapidly changing markets. But starting a business has many risks. Doing at least some planning is not just advisable but necessary, especially when an entrepreneur needs to look for funds from outside sources.

Appendix E discusses business plans in more detail. The Internet also offers a variety of resources for creating business plans. **Table 6.1** lists some of these online resources.

Table 6.1 Online Resources for Preparing a Business Plan

AllBusiness.com www.allbusiness.com	Under the "Finance" tab, select "Business Planning" for links to business plan examples, templates, and tips.
Inc. www.inc.com	Search for "business plans" to get access to articles on how to structure a business plan and how to write a mission statement.
MoreBusiness.com www.morebusiness.com	To see sample plans, select "Business Plans" under "Startup."

Finding Financing

seed capital the initial funding needed to launch a new venture.

A key issue in any business plan is financing. The need for **seed capital**, the funds used to launch a company, depends on the nature of the business. Seed capital can range as high as several million—say, for the purchase of a McDonald's franchise in a lucrative area—or as low as $1,000 for a website design. Many entrepreneurs use personal savings. Some ask for loans from business associates, family members, or even friends to use as startup funds. In fact, 82 percent of startups are self-financed, the greatest source by far.[31]

Debt Financing

debt financing borrowed funds that entrepreneurs must repay.

Entrepreneurs sometimes use **debt financing**, borrowed money that they must repay. Debt financing includes loans from banks, finance companies, credit-card companies, and family or friends. Some entrepreneurs charge business expenses to their personal credit cards, which are relatively easy to obtain. But high interest rates on credit cards mean that this source of funding is expensive. It is usually better to find other methods of funding.

Many banks turn down people who apply for loans to fund startups. The banks are fearful of the high risk of starting a new business. Over the last several years, more and more banks have turned down loan requests. Only a small percentage of startups raise seed capital through bank loans. Much planning and preparation is needed when applying for a bank loan. Bank loan officers want to see a business plan and will evaluate the entrepreneur's credit history. Because a startup has not yet established a business credit history, banks often base lending decisions on the entrepreneurs' personal credit histories. Banks are more willing to make loans to three kinds of entrepreneurs: those who have been in business for a while, those whose businesses show a profit on rising revenues, and those who need funds to finance expansion. Some entrepreneurs find that local community banks or credit unions are more interested in their loan applications than are the major national banks.

Even entrepreneurs who have previously received funding from banks—and have maintained a good relationship with their lenders—have experienced credit difficulties in recent years. A line of credit is an approved loan that a business can borrow from when funds are needed. Without that money, some businesses would not be able to pay for the materials they need to make the products that customers have already ordered. The 2008–10 economic slowdown was made worse by the reduction in credit and (in many cases) the refusal to offer more credit to businesses that could no longer function without normal levels of credit.

Equity Financing

equity financing funds invested in new ventures in exchange for part ownership.

venture capitalists business firms or groups of individuals that invest in new and growing firms in exchange for an ownership share.

In **equity financing**, entrepreneurs exchange a share of ownership in their company for money supplied by one or more investors. Entrepreneurs invest their own money and the funds supplied by the other people and firms that become co-owners of the startups. An entrepreneur does not have to repay equity funds. Instead, the investors share in the success of the business. Sources of equity financing include family and friends, business partners, venture capital firms, and private investors.

Some entrepreneurs team up with a partner who has funds to invest. This arrangement may be good for an entrepreneur who has a great business idea and skills but little or no money. Some investors also have business experience. These investors will be eager to share their knowledge because if the company succeeds, they will succeed. But, like borrowing, equity financing has its downsides. For example, investment partners may not agree on the future direction of the business. When the disagreement happens in a partnership, and the partners cannot resolve their differences, one partner may have to buy out the other to keep operating.

Venture capitalists are business organizations or groups of private individuals that invest in early stage, high-potential, growth companies. Venture capitalists usually back companies

Some entrepreneurs find creative ways to obtain equity financing. Gavin McClurg's venture, Offshore Odysseys, is a sailing expedition aboard a catamaran named *Discovery*. Investors buy timeshare segments for between $20,000 and $30,000. During the journey, they might swim across the equator or paraglide above Tahiti.

in high-technology industries such as biotechnology. In exchange for taking a risk with their own funds, these investors expect high rates of return and a share of the company. Typical terms for accepting venture capital include agreeing on how much the company is worth, how much stock both the investors and the founders will retain, control of the company's board, payment of dividends, and the period of time during which the founders are prohibited from "shopping" for further investments.[32] Venture capitalists want to invest in companies that have a combination of extremely rare qualities: the use of innovative technology, a potential for rapid growth, a well-developed business model, and an impressive management team.

Angel investors are wealthy individuals who invest money directly in new ventures in exchange for an equity share. These investors are a larger source of investment capital for startup firms. In contrast to venture capitalists, angels focus mostly on new ventures. Many angel investors are successful entrepreneurs who want to help would-be business owners get through the familiar difficulties of launching their businesses. Angel investors fund a wide variety of new ventures. Most entrepreneurs have trouble finding wealthy private investors. Angel networks have formed to match business angels with startups in need of capital.

You can learn about entrepreneurship and angel investors by watching CBC's television program *Dragons' Den*.

angel investors wealthy individuals who invest directly in a new venture in exchange for an equity stake.

Government Support for New Ventures

All levels of government support new ventures in many ways, as discussed in Chapter 5. Various local agencies and business incubators offer information, resources, and sometimes even access to financing for entrepreneurs.

Another way to encourage entrepreneurship is through *enterprise zones*, specific geographic areas set aside for economic renewal. Enterprise zones encourage investment, often in troubled areas, by offering tax advantages and incentives to businesses locating within the zone.

Long Plain First Nation's second urban reserve is located in Winnipeg at 480 Madison Street. An *urban reserve* is an economic zone within a municipality. It is an area that the federal government has set aside as First Nation reserve land. This economic zone allows for Aboriginal commercial ventures that enjoy tax exemptions offered to traditional reserves. Yellowquill College moved into a converted two-storey, 25,000-square-foot former Manitoba Hydro office building on the Long Plain urban reserve. Plans for the urban reserve include a gas station, a convenience store, and a five-storey, 80,000-square-foot office tower. Also in the plans is a depot for First Nations buyers to take delivery of tax-free goods purchased in the city.

Many First Nations are located in rural and remote areas. These areas are usually some distance from cities and towns where jobs and wealth are created. The distance creates challenges for First Nations who are trying to be economically self-sufficient. The federal government reports that Canada had 120 urban reserves as of 2008. The Winnipeg urban reserve is Long Plain's second urban reserve. Long Plain has operated an urban reserve in Portage la Prairie since the 1980s.[33]

✓ ASSESSMENT CHECK

6.5.1 What are the two most important considerations when choosing an idea for a new business?

6.5.2 What is the difference between debt financing and equity financing?

6.5.3 What is seed capital?

INTRAPRENEURSHIP

LO 6.6 Explain intrapreneurship.

Established companies try to keep the entrepreneurial spirit alive by encouraging **intrapreneurship**, the process of promoting innovation within their organization. In today's business world, things can change very quickly. Established firms need to innovate continually to hold onto their competitive advantages.

Many companies encourage intrapreneurship. In fact, 30 percent of large firms now set aside funds to support intrapreneurship.[34] Perhaps no business has benefited more from intrapreneurship than 3M. To foster creativity, 3M encourages engineers to "bootleg," or borrow, up to 15 percent of their time from other assignments to explore new product ideas of their choosing. Bootlegging has led to some of 3M's most successful products, including Scotch tape and Post-it notes.[35]

intrapreneurship the process of promoting innovation within the structure of an existing organization.

ASSESSMENT CHECK

6.6.1 Why do large companies support intrapreneurship?

6.6.2 What is a skunkworks?

Established companies such as 3M support intrapreneurial activity in varied ways. In addition to allowing bootlegging time for traditional product development, 3M implements two intrapreneurial approaches: skunkworks and pacing programs. A *skunkworks* project is initiated by an employee who has an idea and then recruits resources from within 3M to turn it into a commercial product. *Pacing programs* are company-initiated projects. They focus on a few products and technologies that 3M sees as having potential for success. The company provides financing, equipment, and people to support such pacing projects.[36]

WHAT'S AHEAD

In upcoming chapters, we look at other trends that are shaping the business world of the twenty-first century. In the next part of *Contemporary Business*, we explore the critical issues of how companies organize, lead, and manage their work processes; manage and motivate their employees; empower their employees through teamwork and enhanced communication; handle labour and workplace disputes; and create and produce world-class goods and services.

RETURN TO INSIDE BUSINESS

Sharing Economy Sparks Start-Ups

Entrepreneurial success is like a recipe for success. Given the right ingredients and business conditions, the entrepreneur is more likely to succeed. Those ingredients include the character of the entrepreneur, the uniqueness of the product, and the price customers are willing to pay. Many small businesses are successful at filling a unique need, or a spot in an industry, similar to the way FlightCar, Uber, and Airbnb have in the "share economy."

QUESTIONS FOR CRITICAL THINKING

1. Develop a "shared economy" business idea that follows the patterns established by FlightCar, Uber, and Airbnb.
2. How would your idea be better than the existing competition?

SUMMARY OF LEARNING OBJECTIVES

LO 6.1 Describe what is an entrepreneur and the different types of entrepreneurs.

Unlike many small-business owners, entrepreneurs typically own and run their businesses with the goal of building significant firms that create wealth and add jobs. Entrepreneurs are visionaries. They see opportunities and take the initiative to gather the resources they need to start their businesses quickly. Both managers and entrepreneurs use the resources of their companies to achieve the goals of their organizations.

A classic entrepreneur sees a business opportunity and sets aside resources to gain access to that market. A serial entrepreneur starts one business, runs it, and then starts and runs more businesses, one after another. A social entrepreneur uses business principles to solve social problems.

ASSESSMENT CHECK ANSWERS

6.1.1 What tools do entrepreneurs use to create a new business? Entrepreneurs combine their ideas and drive with money, employees, and other resources to create a business that meets a need.

6.1.2 How do entrepreneurs differ from managers? Managers direct others to reach an organization's goals. Entrepreneurs have the drive and impatience that make their companies successful. These qualities may hurt their ability to manage.

6.1.3 What do classic entrepreneurs and social entrepreneurs have in common? They both see opportunities and then set aside resources to develop new solutions.

6.1.4 Is a social entrepreneur simply a philanthropist who gives to good causes to help others? A philanthropist usually supports human welfare through charitable donations. A social entrepreneur develops new ways to advance social causes and thus enhance social welfare.

LO 6.2 Explain why people choose to become entrepreneurs.

People choose to become entrepreneurs for many reasons. Four of the common reasons are a desire to be one's own boss, a desire to achieve financial success, a desire for job security, and a desire to improve one's quality of life.

✓ ASSESSMENT CHECK ANSWERS

6.2.1 What are the four main reasons people choose to become entrepreneurs? People usually choose to become entrepreneurs because they want to be their own boss, they believe they will achieve greater financial success, they believe they have more control over job security, and they want to enhance their quality of life.

6.2.2 What factors affect the entrepreneur's job security? An entrepreneur's job security depends on the decisions of customers and investors. It also depends on the cooperation and commitment of the entrepreneur's own employees.

LO 6.3 Discuss factors that support and expand opportunities for entrepreneurs.

Several factors provide support and opportunities for entrepreneurs: a favourable public perception, availability of financing, the falling cost and widespread availability of information technology, globalization, entrepreneurship education, and changing demographic and economic trends.

✓ ASSESSMENT CHECK ANSWERS

6.3.1 To what extent is entrepreneurship possible in different countries, and what opportunities does globalization create for today's entrepreneurs? More than 9 percent of adults worldwide are starting or managing a new business. Globalization makes it possible for entrepreneurs to market their products abroad and to hire international talent. Many of the fastest-growing small Canadian companies have international sales, especially to the United States.

6.3.2 Identify the educational factors that help expand current opportunities for entrepreneurs. Many universities offer majors in entrepreneurship, dozens of others offer an entrepreneurship emphasis, and hundreds more offer courses in how to start a business. Some organizations encourage and teach entrepreneurship, such as the Kauffman Center for Entrepreneurial Leadership, Entreprep, and Students in Free Enterprise.

6.3.3 Describe current demographic trends that suggest new goods and services for entrepreneurial businesses. The aging of the North American population and the growth of two-income families are creating opportunities for entrepreneurs to market new goods and services.

LO 6.4 Identify the traits of successful entrepreneurs.

Successful entrepreneurs share several typical traits, including vision, high energy levels, the need to achieve, self-confidence and optimism, tolerance for failure, creativity, tolerance for ambiguity, and an internal locus of control.

✓ ASSESSMENT CHECK ANSWERS

6.4.1 What do we mean when we talk about an entrepreneur's vision? Entrepreneurs begin with a vision, which is an overall idea for how to make their business idea a success. They then follow this vision with energy and excitement.

6.4.2 Why is it important for an entrepreneur to have a high energy level and a strong need for achievement? Start-up companies usually have a small staff and have a difficult time raising enough capital. The entrepreneur needs to make up the difference by working long hours. A strong need for achievement helps entrepreneurs to enjoy the challenge of reaching difficult goals. It also promotes dedication to personal success.

6.4.3 How do entrepreneurs generally feel about the possibility of failure? They view failure as a learning experience and are not easily discouraged or disappointed when things don't go as planned.

LO 6.5 Summarize the process of starting a new venture.

Entrepreneurs must choose an idea for their business, develop a business plan, obtain financing, and organize the resources they need to operate their startups.

✓ ASSESSMENT CHECK ANSWERS

6.5.1 What are the two most important considerations when choosing an idea for a new business? The two most important considerations are finding something you love to do and are good at doing, and finding an idea that meets a need in the marketplace.

6.5.2 What is the difference between debt financing and equity financing? Debt financing is money borrowed that must be repaid. Equity financing is an exchange of ownership shares in a company for money supplied by one or more investors.

6.5.3 What is seed capital?
Seed capital is the money that is used to start a company.

LO 6.6 Explain intrapreneurship.
Organizations encourage intrapreneurial activity within the company in a variety of ways, including through hiring practices, dedicated programs such as skunkworks, providing access to resources, and giving employees freedom to innovate within established firms.

✓ ASSESSMENT CHECK ANSWERS

6.6.1 Why do large companies support intrapreneurship? Large firms support intrapreneurship to keep an entrepreneurial spirit alive and to promote innovation and change.

6.6.2 What is a skunkworks? A skunkworks project is initiated by an employee who has an idea and then recruits resources from within the company to turn the idea into a commercial product.

BUSINESS TERMS YOU NEED TO KNOW

angel investors 169
classic entrepreneur 155
debt financing 168
entrepreneur 154
equity financing 168
intrapreneurship 169
lifestyle entrepreneur 158
seed capital 168
serial entrepreneur 155
social entrepreneur 156
venture capitalists 168

REVIEW QUESTIONS

1. Identify the three categories of entrepreneurs. How are they different from each other? How might an entrepreneur belong to more than one category?

2. People often become entrepreneurs because they want to be their own boss, and they want to be in control of most or all of the major decisions related to their business. How might these desires relate to potential financial success? Are there any downsides? If so, what are they?

3. How have globalization and information technology created new opportunities for entrepreneurs? Describe current demographic trends that suggest new goods and services for entrepreneurial businesses.

4. Identify the eight characteristics that are attributed to successful entrepreneurs. Which trait or traits do you believe are the most important for success? Why? Are there any traits that might contribute to potential failure? If so, which traits? Why might they contribute to failure?

5. When selecting a business idea, why is it important to follow the advice to "do what makes you happy" and "be true to yourself"?

6. Suppose an entrepreneur is considering buying an existing business or franchise. Which of the eight entrepreneurial traits would most likely apply to this person, and why?

7. Imagine that you and a partner are planning to launch a business that sells backpacks, briefcases, and soft luggage made from recycled materials. You'll need seed capital for your venture. Outline how you would use that seed capital.

8. Describe the two main types of financing that entrepreneurs may seek for their businesses. What are the risks and benefits of each?

9. What is an enterprise zone? Describe what types of businesses might benefit from opening in an enterprise zone. How might their success be interconnected?

10. What is intrapreneurship? How does it differ from entrepreneurship?

PROJECTS AND TEAMWORK APPLICATIONS

1. Interview an entrepreneur. You can do the interview in person, by email, or by phone. The person can be a local shop or restaurant owner, a hair salon owner, a pet groomer, a consultant—any field is fine. Find out why that person decided to become an entrepreneur. Ask whether his or her viewpoint has changed since starting the business. Decide whether the person is a classic, serial, or social entrepreneur. Present your findings to the class.

2. Certain demographic trends can represent opportunities for entrepreneurs—the aging of the North American population,

the increasing diversity of the population, the growth in population of some areas, and the large number of two-income families, to name a few. On your own or with a classmate, choose a demographic trend and brainstorm for business ideas that can profit from the trend. Create a poster or a PowerPoint presentation to present your idea—and its relationship to the trend—to your class.

3. Review the eight characteristics of successful entrepreneurs. Which characteristics do you have? Do you think you would be a good entrepreneur? Why or why not? Create an outline of the traits you believe are your strengths—and the traits that might be your weaknesses.

4. Many entrepreneurs turn a hobby or an area of interest into a business idea. Others get their ideas from situations or daily problems when they believe they have a solution—or a better solution than those already tried. Think about an area of personal interest or a problem you think you can solve with a new good or service. Create the first part of a potential business plan, which is the introduction to your new company and its offerings. Outline briefly what kind of financing you think would work best for your business, and what steps you would take to obtain the funds.

5. Enterprise zones are designed to revitalize economically distressed areas. Choose an area you are familiar with. It may be as close as a local neighbourhood, or as far away as a city where you might like to live. Do some online research about the area. Outline your own plan for an enterprise zone. Include businesses that you think would do well in the area, jobs that might be created, housing creation, and other factors.

WEB ASSIGNMENTS

1. **Tools for entrepreneurs.** American Express has established what it calls "Open Forum" to allow entrepreneurs and small-business owners to communicate with one another and share ideas. Visit the Open Forum website and review the material. Prepare a short report on how Open Forum can help an entrepreneur to start and grow a business.

   www.openforum.com

2. **Venture capitalists.** Venture capital firms are an important source of financing for entrepreneurs. Most actively look for funding proposals. Go to the website shown below to learn more about venture capital. What are some of the famous businesses that were originally financed by venture capitalists?

   www.nvca.org

3. **Getting started.** Visit the website of *Entrepreneur* magazine. Explore the information on how to research a business idea. What are the steps involved in getting a product to market?

   www.entrepreneur.com

Note: Internet Web addresses change frequently. If you don't find the exact sites listed, you may need to access the organization's home page and search from there or use a search engine such as Bing or Google.

PART 2: CASE STUDY Beau's All Natural Brewing Company
Getting Started: Choosing a Location, Building the Plant, and Hiring Employees

In 2006, two years after their initial discussions and a year after seriously starting to put things together, Steve and Tim Beauchesne were ready to begin brewing operations for the key summer sales season. Their business plan initially included a bank loan from the Business Development Bank of Canada along with $150,000 from an investor who would not be involved in operations. When the investor backed out, the Beauchesnes scrambled to pool $100,000 of funds from friends and family along with funds from the mortgaged leather plant to total around $300,000. This was perhaps half the funds needed that would have made starting up easier to handle. But the desire to succeed in their business meant that the decision to move ahead and get busy building the business was carried forward. Beer recipes were tried and tested, and relationships with local restaurants and bars were established. Provincial government approval was granted to sell their beer in the highly regulated industry. Beau's was allowed to sell through the LCBO (Liquor Control Board of Ontario) retail system as well as in bars and restaurants throughout Ontario. The only thing holding things up now was acquiring the equipment for production on a larger scale.

By the spring of 2006, Tim's leather finishing plant was prepared and ready to receive machinery and equipment for its new life as a brewery. Months of searching for equipment was finally rewarded when a full brew system complete with a brew house, fermenters, and brite tanks were sourced from a location in New Hampshire. The brand name of the system was CENTURY, a manufacturer that the Beauchesne's later discovered was no longer in business and perhaps explained the reason they had gotten such a good deal. The whole system was in pristine condition and had the desired 15-barrels capacity the Beauchesne's wanted. There were six fermenting and brite tanks that Steve and Tim felt would do the job of getting Beau's off the ground. They hired truckers specially equipped to move the 10-feet-tall tanks in an upright position to their new home in Vankleek Hill.

Steve and Tim recognized the limitations of their knowledge and skills. Making a small batch of beer in their kitchen was one thing; knowing how to operate large-scale machinery that would produce hundreds of litres was something else. Beau's lucked out when one of the most talented brew masters in the country, Matthew O'Hara, joined them. Matthew gained his knowledge of brewing by working his way up the ranks of well-respected breweries, including Upper Canada Brewing (now owned by Sleeman Breweries), Dennison's Brewing in Toronto, and Montreal's McAuslan Brewing. He developed the unique recipe for Beau's flagship beer, a lagered ale called Lug-Tread. Along with family members and a handful of employees, the Beauchesne's were ready.

To Steve, the local market in the Ottawa region seemed particularly receptive to a new craft beer. He was confident he could succeed in serving the younger beer drinkers he sensed he understood well. Ottawa had a young demographic with two large universities and colleges throughout the trading region. Besides being home, Vankleek Hill, located about 45 minutes south-east of Ottawa, was a good location that would allow for short delivery runs to pubs and restaurants and other venues where their brew would be sold. The Beauchesnes received encouragement from local businesses, government officials, and the Ontario Craft Brewers Association. Vankleek Hill's population of 2,000 appreciated the jobs created and the entrepreneurial risk that was being taken. This all fit with the philosophy guiding the Beauchesnes' business thinking, which focused on building relationships with customers and giving back to their community.

Questions for Critical Thinking

1. Evaluate each of the primary risks discussed in Chapter 5 that Beau's faced as a new business.

2. Why was Vankleek Hill a good location choice?

3. How do Steve and Tim Beauchesne fit the textbook description of entrepreneurs?

2 LAUNCHING YOUR...

ENTREPRENEURIAL CAREER

In Part 2, "Starting and Growing Your Business," you learned the many ways that business owners have achieved their dreams of owning their own company and being their own boss. The two chapters in Part 2 introduced the wide variety of entrepreneurial or small businesses; the forms these businesses can take (sole proprietorship, partnership, or corporation); and the reasons that some new ventures succeed and others fail. You learned that entrepreneurs are visionaries who build firms that create wealth. They share qualities such as vision and creativity, high energy, optimism, a strong need to achieve, and a tolerance for failure. You might wonder how you can use this information. Here are some career ideas and opportunities in the small-business and ebusiness areas.

First, think about the field that attracts you as a future business owner. Try to gain experience in the industry by first working for someone else. The information and skills you learn will be valuable when you start out on your own. Remember that lack of experience is often the leading reason for small-business failure.[1]

Next, look for a good fit between your own skills, abilities, and qualities and a market need, or niche. For example, the number of older people in the population is increasing, and more and more young families find themselves running short on time. As a result, the need for childcare and eldercare services will increase—and so will the opportunities for new businesses in those areas. Watch these trends to find ideas that you can use or adapt.

Do you like the idea of being your own boss but worry about risking your savings to start a new and untried business? Then you might want to think about owning a franchise, such as Quiznos or Tim Hortons. Franchising can be less risky than starting a new business from scratch, but it still means hard work. You need to understand the franchise resources you can access and the franchise responsibilities you will take on. Filling a market need is important for success. To find more information about franchising, access the Business Development Bank of Canada's review of franchising at www.bdc.ca/EN/articles-tools/start-buy-business/buy-business/Pages/making-right-choice.aspx.

Are you skilled in a certain area of business, technology, or science? Consulting firms offer their expertise to clients in private, government, not-for-profit, and foreign business operations. Business consultants influence clients' decisions in marketing, finance, manufacturing, information systems, ebusiness, human resources, and many other areas, including corporate strategy and organization. Technology consultants support businesses in all fields. They might set up a secure website, train employees in the use of new software, manage an off-site help desk, or plan for disaster recovery. Science consulting firms find work in the field of environmental consulting. They help businesses to deal with pollution cleanup and control, habitat protection, and help them to meet government environmental regulations and standards.

But maybe you prefer to tinker with gears and machinery or with computer graphics and code. If you think you have the ideas and creativity to invent something completely new, you need to learn about patents, trademarks, and copyright laws to protect your ideas.[2] Patents, trademarks, and copyright each offer different protections for your work, but none will guarantee success. Again, hard work, persistence, and a little bit of luck will help you succeed.

CAREER ASSESSMENT EXERCISES IN ENTREPRENEURSHIP AND BUSINESS OWNERSHIP

1. Find out whether you have what it takes to be an entrepreneur. Review the material on the Business Development Bank of Canada's website: www.bdc.ca/EN/articles-tools/entrepreneur-toolkit/business-assessments/Pages/self-assessment-test-your-entrepreneurial-potential.aspx

   Answer the questions there. After you've finished, use the scoring guides to see how ready you are to start your own business. What weak areas did your results show? What can you do to strengthen those areas?

2. Find an independent business or franchise in your area. Make an appointment to talk to the owner about his or her startup experience. Prepare a list of questions for a 10- to 15-minute interview. Remember to ask about details, such as the number of hours worked per week, the approximate startup costs, the goals of the business, the available resources, the lessons learned since opening, and the rewards of owning the business. How do the owner's answers differ from what you expected?

3. Search online for information about how to file for a patent, trademark, or copyright. A good starting point is the BDC's website: www.bdc.ca/EN/articles-tools/business-strategy-planning/innovate/Pages/patents-trademarks-copyright-an-overview.aspx

Assume you have an invention you want to protect. Find out what forms are required; what fees are needed; how much time is usually needed to complete the legal steps; and the rights and protections you will gain from the patent, trademark, or copyright.

PART 3
MANAGEMENT: EMPOWERING PEOPLE TO ACHIEVE BUSINESS GOALS

Chapter 7 Management, Leadership, and the Internal Organization

Chapter 8 Human Resource Management: From Recruitment to Labour Relations

Chapter 9 Top Performance through Empowerment, Teamwork, and Communication

Chapter 10 Production and Operations Management

AP Photo/Julio Cortez/The Canadian Press

7 | MANAGEMENT, LEADERSHIP, AND THE INTERNAL ORGANIZATION

LEARNING OBJECTIVES

LO 7.1 Describe *management*.

LO 7.2 Explain the role of vision and ethical standards in business success.

LO 7.3 Summarize the importance of planning and the three types of planning.

LO 7.4 Describe the strategic planning process.

LO 7.5 Describe the two major types of business decisions and the steps in the decision-making process.

LO 7.6 Define *leadership*, and compare different leadership styles.

LO 7.7 Discuss the meaning and importance of corporate culture.

LO 7.8 Identify the five major forms of departmentalization and the four main types of organization structures.

INSIDE BUSINESS

Can John S. Chen Save BlackBerry?

It is hard for many people to understand how Waterloo, Ontario-based BlackBerry Ltd. (formerly Research In Motion Ltd. [RIM]) could fall from the height of success. It was even harder for shareholders and industry analysts who watched as the firm's management seemed unable to cope in a competitive environment where once it was the leader.

By 2012, BlackBerry had an estimated 75 million global subscribers and was generating $20 billion in revenues. The company was profitable, posting more than $3.4 billion in profit in 2011. But analysts could see that the firm was losing customers to new-product offerings from Apple, Google, and others.

The company had early success with its 1998 introduction of the device called the BlackBerry. The product's reliability and the firm's superior customer support made it popular and led to its success. To use a BlackBerry device, wireless service providers need to buy into the system that the firm is selling. The individual customer buys a BlackBerry device, but the wireless service provider must buy the software and other technology from the company. Then, the software and technology together make it possible for customers to use these products and products licensed to other manufacturers by BlackBerry.

The business model worked well. In fact, it still works well in many markets around the world where voice and data (text) communication meet the primary needs of mostly business subscribers. But then Apple introduced the iPhone. Software developers began creating hundreds and hundreds of special applications (apps) to run on the iPhone. BlackBerry's smartphone devices lost their appeal as more and more consumers purchased iPhones instead.

By the time the late Steve Jobs introduced the iPad, Apple's mobile tablet device, BlackBerry was trying to catch up. BlackBerry launched its PlayBook, but it was poorly received. The trend for future growth—especially in the bigger consumer market—pointed away from BlackBerry and toward Apple and other producers. Apple and Google chose to focus on digital content sales. It seemed that BlackBerry's management was losing touch with what customers wanted. The hardware device was less important to generating revenue. Instead, digital content was becoming the source of growth.

By January 2012, unhappy shareholders had seen their stock value fall to $15 per share from highs of more than $150 per share in 2008. The shareholders demanded major leadership changes at the firm. The board of directors removed the two top management figures, who had led BlackBerry's original success. Mike Lazaridis and Jim Balsillie were not out, but they were no longer setting the vision and direction for the company they had built from scratch. Thorsten Heins was named president and chief executive officer replacing Mike Lazaridis. Jim Balsillie stepped down as co-CEO. He initially remained on the board of directors, but then stepped down from that position in late March 2012. Thorsten Heins's time at the helm was brief. He was replaced by John S. Chen, a Silicon Valley success story, in 2013 to dramatically change the company. The board had recognized that time was running out for BlackBerry and drastic change in direction was needed if the company was to have any chance of a future in an industry that it had helped create.[1]

CHAPTER 7 OVERVIEW

Many students in introductory business courses dream about the challenges of a management career. When you ask business students about their career goals, many will say, "I want to be a manager." You may think that being a manager means being the boss. But in today's business world, companies want managers to be more than bosses. They want managers who understand technology, adapt quickly to change, can skillfully motivate employees, and realize the importance of satisfying customers. Managers who can master those skills will be in great demand. Managers who have strong commitments can improve their firms' performance.

This chapter begins by looking at how successful organizations use management to turn visions into reality. It describes the levels of management, the skills that managers need, and the functions that managers perform. The chapter explains how the first of these functions—planning—helps managers in two ways: to meet the challenges of a rapidly changing business environment and to develop strategies that guide a company's future. Other sections of the chapter explore the types of decisions that managers make, the role of managers as leaders, and the importance of corporate culture. The chapter concludes by examining the second function of management—organizing.

LO 7.1 Describe *management*.

management the process of achieving organizational goals through people and other resources.

WHAT IS MANAGEMENT?

Management is the process of achieving organizational goals through people and other resources. The manager's job is to combine human and technical resources in the best way possible to achieve the company's goals.

Management principles and concepts apply to both not-for-profit organizations and for-profit firms. The managerial functions described in this chapter are performed by a city mayor, the president of the YMCA, and a superintendent of schools. Management takes place at many levels, from the level of a manager at a family-owned restaurant to the level of a national sales manager for a major manufacturer.

The Management Hierarchy

Your local grocery store has a fairly simple organization: a store manager, several assistant managers or department managers, and employees who may be baggers, cashiers, or stock clerks. If your grocery store is part of a regional or national chain, it will also have corporate managers who are ranked above the store manager. Loblaw is Canada's largest food distribution company. It operates more than 1,000 grocery stores across Canada. It has headquarters in Brampton, Ontario. Each store has managers for everything, from the meat department to human resources. At Loblaw headquarters, you'll find top-level managers for finance, consumer affairs, real estate, information technology, sales and operations, pharmacy, and other areas.[2]

All these managers combine human and other resources to meet Loblaw goals. But their jobs differ because they work at different levels of the organization.

A firm's management usually has three levels: top, middle, and supervisory. These levels of management form a management hierarchy, as shown in **Figure 7.1**. The hierarchy is the traditional structure found in most organizations. Managers at each level perform different activities.

The highest level of management is *top management*. Top managers include such positions as chief executive officer (CEO), chief financial officer (CFO), and executive vice-president. Top managers spend most of their time developing long-range plans for their organizations. They decide whether to introduce new products, purchase other companies, or enter new geographical markets. Top

Top Management
- Chief Executive Officer
- Chief Financial Officer
- Premier, Mayor

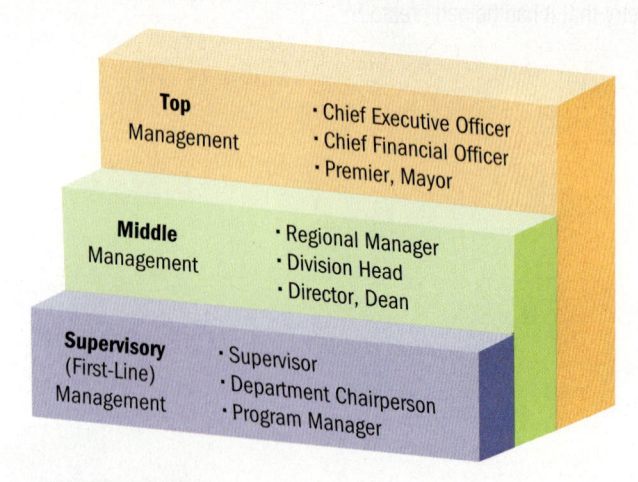

Middle Management
- Regional Manager
- Division Head
- Director, Dean

Supervisory (First-Line) Management
- Supervisor
- Department Chairperson
- Program Manager

FIGURE 7.1 The Management Hierarchy

managers set a direction for their organization. They also inspire the company's executives and employees to achieve their vision for the company's future.

The job isn't easy. Many top managers must steer their firms through an economic downturn, a slump in sales, or a crisis in quality. TD Bank's Ed Clark was recently named outstanding CEO of the Year. This recognition was, in part, because of his success in steering Canada's second-largest bank through one of the worst global financial crises in history (2008–2010) and back to continued growth. The bank's stock market value returned to pre-crisis levels, likely because of two factors: uninterrupted dividend payouts to shareholders and investors' confidence in future growth. In 2012 and 2013, Ed was named to *Barron's* prestigious annual list of the world's 30 best CEOs. He retired from TD Bank in 2014 after 12 years as CEO.[3]

Middle management is the second level in the management hierarchy. It includes general managers, plant managers, division managers, and branch managers. Middle managers focus their attention on specific operations, products, or customer groups. They develop detailed plans and procedures to carry out the firm's strategic plans. For example, suppose top management decides to increase distribution of a product. A sales manager will decide on how many salespeople are needed. Middle managers will focus on the products to be sold and on the customers who will buy the products and lead to the profit growth the CEO expects. The middle managers might budget money for product development, identify new uses for existing products, and improve the ways they train and motivate salespeople. Middle managers are more familiar with day-to-day operations than CEOs. That's why middle managers often come up with new ways to increase sales or solve company problems.

Supervisory management, or first-line management, includes supervisors, section chiefs, and team leaders. These managers assign specific jobs to nonmanagerial employees and assess their performance. Managers at this first level of the hierarchy work directly with the employees who produce and sell the firm's goods and services. They carry out middle managers' plans by motivating workers to accomplish daily, weekly, and monthly goals. In a study of top-ranked customer service firms, all firms had first-line managers who carried out the firms' strategies to provide superior customer service.[4]

For the past six years, TD Canada Trust has ranked highest in customer satisfaction among the big five Canadian retail banks, according to J.D. Power and Associates. The first-line managers make sure that customer service is the main concern for all employees.

Skills Needed for Managerial Success

Managers at every level in the management hierarchy use three basic types of skills: technical, human, and conceptual. All managers must acquire these skills, but the importance of each skill changes at each management level.

Technical skills are the manager's ability to understand and use the techniques, knowledge, tools, and equipment of a specific department or area of study. Technical skills are especially important for first-line managers. They are less important at higher levels of the management hierarchy. But most top executives started out as technical experts. The résumé of a vice-president for information systems probably lists jobs as a computer analyst. A vice-president for marketing usually has a background in sales. Many firms, such as The Home Depot and Dell, have increased their training programs for first-line managers to increase their technical skills and productivity. Cold Stone Creamery operates franchises for its premium ice cream stores in Alberta and Saskatchewan. This company carefully trains managers and crew members in the art of preparing its specialty ice cream for hungry customers. "We set high standards and provide world-class training," says the company.[5]

Human skills are interpersonal skills that help managers to work effectively with people. Human skills include the ability to communicate with, motivate, and lead employees to complete their assigned activities. Managers need human skills to interact with people both inside and outside the organization. People without these skills will probably have a difficult time trying to be a successful manager. Human skills must be adapted to different forms. For example, human skills include mastering and communicating effectively with staff using email, cellphones, pagers, faxes, and text messaging. All these forms of communication are widely used in today's offices. As you can imagine, managers at Cold Stone Creamery ice cream stores need to have excellent human skills, not only with customers but also with employees.

Conceptual skills help a manager to see the organization as a single unit and to understand how each part of the overall organization interacts with other parts. People with conceptual skills can see the big picture by acquiring, analyzing, and interpreting information. Conceptual skills are especially important for top-level managers, who must develop long-range plans for the future direction of their organization. Tony Hsieh sold his own company, LinkExchange, to Microsoft for $265 million. He then joined Zappos as an advisor and later became its CEO. Hsieh's conceptual skills helped Zappos to grow its sales to more than $1 billion annually while also winning praises for being an excellent place to work. Recently, Hsieh sold Zappos to Amazon in a deal worth $1.2 billion.[6]

Managerial Functions

In the course of a typical day, managers meet and talk with people, read, think, and send text or email messages. As they perform these activities, managers carry out four basic functions: planning, organizing, directing, and controlling. Planning activities set out the basics for activity, and the other functions carry out the plans.

Planning

planning the process of looking forward to future events and conditions and deciding on the courses of action for achieving organizational goals.

Planning is the process of looking forward to future events and conditions and deciding on the courses of actions for achieving organizational goals. Effective planning helps a business to focus its vision, avoid costly mistakes, and seize opportunities. Planning should be flexible and responsive to changes in the business environment. It should also involve managers from all levels of the organization. Planning for the future is more important than ever because global competition is getting stronger, technology continues to expand, and firms are bringing new innovations to market faster. For example, a CEO and other top-level managers need to plan for succession—for those who will follow in their footsteps. Some CEOs don't want to do this kind of planning, fearing that it might shorten their time leading a company. Management experts advise firms to plan ahead for the next generation of management, so they can keep the company's position in the marketplace.[7]

Frank Stronach led Magna International from its start in 1969 to become the largest automotive parts manufacturer in North America with sales over $23 billion. Stronach decided to step down as CEO. He announced his decision before a shareholders' vote on his position. Although the company had returned to profitability after the financial crisis, which hit the auto industry hard, many thought that it was time for new leadership at the firm.[8]

Organizing

After plans have been developed, the next step in the management process is **organizing**—the process of blending human and material resources through a formal structure of tasks and authority: arranging work, dividing tasks among employees, and coordinating them to ensure plans are carried out and goals are met. Organizing involves classifying and dividing work into manageable units with a structure that makes sense. Managers staff the organization with the best possible employees for each job. Sometimes, the organizing function requires studying a company's existing structure and deciding whether to restructure it to operate more efficiently, cost effectively, or sustainably.

organizing the process of blending human and material resources through a formal structure of tasks and authority: arranging work, dividing tasks among employees, and coordinating them to ensure plans are carried out and goals are met.

Directing

After an organization has been set up, managers focus on **directing**, or guiding and motivating employees to accomplish organizational goals. Directing can include training (or retraining), setting up schedules, assigning tasks, and monitoring progress. For example, an office manager might need to meet the goal of reducing the office electricity bill. This manager might do the following: assign incandescent light bulbs to be replaced by compact fluorescents, ask employees to turn off the lights when they leave a room, and direct the information technology (IT) staff to program all computer screens to turn off after 15 minutes of inactivity.[9]

Some managers take time to listen to their employees. These managers gain an understanding of their employees, and the employees feel that the manager cares about their work. Weekly meetings with employees allow for the exchange of information, and individuals can make their views known. Such meetings can help to motivate employees and provide an opportunity for comments about the direction the firm is moving.

directing guiding and motivating employees to accomplish organizational goals.

controlling the function of assessing an organization's performance against its goals.

Controlling

The **controlling** function assesses an organization's performance against its goals. Controlling assesses the success of the planning function and provides feedback for future rounds of planning.

Controlling has four basic steps: setting performance standards, monitoring actual performance, comparing actual performance with the standards, and making corrections if needed. For example, according to the Sarbanes-Oxley Act, CEOs and CFOs must monitor the performance of the firm's accounting staff more closely than was done in the past. CEOs and CFOs must personally confirm the truth of financial reports filed with the U.S. Securities and Exchange Commission. Many Canadian firms, such as Magna International, are listed on American stock exchanges. These Canadian firms are also required to comply with Sarbanes-Oxley.

✓ ASSESSMENT CHECK

7.1.1 What is management?

7.1.2 Describe the differences in the jobs of top managers, middle managers, and supervisory managers.

7.1.3 What is the relationship between the manager's planning and controlling functions?

SETTING A VISION AND ETHICAL STANDARDS FOR THE FIRM

LO 7.2 Explain the role of vision and ethical standards in business success.

A business begins with a **vision**, its founder's ability to perceive marketplace needs and what an organization must do to satisfy them. Vision is a focus for a firm's actions. Vision helps to direct the company toward opportunities and sets it apart from its competitors. The current vision for Facebook is not very different from the original vision proposed by founder Mark Zuckerberg—"Giving people the power to share, and make the world more open and connected."[10]

vision the ability to perceive marketplace needs and what an organization must do to satisfy them.

A firm's vision is a focus for its actions. Vision helps to direct the company toward opportunities and sets it apart from its competitors. The current vision for Facebook is not very different from the original vision proposed by founder Mark Zuckerberg—"Giving people the power to share, and make the world more open and connected."

A company's vision must be focused. It must also be flexible enough to adapt to changes in the business environment. The ethical standards set by top management are also important to a firm's long-term relationships with its customers, suppliers, and the general public. Sometimes, ethical standards are made to comply with industry or federal regulations, such as safety or quality standards. Other times, new standards are set after unethical actions have been taken by managers, such as the financial accounting wrongdoings that led to the Sarbanes-Oxley Act. Many firms are now taking a closer look at large compensation packages received by their CEOs and other top executives. Because of public demands, compensation committees are reassessing their guidelines for salaries, bonuses, and other benefits.[11]

The ethical tone set by a top management team can lead to financial and nonfinancial rewards. Setting a high ethical standard does not just keep employees from doing wrong but it also encourages, motivates, and inspires them to achieve goals they never thought possible. Such satisfaction creates a more productive, stable workforce—one that can create a long-term competitive advantage for the organization. In practice, ethical decisions are not always clear, and managers must make difficult decisions. Sometimes, a firm operates in a country where standards differ from our standards in Canada. Other times, a manager might have to make an ethical decision that reduces profits or leads to job losses. You might think that a large firm—because of its size—will have a harder time adopting ethical practices than a small firm. But consider toymaker giant Mattel, which has earned recognition again and again for its ethical standards. Named one of the "World's Most Ethical Companies" by the Ethisphere Institute, Mattel consistently demonstrates high standards. "Our commitment to 'play fair' is at the core of our organization's culture and is the cornerstone of our ethical compliance program," notes chairman and CEO Robert A. Eckert.

Alex Brigham, executive director of the Ethisphere Institute, sees the connection between ethics and good business. "Mattel's promotion of a sound ethical environment shines within its industry and shows a clear understanding that operating under the highest standards for business behaviour goes beyond goodwill and is intimately linked to performance and profitability," he says.[12]

Taking an ethical stand can actually cost a firm in lost revenues and other support. When Google announced a reversal of its original stance on censorship in China—by shutting down operations there and rerouting traffic to an uncensored site in Hong Kong—not only did the company lose business, it found itself standing alone on the issue. Google's decision and the consequences are discussed in the "Solving an Ethical Controversy" feature.

ASSESSMENT CHECK

7.2.1 What is meant by a vision for the firm?

7.2.2 Why is it important for a top executive to set high ethical standards?

SOLVING AN ETHICAL CONTROVERSY

Google Stands Alone: When Ethics and Business Don't Mix

When Google first entered the Chinese market, the firm was criticized. Google had agreed to the censorship guidelines set out by the Chinese government, which controls the distribution of information to the Chinese public. Google made this agreement in the hope that the Chinese government would later relax its stand and allow Chinese citizens to have the same open access to Internet information as others have. But that didn't happen. In fact, the censorship seemed to grow tighter. And it also seemed that someone was using Google to identify Chinese citizens who actively disagreed with the government. So, Google decided to shut down operations in China and rerouted Chinese users to a safe site in Hong Kong. Google received praise from the Internet community for its move to Hong Kong, but received only mild support from the business world.

(continued)

> **SOLVING AN ETHICAL CONTROVERSY** (continued)
>
> **Should the ethical standards set by a business have more weight than undemocratic laws and regulations in the countries where it operates?**
>
> **PRO**
>
> 1. Many multinational firms now have global ethics policies. These policies apply to each country where these firms do business, regardless of national law. Global ethics policies help managers to make consistent decisions, even if they have to lose some profits.
>
> 2. Firms and their employees must always put ethical standards ahead of practices that restrict human rights. "If any corporate executive finds that he or she is actually thinking about putting profit ahead of humanity," argues Mickey Edwards, vice-president of the international not-for-profit Aspen Institute, "it is time for that person to reflect seriously on how and when the moral compass, and one's own claim to humanity, got lost."
>
> **CON**
>
> 1. Ethical standards are not always the same from one country to the next. Google's move may have a negative impact on Chinese consumers. They at least had access to some information when Google was there. "Leaving may look and feel great to those of us in the West, but exiting a market may not always have the desired impact," writes one expert.
>
> 2. Companies that are willing to work with such governments can actually use their influence with consumers to make change happen. For example, companies can create demand for their goods and services. They can also become active in the community through service projects, such as building schools.
>
> **Summary**
>
> Google's exit from China was a clear decision to some people; to others, it was not clear at all. "China is a very important market," noted one analyst. "What's the incentive for a government or another company to join with Google? There is none and that's why you haven't seen it happen." Others point out that China has a market of more than 1 billion consumers, so it is hard to know how open that market will be in the next five or 10 years. And things are getting tougher, not easier for companies wanting to operate in China. "There is a barrage of new rules and regulations for foreign companies operating in China," notes a businessperson with experience in China. "And everybody is trying to figure out what it means."
>
> **Sources:** Alexei Oreskovic and Paul Eckert, "Google Finds Few Allies in China Battle," *Reuters*, March 25, 2010, accessed July 2, 2015, www.reuters.com/article/2010/03/25/us-google-china-analysis-idUSTRE6205FS20100325; Steve Pearlstein and Raju Narisetti, "Doing Right at What Cost?" *The Washington Post*, March 25, 2010, accessed July 2, 2015, http://views.washingtonpost.com/leadership/2010/03/doing_right_at_what_cost/all.html; Aron Cramer and Dunstan Allison Hope, "Google and China: When Should Business Leave on Human Rights Grounds?" *Huffington Post*, March 22, 2010, accessed July 2, 2015, www.huffingtonpost.com/aron-cramer/google-and-china-when-sho_b_508675.html.

IMPORTANCE OF PLANNING

LO 7.3 Summarize the importance of planning and the three types of planning.

Good planning can turn a vision into reality. When Reid Hoffman first got the idea for the professional social network LinkedIn, he was "very interested in this whole notion of each of us as individual professionals who are on the Internet and how that changes the way we do business, our careers, our brand identity. I realized that the world was transforming every individual into a small business." As Hoffman worked on the idea, he thought about how a professional social network could be used. He asked himself and others questions to help develop his plan. "How do you positively influence your brand on the Net? How do you assemble a team fast? Who has the expertise to guide you?" The answers to these questions and more became the plan for LinkedIn.[13]

Types of Planning

Planning can be categorized by scope, or how widely the plan affects other factors. Planning can also be categorized by breadth, or how far into the future the plan extends. For example, some plans are very broad and long range. Other plans are short range and very narrow, affecting only some parts of the organization, not the whole firm. Planning can be divided into four categories: strategic, tactical, operational, and contingency planning. Each step includes more specific information than the step before. Each planning step must also fit into an overall plan, from the mission statement (described in the next section) to objectives to specific plans. This overall plan must also include narrow, functional plans aimed at individual employees and work areas that relate to individual tasks. These plans must fit within the firm's overall plan and help it to reach objectives and achieve its mission.

Strategic Planning

The most far-reaching level of planning is *strategic planning*—the process of deciding on the primary objectives of an organization and then taking action and setting aside resources to achieve those objectives. Generally, strategic planning is done by the top executives in a company. As customers use multiple channels for retail shopping, Home Depot has implemented a strategy called "interconnected retailing." The company wants to create a seamless experience for customers—whether they browse online, open promotional emails on their smartphones, or visit brick-and-mortar locations in person.[14]

As part of its strategic planning, Home Depot has introduced mobile apps with location-based technology that provides shoppers with real-time inventory, pricing, and information about where to find products in a specific store.

Tactical Planning

Tactical planning involves implementing the activities specified by strategic plans. Tactical plans guide the current and near-term activities required to implement overall strategies. As part of Home Depot's strategy to create a multi-channel customer shopping experience, the company has recently introduced an optimized mobile redesign, which integrates location-based technology in smartphones. The technology allows promotions to be sent to in-store shoppers while giving them access to real-time inventory, location, and pricing by store. How-to videos are offered for mobile shoppers doing research on products. The tactical plan keeps customers in contact with the retailer across multiple points of the shopping process.[15]

Operational Planning

Operational planning sets the detailed standards that help to carry out tactical plans. This activity involves choosing specific work targets and assigning employees and teams to carry out plans. Unlike strategic planning, which focuses on the organization as a whole, operational planning deals with developing and implementing tactics in specific functional areas. If customers make purchases online and pick up or return merchandise to the retailer, Home Depot will need staff at its stores to take care of these transactions. This will require additional planning on the part of management that might include additional staffing in shipping, separate customer service teams, and different delivery strategies.

Contingency Planning

Planning cannot foresee every possibility. Even the best plans may face major accidents, natural disasters, and rapid economic downturns. To handle these disruptions, many firms use *contingency planning*. This type of planning helps firms to resume operations as quickly and as smoothly as possible after a crisis. It also makes it easier for them to openly tell the public what happened. Contingency planning activity involves two components: continuing the business and communicating to the public. Many firms have management strategies that make it easier to recover from the loss of data, breaches of security, product failures, and natural disasters such as floods or fire. When a major disaster occurs or business is disrupted, a company can turn to its contingency plan. This plan usually outlines a chain of command for crisis management and assigns specific emergency functions to some or all managers and employees. But a crisis usually occurs on a smaller scale—a product delivery might get lost, a key person might be sick and unable to attend

Chapter 7 Management, Leadership, and the Internal Organization   187

Table 7.1 Planning at Different Management Levels

PRIMARY TYPE OF PLANNING	MANAGERIAL LEVEL	EXAMPLES
Strategic	Top management	Organizational objectives, fundamental strategies, long-term plans
Tactical	Middle management	Quarterly and semi-annual plans, departmental policies and procedures
Operational	Supervisory management	Daily and weekly plans, rules, and procedures for each department
Contingency	Primarily top management, but all levels contribute	Ongoing plans for actions and communications in an emergency

an important meeting, or the electricity might go out for a day. These events also need contingency planning. For example, when British Airways (BA) cabin crews walked off their jobs, the airline had to cancel or delay hundreds of flights. Many travellers were stranded or rerouted. Others tried to find flights on different airlines. By the second day of the strike, many BA flights were back on schedule. BA said that its contingency planning was successful. Because it sensed a possible strike, BA had retrained some on-ground staffers to work as cabin crew. It also leased planes and crew from some of its competitors. "Our contingency plans are continuing to work well . . . around the world," stated an airline spokesperson.[16]

Planning at Different Organizational Levels

Managers spend time planning every day. The total time spent and the type of planning depends on the level of the manager. As shown in **Table 7.1**, top managers, including a firm's board of directors and CEO, spend a great deal of time on long-range planning. Middle-level managers and supervisors focus on short-term, tactical, and operational planning. Employees at all levels can help themselves and their company by making plans to meet their own specific goals.

THE STRATEGIC PLANNING PROCESS

Strategic planning can make the difference between success and failure. Strategic planning forms the basis of many management decisions. Successful strategic planners often follow the six steps shown in **Figure 7.2**: defining a mission, assessing the organization's competitive position, setting organizational objectives, creating strategies for competitive differentiation, implementing the strategy, and assessing the results and refining the plan.

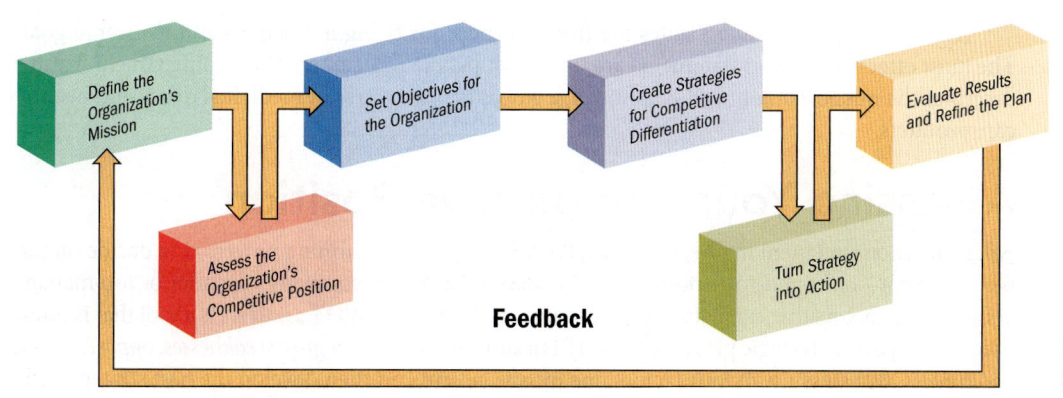

✓ **ASSESSMENT CHECK**

7.3.1 Outline the planning process.

7.3.2 Describe the purpose of tactical planning.

7.3.3 Compare the types of plans made by top managers and middle managers. How does their focus differ?

LO 7.4 Describe the strategic planning process.

FIGURE 7.2 Steps in the Strategic Planning Process

GOING GREEN: JOHNSON & JOHNSON: CARING FOR THE WORLD

In its company statement of values and company credo, Johnson & Johnson promises, "We must maintain in good order the property we are privileged to use, protecting the environment and natural resources." Johnson & Johnson makes consumer products such as Band-Aids, Listerine, and Johnson's Baby Lotion, as well as medical devices and prescription drugs. Doing so can result in a giant carbon footprint made by manufacturing emissions, chemicals in products and processes, and a tremendous use of energy. Yet Johnson & Johnson has put strategies in place to reach its environmental goals.

The firm sets new long-term goals every five years, under its "Healthy Planet" program, for example, using direct purchase of low-impact hydro and wind power, onsite solar power and landfill gas, and purchasing renewable energy certificates. Johnson & Johnson also operates the largest fleet of hybrid and alternative fuel vehicles owned by any corporation in the world.

Part of the "Healthy Planet" program also involves being truthful about green advertising and being specific about sustainability measures. The company is the second-largest producer of solar panels in the United States, and it has received the Leadership in Energy and Environmental Design (LEED) Gold certification for its Spring House research facility in Pennsylvania.

None of these goals could be achieved without support from Johnson & Johnson's leadership. Chairman and CEO Alex Gorsky writes, "I am proud to continue to lead our legacy of commitment to sustainable ideals, born from our Credo commitments and in line with our purpose of caring for the world, one person at a time."

Questions for Critical Thinking

1. What role does the CEO's leadership play in meeting Johnson & Johnson's green goals?
2. How does the company's mission relate to sustainability?

Sources: Johnson & Johnson, accessed February 11, 2014, www.jnj.com; Michael Christel, "J&J's New Lean, Green Lab to Be Key R&D Hub," *PharmaLive*, accessed January 25, 2014, http://blog.rddirections.com; Johnson & Johnson, "To Our Shareholders," Annual Report, accessed January 25, 2014, http://files.shareholder.com/downloads/JNJ/266540474x0x815170/816798CD-60D9-4653-BB5A-50A66FD5B9E7/JNJ_2014_Annual_Report_bookmarked_.pdf; "Partner Profile," Green Power Partnership, accessed January 25, 2014, www.epa.gov.

Defining the Organization's Mission

mission statement a written description of an organization's overall business purpose and aims.

The first step in strategic planning is to translate the firm's vision into a **mission statement**. A mission statement is a written description of an organization's overall business purpose and aims. It is a statement of a firm's reason for being. It can highlight the range of its operations, the market it will serve, and how it will try to set itself apart from competitors. A mission statement guides the actions of employees.

Mission statements can be short or long:

- Starbucks: "To inspire and nurture the human spirit—one person, one cup and one neighbourhood at a time."
- Disney: "We create happiness by providing the finest in entertainment for people of all ages, everywhere."
- Nike: "To bring inspiration and innovation to every athlete in the world."
- Sony: "To experience the joy of advancing and applying technology for the benefit of the public."

A good mission statement states the firm's purpose for being in business and its overall goal. The most effective mission statements are those that people remember. The "Going Green" feature describes the mission of Johnson & Johnson, a global manufacturer of medicinal drugs and healthcare products.

Assessing Your Competitive Position

SWOT analysis SWOT is a short form for *strengths, weaknesses, opportunities*, and *threats*. By assessing all four factors one by one, a firm can then develop the best strategies for gaining a competitive advantage.

After a mission statement has been created, the next step in the planning process is to decide on the firm's current—or hoped-for—position in the marketplace. The company's founder or top managers assess the factors that can help it grow or cause it to fail. The **SWOT analysis** is a tool that is often used in this part of strategic planning. SWOT is a short form for *strengths, weaknesses, opportunities*, and *threats*. By assessing all four factors one by one, a firm can then develop the best strategies for gaining a competitive advantage. The framework for a SWOT analysis is shown in **Figure 7.3**.

Chapter 7 Management, Leadership, and the Internal Organization

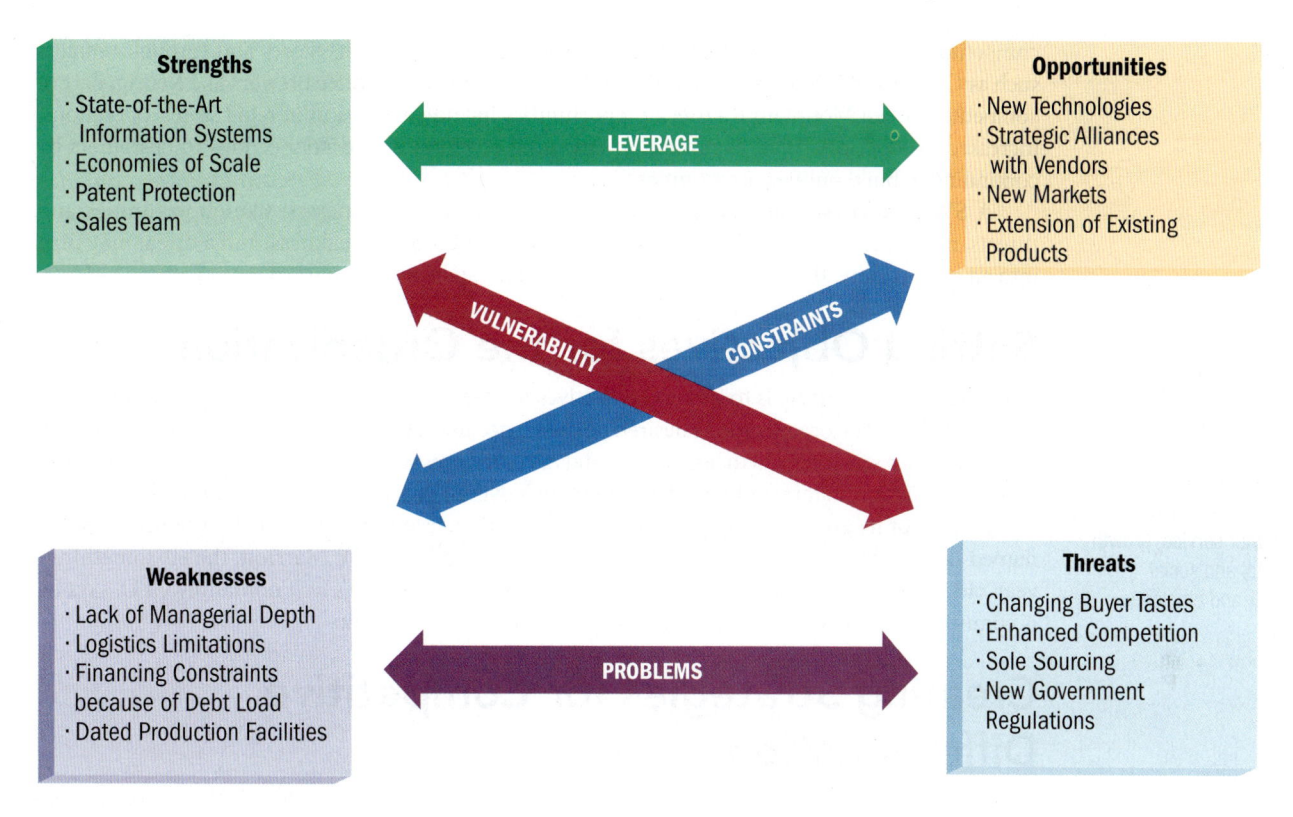

Strengths
- State-of-the-Art Information Systems
- Economies of Scale
- Patent Protection
- Sales Team

Opportunities
- New Technologies
- Strategic Alliances with Vendors
- New Markets
- Extension of Existing Products

Weaknesses
- Lack of Managerial Depth
- Logistics Limitations
- Financing Constraints because of Debt Load
- Dated Production Facilities

Threats
- Changing Buyer Tastes
- Enhanced Competition
- Sole Sourcing
- New Government Regulations

LEVERAGE · VULNERABILITY · CONSTRAINTS · PROBLEMS

FIGURE 7.3 Elements of a SWOT Analysis

To assess a firm's strengths and weaknesses, its managers may look at each functional area, such as finance, marketing, information technology, and human resources. Or they might look at the strengths and weaknesses of each office, plant, or store. Entrepreneurs may use a SWOT analysis to focus on the individual skills and experience they bring to a new business.

For Starbucks, a key strength is consumers' positive view of the company's brand. After all, it gets them to stand in line to pay premium prices for coffee. That positive view comes from Starbucks being one of the best 100 companies to work for according to *Fortune*. It also comes from its socially responsible corporate policies. The company's strategic plans have included various ways to build on Starbucks's strong brand loyalty by attaching it to new products and expanding into new markets. The expansion efforts have included the purchase of Evolution Fresh cold-pressed juices, La Boulange Café and Bakery, and Teavana, a high-end tea store found in shopping malls. Starbucks remains focused on overseas retail expansion; its online, mobile, and digital loyalty program; and its gift card business. Weaknesses include a premium-priced product in a challenging economy, saturating some markets with too many stores, and not paying attention to store design. Starbucks eventually addressed these weaknesses by lowering the price of bagged coffee, closing some stores, and redesigning others.[17]

SWOT analysis continues with an attempt to define the major opportunities and threats the firm is likely to face. Threats might include rising coffee bean prices, trademark infringements, increased competition from local cafes and lower-priced fast-food chains, and increased online shopping, particularly during holiday seasons, thus reducing foot traffic in stores. Starbucks addressed the threat of the challenging economy and lower-priced

Starbucks extends its strong brand loyalty to new products and markets. This activity is one example of the company's strategic turnaround plan.

competitors by beginning to offer less-expensive, instant coffee in its stores and through retailers such as Costco and Walmart. An additional threat includes single coffee brewers like Keurig, part of competitor Green Mountain Roasters. Opportunities include expansion of retail stores' operations, increased product offerings, expansion to emerging economies, and connections to customers by continuing to build online communities.[18]

A SWOT analysis can change. After all, strengths and weaknesses, like opportunities and threats, may shift over time. A strength may eventually become a weakness, and a threat may turn into an opportunity. But the SWOT analysis gives managers a place to start.

Setting Objectives for the Organization

objectives guideposts by which managers define the organization's desired performance in such areas as new-product development, sales, customer service, growth, environmental and social responsibility, and employee satisfaction.

The next step in planning is to develop objectives for the firm. **Objectives** set guideposts by which managers define the organization's desired performance in such areas as new-product development, sales, customer service, growth, environmental and social responsibility, and employee satisfaction. While the mission statement identifies a company's overall goals, objectives are more concrete.

As part of its growth strategy, Marriott Corporation recently opened its first boutique hotel, named *Edition*, in London. "We're trying to get some flash," says J.W. Marriott, the 80-something-year-old son of the company's founder. Arne M. Sorenson, Marriott's first nonfamily CEO, says he is committed to broadening the company's overall business portfolio.[19]

Creating Strategies for Competitive Differentiation

When managers develop a mission statement and set objectives, they help their business to move in a specific direction. But the firm also needs to decide on the strategies it will use to reach its target ahead of the competition. The basic goal of developing a strategy is *competitive differentiation*—the unique mix of a company's abilities and resources that set it apart from its competitors. A firm might differentiate itself, or set itself apart, by being the first to introduce a product. For example, Apple introduced the iPad to a global market, WestJet decided to focus on providing exceptional customer service, and Costco chose to offer bargains. Becel is the leading margarine brand in Canada. The company has a strong commitment to heart health innovation and education. The firm sets itself apart from other brands by highlighting its association with reducing cholesterol through proper diet and exercise.[20]

Implementing the Strategy

After the first four phases of the strategic planning process are complete, managers are ready to put those plans into action. The middle managers or supervisors are often the people who actually implement a strategy. But studies show that many top company officials don't want to give these managers the power to make decisions that could be helpful for the company. Companies that *are* willing to empower employees usually profit from that decision.[21]

Many firms have a strategy of cutting costs and maintaining a high level of customer service. A strategy that makes sense is to cross-train call centre representatives. When customers phone in, they don't need to be transferred to someone else if the person who answers the call has been trained to answer the most frequently asked questions. This idea may seem like an obvious strategy that won't have much effect. But research shows that cross-training can reduce the cost of running a call centre, increase customer satisfaction, and improve employee morale.[22]

Monitoring and Adapting Strategic Plans

✓ **ASSESSMENT CHECK**

7.4.1 What is the purpose of a mission statement?

7.4.2 Which of a firm's characteristics are compared in a SWOT analysis?

7.4.3 How do managers use objectives?

The final step in the strategic planning process is to monitor and adapt plans when the actual performance fails to meet goals. Monitoring involves gathering feedback about performance. Managers might compare actual sales against forecast sales; compile information from surveys; listen to complaints from the customer hot line; interview employees who are involved; and review reports prepared by production, finance, marketing, or other company units. If an Internet advertisement doesn't result in enough customers or sales, managers might look at whether to continue the advertisement, change it, or discontinue it. If a retailer sees that customers buy more jeans when they are displayed near the front door, the display area will probably stay near the door—and may even be made bigger. Managers can continue to use of such tools as SWOT analysis and forecasting to help adapt their objectives and functional plans as changes occur.

MANAGERS AS DECISION MAKERS

LO 7.5 Describe the two major types of business decisions and the steps in the decision-making process.

Managers make decisions every day. Some decisions may involve shutting down a manufacturing plant. Other decisions may deal with adding grilled cheese sandwiches to a lunch menu. **Decision making** is the process of seeing a problem or opportunity, assessing possible solutions, selecting and carrying out the best-suited plan, and assessing the results. Managers make two basic kinds of decisions: programmed decisions and nonprogrammed decisions.

decision making the process of seeing a problem or opportunity, assessing possible solutions, selecting and carrying out the best-suited plan, and assessing the results.

Programmed and Nonprogrammed Decisions

A *programmed decision* involves simple, common, and frequently occurring problems that already have solutions. For example, programmed decisions include reordering office supplies, renewing a lease, and referring to an already-decided-on discount for bulk orders. Programmed decisions are made in advance. The firm sets rules, policies, and procedures for managers and employees to follow on a routine basis. Programmed decisions save managers time and save companies money because new decisions don't have to be made each time the situation arises.

A *nonprogrammed decision* involves a complex and unique problem or opportunity and has important results for the organization. Nonprogrammed decisions include entering a new market, deleting a product from the line, or developing a new product. Apple's decision to develop and launch the iPad was a nonprogrammed decision that involved research and development, finances, technology, production, and marketing. Decisions were made about everything, from what kinds of apps and accessories the iPad would offer, to how much the new device would cost consumers.[23]

Apple made a nonprogrammed decision when it released the iPad. The decision involved a complex and unique opportunity and had important results for the company.

How Managers Make Decisions

In a simple view, decision making is choosing from two or more options, and the chosen option becomes the decision. In a larger view, decision making is a step-by-step process that helps managers to make effective choices. This process begins when someone sees a problem or an opportunity, develops possible ways of taking action, evaluates the options, selects and carries out one option, and assesses the outcome. It's important to remember that managers are *human* decision makers. Managers may follow the decision-making process shown in **Figure 7.4** step-by-step, but the outcome of their decisions depends on many factors: the quality of the information they used and their experience, creativity, and wisdom. Warren Buffett, billionaire investor and CEO of Berkshire Hathaway, empowers his managers to make decisions without his input. See the "Hit & Miss" feature for more on Buffet's management style.

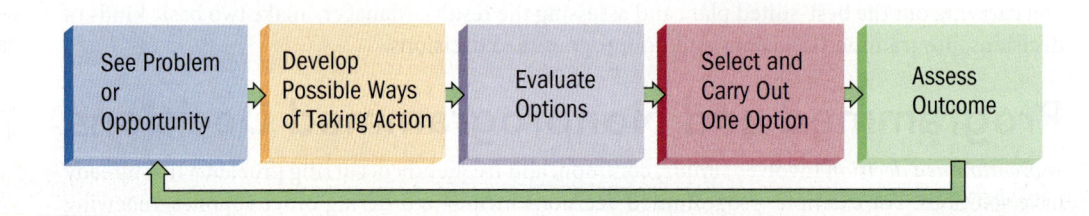

FIGURE 7.4 Steps in the Decision-Making Process

See Problem or Opportunity → Develop Possible Ways of Taking Action → Evaluate Options → Select and Carry Out One Option → Assess Outcome

HIT & MISS

Hands-Off Approach Works for Buffett

Warren Buffett, billionaire investor and CEO of Berkshire Hathaway, is known for his hands-off management style. Buffett prefers to give his chief lieutenants the autonomy to make decisions on their own about the companies they run—even if he doesn't agree with them.

Buffett believes that giving people autonomy motivates them to do the best possible job. In his company's annual letter to shareholders, he writes, "there are managers to whom I have not talked in the last year, while there is one with whom I talk almost daily. Our trust is in people rather than process. A 'hire well, manage little' code suits both them and me."

In Berkshire Hathaway's more than 40 businesses, the CEOs are experienced and competent, and understand Buffett's management approach. Tracy Cool, a 29-year-old business-school graduate, is one of Buffett's most recent recruits and has become one of his most trusted advisors. Cool chairs four of Buffett's subsidiaries, with combined sales exceeding $4 billion and more than 10,000 employees. When Cool hires employees, she tries to hire individuals who are committed to the job, who understand Berkshire's unique culture, and who can function in a hands-off environment. She also believes that making mistakes is a great way to learn, and Buffett is very supportive of his management team. Buffett echoes Cool's comments.

He believes in hiring self-starters who love what they do. "Talented people can accomplish a whole lot," he says.

Questions for Critical Thinking

1. What are the advantages and disadvantages of a hands-off management style like Buffett's approach?

2. Buffett states there are managers to whom he has not talked with over the last year, and those with whom he talks almost daily. As one of Buffett's lieutenants, how often would you communicate with your boss? Explain your reasoning.

Sources: Company website Berkshire Hathaway, accessed January 26, 2014, http://berkshirehathaway.com; Anupreeta Das, "Tracy Britt Cool on Management Lessons from Warren Buffett," *The Wall Street Journal*, October 16, 2013, accessed July 2, 2015, http://blogs.wsj.com/moneybeat/2013/10/16/tracy-britt-cool-on-management-lessons-from-warren-buffett; Noah Buhayar and Laura Colby, "Buffett Leans on 29-Year-Old Cool to Oversee Problems," *Bloomberg Business*, January 21, 2014, accessed July 2, 2015, www.bloomberg.com/news/articles/2014-01-21/buffett-leans-on-29-year-old-cool-to-oversee-problems; Andrew Ross Sorkin, "Warren Buffett, the Delegator in Chief," *The New York Times*, April 23, 2011, accessed July 2, 2015, http://dealbook.nytimes.com/2011/04/23/warren-buffett-the-delegator-in-chief; Timothy R. Clark, "Why We Trust Warren Buffett," *Deseret News*, April 11, 2011, accessed July 2, 2015, www.deseretnews.com/article/705370243/Why-we-trust-Warren-Buffett.html?pg=allwww.deseretnews.com.

Chapter 7 Management, Leadership, and the Internal Organization   193

Making good decisions is never easy. A decision might hurt or help the sales of a product; it might insult or disappoint a customer or co-worker; it might affect the manager's own career or reputation. Managers' decisions can have legal and ethical effects. In Canada, *Corporate Knights Magazine* publishes an annual list of "The Best 50 Corporate Citizens." In the United States, *CRO Magazine* publishes an annual list of "The 100 Best Corporate Citizens." The companies on these lists make decisions that are ethical, environmentally responsible, fair toward employees, and accountable to local communities. These companies also provide responsible goods and services to customers and a healthy return to investors. These organizations prove that good corporate citizenship is good behaviour. The top 10 Canadian corporate citizens named one recent year were Mountain Equipment Co-op, Co-operators Group, Vancouver City Savings Credit Union, Bombardier, Tim Hortons, Mouvement des caisses Desjardins (The Desjardins Group), Teck Resources, Husky Energy, Toronto-Dominion Bank, and Cenovus Energy. The top 10 U.S. corporate citizens named were AT&T, Mattel, Bristol-Myers Squibb, Eaton, Intel, The Gap, Hasbro, Merck & Co., Campbell Soup Company, and Coca-Cola Enterprises.[24]

> **ASSESSMENT CHECK**
>
> 7.5.1 Distinguish between programmed and nonprogrammed decisions.
>
> 7.5.2 What are the steps in the decision-making process?

MANAGERS AS LEADERS

> **LO 7.6** Define *leadership*, and compare different leadership styles.

A manager must show **leadership**, by directing or inspiring others to reach goals. All great leaders do not share the same qualities, but three personal qualities are often mentioned: empathy (the ability to imagine being in someone else's position), self-awareness, and objectivity. Empathy and objectivity may seem like opposites, but they do balance each other. Many leaders share other qualities, such as courage, passion, commitment, innovation, and flexibility.

leadership the ability to direct or inspire people to reach goals.

Leadership involves the use of influence or power. This influence may come from one or more sources. One source of power is the leader's position in the company. A national sales manager has the authority to direct the activities of the sales force. Another source of power is a leader's expertise and experience. A first-line supervisor with expert machinist skills will likely be respected by employees in the machining department. Some leaders derive power from their personalities. Employees may admire a leader because they see a person who is exceptionally kind and fair, humorous, energetic, or enthusiastic. Admiration, inspiration, and motivation are especially important during difficult economic times or when a leader needs to make tough decisions for the company, as was the case at General Motors. See the accompanying "Hit & Miss" feature for an introduction to Mary Barra, the company's first female CEO.

When Doug Conant, former CEO at Campbell Soup Company, took over the company in 2001, the company was decidedly a little boring. Instead of being filled with new ideas, the firm wasn't thinking about doing anything new. Conant looked around the company. It produces one of the best-known brands in the world. Conant was frustrated. "The microwave was invented in 1947, but it took us until 2002 to put together a microwaveable soup pack," he told the company's researchers, marketers, and managers. Conant got to work on updating the world's largest soup company. He cut all products that were not number one or number

Doug Conant, Campbell Soup Company's former CEO, believed that action was the best way to show leadership.

HIT & MISS

GM's First Female CEO Faces Challenges and Opportunities

Mary Barra, GM's first female CEO, knows cars. She has worked for the Detroit automaker for more than 30 years in a variety of positions. She began her GM career as an intern while in college. After graduation, Barra's first job was a plant engineer at the assembly factory in Pontiac, Michigan.

Before being tapped for the CEO post, Barra spent time in several different divisions of the company, including global manufacturing, purchasing, supply chain management, and human resources. Most recently, she headed up the $15 billion global product development group, where she and her team were responsible for the design and engineering of GM vehicles worldwide. *Motor Trend Magazine* recently named the Cadillac CTS Car of the Year, and *Consumer Reports* named the Chevy Impala the best sedan and the Silverado the best pickup truck.

In her new position as CEO, Barra has already faced several challenges, including a safety recall of millions of GM vehicles caused by a faulty ignition switch that resulted in multiple deaths. She appeared before a congressional committee to discuss the recall, authorized an in-depth internal investigation by a former federal prosecutor, and subsequently fired 15 employees for misconduct and incompetence.

Despite the recall and associated issues, Barra continues to see opportunities for GM, particularly in Asia. Of the 2.4 million cars sold in GM's most recent financial quarter, more than 30 percent were sold in China. She plans to continue the company's global expansion with sales of the Chevrolet and Cadillac brands and is optimistic that new product launches will keep the auto giant on a successful business path.

Questions for Critical Thinking

1. How do Barra's previous job experiences at GM help her in her role as the company's CEO?
2. What challenges will Barra encounter as she guides the company's global expansion into other markets?

Sources: Kyle Stock, "GM's Mary Barra Fires 15, Says More Recalls Are Coming," *Bloomberg Business*, June 6, 2014, accessed July 2, 2015, www.bloomberg.com/bw/articles/2014-06-05/gms-mary-barra-fires-15-says-more-recalls-are-coming; Chris Isidore and Katie Lobosco, "GM CEO Barra: 'I Am Deeply Sorry,'" *CNN Money*, April 1, 2014, accessed July 5, 2015, http://money.cnn.com/2014/04/01/news/companies/barra-congress-testimony; Joann Muller, "Exclusive Q&A: GM CEO Mary Barra on Crisis Management, Culture Change and the Future of GM," *Forbes*, May 29, 2014, accessed July 2, 2015, www.forbes.com/sites/joannmuller/2014/05/29/exclusive-qa-gm-ceo-mary-barra-on-crisis-management-culture-change-and-the-future-of-gm; General Motors company website, www.gm.com, accessed February 11, 2014; Sherri Welch, "By Naming Mary Barra CEO, GM Sends Strong Message about Talent, Opportunity," *Crain's Detroit Business*, December 10, 2013, accessed July 2, 2015, www.crainsdetroit.com/article/20131210/NEWS/131219986/analysis-by-naming-mary-barra-ceo-gm-sends-strong-message-about; Tim Higgins, "GM CEO Barra Aims to Accelerate Strategies Set Under Akerson," *Bloomberg Business*, January 23, 2014, accessed July 2, 2015, www.bloomberg.com/news/articles/2014-01-23/gm-s-barra-seeks-to-accelerate-strategy-set-under-akerson; Tim Higgins and Brian Urstadt, "Exclusive: The Inside Story of GM's Comeback and Mary Barra's Rise," *Bloomberg Business*, December 12, 2013, accessed July 2, 2015, www.bloomberg.com/bw/articles/2013-12-12/exclusive-the-inside-story-of-gms-comeback-and-mary-barras-rise.

With more than 30 years of experience at GM, Mary Barra recently became the company's first female CEO.

two in their categories. He poured resources into developing products that offered value, nutrition, and convenience. And he engineered a new focus on two of the world's largest soup-eating nations: China and Russia. Conant believed that action was the best demonstration of leadership. "You can't talk your way out of something you behaved your way into," he says.[25]

Leadership Styles

A person's leadership style depends on how that person uses power to lead others. Leadership styles range from autocratic leadership at one extreme to free-rein leadership at the other extreme. *Autocratic leadership* is centred on the boss. Autocratic leaders make decisions on their own without consulting employees. They make decisions, communicate the decisions to employees, and expect the decisions to be carried out right away.

Democratic leadership includes employees in the decision-making process. This leadership style centres on employees' contributions. Democratic leaders assign projects, ask employees for suggestions, and encourage participation. An important outcome of democratic leadership in business is the concept of *empowerment*, where employees share authority, responsibility, and decision making with their managers.

At the opposite extreme from autocratic leadership is *free-rein leadership*. Free-rein leaders believe in minimal supervision. They allow employees to make most of their own decisions. Free-rein leaders communicate with employees frequently. For its first decade in business, Google was proud of its free-rein leadership style. Engineers were encouraged to pursue any and all ideas, teams formed or disbanded on their own, and employees spent as much or as little time as they wanted to on any given project. But then the firm entered its second decade. Not every innovation was worth pursuing—and some valuable ideas were getting lost. CEO Eric Schmidt noted, "We were concerned that some of the biggest ideas were getting squashed." So the firm set up a process for reviewing new project ideas to focus on those ideas most likely to succeed.[26]

empowerment giving employees shared authority, responsibility, and decision making with their managers.

Which Leadership Style Is Best?

No single leadership style is right for every firm in every situation. Leadership styles sometimes need to be changed for a company to grow. That was the situation for Google. In a crisis, an autocratic leadership style might save the company—and sometimes the lives of customers and employees. That's what happened when US Airways flight 1549 was forced to land in the Hudson River in New York. Quick, autocratic decisions made by pilot Chesley Sullenberger meant that everyone on the flight survived. But US Airways management on the ground used a democratic style of leadership: managers at many levels were empowered to take actions to help the passengers and their families. For example, one executive arrived on the scene with a bag of emergency cash for passengers and credit cards for employees so they could purchase medicines, food, or anything else they needed.[27] Some companies know which leadership style works best for their employees, customers, and business conditions. Those companies are most likely to choose the best leaders for their needs.

✓ **ASSESSMENT CHECK**

7.6.1 How is *leadership* defined?

7.6.2 Identify the styles of leadership as they range from the most to the least amount of employee participation.

CORPORATE CULTURE

An organization's **corporate culture** is its collection of principles, beliefs, and values. The corporate culture is influenced by the leadership style of its managers, the way the firm communicates, and the overall work environment. A corporate culture is typically shaped by the leaders who founded and developed the company and by the leaders who were appointed since the founders left. For example, look at Google. It has grown by leaps and bounds since its launch. The firm tries to continue the culture of innovation, creativity, and flexibility that its co-founders, Larry Page and Sergey Brin, promoted from the beginning. Google now has offices around the world, staffed by thousands of workers who speak many different languages. "We are aggressively inclusive in our hiring, and we favour ability over experience," states the website. "The result is a team that reflects the global audience Google serves. When not at work, Googlers pursue interests from cross-country cycling to wine tasting, from flying to Frisbee."[28]

Managers sometimes use symbols, rituals, ceremonies, and stories to strengthen a corporate culture. The corporate culture at the Walt Disney Company is almost as famous as the Disney characters themselves. In fact, every Disney employee is known as a cast member. All new employees attend training seminars to learn the language, customs, traditions, stories, product lines—everything about the Disney culture and its original founder, Walt Disney.[29]

Corporate cultures can be very strong and lasting. But sometimes they need to change to meet new demands in the business world. A firm that is filled with tradition and bureaucracy might need to shift to a leaner, more flexible culture to respond to shifts in technology or customer

LO 7.7 Discuss the meaning and importance of corporate culture.

corporate culture an organization's collection of principles, beliefs, and values.

HIT & MISS

WestJet Airlines: Most Admired Corporate Culture in Canada

WestJet Airlines was named a J.D. Power 2011 Customer Service champion. The company was also inducted into the Corporate Cultures Hall of Fame after being named one of Canada's Most Admired Corporate Cultures every year from 2005 to 2010. The airline is well known for its reasonable fares, cheerful service, convenient schedules, and genuine interest in its passengers. WestJet is both successful and profitable. It is the business model that other service-oriented businesses study to learn how WestJet sets itself apart through its superior customer service.

WestJet's strategic plan is built on four pillars for long-term success:

- People and Culture: Investing in and fostering the growth, development, and commitment of our people.
- Guest Experience: Consistently and continuously providing an amazing guest experience.
- Revenue and Growth: Achieving an average annual compound growth rate in available seat miles of between four and seven per cent.
- Costs: Achieving a targeted, sustainable profit margin that will be number one among North American airlines.

Together, these pillars describe the corporate focus and culture that directs the firm. WestJet is also known to have a corporate culture filled with humour and energy that spills over to its customers. When you fly WestJet, the hosts tell jokes over the public address system before giving the formal instructions about flight safety. The jokes help to get passengers' attention and create a more relaxed atmosphere for the flight. Employees are empowered and convey the culture of the company to customers. The idea is that if the company's 8,000 employees are happy, they will want to make sure their customers are happy, too. This simple strategy has been very effective. There's another reason employees feel differently about the company they work for. About 85 percent of eligible employees own shares of the company through an employee share purchase plan.

Questions for Critical Thinking

1. How would you describe the principles, beliefs, and values at WestJet?
2. How important is employee ownership to creating and maintaining the corporate culture?

Sources: WestJet website, "About WestJet," accessed January 23, 2012, www.westjet.com/guest/en/about/index.shtml; WestJet, Fact Sheet, accessed January 23, 2012, www.westjet.com/pdf/investorMedia/investorFactSheet.pdf; Canada Newswire, "WestJet Named to Corporate Culture Hall of Fame," February 1, 2010, accessed July 2, 2015, www.newswire.ca/en/story/692931/westjet-named-to-corporate-culture-hall-of-fame; "WestJet Culture Seen as Tops in Country," *Calgary Herald*, October 11, 2006, accessed January 12, 2012, www.canada.com/calgaryherald/news/calgarybusiness/story.html?id=1cec87b5-bbab-4e1 e-a63a-e64f91 b15fa6&k=24339.

ASSESSMENT CHECK

7.7.1 What is the relationship between leadership style and corporate culture?

7.7.2 What is a strong corporate culture?

LO 7.8 Identify the five major forms of departmentalization and the four main types of organization structures.

organization a structured group of people working together to achieve common goals.

demands. A firm that grows quickly—like Google—usually needs to make some adjustments in its culture to make room for more customers and more employees.

In an organization with a strong culture, everyone knows and supports the same principles, beliefs, and values. That's the culture at WestJet Airlines, described in the "Hit & Miss" feature. To reach its goals, a business must also provide structure, which results from the management function of organizing.

ORGANIZATIONAL STRUCTURES

An **organization** is a structured group of people working together to achieve common goals. An organization features three key elements: human interaction, goal-directed activities, and structure. The organizing process is mostly led by managers. It should result in an overall structure that makes it easier for individuals and departments to work together to achieve company goals.

The steps involved in the organizing process are shown in **Figure 7.5**. Managers first decide on the specific activities needed to carry out plans and achieve goals. Next, they group these work activities into a structure that makes sense. Then, they assign work to specific employees and give them the resources they need. Managers coordinate the work of different groups and employees

Chapter 7 Management, Leadership, and the Internal Organization 197

| 1. Decide on the Specific Work Activities Needed to Carry Out Plans and Achieve Objectives | 2. Group All Work Activities into a Pattern or Structure that Makes Sense | 3. Assign Activities to Specific Employees and Give Them the Resources They Need | 4. Coordinate the Activities of Different Groups and Individuals | 5. Evaluate the Results of the Organizing Process |

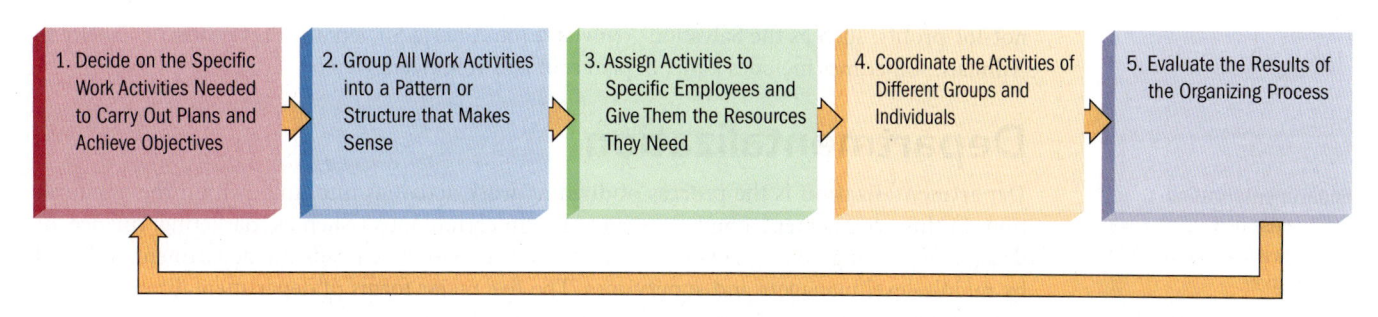

FIGURE 7.5 Steps in the Organizing Process

within the firm. Finally, they evaluate the results of the organizing process to ensure effective and efficient progress toward planned goals. Evaluation sometimes results in changes to the way work is organized.

Many factors can affect the results of organizing. The list includes a firm's goals and competitive strategy, the type of product it offers, the way it uses technology to accomplish work, and its size. Small firms typically create very simple structures. For example, the owner of a dry-cleaning business is often the top manager, who hires several employees to process orders, clean the clothing, and make deliveries. The owner purchases supplies such as detergents and hangers, hires and trains employees, coordinates employees' work, prepares advertisements for the local newspaper, and keeps the accounting records.

As a company grows, its structure becomes more complex. Increased size often means specialization and growing numbers of employees. A larger firm may need to hire many salespeople and a sales manager to direct and coordinate their work, or it may need to organize an accounting department.

An effective structure is clear and easy to understand: employees know what they are expected to do, and they know whom they report to. They also know how their jobs help to achieve the company's mission and overall strategic plan. An *organization chart* can help people to understand the structure of a firm. **Figure 7.6** shows a sample organization chart.

Not-for-profit organizations also organize themselves using formal structures. These structures help them to function efficiently and to carry out their goals. The organizational structure of

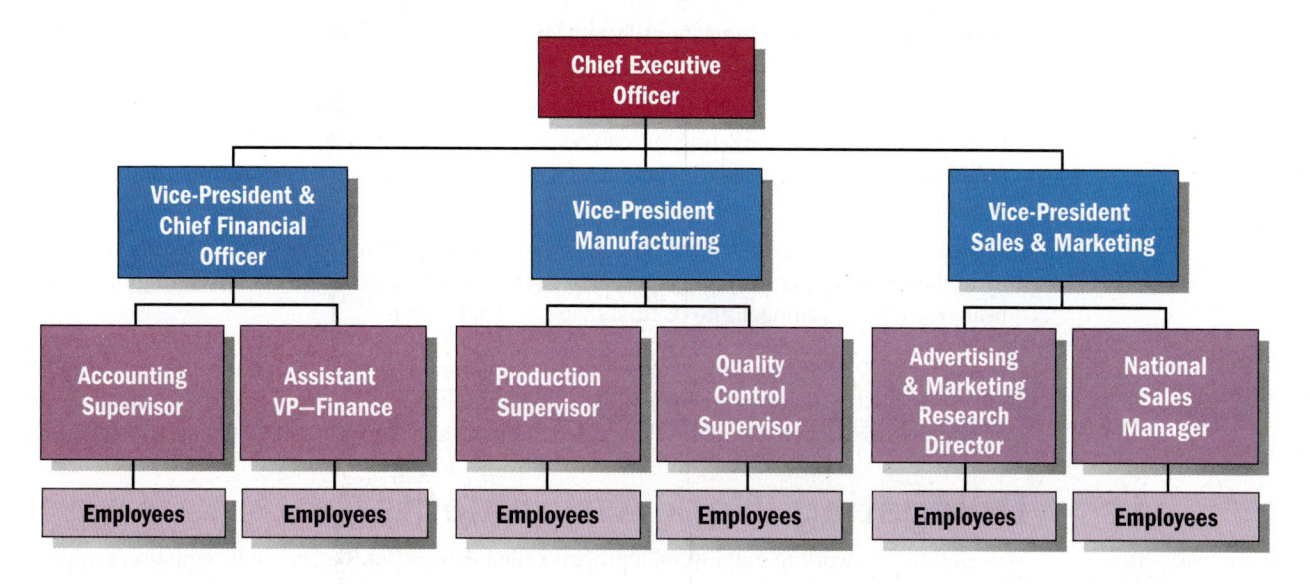

Chief Executive Officer
- **Vice-President & Chief Financial Officer**
  - Accounting Supervisor → Employees
  - Assistant VP—Finance → Employees
- **Vice-President Manufacturing**
  - Production Supervisor → Employees
  - Quality Control Supervisor → Employees
- **Vice-President Sales & Marketing**
  - Advertising & Marketing Research Director → Employees
  - National Sales Manager → Employees

FIGURE 7.6 Sample Organization Chart

not-for-profits, such as the Salvation Army and the Alberta Society for Prevention of Cruelty to Animals, sometimes includes a mix of paid staff and volunteers.

Departmentalization

departmentalization the process of dividing work activities into units within the organization.

Departmentalization is the process of dividing work activities into units within the organization. In this arrangement, employees specialize in certain jobs—such as marketing, finance, or design. Depending on the size of the firm, usually an executive heads the department, followed by middle-level managers and supervisors. The five major forms of departmentalization divide work by product, geographical area, customer, function, and process.

- *Product departmentalization.* This approach organizes work units based on the goods and services a company offers. Activision Blizzard Inc. recently restructured its organization by product. The videogame publisher is now divided into four divisions: "Call of Duty," a military game; internally owned games, such as "Guitar Hero" and "Tony Hawk"; licensed properties; and Blizzard Entertainment, maker of the online game "World of Warcraft."[30]

- *Geographical departmentalization.* This form organizes units by geographical regions within a country or, for a multinational firm, by region throughout the world. Enterprise Rent-A-Car is organized by geography, staffing 7,000 rental locations in the United States, Canada, Germany, Ireland, and England.[31]

These familiar office products represent only one of 3M Corporation's many product lines. Because 3M serves a broad range of customers, it is organized on the basis of customer departmentalization.

- *Customer departmentalization.* Customer departmentalization might be used by a firm that offers a variety of goods and services for different types of customers. For example, 3M's wide range of products is divided among six business units: consumer and office; display and graphics; electro and communications; healthcare; industrial and transportation; and safety, security, and protection services.[32]

- *Functional departmentalization.* Some firms organize work units according to business functions, such as finance, marketing, human resources, and production. An advertising agency may create departments for creative personnel (for example, copywriters), media buyers, and account executives.

- *Process departmentalization.* Some goods and services require multiple work processes to complete their production. A manufacturer may set up separate departments for cutting material, heat-treating it, forming it into its final shape, and painting it.

As **Figure 7.7** shows, a single company may use several forms of departmentalization. When deciding on a form of departmentalization, managers take into account the type of product they produce, the size of their company, their customer base, and the locations of their customers.

Delegating Work Assignments

delegation the managerial process of assigning work to employees.

Managers assign work to employees, a process called **delegation**. For example, employees might be assigned to answer customer calls, scoop ice cream, process returns, make deliveries, open or close a store, cook or serve food, contribute to new-product design, calculate a return on investment,

Chapter 7 Management, Leadership, and the Internal Organization 199

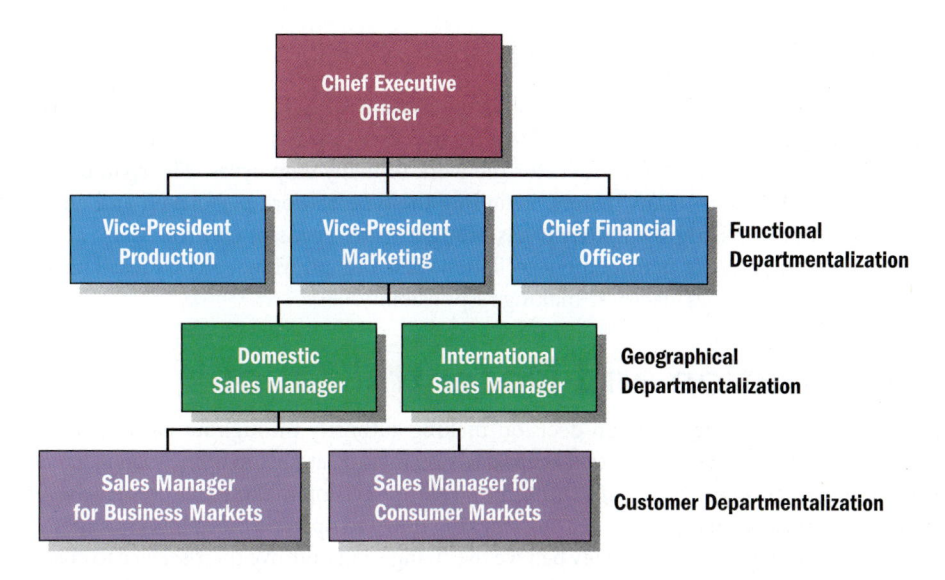

FIGURE 7.7 Different Forms of Departmentalization within One Company

or any of thousands of other tasks. Just as important as the tasks themselves, employees are usually given some authority to make decisions.

Companies like Zappos, the online shoe retailer, give their workers the power to make decisions to better serve their customers. The result is generally happier employees and more satisfied customers.[33] As employees receive more power to make decisions, they also must be accountable for their actions and decisions—that is, they receive credit when things go well and must accept responsibility when things don't go well. Managers also must decide on the best way to delegate responsibilities when employees belong to different age groups, as discussed in the "Career Kickstart" feature.

CAREER KICKSTART

Managing a Multigenerational Workforce

Today's firms employ workers who span a wide range of ages. Management experts warn against stereotyping, or treating people on the basis of an overly simple idea of their characteristics or qualities. The experts do suggest making an effort to understand each group. They suggest taking steps to open up communications so that everyone in the workforce works well together. Baby boomers, those people born between 1946 and 1964, tend to be competitive. Most of them believe that younger employees should work their way up the company ladder. Gen-Xers, born between 1965 and 1977, are more skeptical, independent thinkers. Gen-Yers—also called the Millennials—were born in 1978 or later. They prefer teamwork, feedback, and technology.

Managers can use the following tips to effectively assign work to employees in these groups:

- Offer—and encourage—mentoring, an informal relationship between younger and older employees to guide and advise younger employees. Communication and support that crosses age groups can increase understanding among employees.

- Understand different learning styles and work styles, and make workplace changes to help employees who learn and work differently.

- Involve employees in the workplace through training, education, and career development opportunities.

- Discard strict routines for those who work best without them.

- Use different forms of communication. Older employees may prefer chatting on the phone or in person. Millennials might prefer emails, text messages, or social networking.

- Give everyone an equal voice. Everyone wants to be heard and understood. Offer opportunities for all employees to voice their opinions.

Sources: Sally Kane, "The Multigenerational Workforce," About.com, accessed March 29, 2010, http://legalcareers.about.com/od/practicetips/a/multigeneration.htm; "How to Manage Different Generations," *Wall Street Journal*, accessed March 29, 2010, http://guides.wsj.com/management/managing-your-people/how-to-manage-different-generations; Tammy Erickson, "Finally, Gen X Takes Over," *Harvard Business Review*, January 12, 2009, accessed March 29, 2010, https://hbr.org/2009/01/across-the-ages-in-2009.

Span of Management

The *span of management*, or span of control, is the number of employees a manager supervises. These employees are often referred to as *direct reports*. First-line managers often have the widest spans of management because they monitor the work of many employees. The span of management varies, depending on many factors, including the type of work performed and employees' training. In recent years, a growing trend has brought wider spans of control. Many companies have reduced their layers of management to flatten their organizational structures. This process usually increases employees' decision-making responsibility.

Centralization and Decentralization

How widely should managers assign decision-making authority throughout an organization? A company that emphasizes *centralization* keeps decision making at the top of the management hierarchy. A company that emphasizes *decentralization* shifts decision making to lower levels. A trend toward decentralization has pushed decision making down to operating employees in many companies. Firms decentralize because they believe the change will improve their service to customers. For example, a hotel's front desk clerk is better able to help a guest who needs a crib or a wake-up call than the hotel's general manager.

Types of Organization Structures

The four basic types of organization structures are line, line-and-staff, committee, and matrix. Some companies use one type of structure, but most use a mix of two or more types.

Line Organizations

The oldest and simplest organization structure is a *line organization*. It sets up a direct flow of authority from the chief executive to the employees. The line organization defines a simple, clear *chain of command*—a hierarchy of managers and workers. Everyone knows who is in charge, and decisions can be made quickly. This structure is very effective in a crisis situation. But a line organization also has its downsides. Each manager has complete responsibility for a range of activities. But in a medium-sized or large organization, the manager can't be an expert in all of the tasks. In a small organization, such as a local hair salon or a dentist's office, a line organization is probably the most efficient way to run the business.

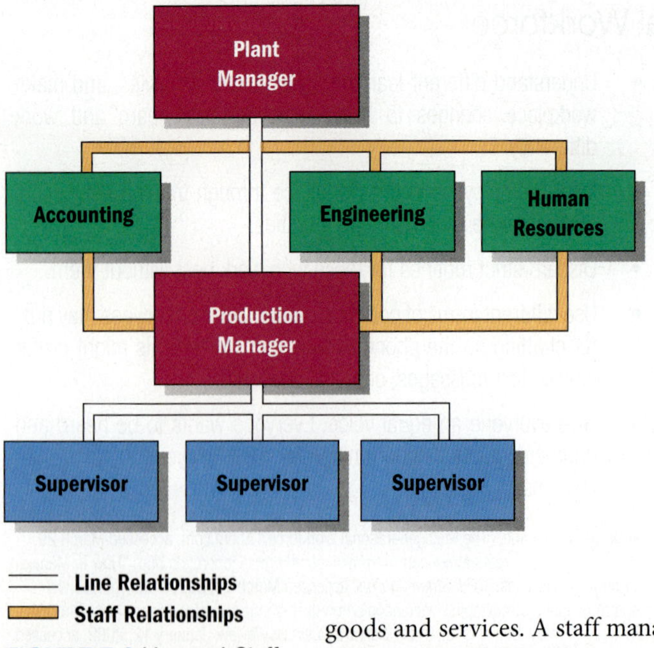

Line-and-Staff Organizations

A *line-and-staff organization* combines the direct flow of authority of a line organization with staff departments that support the line departments. Line departments help to make decisions that affect the firm's core operations. Staff departments lend specialized technical support. **Figure 7.8** shows a line-and-staff organization. Accounting, engineering, and human resources are staff departments. They support the line authority that extends from the plant manager to the production manager and supervisors.

A line manager and a staff manager have different authority relationships. A line manager forms part of the primary line of authority that flows throughout the organization. Line managers work directly with the production, financing, or marketing departments—the areas that are needed to produce and sell goods and services. A staff manager provides information, advice, or technical assistance to help the line managers. Staff managers do not have authority to give orders outside their own departments or to assign actions to the line managers.

FIGURE 7.8 Line-and-Staff Organization

The line-and-staff organization is common in mid-size and large organizations. It is an effective structure because it combines the line organization's rapid decision making and direct communication with the expert knowledge of the staff departments.

Committee Organizations

A *committee organization* is a structure that places authority and responsibility in a group of individuals, not a manager. This model often appears as part of a regular line-and-staff structure.

Committees also work in areas such as new-product development. A new-product committee may include managers from accounting, engineering, finance, manufacturing, marketing, and technical research. Having representatives from all areas involved in creating and marketing products is a good idea. It usually improves both the planning process and employee morale because decisions reflect very different viewpoints.

Committees tend to act slowly and make conservative, or safe, decisions. They may make decisions by compromising, or by coming to an agreement with conflicting interests, instead of choosing the best alternative. The definition of a camel as "a racehorse designed by committee" provides a fitting description of the imperfections of committee decisions.

Matrix Organizations

Some organizations use a matrix or product management design to make their structures more suitable to their business. The *matrix structure* links employees from different parts of the organization who work together on specific projects. **Figure 7.9** shows a matrix structure. A project manager assembles a group of employees from different functional areas. The employees keep their ties to the line-and-staff structure, as shown by the vertical white lines. As the horizontal gold lines show, employees are also members of project teams. When the project is completed, employees return to their "regular" jobs.

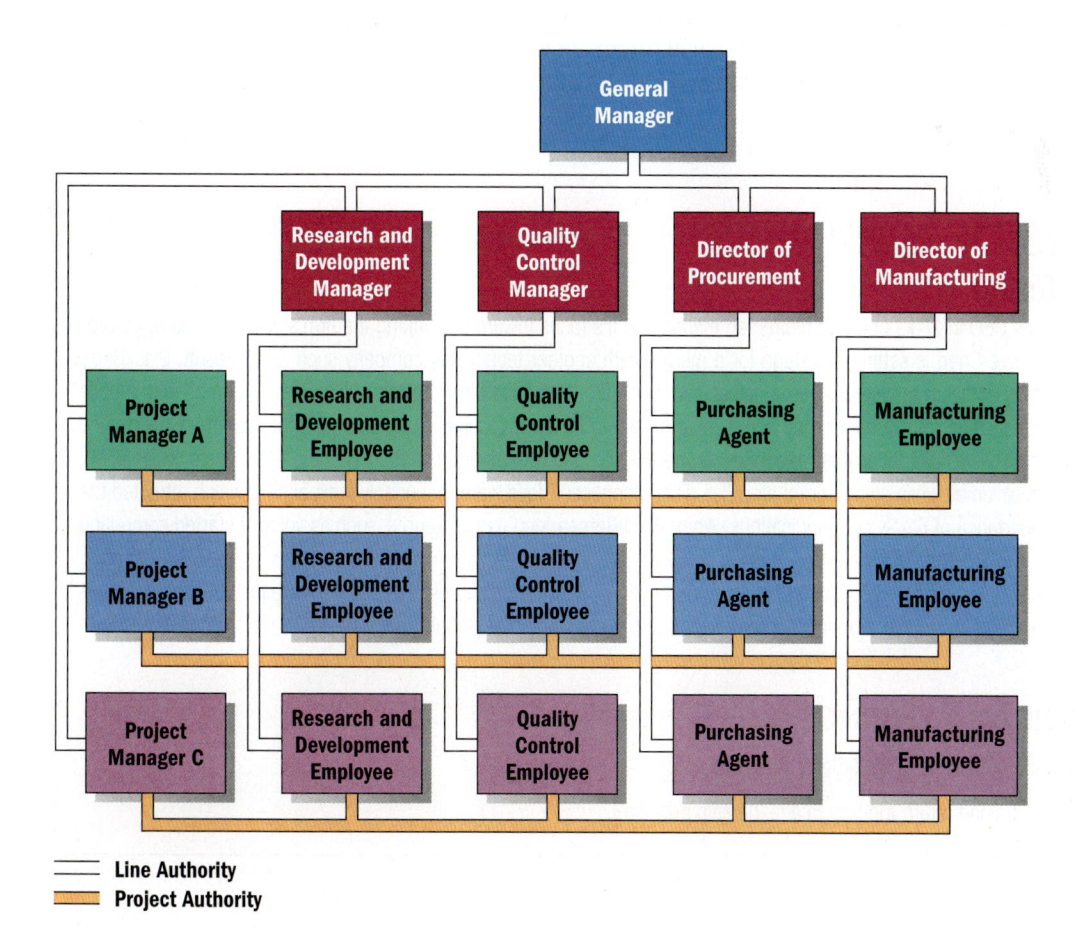

FIGURE 7.9 Matrix Organizations

In the matrix structure, each employee reports to two managers: one line manager and one project manager. Employees who are working on a special project receive instructions from the project manager (horizontal authority), but they continue as employees in their permanent functional departments (vertical authority). The term *matrix* refers to the intersecting grid of horizontal and vertical lines of authority.

The matrix structure is popular at high-technology and multinational corporations, and in hospitals and consulting firms. Dow Chemical and Procter & Gamble have both used matrix structures. The major upsides of the matrix structure come from its flexibility to adapt quickly to rapid changes in the environment. It also focuses resources on major problems or products. The matrix structure also provides an outlet for employees' creativity and initiative. But it challenges project managers to take the skills of specialists from many departments and form a coordinated team. Team members' permanent functional managers must adjust their employees' regular workloads.

The matrix structure is most effective when company leaders give project managers the authority to use whatever resources are available to achieve the project's objectives. Good project managers know how to make the project goals clear and how to keep team members focused. A firm that truly adopts the matrix structure will also encourage a project culture by making sure staffing is adequate, the workload is reasonable, and other company resources are available to project managers.[34]

✓ ASSESSMENT CHECK

7.8.1 What is the purpose of an organization chart?

7.8.2 What are the five major forms of departmentalization?

7.8.3 What does *span of management* mean?

WHAT'S AHEAD

In the next chapter, we focus on the importance of people in shaping the growth and profitability of the organization. We examine how firms recruit, select, train, evaluate, and compensate employees as they try to attract, retain, and motivate a high-quality workforce. The concept of motivation is examined, and we will discuss how managers apply theories of motivation in the modern workplace. The next chapter also looks at the important topic of labour-management relations.

RETURN TO INSIDE BUSINESS

Can John S. Chen Save BlackBerry?

John S. Chen replaced Thorsten Heins as CEO in 2013 and has redirected management's focus toward developing the firm's software and other proprietary technology. Many observers believe Chen is setting the stage for a merger with another technology company such as Microsoft. BlackBerry remains synonymous with leading security software in wireless communications. When first introduced in 1998, the BlackBerry was a hit with mobile business people who liked the value-added feature of a pager they could securely use to instantly receive, read, and reply to email from their office computers. Laptops were larger, more expensive, and not as easy to connect for communicating with others. The BlackBerry is small, costs under $500, and allows business people to receive their email while away from their office. Their connection fees were reasonably inexpensive, which attracted the business market that believed in the importance of timely communications. When BlackBerry added more features, such as voice, it started competing with cellphones.

As we all know now, Apple's iPhone and iPad offered consumers even more functions. Some people questioned the firm's leadership and management decision making. Today, many are watching to see if John Chen can revitalize the company in a global market where many are concerned with secure communications.

QUESTIONS FOR CRITICAL THINKING

1. Is top management responsible for the decline of BlackBerry share value?
2. Can a restructuring of management alone return the firm to a leadership position?

SUMMARY OF LEARNING OBJECTIVES

LO 7.1 Describe *management*.

Management is the process of achieving organizational goals through people and other resources. The management hierarchy usually has three levels: top managers who provide overall direction for company activities, middle managers who carry out the strategies of top managers and direct the activities of supervisors, and supervisors who deal directly with workers. The three basic managerial skills are technical, human or interpersonal, and conceptual. The four basic managerial functions are planning, organizing, directing, and controlling.

✓ ASSESSMENT CHECK ANSWERS

7.1.1 What is management? Management is the process of achieving organizational goals through people and other resources. The manager's job is to combine human and technical resources in the best way possible to achieve the company's goals.

7.1.2 Describe the differences in the jobs of top managers, middle managers, and supervisory managers. Top managers develop long-range plans, set a direction for their organization, and inspire all employees to achieve the company's vision. Middle managers focus their attention on specific operations, products, or customers. They develop plans and procedures to carry out the firm's strategic plans. Supervisory managers deal directly with nonmanagerial employees who produce and sell the firm's goods and services. These managers are responsible for carrying out the plans developed by middle managers and for motivating workers to accomplish immediate goals.

7.1.3 What is the relationship between the manager's planning and controlling functions? Controlling is assessing an organization's performance to decide whether it is achieving its goals. The basic purpose of controlling is to assess the success of the planning function. Controlling also provides feedback for future rounds of planning.

LO 7.2 Explain the role of vision and ethical standards in business success.

Vision is the founder's ability to perceive marketplace needs and what an organization must do to satisfy them. Vision helps to clarify a firm's purpose and the actions it can take to make the most of opportunities. High ethical standards can help build success for a firm through job satisfaction and customer loyalty.

✓ ASSESSMENT CHECK ANSWERS

7.2.1 What is meant by a vision for the firm? A vision is a focus for a firm's actions. Vision helps to direct the company toward opportunities and sets it apart from its competitors.

7.2.2 Why is it important for a top executive to set high ethical standards? High ethical standards often result in a stable workforce, job satisfaction, and customer loyalty.

LO 7.3 Summarize the importance of planning and the three types of planning.

The planning process identifies organizational goals and develops the actions needed to reach those goals. Planning helps a company to turn its vision into action. It also helps it to take advantage of opportunities and to avoid costly mistakes. Strategic planning is a far-reaching process. It takes a broad view of the world to decide on the organization's long-range focus and activities. Tactical planning focuses on the current and short-range activities required to carry out the organization's strategies. Operational planning sets the standards and work targets for functional areas such as production, human resources, and marketing.

✓ ASSESSMENT CHECK ANSWERS

7.3.1 Outline the planning process. Some plans are very broad and long range. These plans focus on the main organizational goals. Other plans are more detailed and show how particular goals will be met. Each planning step—from the mission statement to objectives to specific plans—must fit into an overall plan.

7.3.2 Describe the purpose of tactical planning. The purpose of tactical planning is to decide which short-term activities should be carried out to meet the firm's overall strategy.

7.3.3 Compare the types of plans made by top managers and middle managers. How does their focus differ? Top managers focus on long-range, strategic plans. In contrast, middle-level managers and supervisors focus on short-term, tactical planning.

LO 7.4 Describe the strategic planning process.

The first step in strategic planning is to translate the firm's vision into a mission statement that describes the firm's overall purpose and aims. Next, planners assess the firm's current competitive position using tools such as a SWOT analysis. Managers then set specific objectives. The next step is to develop strategies for reaching objectives that will differentiate the firm, or set it apart, from its competitors. Managers then develop an action plan. This plan outlines the specific ways for carrying out the strategy. Finally, the results achieved by the plan are assessed, and the plan is adjusted as needed.

ASSESSMENT CHECK ANSWERS

7.4.1 What is the purpose of a mission statement? A mission statement is a public description of a firm's purpose, the reason it exists, the customers it will serve, and the way it is different from competitors. A mission statement guides the actions of company managers and employees.

7.4.2 Which of a firm's characteristics are compared in a SWOT analysis? A SWOT analysis assesses a firm's strengths, weaknesses, opportunities, and threats, compared with its competitors. A SWOT analysis helps to decide on a firm's competitive position in the marketplace.

7.4.3 How do managers use objectives? Objectives result from the firm's mission statement. They are used to set performance levels in areas such as profitability, customer service, and employee satisfaction.

LO 7.5 Describe the two major types of business decisions and the steps in the decision-making process.

A programmed decision applies a company rule or policy to solve a frequently occurring problem. A nonprogrammed decision responds to a complex and unique problem that has important results for the organization. The five-step approach to decision making includes seeing a problem or opportunity, developing possible ways of taking action, evaluating the options, selecting and carrying out one option, and assessing the outcome.

ASSESSMENT CHECK ANSWERS

7.5.1 Distinguish between programmed and nonprogrammed decisions. Programmed decisions involve simple problems that occur frequently, such as reordering office supplies. The firm usually sets policies and procedures for dealing with these problems to make the process easier. Nonprogrammed decisions require more individual evaluation. For example, buying real estate or equipment is a nonprogrammed decision that needs some research.

7.5.2 What are the steps in the decision-making process? The decision-making steps are seeing a problem or opportunity, developing possible ways of taking action, evaluating the options, selecting and carrying out one option, and assessing the outcome.

LO 7.6 Define *leadership*, and compare different leadership styles.

Leadership is the ability to direct or inspire others to reach goals. The basic leadership styles are autocratic, democratic, and free-rein leadership. The best leadership style depends on three elements: the leader, the followers, and the situation.

ASSESSMENT CHECK ANSWERS

7.6.1 How is *leadership* defined? Leadership means the ability to direct or inspire people to reach organizational goals. Effective leaders share several personal qualities, such as empathy, self-awareness, and objectivity in dealing with others. Leaders also use the power of their jobs, expertise, and experience to influence others.

7.6.2 Identify the styles of leadership as they range from the least to the most amount of employee participation. At one extreme, autocratic leaders make decisions on their own without consulting employees. At the opposite extreme, free-rein leaders leave most decisions to their employees. In the middle are democratic leaders who ask employees for suggestions and encourage participation.

LO 7.7 Discuss the meaning and importance of corporate culture.

Corporate culture refers to an organization's principles, beliefs, and values. It is typically shaped by a firm's founder and is communicated to all employees through formal programs, such as training, rituals, and ceremonies, and through informal discussions among employees. Corporate culture can influence a firm's success by giving it a competitive advantage.

ASSESSMENT CHECK ANSWERS

7.7.1 What is the relationship between leadership style and corporate culture? The best leadership style to adopt often depends on the organization's corporate culture, its system of principles, beliefs, and values. Corporate culture is influenced by managers' philosophies, the firm's communications networks, its workplace environments, and its practices.

7.7.2 What is a strong corporate culture? A corporate culture is an organization's collection of principles, beliefs, and values. In an organization with a strong culture, everyone knows and supports the same principles, beliefs, and values.

LO 7.8 Identify the five major forms of departmentalization and the four main types of organization structures.

The division of work activities into units within the organization is called *departmentalization*. The units may be based on products, geographical locations, customers, functions, or processes. Most firms implement one or more of four organization structures: line, line-and-staff, committee, and matrix structures.

✓ ASSESSMENT CHECK ANSWERS

7.8.1 What is the purpose of an organization chart? An organization chart is a visual diagram of a firm's structure that shows job positions, job functions, and the reporting hierarchy.

7.8.2 What are the five major forms of departmentalization? Product departmentalization organizes units by the goods and services a company offers. Geographical departmentalization organizes units by geographical regions. Customer departmentalization organizes units by different types of customers. Functional departmentalization organizes units by business functions such as finance, marketing, human resources, and production. Process departmentalization organizes units by the steps or work processes needed to complete production or provide a service.

7.8.3 What does *span of management* mean? The span of management, or span of control, is the number of employees a manager supervises.

BUSINESS TERMS YOU NEED TO KNOW

controlling 183
corporate culture 195
decision making 191
delegation 198
departmentalization 198
directing 183
empowerment 195
leadership 193
management 180
mission statement 188
objectives 190
organization 196
organizing 183
planning 182
SWOT analysis 188
vision 183

REVIEW QUESTIONS

1. What are the three levels of management hierarchy? Which management skills are the most important at each level? Why?

2. Identify the four basic managerial functions. Suppose you were hired to be the manager of a local restaurant. Which managerial functions would the biggest part of your job? Why?

3. Describe the link between a company's vision and its ethical standards. Why is it important for top management to communicate a clear vision and ethical standards for a company?

4. Identify the four types of planning. Suppose you planned a barbecue with your friends. When you woke up on the morning of the party, it was pouring rain. What type of planning would help you to deal with the rain? What are your options for the barbecue?

5. What is the link between a firm's vision and its mission statement? Think about your own dream of a career as an entrepreneur. What is your vision? What might be your mission statement?

6. Define *objectives*. Outline objectives you might have for your own college or university education and your career. How can an outline help you carry out your own career strategy?

7. Identify each of the following as a programmed or nonprogrammed decision:
   a. Reordering printer cartridges
   b. Selecting a cellphone provider
   c. Buying your favourite toothpaste or shampoo
   d. Selecting a college or university to attend
   e. Filling your car with gasoline

8. From what sources does a leader gain power? Which leadership style works best for a manager whose firm is making cost-cutting decisions? Why?

9. Why is a strong corporate culture important to a company's success? How is the corporate culture linked to leadership style?

10. Which type of organization structure provides the most flexibility to respond to changes in the marketplace and to be innovative? What are the downsides of this structure?

PROJECTS AND TEAMWORK APPLICATIONS

1. Imagine that you've been hired as a supervisor at a bakery shop called Claire's Cakes. The founder, Claire, wants to increase production, expand deliveries, and eventually open several more shops. Create a job description for yourself. Include the managerial functions and the skills you'll need to be successful.

2. On your own or with a classmate, write a mission statement for Claire's Cakes. Think about the type of company it is, the products it offers customers (cakes for special occasions), and the type of growth it is planning.

3. Contingency planning requires a combination of looking ahead and being adaptable. Josh James is the founder of Omniture, the Web analytics firm he recently sold to Adobe. James recalls the importance of being adaptable when his company was having difficulties. "There were times when I lay down on the floor at night, close to crying. Then my wife would come over and kick me and say, 'Get up and figure it out.'"[35] Research the news headlines for situations that required contingency planning. Report to the class what the challenge was and how the managers handled it. Discuss whether the planning was effective or successful.

4. Identify a person you think is a good leader. It can be someone you know personally or a public figure. Describe the personal qualities that are most important in making this person an effective leader. Would this person's leadership style work in situations other than his or her current position? Why or why not?

5. Research a firm whose goods or services you purchase or admire. Learn what you can about the organization's culture. Would you be an effective manager in this culture? Why or why not? Share your findings with the class.

WEB ASSIGNMENTS

1. **Strategic planning.** Visit the website listed below. It summarizes Johnson & Johnson's strategic planning philosophy. Read up on several recent acquisitions by Johnson & Johnson. Prepare a brief report to discuss how the acquisitions resulted from the company's strategic planning process.
   www.investor.jnj.com/strategic.cfm

2. **Mission statements.** Go to the websites of two organizations: one for-profit firm and one not-for-profit organization. Print out the mission statements from both organizations. Take the material with you to class to participate in a discussion on mission statements.

3. **Management structure.** Visit the website listed below. Click on "corporate governance" and answer the following questions:
   a. How would you characterize Target's organizational structure?
   b. What is the composition of Target's board of directors?
   http://investors.target.com/phoenix.zhtml?c=65828&p=irol-IRHome

Note: Internet Web addresses change frequently. If you don't find the exact sites listed, you may need to access the organization's home page and search from there or use a search engine such as Bing or Google.

8 HUMAN RESOURCE MANAGEMENT: FROM RECRUITMENT TO LABOUR RELATIONS

LEARNING OBJECTIVES

LO 8.1 Explain the role and responsibilities of human resource management.

LO 8.2 Describe how human resource managers recruit and select employees.

LO 8.3 Discuss how companies develop their employees.

LO 8.4 Describe how firms compensate employees.

LO 8.5 Discuss employee separation and the impact of downsizing and outsourcing.

LO 8.6 Explain the different methods and theories of motivation.

LO 8.7 Discuss labour–management relations.

INSIDE BUSINESS

Canadian Apparel Manufacturing: Seeking Solutions in a Global Marketplace

Until the 1950s, one of the largest players in the Canadian economy was the Canadian apparel (clothing) manufacturing industry. This industry provided jobs to thousands in both large and small businesses. But today, the managers of mostly small firms in a shrinking industry try to deal with increasingly difficult global competitive forces.

In 2011, Canadian manufacturers produced more than $7 billion worth of clothing. Some of it, 24 percent, was exported to the United States. Smaller Canadian producers can take advantage of being located close to American customers, smaller production runs, and quick delivery times. Still, the industry faces increasing difficulties due to rising costs for labour, fabrics, and marketing, and the rising exchange rate on the American dollar. In 2003, the lower-valued Canadian dollar acted as a subsidy for exporters, by keeping the price of Canadian goods low. Then, the value of the Canadian dollar was at a low of US $0.65. Up until late 2014, the Canadian and American dollars were close to being at par: a dollar in one country was very close to being worth a dollar in the other country. This situation presented a challenge to Canadian manufacturers. Canadian businesses also faced heavier competition from lower-costing imports from China and India. As of 2015, the Canadian dollar is around US $0.80.

Each year, about $4 billion worth of clothing is imported into Canada—clothing that once was almost all made in Canada. Today, only 21 percent of all clothing sold in Canada was made in Canada. Canadian clothing manufacturers have moved away from competing against cheaper imported clothing. Some have found success by focusing on higher-quality and higher-priced clothing.

Today, 71 percent of Canadian-made clothing is sold to Canadians, and 24 percent is sold to Americans. Less than 20 years ago, about 70 percent of the textile and clothing products consumed in Canada were made in Canada.

A major factor in the decline of Canadian manufacturing is the dropping of trade barriers. The result was more open trade that shifted jobs in production. As a result of the Uruguay Round of negotiations, World Trade Organization member-countries agreed to remove all quotas between 1995 and 2005. The end of quotas meant Canadian manufacturers lost their protection from imports. According to the Canadian Apparel Federation, the clothing manufacturing industry lost more than 40,000 jobs from 2001 to 2006. Some economists believe that these jobs will never return. Canada will have to replace these jobs if Canadians are to find well-paid employment in the future.

In response, Canadian manufacturers have increased their investment in more efficient machinery and equipment, automated more of the production process, focused on fewer lines of products, and increased their marketing efforts into new markets. Over the past decade, Canadian companies have outsourced more large-scale production runs to China and India where labour costs are much lower.

Canadian retailers sell more than $34 billion worth of apparel merchandise. The revenues for wholesalers and manufacturers are about $10 billion and $7 billion, respectively. Clearly, the clothing industry is a big business that offers huge rewards to those that can compete. Large-scale retailers like Walmart and chain stores like The Gap have, over the years, pushed thousands of smaller independent retailers out of business. Some large retailers have even set up their own wholesaling and manufacturing divisions. The Canadian industry is moving farther away from manufacturing and more toward being a distribution business. The challenge to the surviving Canadian manufacturers is to find a way to compete both in Canada and internationally.

According to Statistics Canada, the industry is made up of some 2,200 manufacturers, mostly small businesses, located primarily in Quebec (51 percent), Ontario (28 percent), British Columbia (12 percent), Alberta (4 percent), and Manitoba (2 percent). Quebec accounts for 58 percent of all industry activity, with more than 1,000 clothing-related businesses located in Montreal, the historical capital of the industry.

More than 32,000 people work in the apparel manufacturing industry. This industry has traditionally provided semi-skilled jobs, such as sewing, for local people and for new immigrants. About 58 percent of businesses employ fewer than 100 people, and 38 percent employ fewer than five people. Only 4 percent of businesses have between 100 and 499 employees, which means they also likely operate on a large manufacturing scale. Smaller manufacturers sometimes outsource certain steps in the production process to other local firms that might specialize in a particular task, or they might invest in labour-saving machinery. But smaller production runs and higher average costs due to outsourcing help explain the very small profit margins—of less than 1 percent. These low profits have led to many business closures.

Research by the apparel industry notes that despite the many challenges, new companies continue to enter this industry. This regeneration, or new growth, has been encouraged by relatively few barriers to entry to the industry, particularly capital investment requirements. Many new companies try to set up based on an idea from an entrepreneur who has identified an unmet need, or niche. New niches continue to be found, and many are successful. Today, approximately 7,000 students are registered in post-secondary apparel programs in Canada. That means new talent will likely continue to find its way into the industry.[1]

CHAPTER 8 OVERVIEW

The very basis of management is the importance of employees to the success of any organization. In this chapter, we explore the important issues of human resource management and motivation. We begin by discussing how organizations attract, develop, and retain employees. Then we describe the concepts, or ideas, behind motivation and how human resource managers apply these concepts to increase employee satisfaction and organizational effectiveness.

We discuss the reasons why labour unions exist. We also focus on legislation that affects labour–management relations. We then discuss the process of collective bargaining and the tools that unions and management use in seeking their objectives.

LO 8.1 Explain the role and responsibilities of human resource management.

HUMAN RESOURCES: THE PEOPLE BEHIND THE PEOPLE

A company is only as good as its workers. At some companies, people come to work each day eager to see each other, to do their very best on the job, to serve their customers, and to help their firm compete. Those companies are very likely to be a success. The best companies value their employees just as much as they value their customers. Without workers, companies would not have any goods or services to offer customers. Firms understand the value of good workers. That's why they do their best to hire top-quality employees and support them. Achieving a high level of job satisfaction and dedication among employees is the goal of **human resource management**, which attracts, develops, and retains the employees who can perform the activities needed to meet organizational objectives. However, when the firm is a small competitor in the Canadian apparel manufacturing industry and has limited financial resources, attracting and keeping top managerial talent can be just one more challenge to face.

Not every firm is large enough to have a separate human resources department. But whoever performs this function generally does the following: plans for staffing needs, recruits and hires workers, provides for training and evaluates performance, decides on compensation and benefits, and oversees employee separation. In accomplishing these five tasks, shown in **Figure 8.1**, human resource managers achieve the following objectives:

1. Providing qualified, well-trained employees for the organization
2. Maximizing employee effectiveness in the organization
3. Satisfying individual employee needs through monetary compensation, benefits, opportunities to advance, and job satisfaction

human resource management the function of attracting, developing, and retaining employees who can perform the activities needed to meet organizational objectives.

FIGURE 8.1 Human Resource Management Responsibilities

- Employee Recruitment and Selection
- Employee Training and Performance Evaluation
- Employee Compensation and Benefits
- Employee Separation
- Planning for Staffing Needs

Core Responsibilities of Human Resource Management

Human resource plans must be based on an organization's overall competitive strategies. Human resource managers work with other managers to predict how many employees a firm or department will need. These managers also decide what skills those workers should bring to the job—and what skills they might learn on the job. Human resource managers are often asked for advice when a firm is thinking about reducing costs by laying off workers or increasing costs by hiring new workers. Human resource managers are also involved in both long-term and short-term planning.

✓ **ASSESSMENT CHECK**

8.1.1 What are the five main tasks of a human resource manager?

8.1.2 What are the three overall objectives of a human resource manager?

RECRUITMENT AND SELECTION

LO 8.2 Describe how human resource managers recruit and select employees.

Human resource managers recruit and help select the right workers for a company. They need to ensure that job candidates bring the needed skills to the job or have the desire and ability to learn these skills. To help in this task, most firms implement the recruitment and selection process shown in **Figure 8.2**.

Finding Qualified Candidates

When the economy dips and jobs are lost, many people compete for a limited number of jobs. A company that develops a great reputation for benefits or their working conditions might receive hundreds of job applications. But even with so many job seekers competing for a small number of job openings, companies often have trouble finding the right person. According to a recent survey, by career website Brandresume.com, firms are currently looking for candidates with these skills: social media management, marketing research, mobile application development, data engineering, and talent acquisition.[2]

The traditional methods of recruiting workers include college and university job fairs, personal referrals, and want ads. Most companies now rely on their websites for recruiting new workers. A firm's website might include a career section that provides general employment information and a listing of open positions. Job seekers are often able to submit a résumé and apply for an open position online. Appendix G, Careers in Contemporary Business, points out that some firms also post job openings on job websites such as Monster.com.

Internet recruiting is a quick, efficient, and inexpensive way to reach a large number of job seekers. Most companies currently use the Internet, including social networking sites, to fill job openings. Using the Internet is also the best way for firms to reach new college and university graduates and workers in their twenties and thirties. The "Hit & Miss" feature describes the growth of employee recruitment via mobile devices.

Recruiting techniques continue to change as technology advances. JobsinPods.com is an online library of podcast interviews with hiring managers and employees at a variety of companies, including Intel and IBM. New podcasts, also called jobcasts, are posted in a blog format, and older podcasts are archived. Some of the people interviewed describe employers' hiring needs, while others talk about what it's like to work at a particular company. Job seekers can also download the podcasts to an iPod and listen to them whenever they want to.[3]

Selecting and Hiring Employees

The human resource manager selects and hires employees, often by working with department managers or supervisors. Every firm must follow provincial and federal employment laws. These laws state that employers cannot discriminate against job applicants, or treat them unfairly, because of their race, religion, colour, sex, national origin, and so forth.

These laws are designed to make the competition for jobs fairer for all job seekers. These laws have also led to many legal cases over the years. For example, UPS Freight recently agreed to pay a $46,000 settlement to a former employee because of religious discrimination. The employee, who is a Rastafarian, was told to shave his beard and cut his hair, which would follow company grooming policy. Because long hair and a beard are part of Rastafarian worship, the employee requested

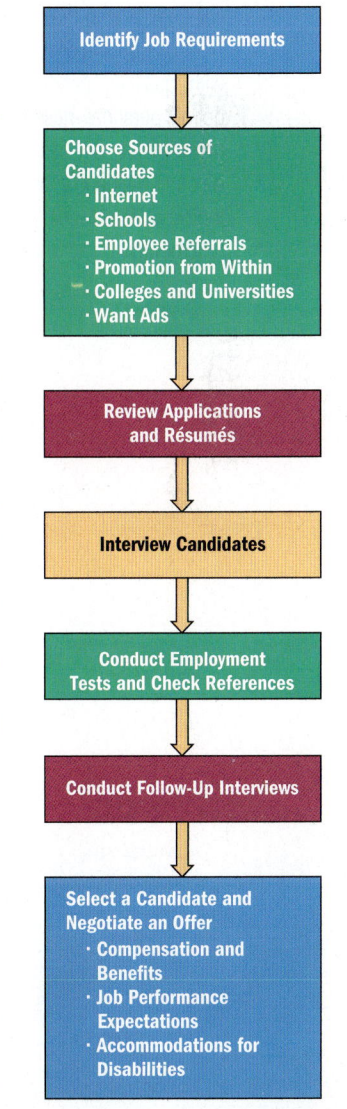

Identify Job Requirements
↓
Choose Sources of Candidates
- Internet
- Schools
- Employee Referrals
- Promotion from Within
- Colleges and Universities
- Want Ads

↓
Review Applications and Résumés
↓
Interview Candidates
↓
Conduct Employment Tests and Check References
↓
Conduct Follow-Up Interviews
↓
Select a Candidate and Negotiate an Offer
- Compensation and Benefits
- Job Performance Expectations
- Accommodations for Disabilities

FIGURE 8.2 Steps in the Recruitment and Selection Process

HIT & MISS

Accenture's Mobile Recruitment Strategy

How would you like to use a mobile app to shop for a new career in much the same way that you shop online for shoes? With more job seekers using mobile devices to search for positions, Accenture, a global management consulting firm, uses mobile career pages and social platforms to compete for workforce talent.

Accenture's career app allows mobile users to receive notifications, read job descriptions, ask questions, sign up for alerts, and search for jobs by location. The app provides published podcasts, insights, and company information for job seekers. Accenture's mobile-friendly approach is a good branding strategy, and it increases the chance that candidates will engage with the company directly.

Using location-based services, Accenture targets and connects with qualified candidates by geographic location. Accenture can deliver personal messages to candidates with the interface they use most: mobile devices. For a faster, more intuitive experience, candidates can video record answers to written interview questions from their mobile devices. Accenture recruiters can watch the videos any time or anywhere, which helps when working around busy schedules.

As mobile surpasses desktop in terms of usage, your next job interview might well be on your mobile device.

Questions for Critical Thinking

1. In the competitive world of recruitment, what are the benefits to Accenture of using a mobile approach?

2. Do you believe that mobile recruiting increases hiring success rates and choosing the right candidate for the job? Discuss its pros and cons.

Sources: Accenture website, "Accenture App for iPhone," accessed February 9, 2014, http://careers.accenture.com/gr-en/Pages/accenture-iphone-application.aspx; Selena Kerley, "Mobile Recruiting: It's Here to Stay," *The Undercover Recruiter*, accessed February 9, 2014, http://theundercoverrecruiter.com/mobile-recruiting-to-stay/; Meghan Biro, "Leadership Is Catching a Mobile Recruiting Wave," *Forbes*, November 10, 2013, accessed July 2, 2015, www.forbes.com/sites/meghanbiro/2013/11/10/leadership-is-catching-a-mobile-recruiting-wave; Lauren Weber, "How Your Smartphone Can Get You a Job," *The Wall Street Journal*, April 24, 2013, accessed July 2, 2015, www.wsj.com/articles/SB10001424127887323551004578441130657837720; Jessica Miller-Merrell, "25 Companies with Careers & Recruiting Apps," *Blogging for Jobs*, April 16, 2013, accessed July 2, 2015, www.blogging4jobs.com/social-media/25-companies-mobile-careers-recruiting-apps/#FfcPjfREP2dYz4p0.97.

---

that the company accommodate, or help him to meet, his religious needs. But instead, UPS fired him, which was a violation, or a breach, of his civil rights to be able to practise his religion.[4] Failure to follow the terms of equal employment opportunity laws can result in costly legal fees, expensive fines, bad publicity, and poor employee morale.

Because of the high cost of such lawsuits and settlements, human resource managers must understand the laws that apply to employment so they can prevent unintended actions that might break these laws. Even the process of interviewing a job candidate must be carried out according to law. For example, an interviewer may not ask job applicants about their marital status, children, race or nationality, religion, age, criminal records, mental illness, medical history, or alcohol and substance abuse. For more information about employment law, visit the websites of the Society for Human Resource Management (www.shrm.org) and Services Canada (www.servicecanada.gc.ca/).

Dealing with hiring restrictions can be a challenge. Some firms try to screen out high-risk employees by requiring drug testing for job applicants. Drug testing is common in industries that deal with public safety—such as air travel and truck driving. But drug testing can lead to strong debates because of privacy issues. Also, positive test results may not be accurate. Another issue is whether employees can be required to speak a particular language in the workplace. Employers may legally establish requirements for specific jobs—true occupational qualifications. For example, a designer of women's clothing can hire only female models to show off new designs.

Recruiting and selecting employees is expensive. There are costs for advertising, interviewing, employment testing, and even medical exams. After an applicant is hired, there are costs for training and for equipment, such as a computer. But a bad hiring decision is even more expensive because the firm has to go through the whole process again to find the right person. One estimate suggests that the total cost of a hiring mistake amounts to 24 times the applicant's annual pay.[5] So it's especially important for human resource managers to make the best choices when it comes to recruitment and selection.

To avoid these mistakes—and to get the right person for the job the first time—many employers require applicants to complete employment tests. These tests may be used to prove the applicant has certain skills, such as mechanical, technical, language, and computer skills. One example is the Wonderlic Basic Skills Test, which measures basic math and verbal skills. The Wonderlic, a cognitive ability test, measures a person's abilities in understanding words, numbers, and logic. Cognitive ability tests accurately predict job performance on many types of jobs.

ASSESSMENT CHECK

8.2.1 Describe several recruiting techniques used by human resource managers.

8.2.2 Is it unfair to firms that some questions cannot be asked during job interviews?

ORIENTATION, TRAINING, AND EVALUATION

LO 8.3 Discuss how companies develop their employees.

After employees are hired, they need to know what is expected of them and how well they are performing. Companies provide this information through orientation, training, and evaluation. A new hire may complete an orientation program prepared by the human resource personnel and the department where the employee will work. During orientation, employees learn about company policies regarding their rights and benefits. They might receive an employee manual that includes the company's code of ethics and code of conduct. And they'll usually receive some form of training.

Training Programs

Training is a good investment for both employers and employees. Training provides workers with an opportunity to build their skills and knowledge. These new skills can also prepare them for new job opportunities within the company. Training also helps employers to keep long-term, loyal, high-performing workers.

On-the-Job Training

One popular teaching method is *on-the-job training*. This type of training prepares employees for job duties by having them perform tasks under the guidance of experienced employees. A variation of on-the-job training is apprenticeship training. An employee who is an apprentice learns a job by working as an assistant to a trained worker. Apprenticeships usually focus on blue-collar trades—such as plumbing and heating services. But many new entrants to white-collar professions also complete apprenticeships. McDonald's has apprenticeship-training programs in its U.K. restaurants as part of an economic stimulus plan launched by the British government. McDonald's offered 6,000 apprenticeships in the first year of its program, increasing the number to 10,000 the following year. "We're letting people know that we're as serious about education as we are about burgers and fries," notes the company's website.[6]

Classroom and Computer-Based Training

Many firms offer some form of classroom instruction, such as lectures, conferences, workshops, or seminars. Ernst & Young, a large tax-service firm, offers a training program called Ernst & Young and You (EYU). This program focuses on classroom learning, experiential learning, and coaching.[7]

Many firms are replacing classroom training with computer-based training programs. These programs can significantly reduce the cost of training. Computer-based training offers consistent presentations. It can also include videos that simulate the work environment, often by using actors in similar situations. Employees can learn at their own pace without having to sign up for a class. Employees can use online training programs for interactive learning. They might work with a mentor or instructor who is located elsewhere; or they might take part in a simulation where they have to make decisions related to their work. In general, human resources managers agree on the value of training. In a study on training, Accenture discovered that for every hour its competitors spent on training, Accenture spent two hours. Accenture invests heavily in its employees because it believes these workers will be able to help their company gain a competitive edge in the marketplace.[8]

Management Development

A *management development program* provides training designed to improve the skills and broaden the knowledge of current or future managers and executives. Training may be aimed at increasing specific technical knowledge or more general knowledge, in areas such as leadership and interpersonal skills. For example, the Conference Board of Canada provides management training in leadership, team development, and strategic implementation. Canadian businesspeople can take the courses online or at selected classroom settings.[9]

Performance Appraisals

The best way for a company—and its employees—to improve is to provide feedback about job performance. Most firms use an annual **performance appraisal** to evaluate an employee's job performance and provide feedback. A performance appraisal can include assessments of everything from attendance to goals met. A manager will use this evaluation to make decisions about compensation, promotion, additional training needs, transfers, or even termination. Performance appraisals are common, but not everyone agrees how useful they are. Some management experts argue that a performance review is based on a single manager's subjective, or personal, opinion, which can be positive or negative. The same experts say that most employees are afraid to speak honestly to their managers during a performance review.[10] If a performance review is to be effective, it should meet the following criteria, or guidelines:

performance appraisal evaluation of and feedback on an employee's job performance.

- Take place several times a year
- Be linked to organizational goals
- Be based on objective measures
- Take place in the form of a two-way conversation[11]

Employees value face-to-face feedback on their job performance. Evaluations that are fair and consistent can improve an organization's productivity and profitability.

Some firms use peer reviews, which have employees assess the job performance of their co-workers. Other firms ask employees to review the job performance of their supervisors and managers. One such performance appraisal is the *360-degree performance review*. This type of appraisal gathers feedback from a review panel of 8 to 12 people, including co-workers, supervisors, team members, people who report to the employee, and sometimes even customers. The idea is to get as much feedback from as many viewpoints as possible. This kind of review involves a lot of work, but employees benefit: they are more involved with the process and they understand more about their own strengths, weaknesses, and roles in the company. Managers also benefit because they get much more in-depth feedback from all parts of the organization. Firms such as Halogen Software, which has headquarters in Kanata, Ontario, offer computer programs to help firms gather and deal with this type of performance review data.[12] A potential weakness of 360-degree performance reviews is their anonymous nature—workers with personal likes and dislikes might try to influence the outcome.

✓ **ASSESSMENT CHECK**

8.3.1 What are the benefits of computer-based training?

8.3.2 What is a management development program?

8.3.3 What are the four criteria, or standards, of an effective performance appraisal?

COMPENSATION

LO 8.4 Describe how firms compensate employees.

Compensation—the amount employees are paid in money and benefits—is one of the most highly charged issues faced by human resource managers. The amount employees are paid, including any benefits they receive, has a huge effect on where people live, what they eat, and how they spend their leisure time. It also has an effect on job satisfaction. Balancing compensation for employees at all job levels can be a challenge for human resource managers.

Everyone likes to read about the companies—or the jobs—that pay their employees the most in cash and benefits. *Fortune* magazine publishes an annual list of "100 Best Companies to Work For." This list includes information on compensation. Top executives at large companies earn millions of dollars, which can be a touchy issue among employees and shareholders.

The terms *wage* and *salary* are often used as if they mean the same thing, but actually the two terms are different. A **wage** is pay that is based on an hourly pay rate or the amount of work accomplished. Typical wage earners are factory workers, construction workers, auto mechanics, retail salespeople, and restaurant wait staff. A **salary** is calculated periodically, often weekly or monthly. Salaried employees receive a set amount of pay that does not rise or fall with the number of hours worked. Wage earners can receive overtime pay, but salaried workers do not. Office personnel, executives, and professional employees usually receive salaries.

An effective compensation system should attract well-qualified workers, keep them satisfied in their jobs, and inspire them to succeed. It's also important to note that certain laws, including minimum wage laws, must be taken into account.

Most firms base their compensation policies on the following factors: (1) what competing companies are paying, (2) government regulation, (3) the cost of living, (4) company profits, and (5) an employee's productivity. Many firms try to find a balance between rewarding workers and

compensation the amount employees are paid in money and benefits.

wage pay based on an hourly rate or the amount of work accomplished.

salary pay calculated on a periodic basis, such as weekly or monthly.

CAREER KICKSTART

How to Ask for a Raise

Have you ever thought about asking for a raise? Just thinking about it might make your hands sweat. You fear rejection—being turned down—or worse, retaliation, such as anger or criticism. But if you know that you are doing a superior job—such as taking the initiative when it's not required—or if it's been more than a year since your last pay increase, then maybe it's time to build a case for a raise. You should be able to at least open the conversation with your boss. Here are a few tips for being successful:

- *Be prepared*. Find out whether your company has a policy for raises. For example, some companies have a pay range or sliding pay scale for each position. If your company has a pay scale, learn where your pay fits on the scale.

- *Gather important data about yourself*. Keep track of your work accomplishments, including extra projects or tasks you've done well. Keep a log of positive feedback from co-workers, other supervisors, and customers. If the praise is already in writing, that's even better.

- *Think through exactly what you want*. Do you want a percentage increase, or a dollar amount? Or maybe you want more vacation time or time off for career education? Make sure your request is reasonable. When you meet with your supervisor, be as specific as possible about what you want.

- *Don't be pushy or hasty in your conversation*. At the same time, state your argument with confidence. Your goal is to get your supervisor to open up to thinking about the possibility of meeting your request.

- If your supervisor turns down your request, *ask for specifics about what you need to do to qualify for the raise*—and when. If possible, ask for a follow-up meeting within a certain period of time, such as two months.

- When you return to your desk or office, *send your supervisor an email thanking him or her for meeting with you*. You can also politely state the results of the conversation. If your request has been granted, make sure your performance lives up to your raise in pay. If your supervisor has put off making a decision, don't give up. Get back to work, document everything, and earn that raise.

Sources: Samantha Mariarz Christmann, "Asking for More: Don't Be Afraid to Ask for a Raise," *Buffalo News*, March 15, 2010, www.buffalonews.com; "How to Negotiate for a Raise—Even in a Bad Economy," *EmploymentDigest.net*, March 4, 2010; Mary Sevinsky, "Is a Raise in Your Future for 2010?" *CareerRealism.com*, January 15, 2010.

FIGURE 8.3 Four Forms of Incentive Compensation

Profit Sharing — Bonus based on company profits	Gain Sharing — Bonus based on productivity gains, cost savings, or quality improvements
Lump-Sum Bonus — One-time cash payment or option to buy shares of company stock based on performance	Pay for Knowledge — Salary increase based on learning new job tasks

employee benefits additional compensation—such as vacation time, retirement savings plans, profit-sharing, health insurance, gym memberships, child and elder care, and tuition reimbursement—paid entirely or in part by the company.

maintaining profits. They do this by linking more of employees' pay to superior performance. Firms try to motivate employees to excel by offering some incentive compensation in addition to salaries or wages. These programs include the following:

- Profit sharing, awards that are bonuses based on company profits
- Gain sharing, whereby companies share the financial value of productivity gains, cost savings, or quality improvements with their workers
- Lump-sum bonuses and stock options, such as one-time cash payments and the right to purchase stock in the company based on performance
- Pay for knowledge, which distributes wage or salary increases as employees learn new job tasks

Figure 8.3 summarizes the four types of incentive compensation programs.

Employee Benefits

In addition to paying wages and salaries, firms also provide benefits to employees and their families as part of their compensation. **Employee benefits** are additional compensation that is paid entirely or in part by the company. Employee benefits can include vacation time, retirement savings plans, profit-sharing, health insurance, gym memberships, child and elder care, and tuition reimbursement. Benefits represent a large portion of an employee's total compensation. Wages and salaries account for around 70 percent of the typical employee's earnings. The other 30 percent takes the form of employee benefits. Pensions and other retirement plans make up a large portion of employee benefits.[13]

Some benefits are required by law. Firms may be required to make pension contributions and payments to unemployment insurance and workers' compensation programs, which protect workers in case of job-related injuries or illnesses. Firms voluntarily provide some other employee benefits, such as child care and health insurance, to help them attract and retain employees.

In general, large companies often pay for supplementary healthcare benefits, leaving employees paying little of the cost. However, with costs increasing each year, employers now offer incentives for

Onsite fitness facilities are a company benefit that improves both the company's health and that of its employees.

workers to live healthier lives. Gym memberships, nutrition programs, wellness visits to the doctor, and smoking-cessation classes are all examples of these incentives. At Qualcomm, a global mobile technologies firm, employee benefits include unlimited sick days, onsite gyms, tuition assistance, and work–life balance programs like job sharing, compressed workweeks, and telecommuting. In addition, Qualcomm provides a generous company matching program on its retirement savings plan and pays 100 percent of the monthly health insurance premiums.[14]

Flexible Benefits

In today's workplaces, employees now represent a wide range of personalities and lifestyles. In response to this increasing diversity, firms are developing creative ways to tailor their benefit plans to employees' needs. One approach sets up *flexible benefit plans*, also called cafeteria plans. These plans offer a choice of benefits, including different types of medical insurance, dental and vision plans, and life and disability insurance. One working spouse can choose medical coverage for the entire family, while the other spouse can use benefit dollars to buy other types of coverage. Typically, each employee receives a set allowance (called flex dollars or credits) to pay for benefits that suit his or her needs. Contributions to cafeteria accounts can be made by both the employee and employer. Cafeteria plans also offer tax benefits to both employees and employers.

Another way to increase the flexibility of employee benefits involves time off from work. Instead of having a set numbers of holidays, vacation days, and sick days, some employers give each employee a bank of *paid time off (PTO)*. Employees can use days from their PTO accounts without having to explain why they need the time. The greatest advantage of PTO is the freedom it gives workers to make their own choices. The greatest disadvantage is that it is an expensive benefit for employers.[15]

Flexible Work

Some firms offer the option of *flexible work plans*. These plans allow employees to adjust their working hours or their places of work according to their needs. Flexible work plan options include flextime, compressed workweeks, job sharing, and home-based work (telecommuting). These benefit programs reduce employee turnover and absenteeism and boost productivity and job satisfaction. Flexible work has become critical in attracting and keeping talented human resources.

Flextime allows employees to set their own work hours within certain limits. For example, instead of scheduling everyone to work between 8:00 a.m. and 5:00 p.m., a manager might decide that all employees must be at work between the core hours of 10:00 a.m. and 3:00 p.m. Outside the core hours, employees can choose to start and end early, or start and end late. Flextime works well in jobs that are independent. But it does not work so well when the employees work in teams or provide direct customer service. Flextime is popular in Europe, where 56 percent of all companies offer some kind of flextime arrangement.[16]

Flexible scheduling is easier to arrange with a small number of employees. But, with the help of web-based software programs, the logistics problems of flexible scheduling can be made easier for larger organizations. Managers can post schedules online; then employees can log in and request certain shifts or schedule changes.[17]

Some companies offer a *compressed workweek*. This plan allows employees to work longer hours on fewer days. Employees might work four 10-hour days and then have three days off each week. These work arrangements not only reduce the number of hours employees spend commuting each week but can stretch out the company's overall workday, providing more availability to customers in other time zones. People who work in hospitals, airlines, and police and fire departments often work several long days, then have several days off.

A *job sharing program* allows two or more employees to divide up the tasks of one job. This plan appeals to more and more people who prefer to work part-time rather than full-time—such as older workers, students, working parents,

Many employees use flextime to mesh their work schedules with opening and closing times at schools and daycare programs.

and people of all ages who want more time for personal interests or leisure. Job sharing requires a lot of cooperation and communication between the partners, but a company can benefit from the talents of both people.

Home-based work programs allow employees to perform their jobs from home instead of at the workplace. These *telecommuters* are connected to their employers through the Internet, voice and video conferencing, and mobile devices. Working from home generally appeals to employees who want freedom. It also appeals to persons with disabilities, older workers, and parents. Companies benefit from telework arrangements because they can expand their pool of talent and increase productivity without increasing costs.[18] Telecommuters need to be self-disciplined and reliable employees. They also need managers who are comfortable with setting goals and managing from afar.[19]

More than 70 percent of Generation Y professionals—those just entering the workforce—are concerned with balancing career with personal life. Most simply reject the idea of sitting in an office cubicle for 8 to 10 hours a day. They want the flexibility to do their jobs anywhere, any time.[20] Their demands place pressure on companies to offer such options as job sharing, compressed workweeks, and telecommuting.

✓ ASSESSMENT CHECK

8.4.1 Explain the difference between *wage* and *salary*.

8.4.2 What are flexible benefit plans? How do they work?

LO 8.5 Discuss employee separation and the impact of downsizing and outsourcing.

EMPLOYEE SEPARATION

Employee separation is a broad term for the loss of an employee for any reason, voluntary or involuntary. Voluntary separation includes workers who resign to take a job at another firm or to start a business. Involuntary separation includes downsizing and outsourcing.

Voluntary and Involuntary Turnover

Turnover occurs when an employee leaves his or her job. Voluntary turnover occurs when the employee decides to resign for his or her own reasons—perhaps to take another job, start a new business, or retire. Some human resource managers will ask the employee for an exit interview to learn why he or she is leaving; this conversation can provide valuable information to a firm. An employee might decide to resign because of lack of career opportunities. The human resource manager who learns of this reason might offer ongoing training.[21] Another employee might resign because of low pay. In that case, the human resource manager might offer a raise. The "Career Kickstart" feature offers some advice on how to ask for a raise. Sometimes, employees choose to resign and accept jobs at other firms because they fear upcoming layoffs. In this case, the human resource manager might be able to put to rest any fears about job security.

Involuntary turnover occurs when employees are terminated because of poor job performance or unethical behaviour in their business practices or in the workplace. Involuntary turnover also occurs when firms are forced to eliminate jobs as a cost-cutting measure, as in the case of downsizing or outsourcing. No matter how necessary a termination may be, it is never easy for either the human resource manager or the employee. The employee may react with anger or tears; co-workers may take sides. Human resource managers should remain calm and professional. They must be educated in employment laws so the termination is handled properly. Some employees who are fired say they have been wrongfully dismissed and file their complaint formally, in a lawsuit.

employee separation a broad term for the loss of an employee for any reason, voluntary or involuntary.

Downsizing

As the economy tightens, companies often face the hard choice of terminating employees to cut costs or streamline the organization. **Downsizing** is the process of reducing the number of employees within a firm by eliminating jobs. Downsizing can be done by offering early retirement or voluntary severance programs. But these options don't always accomplish the goal of downsizing. Read about AOL's recent downsizing effort in the "Hit & Miss" feature.

After downsizing, some firms report improvements in profits, market share, employee productivity, quality, and customer service. But research is beginning to show that downsizing doesn't always lead to those improvements. "Much of the conventional wisdom about downsiz-

downsizing the process of reducing the number of employees within a firm by eliminating jobs.

HIT & MISS

AOL Employees Don't Exit Voluntarily

People don't usually want to leave their jobs, especially when the economy is tighter than usual and unemployment numbers are already high. But that's what AOL asked its workers to do in a recent effort to downsize the company and control costs. AOL asked for 2,500 volunteer separations and received only 1,100. That left a gap of 1,400 workers. The goal was to reduce the firm's workforce by more than 30 percent, from 6,900 to about 4,400.

AOL had been struggling for several years after the merger with Time Warner. It finally spun off as an independent company—but a damaged one. AOL management decided that the only way to turn the company around was to trim as many costs as possible, from every corner of the organization. The turnaround plan, called Project Everest, was led by new CEO Tim Armstrong, a former sales executive for Google. After downsizing the workforce, Armstrong planned to refocus AOL's business in a few select areas, including content, online advertising, and communications. "Project Everest is the completion of phase one of AOL's turnaround," noted a company spokesperson.

If you think all of this sounds a bit cold-hearted and short-sighted, you are not alone. One of the greatest difficulties to a company after layoffs is dealing with the low morale of the remaining workers. Layoffs are distressing to those who are let go and just as traumatic to those who remain. Productivity often slides, as does the image of the company. "There's substantial research into the physical and health effects of downsizing on employees—research that reinforces the notion that layoffs are literally killing people," warns Jeffrey Pfeffer of Stanford University. In the case of AOL, the firm actually hired new salespeople to ensure there would be no breaks in advertising. AOL managers also held meetings with advertisers to tell them of the actions being taken. They also sent notes to some clients containing private contact information for top executives. Despite taking these steps, some advertising clients decided to take their business elsewhere. In an effort to rebuild its business, AOL may have lost one of its most valuable assets—its best people.

Questions for Critical Thinking

1. Was it a good decision for AOL to ask for volunteers to resign before making layoffs? Why or why not?

2. Could AOL managers have better prepared their clients for the downsizing?

Sources: Dustin Ensinger, "Why Layoffs Are Not Beneficial to Companies," *Economy in Crisis*, February 8, 2010, accessed July 2, 2015, http://economyincrisis.org/content/why-layoffs-are-not-beneficial-companies; Nicholas Carlson, "AOL Is Hiring Sales People to Make Sure Layoffs Don't Interrupt Coverage," *Business Insider*, January 13, 2010, accessed July 2, 2015, www.businessinsider.com/aol-is-hiring-sales-people-to-make-sure-layoffs-dont-interrupt-coverage-2010-1; "AOL Layoffs Begin: 1,400 Jobs to Be Slashed," *Mashable.com*, January 11, 2010, accessed July 2, 2015, http://mashable.com/2010/01/11/aol-layoffs-3; Miguel Helft, "AOL Begins 1,200 Layoffs," *The New York Times*, January 11, 2010, accessed August 18, 2015, http://bits.blogs.nytimes.com/2010/01/11/aol-laying-off-1200-this-week; Juan Carlos Perez, "AOL Voluntary Layoff Program Falls Short," *ComputerWorld*, January 5, 2010, accessed July 2, 2015, www.computerworld.com/article/2522579/it-careers/aol-voluntary-layoff-program-falls-short.html.

---

ing—like the fact that it automatically drives a company's stock price higher, or increases profitability—turns out to be wrong," notes Jeffrey Pfeffer of Stanford University.[22] Downsizing can have the following negative effects:

- Anxiety, health problems, and lost productivity among the remaining workers
- Expensive severance packages paid to laid-off workers
- A domino effect on the local economy—unemployed workers have less money to spend, which creates less demand for consumer goods and services, which increases the likelihood of more layoffs and other failing businesses[23]

If downsizing is the only option for company survival, then managers can take steps to make sure it is done the best way possible. If a firm is committed to its workforce as part of its mission, it will do everything it can to support both the workers who must leave and the workers who will stay. For example, Xilinx Inc., a North American semiconductor manufacturer, was recently forced to either shrink its operations or close. The company took several steps to avoid layoffs. First, the company temporarily shut down plants and offered voluntary retirement plans and sabbatical leaves. Human resource managers discussed the situation with employees before making pay cuts.

outsourcing using outside vendors to produce goods or fulfill services and functions that were previously handled in-house or in-country.

✓ **ASSESSMENT CHECK**

8.5.1 What is the difference between voluntary and involuntary turnover?

8.5.2 What is downsizing? How is it different from outsourcing?

LO 8.6 Explain the different methods and theories of motivation.

By taking these steps—with all employees giving up something—the company survived its downturn without any involuntary terminations.[24]

Outsourcing

Another way that firms shrink themselves into leaner organizations is by **outsourcing**. Outsourcing involves using outside vendors to produce goods or fulfill services and functions that were previously handled in-house or in-country. Jobs are transferred from inside a firm to outside the firm. Jobs that are most often outsourced include office maintenance, deliveries, food service, and security. However, other job functions can be also outsourced, including manufacturing, design, information technology (IT), and accounting. In general, companies will try to outsource functions that are not part of their core business so they can save on expenses and remain flexible. In some cases, such as with small Canadian apparel manufacturers, outsourcing some parts of the production process to lower-cost specialists is necessary to survive in a highly competitive business environment. As long as the final product delivered to customers is what was planned, it does not matter who actually did the work.

MOTIVATING EMPLOYEES

One of a manager's main goals is to motivate employees to be loyal to their company and to perform their best on the job. Motivation starts with good employee morale. Morale is the employees' mental view toward their employer and jobs, often including a common sense of purpose.

High employee morale occurs when workers feel they are valued, their opinions are heard, and they are empowered to contribute what they do best. High morale generally results from good management, including an understanding of human needs and an effort to satisfy those needs in ways that move the company forward. In contrast, low employee morale usually signals a poor relationship between managers and employees. It often results in absenteeism, voluntary turnover, and a lack of motivation. Sometimes employees use social media to express frustration with management. See the "Solving an Ethical Controversy" feature about the pros and cons of posting comments online.

Generally speaking, managers use rewards and punishments to motivate employees. Extrinsic rewards are rewards that are external to, or outside of, the work itself, such as pay, fringe benefits, and praise. Intrinsic rewards are feelings related to performing the job, such as feeling proud about meeting a deadline or achieving a sales goal. Punishment involves a negative outcome in response to such undesirable behaviour as being late, skipping staff meetings, or treating a customer poorly.

There are several theories of motivation. All theories relate to the basic process of motivation itself: recognizing a need, moving toward meeting that need, and satisfying that need. For example, if you are hungry, you might be motivated to make yourself a sandwich. Once you have eaten the sandwich, the need is satisfied, and you are no longer hungry. **Figure 8.4** illustrates the process of motivation.

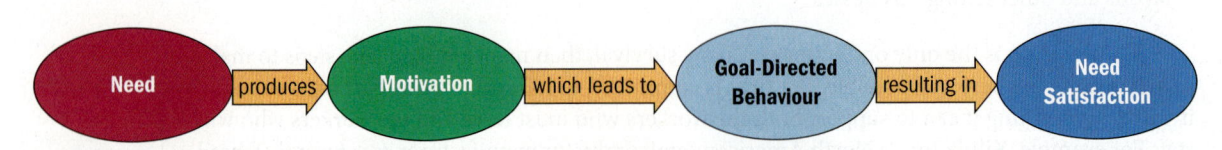

Need → produces → Motivation → which leads to → Goal-Directed Behaviour → resulting in → Need Satisfaction

FIGURE 8.4 The Process of Motivation

SOLVING AN ETHICAL CONTROVERSY

Monitoring Employees' Social Media Activities

A study by the Society for Human Resource Management (SHRM) reveals that more than half of hiring managers report using social media sites to screen and research job applicants. But what happens when companies check out their employees' presence and comments on social media and use this information in the work setting?

Is everything an employee posts online fair game?

PRO

1. In many cases, screening social media information can be helpful in seeing what workers are up to during their tenure with an employer. A well-crafted online profile, a professional presentation, well-written blogs, tweets, and posts can actually make an employee look more favourable and represent his or her employer in a positive light.

2. Employers are using all available tools as part of their HR practices to ensure they have hired the best possible employees. Whatever is found online is fair game—a public profile is just that. It is acceptable for HR managers to search for employees online to learn more about whether they represent the company's best interests.

CON

1. Employers are apt to misinterpret employees' online postings. Information and decisions made about an employee's off-duty behaviour can be misleading and irrelevant.

2. It is inappropriate to obtain information that is unlawful to consider in any workplace or employment decision, such as the applicant's race, marital status, disability, or sexual orientation.

Summary

Social media issues continue to blur the lines between a candidate's private and work life. While social media sites can help confirm an employer's decision with regard to hiring and promoting workers, they can also provide information that confirms an employer's decision not to hire a candidate or to let go an employee if downsizing becomes necessary. Employees need to be mindful that their social media behaviour can be viewed by anyone—even their employer.

Sources: Jacquelyn Smith, "How Social Media Can Help (or Hurt) You in Your Job Search," *Forbes*, April 16, 2013, accessed July 2, 2015, www.forbes.com/sites/jacquelynsmith/2013/04/16/how-social-media-can-help-or-hurt-your-job-search; Sara Jodka, "The Dos and Don'ts of Conducting a Legal, Yet Helpful, Social Media Background Screen," *Law Practice Today*, September 2013, accessed July 2, 2015, www.americanbar.org/content/newsletter/publications/law_practice_today_home/lpt-archives/september13/the-dos-and-donts-of-conducting-a-legal-yet-helpful-social-media-background-screen.html; "More Employers Finding Reasons Not to Hire Candidates on Social Media, Finds CareerBuilder Survey," *CareerBuilder*, June 27, 2013, accessed July 2, 2015, www.careerbuilder.com/share/aboutus/pressreleasesdetail.aspx?sd=6/26/2013&id=pr766&ed=12/31/2013; Robert McHale, "Using Facebook to Screen Potential Hires Can Get You Sued," *Fast Company*, July 20, 2012, accessed July 2, 2015, www.fastcompany.com/1843142/using-facebook-screen-potential-hires-can-get-you-sued.

Maslow's Hierarchy of Needs Theory

Managers can motivate employees by applying the studies of psychologist Abraham H. Maslow. **Maslow's hierarchy of needs** is a widely accepted list of human needs. This list is based on these important assumptions:

- People's needs depend on what they already possess.
- A satisfied need is not a motivator; only needs that remain unsatisfied can influence behaviour.
- People's needs are arranged in a hierarchy of importance; once people satisfy one need, at least partially, another need emerges and demands satisfaction.

Maslow's hierarchy of needs a theory of motivation proposed by Abraham Maslow. According to the theory, people have five levels of needs that they try to satisfy: physiological, safety, social, esteem, and self-actualization.

Maslow proposed that all people have basic needs such as hunger and protection. People must satisfy these basic needs before they can consider higher-order needs, such as social relationships and self-worth. Maslow identified five types of needs:

1. *Physiological needs.* These basic human needs include food, shelter, and clothing. On the job, employers satisfy these needs by paying salaries and wages and providing a heated or cooled workspace.

2. *Safety needs.* These needs refer to desires for physical and economic protection. Companies satisfy these needs by providing benefits such as health insurance and meeting safety standards in the workplace.

3. *Social (belongingness) needs.* People want to be accepted by family, friends, and co-workers. Managers might satisfy these needs by encouraging teamwork and group lunches.

4. *Esteem needs.* People like to feel valued and recognized by others. Managers can meet these needs by offering special awards or privileges.

5. *Self-actualization needs.* These needs drive people to seek fulfillment of their dreams and capabilities. Employers can satisfy these needs by offering challenging or creative projects and opportunities for education and advancement.[25]

According to Maslow, people must satisfy their lower-order needs (physiological and safety needs) before they are motivated to satisfy higher-order needs (social, esteem, and self-actualization needs).

Herzberg's Two-Factor Model of Motivation

More than 50 years ago, Frederick Herzberg—a social psychologist and consultant—came up with a theory of motivation and work that is still popular today. Herzberg surveyed workers to find out when they felt good or bad about their jobs. He learned that certain factors were important to job satisfaction though they might not contribute directly to motivation. These *hygiene factors* (or maintenance factors) refer to aspects of work that do not directly relate to a task but *do* relate to the job environment. These factors include pay, job security, working conditions, status, interpersonal relations, technical supervision, and company policies.

Motivator factors, in contrast, can produce high levels of motivation when they are present. These factors relate directly to specific aspects of a job, including job responsibilities, achievement and recognition, and opportunities for growth. Hygiene factors are extrinsic, or come from outside, while motivators are intrinsic, or come from within. Managers should remember that hygiene factors, though not motivational, can result in satisfaction. Managers who want to motivate employees should emphasize recognition, achievement, and growth. Companies that make the various lists of "best places to work" always have managers who understand what it takes to motivate employees, whether the firm is large or small. Canada's Top Employers is an organization that promotes recognition of best practices. It has a special designation for "Young People." The factors used to decide on rankings include benefits such as tuition assistance and the availability of co-op or work–study programs; mentorship and training programs, including benefits such as bonuses paid when employees complete certain courses or professional designations; and career management program

Everyone, including employees, has a need to belong. Occasional office parties allow workers to relax and socialize, lifting their morale and motivating them to do a good job.

that look for initiatives—such as companywide skills inventories—that can help younger workers to advance faster in the organization.[26]

Expectancy Theory and Equity Theory

Victor Vroom's work led to his **expectancy theory** of motivation. This theory describes the process people use to evaluate the likelihood that their efforts will lead to the results they want and the degree to which they want those results. Expectancy theory suggests that people use three factors to determine how much effort to put forth. First is a person's subjective, or personal, prediction that a certain effort will lead to the desired result. This is the "can do" component of an employee's approach to work. Second is the value of the outcome (reward) to the person. Third is the person's assessment of how likely a successful performance will lead to a desirable reward. Vroom's expectancy theory is summarized in **Figure 8.5**. In short, an employee is motivated if he or she thinks he or she can complete a task. Next, the employee assesses the reward for accomplishing the task and is motivated if the reward is worth the effort.

Equity theory is concerned with an individual's view of fair and equitable treatment. In their work, employees first consider their effort and then their rewards. Next, employees compare their results against the results of their co-workers. As shown in **Figure 8.6**, if employees feel they are under-rewarded for their effort in comparison with others doing similar work, equity theory suggests they will decrease their effort to restore the balance. Conversely, if employees feel they are over-rewarded, they will feel guilty and put more effort into their job to restore equity and reduce guilt.

expectancy theory the process people use to evaluate the likelihood that their efforts will lead to the results they want and the degree to which they want those results.

equity theory an individual's perception of fair and equitable treatment.

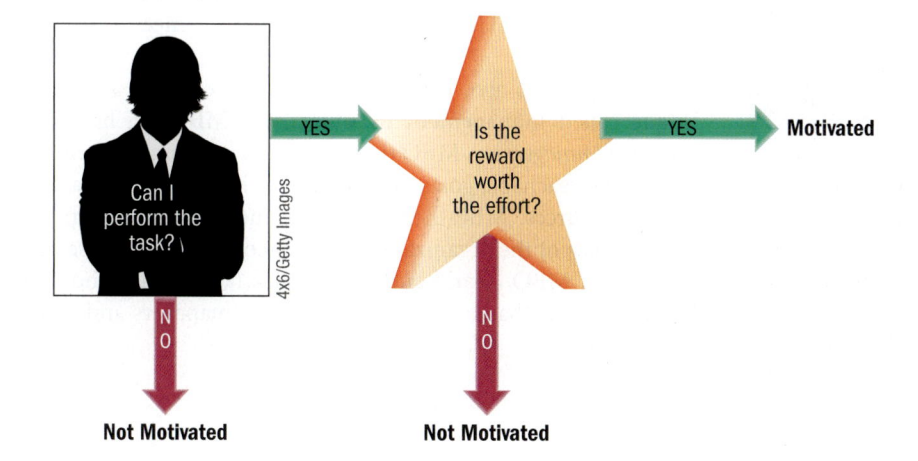

FIGURE 8.5 Vroom's Expectancy Theory

FIGURE 8.6 Equity Theory

Goal-Setting Theory and Management by Objectives

When people have needs, those needs motivate them to direct their behaviour toward something that will satisfy their needs. That something is a goal. A goal is a target, objective, or result that someone tries to accomplish. **Goal-setting theory** says that people will be motivated to the extent to which they accept specific, challenging goals and receive feedback that shows their progress toward goal achievement. As shown in **Figure 8.7**, the basic components of goal-setting theory are goal specificity, goal difficulty, goal acceptance, and performance feedback.

Goal specificity refers to goals that are clear and concrete. A goal such as "we want to reduce our carbon footprint" is vague and hard to relate to a clear target. But, a goal such as "we want to reduce our carbon footprint by 2 percent" gives employees a clear target. Goal difficulty shows how hard the goal is to reach. A more difficult goal, such as "we want to reduce our carbon footprint by 5 percent in three years" can be more motivating than the easier goal.

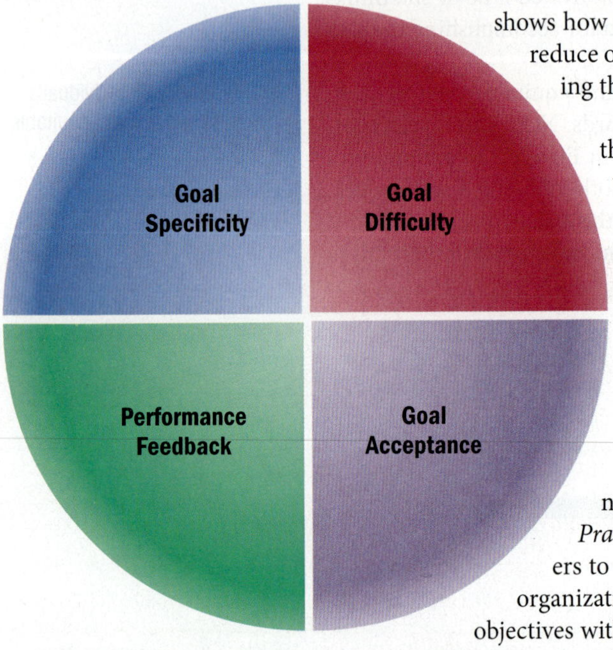

Goal acceptance relates to people's understanding of the goal and their agreement with the goal. People are likely to reject a goal that is too challenging—such as reducing the firm's carbon footprint by 20 percent in two years. Finally, performance feedback is information about performance and how well the goal has been met. Goal setting typically won't work unless performance feedback is provided.

Goals help focus workers' attention on the important parts of their jobs. Goals also energize and motivate people. They create a positive tension between the current state of affairs and the desired state. This tension is satisfied by meeting the goal or rejecting it.

Fifty years ago, Peter Drucker introduced a goal-setting technique called **management by objectives (MBO)** in his book, *The Practice of Management*. MBO is a structured approach that helps managers to focus on reachable goals and to achieve the best results based on the organization's resources. MBO helps motivate individuals by aligning their objectives with the goals of the organization. The outcome is an increase in overall organizational performance. MBO clearly outlines people's tasks, goals, and contributions to the company. MBO is a process that is worked out between managers and employees. MBO principles include the following:

- A series of related organizational goals and objectives
- Specific objectives for each person
- Participative decision making
- A set time period to accomplish goals
- Performance evaluation and feedback

goal-setting theory the idea that people will be motivated to the extent to which they accept specific, challenging goals and receive feedback that shows their progress toward goal achievement.

FIGURE 8.7 Components of Goal-Setting Theory

management by objectives (MBO) a structured approach that helps managers to focus on reachable goals and to achieve the best results based on the organization's resources.

Job Design and Motivation

Today's human resource managers are always looking for ways to motivate employees through their jobs. Jobs can be designed to be more motivating in three ways: through job enlargement, job enrichment, and job rotation.

Job enlargement is a job design that expands an employee's responsibilities by increasing the number and variety of tasks. Redesigning the production process is one way to enlarge a job. For example, on a traditional assembly line, each worker completes the same task over and over again. A firm can redesign the assembly line to a modular work area where employees complete a variety of tasks. These tasks may then result in the production of an entire product.

Job enrichment expands an employee's job duties to empower an employee to make decisions and learn new skills leading toward career growth. A firm might give its managers and sales consultants the power to make decisions about their work, such as how to organize sales presentations and when they prefer to work.

Job rotation involves a system of moving employees from one job to another. Job rotation increases an employee's range of activities. Workers learn more jobs and therefore learn more tasks. The goal is to increase employees' interest in their jobs and to have them learn more about the company. For example, nurses in a hospital might rotate from oncology to the ICU.

Managers' Attitudes and Motivation

A manager's attitude toward his or her employees greatly influences their motivation. Maslow's theory, described earlier, helps managers to understand that employees have a range of needs beyond their paycheques. Psychologist Douglas McGregor, a student of Maslow, studied employee motivation from the viewpoint of managers. McGregor studied managers' interactions with employees. He saw that managers made one of two assumptions about workers' behaviour. McGregor named these two assumptions Theory X and Theory Y. He also showed how these assumptions affect management styles.

- *Theory X* assumes that employees dislike work and try to avoid it whenever possible. Managers must work at getting employees to do their jobs. Theory X managers believe that the average worker prefers to receive instructions, avoid responsibility, and take little initiative. These managers also believe that the average worker views money and job security as the only valid motivators—Maslow's lower order of needs.

- *Theory Y* assumes that the typical person actually likes work and will seek and accept more and more responsibility. Theory Y managers assume that most people can think of creative ways to solve work-related problems. These managers believe in giving employees the opportunity to participate in decision making. The traditional management philosophy relies on external control and constant supervision, but Theory Y views self-control and self-direction as the main motivators—Maslow's higher order of needs.

Management professor William Ouchi proposed another viewpoint on management, labelled *Theory Z*. Theory Z tries to blend the best of American and Japanese management practices. This approach views worker involvement as the key to increased productivity for the company and improved quality of work life for employees. Many Canadian firms have adopted the participation aspect of the Japanese management style. These firms ask workers for suggestions to improve their jobs, and then give them the authority to implement changes.

LABOUR–MANAGEMENT RELATIONS

The North American workplace is far different from what it was a century ago. Then, it was common to have child labour, unsafe working conditions, and a 72-hour workweek. The changed workplace is a result of labour unions, labour legislation, and the collective bargaining process. Today's human resource managers must be educated in labour–management relations, the settling of disputes, and the competitive tactics of unions and management.

Development of Labour Unions

A **labour union** is a group of workers who organize themselves to work toward common goals in the areas of wages, hours, and working conditions.

✓ **ASSESSMENT CHECK**

8.6.1 What are the four steps in the process of motivation?

8.6.2 Explain how goal-setting works.

8.6.2 Describe the three ways that managers design jobs for increased motivation.

LO 8.7 Discuss labour–management relations.

labour union a group of workers who organize themselves to work toward common goals in the areas of wages, hours, and working conditions.

Labour unions are found at the local, national, and international levels. A *local union* represents union members in a specific area, such as a single community. A *national union* is a labour organization consisting of numerous local chapters. An *international union* is a national union with membership outside of Canada, usually in the United States. The International Brotherhood of Teamsters is an international union.

Canadian-based labour groups grew and eventually organized into the country's largest national organization of unions, the Canadian Labour Congress (CLC). The CLC represents about 3 million of the 4.6 million unionized Canadians, about 70 percent of the unionized workforce. In Canada, about 30 percent of the entire workforce is unionized.[27] Some unions belong to more than one of these central union organizations, and some belong to both Canadian and American groups. For example, the United Steel Workers belong to the CLC in Canada and the American Federation of Labour and Congress of Industrial Organizations (AFL-CIO) in the United States.

Labour Relations Board

A labour relations board is a type of judicial organization. It is responsible for overseeing workers' groups that apply to become a union and activities that occur during a labour dispute. Each province has its own labour relations board. People who work in interprovincial communications or transportation are under the legal authority of the national labour board, the Canada Industrial Relations Board. Although some rules vary, they all function in a similar manner.

The Collective Bargaining Process

Labour unions work to increase job security for their members and to improve wages, hours, and working conditions. These goals are achieved primarily through **collective bargaining**, the process of negotiation between management and union representatives.

collective bargaining the process of negotiation between management and union representatives.

Union contracts usually cover a two- or three-year period. They are often the result of weeks or months of discussion, disagreement, compromise, and eventual agreement. After an agreement is reached, the union members must vote to accept or reject the contract. When the contract is rejected, the union members have two choices. They can send union representatives back to the bargaining process with management representatives, or the union members may decide to strike to obtain their demands.

Settling Labour–Management Disputes

We hear about strikes in the news, but most labour–management negotiations result in a signed contract. If a disagreement occurs, it is usually settled through a grievance procedure, mediation, or arbitration. These options are quicker and less expensive than a strike.

The union contract is a guide to relations between the firm's management and its employees. The agreement states the rights of each party. No contract, regardless of how detailed it is, will remove the possibility of disagreement. Disagreements can be the beginning of a *grievance*, a complaint—by a single employee or by the entire union—that management is violating, or is breaking, some portion of the agreed-on contract. Almost all union contracts state that these complaints must be submitted through a formal grievance procedure, such as the process shown in **Figure 8.8**. A grievance might be a disagreement about pay, working hours, or the workplace itself. The grievance procedure usually begins with an employee's supervisor and then moves up the company's hierarchy. If the highest level of management can't settle the grievance, it is submitted to an outside party for mediation or arbitration.

Mediation is the process of settling labour–management disagreements through an impartial, or objective, third party. Although the mediator does not make the final decision, he or she can hear the whole story and make objective recommendations. If the dispute still cannot be settled, then the two parties can turn to *arbitration*. An outside arbitrator is chosen who must be acceptable to both the union and management. The arbitrator will then make a legally binding

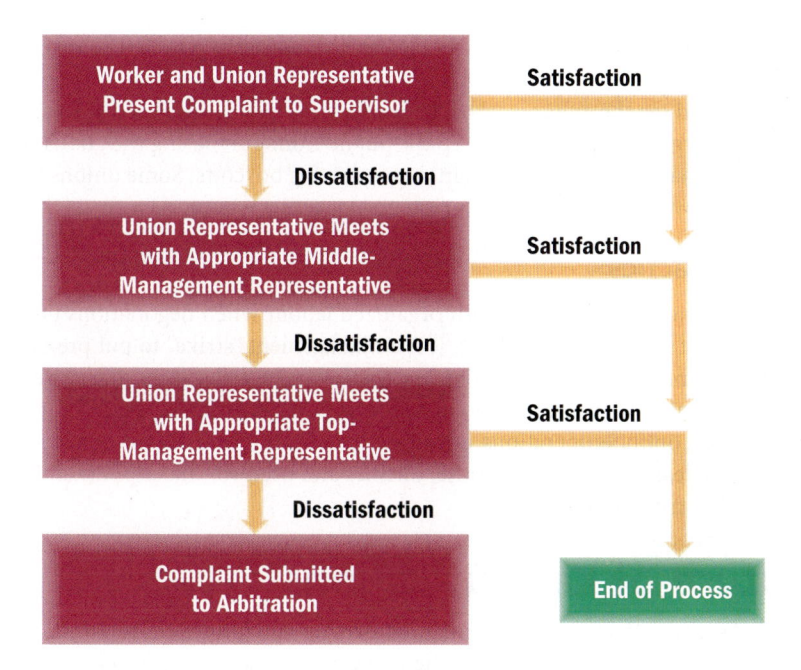

FIGURE 8.8 Steps in the Grievance Procedure

decision. This decision is final. Both parties are legally required to agree to it. Most union negotiations go to arbitration if union and management representatives cannot reach a contract agreement.

Competitive Tactics of Unions and Management

Both unions and management use tactics to make their views known and to win support.

Union Tactics

The union's main tactics are strikes, picketing, and boycotts. The *strike*, or walkout, is one of the labour union's most effective tools. It involves a temporary work stoppage by workers until a dispute has been settled or a contract signed. A strike generally seeks to disrupt business by calling attention to workers' needs and union demands. Strikes can last for days or weeks and can be costly to both sides. The 2004–05 strike by the National Hockey League Players Association against the National Hockey League lasted 310 days, starting September 16, 2004. This strike resulted in the cancellation of the season without the awarding of the Stanley Cup.[28] Although a strike is powerful, it can also damage a wider portion of the local economy. If fans aren't watching games at local sports bars, those businesses will lose profits on nights that normally bring in large crowds.

Picketing involves workers marching in a public protest against their employer. This activity is another effective form of union pressure. Picketing is protected under law as long as it does not involve violence or intimidation. Picketing may accompany a strike, or it may be a protest against what are believed to be unfair labour practices. On a holiday

Picket lines went up at British Airways when members of the cabin crews went on strike. Strikes are a last-ditch tactic that can be costly for the union, hurt an entire industry, and even damage the economy.

weekend during a strike, hundreds of British Airways workers picketed a soccer field near Heathrow airport during a tense standoff. Although planes continued to take off and land over the field, passengers could see the angry workers below.[29]

A *boycott* is an organized attempt to keep the public from purchasing the goods or services of a firm. Some unions have been very successful in organizing boycotts. Some unions fine members who do not obey a boycott.

Management Tactics

Management has tactics for competing with organized labour when negotiations break down. In the past, management has used the lockout. It is a management "strike" to put pressure on union members by closing the firm. But companies usually use one of two tactics: they hire strikebreakers in highly visible fields, such as professional sports, or they transfer supervisors and other non-union employees to continue operations during strikes. In the British Airways strike described earlier, management leased aircraft from other airlines and used volunteer pilots and managers to take the place of the striking cabin crews.[30]

The Future of Labour Unions

Through most of the twentieth century, union membership and influence grew. Industrial workers had a voice in decisions about their wages, benefits, and working conditions. But Canada, the United States, Western Europe, and Japan have shifted from manufacturing economies to information and service economies. As a result, union membership and influence have declined. The largest union in Canada is the Canadian Union of Public Employees (CUPE). It has more than 600,000 government employee members. After the federal government passed the Public Service Staff Relations Act of 1967, all federal, provincial, and municipal employees were able to organize into unions. Soon after, public sector unions began to grow. Today, public sector unions include more than 70 percent of all employees. They make up three of the largest unions in Canada: the Canadian Union of Public Employees (CUPE), the National Union of Public and General Employees (NUPGE), and the Public Service Alliance (PSA).[31]

How can labour unions change so they continue to play a valuable role? They can be more flexible and adapt to a global economy and a diverse workforce. They can respond to the growing need for environmentally responsible business and manufacturing processes. That's what the

---

LABOUR UNIONS AND GREEN CONSTRUCTION

The construction industry has nearly unlimited opportunities to make the world greener. One labour union, the Operative Plasterers' and Cement Masons' International Association (OPCMIA), has already recognized this and is training its members in the use of new green technologies and processes.

The OPCMIA training program, called Green Five, is being incorporated into existing training curricula to reach about 5,400 participants in 70 programs across local chapters, community colleges, vocational/technical schools, and OPCMIA Joint Apprenticeship and Training Centers. The Green Five program trains plasterers and cement masons in the sustainable use and application of concrete, exterior insulation finish systems, and American Clay. The Green Five program includes Green Awareness Training, which deals with energy-efficient building construction in general, addresses the process of energy assessment and retrofitting existing buildings, and provides an overview of environmentally sustainable products and manufacturing processes. Leadership training and "train-the-trainer" courses are offered as well.

Questions for Critical Thinking

1. How does a progressive stance toward green training help secure an important industry role for OPCMIA going forward?

2. Besides construction, what other industries might benefit from unions taking a leadership role in sustainability training? How might these steps benefit workers, unions, and management?

Sources: OPCMIA website, "About OPCMIA," accessed February 16, 2014, www.opcmia.org; Gerry Ryan, "Plasterers and Cement Masons Implement Green Construction Technologies and Training," OPCMIA News, April 27, 2010, accessed July 2, 2015, www.plasterers31.org/news_green_five_program.html; Gerry Ryan, "The Green Five Program," *Green Labor Journal*, accessed February 16, 2014, http://greenlaborjournal.com; David Bradley, "TR10: Green Concrete," *MIT Technology Review*, May/June 2010, accessed July 2, 2015, www2.technologyreview.com/article/418542/tr10-green-concrete.

Operative Plasterers, and Cement Masons, International Association (OPCMIA) is doing, as described in the "Going Green" feature. Unions can set up working relationships with human resource managers and other management officials. They can also recognize the potential for prosperity for everyone—management and union workers included.

> ✓ **ASSESSMENT CHECK**
>
> **8.7.1** What is a labour union? What is collective bargaining?
>
> **8.7.2** What are the three main tactics used by unions to win support for their demands?

WHAT'S AHEAD

One way to recruit and keep a highly motivated workforce is to treat employees well by improving their work environment. Managers can also help employees to reach their full potential in three ways: by empowering them to make decisions, leading them to work effectively as teams, and encouraging clear, positive communication. The next chapter discusses these three ways of improving performance. Companies that apply these three methods benefit from their employees' knowledge, and employees can have a more meaningful role in the company.

RETURN TO INSIDE BUSINESS

Canadian Apparel Manufacturing: Seeking Solutions in a Global Marketplace

Small-business entrepreneurs have always been present in the Canadian garment industry. Entrepreneurs generally learn the business first by working for someone else and then set out on their own. In general, barriers to entry, such as the required financial investment, have remained relatively low, compared with most other manufacturing industries. As anyone in the fashion business will tell you, "You're only as good as your last season." With every new fashion season, the process starts all over again as manufacturers look for the next styles, fabrics, and colours that will bring sales, profits, and sustainability.

QUESTIONS FOR CRITICAL THINKING

1. How can Canadian apparel manufacturers better compete against imports within Canada?
2. How can Canadian apparel manufacturers better compete in international markets?
3. What motivates young people to enter the fashion production business?

SUMMARY OF LEARNING OBJECTIVES

LO 8.1 Explain the role and responsibilities of human resource management.

Human resource managers are responsible for attracting, developing, and retaining the employees who can perform the activities needed to meet organizational objectives. They plan for staffing needs, recruit and hire workers, provide for training and evaluate performance, decide on compensation and benefits, and oversee employee separation.

✓ ASSESSMENT CHECK ANSWERS

8.1.1 What are the five main tasks of a human resource manager? The five main tasks are planning for staffing needs, recruiting and hiring workers, providing for training and evaluating performance, deciding on compensation and benefits, and overseeing employee separation.

8.1.2 What are the three overall objectives of a human resource manager? The three overall objectives are providing qualified, well-trained employees for the organization; maximizing employee effectiveness; and satisfying individual employee needs through monetary compensation.

LO 8.2 Describe how human resource managers recruit and select employees.

Human resource managers use internal and external methods to recruit qualified employees. They may use college and university job fairs, personal referrals, want ads, and other resources. Internet recruiting is now the fastest, most efficient, and least expensive way to reach a large number of job seekers. Firms must abide by employment laws to avoid lawsuits. Before hiring candidates, human resource managers may require employment tests that evaluate certain skills or aptitudes. When all of this is complete, there is a better chance that the right person will be hired for the job.

✓ ASSESSMENT CHECK ANSWERS

8.2.1 Describe several recruiting techniques used by human resource managers. Techniques include college and university job fairs, personal referrals, want ads, company websites, online job sites, and podcast interviews (known as jobcasts) that feature hiring managers and employees talking about work at their companies.

8.2.2 Is it unfair to firms that some questions cannot be asked during job interviews? The firm should only be interested in whether job applicants have the skills or experience to perform a certain job. Any interview questions should be concerned only with the job applicant's abilities. The firm should be free to ask these questions.

LO 8.3 Discuss how companies develop their employees.

New employees often complete an orientation program where they learn about company policies and practices. Training programs provide opportunities for employees to build their skills and knowledge. These new skills can also prepare them for new job opportunities within the company. Training also helps employers to keep long-term, loyal, high-performing employees. Performance appraisals give employees feedback about their strengths and weaknesses and how they can improve.

✓ ASSESSMENT CHECK ANSWERS

8.3.1 What are the benefits of computer-based training? Computer-based training offers consistent presentations and interactive learning. Employees can also learn at their own pace. Computer-based training is also less expensive than other types of training.

8.3.2 What is a management development program? A management development program provides training designed to improve the skills and broaden the knowledge of current and potential executives.

8.3.3 What are the four criteria, or standards, of an effective performance appraisal? A performance appraisal should take place several times a year, be linked to organizational goals, be based on objective measures, and be a two-way conversation.

LO 8.4 Describe how firms compensate employees.

Firms compensate employees with wages, salaries, incentive pay systems, and benefits. Benefit programs vary among firms, but most companies offer healthcare programs, insurance, retirement plans, paid time off, and sick leave. More and more companies offer flexible benefit plans and flexible work plans, such as flextime, compressed workweeks, job sharing, and home-based work.

✓ ASSESSMENT CHECK ANSWERS

8.4.1 Explain the difference between *wage* and *salary*. Wages are based on an hourly pay rate or the amount of work accomplished. Salaries are paid periodically, such as weekly or monthly. Salaries do not rise or fall with the number of hours worked.

8.4.2 What are flexible benefit plans? How do they work? Flexible benefit plans offer a choice of benefits, including different types of medical insurance, dental and vision benefits, and life and disability insurance. Typically, each employee receives a set allowance (also known as flex dollars) to pay for these benefits that suit his or her needs.

LO 8.5 Discuss employee separation and the impact of downsizing and outsourcing.

Employee separation occurs when a worker leaves his or her job, either voluntarily or involuntarily. Sometimes an employee is terminated because of poor job performance or unethical behaviour. Downsizing is the process of reducing the number of employees within a firm by eliminating jobs. Some negative effects of downsizing include anxiety and lost productivity among the remaining workers, expensive severance packages, and a domino effect in the local economy. Outsourcing involves transferring jobs from inside a firm to outside the firm. While some expenses may be cut, a firm may experience a strong negative reaction in job performance and public image.

✓ ASSESSMENT CHECK ANSWERS

8.5.1 What is the difference between voluntary and involuntary turnover? Voluntary turnover occurs when employees leave firms for their own reasons, such as to start their own businesses, take jobs with other firms, move to another community, or retire. Involuntary turnover occurs because of employees' poor job performance or unethical behaviour in their business practices or in the workplace. It can also occur when a company is forced to eliminate jobs.

8.5.2 What is downsizing? How is it different from outsourcing? Downsizing is the process of reducing the number of employees within a firm by eliminating jobs. Downsizing is done to cut overhead costs and streamline the organizational structure. Outsourcing occurs when companies contract with other firms to perform noncore jobs or business functions, such as housekeeping, maintenance, or relocation services. Outsourcing allows companies to focus on what they do best. It can also result in a downsized workforce.

LO 8.6 Explain the different methods and theories of motivation.

Employee motivation starts with high employee morale. According to Maslow's hierarchy of needs, people satisfy lower-order needs (such as food and safety) before moving to higher-order needs (such as esteem and fulfillment). Herzberg's two-factor model of motivation is based on the fulfillment of hygiene factors and motivation factors. Expectancy theory suggests that people use these factors to decide whether to make the effort needed to complete a task. Equity theory refers to a person's view of fair and equitable treatment. Goal-setting theory says that people will be motivated to the extent to which they accept specific, challenging goals. Job design is also used by managers for motivation.

✓ ASSESSMENT CHECK ANSWERS

8.6.1 What are the four steps in the process of motivation? The four steps are need, motivation, goal-directed behaviour, and need satisfaction.

8.6.2 Explain how goal-setting works. People will be motivated to the extent to which they accept specific, challenging goals and receive feedback that shows their progress toward goal achievement.

8.6.3 Describe the three ways that managers design jobs for increased motivation. Jobs can be designed to be more motivating in three ways: through job enlargement, job enrichment, and job rotation. Job enlargement is a job design that expands an employee's responsibilities by increasing the number and variety of tasks. Job enrichment changes the job duties to increase employees' authority in planning their work, deciding how it should be done, and learning new skills that help them grow. Job rotation involves a system of moving employees from one job to another.

LO 8.7 Discuss labour–management relations.

Labour unions have led to improvements in wages, working conditions, and labour laws. Unions achieve these improvements through the collective bargaining process, which results in an agreement. Most labour–management disagreements are settled through the grievance process. Sometimes, third-party mediation or arbitration is needed to settle disagreements.

✓ ASSESSMENT CHECK ANSWERS

8.7.1 What is a labour union? What is collective bargaining? A labour union is a group of workers who organize themselves to work toward common goals in the areas of wages, hours, and working conditions. Collective bargaining is the process of negotiation between management and union representatives.

8.7.2 What are the three main tactics used by unions to win support for their demands? Unions' main tactics are strikes (walk-outs), picketing, and boycotts.

BUSINESS TERMS YOU NEED TO KNOW

collective bargaining 226
compensation 215
downsizing 218
employee benefits 216
employee separation 218
equity theory 223

expectancy theory 223
goal-setting theory 224
human resource management 210
labour union 225
management by objectives (MBO) 224
Maslow's hierarchy of needs 221

outsourcing 220
performance appraisal 214
salary 215
wage 215

REVIEW QUESTIONS

1. Why has Internet recruiting become an important tool for human resource managers?

2. Recruitment and selection are expensive. What steps can human resource managers take to make sure they hire the right person for each job?

3. Give an example of a type of job that would be suitable for on-the-job training. Describe specifically how on-the-job training would work for this job. Include a list of tasks a new hire might learn on the job.

4. What five factors are compensation policies usually based on? Name three employee benefits that are required by law. Name three employee benefits that firms often provide voluntarily.

5. Describe four types of flexible work plans. Identify an industry that would be well suited to each type of plan, and explain why.

6. Why do companies downsize? What are some of the downsides to downsizing? Why do companies outsource? What are some of the downsides to outsourcing?

7. Select three different theories of motivation. Explain how each theory can be used by managers to motivate employees.

8. Suppose a manager of a popular sandwich shop maintains a Theory X view about employees. At the beginning of each workweek, what might this manager tell his or her employees? Now suppose the manager has a Theory Y view, then a Theory Z view. Describe what a manager with each of these views might say to employees.

9. In what major ways have labour laws changed the workplace over the past century? How would today's workplace be different if we did not have these laws?

10. What are mediation and arbitration? Describe a situation that might lead to arbitration.

PROJECTS AND TEAMWORK APPLICATIONS

1. On your own or with a classmate, research firms that provide management training programs. Prepare a presentation about one of these firms. Describe how the firm uses management training programs and some specific details of the program.

2. Choose one of the following companies, or a company that you might like to work for. Research the company's benefits by using the firm's website and a job search website such as Monster.com. Outline the firm's benefits. Decide whether you still want to work for the company, and why. Suggested firms:
   a. Timberland
   b. SAS
   c. NextEra Energy Resources
   d. Kraft Foods
   e. FedEx

3. With a classmate, choose an on-campus job and outline how you would share that job. Create a schedule and division of tasks.

4. Choose what you think would be your dream job five years from now. Using Maslow's hierarchy of needs, create a chart that shows how this job fulfills each level of need.

5. Research one of the major labour laws mentioned in the text. Learn what circumstances led to the proposal and passing of the law. How will this law affect the work world you will enter when you graduate?

WEB ASSIGNMENTS

1. **Human resources (HR) as a profession.** The Conference Board of Canada Human Resources website provides a variety of information. Summarize the highlights presented in one report:

    www.conferenceboard.ca/topics/humanresource/default.aspx

2. **Performance reviews.** The Government of Canada's Office of the Chief Human Resources Officer (OCHRO) is the centre for federal public service employees. Compare the management performance information provided for the employees and executives:

    www.tbs-sct.gc.ca/chro-dprh/hrh-eng.asp

3. **Teamsters.** The Teamsters is one of the North America's largest and oldest labour unions. Go to the union's website (www.teamsters-canada.org) and review the material. When was the union founded? The union originally represented workers in what industry? How many members do the Teamsters currently have?

Note: Internet Web addresses change frequently. If you don't find the exact sites listed, you may need to access the organization's home page and search from there or use a search engine such as Bing or Google.

9 | TOP PERFORMANCE THROUGH EMPOWERMENT, TEAMWORK, AND COMMUNICATION

LEARNING OBJECTIVES

LO 9.1 Describe why and how organizations empower employees.

LO 9.2 Describe the five types of teams in the workplace.

LO 9.3 Describe the characteristics of an effective team and the stages of team development.

LO 9.4 Relate team cohesiveness and norms to effective team performance.

LO 9.5 Describe the factors that can cause team conflict and ways to manage conflict.

LO 9.6 Outline the process of effective communication.

LO 9.7 Compare the basic forms of communication.

LO 9.8 Explain external communication and methods of managing a public crisis.

INSIDE BUSINESS

Pam Cooley and CarShareHFX

"This is what we do as humans. We move people and we move things. How we do this exposes our intelligence and our values."

Social entrepreneur Pam Cooley co-founded CarShareHFX in Halifax in 2008. Cooley has strong organizational and communications skills. She is also devoted to socially responsible causes. These skills and interests helped her to set up a new way of using automobiles. CarShare Atlantic Limited was the first multi-vehicle CarShare service in Atlantic Canada. The Halifax Chamber of Commerce named the firm the Gold New Business of the Year for 2010. Cooley has succeeded in getting the socially responsible message out—CarShare provides a cost-effective alternative to vehicle ownership. Members pay an annual fee and have 24-hour self-service access to the entire fleet of cars. Cars are booked using a phone-in or online reservation system. Society will benefit from having greater mobility and lower traffic congestion and exhaust emissions. By partnering with CarShareHFX, organizations can reduce parking limitations, decrease the number of parking spots they need to build, and save thousands of dollars. Dalhousie University chose to be a partner to help reduce congestion and to make more space available for people, not vehicles.

For the system to work, participants need to have a high level of cooperation with each other. That means clear communications about everything, from what to do if the gas tank runs low to how to deal with finding dents or scratches on the car.

Much of this customer information is explained in simple step-by-step videos and text on the firm's website, http://carsharehfx.ca. The promotional information is aimed at drivers who can benefit from the co-operative model of car sharing rather than car ownership. And it's very persuasive. The highlighted benefits include the freedom from many responsibilities associated with car ownership, such as costs for insurance, maintenance, and parking. Customer members pay only for the time they use a vehicle. All costs are included in the hourly and per kilometre rates.

CarShareHFX vehicles can use privileged parking locations around town, and members can conveniently reserve a car online. This company appeals to a generation of young drivers who are concerned with socially responsible behaviours. But government and corporate organizations, such as Clean Nova Scotia, also want to encourage and participate in the system. Clean Nova Scotia (http://clean.ns.ca) is a not-for-profit organization founded in 1988. It is guided by a board of directors with representation from business, academia, government, and the community. Over the last 20 years, Clean Nova Scotia has become an effective, high-profile organization that works with individuals, government, business, and communities to improve the environment. Clean Nova Scotia spokesperson Derek Gillis is a supporter of CarShareHFX. He sees its role as a way for reducing the size of corporate fleets of vehicles. Gillis argues that the co-operative model could be expanded to include trucks and other vehicles that may not be driven very often. These vehicles could be shared between businesses and governments.

Another targeted customer base for CarShareHFX is property managers and their tenants. The program might also appeal to real estate developers looking both to improve the quality of life for their tenants and to reduce their environmental footprint on new apartment or condominium projects. These developers could partner with CarShareHFX to provide onsite vehicles for tenants to share. This service would provide added value by decreasing demand for parking spaces. The idea fits well with developers who want to improve their green initiatives, including LEED (Leadership in Energy and Environmental Design) certification, the gold seal in environmentally superior construction. Some partners currently offering CarShareHFX benefits to their residents are The Westwood, Southwest Properties, Killam Properties, and King's Wharf developments.

Pam Cooley's ongoing efforts to help build more economically sound, socially responsible opportunities will definitely benefit from her visible success with CarShareHFX.[1]

CHAPTER 9 OVERVIEW

Well-managed large organizations know that teamwork and communication are essential for empowering employees to perform their best. This chapter focuses on how organizations involve employees by sharing information and empowering them to make critical decisions, by having them work in teams, and by encouraging communication. We begin by discussing how managers can empower their employees' decision-making authority and responsibility. Then we explain why and how more and more firms are relying on teams of workers, not individuals, to make decisions and carry out assignments. Finally, we discuss how effective communication helps workers to share information that improves the quality of decision making.

LO 9.1 Describe why and how organizations empower employees.

EMPOWERING EMPLOYEES

empowerment giving employees shared authority, responsibility, and decision making with their managers.

An important component of effective management is the **empowerment** of employees. Organizations promote this goal by giving employees shared authority, responsibility, and decision making with their managers. Empowerment uses the brainpower of all workers to find better ways of doing their jobs, serving customers, and achieving organizational goals. Empowerment frees managers from hands-on control of workers. It motivates workers by adding challenges to their jobs. Empowerment also gives workers a feeling of ownership. Managers empower employees by sharing company information and decision-making authority and by rewarding them for their own performance—and the company's. The topic of employee empowerment is discussed in the "Solving an Ethical Controversy" feature.

Sharing Information and Decision-Making Authority

One of the most effective ways to empower employees is to keep them informed about the company's financial performance. Research suggests that companies should provide regular reports to their employees on key financial information, such as profit-and-loss statements. Firms show their willingness to practise open-book management by using the company's internal website, or intranet, to post financial statements, training schedules, policy documents, and other information. Employees can visit the website and look up the company's cash flow, its design standards, and its basic measures of financial performance. In this way, employees can understand more about the organization's strategic thinking and how their own work fits into the overall plan. Employees who are trained in how to read financial statements can understand how their work contributes to company profits. These employees are better able to direct their work efforts to make use of company resources. Using information technology to empower employees carries some risks. One risk is that private company information may reach competitors. Management must weigh this risk and other risks against the benefits of sharing information with employees.[2]

The second way that companies empower employees is by giving them broad authority to make decisions that carry out a firm's vision and its competitive strategy. Even among non management staff, empowerment extends to decisions and activities usually handled by managers. Employees might be responsible for such tasks as purchasing supplies, making hiring decisions, scheduling production or work hours, overseeing the safety program, and granting pay increases.

Linking Rewards to Company Performance

The ultimate step in convincing employees of their role in the success of their firm is worker ownership. Companies offer worker ownership in two ways: employee stock ownership plans and stock options. **Table 9.1** compares these two methods of employee ownership.

Employee Stock Ownership Plans

About 7 percent of Canadians participate in *employee stock ownership plans (ESOPs)*.[3] These plans are growing in popularity in Canada. ESOPs benefit employees by giving them stock ownership in

SOLVING AN **ETHICAL** CONTROVERSY

Employee Empowerment: Yes or No?

Many firms today recognize the benefits of empowering employees—entrusting them with decision-making authority that may improve sales outcomes, relationships with customers, and the firm's ultimate success. But not all managers are convinced that giving control to their employees is the best way to run a company. They worry about allowing employees to make decisions that could be an expensive lesson if those choices turn out to be wrong.

Should firms empower employees to make decisions that could improve company relationships and overall performance?

PRO

1. Employees who are empowered to make decisions within their job descriptions and their years of expertise can help build both relationships and sales. For example, an employee who has direct contact with customers can market products and solve customer problems more effectively if he or she has the authority to do so. A salesperson who can authorize a return or a discount on the spot can improve a firm's relationship with a customer and ensure repeat business.

2. Empowered employees are motivated to increase their own performance and that of the firm. Workers who are entrusted with making decisions about their own jobs feel a sense of ownership in their company's overall performance. Employees can move their companies into a position of success when they are motivated to display the commitment, initiative, and creativity that decision making requires.

CON

1. When things at a firm go wrong—such as a major product recall or the discovery of poor working conditions at an outsourced facility—customers, investors, and the public immediately turn their attention to the company's leadership. If the company's top management appears unaware of the decision making that led to these mistakes, then customers, investors, and the public quickly lose faith in the firm. Employee decision making can result in this type of communication breakdown within an organization.

2. When employees are empowered but don't receive proper training, customers or suppliers might receive insufficient or inaccurate information. That poor information can lead to failed solutions, damaged relationships, and lost sales.

Summary

Most firms now practise some degree of empowerment among their employees. Some managers, though, are unwilling to pass this kind of decision-making authority to employees. But even those managers who support empowerment agree that employees must be trained in decision-making skills and educated about the goods and services marketed by their firm. The company must create a single and consistent message so all customers are treated fairly by different employees. When empowerment is set up properly, it can be an important force in moving an organization forward.

Sources: George N. Root III, D, "Challenges of Employee Empowerment," *Small Business.Chron.com*, accessed July 2, 2015, http://smallbusiness.chron.com/challenges-employee-empowerment-705.html; Cameron Kauffman, "Employee Involvement: A New Blueprint for Success," *Journal of Accountancy*, May 1, 2010, www.journalofaccountancy.com/issues/2010/may/20092404.html; Bob Reynolds, "Thoughts from the Shower—Pros and Cons to Empowering Your Employees," *Snoitulos Ten*, April 30, 2010, www.snoitulosten.com; Stacy Blackman, "How to Empower Employees with the Illusion of Control," *CBS Money Watch*, April 16, 2009, accessed July 2, 2015, www.cbsnews.com/news/how-to-empower-employees-with-the-illusion-of-control.

TABLE 9.1 Employee Stock Ownership Plans and Stock Options

EMPLOYEE STOCK OWNERSHIP PLANS	STOCK OPTIONS
Company-sponsored trust fund holds shares of stock for employees	Company gives employees the option to buy shares of its stock
Usually covers all full-time employees	Can be granted to one, a few, or all employees
Employer pays for the shares of stock	Employees pay a set price to exercise the option
Employees receive stock shares (or value of stock) when they retire or leave the company	Employees receive shares of stock when (and if) they exercise the option, usually during a set period

Sources: "Employee Stock Options and Ownership (ESOP)," Reference for Business, accessed April 19, 2010, www.referenceforbusiness.com; "Employee Stock Options Fact Sheet," The National Center for Employee Ownership, accessed April 19, 2010, www.nceo.org.

their companies. These stocks can lead to profits when the value of the firm increases. Under ESOPs, the employer buys shares of the company stock on behalf of the employee as a retirement benefit. The accounts continue to grow in value tax-free. When employees leave the company, they can cash in their stock shares. Employees are motivated to work harder and smarter because, as part owners, they share in their firm's financial success. About 60 percent of surveyed companies that offer ESOPs report an increase in employee productivity. The most definitive study in Canada was done by the Toronto Stock Exchange. It compared ESOP versus non-ESOP public companies. ESOP companies scored better than non-ESOP companies on several factors: their five-year profit growth was 123 percent higher, net profit margin was 95 percent higher, productivity measured by revenue per employee was 24 percent higher, return on average total equity was 92.3 percent higher, and return on capital was 65.5 percent higher.[4]

When ESOPs are used for retirement funds, they must follow government regulations designed to protect pension benefits. Because ESOPs can be expensive to set up, they are more common in larger firms than in smaller firms. ESOPs have one danger: if the majority of an employee's retirement funds are in company stock and the value falls dramatically, the employee may lose financially.[5]

Stock Options

Another popular way for companies to share ownership with their employees is by offering *stock options*, or the rights to buy a specified amount of company stock at a given price within a given time period. In an ESOP, the company holds stock for the benefit of employees. In stock options, employees can own the stock themselves if they choose to exercise, or use, their options by purchasing stock. For example, an employee receives an option on 100 shares at $10 per share. The stock price increases to $20 per share. The employee can choose to exercise, or use, the option to buy those 100 shares at $10 each. The employee can then sell the stocks at the market price of $20 per share, and keep the difference. If the stock price never increases above the option price, the employee doesn't need to exercise the option.[6]

Options were once limited to senior executives and members of the board of directors, but some companies now offer stock options to all employees. An estimated 11 million employees in thousands of North American companies hold stock options.[7] Of all the stock options issued by these corporations, about one-third go to the top five executives at each firm. Much of the remainder goes to other executives and managers, who make up only about 2 percent of the workforce. Solid evidence suggests that stock options motivate regular employees to perform better. Some people argue that for stock options to be most effective as motivators, they need to be offered to a much broader range of employees.

Stock options have turned hundreds of employees into millionaires at such firms as Tim Hortons, The Home Depot, Microsoft, and Google. But their success stories don't mean that everyone can make money through stock options. Remember that stock prices drop during economic downturns. And, similar to ESOPs, employees face risks when they rely on a single company's stock to provide for their retirement. In addition to stock options and ESOPs, many firms offer their executives other perks, or special privileges.

✓ ASSESSMENT CHECK

9.1.1 What is empowerment?

9.1.2 What kinds of information can companies provide to employees to help them share decision-making responsibility?

9.1.3 How do employee stock ownership plans and stock options reward employees and encourage empowerment?

LO 9.2 Describe the five types of teams in the workplace.

TEAMS

A **team** is a group of people with certain skills who share a common purpose, approach, and performance goals. All team members hold themselves responsible and accountable for reaching their objectives. Teams are widely used in business and in many not-for-profit organizations, such as hospitals and government agencies. Teams are one of the most frequently discussed topics in employee training programs because teams require that people learn how to work well together. Many firms emphasize the importance of teams during their hiring processes. For example, job applicants are often asked about their previous experiences as team members. Companies want to hire people who can work well with others. Combining all of their talents and ideas will achieve more than they could achieve working alone. **Figure 9.1** outlines five basic types of teams: work teams, problem-solving teams, self-managed teams, cross-functional teams, and virtual teams.

team a group of people with certain skills who share a common purpose, approach, and performance goals.

About two-thirds of firms use **work teams**. These teams are relatively permanent groups of employees. In this approach, people with complementary skills perform the day-to-day work of the organization. A work team might include all the workers involved in assembling and packaging a product—anything from cupcakes to cars.

In contrast to work teams, a **problem-solving team** is a temporary combination of workers who gather to solve a specific problem. After this problem is solved, the team is no longer needed and is disbanded. Problem-solving teams differ from work teams in important ways. Work teams are permanent groups designed to handle any business problem that arises, but problem-solving teams have specific missions. Toyota faced serious quality problems—unintended acceleration, faulty brakes, and questions about their tires. The company was forced to recall thousands of vehicles. Toyota formed rapid-response Swift Market Analysis Response Teams (SMART) to deal with the technical problems. These teams were made up of field technology specialists, engineers from manufacturing and design, and product engineers from North America. Specialists from Japan were on call, available when they were needed. Together, the SMART members worked with dealers across North America to contact customers and arrange for onsite analyses of each problem vehicle to figure out what went wrong and why. Teams were encouraged to "listen and react" to customers' descriptions of their experiences as part of their investigation.[8] Typically when a problem is solved, the team is no longer needed and disbands. In other cases, the team may develop a more permanent role within the firm.

A **self-managed team** is a work team that has the authority to decide how its members will complete their daily tasks. A self-managed team works most effectively when it combines employees with a range of skills and functions. Members are cross-trained to perform each other's jobs as needed. Distributing decision-making authority in this way can mean that members can concentrate on satisfying customers. Whole Foods Market has a structure that is based on self-managed work teams. Company managers decided that Whole Foods could be most innovative if employees made decisions themselves. Every employee is part of a team, and each store has about 10 teams handling separate functions, such as groceries, bakery, and customer service. Each team handles responsibilities such as setting goals, hiring and training employees, scheduling team members, and purchasing goods to stock. Teams meet at least monthly to review goals and performance, solve problems, and explore new ideas. Whole Foods awards bonuses based on the teams' performance relative to their goals.[9]

A **cross-functional team** is a team made up of members from different functions, such as production, marketing, and finance. Cross-functional teams usually work on specific problems or projects, but they can also serve as permanent work teams. The value of cross-functional teams is their different perspectives and the range of skills that they bring to a work effort. At Harley-Davidson, cross-functional teams work to find new ways to enhance the unique sound of its motorcycles while reducing unwanted noise. "We're aggressively moving from a tribal way of working to a cross-functional approach," notes Alex Bozmoski, manager of the cross-functional teams.[10]

Virtual teams are groups of geographically or organizationally separated co-workers who use telecommunications and information technologies to accomplish an organizational task. Because they use email, video conferencing, and group communication software, members of virtual teams rarely meet face to face. The main advantage of virtual teams is their flexibility. Employees can work with each other regardless of physical location, time zone, or their organizational relationship. Because of their very nature, virtual teams that are scattered across the globe can be difficult to manage. Firms that are committed to virtual teams believe that the benefits outweigh the drawbacks.

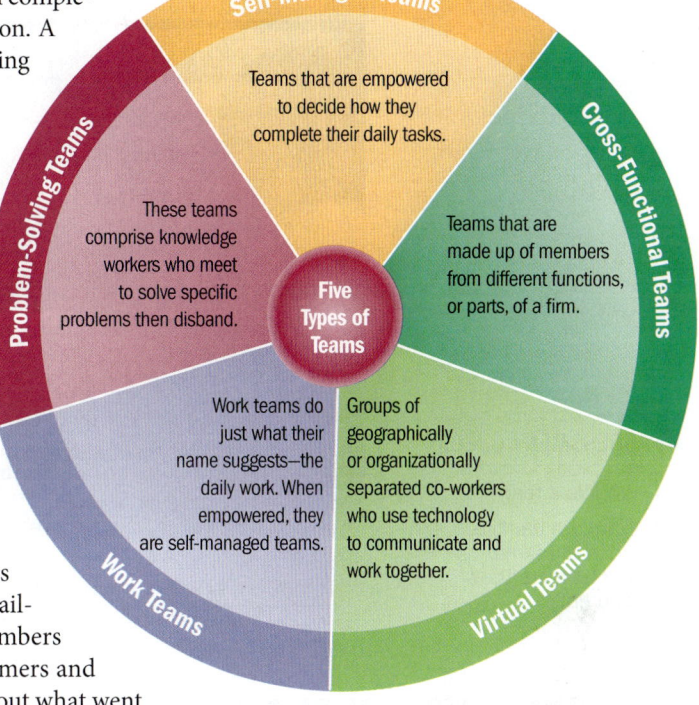

FIGURE 9.1 Five Types of Teams

Five Types of Teams:
- **Self-Managed Teams**: Teams that are empowered to decide how they complete their daily tasks.
- **Cross-Functional Teams**: Teams that are made up of members from different functions, or parts, of a firm.
- **Virtual Teams**: Groups of geographically or organizationally separated co-workers who use technology to communicate and work together.
- **Work Teams**: Work teams do just what their name suggests—the daily work. When empowered, they are self-managed teams.
- **Problem-Solving Teams**: These teams comprise knowledge workers who meet to solve specific problems then disband.

work teams relatively permanent groups of employees with complementary skills who perform the day-to-day work of organizations.

problem-solving team a temporary combination of workers who gather to solve a specific problem and then disband.

self-managed team a work team that has the authority to decide how its members complete their daily tasks.

cross-functional team a team made up of members from different functions, such as production, marketing, and finance.

virtual teams groups of geographically or organizationally separated co-workers who use telecommunications and information technologies to accomplish an organizational task.

ASSESSMENT CHECK

9.2.1 What is a team?

9.2.2 What are the five types of teams, and how are they different?

Members of a virtual team rarely meet in person, but they stay in touch through new technologies, such as video conferencing. In today's global marketplace, the flexibility of virtual teams is a distinct advantage.

LO 9.3 Describe the characteristics of an effective team and the stages of team development.

TEAM CHARACTERISTICS

Effective teams share several characteristics. They must be an appropriate size to accomplish their work. In addition to size, teams also can be sorted according to the similarities and differences among team members, called *level* and *diversity*. We discuss these three characteristics next.

Team Size

Teams can range in size from as small as two people to as large as 150 people. Most teams, though, have fewer than 12 members. Although no ideal size limit applies to every team, research on team effectiveness shows that teams achieve their best results with six or seven members. A group of this size is big enough to benefit from a variety of diverse skills, yet small enough that members can communicate easily and feel part of a small and supportive group.

Groups smaller or larger than six or seven can be effective, but they create added challenges for team leaders. Participants in small teams of two to four members often show a desire to get along with each other. They tend to like informal relationships marked by discussions of personal topics, and they make only limited demands on team leaders. A large team with more than 12 members poses a different challenge for team leaders. With this size of group, decision making may work slowly. Participants may also feel less committed to the team goals. Larger teams also tend to lead to disagreements, absenteeism, and membership turnover. Subgroups may form, leading to possible disagreements about various functions. As a general rule, a team of more than 20 people should be divided into sub-teams, each with its own members and goals.

Team Level and Team Diversity

team level the team's average level of ability, experience, personality, or any other factor.

team diversity the team's differences in ability, experience, personality, or any other factor.

Team level is the team's average level of ability, experience, personality, or any other factor. Businesses consider team level when they need teams with a particular set of skills to do their jobs well. For example, an environmental engineering firm might put together a team with a high level of experience to write a proposal for a large contract.

Team level represents the average level or capability on a team. **Team diversity** represents the team's differences in ability, experience, personality, or any other factor. Strong teams have

Chapter 9 Top Performance Through Empowerment, Teamwork, and Communication   241

talented members—as shown by their team level. They also have members who are different in terms of their ability, experience, or personality. Team diversity is an important consideration for teams that must complete a wide range of different tasks or complex tasks. For example, the British Broadcasting Corporation (BBC) routinely creates teams for events such as the FIFA World Cup or the Olympic Games. These teams involve production and broadcast groups larger than 100 people, many of whom are part-time employees. The team members typically come from more than 15 different countries. Their skills can range from those of an electrician to those of a statistician, and from scheduling to producing. Because an event at the sports venues takes place only once, the BBC teams have one chance to get it right.[11] Ernst & Young, a global firm that provides financial services, relies on team diversity, as described in the "Hit & Miss" feature.

Strong teams not only have talented members but also members who are different in their ability, experience, or personality. Team diversity is an important consideration for teams that need to complete a wide range of different tasks or complex tasks. For example, the British Broadcasting Corporation (BBC) routinely creates teams for events such as the FIFA World Cup or the Olympic Games.

HIT & MISS

Team Diversity at Ernst & Young

Ernst & Young has seen it all—economic booms and busts, including the recent recession and fallout from the financial industry. But the company that provides tax, transaction, and advisory services is surviving. It is doing well partly because of its new outlook about the business environment and how it will operate. One focus is how its 144,000 employees can contribute their talents more fully to the company's future.

Specifically, Ernst & Young is changing the way it uses teams. A recent company survey was titled, "The New Global Mindset: Driving Innovation through Diverse Perspective." The survey's results found that companies operating in 25 or more countries base only 5 percent of their senior leadership in those countries. These companies are failing to make the most of the diverse cultures and ideas that could move them forward. "The economic crisis has mandated that companies rethink the way they do business," observes James S. Turley, chairman and CEO of Ernst & Young. "Company leaders need to consider how a lack of diverse perspectives—at the top of their organization and at the individual team level—might affect plans for global growth, new products, or mergers and acquisitions."

Ernst & Young has come up with a strategy for its new team diversity. Managers who are planning or leading teams should consider the following:

- *The mindset.* Managers must think about what needs to happen so that a true cultural change can occur within the organization.

- *The talent.* Managers should search every corner of the organization for true talent—it might be in the cafeteria, at an assistant's desk, or in the human resources office.

- *Anticipation.* Creative managers need to use the diverse talents of team members to identify new products and services that could be the next "big thing."

- *Consensus.* Total agreement among team members isn't always necessary. In fact, disagreement can boost a team's energy and force people to come up with new and better ideas and solutions.

"We all know that innovation is critical to economic recovery," says Beth Brooke, global vice chair of Ernst & Young. "In today's environment, the business leaders who have a truly global mindset and can integrate diverse perspectives will be the ones best positioned to drive innovation and long-term success."

Questions for Critical Thinking

1. Why is team diversity so critical for a global firm like Ernst & Young?

2. Think about the nature of Ernst & Young's business. What level would you expect Ernst & Young's teams to operate at? Why?

Sources: Ernst & Young, "LLP Diversity Award," *BAP Forums*, accessed April 19, 2010, www.bap.org; "Diversity Drives Innovation," January 27, 2010, Ernst & Young website, www.ey.com; James S. Turley, "The New Global Mindset," *Bloomberg Businessweek*, January 26, 2010, www.businessweek.com/managing/content/jan2010/ca20100126_437043.htm; "Ernst & Young LLP Starts 2010 with a Three-Day Event for Minority Students and a Faculty Roundtable Focused on Campus Diversity," *PR Newswire*, January 6, 2010, accessed July 2, 2015, www.prnewswire.com/news-releases/ernst-young-llp-starts-2010-with-a-three-day-event-for-minority-students-and-a-faculty-roundtable-focused-on-campus-diversity-80814047.html.

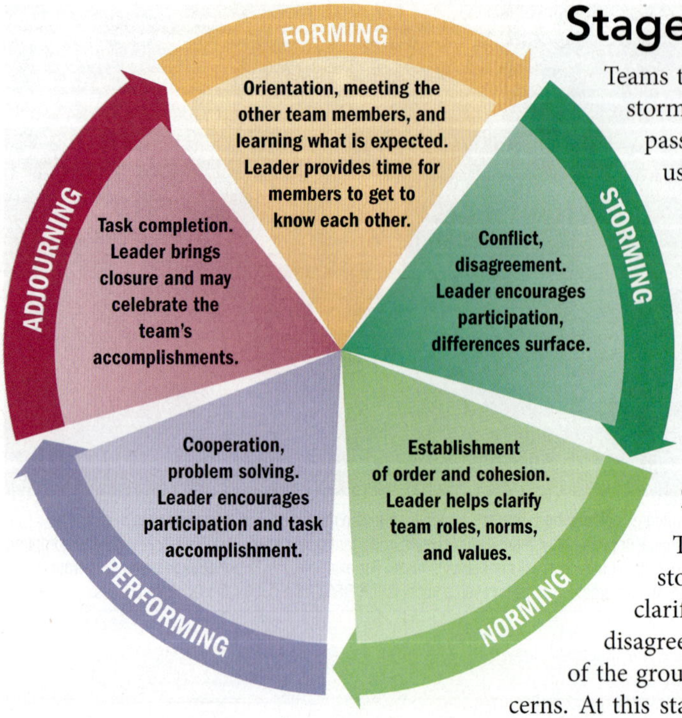

Stages of Team Development

Teams typically progress through five stages of development: forming, storming, norming, performing, and adjourning. Not every team passes through each of these stages, but teams that use each step are usually better performers. These stages are shown in **Figure 9.2**.

Stage 1: Forming

Forming is the orientation period when team members get to know each other and learn what behaviours are acceptable to the group. Team members begin with curiosity about what they are expected to do and whether they will fit in with the group. An effective team leader provides time for members to get to know each other.

Stage 2: Storming

The personalities of team members begin to emerge at the storming stage. Individual personalities come out, as members clarify their roles and expectations. Conflicts may arise, as people disagree about the team's mission and compete for position and control of the group. Subgroups may form because of common interests or concerns. At this stage, the team leader must encourage everyone to participate. Members need to work through their uncertainties and conflicts. Teams must move beyond this stage to achieve productivity.

FIGURE 9.2 Stages of Team Development

Stage 3: Norming

During the norming stage, members resolve their differences, accept each other, and reach broad agreement about the roles of the team leader and other participants. This stage is usually brief. The team leader can use this stage to emphasize the team's unity and the importance of its objectives.

Stage 4: Performing

While performing, members focus on solving problems and accomplishing tasks. They interact frequently and handle conflicts constructively. The team leader encourages all members to contribute. He or she should try to ensure everyone is involved.

Stage 5: Adjourning

The team adjourns after members have completed their assigned task or solved the problem. During this phase, the focus is on wrapping up and summarizing the team's experiences and accomplishments. The team leader may recognize the team's accomplishments with a celebration, perhaps handing out plaques or awards.

✓ ASSESSMENT CHECK

9.3.1 Explain team level and team diversity.
9.3.2 Explain how teams progress through the stages of team development.

LO 9.4 Relate team cohesiveness and norms to effective team performance.

TEAM COHESIVENESS AND NORMS

team cohesiveness the extent to which team members feel attracted to the team and motivated to remain part of it.

Teams tend to maximize productivity when they form highly cohesive, or unified, units. **Team cohesiveness** refers to the extent to which members feel attracted to the team and motivated to remain part of it. This cohesiveness, or feeling of unity, typically increases when members interact frequently, share common attitudes and goals, and enjoy being together. Cohesive groups have a better chance of retaining their members than groups that do not achieve cohesiveness. As a result, cohesive groups typically experience lower turnover. Team cohesiveness promotes cooperative behaviour, generosity, and a willingness of team members to help each other. When team cohesiveness is high, team members are more motivated to contribute to the team because they want the approval of other team members.

Not surprisingly, studies have clearly shown that cohesive teams quickly achieve high levels of performance and consistently perform better than groups that are not cohesive.

Team-building retreats are sometimes used to encourage team cohesiveness and improve team members' satisfaction and retention. Team retreats allow members to participate in team-building exercises and games away from the office. These retreats provide time and space for people to get to know each other outside of the workplace. These retreats can lead to team members creating bonds with each other. When these bonds return with team members to the workplace, they can lead to benefits for a long period of time.[12] Team training can also build cohesion by cross-training team members in others' roles or by training team members to develop the skills needed to support the team task.[13]

A **team norm** is a standard of conduct shared by team members that guides their behaviour. Norms are not formal written guidelines; they are informal standards that identify key values and clarify team members' expectations. Team norms include standards of conduct during meetings and a shared vision for the team. Norms can be positive or negative. In highly productive teams, positive norms contribute to constructive work and the accomplishment of team goals. Negative norms can contribute to reduced work effort, reduced quality, and poor job attendance.

team norm a standard of conduct shared by team members that guides their behaviour.

✓ ASSESSMENT CHECK

9.4.1 How does cohesiveness affect teams?

9.4.2 Explain how team norms positively and negatively affect teams.

TEAM CONFLICT

Conflict occurs when one person's, or one group's, needs do not match those of another, and one side may try to block the other side's intentions or goals. Conflict and disagreement are to be expected in most teams. But that shouldn't be a surprise. People who work together are naturally going to disagree about what to do and how to do it. What causes conflict in teams? Almost anything can lead to conflict, but the main cause of team conflict is disagreement over goals and priorities. Other common causes of team conflict include disagreements over task-related issues, personalities that can't get along, being overtired and overstressed, and team diversity.

Earlier in this chapter, we discussed how teams can experience diversity among their members. Diversity brings stimulation, challenge, and energy, but it can also lead to conflict. The job of the manager is to create an environment where differences are appreciated, and a team of diverse individuals can work productively together. Diversity awareness training programs can reduce conflict by bringing these differences out in the open and identifying the unique talents of diverse individuals.

Most people think conflict should be avoided, but management experts know that conflict can actually improve team performance. The key to dealing with conflict is making sure that the team experiences the right kind of conflict. **Cognitive conflict** focuses on problem-related differences of opinion. Resolving these differences strongly improves team performance. In cognitive conflict, team members disagree because their different experiences and expertise lead them to different views of the problem and its solutions. People in a cognitive conflict have a willingness to examine, compare, and resolve their differences to produce the best possible solution. By contrast, **affective conflict** refers to the emotional reactions that can occur when disagreements become personal instead of remaining professional. These differences can strongly decrease team performance. Affective conflict often results in hostility, anger, resentment, distrust, cynicism, and apathy. It can make people uncomfortable, cause them to withdraw, decrease their commitment to a team, lower the satisfaction of team members, and decrease team cohesiveness. Unlike cognitive conflict, affective conflict weakens team performance by preventing teams from taking part in activities that are needed to achieve team effectiveness.

Managers can learn to manage team conflict. They can even make conflict work for them. The team leader's most important contribution to conflict resolution may be encouraging good

LO 9.5 Describe the factors that can cause team conflict and ways to manage conflict.

conflict the outcome when one person's, or one group's, needs do not match those of another, and one side may try to block the other side's intentions or goals.

cognitive conflict a disagreement that focuses on problem- and issue-related differences of opinion.

affective conflict a disagreement that focuses on individuals or personal issues.

ASSESSMENT CHECK

9.5.1 What is cognitive conflict, and how does it affect teams?

9.5.2 Explain affective conflict and its impact on teams.

LO 9.6 Outline the process of effective communication.

communication a meaningful exchange of information through messages.

communication and making it possible. Then, teammates will respect each other and are free to disagree with each other. Ongoing, effective communication means that team members view each other accurately, understand what is expected of them, and obtain the information they need. Organizations can extend this strategy by looking at situations or conditions in the workplace that might be causing conflict. Solving a single conflict isn't helpful if the team or the company has deeper problems. Employees can learn to become better team members through team-building exercises, listening exercises, and role-playing.[14]

THE IMPORTANCE OF EFFECTIVE COMMUNICATION

China, India, and Mexico are home to businesses that provide goods and services to companies and consumers in North America. But as the number of players involved in the production process increases, the harder it is to coordinate communication. Japanese Toyota found itself in the middle of miscommunications when it tried to document a consistent timeline for the discovery and reporting of unintended acceleration in some of its vehicles. Everyone was talking about the cause—loose floor mats, stuck gas pedals, and electronics. But then it came out that European dealers had received information and repair kits from Toyota months earlier.[15]

Communication can be defined as a meaningful exchange of information through messages. Few businesses can succeed without effective communication. As shown by the Toyota example, miscommunication can result in damage to the company. Toyota was ordered to pay a record-breaking $16.4 million in fines for its failure to communicate the safety problems quickly enough.[16]

Managers spend about 80 percent of their time—6 hours and 24 minutes of every eight-hour day—in direct communication with others, whether on the telephone, in meetings, via email, or in individual conversations. Company recruiters rate effective communication—listening, conversing, and giving feedback—as the most important skill they look for when hiring new employees. In this last half of the chapter, you'll learn about the communication process, the basic forms of communication, and ways to improve communication within organizations.

The Process of Communication

Every communication follows a step-by-step process that includes interactions among six elements: sender, message, channel, audience, feedback, and context. This process is shown in **Figure 9.3**.

In the first step, the *sender* composes the message and sends it through a communication carrier, or channel. Encoding a message means that the sender translates its meaning into

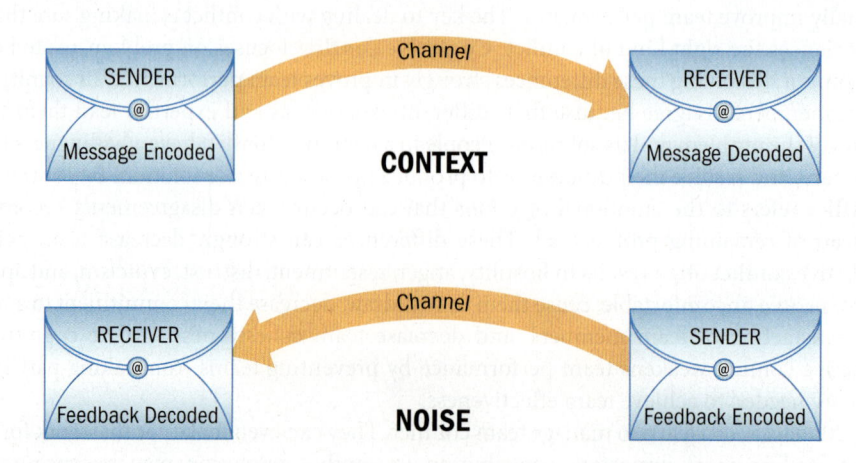

FIGURE 9.3 The Communication Process

understandable terms and puts it in a form so the message can be sent through a chosen channel. The sender can communicate a particular message through many different channels, including face-to-face conversations, phone calls, and email or texting. A promotional message to the firm's customers may be communicated through such forms as radio and television ads, billboards, magazines and newspapers, sales presentations, and social media such as Facebook and Twitter. The audience consists of the people who receive the message. In decoding, the receiver of the message interprets its meaning. Feedback from the audience—in response to the sender's communication—helps the sender to know whether the audience has correctly interpreted the intended meaning of the message.

Every communication takes place in a situational or cultural context. The *context* can exert a powerful influence on how well the process works. For an example of a situational context, consider that a conversation between two people in a quiet office may be a very different experience from the same conversation held at a noisy party. For an example of a cultural context, consider that a Canadian who orders chips in an English tavern will likely receive French fries.

Anthropologists classify cultures as low context or high context. Communication in *low-context cultures* tends to rely on written and verbal messages. Examples of low-context cultures include Switzerland, Austria, Germany, Canada, and the United States. In contrast, communication in *high-context cultures* depends not only on the message itself but also on the conditions that surround it, including nonverbal cues, past and present experiences, and personal relationships between the parties. High-context cultures include Japan, Latin America, and India. Westerners must carefully match their own low-context style to the expectations of colleagues and clients from high-context countries. North Americans tend to favour direct interactions and want to "get down to business" soon after shaking hands or sitting down to a business dinner. Businesspeople in Mexico and Asian countries prefer to become acquainted before discussing details. When conducting business in these cultures, wise visitors allow time for relaxed meals when business-related topics are avoided.

Senders must pay attention to audience feedback. They should even ask for feedback if none is offered. Feedback clarifies whether the communication's intended message was properly received. Feedback can show whether the receiver heard the message and was able to decode it accurately. Even when the receiver tries to understand, the communication may fail if the message contained slang or words that are unclear.

Noise during the communication process is any interference with the transmission of messages and feedback. Noise can result from simple physical factors, such as the poor reception of a cellphone or static that drowns out a radio commercial. Noise can also be caused by more complex differences in people's attitudes and viewpoints. Even when people are sent the same communications, they can have very different understandings of the message because of communication noise.

Noise during the communication process can result from simple physical factors, such as the poor reception of a cellphone or static that drowns out a radio commercial. Even when people are sent the same communications, they may have very different understandings of the message because of communication noise.

Noise can be present at any point in the communication process. Managers must learn how to cut through noise when communicating with employees. Managers at iLEVEL, a digital communications agency, found a creative way to cut through noise when communicating its plans to move from a paper-based process to an online system. First, the managers distributed "i" character mugs to office staff. Then they sent messages to employees' mobile phones. Those with iPhones received animated messages. New hires and prospective employees without company phones received a USB stick with the messages. "The communications felt really innovative and it was good using digital media because at the end of the day, that's what we're about as a company," says James Miller, the company's human resource director. "People have found it really good fun and I'm really, really pleased with the concept we have come up with."[17]

✓ ASSESSMENT CHECK

9.6.1 What is the difference between communication in low-context and high-context cultures?

9.6.2 In the context of the communication process, what is noise?

LO 9.7 Compare the basic forms of communication.

BASIC FORMS OF COMMUNICATION

Managers and co-workers communicate in many different ways. They make phone calls, send email, hold a staff meeting, or chat in the hallway. They also communicate with facial expressions, gestures, and other body language. Small variations can change how a message is received. As **Table 9.2** shows, communication takes different forms: oral and written, formal and informal, and nonverbal.

TABLE 9.2 Forms of Communication

FORM	DESCRIPTION	EXAMPLES
Oral communication	Communication transmitted through speech	Personal conversations, speeches, meetings, voice mail, telephone conversations, video conferences
Written communication	Communication transmitted through writing	Letters, memos, formal reports, news releases, email, faxes, online discussion groups, Internet messaging
Formal communication	Communication transmitted through the chain of command within an organization to other members or to people outside the organization	Internal—memos, reports, meetings, written proposals, oral presentations, meeting minutes External—letters, written proposals, oral presentations, speeches, news releases, press conferences
Informal communication	Communication transmitted outside formal channels without regard for the organization's hierarchy of authority	Rumours spread informally among employees via the grapevine
Nonverbal communication	Communication transmitted through actions and behaviours rather than through words	Gestures, facial expressions, posture, body language, dress, makeup

Oral Communication

Managers spend a lot of time using oral communication, both in person and on the phone. Some people prefer to communicate this way, believing that using oral communication means that messages are received more accurately. Face-to-face oral communication allows people to combine words with other cues, such as facial expressions and tone of voice. Oral communication over the telephone lacks visual cues, but people receiving the message can hear the tone of voice. People can also provide immediate feedback by asking questions or restating the message. Because oral communication is immediate, it has drawbacks. If one person is upset or nervous during a conversation, noise enters the communication process. A hurried manager might brush off an employee who has an important message to deliver. A frustrated employee might say some harsh words to an unsupportive supervisor instead of thinking before speaking.

An important part of oral communication is **listening**—receiving a message and interpreting its intended meaning by accurately grasping the facts and feelings the message conveys. Listening may be the most important communication skill, but most of us don't use it enough—or as well as we should.

Listening may seem easy because the listener appears to make no effort. But the average person talks at a rate of 150 words per minute, while the brain can handle up to 400 words per minute. This gap can lead to boredom, inattention, and misinterpretation. In fact, immediately after listening to a message, the average person can recall only half of it. After several days, a listener can recall only 25 percent or less.

listening receiving a message and interpreting its intended meaning by grasping the facts and feelings the message conveys.

Certain types of listening behaviours are common in both business and personal interactions:

- *Cynical or defensive listening.* This type of listening occurs when the receiver of a message feels that the sender is trying to gain some advantage from the communication.

- *Offensive listening.* In this type of listening, the receiver tries to catch the speaker in a mistake or contradiction.

- *Polite listening.* In this mechanical type of listening, the receiver listens to be polite. The listener does not expect to contribute to the communication. Polite listeners usually don't pay attention. They spend their time thinking about what they want to say when the speaker finishes.

- *Active listening.* This form of listening requires involvement with the information and empathy with the speaker's situation. In both business and personal life, active listening is the basis for effective communication.

Listening may seem easy because the listener appears to make no effort. But the average person talks at a rate of 150 words per minute, while the brain can handle up to 400 words per minute. This gap can lead to boredom, inattention, and misinterpretation.

An especially important goal for business leaders is to learn to be an active listener. Effective communication is essential to their role. Listening is hard work, but it pays off with increased learning, better interpersonal relationships, and greater influence.[18] Both managers and employees can develop skills to make them better listeners, as described in the "Career Kickstart" feature.

CAREER KICKSTART
Tune Up Your Listening Skills

Smart managers know that good listening is important to business success. Tuning in to employees, customers, and competitors can provide valuable insight and information. Listening means paying attention to verbal and nonverbal cues. It means turning off your cellphone during a face-to-face conversation or meeting. It involves strategies for understanding the message that is conveyed. Here are a few tips for improving your listening skills:

- *Be attentive.* If it is culturally appropriate, maintain eye contact with the speaker, but don't stare. Nod your head to show that you are listening. Block out distractions such as background noise and unrelated thoughts.

- *Keep an open mind.* Hear the other person all the way through, even if you are certain you will disagree. You will show respect for the speaker, and your own reply will be better informed.

- *Don't interrupt.* Even if you are absolutely certain of what the person is going to say—or if you are sure you have a solution or answer—wait until the speaker is finished. Then, you can ask a question or make your point.

- *Ask questions.* Ask at least one question or paraphrase portions of the speaker's discussion to ensure that you understand the other person's point.

- *Be empathetic.* Laugh or be consoling when it is suitable. You don't have to agree with the speaker, but even in the heat of disagreement, you can show empathy.

Sources: Norma Chew, "Are You a Good Listener?" *Associated Content*, accessed April 19, 2010, www.associatedcontent.com; Dianne Schilling, "Listening Skills: 10 Steps to Effective Learning", *Forbes*, November 9, 2012, www.forbes.com/sites/womensmedia/2012/11/09/10-steps-to-effective-listening; "Are You an Active Listener?" *New Horizons*, February 16, 2010, www.newhorizons123.com.

Written Communication

Channels for written communication include reports, letters, memos, online discussion boards, social media, emails, and text messages. Many of these channels permit only delayed feedback and create a record of the message. The sender of a written communication needs to prepare the message carefully. The sender should also review the message to avoid misunderstandings, especially before pressing the "send" button.

Effective written communication reflects its audience, the channel carrying the message, and a suitable degree of formality. When writing a formal business document, such as a complex marketing research report, a manager must plan in advance and carefully construct the document. The process of writing a formal document involves planning, research, organization, composition and design, and revision. Written communication via email may call for a less formal writing style, including short sentences, phrases, and lists.

Email is a very effective communication channel, especially for delivering straightforward messages and information. Email's effectiveness also leads to its biggest problem: too much email! Many workers find their valuable time is used up dealing with email. To relieve this task and leave more time for the most important tasks, some companies are looking at ways to reduce the time employees spend sending and reading email and other online data. To meet this need, some firms provide specialized software and services. OpenText Corporation, a company headquartered in Waterloo, Ontario, provides content management solutions to clients, including solutions related to email.[19]

Two other email issues are security and retention. Because email messages are often informal, senders sometimes forget that they are creating a written record. Even if the recipient deletes an email message, other copies exist on company email servers. Emails on company servers can be used as evidence in a legal case or to build a case for disciplinary action.

Formal Communication

A *formal communication channel* carries messages that flow within the chain of command structure defined by an organization. The most familiar channel is downward communication. This channel carries messages from someone who holds a senior position in the organization to subordinates, or the people below. Managers may communicate downward by sending employees email messages, leading discussions at department meetings, giving employees policy manuals, posting notices on bulletin boards, and reporting news in company newsletters. The most important factor in formal communication is to be open and honest. "Spinning" bad news to make it look better almost always doesn't work. In a work environment that has open communication, employees feel free to express opinions, offer suggestions, and even voice their complaints. Research has shown that open communication has the following seven characteristics:

1. *Employees are valued.* Employees are happier and more motivated when they feel they are valued and their opinions are heard.
2. *A high level of trust exists.* Telling the truth maintains a high level of trust. Trust forms the foundation for open communication, which can lead to employee motivation and retention.
3. *Conflict is invited and resolved positively.* Conflict encourages innovation and creativity.
4. *Creative dissent is welcomed.* When employees can express their creative ideas, they feel they are contributing to the company and improving performance.
5. *Employee input is requested.* The key to any company's success is input from employees. Seeking employees' feedback gives them a sense of involvement and improves working relations.
6. *Employees are well informed.* Employees feel valued when they are kept informed about what is happening within the organization.
7. *Feedback is ongoing.* Both positive and negative feedback must be ongoing. Feedback should be provided in a way that builds relationships rather than assigns blame.[20]

Many firms also define formal channels for upward communications. These channels encourage communication from employees to supervisors and upward to top management levels. Some examples of upward communication channels are employee surveys, suggestion boxes, and systems for employees to propose ideas for new products or voice complaints. Upward communication is also needed for managers to evaluate the effectiveness of downward communication. **Figure 9.4** shows the different forms of formal and informal organizational communication.

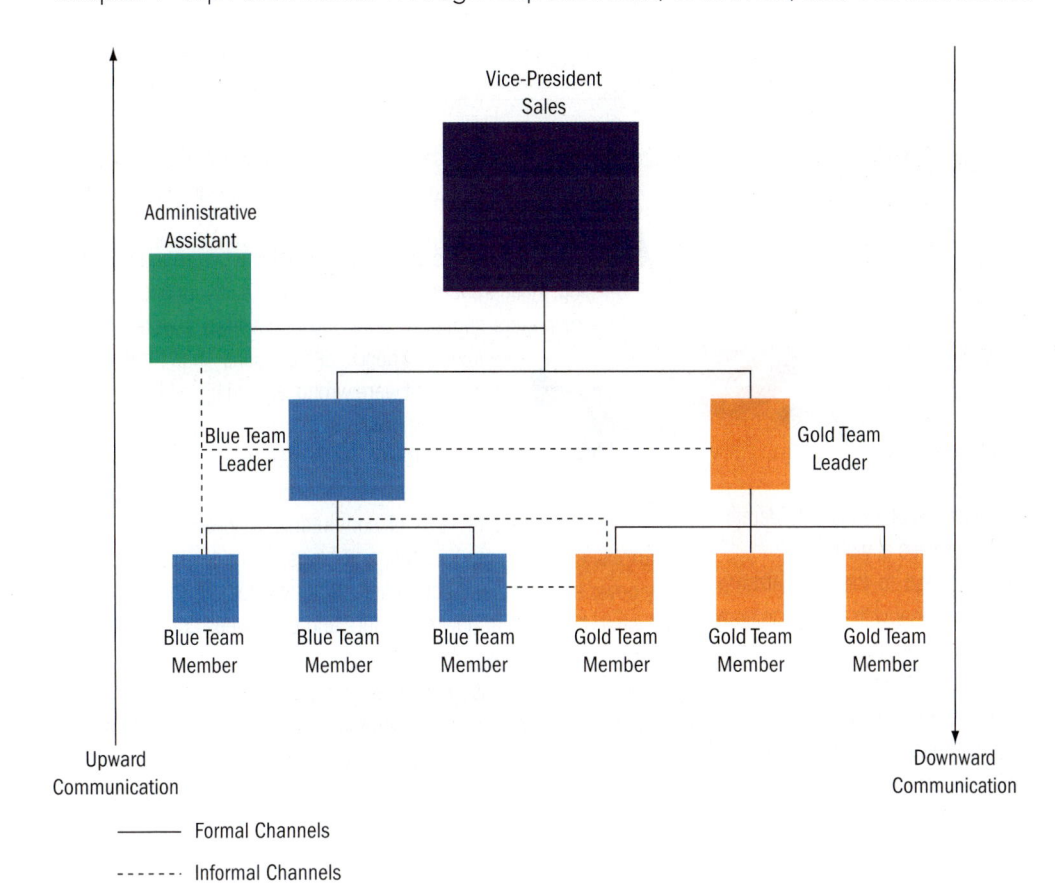

FIGURE 9.4 Formal and Informal Channels of Communication

Informal Communication

Informal communication channels carry messages outside the formally authorized channels of an organization's hierarchy. A familiar example of an informal channel is the **grapevine**, an internal channel that passes information from unofficial sources. All organizations, large or small, have grapevines. Grapevines spread information with speed and economy—and they are surprisingly reliable. But company communications must be managed effectively so that the grapevine is not the main source of information. When properly encouraged, the grapevine can help managers in three ways: to get a feel for the morale of companies, to understand the anxieties of the workforce, and to evaluate the effectiveness of formal communications. Managers can improve the quality of information passing through the company grapevine by sharing what they know, even if it is early or partial information. By feeding information to selected people, smart leaders can harness the power of the grapevine.

The main drawback of this communication channel is gossip, which usually travels along the grapevine. People who gossip often spread misinformation and weaken morale. A manager should deal directly with the gossiper, taking action that suits the severity of the situation. The manager can then use the grapevine and other communication channels to spread accurate information about the company.[21]

Organizations are becoming more decentralized and more spread out globally. That means that more than ever, informal communication provides an important source of information, through email, texting, and social media. Henry Mintzberg, a McGill University professor, believes that informal communications are essential to good managerial decision making. The "Hit & Miss" feature discusses Mintzberg's studies.

grapevine an internal information channel that passes information from unofficial sources.

Nonverbal Communication

So far, this section has discussed different forms of verbal communication, or communication that uses words to convey meaning. Equally important is *nonverbal communication*, which transmits messages through actions and behaviours. Nonverbal actions that become communication cues

HIT & MISS

Henry Mintzberg: Observing What Managers Do

McGill University management professor Henry Mintzberg enjoys a well-deserved international reputation for his scholarly work on how managers behave in the workplace. Mintzberg is noted for his study published in 1980. In that study, he reported what managers did while they worked. Mintzberg gathered data by following several senior managers while they were busy at their jobs. Mintzberg found that managers showed several common working methods and played clearly identifiable managerial roles to achieve their objectives at work.

To show the methods managers tended to follow, Mintzberg drew a picture of the fast-paced, driven manager with little or no time to spare. Coffee breaks and lunch were opportunities for meetings and informal communication with people. Work was never one continuous task; instead, it was choppy, constantly interrupted by other tasks, such as phone calls and short conversations with people who entered the office without an appointment. Mintzberg also recognized the existence of a critical network of people. These were the people that managers talked with regularly. Managers also counted on these people to help achieve their work goals.

Mintzberg observed and classified three primary behaviour roles of managers. Interpersonal roles included leadership and managerial actions that connected people in the organizations; informational roles involved the collection and distribution of information; and decisional roles included negotiation, designing change within the organization, and other activities related to decision making.

These role descriptions helped to provide insights into the work managers did and the skills they would need to be successful. The Mintzberg study also helped to show how work actually got done in a modern corporation, which dismissed many myths about corporate culture.

Today, Mintzberg has triggered more discussion and debate. He argues that formal evidence-based performance output data (for example, unit sales) are usually too dated for managers to use to make good decisions. Mintzberg believes that managers should put their faith in the flow of informal information, opinions, and even hearsay. Of course, many disagree with this view and strongly support using formal communication reports to guide managerial decision making.

Mintzberg's study was thought to be groundbreaking. Researchers had always made assumptions about how managers communicated and behaved in a work environment. Those assumptions had seemed logical, but were wrong, according to Mintzberg. Technology plays a big role in how we communicate today. Team members who are not in the same physical location may communicate through the use of computerized videoconferencing, smartphones, social media sites, and blogs. Some team members may never actually meet face to face. What will today's researchers find when they look at how managers and employees actually work in today's electronic environment?

Mintzberg's recent commentary suggests that managers should pay more attention to informal communications, not wait for formal evidence-based performance output data (for example, unit sales). His viewpoint speaks to the changes that are taking place in management communications and decision making.

Questions for Critical Thinking

1. How much value should higher management place on postings to the corporate blog, where any of a firm's managers can comment on their current thoughts, opinions, and activities?

2. How can a firm improve communications within a team of managers located across Canada who have never met face to face?

Sources: Henry Mintzberg, *Managing* (San Francisco: Berrett-Koehler, 2009); Henry Mintzberg, *The Nature of Managerial Work*, (New York: Harper & Row, 1973; reprinted by Prentice-Hall, 1983); Ingo Keilitz, "Henry Mintzberg Misses the Mark on Performance Measurement Data," *Made2Measure Blog*, November 15, 2009, accessed July 2, 2015, http://made2measure.blogspot.com/2009/11/henry-mintzberg-misses-mark-on.html; Proven Models website, accessed January 30, 2012, www.provenmodels.com/88/ten-managerialroles/mintzberg-henry; Karl Moore, "Porter or Mintzberg: Whose View of Strategy Is the Most Relevant Today?" *Forbes*, March 28, 2011, accessed July 2, 2015, www.forbes.com/sites/karlmoore/2011/03/28/porter-or-mintzberg-whose-view-of-strategy-is-the-most-relevant-today; Henry Mintzberg, "The Manager's Job: Folklore and Fact," *Harvard Business Review*, July–August 1975, pp. 49–61; K.M. Bartol and D.C. Martin, *Management* (New York: McGraw-Hill Inc. 1991), pp. 10–14.

---

include gestures, posture, eye contact, tone and volume of voice, and even clothing choices. Nonverbal cues can have more impact on communications than many people realize. In fact, some people estimate that 70 percent of interpersonal communication is conveyed through nonverbal cues. Top salespeople are particularly good at reading and using these cues. For example, they practise "mirroring" a customer's gestures and body language to show agreement.[22]

Powerful messages are even conveyed through the amount of personal space, or the physical distance, between people who are communicating. **Figure 9.5** shows the four zones of personal space and social interaction: intimate, personal, social, and public. In North America, most business

FIGURE 9.5 Influence of Personal Space in Nonverbal Communication

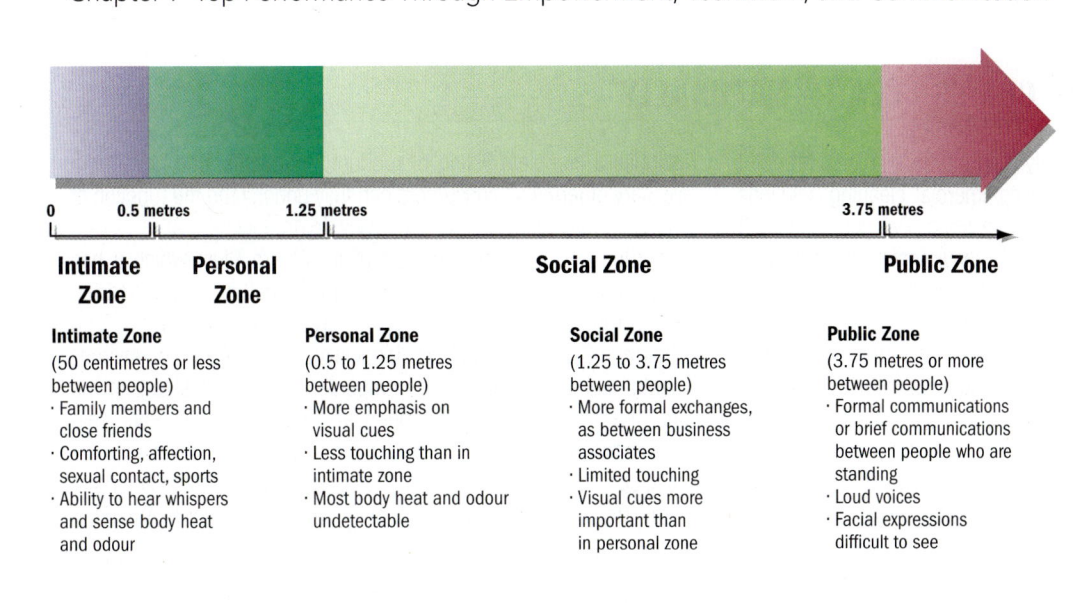

Intimate Zone (50 centimetres or less between people)
- Family members and close friends
- Comforting, affection, sexual contact, sports
- Ability to hear whispers and sense body heat and odour

Personal Zone (0.5 to 1.25 metres between people)
- More emphasis on visual cues
- Less touching than in intimate zone
- Most body heat and odour undetectable

Social Zone (1.25 to 3.75 metres between people)
- More formal exchanges, as between business associates
- Limited touching
- Visual cues more important than in personal zone

Public Zone (3.75 metres or more between people)
- Formal communications or brief communications between people who are standing
- Loud voices
- Facial expressions difficult to see

conversations occur within the social zone, roughly between 1.25 and 3.75 metres apart. If one person tries to approach closer than that, the other will likely feel uncomfortable or even threatened.

Understanding nonverbal cues can be especially challenging for people from different cultural backgrounds. Cultural ideas of personal space differ widely throughout most of the world. For example, most Latin Americans have business conversations while standing very close to the person they are talking to. Many North Americans find the space uncomfortably close. North Americans often step back to keep their personal space a little wider, but Latin Americans see that gesture as a sign of cold and unfriendly relations. To protect their personal space, some North Americans use desks or tables to separate themselves from their Latin American colleagues. Of course, these people risk their colleagues moving around the furniture to reduce the uncomfortable distance.

People send nonverbal messages even when they try not to. Nonverbal cues can show a person's true feelings and thoughts, which may differ from what they are saying. Generally, when verbal and nonverbal cues conflict, receivers of the communication tend to believe the nonverbal content. In job interviews, managers watch for nonverbal behaviour. When looking to hire people with good attitudes and a team orientation, many firms have several job applicants meet in group sessions. When one applicant gives a good answer, and another applicant frowns or looks discouraged, that nonverbal behaviour suggests that a person may not be a strong team player.

✓ ASSESSMENT CHECK

9.7.1 Define the four common listening behaviours.

9.7.2 What are the differences between formal and informal communication?

EXTERNAL COMMUNICATION AND CRISIS MANAGEMENT

LO 9.8 Explain external communication and methods of managing a public crisis.

External communication is an exchange of information using messages sent between an organization and its major audiences: customers, suppliers, other firms, the general public, and government officials. Businesses use external communication to keep their operations going, to maintain their positions in the marketplace, and to build customer relationships by supplying information such as changes to products and prices. Every communication with customers—including sales presentations and advertisements—should create goodwill and contribute to customer satisfaction. Firms such as Clorox use their websites to publish good news about their company, as described in the "Going Green" feature. An important function of external communication is informing the public about new initiatives for environmentally friendly processes, community projects, and the firm's other socially responsible activities.

However, companies can experience a public relations crisis that threatens their reputation or goodwill. Nestlé is one of the world's largest food producers. It faced a crisis when Greenpeace

external communication a meaningful exchange of information through messages sent between an organization and its major audiences.

Going Green: CLOROX COMES CLEAN—NATURALLY

You've probably seen the Green Works brand of household and commercial cleaning solutions at your local grocery store. But you might not know that these natural, environmentally responsible cleaners are made by the same people who make bleach. Clorox is committed to following through on initiatives to reduce its impact on the environment by changing both its manufacturing processes and the ingredients in its products. To accomplish this, the firm has established a department of Environmental Sustainability Strategy and an Eco Office. Clorox's line of Green Works products meets strict environmental standards for ingredients, fragrances, packaging, and manufacturing processes. Clorox is also working on similar efforts to improve its traditional products.

One of the first pieces of external communication about its new focus on product ingredients was a list of ingredients, so consumers would know more about the products they were buying. The list has grown in detail. Clorox now provides more detailed information about its safety processes, the guidelines it uses to screen ingredients, and information on fragrances (a major ingredient in cleaning solutions). Clorox asks all fragrance suppliers to agree to increasingly strict fragrance standards. Clorox is the first major consumer-packaged-goods company to provide such detail to let consumers know exactly what its products contain and how they are made.

To spread the word farther, Clorox recently launched its own Corporate Social Responsibility (CSR) website. It provides information about Clorox's processes and products. The site is easy to use, includes a complete listing of product ingredients, and provides a glossary of terms so consumers can fully understand the function of each ingredient in a product (see www.trygreenworks.ca).

Clorox has gained the trust of the Sierra Club, which it has partnered with on some of its programs. Together, Clorox and the Sierra Club praise the benefits of green cleaning. Sierra Club Chairman Carl Pope said that Clorox is showing the kind of environmental leadership that more companies should be taking. In the time that the Sierra Club has been working with Clorox, Pope said he's seen solid progress in things such as creating innovative products, communicating ingredients to consumers, and transitioning to eliminate the transportation of chlorine from its North American supply chain.

Questions for Critical Thinking

1. Clorox uses its CSR website to publish information and news about its green processes and products. How can the company use a social network, such as Facebook, to increase its online external communication?
2. Is there a downside to using the Internet for this type of communication? Why or why not?

Sources: Clorox website, www.cloroxcsr.com, accessed April 29, 2010; "2010 Best Companies for America's Children," *Working Mother*, accessed April 29, 1010, www.workingmother.com; "Clorox's New CSR Web Site Features Upgraded 'Ingredients Inside' Product Information," *CSRwire*, February 1, 2010, www.csrwire.com.

---

reported that the firm was importing palm oil from suppliers who were damaging the rainforests in Indonesia, home to endangered orangutans and other species at risk. Outraged consumers raced to Nestlé's Facebook page to add their angry comments. Nestlé's response to the problem turned angry, including scolding the Facebook visitors for their aggression. This response angered consumers further, until Nestlé's Facebook moderator apologized "for being rude."[23]

How a company such as Nestlé handles a crisis can affect whether its reputation will be restored. Deciding on a plan of action and dealing with facts and rumours immediately can make the difference between regaining trust and allowing the disaster to grow. The following communication steps can help calm a public relations crisis:

1. When a crisis occurs, a firm should respond quickly. Executives should prepare a written statement—and stick to it. The statement should mention the time, place, and the initial description of what occurred (not the cause), and the number and status of the people involved.

2. As soon as possible, top company management should appear in public with news media present, if possible. The public will hold top management responsible, so it's best that top managers respond to reporters' questions.

3. When answering questions at an initial press conference or in an interview, the management representative must stick to the facts. If the press conference is held immediately, many details about the event, the cause, and the people involved may not yet be known; the spokesperson should not speculate, or create theories, about these details. As information becomes available, the firm can provide accurate updates.

4. If a question is currently unanswerable, the executive can offer to find out the answer. This answer should be quickly found and relayed as soon as possible. It's not a good idea to answer a question by saying, "No comment." It is much better to say, "I don't know."
5. The firm should recognize that problems exist, explain solutions, and welcome feedback. If a question or factual statement puts the organization in a negative light, the manager should accept that there is a problem, and then explain how the firm is correcting it.
6. The press conference or interview will be most effective if the executive speaks briefly and clearly and provides visual images. If available, a video with positive images—such as thriving rainforests—can be useful.[24]

The crisis faced by Nestlé—the claim that it was purchasing palm oil from a supplier that was contributing to the destruction of rainforests—was made worse by the criticism posted on social media sites. Nestlé announced it would immediately stop purchasing oil from this supplier and added that this supplier represented only 1.25 percent of its total palm oil use. Still, debate over the company's environmental practices continued online. Nestlé spokesperson Nina Backes notes that in these instances it is difficult "to show that we are listening, which we obviously are, while not getting into a shouting match." Daniel Kessler, press officer at Greenpeace, admits that social media present a new challenge for companies trying to manage their external communication. "This is the place where major corporations are very vulnerable," he remarks.[25]

Businesses use external communication to keep their operations going, to maintain their positions in the marketplace, and to build customer relationships. Every communication with customers—including advertisements—should create goodwill and contribute to customer satisfaction.

WHAT'S AHEAD

Today's consumers expect the products they buy to be of the highest value for the price. Firms ensure this value by developing efficient systems for producing goods and services and by maintaining high quality. The next chapter examines the ways in which businesses produce world-class goods and services, efficiently organize their production facilities, purchase what they need to produce their goods and services, and manage large inventories to maximize efficiency and reduce costs.

✓ **ASSESSMENT CHECK**

9.8.1 What is external communication?

9.8.2 What is the first thing a company should do when a public crisis occurs?

RETURN TO INSIDE BUSINESS

Pam Cooley and CarShareHFX

When Pam Cooley was developing the CarShareHFX concept in the Halifax area, she needed to communicate a message that would attract a particular targeted customer or intermediary. An obvious message to users, both individuals and businesses, is the advantage of saving money and simplifying car ownership. The message directed to real estate developers and property management firms was a little different. For these customers, CarShareHFX partnerships provide a value-added competitive advantage by reducing the number of parking spots needed for residents. For example, a retired couple living in the city core might only occasionally need to use a second vehicle. Instead of paying for a second car that isn't used much, the couple can use a CarShare car that they can access from their building's garage.

QUESTIONS FOR CRITICAL THINKING

1. Identify other potential users that might benefit from the car-sharing model.
2. What message would you use to gain their participation?

SUMMARY OF LEARNING OBJECTIVES

LO 9.1 Describe why and how organizations empower employees.

Organizations empower employees by giving them shared authority and responsibility to make decisions about their work with their managers. Empowerment tries to use the brainpower of all workers to find better ways of doing their jobs, serving customers, and achieving organizational goals. Empowerment often includes linking rewards to company performance through employee stock ownership plans (ESOPs) and stock options.

✓ ASSESSMENT CHECK ANSWERS

9.1.1 What is empowerment? Empowerment is giving employees shared authority and responsibility to make decisions about their work with their managers.

9.1.2 What kinds of information can companies provide to employees to help them share decision-making responsibility? One of the best ways to get employees to share decision-making responsibility is for executives to share information about company performance, particularly financial performance.

9.1.3 How do employee stock ownership plans and stock options reward employees and encourage empowerment? Employee stock ownership plans (ESOPs) benefit employees by giving them ownership stakes in their companies. Employees are motivated to work harder and smarter because they share in their firm's financial success. In an ESOP, the company holds stock for the benefit of employees (when employees leave the company, they cash in their stock). Stock options give employees a chance to own the stock themselves if they exercise, or use, their options by purchasing the stock.

LO 9.2 Describe the five types of teams in the workplace.

The five basic types of teams are work teams, problem-solving teams, self-managed teams, cross-functional teams, and virtual teams. Work teams are permanent groups of co-workers who perform the day-to-day tasks needed to operate the organization. Problem-solving teams are temporary groups of employees who gather to solve specific problems and then disband. Self-managed teams have the authority to make decisions about how their members complete their daily tasks. Cross-functional teams are made up of members from different units, such as production, marketing, and finance. Virtual teams are groups of geographically or organizationally separated co-workers who use telecommunications and information technologies to accomplish an organizational task.

✓ ASSESSMENT CHECK ANSWERS

9.2.1 What is a team? A team is a group of employees who share a common purpose, approach, and set of performance goals.

9.2.2 What are the five types of teams, and how are they different? Work teams are permanent, while problem-solving teams are temporary. Unlike work teams, self-managed teams have the authority to change how they get their work done. Cross-functional teams are composed of people from different work functions, while virtual teams are composed of people from different locations who use technology to communicate and work together.

LO 9.3 Describe the characteristics of an effective team and the stages of team development.

Three important characteristics of a team are its size, team level, and team diversity. The ideal team size is about six or seven members. Team level is the team's average level of ability, experience, personality, or any other factor. Team diversity represents the team's differences in ability, experience, personality, or any other factor. Team diversity is an important consideration for teams that must complete a wide range of different tasks or complex tasks. Teams pass through five stages of development: (1) forming is the orientation period when members get to know each other and learn what behaviours are acceptable to the group; (2) storming is the stage when individual personalities come out, as members clarify their roles and expectations; (3) norming is the stage when differences are resolved, members accept each other, and they agree about the roles of the team leader and other participants; (4) performing is characterized by problem solving and a focus on task accomplishment; (5) adjourning is the final stage, with a focus on wrapping up and summarizing the team's experiences and accomplishments.

✓ ASSESSMENT CHECK ANSWERS

9.3.1 Explain team level and team diversity. Team level represents the team's average level or capability. Team diversity represents the team's differences in ability, experience, personality, or any other factor.

9.3.2 Explain how teams progress through the stages of team development. Teams pass through five stages of development: forming, storming, norming, performing, and adjourning.

LO 9.4 Relate team cohesiveness and norms to effective team performance.

Team cohesiveness is the extent to which team members feel attracted to the team and motivated to remain on it. Team norms are the standards of conduct shared by team members that guide their behaviour. Highly cohesive teams whose members share certain standards of conduct tend to be more productive and effective.

ASSESSMENT CHECK ANSWERS

9.4.1 How does cohesiveness affect teams? Members of cohesive teams interact frequently, share common attitudes and goals, have high morale, and are likely to help each other. Cohesive teams also perform better.

9.4.2 Explain how team norms positively and negatively affect teams. Norms are informal standards that identify key values and clarify team members' expectations. Norms can be positive or negative. Positive norms contribute to constructive work and the accomplishment of team goals. Negative norms can, for example, contribute to reduced work effort, reduced quality, and poor job attendance.

LO 9.5 Describe the factors that can cause team conflict and ways to manage conflict.

Conflict and disagreement are to be expected in most teams. Conflict can come from many sources: disagreements about goals and priorities, task-related issues, personalities that can't get along, scarce resources, and being overtired and overstressed. The key to dealing with team conflict is not avoiding it, but making sure that the team experiences the right kind of conflict. Cognitive conflict focuses on problem-related differences of opinion. Resolving these differences strongly improves team performance. By contrast, affective conflict refers to the emotional reactions that can occur when disagreements become personal instead of remaining professional. These differences can strongly decrease team performance. A team leader can manage team conflict by encouraging good communication so team members view each other accurately, understand what is expected of them, and obtain the information they need.

ASSESSMENT CHECK ANSWERS

9.5.1 What is cognitive conflict, and how does it affect teams? In cognitive conflict, team members disagree because their different experiences and expertise lead them to different views of the problem and its solutions. People in a cognitive conflict have a willingness to examine, compare, and resolve their differences to produce the best possible solution.

9.5.2 Explain affective conflict and its impact on teams. Affective conflict often results in hostility, anger, resentment, distrust, cynicism, and apathy. It can make people uncomfortable, cause them to withdraw, decrease their commitment to a team, lower the satisfaction of team members, and decrease team cohesiveness.

LO 9.6 Outline the process of effective communication.

Managers spend about 80 percent of their time in direct communication with others. Company recruiters consistently rate effective communication—listening, conversing, and giving feedback—as the most important skill they look for when hiring new employees. The communication process follows a step-by-step process that involves interactions among six elements: sender, message, channel, audience, feedback, and context. The sender composes the message and sends it through the channel. The audience receives the message and interprets its meaning. The receiver gives feedback to the sender. The communication takes place in a situational or cultural context.

ASSESSMENT CHECK ANSWERS

9.6.1 What is the difference between communication in low-context and high-context cultures? Communication in low-context cultures tends to rely on written and verbal messages. By contrast, communication in high-context cultures depends not only on the message itself but also on the conditions that surround it, including nonverbal cues, past and present experiences, and personal relationships between the parties.

9.6.2 In the context of the communication process, what is noise? Noise is any interference with the transmission of messages and feedback. Noise can result from physical factors such as poor reception of a cellphone or differences in people's attitudes and perceptions.

LO 9.7 Compare the basic forms of communication.

People exchange messages in many ways. Their communication takes many forms: oral and written, formal and informal, verbal and nonverbal. Effective written communication reflects its audience, its channel, and a suitable degree of formality. Formal communication channels carry messages within the chain of command. Informal communication channels, such as the grapevine, carry messages outside the formal chain of command. Nonverbal communication plays a larger role than most people think. Sometimes, verbal and nonverbal cues conflict. When that happens, the receiver of a message tends to believe the meaning conveyed by nonverbal cues.

ASSESSMENT CHECK ANSWERS

9.7.1 Define the four common listening behaviours. Cynical listening occurs when the receiver of a message feels that the sender is trying to gain some advantage from the communication. Offensive listening occurs when the receiver tries to catch the speaker in a mistake or contradiction. Polite listening occurs when the receiver is thinking about what he or she wants to say when the speaker finishes. Active listening requires involvement with the information and empathy with the speaker's situation.

9.7.2 What are the differences between formal and informal communication? Formal communication occurs within the formal chain of command defined by an organization. Informal communication occurs outside the organization's hierarchy.

LO 9.8 Explain external communication and methods of managing a public crisis.

External communication is an exchange of information using messages sent between an organization and its major audiences: customers, suppliers, other firms, the general public, and government officials. Every communication with customers should create goodwill and contribute to customer satisfaction. However, companies can experience a public crisis that threatens their reputations or goodwill. To manage a public crisis, businesses should respond quickly and honestly, and a member of top management should be available to answer questions.

✓ ASSESSMENT CHECK ANSWERS

9.8.1 What is external communication? External communication is an exchange of information using messages sent between an organization and its major audiences.

9.8.2 What is the first thing a company should do when a public crisis occurs? The firm should respond quickly by preparing a written statement. This statement should include the time, place, description of the event, and the number and status of people involved.

BUSINESS TERMS YOU NEED TO KNOW

affective conflict 243	empowerment 236	self-managed team 239	team norm 243
cognitive conflict 243	external communication 251	team 238	virtual teams 239
communication 244	grapevine 249	team cohesiveness 242	work teams 239
conflict 243	listening 246	team diversity 240	
cross-functional team 239	problem-solving team 239	team level 240	

REVIEW QUESTIONS

1. How do companies benefit from empowering their employees? How do employees benefit from empowerment?
2. Suppose that a shoe manufacturer wants to use teams to decide how to improve its environmental standards for products and processes. What type (or types) of teams would be best for this initiative? Why?
3. How do team level and team diversity affect team performance?
4. What are the characteristics of an effective team? Why are these features so significant?
5. At what stages of development might a team not be able to move forward? How should a team leader or manager deal with this situation?
6. Describe the norms associated with your business class. How do these norms influence the way you behave?
7. What steps can managers take to manage team conflict?
8. In what ways is context a powerful influence on the effectiveness of communication? Describe a situation where situational or cultural context affected one of your communication processes.
9. What are the upsides and downsides of oral and written communication?
10. What is the role of external communication? Why is external communication important to companies?

PROJECTS AND TEAMWORK APPLICATIONS

1. Empowerment is having the power and authority to make decisions. For this project, the teacher steps back and allows the class to plan and carry out a day of classes. The students might appoint a leader, divide into teams (to plan a lecture, decide on an assignment, plan a field trip, and other activities). It's completely up to the students how they organize and carry out the day's classes. In the next class, discuss the experience—including any upsides and downsides of empowerment.

2. Divide the class into teams of relatively equal size. Each team can select one of the following two problems to solve or use another problem: arranging for a speaker or expanding the vegetarian menu in the cafeteria. The students do not need to complete the entire problem-solving process. Each team should go through the forming stage of team development and establish norms. Each team should outline a plan for accomplishing the group's task. Is each team cohesive? Why or why not?

3. Try this listening exercise with a partner. First, spend a few minutes writing a paragraph or two about the most important thing that happened to you this week. Second, read your paragraph out loud to your partner. Next, have your partner read his or her paragraph. Finally, take turns stating the most important points in the other person's story. See how well you listened to each other.

4. On your own or with a classmate, visit your school's library, a mall, or anywhere that people gather. Take 10 or 15 minutes to observe the nonverbal cues that people give each other: Does the librarian smile at students? What is the body language of students in groups? Notice any changes in nonverbal communication when someone joins a group or leaves it. After you leave the area, jot down as many of your observations as you can.

5. Choose a company you are familiar with or whose products you use. Research the company's products and its socially responsible and sustainability initiatives (for example, see whether the firm has set a goal to reduce its energy consumption). Create an advertisement that focuses on one of these initiatives as an example of the company's positive external communication.

WEB ASSIGNMENTS

1. **Team-building exercises.** The website Teampedia is "a collaborative encyclopedia of free team building activities, free icebreakers, teamwork resources, and tools for teams that anyone can edit!" Find some team-building activities to help break down stereotypes.

    www.teampedia.net/wiki/index.php?title=Main_Page

2. **Writing better business letters.** Using a search engine, such as Google or Bing, search for websites that offer tips and suggestions to improve letter-writing skills. (One such website is shown below.) Select two of these sites and review the material. Prepare a brief summary.

    www.letterwritingguide.com

3. **Employee stock ownership plans.** Visit the website of the ESOP Association (www.esopassociation.org). Go to "Learn about ESOPs," then click on "Use of ESOPs." Print out the material and bring it to class to participate in a class discussion on employee stock ownership plans.

Note: Internet Web addresses change frequently. If you don't find the exact sites listed, you may need to access the organization's home page and search from there or use a search engine such as Bing or Google.

10 | PRODUCTION AND OPERATIONS MANAGEMENT

LEARNING OBJECTIVES

LO 10.1 Explain the strategic importance of production.

LO 10.2 Describe the four main categories of production processes.

LO 10.3 Explain the role of technology in the production process.

LO 10.4 Identify the factors involved in a plant location decision.

LO 10.5 Outline the job of production managers.

LO 10.6 Identify the steps in the production control process.

LO 10.7 Discuss the importance of quality control.

INSIDE BUSINESS

Building a 3D Future at GE

General Electric (GE), one of the world's largest manufacturers, is creating parts for its jet engines using a new technology called 3D printing or additive manufacturing. Unlike many conventional manufacturing processes that are subtractive—for example, drilling a hole in a block of metal—3D printing is an additive manufacturing process that creates the metal block around the hole. Expected to be one of the biggest changes in industrial production methods in decades, 3D printing is a process that is capable of creating almost any solid shape.

As with a 2D printer, the 3D printing process begins with the creation of a product design on a computer. Designers use computer-aided design (CAD) programs to specify the product size, shape, tolerances, colour, and materials. This information is then transferred to a 3D printer, which creates the shape from plastic or metal material one layer at a time. One method uses thin layers of powdered metals or plastics with an epoxy to adhere the powder particles together. Other methods use extruded plastics or a liquid material that solidifies when exposed to ultraviolet light to make the desired solid shapes.

This process allows firms like GE to create structures that were unimaginable just a few years ago. For its advanced jet engine, the LEAP-1, GE has created a new fuel nozzle using 3D printing. What had been a 20-piece assembly is now a single metal part printed in one piece that is 25 percent lighter than the original version. Printing in one piece also gives the new fuel nozzle a life estimated to be five times greater than the 20-piece assembly. And the design and prototyping time required for building these types of structures is greatly reduced, as engineers can design and fabricate test products in a matter of hours.

Maybe best of all, the cost of producing complex fuel nozzles via 3D printing is 20 percent less than a conventionally made one, according to GE. This translates into lower labour costs because less time is spent assembling and inspecting the various parts of the fuel nozzles. GE believes that 3D printing is the manufacturing technology of the future and estimates it will produce more than 40,000 fuel nozzles annually using this new process.[1]

CHAPTER 10 OVERVIEW

Businesses satisfy their commitment to society by producing and marketing the goods and services that people want. They create what economists call *utility*—the want-satisfying power of a good or service. Businesses can create or improve four basic kinds of utility: time, place, ownership, and form. A firm's marketing department creates time, place, and ownership utility by offering products to customers at a time and place that are convenient for purchase.

Production creates form utility by converting raw materials and other inputs into finished products, such as GE's 3D fuel nozzles. **Production** uses resources, including workers and machinery, to convert materials into finished goods and services. This process can either make major changes to raw materials or combine two or more already finished parts into new products. The task of **production and operations management** is to oversee the firm's production process by managing the people and machinery that convert materials and resources into finished goods and services. This process is shown in **Figure 10.1**.

People sometimes use the terms *production* and *manufacturing* to mean the same thing, but the two are actually different. Production is used in both manufacturing and nonmanufacturing industries. For example, fishing and mining companies are involved in production, as are firms that deliver packages or offer hotel rooms. **Figure 10.2** lists five examples of production systems for goods and services.

The production process can result in a tangible good such as a car or an intangible service such as cable television. The production process always converts inputs into outputs. A cabinetmaker combines wood, tools, and skill to create finished kitchen cabinets. A transit system combines buses, trains, and employees to create its output: passenger transportation. Both production processes create a useful good or service.

This chapter describes the process of producing goods and services. It looks at the importance of production and operations management. It also discusses the new technologies that are changing the production function. The chapter then discusses the tasks of the production and operations manager, the importance of quality, and the methods businesses use to ensure high quality.

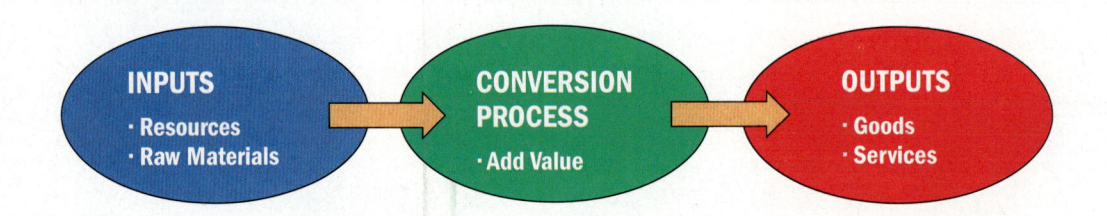

production the use of resources, such as workers and machinery, to convert materials into finished goods and services.

production and operations management the process of overseeing the production process by managing the people and machinery that convert materials and resources into finished goods and services.

FIGURE 10.1 The Production Process: Converting Inputs into Outputs

INPUTS
- Resources
- Raw Materials

→

CONVERSION PROCESS
- Add Value

→

OUTPUTS
- Goods
- Services

LO 10.1 Explain the strategic importance of production.

THE STRATEGIC IMPORTANCE OF PRODUCTION

Production is a vital business activity, as are marketing and finance. Without products to sell, companies cannot generate money to pay their employees, lenders, and shareholders. And without the profits from products, firms quickly fail. The production process is just as important in not-for-profit organizations, such as The Hospital for Sick Children (SickKids) and Goodwill Industries. These organizations offer goods or services that are tied to their existence. When production and operations management are effective, they can lower a firm's costs of production, increase the quality of its goods and services, allow it to be dependable when meeting customer demands, and enable it to renew itself by providing new products. Let's look at the differences among three kinds of production: mass, flexible, and customer-driven production.

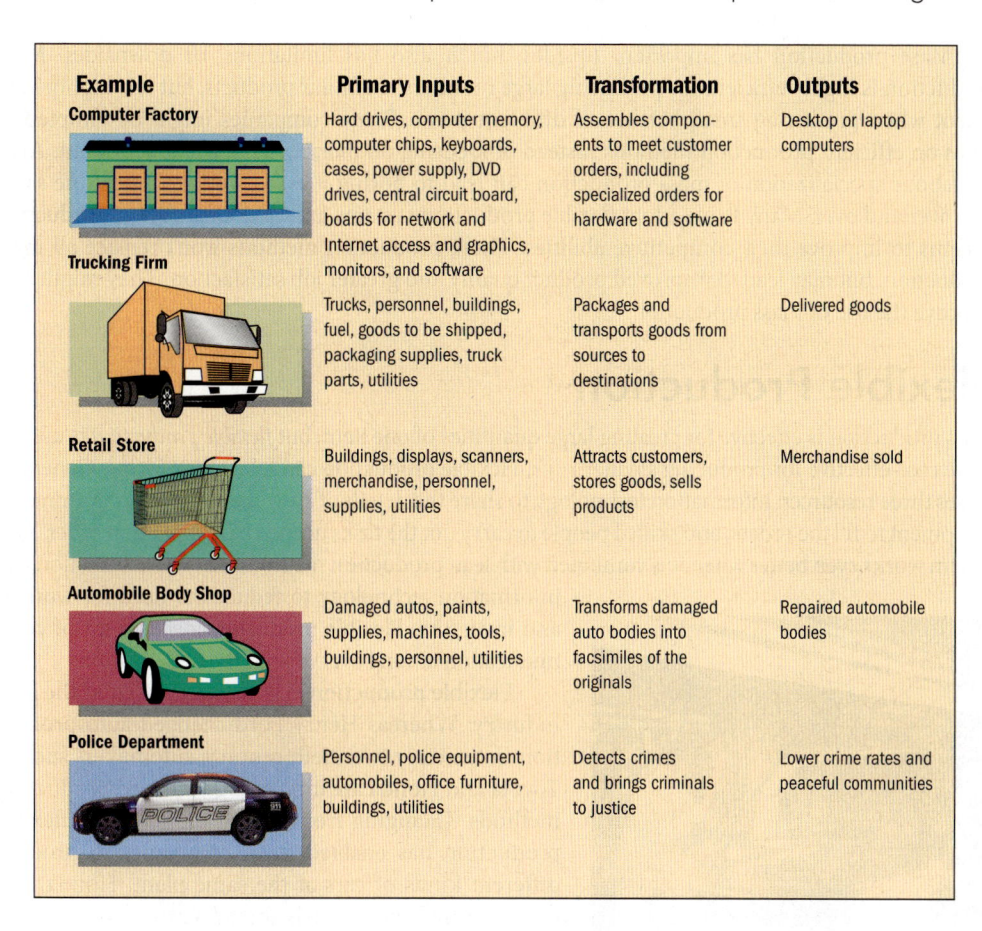

Example	Primary Inputs	Transformation	Outputs
Computer Factory	Hard drives, computer memory, computer chips, keyboards, cases, power supply, DVD drives, central circuit board, boards for network and Internet access and graphics, monitors, and software	Assembles components to meet customer orders, including specialized orders for hardware and software	Desktop or laptop computers
Trucking Firm	Trucks, personnel, buildings, fuel, goods to be shipped, packaging supplies, truck parts, utilities	Packages and transports goods from sources to destinations	Delivered goods
Retail Store	Buildings, displays, scanners, merchandise, personnel, supplies, utilities	Attracts customers, stores goods, sells products	Merchandise sold
Automobile Body Shop	Damaged autos, paints, supplies, machines, tools, buildings, personnel, utilities	Transforms damaged auto bodies into facsimiles of the originals	Repaired automobile bodies
Police Department	Personnel, police equipment, automobiles, office furniture, buildings, utilities	Detects crimes and brings criminals to justice	Lower crime rates and peaceful communities

FIGURE 10.2 Typical Production Systems

Mass Production

Canada began as a colonial supplier of raw materials to Europe and has become an industrial giant. Much of this change has resulted from **mass production**, a system for manufacturing products in large quantities by using effective combinations of employees with *specialized skills*, *mechanization*, and *standardization*. Because of mass production, outputs (goods and services) are available in large quantities at lower prices than individually made items. Mass production has brought us cars, computers, televisions, books, and even homes.

Mass production begins with the specialization of labour skills, by dividing work into its simplest forms so that each worker can focus on one task. By separating jobs into small tasks, managers create the right conditions for high productivity through mechanization. In mechanization, machines do much of the work previously done by people. Standardization, the third element of mass production, involves producing identical, interchangeable goods and parts. Standardized parts make it easier to replace substandard or worn-out parts. For example, if your car's windshield wiper blades wear out, you can easily buy replacements at a local auto parts store, such as Canadian Tire.

These principles of specialization, mechanization, and standardization led to development of the *assembly line*. This manufacturing method moves the product along a conveyor belt past many workstations, where workers perform specialized tasks, such as welding, painting, installing individual parts, and tightening bolts. Henry Ford's application of the assembly line greatly changed auto assembly. Before the assembly line, Ford's workers took 12 hours to assemble a Model T car. With an assembly line, the same car could be made in just 1.5 hours. Not surprisingly, many other industries soon adopted the assembly-line process.

mass production a system for manufacturing products in large quantities by using effective combinations of employees with specialized skills, mechanization, and standardization.

Mass production has important upsides, but it also has limitations, or downsides. Mass production is highly efficient for producing large numbers of similar products, but it is highly inefficient when producing small batches of different items. Some companies might be tempted to focus on efficient production methods instead of focusing on making what customers want. Also, the labour specialization of mass production can lead to boring jobs, as workers repeat the same task over and over. Many firms adopt flexible production systems and customer-driven production systems to improve their competitive abilities. These production methods won't replace all mass production, but may lead to improved product quality and greater job satisfaction. They might also improve the use of mass production.

Flexible Production

Mass production is effective for creating large quantities of one item, but *flexible production* is usually more cost-effective for producing smaller runs. Flexible production can take many forms. Generally, it uses three resources: information technology to share the details of customer orders, programmable equipment to fill the orders, and skilled people to carry out the tasks needed to complete an order. This system works even better when it is combined with lean production methods that use automation and information technology to reduce the need for workers and inventory. Flexible production needs a lot of communication among everyone in the organization.

Flexible production is now widely used in the auto industry. Whereas Henry Ford changed auto production in the early twentieth century, automakers such as Toyota and Honda are innovating with new production methods. Changing from mass production to flexible production has enabled these companies to produce different kinds of cars at the same plant. Honda now builds 15 different models spread across four plants in North America. "Using our flexible manufacturing capacity, we plan to continue to maintain our local production levels at approximately 80 percent of our annual sales," states a company spokesperson.[2] Honda's news is good news for North American workers and consumers.

This Honda auto plant uses flexible production techniques to produce different models. The auto industry developed mass production methods, but now finds more efficiency in flexible production.

Customer-Driven Production

A *customer-driven production* system assesses customer demands to make a connection between the products that are manufactured and the products people want to buy. Many firms use this approach with great success. One method is to set up computer links between factories and retailers' scanners. Data about sales are then used to create short-term forecasts and design production schedules to meet those forecasts. Another approach to customer-driven production systems is to wait until a customer orders a product and then produce it—whether it's a taco or a computer. Shibui Designs creates custom-made dresses in high-end fabrics for female executives and other women over 40. Each item of clothing is made to fit a single customer's measurements. Founder Elizabeth Nill, who is over 60, started the business because she couldn't find clothing that fit well. "I don't have the body of a model, and the bulges are real. Truly made classic clothing that is custom made-to-measure helps camouflage these inevitable imperfections and makes me feel more elegant." Nill's customers agree.[3]

✓ ASSESSMENT CHECK

10.1.1 What is mass production?

10.1.2 What is the difference between flexible production and customer-driven production?

LO 10.2 Describe the four main categories of production processes.

PRODUCTION PROCESSES

It probably won't surprise you that an Apple iPad and a litre of gasoline use different production processes and take different amounts of time to make. Production processes use either an analytic or a synthetic system; time requirements use either a continuous or an intermittent process.

An analytic production system reduces a raw material to its component, or individual, parts to extract one or more marketable products. Petroleum refining breaks down crude oil into several marketable products, including gasoline, heating oil, and aviation fuel. When corn is processed, it results in marketable food products, including animal feed and corn-based sweetener.

A synthetic production system is the reverse of an analytic system. It combines two or more raw materials or parts, or transforms raw materials, to produce finished products. Canon's assembly line produces a camera by assembling various parts such as a shutter or a lens cap. Other synthetic production systems make drugs, chemicals, computer chips, and canned soup.

A continuous production process creates finished products over a long period of time. The steel industry is a good example. Its blast furnaces never completely shut down except for repairs. Other firms that use continuous production are petroleum refineries, chemical plants, and nuclear power facilities. A shutdown can damage sensitive equipment and lead to a costly outcome.

An intermittent production process creates products in short production runs. Machines may be shut down frequently or may be changed so they produce different products. Most services result from intermittent production systems. For example, accountants, plumbers, and dentists do not try to standardize their services because each customer offers a different situation that needs an individual approach. But some companies, such as Mr. Lube (auto service), H&R Block (tax preparation service), and GreenLawn (lawn-care service), offer standardized services. This offering is part of a strategy to operate more efficiently and to compete by offering lower prices. McDonald's is well known for its nearly continuous production of food. This company has moved toward a more intermittent production model. The fast-food chain invested millions of dollars in new cooking equipment to set up kitchens for preparing sandwiches quickly to order. McDonald's prefers this method instead of producing large batches ahead of time and then keeping them warm under heat lamps.

ASSESSMENT CHECK

10.2.1 What are the two main production systems?

10.2.2 What are the two time-related production processes?

TECHNOLOGY AND THE PRODUCTION PROCESS

LO 10.3 Explain the role of technology in the production process.

Production changes rapidly as computer technologies continue to develop. Many manufacturing plants are now known as "lights out" facilities. These facilities are completely automated. That means no workers are needed to build or make the products. This type of manufacturing plant means a big change in the types of jobs available in manufacturing. It also means that companies can design, produce, and adapt products more quickly to meet customers' changing needs.

Green Manufacturing Processes

More and more manufacturing firms are investing resources into developing processes that result in less waste, lower energy use, and little or no pollution. Companies as big as Walmart and as small as your local café are learning to operate in a more sustainable manner. Some companies may use biofuel to power a fleet of delivery trucks or may stop using unnecessary packaging. Firms are proud of the steps they take to be more sustainable. Seventh Generation makes household goods and cleaning products. This company has used sustainable manufacturing processes since it started. The firm's approach is to look at its operations as a whole, by considering the entire impact of its processes and products on the environment. Seventh Generation consistently assesses its processes and makes changes. For example, it might cut emissions from its distribution system or redesign its packages. "It's the best insurance any company can have for long-term success," notes co-founder and top executive Jeffrey Hollender.[4] The "Going Green" feature describes energy firms that are working on new methods for drilling for natural gas. The new methods are much less damaging to the environment than traditional methods.

GOING GREEN

DRILLING FOR NATURAL GAS—CLEAN ALTERNATIVES

Drilling for natural gas doesn't usually lead to images of an undisturbed landscape. In fact, studies by the government and by private environmental groups show that the main method for extracting natural gas from the earth—hydraulic fracturing—can result in contaminated water supplies. Hydraulic fracturing involves injecting millions of litres of water, sand, and chemicals deep into the ground to crack open the beds of shale that contain natural gas. Then, the gas can rise to the surface. Environmental scientists and the people who live near the drilling sites are concerned about two things: the amount of water being used and the possible contamination of their water supplies by the chemicals used in the process. These concerns have been voiced in many communities across Canada. In Quebec, the provincial government decided to go ahead with its planned natural gas development. The Quebec government's handling of the decision and how it dealt with public opinion led to much criticism.

But many energy companies *are* paying attention to these concerns—including those that drill for oil and natural gas. Environmental Technologies Ltd. makes a nontoxic alternative to the toxic chemicals. This firm says that its product kills bacteria just as effectively as the toxic chemicals. Ecosphere Technologies Inc. claims antibacterial chemicals aren't needed because its product can completely kill the bacteria at the surface before water is injected into the gas wells. Ecosphere also reduces water use and water waste by helping energy producers to reuse the water used in hydraulic fracturing. That means companies no longer need to pay to ship millions of litres of waste water to treatment plants or disposal sites.

None of these firms suggests that the drilling should stop. Instead, the firms are researching and developing greener technologies. New companies—and divisions or subsidiaries of the larger energy firms—are forming rapidly to take advantage of this business opportunity.

Questions for Critical Thinking

1. What type of production system is used by natural gas drilling companies? Explain your answer.

2. Do you predict that the firms that are investing in greener processes will ultimately be successful? Why or why not?

Sources: Marianne White, "Quebec Moved Too Fast on Shale Gas: Watchdog," *Montreal Gazette*, March 31, 2011, accessed April 14, 2011, http://www.montrealgazette.com/news/decision-canada/Quebec+moved+fast+shale+watchdog/4532660/story.html#ixzz1JW9Ku1zL; "Hydraulic Fracturing," EPA website, accessed April 29, 2010, www.epa.gov; "Sustainable Technology," Baker Hughes website, accessed April 29, 2010, www.bakerhughes.com/company/corporate-social-responsibility/sustainable-technology; Ben Casselman, "Firms See 'Green' in Natural-Gas Production," *The Wall Street Journal*, March 30, 2010, www.wsj.com/articles/SB10001424052748704094104575143771963721284; "EPA Launches Hydraulic Fracturing Study," *Environmental Leader*, March 19, 2010, www.environmentalleader.com/2010/03/19/epa-launches-hydraulic-fracturing-study.

LEED (Leadership in Energy and Environmental Design) a voluntary certification program administered by the Canada Green Building Council, aimed at promoting the most sustainable construction processes available.

Firms that are involved in building construction—or are thinking of building new offices or manufacturing plants—are turning their attention to **LEED (Leadership in Energy and Environmental Design)** certification. LEED is a voluntary certification program offered by the Canada Green Building Council (CaGBC). It is aimed at promoting the most sustainable construction processes available. The LEED certification process is tough. It involves meeting standards in energy savings, water efficiency, carbon dioxide (CO_2) emissions reduction, improved indoor environmental quality (including air and natural light), and other categories.[5]

Robots

More and more manufacturers have freed workers from boring and sometimes dangerous jobs by replacing them with robots. A *robot* is a machine that can be programmed to perform tasks that require the repeated use of materials and tools. Robots can repeat the same tasks many times without changing their movements. Many factories use robots to stack their products on pallets and shrink-wrap them for shipping. Consolidated Technologies Inc. is located in Vaudreuil, Quebec, near Montreal. It produces robotic corrugated paper-box assemblers and product-packaging machines. One machine can assemble more than 120 cartons per minute. Another machine fills the cartons at a rate of 20 cases of products per minute. Both machines work much faster than humans.[6]

In the past, robots were most common in automotive and electronics manufacturing. Today, more and more industries are adding robots to their production lines. Because of improvements in technology, robots are now less expensive and more useful than they once were. Firms operate many different types of robots. The simplest is a pick-and-place robot. It moves in only two or three directions, picking up one item from one spot and placing it in another spot. So-called field robots assist people in nonmanufacturing, often dangerous, environments, such as nuclear power plants, the International Space Station, and even on battlefields. Police use remote-controlled robots to pick up and deal with suspected bombs. The same technology can also be used in factories. By using vision systems, infrared sensors, and bumpers on mobile platforms, robots can move parts or finished goods from one place to another. They can either follow or avoid people, whichever is needed to do the job. For example, machine vision systems are used for complex applications, such as quality assurance in the manufacturing of medical devices. Innovations in machine vision parts, such as cameras, lighting systems, and processors have greatly improved what these systems can do.

Robots are used in manufacturing as well as in many other fields. In auto manufacturing, robots can perform a variety of tasks that have freed workers from boring and sometimes dangerous jobs.

Computer-Aided Design and Manufacturing

Computer-aided design (CAD) is a process used by engineers to design parts and entire products on the computer. Engineers who use CAD can work faster and with fewer mistakes than those who use traditional drafting systems. An engineer can use an electronic pen to sketch three-dimensional (3D) designs on an electronic drafting board or directly on the computer screen. The engineer can then use software tools to make major and minor design changes. The computer can also analyze the results for certain characteristics or problems. Engineers can put a new car design through a simulated road test to project its real-world performance. For example, if they find a problem with weight distribution, the necessary changes can be made virtually—without actually test-driving the car. With advanced CAD software, creating a prototype, or a trial model, is as much "virtual" as it is "hands-on." Actual prototypes or parts aren't built until the engineers are satisfied that the virtual designs are as perfect as they can be. Dentistry has also benefited from CAD, which can design and create, at the dentist's office, such products as caps and crowns that perfectly fit a patient's mouth or jaw.[7]

The process of **computer-aided manufacturing (CAM)** picks up where the CAD system leaves off. A manufacturer can use CAM to analyze the steps that a machine must take to produce a needed product or part. Electronic signals send instructions to the processing equipment to perform the needed production steps in the correct order. Both CAD and CAM technologies are now used together at most modern production facilities. These so-called CAD/CAM systems are linked electronically so they can automatically transfer computerized designs to the production facilities. These systems save both time and effort. They also allow firms to produce parts that need more precise manufacturing.

computer-aided design (CAD) a process used by engineers to design parts and entire products on the computer. Engineers who use CAD can work faster and with fewer mistakes than those who use traditional drafting systems.

computer-aided manufacturing (CAM) a computer tool that a manufacturer uses to analyze CAD output and the steps that a machine must take to produce a needed product or part.

Flexible Manufacturing Systems

A **flexible manufacturing system (FMS)** is a production facility that workers can quickly change to manufacture different products. The typical system uses computer-controlled machining centres to produce metal parts, robots to handle the parts, and remote-controlled carts to deliver the materials. All steps of the process are linked by electronic controls that direct activities at each stage of manufacturing. The system can even replace broken or worn-out drill bits and other tools.

Flexible manufacturing systems have been improved by powerful new software that allows machine tools to be reprogrammed while they are running. This capability means that the same

flexible manufacturing system (FMS) a production facility that workers can quickly change to manufacture different products.

computer-integrated manufacturing (CIM) an integrated production system that uses computers to help workers design products, control machines, handle materials, and control the production function.

machine can make hundreds of different parts, and the operator doesn't need to shut the machine down to load each new program. The software also connects to the Internet to receive updates and to control machine tools at other sites. The software resides on a company's computer network. That means that engineers can use the software to locate production problems any time, from anywhere they can access the network. Nissan Motor Company recently expanded its flexible manufacturing system to join its plants in emerging markets, including China, Thailand, and India. In general, Nissan's expanded FMS cuts its new-vehicle lead time and investment in half. But the new system is not without its flaws that will take time to work out.[8]

Computer-Integrated Manufacturing

Companies use robots, CAD/CAM, FMS, computers, and other technologies together to apply **computer-integrated manufacturing (CIM)**. This integrated production system uses computers to help workers design products, control machines, handle materials, and control the production function. This type of manufacturing does not always lead to more automation and fewer people than other options. But it does involve a new type of automation that is organized around the computer. The key to CIM is a centralized computer system running software that integrates and controls separate processes and functions. The advantages of CIM include increased productivity, decreased design costs, increased equipment utilization, and improved quality.

CIM is widely used in the printing industry to coordinate thousands of printing jobs, some very small. CIM saves money by combining many small jobs into one larger job and by automating the printing process from design to delivery. Global printing company manroland uses CIM to provide printing solutions for its business customers. One of its products, PrintValue, offers a complete line of solutions for every aspect of a pressroom.[9]

✓ ASSESSMENT CHECK

10.3.1 List some of the reasons businesses invest in robots.

10.3.2 What is a flexible manufacturing system (FMS)?

10.3.3 What are the major benefits of computer-integrated manufacturing (CIM)?

LO 10.4 Identify the factors involved in a plant location decision.

THE LOCATION DECISION

The decision of where to locate a production facility depends on transportation, human, and physical factors, as shown in **Table 10.1**. Transportation factors include the closeness to markets and raw materials and the availability of transportation options for both inputs and outputs. Automobile assembly plants are usually located near major rail lines. Inputs—such as engines, plastics, and metal

TABLE 10.1 Factors in the Location Decision

LOCATION FACTOR	EXAMPLES OF AFFECTED BUSINESSES
Transportation	
Closeness to markets	Baking companies and manufacturers of other perishable products, dry cleaners, hotels, other services
Closeness to raw materials	Paper mills
Availability of transportation options	Brick manufacturers, retail stores
Physical Factors	
Water supply	Computer chip fabrication plants
Energy	Aluminum, chemical, and fertilizer manufacturers
Hazardous wastes	All businesses
Human Factors	
Labour supply	Auto manufacturers, software developers
Local zoning regulations	Manufacturing and distribution companies
Community living conditions	All businesses
Taxes	All businesses

Deciding where to locate a production facility can often depend on the weather. Some theme parks, such as Walt Disney World, are located in warm climates so they can attract visitors year round.

parts—arrive by rail, and the finished vehicles are shipped out by rail. Shopping malls are often located next to major streets and freeways in suburban areas because most shoppers arrive by car.

Physical variables include such issues as weather, water supplies, available energy, and options for disposing of hazardous waste. Theme parks, such as Walt Disney World, are often located in warm climates so they can attract visitors year round. A manufacturing business that wants to locate near a community must prepare an *environmental impact study*. This study analyzes how a proposed plant will affect the quality of life in the surrounding area. Regulatory agencies usually need these studies to report on the impact on transportation facilities; energy requirements; water and sewage treatment needs; the effects on natural plant life and wildlife; and any possible water, air, and noise pollution.

Human factors in the location decision include an area's labour supply, local regulations, taxes, and living conditions. Management considers local labour costs and the availability of workers with the needed qualifications. Software makers and other computer-related firms concentrate in areas that have the technical talent they need, including California's Silicon Valley, Boston, Toronto, Montreal, and Austin, Texas. By contrast, some labour-intensive industries have located their plants in rural areas, where there is readily available labour and few other high-wage jobs. Some firms that have headquarters in Canada, the United States, and other industrialized countries have moved their production offshore in search of low wages. But no matter what type of industry a firm is in, when deciding on a location, a production and operations manager must consider the following factors:

- Closeness to suppliers, warehouses, and service operations
- Costs of insurance and taxes
- Availability of employee needs such as housing, schools, mass transportation, day care, shopping, and recreational facilities
- Size, skills, and costs of the local labour force
- Enough space for current and future needs of the firm

- Distance to the market for goods
- Receptiveness of the community
- Economical transportation for incoming materials and supplies and for outgoing finished goods
- Climate and environment that matches the industry's needs and employees' lifestyle
- Amount and cost of energy services
- Government incentives

A recent trend in location strategy is bringing production facilities closer to the final markets where the goods will be sold. One reason is the reduced time and cost for shipping. Another reason is a closer cultural relationship between the parent company and the supplier (in cases where production remains overseas). This trend has led some business developers to label Central America "the new Asia."[10] German automaker Volkswagen decided to build a $1 billion manufacturing plant in North America to make its new midsize sedan. Volkswagen expects to roll 150,000 vehicles out of the plant each year. The plant site includes the possibility of a major expansion that would further increase production capacity. CEO Stefan Jacoby notes that the plant is part of Volkswagen's overall strategy for capturing more of the North American auto market.[11]

Governments sometimes offer incentives to businesses that are willing to locate in their region. These incentives may take the form of tax breaks, agreements to improve infrastructure, and similar activities. Sometimes, location is all about bringing the right people together in the centre of the action. The "Hit & Miss" feature describes how Mexico has become a major hub for automobile manufacturing.

ASSESSMENT CHECK

10.4.1 How does an environmental impact study affect the location decision?

10.4.2 What human factors contribute to the location decision?

HIT & MISS

Mexico Becomes a Major Hub for Auto Manufacturing

When it comes to automobile manufacturing, you probably do not think about Mexico as the destination for billions of investment dollars—but it is. Most automakers, including Ford, General Motors, and Chrysler, have increased their manufacturing assembly lines in Mexico. The country's proximity to the United States and its highly skilled workers match their American and Canadian counterparts at a fraction of the wage cost.

Mexico has become the fastest-growing country worldwide for auto assembly and parts production. General Motors is making its iconic Silverado pickup trucks in central Mexico's Guanajuato state. Audi will invest $1.3 billion to build its assembly plant in the state of Puebla, where it will build its luxury vehicles—a first for Mexico. And Mexico is ground zero for Nissan's expansion plans in the Americas. Honda and Mazda are also adding manufacturing facilities in the country, which has shot past Canada to become the second-largest auto producer in North America.

A German-engineered BMW made in Mexico? The company recently announced a billion-dollar investment to build a new plant there to produce 150,000 vehicles annually, and Toyota recently announced it was going to build a billion-dollar plant in Guanajuato, Mexico, to take over production of the subcompact Corolla, currently assembled in Cambridge, Ontario. The Cambridge plant will be refurbished to build more expensive vehicles.

Questions for Critical Thinking

1. How does this business boom in Mexico impact the future of autoworkers in the United States and Canada?

2. About 80 percent of the cars made in Mexico are for export to the United States and Canada. Do you foresee Mexico's growth trend continuing? Why or why not?

Sources: *FinancialPost.com*, "Toyota moves Corolla production to Mexico with new plant, retools Ontario factory for other models," April 15, 2015, accessed April 15, 2015, http://business.financialpost.com/news/transportation/toyota-moves-corolla-production-to-mexicowith-new-plant-retools-ontario-factory-for-other-models; Nick Parker, "BMW's Billion-Dollar Bet on Mexico," CNN Money, accessed July 13, 2014, http://money.cnn.com; Chris Anderson, "Mexico: The New China," The New York Times, accessed February 24, 2014, www.nytimes.com; Harold L. Sirkin, "The New Mexico," Bloomberg Businessweek, accessed February 24, 2014, www.businessweek.com; Philip LeBeau, "Mexico Stakes Claim as Hottest Hub for Auto Production," CNBC, accessed February 24, 2014, www.cnbc.com; Ben Klayman, "Auto Industry Love for Mexico Grows with New Audi Plant," Reuters, accessed February 24, 2014, www.reuters.com; Juan Montes, "BMW Considers First Plant in Mexico," The Wall Street Journal, accessed February 24, 2014, http://online.wsj.com.

THE JOB OF PRODUCTION MANAGERS

LO 10.5 Outline the job of production managers.

Production and operations managers supervise the work of people and machinery to convert inputs (materials and resources) into finished goods and services. As **Figure 10.3** shows, these managers perform four major tasks.

1. Planning the overall production process
2. Selecting the best layout for the firm's facilities
3. Carrying out the production plan
4. Controlling the manufacturing process to maintain the highest possible quality

Part of the control process involves continuous assessment of the results. If problems occur, managers return to the first step and make adjustments.

PRODUCTION MANAGEMENT TASKS

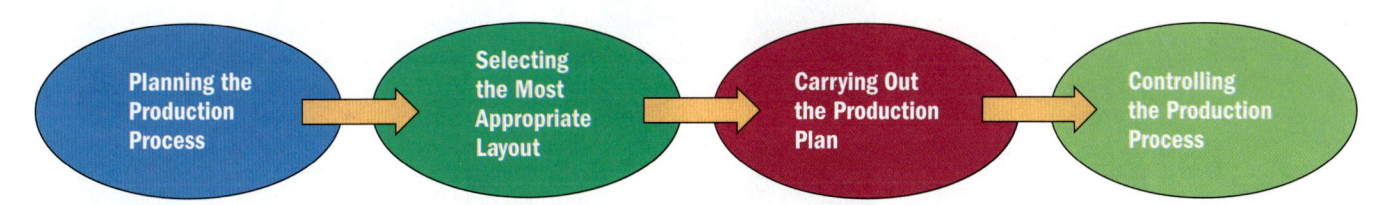

Planning the Production Process → Selecting the Most Appropriate Layout → Carrying Out the Production Plan → Controlling the Production Process

FIGURE 10.3 Tasks of Production Managers

Planning the Production Process

Production planning begins by choosing the goods or services to offer to customers. This decision is the essence, or core, of every company's reason for operating. Other decisions follow product planning, such as machinery purchases, pricing decisions, and selection of retail outlets. In product planning, it's not enough to plan products that satisfy customers. Products must satisfy customers *and* be produced as efficiently and inexpensively as possible. Market research is used to gather consumer reactions to proposed products. It is also used to estimate potential sales and profitability. Production departments focus on planning the production process in two ways: (1) by converting original product ideas into final specifications and (2) by designing the most efficient facilities to produce those products.

Production managers need to understand how a project fits into the company's structure because it can affect the success of the project. In a traditional manufacturing organization, each production manager has a specific area of authority and responsibility, such as purchasing or inventory control. One downside to this structure is that it may actually mean that the purchasing manager will compete against the inventory control manager. More organizations have moved toward team-oriented structures. Some organizations assign team members to specific projects, with all team members reporting to the production manager. Each team is responsible for the quality of its products and has the authority to make changes to improve performance and quality. The two approaches have two major differences: all workers on teams are responsible for their output, and teamwork avoids the competitiveness between managers often found in traditional structures.

Selecting the Facility Layout

The next production management task is selecting the best layout for the facility. An efficient facility layout can reduce material handling, decrease costs, and improve product flow through the facility. This decision requires managers to consider all phases of production and the inputs needed at each step. **Figure 10.4** shows three common layout designs: process, product, and fixed-position layouts. It also shows a customer-oriented layout typical of service providers' production systems.

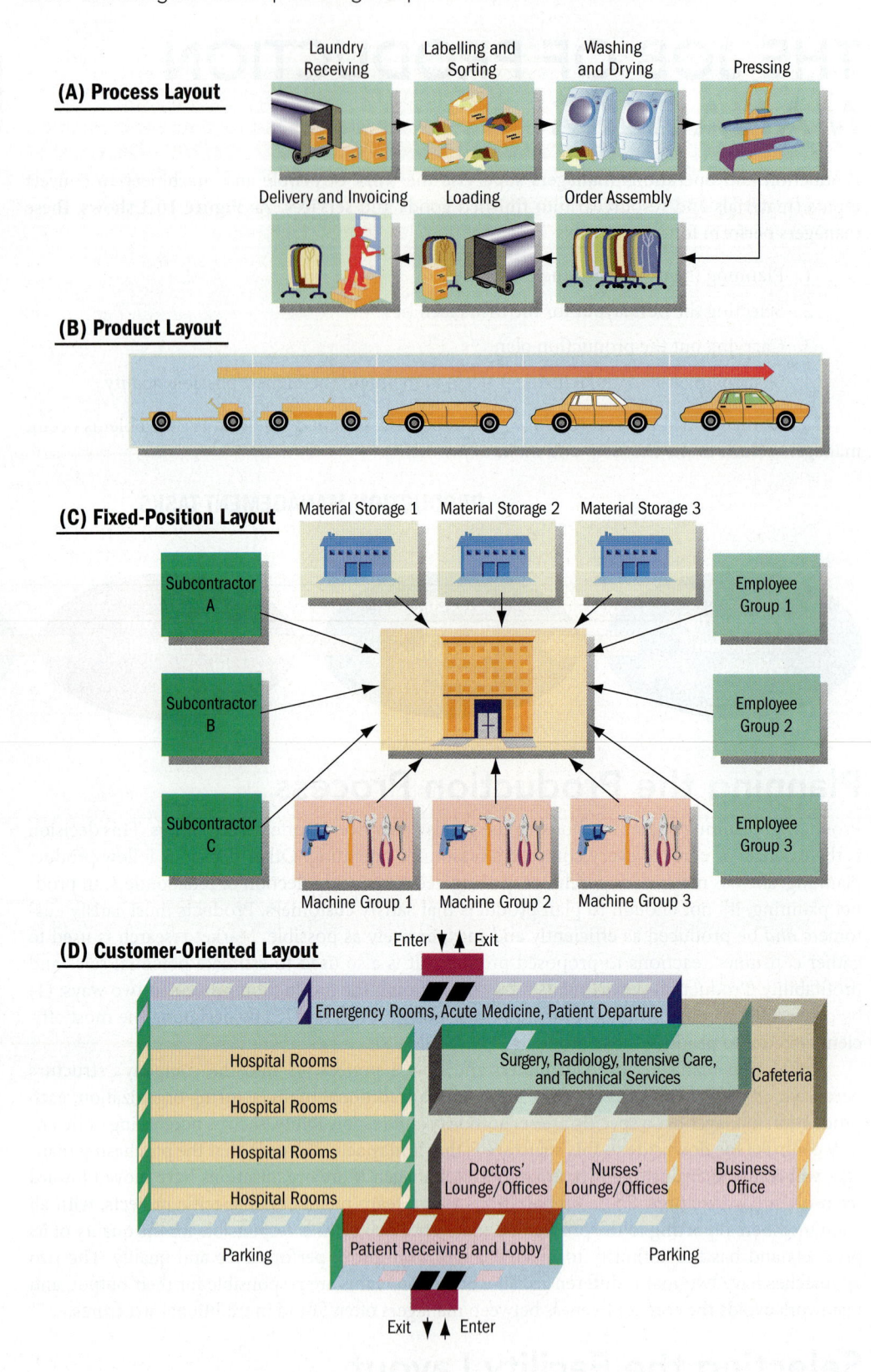

FIGURE 10.4 Basic Facility Layouts

A *process layout* groups machinery and equipment according to their functions. The work in process moves around the plant to reach different workstations. A process layout often makes it easier to produce a variety of nonstandard items in relatively small batches.

Its purpose is to process goods and services that have a variety of functions. For example, a typical machine shop has separate departments where machines are grouped by functions such as grinding, drilling, pressing, and lathing. *Process layouts* can suit a variety of production functions and use general-purpose equipment that can be less costly than specialized equipment to purchase and maintain.

A *product layout*, also called an assembly line, sets up production equipment along a product-flow line. The work in process moves along this line past workstations. This type of layout efficiently produces large numbers of similar items, but it may be inflexible, with room for only a few product variations. Although product layouts date back at least to the Model T assembly line, companies are improving this approach with modern touches. Many auto manufacturers continue to use a product layout, but robots perform many of the activities that humans once did. Automation solves one of the major drawbacks of this system—unlike humans, robots don't get bored doing a dull, repetitive job. European automaker Holland Car PLC uses an assembly-line approach called complete knockdown (CKD). In this assembly line, all the auto parts are imported in pieces to be welded, painted, and assembled at its facility in Ethiopia.[12]

A *fixed-position layout* places the product in one spot. The workers, materials, and equipment go to the product's location. This approach suits very large, bulky, heavy, or fragile products. For example, a bridge cannot be built on an assembly line. Fixed-position layouts are used in several industries, including construction, shipbuilding, aircraft and aerospace, and oil drilling. In all of these industries, the nature of the product generally dictates a fixed-position layout.

Service organizations must also decide on suitable layouts for their production processes. A service firm should arrange its facilities to enhance the interactions between customers and its services—also called a *customer-oriented layout*. If you think of patients as inputs, a hospital uses a form of the process layout. Banks, libraries, dental offices, and hair salons also use process layouts. Sometimes the details surrounding a service require a fixed-position layout. For example, doctors, nurses, and medical devices are brought to patients in a hospital emergency room.

Carrying Out the Production Plan

After production managers plan the production process and select the best layout, the next task is to carry out the production plan. This activity involves (1) deciding whether to make, buy, or lease products or parts; (2) selecting the best suppliers for materials; and (3) controlling inventory to keep enough supplies in stock, but not too much.

Make, Buy, or Lease Decision

Every producer faces a **make, buy, or lease decision**—whether to manufacture a product or part in-house, buy it from an outside supplier, or lease it. This decision is critical in many contemporary business situations.

Several factors affect the make, buy, or lease decision, including the costs of leasing or purchasing parts from outside suppliers compared with the costs of producing the parts in-house. The decision sometimes depends on whether outside suppliers can meet a firm's standards for quality and quantity. The need for confidentiality sometimes affects the decision, as does the short- or long-term duration of the firm's need for supplies. A firm might not yet have the technology to produce certain components or materials, or the technology might be too costly. The "Hit & Miss" feature describes some of the difficult production decisions Harley-Davidson had to make to help it rebound from a sluggish economy.

When a firm decides to buy goods from outside suppliers, production managers should still keep a relationship going with other supply sources. Having an alternative supplier means that the firm can get the materials it needs even during strikes or when quality-assurance problems or other situations affect the inputs. Outsourcing has its downsides, too. Companies say the main reason they use outsourcing is to reduce costs and focus on their core business activities. But outsourcing can also lead to layoffs and a decrease in the quality of the firm's outputs.[13]

make, buy, or lease decision choosing whether to manufacture a product or part in-house, buy it from an outside supplier, or lease it.

HIT & MISS

Harley-Davidson Turns Lean

For more than a century, Harley-Davidson, the iconic motorcycle brand, has embodied everything American. In its heyday, Harley-Davidson had such a following that consumers would wait patiently for 18 months to get their hands on a new bike. More recently, however, a combination of a slow economy and global competition created some tough decisions for the company. Like other manufacturers that opted for low-cost overseas or domestic nonunion production, the company was forced to decide whether to eliminate its union. Rather than scrap the union, the company redesigned the production system to allow for fewer workers in its York, Pennsylvania, plant—with the union's blessing. In addition, Harley-Davidson tore down the York plant and built a brand-new one. Instead of replacing experienced employees with state-of-the-art robotic technology, the company developed a lean manufacturing operation, complete with teams of five to six workers who manually build each of its core four motorcycle styles, complete with more than 1,200 customizable options.

With its lean manufacturing process and new facility, the company has reduced costs by $100 million while increasing quality and customer demand. In addition, it retained the union—experienced workers who are able to solve problems and search for better ways to make motorcycles that robots cannot. With a new motorcycle starting on the assembly line every 80 seconds, Harley-Davidson remains optimistic that its H.O.G. members (Harley Owner's Group) worldwide will continue to be happy, while now only waiting a few weeks for a new bike.

Questions for Critical Thinking

1. What do you think might have been the outcome had the company decided to follow other manufacturers overseas in pursuit of lower production costs?

2. Discuss the relationship between the iconic Harley-Davidson brand and the company's production decisions.

Sources: Company website, "Harley Owners Group," www.Harley-Davidson.com, accessed February 5, 2014; Adam Davidson, "Building a Harley Faster," The New York Times, accessed February 5, 2014; www.nytimes.com; Ginger Christ-Martin, "2013 IW Best Plants Winner: Harley-Davidson—Driving a Future of Excellence," Industry Week, accessed February 5, 2014, www.industryweek.com; James Hagerty, "Harley Goes Lean to Build Hogs," The Wall Street Journal, accessed February 5, 2014, http://online.wsj.com.

Selection of Suppliers

After a company decides what inputs to buy, it must choose the best suppliers for its needs. To make this choice, production managers compare several factors: quality, prices, dependability of delivery, and services offered by competing companies. Different suppliers may offer the same quality and the same prices. The final decision often depends on the firm's past experience with each supplier, speed of delivery, warranties on purchases, and other services.

When a firm is planning for a major purchase, negotiations with suppliers may take several weeks or months. The buying decision may need several managers to look at all the options before the final selection is made. For example, the selection of a supplier for an industrial drill press may require a joint decision by the production, engineering, purchasing, and quality-control departments. These departments often must sort out their different views before they agree on a purchasing decision.

The Internet provides powerful tools for finding and comparing suppliers. Buyers can log on to business exchanges to compare specifications, prices, and availability. Ariba offers online software and other tools that organizations can use to source $120 billion worth of goods and services from suppliers around the world.[14]

Firms often purchase raw materials and parts on long-term contracts. If a manufacturer needs a continuous supply of materials, a one-year or two-year contract with a supplier can ensure availability. Today, many firms build long-term relationships with suppliers and reduce the number of companies they deal with. At the same time, many organizations ask their suppliers to expand their roles in the production process.

Production managers use networking to learn about suppliers and to get to know them personally. Managers also meet suppliers, competitors, and colleagues at trade shows, conferences,

CAREER KICKSTART

Making the Most of Business Meetings

Some people love business meetings because they are a nice change from boring tasks. Others find meetings to be tiresome disruptions from more important work they need to do. But business meetings are sometimes necessary. You might enjoy meetings more if you look at how they can help you to build your career. Think of all meetings—including staff meetings, sales meetings, appointments with customers, and conferences with colleagues—as part of your overall networking strategy. Use these tips to make the most of your next business meeting:

- *Be on time.* Being on time shows that you value your own time and that of others. It also shows that you take the meeting seriously.

- *Turn off your cellphone and any other electronic devices.* Unless you are a doctor on call for emergencies, keep your cellphone turned off. Beeps and ringtones can distract others. They also show that your attention is elsewhere.

- *Pay attention.* Listen actively to what others are saying. Take notes when it is suitable.

- *Participate.* Ask questions and make brief points when appropriate. Stay on the subject. Avoid controlling a discussion.

- *Conduct yourself professionally.* Be polite to others at the meeting. Thank the others for their time at the end of the meeting.

- *Exchange business cards.* At the end of the meeting, exchange business cards or contact information with others that you may want to contact later.

Sources: Karyn Hill, "Business Meeting Etiquette—5 Essential Tips," Business Coach site, accessed April 26, 2010, www.bellaonline.com; Donna Reynolds, "Practice Business Meeting Etiquette," *How To Do Things*, accessed April 26, 2010, www.howtodothings.com, accessed April 26, 2010; Shaun Mangan, "7 Tips for More Effective Business Meetings," *Ezine Articles*, accessed April 26, 2010, http://ezinearticles.com.

---

and seminars, and other meetings. The "Career Kickstart" feature provides tips for making the most of these meetings.

Inventory Control

Production and operations managers are responsible for **inventory control**. They need to balance the costs of storing inventory with the need to have stock on hand to meet demand. Several costs are involved in storing inventory: warehousing costs, taxes, insurance, and maintenance. Firms waste money if they store more inventory than they need. But having too little inventory may lead to a shortage of raw materials, parts, or goods that can be sold. The outcome can be delays and unhappy customers.

Firms lose business when they keep missing promised delivery dates or turn away orders. When farmer Jay Armstrong ordered a combine attachment—just as his family had done for 50 years—the dealer told Armstrong he wouldn't receive the equipment until August, when the farm's growing season would nearly be over. Armstrong was forced to make his purchase from a competitor, who promised delivery in May.[15]

Efficient inventory control can save money. Many firms use *perpetual inventory* systems to continuously assess the amount of their stock and where it is stored. These inventory control systems usually rely on computers, and many automatically generate orders when stock is low. Many grocery stores link their scanning devices to perpetual inventory systems that reorder goods without the need for a human. When the system records a shopper's purchase, it reduces the inventory count stored in the computer. When inventory drops to a certain level, the system automatically reorders the merchandise. Canada's largest supermarket chain, Loblaw, uses a software system designed by SAP. The network of more than 1,000 corporate and franchised Loblaw stores use the SAP system to manage stock. The system is responsible for ordering and receiving inventory. It also counts and selects inventory in the stockrooms. The software can update and confirm the perpetual inventory balances.[16]

Some companies hand over their inventory control functions to suppliers. This concept is known as *vendor-managed inventory*. At Dell Computer assembly plants, almost all the parts suppliers also handle Dell's inventory control functions.

inventory control a function that balances the costs of storing inventory with the need to have stock on hand to meet demand.

JIT systems are being used in a wide range of industries, including the medical supplies field.

Just-in-Time Systems

just-in-time (JIT) system a broad management philosophy that reaches beyond the narrow activity of inventory control to affect the entire system of production and operations management.

A **just-in-time (JIT) system** is based on a broad management philosophy that reaches beyond the narrow activity of inventory control. A JIT system affects all production and operations management. A JIT system tries to use only items that add value to operations activities. It does this by providing the right part at the right place at just the right time—just before it is needed in production.

JIT systems are used in a wide range of industries, including the medical supplies field. Hospitals can use a JIT system to manage the distribution of supplies, equipment, and clinical materials. Hospitals partner with their key distributors to keep an inventory of certain emergency supplies on hand. Other supplies are distributed on a JIT basis, which saves time and money.[17]

Production that uses a JIT system shifts most of the responsibility for carrying inventory to suppliers. The suppliers use forecasts to decide how much inventory to carry. They keep stock on hand to respond to manufacturers' needs. When suppliers do not keep enough high-quality parts on hand, the purchasers may hand them penalties. When manufacturers underestimate demand for a product, the JIT system may have trouble adapting. Strong demand can overtax JIT systems. Suppliers and their customers may struggle to keep up with orders without having an inventory of goods to meet the extra demand.

Materials Requirement Planning

materials requirement planning (MRP) a computer-based production planning system that ensures a firm has all the parts and materials it needs to produce its output at the right time and place and in the right amounts.

Effective inventory control requires efficiency. It also needs careful planning to ensure the firm has all the inputs it needs to make its products. How do production and operations managers work through all of this information? They use **materials requirement planning (MRP)**, a computer-based production planning system that ensures a firm has all the parts and materials it needs to produce its output at the right time and place and in the right amounts.

Production managers use MRP programs to create schedules that list the specific parts and materials needed to produce an item. These schedules show the exact quantities needed. They also show the dates to order those quantities from suppliers so that they will be delivered at the correct time in the production cycle. A small company might get by without an MRP system. If a firm makes a simple product with only a few parts, a production manager can phone in an order for an overnight delivery of crucial parts. But for a complex product, such as a high-definition TV or aircraft, longer lead times are needed.

The Allan Candy Company is a large Canadian candy manufacturer. It uses MRP software from Microsoft to streamline and integrate all of its processes. The software figures out which materials are needed and automatically generates the purchase orders. CEO Steven Dakowsky believes this system gives his firm a competitive edge in the candy market. "I believe in the power of technology and that it is a differentiating factor, especially for companies our size," he says. "So, for me, it is critically important that we are ahead of the game."[18]

> **ASSESSMENT CHECK**
>
> 10.5.1. List the four major tasks of production and operations managers.
>
> 10.5.2 What is the difference between a traditional manufacturing structure and a team-based structure?
>
> 10.5.3 What factors affect the make, buy, or lease decision?

CONTROLLING THE PRODUCTION PROCESS

LO 10.6 Identify the steps in the production control process.

The final task of production and operations managers is controlling the production process to maintain the highest possible quality. **Production control** creates well-defined procedures for coordinating people, materials, and machinery to provide the greatest production efficiency. Suppose that a watch factory must produce 80,000 watches during October. Production control managers divide this total into a daily production assignment of 4,000 watches for each of the month's 20 working days. Next, they decide on the number of workers, raw materials, parts, and machines the plant needs to meet the production schedule. This work is much like the work of a manager in a service business such as a restaurant. A restaurant manager must estimate how many dinners will be served each day. The manager then decides what food to buy and how many people are needed to prepare and serve the food.

production control creating well-defined procedures for coordinating people, materials, and machinery to provide the greatest production efficiency.

Figure 10.5 shows production control as a five-step process: planning, routing, scheduling, dispatching, and follow-up. These steps are part of the firm's overall emphasis on total quality management.

Planning → Routing → Scheduling → Dispatching → Follow-Up

FIGURE 10.5 Steps in Production Control

Production Planning

The first step of production control is *production planning*. In this step, managers decide on the amount of resources (including raw materials and other items) needed to produce a certain output. The production planning process leads to a list of all needed parts and materials. Purchasing staff can compare this list with the firm's perpetual inventory data to identify which items need to be purchased. Employees or automated systems set up the delivery schedules so the needed parts and materials will arrive when they are needed during the production process. Production planning also ensures the availability of needed machines and personnel. At the Wilson Sporting Goods Company factory in Ohio, there's a special excitement leading up to the Super Bowl each year. Workers there have made every football that has ever been used in a Super Bowl game. Each January, construction on the balls begins. The footballs are about 70 percent complete before the final playoff games are decided. When workers know which two team names will be printed on the balls, production speeds up. The plant makes about 120 official game balls and about 6,000 versions for sale to fans. "The market determines how many balls we will make," notes Gregory Miller, the plant controller.[19]

Material inputs contribute to service-production systems, but production planning for services tends to focus on human resources more than materials.

Routing

The second step of production control is *routing*. In this step, the manager decides on the sequence of work throughout the facility, who will perform each part of the work, and where the work will be done. Routing choices depend on two factors: the nature of the good or service and the facility layout. As discussed earlier in the chapter, the common layout designs are product, process, fixed-position, and customer-oriented layouts. Some routing decisions make sense, such as dipping an automobile body into a rust-proofing bath before painting it. Other decisions may need more study. For example, what is the best sequence when mixing ingredients to make a salad dressing?

Scheduling

The next stage of production control is the *scheduling* phase. In this stage, managers develop timetables that show how long each operation in the production process takes and when workers should perform it. Efficient scheduling means that production will meet the delivery schedules and make efficient use of resources.

Scheduling is important whether the product is complex or simple to produce and whether it is a good or a service. A pencil is simpler to produce than a computer, but each production process has scheduling needs. A stylist may take 25 minutes to complete each haircut using just one or two tools, but every day a hospital schedules procedures and treatments, from x-rays to surgery to follow-up appointments. Sleepmaster is a medium-sized firm that recently moved some of its production from its Australian headquarters to China. But the company's MRP system had very little capacity for scheduling, and the workers in China did not know how to use the technology. Sleepmaster's operations manager set up a new scheduling program called Resource Manager. The new program is easier to use and organize, costs little to operate, and has support available via Skype.[20]

Production managers use several analytical methods for scheduling. One of the oldest methods is the *Gantt chart*. This method tracks projected and actual work progress over time. Many people use Gantt charts, like the one shown in **Figure 10.6**. One glance at the chart quickly shows the progress of any project. Gantt charts are most effective for scheduling simple projects.

A complex project might require a *PERT (program evaluation and review technique) chart*. This chart tries to reduce the number of delays by coordinating all parts of the production process. PERT was first developed for the military and has been adapted for use in industry. The simplified PERT diagram in **Figure 10.7** shows the schedule for purchasing and installing a new robot. The heavy gold line indicates the *critical path*—the sequence of operations that requires the longest time for completion. In this case, the project cannot be completed in less than 17 weeks.

A PERT network may be made up of thousands of events and may take place over months of time. Complex computer programs help production managers to develop a PERT network and to find the critical path among all the events and activities. This type of complex production planning is needed when constructing a huge office building.

In the routing phase of production control, managers decide on the sequence of work throughout the facility, who should perform each operation in the production process, and where it should be done.

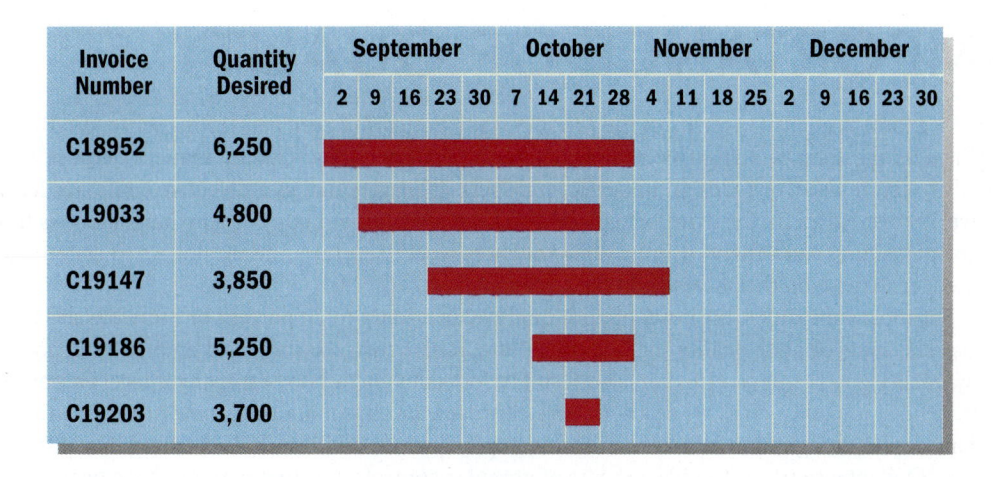

FIGURE 10.6 Sample Gantt Chart

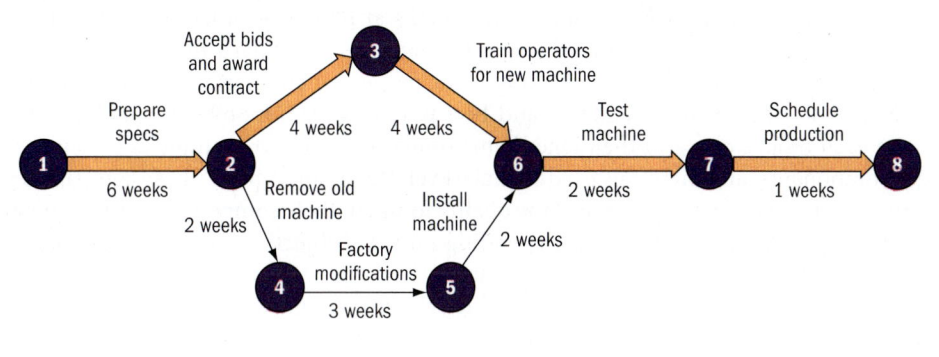

FIGURE 10.7 PERT Diagram for the Purchase and Installation of a New Robot

Dispatching

In the *dispatching* phase of production control, management instructs each department on the work it needs to do and how long it has to do the work. The dispatcher authorizes performance, provides instructions, and lists job priorities. Dispatching may be the responsibility of a manager or a self-managed work team.

Follow-Up

Sometimes even the best plans fail. That's why production managers need to be aware of any problems. In the *follow-up* phase of production control, managers and employees, or team members, spot problems in the production process and come up with solutions. Problems can take many forms: machinery malfunctions, delayed shipments, and absent employees can all affect production. The production control system must identify and report these delays to managers or work teams so they can adjust schedules and correct the underlying problems.

✓ **ASSESSMENT CHECK**

10.6.1 What five steps are involved in controlling the production process?

10.6.2 What is the difference between a PERT chart and a Gantt chart?

LO 10.7 Discuss the importance of quality control.

quality the state of being free of deficiencies or imperfections.

IMPORTANCE OF QUALITY

Next we look at quality in terms of the production of goods and services. In this sense, **quality** is defined as the state of being free of deficiencies or imperfections. Quality matters because it is costly to fix, replace, or redesign imperfect products. If Seagate makes a defective computer hard drive, it must either fix the drive or replace it to keep a customer happy. If Air Canada books too many passengers for a flight, it must offer vouchers worth several hundred dollars to encourage passengers to give up their seats and take a later flight.

For most companies, the costs of poor quality can add up to 20 percent or more of sales revenue. The costs of poor quality include downtime, repair costs, rework, and employee turnover. Low-quality goods and services can also result in lost sales and a poor company image. Facebook experienced a quality crisis when users were confused and upset about its new privacy settings. "Many of you thought our controls were too complex," wrote CEO Mark Zuckerberg in a letter to users. "Our intention was to give you lots of granular controls, but that may not have been what many of you wanted. We just missed the mark."[21]

benchmarking the process of looking at how well other companies perform business functions or tasks and using their performance as a standard for measuring another company's performance.

Companies can use benchmarking to ensure that they always produce high-quality products. When a company uses **benchmarking**, it looks at how well other companies perform business functions or tasks and uses their performance as a standard for measuring its own performance. In other words, benchmarking is the process of comparing one firm's standards and practices to other firms' standards and best practices. Automobile companies routinely purchase each other's cars and then take them completely apart to examine and compare the design, components, and materials used to make even the smallest part. These companies then make improvements to match or exceed the quality found in their competitors' cars. Companies may use many different benchmarks, depending on their objectives. For example, organizations that want to make more money may compare their operating profits or expenses to those of other firms. Retailers concerned with productivity may want to benchmark their sales per square metre.

When a firm is benchmarking, it needs to decide what it wants to accomplish, what it wants to measure, and which company can provide the most useful benchmarking information. A firm might choose a direct competitor for benchmarking, or it might choose a company in an entirely different industry that has processes the firm wants to study and copy.[22]

Quality Control

quality control measuring output against quality standards.

Quality control involves measuring output against quality standards. Firms use quality control to spot defective or imperfect products and to avoid delivering poor-quality goods to customers. Quality standards should be set high enough to meet customer expectations. A 90 or 95 percent success rate might seem to be good, but would you want your phone service or Internet network to work only 90 percent of the time? You would likely feel frustrated, and you would probably switch your phone service or your Internet service provider.

Manufacturing firms can check on quality levels by using visual inspections, electronic sensors, robots, and x-rays. Service organizations can gather quality-control information from surveys. Negative feedback from customers or a high rejection rate on a product or part may mean that production is not meeting quality standards. Firms that outsource their operations face a greater challenge in checking on quality levels. They also have a tougher time assuring customers of the quality of their goods or services, especially when they are highly visible companies, such as airlines. The "Solving an Ethical Controversy" feature discusses the quality of multivitamins manufactured in China for North American companies.

A typical factory can spend up to half its operating budget identifying and fixing mistakes. That means that a company should not rely just on inspections to meet its quality goals. Instead, production managers should identify all processes involved in producing goods and services and then work to increase the efficiency of these processes. They need to find and correct the causes of problems in the processes. A company needs to focus its efforts on better designs of products and processes and to set clear quality targets. These efforts can lead to higher-quality, error-free production.

The Six Sigma concept to achieving quality goals is used by more and more large organizations, including Rogers Communications, the Ontario Lottery and Gaming Corporation, General Electric, Heinz, 3M, and Sears. When a company uses *Six Sigma*, it tries to make error-free products 99.9997 percent of the time. That means it is allowed to make only 3.4 errors for every 1 million opportunities. The goal of Six Sigma programs is for companies to eliminate nearly all defects in output, processes, and transactions.[23]

ISO Standards

For many organizations, an important measure of quality is being able to meet the standards of the **International Organization for Standardization**, known as **ISO** for short. ISO doesn't stand for anything; that is, it is not an acronym but is a shorter name from the Greek word *isos*, meaning "equal." ISO started in 1947 and is a network of national standards bodies from 163 countries. Its mission is to develop and promote international standards for business, government, and society. The aim is to improve and encourage global trade and cooperation. ISO has developed voluntary standards for all sorts of tasks, from the format of banking and telephone cards to freight containers to paper sizes to metric screw threads. The Standards Council of Canada (SCC) is the Canadian member body, and the American National Standards Institute is the U.S. member. Canadian firms typically deal with both bodies.

The ISO 9000 standards help organizations to ensure that their products and services (1) are of high quality and (2) provide a basis for continual improvement. The ISO 14000 standards for

International Organization for Standardization (ISO) an international organization whose mission is to develop and promote international standards for business, government, and society. The aim is to improve and encourage global trade and cooperation.

SOLVING AN **ETHICAL** CONTROVERSY

Multivitamins Produced in China: Are Stricter Quality Controls Necessary?

Chinese-made multivitamins reportedly contain dangerous levels of lead and toxic bacteria—and are showing up in North American stores. Some people have called for stricter quality standards.

PRO

1. According to the Chinese Ministry of Commerce, 85 percent of Chinese citizens rank quality concerns high for food and drugs made in their own country. Tighter controls would also benefit Chinese consumers.

2. Vitamins stamped "Made in Germany" or "Made in the USA" might still contain ingredients from China. Because it has already been demonstrated that these products contain high levels of toxic substances, tighter quality controls must be put into place.

CON

1. Many vitamins contain ingredients from multiple sources, so it is impossible to target China as the sole source of contamination.

2. Chinese production offers companies good value. With lower-cost labour and other services, savings can be passed along to the consumer.

Summary

Despite ongoing concerns, Swiss manufacturer Lonza recently announced it would locate its vitamin B3 manufacturing in China. Meanwhile, China is considering new production regulations on vitamin C—but with an emphasis on pricing power.

Sources: Steve Kelman, "Secret Chinese Vitamins," Federal Computer Week, accessed February 4, 2014, www.fcw.com; "Lonza to Build Vitamin B3 Plant in China," All about Feed, accessed February 4, 2014, www.allaboutfeed.net; "New Multivitamins Target Concern over China's Quality Problems," Bio-Medicine, accessed February 4, 2014, http://news.bio-medicine.org.

Many consumers prefer to buy from companies that are ISO certified.

environmental management help organizations to ensure that their operations (1) cause as little harm as possible to the environment and (2) continually improve their environmental performance.

ISO 9001:2008 and ISO 14001:2004 respectively give the requirements for a quality management system and an environmental management system. Both can be used for certification. An organization gains certification when its management system (the way it manages its processes) is independently audited by a certification body (also known in North America as a registration body, or registrar) and is confirmed as meeting the requirements of the standard. The organization is then issued with an ISO 9001:2008 or an ISO 14001:2004 certificate.

Certification is not a requirement of either standard. An organization can follow ISO standards to gain benefits for the organization and its customers—without certification. But many organizations want to be certified because many managers, consumers, and shareholders see an independent audit as adding confidence to a firm's abilities. Business partners, customers, suppliers, and shareholders may prefer to deal with certified organizations. Certifications need to be renewed every few years, which means audits are also needed every few years.

The ISO itself develops standards but does not carry out the auditing and certification. These tasks are done independently of ISO by hundreds of certification organizations around the world. The certificates they issue carry their own logo, not that of the ISO because the ISO does not approve or control the activities of the certification organizations.

Many organizations report significant benefits from using ISO's management system standards, such as increased efficiency, better teamwork, improved customer satisfaction, and reduced consumption of resources.[24]

✓ ASSESSMENT CHECK

10.7.1 What are some ways that a company can track the quality of its output?

10.7.2 List some of the benefits of ISO 9000 certification.

WHAT'S AHEAD

Maintaining high quality is an important part of satisfying customers. The business function of marketing also has the objectives of product quality and customer satisfaction. The next part consists of three chapters that explore the many activities involved in customer-driven marketing. These activities include product development, distribution, promotion, and pricing.

RETURN TO INSIDE BUSINESS

Building a 3D Future at GE

3D printing technology is changing the way many industries think about production planning and inventory control. Instead of mass production of rarely needed parts, customized products can be made with short production runs on a demand basis eliminating inventory and storage costs. This emerging technology is also providing opportunities for small businesses that can service industries who only require occasional production services much the way a printing service company works today.

QUESTIONS FOR CRITICAL THINKING

1. Which industries would likely do well to adopt 3D technology production?
2. How might 3D technology development affect management relations with employees?

SUMMARY OF LEARNING OBJECTIVES

LO 10.1 Explain the strategic importance of production.

Production and operations management is a vital business function. A company needs a quality good or service to create profits; otherwise, it soon fails. The production process is also important in not-for-profit organizations. These organizations offer goods or services that are tied to why they exist. Production and operations management plays an important strategic role. It can lower the costs of production, increase output quality, and allow the firm to respond flexibly and dependably to customers' demands.

✓ ASSESSMENT CHECK ANSWERS

10.1.1 What is mass production? Mass production is a system for manufacturing products in large quantities by using effective combinations of mechanization, standardization, and employees with specialized skills.

10.1.2 What is the difference between flexible production and customer-driven production? Flexible production generally involves using three resources: information technology to receive and share orders, programmable equipment to fill the orders, and skilled people to carry out tasks needed to complete an order. Customer-driven production assesses customer demands to make a connection between the products that are manufactured and the products people want to buy.

LO 10.2 Describe the four main categories of production processes.

The four main categories of production processes are the analytic production system, the synthetic production system, the continuous production process, and the intermittent production process. The analytic production system reduces a raw material to its component, or individual, parts to extract one or more marketable products. The synthetic production system combines two or more raw materials or parts to produce finished products. The continuous production process creates finished products over a long period of time. The intermittent production process creates products in short production runs.

✓ ASSESSMENT CHECK ANSWERS

10.2.1 What are the two main production systems? The two main production systems are analytic production and synthetic production. An analytic production system reduces a raw material to its component, or individual, parts to extract one or more marketable products. A synthetic production system combines two or more raw materials or parts, or transforms raw materials, to produce finished products.

10.2.2 What are the two time-related production processes? The two time-related production processes are the continuous production process and the intermittent production process. The continuous production process creates finished products over a long period of time. The intermittent production process creates products in short production runs.

LO 10.3 Explain the role of technology in the production process.

Computer-driven automation allows companies to design, create, and adapt products quickly. Companies can also produce products in ways that meet customers' changing needs. Important design and production technologies include robots, computer-aided design (CAD), computer-aided manufacturing (CAM), and computer-integrated manufacturing (CIM). Many manufacturing firms invest resources into developing processes that result in less waste, lower energy use, and little or no pollution.

✓ ASSESSMENT CHECK ANSWERS

10.3.1 List some of the reasons businesses invest in robots. Businesses use robots to free workers from sometimes dangerous jobs and to move heavy items from one place to another in a factory.

10.3.2 What is a flexible manufacturing system (FMS)? An FMS is a production facility that workers can quickly change to manufacture different products.

10.3.3 What are the major benefits of computer-integrated manufacturing (CIM)? The main benefits are increased productivity, decreased design costs, increased equipment utilization, and improved quality.

LO 10.4 Identify the factors involved in a plant location decision.

The factors for choosing the best site for a production facility fall into three categories: transportation, human, and physical factors. Transportation factors include the availability of transportation options and the closeness to markets and raw materials. Physical variables involve such issues as water supply, available energy, and options for disposing of hazardous wastes. Human factors include the area's labour supply, local regulations, taxes, and living conditions.

✓ ASSESSMENT CHECK ANSWERS

10.4.1 How does an environmental impact study affect the location decision? An environmental impact study analyzes how a proposed plant will affect the quality of life in the surrounding area. The study reports on how transportation, energy use, water and sewer treatment needs, and other factors will affect plants, wildlife, water, air, and other features of the natural environment.

10.4.2 What human factors contribute to the location decision? Human factors in the location decision include an area's labour supply, labour costs, local regulations, taxes, and living conditions.

LO 10.5 Outline the job of production managers.

Production and operations managers use people and machinery to convert inputs (materials and resources) into finished goods and services. Four major tasks are involved. First, the managers must plan the overall production process. Next, they must select the best layout for their facilities. Then they carry out their production plans. Finally, they control the production process and assess the results to maintain the highest possible quality.

Carrying out the production plan involves deciding whether to make, buy, or lease products or parts; selecting the best suppliers for materials; and controlling inventory to keep enough supplies in stock, but not too much.

✓ ASSESSMENT CHECK ANSWERS

10.5.1 List the four major tasks of production and operations managers. The four tasks are planning overall production, selecting a layout for the firm's facilities, carrying out the production plan, and controlling manufacturing to achieve high quality.

10.5.2 What is the difference between a traditional manufacturing structure and a team-based structure? In the traditional structure, each manager is responsible for a specific area. In a team-based structure, all workers are responsible for their output.

10.5.3 What factors affect the make, buy, or lease decision? Several factors affect this decision, including the need for confidentiality, whether outside suppliers can meet a firm's standards, and the costs of leasing or purchasing parts from outside suppliers compared with the costs of producing them in-house.

LO 10.6 Identify the steps in the production control process.

The production control process has five steps: planning, routing, scheduling, dispatching, and follow-up. Quality control is an important consideration throughout this process. Coordination of each of these phases should result in high production efficiency and low production costs.

✓ ASSESSMENT CHECK ANSWERS

10.6.1 What five steps are involved in controlling the production process? The five steps are planning, routing, scheduling, dispatching, and follow-up.

10.6.2 What is the difference between a PERT chart and a Gantt chart? PERT charts try to reduce the number of delays by coordinating all parts of the production process. PERT charts are used for more complex projects. Gantt charts track projected and actual work progress over time. Gantt charts are used for scheduling simple projects.

LO 10.7 Discuss the importance of quality control.

Quality control involves measuring goods and services against quality standards. Firms use quality control to spot defective or imperfect products and to avoid delivering poor-quality goods to customers. Devices for monitoring quality levels of the firm's output include visual inspection, electronic sensors, robots, and x-rays. Companies can increase the quality of their goods and services by using Six Sigma techniques and by becoming ISO 9000 and 14000 certified.

✓ ASSESSMENT CHECK ANSWERS

10.7.1 What are some ways that a company can track the quality of its output? Companies can track quality by using benchmarking, quality control, Six Sigma, and ISO standards.

10.7.2 List some of the benefits of ISO 9000 certification. These standards show how a company can ensure that its products meet customers' requirements. Studies show that business partners, customers, suppliers, and shareholders prefer to deal with companies that are ISO 9000 certified.

BUSINESS TERMS YOU NEED TO KNOW

benchmarking 278

computer-aided design (CAD) 265

computer-aided manufacturing (CAM) 265

computer-integrated manufacturing (CIM) 266

flexible manufacturing system (FMS) 265

International Organization for Standardization (ISO) 279

inventory control 273

just-in-time (JIT) system 274

LEED (Leadership in Energy and Environmental Design) 264

make, buy, or lease decision 271

mass production 261

materials requirement planning (MRP) 274

production 260

production and operations management 260

production control 275

quality 278

quality control 278

REVIEW QUESTIONS

1. What is utility? How does production create utility?

2. Why is production such an important business activity? How does production create value for the company and its customers?

3. Why are firms moving toward flexible production and customer-driven production instead of mass production? Describe a product that is better suited to flexible production or customer-driven production than mass production. Explain your choice.

4. Identify whether an analytic production system or a synthetic production system applies to each of the following products:
    a. logging
    b. medical care
    c. cotton farming
    d. fishing
    e. construction

5. The home construction industry and the dental industry benefit from the use of CAD. Both industries can also benefit from using CAM—to manufacture home construction parts and to create dental implants and crowns. Choose another industry that would benefit from the use of both CAD and CAM systems. Explain how the industry can use both systems.

6. The Vancouver Aquarium is the largest aquarium in Canada and one of the five largest in North America. What specific factors might have contributed to the selection and success at this location?

7. What is the best facility layout for each of the following?
    a. movie rental shop
    b. a nail salon
    c. a car wash
    d. a sandwich shop

8. What factors might be involved in selecting suppliers for a steakhouse restaurant?

9. What is inventory control? Why is the management of inventory crucial to a company's success?

10. What is benchmarking? How can it help a firm improve the quality of its goods and services?

PROJECTS AND TEAMWORK APPLICATIONS

1. Imagine that you recently became the owner of a popular ice cream shop. You want to attract more customers and expand the business. What type of production process—continuous or intermittent—is better for your business? Create a plan that shows the details of how you will use this process and why it will help you to meet your goals as a business owner.

2. On your own or with a classmate, imagine that you've been hired to help a business group design a shopping mall. Using the location factors discussed in the chapter, recommend where the mall should be located—and why. Present your plan to the class.

3. On your own or with a classmate, select one of the following businesses and sketch out or describe the layout that would be best for attracting and serving customers:
    a. a Mexican restaurant
    b. a home furnishings store
    c. a pet store
    d. a motorcycle dealership
    e. a dentist office

4. Suppose you and your best friend decide to start a house-painting service. Draft a production plan for your business, including the following decisions: (a) make, buy, or lease; (b) suppliers; and (c) inventory control.

5. Choose two firms to compare (one firm should provide a good benchmarking opportunity for its production processes). The benchmarking firm doesn't need to be in the same industry as the other firm. Present your decisions to the class and explain why you made both choices.

WEB ASSIGNMENTS

1. **Just-in-time inventory management systems.** Go to the websites listed below to learn more about just-in-time inventory management systems. Make some notes on what you learned and bring them to class to participate in a class discussion.

   www.wisegeek.com/what-is-a-just-in-time-inventory.htm
   www.smcdata.com/software-choices/just-in-time-inventory-control-systems-1.html

2. **Plant location decision.** Using an Internet news service, such as Google news (http://news.google.com) or Yahoo! news (http://news.yahoo.com), search for news about a recent decision on a plant location. An example is Toyota's recent decision to expand its production facilities in Woodstock and Cambridge, Ontario. Research the decisions. Prepare a brief report that shows the factors that the firm considered in making its decision to expand in Canada.

   www.theglobeandmail.com/report-on-business/toyota-eyes-expansion-of-ontario-plants/article2341364

3. **ISO certification.** Visit the website of the International Organization for Standardization (www.iso.org). Click on one of the popular standards and summarize the information presented.

Note: Internet Web addresses change frequently. If you don't find the exact sites listed, you may need to access the organization's home page and search from there or use a search engine such as Bing or Google.

PART 3: CASE STUDY Beau's All Natural Brewing Company

Managing the Pains of Early Growth

Steve Beauchesne had written over 100 business plans while working for an Ontario government agency. He understood the importance of thinking out the details in a strategic plan that would guide management before launching the business. Once the business was functional, time would be in short supply, especially since he and his small team would be doing everything necessary to kickstart the brewery. Looking back, 70 hour workweeks were the norm for Steve and Tim. No one else managing the firm had as much invested in the brewery and no one else was as motivated to make Beau's succeed.

From the beginning Steve and Tim were guided by a desire to make Beau's different than its competitors in ways that would guide how the company would be managed and seen by their customers and employees. Their mission statement focuses on five key ideas: quality beer production, local focus, family run, organic and sustainable, and a DIY-entrepreneurial spirit. Each of these ideas would be the starting point for their future SWOT analyses and efforts to develop competitive advantage over their competitors.

Quality Beer Production

Steve and Tim believed that the beer they produced had to be unique and offer an alternative taste to the traditional beers produced by the big brewers. They also believed their beer had to be more than different—it had to be "better" if they were going to establish themselves as an alternative to the craft brew customer. Beau's efforts have been recognized by the dozens of industry awards earned in competitions.

Local Focus

Beau's is managed with a strong and active commitment to the community it serves, supporting more than 100 independent arts and music, community building, and charitable organizations every year. Giving back to the community reflects the understanding that the Beauchesne's are also members of the community. Beginning with the handful of employees hired to start the company, new employees are made welcome to a growing fun place to work.

Family Run

Like Beau's, most of the customers Steve and Tim called on to introduce their beer were also family-owned restaurants, pubs, and bars. According to Steve, there was instant recognition of the family effort to get Beau's started and help it grow. Letting retailers and their customers know that Beau's was the real-deal family-run business was a distinguishing plus for the firm.

Organic and Sustainable

Perhaps Steve and Tim's commitment to brewing outstanding award-winning beer is explained by their use of only the finest-quality certified organic ingredients. These ingredients may cost more, but they

(continued)

PART 3: CASE STUDY Beau's All Natural Brewing Company

help make for better beer taste and are worth the extra expense, according to Steve. This way of thinking also guides managerial decision making when it comes to issues related to sustainability and the environment. For example, the company uses enviro-friendly packaging and solar-generated electricity to run the plant.

DIY-Entrepreneurial Spirit

Starting any business is a challenge. Especially when there are so many tasks to be concerned with and many of those that require specialized expertise and knowledge. As mentioned in part two of the case study, Beau's lucked out when one of the most talented brew masters in the country, Matthew O'Hara, joined them. Matthew developed Beau's flagship beer, a lagered ale called Lug Tread, and hasn't stopped experimenting with new recipes. In fact, the spirit of developing new ideas for products or marketing is part of the DIY (do-it-yourself) culture at Beau's where everyone is encouraged to explore their interests. "When someone comes forward with an idea we encourage them to run with it. Rather than going outside the company, we allocate a bit of money to test the idea out, and if it works we allocate more money and resources the next time," according to Steve. As a result, the 130 employees understand there are opportunities to develop their interests and grow with the firm.

As the firm grew from humble beginnings and a handful of employees into a going concern with over 130 employees, Steve and Tim have gradually expanded the organization structure with defined managerial lines of command and communications. Although the family-oriented open management style is still at the core of the firm's culture, the challenge remains to move forward without undermining what works so well today.

Questions for Critical Thinking

1. As the company continues to grow, how can Steve and Tim maintain the corporate culture and core values that are at the heart of their success?

2. Going forward, what do you think an ideal organization structure would look like?

3. How can Steve and Tim maintain control over decision making as the firm grows?

3 LAUNCHING YOUR...

MANAGEMENT CAREER

Part 3, "Management: Empowering People to Achieve Business Goals," covers Chapters 7 through 10. These four chapters discuss management, leadership, and the internal organization; human resource management, motivation, and labour–management relations; improving performance through empowerment, teamwork, and communication; and production and operations management. In those chapters, you read about top executives and company founders who directed their companies' strategy and led others in their day-to-day tasks to keep them on track. You also read about middle managers who make plans to turn the strategies into realities, and supervisors who work directly with employees to create strong teams that satisfy customers. A variety of jobs are available to people who choose management careers. And the demand for managers will continue to grow.

So what kinds of jobs can you choose from if you decide on a management career? As you learned in Chapter 7, three types of management jobs exist: supervisory managers, middle managers, and top managers. Supervisory management, or first-line management, includes positions such as supervisor, office manager, department manager, section chief, and team leader. Managers at this level work directly with the employees who produce and sell a firm's goods and services.

Middle management includes positions such as general managers, plant managers, division managers, and regional or branch managers. These managers are responsible for setting objectives that work with top management's goals. They also plan and carry out strategies for meeting those objectives.

Top managers include such positions as chief executive officer (CEO), chief operating officer (COO), chief financial officer (CFO), chief information officer (CIO), and executive vice-president. Top managers spend most of their time developing long-range plans, setting a direction for their organization, and inspiring a company's executives and employees to achieve their vision for the company's future. Top managers travel frequently between local, national, and global offices so they can meet and work with customers, suppliers, company managers, and employees.

Most managers start their careers in sales, production, or finance. If you are interested in a management career, you will likely start in a similar entry-level job. When you perform that job and other jobs well, you may be considered for a supervisory position. Then, if you are interested in supervising others and you have the technical, human, and conceptual skills to succeed, you'll begin your management career path. But what kinds of supervisory management jobs are available? Let's review the exciting possibilities.

Administrative services managers manage basic services that all organizations need—such as clerical work, payroll, travel, printing and copying, data records, telecommunications, security, parking, and supplies.

Construction managers plan, schedule, and coordinate the building of homes, commercial buildings such as offices and stores, and industrial facilities such as manufacturing plants and distribution centres. While administrative service managers work in offices, construction managers usually work on building sites with architects, engineers, construction workers, and suppliers.

Food service managers run restaurants and services that prepare and offer meals to customers. They coordinate workers and suppliers in kitchens, dining areas, and banquet operations; are responsible for those who order and purchase food inventories; maintain kitchen equipment; and recruit, hire, and train new workers. Food service managers can work for restaurant chains such as Swiss Chalet, for small locally owned restaurants, or for corporate food service departments in organizations.

Human resource managers help organizations to follow federal and provincial labour laws; effectively recruit, hire, train, and retain talented workers; administer corporate pay and benefits plans; develop and administer organizational human resource policies; and, when necessary, participate in contract negotiations or handle disputes. Human resource management jobs vary widely, depending on how specialized the requirements are.

Lodging managers work in hotels and motels but also help run camps, ranches, and recreational resorts. They may supervise employees that work in guest services, the front desk, the kitchen, the restaurant, banquets, house cleaning, and building maintenance. Because they are expected to help satisfy customers around the clock, they often work long hours and may be on call when not at work.

Medical and health services managers work in hospitals, nursing homes, doctors' offices, and corporate and university settings. They run departments that offer clinical services; ensure that provincial and federal laws are followed; and handle decisions related to the management of patient care, nursing, surgery, therapy, medical records, and financial payments.

Purchasing managers lead and control organizational supply chains that ensure companies purchase materials at reasonable prices and have the materials they need to produce the goods and services they sell. They also oversee deliveries when and where they are needed. Purchasing managers work with wholesale and retail buyers, to buy goods that are then resold to others; purchasing agents, who buy supplies and raw materials for their organizations; and contract specialists, who negotiate and supervise purchasing contracts with key suppliers and vendors.

Production managers direct and coordinate operations that manufacture goods. They work with employees who produce parts and assemble products and help decide which new machines should be purchased and when existing machines need maintenance. They are also responsible for meeting production goals that specify the quality, cost, schedule, and quantity of units to be produced.

The website "Living in Canada" provides a survey of salaries paid for a wide variety of managerial and other positions. You can find out more about managerial salaries by visiting www.livingin-canada.com/wages-for-management-jobs-canada.html. The average manager's salary appears to be about $60,000 per year.[1]

CAREER ASSESSMENT EXERCISES IN MANAGEMENT

1. The Canadian Institute of Management (CIM) is a not-for-profit professional organization that provides a range of management development and educational services to individuals, companies, and government agencies. Access the CIM's website at www.cim.ca. Write a one-page summary of CIM's services.

2. Go online to a business news service, such as Yahoo! News or Google News, or look at the business section of your local newspaper. Find a story relating to a first-line supervisor, a middle manager, or a top executive. Write a summary of that person's duties. What decisions does the manager make? How do those decisions affect the manager's organization?

3. From the descriptions above, pick a management position that interests you. Research the career field. What skills do you have that would make you a good candidate for a management position in that field? What work and other experience do you need to help you get started? List your strengths and weaknesses. Draw up a plan to improve your strengths.

PART 4
MARKETING MANAGEMENT

Chapter 11 Customer-Driven Marketing

Chapter 12 Product and Distribution Strategies

Chapter 13 Promotion and Pricing Strategies

11 CUSTOMER-DRIVEN MARKETING

LEARNING OBJECTIVES

LO 11.1 Explain what marketing is and how it creates utility.

LO 11.2 Discuss the evolution of the marketing concept.

LO 11.3 Describe not-for-profit marketing and nontraditional marketing.

LO 11.4 Outline the basic steps in developing a marketing strategy.

LO 11.5 Describe the marketing research function.

LO 11.6 Discuss the methods used to segment consumer and business markets.

LO 11.7 Outline the determinants of consumer behaviour.

LO 11.8 Discuss the benefits of, and tools for, relationship marketing.

INSIDE BUSINESS

Handmade Items: Etsy.com Has Them All

Lisa Lutz, of Kelowna, British Columbia, promotes her handmade beaded jewellery and accessories from her own website, BeadCrazed.com. But she sells to customers online through her personal Etsy.com shop. Unique, handmade items have always been popular alternatives to mass-market products. Not very long ago, many craftspeople physically carried their creations to craft fairs or sold their work through friends and associates. Some still do, but now they also have access to potentially unlimited global markets through websites such as ArtFire, 1000 Markets, and Etsy.

Unlike eBay, where independent artisans compete directly with mass producers and importers, Etsy caters to customers who are looking for one-of-a-kind jewellery, a handmade quilt, or a pair of hand-carved bookends. Think of a craft fair online. Artisans use these sites to set up online "shops"; many have shops at more than one website to increase their exposure. These sites also carry knitted goods, clothing for adults and children, vintage items, photographs and other visual artworks, paper goods, spices and other food items, services such as custom DVDs of your special event, and craft supplies for making your own project. Shoppers can see photographs of individual items and ratings of different sellers. They also can choose from various payment options.

Etsy is now the largest online artisan and vintage market. Etsy got a boost from the craft boom. But when the collapse of the job market drove many hobbyists to try to make a living from their crafts, Etsy's membership soared. Etsy now has 19.8 million active buyers connecting to 1.4 million active sellers listing 29 million items. In a recent year, it had gross sales of $1.93 billion from which the company of 650 employees generated revenues of $195 million. Looking for a piece of jewellery, maybe a new ring? A jewellery search on Etsy turned up 86,237 rings on 4,107 pages. Their prices range from pennies to almost a hundred thousand dollars for an opulent diamond engagement ring. The Etsy community spans the globe with buyers and sellers coming from more than 150 countries, including Canada.

Opening an online shop is cheaper and easier than opening a bricks-and-mortar store. Most websites allow sellers to set up shop for free, charge a small fee to post an item, and take a percentage of each sale. For example, Etsy charges 20 cents to post one item for four months, and takes 3.5 percent when that item is sold. That isn't very much, but if sellers want their items to stay high in search results, they need to renew the listings often. Some sellers renew their listings daily, so the fees can add up. Etsy also offers sellers a support system through blogs and links to social networking sites such as Facebook and Twitter. It is working to improve its search functions and is planning to set up a customer service phone line.

Many people dream of quitting their day jobs to make a living from selling their handmade products online, but selling online is not easy and is getting harder. Competition has become extreme as more artisans are joining these websites. Working from home or a studio often means spending long hours knitting or sewing or making jewellery—especially during the holiday rush—then more long hours standing in line at the post office waiting to ship the items sold. And of course, sellers have to spend time promoting their products in every possible medium, from blogs to magazines to, yes, that network of friends and associates.[1]

CHAPTER 11 OVERVIEW

Business success in the twenty-first century is directly tied to a company's ability to identify and serve its target markets. In fact, all organizations—profit-oriented and not-for-profit, manufacturing, and retailing—*must* serve customer needs to succeed. And that's what Etsy does by offering a wide range of unique, handmade items. Marketing is the link between the organization and the people who buy and use its goods and services. Organizations use marketing to figure out buyer needs. They also use marketing to show that they can meet those needs by supplying a quality product at a reasonable price. Marketing is the path to developing loyal, long-term customers.

Consumers purchase goods for their own use and enjoyment. Business purchasers look for products for their firms to use in their business operations. Both types of buyers may seem to be made up of a large number of similar people. But marketers see the separate wants and needs for each group. Buyers can be manufacturers, Web surfers, and shoppers in the grocery aisles. Companies gather huge amounts of data on every detail of consumer lifestyles and buying behaviours. Marketers use the data to understand the needs and wants of both final customers and business buyers. When buyers can satisfy customers, they are on their way toward building relationships with them. But it's not always easy. To start a relationship with the buying public, Whole Foods CEO John Mackey invites emails from consumers who may—or may not—be customers. Mackey spent several weeks in an email debate with an animal welfare activist about Whole Foods selling duck meat from a particular source. Mackey then asked the activist to help rewrite his firm's policies on farm animal treatment. This relationship developed through direct communication between the CEO and a consumer. Mackey's open email invitation helps Whole Foods to build a relationship with customers who have certain food-source concerns.

This chapter begins with an examination of the marketing concept and how businesspeople develop a marketing strategy. We then turn to marketing research techniques and an explanation of how businesses apply data to market segmentation to better understand customer behaviour. The chapter closes with a detailed look at the important role customer relationships play in today's highly competitive business world.

WHAT IS MARKETING?

LO 11.1 Explain what marketing is and how it creates utility.

marketing an organizational function and set of processes for creating, communicating, and delivering value to customers and for managing customer relationships in ways that benefit the organization and its stakeholders.

To succeed, every organization must serve customer needs—from profit-seeking firms such as McDonald's and Bell Canada to not-for-profits such as the Make-a-Wish Foundation of Canada and the Canadian Cancer Society. According to the American Marketing Association, **marketing** is "an organizational function and a set of processes for creating, communicating, and delivering value to customers and for managing customer relationships in ways that benefit the organization and its stakeholders."[2] Marketing techniques don't just sell goods and services, they also help people support ideas or viewpoints and educate others. The Canadian Diabetes Association mails out questionnaires that ask, "Are you at risk for diabetes?" The documents help educate the general public about this widespread disease by listing its risk factors and common symptoms and by describing the work of the association.

The best marketers not only give consumers what they want but anticipate and expect consumers' needs even before consumers see those needs themselves. Ideally, marketers can get ahead of the competition by helping consumers create a link between their new need and the fulfillment of that need by the marketers' products. ScotiaBank and Bank of Montreal promote pre-approved mortgages at low interest rates so customers know what they can borrow before they shop for a house. NetJets offers fractional (or shared) jet ownership to executives who want the luxury and flexibility of private ownership without the cost of owning their own plane. Samsung offers its next generation of high-definition TV with its trademarked Internet@TV. Owners connect their televisions to their home Internet connection, then add widgets to track the weather, check eBay, view Flickr albums, and check for Twitter updates—all in real time. Consumers can also sign up for Video-on-Demand service through Rogers, Bell, and other service providers. "Get the best of the Web right on your TV!" their promotion says.

The best marketers give consumers what they want and anticipate their needs. NetJets offers fractional (shared) jet ownership to executives who want the luxury and flexibility of private ownership without the cost of owning their own plane.

As these examples show, marketing is more than just selling. Marketing is a process that begins with discovering unmet customer needs and continues with several tasks: researching the potential market; producing a good or service that can satisfy the targeted customers; and promoting, pricing, and distributing that good or service. Throughout the entire marketing process, a successful organization focuses on building customer relationships.

When two or more parties benefit from trading something of value (such as goods, services, or cash), they have entered into an **exchange process**. When you purchase a cup of coffee, the other party in the exchange may be a convenience store clerk, a vending machine, or a Tim Hortons server. The exchange seems simple—you hand over some money, and you receive your cup of coffee. But the exchange process is more complex. The exchange happens because you felt the need for a cup of coffee. It also happens because you saw the convenience store or the vending machine. You might not choose Tim Hortons unless you had heard of the brand. Because of marketing, your desire for a flavoured blend, a decaf, or a plain black coffee is identified—and the coffee manufacturer's business is successful.

exchange process an activity in which two or more parties trade something of value (such as goods, services, or cash) that satisfies each other's needs.

How Marketing Creates Utility

Marketing affects many parts of an organization. It also affects an organization's dealings with its customers. **Utility** is the ability of a good or service to satisfy the wants and needs of customers. A company's production function creates *form utility* by converting raw materials, component parts, and other inputs into finished goods and services. But the marketing function creates three types of utility: time utility, place utility, and ownership utility. *Time utility* is created by making a good or service available when customers want to purchase it. *Place utility* is created by making a product available in a location convenient for customers. *Ownership utility* refers to an organized

utility the power of a good or service to satisfy a want or need.

HIT & MISS

Beyoncé Thrills Fans and Surprises Marketers

Grammy Award–winning entertainer Beyoncé recently took the music industry—and marketing strategists—by storm. Without any advance warning, she released a new self-titled album by simply posting a trailer on her Instagram account with the caption "Surprise!" Beyoncé announced her latest release exclusively on iTunes. And in its first three days, consumers downloaded the album with its 14 songs and 17 videos more than 828,000 times.

Stunned by this approach, some executives believe that Beyoncé has changed music marketing forever. Others think her strategy worked because the singer's superstar brand allowed her to bypass traditional marketing channels. Some marketing experts have compared Beyoncé's album release to a form of relationship marketing. Beyoncé's surprise announcement about her new album catapulted its release to the top of iTune's all-time downloads list because she has a very loyal fan base with whom she has built a rock-solid relationship.

Questions for Critical Thinking

1. How will Beyoncé's move to bypass traditional marketing channels impact future projects?
2. What is the downside to Beyoncé's marketing strategy?

Sources: "Did Beyoncé's Album Just Prove Marketing Is Dead?" *CNBC*, December 17, 2013, accessed July 3, 2015, www.cnbc.com/id/101277017; Lyneka Little, "Target Doesn't Plan on Carrying New Beyoncé Album," *Wall Street Journal*, December 17, 2013, accessed July 3, 2015, http://blogs.wsj.com/speakeasy/2013/12/17/target-doesnt-plan-on-carrying-new-beyonce-album; Abigail Tracy, "Beyoncé Shows How Social Media Is Changing Marketing," *Inc.*, December 16, 2013, accessed July 3, 2015, www.inc.com/abigail-tracy/beyonce-shows-the-true-power-of-social-media.html; Lyneka Little, "Beyoncé Surprises Fans with Sudden Release of New 'Visual Album,'" *Wall Street Journal*, December 13, 2013, accessed July 3, 2015, http://blogs.wsj.com/speakeasy/2013/12/13/beyonce-surprises-fans-with-sudden-release-of-new-visual-album.

---

transfer of goods and services from the seller to the buyer. Some firms can create all three forms of utility. Target was the first American retailer to offer bar-coded, scannable mobile coupons direct to cellphones. Guests can sign on to the program either on their personal computers or on their cellphones. Each month, they receive either an email or a text message with a link to a mobile website page where they find offers for various products. They can use the mobile coupons at any Target store because Target is the first retailer to have point-of-sale scanning technology for the coupons in all of its stores.[3] Technology is also having a major impact on the entertainment industry. See the "Hit & Miss" feature for more details.

ASSESSMENT CHECK

11.1.1 What is utility?

11.1.2 Identify how marketing creates utility.

LO 11.2 Discuss the evolution of the marketing concept.

EVOLUTION OF THE MARKETING CONCEPT

Marketing has always been a part of business, from the earliest village traders to large twenty-first century organizations that produce and sell complex goods and services. Over time, marketing activities have evolved through the five eras shown in **Figure 11.1**: the production, sales, marketing, relationship, and now the social era. These eras run similar to some of the time periods discussed in Chapter 1.

For centuries, organizations of the *production era* stressed their efficiency in producing quality products. Their philosophy could be summed up by the remark, "A good product will sell itself." This focus on production continued into the twentieth century, then it gradually gave way to the *sales era*. In the sales era, businesses assumed that consumers would buy as a result of energetic sales efforts. Organizations didn't fully recognize the importance of their customers until the *marketing era* of the 1950s. Then, organizations began to adopt a consumer orientation. This focus has grown stronger in recent years, leading to the *relationship era* in the 1990s. In the relationship era, companies focus on customer satisfaction and building long-term business relationships. Today, the social era continues to grow exponentially, thanks to the Internet and social media sites

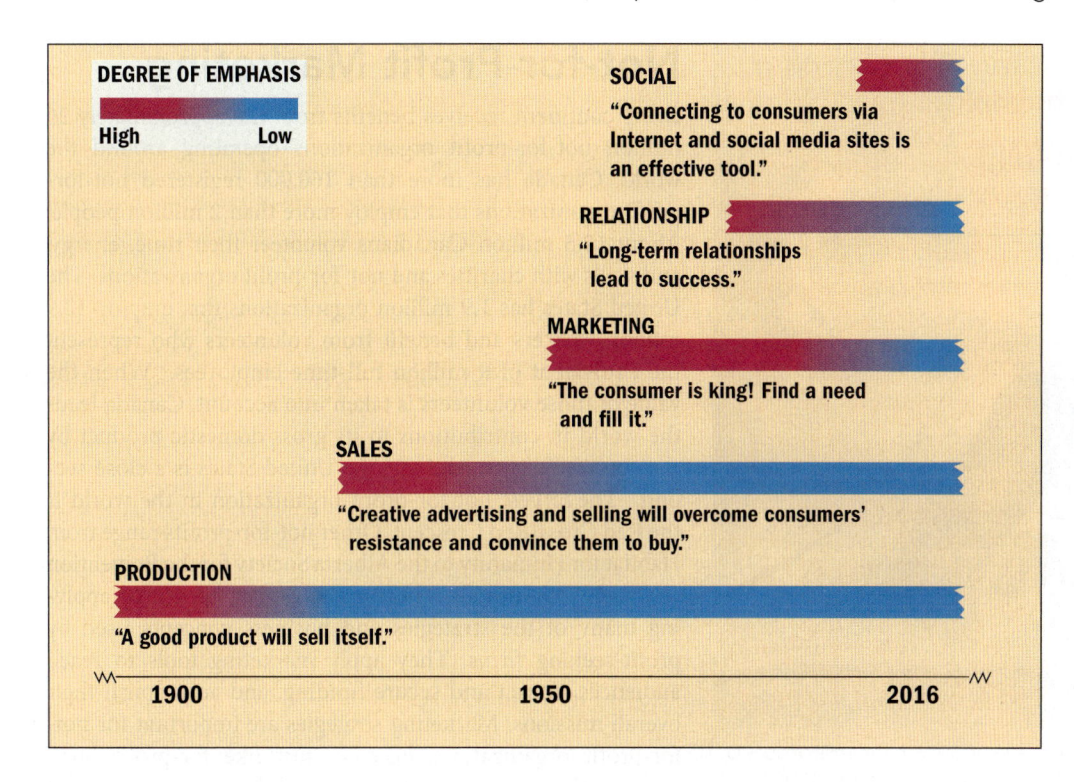

FIGURE 11.1 Five Eras in the History of Marketing

DEGREE OF EMPHASIS
High — Low

SOCIAL
"Connecting to consumers via Internet and social media sites is an effective tool."

RELATIONSHIP
"Long-term relationships lead to success."

MARKETING
"The consumer is king! Find a need and fill it."

SALES
"Creative advertising and selling will overcome consumers' resistance and convince them to buy."

PRODUCTION
"A good product will sell itself."

1900 — 1950 — 2016

like Facebook, Twitter, and LinkedIn. Companies now routinely use mobile, social media, and the Web as a way of marketing their goods and services to consumers.

Emergence of the Marketing Concept

The term **marketing concept** refers to a companywide customer focus with the goal of achieving long-term success. The basic idea of the marketing concept is that marketplace success begins with the customer. A firm should analyze each customer's needs and then work backward to offer products that fulfill those needs. The emergence of the marketing concept can be explained best by the shift from a *seller's market,* a market with a shortage of goods and services, to a *buyer's market,* a market with too many goods and services. During the 1950s, North America became a strong buyer's market. As a result, companies were forced to satisfy customers rather than just producing and selling goods and services.

Today, much competition among firms centres on the effort to satisfy customers. Apple's iPhone followed on the heels of its wildly successful iPod. Apple introduced the iWatch, which has launched a new category of "wearable" devices that connect to iPhones. As with other devices, an entire industry of programmers has sprung up to take advantage of the Apple software platform to produce apps that will cater to a variety of customers' needs and wants.[4]

marketing concept a companywide consumer focus on promoting long-term success.

ASSESSMENT CHECK

11.2.1 What is the marketing concept?

11.2.2 How is the marketing concept tied to the relationship and social eras of marketing?

NOT-FOR-PROFIT AND NONTRADITIONAL MARKETING

LO 11.3 Describe not-for-profit marketing and nontraditional marketing.

The marketing concept has traditionally been associated with profit-seeking organizations. But today the marketing concept is also applied to the not-for-profit sector and to other nontraditional areas, such as religious organizations and political campaigns.

Not-for-Profit Marketing

Every continent receives benefits from the approximately 20 million not-for-profit organizations operating around the world. Canada has more than 160,000 registered not-for-profit organizations that employ more than 2 million people. About 12.5 million Canadians volunteer their time, energy, and skills with charities and not-for-profit organizations. The United States has 1.9 million organizations that employ 12.9 million workers and benefit from volunteers who represent the equivalent of 9 million full-time employees.[5] When the value of those volunteers is taken into account, Canada leads the world in contributions to its gross domestic product by not-for-profit organizations; the United States is a close second.[6] The largest not-for-profit organization in the world is the Red Cross/Red Crescent. Other not-for-profits range from Habitat for Humanity to the Alberta Society for the Prevention of Cruelty to Animals. These organizations benefit by applying many of the strategies and business concepts used by profit-seeking firms. They apply marketing tools to reach audiences, attract and secure funding, and accomplish their overall missions. Marketing strategies are important for not-for-profit organizations because, just like for-profit businesses, they also compete for dollars. Not-for-profit organizations compete for dollars from individuals, foundations, and corporations.

Not-for-profit organizations operate in both public and private sectors. Public groups include government units and agencies that receive tax funding. For example, a municipal swimming pool receives funding from the local municipal government and might be operated by volunteers. The private not-for-profit sector comprises many different types of organizations, including the Canadian Olympic Committee and the Canadian Medical Association. Although some private not-for-profits generate surplus revenue, their primary goals are not about earning profits. If they earn funds beyond their expenses, they invest the excess in their organizational missions.

Celebrities are particularly visible in their campaigns for not-for-profit organizations—both their own organizations and those of others. The actress Reese Witherspoon is the Avon Global Ambassador and Honorary Chairperson of the Avon Foundation for Women. Witherspoon helped present a $500,000 grant to the Fund for Global Women's Leadership. The grant was intended to help the worldwide movement to end violence toward women.[8]

Nontraditional Marketing

Not-for-profit organizations often use one or more of five major categories of nontraditional marketing: person marketing, place marketing, event marketing, cause marketing, and organization marketing. **Figure 11.2** shows examples of these types of marketing. As described in the "Going Green" feature, an organization uses each of these types of marketing to connect with the audience that is most likely to offer time, money, or other resources. In some cases, the effort may reach the market the organization intends to serve. In the case of ice cream maker Häagen-Dazs, the company has chosen to support research related to the disappearing honey bee.

In some cases, not-for-profit organizations form a partnership with a for-profit company to promote the firm's message or to distribute its goods and services. This partnership usually benefits both organizations. Scotiabank is the title sponsor for the annual Rat Race for the United Way Toronto.[7]

FIGURE 11.2 Categories of Nontraditional Marketing

GOING GREEN: HÄAGEN-DAZS FOCUSES ON HONEY BEE RESEARCH

You may not immediately make an association between premium ice cream and honey bees. Pollinating many of the fruits, vegetables, and nuts we eat, honey bees are integral to more than half of the all-natural fruits, nuts, and berries used to produce Häagen-Dazs ice creams, sorbets, and frozen yogurts. Mysteriously, honey bees have been disappearing over the last decade.

Häagen-Dazs decided to take action by contributing to research to preserve honey bee colonies. The company has created the Häagen-Dazs Ice Cream Bee Board to provide insight and consultation into the causes of colony collapse disorder (CCD), which occurs when bees mysteriously die after leaving their hives.

Scientists and researchers are not certain what causes CCD. Environmental factors like chemical exposure, parasites, and pesticides are believed to be contributors, along with viruses, mites, and poor nutrition.

To date, Häagen-Dazs has contributed over $700,000 to support a California-based honey bee research facility, one of the largest of its kind in North America. In addition, the company has made a gift of $250,000 to Penn State University to provide funds for research, education, outreach, and student training. "We want to keep these little heroes buzzing. We hope you'll join our mission," reads the Häagen-Dazs website.

Questions for Critical Thinking

1. Häagen-Dazs has introduced an ice cream flavour called Vanilla Honey Bee, and partial proceeds go to CCD research. How can the company make consumers aware of its efforts to save the bees?

2. Discuss how Häagen-Dazs is attempting to use cause marketing. Whose interests are being served in the company's attempt to save honey bees?

Sources: Häagen-Dazs, "Honey, Please Don't Go," accessed February 9, 2014, www.haagendazs.us/Learn/HoneyBees/; University of California, Davis, "Laidlaw Facility: Häagen-Dazs Honey Bee Haven," accessed February 9, 2014, http://beebiology.ucdavis.edu; Michael Wines, "Bee Deaths May Stem from Virus, Study Says," *New York Times*, January 14, 2014, accessed www.nytimes.com/2014/01/22/us/bee-deaths-may-stem-from-virus-study-says.html?_r=0; Parija B. Kavilanz, "Disappearing Bees Threaten Ice Cream Sellers," *CNNMoney*, February 20, 2008, accessed July 3, 2015, http://money.cnn.com/2008/02/17/news/companies/bees_icecream.

Person Marketing

Person marketing refers to efforts designed to attract the attention, interest, and preference of a target market toward a person. Campaign managers for a political candidate conduct marketing research to identify groups of voters and financial supporters. They design advertising campaigns, fundraising events, and political rallies to reach that target group. In another example of person marketing, Canon Canada's television advertising campaign spokeswoman Avril Lavigne showed her creative use of Canon's PowerShot camera to a young potential market that knew her more for her musical talents. The message was clear—PowerShot makes creative photography simple and easy, even for people who know very little about the mechanics of a camera.

Many successful job seekers use the tools of person marketing. They research the wants and needs of prospective employers, and they identify ways they can meet those wants and needs. They look for employers through a variety of channels and send messages that focus on how they can benefit the employer.

person marketing efforts that are designed to attract the attention, interest, and preference of a target market toward a person.

Place Marketing

As the term suggests, **place marketing** attempts to attract people to a particular area, such as a city, region, or country. This marketing may focus on a place that may appeal to consumers as a tourist destination or to businesses as a desirable business location. A strategy for place marketing often includes advertising.

Place marketing may be combined with event marketing, such as the Olympics. For example, Vancouver used three mythical cartoon critters, named Quatchi, Miga, and Sumi, to promote the Olympic and Paralympic Winter Games. Merchandise featuring the mascots was available for sale to the public for more than two years before the actual games took place.[9]

place marketing an attempt to attract people to a particular area, such as a city, region, or country.

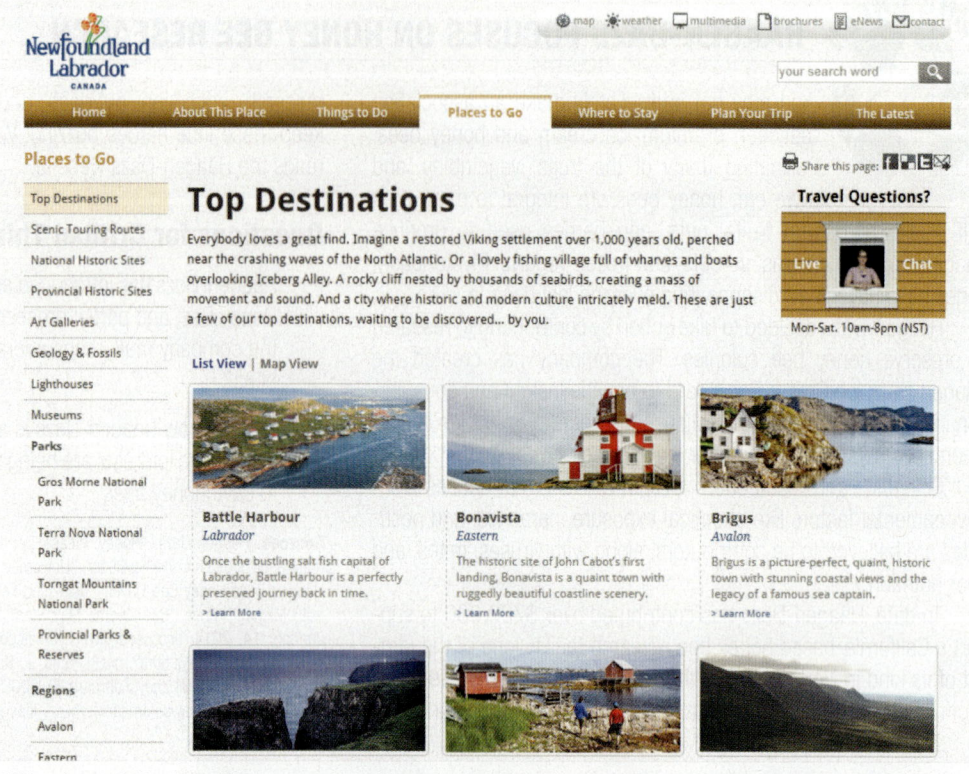

This webpage sightseeing guide is an example of *place marketing*. It is published by the government of Newfoundland and Labrador to encourage tourism.

Event Marketing

event marketing marketing or sponsoring of short-term events such as athletic competitions and cultural and charitable performances.

Event marketing refers to marketing or sponsoring short-term events such as athletic competitions and cultural and charitable performances. The Canadian Diabetes Association sponsors "Walk, Run, Cycle for Diabetes" events throughout the year. This event offers Canadian communities an opportunity to get active while also raising awareness and funds for the Canadian Diabetes Association. These volunteer-led events target local communities, promote a healthy and active lifestyle, and are dedicated to exposing the reality of diabetes and the importance of the cause.[10]

Event marketing often leads to partnerships between not-for-profit and for-profit organizations. Many businesses sponsor events such as 10K runs to raise funds for health-related charities. These occasions require a marketing effort to plan the event and attract participants and sponsors. Events may be intended to raise money or awareness, or both.

Cause Marketing

cause marketing marketing that promotes a cause or social issue, such as preventing child abuse, anti-littering efforts, and stop-smoking campaigns.

Cause marketing is marketing that promotes awareness of a cause or social issue or raises money for a cause or social issue, such as drug abuse prevention or childhood hunger. Cause marketing tries to educate the public and may or may not try to raise funds. An advertisement often contains a phone number or website address where people can get more information about the organization or issue. People can either donate money or take other actions of support. The Royal Bank of Canada sponsors the University of Western Ontario's Alternative Spring Break program. This program provides funds that help young adults and student volunteers participate in community activities in Canada and in other locations in need. Projects range from rebuilding housing damaged by natural disaster to teaching health care and English to children.[11]

For-profit companies look for ways to contribute to their communities by joining forces with charities and causes to provide financial resources, marketing resources, and human resources. Timberland is well known for participating in the City Year program, where young adults contract to perform a year of volunteer service in their communities. For-profit firms can also combine their goods and services with a cause. Seventh Generation makes household cleaning and paper products and is committed to educating consumers about how "green" products can make their homes healthier and safer.[12]

Organization Marketing

The final category of nontraditional marketing, **organization marketing,** focuses on an organization. It influences consumers to accept the goals of an organization, receive the services of an organization, or contribute in some way to an organization. Examples of organizations that use marketing include the college or university you are attending, the Canadian Cancer Society, and Oprah Winfrey's Angel Network. These organizations use their own websites, advertise in magazines, and send mail directly to consumers in their efforts to market their organizations. The Angel Network was established by Oprah Winfrey more than a decade ago to "encourage people around the world to make a difference in the lives of others." The organization runs its own charitable projects and supports the projects of other not-for-profits such as Habitat for Humanity.[13]

organization marketing a marketing strategy that influences consumers to accept the goals of an organization, receive the services of an organization, or contribute in some way to an organization.

✓ **ASSESSMENT CHECK**

11.3.1 Why do not-for-profit organizations use marketing?

11.3.2 What are the five types of nontraditional marketing used by not-for-profit organizations?

DEVELOPING A MARKETING STRATEGY

LO 11.4 Outline the basic steps in developing a marketing strategy.

In any successful organization, for-profit or not-for-profit, decision makers follow a two-step process to develop a *marketing strategy*. First, decision makers study and analyze all possible target markets and choose the most suitable market. Second, they create a marketing mix to satisfy the chosen market. **Figure 11.3** shows the relationships among the target market, the marketing mix variables, and the marketing environment. This section describes the development of a marketing strategy that is designed to attract and build relationships with customers. Sometimes, in an effort to attract customers, marketers use questionable methods, as described in the "Solving an Ethical Controversy" feature.

Earlier chapters of this book introduced many environmental factors that affect the success or failure of a firm's business strategy, including today's rapidly changing and highly competitive world of business, a wide range of social and cultural factors, economic challenges, political and legal factors, and technological innovations. Although these external forces often operate outside managers' control, marketers must still consider the impact of environmental factors on their decisions.

A marketing plan is a key part of a firm's overall business plan. The marketing plan outlines a firm's marketing strategy. It also includes information about the target market, sales and revenue goals, the marketing budget, and the timing for implementing the elements of the marketing mix.

Selecting a Target Market

The two elements of a marketing strategy are best described by the expression "find a need and fill it." A firm's marketers study the individuals and business decision makers in its potential market to find a need. A market consists of people who have purchasing power, a willingness to buy, and the authority to make purchase decisions.

Markets can be classified by type of product. Consumer products—often known as **business-to-consumer (B2C)** products—are goods and services that are purchased by end users. Some examples

business-to-consumer (B2C) product a good or service that is purchased by end users.

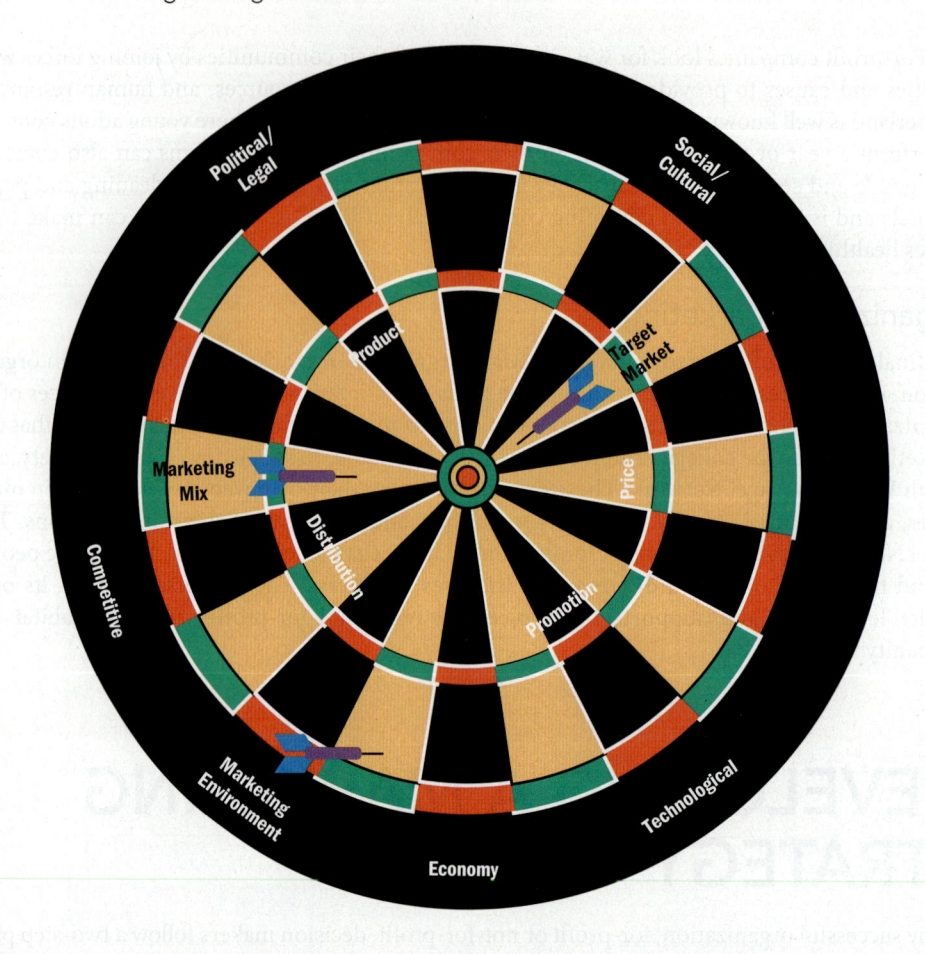

FIGURE 11.3 Target Market and Marketing Mix within the Marketing Environment

---

SOLVING AN **ETHICAL** CONTROVERSY

When Free Credit Reports Aren't Free

When times are tough and credit is tight, consumers are more likely to want to look up their credit scores and see what they can do about them. In Canada, the way that credit reporting companies handle a person's personal information is governed by the federal Personal Information Protection and Electronic Document Act (PIPEDA) and Credit Reporting Act and by such provincial acts as the Personal Information Protection Act (PIPA). In the United States, the Fair Credit Reporting Act (FCRA) governs the industry, which deals with the three major consumer reporting companies in North America—Equifax, Experian, and TransUnion. Credit reporting companies often advertise offers for a free credit report on the Internet. But many offers have hidden costs or will lead customers to other services that have costs.

Should firms be allowed to use the word *free* when advertising for credit reports if the service contains hidden costs?

PRO

1. If the credit score itself is free, but related services are not, then the advertising is truthful. Ty Taylor, the president of Experian's Consumer Direct Division, says, "You get a free credit report and free score for test-driving our services."

2. Some promotional offers include free credit scores, with a tie-in to additional services for a fee. Other industries make similar offers for a free month of phone, cable, or Internet service.

CON

1. The word *free* is a powerful invitation in advertising. Some companies provide "free" reports, then bill consumers for services they have to cancel.

2. Consumer advocates say that firms work on people's fears. Edgar Dworsky, the founder of ConsumerWorld.org and former member of Experian's consumer advisory panel, says, "Does the average person really need to see their credit reports more than once every four months? Do you need to look at it daily? That's paranoia."

(continued)

> **SOLVING AN ETHICAL CONTROVERSY** (continued)
>
> **Summary**
> Most consumers know that the use of the word *free* in any advertising is generally attached to some kind of cost at some point in time. However, should consumers have to figure out exactly when they might be charged a cost for their dealings with consumer reporting companies—or with any company?
>
> **Sources:** Federal Trade Commission, "Free Annual Credit Reports," accessed February 11, 2014, www.consumer.ftc.gov/articles/0155-free-credit-reports; Ron Lieber, "Free Credit on Credit? No Longer," *New York Times*, April 17, 2010, accessed February 11, 2014, www.nytimes.com/2010/04/08/your-money/credit-scores/08credit.html; Joe Taylor Jr., "New Laws Crack Down on Free Credit Report Marketing," *CardRatings*, updated March 22, 2015, accessed February 11, 2014, www.cardratings.com/free-credit-report-legislation.html; Michelle Singletary, "Free Credit Reports Get Easier to Find," *Washington Post*, March 4, 2010, accessed February 11, 2014, www.boston.com/business/personalfinance/articles/2010/03/04/free_credit_reports_get_easier_to_find.

are ice skates, tomato sauce, and a haircut. Business products—or **business-to-business (B2B)** products—are goods and services purchased to be used, either directly or indirectly, in making other goods that will be resold. Some products can fit either classification depending on who buys them and why. For example, a computer and a credit card can be used by both a business and a consumer.

A **target market** is the group of possible customers that an organization directs its marketing efforts toward. Customer needs and wants differ, and no single organization can satisfy everyone. For example, *Popular Science* is a magazine geared toward readers who are interested in science and technology, whereas *Bon Appétit* is aimed at readers who are interested in fine food and cooking.

Decisions about marketing involve strategies for four areas of marketing activity: product, distribution, promotion, and pricing. A firm's **marketing mix** blends the four strategies to fit the needs and preferences of a specific target market. Marketing success depends not on the four individual strategies but on their unique combination.

Product strategy involves more than just designing a good or service by adding needed qualities. It also includes decisions about package design, brand names, trademarks, warranties, product image, new-product development, and customer service. Think about your favourite pair of jeans. Do you like them because they fit the best, or do other qualities—such as styling and overall image—play a role in your brand preference? *Distribution strategy*, the second marketing mix variable, ensures that customers receive their purchases in the proper quantities at the right times and locations. *Promotional strategy*, another marketing mix element, effectively blends advertising, personal selling, sales promotion, and public relations to achieve its goals of informing, persuading, and influencing purchase decisions.

Pricing strategy, the final mix element, is also one of the most difficult areas of marketing decision making. Firms need to set profitable and justifiable prices for their product offerings. Such actions must sometimes comply with government regulation and may receive considerable public criticism. They also represent a powerful competitive strategy. Pricing strategies frequently lead to responses by the other firms in the industry, which may match price changes to avoid losing customers. Think about your jeans again. Would you continue to purchase them if they were priced much higher or much lower?

business-to-business (B2B) product a good or service purchased to be used, either directly or indirectly, in the production of other goods for resale.

target market a group of people that an organization markets its goods, services, or ideas toward, using a strategy designed to satisfy this group's specific needs and preferences.

marketing mix a blending of the four elements of marketing strategy—product, distribution, promotion, and pricing—to satisfy chosen customer segments.

Developing a Marketing Mix for International Markets

Marketing a good or service in foreign markets means deciding whether to offer the same marketing mix in every market (*standardization*) or to develop a unique mix to fit each market (*adaptation*). Standardizing the marketing mix can have upsides such as reliable marketing performance and low costs. This approach works best with B2B goods, such as steel, chemicals, and aircraft. These products need little sensitivity to a nation's culture.

Adaptation allows marketers to vary their marketing mix to suit local competitive conditions, consumer preferences, and government regulations. Consumer products tend to be more culture dependent than business products. For that reason, they often need adaptation. SUBWAY, which already has 144 stores in China, plans to open 500 new stores there.

In contrast, adaptation lets marketers vary their marketing mix to suit local competitive conditions, consumer preferences, and government regulations. Consumer tastes are often shaped by local cultures. Consumer products tend to be more culture dependent than business products. For that reason, they often need adaptation. SUBWAY, which already has 425 stores in China, plans to open 600 new stores in the next few years. SUBWAY hopes to match the Chinese presence of McDonald's in 10 years, and with 40,000 stores worldwide has surpassed McDonald's 33,000 units. As SUBWAY opens stores in different regions, it plans to adapt its menu to local tastes with such offerings as Beijing roast duck sandwiches and "hot spicy Szechuan sauce." Why do these firms go out of their way to adapt to Chinese preferences? China is a market with 1.3 billion potential consumers.[14]

Marketers also try to build adaptability into the designs of standardized goods and services for international and domestic markets. *Mass customization* allows a firm to mass-produce goods and services while also adding unique features to individual or small groups of orders. For example, online firm Blank Label (www.blanklabel.com) specializes in custom-made men's dress shirts. Customers can choose their own fabric, style, individual features, and size. Spreadshirt (www.spreadshirt.com) specializes in customized casual wear, accessories, and even personalized underwear.[15]

ASSESSMENT CHECK

11.4.1 Distinguish between consumer products and business products.

11.4.2 What are the steps in developing a marketing strategy?

LO 11.5 Describe the marketing research function.

marketing research the process of collecting and evaluating information to support marketing decision making.

MARKETING RESEARCH

Marketing research involves more than just collecting data. Researchers must decide how to collect data, interpret the results, convert the data into decision-oriented information, and communicate those results to managers for use in decision making. **Marketing research** is the process of collecting and evaluating information to help marketers make effective decisions. It links business decision makers to the marketplace by providing data about potential target markets that help them design effective marketing mixes.

Obtaining Marketing Research Data

Marketing researchers need both internal and external data. Firms generate *internal data* within their organizations. Financial records provide useful information, such as changes in unpaid bills; inventory levels; sales generated by different categories of customers or product lines; profitability of particular divisions; or comparisons of sales by territories, salespeople, customers, or product lines.

Researchers gather *external data* from outside sources, including previously published data. Trade associations publish reports on activities in specific industries. Advertising agencies collect information on the audiences reached by various media. National marketing research firms offer information through subscription services. Some professional research firms specialize in specific markets, such as youth or ethnic groups. This information helps companies to make decisions about developing or modifying products. The largest consumer-goods manufacturer in the world, Procter & Gamble, has excelled in marketing research for a long time; it created its own marketing research department in 1923 and began conducting its research online in 2001. To help the company recover from the global recession and focus on the future, the company's CEO, A.G. Lafley, continues to rely on his inquisitive nature and commitment to understanding how consumers live. Early in his career, Lafley spent time in households in various countries to observe and listen and to understand what delights customers. As the consumer products giant moves forward with expansion plans to reach customers in developing regions, Procter & Gamble continues its sharply focused marketing research efforts.[16]

Secondary data, or previously published data, are low cost and easy to obtain. Government publications are excellent data sources, and most are available online. The most frequently used government statistics are census data, which contain the population's age, gender, education level, household size and composition, occupation, employment status, and income. Even private research firms such as TRU-Insight (formerly Teenage Research Unlimited), which studies the purchasing habits of teens, provide some free information on their websites. This information helps firms evaluate consumers' buying behaviour, look ahead to possible changes in the marketplace, and identify new markets.[17]

Even though secondary data are a quick and inexpensive resource, this information sometimes is not specific or current enough for marketing researchers' needs. Researchers may decide that they need to collect *primary data*—data collected firsthand through such methods as observation and surveys.

Observational studies view the actions of consumers either directly or by using mechanical devices. More retailers are watching their customers by way of video cameras. This kind of observation can solve problems such as widening a too-narrow aisle to allow shoppers easier access. But such close observation has also raised privacy concerns.[18] Procter & Gamble spends about $200 million on consumer observation each year and says it is the firm's most important type of marketing research. Retired CEO Robert McDonald said, "If we can continue to innovate and continue to mind consumer needs and delight consumers, that ability outweighs any macroeconomic force."[19]

Observing customers cannot provide all the information a marketing researcher needs. For example, a researcher might observe a customer buying a red sweater, but have no idea why the purchase was made—or for whom. When researchers need information about consumers' attitudes, opinions, and motives, they need to ask the consumers themselves. They may conduct surveys by telephone, in person, online, or in focus groups.

A *focus group* gathers 8 to 12 people in a room or over the Internet to discuss a specific topic. A focus group can lead to new ideas, address consumers' needs, and even point out flaws in existing products. Campbell Soup Company held nationwide focus groups in which respondents reviewed ingredients from two soups. Two of three focus group participants overwhelmingly chose the Campbell's brand. Marketing researchers have also begun to take advantage of mobile marketing and social media outlets such as Facebook, Twitter, and blogs.[20]

Applying Marketing Research Data

Market researchers now collect information that is more accurate than in the past. That means the resulting marketing strategies are also more effective. One field of research, known as **business intelligence**, uses various activities and technologies to gather, store, and analyze data to make better competitive decisions. Unilever, maker of consumer products including Dove soap, Axe deodorant, and Ben and Jerry's ice cream, has a highly regarded global research staff and values input from outside sources. The company has adopted a crowdsourced, open-idea platform, where external contributions are sought for diverse projects. Unilever's "challenges and wants" webpage solicits ideas for new designs and technologies to help improve the way its products are made. If Unilever decides to pursue a submitted idea, the originator might benefit financially.[21]

business intelligence a field of research that uses activities and technologies for gathering, storing, and analyzing data to make better competitive decisions.

Data Mining

data mining the use of computer searches of customer data to detect patterns and relationships.

data warehouse a customer database that allows managers to combine data from several different organizational functions.

After a company has built a database, marketers must be able to analyze the data and use the information it provides. **Data mining** is part of the broader field of business intelligence. It refers to the task of using computer-based technology to evaluate data in a database and identify useful trends. These trends or patterns may suggest models of real-world business activities. Accurate data mining can help researchers forecast recessions and pinpoint sales prospects.

Data mining uses a **data warehouse**, a sophisticated customer database that allows managers to combine data from several different organizational functions. Rapleaf Inc. collects publicly available personal information from social networking sites such as Facebook, Twitter, and other forums. Rapleaf then sells this information to airlines and credit card companies that view those individuals as potential customers. Such information can include everything from your blogging or posting habits to your credit rating. Among the issues arising from data mining are ownership of Web user data, the targeting capabilities of the Web, government supervision—and, of course, privacy.

Some observers feel that privacy norms are changing. They see confidentiality giving way to increasing openness.[22] Playnomics's segmentation technology and predictive analysis mine and analyze the behaviour of online and app game players by tracking the number of hours they spend on games and creating behavioural profiles. App and game developers pay a monthly fee for the resulting data. The company's CEO says providing information about user activity gives marketers a way to find and engage the right player for greater retention and increased revenues.[23]

✓ ASSESSMENT CHECK

11.5.1 What is the difference between primary data and secondary data?

11.5.2 What is data mining?

LO 11.6 Discuss the methods used to segment consumer and business markets.

MARKET SEGMENTATION

market segmentation the process of dividing a total market into several relatively similar groups.

Market segmentation is the process of dividing a market into several relatively similar groups. Both for-profit and not-for-profit organizations use segmentation to help them reach desirable target markets. Market segmentation is often based on the results of research, which tries to identify trends among certain groups of people. For instance, one recent survey revealed that social media use among Internet-using baby boomers—those North Americans between 50 and 64 years old—grew from 52 to 65 percent. Younger adults—those under age 30—are still the heaviest users, with 90 percent visiting a social networking site on any given day. Overall, 73 percent of adult Internet users visit social networking sites, but the rise in use by older consumers is important information for businesses.[24] This kind of information helps marketers to decide what types of products to develop and to whom these products should be marketed.

Market segmentation attempts to isolate the traits that set a certain group of customers apart from the overall market. However, segmentation doesn't automatically produce marketing success. **Table 11.1** lists several criteria that marketers should consider. The effectiveness of a segmentation strategy depends on how well the market meets these criteria. Once marketers identify a market segment to target, they can create an appropriate marketing strategy.

Table 11.1 Criteria for Market Segmentation

CRITERION	EXAMPLE
A segment must be a measurable group.	Data can be collected on the dollar amount and number of purchases made by college and university students.
A segment must be accessible for communication.	More and more seniors are now online, so many more seniors can now be reached through Internet channels.
A segment must be large enough to offer profit potential.	In a small community, a store carrying only large-size shoes might not be profitable. For similar reasons, a specialty retail chain may prefer to locate in a large market.

Companies that can identify trends in consumer preferences before their rivals can benefit greatly; those that miss the boat generally suffer the consequences. There is an expanding opportunity for mobile apps and Internet-based services to make their way into consumers' cars. Pandora Internet Radio is now being used in 5 million cars and 100 models through its partnerships with auto brands and stereo manufacturers. Apple hopes to integrate Siri technology and maps into car navigation systems, and Ford already uses voice, steering wheel, or touchscreen-activated controls for mobile apps.[25]

How Market Segmentation Works

The first segmentation distinction involves whether a firm offers goods and services to customers for their own use or to purchasers who will use them directly or indirectly in providing other products for resale (the so-called B2B market). Depending on whether their firms offer consumer or business products, marketers segment their target markets differently. Four common bases for segmenting consumer markets are geographical segmentation, demographic segmentation, psychographic segmentation, and product-related segmentation. By contrast, business markets can segment on three criteria: customer-based segmentation, end-use segmentation, and geographical segmentation. **Figure 11.4** illustrates the segmentation methods for these two types of markets.

Segmenting Consumer Markets

Market segmentation has been practised since people first began selling products. Tailors made some clothing items for men and others for women. Tea was imported from India for tea drinkers in England and other European countries. In addition to demographic and geographical segmentation, today's marketers also define customer groups based on product-related differences and criteria that are psychographic—relating to lifestyle and values.

Geographical Segmentation

The oldest segmentation method is **geographical segmentation**—dividing a market into similar groups on the basis of their locations. Geographical location does not guarantee that consumers in a certain region will all buy the same kinds of products, but it does provide some information about needs. For example, people who live in the suburbs buy more lawn-care products than those

geographical segmentation dividing an overall market into similar groups on the basis of their locations.

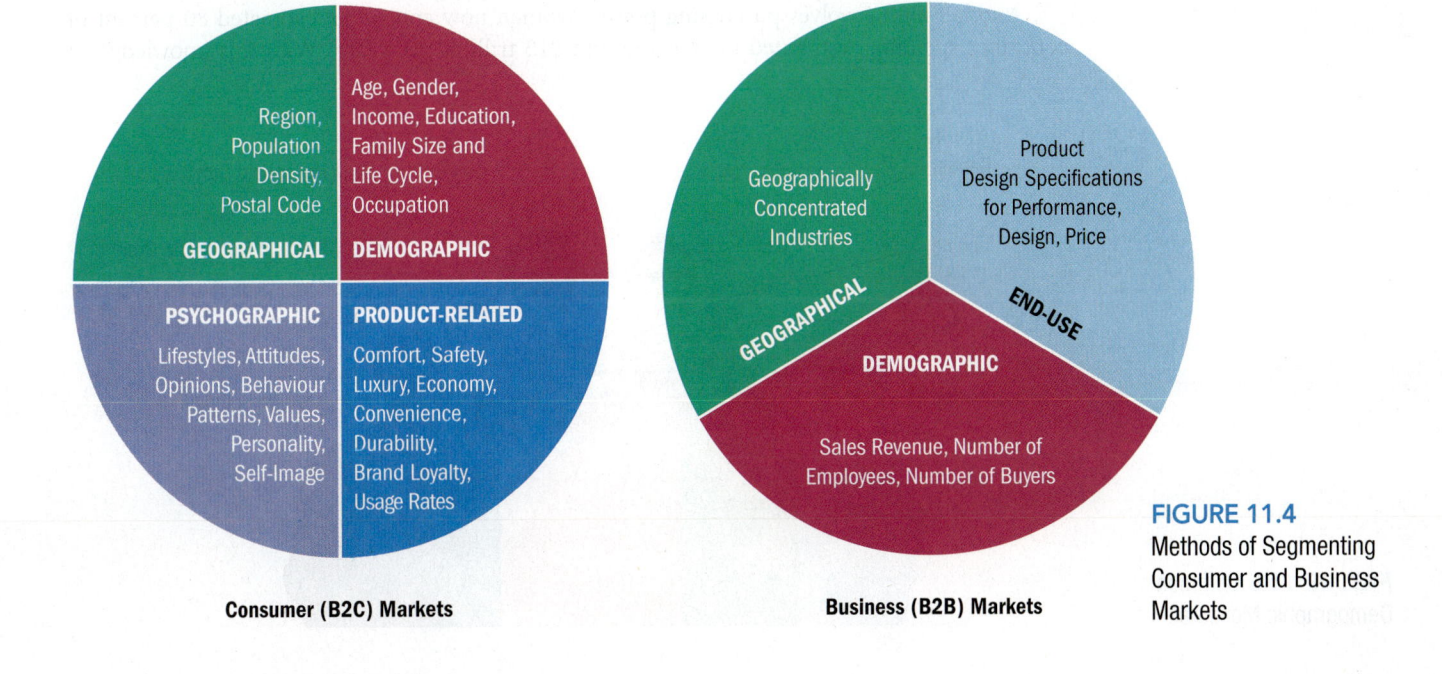

FIGURE 11.4 Methods of Segmenting Consumer and Business Markets

Consumer (B2C) Markets:
- GEOGRAPHICAL: Region, Population Density, Postal Code
- DEMOGRAPHIC: Age, Gender, Income, Education, Family Size and Life Cycle, Occupation
- PSYCHOGRAPHIC: Lifestyles, Attitudes, Opinions, Behaviour Patterns, Values, Personality, Self-Image
- PRODUCT-RELATED: Comfort, Safety, Luxury, Economy, Convenience, Durability, Brand Loyalty, Usage Rates

Business (B2B) Markets:
- GEOGRAPHICAL: Geographically Concentrated Industries
- END-USE: Product Design Specifications for Performance, Design, Price
- DEMOGRAPHIC: Sales Revenue, Number of Employees, Number of Buyers

who live in city centres. But many people in the suburbs choose instead to purchase the services of a lawn maintenance firm. Consumers who live where winter is more severe are more likely than those who live in warmer areas to buy ice scrapers, snow shovels, and snow blowers. They are also more likely to contract with firms to remove the snow from driveways. Marketers also look at the size of the population of an area and who lives there—are the residents old or young? Do they reflect an ethnic background? What is the level of their income?

Job growth and migration patterns are also important to consider. Some businesses combine areas or even entire countries that share similar population and product-use patterns, instead of treating each as an independent segment.

Demographic Segmentation

demographic segmentation dividing markets on the basis of various demographic or socioeconomic characteristics, such as gender, age, income, occupation, household size, stage in family life cycle, education, or ethnic group.

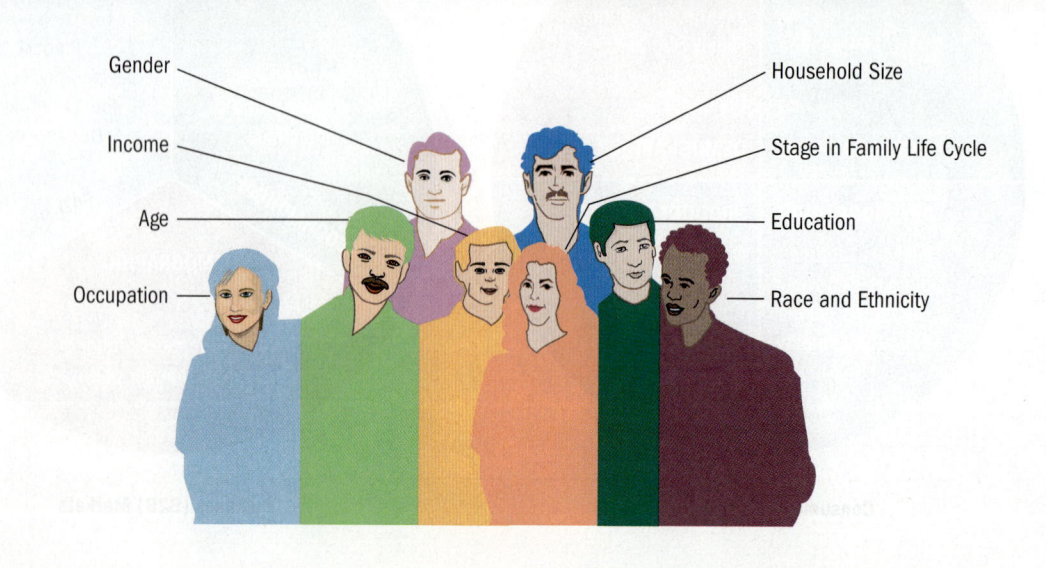

The most common method of market segmentation is **demographic segmentation**. This type of segmentation separates markets on the basis of various demographic or socioeconomic characteristics. Common demographic measures include gender, income, age, occupation, household size, stage in the family life cycle, education, and racial or ethnic group. Statistics Canada and the U.S. Census Bureau are the best sources of demographic information for their markets. **Figure 11.5** lists some of the measures used in demographic segmentation.

North American police departments are a highly specialized occupational demographic group. Popular for its durability, the Ford Crown Victoria has long held 75 percent of the patrol-car market share. Ford has phased out the "Crown Vic," replacing it with the Police Interceptor, modelled on the Taurus sedan but modified for the extreme circumstances of police work. The Interceptor's fuel efficiency is 25 percent better than the Crown Vic's. Its 365-horsepower engine outguns the Crown Vic's by 115 horsepower. Its newest model, the Explorer Police Interceptor, has a 3.5-liter, twin turbocharged engine, which helps the company compete with similar models from GM and Dodge.[26]

Gender used to be a simple way to define markets for certain products—jewellery and skin care products for women; tools and motorcycles for men. Much of that has changed—dramatically. Men now buy jewellery and skin care products, and women buy tools and motorcycles. But marketers have also found that even though these shifts have blurred the lines between products, there are still differences in the *way* that women and men shop. A recent study of online shopping habits revealed that men are more likely to make a purchase from a desktop or laptop computer, while women are more likely to use a mobile device to complete a purchase. Marketers should be sure a website has an easy-to-use mobile interface. Other data suggests that women were slightly more intent on getting the best available price, so easy page-browsing and in-page price comparisons from a mobile device should be a top priority.[27]

Another shift involves purchasing power. Women now control an estimated 80 percent of consumer spending, estimated between $5 and $15 trillion per year.[28] With this knowledge in

FIGURE 11.5 Common Demographic Measures

hand, Amazon purchased online retailer Zappos and launched a program called Amazon Mom, a free membership program for parents of small children.[29]

Age may be the most unstable factor in demographic segmentation in Canada and the United States because of our rapidly aging population. Of the 340-plus million people who live in North America, more than one-third will be age 55 or older by the year 2020.[30] Because of these statistics, marketers for travel and leisure products, and marketers for retirement and business investments, are working hard to attract the attention of this age group, the aging baby boomers—those born between 1946 and 1964. Active-adult housing communities are one result of these efforts. Some developers have built communities with a resort-style atmosphere in desirable locations such as Whistler, British Columbia, ski country or the outskirts of a large city such as Toronto or Montreal. But, because of the recession, many such communities have actually seen their populations decrease. According to Mark Mather, associate vice-president of the Population Reference Bureau, "Baby boomers helped fuel housing and population growth in retirement areas earlier in the decade, and now they are playing an important role in the decline."[31]

The millennials are a rapidly growing consumer market. They are characterized as tech-savvy shoppers who influence the purchases of their families and friends.

Teens are another rapidly growing market. The entire scope of Generation Y—those born between 1976 and 1997—takes in about one-third of the total North American population. These consumers, often called the millennials, are tech-savvy shoppers. They influence not only their own purchases but also those of their families and friends. They are educated consumers who comparison shop and usually avoid impulse purchases, partly because of the recession and partly because they are spending their own money. According to a Nielsen survey, compared with older generations, such as the "greatest generation" (those who lived through World War II) and the baby boomers, Generation Y consumers shop less often but when they do shop, they buy more, preferring megastores and big box-retailers.[32]

Statistics can be helpful, but they don't tell the whole story. To serve customers well, marketers must also learn where people live, how old they are, what languages they speak, how much income they have, and their cultural tastes and preferences. Sometimes, marketers must do intensive research to reach a particular age group or gender group, or both, as described in the "Hit & Miss" feature.

HIT & MISS

Disney XD TV: Marketing to Boys

Disney marketing aimed at young girls has been highly successful. Just think of the "Princesses" products, the Jonas Brothers, and *High School Musical*. But the Disney Channel audience is 40 percent male. *(Pirates of the Caribbean* and *Toy Story* have both had successful sequels.)

In North America, about 10 percent of the population are males aged 5 to 19 years old. Worldwide, boys (or their parents) spend $50 billion every year on clothes, toys, and video games.

Recently, Disney bought Marvel Entertainment. It is hoping that Marvel's superheroes will draw viewers to Disney's XD TV channel. The channel is aimed at boys but doesn't exclude girls from its offerings of animation, action-adventure, comedy, movies, sports-themed shows, and music videos. The Disney XD website provides access to games, videos, and TV episodes.

How did Disney research a demographic that is known for not talking about their feelings? It hired a team of social scientists, who learned the following:

- Boys identify with main characters who are trying to grow, and they want to see more characters like themselves in TV shows.
- Boys personalize the undersides of their skateboards and carry them so the tag shows.
- Boys like to share small accomplishments.

(continued)

> **HIT & MISS** *(continued)*
>
> - Boys shuttle quickly from one activity to another, moving from TV to video games to sports, and so on.
> - Boys want more variety and reality in TV shows, not just all action or all cartoons.
>
> Disney used these results to add a trophy room to the games page at the XD website and by advising its actors to carry their skateboards so the tagging showed, for realism. Viewership at XD increased more than 25 percent—but most of the new audience was girls. Boys aged 6 to 14 increased only 10 percent. The economic downturn also hurt advertising, but didn't discourage Rich Ross, the president of Disney Channels Worldwide. "We've seen cultural resonance, and it doesn't come overnight," he said.
>
> **Questions for Critical Thinking**
>
> 1. What type(s) of segmentation strategy is Disney applying? Will it be effective? Why or why not?
> 2. What steps can Disney take to increase viewership of Disney XD among boys?
>
> **Sources:** Disney XD, accessed April 17, 2015, www.disneyxd.ca; Disney, accessed April 11, 2010, http://disney.com; Tom Lowry and Ronald Grover, "Disney's Marvel Deal and the Pursuit of Boys," *Bloomberg Business*, March 9, 2010, accessed July 3, 2015, www.bloomberg.com/bw/magazine/content/09_38/b4147066139865.htm; Seth Lubove and Andy Fixmer, "Disney Beefs Up Marketing to Boys," *Ledger*, March 4, 2010, accessed July 3, 2015, www.theledger.com/article/20100304/news/3045052.

Psychographic Segmentation

psychographic segmentation dividing consumer markets into groups with similar attitudes, values, and lifestyles.

Lifestyle is the sum of a person's needs, preferences, motives, attitudes, social habits, and cultural background. In recent years, marketing researchers have tried to put together lifestyle portraits of consumers. This effort has led to another strategy for segmenting target markets, **psychographic segmentation**, which divides consumer markets into groups with similar psychological characteristics, values, and lifestyles.

Psychographic studies are used to evaluate motivations for purchases of hundreds of goods and services, ranging from soft drinks to healthcare services. Firms use the resulting data to tailor their marketing strategies to carefully chosen market segments. A frequently used way of developing psychographic profiles uses *AIO statements*—people's verbal descriptions of their various attitudes, interests, and opinions. Researchers survey a sample of consumers, asking them whether they agree or disagree with each statement. The answers are then organized and analyzed for use in identifying various lifestyle categories.

Another way to get consumers to provide current information about their lifestyles is for organizations to create *blogs* in the hope that consumers may respond. Companies including Lululemon Athletica, *Globe and Mail*, and Microsoft have hired bloggers to run online Web journals as a way to connect with consumers and receive information from them. Other firms encourage employees at all levels to use blogs to communicate with consumers. General Motors has several blogs at its GMblogs.com site, each set up for a specific brand or consumer interest. The FastLane blog discusses GM cars and trucks and invites consumers to offer their thoughts and ideas. Chevrolet Voltage is aimed at fans of the Volt and other electric vehicles. The Lab is where GM's advanced design team talks about its work and invites feedback from community members.[33] Although demographic classifications such as age, gender, and income are relatively easy to identify and measure, researchers also need to define psychographic categories. Marketing research firms often conduct wide studies of consumers and then share their psychographic data with clients. Businesses sometimes look to studies done by sociologists and psychologists to help them understand their customers. For example, while children may belong to one age group and their parents to another, both live certain lifestyles together. Recent marketing research shows that today's parents are willing and able to spend more on goods and services for their children than parents were willing and able to spend a generation or two ago. Spending on toys and video games for children topped $38 billion for a recent year in North America.[34] These are just a few trends identified by the researchers, but they provide valuable information to firms that may be considering developing games, designing the interiors of family vehicles, or offering new wireless plans.

Product-Related Segmentation

product-related segmentation dividing consumer markets into groups that are based on benefits sought by buyers, usage rates, and loyalty levels.

Sellers who use **product-related segmentation** divide a consumer market into groups that are based on buyers' relationships to the good or service. The three most popular approaches to product-related segmentation are based on benefits sought, usage rates, and brand loyalty levels.

WRAP DRESS

$99.00 USD

COLOR: Black
SIZE: XS
QUANTITY: 1   [Buy Now]

Flattering, always a classic and always on trend. Designed for the seated frame, hemline in the back has more length than usual, so it matches length in the front when seated. Easy dressing with simple wrap and tie. Stretch fabric for added comfort and fit.

Full-length sleeves.

V-neck.

Tie closure.

95% rayon, 5% spandex.

Machine wash warm, tumble dry low, medium iron.

Share: f Facebook   Twitter   Pinterest

PARKA

$529.00 USD

COLOR: Black
SIZE: S
QUANTITY: 1   [Reserve]

The ultimate in warmth and style. Longer in the front to drape smoothly over your lap. Hemline at back finishes at the seat of your chair, makes it easier to get dressed while seated. Water-resistant shell. Lined with Kasha and Thinsulate for serious warmth. Hood with removable coyote fur-trim.

Two front pockets.

Elastic cuffs.

Zipper & Velcro closures.

Hood.

Removable coyote fur trim.

Shell: 100% nylon.

Fill: Thinsulate.

Canadian businesses can compete in a crowded fashion industry by developing and producing products that cater to niche markets. IZ Collection produces adaptive fashions for wheelchair users. Its clothing is cut and designed to fit a seated body shape, while maintaining comfort and style.

Courtesy of IZ Collection

Segmenting by *benefits sought* focuses on the qualities that people look for in a good or service and the benefits they expect to receive. As more firms shift toward consumer demand for products that are eco-friendly, marketers find ways to emphasize the benefits of these products. Home-goods retailer Crate & Barrel has begun to offer tables and chairs made of mango wood. The wood is harvested only after the trees can no longer produce fruit. Consumers can also select a sofa whose cushions are made of recycled fibres that are filled with a natural, soy-based foam. According to the company's website, "While our collection has featured renewable woods and sustainable materials for a number of years, we are now introducing important initiatives that will help make our homes more thoughtful environments."[35]

Consumer markets can also be segmented according to the amounts of a product that people buy and use. Segmentation by *product usage rate* usually defines such categories as heavy users, medium users, and light users. The 80/20 principle states that roughly 80 percent of a product's revenues come from only 20 percent of its buyers. Companies can now pinpoint which of their customers are the heaviest users and even the most profitable customers. Companies then direct most of their marketing efforts to those customers.

The third technique for product-related segmentation divides customers by *brand loyalty*—the degree to which consumers recognize, prefer, and insist on a particular brand. Marketers define groups of consumers with similar degrees of brand loyalty. They then try to tie loyal customers to a good or service by giving away premiums, anything from a logo-imprinted T-shirt to a pair of tickets to a concert or sports event.

Segmenting Business Markets

In many ways, the segmentation process for business markets is like the segmentation process for consumer markets. But some specific methods are different. Business markets can be divided in three ways: through geographical segmentation; demographic, or customer-based, segmentation; and end-use segmentation.

Geographical segmentation methods for business markets are like the geographic segmentation methods used for consumer markets. Many B2B marketers target geographically concentrated industries, such as aircraft manufacturing, automobiles, and oil field equipment. The marketing mix may need to be changed to adapt to the customer needs, languages, and other variables of a different location. These changes will likely be needed when the company is marketing itself internationally.

Demographic, or customer-based, segmentation begins with a good or service being designed to suit a specific organizational market. Sodexho Marriott Services is the largest provider of food services in North America. Its customers include healthcare institutions, business and government offices, schools, colleges, and universities. Within these broad business segments, Sodexho identifies more specific segments, which might include government offices on the west coast or universities that have culturally diverse populations—and their different food preferences or dining styles. Sodexho uses survey data that cover students' lifestyles, attitudes, preferences for consumer products in general, services, and media categories. In addition, Sodexho uses targeted surveys that identify preferences for restaurant brands or certain foods, meal habits, and the amount spent on meals. Marketers evaluate the data, which sometimes reveal surprising trends. At one university, students said that they liked foods with an international flavour. So Sodexho adapted its offerings.[36]

To make it easier to focus on a specific type of business customer, the federal government has developed a system for subdividing the business marketplace into detailed segments. The six-digit *North American Industry Classification System (NAICS)* provides a common classification system used by the United States, Canada, and Mexico, the member nations of the North American Free Trade Agreement (NAFTA). This system divides industries into broad categories such as agriculture, forestry, and fishing; manufacturing; transportation; and retail and wholesale trade. Each major category is further subdivided into smaller segments, such as gas stations with convenience food and warehouse clubs. The smaller segments provide more detailed information and make it easier to compare data among the member nations.

Another way to group firms by their demographics is to segment them by size, such as by their sales revenues or number of employees. Some firms collect data from visitors to its website and use the data to segment customers by size. Modern information processing also means that companies can segment business markets based on how much they buy, not just how big they are.

End-use segmentation focuses on the precise way a B2B purchaser will use a product. This method is similar to the benefits-sought segmentation used for consumer markets. End-use segmentation helps small and mid-size companies target specific end-user markets instead of competing directly with large firms for wider customer groups. A company might also design a marketing mix based on certain criteria for making a purchase.

end-use segmentation a marketing strategy that focuses on the precise way a B2B purchaser will use a product.

✓ ASSESSMENT CHECK

11.6.1 What is the most common form of segmentation for consumer markets?

11.6.2 What are the three approaches to product-related segmentation?

11.6.3 What is end-use segmentation in the B2B market?

CONSUMER BEHAVIOUR

A fundamental marketing task is to find out why people buy one product and not another. The answer requires an understanding of **consumer behaviour**: the activities of end consumers that are directly involved in obtaining, consuming, and disposing of products, and the decision processes before and after these activities.

LO 11.7 Outline the determinants of consumer behaviour.

consumer behaviour end consumers' activities that are directly involved in obtaining, consuming, and disposing of products, and the decision processes before and after these activities.

Determinants of Consumer Behaviour

Businesses study people's purchasing behaviour to identify their attitudes toward products and to learn how they use products. This information also helps marketers reach their targeted customers. Both personal and interpersonal factors affect the way buyers behave. Personal influences on consumer behaviour include individual needs and motives, perceptions, attitudes, learned experiences, and self-concept. For example, people are constantly looking for ways to save time, so firms do everything they can to provide goods and services that are designed for convenience. But when it comes to products such as dinner foods, consumers don't just want convenience—they also want the flavour of a home-cooked meal and quality time with their families. So companies such as Stouffer's offer frozen lasagna and manicotti in family sizes, and grocery stores have entire sections of freshly prepared take-out meals, including roast turkey and filet mignon.

McDonald's is betting that consumers who drink premium coffee beverages will also like to buy them at bargain prices. In many locations, McDonald's has placed McCafé coffee bars near the cash register. These coffee bars offer cappuccinos, lattes, and mochas. Most McDonald's stores now serve these beverages, putting the company in direct competition with Starbucks.[37]

The interpersonal determinants of consumer behaviour include cultural, social, and family influences. In the area of convenience foods, cultural, social, and family influences come into play as much as an individual's need to save time. Marketers understand that many consumers value the time they spend with their families and want to provide them with good nutrition. Marketers often emphasize these values when advertising convenience food products.

Sometimes external events influence consumer behaviour. One study suggests that because of the recession, consumers may have permanently changed their buying and spending behaviour. The survey found that 72 percent of consumers said that they had significantly or somewhat changed their shopping habits; only 7 percent said they had made no change. Manufacturers and retailers—and especially small businesses—will need to create new marketing strategies in response to these challenges.[38]

Determinants of Business Buying Behaviour

When business buyers need to make a purchase, they have to deal with their own preferences, which may not be their firm's preference. They must also deal with a variety of influences from their organizations because many people can be involved in the decision to purchase B2B products. For example, a design engineer may help set the specifications that potential suppliers must meet. A procurement manager may invite selected companies to bid on a purchase. A production supervisor may evaluate the operational qualities of the proposals that the firm receives, and the vice-president of manufacturing may head a committee making the final decision.

Steps in the Consumer Behaviour Process

Consumer decision making follows the sequential process shown in **Figure 11.6**. Interpersonal and personal influences affect every step. The process begins when the consumer recognizes a problem or opportunity. For example, if someone needs a new pair of shoes, that need becomes a problem to solve. If you receive a promotion at work and a 20 percent salary increase, that change may lead to a purchase opportunity.

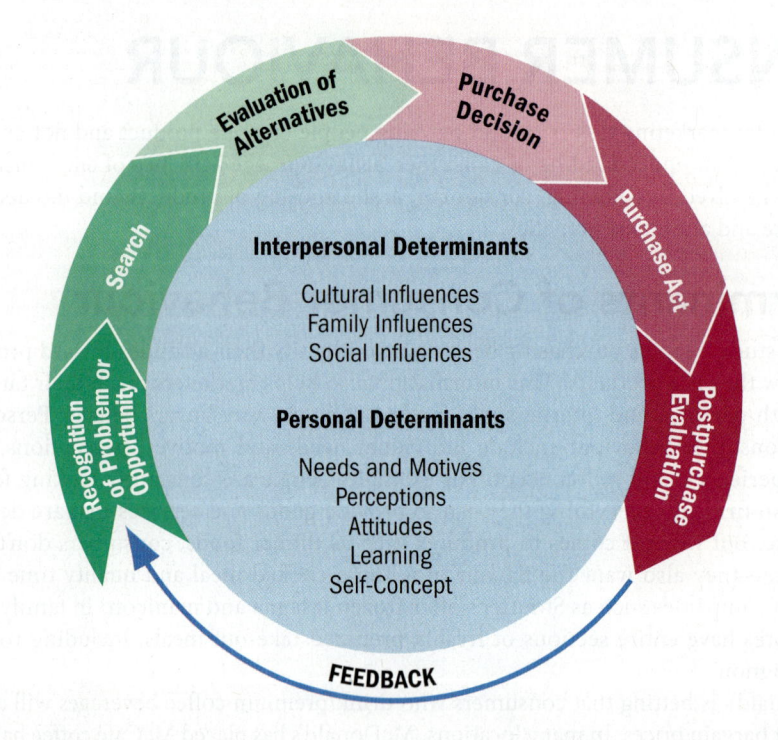

FIGURE 11.6 Steps in the Consumer Behaviour Process

Diagram shows a circular process with outer steps: Recognition of Problem or Opportunity → Search → Evaluation of Alternatives → Purchase Decision → Purchase Act → Postpurchase Evaluation → FEEDBACK. Inner circle lists:

Interpersonal Determinants
- Cultural Influences
- Family Influences
- Social Influences

Personal Determinants
- Needs and Motives
- Perceptions
- Attitudes
- Learning
- Self-Concept

✓ **ASSESSMENT CHECK**

11.7.1 Define *consumer behaviour*.

11.7.2 What are some determinants of consumer behaviour?

LO 11.8 Discuss the benefits of, and tools for, relationship marketing.

relationship marketing developing and maintaining long-term, cost-effective exchange relationships with partners.

To solve the problem or take advantage of the opportunity, the consumer looks for information about his or her intended purchase and evaluates options, such as the available brands. The goal is to find the best response to the problem or opportunity.

In the end, the consumer usually reaches a decision and completes the transaction. Later, the customer evaluates the experience by making a postpurchase evaluation. Feelings about the experience serve as feedback that will affect future purchase decisions. The various steps in the sequence are affected by both interpersonal and personal factors.

RELATIONSHIP MARKETING

The past decade has brought rapid change to most industries. Customers have become better informed and more demanding purchasers by closely comparing competing goods and services. They expect, even demand, new benefits from the companies that supply them. These expectations make it harder for firms to gain a competitive advantage on the basis of product features alone.

In today's hypercompetitive era, businesses need to find new ways of relating to customers to maintain long-term success. Businesses are developing strategies and tactics that create closer relationships with their customers, suppliers, and even employees. As a result, many firms are turning their attention to relationship marketing. **Relationship marketing** goes beyond an effort toward making the sale. This type of marketing develops and maintains long-term, cost-effective exchange relationships with partners. These partners include individual customers, suppliers, and employees. As its ultimate goal, relationship marketing seeks to achieve customer satisfaction.

When businesses manage their relationships instead of just completing sales transactions, they can often develop creative partnerships. But customers will enter into relationships with firms only when they are assured that the relationship will be of benefit to them. As the intensity of commitment increases, so does the likelihood of a business continuing a long-term relationship with its customers. Businesses build relationships by partnering with customers, suppliers, and other businesses. Timberland, maker of footwear and clothing, creates many partnerships that foster long-term relationships. Timberland partners with not-for-profit organizations such as CARE, City Year, and Clean Air–Cool Planet to complete service projects for communities and the environment.

Through its Serv-a-Palooza, hundreds of Timberland employees sign up for volunteer tasks in their communities. Those opportunities even extend to customers who have expressed an interest in participating in programs in their own regions. If you want to volunteer for a food drive or to help restore a marsh, just log on to the Timberland website to see what's available. All of these activities help build relationships with customers, communities, and other organizations.[39]

Benefits of Relationship Marketing

Relationship marketing helps all parties involved. Businesses that create solid relationships with suppliers and customers protect themselves against competitors. These businesses are also often rewarded with lower costs and higher profits than they would generate on their own. Long-term agreements with a few high-quality suppliers can reduce a firm's production costs. Unlike one-time sales, these ongoing relationships encourage suppliers to offer customers preferred treatment. For example, suppliers might quickly correct any quality problems and be willing to adjust shipments to accommodate changes in orders.

Encouraging good relationships with customers can be a vital strategy for a firm. By identifying current purchasers and maintaining positive relationships with them, organizations can efficiently target their best customers. Studying current customers' buying habits and preferences can help marketers to identify potential new customers and establish ongoing contact with them. Attracting a new customer can cost five times as much as keeping an existing customer. Long-term customers do not just reduce marketing costs; they usually buy more, require less service, refer other customers, and provide valuable feedback. Together, these elements contribute to a higher **lifetime value of a customer**—the revenues and intangible benefits (such as referrals and customer feedback) from the customer over the life of the relationship, minus the amount the company must spend to acquire and serve that customer. Keeping that customer may occasionally require some extra effort, especially when the customer has become upset or dissatisfied with a good or service. But good marketers can overcome this particular challenge, as described in the "Career Kickstart" feature.

lifetime value of a customer the revenues and intangible benefits (such as referrals and customer feedback) from a customer over the life of the relationship, minus the amount the company must spend to acquire and serve that customer.

CAREER KICKSTART

Calming the Angry Customer

In any business, an angry customer is a challenge. An upset customer represents not only an immediate problem but also a potential loss of future business. The customer may be upset over poor service or a broken product, frustrated by lack of attention from the company, or just plain demanding. You, the businessperson, should look at this customer not as a disruption but as an opportunity to see your company from the outside. With a little bit of common sense, good personal skills, and knowledge of your company and its products, you can turn the customer's dissatisfaction into satisfaction.

- *Remain calm and professional.* The customer isn't angry with you personally. Let the customer speak first, and listen carefully as he or she states the problem. Make written notes. Acknowledge the customer's anger, then assure him or her that you will correct the situation.

- *Repeat the customer's stated problem.* Using your own words assures the customer that you have been listening. For example, you might say, "The shoes you received were the right colour but the wrong size." Make sure you understand the problem before offering a solution.

- *Focus on the solution.* Having procedures in place beforehand can help you resolve a problem quickly. If you can't solve the problem yourself, immediately refer it to someone who can. Fast action will let the customer know that you are on his or her side.

- *Thank the customer for his or her patience.* By bringing the problem to your attention, the customer is actually giving you an opportunity to improve service to all your clients.

- *Follow up.* If appropriate, send an email or make a phone call to make sure the correct pair of shoes arrived. Your professionalism will strengthen the customer's relationship with your firm—and positive word of mouth may even bring you new customers.

Sources: Lynne McClure, "Handling Customers," *Impact Publications*, accessed February 25, 2014, www.impactpublications.com; Katy Tynan, "Conflict Management Part 2—Calming an Irate Customer," *Ezinearticles.com*, accessed February 25, 2014, http://ezinearticles.com/?Conflict-Management-Part-2---Calming-an-Irate-Customer&id=3656834; "How to Calm an Angry Customer," *Business Knowledge Source*, accessed February 25, 2014, http://businessknowledgesource.com/blog/how_to_calm_an_angry_customer_024261.html.

Businesses also benefit from having strong relationships with other companies. Purchasers who repeatedly buy from one business may find that they save time and gain service quality as the business learns more about their specific needs. Some relationship-oriented companies also customize items based on customer preferences. Because many businesses reward loyal customers with discounts or bonuses, some buyers may even find that they save money by developing long-term relationships. Alliances, or working with other firms, to serve the same customers also can be rewarding. The partners combine their capabilities and resources to accomplish goals that they could not reach on their own. Alliances with other firms may also help businesses to develop the skills and experience they need to improve service to current customers or to successfully enter new markets.

Tools for Nurturing Customer Relationships

Relationship marketing has important benefits for both customers and businesses. Most relationship-oriented businesses quickly learn that some customers generate more profitable business than others. The 80/20 principle mentioned earlier in the chapter suggests that 20 percent of a firm's customers account for 80 percent of its sales and profits. A customer in that category has a higher lifetime value than a customer who buys only once or twice, or a customer who makes small purchases.

Businesses shouldn't ignore any customer, but they do need to distribute their marketing dollars wisely. A firm may choose to customize goods or services for high-value customers while working to increase repeat sales of standardized products to less valuable customers. Differentiating between these two groups also helps marketers to focus on each group in an effort to increase their commitment.

Frequency Marketing and Affinity Marketing Programs

Firms try to build and protect customer relationships by using popular techniques, including frequent-buyer or frequent-user programs. These so-called **frequency marketing** programs reward purchasers with cash, rebates, merchandise, or other premiums. Frequency programs have grown more sophisticated over the years. They offer more personalization and customization than in the past. Airlines, hotel groups, restaurants, and many retailers, including grocery stores, use frequency programs. Customers who join the Marriott Rewards program have the option to spend their earned points at nearly 3,000 hotels, resorts, spas, and golf locations in 67 countries and territories worldwide.[40]

Affinity programs are another tool for building emotional links with customers. An affinity program is an organization's marketing effort that targets people who share common interests and activities. Affinity programs are common in the credit card industry. For example, a person can sign up for a credit card that is printed with the logo of a favourite charity, a sports or entertainment celebrity, or a photograph of his or her college or university. MBNA Canada Bank is the largest independent credit card issuer in the world and offers an affinity MasterCard credit card for the University of Toronto.

Many businesses also use co-marketing and co-branding. In a **co-marketing** deal, two businesses jointly market each other's products. When two or more businesses link their names to a single product, **co-branding** occurs. Sometimes, two unlikely businesses team up. When that happens, the marketing sparks can fly—and two very different groups of consumers may come together to buy the same product. For example, Nike and Apple have marketed the Nike + iPod Sport kit. To use this kit, a runner

frequency marketing a marketing initiative that rewards frequent purchases with cash, rebates, merchandise, or other premiums.

affinity program a marketing effort sponsored by an organization that targets people who share common interests and activities.

co-marketing a cooperative arrangement where two businesses jointly market each other's products.

co-branding a cooperative arrangement where two or more businesses team up to closely link their names on a single product.

Affinity programs are a tool for building emotional links with customers. These programs are common in the credit card industry. For example, MBNA Canada Bank offers an affinity MasterCard credit card for the University of Toronto.

inserts a special sensor into a built-in pocket in a Nike + shoe. The sensor matches the runner's activity with workout data and music that plays through the iPod. Consumers can also purchase specially designed Nike workout clothing that has pockets designed to hold an iPod nano itself.[41]

One-on-One Marketing

The ability to customize products and rapidly deliver goods and services is increasingly dependent on technology, such as computer-aided design and computer-aided manufacturing (CAD/CAM). The Internet offers a way for businesses to connect with customers in a direct and personal manner. Companies can take orders for customized products, gather data about buyers, and predict what items a customer might want in the future. Computer databases provide strong support for effective relationship marketing. Marketers can maintain databases on customer tastes, price-range preferences, and lifestyles. They can also quickly obtain names and other information about possible customers. Amazon.com greets each online customer with a list of suggested books he or she might like to purchase. Many online retailers send their customers emails about upcoming sales, new products, and special events.

Small and large companies often use *customer relationship management (CRM)* software technology to help them gather, sort, and interpret data about customers. Software firms develop this software to help businesses build and manage their relationships with customers. For example, QueueBuster is a software product that offers callers the choice of receiving an automated return call instead of waiting on hold for the next available representative. After putting the software in place, travel agency STA reported that its customer satisfaction ratings had improved to 98 percent. This simple solution to customers' frustration helped STA to build customer loyalty. It also helped save STA from lost business.[42]

✓ ASSESSMENT CHECK

11.8.1 What is the lifetime value of a customer?

11.8.2 Discuss the increasing importance of one-on-one marketing efforts.

WHAT'S AHEAD

The next two chapters examine each of the four elements of the marketing mix that marketers use to satisfy their selected target markets. Chapter 12 focuses on products and their distribution through various channels to different outlets. Chapter 13 covers promotion and the various methods marketers use to communicate with their target customers, and strategies for setting prices for different products.

RETURN TO INSIDE BUSINESS

Handmade Items: Etsy.com Has Them All

Lisa Lutz creates her own jewellery and uses Etsy.com to help build her brand recognition and distribution. She also uses Facebook and other social media platforms such as blogs to link online readers back to her business, Bead Crazed, and its website at www.beadcrazed.com/. She writes online, "I love to learn and have taken classes in wirework, ArtClay silver and metalsmithing. While looking for the 'perfect' bead, I discovered lampworking. My hobby quickly turned into a bead crazed obsession, and I have been making lampwork beads for about 4 years now." Although she is a full-time medical technician in microbiology and mother of four, she says that she is happily busy producing and selling her creations online as well as creating customized pieces for customers.

QUESTIONS FOR CRITICAL THINKING

1. How can Bead Crazed and Lisa Lutz generate more attention online?
2. Does Lutz have an advantage producing and selling jewellery online instead of some other art form?
3. What sort of customer is drawn to the artisans selling on Etsy.com?

SUMMARY OF LEARNING OBJECTIVES

LO 11.1 Explain what marketing is and how it creates utility.

Utility is the ability of a good or service to satisfy the wants and needs of customers. The production function creates form utility by converting inputs to finished goods and services. Marketing creates three types of utility—time utility, place utility, and ownership utility—by making the product available when consumers want to buy it, where consumers want to buy it, and arranging for an organized transfer of ownership.

✓ ASSESSMENT CHECK ANSWERS

11.1.1 What is utility? Utility is the ability of a good or service to satisfy the wants and needs of customers.

11.1.2 Identify how marketing creates utility. Marketing creates time utility by making a good or service available when customers want to purchase it, place utility by making the product available in a convenient location, and ownership utility by transferring the product from the buyer to the seller.

LO 11.2 Discuss the evolution of the marketing concept.

The marketing concept refers to a companywide customer focus with the goal of achieving long-term success. This concept is much needed in today's marketplace, which is mainly a buyer's market, where buyers can choose from many goods and services. Marketing now centres on satisfying customers and building long-term relationships with them.

✓ ASSESSMENT CHECK ANSWERS

11.2.1 What is the marketing concept? The marketing concept is a companywide customer focus with the goal of achieving long-term success. According to the marketing concept, success begins with the customer.

11.2.2 How is the marketing concept tied to the relationship and social eras of marketing? Most marketing now centres on the satisfaction of customers and building long-term relationships with them through several channels including the Internet and social media, rather than simply producing and selling goods and services.

LO 11.3 Describe not-for-profit marketing and nontraditional marketing.

Not-for-profit organizations use marketing just as for-profit firms do. Not-for-profit organizations operate in both the public and private sectors. They use marketing to attract volunteers and donations, to make people aware of their existence, and to achieve certain goals for society. Not-for-profit organizations may use several types of nontraditional marketing—person, place, event, cause, or organization marketing. They may use only one type of marketing or a combination of two or more types.

✓ ASSESSMENT CHECK ANSWERS

11.3.1 Why do not-for-profit organizations use marketing? Not-for-profit organizations use marketing to attract volunteers and donors, communicate their message, and achieve their societal goals.

11.3.2 What are the five types of nontraditional marketing used by not-for-profit organizations? The five types of nontraditional marketing are person, place, event, cause, and organization marketing.

LO 11.4 Outline the basic steps in developing a marketing strategy.

All organizations develop marketing strategies to reach their customers. This process involves two steps: first, analyzing the overall market and selecting a target market; and, second, developing a marketing mix that blends elements related to product, distribution, promotion, and pricing decisions.

✓ ASSESSMENT CHECK ANSWERS

11.4.1 Distinguish between consumer products and business products. Business products are goods and services purchased to be used, either directly or indirectly, in the production of other goods for resale. Consumer products are goods and services purchased by the end users.

11.4.2 What are the steps in developing a marketing strategy? The steps in developing a marketing strategy are analyzing the overall market, selecting a target market, and developing a marketing mix.

LO 11.5 Describe the marketing research function.

Marketing research is the information-gathering function that links marketers to the marketplace. It provides valuable information about potential target markets. Firms may generate internal data or gather external data. They may use secondary data or conduct research to obtain primary data. Data mining involves computer searches through customer data to detect patterns or relationships. It is a helpful tool in forecasting various trends such as sales revenues and consumer behaviour.

ASSESSMENT CHECK ANSWERS

11.5.1 What is the difference between primary data and secondary data? Primary data are collected firsthand through observation or surveys. Secondary data are previously published facts that are inexpensive to retrieve and easy to obtain.

11.5.2 What is data mining? Data mining involves using computer searches of customer data to evaluate the data and identify useful trends that may suggest models of real-world business activities.

LO 11.6 Discuss the methods used to segment consumer and business markets.

Consumer markets can be divided according to four criteria: geographical factors; demographic characteristics, such as age and family size; psychographic variables, which involve behavioural and lifestyle profiles; and product-related variables, such as the benefits consumers look for when buying a product or the degree of brand loyalty they feel toward it. Business markets are segmented according to three criteria: geographical characteristics, customer-based specifications for products, and end-user applications.

ASSESSMENT CHECK ANSWERS

11.6.1 What is the most common form of segmentation for consumer markets? The most commonly used consumer market segmentation method is demographics.

11.6.2 What are the three approaches to product-related segmentation? The three approaches to product-related segmentation are by benefits sought, product usage rate, and brand loyalty.

11.6.3 What is end-use segmentation in the B2B market? End-use segmentation focuses on the precise way a B2B purchaser will use a product.

LO 11.7 Outline the determinants of consumer behaviour.

Consumer behaviour refers to end consumers' activities that have direct effects on obtaining, consuming, and disposing of products, and the decision processes before and after these actions. Personal influences on consumer behaviour include an individual's needs and motives, perceptions, attitudes, learned experiences, and self-concept. The interpersonal determinants include cultural influences, social influences, and family influences. Many people within a firm may take part in business purchase decisions, so business buyers must consider a variety of organizational influences in addition to their own preferences.

ASSESSMENT CHECK ANSWERS

11.7.1 Define *consumer behaviour*. Consumer behaviour refers to end consumers' activities that are directly involved in obtaining, consuming, and disposing of products, and the decision processes before and after these actions.

11.7.2 What are some determinants of consumer behaviour? Determinants of consumer behaviour include both personal influences and interpersonal influences. Personal influences include an individual's needs and motives; perceptions, attitudes, and experiences; and self-concept. Interpersonal influences include cultural, social, and family influences.

LO 11.8 Discuss the benefits of, and tools for, relationship marketing.

Relationship marketing is an organization's attempt to develop long-term, cost-effective links with individual customers for mutual benefit. Encouraging good relationships with customers can be part of a firm's vital strategy. By identifying current purchasers and encouraging a positive relationship with them, an organization can efficiently target its best customers, fulfill their needs, and create loyalty. Information technologies, frequency and affinity programs, and one-on-one efforts all help build relationships with customers.

ASSESSMENT CHECK ANSWERS

11.8.1 What is the lifetime value of a customer? The lifetime value of a customer is the total of the revenues and intangible benefits from the customer over the life of the customer's relationship with a firm, minus the amount the company must spend to acquire and serve the customer.

11.8.2 Discuss the increasing importance of one-on-one marketing efforts. One-on-one marketing is increasing in importance as consumers demand more customization in goods and services. One-on-one marketing is also increasingly dependent on technology such as computer-aided design and computer-aided manufacturing (CAD/CAM). The Internet also offers a way for businesses to connect with customers in a direct and personal manner.

BUSINESS TERMS YOU NEED TO KNOW

affinity program 314
business intelligence 303
business-to-business (B2B) product 301
business-to-consumer (B2C) product 299
cause marketing 298
co-branding 314
co-marketing 314
consumer behaviour 311

data mining 304
data warehouse 304
demographic segmentation 306
end-use segmentation 310
event marketing 298
exchange process 293
frequency marketing 314
geographical segmentation 305

lifetime value of a customer 313
marketing 292
marketing concept 295
marketing mix 301
marketing research 302
market segmentation 304
organization marketing 299
person marketing 297

place marketing 297
product-related segmentation 308
psychographic segmentation 308
relationship marketing 312
target market 301
utility 293

REVIEW QUESTIONS

1. Define the four different types of utility and explain how marketing contributes to the creation of utility. Then choose one of the following companies and describe how it creates each type of utility with its goods or services:
    a. Burger King
    b. Polo Ralph Lauren
    c. Indigo bookstore
    d. Supercuts hair salons
    e. Adobe Systems

2. Describe the shift from a seller's market to a buyer's market. Why was this move important to marketers?

3. Describe how an organization might combine person marketing and event marketing. Give an example.

4. Describe how an organization might combine cause marketing and organization marketing. Give an example.

5. Identify each of the following as a consumer product or a business product, or classify it as both:
    a. a cup of coffee
    b. iPad
    c. gasoline
    d. a boat trailer
    e. hand sanitizer
    f. hair gel

6. Identify and describe the four strategies that blend to create a marketing mix.

7. What is a target market? Why is target market selection usually the first step in the development of a marketing strategy?

8. Identify the two strategies that a firm can use to develop a marketing mix for international markets. What are the upsides and downsides of each?

9. Describe the types of data that might be gathered by someone who is thinking of starting an accounting service. How might this businessperson use the data in making the startup decision?

10. Explain each of the methods used to segment consumer and business markets. Which methods are most effective for each of the following and why? (Note that more than one method might be suitable.)
    a. a grocery store featuring organic foods
    b. hair-care products
    c. a tour bus company
    d. a line of baby food
    e. dental insurance
    f. a dry cleaner

11. What are the three major determinants of consumer behaviour? Give an example of how each one might influence a person's purchasing decision.

12. What are the benefits of relationship marketing? Describe how frequency and affinity programs work toward building relationships.

PROJECTS AND TEAMWORK APPLICATIONS

1. On your own or with a classmate, choose one of the following products and create an advertisement that illustrates how your firm creates time, place, and form utility in its delivery of the product to the customer.

   a. an auto repair service

   b. hiking tours

   c. a craft supply store

   d. a pet-sitting service

2. Choose one of the following not-for-profit organizations or find one on your own. Research the organization online to learn more about it. Outline your proposal for a fundraising event. You can base your event on the chapter discussion of nontraditional marketing, such as cause marketing or organization marketing.

   a. Alberta Society for the Prevention of Cruelty to Animals

   b. Prostate Cancer Foundation

   c. Canadian Red Cross

   d. Salvation Army

3. As a marketer, you may be able to classify your firm's goods and services as both business and consumer products. Your company's sales will likely increase because you will build relationships with a new category of customers. On your own or with a classmate, choose one of the following products, and outline a marketing strategy for attracting the classification of customer that is *opposite* from the one listed in parentheses.

   a. a hybrid car (consumer)

   b. an LCD TV (consumer)

   c. a limousine service (business)

   d. office furniture (business)

4. Think of two situations where you were a customer: one situation when you were satisfied with the merchandise you received and one situation when you were not satisfied. List the reasons you were satisfied in the first case and list the reasons you were not satisfied in the second case. Did the failure occur because the seller did not understand your needs?

5. Co-marketing and co-branding are techniques that organizations often use to market their own and each other's products, such as Nike running shoes and the Apple iPod. On your own or with a classmate, choose two firms with goods and/or services you think would work well together for co-marketing separate products or co-branding a single product. Create an advertisement for your co-marketing or co-branding effort.

WEB ASSIGNMENTS

1. **Demographic trends**. The Canadian Census and the *Statistical Abstract of the United States* are excellent sources of demographic and economic data. Visit the websites listed below. On the StatsCan website, click on "By topic" from the list on the left and then view the population data. On the U.S. website, scroll down the list on the left and select "Population." What do the Canadian and American populations currently look like in terms of age and race? What will the population look like in the decades to come?

   www12.statcan.ca/census-recensement/index-eng.cfm
   www.census.gov/compendia/statab

2. **Market segmentation**. Go to the website of Canon Canada and review the company's range of product offerings. Prepare a brief report on how Canon segments its markets.

   www.canon.ca

3. **Customer loyalty programs**. Airlines and hotel chains offer customer loyalty programs. Pick an airline and hotel chain and print out information on the firm's customer loyalty program (two examples are listed here). Bring the material to class to participate in a discussion on this topic.

   www.westjet.com/guest/en/rewards/index.shtml
   www.marriott.com/rewards/rewards-program.mi

Note: Internet Web addresses change frequently. If you don't find the exact sites listed, you may need to access the organization's home page and search from there or use a search engine such as Bing or Google.

12 | PRODUCT AND DISTRIBUTION STRATEGIES

Echo/Getty Images

LEARNING OBJECTIVES

LO 12.1 Explain product strategy and how to classify goods and services.

LO 12.2 Describe the four stages of the product life cycle and their marketing implications.

LO 12.3 Explain how firms identify their products.

LO 12.4 Outline the major components of an effective distribution strategy.

LO 12.5 Explain the concept of wholesaling.

LO 12.6 Describe the types of retailers and retail strategies used.

LO 12.7 Discuss distribution channel decisions and logistics.

INSIDE BUSINESS

Montreal's Fitness City Complex: Bringing Fitness Businesses Together Under One Roof

It is a well-established business model—bring competing businesses together at one location for the convenience of the customer. If customers don't find what they are looking for at one business, they can easily check out the others. That's why we often find car dealerships grouped together in a "car-shopping district." Customers can easily visit a few car dealers and compare their products before making a purchase decision. Car dealerships outside of the main car-shopping district need to offer something very special if they expect shoppers to travel to their business.

This clustering, or grouping, strategy is familiar to us. We see it in large cities in their restaurant districts, fashion districts, and theatre districts. The same idea might be successful for other businesses, too. Think about the possibilities for businesses that do not compete directly, but complement each other by offering related services. These businesses tend to be scattered. Because of their locations, they are not very visible to potential customers. But, by clustering together in one location, customers of one business are more likely to become customers of a complementary business.

An example of this kind of strategic thinking is Fitness City, located near the Trans-Canada Highway in Montreal's suburban area known as the West Island. Fitness City instantly became the largest fitness facility in Quebec when it recently opened its doors. The facility brings together a variety of fitness businesses under one 73,000-square-foot roof to serve customers who are both fitness-conscious and health-conscious.

Fitness City's largest fitness provider is Monster Gym, which takes up 45,000 square feet. Monster Gym has been owned and managed by Carmine Petrillo for more than 20 years. His original gym would have been considered large enough at 8,000 square feet. But the move to the new building provides space to offer even more facilities to Monster Gym's 6,000 members. Monster Gym acts as the "anchor" for the complex because of its 24/7 operating hours, its size, and its large and diverse clientele.

As members walk through the building's main entrance, they pass Cielos Studios, the 9,000-square-foot space dedicated to yoga, Pilates, pole dancing, Zumba, tai chi, erotic dance, meditation, and other equipment-free classes. Like Monster Gym, Cielos was an established West Island business that brought along its diverse customers when it relocated to Fitness City.

The same scenario was true for Grant Brothers Boxing and MMA Gyms, operated by former Canadian Middleweight Champion Otis Grant and his brother Howard, a 1988 Olympian and former Canadian Lightweight Champion. (Another brother, Ryan, operates a Grant Brothers Boxing Gym in Toronto.) These gyms offer boxing, which tends to attract young men. They also offer kick-boxing, which appeals to women because of the aerobic workout and defensive training. According Howard Grant, men and women are often more likely to try boxing and other classes when they see someone of their own age in the ring working out. This is especially true for young adults who look at boxing and other contact sports as part of an overall effort to build and discipline both their bodies and their minds.

The Fitness City complex also offers the services of the Nuance Spa and massage facility, professional physiotherapists, dieticians, trainers, and coaches to help fitness-minded individuals reach their goals. Le Bistro Fit is the new restaurant located in the centre of the complex. It provides healthy meals and beverages for clients to enjoy after their workouts. Each of these individually owned businesses hopes to gain new customers—and revenue—from the mix of clientele that use the complex. In time, each business will see how much it benefits from the success of its neighbours.[1]

CHAPTER 12 OVERVIEW

In this chapter we examine the many ways that organizations design and carry out marketing strategies that address customers' needs and wants. Two of the most powerful tools are strategies that relate to products (which include both goods and services) and strategies that relate to the distribution of those products.

As the Fitness City complex shows, successful companies are deeply aware of their customers' needs. Fitness City continues to build business by adding new service providers, such as food supplements stores and more martial arts specialists. The creation of new products is the lifeblood, or life force, of an organization. Companies must constantly develop new products to ensure their survival and long-term growth.

This chapter focuses on the first two elements of the marketing mix: product and distribution. We begin our discussion of product strategy by describing the classifications of goods and services, customer service, product lines and the product mix, and the product life cycle. Companies often shape their marketing strategies differently depending on the stage of the product life cycle: when they are introducing a new product, when the product has established itself in the marketplace, and when the product is declining in popularity. We also discuss product identification through brand name and distinctive packaging. We then look at how companies foster, or encourage, loyalty to their brands to keep customers coming back for more.

Distribution is the second mix variable discussed. It focuses on moving goods and services from producer to wholesaler to retailer to buyers. Managing the distribution process includes making decisions such as what kind of wholesaler to use and where to offer products for sale. Retailers can range from specialty stores to factory outlets and everything in between. To succeed, retailers must choose suitable customer service, pricing, and location strategies. The chapter ends with a look at logistics, the process of coordinating the flow of information, goods, and services among suppliers and on to final consumers.

PRODUCT STRATEGY

LO 12.1 Explain product strategy and how to classify goods and services.

product a bundle of physical, service, and symbolic characteristics designed to satisfy consumer wants.

What is a product? Most people answer this question by listing a product's physical features. But marketers take a broader view. To marketers, a **product** is a bundle of physical, service, and symbolic characteristics designed to satisfy consumer wants. The chief executive officer of a major tool manufacturer once startled his shareholders when he said, "Last year our customers bought over 1 million quarter-inch drill bits, and none of them wanted to buy the product. They all wanted quarter-inch holes." Product strategy involves much more than just producing a good or service; it focuses on the benefits of a good or service. The marketing conception of a product includes decisions about package design, brand name, trademarks, warranties, product image, new-product development, and customer service. For example, think about your favourite soft drink. Do you like it for its taste alone? Or are you attracted by other qualities, such as clever ads, attractive packaging, overall image, and ease of purchase from vending machines and other convenient locations? These other qualities may influence your choice more than you think.

Classifying Goods and Services

Marketers have found it useful to classify goods and services as either B2C or B2B, depending on whether the purchasers of the particular item are consumers or businesses. These classifications can be subdivided further. Each classification type needs a different competitive strategy.

Classifying Consumer Goods and Services

Consumer goods and services—that is, goods and services used by end consumers who purchase products for their own use and enjoyment and not for resale—are usually classified on the basis of how consumers buy them. Convenience products are items that *consumers purchase* frequently, immediately, and with little effort. For example, such convenience products as newspapers, snacks, candy, coffee, and bread are usually for sale in gas-station stores, vending machines, and local newsstands.

Shopping products are those products that are usually purchased only after the buyer has compared competing products in competing stores. A person who wants to buy a new sofa or dining room table may visit many stores, examine dozens of pieces of furniture, and spend days making the final decision. *Specialty products* are the third category of consumer products. These are products that a purchaser is willing to make a special effort to obtain. The purchaser is already familiar with the item and considers it to have no reasonable substitute. For example, the nearest Mini Cooper dealer may be 75 kilometres away, but if you have decided you want one, you will make the trip.

Note that a shopping product for one person may be a convenience item for someone else. Each item's product classification is based on the buying patterns of most of the people who purchase it.

The interrelationship of the marketing mix factors is shown in **Figure 12.1**. Marketing decision makers need to know the best classification for a specific product. Knowing the most suitable classification helps marketers to understand how the other mix variables will adapt to create a profitable, customer-driven marketing strategy.

Buying a *specialty product* takes extra effort. The Fiat 500 is sold in a limited number of places.

Classifying Business Goods

Business products are goods and services such as paycheque services and huge multifunction copying machines used in operating an organization. They also include machinery, tools, raw materials, components, and buildings used to produce other items for resale. While consumer products are classified by how consumers buy them, business products are classified by their basic characteristics

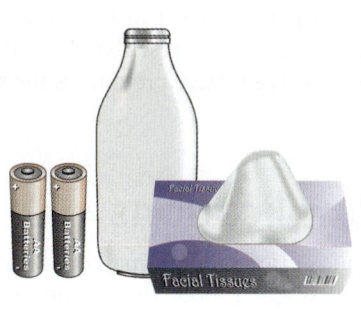

Marketing Strategy Factor	Convenience Product	Shopping Product	Specialty Product
• Purchase Frequency	• Frequent	• Relatively infrequent	• Infrequent
• Store Image	• Unimportant	• Very important	• Important
• Price	• Low	• Relatively high	• High
• Promotion	• By manufacturer	• By manufacturer and retailers	• By manufacturer and retailers
• Distribution Channel	• Many wholesalers and retailers	• Relatively few wholesalers and retailers	• Very few wholesalers and retailers
• Number of Retail Outlets	• Many	• Few	• Very small number; often one per market area

FIGURE 12.1 Marketing Impacts of Consumer Product Classification

and by how they are used. Products that are long lived and relatively expensive are called *capital items*. Less costly products that are consumed within a year are referred to as *expense items*.

B2B products have five basic categories: installations, accessory equipment, component parts and materials, raw materials, and supplies. *Installations* are major capital items, such as new factories, heavy equipment and machinery, and custom-made equipment. Installations are expensive and often involve buyer and seller negotiations that may last for more than a year before a purchase is made. Purchase approval often involves the agreement of many different people—production specialists, purchasing department representatives, and members of top management.

Although *accessory equipment* also includes capital items, these items are usually less expensive and shorter lived than installations, and involve fewer decision makers. Examples include hand tools and fax machines. *Component parts and materials* are finished business goods that become part of a final product, such as disk drives that are sold to computer manufacturers or batteries purchased by automakers. *Raw materials* are farm and natural products used to produce other final products. Examples include milk, wood, leather, and soybeans. *Supplies* are expense items used in a firm's daily operation that do not become part of the final product. Supplies are often referred to as MRO (maintenance, repair, and operating supplies). They include paper clips, light bulbs, and copy paper.

Classifying Services

Services can be classified as either B2C or B2B. Examples of services for consumers include childcare and eldercare centres and auto detail shops. Examples of services for businesses include the Pinkerton security patrol at a local factory and Kelly Services' temporary office workers. Sometimes, a service works in both consumer and business markets. For example, when ServiceMaster cleans the upholstery in a home, it is a B2C service, but when it spruces up the painting system and robots in a manufacturing plant, it is a B2B service.

Services can also be convenience products, shopping products, or specialty products. Which type of product it is will depend on the buying patterns of customers. Services can be distinguished from goods in several ways. First, services are intangible, or immaterial; in contrast, goods are tangible, or material. In addition, services are perishable, or short-lived, because firms cannot store them in inventory. They are also difficult to standardize because they must meet individual customers' needs. Finally, from a buyer's perspective, the service provider is the service; the two are inseparable in the buyer's mind.

Marketing Strategy Implications

The consumer-product classification system is a useful tool in marketing strategy. As shown in Figure 12.1, a new refrigerator is classified as a shopping good. That classification gives its marketers a better idea of how it needs to be promoted, priced, and distributed.

Each group of business products needs a different marketing strategy. Most installations and many component parts are marketed directly from manufacturer to business buyer. That means the promotional emphasis is on personal selling, not on advertising. In contrast, marketers of supplies and accessory equipment rely more on advertising because their products are often sold through an intermediary, such as a wholesaler. Producers of installations and component parts may involve their customers in new-product development, especially when the business product is custom made. Finally, firms selling supplies and accessory equipment place greater emphasis on competitive pricing strategies than do other B2B marketers, who tend to focus more on product quality and customer service.

Product Lines and Product Mix

Few firms do business with only a single product. If their first market entry is successful, they tend to increase their chances for profit and growth by adding new offerings. The iPhone and iPad, with their touch-screen technology and apps, have expanded Apple's product line.

PepsiCo product mix includes Rockstar energy drinks, which are distributed in the United States and Canada by various Pepsi bottling enterprises.

Although most main-stream knowledge workers will probably continue to use conventional computers for some time, touch-screen technology is fast becoming a standard feature in consumer electronics.[2]

A company's **product line** is a group of related products that share physical similarities or are targeted toward a similar market. A **product mix** is the assortment of product lines and individual goods and services that a firm offers to consumers and business users. The Coca-Cola Company and PepsiCo both have product lines that include old standards—Coke Classic and Diet Coke, Pepsi and Diet Pepsi. But recently, Rockstar Energy Drink switched distributors from The Coca-Cola Company to PepsiCo, as a result of The Coca-Cola Company's distribution agreement with competitor Monster energy drink. As part of a multiyear agreement, Rockstar energy drinks are distributed in the United States and Canada by Pepsi Bottling Group, PepsiAmericas, and Pepsi Bottling Ventures, as well as other independent Pepsi bottlers.[3]

Marketers must continually assess their product mix for a few reasons: to ensure company growth, to satisfy changing consumer needs and wants, and to adjust to competitors' offerings. To remain competitive, marketers look for gaps in their product lines and fill them with new offerings or modified versions of existing products. A helpful tool that is frequently used in making product decisions is the product life cycle.

product line a group of related products that share physical similarities or are targeted toward a similar market.

product mix the assortment of product lines and individual goods and services that a firm offers to consumers and business users.

✓ **ASSESSMENT CHECK**

12.1.1 How do consumer products differ from business products?

12.1.2 Differentiate among convenience products, shopping products, and specialty products.

PRODUCT LIFE CYCLE

After a product is on the market, it usually goes through four stages known as the **product life cycle**: introduction, growth, maturity, and decline. As **Figure 12.2** shows, industry sales and profits vary depending on the product's life-cycle stage.

Product life cycles are not set in stone; that is, not all products follow this pattern precisely, and some products may spend different amounts of time in each stage. But the idea of a product life cycle helps the marketing planner to look ahead to new developments throughout the various stages of a product's life. Profits take on a predictable pattern through the stages, and the promotional focus shifts from communicating product information in the early stages to heavy brand promotion in the later stages.

LO 12.2 Describe the four stages of the product life cycle and their marketing implications.

product life cycle the four basic stages in the development of a successful product—introduction, growth, maturity, and decline.

Stages of the Product Life Cycle

In the *introduction stage*, the firm tries to promote demand for its new offering; inform the market about it; give free samples to entice consumers to make a trial purchase; and explain its features, uses, and benefits. Sometimes companies partner at this stage to promote new products. California-based Fuhu is the maker of the Nabi, a first-of-its-kind Android tablet for children. The company

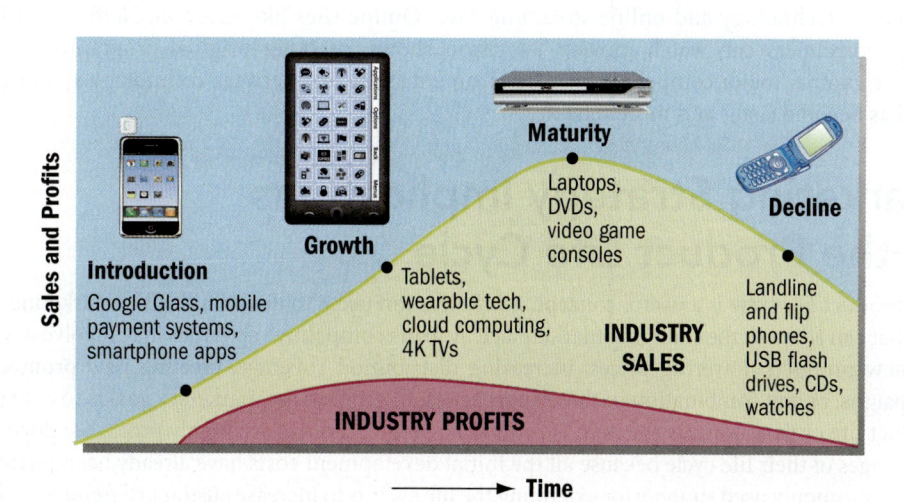

FIGURE 12.2 Stages in the Product Life Cycle

sees the Nabi as a distribution channel for content geared to children and has signed agreements with Nickelodeon and Disney. With retailers Walmart, Target, and Best Buy on board to sell the tablet, the company is developing an audio dock attachment that converts the Nabi into a karaoke machine. Fuhu has announced it will produce an original animated TV series on the BabyFirst cable network that will feature a character modelled after its Nabi tablet.[4]

New-product development costs and extensive introductory promotional campaigns to acquaint prospective buyers with the merits of the innovation, though essential to later success, are expensive and commonly lead to losses in the introductory stage. Some firms are seeking to lower these costs through ultra-low-cost product development, which involves meeting customer needs with the lowest-cost innovations possible, designing from scratch with a stripped-down budget, and the simplest engineering possible. But all these expenditures are necessary if the firm is to profit later.

During the *growth stage*, sales climb quickly as new customers join early users who now are repurchasing the item. Word-of-mouth referrals and continued advertising and other special promotions by the firm induce others to make trial purchases. At this point, the company begins to earn profits on the new product. This success encourages competitors to enter the field with similar offerings, and price competition develops. After its initial success with the Kindle, Amazon faced competition from Barnes & Noble's Nook. Amazon rushed to launch its Kindle for the iPad app, then Barnes & Noble countered with its Nook Color. Since then, the tablet market has become increasingly crowded, with the iPad still dominating the sector. Recent statistics reveal Apple with a 37 percent share of the tablet market, Samsung with 18 percent, and Amazon with 3 percent.[5]

In the *maturity stage,* industry sales at first increase, but they eventually reach a saturation level at which further expansion is difficult. Competition also intensifies, increasing the availability of the product. Firms concentrate on capturing competitors' customers, often dropping prices to further the appeal. Smartphones are in the maturity stage: competitors compete not only on price but also on features such as operating systems, size, weight, battery life, camera and video specifications, and messaging. When flat-screen TVs reached the maturity stage, companies tried to entice customers to buy new ones by offering even bigger screen sizes than before, topping the 90-inch mark. Today, there are continuing developments in colour accuracy, higher resolution, and brighter displays for better screen visibility.[6]

Sales volume fades late in the maturity stage, and some of the weaker competitors leave the market. During this stage, firms promote mature products aggressively to protect their market share and to distinguish their products from those of competitors.

Sales continue to fall in the *decline stage,* the fourth phase of the product life cycle. Profits decline and may become losses as further price cutting occurs in the reduced overall market for the item. Competitors gradually exit, making some profits possible for the remaining firms in the shrinking market. The decline stage usually is caused by a product innovation or a shift in consumer preferences. Sometimes technology change can accelerate the decline stage for a product. For example, at one time more than 90 percent of U.S. homes contained at least one DVD player. Once touted as the ultimate in DVD technology, high-definition DVDs have now been superseded by Blu-ray technology and online streaming sites. Online sites like Amazon, Netflix, and Hulu, where consumers can watch movies, television shows, or other original programming, have become another major competitor for entertainment as the link between technology and distribution has become faster and more reliable.[7]

Marketing Strategy Implications of the Product Life Cycle

The product life cycle is a useful concept. Marketers can use it to design a flexible marketing strategy that can adapt to the changing marketplace. A firm's competitive activities may involve developing new products, lowering prices, increasing distribution coverage, creating new promotional campaigns, or any combination of these approaches. In general, the marketer's goal is to extend the product life cycle as long as the item is profitable. Some products are highly profitable during the later stages of their life cycle because all the initial development costs have already been recovered.

A commonly used strategy for extending the life cycle is to increase customers' frequency of use. (See the "Hit & Miss" feature for a description of Canadian Tire's life cycle and the current upgrades

HIT & MISS

Canadian Tire: Changing with the Times

From coast to coast across Canada, the long-respected Canadian Tire Corporation is a retailing institution. About 85 percent of Canadians live within a 15-minute drive of a store. More than 10,000 Canadians have their cars serviced there every day. Canadian Tire is visited by 40 percent of the adult population at least once a week. It is the most visited nongrocery retailer in the country. Not surprising, Canadian Tire is the top national retailer in gardening, home appliances, home-improvement products, power tools—and, of course, auto parts and accessories. Today, Canadian Tire has 487 associated dealer-owned and corporate-owned stores across Canada employing more 68,000 people.

But it wasn't always this way. It may be hard to imagine, but in 1922 Ontario had about 200,000 automobiles. The same year, brothers John W. and Alfred J. Billes bought the Hamilton Tire & Garage Ltd. in Toronto. Just when Canadians were starting to think about the automobile as a serious form of personal transportation, the Billes brothers were offering parts, a repair service, storage in the winter, and fuel to keep local motorists on the move. As the popularity of automobiles ownership increased, companies like Canadian Tire competed for the attention of customers who would need services for their automobiles and farm vehicles. The Canadian Tire Corporation has grown tremendously. Over the years, it has become a retail centre for auto, sports, leisure, and home products.

The Canadian Tire catalogue was first introduced in 1928 to reach customers in rural and remote areas of the country. The catalogue is still popular today: 9 million copies are printed each year. One thing may be more appreciated by Canadians than the convenience of their local Canadian Tire store or catalogue—finding a stack of Canadian Tire money in their glove compartment. Canadian Tire money was first introduced in 1961 to reward cash-paying customers and to encourage return visits. It has proven to be a huge success as a customer-loyalty plan.

Today, Canadian Tire stores in major city centres and regional shopping malls don't look anything like the small retailer that seemed to show up in every small Canadian town, where it sold sports gear and provincial hunting and fishing licences. The pace of store renovations has been increased to attract more shoppers after early results showed customers' quick acceptance of the new look and product selections. Canadian Tire has introduced financial services, including bank savings accounts, guaranteed investment certificates, credit cards, and mortgages. In 2002, the company acquired Mark's Work Wearhouse casual clothing. In 2011, it bought The Forzani Group of sports shops. Both acquisitions have helped position the firm for future revenue growth. As customers continue to respond to new, larger store formats, Canadian Tire earnings and profits reach ever higher levels. In 2014, gross revenues rose to $12.4 billion. From humble beginnings, the Billes's small family enterprise has grown to become the huge Canadian franchise corporation we know today.

Questions for Critical Thinking

1. What are the greatest challenges facing Canadian Tire today?
2. Which future retailing acquisition would fit well within the Canadian Tire organization?

Sources: Canadian Tire, accessed April 20, 2015, http://corp.canadiantire.ca/EN/Pages/default.aspx; Canadian Tire Annual Report 2014, accessed April 26, 2015, http://corp.canadiantire.ca/EN/Investors/Documents/2014%20Annual%20Report-EN.pdf.

---

the store is making to attract new customers.) Walmart and Shoppers Drug Mart (Pharmaprix in Quebec) offer grocery sections in their stores. Both firms added groceries to increase the frequency of shopper visits. Another strategy is to add new users. Marketers for Old Spice grooming products decided that Old Spice didn't need to be an old-fashioned product. They came up with a campaign to freshen up the product line's image and attract younger men. The new campaign was called "The Man Your Man Could Smell Like." It cleverly poked fun at the idea that merely using Old Spice would make younger men irresistible to women—while promising, with a wink, that it would.[8]

Arm & Hammer used a third approach: it found new uses for its products. The original use of the firm's baking soda was for baking. But Arm & Hammer now promotes its newer uses as a toothpaste, refrigerator freshener, and flame extinguisher. A fourth product life cycle extension strategy is changing package sizes, labels, and product designs. Changing the product design can often mean finding a way to give it an online application. For example, Mattel's doll sales had declined almost 20 percent. The toymaker increased sales by teaming its Barbie doll with the White House Project and the Take Our Daughters and Sons to Work Foundation. Consumers were invited to celebrate Barbie's 125th career by voting online to choose from among architect, computer engineer, environmentalist, news anchor, and surgeon. The winners, announced at the New York Toy Fair, were Computer Engineer Barbie (by popular vote) and News Anchor Barbie (by girls' vote). Both were part of Barbie's "I Can Be" series.[9]

Stages in New-Product Development

New-product development is expensive, time-consuming, and risky. Only about one-third of all new products become success stories. Products can fail for many reasons. Some have not been properly developed and tested, some are poorly packaged, and others don't have enough promotional support or distribution or do not satisfy a consumer need or want. Even successful products reach the end of the decline stage and must be replaced with new-product offerings.

Most of today's newly developed items are aimed at satisfying specific consumer demands. New-product development is more efficient and cost effective because marketers use a systematic, or organized, approach to develop new products. As **Figure 12.3** shows, the new-product development process has six stages. Each stage requires a "go/no-go" decision by management before moving on to the next stages. The development of new products needs large investments in both time and money. The sooner that decision makers can identify a weak product and drop it from further steps, the less time and money will be wasted.

The starting point in the new-product development process is generating ideas for new offerings. Ideas come from many sources, including customer suggestions, suppliers, employees, research scientists, marketing research, inventors outside the firm, and competitive products. The most successful ideas are directly related to satisfying customer needs. Procter & Gamble recently expanded its Febreze home collection by adding the Flameless Luminary In-Home Scent Delivery System. Instead of lighting a potentially dangerous candle, consumers can use a battery-operated, flameless light that distributes fragrance from a decorative, scented shade. The light automatically turns off after four hours. The design was a finalist in the Consumer Packaged Goods—Household Segment category of the Edison Best New Product Awards.[10]

In the second stage, screening removes ideas that do not work with overall company goals or that cannot be developed given the company's resources. Some firms hold open discussions of new-product ideas with specialists who work in different functional areas in the organization.

During the concept development and business analysis phase, further screening occurs. The analysis involves assessing the new product's potential sales, profits, growth rate, and competitive strengths. It also tries to determine whether the new product fits with the company's product, distribution, and promotional resources. At this stage, some companies use *concept testing*—marketing research designed to attract consumers' first reactions to new-product ideas. For example, potential consumers might be asked about proposed brand names and other methods of product identification. *Focus groups* are formal sessions where consumers meet with marketers to discuss what they like or dislike about current products. Sometimes the consumers can test or sample a new offering to provide immediate feedback.

Next, an actual product is developed, subjected to a series of tests, and revised. At this stage, developers may create functioning prototypes, or test models, or detailed descriptions of the product. These designs are the joint responsibility of the firm's development staff and its marketers. The marketers provide feedback on consumer reactions to the proposed product design, colour, and other physical features.

Test marketing introduces a new product and a complete marketing campaign to a selected city or TV coverage area. When marketers look for a test location, they prefer a location or television coverage area with a manageable size, where residents match their target market's demographic profile. During the test marketing stage, the item is sold in a limited area while the company examines both consumer responses to the new offering and the marketing effort used to support the product. Test market results can help managers to decide on the product's likely performance in a full-scale introduction. Some firms skip test marketing because of concerns that the test could reveal their

Funnel stages:
- Generate New Product Ideas
- Screening
- Concept Development and Business Analysis
- Product Development
- Test Marketing*
- Commercialization

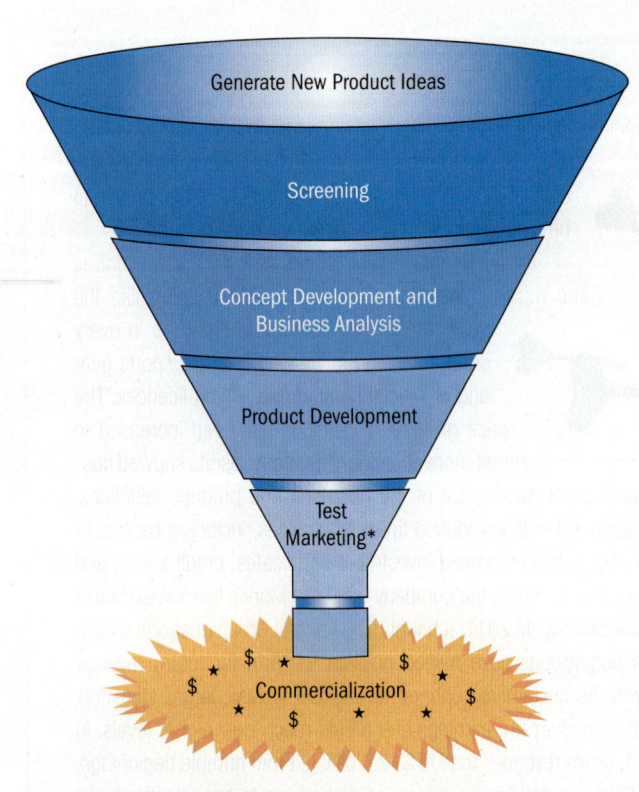

* Some firms skip this step and move directly from product development to commercialization.

FIGURE 12.3 Process for Developing New Goods and Services

test marketing the introduction of a new product and a complete marketing campaign to a selected city or TV coverage area.

Table 12.1 Examples of Products That Failed

PRODUCT	WHY IT FLOPPED
New Coke	Facing stiff competition from other soft drink producers in the mid-1980s, executives at The Coca-Cola Company stopped production on the original Coke and introduced a new, sweeter formula of the soft drink. Consumers were outraged and flooded the company with complaints. Three months later, the company went back to the original Coke formula.
Sony Betamax	Sony's Betamax video recorder was introduced in the mid-1970s. Soon after, a rival company introduced VHS technology, which became the standard for video recordings, and several other competitors introduced VHS machines quickly. Because Sony chose not to license its Betamax technology, and the two technologies were not compatible, consumers needed to choose between Betamax and VHS. As a result, Sony lost its market share.
Pepsi A.M. and Crystal Pepsi	In the late 1980s, Pepsi A.M. was marketed as an alternative to coffee for people who wanted a caffeinated beverage in the morning. Crystal Pepsi was introduced about the same time and was a clear cola drink. Neither product caught on with consumers.
Harley-Davidson Perfume	Fans of the Harley-Davidson brand are considered very loyal to the motorcycle maker. Trying to leverage this loyalty and extend its brand, the company introduced perfume, but consumers didn't buy it.
Colgate Kitchen Entrees	Colgate tried to capitalize on its popular brand by introducing a line of frozen dinners in the early 1980s. Unfortunately, consumers thought of Colgate as a toothpaste brand and not a food company.

Sources: "Top 25 Biggest Product Flops of All Time," *Daily Finance*, accessed March 12, 2014, www.dailyfinance.com/photos/top-25-biggest-product-flops-of-all-time; Len Penzo, "10 Grocery Products That Flopped," accessed March 12, 2014, http://lenpenzo.com/blog/id12478-10-grocery-store-products-that-flopped.html; "Top 10 Bad Beverage Ideas," *Time*, accessed March 12, 2014, http://content.time.com/time/specials/packages/article/0,28804,1913612_1913610_1913608,00.html.

product strategies to the competition. Also, many expenses are involved in doing limited production runs of complex products such as a new auto or refrigerator. Sometimes, these costs are so high that the test marketing stage is skipped, and the development process moves directly to the next stage.

In the final stage, commercialization, the product is made available in the marketplace. This stage is also known as a product launch. Much planning goes into this stage. The firm's strategies for distribution, promotion, and pricing must all work together to support the new product. The videogame-maker Electronic Arts (EA) announced a new distribution strategy for future games. EA will release premium downloadable content (PDLC) for a game before releasing the complete, packaged version. The PDLC will be priced at $15 and will include three to four hours of playing time. The company will invite comments from reviewers and players. It will then make changes to the final version before releasing it for sale.[11]

New-product development is a vital process for twenty-first-century firms: firms need a steady stream of new products to offer their customers; the risks of product failure can be very expensive; and tens of millions of dollars are needed to complete a successful new-product launch. But, as **Table 12.1** shows, success is not guaranteed until the new product achieves customer acceptance. Microsoft introduced a new operating system, Windows Vista, but it never caught on. The next version of Windows, Windows 7, did much better. Another company, DigiScent, launched a new computer device. It was intended to bring the sense of smell to online shopping or browsing. But DigiScent didn't think through its plan carefully. Consumers rejected the idea of having to deal with unwanted aromas. Consumers also gave a thumbs-down on the product's name—iSmell.[12]

ASSESSMENT CHECK

12.2.1 What are the stages of the product life cycle?

12.2.2 What are the marketing implications of each stage?

PRODUCT IDENTIFICATION

LO 12.3 Explain how firms identify their products.

A major part of developing a successful new product is choosing how to identify the product and distinguish it from other products. Both tangible goods and intangible services are identified by brands, brand names, and trademarks. A **brand** is a name, term, sign, symbol, design, or some combination that identifies the products of one firm and shows how they differ from competitors' products. Tropicana, Pepsi, and Gatorade are all made by PepsiCo, but the unique combinations of names and symbols used to market these products sets them apart from other similar products.

brand a name, term, sign, symbol, design, or some combination that identifies the products of one firm and shows how they differ from competitors' offerings.

brand name the part of the brand that is made up of words or letters that form a name. It is used to identify a firm's products and show how they differ from the products of competitors.

trademark a brand that has been given legal protection.

A **brand name** is that part of the brand that is made up of words or letters that form a name. It is used to identify a firm's products and show how they differ from the products of competitors. The brand name is the part of the brand that can be spoken. Many brand names are well known around the world, such as Coca-Cola, McDonald's, American Express, Google, and Nike. McDonald's brand mark, the "golden arches," is also familiar around the world. In 2013, Research In Motion changed its corporate name to BlackBerry, the brand for which it was recognized around the world.

A **trademark** is a brand that has been given legal protection. The protection is granted only to the brand's owner. Trademark protection includes the brand name, design logos, slogans, packaging elements, and product features such as colour and shape. A well-designed trademark, such as the Nike "swoosh," can make a difference in how positively consumers perceive a brand.

Selecting an Effective Brand Name

Good brand names are easy to say, easy to recognize, and easy to remember: Crest, Visa, and Dell are good examples. Global firms face a real problem when selecting brand names. An excellent brand name in one country may be a poor choice in another country. Most languages have a short *a*, so *Coca-Cola* is easy to say almost anywhere. But an advertising campaign for E-Z washing machines failed in the United Kingdom. The British pronounce *z* as "zed." They are not as familiar with American "pronunciation" as Canadians are.

Brand names should also send the right image to the buyer. One effective way to create a name is to link the product with its positioning strategy. The name Purell reinforces the concept of sanitizing hands to protect against germs. Dove soap and beauty products link to the idea of mildness. Taster's Choice instant coffee links to its promotional claim "Tastes and smells like ground roast coffee."

Brand names also must be legally protectable. Trademark law does not allow brand names that contain words in general use, such as *television* or *automobile*. Generic words—words that describe a type of product—cannot be used exclusively by any organization. But sometimes a brand name becomes so popular that it passes into common language and turns into a generic word. Then, the company can no longer use it as a brand name. A long time ago, aspirin, linoleum, and zipper were exclusive brand names. But these words have become generic terms and no longer have legal protection.

To be effective, *brand names* must be easy for consumers to say, recognize, and remember.

Brand Categories

A brand that is offered and promoted by a manufacturer is known as a *manufacturer's* (or *national*) *brand*. Examples are Tide, Cheerios, Windex, Fossil, and Nike. But not all brand names belong to manufacturers; some are the property of retailers or distributors. A *private* (or *store*) *brand* identifies a product that is not linked to the manufacturer; instead, it carries a wholesaler's or retailer's label. Two examples are Sears's Craftsman tools and Loblaw's President's Choice foods.

Another branding decision that marketers must make is whether to use a family branding strategy or an individual branding strategy. A *family brand* is a single brand name used for several related products. Lululemon, Kraft, KitchenAid, Johnson & Johnson, Hewlett-Packard, and Arm & Hammer use a family name for their entire line of products. When a firm using family branding introduces a new product, both customers and retailers recognize the familiar brand name. The promotion of individual products within a product line benefits all the products because the family brand is well known.

Other firms use an *individual branding* strategy by giving a different brand name to each product within a product line. For example, Procter & Gamble has individual brand names for its different laundry detergents—Tide, Cheer, and Gain. Each brand targets a unique market segment. Consumers who want a cold-water detergent can choose Cheer over Tide or Gain, instead of purchasing a competitor's brand. Individual branding also builds competition within a firm and enables the company to increase its overall sales.

Brand Loyalty and Brand Equity

Brands achieve different levels of consumer familiarity and acceptance. For example, a homeowner may insist on Andersen windows when renovating, but may not prefer any brand when buying a loaf of bread. Consumer loyalty can increase a brand's value, so marketers try to strengthen brand loyalty. When a brand image suffers, marketers try to recreate a positive image.

Brand Loyalty

Marketers measure brand loyalty in three stages: brand recognition, brand preference, and brand insistence. *Brand recognition* is brand acceptance that is strong enough that the consumer is aware of the brand, but not strong enough to lead a customer to prefer it over other brands. A consumer might have heard of L'Oréal hair care products, without necessarily preferring those products to Redken products. Marketers can often increase brand recognition through advertising, free samples, and discount coupons.

Brand preference occurs when a consumer chooses one firm's brand over a competitor's. At this stage, the consumer usually uses his or her previous experience when selecting the product. Furniture and other home furnishings fall into this category. Suppose a shopper purchased an IKEA dining room table and chairs and was satisfied with them. This shopper is likely to return to IKEA to purchase a bedroom set. While there, this shopper might also pick up a set of mixing bowls for the kitchen or a lamp for the family room—because this shopper knows and likes the IKEA brand.

During Design Week in New York City, IKEA installed this clever display, which is meant to look like a bus stop. IKEA, the retailer of affordable, well-designed contemporary furniture enjoys *brand insistence*—the ultimate expression of brand loyalty. For devoted IKEA fans, no other brand will do.

Brand insistence is the ultimate degree of brand loyalty. Consumers who have brand insistence will look for a product at another outlet, special-order it from a dealer, order by mail, or search the Internet. Shoppers who insist on IKEA products for their homes may drive an hour or two—making a day excursion of the venture—to visit an IKEA store. The combination of value for the money and the concept of IKEA as a shopping destination have given the brand a unique appeal for shoppers.[13]

Brand-building strategies were once limited to consumer goods, but they are becoming more important for B2B brands. Intel, Xerox, IBM, and service providers such as ServiceMaster and Cisco are among the suppliers who have built brand names among business customers.

Brand Equity

Brand loyalty is at the heart of **brand equity**, the added value that a respected and successful name gives to a product. This value results from a combination of factors: awareness, loyalty, perceived quality, and feelings or images the customer associates with the brand. High brand equity offers financial advantages to a firm because the product represents a large market share. High brand equity can also reduce price sensitivity, which can lead to higher profits. **Figure 12.4** shows the world's 10 most valuable brands and their estimated worth.

Brand awareness is high when the product is the first one that comes to mind when you hear a product category. If someone says "coffee," do you think of Starbucks, Dunkin' Donuts, or Tim Hortons? Brand association is the link between a brand and other favourable images.

Large companies usually assign the task of managing a brand's marketing strategies to a *brand manager*, also called a *product manager*. This marketing professional plans and puts in place the other promotional, pricing, distribution, and product arrangements that lead to strong brand

brand equity the added value that a respected and successful name gives to a product.

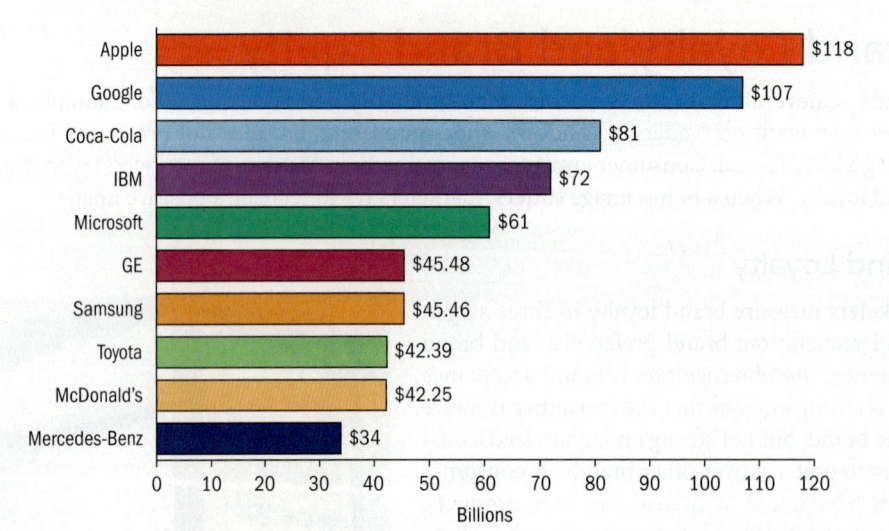

FIGURE 12.4 The World's Ten Most Valuable Brands and Their Worth (in billions of dollars)

Source: Data from "Best Global Brands 2014," *Interbrand*, http://interbrand.com/best-brands/best-global-brands/2014/ranking.

Apple	$118
Google	$107
Coca-Cola	$81
IBM	$72
Microsoft	$61
GE	$45.48
Samsung	$45.46
Toyota	$42.39
McDonald's	$42.25
Mercedes-Benz	$34

category advisor the individual that the business customer assigns as the major supplier to deal with all the other suppliers for a project. The category advisor also presents the entire package to the business buyer.

equity. A *category manager*, a newer type of professional, oversees an entire group of products. Unlike traditional brand managers or product managers, category managers have profit responsibility for their product group. These managers are assisted by associates, usually called *analysts*. Part of the shift to category management was started by large retailers. They realized they could benefit from the marketing power of large grocery and household goods producers such as Kraft and Procter & Gamble. As a result, producers began to focus their attention on in-store merchandising instead of mass-market advertising. A few years ago, Kraft reorganized its sales force so that each representative was responsible for a retailer's needs instead of just promoting a single brand.

A **category advisor** functions in the B2B context. This individual is the major supplier that a business customer assigns to deal with all the other suppliers for a project. The category advisor also presents the entire package to the business buyer.

Packages and Labels

Packaging and labels are needed for product identification. They also play an important role in a firm's overall product strategy. Packaging affects an item's durability, image, and convenience. It is also one of the biggest costs in many consumer products. Consumer demand has led to smaller, more environmentally friendly packages. Box manufacturers and chemical companies are working to create more compact packaging that is made from renewable sources and is recyclable. As explained in the "Going Green" feature, Frito-Lay introduced compostable packaging for its SunChips multigrain snacks. One-third of North America's waste consists of containers and packaging, much of it from fast-food chains. Quiznos recently launched its "Eat Toasty, Be Green" campaign to introduce its new, environmentally friendly packaging. The restaurant chain now uses 100 percent compostable, wax-coated paper cups; salad containers made of renewable sugar cane; napkins made from 100 percent recycled materials; and plastic lids made from 30 percent recycled polyethylene terephthalate (PET) bottles. Even the employees' uniforms were changed—the hats and aprons are now made from 100 percent recycled soda bottles.[14]

Choosing the right package is especially important in international marketing. Marketers need to be aware of language variations and cultural preferences. Consumers in African nations

Consumer demand has led to more environmentally friendly packages. Box manufacturers and chemical companies are working to create more compact packaging that is made from renewable sources and is recyclable. Frito-Lay introduced compostable packaging for its SunChips multigrain snacks.

GOING GREEN

SUNCHIPS INTRODUCES GREENER PACKAGING

Everybody loves to snack on chips. But nobody can love what happens to the empty bag. It eventually ends up in a landfill—and may never decompose. Frito-Lay's brand SunChips aimed to change all that. On Earth Day 2009, it introduced what it called "the world's first compostable chip bag."

In a recent survey, 75 percent of those questioned thought that recyclable packaging was "somewhat important," and 51 percent felt that compostable packaging was "somewhat important." A recyclable item can be used repeatedly, whereas a compostable item breaks down in the presence of water and oxygen.

The company had to meet the challenge of developing packaging that was ecologically sound while also preserving the contents. After four years of research and testing, the company had a bag made of more than 90 percent plant-based, and therefore renewable, materials. The outer layer is made of corn-based polylactic acid (PLA). Although the bag is 100 percent compostable, researchers are working on an environmentally friendly inner layer that will keep the contents crisp and edible. Frito-Lay makes it clear that the bag decomposes most quickly—in about 14 weeks—in a hot, active composting bin. If the bag is simply left on the ground, it will still break down, but less quickly.

The new bag sounds a little different from its old packaging. But Frito-Lay assured its customers that SunChips still taste the same. It even promoted the difference as the "new sound of green" and included a clip of the sound on its website, along with a link to Facebook.

The Biodegradable Products Institute certified the new packaging, but getting North Americans to recognize the need for composting is another matter. A Frito-Lay executive acknowledged the challenge—and the opportunity to educate consumers. What was not expected was an 11 percent drop in sales and public ridicule over the "noise" made when consumers handled the new packaging material. Marketers learned a hard lesson: Although the socially responsible green packaging was popular with most consumers and most of society, many customers avoided the product because of this effect. As a result, the company returned to the original packaging for all but the original flavour chips. Frito-Lay continues to search for new materials that are not quite so noisy.

Questions for Critical Thinking

1. What role did the new, compostable packaging play in the overall marketing strategy for SunChips?

2. How do you think SunChips can most effectively educate North Americans about the importance of composting?

Sources: Bruce Horovitz, "Frito-Lay Sends Noisy, 'Green' SunChips Bag to the Dump," *USA Today*, October 5, 2010, accessed May 9, 2012, www.usatoday.com/money/industries/food/2010-10-05-sunchips05_ST_N.html; SunChips, accessed April 20, 2015, www.sunchips.com; Kate Galbraith, "A Compostable Chips Bag Hits the Shelves," *New York Times*, March 16, 2010, http://green.blogs.nytimes.com/2010/03/16/a-compostable-chips-bag-hits-the-shelves/?_r=0; Kathryn Siranosian, "New SunChips Bag: 90% Plant-Based, 100% Compostable," *Triple Pundit*, February 22, 2010, www.triplepundit.com/2010/02/new-sunchips-bag-compostable.

---

often prefer bold colours, but use of the country's flag colours can lead to problems. Some countries don't like to see other uses of their flag. Also, Africans often associate red with death or witchcraft. Package size can vary depending on a country's purchasing patterns and market conditions. In countries where many people have only small refrigerators, consumers may want to buy their beverages one at a time instead of in six-packs. Package weight is another important issue because shipping costs are often based on weight.

Labelling is another important part of the packaging process. In Canada, companies must meet labelling laws by providing enough information so that consumers can compare competitive products. In the case of food packaging, labelling must include nutritional information. Marketers who ship products to other countries must meet the labelling requirements in those nations. They need to know the answers to the following questions:

- Does the information on the labels need to be in more than one language?
- Do ingredients need to be listed?
- Do the labels give enough information about the product to meet government standards?

Another important part of packaging and labelling is the *universal product code (UPC)*. This bar code is read by the optical scanners that link the UPC to a product and print the name of the item and the price on a receipt. For many stores, these identifiers are useful for packaging and labelling, for simplifying and speeding retail transactions, and for evaluating customer purchases and controlling inventory. Radio-frequency identification (RFID) technology uses embedded chips that can broadcast their product information to receivers. It is unlikely, however, that they will replace bar codes.

✓ ASSESSMENT CHECK

12.3.1 Differentiate among a brand, a brand name, and a trademark.

12.3.2 Define *brand equity*.

LO 12.4 Outline the major components of an effective distribution strategy.

DISTRIBUTION STRATEGY

The second element of the marketing mix is the **distribution strategy**. This strategy is a plan that deals with the marketing activities and institutions that get the right good or service to the firm's customers. Distribution decisions involve selecting the suitable types of transportation, warehousing, inventory control, order processing, and marketing channels. Marketing channels are usually made up of intermediaries such as retailers and wholesalers that move a product from producer to final purchaser.

Two major parts of an organization's distribution strategy are distribution channels and physical distribution. **Distribution channels** are the paths that products—and their legal ownership—follow from producer to consumer or business user. All organizations use these channels to distribute their goods and services. **Physical distribution** is the actual movement of products from producer to consumers or business users. Physical distribution covers a broad range of activities, including customer service, transportation, inventory control, materials handling, order processing, and warehousing. As explained in the "Hit & Miss" feature, Gourmet Chips and Sauces, a Montreal food distributor, is building a distribution network of retailers across Canada for its imported and domestic lines of all-natural extremely hot products.

distribution strategy a plan that deals with the marketing activities and institutions that get the right good or service to the firm's customers.

distribution channels the paths that products—and their legal ownership—follow from producer to consumers or business users.

physical distribution the actual movement of products from producer to consumers or business users.

Distribution Channels

Marketers' first decision in distribution channel selection is to choose which type of channel will best meet both their firm's marketing objectives and the needs of their customers. As shown in **Figure 12.5**, marketers can choose to use either a *direct distribution channel* or a *marketing intermediary*. A distribution channel carries goods directly from producer to the consumer or business user. A *marketing intermediary* (also called a *middleman*) is a business firm that moves goods from their producers to consumers or business users. It usually involves several different marketing intermediaries. Marketing intermediaries help the distribution channel operate smoothly through

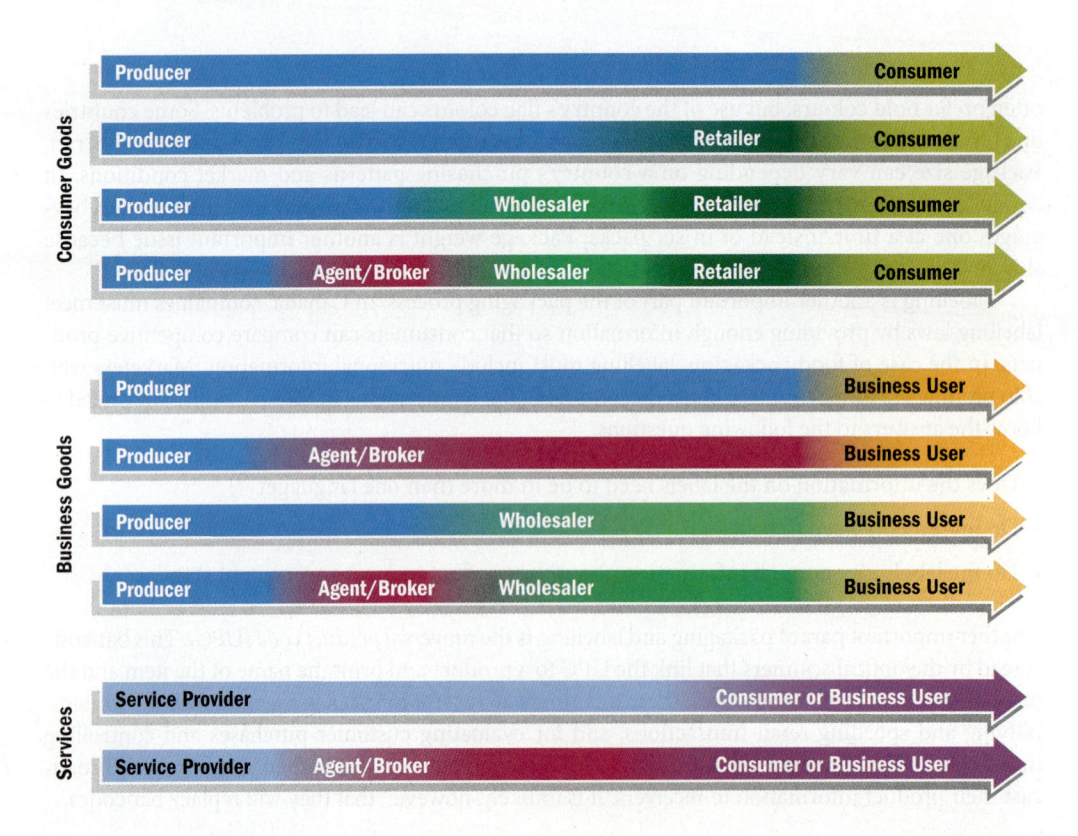

Consumer Goods
- Producer → Consumer
- Producer → Retailer → Consumer
- Producer → Wholesaler → Retailer → Consumer
- Producer → Agent/Broker → Wholesaler → Retailer → Consumer

Business Goods
- Producer → Business User
- Producer → Agent/Broker → Business User
- Producer → Wholesaler → Business User
- Producer → Agent/Broker → Wholesaler → Business User

Services
- Service Provider → Consumer or Business User
- Service Provider → Agent/Broker → Consumer or Business User

FIGURE 12.5 Alternative Distribution Channels

HIT & MISS

Gourmet Chips & Sauces Targets a Niche Market

The "heat levels" of these products differ. Some are mild, like Aubrey D.'s Condiments, Sweet Death, Jalapeño Death Sauces, and Chipotle Death Rain Potato Chips. Others are insanely hot, like Ultra Death Sauce and XXX Hot Habañero Salsa. And when Gourmet Chips & Sauces talks about the "heat level," they're talking about the "extreme end" of the market. With every bite, warning labels and fire alarm bells go off.

The gourmet market for high-quality "extremely hot" and spicy chips and sauces is small when compared with the variety and sales volumes offered by the industry's leaders, such as PepsiCo. PepsiCo leads the market by selling products with highly visible and recognizable brands such as Frito-Lay, Tostitos, and Doritos.

To compete with companies like PepsiCo, smaller firms can choose to focus on a niche in the marketplace. They can try to set themselves apart to attract customers who want something that is different from all the mass-market products.

Montreal-based Gourmet Chips & Sauces produces its own line of Aubrey D.'s Gourmet Condiments. It also imports a select line of Blair's sauces and chips from the United States and distributes this product for sale across Canada. This line of hot and spicy potato chips and sauces are all handcrafted to ensure top quality. They are made from natural ingredients, contain no preservatives or trans fats, and are gluten-free. The chips are kettle-cooked in canola or sunflower oil. Along with the sauces, they are a healthier alternative to the mass-market snacks typically found.

The limited distribution is a problem. Customers need to make more of an effort to buy these products, compared with the PepsiCo products that seem to be for sale everywhere. But the limited distribution has led to a growing niche market of premium customers and retailers who recognize the superior quality and unique product value. As a result, many customers who have tried the products are prepared to spend time looking for them. They are also prepared to pay a small premium in price. Retailers want to offer their customers something unique. The premium price is also a welcome contribution to their businesses.

Questions for Critical Thinking

1. How can Gourmet Chips & Sauces build its distribution network of grocery and convenience stores across Canada?
2. What other products could the firm add to its line?

Sources: Gourmet Chips & Sauces, accessed April 20, 2015, www.gourmetchip.com; interviews with company owner, Aubrey Zelman, March 15, 2015, and November 15, 2011.

---

several activities: buying, selling, storing, and transporting products; sorting and grading bulky items; and providing information to other channel members. The two main categories of marketing intermediaries are wholesalers and retailers.

No one channel suits every product. The best channel depends on the circumstances of the market and on customer needs. The most suitable channel choice may also change over time as new opportunities arise and marketers try to maintain their competitiveness.

Direct Distribution

The shortest and simplest way to connect producers and customers is by direct contact between the two parties. This method is most commonly used in the B2B market. Other examples of direct distribution occur when consumers buy fresh fruits and vegetables at roadside stands or farmers markets. Direct distribution can also be found in services, such as banking, 10-minute oil changes, and ear piercing.

Direct distribution is often found in the marketing of relatively expensive, complex products that may require demonstrations. Direct contacts between producers and business buyers are used to market most major B2B products, such as installations, accessory equipment, component parts, business services, and even raw materials. The Internet has also made direct distribution an attractive option for many retail companies and service providers. FedEx customers have long used online tools to track conventional shipments. FedEx's new International Priority Direct Distribution service allows users to ship more than one package from a single country of origin to different recipients in a single destination country. The packages are cleared through customs as a single shipment. In addition, multiple shipments to multiple recipients in multiple European

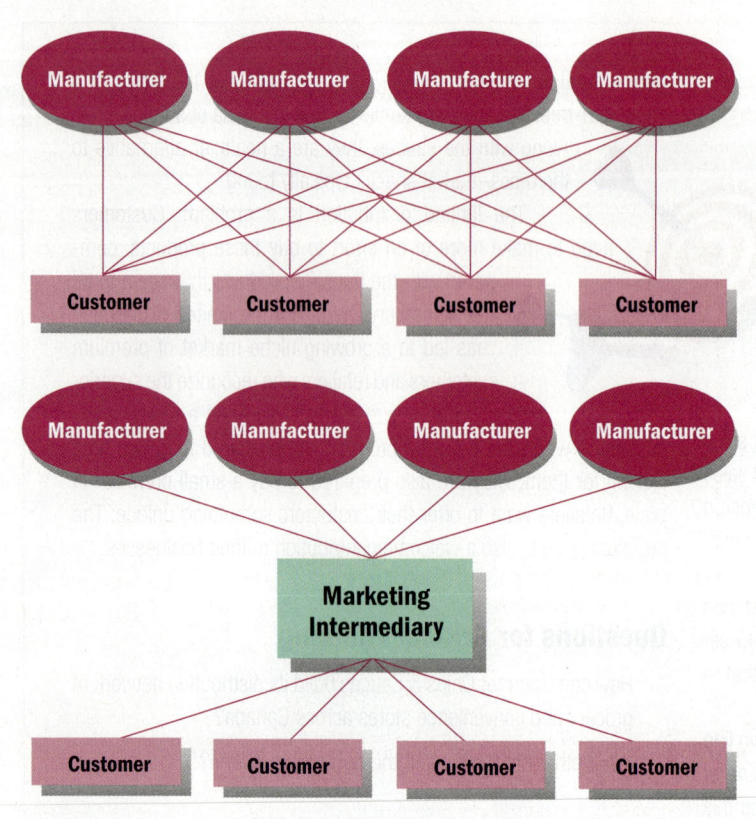

Distribution Channels Using Marketing Intermediaries

Direct channels allow producers to have simple and straightforward connections with their customers. But the list of channel alternatives in Figure 12.5 suggests that direct distribution is not always the best choice. Some products sell in small quantities for relatively low prices to thousands of widely scattered consumers. Makers of such products cannot cost-effectively contact each of their customers. Instead, they distribute products through specialized intermediaries called *wholesalers* and *retailers*.

You might think that adding intermediaries to the distribution process would increase the final cost of products. But adding intermediaries often lowers consumer prices. Intermediaries such as wholesalers and retailers often add significant value to a product as it moves through the distribution channel. They add value by creating utility, providing additional services, and reducing costs.

Marketing utility is created when intermediaries help ensure that products are available for sale when and where customers want to purchase them. For example, if you want something warm to eat on a cold winter night, you don't call Campbell's Soup and ask them to ship a can of chicken noodle soup. Instead, you go to the nearest grocery store, where you find utility in the form of product availability—a can of Campbell's chicken noodle soup on the grocery store shelf. Intermediaries perform important services such as transporting merchandise to convenient locations. Finally, a marketing intermediary represents numerous producers, which can cut the costs of buying and selling. As **Figure 12.6** illustrates, four manufacturers each selling directly to four consumers requires 16 separate transactions. Adding a marketing intermediary, such as a retailer, cuts the number of necessary transactions to eight.

FIGURE 12.6 Reducing Transactions through Marketing Intermediaries

✓ ASSESSMENT CHECK

12.4.1 Define *distribution channels*.

12.4.2 What is a marketing intermediary?

LO 12.5 Explain the concept of wholesaling.

WHOLESALING

A **wholesaler** is a distribution channel member that sells primarily to retailers, other wholesalers, or business users. For example, Sysco is a wholesaler that buys food products from producers and then resells them to restaurants, hotels, and other institutions in the United States and Canada.

Wholesaling is a crucial part of the distribution channel for many products, especially consumer goods and business supplies. Wholesaling intermediaries can be classified on the basis of ownership: some are owned by manufacturers, some are owned by retailers, and others are independently owned. Statistics Canada reports that Canada has approximately 111,500 wholesale enterprises located mostly in Ontario (39 percent) and Quebec (23 percent). The United States has about 486,000 wholesalers, and two-thirds of them have fewer than 20 employees. In many product categories, Canadian wholesalers compete with American wholesalers for customers anywhere in North America.[16]

wholesaler a distribution channel member that sells primarily to retailers, other wholesalers, or business users.

Manufacturer-Owned Wholesaling Intermediaries

A manufacturer's marketing manager may decide to distribute goods directly through company-owned facilities to control distribution or customer service. Firms operate two main types of manufacturer-owned wholesaling intermediaries: sales branches and sales offices.

Sales branches stock the products they distribute and fill orders from their inventories. They also provide offices for sales representatives. Sales branches are common in the chemical, petroleum products, motor vehicle, and machine and equipment industries.

A *sales office* is exactly what its name implies: an office for a producer's salespeople. Manufacturers set up sales offices in various regions to support local selling efforts and improve customer service. Some kitchen and bath fixture manufacturers maintain showrooms to display their products. Builders and decorators can visit these showrooms to see how the finished items will look. Unlike sales branches, sales offices do not store any inventory. When a customer orders from a showroom or other sales office, the merchandise is delivered from a separate warehouse.

Independent Wholesaling Intermediaries

An independent wholesaling intermediary is a business that represents several different manufacturers and sells to retailers, manufacturers, and other business accounts. Independent wholesalers can be either merchant wholesalers or agents and brokers, depending on whether they take title to (legal ownership of) the products they handle.

Merchant wholesalers, like apparel wholesaler WholesaleSarong.com, are independently owned wholesaling intermediaries. They take title to, or legal ownership of, the goods they handle. Within this category, a *full-function merchant wholesaler* provides an assortment of services for retailers or industrial buyers, such as warehousing, shipping, and even financing. A subtype of full-function merchant is a *rack jobber*. This type of firm stocks, displays, and services specific retail products, such as paperback books or greeting cards in a drugstore or supermarket. The retailer usually receives a commission that is based on actual sales. This commission is considered to be payment for providing merchandise space to a rack jobber.

A *limited-function merchant wholesaler* also takes legal title to the products it handles, but it provides fewer services to the retailers it sells to. Some limited-function merchant wholesalers only warehouse products and do not offer delivery services. Others may warehouse products and deliver them but provide no financing. One type of limited-function merchant wholesaler is a *drop shipper*. Drop shippers operate in the coal and lumber industries and in other industries that deal in bulky products, where no single producer can provide a complete assortment. Drop shippers provide access to many related goods by contacting numerous producers and negotiating the best possible prices. To control costs, producers usually ship such products directly to the drop shipper's customers.

Another category of independent wholesaling intermediaries consists of *agents* and *brokers*. They may or may not take physical possession of the goods they handle, but they never take title, or ownership. They work mainly to bring buyers and sellers together. Stockbrokers, such as Scotiabank's ScotiaMcLeod investment dealers, and real estate agents, such as RE/MAX realtors, perform functions similar to those of agents and brokers, but at the retail level. They do not take title to the sellers' property; instead, they create time and ownership utility for both buyer and seller by helping to carry out buying and selling transactions.

Manufacturers' reps act as independent sales forces by representing the manufacturers of related but noncompeting products. These agent intermediaries are sometimes referred to as *manufacturers' agents*. They receive commissions that are based on a percentage of the sales they make.

Retailer-Owned Cooperatives and Buying Offices

Retailers sometimes work together to form their own wholesaling organizations. Such organizations can take the form of either a buying group or a cooperative. The retailers set up the new operation to reduce costs or to provide some service that is not readily available in the marketplace.

ASSESSMENT CHECK

12.5.1 Define *wholesaling*.

12.5.2 Differentiate between a merchant wholesaler and an agent or broker in terms of title to the goods.

For example, to achieve cost savings through quantity purchases, independent retailers may form a buying group that negotiates bulk sales with manufacturers. Federated Co-operatives Limited (FCL) is a Western Canada-based cooperative that is owned by approximately 250 retail cooperatives. These retail co-ops are the "members" of FCL. FCL provides central wholesaling, manufacturing, and administrative services to its member owners. Together, FCL and its member owners are known as the Co-operative Retailing System (CRS).[17] In a cooperative, an independent group of retailers may decide to work together to share functions such as shipping or warehousing.

LO 12.6 Describe the types of retailers and retail strategies used.

retailers distribution channel members that sell goods and services to individuals for their own use, not for resale.

RETAILING

Retailers, in contrast to wholesalers, are distribution channel members that sell goods and services to individuals for their own use, not for resale. Consumers usually buy their food, clothing, shampoo, furniture, and appliances from some type of retailer. Your grocery store may have bought some of its dairy products from a cooperative wholesaler, such as Quebec-based Agropur, and then resold them to you.

Retailers are the final link—the so-called "last three feet"—of the distribution channel. Retailers are often the only channel members that deal directly with consumers. That means retailers need to remain alert to changing consumer needs. For example, soaring gas prices affect consumers' budgets: they may make fewer trips to the mall and may cut back on nonessential purchases. As a result, retailers may need to offer special sales or events to encourage customers to visit their shops. Retailers also need to keep pace with developments in the fast-changing business environment, such as disruptions in the delivery of supplies because of widespread wildfires or storms.

Nonstore Retailers

Retailers are divided into two categories: store retailers and nonstore retailers. As **Figure 12.7** illustrates, nonstore retailing includes four forms: direct-response retailing, Internet retailing, automatic merchandising, and direct selling. *Direct-response retailing* reaches consumers through catalogues; telemarketing; and even magazine, newspaper, and television ads. Shoppers order goods by mail, telephone, computer, and fax machine. Their purchases are delivered to their home, or shoppers pick up their purchases at a local store.

Internet retailing is the second form of nonstore retailing. Tens of thousands of retailers have set up shop online. Internet sales are growing at a rate of about 5 percent a year (as total retail sales decline). Today, North American online sales account for about 6 percent of total retail sales.[18] Hundreds of Internet enterprises shut down during the first few years of the twenty-first century. The firms that survived have stronger business models than those that failed. Two examples of successful pure dot-com businesses are Amazon and eBay. Retailing has seen a major shift: many traditional bricks-and-mortar retailers have set up online shopping through their own websites to compete with pure dot-com start-ups. Best Buy and Walmart report strong online sales. Shopping sites are among the most popular Internet destinations, and the most common products purchased online include electronics, clothing, household goods, and office supplies.

The last two forms of nonstore retailing are automatic merchandising and direct selling. *Automatic merchandising* provides convenience through the use of vending machines. Automated teller machines (ATMs) may soon join vending machines as banks find new ways to compete for customers. In the United States, NCR Corporation, a leading manufacturer of ATMs, will soon be putting human tellers on its screens. The new interactive teller includes human help to assist customers with transactions in English or Spanish, with more languages to be added in the future. Bank of

FIGURE 12.7 Types of Nonstore Retailing

Nonstore Retailers

- **Direct-Response Retailing Examples:** sales through catalogues; telemarketing; and magazine, newspaper, and television ads
- **Internet Retailing Examples:** sales through virtual storefronts, Web-based sellers, and the websites of bricks-and-mortar retailers
- **Automatic Merchandising Examples:** sales of such consumer products as candy, soft drinks, ice, chewing gum, sandwiches, and soup through vending machines
- **Direct Selling Examples:** direct manufacturer-to-consumer sales through party plans and direct contact by Amway, Home & Garden Party decorations, and Electrolux vacuum cleaner salespeople

America hopes the use of remote tellers at its ATMs will help build deeper customer relationships.[19] *Direct selling* includes direct-to-consumer sales by Pampered Chef kitchen representatives and salespeople for Silpada sterling silver jewellery through party-plan selling methods. Both are forms of direct selling.

Companies that once used telemarketing to attract new customers have been faced with consumer resistance to intrusive phone calls. Among the growing barriers are caller ID, call-blocking devices such as the TeleZapper, and the National Do Not Call List (DNCL). The DNCL makes it illegal for most companies to call people who have registered their phone number. As a result, many companies, including telecommunications and regional utilities, now send direct-mail pieces to promote such services as phones, cable television, and natural gas.

Bank of America hopes the use of remote human tellers at its ATMs will build stronger customer relationships.

Store Retailers

In-store sales still result in more sales than nonstore retailing such as direct-response retailing and Internet selling. Store retailers range in size from tiny newsstands to multi-storey department stores and large warehouse-style retailers such as Costco. **Table 12.2** lists the different types of store retailers with examples of each type. Clearly, retailing can take many approaches. Retail outlets must choose among these approaches to sell a variety of services and product lines offered at a range of prices.

Table 12.2 Types of Retail Stores

STORE TYPE	DESCRIPTION	EXAMPLE
Specialty store	Offers a complete selection in a narrow line of merchandise	Choices Markets, Bass Pro Shops, Golf Town, Williams-Sonoma
Convenience store	Offers staple convenience goods, easily accessible locations, extended store hours, and rapid checkouts	7-Eleven, Boni Soir, Mac's
Discount store	Offers wide selection of merchandise at low prices; off-price discounters offer designer or brand-name merchandise	Walmart, Giant Tiger, Army & Navy
Warehouse club	Large, warehouse-style store selling food and general merchandise at discount prices to membership card-holders	Costco, DirectBuy
Factory outlet	Manufacturer-owned store selling seconds, production overruns, or discontinued lines	Adidas, Tommy Hilfiger, Pottery Barn, Ralph Lauren
Supermarket	Large, self-service retailer offering a wide selection of food and nonfood merchandise	Safeway, Whole Foods Market, Loblaw
Supercentre	Giant store offering food and general merchandise at discount prices	Walmart Supercentre, Real Canadian Superstore
Department store	Offers a wide variety of merchandise selections (furniture, cosmetics, housewares, clothing) and many customer services	Hudson's Bay

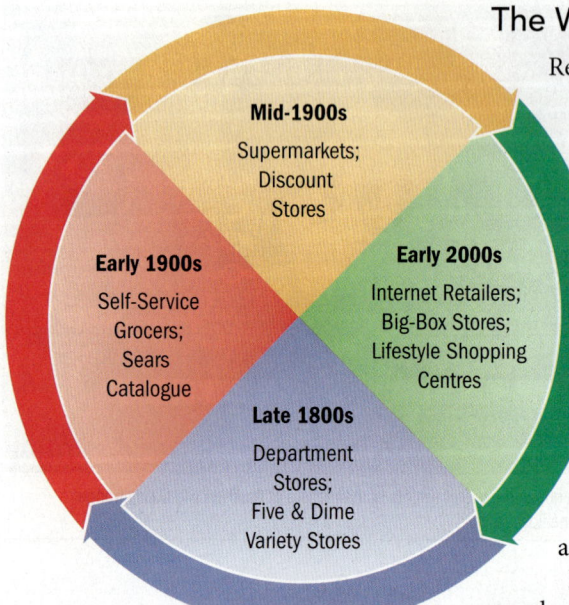

The Wheel of Retailing

Retailers face constant change as new stores replace older stores. In a process called the *wheel of retailing*, new retailers enter the market by reducing services so they can offer lower prices. For example, supermarkets and discount stores gained their market position by offering low prices and limited service. Some of these new retailers slowly add services as they grow. In a few years, they become "older stores" and are the targets of new retailers.

As **Figure 12.8** illustrates, most major developments in retailing appear to fit the wheel pattern. The low-price, limited-service strategy describes supermarkets, catalogue retailers, discount stores, Internet retailers, and "big-box" stores, such as PetSmart and Office Depot. Corner grocery stores have led to supermarkets and then to warehouse clubs such as Costco. Department stores have lost market share to discount clothing retailers such as Target and Winners. Independent bookstores have lost business to giant chains such as Chapters Indigo and online-only sellers such as Amazon.ca and Buy.ca.

But the wheel of retailing does not fit every pattern of retail evolution. For example, automatic merchandising has always been a relatively high-priced retail method. The wheel of retailing has benefits for retailers. It gives retail managers a general idea of what to expect during the evolution of retailing. It also shows that business success involves the "survival of the fittest." Retailers that fail to change will fail to survive.

FIGURE 12.8 The Wheel of Retailing

- Mid-1900s: Supermarkets; Discount Stores
- Early 1900s: Self-Service Grocers; Sears Catalogue
- Early 2000s: Internet Retailers; Big-Box Stores; Lifestyle Shopping Centres
- Late 1800s: Department Stores; Five & Dime Variety Stores

How Retailers Compete

Retailers compete with each other in many ways. Nonstore retailers focus on making the shopping experience as convenient as possible. Shoppers at store retailers such as Holt Renfrew enjoy a luxurious atmosphere and personal service.

Like manufacturers, retailers must develop marketing strategies that are based on goals and strategic plans. Successful retailers use images that alert consumers to the stores' identities and the shopping experiences they provide. To create that image, all parts of a retailer's strategy must work together and complement each other. Retailers must first identify their target markets, and then choose the strategies for merchandising, customer service, pricing, and location that will attract customers in their target market segments.

Identifying a Target Market

The first step in developing a competitive retailing strategy is to select a target market. This choice requires careful evaluation of the market segment's size, profit potential, and its current level of competition. For example, bargain stores, such as Dollar Store, target consumers who are extremely price-conscious; while convenience stores, such as 7-Eleven, target consumers who want an easy way to purchase items they buy frequently. Seventh Generation makes "green" products for household cleaning and personal care. It began as a mail-order company, then started selling at natural-food stores. It grew into a major business whose products were featured at supermarkets nationwide and at Amazon.ca. Seventh Generation is committed to increasing consumer awareness of environmentally safe cleaning and household products. It recently began its "Protecting Planet Home" campaign. The company plans to build on its 45 percent profits by launching its first national marketing campaign online, in print, and in TV commercials. The company's goal is to get 45 percent of North American households to try at least one Seventh Generation product.[20]

Seventh Generation identified its *target market* as those people who are committed to using environmentally safe products for household cleaning.

Selecting a Product Strategy

Next, the retailer must develop a product strategy to decide on the best mix of merchandise to carry to satisfy its target market. Retail strategists must decide on the general product categories, product lines, and the variety to offer. Sometimes this decision involves expanding or reducing the product mix. Almost 20 years ago, Under Armour began making tee shirts to help athletes stay cool and dry. Since then, the company has expanded its brand to include women's and children's clothing, as well as football cleats and running shoes.[21]

Shaping a Customer Service Strategy

A retailer's customer service strategy focuses on attracting and retaining target customers to maximize sales and profits. Some stores offer a wide variety of services, such as gift wrapping, alterations, returns, interior design services, and delivery. Other stores offer only basic customer service, and they feature their low prices instead. Some grocery shoppers find convenience online, by using a service that selects grocery items, packs the products, and delivers the purchases to the door. Other grocery shoppers choose to visit a bricks-and-mortar store and make their own selections.

Selecting a Pricing Strategy

Retailers base their pricing decisions on their costs of purchasing products from other channel members and offering services to customers. Pricing can play a major role in consumers' view of a retailer. Consumers don't always choose the lower-priced products. For example, Loblaw offers three choices: high-quality products under its President's Choice private brand, lower-priced no-name brands, and higher-priced national brands. Loblaw provides these options, and customers can choose the products they prefer. Pricing strategy is covered in more detail in Chapter 13.

Choosing a Location

A good retail location can often make the difference between success and failure. The location decision depends on the retailer's size, financial resources, product offerings, competition, and, of course, its target market. The decision is also influenced by traffic patterns, the visibility of the store's signage, parking, and the location of complementary stores. Consider the competition between PetSmart and Mondou. Mondou tends to have smaller stores than PetSmart and in greater numbers. Their stores are mostly located in strip malls. In contrast, PetSmart's strategy is to build bigger "power centres" right beside other large discount chains. Some PetSmart stores offer added pet services—adoption, grooming, daycare, and boarding. Mondou stores are thought of more as "convenience stores" for pet supplies—especially food. Both companies have implemented "green" initiatives.[22]

A *planned shopping centre* is a group of retail stores that have been planned, coordinated, and marketed as a unit to shoppers in a geographical trade area. By providing single convenient locations and free parking, shopping centres have replaced downtown shopping in many cities. But time-pressed consumers are always looking for more efficient ways to shop, including using catalogues, Internet retailers, and one-stop shopping at large free-standing stores such as Walmart Supercentres. To lure more customers, shopping centres are now marketing themselves as entertainment destinations, by offering movie theatres, art displays, carousel rides, and musical entertainment. The West Edmonton Mall includes a water park and indoor arena. The giant Mall of America in Bloomington, Minnesota, features a seven-acre amusement park and an aquarium.

Shopping malls attract teens, who often meet there to socialize with friends. Businesses want to welcome their teen customers, but sometimes the group of teens hanging around the mall causes difficulties for other customers and some retailers, as described in the "Solving an Ethical Controversy" feature.

In recent years, some large regional malls have seen a growing shift in shopping centre traffic to smaller strip centres and name-brand outlet centres. Many consumers have also shifted their

SOLVING AN ETHICAL CONTROVERSY

Teens at the Mall: Good or Bad for Business?

Some shopping malls have banned unsupervised minors on weekend evenings. Others have initiated a total ban on unaccompanied teens. However, teenagers also spend money at malls. Some merchants who once complained about groups of unsupervised teens have now pinned their revenue hopes on these young spenders.

Should malls lift curfews on teenagers to boost business?

PRO

1. Some studies suggest teenage spending has increased, contrary to expectations after several years of declining figures.
2. Most teenagers are well behaved and should not be banned as a group because of the bad behaviour of a few.

CON

1. Some merchants are still wary because some parents ignore their childrens' bad behaviour.
2. The attractiveness of teenage spending has to be weighed against the reality of crowd behaviour. Malls provide a venue for teen fights, flash mobs, and other disturbances.

Summary

Just as adults spent much less during the recent recession, so did their children. Teenagers have now returned in some measure to previous spending habits, particularly if they are carrying credit cards. Mall owners and civic leaders will need to find a balance between maintaining order and encouraging tomorrow's consumers.

Sources: Thomas Tracy and Mark Morales, "Brooklyn Mall Lifts Ban on Teens after Post-Christmas Flash Mob Trouble," *New York Daily News*, accessed February 15, 2014, www.nydailynews.com/new-york/brooklyn/brooklyn-mall-lifts-ban-teens-flash-mob-trouble-article-1.1561067; Pattie Kate, "What Are the Characteristics of Teenage Spending?" *wiseGEEK*, accessed February 14, 2014, www.wisegeek.com/what-are-the-characteristics-of-teenage-spending.htm; Andrea Chang, "Free-Spending Teens Return to Malls," *Los Angeles Times*, accessed February 14, 2014, http://articles.latimes.com/2010/mar/28/business/la-fi-cover-teen-spending28-2010mar28; Erica Shaffer, "City Leaders Recommend Total Ban of Unsupervised Teens at Mall," *Toledo News NOW*, accessed February 14, 2014, www.toledonewsnow.com/story/12008127/city-leaders-recommend-total-ban-of-unsupervised-teens-at-mall; Fran Daniel, "Mall May Limit Teens: Policy Expected to Require Parental Supervision on Friday, Saturday Evenings," *Winston-Salem Journal*, accessed February 14, 2014, www.journalnow.com/business/mall-may-limit-teens-policy-expected-to-require-parental-supervision/article_d893f606-4926-5a40-8004-04e9a01acf4d.html.

shopping to so-called *lifestyle centres*. These open-air complexes house retailers that often focus on specific shopper segments and specific product interests.

Building a Promotional Strategy

A retailer designs advertisements and develops other promotions for two reasons: to create demand and to provide information, such as the store's location, its offerings, prices, and hours. When a recent year proved to be difficult, Starbucks turned to social media for a new promotional strategy. The chain launched MyStarbucksIdea.com. Customers could log onto this forum to ask questions, offer suggestions, and even voice their dislikes. The site's 180,000 registered users have offered 100,000 ideas; Starbucks has carried out 150 of the suggestions. The Starbucks Facebook page has some 36 million fans; the chain also has 7 million Twitter followers. Charles Bruzzo, the chain's vice-president for brand, content, and online, says the company is seeing the beginning of an "intersection between digital and physical."[23]

Nonstore retailers provide their phone numbers and website addresses as part of their promotional strategy. More recently, online retailers have scaled back their big advertising campaigns and worked to build traffic through word of mouth and clever promotions. Promotional strategy is also discussed in depth in Chapter 13.

Creating a Store Atmosphere

A successful retailer designs its merchandising, pricing, and promotion strategies to work with *store atmospherics*, the physical characteristics of a store and its services. The idea is to positively influence consumers' views of the shopping experience. Atmospherics begin with the store's exterior. Eye-catching architectural elements and signage are used to attract customer attention and interest. Interior atmospheric elements include the store layout, merchandise presentation, lighting, colour, sound, and cleanliness. For example, a high-end store like Holt Renfrew may feature high ceilings that highlight tasteful and well-designed displays of high-quality goods. In contrast, Costco stocks an ever-changing offering of moderately priced products in its warehouse-like settings decorated with industrial-style display hardware.

> ✓ **ASSESSMENT CHECK**
> **12.6.1** Define *retailer*.
> **12.6.2** What are the elements of a retailer's marketing strategy?

DISTRIBUTION CHANNEL DECISIONS AND LOGISTICS

LO 12.7 Discuss distribution channel decisions and logistics.

Every firm faces two major decisions when choosing how to distribute its goods or services: selecting a specific distribution channel and deciding on the level of distribution intensity. When deciding which distribution channel is most efficient, business managers need to consider four factors: the market, the product, the producer, and the competition. These factors are often interrelated and may change over time. In today's global business environment, strong relationships with customers and suppliers are important for survival. One way to help strengthen such relationships online is through the effective use of social media, as explained in the "Career Kickstart" feature.

CAREER KICKSTART

Effective Use of Social Media for Your Small Business

More and more entrepreneurs are using social networking media to promote their small or medium-size businesses. Facebook, Twitter, LinkedIn, and many blogs and forums offer endless marketing opportunities. A recent survey found that 70 percent of small businesses planned to increase their use of social media. Seventy-nine percent did not plan to run TV commercials, and 70 percent didn't use radio ads. Just as in the real business world, good manners, common courtesy, and common sense will take you far in the virtual business world. Here are a few tips for effective use of social media:

1. *Even though you join social networks to promote your business, don't make it too obvious.* Instead of promoting yourself or your business nonstop, post carefully worded messages to show that you have something of value to offer to interested people. Otherwise, you risk being considered a spammer.

2. *Be aware that you are in social networks for the long haul.* Group members or forum members are real people with real interests and ideas. Get to know the members of your forums. Learn about their interests and how the community, as a whole, works. Virtual networks of "friends" have unwritten rules, just as real networks do.

3. *It's not the numbers that count.* Getting your brand known or achieving other marketing goals doesn't depend on how many Twitter followers you have; it depends on how you connect with them.

4. *Be careful of what you say.* Avoid vulgar language, off-colour jokes, or any hint of racial or gender bias. Don't bring up religion, politics, or other sensitive subjects. Leave any strong opinions out of your marketing profile.

5. *Remember that your customers will be discussing you on their own networks.* Your reputation may travel farther than you know!

Sources: Mickie Kennedy, "Do You Have Good Social Media Manners?" *eReleases,* March 23, 2010, www.ereleases.com/prfuel/good-social-media-manners; Michelle Bowles, "5 Social Media Tips for ecommerce Marketing," Top Rank Online Marketing Blog, March 12, 2010, www.toprankblog.com/2010/03/ecommerce-marketing-social-media-tips; Kim States, "Five Social Media Tips to Connect Small Businesses," *Inside Tucson Business,* January 2, 2010, www.insidetucsonbusiness.com/news/small_business/five-social-media-tips-to-connect-small-businesses/article_45cf1623-afdf-52e4-960f-9fb516a0ae36.html.

Selecting Distribution Channels

Market factors may be the most important consideration when choosing a distribution channel. When a firm needs to reach a target market of a small number of buyers or buyers within a small geographical area, the best option may be a direct channel. In contrast, if the firm must reach customers who live in a wide geographical area or who make frequent small purchases, then the channel may need to use marketing intermediaries to make goods available when and where customers want them.

In general, most standardized products or items with low unit values use relatively long distribution channels. On the other hand, products that are complex, expensive, custom made, or perishable move through shorter distribution channels involving few—or no—intermediaries. The increasing use of ecommerce is resulting in changes in traditional distribution practices. The European Commission recently issued an interesting set of rules, effective until 2022. These rules allow makers of goods with less than a 30 percent market share—usually high-end manufacturers—to block Internet-only retailers from carrying their products. The commission declared that "suppliers should normally be free to decide on the number and type of distributors they want to have in their distribution systems . . . More generally, suppliers may only want to sell to distributors that have one or more physical points of present [actual "bricks-and-mortar" stores] where the suppliers' goods can be touched, smelled, tried, etc." The European Alliance—which represents luxury goods manufacturers such as Louis Vuitton Moët Hennessey (LVMH), Gucci, and Burberry—lobbied for and welcomed the new rules as a way to protect the quality image of their products. Online-only retailers, such as Amazon, eBay, and their European equivalents, called for a reversal of the "bricks-and-mortar" requirement and warned that some manufacturers would use the new rules to "restrict the availability" of their products online and thus keep prices high.[24]

But the Greek entrepreneur Stelios Haji-Ioannou finds the Internet to be the perfect channel for easyGroup, the private investment group for his "easy" brand. The company represents a variety of businesses with the "easy" tag—easyJet.com, easyCar.com, easyJobs.com, easyPizza.com, and even an easyBus route between Gatwick Airport and London. Each business offers a no-frills, low-cost approach to services that consumers can order online. EasyJet is one of Europe's biggest Internet retailers, selling 95 percent of its seats online.[25]

Some producers offer a broad product line and have the financial and marketing resources to distribute and promote their products. These producers are more likely than others to choose a shorter channel. Instead of depending on marketing intermediaries, financially strong manufacturers with broad product lines typically use their own sales representatives, warehouses, and credit departments to serve both retailers and consumers.

In many cases, startup manufacturers turn to direct channels for two reasons: because they can't get intermediaries to carry their products or because they want to extend their sales reach. Some companies use direct channels to carry intangible goods. For example, in New York City, Art Meets Commerce uses the Internet and social networking to promote small Broadway and off-Broadway shows that have tight marketing budgets. The company posts short videos of its clients' shows on YouTube. It also uses Facebook and Twitter to increase traditional word-of-mouth publicity. When celebrities see the shows and post favourable tweets, their followers may also feel encouraged to see the shows.[26]

Competitive performance is the fourth key consideration when choosing a distribution channel. A producer loses customers when an intermediary fails to deliver the promotion or product. Channels used by established competitors and new market entries also can influence decisions. Sometimes a joint venture between competitors can work well. For example, Best Buy and Apple have teamed up to sell their products under the same roof. Under the agreement, Apple controls its own retail space within Best Buy stores. Although Apple has a well-established retail business, it can't match the size of electronics giant Best Buy. Best Buy benefits by generating more traffic from customers who want to see and buy Apple's innovative products in convenient locations. The strategy has worked well—specifically, sales of Macs have increased. Best Buy was the only non-Apple retailer in North America to carry the iPad. All of Best Buy's 673 stores with Apple shops sold out their stock of iPads in four days.[27]

Selecting Distribution Intensity

A second key distribution decision involves *distribution intensity*—the number of intermediaries or outlets a manufacturer uses to distribute its goods. Your community may have only one BMW dealership, but you can likely find Coca-Cola everywhere—in grocery stores, convenience stores, gas stations, vending machines, and restaurants. BMW has chosen a different level of distribution intensity from that used by Coca-Cola. In general, market coverage has three different intensity levels:

1. *Intensive distribution* involves placing a firm's products in nearly every available outlet. Intensive distribution usually suits low-priced convenience goods such as milk, newspapers, and soft drinks. This kind of market coverage requires cooperation from many intermediaries, including wholesalers and retailers.

Exclusive distribution limits market coverage in a specific geographical region. This approach suits relatively expensive specialty products such as Rolex watches. Retailers are carefully selected to enhance the product's image to the market.

2. *Selective distribution* involves a manufacturer selecting only a limited number of retailers to distribute its product lines. Selective distribution can reduce total marketing costs and establish strong working relationships within the channel.

3. *Exclusive distribution* is at the opposite extreme from intensive distribution. This distribution strategy limits market coverage in a specific geographical region. This approach suits relatively expensive specialty products such as Rolex watches. Retailers are carefully selected to enhance the product's image to the market and to ensure that well-trained personnel will contribute to customer satisfaction. Producers may give up some market coverage by granting an exclusive territory to a single intermediary. But the decision usually pays off by developing and maintaining an image of quality and prestige.

When companies are clearing out excess inventory, even high-priced retailers may look to discounters to help them move the merchandise from their warehouses. For example, to satisfy consumers' taste for luxury goods, designer outlet malls offer shoppers a chance to buy originally high-priced items at lower prices. And online vendors like Montreal-based Beyond the Rack provide distributors and manufacturers the opportunity to clear excess merchandise inventories quickly. After all, their fashion-driven shoppers are searching online for the next great deal.[28]

Logistics and Physical Distribution

A firm's choice of distribution channels creates the final link in the **supply chain**, the complete sequence of suppliers that help to create a good or service and deliver it to business users and final consumers. The supply chain begins when the raw materials used in production are delivered to the producer. The supply chain continues with the actual production activities that create finished goods. Finally, the finished goods move through the producer's distribution channels to end customers.

The process of coordinating the flow of goods, services, and information among members of the supply chain is called **logistics**. The term originally referred to strategic movements of military troops and supplies. Today, it describes all of the business activities involved in the supply chain with the ultimate goal of getting finished goods to customers.

Physical Distribution

Physical distribution is a major focus of logistics management. It was identified earlier in the chapter as one of the two basic dimensions of distribution strategy. Physical distribution refers to the activities aimed at efficiently moving finished goods from the production line to the consumer or business

supply chain the complete sequence of suppliers that help to create a good or service and deliver it to business users and final consumers.

logistics the process of coordinating the flow of goods, services, and information among members of the supply chain.

Physical Distribution

Marketer → Customer Service · Transportation · Warehousing · Materials Handling · Inventory Control · Order Processing → Customers

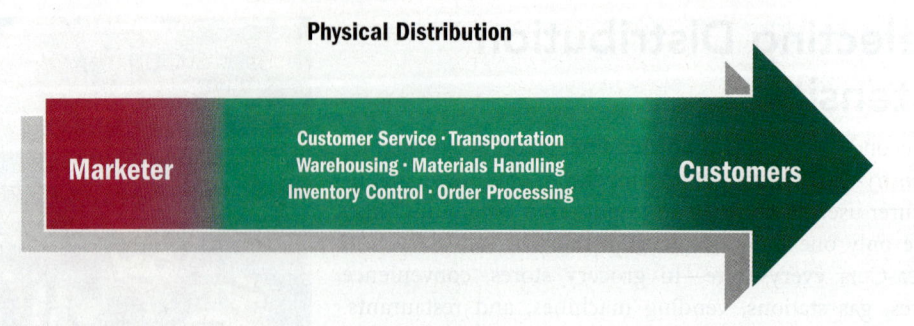

FIGURE 12.9 Elements of a Physical Distribution System

buyer. As **Figure 12.9** shows, physical distribution is a broad concept that includes transportation and many other elements that help link buyers and sellers. An effectively managed physical distribution system can increase customer satisfaction by ensuring reliable movements of products through the supply chain. For example, Walmart studies how quickly goods can be shelved after they arrive at the store. Walmart executives know that strategies that may seem to be efficient in the warehouse, such as completely filling pallets with goods, can actually be time-consuming or costly in the store aisles.

Radio-frequency identification (RFID) technology relies on a computer chip. This chip is implanted on a product or its packaging and emits a low-frequency radio signal to identify the item. The radio signal doesn't need a direct line of sight to register on the store's computers the way a bar code does. That means a hand-held RFID reader can scan crates and cartons before they are unloaded. Because the chip can store information about the product's progress through the distribution channel, RFID can help retailers to better manage inventories, maintain stock levels, reduce loss, track stolen goods, and cut costs. The technology is similar to what is already used to identify lost pets and to help some vehicles move more quickly past toll booths. Walmart, Target, and the German retailer Metro Group already require their suppliers to use RFID technology. Automakers use RFID technology to improve their production processes by tracking parts and other supplies. A new version of the RFID chip can be printed on paper or plastic. The use of RFID technology has led to privacy and counterfeiting concerns. Recently, one company developed a process that uses unique silicon "fingerprints" to generate unclonable RFID chips.[29]

Warehousing is the physical distribution activity that involves the storage of products. *Materials handling* is moving items within factories, warehouses, transportation terminals, and stores. Inventory control involves managing inventory costs, such as storage facilities, insurance, taxes, and handling. The physical distribution activity of *order processing* includes preparing orders for shipment and receiving orders when shipments arrive.

The wide use of electronic data interchange (EDI) and the constant pressure on suppliers to improve their response time have led to **vendor-managed inventory**. It is the process in which the producer and the retailer agree that the producer (or the wholesaler) will decide how much of a product a buyer needs and automatically ship new supplies when needed.

The form of transportation used to ship products depends on the kind of product, the distance involved, and the cost. The logistics manager can choose from several companies and types of transportation. **Table 12.3** shows the five major transport modes: trucks (with about 75 percent

vendor-managed inventory the process in which the producer and the retailer agree that the producer (or the wholesaler) will decide how much of a product a buyer needs and automatically ship new supplies when needed.

Table 12.3 Comparison of Transportation Modes

MODE	SPEED	DEPENDABILITY IN MEETING SCHEDULES	FREQUENCY OF SHIPMENTS	AVAILABILITY IN DIFFERENT LOCATIONS	FLEXIBILITY IN HANDLING	COST
Truck	Fast	High	High	Very Extensive	Average	High
Rail	Average	Average	Low	Low	High	Average
Water	Very slow	Average	Very low	Limited	Very high	Very low
Air	Very fast	High	Average	Average	Low	Very high
Pipeline	Slow	High	High	Very limited	Very low	Low

of total expenditures), railroads (approximately 12 percent), water carriers (6 percent), air freight (4 percent), and pipelines (3 percent). The faster methods usually cost more than the slower methods. When choosing the most suitable method of transportation, the important factors include speed, reliable delivery, shipment frequency, location availability, handling flexibility, and cost.

About 26.4 million trucks operate in the United States, and about 700,000 operate in Canada. They carry most finished goods all or part of the way to the consumer. Nearly 3 million of the U.S. trucks are tractor trailers.[30] Another major form of transportation is the railroads, which compete with many truck routes despite their recent loss of market share. The 565 freight railroads in the United States, Canada, and Mexico operate across more than 325,000 kilometres of track and earn almost $75 billion in revenues. Seventy percent of all autos manufactured in North America travel to their destinations by train. A freight train needs only 3.8 litres of diesel fuel to transport 1 tonne of cargo almost 685 miles.[31]

Customer Service

Customer service is a major part of both product and distribution strategies. *Customer service standards* measure the quality of service a firm provides for its customers. Managers often set quantitative guidelines—for example, that all orders be processed within 24 hours after they are received or that salespeople approach shoppers within two minutes after they enter the store. Sometimes customers set their own service standards and then choose suppliers that meet or exceed those standards.

The customer service portions of product strategy include warranty and repair service programs. *Warranties* are firms' promises to repair a defective product, refund money paid, or replace a product if it proves unsatisfactory. Repair services are also important. Consumers want to know that help is available if something goes wrong. For example, shoppers for home computers often choose retailers that feature low prices *and* offer repair services and tech support centres. Products with poor after-sales service quickly disappear from the market as a result of word-of-mouth criticism.

Consumers' complaints of the impersonal service they received at websites led dot-coms to take several steps to "humanize" their customer interactions and deal with complaints. Many websites include help button icons that link the visitor to a company representative.

✓ ASSESSMENT CHECK

12.7.1 What is distribution intensity?
12.7.2 Define *supply chain*.
12.7.3 What do customer service standards measure?

WHAT'S AHEAD

This chapter covered two of the elements of the marketing mix: product and distribution. It introduced the key marketing tasks of developing, marketing, and packaging want-satisfying goods and services. It also focused on three major parts of an organization's distribution strategy: the design of efficient distribution channels; wholesalers and retailers who make up many distribution channels; and logistics and physical distribution. We now turn to the remaining two elements of the marketing mix—promotion and pricing—in Chapter 13.

RETURN TO INSIDE BUSINESS

Montreal's Fitness City Complex—Bringing Fitness Businesses Together Under One Roof

The concept of clustering fitness businesses under one roof has proven to be successful. Soon after Fitness City opened, a new tenant launched a CrossFit centre catering to a new method of working out with motivational support from group members. This business is a welcomed addition to Fitness City and undoubtedly will benefit from its location at the main entrance of the complex.

The owners of Fitness City continue to seek new tenants that can benefit from the fitness-oriented customers who regularly spend time—and money—at the complex. One idea is to expand health and wellness services by providing space where professionals such as dieticians and physiotherapists can meet with their clients.

QUESTIONS FOR CRITICAL THINKING

1. Which other health-related and wellness-related professionals should be considered as tenants?
2. How can these professional services be marketed within the complex?

SUMMARY OF LEARNING OBJECTIVES

LO 12.1 Explain product strategy and how to classify goods and services.

A product is a bundle of physical, service, and symbolic characteristics designed to satisfy consumer wants. The marketing concept of a product includes the brand, product image, warranty, service attributes, packaging, labelling, and the physical or functional characteristics of the good or service.

Goods and services can be classified as consumer (B2C) or business (B2B) products. Consumer products are those goods and services purchased by end consumers for their own use. They can be convenience products, shopping products, or specialty products, depending on how consumers buy them. Business products are those products purchased for use either directly or indirectly in the production of other goods and services for resale. They can be classified as installations, accessory equipment, component parts and materials, raw materials, and supplies. This classification is based on how the items are used and product characteristics. Services can be classified as either consumer or business services.

A product mix is the assortment of goods and services a firm offers to individual consumers and B2B users. A product line is a series of related products.

✓ **ASSESSMENT CHECK ANSWERS**

12.1.1 How do consumer products differ from business products? Business products, such as drill presses, are sold to firms or organizations. Consumer products, such as personal-care items, are sold to end users.

12.1.2 Differentiate among convenience products, shopping products, and specialty products. Convenience products are items the consumer seeks to purchase frequently, immediately, and with little effort. Shopping products are typically purchased after the buyer has compared competing products in competing stores. Specialty products are those products that a purchaser is willing to make a special effort to obtain.

LO 12.2 Describe the four stages of the product life cycle and their marketing implications.

Every successful new product passes through four stages in its product life cycle: introduction, growth, maturity, and decline. In the introduction stage, the firm attempts to create demand for the new product. In the product's growth stage, sales climb, and the company earns its first profits. In the maturity stage, sales reach a saturation level. In the decline stage, both sales and profits decrease. Marketers sometimes use strategies to extend the product life cycle, such as increasing the frequency of use; adding new users; finding new uses for the product; and changing package size, labelling, or product quality.

The new-product development process for most products has six stages: idea generation, screening, concept development and business analysis, product development, test marketing, and commercialization. At each stage, marketers must decide whether to continue to the next stage, make changes to the new product, or discontinue the development process. Some new products may skip the test marketing stage for various reasons: because they want to quickly introduce a new product with excellent potential, because of a desire not to reveal new-product strategies to competitors, or because of the high costs involved in limited production runs.

✓ **ASSESSMENT CHECK ANSWERS**

12.2.1 What are the stages of the product life cycle? The product life cycle has four stages: introduction, growth, maturity, and decline. In the introduction stage, the firm tries to attract demand for the new product. In the product's growth stage, sales climb, and the company earns its first profits. In the maturity stage, sales reach a saturation level. In the decline stage, both sales and profits decline.

12.2.2 What are the marketing implications of each stage? Marketers sometimes use strategies to extend the product life cycle, including increasing frequency of use, adding new users, finding new uses for the product, and changing package size, labelling, or product quality.

LO 12.3 Explain how firms identify their products.

Products are identified by brands, brand names, and trademarks. All three are important elements of product images. Effective brand names are easy to say, easy to recognize, and easy to remember. They also project the right images to buyers. Brand names cannot contain generic words. Under certain circumstances, companies can lose the exclusive rights to their brand names if common use transforms the brand names into generic terms for product categories. Some brand names belong to retailers or distributors, not to manufacturers. Brand loyalty is measured in three degrees: brand recognition, brand preference, and brand insistence. Some marketers use family brands to identify several related items in a product line. Other marketers use individual branding strategies by giving a different brand name to each product within a product line.

✓ **ASSESSMENT CHECK ANSWERS**

12.3.1 Differentiate among a brand, a brand name, and a trademark. A brand is a name, term, sign, symbol, design, or some combination used to identify the products of one firm and show how they differ from competitive offerings. A brand name is that part of the brand consisting of words or letters. It is used to identify a firm's products and show how they differ from the products of competitors. A trademark is a brand that has been given legal protection.

12.3.2 Define *brand equity*. Brand equity is the added value that a respected and successful brand name gives to a product.

LO 12.4 Outline the major components of an effective distribution strategy.

A firm must decide whether to move products through direct or indirect distribution. After making this decision, the company needs to identify which types of marketing intermediaries, if any, will distribute its goods and services. The Internet has made direct distribution an attractive option for many retail companies.

✓ ASSESSMENT CHECK ANSWERS

12.4.1 Define *distribution channels*. Distribution channels are the paths that products, and their legal ownership, follow from producer to consumer or business user.

12.4.2 What is a marketing intermediary? A marketing intermediary (also called a middleman) is a business firm that moves goods from their producers to the consumers or business users.

LO 12.5 Explain the concept of wholesaling.

Wholesaling is a crucial part of the distribution channel for many products, especially consumer goods and business supplies. Wholesaling intermediaries can be classified on the basis of ownership: some are owned by manufacturers, some are owned by retailers, and others are independently owned. Firms operate two main types of manufacturer-owned wholesaling intermediaries: sales branches and sales offices.

An independent wholesaling intermediary is a business that represents several different manufacturers and sells to retailers, manufacturers, and other business accounts. Independent wholesalers can be either merchant wholesalers or agents and brokers, depending on whether they take title to (legal ownership of) the products they handle.

Retailers sometimes work together to form their own wholesaling organizations. Such organizations can take the form of either a buying group or a cooperative.

✓ ASSESSMENT CHECK ANSWERS

12.5.1 Define *wholesaling*. Wholesaling is a crucial part of the distribution channel for many products, especially consumer goods and business supplies.

12.5.2 Differentiate between a merchant wholesaler and an agent or broker in terms of title to the goods. Merchant wholesalers are independently owned wholesaling intermediaries that take title to the goods they handle. Agents and brokers may or may not take physical possession of the goods they handle, but they never take title, or ownership. They work mainly to bring buyers and sellers together.

LO 12.6 Describe the types of retailers and retail strategies used.

Retailers, in contrast to wholesalers, are distribution channel members that sell goods and services to individuals for their own use, not for resale. Nonstore retailing includes four forms: direct-response retailing, Internet retailing, automatic merchandising, and direct selling. Store retailers range in size from tiny newsstands to multi-storey department stores and warehouse-style retailers such as Costco.

The first step in developing a competitive retailing strategy is to select a target market. Next, the retailer must develop a product strategy to determine the best mix of merchandise to carry to satisfy that market. A retailer's customer service strategy focuses on attracting and retaining target customers to maximize sales and profits. Retailers base their pricing decisions on their costs of purchasing products from other channel members and offering services to customers. A good retail location can often make the difference between success and failure. A retailer designs advertisements and develops other promotions to stimulate demand and to provide information such as the store's location, merchandise offerings, prices, and hours. A successful retailer closely matches its merchandising, pricing, and promotion strategies with store atmospherics—the physical characteristics of a store and its amenities. A good match can help to influence consumers' perceptions of the shopping experience.

✓ ASSESSMENT CHECK ANSWERS

12.6.1 Define *retailer*. A retailer is a distribution channel member that sells goods and services to individuals for their own use, not for resale.

12.6.2 What are the elements of a retailer's marketing strategy? Retailers must first identify their target markets, and then choose the strategies for merchandising, customer service, pricing, and location that will attract customers in their target market segments.

LO 12.7 Discuss distribution channel decisions and logistics.

Marketers can choose either a direct distribution channel or an indirect distribution channel. A direct distribution channel moves goods directly from the producer to the consumer. An indirect distribution channel uses marketing intermediaries to make goods available when and where customers want them. Ideally, the choice of a distribution channel should support a firm's overall marketing strategy. Before selecting distribution channels, firms must consider their target markets, the types of goods being distributed, their own internal systems and concerns, and competitive factors.

A second key distribution decision involves distribution intensity. The business must decide on the market coverage needed to achieve its marketing strategies: intensive distribution, selective distribution, or exclusive distribution.

ASSESSMENT CHECK ANSWERS

12.7.1 What is distribution intensity? Distribution intensity is the number of intermediaries or outlets a manufacturer uses to distribute its goods.

12.7.2 Define *supply chain*. A supply chain is the sequence of suppliers that help in creating a good or service and delivering it to business users and end consumers.

12.7.3 What do customer service standards measure? Customer service standards measure the quality of service a firm provides for its customers.

BUSINESS TERMS YOU NEED TO KNOW

brand 329	distribution strategy 334	product line 325	trademark 330
brand equity 331	logistics 345	product mix 325	vendor-managed inventory 346
brand name 330	physical distribution 334	retailers 338	wholesaler 336
category advisor 332	product 322	supply chain 345	
distribution channels 334	product life cycle 325	test marketing 328	

REVIEW QUESTIONS

1. Classify each of the following products as either a business-to-consumer (B2C) product or a business-to-business (B2B) product. Then choose one product and describe how it can be classified as both a B2C product and a B2B product.
    a. *Runner's World* or *Esquire* magazine
    b. A six-pack of apple juice
    c. A limousine service
    d. Tech support for a communications system
    e. A golf course
    f. A Thai restaurant

2. What is the relationship between a product line and a product mix? Give an example of each.

3. Identify and briefly describe the six stages of new-product development.

4. What is the difference between a manufacturer's brand and a private brand? What is the difference between a family brand and an individual brand?

5. What are the three stages of brand loyalty? Why is it so important to marketers to reach the last stage of brand loyalty?

6. What are the upsides of direct distribution? When is a producer most likely to use direct distribution?

7. What is the wheel of retailing? How has the Internet affected the wheel of retailing?

8. Identify and briefly describe the four different types of nonstore retailers. Give an example of at least one type of good or service that would be suited to each type of nonstore retailer.

9. What are the three intensity levels of distribution? Give an example of two products for each level.

10. Define *logistics*. How does it relate to physical distribution?

PROJECTS AND TEAMWORK APPLICATIONS

1. On your own or with a classmate, choose one of the following goods or services. Decide whether you want to market it as a consumer product or a business product. Create a brand name and marketing strategy for your product.
    a. A lawn mower repair service
    b. A hardware store
    c. A soft drink
    d. An English-language class
    e. An accounting firm

2. Choose one of the following products that is in either the maturity stage or the decline stage of its life cycle (or select one of your own). Develop a marketing strategy for extending the product's life cycle.

   a. Popcorn
   b. A fast-food restaurant chain
   c. A newspaper
   d. Music CDs
   e. Paper stationery or notecards

3. Where do you do most of your shopping—in stores or online? Choose your favourite retailer and analyze why you like it. Outline your reasons for shopping there. Suggest two or three areas for improvement.

4. Choose one of the following products. Select a distribution intensity for the product. Describe specifically where and how the product would be sold. Describe the reasons for your strategy.

   a. A line of furniture manufactured from recycled or reclaimed materials
   b. Custom-designed jewellery
   c. A house-painting service
   d. Handicraft supplies
   e. A radio talk show

WEB ASSIGNMENTS

1. **Product classification.** Review the chapter's discussion on product classification. Visit the website of Johnson & Johnson (www.jnj.com) and click on "Our Products." Classify Johnson & Johnson's wide range of products.

2. **Shopping centres.** The West Edmonton Mall in Edmonton is North America's largest shopping centre. Go to the mall's website (www.wem.ca) to learn more about it. Make a list of five interesting facts you learned about the West Edmonton Mall.

3. **Railroad statistics.** Visit the website of the Railway Association of Canada (www.railcan.ca). Review the material and answer the following questions:

   a. How big is the railway industry in Canada?
   b. How many people do railroads employ?
   c. How much freight did railroads carry during the most recent year for which data are available?

Note: Internet Web addresses change frequently. If you don't find the exact sites listed, you may need to access the organization's home page and search from there or use a search engine such as Bing or Google.

13 | PROMOTION AND PRICING STRATEGIES

LEARNING OBJECTIVES

LO 13.1 Discuss how integrated marketing communications relates to a firm's overall promotional strategy.

LO 13.2 Summarize the different types of advertising.

LO 13.3 Outline sales promotion.

LO 13.4 Describe pushing and pulling promotional strategies.

LO 13.5 Outline the different types of pricing objectives in the marketing mix.

LO 13.6 Describe how firms set prices in the marketplace and the four alternative pricing strategies.

LO 13.7 Discuss consumer perceptions of price.

INSIDE BUSINESS

WorkSafeBC: Promoting Safety to Young Workers

WorkSafeBC is an insurance agency serving more than 200,000 employers and 2.3 million workers in British Columbia. It is a workers' compensation board that helps workers who have injuries related to the workplace. WorkSafeBC is a quasi-government agency, which means it operates under the guidance of the BC provincial government but is separate from the government. In a recent year, premiums collected from employers totalled about $1 billion and payouts for claims were more than $1.3 billion. About 137,000 claims were made, resulting in 2.8 million lost workdays. The top three causes of injuries that led to lost workdays were strains (excluding back strains) at 1,118,000 days, back strains at 567,000 days, and fractures at 456,000 days. Although the average age of an injured worker is 41 years, 12 percent of young men under age 25 (about 6,300) reported injuries. The agency performance can be improved by reducing the number and the seriousness of worker injuries. One way to achieve this goal is to change people's attitudes toward workplace safety—especially the attitudes of younger men, who are more likely than any other population group to experience an injury.

Back in 2001, Vancouver-based Wasserman & Partners Advertising Inc. first won the contract to create a new promotional program for BC's Workers' Compensation Board (WCB). The agency began with a basic recommendation—make WorkSafeBC the public face of the organization. A total rebrand was needed. The WCB brand referred to claims, insurance, and administration, but it didn't have the heart or the belief that anyone or anything could change workplace behaviour. It also did not capture the passion within the organization that was focused on safety and accident prevention in the workplace.

WorkSafeBC's goal was to change social attitudes toward safety in the workplace. By doing this, it was hoped that workers would learn that work injuries can be avoided. Since putting the rebrand strategy in place, the organization's corporate reputation has increased. WorkSafeBC has a proud internal culture and focus. Statistics show that its promotional campaigns are changing attitudes toward workplace safety—and reducing injuries.

Before developing promotional ideas, research was done to better understand the target audience. This generation of consumers believes that it's cool to care about something; the agency wanted to find an opportunity to use that desire to make a change for the good. This audience also feels in control of their culture, instead of being consumers of culture. They don't want to be spoken at, they want to engage. They are connected 24/7. Technology and community are both important.

Unlike most other safety campaigns that target youth, the firm rejected the traditional "shock and awe" approach of scaring young people into working safely. According to Alvin Wasserman, president and creative strategist:

"Shock and awe" catches attention, but in our current culture of violence as entertainment, it's too easy to say "That's not me" and it doesn't provide tangible information on what to do. Research shows that it is ineffective in changing behaviour. A successful social marketing campaign presents the magnitude of the problem but also gives the audience something tangible to do in order to address the problem. To develop our approach we asked ourselves and our target audience what would be the first step to making the work environment safer. The answer—ask for help if you don't know what to do.

The strategy developed was to tap into the target audience's desire to make a difference. This strategy led to the launch of the Raise Your Hand campaign, as a blueprint, or a plan, for a young worker movement that focuses on workplace safety and rights: the right to know about hazards at your job and how to protect yourself; the right to participate in making sure your job and workplace are safe and healthy; and the right to refuse unsafe work. The idea was to help create a social environment where all young workers in BC would ask for help to be safer on the job and would feel free to "raise their hand" when the workplace did not appear to be safe.

Raise Your Hand engages with young workers by showing up at all of the popular summertime youth cultural events throughout the province. From music events to major sporting events, the Raise Your Hand team is there. In the fall, Raise Your Hand participates in campus crawls at universities and colleges throughout BC to reach more young people.

But connecting online has always been a major strategy of the campaign. The interactivity of rich media online ads has led to record website results. WorkSafeBC's online presence includes distribution strategies that use social media sites such as Facebook, YouTube, and Twitter.[1]

CHAPTER 13 OVERVIEW

This chapter focuses on the different types of promotional activities and how prices are decided on for goods and services. **Promotion** is the function of informing, persuading, and influencing a purchase decision. This activity is as important to not-for-profit organizations as it is to for-profit companies.

Some promotional strategies try to develop *primary demand*, or consumer desire, for a general product category. The objective of such a campaign is to stimulate sales for an entire industry so that individual firms benefit from the total market growth. A popular example is the dairy industry's "Got Milk?" campaign. Print and television messages about the nutritional benefits of milk feature various celebrities. Another very successful promotional campaign aimed at increasing per-capita consumption is the long-running "Get Cracking" campaign by the Egg Farmers of Ontario. This promotion emphasizes the many easy meal preparations that use eggs.

In contrast, most promotional strategies try to stimulate *selective demand*—desire for a specific brand. Just about every adult needs banking and financial services. TD Canada Trust wants consumers to pick its firm from among the many competitors in the marketplace. Banks tend to promote their friendly customer services, expertise, and convenient locations to set themselves apart from competitors. For most customers, the bank brand is understood in terms of the people they actually come in contact with at their local branch. Marketers choose from among many promotional options to communicate with potential customers. Marketing messages can be communicated through a television or radio commercial, a newspaper or magazine ad, a website, a direct-mail flyer, or a sales call. Each marketing message reflects the product, place, person, cause, or organization promoted in the content. Marketers use **integrated marketing communications (IMC)** to coordinate all promotional activities—media advertising, direct mail, personal selling, sales promotion, and public relations—to produce a unified, customer-focused promotional strategy. This coordination is designed to avoid confusing the consumer and to focus positive attention on the promotional message.

This chapter begins by explaining the role of IMC, and then discusses the objectives of promotion and the importance of promotional planning. Next, it examines the elements of the promotional mix: advertising, sales promotion, personal selling, and public relations. Finally, the chapter addresses pricing strategies for goods and services.

promotion the function of informing, persuading, and influencing a purchase decision.

integrated marketing communications (IMC) the coordination of all promotional activities—media advertising, direct mail, personal selling, sales promotion, and public relations—to produce a unified, customer-focused promotional strategy.

LO 13.1 Discuss how integrated marketing communications relates to a firm's overall promotional strategy.

INTEGRATED MARKETING COMMUNICATIONS

An integrated marketing communications strategy focuses on customer needs to create a unified promotional message in the firm's ads, in-store displays, product samples, and presentations by company sales representatives. To gain a competitive advantage, marketers that use IMC need a broad view of promotion. Media options continue to increase, and marketers cannot rely on traditional broadcast, print media, and direct mail. Marketing plans must include all forms of customer contact. Packaging, store displays, sales promotions, sales presentations, and online and interactive media also communicate information about a brand or organization. Marketers that use IMC create a unified personality and message for the good, brand, or service they promote. Coordinated activities also increase the effectiveness of reaching and serving target markets.

Marketing managers set the goals and objectives for the firm's promotional strategy, while keeping in mind the firm's overall organizational objectives and marketing goals. Using these objectives, marketers weave the various elements of the strategy—personal selling, advertising, sales promotion, publicity, and public relations—into an integrated communications plan. This document becomes a central focus of the firm's total marketing strategy to reach its selected target market. Feedback, including marketing research and sales reports, completes the strategy by identifying any activities that differ from the plan and suggesting improvements.

The job-search engine Monster.com combined several marketing promotions to create its stepped-up IMC campaign "Get a Monster Advantage." The campaign's first TV commercial featured a down-on-his-luck boogeyman who goes to Monster.com to find the perfect new job. A second commercial, featuring another character, aired during a recent Super Bowl game. Other spots were aired on national cable networks and were extended to social media. Humorous interactive links on sites such as Facebook and advertising on other sites further reached out to the online audience. Print ads appeared in the *Wall Street Journal,* in more than 100 regional daily newspapers, in monthly business publications, and in human resource publications, such as *HR Executive, Wired,* and *Fast Company.*[2]

The Promotional Mix

Every organization creates a marketing mix by combining product, distribution, promotion, and pricing strategies. In a similar way, each organization also needs to blend the many types of promotion into a unified and organized plan. The **promotional mix** is the combination of personal selling and nonpersonal selling that marketers use to meet the needs of a firm's target customers and to effectively and efficiently communicate its message to them. **Personal selling** is the most basic form of promotion: a direct person-to-person promotional presentation to a potential buyer. The buyer–seller communication can occur in several ways: during a face-to-face meeting, or by telephone, videoconference, or an interactive computer link.

Nonpersonal selling consists of advertising, sales promotion, direct marketing, and public relations. Advertising is the best-known form of nonpersonal selling, but sales promotion accounts for about half of the money spent on nonpersonal selling. Spending is increasing for sponsorships, which involve marketing messages that are delivered in association with another activity, such as a golf tournament or a benefit concert. Marketers need to be careful about the types of promotion they choose because they risk alienating, or isolating, the very people they are trying to reach.

Each element in the promotional mix offers its own advantages and disadvantages, as **Table 13.1** shows. When a firm selects the most effective combination of promotional mix elements, it may reach its promotional objectives. The spending levels within the promotional mix vary by industry. Manufacturers of many business-to-business (B2B) products typically spend more on personal selling than on advertising because those products—such as a new telecommunications system—may require a significant investment. Consumer-goods marketers may focus more on advertising and sponsorships. Later sections of this chapter discuss how the parts of the mix contribute to effective promotion.

promotional mix the combination of personal and nonpersonal selling that marketers use to meet the needs of a firm's target customers and to effectively and efficiently communicate its message to them.

personal selling the most basic form of promotion: a direct person-to-person promotional presentation to a potential buyer.

nonpersonal selling forms of selling such as advertising, sales promotion, direct marketing, and public relations.

Table 13.1 Comparing the Elements of the Promotional Mix

ELEMENT	ADVANTAGES	DISADVANTAGES
Advertising	Reaches large consumer audience at low cost per contact	Difficult to measure effectiveness
	Allows strong control of the message	Limited value for closing sales
	Message can be modified to suit different audiences	
Personal selling	Message can be tailored for each customer	High cost per contact
	Produces immediate buyer response	High expense and difficulty of attracting and retaining effective salespeople
	Effectiveness is easily measured	
Sales promotion	Attracts attention and creates awareness	Difficult to differentiate from similar programs of competitors
	Effectiveness is easily measured	Nonpersonal appeal
	Produces increases in short-term sales	
Public relations	Improves trust in a product or firm	Difficult to measure effectiveness
	Creates a positive attitude about the product or company	Often devoted to nonmarketing activities
Sponsorships	Viewed positively by consumers	Difficult to control message
	Enhances brand awareness	

Objectives of Promotional Strategy

Promotional strategy objectives vary among organizations. Some organizations use promotion to expand their markets, while other organizations use promotion to defend their current positions. As **Figure 13.1** illustrates, common objectives include providing information, differentiating a product, increasing sales, stabilizing sales, and highlighting a product's value.

Marketers often pursue more than one promotional objective at the same time. For example, to promote its Microsoft Office software, Microsoft needs to convince two groups that the product is a worthwhile investment: business owners, who buy the software, and the business owners' employees, who use the software.

FIGURE 13.1 Five Major Promotional Objectives

Pie chart segments:
- **DIFFERENTIATE PRODUCT** — Example: Television ad comparing performance of two leading laundry detergents
- **PROVIDE INFORMATION** — Example: Print ad describing features and availability of a new breakfast cereal
- **STABILIZE SALES** — Example: Even out sales patterns by promoting low weekend rates for hotels, holding contests during slow sales periods, or advertising cold fruit soups during summer months
- **INCREASE SALES** — Example: End-of-aisle grocery displays, or "end caps," to encourage impulse purchases
- **HIGHLIGHT PRODUCT VALUE** — Example: Warranty programs and guarantees that make a product more attractive than its major competitors

positioning a concept whereby marketers try to establish their products in the minds of customers by communicating to buyers the meaningful differences about the attributes, price, quality, or use of a good or service.

Providing Information

A major portion of advertising is information-oriented. Credit card ads provide information about benefits and rates. Ads for hair-care products include information about benefits such as shine and volume. Ads for breakfast cereals often mention nutritional information. Television ads for prescription drugs, a nearly $3 billion industry in North America, are sometimes criticized for relying on emotional appeals rather than providing information about the causes, risk factors, and the prevention of disease.[3] But print advertisements for drugs often contain an entire page of warnings, side effects, and usage guidelines.

Differentiating a Product

Promotion can also be used to differentiate a firm's offerings from the competition. By using a concept called **positioning**, marketers try to establish their products in the minds of customers. The idea is to communicate to buyers some meaningful differences about the attributes, price, quality, or use of a good or service.

When you set out to purchase a car, you can choose from hundreds of brands. How do you decide which car to buy? Carmakers do their best to differentiate their vehicles by style, performance, safety features, and price. They must make their vehicles stand out to individual consumers. General Motors intends its new Chevrolet Cruze compact car to replace the discontinued Cobalt model. Traditionally, compact cars have been less expensive than midsize cars but are also known for being pretty ordinary, or average. The Cruze costs more than the Cobalt, but GM is promoting its higher quality and—especially—its high-quality safety engineering and safety features. A version of the Cruze has been on sale in other countries for a few years. The Cruze received the highest crash-safety score ever in the European New Car Assessment Program.[4]

Increasing Sales

Increasing sales volume is the most common objective of a promotional strategy. Naturalizer became the third-largest seller of women's dress shoes by appealing to baby boomers. But as these women have grown older, they have bought fewer pairs of shoes each year. Naturalizer wants to keep these customers but also wants to attract the younger generation. The firm developed a new line of trendy shoes. The promotional strategy included ads in magazines read by younger women—such as *Elle* and *Marie Claire*—featuring young women in beach attire and Naturalizer shoes. The response to this strategy was a large increase in Naturalizer's sales in department stores.

Stabilizing Sales

Sales stabilization is another goal of promotional strategy. During slow sales periods, some firms use employee sales contests. These contests are meant to motivate salespeople by offering prizes such as vacations, TVs, smartphones, and cash to those who meet certain sales goals. During the off-season, companies may try to stimulate sales from customers by distributing sales promotion materials, such as calendars, pens, and notepads. Jiffy Lube puts that little sticker on your windshield to remind you when to have your car's next oil change. The regular visits help to stabilize sales. A stable sales pattern brings several advantages. It evens out the production cycle and reduces some management and production costs. It also simplifies financial, purchasing, and marketing planning. An effective promotional strategy can contribute to these goals.

Highlighting the Product's Value

Some promotional strategies improve a product's value by explaining the hidden benefits of ownership. For example, carmakers offer long-term warranty programs, and life insurance companies promote certain policies as investments. The creation of brand awareness and brand loyalty improves a product's image and increases its desirability. Advertising that includes luxurious images supports the reputation of premium brands such as Jaguar, Tiffany, and Rolex.

Promotional Planning

Today's marketers can promote their products in many ways, and the lines between the different elements of the promotional mix are blurring. Consider the practice of **product placement**. A growing number of marketers pay placement fees to have their products showcased in various media, ranging from newspapers and magazines to television and movies. The Superman movie *Man of Steel* holds the current record for the number of product placements, with more than 100 companies paying $160 million or about 75 percent of the film's total budget. Brands skillfully integrated into the movie include Sears, IHOP, and 7-Eleven. Product placement can be subtle, as was shown in the TV series *24*, where the lead character, Jack Bauer, drove a Chevrolet. One of the longest-running product placements is Coca-Cola on *American Idol*.[5]

Another type of promotional planning must be considered by firms with small budgets. **Guerrilla marketing** involves innovative, low-cost marketing efforts designed to get consumers' attention in unusual ways. Guerrilla marketing is an increasingly popular tactic for marketers, especially those with limited promotional budgets. Cathay Pacific, a Hong Kong airline, surprised travellers during a recent holiday season by staging a 300-person flash mob at Hong Kong International Airport, which included ground staff, cabin crew, and even pilots. The unannounced dance took place to the tune of "All I Want for Christmas Is You" in the middle of the busy airport.[6]

product placement a form of promotion where marketers pay placement fees to have their products featured in various media, from newspapers and magazines to television and movies.

guerrilla marketing innovative, low-cost marketing efforts designed to get consumers' attention in unusual ways.

Energy drink maker Red Bull used a space stunt as a guerilla marketing tactic to launch Felix Baumgartner from a capsule approximately 24 miles above New Mexico. Baumgartner's space suit was covered with Red Bull logos.

ASSESSMENT CHECK

13.1.1 What is the objective of an integrated marketing communications program?

13.1.2 Why do firms pursue multiple promotional objectives at the same time?

13.1.3 What are product placement and guerrilla marketing?

Marketers for larger companies have caught on and are using guerrilla approaches as well. In addition to online viral campaigns, there is a new breed of guerrilla tactics being used by leading brands like Red Bull. Maker of energy drinks, Red Bull made a huge scene during a Formula 1 event when a driver made a pit stop in the London race. In another guerrilla marketing move, Red Bull's space stunt, complete with the slogan, "Red Bull Gives You Wings," includes Felix Baumgartner's parachute jump from a capsule at the edge of space—24 miles above Roswell, New Mexico. Baumgartner's spacesuit was branded with Red Bull's logo, and the marketing event was viewed live by millions on YouTube.[7]

From this overview of the promotional mix, we now turn to discussions of each of its elements. The following sections detail the major promotional mix elements of advertising, sales promotion, personal selling, and public relations.

LO 13.2 Summarize the different types of advertising.

ADVERTISING

Consumers receive thousands of marketing messages each day, many of them in the form of advertising.[8] Advertising is the most visible form of nonpersonal promotion—and the most effective for many firms. **Advertising** refers to paid nonpersonal communication usually targeted at large numbers of potential buyers. Although we often think of advertising as a typically North American function, it is a multibillion-dollar global activity. In a recent year, global ad spending was expected to reach $500 billion—an all-time high. The surge is primarily a result of the growth of mobile technologies and the use of social media. Global ad spending is expected to reach levels experienced prior to the global recession. In addition, consumer electronics and technology is the fastest-growing ad category among the top 100 global firms.[9] More than $10 billion is spent on advertising every year in Canada. According to Statistics Canada, about 5,000 advertising agencies are among nearly 12,000 firms involved in advertising and related services. Advertising agencies account for about 40 percent of advertising revenues generated, with the most being revenues sourced in Ontario (57 percent), Quebec (23 percent), and British Columbia (8 percent).[10]

advertising paid nonpersonal communication usually targeted at large numbers of potential buyers.

Product advertising consists of messages designed to sell a particular good or service.

Advertising expenditures vary among industries, companies, and media. The top five categories for global advertisers are consumer goods, health care, industry and services (business services, property, institutions, power, and water), media, and telecommunications. Personal-care marketers make up 25 percent of global ad spending in a recent year, and the three biggest global advertisers are consumer product companies, Procter & Gamble, Unilever, and L'Oréal. Because advertising expenditures are so great, and because consumers around the world are bombarded with messages, advertisers need to be increasingly creative and efficient at attracting consumers' attention.[11]

product advertising messages designed to sell a particular good or service.

institutional advertising messages that promote concepts, ideas, or philosophies. It can also promote goodwill toward industries, companies, organizations, or government entities.

Types of Advertising

The two basic types of advertisements are product ads and institutional ads. **Product advertising** consists of messages designed to sell a particular good or service. Advertisements for BlackBerry PlayBooks, Apple iPods, and Capital One credit cards are examples of product advertising. **Institutional advertising** involves messages that promote concepts, ideas, or philosophies. It can also promote goodwill toward industries, companies, organizations, or government entities. Each year, the Juvenile Diabetes Research Foundation promotes its "Walk for the Cure," a fundraising event. Your college or university may advertise in local papers or on news shows to promote its activities.

Cause advertising is a form of institutional advertising that is growing in importance. This type of advertising promotes a specific viewpoint on a public issue. It uses advertising to influence public opinion and the political process about such issues as literacy, hunger and poverty, and alternative energy sources. Both not-for-profit organizations and businesses use cause advertising, which is sometimes called *advocacy advertising*. As part of Avon's corporate responsibility, the Avon Foundation promotes its Speak Out Against Domestic Violence program. The ads feature a celebrity endorsement from Reese Witherspoon.[12]

cause advertising a form of institutional advertising that promotes a specific viewpoint on a public issue as a way to influence public opinion and the political process.

Advertising and the Product Life Cycle

Advertising is designed to inform, persuade, or remind. Both types of advertising—product advertising and institutional advertising—belong to one of these three categories depending on the advertising objectives. For example, a firm uses *informative advertising* to build initial demand for a product in the introductory, or beginning, phase of the product life cycle. Highly publicized new-product entries attract the interest of potential buyers. The buyers then look for information about the advantages of the new products over existing products, the new products' warranties, their prices, and locations that offer the new products. Ads for new cellphones try to attract new customers by boasting about their new features, colours, designs, and pricing options.

Persuasive advertising tries to improve the competitive status of a product, institution, or concept. This type of advertising is usually used in the growth and maturity stages of the product life cycle. *Comparative advertising* is one of the most popular types of persuasive product advertising. This type of advertising compares products directly with their competitors—either by naming the competing product or by suggesting it. For example, Tylenol advertisements mention the possible stomach problems that the generic drug aspirin could cause, and then states that its pain reliever does not irritate the stomach. But advertisers need to be careful when they name competing brands; they risk leaving themselves open to controversy or even legal action. Notice that Tylenol does not mention a specific aspirin brand in its promotions.

Reminder-oriented advertising is often used for products in the late maturity or decline stages of the product life cycle. This advertising is used to maintain awareness of the importance and usefulness of a product, concept, or institution. For example, Triscuits have been around for a long time, but Nabisco tries to increase sales by using up-to-date advertising that appeals to health and fitness-conscious consumers. The advertising mentions its new no-trans-fat formula.

Advertising Media

Marketers must choose how to allocate their advertising budgets among various media. All media offer advantages and disadvantages. Cost is an important consideration in media selection, but marketers must also choose the media best suited for communicating their message. As **Figure 13.2** indicates, the three leading media outlets for advertising are television, the Internet, and newspapers. Advertising executives have observed that firms are rethinking traditional ad campaigns and incorporating new media, as well as updated uses of traditional media. Less than a decade ago, the Internet ranked sixth in global ad media behind TV, newspapers, magazines, radio, and outdoor advertising. Today, it is second behind television and ahead of newspapers. Global Internet ad spending has surpassed the 20 percent mark, and over the next several years, analysts expect the Internet to account for more than 27 percent of global ad spending.[13]

Television

Television continues to be one of North America's leading national advertising media. Television advertising can be classified as network ads, national ads, local ads, or cable ads. Despite a decline in audience share

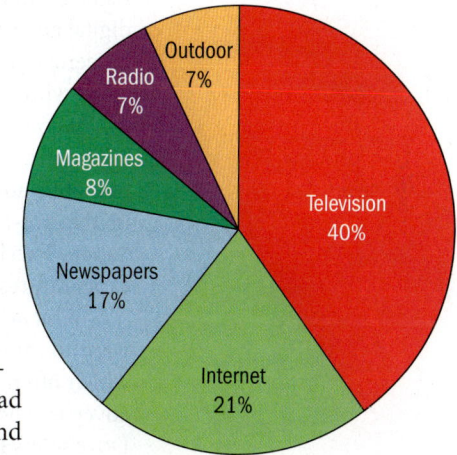

FIGURE 13.2 Dividing Up the Advertising Media Pie

- Television 40%
- Internet 21%
- Newspapers 17%
- Magazines 8%
- Radio 7%
- Outdoor 7%

Sources: "Executive Summary: Advertising Expenditure Forecasts December 2013," *ZenithOptimedia*, accessed February 20, 2014, www.zenithoptimedia.com/wp-content/uploads/2013/12/Adspend-forecasts-December-2013-executive-summary.pdf; "TV Remains the Reigning Champ, but Display Internet Ads Are the MVPs of 3Q," Nielsen, accessed February 20, 2014, www.nielsen.com/us/en/insights/news/2014/tv-remains-the-reigning-champ-but-display-internet-ads-are-the-mvps-of-3q.html.

and growing competition from cable, network television remains the easiest way for advertisers to reach large numbers of viewers—10 million to 20 million North Americans with a single commercial. Automakers, fast-food restaurants, and food manufacturers are heavy users of network TV advertising.

About 80 percent of Canadian households (11.5 million subscribers) and 32 percent of U.S. households with TVs subscribe to cable television. They are attracted to the more than 800 channels available through cable or satellite services. But the cable and satellite networks are facing new competition. One survey indicates that 60 percent of North American homes have one or more videogame consoles. People are using the consoles to download apps and video-on-demand offerings. And a growing number of viewers are discontinuing their cable service and opting instead for online services such as Netflix, Hulu, Apple's iTunes, and the networks' own websites. Recently, 1.3 million people watched at least part of the Masters Golf Tournament online, double the number who watched online the previous year. People still prefer free, advertising-supported downloads, although online network advertising made up only 2.5 percent of the $62 billion in annual North American advertising revenues. But the number of homes with digital video recorders (DVRs) and high-definition (HD) televisions is increasing steadily. Recent research suggests that even people who can use their DVRs to skip TV ads don't always do so. According to the Nielsen Company, many DVR users still watch shows at their scheduled times and watch the ads; even those who record shows for later viewing watch almost half the ads they could skip. As more people watch playbacks of their favourite shows, the networks' ratings—and commercial watching—increase too.[14]

Although—or perhaps because—television reaches the greatest number of consumers at once, it is the most expensive advertising medium. The Super Bowl is widely known for its hefty advertising price tag—and its ability to reach over 100 million people in a three-hour period. Firms such as Budweiser, Frito-Lay, GoDaddy, T-Mobile, and The Coca-Cola Company paid as much as $4 million for a 30-second spot during a recent game, although some of the advertisers posted their ads online in the days leading up to the game. Intuit, a software developer for small businesses, recently sponsored a contest called "Small Business Big Game." The winner was awarded a 30-second commercial spot on the Super Bowl broadcast. Oakland, California–based GoldieBlox, maker of toys intended to get girls interested in science and engineering, has experienced phenomenal success as the winning entry, with more than 100 million viewers exposed to its unique products.[15]

Internet Advertising

The digital ad market is growing faster than the rest of the advertising sector due mainly to the rising number of smartphones and tablets in use and increased social media usage. North American digital advertising, including mobile, rose to about $27 billion in a recent year, making up almost 25 percent of all advertising revenues. Ad types include search and banner, the largest category, along with classified, rich media, video, lead generation, sponsorship, and email.

Second to TV ads in terms of overall dollars, digital ad revenues are expected to reach $42 billion in a few years. Spending on ads delivered to desktops and laptops has slowed in comparison to mobile advertising, which has doubled over the last few years and is expected to top $10 billion in the not-too-distant future. The five companies that dominate digital advertising—Google, Yahoo, Facebook, Microsoft, and AOL—accounted for more than 64 percent of all digital ad expenditures in a recent year.[16]

Viral advertising creates a message that is novel or entertaining enough for consumers to forward to others, spreading it like a virus. The great advantage is that spreading the word online, which often relies on social networking sites such as Facebook, YouTube, and Twitter, costs the advertiser nothing. Although viral marketing can be risky, the best campaigns are edgy or funny. Dove soap's Beauty Sketches campaign, one of the biggest online viral sensations ever, sent the following message to women: "You are more beautiful than you think." The campaign compares a woman's description of herself to a description made by strangers through a series of sketches created by an FBI-trained artist. The stranger's description was typically more attractive than what the women themselves described—with the point being that women tend to be overly critical about the way they look. The viral campaign generated close to 30 million views and 660,000 Facebook shares during its first 10 days online.[17]

Newspapers

As companies shift advertising dollars to other platforms, newspaper print advertising revenues continue to fall. Although one advantage of newspaper advertising is the ease with which marketers can easily tailor ads to local tastes and preferences, a disadvantage comes from the relatively short life span—people usually discard their newspapers soon after reading them. Retailers and automobile dealers rank as the biggest newspaper advertisers. Most newspapers now have websites, which have offset some of the declines in advertising dollars.[18]

Radio

Despite the proliferation of other media, the average North American household owns a number of radios—including those in cars—and this is a market penetration that makes radio, which relies on commercial sponsorship, an important advertising medium. Advertisers like the captive audience of listeners at work or as they commute to and from work. As a result, morning and evening drive-time shows command higher ad rates for airtime. In major markets, many stations, depending on their format, serve different demographic groups with targeted programming. Internet radio programming also offers opportunities for more focused targeting.

A recent study of several music-sharing sites reveals that more than half of people 12 years and older listen to online radio through a computer or smartphone. The top reasons cited for listening to online radio include better variety of music and the ability to skip songs.

Projected ad spending estimates for Internet radio, which includes news, sports, talk, and various music genres, will reach $1.31 billion over the next few years with the number of monthly listeners projected to be over 175 million. Recent marketing research shows that the percentage of people listening to Internet radio will soon surpass traditional platforms like AM and FM stations.[19]

Magazines

Magazines include consumer publications and business trade journals. *Time, Reader's Digest,* and *Sports Illustrated* are consumer magazines. *Advertising Age* and *Oil & Gas Journal* are trade publications.

Magazines sometimes customize their publications and target advertising messages to different regions of the country. One method places local advertising in regional editions of the magazines. Other magazines attach wraparounds—half-size covers on top of full-size covers. These wraparounds highlight articles that relate to particular geographic areas; different wraparounds appear in different parts of the country.

Magazines are a natural choice for targeted advertising. Media buyers study demographics of subscribers and select magazines that attract the desired readers. For example, American Express advertises in *Fortune* and *Forbes* to reach businesspeople. PacSun clothes and Clearasil skin medications are advertised in *Teen Vogue*.

Direct Mail

The average North American household receives about 550 pieces of direct mail each year, including 100 catalogues. The huge growth in the variety of direct-mail offerings and the convenience they offer today's busy, time-pressed shoppers has made direct-mail advertising a multibillion-dollar business. Even consumers who like to shop online often page through a catalogue before placing an online order. Although direct-mail advertising is expensive per person, a small business may be able to afford a limited direct-mail campaign but not a television or radio ad. For businesses with a small advertising budget, a carefully targeted direct-mail effort can be highly effective. Email is a low-cost form of direct marketing. Marketers can target the most interested Internet users by offering website visitors an option to register to receive email. Companies like Amazon.ca, The Home Depot, and Abercrombie & Fitch routinely send emails to regular customers.

Address lists are at the heart of direct-mail advertising. Direct-mail marketers use data-mining techniques to segment markets. They then create profiles that show the types of consumers who are likely to buy their products or donate to their organizations. Catalogue retailers sometimes experiment by sending direct-mail pieces randomly to people who subscribe to particular magazines. Then, they analyze the orders received from the mailings and develop profiles of purchasers. Finally, they rent lists of subscriber names that match the profiles they have developed.

Studies have shown that most consumers are annoyed by the amount of so-called "junk mail" they receive every day, including catalogues, advertising postcards, and flyers. Among Internet users, a major pet peeve is *spam,* or junk email. Many local governments have outlawed sending email promotions without legitimate return addresses, although it is difficult to track down and charge offenders.

The Canadian Marketing Association (CMA; www.the-cma.org) helps marketers by offering its members guidelines on ethical business practices. The American-based Direct Marketing Association (DMA; www.the-dma.org) also provides consumer information at its website. The DMA and Canada Post offer services for consumers to opt out of receiving unsolicited direct mail.

Outdoor Advertising

In one year, outdoor advertising accounted for more than $6.7 billion in North American advertising spending.[20] Most spending on outdoor advertising is for billboards, but spending is growing fast for other types of outdoor advertising, such as signs in transit stations, stores, airports, and sports stadiums. Advertisers are exploring new forms of outdoor media that involve technology: computerized paintings, video billboards, "trivision" that displays three revolving images on a single billboard, and moving billboards mounted on trucks, as well as advertising on taxi tops. To see how some NBA teams are using advertising on their courts, see the "Hit & Miss" feature. Other innovations include ads displayed on the Goodyear blimp, using an electronic system that offers animation and video. Digital, electronic, or LED billboards, introduced less than two decades ago, provide an effective medium for advertisers who want to reach their segment with timely and relevant messages. Digital billboards are dynamic, with content updating every 4 to 10 seconds, with multiple advertisers and messages. But outdoor advertising has several disadvantages. The medium requires brief messages, and billboards are often attacked by preservation and conservation groups.

Advertisers are exploring new forms of outdoor media that involve technology, such as computerized paintings and electronic billboards. At 24 million pixels, this eight story high, one-block long digital billboard in Times Square is the largest and highest resolution sign. Advertisers such as Google pay over $2.5 million USD a month.

HIT & MISS

NBA Says Yes to Floor Ads

Instead of putting corporate logos on its jerseys, the NBA has allowed floor advertising on the courts of its 30 teams. The floor ad space is the idea of NBA commissioner Adam Silver, and it will be evaluated over time to determine if there will be a permanent location to sell ad space in the future. While corporate logos on NBA jerseys would generate about $100 million annually, the NBA management projects the "real estate" on the court floor to be worth far more money from television advertising and exposure.

NBA teams received approval to sell space on part of the basketball court known as the apron—space that covers the out-of-bounds area on the sidelines between the baselines, in front of team benches, and the coaches' box where teams already advertise their websites or Twitter handles. There is a catch, however. Company logos must be removable decals and can only be affixed during games televised locally.

So far, three teams have signed up. The Indiana Pacers signed a deal with the state's Economic Development Corporation; JP Morgan Chase will be on the floor at Madison Square Garden during New York Knicks games, and the Miami Heat has signed a deal with Samsung. Samsung is also one of the NBA's newest league partners, recently signing a reported three-year, $100 million deal. The Toronto Raptors were the first team to experiment with technology that creates a 3D optical illusion of its logo on the baseline, which could potentially be extended to corporate sponsor logos.

While pricing varies among the 30 teams, it is rumoured that one top franchise has an asking price of $3 million for the ad space on the court. Front Row Marketing Services, a company that tracks what appears on-screen in sports broadcasts, estimates that the prime floor space might fetch anywhere between $450,000 and $2.5 million per year, depending on the franchise.

Questions for Critical Thinking

1. Although ad space sales have been slow initially, observers believe that some teams are holding out for blue chip companies that appear to be a good fit for the team. What types of sponsors would be the best fit with top NBA franchises?

2. While this is a unique marketing opportunity for a corporate sponsor, some argue that the cost is on par with national advertising fees for games that will only be televised locally. So far, nationally televised regular season games, NBA All-Star weekend, and playoff games are not included. How would you evaluate the cost versus the marketing exposure?

Sources: Ira Boudway, "Slow Sales at the Outset for NBA Floor Space," *Bloomberg Business*, accessed February 16, 2014, www.bloomberg.com/bw/articles/2013-12-02/slow-sales-at-the-outset-for-nba-floor-space; Darren Rovell, "Limited Use of Ads on Court OK'd," *Hotbox Sports*, accessed February 16, 2014, http://news.hotboxsports.com/NBA/article/30799; Philip Johnson, "The NBA Expects To Make $100 Million with On-Court Ads Next Season," *Business Insider*, accessed February 16, 2014, www.businessinsider.com/nba-on-court-ads-first-time-next-season-2013-6; YouTube, "Toronto Raptors Show Off New 3-D Illusion," accessed April 20, 2015, www.youtube.com/watch?v=Fqc92khwhwU.

Sponsorship

Marketers can use one of the hottest trends in promotion to integrate several elements of the promotional mix. **Sponsorship** involves providing funds for a sporting or cultural event in exchange for a direct association with the event. Sports sponsorships attract two-thirds of all sponsorship dollars in North America. Entertainment, festivals, causes, and the arts divide up the remaining third of sponsorship dollars. Firms may also sponsor charitable or other not-for-profit awards or events such as the CIBC-sponsored Canadian Breast Cancer Foundation's Run for the Cure.

Sponsors benefit in two major ways: they gain exposure to the event's audience and they gain association with the image of the activity. If a celebrity is involved, sponsors usually earn the right to use the celebrity's name and the name of the event in advertisements. They can set up signs at the event, offer sales promotions, and similar activities. Sponsorships play an important role in relationship marketing, by bringing together the event, its participants, and the sponsoring firms. Spending on sponsorships is expected to soon increase to $20.6 billion.[21]

sponsorship providing funds for a sporting or cultural event in exchange for a direct association with the event.

Other Media Options

As consumers filter out familiar advertising messages, marketers look for new ways to catch their attention. Many firms use the major media, but some firms promote through other means, such as infomercials and specialized media. **Infomercials** are a form of broadcast direct marketing, also

infomercials a form of broadcast direct marketing; 30-minute programs resemble regular TV programs, but sell goods or services.

ASSESSMENT CHECK

13.2.1 What are the two basic types of advertising? Into what three categories do they fall?

13.2.2 What is the leading advertising medium in North America?

13.2.3 In what two major ways do firms benefit from sponsorship?

called *direct-response television (DRTV)*. These 30-minute programs resemble regular television programs but sell goods or services, such as exercise equipment, skin-care products, or kitchenware. The long format allows an advertiser to thoroughly present product benefits, increase awareness, and make an impact on consumers. Advertisers also receive immediate responses in the form of sales or inquiries because most infomercials feature toll-free phone numbers. Infomercial stars may become celebrities, attracting more customers wherever they go. The most effective infomercials tend to be for auto-care products, beauty and personal-care items, investing and business opportunities, collectibles, fitness and self-improvement products, housewares, and electronics.[22]

Advertisers use just about any medium they can find. A more recent development is the use of automated teller machines (ATMs) for advertising. Some ATMs can play 15-second commercials on their screens, and many can print advertising messages on receipts. An ATM screen has a captive audience because the user must watch the screen to complete a transaction. Directory advertising includes the familiar Yellow Pages listings in telephone books. Advertising is also available in thousands of other types of directories; most such advertising is for business-related promotions. Besides local and regional directories, publishers also produce special printed and online versions of the Yellow Pages specifically for ethnic groups.

LO 13.3 Outline sales promotion.

SALES PROMOTION

sales promotion forms of promotion such as coupons, product samples, and rebates that support advertising and personal selling.

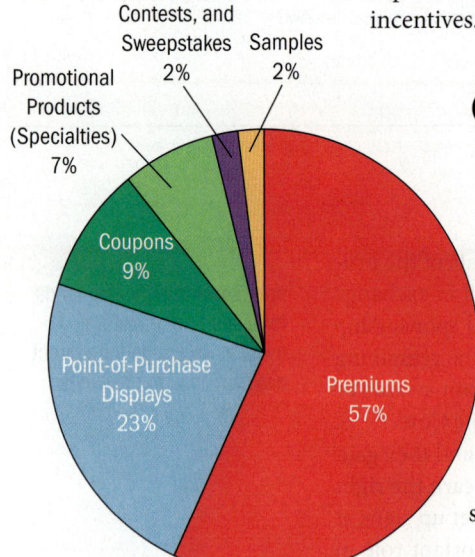

Sales promotion was traditionally viewed as a supplement, or add-on, to a firm's sales or advertising efforts. But sales promotion has emerged as an important part of the promotional mix. Promotion now accounts for more than half as many marketing dollars as are spent on advertising, and promotion spending is rising faster than ad spending. **Sales promotion** consists of forms of promotion such as coupons, product samples, and rebates that support advertising and personal selling.

Both retailers and manufacturers use sales promotions to offer consumers extra incentives to buy. Sales promotions can lead to the short-term advantage of increased sales. But sales promotions can also help marketers build brand equity and improve their customer relationships. Examples of sales promotion include samples, coupons, contests, displays, trade shows, and dealer incentives.

Consumer-Oriented Promotions

The goal of a consumer-oriented sales promotion is to get new and existing customers to try products, and ultimately, to buy products. Marketers want to increase sales of complementary products, increase impulse purchases, and encourage repeat business by rewarding product purchasers. **Figure 13.3** illustrates how marketers allocate their consumer-oriented spending among the categories of promotions. Total promotions spending in the North America exceeded $584 billion in a recent year, reflecting opportunities for other businesses to produce promotional products for various campaigns.[23]

Promotions can also be used to popularize an idea, such as the growing awareness of plastic shopping bags and the pollution they contribute to the environment. The "Going Green" feature discusses the growing trend of banning plastic shopping bags.

Premiums, Coupons, Rebates, and Samples

Nearly six of every 10 sales promotion dollars are spent on *premiums*—items given away for free or at a reduced price when another product is purchased. For example, cosmetics companies, such as Clinique, offer sample kits with purchases of their products. Fast-food restaurants are also big users of premiums. McDonald's and Burger King include a toy with the purchase of every children's meal. The toys are often tie-ins with new movies or popular cartoon shows. Marketers generally choose premiums that are likely to get consumers thinking about and caring about the brand and

FIGURE 13.3
Spending on Consumer-Oriented Promotions

Games, Contests, and Sweepstakes 2%
Samples 2%
Promotional Products (Specialties) 7%
Coupons 9%
Point-of-Purchase Displays 23%
Premiums 57%

Sources: Data from Kathleen M. Joyce, "Higher Gear," *Promo Magazine*, accessed April 26, 2010, http://promomagazine.com.

GOING GREEN

HOW MUCH WOULD YOU PAY FOR A PLASTIC SHOPPING BAG?

Many stores in Toronto, Montreal, Vancouver, and other Canadian cities now collect a tax or charge about five cents for giving customers a plastic shopping bag at the checkout counter. This cost is meant to discourage the use of plastic bags and instead encourage the use of longer-lasting reusable and recyclable bags.

In North America, it is estimated that almost 4 billion tons of plastic waste—in the form of bags, sacks, and wrapping—were generated in one year. The plastic is made from oil and can take 1,000 years to break down. Only about 1 percent of this waste is ever recycled.

A growing number of people want to reduce these statistics. For example, more city governments have banned the use of plastic bags, required certain retailers to accept plastic bags for recycling, or imposed a tax on plastic.

But such laws have not always been met with approval. In eco-friendly Seattle, voters overturned a law charging 20 cents per plastic bag, perhaps because they were already recycling and reusing the bags. Big retailers like Walmart and Loblaw sell reusable bags for about a dollar. These bags carry the store's logo and name and promote the use of reusable bags. Some retailers have reacted to customer complaints and have stopped charging for plastic bags.

Questions for Critical Thinking

1. Can stores that provide eco-friendly shopping bags or other ways to reduce the polluting effects of plastic gain promotional benefits from their efforts? How can cities that ban or tax plastic bags promote their actions?

2. What other ways can you think of to promote the idea of recycling plastic bags or reducing their use?

Sources: "NYCWasteLe$$," Plastic Bag Recycling, accessed May 11, 2010, www.nyc.gov; Dave Gram, "Vt. Plastic Bag Tax Proposal Seen Coming Too Late," *Rutland Herald,* April 16, 2010, www.rutlandherald.com/article/20100416/NEWS04/4160363; Melissa Eddy, "Plastic Bag Ban: Would You Pay 5 Cents for a Bag?" *Huffington Post,* February 22, 2010, www.huffingtonpost.com/2010/02/22/plastic-bags-ban-would-yo_n_471228.html; Steve Painter, "3 Wal-Marts Testing Purge of Plastic Bags," *Arkansas Online,* January 24, 2010, www.arkansasonline.com/news/2010/jan/24/3-wal-marts-testing-purge-plastic-bags-20100124; Stephen Messenger, "Washington D.C.'s Plastic Bag Tax Takes Effect This Week," *TreeHugger.com,* January 3, 2010, www.treehugger.com.

---

the product. People who purchase health foods at a grocery store may find an offer for a free personal training session at a local health club printed on the back of their sales receipt.

Customers redeem *coupons* for small price discounts when they purchase the promoted products. Such offers may persuade a customer to try a new or different product. Some large supermarket chains double the face value of manufacturers' coupons. Coupons have the downside of focusing customers on price instead of brand loyalty. Some consumers complain that clipping or printing out coupons is too time-consuming, but others enjoy the savings, especially when money is tight and prices seem high.

Industrywide coupon redemption remained steady in a recent year at 2.9 billion coupons redeemed, while distribution grew more than 3 percent over the previous year. Of the coupons distributed, approximately 40 percent were for food products. As marketers continue to leverage technology when offering coupons, digital coupon redemption increased more than 140 percent in a recent year. Overall, the use of digital coupons continues to grow faster than traditional coupons. Approximately 87 percent of traditional coupons are distributed through free-standing inserts in the newspaper—and represent 41 percent of the coupons redeemed. Some people predict that the growing use of paperless mobile coupons, which consumers access on their smartphones while shopping could make clippable or printed-out coupons obsolete.[24]

Rebates offer cash back to consumers who mail in required proofs of purchase. Today, firms have simplified the rebate mail-in requirement by offering consumers the opportunity to submit rebates online. Rebates help packaged-goods manufacturers increase purchase rates, promote multiple purchases, and reward product users. Other types of companies also offer rebates, especially for electronics, computers and their accessories, and automobiles. Processing rebates gives marketers a way to collect data about their customers, but many shoppers find it awkward to collect the required receipts, forms, and universal product codes (UPCs) and then wait several weeks for the refund. In the past, many manufacturers counted on the fact that consumers would not follow through on rebates.[25]

A *sample* is a gift of a product distributed by mail, door to door, in a demonstration, or inside packages of another product. On any given day, you might receive a sample moisturizer, a bar of soap, or a packet of laundry detergent. Out of every four consumers who receive samples, three will try them.

Games, Contests, and Sweepstakes

Contests, sweepstakes, and games offer cash, merchandise, or travel as prizes to participating winners. Firms often sponsor these activities to introduce new goods and services and to attract new customers. Games and contests require entrants to solve problems or write essays, and they must sometimes provide a proof of purchase. Sweepstakes choose winners by chance and require no product purchase. Consumers typically prefer sweepstakes because they are easy; games and contests require more effort. Companies like sweepstakes, too, because they are inexpensive to run and the number of winners is decided at the beginning. With games and contests, the company doesn't know how many people will correctly complete a puzzle or gather the right number of symbols from scratch-off cards. Sweepstakes, games, and contests can reinforce a company's image and advertising message. But consumer attention may focus on the promotion instead of on the product.

In recent years, court rulings and legal restrictions have limited the use of games and contests. Companies must proceed carefully when advertising their contests and games and the prizes they award. Marketers must show the chances of winning and avoid false promises, such as suggesting that a consumer has already won.

Specialty Advertising

specialty advertising promotional items that prominently display a firm's name, logo, or business slogan.

Have you received any free pens, T-shirts, or refrigerator magnets imprinted with a business name? These offers are examples of **specialty advertising** or *advertising specialties*. This type of sales promotion involves the gift of useful merchandise carrying the name, logo, or slogan of a profit-seeking business or a not-for-profit organization. Because those products are useful and sometimes personalized with recipients' names, people tend to keep and use them, giving advertisers repeated exposure. Advertising specialties were originally designed to identify and create goodwill for advertisers. Now they generate sales leads and develop traffic for stores and trade show exhibitors. Like premiums, these promotions should reinforce the brand's image and its relationship with the recipient.

Trade-Oriented Promotions

trade promotion sales promotion geared to marketing intermediaries, not to final consumers.

Sales promotion techniques can also contribute to campaigns directed to retailers and wholesalers. **Trade promotion** is sales promotion geared to marketing intermediaries, not to consumers. Marketers use trade promotion to encourage retailers to stock new products, continue carrying existing products, and promote both new and existing products effectively to consumers. Successful trade promotions offer financial incentives. They require careful timing, attention to costs, and should be easy for intermediaries to apply. These promotions should bring quick results and improve retail sales. Major trade promotions include point-of-purchase advertising and trade shows.

point-of-purchase (POP) advertising displays or demonstrations that promote products when and where consumers buy them, such as in retail stores.

Point-of-purchase (POP) advertising consists of displays or demonstrations that promote products at checkout areas or in the location where consumers buy the item, such as in retail stores. Displays are in various forms, including shelf-mounted signs and hanging posters. Sunscreen, painting supplies, and snacks are typically displayed this way. POP displays can have a significant impact on sales, as an estimated 70 percent of purchase decisions are made within the retail store itself. Recently, electronic, dynamically updated POP displays have been used to present targeted product information and instant coupons. Marketing research has shown that consumers are more likely to purchase certain products when such displays are present. About 78 percent of Facebook's daily users visit the site via mobile and tablet devices, and 41 percent of ad revenue comes from small screens over laptops and desktops. Location-based advertising will be directed primarily to smartphones.[26]

Manufacturers and other sellers often exhibit at *trade shows* to promote goods or services to members of their distribution channels. These shows are often organized by industry trade associations. Each year, thousands of trade shows attract millions of exhibitors and hundreds of millions of attendees. Such shows are particularly important in fast-changing industries like those for computers, toys, furniture, and fashions. The International Consumer Electronics Show, which is held annually in Las Vegas and attracts more than 3,200 exhibitors and 150,000 attendees, is the largest. Other trade shows are in the construction, consumer goods, energy, entertainment, manufacturing, and sports and outdoors industries. Trade shows are especially effective for introducing new products and generating sales leads.[27]

Personal Selling

Many companies consider personal selling—a person-to-person promotional presentation to a potential buyer—to be the key to marketing effectiveness. Unless a seller matches a firm's goods or services to the needs of a certain client or customer, none of the firm's other activities produces any benefits. Today, sales and sales-related jobs employ about 16 million North American workers and are expected to grow.[28] Businesses often spend five to 10 times as much on personal selling as on advertising. Personal selling includes the significant costs of hiring, training, benefits, and salaries. Because of these costs, businesses are very concerned with the effectiveness of their sales personnel. One of their continuing concerns is with the way representatives communicate with others.

How do marketers decide whether to make personal selling the main focus of their firm's marketing mix? In general, firms are likely to focus on personal selling instead of advertising or sales promotion under four conditions:

1. Customers are relatively few in number and are geographically concentrated.
2. The product is technically complex, involves trade-ins, or requires special handling.
3. The product carries a relatively high price.
4. The product moves through direct distribution channels.

Personal selling involves a person-to-person promotional presentation to a potential buyer. At a cosmetics counter, the salesperson provides a free makeup demonstration to reinforce the message of how a company's products enhance a person's looks.

A good example is selling Piper Cub airplanes. Airplane buyers tend to be wealthy people who value their freedom and privacy—and the luxury of owning their own plane. "It is a way of life I am selling," says veteran sales rep Bruce Keller, "not just aluminum. I want the customer to share that with me. If you look at my airplane and you sit in it, you are going flying."[29]

The sales functions of most companies are going through rapid change. Compared to the past, today's salespeople are more concerned with creating long-term buyer–seller relationships and acting as consultants to their customers. After the recession, salespeople faced a new challenge—consumers who haggle over prices, even on retail items. One survey found that 88 percent of those questioned had haggled over at least one price in the past six months. The survey found that hagglers had better than a 75 percent success rate in making deals on clothing, appliances, and jewellery.[30] The Great Depression of the 1930s was the last time North Americans engaged in serious amounts of haggling. Today's consumers have advantages that would surprise their grandparents. Anyone with a smartphone can search online for competing prices of merchandise while standing in a retail store. Many consumers have become savvy online shoppers, searching for bargains on websites like Overstock, eBay, Expedia, Orbitz, and Priceline.

Personal selling can occur in several settings; each setting can involve either business-to-business (B2B) or business-to-consumer (B2C) selling. *Field selling* refers to sales representatives who make sales calls on prospective customers at their businesses. Companies that sell major industrial equipment typically rely on field selling. *Over-the-counter selling* describes sales activities in retailing and some wholesale locations, where customers visit the seller's facility to purchase items. *Telemarketing* sales representatives make their presentations over the phone. A later section reviews telemarketing in more detail.

Sales Tasks

All sales activities involve helping customers in some way. A salesperson's work can vary from one company or situation to another, but all sales work usually includes a mix of three basic tasks: order processing, creative selling, and missionary selling.

Order Processing **Order processing** is used in both field selling and telemarketing, but this form of selling is most often related to retail and wholesale firms. In order processing, the salesperson identifies customer needs, points out merchandise to meet those needs, and processes the order. Route-sales personnel process orders for such consumer goods as bread, milk, soft drinks, and snack foods. They check each store's stock, report inventory needs to the store manager, and complete the sale. Most of these jobs include at least minor order-processing functions.

order processing a form of selling used mostly at the wholesale and retail levels; involves identifying customer needs, pointing out products that meet those needs, and completing orders.

Creative Selling Sales representatives for most business products and some consumer items perform **creative selling**, a persuasive type of promotional presentation. Creative selling promotes a good or service whose benefits are not readily seen or whose purchase decision requires a close look at other options. Creative selling is used to sell intangible products such as insurance, but can also be used to sell tangible goods.

creative selling a persuasive type of promotional presentation.

Many retail salespeople just process orders, but many consumers want more customer service. That's where creative selling comes in. For example, training sales staff at women's clothing stores might include holding seasonal wardrobe-building workshops. After attending such a workshop, the sales staff can better help customers select and purchase coordinating clothing, accessories, and shoes. Customers might not have purchased these items if they hadn't received such advice.

Missionary Selling Sales work also includes an indirect form of selling, where the representative promotes goodwill for a company or gives the customer technical or operational help. This practice is called **missionary selling**. Many businesses that sell technical equipment, such as Oracle and Fujitsu, provide systems specialists who act as consultants to customers. These salespeople work to solve problems and sometimes help their clients with questions not directly related to their employers' products. Other industries also use missionary selling techniques. Pharmaceutical company representatives—called *detailers*—visit physicians to describe the firm's latest offerings. Some firms are also finding success with less direct methods, including web-based sales calls after office hours. The large pharmaceutical maker Pfizer recently cut back its sales force and is turning toward electronic marketing. The company has found electronic detailing especially helpful. It allows doctors to access the latest information on drugs when and where they choose. The information can also be strictly controlled, and the company runs much less risk of its salespeople being accused of marketing drugs for off-label uses—that is, for treating conditions other than those they were originally intended to help.[31] The actual sales, in any case, are handled through pharmacies, which fill the prescriptions.

missionary selling an indirect form of selling where the representative promotes goodwill for a company or provides technical or operational assistance to the customer.

Telemarketing **Telemarketing** refers to personal selling by telephone. It provides a firm's marketers with a high return on their expenses, an immediate response, and an opportunity for a personalized two-way conversation. Many firms use telemarketing because expense or other factors keep salespeople from meeting many potential customers in person. Telemarketers can use databases to target prospects based on population data. Telemarketing takes two forms: outbound and inbound. A sales representative who calls you is practising *outbound telemarketing*. On the other hand, *inbound telemarketing* occurs when you call a toll-free phone number to get product information or place an order.

telemarketing personal selling by telephone, which provides marketers with a high return on their expenses, an immediate response, and an opportunity for a personalized two-way conversation.

Outbound telemarketers must follow various legal requirements and industry guidelines that guide their behaviour. In general, telemarketers must disclose what they are selling and the organization they represent before making their presentations. Calls are limited to between 9 A.M. and 9:30 P.M. on weekdays and between 10 A.M. and 6 P.M. on weekends. Sellers must also inform the customer about the details of exchange policies. Recent legislation requires telemarketers to respect lists of people who do not want to receive calls. Consumers who want to be on the list must call a special number or visit a website to register. Telemarketers must stop calling registered numbers within 31 days or face stiff fines.[32] Charities, surveys, and political campaign calls are exempt from these restrictions. Also, businesses that already have a relationship with consumers can make telemarketing calls. These businesses include the bank where customers have accounts or the dealership where they bought their car.

The Sales Process

The sales process typically follows the seven-step sequence illustrated in **Figure 13.4**: prospecting and qualifying, the approach, the presentation, the demonstration, handling objections, closing, and the follow-up. Remember the importance of flexibility; a good salesperson will vary the sales process to suit a customer's responses and needs. The process of selling to a potential customer who is unfamiliar with a company's products differs from the process of serving a long-time customer.

Prospecting, Qualifying, and Approaching At the prospecting stage, salespeople identify potential customers. Salespeople may look for leads for prospective sales from such sources as existing customers, friends and family, and business associates. The qualifying process identifies potential customers who have the financial ability and authority to buy.

Companies use different ways to identify and qualify prospects. Some companies rely on business development teams to do this work. They use the responses from direct mail to provide leads to sales reps. Other companies believe in personal visits from sales representatives; others use email, which is inexpensive and usually has a good response rate. Many B2B firms use electronic social media such as electronic newsletters, web events, virtual trade shows, podcasts, videos, online demonstrations, and blogs.[33]

Before making the first contact with a customer, successful salespeople make careful preparations, by analyzing available data about a prospective customer's product lines and other related information. These salespeople know that a good first impression can influence a customer's attitude toward the selling company and its products.

Presentation and Demonstration At the presentation stage, salespeople communicate promotional messages. They may describe the major features of their products, highlight the advantages, and give examples of satisfied consumers. A demonstration is a critical step in the sales process. It helps to reinforce the message that the salesperson has been communicating. For example, department-store shoppers can get a free makeover at the cosmetics counter. And anyone looking to buy a car will take it for a test drive before deciding whether to purchase it.

Some products are too large to transport to prospective buyers or require a special installation to demonstrate. Sales representatives can demonstrate these products for customers by using laptop computers, multimedia presentations, web conferences, podcasts, and graphic programs like SmartDraw.[34] Services, which are intangible, can't be demonstrated in the same way. Salespeople may find it helpful to show a presentation that includes testimonials from satisfied customers or graphs illustrating results.

Handling Objections Some salespeople fear potential customers' objections because they view their questions as criticism. But a good salesperson can use objections as an opportunity to answer

Step 7 Follow-Up Thank the Customer and Begin the Process of Maintaining Mutually Beneficial Relationships That Result in Future Sales

Step 6 Closing Ask for the Order

Step 5 Handling Objections Answer the Prospect's Questions

Step 4 Demonstration Involve the Customer in the Presentation

Step 3 Presentation Tell the Product's Story

Step 2 Approach Prepare for the Sales Interview

Step 1 Prospecting & Qualifying Identify Potential Customer

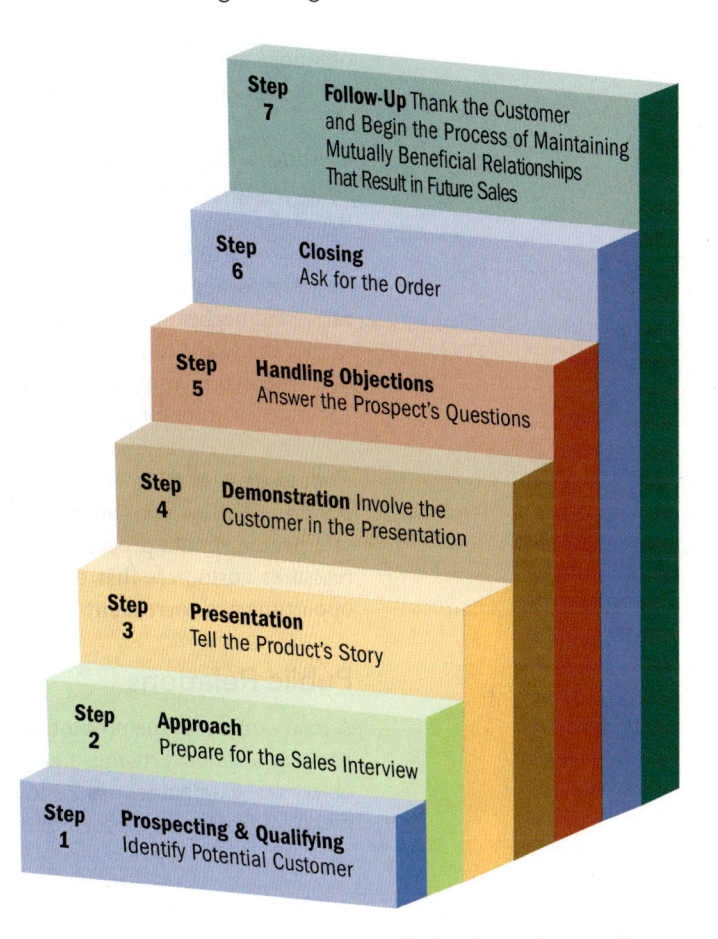

FIGURE 13.4 Seven Steps in the Sales Process

questions and explain how the product will benefit the customer. As a general rule, the key is to sell the benefits, not the features: How will this product help the customer?

Closing The critical point in the sales process is the closing. This is the time when the salesperson asks the prospect to buy. If the presentation has matched the product benefits to customer needs, the closing should be a natural conclusion. If there are some bumps in the process, the salesperson can try some different techniques, such as offering alternative products, offering a special incentive for purchase, or restating the product benefits. The ideal outcome of this interaction is closing the sale—and beginning a relationship where the customer builds loyalty to the brand or product. But even if the sale is not closed, the salesperson should still think of the interaction as the beginning of a potential relationship. The prospect might become a customer in the future. See the "Career Kickstart" feature for tips on how to close the big sale.

Follow-up A salesperson's actions after the sale may lead to the customer making another purchase. Follow-up is an important part of building a long-lasting relationship. After closing, the salesperson should process the order efficiently. By calling soon after a purchase, the salesperson reassures customers that they made the right decision to buy. The salesperson also creates an opportunity to correct any problems.

Public Relations

A final element of the promotional mix is public relations (PR). Public relations includes publicity and supports advertising, personal selling, and sales promotion, usually by pursuing broader objectives. Companies use PR to try to improve their image with the public by distributing specific messages or ideas to target audiences. Cause-related promotional activities are often backed up by

CAREER KICKSTART

How to Negotiate in a Difficult Economy

Tips for Closing the Next Big Sale

If you enjoy competition, the thrill of victory, and rewards commensurate with your performance, a sales career might be for you. There is no better feeling than closing a deal—and the potential rewards that come with a close. However, with victory comes a fair share of rejection. Here are some tips for closing a sale:

- *Know your customer.* Review everything the customer has told you about the business and the challenges or issues that need to be resolved.

- *Listen.* Always be the best listener you can be. Listening allows you to develop an effective solution, and selling a solution helps close the deal.

- *Be patient.* Whether it is for a large, multimillion dollar deal or not, building solid relationships takes time, sometimes even years.

- *Create value.* Positioning your goods or services to meet customer needs is at the heart of selling. Part of the sales process involves identifying a customer's objectives, strategy, decision process, and timing. It also involves showing the customer how your good or service will help overcome issues or challenges. Ask probing questions and obtain honest feedback.

- *Summarize the benefits.* Have the conviction and confidence that your good or service will help solve the customer's problem. Provide a final summary with the benefits of your good or service. This is also the time for your customer to bring up any objections.

- *Know how to ask for the business.* There comes a time when it simply makes sense to ask your customer for the sale. If your solution is well thought out, organized, and targeted, asking for the sale should be a time for both parties to agree to move forward.

If you don't succeed and the customer doesn't buy, remember that the last impression is almost as important as the first and be gracious and professional. Most important, always follow up.

Sources: Thomas Phelps, "Why Choose a Career in Sales," About.com, accessed February 16, 2014, http://salescareers.about.com; Geoffrey James "How to Close a Sale," Inc., accessed February 16, 2014, www.inc.com; Sloan Brothers, "5 Tips for Closing a Sales Deal," Startup Nation, accessed February 16, 2014, www.startupnation.com.

public relations and publicity campaigns. In addition, PR helps a firm to increase awareness of goods and services and then builds a positive image of those goods and services.

Public relations refers to an organization's communications and relationships with its various public audiences, such as customers, vendors, news media, employees, shareholders, the government, and the general public. Many of these communication efforts have marketing purposes. Public relations is an efficient, indirect communications channel for promoting products. It can publicize products and help create and maintain a positive image of the company.

The public relations department links a firm with the media. It provides the media with news releases and video and audio clips. It also holds news conferences to announce new products, the formation of strategic alliances, management changes, financial results, and other developments. Publications issued by the department include newsletters, brochures, and reports.

Publicity

The type of public relations that is tied most closely to promoting a company's products is **publicity**—the nonpersonal stimulation of demand for a good, service, place, idea, event, person, or organization by unpaid placement of information in print or broadcast media. Press releases and news coverage generate publicity. Ironically, criticism can sometimes also generate publicity. Spirit Airlines recently got a lot of negative publicity when it started charging fees for carry-on luggage—but the airline's bookings increased 50 percent. The increased bookings resulted from the airline having installed "pre-reclined" seats on its new planes. The new seats meant the airline could add more seating and lower its airfares. Even though "pre-reclined" is a poor name—the seats don't recline but stay permanently upright—some observers say that consumers looking for the cheapest airfares will continue to book on Spirit.[35]

Publicity also benefits not-for-profit organizations when they receive coverage of events such as the 17th Annual Head and Neck Cancer Fundraising Gala for McGill University's Department of Otolaryngology. The event was highly publicized because of the attendance and support of actor and producer Michael Douglas. Douglas has a vacation home in the resort area of Mont Tremblant. When he called his doctor in New York complaining about severe pain, his doctor referred him to his friend and colleague, Dr. Saul Frenkiel, at the Jewish General Hospital in Montreal. Frenkiel diagnosed Douglas as having a tumour. But other health professionals had examined Douglas for the same symptoms and had missed the tumour. After successful treatment in the United States, a grateful Douglas asked how he could show his gratitude. Someone suggested he could help with fundraising. That's how Douglas became the honouree at the event, which raised $2 million. It is an extraordinary amount for what is generally considered to be a little known area of cancer research and treatment. Besides the funds for research, the publicity has helped raise awareness in the general public about this cancer's risks and treatments.[36] When a for-profit firm teams up with a not-for-profit firm in a fundraising effort, the relationship usually generates good publicity for both organizations.

public relations an organization's communications and relationships with its various public audiences.

publicity the nonpersonal stimulation of demand for a good, service, place, idea, event, person, or organization by unpaid placement of information in print or broadcast media.

✓ **ASSESSMENT CHECK**

13.3.1 Why do retailers and manufacturers use sales promotions?

13.3.2 When does a firm use personal selling instead of nonpersonal selling?

13.3.3 How do public relations serve a marketing purpose?

PUSHING AND PULLING STRATEGIES

LO 13.4 Describe pushing and pulling promotional strategies.

Marketers can choose between two general promotional strategies: a pushing strategy or a pulling strategy. A **pushing strategy** uses personal selling to market an item to wholesalers and retailers in a company's distribution channels. Companies promote the product to members of the marketing channel, not to end users. Sales personnel explain to marketing intermediaries why they should carry particular merchandise. They usually support their promotion by offering special discounts and promotional materials. Some marketers also offer **cooperative advertising** allowances, by sharing with channel partners the cost of local advertising of their firm's product or product line. All these strategies are designed to motivate wholesalers and retailers to push the good or service to their own customers.

pushing strategy personal selling to market an item to wholesalers and retailers in a company's distribution channels.

cooperative advertising allowances that marketers provide to share with channel partners the cost of local advertising of their firm's product or product line.

pulling strategy promotion of a product by generating consumer demand for it, mainly through advertising and sales promotion appeals.

✓ ASSESSMENT CHECK

13.4.1 Give an example of a pushing strategy.

13.4.2 Give an example of a pulling strategy.

A **pulling strategy** tries to promote a product by generating consumer demand for it, mainly through advertising and sales promotion appeals. Potential buyers will then request that their suppliers—retailers or local distributors—carry the product, which pulls it through the distribution channel. Dove used this strategy when it launched its new Men 1 Care line of men's personal-care products during a recent Super Bowl. The 30-second commercial, with its tagline "Be comfortable in your own skin," generated a large online response. Many consumers searched such terms as "Super Bowl," "ad," and "men" to find retailers that stocked the products.[37]

Most marketing situations require combinations of pushing and pulling strategies, although the main emphasis can vary. Consumer products usually depend more heavily on pulling strategies; and B2B products usually favour pushing strategies.

LO 13.5 Outline the different types of pricing objectives in the marketing mix.

PRICING OBJECTIVES IN THE MARKETING MIX

Products offer utility, or want-satisfying power. As consumers, we decide how much value we associate with each product. For example, after a major storm, we may value electricity, food, and water above everything else. If we commute a long distance or are planning a vacation, fuel may be of greater concern. All consumers have limited amounts of money and a variety of possible uses for it. The **price**—the exchange value of a good or service—becomes a major factor in consumer buying decisions.

price the exchange value of a good or service.

Businesspeople try to meet certain objectives through their pricing decisions. Pricing objectives vary from firm to firm, and many companies have multiple pricing objectives. Some firms try to improve profits by setting high prices; others set low prices to attract new business. As **Figure 13.5** illustrates, the four basic categories of pricing objectives are (1) profitability, (2) volume, (3) meeting competition, and (4) prestige.

Profitability Objectives

Profitability objectives are the most common goals listed in most firms' strategic plans. Marketers know that profits are the revenue the company brings in, minus its expenses. Usually a big difference exists between revenue and profit. Most automakers try to produce at least one luxury vehicle. They can charge $50,000 or more for it instead of relying entirely on the sale of cars priced at $15,000 to $25,000.

Some firms maximize profits by reducing costs instead of increasing prices. Companies can maintain prices and increase profitability by operating more efficiently or by changing the product to make it less costly to produce. One strategy is to maintain a steady price while reducing the size or amount of the product in the package. Manufacturers of candy, coffee, and cereal often use this strategy.

FIGURE 13.5 Pricing Objectives

- **Profitability** "We want profits to increase by 10 percent a year through 2020."
- **Volume** "By 2020, we plan to achieve a 28 percent share of the personal watercraft market."
- **Meeting Competition** "We will meet their prices and achieve profit and volume growth by offering better customer service."
- **Prestige** "The new perfume has an exquisite package, a beautiful label, and one of the highest retail prices."

profitability objectives common goals that are included in the strategic plans of most firms.

volume objectives pricing decisions that are based on market share, the percentage of a market controlled by a certain company or product.

Volume Objectives

A second approach to pricing strategy—**volume objectives**—bases pricing decisions on market share, the percentage of a market controlled by a certain company or product. One firm may want to have a 25 percent market share in a certain product category; another firm may want to maintain or expand its market share for specific products. As a market becomes oversupplied—like the PC market—firms need to find ways to get consumers to upgrade or try new products. Setting a lower price can meet that objective, as long as the firm still makes a profit. Many PC makers—and retailers—have begun to offer their products at lower prices, especially at the start of the school year.[38]

Pricing to Meet Competition

A third set of pricing objectives tries to meet competitors' prices so that price becomes a nonissue. In many lines of business, firms set their own prices to match the prices set by established industry leaders. But companies cannot legally work together to agree on prices.

Price is a highly visible element of a firm's marketing mix. Some businesses may be tempted to use a product's price to gain an advantage over competitors. Sometimes the race to match competitors' prices results in a *price war,* which has happened in the airline and fast-food industries. Because some competitors can match a price cut, many marketers try to avoid price wars by using other strategies, such as adding value, improving quality, educating consumers, and building relationships.

Although price is a major element of the marketing mix, it is not the only one. Electronic readers such as the Kindle and the iPad are in a fierce pricing competition for digital books, as the "Solving an Ethical Controversy" feature explains.

Prestige Objectives

The final category of objectives takes in the effect of prices on prestige. **Prestige pricing** sets a relatively high price to develop and maintain an image of quality and exclusiveness. Marketers set such objectives because they recognize the role of price in communicating an overall image for the firm

prestige pricing setting a relatively high price to develop and maintain an image of quality and exclusiveness.

SOLVING AN **ETHICAL** CONTROVERSY

Free E-books: Good or Bad for Business?

When Amazon's Kindle electronic reader first became available, Amazon charged consumers $9.99 for each e-book they purchased. Publishers insisted that that price was too low to keep their business profitable. But Amazon actually gave some e-books away for free, including those of living authors who earn an income from their writing.

Amazon explained that the free e-books were a way to get consumers to read some unfamiliar writers. The hope was that customers would then buy other works by those writers. But some publishers delay publication of electronic editions for several months after the hardcover books have been issued, in the same way they delay publishing paperback editions.

Should e-books be given away for free?

PRO

1. Some publishers view free e-books as promotions to generate buzz about new or unknown authors.
2. Some publishers that give away e-books on a regular basis have noticed an increase in sales, which, as one executive says, is "all found money."

CON

1. "It is illogical to give books away for free," said David Young of Hachette Book Group, which publishes Stephenie Meyer's *Twilight* series.
2. The relatively low price of e-books may discourage consumers from buying actual books with suggested retail prices of $25 or more.

Summary

Both Amazon's Kindle and Barnes & Noble's Nook continue to offer free e-books. In addition, both offer the capability for customers to lend e-books to friends and family for 14 days by simply inputting a name and email address. Although some publishers might cringe at these practices, it is likely that the trend will continue.

Sources: Hillel Italie, "Amazon Escalates Standoff with Hachette," *USA Today*, accessed June 17, 2014, www.usatoday.com/story/money/business/2014/05/23/amazon-escalates-standoff-with-publisher-hachette/9507621; Alec Liu, "Kindle, Nook, Whatever: Here's How to Get Free E-Books," *Fox News*, accessed February 21, 2014, www.foxnews.com/tech/2011/01/27/kindle-nook-heres-free-e-books; Stan Schroeder, "The E-Book Price War Isn't Over Yet," *Mashable*, accessed February 21, 2014, http://mashable.com/2010/02/18/ipad-ebook-prices; Motoko Rich, "Apple's Prices for E-Books May Be Lower Than Expected," *New York Times*, accessed February 21, 2014, www.nytimes.com/2010/02/18/technology/18apple.html?_r=0; "With Kindle, the Best Sellers Don't Need to Sell," *Hindustantimes*, accessed February 21, 2014, www.hindustantimes.com/world-news/with-kindle-the-best-sellers-don-t-need-to-sell/article1-501400.aspx; "The Kindle Pricing Strategy & the Kindle Pricing History," *Ask Deb*, accessed February 21, 2014, www.askdeb.com.

Prestige pricing sets a relatively high price to develop and maintain an image of quality and exclusiveness. People expect to pay more for a Louis Vuitton bag, just like the rock star in this ad.

and its products. People expect to pay more for a Lexus, a Louis Vuitton purse, or a Caribbean vacation on St. Kitts or Nevis. Despite a recession, the British retailer Selfridges has seen a 60 percent increase in sales of "must-have" handbags by the luxury brand Mulberry. Mulberry even has waiting lists for some of its styles.[39]

Scarcity can also create prestige. Products that are limited in distribution or products that are so popular that they become scarce generate their own prestige. Businesses can then charge more for them. Apple iPhones and iPads always seem to be in short supply when new models are introduced. Eager buyers can be seen camping outside retail locations the day before, in hopes of being among the first to own the latest technological gadgets.

✓ **ASSESSMENT CHECK**

13.5.1 Define *price*.
13.5.2 What is a second approach to pricing strategy?

LO 13.6 Describe how firms set prices in the marketplace and the four alternative pricing strategies.

PRICING STRATEGIES

People from different areas of a company contribute their expertise to set the most strategic price for a product. Accountants, financial managers, and marketers provide relevant sales data, cost data, and customer feedback. Designers, engineers, and systems analysts also contribute important information.

Prices are determined in two basic ways: by applying the concepts of supply and demand discussed in Chapter 3 and by completing cost-oriented analyses. Economic theory assumes that a market price will be set at the point where the amount of a product desired at a given price equals the amount that suppliers will offer for sale at that price. In other words, the market price occurs at the point where the amount demanded and the amount supplied are equal. Online auctions, such as those on eBay, are a popular application of the demand-and-supply approach.

Price Determination in Practice

Economic theory might lead to the best pricing decisions, but most businesses do not have all the information they need to make those decisions. Most businesses use **cost-based pricing** formulas. These formulas calculate total costs per unit and then add markups to cover overhead costs and generate profits.

Cost-based pricing totals all costs associated with offering a product in the market, including research and development, production, transportation, and marketing expenses. An added amount, the markup, then covers any unexpected or overlooked expenses and provides a profit.

cost-based pricing calculating total costs per unit and then adding markups to cover overhead costs and generate profits.

The total is the selling price. The actual markup used varies depending on such factors as brand image and type of store. The typical markup for clothing is determined by doubling the wholesale price (the cost to the merchant) to arrive at the retail price for the item.

Breakeven Analysis

Businesses often do a **breakeven analysis** to calculate the minimum sales volume a product must generate at a certain price level to cover all costs. This method involves looking at various costs and total revenues. *Total cost* is the sum of total variable costs and total fixed costs. *Variable costs* change with the level of production, as labour and raw materials do. *Fixed costs* such as insurance premiums and utility rates charged by water, natural gas, and electric power suppliers remain stable regardless of the production level. *Total revenue* is calculated by multiplying price by the number of units sold.

breakeven analysis the pricing-related technique used to calculate the minimum sales volume a product must generate at a certain price level to cover all costs.

Finding the Breakeven Point

The *breakeven point* is the level of sales that will generate enough revenue to cover all of the company's fixed and variable costs. It is the point where total revenue just equals total costs. Sales beyond the breakeven point will generate profits; sales volume below the breakeven point will result in losses. This is illustrated in **Figure 13.6**.

The following formulas give the breakeven point in units and dollars:

$$\text{Breakeven Point (in units)} = \frac{\text{Total fixed costs}}{\text{Contribution to fixed costs per unit}}$$

$$\text{Breakeven Point (in dollars)} = \frac{\text{Total fixed costs}}{1 - \text{Variable cost per unit}/\text{Price}}$$

As an example, a product sells for $20. It has a variable cost of $14 per unit and produces a $6 per-unit contribution to fixed costs. If the firm has total fixed costs of $42,000, then it must sell 7,000 units to break even on the product. The calculation of the breakeven point in units and dollars is as follows:

$$\text{Breakeven Point (in units)} = \frac{\$42{,}000}{\$20 - \$14} = \frac{\$42{,}000}{\$6} = 7{,}000 \text{ units}$$

$$\text{Breakeven Point (in dollars)} = \frac{\$42{,}000}{1 - \$14/\$20} = \frac{\$42{,}000}{1 - 0.7} = \frac{\$42{,}000}{0.3} = \$140{,}000$$

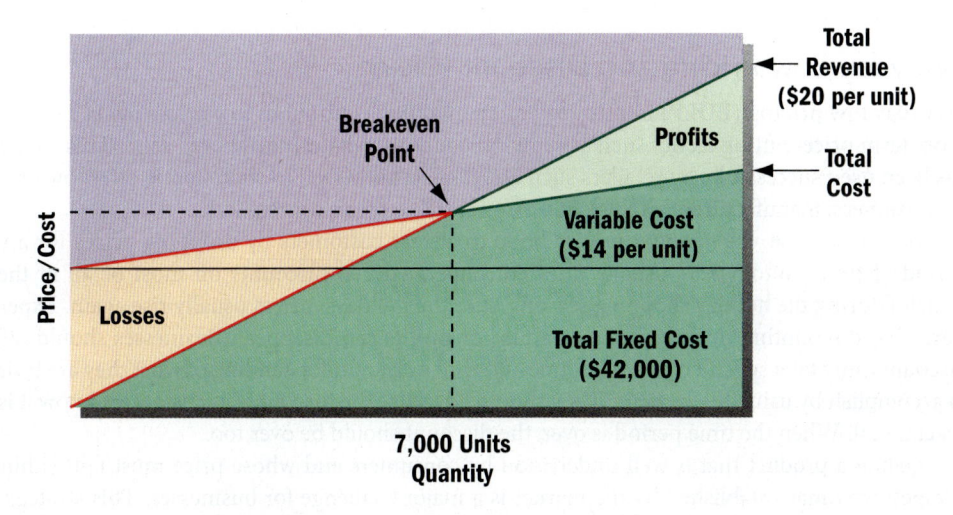

FIGURE 13.6 Breakeven Analysis

Marketers use breakeven analysis to calculate the profits or losses that would result from several different proposed prices. Because different prices produce different breakeven points, marketers can compare their calculations of required sales to break even with the sales estimates from marketing research studies. This comparison can identify the best price—the price that would attract enough customers to exceed the breakeven point and earn profits for the firm.

Most firms want to know whether enough customers will buy the number of units the firm needs to sell at a particular price to break even. They develop estimates of consumer demand through surveys of likely customers, interviews with retailers that would sell the product, and reviewing prices charged by competitors. The breakeven points for several possible prices are then calculated and compared with sales estimates for each price. This practice is referred to as *modified breakeven analysis*.

Alternative Pricing Strategies

The strategy a company uses to set its prices should grow out of the firm's overall marketing strategy. In general, firms can choose from four alternative pricing strategies: skimming, penetration, discount or everyday low pricing, and competitive pricing.

Skimming Pricing

skimming pricing a strategy that sets an intentionally high price relative to the prices of competing products.

A **skimming pricing** strategy sets an intentionally high price relative to the prices of competing products. The term comes from the expression "skimming the cream." This pricing strategy often works when introducing a distinctive good or service that has little or no competition, but it can also be used at other stages of the product life cycle. A skimming strategy can help marketers set a price that separates a firm's high-end product from those of competitors. It can also help a firm recover its product development costs before competitors enter the field. This strategy is often used with prescription drugs.

Penetration Pricing

penetration pricing a strategy that sets a low price as a major marketing tactic.

A **penetration pricing** strategy sets a low price as a major marketing tactic. Businesses may price new products much lower than competing products when they enter new industries that have dozens of competing brands. Once the new product achieves some market success, through purchases encouraged by its low price, marketers may increase the price to the level of competing products. But stiff competition can prevent the price increase.

Everyday Low Pricing and Discount Pricing

everyday low pricing (EDLP) a strategy of maintaining continuous low prices instead of using short-term price-cutting tactics such as cents-off coupons, rebates, and special sales.

Everyday low pricing (EDLP) is a strategy of maintaining continuous low prices instead of using short-term price-cutting tactics such as cents-off coupons, rebates, and special sales. This strategy has been used successfully by retailers such as Walmart and GNC to consistently offer low prices to consumers; manufacturers also use EDLP to set stable prices for retailers.

Businesses that use *discount pricing* hope to attract customers by dropping prices for a set period of time. Automakers usually offer consumers special discounts on most or all of their vehicles during the holiday shopping season. After the holidays, prices usually rise again. Experts warn that discounting must be done carefully, or profits can disappear. Businesses should offer discounts only for a specified period of time and with a clear understanding of what they are trying to accomplish by using the strategy. They should advertise the discount, so customers know it is a special deal. When the time period is over, the discount should be over too.

Selling a product that is well understood by consumers and whose price must fall within a competitive range established by the market is a major challenge for businesses. This strategy is discussed in the "Hit & Miss" feature.

Chapter 13 Promotion and Pricing Strategies 377

Stores such as Walmart use an everyday low pricing strategy of maintaining continuous low prices instead of using short-term price-cutting tactics such as cents-off coupons, rebates, and special sales.

HIT & MISS

A Bis Gourmet—Quality Fast Food At Competitive Prices

A bis, the Latin term for "encore or to repeat a pleasurable experience," suggests the company philosophy that customers will come back for more after tasting the difference quality can make to something as simple as a sandwich.

A Bis Gourmet hand produce and deliver over 20,000 fresh sandwich products, parfait cups, fresh leaf and pasta salads each and every day. The reason for their success is attention to quality, consistency, and customer service. From locations in Montreal, Ottawa, and Toronto, dedicated staff prepare preservative free, high-quality food, wrapped in eco-friendly individual serving containers for sale to customers on-the-go through retail convenience stores.

The market price for these sorts of food items is competitive and A Bis Gourmet must be careful to control costs while delivering the superior quality products and taste it promises its retail distributors. This competitive differentiation allows A Bis Gourmet to confidently promote their brand as a superior choice for retail distributors to offer their customers—and keep them coming back for more too.

Questions for Critical Thinking

1. How much "extra" do think customers would be willing to pay for higher quality sandwiches at say, a convenience store located on the ground floor of a downtown office building?

2. How would you suggest A Bis Gourmet develop new customized menu items in conjunction with retailers that would sell them exclusively?

Sources: A Bis Gourmet, accessed April 20, 2015, www.abisgourmetqc.ca.

Competitive Pricing

Many organizations rely heavily on price as a competitive tactic, but even more organizations use **competitive pricing** strategies. These firms try to reduce the emphasis on price competition by matching other firms' prices and by focusing their own marketing efforts on the product, distribution,

competitive pricing a strategy that tries to reduce the emphasis on price competition by matching other firms' prices and by focusing their own marketing efforts on the product, distribution, and promotional elements of the marketing mix.

> **ASSESSMENT CHECK**
>
> 13.6.1 What is a cost-based pricing formula?
>
> 13.6.2 Why do companies implement competitive pricing strategies?

LO 13.7 Discuss consumer perceptions of price.

CONSUMER PERCEPTIONS OF PRICES

How do you perceive, or view, prices for certain products? Marketers need to consider how customers perceive prices. If large numbers of potential buyers consider a price to be too high or too low, businesses must correct the situation. When setting prices, marketers consider price–quality relationships and the use of odd pricing.

Price–Quality Relationships

Research shows that a consumer's perception of product quality is closely related to an item's price. Most marketers believe that this perceived price–quality relationship remains steady over a relatively wide range of prices, although extremely high or low prices have less credibility. The price–quality relationship can critically affect a firm's pricing strategy.

Many consumers associate prestige, quality, and high price as being related. That is, they believe that paying a high price for an item such as an Infiniti car or a Chanel bag will convey prestige and ensure quality. Others believe that eating at an expensive restaurant means the food will be better than food served at a modestly priced restaurant. The opposite is also true. Many consumers may view an extremely low price as an indication that corners have been cut and quality will be poor. Interestingly, a recent study noted that California wines made from organically grown grapes are less expensive than those made from nonorganic grapes. But this price difference actually seemed to be a disadvantage for the organic wines: labelling a wine as "made from organically grown grapes" drove the price down, but the same wine without the certification notice sold for more. Many factors may contribute to this situation. In the 1970s and 1980s, when organic wines were first produced, the reds gained a bad reputation: many of them quickly turned to vinegar because they were made without preservatives. Some consumers still remember this. Also, "green" consumers are aware of the benefits of organically grown fruits and vegetables, but the benefits of organically grown wines are not so well known. Growers need to communicate to consumers that, in this case at least, price and quality don't necessarily go together.[40]

odd pricing a pricing method that uses uneven amounts to make prices appear to be less than they really are.

Odd Pricing

Have you ever wondered why retailers set prices like $1.99 instead of $2 or $9.95 instead of $10? **Odd pricing** is a pricing method that uses uneven amounts to make prices appear to be less than they really are. Before the age of cash registers and sales taxes, retailers reportedly followed this practice to force clerks to make correct change as part of their cash control efforts. But odd pricing is commonly used today because many retailers believe that consumers prefer uneven amounts or amounts that sound less than they really are. Some retailers also use this method to identify items that have been marked down. The odd price lets people know the item is on sale.

> **ASSESSMENT CHECK**
>
> 13.7.1 How does the price–quality relationship affect a firm's pricing strategy?
>
> 13.7.2 Why is odd pricing used?

WHAT'S AHEAD

The chapters in Part 4 have explained the main principles of marketing management. These chapters also described how each principle fits a firm's overall business strategy. Part 5 will help you understand how companies manage the technology and information that businesses can use to create value for their customers and improve their competitiveness in the marketplace.

RETURN TO INSIDE BUSINESS

WorkSafeBC: Promoting Safety to Young Workers

For the first two years, Raise Your Hand was expressed simply by using photos of raised hands. Each hand was connected to a story contributed by a young worker. As more and more young workers participated, the website changed daily. The campaign grew to further express the feel of a grassroots movement. It then built on the stories, to give something back to young workers in the form of an empowering message about how to exercise their workplace rights.

Postings to YouTube and other social media sites have exceeded expectations, as measured by the number and quality of stories, event and online interactions, and click-through rates.

QUESTIONS FOR CRITICAL THINKING

1. How would you continue the success of this online program?
2. Describe the concept for a new online promotional campaign.

SUMMARY OF LEARNING OBJECTIVES

LO 13.1 Discuss how integrated marketing communications relates to a firm's overall promotional strategy.

When a firm practises integrated marketing communications, it coordinates promotional activities to produce a unified, customer-focused message. IMC identifies consumer needs and shows how a company's products meet those needs. Marketers select the promotional media that work best to target and reach customers. The programs rely on teamwork and careful promotional planning to coordinate IMC strategies.

A company's promotional mix combines personal selling and nonpersonal selling. Nonpersonal selling includes advertising, sales promotion, and public relations. By selecting the most suitable combination of promotional mix elements, marketers try to achieve the firm's five major promotional objectives: providing information, differentiating a product, increasing demand, stabilizing sales, and highlighting the product's value.

✓ ASSESSMENT CHECK ANSWERS

13.1.1 What is the objective of an integrated marketing communications program? An IMC strategy focuses on customer needs to create a unified promotional message about a firm's goods or services.

13.1.2 Why do firms pursue multiple promotional objectives at the same time? Firms pursue multiple promotional objectives because they may need to convey different messages to different audiences.

13.1.3 What are product placement and guerrilla marketing? Product placement involves paying a fee to have a product featured in certain media. Guerrilla marketing refers to innovative, low-cost marketing efforts designed to get consumers' attention in unusual ways.

LO 13.2 Summarize the different types of advertising.

Advertising is the most visible form of nonpersonal promotion. Advertising is designed to inform, persuade, or remind. Product advertising promotes a good or service, while institutional advertising promotes a concept, idea, organization, or philosophy. Television, newspapers, and magazines are the largest advertising media categories. Other advertising media include direct mail, radio, and outdoor advertising. Interactive advertising directly involves the consumer, who controls the flow of information.

ASSESSMENT CHECK ANSWERS

13.2.1 What are the two basic types of advertising? Into what three categories do they fall? The two basic types are product and institutional. They fall into the categories of informative, persuasive, and reminder-oriented advertising.

13.2.2 What is the leading advertising medium in North America? According to the most recent statistics listed in Figure 13.2, television is the leading advertising medium in North America.

13.2.3 In what two major ways do firms benefit from sponsorship? Firms benefit from sponsorship in two ways: they gain exposure to the event's audience, and they gain from their association with the activity's positive image.

LO 13.3 Outline sales promotion.

Sales promotion accounts for more expenses than advertising. Consumer-oriented sales promotions include coupons, games, rebates, samples, premiums, contests, sweepstakes, and promotional products. This type of sales promotion offers consumers an extra incentive to buy a product. Point-of-purchase advertising displays and trade shows are sales promotions directed to the trade markets. Personal selling involves face-to-face interactions between the seller and buyers. The primary sales tasks are order processing, creative selling, and missionary selling. Public relations is nonpaid promotion that seeks to enhance a company's public image.

ASSESSMENT CHECK ANSWERS

13.3.1 Why do retailers and manufacturers use sales promotions? Retailers and manufacturers use sales promotions to offer consumers extra incentives to buy their products

13.3.2 When does a firm use personal selling instead of nonpersonal selling? Personal selling is generally used when there are few customers who are geographically concentrated, the product is technically complex or requires special handling, the price is high, or the product moves through direct distribution channels.

13.3.3 How do public relations serve a marketing purpose? Public relations are an efficient, indirect communications channel for promoting products. It can publicize products and help create and maintain a positive image of the company.

LO 13.4 Describe pushing and pulling promotional strategies.

A pushing strategy relies on personal selling to market a product to wholesalers and retailers in the company's distribution channels. A pulling strategy promotes the product by generating consumer demand for it, through advertising and sales promotion.

ASSESSMENT CHECK ANSWERS

13.4.1 Give an example of a pushing strategy. A pushing strategy is used by drug manufacturers, who used to market only to physicians and hospitals. Today, drug manufacturers also use a pulling strategy by marketing directly to patients through advertising, which encourages patients to ask their doctors about the medications.

13.4.2 Give an example of a pulling strategy. Pulling strategies are used by retailers and by manufacturers of consumer goods such as cosmetics, automobiles, and clothing.

LO 13.5 Outline the different types of pricing objectives in the marketing mix.

Pricing objectives can be classified as profitability, volume, meeting competition, and prestige. Profitability objectives are the most common goals. Volume objectives base pricing decisions on market share. Meeting competitors' prices makes price a nonissue in competition. Prestige pricing sets a high price to develop and maintain an image of quality or exclusiveness.

ASSESSMENT CHECK ANSWERS

13.5.1 Define *price*. Price is the exchange value of a good or service.

13.5.2 What is a second approach to pricing strategy? A second approach to pricing strategy is volume objectives. This pricing strategy bases pricing decisions on market share.

LO 13.6 Describe how firms set prices in the marketplace and the four alternative pricing strategies.

Economic theory determines prices by using the law of demand and supply. But most firms use cost-based pricing, which adds a markup after totalling all costs. Firms usually do a breakeven analysis to calculate the minimum sales volume a product must generate at a certain price to cover all costs. The four alternative pricing strategies are skimming, penetration, everyday low pricing and discounting, and competitive pricing. A skimming strategy sets a high price initially to recover costs and then lowers the price. A penetration strategy sets a lower price and then raises it later. Everyday low pricing and discounting offer a lower price for a period of time. Competitive pricing matches other firms' prices and highlights a product's nonprice benefits.

ASSESSMENT CHECK ANSWERS

13.6.1 What is a cost-based pricing formula? A cost-based pricing formula calculates the total costs per unit and then adds markups to cover overhead costs and generate profits.

13.6.2 Why do companies implement competitive pricing strategies? Companies use competitive pricing strategies to reduce the emphasis on price competition by matching other firms' prices and by focusing their own marketing efforts on the product, distribution, and promotional elements of the marketing mix.

LO 13.7 Discuss consumer perceptions of price.

When setting prices, marketers must consider how consumers perceive the price–quality relationship of their products. Consumers may be willing to pay a higher price if they perceive a product to be of superior quality. Marketers often use odd pricing to convey a message to consumers.

✓ ASSESSMENT CHECK ANSWERS

13.7.1 How does the price–quality relationship affect a firm's pricing strategy? Consumers believe that the price of an item reflects its quality, except in extreme cases. A firm must try to set its prices accordingly.

13.7.2 Why is odd pricing used? Retailers believe that consumers prefer prices that have uneven amounts or amounts that sound like less than they really are. Odd pricing may also be used to indicate a sale item.

BUSINESS TERMS YOU NEED TO KNOW

- advertising 358
- breakeven analysis 375
- cause advertising 359
- competitive pricing 377
- cooperative advertising 371
- cost-based pricing 374
- creative selling 368
- everyday low pricing (EDLP) 376
- guerrilla marketing 357
- infomercials 363
- institutional advertising 358
- integrated marketing communications (IMC) 354
- missionary selling 368
- nonpersonal selling 355
- odd pricing 378
- order processing 368
- penetration pricing 376
- personal selling 355
- point-of-purchase (POP) advertising 366
- positioning 356
- prestige pricing 373
- price 372
- product advertising 358
- product placement 357
- profitability objectives 372
- promotion 354
- promotional mix 355
- publicity 371
- public relations 371
- pulling strategy 372
- pushing strategy 371
- sales promotion 364
- skimming pricing 376
- specialty advertising 366
- sponsorship 363
- telemarketing 368
- trade promotion 366
- volume objectives 372

REVIEW QUESTIONS

1. What is the purpose of integrated marketing communications?
2. What are the five major objectives of a promotional strategy?
3. Identify and define each of the three categories of advertising based on their purpose. Which of the three categories of advertising would marketers likely use for the following products?
    a. Deodorant
    b. An electronic reader
    c. Organic produce
    d. Healthcare insurance
4. What are the benefits of online and interactive advertising? What might be some drawbacks?
5. For each of the following, describe potential benefits and drawbacks of a sponsorship relationship:
    a. Royal Bank of Canada and professional golfer Jason Day
    b. Bell Canada and Montreal International Jazz Festival
6. If you were a marketer for Rolex, what kind of sales promotion might you use for high-end watches?
7. In what situations are firms likely to emphasize personal selling?
8. Describe the seven-step sales process.
9. Define the four basic categories of pricing objectives.
10. What are the four alternative pricing strategies used by marketers? Give an example of the circumstances under which each might be selected.

PROJECTS AND TEAMWORK APPLICATIONS

1. Choose a product that you purchased recently. Identify the various media that were used to promote the product and analyze the promotional mix. Do you agree with the company's marketing strategy, or would you suggest changes to the promotional mix? Why? Create your own print ad for the product you chose, using any business strategies or knowledge you have learned in this course so far.

2. Evaluate the price of the product you selected in the exercise above. What pricing strategy is the manufacturer using? Do you think the price is fair? Why or why not? Choose a different strategy; develop a new price for the product based on the new strategy. Ask your classmates whether they would purchase the product at the new price. Why or why not?

3. Some schools receive financial benefits by allowing companies to promote their goods and services to students. Others have decided against this practice, and some schools ban this type of promotion. Find some examples of corporate sponsors in public elementary and high schools and on college and university campuses. With your class, discuss the pros and cons of promotion in public schools and on college and university campuses. In your view, is there a difference between a public school and a college or university campus? Why or why not?

4. On your own or with a classmate, research a recent issue that has caused a business, a not-for-profit organization, or a government agency to suffer from bad publicity. Evaluate the situation, outlining the steps the organization might take to build better public relations.

5. You are the marketing manager at a company that is introducing a new line of video games. How would you set the prices for the new products?

WEB ASSIGNMENTS

1. **Top advertisers.** *Advertising Age* compiles data annually on the top national advertisers. Visit the website listed below to access the most recent year. Answer the following questions:
   a. Who were the top 10 advertisers that year?
   b. How much did they spend on advertising?
   c. What was the most advertised brand that year?

   http://adage.com/datacenter/#advertising_spending

2. **Online coupon fraud.** Go to the websites listed to learn about online coupon fraud. Prepare a brief report. Make sure to answer the following questions: How big a problem is online coupon fraud? What changes have marketers made to try to reduce online coupon fraud?

   www.newser.com/story/35962/hackers-spread-coupon-scam.html

   http://online.wsj.com/article/SB124641121217977575.html

   http://multichannelmerchant.com/retail/news/0308-curtailing-online-coupon-fraud

3. **Yield management.** Assume you want to fly from St. John's, Newfoundland and Labrador, to Victoria, British Columbia. Visit some travel sites. Search for fares. Change such factors as advance purchase, day of departure, time of departure, and so on. What did this exercise teach you about yield management?

   www.expedia.ca
   www.ca.kayak.com
   www.travelocity.ca

Note: Internet Web addresses change frequently. If you don't find the exact sites listed, you may need to access the organization's home page and search from there or use a search engine such as Bing or Google.

PART 4 CASE STUDY Beau's All Natural Brewing Company
Building Brand Awareness

Strategic planning today is built upon historical industry knowledge—primarily about competitors and customers that have come before your company. Although many things change over time, industry knowledge is cumulative and often reflects trends in behaviours that may have started long ago. Having researched and written over 100 business plans in his career with the Ontario government before starting up Beau's, Steve Beauchesne was familiar with the importance of industry research. He learned to follow proven strategies in some cases but in others, he found "there were myths about what had to be done, or else."

The first Canadian craft beer venture is generally credited to John Mitchell and Frank Appleton in British Columbia. In the early 1980s, strict provincial control of beer sales prevented a brewery owner from owning a licensed establishment serving beer as well. As a result, only large producers like Molson, Labatt, Carling, and O'Keefe provided product to the beer market. After successfully lobbying politicians to change the laws, Mitchell and Appleton were able to do both.

Mitchell was originally from Britain and was familiar with the brewpub model where local pubs produced and sold their products along with quality food. Appleton knew about craft brewing and taught Mitchell the techniques. Shortly after developing their signature "Bay Ale," the two turned their Troller Pub in Horseshoe Bay, BC in West Vancouver into Canada's first brewpub. They learned what customers liked directly from customer feedback. If it sold well and customers asked for more, they brewed more. In many ways, this empirical research model still drives how craft brewers research customer preferences and plan growth. They have learned that the best way to know what to brew is from customer tasting and feedback. This demands a distribution network that provides a presence in the bars, restaurants and other venues and servers familiar with the competing brands. Distribution means availability and sales will follow.

Generally, each craft brewer would boost its bestselling and banner beer brand and attempt to grow sales and customers through development of other blends. Steve and Tim had developed various brews as hobbyists and had hit on several recipes that they felt were outstanding. Informal testing among friends and family convinced them that these brews would be well received if they could gear up production and provide a distribution network where customers could buy.

Craft beer marketing generally focuses on a unique recipe, freshness of the brew, use of organic ingredients, and the absence of preservatives. There is also a cultural difference in the way the business and its products are offered to customers. The breweries, which are also primary points of sale to customers, are generally presented as fun places to tour, see how the beer is made, and shop. The brewery tour also allows the firm to promote their pride in the production process and develop closer relationships with customers and the communities served.

The primary challenge facing every new business is generating brand recognition by the target market of potential customers. Craft beer customers don't order brands they have never heard of or know nothing about. They are different from regular "big brewery" customers in several ways. For instance, determinants that influence how customers learn about new beers entering the marketplace are different. Whereas big brewery customers are typically made aware of new brands through large-scale advertising campaigns in multiple media platforms, craft beer customers are generally introduced to new brands and breweries by their local bar or restaurant server. So the first order of business Steve and Tim faced, and continue to face as the firm expands into new markets throughout Ontario, Quebec, and the United States, is to establish brand recognition. Once the potential customer understands what the Beau's brand means and is presented with the opportunity to taste the difference themselves—as Steve says, "We've won them over."

Learning how to generate awareness, promote trial tasting, and building brand loyalty with customers is an ongoing effort as conditions are often different in different markets, and craft beer customers don't all behave in the same way. Beau's marketing team has learned to grow sales by trying different low budget strategies and has avoided the industry myth that demands heavy advertising spending to succeed. Instead, great success has come from small promotional events, which often can generate publicity in the local media. For example, Oktoberfest is a popular annual event at Beau's brewery in Vankleek Hill that recently brought together 19,000 visitors and raised over $95,000 for community charities.

This way of thinking and learning from others in the craft beer industry seems to be working as sales recently surpassed 3.5 million litres. With the Ontario government seemingly more open to relaxing strict retail-sales control of beer, Beau's is exploring new ways to generate growth.

Questions for Critical Thinking

1. What other marketing ideas would you suggest Beau's try?
2. How can Beau's communicate with customers who are too far away to actually have direct contact with the Beau's brewery staff?
3. What does the Beau's logo and labels communicate about the company, in your mind?

4 LAUNCHING YOUR...

MARKETING CAREER

In Part 4, "Marketing Management," you learned about the goals and functions of marketing. The three chapters in this part emphasized the central role of customer satisfaction in defining value and developing a marketing strategy in traditional and nontraditional marketing settings. You learned about the role of marketing research and the need for relationship marketing in today's competitive environment. You discovered how new products are developed and how they change through the four stages of the product life cycle, from introduction through growth and maturity to decline. You also learned about the role of different channels in creating effective distribution strategies. Finally, you saw the impact of integrated marketing communications on the firm's promotional strategy, the role of advertising, and how pricing affects consumer behaviour. You may have read about some marketing tasks and functions that sounded especially interesting. Here are a few ideas about careers in marketing.

The first thing to remember is that marketing is more than personal selling and advertising. For example, are you curious about why people behave the way they do? Are you good at spotting trends? Marketing research analysts look for answers to a wide range of questions about business competition, customer preferences, market trends, and past and future sales. They often design and conduct their own consumer surveys, using the telephone, mail, the Internet, or personal interviews and focus groups. They collect the data and analyze it. Their recommendations become input for managerial decisions, such as whether to introduce new products, redesign current products, enter new markets, or discontinue products or markets where profitability is low. Marketing researchers may be included in a new-product development team, where they work directly with scientists, production and manufacturing personnel, and finance employees. Marketing researchers are often asked to help clients put their recommendations in place. With today's highly competitive economy, jobs in this area are expected to grow.

Another career path in marketing is sales. Do you work well with others? Are you good at reading other people's feelings? Are you a self-starter? If so, being a sales representative might be for you. Selling jobs exist in every industry. Many of these jobs use a combination of salary and performance-based commissions, so they can pay very well. Sales jobs are also often a first step on the ladder to upper-management positions. Sales representatives work for wholesalers and manufacturing companies (and even for publishers such as the one that produces this book). They sell automobiles, computer systems and technology, pharmaceuticals, advertising, insurance, real estate, commodities and financial services, and all kinds of consumer goods and services.

If you're interested in mass communications, you should know that print and online magazines, newspapers, and broadcast companies generate most of their revenue from advertising. Sales representatives who sell space and time slots in the media contribute to the success of these firms. If you like to travel, consider that many sales jobs involve travel.

Advertising, marketing management, and public relations are other categories of marketing. In large companies, marketing managers, product managers, promotion managers, and public relations managers often work long hours under pressure; they may travel frequently or transfer between jobs at headquarters and positions in regional offices. Their responsibilities include directing promotional programs, supervising advertising campaigns and budgets, and conducting communications such as press releases with the firm's public audiences. Thousands of new positions are expected to open up in the next several years; the field is expected to grow 14 percent over the next decade. Growth of the Internet and new media has increased demand for advertising and public relations specialists.

Advertising and public relations firms employ thousands of people. Most advertising firms develop specialties; many of the largest advertising firms work internationally. Online advertising is one area where new jobs will be opening in the future, especially as more and more client firms expand their online sales operations.

CAREER ASSESSMENT EXERCISES IN MARKETING

1. Select a field that interests you. Use the Internet to research the types of sales positions available in that field. Locate a few entry-level job openings and see what career steps that position can lead to. (You might want to start with a popular job-posting site such as Monster.ca.) Note the job requirements, the starting salary, and the form of compensation—straight salary or salary plus commission? Write a one-page summary of your findings.

2. Use the Internet to identify and research two or three of the leading advertising agencies in Canada, such as Cossette Communications or Wasserman & Partners. What are some of their recent ad campaigns? Who are their best-known clients? Where do the agencies have offices? What job openings do they currently list, and what qualifications do they ask for? Write a brief report comparing the agencies you selected, decide which agency you would prefer to work for, and give your reasons.

3. Test your research skills. Choose an ordinary product, such as toothpaste or soft drinks. Design a survey to find out why people chose the brand they most recently purchased. For instance, suppose you wanted to find out how people choose their shampoo. List as many decision criteria as you can think of, such as availability, scent, price, packaging, benefits from use (conditioning, dandruff-reducing, and so on), brand name, and ad campaign. Ask eight to 10 friends to rank these decision factors, and note some simple demographics about your research subjects such as their age, gender, and occupation. Chart your results. What did you learn about how your friends made their purchase decision? Did any of your findings surprise you? How could you have improved the survey?

PART 5
MANAGING TECHNOLOGY AND INFORMATION

Chapter 14 Using Technology to Manage Information

14 USING TECHNOLOGY TO MANAGE INFORMATION

LEARNING OBJECTIVES

LO 14.1 Distinguish between data and information, and discuss the role of information systems in business.

LO 14.2 Describe the components and types of information systems.

LO 14.3 Outline how computer hardware and software are used to manage information.

LO 14.4 Describe networking and telecommunications technology and the types of computer networks.

LO 14.5 Outline the security and ethical issues affecting information systems.

LO 14.6 Explain how companies plan for, and recover from, information systems disasters.

LO 14.7 Review the trends in information systems.

INSIDE BUSINESS

Stock-Trak: Learning about the Stock Market through Simulation

What's the best way to learn about the stock market—a complicated business environment that involves rapidly changing information and special terms that only those involved seem to understand? More importantly, how can someone develop good trading skills, gain a sense of how stocks behave in real time, and experience what they would do in a situation—without actually risking any money?

According to Tom Reti and Mark Brookshire, executives at Stock-Trak Global Portfolio Simulations, there is no better way to learn about investment trading than real-life experience. To get that experience without risking any money, Stock-Trak provides a web-based stock market simulation and training products package. Stock-Trak has sold its products to the academic and financial services markets and to the general public.

Wall Street Survivor (www.wallstreetsurvivor.com) is part of Stock-Trak's consumer division; it targets online investing, trading, and game enthusiasts with an investment-oriented simulation and contest website. Anyone interested in learning and developing their trading skills can sign up and experience online trading without the risk of losing real money. Real-time data are provided so that learners can see the immediate results of their decisions. Learners can also use a variety of learning materials and supplements, such as discussion forums with other learners and tutorials to improve their trading skills. Contest prizes make the experience more exciting and competitive while avoiding the risk of losing money. Stock-Trak's co-branding with newspapers and other media has proven very successful, as shown by the website www.marketwatch.com/game/. If you've ever seen a stock market investment contest, chances are good that Stock-Trak provided the simulation and learning environment.

In the academic market, more than 60,000 students at colleges and universities in 30 countries have used the simulation to learn about trading stocks, options, futures, bonds, and mutual funds. Dedicated websites such as http://nipissing.stocktrak.com/home.aspx at Ontario's Nipissing University are typical of websites Stock-Trak has set up for other universities, such as Montreal's McGill University, the University of Toronto, New York University, Yale University, and Columbia University.

The third market for Stock-Trak is the growing financial services industry that uses simulation training for employees before putting them to work trading with real client's money. Stock-Trak has been providing training to employees of Scottrade Inc. since 2008. Under the terms of their agreement, Stock-Trak manages a web-based employee education and training simulator used by employees of Scottrade's 375 branch offices. Each quarter, new hires are given simulated cash to manage. They are tested for their knowledge of the stock and option markets and their ability to successfully use the various tools and techniques learned through Scottrade's training program.

Stock-Trak has three office locations in Montreal, Quebec; Mississauga, Ontario; and Atlanta, Georgia.[1]

CHAPTER 14 OVERVIEW

This chapter explores how businesses manage information as a resource and how they use technology to help in this task. Today, nearly all business functions—from human resources to production to supply chain management—rely on information systems. The chapter begins by looking at the differences between information and data and then defines an information system. The components of information systems are presented, and two major types of information systems are described. The chapter also discusses databases, which are important to all organizations and are the heart of all information systems. Then the chapter looks at the computer hardware and software that drive information systems. Today, specialized networks make information access and information transmission work smoothly; so the chapter examines different types of telecommunications and computer networks to see how businesses are using them for competitive advantage. The chapter then turns to a discussion of the ethical and security issues affecting information systems, followed by a description of how organizations plan for, and recover from, information system disasters. A review of the current trends in information systems concludes the chapter.

LO 14.1 Distinguish between data and information, and discuss the role of information systems in business.

DATA, INFORMATION, AND INFORMATION SYSTEMS

Every day, businesspeople ask themselves questions such as the following:

- How well is our product selling in Calgary compared to Halifax? Have sales among consumers aged 25 to 45 increased or decreased in the past year?
- How will rising energy prices affect production and distribution costs?
- If employees can access the benefits system through our network, will our benefit costs increase or decrease?
- How can we communicate more efficiently and effectively with our workforce that is spread out across the country?

data raw facts and figures that may or may not be meaningful to a business decision.

information knowledge gained from processing data.

An effective information system can help answer these and many other questions. **Data** consist of raw facts and figures that may or may not be relevant, or meaningful, to a business decision. **Information** is knowledge gained from processing those facts and figures. For example, businesspeople need to gather demographics, or population data, about a target market or the specifications of a certain product. But the data are useless unless they are transformed into relevant information that can be used to make a competitive decision. For example, data might be the sizes of various demographic groups. Information drawn from those data could be how many of those individuals are potential customers for a firm's products. Technology has advanced so quickly that all businesses—large or small, in large cities or in remote areas, now have access to data and information that can make them competitive in a global arena.

information system an organized method for collecting, storing, and communicating past, present, and projected information on internal operations and external intelligence.

chief information officer (CIO) the executive responsible for managing a firm's information systems and related computer technologies.

An **information system** is an organized method for collecting, storing, and communicating past, present, and projected information on internal operations and external intelligence. Most information systems today use computer and telecommunications technology. A large organization typically assigns responsibility for managing its information systems and related operations to an executive called the **chief information officer (CIO)**. The CIO often reports directly to the firm's chief executive officer (CEO). An effective CIO can understand and control technology so that the company can use one seamless operation to communicate both internally and externally. But small companies rely just as much on information systems as do large ones, even if they do not assign a full-time manager to this area.

Today's CIO, closely connected to the company's overall business strategies and marketing efforts, is concerned with how cloud-delivered business services of software and data are transmitted to enterprises, with a focus on sales, customer interfaces, and "consumerization," the reorientation of goods and service designs around the individual end user. Yesterday's CIO, focused on installation and design of software, has become increasingly aware of the need for data security, systems availability, and responsiveness. Their expertise makes CIOs and former CIOs good candidates for corporate boards.[2]

Information systems can be designed to assist many business functions and departments—from marketing and manufacturing to finance and accounting. They can manage a huge flood of information by organizing data in a logical and accessible manner. A company can use the system to monitor all areas of its operations and business strategy and to identify problems and opportunities. Information systems gather data from inside and outside the organization; they then process the data to produce information that is meaningful to all aspects of the organization. The processing steps can include storing data for later use, classifying and analyzing it, and retrieving it easily when needed.

Many companies—and nations—combine high-tech and low-tech solutions to manage the flow of information. Email, wireless communications, and videoconferencing are increasingly common. But they haven't totally replaced paper memos, phone conversations, and face-to-face meetings. Information can make the difference between staying in business and going bankrupt. The right information can help a firm keep up to date with changing consumer demands, competitors' activities, and government regulations. A firm can then apply this information to fine-tune existing products, develop new products, and maintain effective marketing.

ASSESSMENT CHECK

14.1.1 Distinguish between data and information.

14.1.2 What is an information system?

COMPONENTS AND TYPES OF INFORMATION SYSTEMS

LO 14.2 Describe the components and types of information systems.

The definition of *information system* in the previous section does not specifically mention the use of computers or technology. Information systems have been around since the beginning of civilization. Of course, by today's standards, the early information systems were very low-tech. Think about your college or university library. At one time, the library probably had a card catalogue to help students find information. The card catalogue was an information system because it stored data about books and periodicals in an organized manner on index cards. Library users could flip through the cards and locate library materials by author, title, or subject. But the process could be difficult and time-consuming.

When today's businesspeople think about information systems, they most likely think about **computer-based information systems**. These systems rely on computer and related technologies to store information electronically in an organized, accessible manner. Instead of a card catalogue, your college or university library probably uses a computerized information system. Users can search through library holdings quickly and easily.

Computer-based information systems consist of four components and technologies:

- Computer hardware
- Computer software
- Telecommunications and computer networks
- Data resource management

Computer hardware consists of machines that range from supercomputers to smartphones. It also includes the input, output, and storage devices needed to support computing machines. Software includes operating systems, such as Microsoft's Windows 8 or Linux, and application programs, such as Adobe Acrobat and Customer Relationship Management, or CRM. Consumer software includes Dropbox and Evernote, while enterprise software includes Salesforce.com and Workday. In addition, mobile software consists primarily of iOS and Android operating systems. Telecommunications and computer networks encompass the hardware and software needed to provide wired or wireless voice and data communications. This includes support for external networks such as the Internet and private internal networks. Data resource management involves developing and maintaining an organization's databases so that decision makers are able to access the information they need in a timely manner.

In the case of your college or university library, the computer-based information system is usually made up of computer hardware, such as monitors and keyboards, which are linked to the library's network and a database containing information on the library's holdings. Specialized software allows users to access the database. The library's network is likely also connected to a larger private network and the Internet. These connections give users remote access to the library's database and access to other computerized databases, such as LexisNexis.

computer-based information systems information systems that use computer and related technologies to store information electronically in an organized, accessible manner.

database a centralized integrated collection of data resources.

Databases

The heart of any information system is its **database**, a centralized integrated collection of data resources. A company designs its databases to meet specific information processing and retrieval needs of its workforce. Businesses obtain databases in many ways. They can hire a staff person to build them onsite, hire an outside source to build them, or buy packaged database programs from specialized vendors, such as Oracle. A database acts as an electronic filing cabinet. It is capable of storing large amounts of data and retrieving a specific piece of data within seconds. A database should be continually updated; otherwise, a firm may find itself with data that are outdated and possibly useless. One problem with databases is that they often contribute to information overload—too much data for people to absorb or data that are irrelevant, or not meaningful, to decision making. Computer processing speed and storage capacity are increasing rapidly, and data have become more abundant—that is, there is more data and it is more easily available. As a result, businesspeople need to be careful that their databases contain only the facts they need. If they aren't careful, much time can be wasted wading through unnecessary data. Another challenge with databases is keeping them safe, as the "Hit & Miss" feature describes.

Decision makers can also look up data online. Online systems give access to large amounts of government data, such as economic data from Statistics Canada. One of the largest online databases is that of the Canadian Census. The Canadian Census of Population is conducted every five years. It collects data on households across Canada and tries to count everyone in the country. Selected participants fill out forms, answering questions about marital status, place of birth, ethnic background, citizenship, workplaces, commuting time, income, occupation, type of housing, number of telephones and vehicles, and even the number of grandparents who are caregivers. Although certain restrictions limit how people can access and use specific census data, the general public may access the data through Statistics Canada's website. Another

A library's *computer-based information system* is generally made up of computer hardware linked to the library's network and a database of information on the library's holdings. Specialized software allows users to access the database.

HIT & MISS

Business Intelligence Software Helps with Information Overload

According to research, about 60 percent of Canadian companies use business intelligence software to help managers deal with all the data they need to process and understand. Sales of analytical software are growing at a 10 percent rate and approaching $11 billion annually.

More than half of executives reported feeling weighed down by the volume of data processing and analysis that they need to do as part of their decision-making responsibilities. But these tasks can be made easier by using software that processes large volumes of data and can produce guidance for management.

For example, most businesses have little if any understanding of their mobile, wireless, and data communications usage. They receive invoices from large telecommunications companies, such as Bell Canada, Rogers, or TELUS, and simply pay the bills. They have no way of knowing if they are paying for unneeded services or if they are overpaying for the services they use. A business intelligence software solution can now help large corporations to save time and money.

Etelesolv is a startup consulting firm in Lachine, Quebec. Its TeleManager system provides managers with details of costs and usage to help them control costs, such as an employee who runs up excessive charges. According to Etelesolv's president, Christopher Thierry, the software identified $800,000 of potential savings for one client.

The young company's clients include RBC Financial Group, Canada Post, RONA, GazMet, and Sun Life Financial. But even smaller firms need help with analyzing and reconciling their telecommunications invoices.

Questions for Critical Thinking

1. What other areas of managerial decision making involve large volumes of data and would likely benefit from a software solution?
2. How might software firms price their software solutions to different companies?

Sources: Etelesolv, accessed May 19, 2011, www.etelesolv.com; Peter Hadekel, "Solving Telecom Mysteries," *Montreal Gazette,* April 7, 2011, B1–B2; Matt Hartley, "Information Overload Burden to Execs: Poll," *National Post,* May 16, 2011, A2.

source of free information is company websites. Anyone who is interested can visit firms' home pages to look for information about customers, suppliers, and competitors. Trade associations and academic institutions also maintain websites with related information.

Types of Information Systems

Many different types of information systems exist. In general, information systems fall into one of two broad categories: operational support systems or management support systems.

Operational Support Systems

Operational support systems are designed to produce a variety of information on an organization's activities for both internal and external users. Examples of operational support systems include transaction processing systems and process control systems. **Transaction processing systems** record and process data from business transactions. For example, major retailers use point-of-sale systems, which link electronic cash registers to the retailer's computer centres. Sales data are transmitted from cash registers to the computer centre either immediately or at regular intervals. **Process control systems** monitor and control physical processes. For example, a steel mill may have electronic sensors linked to a computer system to monitor the entire production process. The system makes necessary changes and alerts operators to potential problems.

Commercial airplane manufacturer Airbus relies on an advanced information system. It uses RFID (radio-frequency identification) technology to track parts and tools used in the production and maintenance of its products, including its new A350 XWB planes. The high-memory RFID tags are placed on parts. The information system then follows the parts from warehouses to production facilities to the specific production lines where they are attached to aircraft. The system also tracks how and where tools are used. Airbus expects the information system to improve overall supply chain management, reduce required inventory levels, and increase productivity.[3]

Management Support Systems

Management support systems are information systems that are designed to provide support for effective decision making. Several different types of management support systems are available. A **management information system (MIS)** is designed to produce reports to managers and other professionals.

A **decision support system (DSS)** gives direct support to businesspeople during the decision-making process. For example, a marketing manager might use a decision support system to analyze

operational support systems information systems designed to produce a variety of information on an organization's activities for both internal and external users.

transaction processing systems operational support systems that record and process data from business transactions.

process control systems operational support systems that monitor and control physical processes.

management support systems information systems that are designed to provide support for effective decision making.

management information system (MIS) an information system that is designed to produce reports to managers and other professionals.

decision support system (DSS) an information system that gives direct support to businesspeople during the decision-making process.

The complex process of airline production and maintenance is critical to passenger safety. Many airlines use an *operational support system* to track parts, schedule inspections, and manage inventory levels.

executive support system (ESS) an information system that lets senior executives access the firm's primary databases, often by touching the computer screen, pointing and clicking a mouse, or using voice recognition.

expert system a computer program that imitates human thinking through complicated sets of "if-then" rules.

✓ ASSESSMENT CHECK

14.2.1 List the four components of a computer-based information system.

14.2.2 What is a database?

14.2.3 What are the two general types of information systems? Give examples of each.

LO 14.3 Outline how computer hardware and software are used to manage information.

how a product's price change will affect sales and profits. MEI Computer Technology Group provides North American consumer-products producers with a comprehensive sales and trade promotions tracking software called TradeInsight. This software provides real results that are linked to specific promotional efforts, such as an advertising campaign, a special coupon, or another marketing tactic. Clients such as Kellogg's, Heinz, and L'Oreal can track the impact of their promotional spending on sales. They can then use this information when planning their future promotional strategies.[4]

An **executive support system (ESS)** lets senior executives access the firm's primary databases, often by touching the computer screen, pointing and clicking a mouse, or using voice recognition. In the typical ESS, users can choose from many kinds of data, such as the firm's financial statements and sales figures or stock market trends for the company and for the industry as a whole. Managers can start by looking at summaries, and then access more detailed information when needed.

Finally, an **expert system** is a computer program that imitates human thinking through complicated sets of "if-then" rules. The system applies human knowledge in a specific subject area to solve a problem. Expert systems are used for a variety of business purposes: to set credit limits for credit card applicants, to monitor machinery in a plant to detect potential problems or breakdowns, to arrange mortgage loans, and to design plant layouts. They are typically developed by capturing the knowledge of recognized experts in a field whether within a business itself or outside it.

COMPUTER HARDWARE AND SOFTWARE

It may be hard to believe, but only a few decades ago computers were thought of as exotic curiosities, used only for very specialized applications and understood by only a few people. The first commercial computer, UNIVAC I, was sold to the U.S. Census Bureau in the early 1950s. It cost $1 million, took up most of a room, and could perform about 2,000 calculations per second.[5] The invention of transistors and then integrated circuits (microchips) quickly led to smaller and more powerful devices. By the 1980s, computers could perform several million calculations per second. Now, computers perform billions of calculations per second, and some fit in the palm of your hand.

The first personal computers were introduced in the late 1970s and early 1980s. Then, the idea of a computer on every desk, or in every home, seemed unbelievable and not very likely. Today, computers have become a must-have for both businesses and households. Not only have computers become much more powerful and faster over the past 35 years, but they are also less expensive. IBM's first personal computer (PC), introduced in 1981, cost well over $5,000. Today, a PC can sell for less than $400.

Types of Computer Hardware

hardware all tangible, or physical, elements of a computer system.

Hardware consists of all tangible, or physical, elements of a computer system—the input devices, the components that store and process data and perform calculations, and the output devices that present the results to users. Input devices allow users to enter data and commands for processing, storage, and output. The most common input devices are the keyboard and mouse. Storage and processing components include the hard drive and various other storage components, such as DVD drives and flash memory devices. Flash memory devices are becoming increasingly popular because they are small and can hold large amounts of data. Some, called thumb drives, can even fit on a keychain. To gain access to the data they hold, users plug the drives into a USB (universal serial bus) port, standard on today's computers. Output devices, such as monitors and printers, are the hardware elements that transmit or display documents and other results of a computer system's work.

Different types of computers have varying memory capacities and processing speeds. These differences define four broad classifications: mainframe computers, midrange systems, personal computers, and hand-held devices. A mainframe computer is the largest computer system. It has the greatest storage capacity and the fastest processing speeds. Especially powerful mainframes called *supercomputers* can handle extremely rapid, complex calculations that involve thousands of variables, such as weather modelling and forecasting. Today's supercomputers can perform a trillion or more calculations per second.

Midrange systems consist of high-end network servers and other types of computers that can handle large-scale processing needs. They are less powerful than mainframe computers but more powerful than most personal computers. A **server** is the heart of a midrange computer network. It supports applications and allows networked users to share output devices, software, and databases. Many Internet-related functions at organizations are handled by midrange systems. Midrange systems are also commonly used in process control systems, computer-aided manufacturing (CAM), and computer-aided design (CAD).

server the heart of a midrange computer network.

Once the centre of the digital universe, a full-scale Windows or Mac OS personal desktop computer was the way most people accessed the Internet, wrote papers, played games, organized music and photos, and more. While some believe the PC is on its way to extinction and ownership rates have declined, PCs are still popular in homes, businesses, schools, and government agencies.

While millions of desktop computers remain on the job, laptops—including notebooks and netbooks—have surpassed desktop units in sales. The increasing popularity of these computers can be explained by smaller, lighter, more powerful computing, and by their improved displays, faster processing speeds, ability to handle more intense graphics, larger storage capacities, and more durable designs. Business owners, managers, salespeople, and students all benefit from their portability and instantaneous access to information.

Prices for full-size laptops, notebooks, and net-books vary greatly—a netbook can be purchased for an average of $350 to $500 or a MacBook Pro laptop for between $1,500 and $3,500. A netbook does not have the computing capacity of a larger, more expensive notebook, but it can perform basic tasks such as search, email, word processing, and spreadsheet calculations.

Hand-held devices such as smartphones are even smaller. The most popular smartphones today are powered by Google's Android and Apple's iOS mobile operating systems. Smartphones like the iPhone and Samsung's Galaxy essentially combine a mobile phone with more advanced computing capabilities than their predecessor, the basic cellphone. While smartphones can be terrific tools that boost productivity, some people overuse or even misuse them. See the "Career Kickstart" feature which describes some of the dos and don'ts of smartphone use in the business environment.

Two other devices—tablets and e-readers—are taking major market share from laptops. According to Pew Research Center's Internet and American Life Project, more than a third of U.S. adults now own a tablet.[6] In addition to the Apple iPad, the top selling tablet, there are a proliferation of tablet models on the market, including those from Google, Samsung, Amazon, and Sony. E-readers such as Amazon's Kindle continue to expand their market share. Currently, about 32 percent of U.S. adults own an e-reader. A hybrid device, called a phablet, is a cross between a smartphone and a tablet, with a screen larger than a smartphone but smaller than a

Using smartphones and tablets can boost productivity, but some people overuse or misuse them.

CAREER KICKSTART

Courteous Communications via Mobile Devices

The number of smartphone users worldwide is expected to reach 4.5 billion over the next few years. With so many of us communicating instantly—and almost constantly—it is more important than ever to be courteous, or well-mannered, whether speaking or emailing on a hand-held device.

1. *Be aware of your surroundings—and your neighbours.* If you're in a meeting or another place where a phone conversation would be unsuitable, turn off your ring tone. If the call or email simply can't wait, excuse yourself and leave the room to respond.

2. *Lower your voice when taking a call in a public area.* If you are in an area that is quieter than your speaking voice, it's better to find another area more suitable for having a conversation.

3. *When sending email or texting, don't overabbreviate.* A business message can be short without being cute or, worse, hard to understand. It is just as easy to key in "See you at 3" as "cu@3."

4. *Before sending a text message or email, read it over carefully.* Typos and grammatical errors don't look professional in a business message.

5. *Be careful about your Facebook photos.* Now that smartphones let users link all their contact information, your photo may appear on the other person's phone when you call. And people beyond those on your Facebook friends list will see it. Be sure your photo is suitable for both friends and business callers.

Sources: "Smartphone Users Worldwide Will Total 1.75 Billion in 2014," eMarketer, accessed February 27, 2014, www.emarketer.com; Christopher Elliott, "E-Mail Etiquette for Wireless Devices," Microsoft Small Business Center, accessed February 25, 2014, www.microsoft.com; Taya Flores, "Cell Phone Etiquette Is Important," JC Online, accessed February 25, 2014, www.jconline.com; Mike Elgan, "Here Comes the New Cell Phone Etiquette," IT World, accessed February 25, 2014, www.itworld.com.

---

tablet. In the next few years, analysts predict that more than half of the smart connected devices sold will be tablets, followed by laptops and desktops. In a recent quarter, tablet sales surpassed desktop and laptop sales combined.[7]

In addition to smartphones, specialized hand-held devices are used in a variety of businesses for different applications. Some restaurants, for example, have small wireless devices that allow servers to swipe a credit or debit card and print out a receipt right at the customer's table. Drivers for UPS and FedEx use special hand-held devices to track package deliveries and accept delivery signatures. As each package is delivered, the information is transmitted to the delivery firm's network, and the sender can check online to see the delivery information and even the recipient's signature.

Computer Software

software all the programs, routines, and computer languages that control a computer and tell it how to operate.

Software includes all of the programs, routines, and computer languages that control a computer and tell it how to operate. The *operating system* is the software that controls the basic workings of a computer system. More than 90 percent of personal computers use a version of Microsoft's popular Windows operating system. Personal computers made by Apple use the Mac operating system. Most hand-held devices use either the Palm or Symbian operating system or a special version of Windows called Windows Mobile. But the Droid, iPhone, and BlackBerry models have their own operating systems. Other operating systems include Unix, which runs on many midrange computer systems, and Linux, which runs on both PCs and midrange systems.

Application software is a software program that performs the specific tasks that the user wants to carry out—such as writing a letter or looking up data. Examples of application software include Adobe Acrobat, Microsoft PowerPoint, and Quicken. **Table 14.1** lists the major categories of application software. Most application programs are stored on individual computers. But the future of applications software is constantly changing. Some believe much of it will become web-based, with the programs themselves stored in the "cloud," on Internet-connected servers. Others disagree, arguing that most computer users will not want to rely on an Internet connection to perform such tasks as preparing a spreadsheet using Microsoft Excel. The "Going Green" feature explains how some observers believe that cloud computing might help reduce greenhouse gases.

✓ ASSESSMENT CHECK

14.3.1 List two input and two output devices.

14.3.2 Why are notebook computers so popular?

14.3.3 What is software? List the two categories of software.

Table 14.1 **Common Types of Application Software**

TYPE	DESCRIPTION	EXAMPLES
Word processing	Programs that input, store, retrieve, edit, and print various types of documents.	Microsoft Word, Pages (Apple)
Spreadsheets	Programs that prepare and analyze financial statements, sales forecasts, budgets, and similar numerical and statistical data.	Microsoft Excel, Numbers (Apple)
Presentation software	Programs that create presentations. Users can create bulleted lists, charts, graphs, pictures, audio, and even short video clips.	Microsoft PowerPoint, Keynote (Apple)
Desktop publishing	Software that combines high-quality type, graphics, and layout tools to create output that can look as attractive as documents produced by professional publishers and printers.	Adobe Acrobat, Microsoft Publisher
Financial software	Programs that compile accounting and financial data to create financial statements, reports, and budgets; they perform basic financial management tasks such as balancing a chequebook.	Quicken, QuickBooks
Database programs	Software that searches and retrieves data from a database; it can sort data based on various criteria.	Microsoft Access, Approach
Personal information managers	Specialized database programs that allow people to track communications with personal and business contacts; some combine email capability.	Microsoft Outlook, Lotus Organizer
Enterprise resource planning	Integrated cross-functional software that controls many business activities, including distribution, finance, and human resources.	SAP Enterprise Resource Planning

GOING GREEN

CAN CLOUD COMPUTING ALSO BE "GREEN" COMPUTING?

The increase in cloud computing has some observers hoping it will also decrease the emission of greenhouse gases. But others are growing concerned that cloud computing will cause emissions to increase because it will lead to larger and larger data storage centres that use more energy.

The environmental organization Greenpeace issued the "Cool IT Challenge" to the IT sector. Greenpeace urges firms to reduce emissions by using renewable electricity to power their data centres. Greenpeace also wants firms to pressure utility companies to improve their access to renewable energy. In a report, Greenpeace said that IT energy solutions can even encourage the growth of local, decentralized energy centres as opposed to large grids. These smaller, local networks could result in better energy choices for consumers, improved energy efficiency, and greater use of renewable energy.

Greenpeace has published a chart that rates major data centres' use of power sources. Google's data centre in Oregon was the leading user of renewable energy: almost 51 percent of its energy comes from renewable sources, not from coal and nuclear power.

The Green Grid is a group of IT companies interested in improving energy efficiency. It launched a downloadable tool that helps IT professionals lower their overall energy use by using outside air and water to cool their data centres at little or no cost.

Even Greenpeace has come under fire for relying on coal and nuclear energy at some of its data centres, due to long-term agreements with local utilities. Gary Cook, one of the Cool IT Campaign's policy advisors, said, "We're definitely trying to run the greenest operation we can . . . We're in the process of reworking some of our IT infrastructure, and we'll clean that up."

Questions for Critical Thinking

1. Why do devices that rely on cloud computing, such as smartphones or the iPad, contribute to increased greenhouse gas emissions?

2. Will the data centres' voluntary actions be enough to lower greenhouse gas emissions? Why or why not?

Sources: Greenpeace, accessed May 22, 2010, www.greenpeace.org; The Green Grid, accessed May 22, 2010, www.thegreengrid.org; GreenerComputing Staff, "Green Grid Offers Tools for Free Data Center Cooling," *GreenBiz*, April 12, 2010, www.greenbiz.com/news/2009/04/12/green-grid-offers-tools-free-data-center-cooling; Rich Miller, "Greenpeace: Cloud Contributes to Climate Change," *Data Center Knowledge*, March 30, 2010, www.datacenterknowledge.com/archives/2010/03/30/greenpeace-cloud-contributes-to-climate-change; Matthew Wheeland, "Cloud Computing Is Efficient, But It's Not Green—Yet," *GreenBiz*, March 30, 2010, www.greenbiz.com/blog/2010/03/30/cloud-computing-efficient-but-not-green-yet; Rich Miller, "Greenpeace's Hosting: Not 'Truly Green,'" *Data Center Knowledge*, March 3, 2010, www.datacenterknowledge.com/archives/2010/03/03/greenpeaces-hosting-not-truly-green.

LO 14.4 Describe networking and telecommunications technology and the types of computer networks.

COMPUTER NETWORKS

As mentioned earlier, nearly all computers today are linked to networks. In fact, if your PC has Internet access, you're linked to a network. Local area networks and wide area networks allow businesses to communicate, transmit and print documents, and share data. These networks require businesses to install special equipment and connections between office sites. But Internet technology has also been applied to internal company communications and business tasks, by using a ready-made network. Among these new Internet-based applications are intranets, virtual private networks (VPNs), and voice over Internet protocol (VoIP). Each has contributed to the effectiveness and speed of business processes, so we discuss them next.

Local Area Networks and Wide Area Networks

Most organizations connect their offices and buildings by creating **local area networks (LANs)**, computer networks that connect machines within limited areas, such as a building or several nearby buildings. LANs are useful because they link computers and allow them to share printers, documents, and information. LANs also provide access to the Internet. **Figure 14.1** shows what a small-business computer network might look like.

Wide area networks (WANs) tie larger geographical regions together by using telephone lines, microwave transmission, and satellite transmission. One familiar WAN is long-distance telephone service. Companies such as Bell Canada and TELUS provide WAN services to businesses and consumers. Firms also use WANs to conduct their own operations. Typically, companies link their own network systems to outside communications equipment and services for transmission across long distances.

local area networks (LANs) computer networks that connect machines within limited areas, such as a building or several nearby buildings.

wide area networks (WANs) computer networks that tie larger geographical regions together by using telephone lines and microwave and satellite transmission.

Wi-Fi a wireless network that connects various devices and allows them to communicate with one another through radio waves.

Wireless Local Networks

A wireless network allows computers, printers, and other devices to be connected without the need for cables that physically link the devices. The current standard for wireless networks is called Wi-Fi, popularly thought to stand for *wireless fidelity*. **Wi-Fi** is a wireless network that connects various devices and allows them to communicate with one another through radio waves. Any PC that has a Wi-Fi receptor can connect with the Internet at so-called hot spots—locations with a wireless router and a high-speed Internet modem. There are hundreds of thousands of hot spots around the world. They are found in a variety of places, including college and university campuses, airports, libraries, and coffee shops. Some locations provide free access, while others charge a fee.

Many believe that Wi-Fi will soon be followed by *Wi-Max*. Unlike Wi-Fi's relatively limited geographic coverage area—generally around 90 metres—a single Wi-Max access point can provide coverage over many kilometres. In addition, cellphone service providers, such as Bell Canada and Rogers, offer broadband network cards for notebook PCs. These devices allow users to access the provider's mobile broadband network from nearly any location where cellphone reception is available.

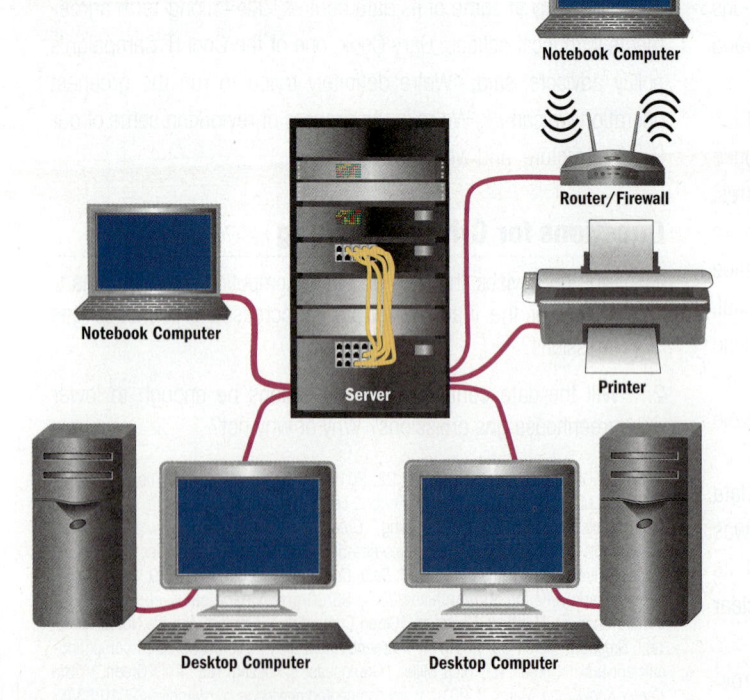

FIGURE 14.1 A Local Area Network

Wi-Fi connections are often called *hot spots*—locations with a wireless router and a high-speed Internet modem. There are hundreds of thousands of hot spots around the world. They are found in a variety of places, including college and university campuses, airports, libraries, and coffee shops.

Intranets

One way to share information in an organization is to set up a company network similar to the Internet. This type of network is called an **intranet**. Intranets are similar to the Internet, but they limit access to authorized users, often an employee group. Intranet users access the system by entering a password. An intranet blocks outsiders who don't have valid passwords by using software and hardware known as a **firewall**. Firewalls limit data transfers to certain locations. They also track system use so that managers can identify threats to the system's security, including attempts to log on with invalid passwords. Highly advanced software will immediately alert system administrators to suspicious activities but will allow authorized personnel to use smart cards to connect from remote terminals.

Intranets solve the problem of linking different types of computers. Like the Internet, intranets can link computers that run different kinds of operating systems. Intranets are relatively easy and inexpensive to set up because most businesses already have some of the required hardware and software. For example, a small business can purchase a digital subscriber line (DSL) router and a few cables to create an intranet using phone jacks and internal phone lines. All the business's computers will be linked to each other and to the Internet.

Intranets also support teamwork among employees who travel or work from home. Any intranet member with the right identification, a PC, and an Internet connection can link to the intranet and gain access to group calendars, email, documents, and other files. Intranets can also be used for videoconferencing and other forms of virtual meetings. Jetstar, an airline serving the Asia-Pacific region, has more than 3,000 employees. But three-quarters of them—pilots, cabin crews, and airport staff—will never set foot in the home office. Pilots can visit the company's intranet to access the latest safety information, and home office employees can go online to update the staff directory and transfer paper forms. Corporate and staff communications are transmitted to all employees via Jetstar's intranet. These communications help to build a sense of community among people who may rarely meet in person.[8]

intranet a computer network that is similar to the Internet but limits access to authorized users.

firewall a type of security system for computers that limits data transfers to certain locations; it also tracks system use so that managers can identify threats to the system's security, including attempts to log on with invalid passwords.

Virtual Private Networks

virtual private networks (VPNs) secure connections between two points on the Internet.

To gain increased security for Internet communications, companies often turn to **virtual private networks (VPNs)**, secure connections between two points on the Internet. These VPNs use firewalls and programs that encrypt, or encode, data to make them more secure during transit. The data are then decrypted, or decoded at the receiving end. In very general terms, a VPN can include a range of networking technologies, from secure Internet connections to private networks from service providers like IBM. A VPN is cheaper for a company to use than leasing several of its own lines. It might take months to install a leased line in some parts of the world, but a new user can be added to a VPN in a day. Because a VPN uses the Internet, it can be wired, wireless, or a combination of the two.

VoIP

VoIP an alternative to traditional telecommunication services provided by companies such as Bell Canada and TELUS; uses the Internet instead of telephone lines to transmit messages.

VoIP stands for *voice over Internet protocol*. It is an alternative to traditional telecommunication services provided by companies such as Bell Canada and TELUS. The VoIP telephone is not connected to a traditional phone jack but is connected to a personal computer that has a broadband connection. Special software transmits phone conversations over the Internet, instead of through telephone lines. A VoIP user can access the phone as usual. People can use VoIP to place and receive calls to and from others who have traditional telephone connections (either landline or wireless).

A growing number of consumers and businesses are using VoIP, mainly because of its cost savings and extra features. As technology continues to advance, demand for VoIP has increased. Videotron provides VoIP service to Quebec customers, in addition to providing Internet and cable television services. Google announced it is developing its own VoIP service. The various VoIP providers are working together with the goal of creating a single VoIP standard to permit seamless roaming worldwide. This new standard might develop soon, especially since Microsoft acquired the global leader in VoIP technology—Skype.[9]

VoIP has many advantages. But there are also several potential downsides to replacing traditional telephony with Internet telephony. For one thing, an Internet phone service is only as reliable as the broadband connection. If your broadband connection goes out, so will your phone service. Also, without suitable protection, VoIP can expose a phone system to threats that can affect the rest of the Internet, such as worms and viruses.

✓ ASSESSMENT CHECK

14.4.1 What is a LAN?

14.4.2 What are the differences between an intranet and a VPN?

14.4.3 Briefly explain how VoIP works.

LO 14.5 Outline the security and ethical issues affecting information systems.

SECURITY AND ETHICAL ISSUES AFFECTING INFORMATION SYSTEMS

Many security and ethical issues affect information systems. Information systems are becoming more important as business assets; they are also becoming harder and more expensive to replace. Damage to information systems or theft of data can have disastrous results. When computers are connected to a network, a problem at any individual computer can affect the entire network. Two of the major security threats are cybercrime and so-called malware.

Cybercrime

Computers provide efficient ways for employees to share information. But they may also allow access to information by people who may have criminal intentions. Or they may allow access to private information by pranksters—who have no purpose other than to see whether they can break into a system. Common cybercrimes involve stealing or altering data in several ways:

- Employees or outsiders may change or create data to produce inaccurate or misleading information.

- Employees or outsiders may alter computer programs to create false information or illegal transactions or to insert viruses.
- Unauthorized people can access computer systems for their own benefit or knowledge or just to see if they can figure out how to get in.

Individuals, businesses, and government agencies are all vulnerable to computer crime. Computer hackers are unauthorized users. They sometimes work alone and sometimes work in groups. Hackers sometimes break into computer systems just to show that they can do it; other times, they have more disturbing reasons. A survey reported that although computer crimes have decreased slightly, many computer crimes may go undetected. Why? Because firms focus on discouraging hackers and blocking pornography but leave themselves open to cybercriminals who are developing increasingly advanced tools. Even Apple computers, which are normally protected from cybercrime, are becoming vulnerable: more and more Mac users now store data in the "cloud"—that is, on the Internet itself, not on their hard drives. Although there is no single uniform system for reporting cybercrime, the Internet Engineering Task Force (IETF) is working toward a common format that will have reliable time stamps, will be available in different languages, and will allow users to attach samples of malicious code. These automated tools will be able to analyze massive amounts of data much faster than human analysts.[10]

Information system administrators use two basic protections against computer crime: they try to prevent access to their systems by unauthorized users and they try to prevent the viewing of data by unauthorized system users. The simplest method of preventing access requires an authorized user to enter a password. The company may also install firewalls, described earlier. To prevent system users from reading sensitive information, the company may use encryption software, which encodes, or scrambles, messages. To read encrypted messages, users must use an electronic key to convert the messages to regular text. But, as fast as software developers invent new and more advanced protective measures, hackers seem to break through their defences. As a result, computer security is an ongoing battle.

Consumers with credit cards are particularly at risk from hackers. Luxury retailer Neiman Marcus discovered that hackers had breached its cyber-security system, which compromised customer credit card data. It is important for payment-processing companies used by major credit card companies to put protections in place so that consumer credit and debit card information remain safe.[11]

Another form of computer theft is as old as crime itself: theft of equipment. Because computers may contain important information for a business, employees need to be especially careful not to leave laptops unattended or within easy reach of others.

As computer hardware becomes smaller, it also becomes more at risk to theft. Hand-held devices, for instance, are particularly susceptible to theft. At an estimated cost of $30 billion annually, one in three robberies now involves smartphones.[12] Many notebook computers and hand-held devices contain special security software or passwords that make it difficult for a thief, or any unauthorized person, to access the computer's data. Find My iPhone was introduced for iOS users to locate their device and remotely delete data in the event it was lost or stolen. Apple updated its operating system to include software with an activation lock to prevent access to confidential information in the event of theft—similar to a kill switch feature.[13]

Luxury retailer Neiman Marcus is among those retailers who have faced a cybersecurity breach, compromising its customers' credit and debit card information.

© Kristoffer Tripplaar/Alamy

Computer Viruses, Worms, Trojan Horses, and Spyware

Viruses, worms, Trojan horses, and spyware are collectively referred to as **malware**—malicious software programs designed to infect computer systems. These programs can destroy data, steal sensitive information, and even make it impossible to operate a computer. Malware has been

malware any malicious software program designed to infect computer systems.

discovered in advertisements on major sites such as Yahoo and Google. Malware is proliferating; according to estimates, companies are spending more than $100 billion annually to deal with malware-related cyberattacks.[14] Law enforcement has made some progress against cybercrime. But some observers predict that cybercriminals may soon target social-networking sites such as Facebook and Twitter.[15]

Computer **viruses** are malicious software programs that attach themselves to other programs (called *hosts*) and change them or destroy data. According to the computer security company Symantec, almost 3 million computer viruses are currently active worldwide.[16] Viruses can be programmed to become active immediately or to remain inactive for a period of time, and then later activate themselves and cause problems. A virus can reproduce by copying itself onto other programs stored on the same drive. It spreads as users install infected software on their systems or exchange files with others, usually by email, by accessing electronic bulletin boards, by trading disks, or by downloading programs or data from unknown sources on the Internet.

viruses malicious software programs that attach themselves to other programs (called *hosts*) and change them or destroy data.

A **worm** is a small piece of software that uses a security hole in a network to replicate, or copy, itself. A copy of the worm scans the network for another machine that has a specific security hole. It copies itself to the new machine using the security hole and then also starts the same process of copying itself from that machine. Unlike viruses, worms don't need host programs to damage computer systems.

worm a small piece of software that uses a security hole in a network to replicate itself.

A **botnet** is a network of PCs that have been infected with one or more data-stealing viruses. Computer criminals tie the infected computers into a network, often without the owners being aware of it, and sell the botnet on the black market. The cybercriminals or others then use the botnet to commit identity theft, send spam, buy blocks of concert tickets for scalping, and attack the Internet itself. About 4,000 to 6,000 botnets are active today. Spanish authorities brought down the Mariposa botnet, the world's largest botnet to date—a network of 12.7 million infected computers. Some of the computers were inside *Fortune* 1000 companies and major banks. Although the authorities made some arrests, the creator of the Mariposa botnet has not been caught.[17]

botnet a network of PCs that have been infected with one or more data-stealing viruses.

A **Trojan horse** is a program that claims to do one thing but in reality does something else, usually something malicious. For example, a Trojan horse might claim to be a game. But when a user clicks on the Trojan horse to launch it, the program might erase the hard drive or steal personal data stored on the computer.

Trojan horse a program that claims to do one thing but in reality does something else, usually something malicious.

Spyware is software that gathers user information through the user's Internet connection without his or her knowledge, usually for advertising purposes. Spyware applications are typically bundled with other programs downloaded from the Internet. Once installed, the spyware monitors user activity on the Internet and transmits that information in the background to someone else.

spyware software that gathers user information through the user's Internet connection without his or her knowledge, usually for advertising purposes.

Attacks by malware are not limited to computers and computer networks. Users of smartphones have also been affected. Smartphone users have reported a sharp increase in viruses, worms, and other forms of malware.[18] A malware scare known as Backdoor AndroidOS.Obad.a is a Trojan horse that infects the handsets of unsuspecting users. It duplicates itself, installs additional malware, distributes malicious software to other phones via Bluetooth, and performs remote commands in the Android handset, while racking up enormous charges to premium-rate phone numbers.[19]

As viruses, worms, botnets, and Trojan horses become more complex, the technology to fight them must also become more complex. The simplest way to protect against computer viruses is to install one of the many available antivirus software programs, such as Norton AntiVirus and McAfee VirusScan. These programs also protect against worms and some Trojan horses. Antivirus software programs continuously monitor systems for viruses and automatically get rid of any they spot. Users should regularly update their antivirus software by downloading the latest virus definitions. Computer users should also install and regularly update antispyware programs because many Trojan horses are forms of spyware.

But management must begin to emphasize security at a deeper level: during software design, in corporate servers, at web gateways, and through Internet service providers. Because more than 90 percent of the world's PCs run on Microsoft operating systems, a single virus, worm, or Trojan horse can quickly spread among PCs. Individual computer users should carefully choose the files they load onto their systems, scan their systems regularly, keep their antivirus software up to date, and install only software from known sources. They should also be very careful when opening email attachments from unknown sources because many viruses, worms, and Trojan horses are spread that way.

Information Systems and Ethics

The scope and power of today's information systems raise many ethical issues and concerns. These ethical issues affect both employees and organizations. For example, organizations often have specific ethical standards and policies regarding the use of information systems by employees and vendors. These standards include obligations to protect system security and the privacy and confidentiality of data. Policies may also cover employees' personal use of computers and related technologies, both hardware and software.

Ethical issues also involve an organization's use of information systems. Organizations have an obligation to protect the privacy and confidentiality of data on employees and customers. Employment records contain sensitive personal information, such as bank account numbers. If this information is not protected, it could lead to identity theft. Another ethical issue is the use of computer technology to monitor employees while they are working. The "Solving an Ethical Controversy" feature debates the issue of employee monitoring.

ASSESSMENT CHECK

14.5.1 Explain computer hacking.
14.5.2 What is malware?
14.5.3 How does a computer virus work?

SOLVING AN **ETHICAL** CONTROVERSY

Should Employers Monitor Employees' Internet Use?

According to an American Management Association/ePolicy Institute survey, two-thirds of employers monitor employees' use of the Internet. Technology now allows employers to check which websites their employees visit on company time, the pattern of keystrokes on individual computers, and the amount of time spent online. Employers can even use GPS-enabled phones to track employees.

For most employees, on-the-job access to the Internet and email is a necessity. In some workplaces, employees need to do a certain amount of Internet surfing for research purposes. A company's Facebook page can be either a powerful marketing tool or a liability if employees use their own social media sites to complain about the company.

Should employers monitor their employees' time online?

PRO

1. Surveys estimate that employees spend between one and two hours every day online for personal use. Some employees perform innocent tasks such as banking, but others visit inappropriate websites. Either way, those online hours mean lost productivity for the company.

2. Inappropriate use of office computers can leave a company vulnerable to hacking, viruses, and other security threats.

CON

1. Some employers are concerned that if they monitor employees, they could risk losing a workplace atmosphere of trust, commitment, and motivation.

2. Employees have a reasonable concern about privacy, especially if they have not been informed beforehand that their online activities are being monitored.

Summary

Although the law clearly gives employers the right to monitor computer activity, many debate the acceptable range of monitoring a worker's use of a company-provided device. Most analysts suggest that companies should establish clear policies on computer, Internet, and email use. They should train employees, have them sign a document stating that they understand the policies, and then trust their employees to do the right thing.

Sources: Pamela S. Stevens, "Employee Monitoring Software Review 2014," *Top Ten Reviews*, accessed March 20, 2014, http://employee-monitoring-software-review.toptenreviews.com; "How Do Employers Monitor Internet Usage at Work," *wiseGEEK*, accessed March 20, 2014, www.wisegeek.org/how-do-employers-monitor-internet-usage-at-work.htm; Susan M. Heathfield, "Electronic Surveillance of Employees," About.com, accessed March 20, 2014, http://humanresources.about.com/od/technology/a/surveillance.htm; Karen Codere, "Managing Social Media in the Workplace," *Business Ledger*, May 10, 2010, accessed March 20, 2014, http://dhbusinessledger.com/Content/Dot-com/Dot-com/Article/Managing-social-media-in-the-workplace/44/108/62; Laura Petrecca, "More Employers Use Tech to Track Workers," *USA Today*, March 17, 2010, accessed March 20, 2014, http://usatoday30.usatoday.com/money/workplace/2010-03-17-workplaceprivacy15_CV_N.htm.

LO 14.6 Explain how companies plan for, and recover from, information systems disasters.

DISASTER RECOVERY AND BACKUP

Even the most advanced computer information systems can be disrupted by natural disasters, power failures, equipment malfunctions, software glitches, human error, and terrorist attacks. These disruptions can cost businesses and other organizations billions of dollars. Even more serious outcomes can occur. For example, one study found that more than 93 percent of firms that lost their data centres for 10 days or more went bankrupt within six months.[20]

Disaster recovery planning is a critical function of all organizations. It refers to planning how to prevent computer system failures and planning how to continue operations if computer systems do fail. Disaster prevention programs can avoid some costly problems. The most basic precaution is routinely backing up software and data—at the organizational level and the individual level. But the organization's data centre cannot be the only place where critical data is stored because a single location is vulnerable to threats from both natural and human-caused disasters. As a result, offsite data backup is a necessity, whether in a separate physical location or online on the Internet itself. Companies that do online backups store the encrypted data in secure facilities that also have their own backups. The initial backup may take a day or more, but later backups will take far less time because they usually involve backing up only new or revised files.

According to security experts, an organization has five important tasks when considering offsite data storage. First is planning. The organization needs to decide what data need to be protected. Priority should be given to data that would lead to extreme legal or business consequences if it were lost. Second, a backup schedule must be set up and closely followed. Third, when data are transmitted offsite, they must be protected by the highest level of security possible. Fourth, care should be taken in selecting the right security vendor. Dozens of vendors offer different services in different areas of expertise. Finally, the backup system should be continually tested and evaluated.

✓ **ASSESSMENT CHECK**

14.6.1 What types of disasters are information systems vulnerable to?

14.6.2 List an organization's tasks when it is considering offsite data storage.

LO 14.7 Review the trends in information systems.

INFORMATION SYSTEM TRENDS

Computer information systems are continually and rapidly changing. Firms that want to keep their information systems up to date must keep up to date with changes in technology. Some of the most significant trends in information systems include the growing demands of the so-called distributed workforce, the increased use of application service providers, on-demand computing, and cloud and grid computing.

The Distributed Workforce

As discussed in earlier chapters, many companies are relying more and more on a *distributed workforce*—employees who no longer work in traditional offices but work in *virtual offices,* including at home. Information technology (IT) makes a distributed workforce possible. Computers, networks, and other components of information systems make it possible for many workers to do their jobs almost anywhere. For example, none of JetBlue's reservations agents work in offices; they all work at home, connected to the airline's information system. JetBlue is not alone in its use of home-based workers. Boeing, Starbucks, Agilent Technologies, Sun Microsystems, and many other companies maintain virtual offices with thousands of workers. According to research, about 10 percent of North American full-time wage and salary workers work at home on any given day. Of the self-employed workforce, more than one-third work at home on any given day.[21] Statistics show that most at-home workers use computers and related technologies. Virtual offices can range from a mailing address, mail forwarding, and a phone answering service to a full office, usually leased by the month. The increasing demands of the distributed workforce will likely lead to more innovative and increasingly powerful information systems.

Application Service Providers

Many firms find that it makes sense to outsource at least some of their information technology functions. Because of the increasing cost and complexity of obtaining and maintaining information systems, many firms hire an **application service provider (ASP)**, an outside supplier that provides both the computers and the application support for managing an information system. An ASP can simplify complex software for its customers so that it is easier for them to manage and use. When an ASP relationship is successful, the buyer can then devote more time and resources to its core businesses instead of trying to manage its information systems. Firms that use an ASP can also make their technology dollar stretch farther. Smaller companies who use an ASP can now access the kind of information power that was previously available only to larger organizations. Even large companies turn to ASPs to manage some or all of their information systems. Recently, Microsoft outsourced much of its internal information technology services to Infosys Technology to save money and to streamline, simplify, and support its services.[22]

Companies that decide to use ASPs should check the backgrounds and references of these firms before hiring one to manage critical systems. Customers should also ensure that the service provider has strong security measures to block computer hackers or other unauthorized access to the data, that its data centres are running reliably, and that adequate data and applications backups are maintained.

Continued technological advances in data storage and cloud computing allow businesspeople to work on their laptops, tablets, or smartphones from anywhere in the world.

On-Demand, Cloud, and Grid Computing

Another trend is **on-demand computing**, also called *utility computing*. Instead of purchasing and maintaining expensive software, firms rent the software time from application providers. They pay only for their usage of the software, similar to purchasing electricity from a utility. On-demand computing is especially useful for firms that have annual peaks in demand or have seasonal increases in their use of an application. By renting the service they need only when they need it, customers can avoid buying software that is not needed frequently. By using on-demand computing, companies remain current with the most efficient software and avoid having to purchase huge upgrades.

Cloud computing uses powerful servers to store application software and databases. Users access the software and databases via the Web. They can use any Internet-connected device, such as a PC or a smartphone. The software as a service (SaaS) movement is an example of cloud computing. The "Hit & Miss" feature describes how Cisco Systems provides security for cloud-based applications.

Small and medium-size companies occasionally find themselves with jobs that require more computing power than their current systems offer. A cost-effective solution for these firms may be **grid computing**, a network of smaller computers running special software. The software breaks down a large, complex job into smaller tasks and then distributes the tasks to the networked computers. The software then reassembles the results of the individual tasks into the finished job. By combining multiple small computers, grid computing creates a virtual mainframe or even a supercomputer.

application service provider (ASP) an outside supplier that provides both the computers and the application support for managing an information system.

on-demand computing the use of software time from application providers; firms pay only for their usage of the software, not for purchasing or maintaining the software.

cloud computing the use of powerful servers that store application software and databases that users access by using any Internet-connected device, such as a PC or a smartphone.

grid computing a network of smaller computers that run special software.

✓ ASSESSMENT CHECK

14.7.1 What is an application service provider?

14.7.2 Explain on-demand computing.

HIT & MISS

Cisco Systems Tackles Cloud Security

More and more businesses are managing increasing amounts of email and storing increasing amounts of data. Many save money and physical space by turning to cloud computing and storage, including software as a service (SaaS). Instead of installing software on site, a business can use SaaS to access software over the Internet either by subscription or by using a "pay as you go" plan. These businesses also need to protect their databanks from computer crime. In a traditional local area network, security applications are relatively easy to set up at the network's borders. But this challenge is made more difficult by the borderless environment of cloud computing and because of increasing threats to online security.

Cisco Systems has responded by developing security applications for cloud-based computing. One application directs a business's web traffic to security towers located in 100 countries around the world. These locations use layers of antivirus and antimalware utilities to scan websites and quickly block access to any websites that have been infected.

Another application offers both cloud-based and on-site email security. The cloud-based application deletes spam and viruses. The on-site application provides data-loss prevention, email encryption, and other services. Another email encryption service provides cloud-based encryption for locally stored messages.

Other applications support security for off-site workers who use desktops computers, laptops, tablets, and smartphones. One feature addresses the problem that occurs when an employee leaves a business. With one click of the mouse, an administrator can disable the departing employee's access to every SaaS application he or she ever used. And the administrator can use another click to set up access for a new employee.

As the vice-president and general manager of Cisco's security technology unit states, "Securing the cloud is highly challenging. But it is one of the top challenges that the industry must rise to meet."

Questions for Critical Thinking

1. What are some pros and cons of storing data "in the cloud"?
2. Why is it important to block a former employee's access to company data, email, or applications?

Sources: Company website, *News@Cisco* press release, accessed June 4, 2010, www.cisco.com; James Urquhart, "Cloud Computing and the Economy," *CNET News*, April 13, 2010, http://news.cnet.com; Margaret Steen, "Cloud Services and SaaS: A Smarter Way to Do Business," *Cisco News*, March 29, 2010, http://newsroom.cisco.com; Stuart Young, Andy Taylor, and James Macaulay, "Small Businesses Ride the Cloud: SMB Cloud Watch—U.S. Survey Results," Cisco Internet Business Solutions Group, February 2010, www.cisco.com; Mike Kirkwood, "Rulers of the Cloud: Will Cloud Computing Be the Second Coming of Cisco?" *ReadWriteWeb*, February 19, 2010, www.readwriteweb.com.

WHAT'S AHEAD

Part 5 was devoted to managing technology and information. Part 6 is about managing financial resources in contemporary business, and the next chapter, "Understanding Accounting and Financial Statements," focuses on accounting, financial information, and financing reporting. Accounting is the process of measuring, interpreting, and communicating financial information to enable people inside and outside the firm to make informed decisions. The chapter describes the functions of accounting and role of accountants; the steps in the accounting cycle; the types, functions, and components of financial statements; and the role of budgets in an organization.

RETURN TO INSIDE BUSINESS

Stock-Trak: Learning about the Stock Market through Simulation

A major competitive advantage for Stock-Trak is its use of real-time financial information to provide learners with a web-based stock market simulation. Price changes and analytical reports are sent online to users with little delay, only slightly behind the time that the same data and information are provided to real traders. Stock-Trak traders pay large subscription fees to receive this information so they can learn to make more intelligent trading decisions. The simulation provides a real-time learning experience that is as close to reality as the learner can expect to get. Stock-Trak is looking for ways to grow its business, such as by partnering with organizations that can deliver a large group of users.

QUESTIONS FOR CRITICAL THINKING

1. Which other organizations or groups should Stock-Trak consider partnering with? Why?
2. What other educational products or services could Stock-Trak develop?

SUMMARY OF LEARNING OBJECTIVES

LO 14.1 Distinguish between data and information, and discuss the role of information systems in business.

Businesspeople need to understand the difference between data and information. Data are raw facts and figures that may or may not be relevant, or meaningful, to a business decision. Information is knowledge gained from processing those facts and figures. An information system is an organized method for collecting, storing, and communicating past, present, and projected information on internal operations and external intelligence. Most information systems today use computer and telecommunications technology.

✓ ASSESSMENT CHECK ANSWERS

14.1.1 Distinguish between data and information. Data consist of raw facts and figures that may or may not be relevant to a decision. Information is the knowledge gained from processing data.

14.1.2 What is an information system? An information system is an organized method for collecting, storing, and communicating past, present, and projected information on internal operations and external intelligence.

LO 14.2 Describe the components and types of information systems.

When people think about information systems, they generally think of computer-based systems—information systems that use computers and related technologies. Computer-based information systems rely on four components: computer hardware, software, telecommunications and computer networks, and data resource management. The heart of an information system is its database, a centralized integrated collection of data resources. Information systems fall into one of two broad categories: operational support systems or management support systems. Operational support systems are designed to produce a variety of information for users. Examples include transaction processing systems and process control systems. Management support systems are designed to support effective decision making. They include management information systems, decision support systems, executive support systems, and expert systems.

✓ ASSESSMENT CHECK ANSWERS

14.2.1 List the four components of a computer-based information system. The four components of a computer-based information system are computer hardware, software, telecommunications and computer networks, and data resource management.

14.2.2 What is a database? A database is a centralized, integrated collection of data resources.

14.2.3 What are the two general types of information systems? Give examples of each. The two categories of information systems are operational support systems (such as transactions processing systems and process control systems) and management support systems (such as management information systems, decision support systems, executive support systems, and expert systems).

LO 14.3 Outline how computer hardware and software are used to manage information.

Hardware consists of all tangible, or physical, elements of a computer system, including input and output devices. Major categories of computers include mainframes, supercomputers, midrange systems, personal computers (PCs), and hand-held devices. Computer software provides the instructions that tell the hardware what to do. The operating system is the software that controls the basic workings of the computer. Other programs, called application software, perform specific tasks that users want to complete.

✓ ASSESSMENT CHECK ANSWERS

14.3.1 List two input devices and two output devices. Input devices include the keyboard and mouse. Output devices include the monitor and printer.

14.3.2 Why are notebook computers so popular? Notebook computers represent more than half of all new personal computers sold. Their increased popularity is due to better displays, lower prices, more rugged designs, increasing computing power, and slimmer designs.

14.3.3 What is software? List the two categories of software. Computer software provides the instructions that tell the hardware what to do. The two categories of software are the operating system and application software. The operating system is the software that controls the basic workings of the computer. Application software performs the specific tasks that users want to complete.

LO 14.4 Describe networking and telecommunications technology and the types of computer networks.

Local area networks connect computers within a limited area. Wide area networks tie larger geographical regions together by using telephone lines, microwave transmission, or satellite transmission. A wireless network allows computers to communicate through radio waves. Intranets allow employees to share information on a company network. Access to an intranet is restricted to authorized users and is protected by a firewall. Virtual private networks (VPNs) provide a secure Internet connection between two or more points. VoIP—voice over Internet protocol—uses a personal computer running special software and a broadband Internet connection to make and receive telephone calls over the Internet, instead of using traditional telephone networks.

✓ ASSESSMENT CHECK ANSWERS

14.4.1 What is a LAN? A LAN is a local area network, a computer network that connects machines within a limited area, such as a building or several nearby buildings.

14.4.2 What are the differences between an intranet and a VPN? An intranet is a computer network similar to the Internet. Unlike the Internet, access to an intranet is limited to employees or other authorized users. A virtual private network (VPN) is a secure connection between two points on the Internet.

14.4.3 Briefly explain how VoIP works. The VoIP phone is connected to a personal computer that has a broadband connection. Special software transmits phone conversations over the Internet. A VoIP user can place and receive calls to and from others who have traditional telephone connections (either landline or wireless).

LO 14.5 Outline the security and ethical issues affecting information systems.

Many security and ethical issues affect information systems. Two of the main security threats are cybercrime and malware. Cybercrimes range from hacking—unauthorized access to an information system—to the theft of hardware. Malware is any malicious software program designed to infect computer systems. Examples include viruses, worms, botnets, Trojan horses, and spyware. Ethical issues affecting information systems include the proper use of the systems by authorized users. Organizations also have an obligation to employees, vendors, and customers to protect the security and confidentiality of the data stored in information systems.

✓ ASSESSMENT CHECK ANSWERS

14.5.1 Explain computer hacking. Computer hacking refers to unauthorized people gaining illegal access to a computer system. Sometimes the hackers' purpose is just to see whether they can get into the system. Other times, hackers have more disturbing reasons, such as stealing or altering data.

14.5.2 What is malware? Malware is any malicious software program designed to infect computer systems.

14.5.3 How does a computer virus work? A virus is a program that attaches itself to another program (called a host). The virus then changes the host, destroys data, or even makes it impossible to operate the computer system.

LO 14.6 Explain how companies plan for, and recover from, information systems disasters.

Information system disasters may be caused by humans or may result from natural causes. Such disasters can cost businesses billions of dollars. The impact of a disaster can be decreased by routinely backing up software and data, both at an organizational level and at an individual level. Organizations should back up critical data at an offsite location. Some organizations may also want to invest in extra hardware and software sites, which can be accessed during emergencies.

✓ ASSESSMENT CHECK ANSWERS

14.6.1 What types of disasters are information systems vulnerable to? Even the most powerful and advanced computer information systems can be disrupted by natural disasters, power failures, equipment malfunctions, software glitches, human error, and even terrorist attacks.

14.6.2 List an organization's tasks when it is considering offsite data storage. The five tasks are planning and deciding which data to back up, establishing and following a backup schedule, protecting data when they are transmitted offsite, choosing the right vendor, and continually testing and refining the backup system.

LO 14.7 Review the trends in information systems.

Computer information systems are continually and rapidly evolving. Some of the most significant trends are the increasing demands of the distributed workforce, the increased use of application service providers, on-demand computing, and grid computing. Many people now work in virtual offices, including at home. Information technology makes this work arrangement possible. Application service providers allow organizations to outsource many of their IT functions. Instead of buying and maintaining expensive software, users of on-demand computing rent software time from outside vendors and pay only for their usage. Grid computing consists of a network of smaller computers running special software creating a virtual mainframe or even supercomputer.

✓ ASSESSMENT CHECK ANSWERS

14.7.1 What is an application service provider? An application service provider (ASP) is an outside vendor that provides both the computers and the application support for managing an information system. By using an ASP, the organization can effectively outsource some, or all, of its IT functions.

14.7.2 Explain on-demand computing. Instead of purchasing and maintaining expensive software, some organizations use on-demand computing. In this arrangement, software is rented from a vendor and the organization only pays for its actual usage.

BUSINESS TERMS YOU NEED TO KNOW

- application service provider (ASP) 405
- botnet 402
- chief information officer (CIO) 390
- cloud computing 405
- computer-based information systems 391
- data 390
- database 392
- decision support system (DSS) 393
- executive support system (ESS) 394
- expert system 394
- firewall 399
- grid computing 405
- hardware 394
- information 390
- information system 390
- intranet 399
- local area networks (LANs) 398
- malware 401
- management information system (MIS) 393
- management support systems 393
- on-demand computing 405
- operational support systems 393
- process control systems 393
- server 395
- software 396
- spyware 402
- transaction processing systems 393
- Trojan horse 402
- virtual private networks (VPNs) 400
- viruses 402
- VoIP 400
- wide area networks (WANs) 398
- Wi-Fi 398
- worm 402

REVIEW QUESTIONS

1. Distinguish between data and information. Why is this difference important to businesspeople who manage information?
2. What are the four components of an information system?
3. Describe the two different types of information systems, and give an example of how each type might help a specific business.
4. Explain decision support systems, executive support systems, and expert systems.
5. What are the major categories of computers? What is a server?
6. What is an intranet? Give specific examples of the benefits for firms that have their own intranets.
7. What steps can organizations and individuals take to prevent cybercrime?
8. How does a computer virus work? What can individuals and organizational computer users do to reduce the likelihood of acquiring a computer virus?
9. Why is disaster recovery important for businesses? Relate your answer to a natural disaster such as a hurricane or fire.
10. Describe four information system trends.

PROJECTS AND TEAMWORK APPLICATIONS

1. Suppose you've been hired to design an information system for a midsize retailer. Describe what that information system might look like, including the necessary components. Would the system be an operational support system, a management support system, or both?
2. Select a local company and contact the person in charge of its information system for a brief interview. Ask that individual to outline his or her company's information system. Ask the person what he or she likes most about the job. Did this interview make you more or less interested in a career in information systems?
3. Working with a partner, research the current status of Wi-Max. Prepare a short report on its growth, its current uses, and its future for business computing.
4. Your supervisor has asked for your advice. She isn't sure the company's information system needs any major safeguards because the company has very little web presence beyond a simple home page. But employees use email to contact suppliers and customers. List the threats that the company's information system is vulnerable to. What types of protection would you suggest?
5. Has your computer ever been hacked or attacked by a virus? What steps did you take to recover lost files and data? How would you prevent something similar from happening again?

WEB ASSIGNMENTS

1. **Enterprise resource planning (ERP).** SAP is one of the world's largest enterprise resource planning software companies. Visit the firm's website (www.sap.com) and click on "Customer Testimonials." Choose one of the customers listed and read its testimonial. Prepare a brief summary and explain how this exercise improved your understanding of the business applications of ERP software.

2. **Computer security.** Visit McAfee's website. Review the items for security awareness under "Threat Center" and discuss them in terms of how companies and consumers can prevent cybercrimes. www.mcafee.com/us/business-home.aspx

3. **Cloud computing.** IBM is one of the largest providers of cloud computing. Visit the IBM website (www.ibm.com) and click on "Solutions" and then select "Cloud computing." Print out the material and bring it to class to participate in a class discussion.

Note: Internet web addresses change frequently. If you don't find the exact sites listed, you may need to access the organization's home page and search from there or use a search engine such as Bing or Google.

PART 5: CASE STUDY — Beau's All Natural Brewing Company
Using Technology to Manage Communications and Information

Without the array of communications technologies available at Beau's, employees would probably have a much harder time keeping track of sales, transportation logistics, and production scheduling. When Steve was told by some retailers they were out of stock and had nothing sell, he knew Beau's was missing sales opportunities they had already won but could not fulfill. Although delivery schedules worked out at the warehouses and supplemented with emergency deliveries to keep customers stocked worked well enough at the beginning, Steve knew the system was in need of better communications technologies between drivers, warehouses, and customer order takers.

The solution was a tablet device that delivered instructions to drivers while they were on their routes. Adjustments could be made to juggle delivery schedules and emergency deliveries in real time—and the high costs that went with modifications were reduced substantially. Technology allowed for better customer service, fewer headaches, and freed up resources for other tasks. According to Steve, "It was money well spent. We would have had an impossible time growing the distribution network using the old clipboard and cellphone technology. Today, with over 2,000 point-of-sale systems at restaurants, bars, Ontario Liquor Control Board Stores (LCBO) and warehouses in Ottawa, Trenton, and Toronto, the only way we can keep our drivers delivering what customers need, when they need it, is with an integrated online ordering system that connects with each driver through his mobile tablet. Our drivers are able to better serve and maintain contact with the customers they deliver to by making decisions and entering data on the go. We found through our system that by having our trucks carry some extra inventory, drivers were able to spontaneously fill empty shelves at LCBOs when competitors were late or unable to complete promised deliveries. As a result, we picked up 8% more sales simply because we had extra product available beyond what the LCBO had ordered for that delivery."

A second area where technology is enabling the company to serve customers better is through the Internet. Orders can be placed online and customers may choose to come by the brewery for pick up or have Beau's delivery service drop off orders at residences and pick up empty bottles for a fee in selected zones of Ottawa. The service is run in conjunction with BottleWorks, a charitable fundraiser for Operation Come Home. BottleWorks is a commercial empty-bottle pick-up service for local Ottawa restaurants, bars, hotels, condominiums, and conference facilities. It is a social enterprise that employs at-risk youth age 16 and up for a 12-week period to assist with the bottle collection and administrative work.

As much as Beau's computerized systems can display reports on sales, expense, and other common requests for data and information, it does not provide information that would help the company with planning and understanding customer behaviour better. As Steve explained, "What would be really good to know is whether the customer who bought our beer today was a new customer or an

(continued)

PART 5: CASE STUDY Beau's All Natural Brewing Company

established customer who is loyal to one of our brands. Does this customer buy only one or two of our brands or do they rotate through a wider variety of beers we are offering throughout the year? Many of our products are "seasonal" and won't be back until the season returns next year. We might be missing the opportunity to introduce a new "winner" brand but can't know from a short selling season. I wish I knew some of the answers to these questions."

Questions for Critical Thinking

1. How would you use technology do find out some of the answers to these questions?
2. After reviewing Beau's website at www.beaus.ca, evaluate the strengths and weaknesses from a customer information-gathering point of view.
3. How would you change the website to increase information flow to Beau's?

5 LAUNCHING YOUR...

INFORMATION TECHNOLOGY CAREER

Part 5, "Managing Technology and Information," consists of Chapter 14. This chapter discussed using computers and related technology to manage information. We discussed well-known technology companies such as Google and Oracle and many smaller organizations that use computer technology to manage information. These examples show that all organizations need to manage technology and information. The complexity and scope of technology and information are likely to increase in the years ahead. As a result, the demand for information systems professionals is expected to grow.

According to research, employment in occupations such as computer software engineering, software support specialists, and network systems administrators is expected to grow faster than the average for all occupations in the next decade. Of the top five occupations where employment is expected to grow the fastest over the next few years, two occupations are related to information systems.[1]

What types of jobs are available in information systems? What are the working conditions like? What are the career paths? Experience in information systems can lead to a wide variety of jobs. In some cases, you'll work in the information systems department of a business such as Enbridge. In other cases, you may work for a specialized information systems firm, such as IBM. A specialized firm provides information services to governments, not-for-profit organizations, and businesses.

Information systems is a popular business major, and many entry-level positions are available each year. Many information systems graduates spend their entire careers in this field, while some move into other areas. People who began their careers in information systems are well represented in senior management positions. Let's look briefly at some of the specific jobs you might find after earning a degree in information systems.

Technical support specialists are trouble shooters who monitor the performance of computer systems; provide technical support and solve problems for computer users; install, modify, clean, and repair computer hardware and software; and write training manuals and train computer users.

Network administrators design, install, and support an organization's computer networks, including its local area network, wide area network, Internet, and intranet systems. They provide administrative support for software and hardware users and ensure that the design of an organization's computer networks and all of the components fit together efficiently and effectively.

Computer security specialists plan, coordinate, and implement an organization's information security. They educate users about how to protect computer systems, install antivirus and similar software, and monitor the networks for security breaches. The role and importance of computer security specialists have increased in response to the growing number of attacks on networks and data.

CAREER ASSESSMENT EXERCISES IN INFORMATION SYSTEMS

1. Assume you're interested in a career as a systems administrator. Go to the following website: www.itworldcanada.com. Prepare a brief report outlining the responsibilities of a systems administrator, the employers that hire for these positions, and the educational background needed.

2. Examine the website for TradeInsight: www.tradeinsight.com. Read a few of the case studies. Write a brief report about how the firm's software helps clients to better understand their sales and marketing data.

PART 6
MANAGING FINANCIAL RESOURCES

Chapter 15 Understanding Accounting and Financial Statements

Chapter 16 The Financial System

Chapter 17 Financial Management

15 | UNDERSTANDING ACCOUNTING AND FINANCIAL STATEMENTS

LEARNING OBJECTIVES

LO 15.1 Explain the functions of accounting and identify the three basic accounting activities.

LO 15.2 Describe the various types of accounting professionals.

LO 15.3 Discuss the foundation of the accounting system.

LO 15.4 Outline the steps in the accounting cycle.

LO 15.5 Explain the functions and major components of the four principal financial statements.

LO 15.6 Discuss how financial ratios are used to analyze a company's financial strengths and weaknesses.

LO 15.7 Describe the role of budgets in a business.

LO 15.8 Outline the accounting issues facing global business.

INSIDE BUSINESS

Cooking the Books

Imagine it is a few weeks after year end. The financial statements have been prepared by a team of experienced accountants. They've also been audited by another team of experienced auditors. This *must* mean that the statements are correct. After all, how complicated can accounting be? The numbers are either right or wrong.

These are common misconceptions—or misunderstandings—about the nature of accounting information. Accountants have quite a bit of flexibility when preparing financial statements, but they always need to stay within the limits of generally accepted accounting principles.

Accountants make choices about *when* to recognize, or record, revenue and expenses on the financial statements. For example, suppose the publisher of this textbook sells 100 copies of the textbook to your school bookstore with the option to return any books not purchased by students. When will the publisher's accountant recognize, or record, the revenue? Is it recognized when the books are delivered, or when the books are sold to students? Accountants also estimate how much bad debt or depreciation expense to charge against income in a given year. For example, when a company buys a delivery van, over how many years is the van depreciated? The more years the van is depreciated over, the lower the expense each year. Many people who prepare financial statements choose policies and make estimates at the high or low end of the acceptable ranges. Sometimes the decision comes down to an individual's personal motivations. Some individuals may want to increase their bonus, which may be tied to the company's net income; or they may want to lower their income taxes, which may also be based on net income.

Some financial statement preparers go far beyond the prescribed ranges. They commit fraud by changing the statements and providing false information for their personal gain. One well-known Canadian fraud case involved Livent co-founders Garth Drabinsky and Myron Gottlieb. Both were found guilty of forgery and defrauding their investors of more than $400 million. The two ran Livent, a theatre production company that produced some of Canada's best-known theatrical productions, including Canada's longest running musical at the time, *The Phantom of the Opera*. Part of the Livent scheme involved moving expenses from one period to another, or allocating expenses to certain shows that they did not relate to. Drabinsky was sentenced to seven years, and Gottlieb was sentenced to six years. They were released on $350,000 bail while waiting to file an appeal.

In the United States, the energy company Enron filed for bankruptcy in 2001. The Enron case was known as one of the world's biggest audit failures. Enron hid billions of dollars in debt by not recording it on the financial statements. Shortly after the Enron case, another fraud case was revealed. It was discovered that corporate executives at the telecommunications company WorldCom were also "cooking the books." They had been recording many expenses as assets and had inflated revenues by using creative accounting. These well-known accounting scandals resulted in the world's largest bankruptcies at the time.

These major fraud cases led to the creation of increased regulatory legislation, such as the Sarbanes-Oxley Act in the United States and Bill 198 in Canada. Canadian, American, and global companies are now required to spend billions of dollars to remain in compliance with these new legislations.[1]

CHAPTER 15 OVERVIEW

Accounting professionals prepare the financial information that organizations present in their annual reports. Whether you begin your career by working for a company or by starting your own firm, you need to understand what accountants do. You also need to understand why their work is so important in contemporary business.

Accounting is the process of measuring, interpreting, and communicating financial information to enable people inside and outside the firm to make informed decisions. In many ways, accounting is the language of business. Accountants gather, record, report, and interpret financial information in a way that describes the status and operation of an organization and aids in decision making.

Millions of men and women around the world are employed as accountants. In Canada, more than 200,000 people work as accountants or auditors.[2] Accounting is one of the most in-demand disciplines on university campuses. Part of the attraction is the availability of jobs and the high starting salaries for talented graduates. In Canada, salaries for Chartered Professional Accountants (CPAs) average more than $141,000 per year.[3]

This chapter begins by describing who uses accounting information. We then discuss business activities that involve accounting statements: financing, investing, and operations. Next, we explain the accounting process, define double-entry bookkeeping, and present the accounting equation. We then discuss how information about financial transactions is developed into financial statements. Next we look at the methods of interpreting these statements and the role of budgeting when planning and controlling a business. The chapter concludes with a discussion of the impact of financial information in global business.

accounting the process of measuring, interpreting, and communicating financial information to support internal and external business decision making.

LO 15.1 Explain the functions of accounting and identify the three basic accounting activities.

USERS OF ACCOUNTING INFORMATION

Both people inside an organization and people outside an organization use accounting information to help them make business decisions. **Figure 15.1** lists the users of accounting information and how they apply that information.

The major users of accounting information are managers at a business, owners, creditors (including banks), government agencies, and not-for-profit organizations. Accounting information helps them to plan and control daily and long-range operations. Business owners and boards of directors at not-for-profit groups also use accounting data to track managers' progress in operating the organizations. Union officials use accounting data in contract negotiations, and employees refer to it as they monitor their firms' productivity and profitability performance.

Users	Applications
Owners, Shareholders, Potential Investors, Creditors	To Evaluate Operations of the Firm / To Make Investment Decisions
Management	To Plan and Control
Employees, Union Officials	To Use in Contract Negotiations
Lenders, Suppliers	To Evaluate Credit Ratings
Government Agencies, Economic Planners, Consumer Groups	To Evaluate Tax Liabilities / To Approve New Issues of Stocks and Bonds

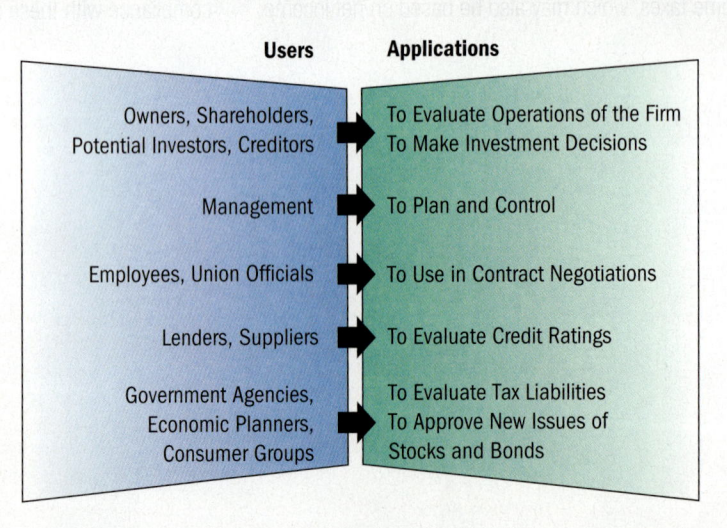

FIGURE 15.1 Users and Applications of Accounting Information

Some companies want employees to understand how their work affects the company's bottom line. These companies share sensitive financial information with their employees and teach them how to understand and use financial statements. People who support *open-book management* believe that allowing employees to view financial information helps them to better understand how their work contributes to the company's success, which, in turn, benefits the employees.

Outside a firm, potential investors evaluate accounting information to help them decide whether to buy a firm's shares. As we'll discuss later in the chapter, any company whose shares are traded publicly must report its financial results on a regular basis. That means that anyone can look up RONA's sales last year or how much money Tim Hortons made during the last quarter. Bankers and other lenders use accounting information to evaluate a potential borrower's financial soundness. The Canada Revenue Agency (CRA) and provincial tax officials use it to calculate a company's tax liability. Citizens' groups and government agencies use accounting information to assess the efficiency of such operations as Alberta Health Services, BC Hydro, and the Art Gallery of Ontario.

Accountants play important roles in business and in many other aspects of society. Their work influences each of the business environments discussed earlier in this book. Accountants clearly provide important information to help managers deal with the competitive and economic environments in which their companies do business.

Some other accounting contributions are less obvious, or less noticed, such as helping others to understand, predict, and react to the technological, regulatory, and social and cultural environments. For example, every year thousands of volunteers help Canadians complete their income tax returns. One of the largest organized programs is the Community Volunteer Income Tax Program (CVITP), organized by the CRA. Through this program, more than 16,000 volunteers help more than half a million Canadians complete their provincial and federal tax returns.

Accountants play an important role in business and other areas of society by providing services to businesses, individuals, government agencies, and not-for-profit organizations.

Business Activities Involving Accounting

The natural progression of a business begins with financing. All the steps after financing, including investing, lead to operating the business. All organizations, whether for-profit and not-for-profit, perform these three basic activities, and accounting plays a key role in each:

1. Financing activities provide necessary funds to start a business and expand it after it begins operating.

2. Investing activities provide valuable assets that are needed to run a business.

3. Operating activities focus on selling goods and services, but they also view expenses as important elements of sound financial management.

Brian Hill, CEO of Vancouver-based Aritzia, performed all three activities during the startup and growth of his high-fashion chain. Aritzia targets women between the ages of 15 and 30. Hill's success in Canada led to a major U.S. expansion. Hill could have tried to finance the expansion himself, as he had done before. But he wanted to avoid the financial risk that he had taken on earlier when Aritzia was growing. Hill decided to seek financing from Berkshire Partners, who took a majority stake in the company. Aritzia recently moved toward a more vertically integrated model. He chose this model to benefit from "a bigger piece of the pie" by cutting out a third-party retailer. He also made this choice for strategic reasons: Hill believes that part of Aritzia's success is that the company understands customers' needs. He feels that if he and his company are involved at the point of sale, they will have a better feel for the needs of the customers. This strategy has proven very successful thus far.[4]

✓ **ASSESSMENT CHECK**

15.1.1 Define *accounting*.

15.1.2 Who uses accounting information?

15.1.3 What three business activities involve accounting?

ACCOUNTING PROFESSIONALS

LO 15.2 Describe the various types of accounting professionals.

Accounting professionals work in many areas in and for business firms, government agencies, and not-for-profit organizations. They can be classified as public accountants, management accountants, government accountants, and not-for-profit accountants.

Public Accountants

public accountant an accountant who provides accounting services to other organizations.

A **public accountant** provides accounting services to individuals or business firms for a fee. Most public accounting firms provide three basic services to clients: (1) auditing, or examining, financial records; (2) tax preparation, planning, and related services; and (3) management consulting. Because public accountants are not employees of a client firm, they can provide unbiased advice about a firm's financial condition.

Canada has hundreds of public accounting firms, but just a few firms attract the largest share of the industry. The four largest public accounting firms—Deloitte, Ernst & Young, KPMG, and PricewaterhouseCoopers—collect almost $5 billion annually from Canadian clients. In contrast, the Toronto-based Grant Thornton, the nation's fifth-largest accounting firm, has annual revenues of approximately $500 million.[5]

Some years ago, public accounting firms were criticized for providing management consulting services to the same firms they audited. Critics argued that when a public accounting firm does both—auditing and management consulting—a conflict of interest is created. This conflict of interest may weaken confidence in the quality of the financial statements that accounting firms audit. The bankruptcies of some high-profile firms increased pressure on public accounting firms to end the practice. Legislation also set strict limits on the types of consulting services auditors can provide. For example, an accounting firm that audits a company's books cannot provide any other services to that company, including tax services. As a result, three of the four largest public accounting firms either sold large portions of their consulting practices or created separate consulting companies. PricewaterhouseCoopers, for example, sold much of its consulting business to IBM. The accounting firms now focus on providing auditing and tax services.

As the "Hit & Miss" feature outlines, more and more public accountants are also being certified as *forensic accountants*. Some smaller public accounting firms have chosen to specialize in forensic accounting. These professionals and the firms that employ them focus on uncovering potential fraud in many different organizations.

Chartered Professional Accountants (CPAs) are Canada's most recognized group of professional accountants. They demonstrate their accounting knowledge by meeting provincial requirements for education and experience and by successfully completing thorough testing in accounting theory and practice, auditing, law, finance, strategy, and taxation. Other recognized accountants meet specified educational and experience requirements and pass certification exams to earn the title *Certified Fraud Examiner (CFE)* or *Certified Internal Auditor (CIA)*.

Management Accountants

An accountant who is employed by a business other than a public accounting firm is called a *management accountant*. A management accountant collects and records financial transactions and prepares financial statements used by the firm's managers in decision making. Management accountants provide timely, relevant, accurate, and concise information that executives can use to operate their firms more effectively and more profitably than without this input. A management accountant prepares financial statements and plays a major role in interpreting them. A management accountant should be able to provide answers to many important questions:

- Where is the company going?
- What opportunities are in the company's future?
- Will certain situations expose the company to excessive risk?
- Does the firm's information system provide detailed and timely information to all levels of management?

HIT & MISS

Forensic Accountants: Fraud Busters

When you think of an accountant, do you picture someone poring over stacks of ledgers or computer printouts, calculator in hand? Much of accounting *does* involve ledgers and printouts, but forensic accounting is a little different. Forensic accountants don't take a company's accounting numbers at face value—they are crime fighters who look at what's happening behind those numbers. Forensic accountants work in a growing field. They investigate such white-collar crimes as business fraud, improper financial reporting, and illegal investment schemes.

Forensic accounting is accounting that is done in preparation for legal review. Forensic accountants take a skeptical view. They investigate below the surface of an organization's accounting system to find out what actually happened. They may also testify as expert witnesses if a case goes to trial. In Canada, forensic accountants typically need a professional accounting designation such as CPA and further training in investigative techniques. Forensic accountants may have a Certified Fraud Examiner (CFE) designation or a diploma in forensic accounting (DIFA).

Nortel Networks was once a large Canadian telecommunications company. It went through multiple financial statement restatements before completely collapsing. As a result, former CEO Frank Dunn, former CFO Douglas Beatty, and former corporate controller Michael Gollogly were charged with fraud, falsification of accounts and documents, and involvement in issuing a false prospectus. Such scandals can have far-reaching and disastrous effects on a firm. Nortel's stock once traded at as high as $124.50 per share and represented more than one-third of the TSE 300 index, the Toronto Stock Exchange's index of 300 influential stocks. After news broke on the accounting charges, Nortel stock became penny stock, trading at less than $1.00 per share. Nortel ceased operations in June 2009.

Al Rosen is one of Canada's best known (and possibly its most outspoken) forensic accountants. He said, "You can churn out all sorts of rubbish in quarterly and annual reports . . . and guess what the newspapers do with their databases? They take this crap, they do all this analysis, and they're playing with bogus numbers."

Questions for Critical Thinking

1. Describe how a shift in the economy has created a new career path for accounting students.

2. How can forensic accounting change the world of business?

Sources: "The Wild Ride of Canada's Most-Watched Stock," *CBC News*, February 27, 2008, accessed May 18, 2011, www.cbc.ca/news/background/nortel/stock.html; CICA, "The CICA Alliance for Excellence in Investigative and Forensic Accounting," accessed May 18, 2011, www.cica.ca/focus-on-practice-areas/forensic-accounting/the-alliance-for-excellence-in-investigative-and-forensic-accounting/index.aspx; "RCMP Lay Fraud Charges against Former Nortel Execs," *CTV News*, June 19, 2008, accessed May 18, 2011, www.ctv.ca/CTVNews/TopStories/20080619/rcmp_nortel_080619/; David Berman, "Lie Detector," *MoneySense*, December/January 2002, accessed May 18, 2011, www.canadianjusticereviewboard.ca/CJRB_director_Al_Rosen.htm.

Management accountants often specialize in different aspects of accounting. For example, a cost accountant decides on the costs of goods and services and helps to set their prices. An internal auditor examines the firm's financial practices to ensure that its records include accurate data and that its operations comply with federal, provincial, and local laws and regulations. A tax accountant works to minimize a firm's tax bill and handles its federal and provincial tax returns.

Management accountants are usually involved in the development and enforcement of organizational policies on such items as employee travel. As part of their job, many employees travel and accumulate frequent flyer miles and hotel reward points. Some organizations have strict policies over the personal use of these travel points, but many do not.

In recent years, the federal regulations for accounting and public reporting have changed. The need to adapt to the new regulations has increased the demand for management accountants. As a result, salaries for these professionals are rising.

Government and Not-for-Profit Accountants

Federal, provincial, and local governments also need accounting services. Government accountants and those who work for not-for-profit organizations perform professional services similar to the services provided by management accountants. Accountants in government and not-for-profit sectors are concerned primarily with how efficiently the organizations work to meet their objectives. Many government agencies employ accountants, including the CRA, the Canadian Security

ASSESSMENT CHECK

15.2.1 List the three services offered by public accounting firms.

15.2.2 What tasks do management accountants perform?

Intelligence Service (CSIS), the Province of Manitoba, and the City of St. John's in Newfoundland and Labrador. The federal government employs hundreds of accountants.

Accountants also work for not-for-profit organizations, such as churches, labour unions, charities, schools, hospitals, and universities. The not-for-profit sector is one of the fastest-growing segments of accounting practice. More not-for-profits are publishing their financial information because donors want more accountability from these organizations. Donors are interested in how the groups spend the money they raise.

LO 15.3 Describe the foundation of the accounting system.

THE FOUNDATION OF THE ACCOUNTING SYSTEM

Accountants need to provide reliable, consistent, and unbiased information to decision makers. To help them in this task, accountants follow guidelines, or standards, known as **generally accepted accounting principles (GAAP)**. These principles outline the conventions, rules, and procedures for deciding on the acceptable accounting and financial reporting practices at a particular time. GAAP includes International Financial Reporting Standards (IFRS), Accounting Standards for Private Enterprises (ASPE), accounting standards for not-for-profit organizations, accounting standards for pension plans, and accounting standards for governments.

generally accepted accounting principles (GAAP) principles that outline the conventions, rules, and procedures for deciding on the acceptable accounting practices at a particular time.

All GAAP standards are based on several basic qualitative characteristics: consistency, relevance, representational faithfulness, reliability, timeliness, understandability, verifiability, and comparability. *Consistency* means that all data should be collected and presented in the same manner across all periods. Any change in how specific data are collected or presented must be noted and explained. *Relevance* states that all information being reported should be appropriate and assist users in evaluating financial information. *Representational faithfulness* means that financial information should reflect the substance of the economic activity during the reporting period. *Reliability* implies that the accounting data in financial statements are dependable and can be verified by an independent party, such as an outside auditor. *Timeliness* states that financial information should be made available within a time period that allows the financial information to be useful in decision making. *Understandability* requires that financial information be clearly presented to users. *Verifiability* means that other independent and knowledgeable individuals would agree that the financial information is fairly presented. Finally, *comparability* ensures that one firm's financial statements can be compared with those of similar businesses.

In Canada, the **Accounting Standards Board (AcSB)** is primarily responsible for evaluating and setting GAAP related to pension plans and to private and not-for-profit businesses. The Public Sector Accounting Board (PSAB) is responsible for accounting standards for governments.

Accounting Standards Board (AcSB) the organization that interprets and modifies GAAP in Canada for private and not-for-profit businesses.

Canadian public companies are required to use International Financial Reporting Standards (IFRS). These standards allow for financial statements to be more easily compared from country to country. This level of comparability is required because of the increase in worldwide trade. The idea of a uniform set of global accounting rules is gaining interest, mainly as a result of the expansion of the European Union and the signing of cross-national trade agreements, such as the North American Free Trade Agreement (NAFTA). Also, more investors are buying shares in foreign multinational corporations, and they need a practical way to evaluate firms in other countries. To assist global investors, more and more firms are reporting their financial information by using international accounting standards. This practice helps investors to make informed decisions.

International Financial Reporting Standards (IFRS) the standards and interpretations adopted by the IASB.

International Financial Reporting Standards (IFRS) are the standards and interpretations adopted by the **International Accounting Standards Board (IASB)**. The use of IFRS is widespread and growing. More than 120 countries require, permit the use of, or have a policy of working with IFRS, including India, Australia, Canada, Hong Kong, and member countries of the European Union.

International Accounting Standards Board (IASB) the organization that promotes worldwide consistency in financial reporting practices.

How does IFRS differ from ASPE? IFRS and ASPE share many similarities, but also have some important differences. For example, under ASPE firms report plant, property, and equipment on the balance sheet at the historical cost minus depreciation; under IFRS, firms have the option to report plant, property, and equipment on the balance sheet at current market value. The IFRS

CAREER KICKSTART

Tips for Complying with the Corruption of Foreign Public Officials Act

The Corruption of Foreign Public Officials (CFPO) Act is meant to prevent the bribery of foreign officials for the purpose of gaining or keeping business in another country. More companies now do business overseas, so they are naturally concerned about being at risk to violations of this law. Enforcement of this act is at an all-time high and is expected to remain high. Penalties are severe, including fines and prison time for anyone convicted. The following are some ways that global firms can improve their compliance and reduce their risk:

1. Assess your firm's risk under the CFPO Act, country by country. Does your firm do business with any government-owned foreign firms or with any foreign government officials? What are the risks of corruption and bribery?

2. Set up a policy for your firm's employees—in Canada and abroad—to comply with the CFPO Act. The policy should cover gifts and payments to foreign officials, charitable donations, accurate and complete records, and other areas at risk.

3. Train your employees in the policies of the CFPO Act. Include these policies in your company's overall compliance process. Have your human resources department make these policies part of new-employee orientation.

4. Have a compliance team in place to monitor compliance to the act and to be on the watch for potential risks. The team should include company lawyers, accountants, and auditors. The team should be empowered to make both in-house and external investigations.

5. Plan any international investigations carefully. Many foreign countries do not apply the attorney-client privilege to company lawyers and employees.

Sources: Department of Justice, "The Corruption of Foreign Public Officials Act: A Guide," May 1999, accessed May 27, 2011, www.justice.gc.ca/eng/dept-min/pub/cfpoa-lcape/index.html; "Foreign Corrupt Practices Act," Ernst & Young, accessed June 1, 2010, www.ey.com; U.S. Department of Justice, "Foreign Corrupt Practices Act: An Overview," accessed June 1, 2010, www.justice.gov; Gary Sturisky, "2010 Compliance Challenges: Three More Areas That Matter," *Corporate Compliance Insights*, March 4, 2010, accessed June 1, 2010, www.corporatecomplianceinsights.com; Brian Loughman, Aaron Marcu, and Kerry Schalders, "Top Ten Tips for FCPA Compliance," Association of Corporate Counsel, March 1, 2010, accessed June 1, 2010, www.acc.com; Nina Gross, "Foreign Corrupt Practices Act: Leading Practices to Consider," Deloitte, January 29, 2010, accessed June 1, 2010, www.deloitte.com.

---

option gives a clearer picture of the real value of a firm's assets. Many accounting experts believe that, overall, IFRS is less complicated than traditional GAAP and more transparent.[6]

In the United States, the **Financial Accounting Standards Board (FASB)** sets GAAP. The FASB is currently working with the IASB on a project to work toward IFRS. The United States is one of the few developed countries not currently using IFRS.

In response to accounting fraud and questions about the independence of auditors, the U.S. government enacted the Sarbanes-Oxley Act in 2002, commonly known as SOX. SOX then created the Public Company Accounting Oversight Board. This five-member board has the power to set audit standards and to investigate and approve the accounting firms that certify the books of publicly traded firms. All Canadian companies that have publicly traded stock or debt on a U.S. stock exchange must comply with SOX. In Canada, Bill 198 requires similar provisions as SOX for Canadian companies.

SOX and Bill 198 also added to the reporting requirements for publicly traded companies. For example, senior executives, including the chief executive officer (CEO) and chief financial officer (CFO), must personally certify that the financial information reported by the company is correct. As noted earlier, these additional requirements have increased the demand for accounting professionals, especially managerial accountants. One result of this increased demand has been higher salaries.

It is expensive for firms to meet GAAP standards and the requirements of SOX and Bill 198. For example, audits can cost millions of dollars each year. These expenses can be especially difficult for small businesses. Some people have suggested making changes to GAAP and SOX for smaller firms. They argue that some accounting rules were designed for larger companies. As a result, Canada has multiple sets of standards, such as the Accounting Standards for Private Enterprises (ASPE), which are set by the AcSB.

The **Corruption of Foreign Public Officials Act** is a federal law that prohibits Canadian citizens and companies from bribing foreign officials to win or continue business. The law was later extended to make foreign officials subject to penalties if they cause similar corrupt practices to occur within Canada or its territories. The "Career Kickstart" feature provides some tips on complying with this act.

Financial Accounting Standards Board (FASB) the organization that interprets and modifies GAAP in the United States.

Corruption of Foreign Public Officials Act a federal law that prohibits Canadian citizens and companies from bribing foreign officials to win or continue business.

✓ ASSESSMENT CHECK

15.3.1 Define *GAAP*.

15.3.2 What is the role played by the AcSB?

LO 15.4 Outline the steps in the accounting cycle.

THE ACCOUNTING CYCLE

Accounting deals with a firm's financial transactions with its employees, customers, suppliers, owners, and with bankers and various government agencies. For example, payroll cheques result in a cash outflow to employees. A payment to a supplier results in the delivery of needed materials for the production process. Customers use cash, cheques, and credit to purchase goods, which generate business funds to cover the costs of operations and to earn a profit. Prompt payment of bills keeps the firm's credit rating high and helps its future ability to earn a profit. Accountants gather data on individual buying and selling transactions and convert these data to financial statements through a process called the **accounting cycle**.

Figure 15.2 shows the activities involved in the accounting cycle: recording, classifying, and summarizing transactions. Any transaction that has a financial impact on the business, such as wages or payments to suppliers, should be recorded. These transactions are recorded in journals, which list the transactions in the order they occurred. Journal listings are then posted to ledgers. A ledger shows increases or decreases in specific accounts, such as cash or wages. Ledgers are used to prepare the financial statements, which summarize the financial transactions. Management and other interested parties use the resulting financial statements for many different purposes.

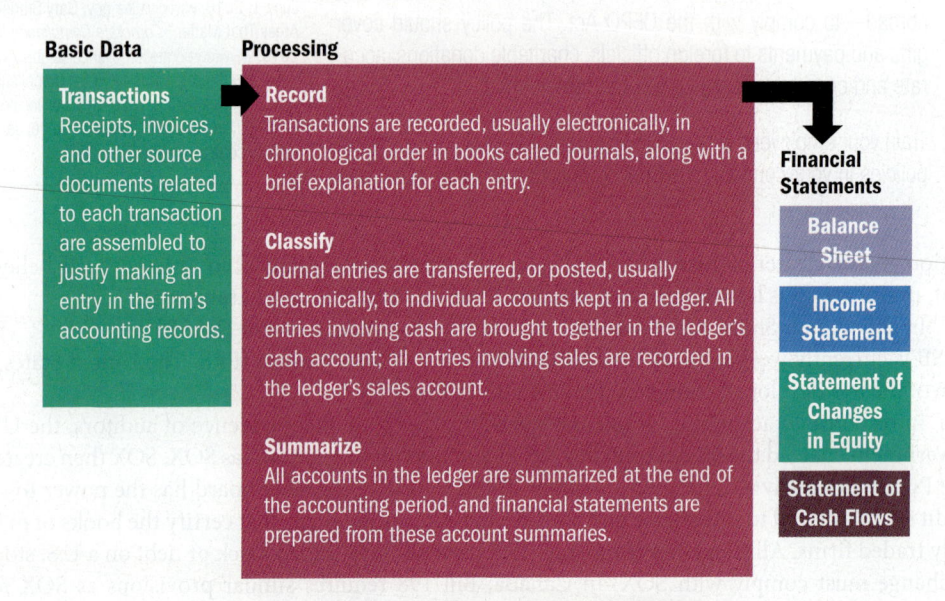

accounting cycle the set of activities involved in converting information and individual transactions into financial statements.

Basic Data

Transactions
Receipts, invoices, and other source documents related to each transaction are assembled to justify making an entry in the firm's accounting records.

Processing

Record
Transactions are recorded, usually electronically, in chronological order in books called journals, along with a brief explanation for each entry.

Classify
Journal entries are transferred, or posted, usually electronically, to individual accounts kept in a ledger. All entries involving cash are brought together in the ledger's cash account; all entries involving sales are recorded in the ledger's sales account.

Summarize
All accounts in the ledger are summarized at the end of the accounting period, and financial statements are prepared from these account summaries.

Financial Statements
- Balance Sheet
- Income Statement
- Statement of Changes in Equity
- Statement of Cash Flows

FIGURE 15.2 The Accounting Cycle

The Accounting Equation

Three fundamental terms appear in the accounting equation: assets, liabilities, and owners' equity. An **asset** is anything with future benefit owned or controlled by a business. Assets include land, buildings, supplies, cash, accounts receivable (amounts owed to the business as payment for credit sales), and marketable securities.

Tangible assets, such as equipment, buildings, and inventories, are the most common assets. But a firm's most important assets may be its intangible assets, such as patents and trademarks. These assets are especially important for companies such as computer software firms, biotechnology companies, and pharmaceutical companies. For example, Johnson & Johnson—which has both biotechnology and pharmaceutical operations—reported more than $40 billion in intangible assets (including goodwill) in one recent year, out of a total of almost $133 billion in assets.[7]

asset anything with future benefit owned or controlled by a firm.

Two groups have claims against the assets of a firm: creditors and owners. A **liability** of a business is anything owed to creditors—that is, the claims of a firm's creditors. When a firm borrows money to purchase inventory, land, or machinery, the claims of creditors are shown as accounts payable, notes payable, or long-term debt. Wages and salaries owed to employees are also liabilities (known as *wages payable* or *accrued wages*).

Owners' equity is the owners' initial investment in the business plus any profits that were not paid to owners. A strong owners' equity position is often used as evidence of a firm's financial strength and stability.

The **accounting equation** (also called the *accounting identity*) states that assets must equal liabilities plus owners' equity. This equation reflects the financial position of a firm at any point in time:

$$\text{Assets} = \text{Liabilities} + \text{Owners' Equity}$$

Tangible assets, such as buildings, equipment, and inventories, may look impressive. But they are sometimes less important to a company than its intangible assets, such as patents and trademarks.

liability a claim against a firm's assets by creditors.

owners' equity the funds that owners invest in the business plus any profits not paid to owners in the form of cash dividends.

accounting equation the relationship that should reflect a firm's financial position at any time: assets should always equal the sum of liabilities and owners' equity.

double-entry bookkeeping the process used to record accounting transactions; each individual transaction is always balanced by another transaction.

Because financing comes from either creditors or owners, the right side of the accounting equation also represents the business's financial structure.

The accounting equation also illustrates **double-entry bookkeeping**—the process used to record accounting transactions. Because assets must always equal liabilities plus equity, each transaction must have two or more effects on the accounts. For example, if a company increases an asset, one of the following must also happen: another asset must decrease, a liability must increase, or owners' equity must increase. That is, if a company uses cash to purchase inventory, one asset (inventory) is increased while another asset (cash) is decreased by the same amount. Following the same idea, a decrease in an asset must be balanced by either an increase in another asset, a decrease in a liability, or a decrease in owners' equity. If a company uses cash to repay a bank loan, both an asset (cash) and a liability (bank loans) decrease by the same amount.

Two simple numerical examples will help to explain the accounting equation and double-entry bookkeeping.

First, assume the owner of a photo studio uses her own funds to buy a new camera system for $5,000. The accounting transaction would look like the following:

Increase plant, property, and equipment (an asset) by $5,000

Increase owners' equity by $5,000

So the left side of the accounting equation increases by $5,000 and is balanced by a $5,000 increase on the right side.

Second, assume a firm has a $100,000 loan from a bank and decides to pay it off using some of its cash. The transaction would be recorded as follows:

Decrease bank loan (a liability) by $100,000

Decrease cash (an asset) by $100,000

In this second example, the left side and right side of the accounting equation both decrease by $100,000.

The relationship described by the accounting equation is the basis for developing the firm's financial statements. Three financial statements form the foundation: the balance sheet, the income statement, and the statement of changes in equity. The information in these statements is calculated using the double-entry bookkeeping system and reflects the basic accounting equation. A fourth statement, the statement of cash flows, focuses on the sources and uses of cash in a firm's operating, investing, and financing activities.

The Impact of Computers and the Internet on the Accounting Process

For hundreds of years, bookkeepers have manually recorded, or posted, accounting transactions as entries in journals. They then transferred the information, or posted it, to individual accounts listed in ledgers. Computers have simplified the process, making it both faster and easier. For example, point-of-sale terminals in retail stores perform several functions each time they record sales. These terminals recall product prices from a computer system's memory and keep inventory counts of individual items. They also do the data entry functions that were once entered manually.

Accounting software programs are used widely in both large and small businesses. They allow a do-it-once approach: A single sales entry is automatically converted into a journal entry, which is stored until needed. Decision makers can then instantly access up-to-date financial statements and financial ratios. Improvements in accounting software continue to make the process faster and easier. CPS is a Canadian company that sells and services machines. Recently CPS decided to use Sage 300 ERP and Sage CRM to integrate its databases and track its sales processes. This new system means that managers no longer need to wait for reports because they can access the data at any time. Those who use information on outside sales can now access and share information with management, accounting, and those who use inside sales figures. All the operational data is integrated with CPS's accounting data to reduce the number of duplicate entries.[8]

The accounting needs of entrepreneurs and small businesses differ from the needs of larger firms. Some accounting software programs, such as QuickBooks and Sage 50 (formerly Sage Simply Accounting), have been designed specifically for entrepreneurs and small businesses. To facilitate ease of use and maintenance, many cloud computing solutions have been introduced, like FreshBooks. Software programs designed for larger firms, such as products from Oracle and SAP, often need more sophisticated computer systems.

For firms that conduct business worldwide, software producers have introduced new accounting programs that handle all of a company's accounting information for every country where it operates. The software also handles other languages and currencies and can deal with the financial, legal, and tax requirements of each nation where the firm does business.

The Internet also influences the accounting process. Several software producers offer Web-based accounting products designed for small and medium-sized businesses. These products allow users to access their complete accounting systems from anywhere using a standard Web browser. The "Going Green" feature explains how Deloitte is integrating sustainability into its infrastructure and its business services.

✓ ASSESSMENT CHECK

15.4.1 List the steps in the accounting cycle.

15.4.2 What is the accounting equation?

15.4.3 Briefly explain double-entry bookkeeping.

DELOITTE EDUCATES ITSELF—AND OTHERS—ON SUSTAINABILITY

Deloitte is one of the Big Four accounting and auditing firms. Recently, the company made two decisions: to make its own internal operations greener and to offer its clients training in green practices. It seems logical that a firm specializing in financial reporting would enter the area of nonfinancial reporting as the business world begins to value green practices. Firms once thought of "going green" as good public relations but not so good financially. But many firms now see the importance of sustainability in an increasingly energy-limited world.

Kathryn Pavlovsky is a co-leader of Deloitte's Enterprise Sustainability Group. She says, "Nonfinancial reporting is evolving from voluntary communications to mandatory compliance, and the environmental regulatory and financial reporting worlds are

(continued)

GOING GREEN (continued)

converging." The move to add sustainable activities to a company's nonfinancial reporting has been encouraged by many factors: the recent recession, activism from shareholders, and changing consumer attitudes and behaviours. Also, technological advances have made green practices more realistic and affordable.

Deloitte's corporate responsibility policy declares that the company will "advocate the sustainable use of natural resources and the environment." The company began its internal greening campaign by surveying its employees. Called "How Green Is Your Footprint?" the survey measured "greenness" on an individual basis within the business environment. It then suggested how each employee could improve his or her performance. A second survey, "How Green Is Your *Other* Footprint?" helps employees to measure their sustainability practices at home.

Deloitte also established a Green Leadership Council (GLC) to maintain contact between the various company regions and management. The GLC educates employees about important green issues and promotes a unified message to all the company's offices. Deloitte employees now conduct virtual meetings and conferences whenever possible. When employees need to travel, the company travel arrangements include car rentals and hotel options considered to be green. Deloitte has also adopted Leadership in Energy and Environmental Design (LEED) standards when building new offices and retrofitting existing offices. The company focuses on purchasing supplies that have a minimal impact on the environment, and it has worked with its suppliers to reach greater levels of sustainability.

Deloitte's Center for Sustainability Performance (CSP) advises businesses on how to reduce their environmental impact and remain profitable. Among the areas covered are planning and strategy, revenue generation, tax incentives, and competitive branding. The CSP also explores sustainability opportunities for employees, offices, IT infrastructure, and communities. The CSP's activities include on-site training for client firms, research and development in sustainability measurement and reporting, publication of reports on these topics for corporate sustainability managers, and consulting and sales support.

One of the CSP's recent workshops for clients was "Sustainability Measurement and Reporting: Tools, Methods, and Metrics." The course was designed to help clients become familiar with the current methods for measuring and reporting their own sustainability. It also provided a preview of new developments in these areas. According to Mark W. McElroy, the CSP's director, the course covered "tools, methods, and metrics across all dimensions of corporate social responsibility and sustainability performance, including carbon, water, solid waste, social impacts, triple bottom line, and non-financial measurement and reporting in general, both from an enterprise and product life cycle perspective."

To further develop its internal greening efforts, Deloitte recently introduced its Green Sync tool. It is intended to promote employee and stakeholder involvement. Johanne Gelinas is a partner with Deloitte Canada's corporate responsibility and sustainability practice. She says, "Executives will always be challenged about where to spend time and resources. By adopting a strategic approach to corporate responsibility, they can start to identify environmental, social and governance initiatives that can also improve shareholder value."

Questions for Critical Thinking

1. Why would Deloitte find it relatively easy to expand from financial reporting to nonfinancial reporting?

2. How would you answer the question "How big is *your* carbon footprint?" What can you do to make your home or your workplace greener?

Sources: Deloitte, accessed June 1, 2010, www.deloitte.com; Deborah Fleischer, "Deloitte: Best Practices for Going Green," *Triple Pundit*, February 1, 2010, accessed June 1, 2010, www.triplepundit.com; Deborah Fleischer, "Deloitte: Green Training on Sustainability Measurement and Reporting," *Green Impact*, January 4, 2010, accessed June 1, 2010, http://greenimpact.com; "Deloitte Launches Center for Sustainability Performance," press release, August 10, 2009, accessed June 1, 2010, www.csrwire.com; Deloitte, "Sustainability & Climate Change," accessed May 17, 2012, www.deloitte.com/us/sustainability.

FINANCIAL STATEMENTS

LO 15.5 Explain the functions and major components of the four principal financial statements.

Financial statements provide managers with the information they need to evaluate the firm's profitability, its overall financial health, and its liquidity position—the ability to meet its current obligations and needs by converting assets into cash. Managers can base their decisions on information in the balance sheet, the income statement, the statement of changes in equity, and the statement of cash flows. Managers interpret the data in these statements so they can communicate the appropriate information to internal decision makers and to interested parties outside the organization.

Of the four financial statements, the only permanent statement is the balance sheet: Its amounts are carried over from year to year. The income statement, statement of changes in equity, and statement of cash flows are temporary statements because they are closed out at the end of each year and therefore are not cumulative in nature.

Public companies report their financial statements at the end of each three-month period and at the end of each fiscal year. Annual statements must be examined and verified by the firm's outside auditors. These financial statements are public information available to anyone. The "Solving an Ethical Controversy" feature discusses the problem of financial fraud.

SOLVING AN ETHICAL CONTROVERSY

Should Whistle-Blowers Be Rewarded?

The U.S. Sarbanes-Oxley Act of 2002 (SOX) and Canada's Bill 198 were intended to reduce fraud. Both require CEOs and CFOs to sign off on the accuracy of their companies' financial statements. But most reported fraud is revealed by anonymous whistle-blowers or by journalists, auditors, or others.

The Public Servants Disclosure Protection Act protects Canadians who report misconduct in the government. But unlike in the United States, this legislation does not financially reward whistle-blowers. In the United States, the False Claims Act allows citizens to file lawsuits alleging fraud against the federal government. The biggest settlements have involved hospital chains and drug manufacturers; the largest fine was $1.4 billion. Some whistle-blowers have collected almost $47 million in rewards. The U.S. Foreign Corrupt Practices Act (FCPA) may also result in huge rewards. But whistle-blowers are not always successful; some have been fired, forced to quit, or demoted.

Should whistle-blowers be rewarded for reporting financial fraud in Canada?

PRO

1. A recent survey found that "a strong monetary incentive to blow the whistle does motivate people with information to come forward."

2. People who commit fraud can face strict penalties, such as those outlined under SOX, Bill 198, the FCPA, and the Corruption of Foreign Public Officials Act. One survey reported that 83 percent of fraud examiners believe that internal corporate controls on fraud will actually decline.

CON

1. Some observers feel that some "whistle-blower-friendly" provisions of the FCPA in the United States may discourage accused firms from simply settling with the federal government and paying a fine to avoid costly legal procedures.

2. Not all whistle-blowers are innocent. A former UBS banker exposed tax evasion at the firm but was sentenced to prison because he did not reveal that he had participated in the fraud himself.

Summary

In the United States, legislation before Congress would require the Securities and Exchange Commission (SEC) to award whistle-blowers up to 30 percent of fines the government collects on the basis of "original information." Some observers worry that these changes could result in a "race to disclose" between companies that self-report and current or former employees. Canada has not seen any similar movements to financially reward whistle-blowers.

Sources: Parliament of Canada, "Bill C-25, The Public Servants Disclosure Protection Act," accessed June 3, 2011, www.parl.gc.ca/About/Parliament/LegislativeSummaries/bills_ls.asp?ls=c25&Parl=37&Ses=3; "Sarbanes-Oxley Can Help Curb Company Fraud," McGladrey, accessed June 1, 2010, http://rsmmcgladrey.com; Michael Connor, "Finance Reform Bill Could Increase Big Payouts to Whistleblowers," *Business Ethics*, May 2, 2010, accessed June 1, 2010, http://business-ethics.com; "Whistleblowers Making Money Thanks to Law," *NewsChannel8*, May 1, 2010, accessed June 1, 2010, http://cfc.news.8.net; Deloitte, "Poll: More Financial Statement Fraud Expected to Be Uncovered in 2010, 2011," *Corporate Compliance Insights*, April 28, 2010, accessed June 1, 2010, www.corporatecomplianceinsights.com; James Hyatt, "Who Detects Corporate Fraud? (Tip: It's Not Usually the SEC . . .)," *Business Ethics*, February 16, 2010, accessed June 1, 2010, http://business-ethics.com; Michael Rubinkam, "UBS Tax Evasion Whistle-Blower Reports to Federal Prison," *USA Today*, January 8, 2010, accessed June 1, 2010, www.usatoday.com; Free Advice, accessed August 13, 2014, http://employment-law.freeadvice.com/employment-law/employment-law/largest-whistleblower-lawsuit.htm.

A fiscal year does not need to be the same as the calendar year. Many companies set different fiscal years. For example, the Starbucks fiscal year runs from October 1 to September 30 of the following year. Nike's fiscal year consists of the 12 months between June 1 and May 31. By contrast, GE's fiscal year is the same as the calendar year, running from January 1 to December 31.

The Balance Sheet

balance sheet a statement of a firm's financial position—what it owns and claims against its assets—at a particular point in time.

A **balance sheet** (or *statement of financial position* under IFRS) shows a firm's financial position on a particular date. It is similar to a photograph of the firm's assets, liabilities, and owners' equity at a specific moment in time. Balance sheets must be prepared at regular intervals because a firm's managers and other internal parties often need this information every day, every week, or at least every month. External users, such as shareholders and industry analysts, may use this information less often, maybe every quarter (every three months) or once a year.

The balance sheet follows the accounting equation. On the left side of the balance sheet are the firm's assets—what it owns. These assets are shown in a downward order of liquidity. In other words, the assets with the highest ability to be converted to cash are shown first; that's why cash is always listed first on the asset side of the balance sheet. The assets represent how management has used its available funds.

On the right side of the equation are the claims against the firm's assets. Liabilities and owners' equity show the sources of the firm's assets. They are listed in the order they are due. Liabilities include the claims of creditors—the financial institutions or bondholders that have loaned the firm money; suppliers that have provided goods and services on credit; and others to be paid in the future, such as federal, provincial, and municipal tax authorities. Owners' equity represents the owners' claims against the firm's assets; in the case of a corporation, owners' equity represents the claims of shareholders. Owners' equity also includes any excess of all assets over liabilities.

Figure 15.3 shows the balance sheet for Diane's Java, a small coffee wholesaler. The accounting equation is illustrated by the three classifications of assets, liabilities, and owners' equity on the company's balance sheet. Remember, total assets must always equal the sum of liabilities and owners' equity. In other words, the balance sheet must always balance.

The balance sheet is the only permanent statement of the four financial statements. It shows the firm's financial position on a particular date, and its amounts are carried over from year to year.

The Income Statement

The **income statement** is a financial record of a company's revenues, expenses, and profits over a specific time period. In contrast, a balance sheet shows a firm's financial record at one specific point in time. You can think of the income statement as a video, while the balance sheet is more like a photograph. The income statement summarizes a firm's financial performance over a specific time period, usually a quarter (three months) or a year.

The income statement also helps decision makers focus on overall revenues and the costs needed to generate these revenues. Managers of a not-for-profit organization use the income statement to check whether the revenues from contributions and other sources will cover the organization's operating costs. Finally, the income statement provides many basic data used to calculate the financial ratios that managers use in planning and controlling activities. **Figure 15.4** shows the income statement for Diane's Java.

An income statement is also called a *profit-and-loss statement*, a *P&L statement*, or under IFRS a *statement of comprehensive income*. It begins with total sales or revenues generated during a year, quarter, or month. The following lines then deduct all of the costs related to producing the revenues. Typical costs include operating expenses, interest, and taxes. After all costs have been subtracted, the remaining net income may be distributed to the firm's owners (the shareholders, proprietors, or partners) or reinvested in the company as retained earnings. The final figure on the income statement—net income after taxes—is the so-called *bottom line*.

Keeping costs under control is an important part of running a business. But too often companies focus more on increasing revenue than on controlling costs. It doesn't matter how much money a company collects in revenues—it won't stay in business for long unless it earns a profit.

income statement a financial record of a company's revenues, expenses, and profits over a specific period of time.

① Current Assets:
Cash and other liquid assets that can or will be converted to cash within one year.

② Plant, property, and equipment (net):
Physical assets expected to last for more than one year; shown net of accumulated depreciation.

③ Value of assets such as patents and trademarks.

④ Current Liabilities:
Claims of creditors that are to be repaid within one year; accruals are expenses, such as wages, that have been incurred but not yet paid.

⑤ Long-term debt:
Debts that come due one year or longer after the date on the balance sheet.

⑥ Owners' (or Shareholders') equity:
Claims of the owners against the assets of the firm; the difference between total assets and total liabilities.

Diane's Java

Balance Sheet
As at December 31, 2017

($ thousands)	2017	2016
Assets		
Current Assets ①		
Cash	$ 800	$ 600
Short-term investments	1,250	940
Accounts receivable	990	775
Inventory	2,200	1,850
Total current assets	5,240	4,165
Plant, property, and equipment (net) ②	3,300	2,890
Goodwill and other intangible assets ③	250	250
Total Assets	8,790	7,305
Liabilities and Shareholders' Equity		
Current Liabilities ④		
Accruals	$ 350	$ 450
Accounts payable	980	900
Notes payable	700	500
Total current liabilities	2,030	1,850
Long-term debt ⑤	1,100	1,000
Total liabilities	3,130	2,850
Shareholders' equity ⑥	5,660	4,455
Total Liabilities and Equity	8,790	7,305

FIGURE 15.3 Diane's Java Balance Sheet (Fiscal Year Ending December 31, 2017)

Chapter 15 Understanding Accounting and Financial Statements 431

① Operating Activities: The nuts and bolts of day-to-day activities of a company carrying out its regular business; increases in accounts receivable and inventory are like uses of cash, while increases in accruals and accounts payables are like sources of cash; in financially healthy firms, net cash flow from operating activities should be positive.

② Investing Activities: Transactions to accumulate or use cash in ways that affect operating activities in the future; often a use of cash.

③ Financing Activities: Ways to transfer cash to or from creditors and to or from owners; can be either positive or negative.

④ Net Cash Flow: The sum of cash flow from operating, investing, and financing activities; a reconcilement of cash from the beginning to the end of the accounting period (one year in this example).

Diane's Java
Statement of Cash Flows
For the Year Ended December 31, 2017

($ thousands)	2017
Cash Flow from Operating Activities	
① Net income	$1,927
Depreciation	350
Change in accounts receivable	(215)
Change in inventory	(350)
Change in accruals	(100)
Change in accounts payable	80
Total cash flow from operating activities	1,692
② Cash Flow from Investing Activities	
Capital expenditures	(760)
Change in short-term investments	(310)
Total cash flow from investing activities	(1,070)
③ Cash Flow from Financing Activities	
Cash dividends	(460)
Sale/repurchase of shares	(262)
Change in notes payable	200
Change in long-term debt	100
Total cash flow from financing activities	(422)
④ Net Cash Flow	200
Cash (beginning of year)	600
Cash (end of year)	800

FIGURE 15.6 Diane's Java Statement of Cash Flows (Fiscal Year Ending December 31, 2017)

FINANCIAL RATIO ANALYSIS

LO 15.6 Discuss how financial ratios are used to analyze a company's financial strengths and weaknesses.

Accounting professionals have important responsibilities beyond preparing financial statements. They also help managers interpret the statements by comparing data on the firm's current activities to data for previous periods and to data on other companies in the same industry. *Ratio analysis* is one of the most commonly used tools. It measures a firm's liquidity, profitability, and reliance on debt financing and how effectively management uses the firm's resources. This analysis also allows comparisons with other firms and with the firm's own past performance.

Ratios help managers by interpreting actual performance and making comparisons to what should have happened. Managers compare their firm's ratios with ratios of similar companies to understand their firm's performance compared with competitors' results. These industry standards are important measures and help to focus on problem areas—and areas of excellence. Ratios for the current accounting period can be compared with similar calculations for previous periods to spot developing trends. Ratios can be classified according to their specific purposes. The four major categories of financial ratios are summarized in **Table 15.1**. The ratios for Diane's Java for the 2016 and 2017 fiscal years are shown in **Table 15.2**.

Table 15.1 Major Categories of Financial Ratios

CATEGORY	RATIO	DESCRIPTION
Liquidity ratios	Current ratio	Current assets divided by current liabilities
	Quick (acid-test) ratio	Current assets (minus inventory and prepaid expenses) divided by current liabilities
Activity ratios	Inventory turnover	Cost of goods sold divided by average inventory
	Receivables turnover	Credit sales divided by average accounts receivable
	Total asset turnover	Revenue or sales divided by average total assets
Leverage ratios	Debt ratio	Total liabilities divided by total assets
	Long-term debt to equity	Long-term debt divided by owners' equity
Profitability ratios	Gross profit margin	Gross profit divided by revenue or sales
	Net profit margin	Net profit divided by revenue or sales
	Return on equity	Net profit divided by average owners' equity

Table 15.2 Financial Ratios for Diane's Java

FINANCIAL RATIO	2017 FISCAL YEAR	2016 FISCAL YEAR
Current ratio	2.58	2.25
Quick ratio	1.50	1.25
Inventory turnover	5.12	5.03
Receivables turnover	19.60	19.32
Total asset turnover	2.15	2.15
Gross profit margin	40.0%	38.0%
Net profit margin	11.1%	10.0%
Return on equity	38.1%	36.6%
Debt ratio	35.6%	39.0%
Long-term debt to equity	19.4%	22.4%

Liquidity Ratios

Liquidity ratios measure a firm's ability to meet its short-term obligations, such as loans, when they are due. An increase in liquidity reduces the likelihood that a firm will need to raise funds to repay loans. On the other hand, firms with low liquidity may have to choose between defaulting (failing to pay) and borrowing from high-cost lending sources to meet their short-term financial obligations.

Two commonly used liquidity ratios are the current ratio and the acid-test ratio, also called the quick ratio. The *current ratio* compares current assets to current liabilities. It provides executives with information about the firm's ability to pay its current debts as they mature or as payments are due. The current ratio of Diane's Java is computed as follows (unless indicated, all amounts from the balance sheet or income statement are in thousands of dollars):

$$\text{Current ratio} = \frac{\text{Current assets}}{\text{Current liabilities}} = \frac{5{,}240}{2{,}030} = 2.58$$

In other words, Diane's Java has $2.58 of current assets for every $1.00 of current liabilities. In general, a current ratio of 2:1 is considered to provide satisfactory liquidity. This rule of thumb, or guideline, must be considered along with other factors, such as the nature of the business, the season, and the quality of the company's management team. Diane's Java's management and others are likely to evaluate this ratio of 2.58:1 by comparing it with ratios for previous operating periods and with industry averages.

The *acid-test (or quick) ratio* measures the ability of a firm to meet its debt payments on short notice. This ratio compares quick assets—the most liquid current assets—against current liabilities. Quick assets generally consist of cash and equivalents, short-term investments, and accounts receivable. In general, quick assets equal total current assets minus inventory and prepaid expenses.

Diane's Java's current balance sheet lists total current assets of $5.24 million and inventory of $2.2 million. Therefore, its quick ratio is calculated as follows:

$$\text{Acid-test ratio} = \frac{\text{Current assets} - \text{Inventory} - \text{Prepaid expenses}}{\text{Current liabilities}} = \frac{(5{,}240 - 2{,}200 - 0)}{2{,}030} = 1.50$$

Because the traditional rule of thumb for an adequate acid-test ratio is around 1:1, Diane's Java appears to have a strong level of liquidity. However, the same cautions apply here as for the current ratio: The ratio should be compared with industry averages and data from previous operating periods to decide whether it is adequate for the firm.

Activity Ratios

Activity ratios measure how effectively management uses the firm's resources. One of the most frequently used activity ratios is the *inventory turnover ratio*. This ratio indicates the number of times merchandise moves through a business:

$$\text{Inventory turnover} = \frac{\text{Cost of goods sold}}{\text{Average inventory}} = \frac{10{,}370}{[(2{,}200 + 1{,}850)]/2} = 5.12$$

Average inventory for Diane's Java is calculated by adding the inventory as of December 31, 2017 ($2.2 million) to the inventory as of December 31, 2016 ($1.85 million) and dividing it by 2. Comparing the 5.12 inventory turnover ratio with industry standards provides a measure of the firm's efficiency. Note that inventory turnover can vary widely depending on the products a company sells and the industry it operates in.

When a company sells a large portion of its products on credit, it can learn useful information by measuring its *receivables turnover*. Receivables turnover can be calculated as follows:

$$\text{Receivables turnover} = \frac{\text{Credit sales}}{\text{Average accounts receivable}}$$

Because Diane's Java is a wholesaler, let's assume that all of its sales are credit sales. Average receivables equals the simple average of 2017's receivables and 2016's receivables. The receivables turnover for Diane's Java is calculated as follows:

$$\text{Receivables turnover} = \frac{17{,}300}{[(990+775)/2]} = 19.60$$

The average age of receivables is calculated by dividing 365 by the receivables turnover. The average age of Diane's Java's receivables is 18.62 days. Assume Diane's Java expects its retail customers to pay outstanding bills within 30 days of the date of purchase. Given that the average age of its receivables is less than 30 days, Diane's Java appears to be doing a good job collecting its credit sales.

Another measure of efficiency is *total asset turnover*. It measures the amount of sales generated by each dollar invested in assets. The calculations for Diane's Java's total asset turnover are as follows:

$$\text{Total asset turnover} = \frac{\text{Sales}}{\text{Average total assets}}$$

$$= \frac{17{,}300}{[(8{,}790+7{,}305)/2]} = 2.15$$

Average total assets for Diane's Java equals total assets as of December 31, 2017 ($8.79 million) plus total assets as of December 31, 2016 ($7.305 million) divided by 2.

Diane's Java generates about $2.15 in sales for each dollar invested in assets. Although a higher ratio generally shows that a firm is operating more efficiently, care must be taken when comparing firms that operate in different industries. Some industries require a higher investment in assets than other industries.

Profitability Ratios

Some ratios measure the organization's overall financial performance by evaluating its ability to generate revenues that are greater than its operating costs and other expenses. These measures are called *profitability ratios*. To compute these ratios, accountants compare the firm's earnings with total sales or investments. Over a period of time, profitability ratios may show the effectiveness of management in operating the business. Three important profitability ratios are *gross profit margin*, *net profit margin*, and *return on equity*:

$$\text{Gross profit margin} = \frac{\text{Gross profit}}{\text{Sales}} = \frac{6{,}930}{17{,}300} = 40.0\%$$

$$\text{Net profit margin} = \frac{\text{Net income}}{\text{Sales}} = \frac{1{,}927}{17{,}300} = 11.1\%$$

$$= \frac{\text{Net income}}{\text{Average equity}} = \frac{1{,}927}{[(5{,}660+4{,}455)/2]} = 38.1\%$$

All these ratios show positive evaluations of the current operations. For example, the net profit margin indicates that the firm realizes a profit of slightly more than 11 cents on each dollar of merchandise it sells. Although this ratio varies widely among business firms, Diane's Java compares well with wholesalers in general, which have an average net profit margin of around 5 percent. But, for a better interpretation of the results, this ratio, like the other profitability ratios, should be evaluated in relation to profit forecasts, past performance, or more specific industry averages. Similarly, although the firm's return on equity of almost 38 percent appears outstanding, any analysis should also consider the degree of risk in the industry.

Leverage Ratios

Leverage ratios measure how much a firm relies on debt financing. These ratios provide interesting information to potential investors and lenders. If management has taken on too much debt to finance the firm's operations, it may face difficulty in meeting future interest payments and repaying outstanding loans. As we discuss in Chapter 17, borrowing money does have advantages. But relying too much on debt financing may lead to bankruptcy. More generally, both investors and lenders may prefer to deal with firms whose owners have invested enough of their own money to avoid having to borrow funds. The *debt ratio* and the *long-term debt to equity* ratio help interested parties evaluate a firm's leverage:

Walmart Inc. President and CEO Doug McMillon addresses shareholders at a meeting and discusses various topics, including the company's return on equity. Return on equity is one measure of a company's profitability.

$$\text{Debt ratio} = \frac{\text{Total liabilities}}{\text{Total assets}} = \frac{3,130}{8,790} = 35.6\%$$

$$\text{Long-term debt to equity} = \frac{\text{Long-term debt}}{\text{Owners' equity}} = \frac{1,100}{5,660} = 19.4\%$$

When the debt ratio (the ratio of total liabilities to total assets) is greater than 50 percent, it shows that a firm is relying more on borrowed money than on owners' equity. Because Diane's Java's debt ratio is 35.6 percent, the firm's owners have invested considerably more than the total liabilities shown on the balance sheet. Also, the firm's long-term debt to equity ratio is only 19.4 percent, which shows that Diane's Java has only about 19.4 cents in long-term debt for every dollar in equity. The long-term debt to equity ratio also shows that Diane's Java hasn't relied much on borrowed money.

The four categories of financial ratios relate balance sheet and income statement data to one another, help management focus on a firm's strengths and weaknesses, and show the areas in need of further investigation. Large, multiproduct firms that operate in different markets use their information systems to update their financial ratios every day or even every hour. Each company's management must decide on a suitable review schedule to avoid the costly and time-consuming mistake of excessive monitoring.

Managers, investors, and lenders should pay close attention to how accountants apply accounting rules when preparing financial statements. GAAP gives accountants some flexibility in reporting certain revenues and expenses. Public companies are required to disclose, in footnotes to the financial statements, how the various accounting rules were applied.

✓ **ASSESSMENT CHECK**

15.6.1 List the four categories of financial ratios.

15.6.2 Define the following ratios: *current ratio, inventory turnover, net profit margin,* and *debt ratio*.

BUDGETING

The financial statements discussed in this chapter focus on past business activities. But these same financial statements also provide the basis for planning in the future. A **budget** is a planning and controlling tool. It is the organization's plan for how it will raise and spend money during a specific period of time. Specifically, it shows the firm's expected sales revenues, operating expenses, cash receipts, and cash expenses. It quantifies the firm's plans for a specified future period. The budget

LO 15.7 Describe the role of budgets in a business.

budget an organization's plans for how it will raise and spend money during a specific period of time.

can be thought of as a short-term financial plan. It becomes the standard that actual performance is compared against.

Budget preparation is often a time-consuming task. It may involve many people from various departments within the organization. The complexity of the budgeting process varies with the size and complexity of the organization. Large corporations such as Magna International, RBC, and Rogers maintain complex and sophisticated budgeting systems. Their budgets serve as planning and controlling tools and help managers to integrate their numerous divisions. Budgeting in both large and small firms is similar to household budgeting in its purpose: to match income and expenses in a way that accomplishes goals and schedules cash inflows and outflows.

The accounting department is an organization's financial centre. It provides much of the data for budget development. The overall master budget, or operating budget, is composed of many individual budgets for each of the firm's separate units. These individual budgets typically include the production budget, cash budget, capital expenditures budget, advertising budget, and sales budget.

Technology has improved the efficiency of the budgeting process. The accounting software products discussed earlier—like QuickBooks—all include budgeting features. The software modules designed for specific businesses are often available from third parties. Many banks now offer their customers personal financial management tools (PFMs) developed by software companies. One such tool is Quicken, Canada's most-used money management program from Intuit.[9]

One of the most important budgets prepared by firms is the *cash budget*. The cash budget tracks the firm's cash inflows and outflows. It is usually prepared each month. **Figure 15.7**

Birchwood Paper Company
Four-Month Cash Budget

($ thousands)	May	June	July	August
Gross sales	$1,200.0	$3,200.0	$5,500.0	$4,500.0
Cash sales	300.0	800.0	1,375.0	1,125.0
One month prior	600.0	600.0	1,600.0	2,750.0
Two months prior	300.0	300.0	300.0	800.0
Total cash inflows	1,200.0	1,700.0	3,275.0	4,675.0
Purchases				
Cash purchases	1,040.0	1,787.5	1,462.5	390.0
One month prior	390.0	1,040.0	1,787.5	1,462.5
Wages and salaries	250.0	250.0	250.0	250.0
Office rent	75.0	75.0	75.0	75.0
Marketing and other expenses	150.0	150.0	150.0	150.0
Taxes		300.0		
Total cash outflows	1,905.0	3,602.5	3,725.0	2,327.5
Net cash flow				
(Inflows − Outflows)	(705.0)	(1,902.5)	(450.0)	2,347.5
Beginnning cash balance	250.0	150.0	150.0	150.0
Net cash flow	(705.0)	(1,902.5)	(450.0)	2,347.5
Ending cash balance	(455.0)	(1,752.5)	(300.0)	2,497.5
Target cash balance	150.0	150.0	150.0	150.0
Surplus (deficit)	(605.0)	(1,902.5)	(450.0)	2,347.5
Cumulative surplus (deficit)	(605.0)	(2,507.5)	(2,957.5)	610.0

FIGURE 15.7 Four-Month Cash Budget for Birchwood Paper Company

illustrates a sample cash budget for Birchwood Paper, a small paper products company. The company has set a $150,000 target cash balance. The cash budget shows the months when the firm will need temporary loans—May, June, and July. It also shows the size of loan the company will need (close to $3 million). The document also shows that Birchwood will generate a cash surplus in August, when it can begin repaying the short-term loan. Finally, the cash budget produces a tangible standard against which to compare actual cash inflows and outflows.

✓ **ASSESSMENT CHECK**

15.7.1 What is a budget?

15.7.2 How is a cash budget organized?

INTERNATIONAL ACCOUNTING

LO 15.8 Outline the accounting issues facing global business.

Today, accounting procedures and practices must be adapted to work in an international business environment. For example, Air Canada generates more than half of its annual revenues from sales outside of Canada. Nestlé, the giant chocolate and food products firm, operates throughout the world. It derives 98 percent of its revenues from outside Switzerland, its home country. Global firms must reliably translate the financial statements of the firm's international affiliated firms, branches, and subsidiaries and convert data about foreign currency transactions to dollars. Also, foreign currencies and exchange rates influence the accounting and financial reporting processes of firms operating internationally.[10]

As market economies have developed in such countries as Poland and China, the demand for accountants has increased. The "Hit & Miss" feature describes recent developments in the accounting profession in China and Hong Kong.

HIT & MISS

Accounting: Hong Kong Meets China

Hong Kong was a British colony for almost 200 years. In 1997, Britain transferred Hong Kong to the People's Republic of China. China's rise to global power has led to difficulties in combining its financial environment with that of Hong Kong. Even after the transfer, Hong Kong and mainland China kept two separate accounting systems with different standards and different qualifying examinations. Hong Kong accounting is based on international standards and is conducted in English; Chinese accounting is not.

At the beginning of 2010, Hong Kong accepted Chinese accounting standards. This step shows China's growing attractiveness to international investors. It also advances China's ambition to be part of the international financial system. Until recently, the Chinese accounting system was known for its "book-cooking" scandals. As Hong Kong's transition to Chinese standards continues, Hong Kong accountants risk losing much of their business to Chinese firms.

Tim Lui is a tax partner at the Hong Kong branch of the worldwide accounting firm PricewaterhouseCoopers. He believes that in the short run, at least, Hong Kong accountants have a competitive edge because of their training and international perspective. Foreign investors will be glad to see that Chinese companies will be audited by large, international accounting firms. But he warns against underestimating the Chinese market: "The mainland's development is robust and fast and the market is immense."

Another concern is that small and medium-sized Hong Kong accounting firms simply aren't big enough to succeed in China, especially in Shanghai, China's business and accounting centre. Robert Sawhney of SRC Associates Ltd., a Hong Kong accounting firm, urges smaller firms to market themselves more aggressively and to update their training strategies. He says, "There is substantial scope for Asian accounting firms to provide services to other organizations and in niche areas."

Questions for Critical Thinking

1. How might the mix of Chinese and internationally accepted accounting methods affect Chinese firms' operations and ethical standards?

2. What can Hong Kong accounting firms do to increase their business in mainland China?

Sources: Robert C. Sawhney, "The Competitiveness of Hong Kong & Asian Accounting Firms," White Paper, March 2010, www.srchk.com; "The Demand for Accountants Is Always There," *China Daily*, January 8, 2010; Alison Leung, "China Auditors Set to Take on Hong Kong Stock Market," *Reuters*, December 30, 2009.

Exchange Rates

As defined in Chapter 4, an exchange rate is the value of one country's currency in terms of the currencies of other countries. Currencies can be treated as if they are goods to be bought and sold. Like the price of any product, currency prices change according to supply and demand. But unlike many products, currency prices change daily—or more often. Exchange rate fluctuations, or ups and downs, complicate accounting entries and accounting practices.

Accountants who deal with international transactions must take care when recording their firms' foreign sales and purchases. Today's sophisticated accounting software helps firms handle all of their international transactions within a single program. An international firm's consolidated financial statements must show any gains or losses caused by changes in exchange rates during specific periods of time. Financial statements that cover operations in two or more countries need to treat fluctuations consistently to allow for comparison.

In Canada, GAAP requires firms to adjust their earnings to reflect changes in exchange rates. A weakening dollar generally increases the earnings of a Canadian firm that has international operations: The same units of a foreign currency will translate into more Canadian dollars. A strengthening dollar will have the opposite effect on earnings—the same number of units of a foreign currency will translate into fewer dollars. In one recent year, for example, currency fluctuations caused an $11 million drop in earnings from the same quarter of the previous year for PPG, the world's second-largest paint manufacturer.[11]

In Pakistan, a truck driver delivers Nestlé food products. Because the Swiss corporation operates around the world, its profits and its financial statements are affected by foreign exchange rates.

✓ ASSESSMENT CHECK

15.8.1 How are financial statements adjusted for exchange rates?

WHAT'S AHEAD

This chapter describes the role of accounting in an organization. Accounting is the process of measuring, interpreting, and communicating financial information to interested parties both inside and outside the firm. The next two chapters discuss the finance function of an organization. Finance deals with planning, obtaining, and managing the organization's funds to accomplish its objectives in the most efficient and effective manner possible. Chapter 16 outlines the financial system, the system used to transfer funds from savers to borrowers. Organizations rely on the financial system to raise funds for expansion or operations. The chapter includes a description of financial institutions, such as banks; financial markets, such as the Toronto Stock Exchange; financial instruments, such as stocks and bonds; and the role of the Bank of Canada. Chapter 17 discusses the role of finance and the financial manager in an organization.

RETURN TO INSIDE BUSINESS

Cooking the Books

Many feel that accounting information is "black and white"—that is, it is either right or wrong with no in-between shades of grey. But as described in the stories of accounting fraud, many accountants and high-level executives risk stiff prison sentences when "cooking the books."

QUESTIONS FOR CRITICAL THINKING

1. How is it possible that what seems to be straightforward financial information can be altered by corporate executives who claim it conforms to GAAP?
2. Why do corporate executives risk prison sentences by preparing questionable financial statements?

SUMMARY OF LEARNING OBJECTIVES

LO 15.1 Explain the functions of accounting and identify the three basic accounting activities.

Accountants measure, interpret, and communicate financial information to people inside and outside the firm to support informed decision making. Accountants gather, record, and interpret financial information for management. They also provide financial information on the status and operations of the firm for evaluation by outside individuals, such as government representatives, shareholders, potential investors, and lenders. Accounting plays key roles in financing activities, which help to start and expand an organization; investing activities, which provide the assets a company needs to continue operating; and operating activities, which focus on selling goods and services and paying expenses incurred in regular operations.

✓ ASSESSMENT CHECK ANSWERS

15.1.1 **Define *accounting*.** Accounting is the process of measuring, interpreting, and communicating financial information that describes the status and operation of an organization and aids in decision making.

15.1.2 **Who uses accounting information?** Managers in all types of organizations use accounting information to help them plan, assess performance, and control daily and long-term operations. Outside users of accounting information include government officials, investors, creditors, and donors.

15.1.3 **What three business activities involve accounting?** The three activities involving accounting are financing, investing, and operating activities.

LO 15.2 Describe the various types of accounting professionals.

Public accountants provide accounting services to other firms or individuals for a fee. They perform the following activities: auditing, tax return preparation, management consulting, and accounting system design. Management accountants are employed by a firm, where they collect and record financial transactions, prepare financial statements, and interpret financial data for managers. Government and not-for-profit accountants perform many of the same functions as management accountants. But instead of dealing with profits and losses, they look at how effectively the organization or agency is operating.

✓ ASSESSMENT CHECK ANSWERS

15.2.1 **List the three services offered by public accounting firms.** The three services offered by public accounting firms are auditing, management consulting, and tax services.

15.2.2 **What tasks do management accountants perform?** Management accountants work for an organization. They are responsible for collecting and recording financial transactions and for preparing and interpreting financial statements.

LO 15.3 Discuss the foundation of the accounting system.

The foundation of the accounting system in Canada is GAAP (generally accepted accounting principles), a set of guidelines or standards that accountants follow. Companies that trade on a public stock exchange are required to use IFRS (International Financial Reporting Standards). Some basic qualitative characteristics of the financial statements are consistency, relevance, representational faithfulness, reliability, timeliness, understandability, verifiability, and comparability. The Accounting Standards Board (AcSB) is an independent body made up of accounting professionals. The AcSB is primarily responsible for evaluating, setting, and modifying GAAP.

✓ ASSESSMENT CHECK ANSWERS

15.3.1 **Define *GAAP*.** GAAP stands for generally accepted accounting principles. It is a set of standards, or guidelines, that accountants follow when recording and reporting financial transactions.

15.3.2 **What is the role played by the AcSB?** The Accounting Standards Board (AcSB) is an independent body made up of accounting professionals. It is primarily responsible for evaluating, setting, and modifying Canadian GAAP related primarily to private and not-for-profit organizations. Note that publicly accountable organizations are required to follow IFRS.

LO 15.4 Outline the steps in the accounting cycle.

The accounting process involves recording, classifying, and summarizing data about financial transactions. This information is used to produce financial statements for the firm's managers and other interested individuals. Transactions are recorded chronologically, in the order they occur, in journals; then posted in ledgers; and then summarized in accounting statements. Today, most of this activity takes place electronically. The basic accounting equation states that assets (what a firm owns) must always equal liabilities (what a firm owes creditors) plus owners' equity (the owners' investments in the firm). This equation also illustrates double-entry bookkeeping, the process used to record accounting transactions. In double-entry bookkeeping, each individual transaction must be balanced by another transaction.

✓ ASSESSMENT CHECK ANSWERS

15.4.1 **List the steps in the accounting cycle.** The accounting cycle involves the following steps: recording transactions, classifying the transactions, summarizing the transactions, and using the summaries to produce financial statements.

15.4.2 What is the accounting equation? The accounting equation states that assets (what a firm owns) must always equal liabilities (what a firm owes) plus owners' equity (the owners' investments in the firm). An increase or decrease in an asset must be balanced by an increase or decrease in liabilities, owners' equity, or both.

15.4.3 Briefly explain double-entry bookkeeping. Double-entry bookkeeping requires every transaction to be balanced by another transaction.

LO 15.5 Explain the functions and major components of the four principal financial statements.

The balance sheet shows a firm's financial position on a particular date. The three major classifications of balance sheet data are the elements of the accounting equation: assets, liabilities, and owners' equity. The income statement shows the results of a firm's operations over a specific time period. It focuses on the firm's activities—its revenues and expenditures—and the resulting profit or loss during the period. The major entries in the income statement are revenues, cost of goods sold, expenses, and profit or loss. The statement of changes in equity shows the change in owners' equity from the end of the previous year to the end of the current year. Finally, the statement of cash flows shows a firm's cash receipts and cash payments during an accounting period. It outlines the sources and uses of cash in the basic business activities of operating, investing, and financing.

✓ ASSESSMENT CHECK ANSWERS

15.5.1 List the four financial statements. The four financial statements are the balance sheet, the income statement, the statement of changes in equity, and the statement of cash flows.

15.5.2 How is the balance sheet organized? Assets (what a firm owns) are shown on one side of the balance sheet and are listed in a downward order based on their convertibility into cash. On the other side of the balance sheet are claims to assets, liabilities (what a firm owes) and owners' equity (the owners' investments in the firm). Claims are listed in the order in which they are due. For example, liabilities are listed before owners' equity. Assets always equal liabilities plus owners' equity.

15.5.3 Define *accrual accounting*. Accrual accounting records revenues and expenses when they occur, not when cash actually changes hands. Most companies use accrual accounting to prepare their financial statements.

LO 15.6 Discuss how financial ratios are used to analyze a company's financial strengths and weaknesses.

Liquidity ratios measure a firm's ability to meet its short-term obligations. Examples are the current ratio and the quick ratio, also called the acid-test ratio. Activity ratios, such as the inventory turnover ratio, the accounts receivable turnover ratio, and the total asset turnover ratio, measure how effectively a firm uses its resources. Profitability ratios assess the overall financial performance of the business. Examples are the gross profit margin, the net profit margin, and the return on owners' equity. Leverage ratios, such as the total liabilities to total assets ratio and the long-term debt to equity ratio, measure the extent to which the firm relies on debt to finance its operations. Financial ratios help managers and outside evaluators compare a firm's current financial information with that of previous years and with results for other firms in the same industry.

✓ ASSESSMENT CHECK ANSWERS

15.6.1 List the four categories of financial ratios. The four categories of ratios are liquidity, activity, profitability, and leverage.

15.6.2 Define the following ratios: *current ratio, inventory turnover, net profit margin*, and *debt ratio*. The current ratio equals current assets divided by current liabilities; inventory turnover equals cost of goods sold divided by average inventory; net profit margin equals net income divided by sales; and the debt ratio equals total liabilities divided by total assets.

LO 15.7 Describe the role of budgets in a business.

Budgets are financial guidelines for future periods. They show a firm's expected sales revenues, operating expenses, cash receipts, and cash expenses. They reflect management's expected outcomes for the future and are based on plans that have been made. Budgets are important tools for planning and controlling. They provide standards against which actual performance can be measured. One important type of budget is the cash budget, which estimates cash inflows and outflows over a period of time.

✓ ASSESSMENT CHECK ANSWERS

15.7.1 What is a budget? A budget is a planning and control tool that reflects the firm's expected sales revenues, operating expenses, cash receipts, cash expenses.

15.7.2 How is a cash budget organized? Cash budgets are usually prepared monthly. Cash receipts are listed first. They include cash sales and the collection of past credit sales. Cash outlays, or cash expenses, are listed next. These include cash purchases, payment of past credit purchases, and operating expenses. The difference between cash receipts and cash outlays is net cash flow.

LO 15.8 Outline the accounting issues facing global business.

One accounting issue that affects global business is exchange rates. An exchange rate is the value of one country's currency in terms of the currencies of other countries. Daily changes in exchange rates affect the accounting entries for the sales and purchases of firms dealing in international markets. These fluctuations, or ups and downs, create either losses or gains for companies.

✓ ASSESSMENT CHECK ANSWERS

15.8.1 How are financial statements adjusted for exchange rates? An exchange rate is the value of one country's currency in terms of the currencies of other countries. Fluctuations, the ups and downs, of exchange rates create either gains or losses for global companies. Data about international financial transactions must be translated into the currency of the country where the parent company resides.

BUSINESS TERMS YOU NEED TO KNOW

accounting 416
accounting cycle 422
accounting equation 423
Accounting Standards Board (AcSB) 420
accrual accounting 430
asset 422
balance sheet 426
budget 435
Corruption of Foreign Public Officials Act 421
double-entry bookkeeping 423
Financial Accounting Standards Board (FASB) 421
generally accepted accounting principles (GAAP) 420
income statement 427
International Accounting Standards Board (IASB) 420
International Financial Reporting Standards (IFRS) 420
liability 423
owners' equity 423
public accountant 418
statement of cash flows 429
statement of changes in equity 429

REVIEW QUESTIONS

1. Define *accounting*. Who are the major users of accounting information?
2. What are the three major business activities where accountants play a major role? Give an example of each.
3. What does the term *GAAP* mean? Briefly explain the role of the Accounting Standards Board.
4. What is double-entry bookkeeping? Give a brief example.
5. List the four major financial statements. Which financial statements are permanent and which are temporary?
6. What is the difference between a current asset and a long-term asset? Why is cash typically listed first on a balance sheet?
7. List and explain the major items found on an income statement.
8. What is accrual accounting? Give an example of how accrual accounting affects a firm's financial statement.
9. List the four categories of financial ratios and give an example of each. What is the purpose of ratio analysis?
10. What is a cash budget? Briefly outline what a simple cash budget might look like.

PROJECTS AND TEAMWORK APPLICATIONS

1. Contact a local public accounting firm and set up an interview with one of the accountants. Ask the accountant about his or her educational background, why he or she was attracted to the accounting profession, and what he or she does during a typical day. Prepare a brief report on your interview. Do you want to learn more about the accounting profession? Are you more interested or less interested in a career in accounting after your interview? Why?
2. Suppose you work for a Canadian firm that has extensive operations in various countries. You are preparing your firm's financial statements and you need to restate data from the various currencies to Canadian dollars. Which financial statements and which parts of these statements will be affected?
3. Identify two public companies operating in different industries. Collect at least three years' worth of financial statements for the firms. Calculate the financial ratios listed in Table 15.1. Prepare an oral report that summarizes your findings.
4. You've been appointed treasurer of a local not-for-profit organization. You want to improve the quality of financial reporting to

existing and potential donors. What kinds of financial statements do you ask the organization's accountant to prepare? Why do you think better-quality financial statements might help reassure donors?

5. Use the format of Figure 15.7 and adapt it to prepare your personal cash budget for next month. Keep in mind the following suggestions as you prepare your budget:
   a. *Cash inflows.* Your sources of cash include your payroll earnings, if any; gifts; scholarships; tax refunds; dividends and interest; and income from self-employment.
   b. *Cash outflows.* When estimating next month's cash outflows, include any of the following that may apply to your situation:
      i. Household expenses (rent or mortgage, utilities, maintenance, home furnishings, telephone/cellphone, cable TV, household supplies, groceries)
      ii. Education (tuition, fees, textbooks, supplies)
      iii. Work (transportation, clothing)
      iv. Clothing (purchases, cleaning, laundry)
      v. Automobile (auto payments, fuel, repairs) or other transportation (bus, train)
      vi. Insurance premiums
         - Renters (or homeowners)
         - Auto
         - Health
         - Life
      vii. Taxes (income, real estate)
      viii. Savings and investments
      ix. Entertainment/recreation (health club, vacation/travel, dining, movies)
      x. Debt (credit cards, instalment loans)
      xi. Miscellaneous (charitable contributions, childcare, gifts, medical expenses)
   c. *Beginning cash balance.* This amount can be based on a minimum cash balance you keep in your chequing account. It should include only the cash available for your use; investments in retirement plans should not be included.

WEB ASSIGNMENTS

1. **International Accounting Standards Board (IASB).** The IASB is responsible for setting and modifying international accounting rules. Go to the IASB's website (www.iasb.org); click on "About Us" and select "About the Organisation." Print out the material and bring it to class to participate in a class discussion on the IASB.

2. **Chartered Professional Accountant (CPA).** As noted in the chapter, many business professionals often seek the CPA designation. Visit the website of CPA Ontario (www.cpaontario.ca). Click on "Students/Education," and then "CPA Certification Program." What are the educational and experiential requirements to obtain a CPA? How many exams does a CPA candidate need to pass? What do these exams cover?

3. **Financial reporting requirements.** The chapter discussed the financial reporting requirements of Canadian companies, including public companies whose shares are traded on a stock exchange. Visit the website listed below and type in the name of a public company. Then click on "financials" to view the firm's current financial statements. Prepare a brief report comparing those statements to the ones shown in the chapter.
   www.google.com/finance

Note: Internet addresses change frequently. If you don't find the exact sites listed, you may need to access the organization's home page and search from there or use a search engine such as Bing or Google.

16 | THE FINANCIAL SYSTEM

LEARNING OBJECTIVES

LO 16.1 Outline the structure and importance of the financial system.

LO 16.2 List the various types of securities.

LO 16.3 Define *financial market* and distinguish between primary and secondary financial markets.

LO 16.4 Describe the characteristics of the major stock exchanges.

LO 16.5 Discuss how financial institutions are organized and how they function.

LO 16.6 Explain the functions of the Bank of Canada and the tools it uses to carry out these functions.

LO 16.7 Describe the regulation of the financial system.

LO 16.8 Describe the global financial system.

INSIDE BUSINESS

Canada Weathers the Credit Crisis

In 2008, much of the world's financial systems melted. But Canada's financial systems were largely unaffected. Europe, Greece, and Italy felt a significant impact of the global credit crisis. In the United States, interest rates were low and borrowing was high. The greater access to financing increased both the demand for housing and housing prices. U.S. banks became very aggressive. They tempted clients, including many high-risk clients, by offering very low down payments and low interest rates for the first few years of their mortgage. These mortgages were then packaged and sold to investors who felt assured that the collateral, or security, behind the mortgages (the homes) would reduce any risk of default on the mortgage. The main problem began after clients completed the first few years of low-interest mortgage payments. Their mortgage rates then increased, causing their monthly payments to also increase. Many clients were forced to default on their payments or sell their homes. The increase of homes on the market led to a reverse effect on prices—the "bubble" burst. The result was a high proportion of "toxic" mortgages, which had a higher value than the homes themselves. For example, homes valued at less than $250,000 had mortgages of more than $500,000. This situation was a disaster for creditors. Some lost half or more of their investment.

Why weren't Canadians affected in the same way? And why were Canadian banks rated the strongest in the world by the World Economic Forum? For starters, Canada's financial system is much more regulated than the U.S. banking system. And, by nature, Canadians tend to be less financially aggressive than Americans. Canadian banks have many more checks and balances related to confirming income, job status, and sales contracts. Canadian *consumers* also carry less debt on average than Americans (20 percent versus 26 percent, respectively). That explains why Canadians had fewer subprime mortgages: one in twenty in Canada versus one in six in the United States.

In Canada, housing values just before the 2008 financial crisis were about 200 percent of what they were in 1989, compared with 260 percent in the United States. During the crisis, the value of U.S. homes dropped to approximately 220 percent of their 1989 values, while little change was felt in Canada. The same type of housing bubble is highly unlikely in Canada because Canadians are generally financially conservative, both on the buyer's side and the lender's side. As a result, Canadian homes are rarely valued at less than their mortgage, which was a problem for Americans after the housing bubble burst. The Canada Mortgage and Housing Corporation (CMHC) is owned by the Canadian government. It insures mortgages for higher-risk clients who have low down payments.

Finally, Canadians receive no tax incentive for having a mortgage, whereas mortgage interest is a tax deduction in the United States, providing another reason for Americans to have a mortgage. In Canada, "a mortgage is seen as something you want to get rid of as fast as possible," says Peter Dungan, an economist at the Rotman School of Management at the University of Toronto. It is clear that no single factor preserved the financial system in Canada during the financial meltdown. Instead, a combination of financial conservatism and government policy helped Canadians to weather the crisis.[1]

CHAPTER 16 OVERVIEW

Businesses, governments, and individuals often need to raise capital, or money. For example, suppose a businessperson forecasts a sharp increase in sales for the coming year. This expected sales increase requires additional inventory. If the business lacks the cash to purchase the needed inventory, it may turn to a bank for a short-term loan. On the other hand, some individuals and businesses have incomes that are greater than their current expenses. They may want to earn interest on the extra funds. For example, suppose your income this month is $3,000, but your expenses are only $2,500. You can deposit the extra $500 in a bank account and receive interest.

The two transactions described above are small parts of what is known as the **financial system**, the mechanism by which money flows from savers to users. Almost all businesses, governments, and individuals participate in the financial system. A well-functioning financial system is vital to a nation's economic health. The financial system is the topic of this chapter.

We begin by describing the financial system and its components in more detail. We then outline the major types of financial instruments, such as bonds and stocks (also known as shares). Next we discuss financial markets, where financial instruments are bought and sold. We then describe the world's major stock markets.

Next, banks and other financial institutions are described in depth. We detail the structure and responsibilities of the Bank of Canada and the tools it uses to control the supply of money and credit. The chapter concludes with an overview of the major laws and regulations affecting the financial system and a discussion of today's global financial system.

financial system the mechanism by which money flows from savers to users.

LO 16.1 Outline the structure importance of the financial system.

UNDERSTANDING THE FINANCIAL SYSTEM

Households, businesses, government, financial institutions, and financial markets together form what is known as the financial system. A simple diagram of the financial system is shown in **Figure 16.1**.

On the left are savers—those who have excess funds. For different reasons, savers choose not to spend all of their current income, so they have a surplus of funds. Users are the opposite of savers; their spending needs are greater than their current income, so they have a shortfall. They need to obtain additional funds to make up the difference. Savings are provided by some households, businesses, and the government, but some other households, businesses, and the government are borrowers. Households may need money to buy automobiles or homes. Businesses may need money to purchase inventory or build new production facilities. Governments may need money to build highways and courthouses.

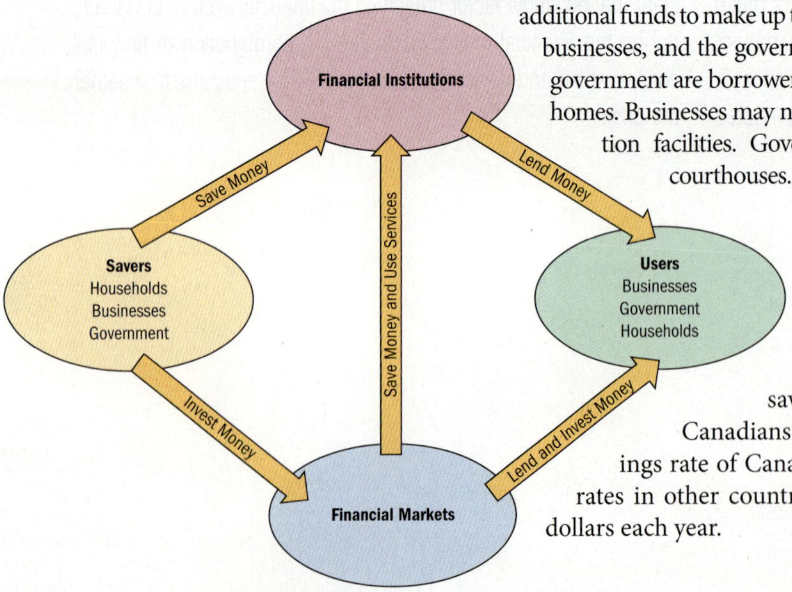

In Canada, households are generally net savers. That means that, as a whole, households save more money than they use. Businesses and governments are net users. That means that they generally use more funds than they save. You may be surprised that households provide most of the net savings in the Canadian financial system. After all, Canadians do not have a reputation for being thrifty. The savings rate of Canadian households is low compared with the savings rates in other countries, but Canadian households still save billions of dollars each year.

How much an individual saves depends on many factors. One of the most important factors is the person's age. As people age, they often move from being net borrowers to being net savers.

FIGURE 16.1 Overview of the Financial System and Its Components

When you graduate from university or college and begin a career, you likely have very little savings. In fact, you may be in debt. In the early years of your career, you may spend more than you make as you buy major assets, like a home. In these early career years, your *net worth*—the difference between what you own and what you owe—is very low and may even be negative. But as your career progresses and your income rises, you will begin to build financial savings to fund retirement and other needs. Your net worth will also increase. It will continue to increase until you retire and begin drawing on your retirement savings.

Funds can be transferred between savers and users in two ways: directly and indirectly. A direct transfer means that the user raises the needed funds directly from savers. Direct transfers *do* occur, but most funds flow through either financial markets or financial institutions. For example, assume a local school district needs to build a new high school. The district does not have enough cash to pay for the school construction costs, so it sells bonds to investors (savers) in the financial market. The district uses the funds from the sale to pay for the new school. In return, the bond investors receive interest each year for the use of their money.

The other way that funds can be transferred indirectly is through financial institutions—for example, through a commercial bank such as TD Canada Trust or Scotiabank. The bank pools, or combines, customer deposits and uses the funds to make loans to businesses and households. These borrowers pay the bank interest, and the bank, in turn, pays its depositors interest for the use of their money.

The accompanying "Going Green" feature describes how TD Bank has started to transform all its branches so that they will be "carbon neutral."

✓ ASSESSMENT CHECK

16.1.1 What is the financial system?

16.1.2 In the financial system, who are the borrowers and who are the savers?

16.1.3 List the two most common ways that funds are transferred between borrowers and savers.

Going Green — TD BANK: "AS GREEN AS OUR LOGO"

TD Bank's square, green logo is a familiar sight from Vancouver to Florida. TD Bank announced that it was the first North American bank to go carbon neutral in the United States. The bank achieved carbon neutrality by reducing waste, using alternative sources of energy, and building environmentally friendly buildings from sustainable materials. With 1,300 branches, or "stores," TD has used its resources to pursue an aggressive "green" policy.

To demonstrate its goal of carbon neutrality, TD bank unveiled a new prototype store. The 3,800-square-foot building is designed to reduce energy use by 50 percent compared with earlier models. Each new store will make up to 20 percent of its own electricity through solar panels on the roof. To keep interior temperatures comfortable, the windows will have specially coated glass that reflects or absorbs heat energy. Sensors will control lighting over the course of the day. The drive-through facility will feature a translucent solar canopy. Outside, the landscaping will include drought-resistant plants and water-efficient plumbing.

Among other measures, TD Bank has bought a block of wind energy large enough to run its 2,300 automated teller machines (ATMs). It plans to encourage its customers to save energy by signing up for online banking and paperless statements. TD Bank has also located many of its branches near public transportation.

TD Bank's first fully green office opened in Queens Village, New York. Since opening this branch, TD has opened 71 LEED (Leadership in Energy and Environmental Design) Certified branches, including one branch in Florida that generates more electricity than it uses. The bank eventually plans to have all of its offices meet LEED standards.

In Canada, TD Financial Group has established the TD Friends of the Environment Foundation. It has provided over $66 million to support more than 22,000 environmental projects and programs.

Fred Graziano, TD Bank's head of regional commercial banking, says, "We're taking the environment seriously and we strongly believe this is the right thing to do for our business, customers, employees and the community. We want TD Bank to be as green as our logo."

Questions for Critical Thinking

1. Why does "going green" make good business sense for TD Bank?

2. Think about your own banking practices. What steps can you take to be greener?

Sources: TD Bank, accessed February 22, 2012, www.tdbank.com; James Comtois, "TD Bank's First Green Branch Sprouts in Queens," *Oram's New York Business.com*, February 22, 2012, www.crainsnewyork.com; Patrick Lo, "TD Bank Goes Carbon Neutral," *Green Street Journal*, March 16, 2010, www.gsjournal.com; "TD Bank Goes Carbon Neutral, Unveils 'Green Store' Prototype," *Environmental Leader*, February 22, 2012, www.environmentalleader.com; "TD Bank, America's Most Convenient Bank, Announces It's Now Carbon Neutral and Unveils New 'Green Store' Prototype Design," press release, February 18, 2010, http://multivu.prnewswire.com; TD Friends of the Environment Foundation, "Helping Canadians Make a Difference," accessed July 4, 2011, www.fef.td/about.jsp; TD Bank, accessed August 13, 2014, www.tdbank.com/aboutus/about_us.html and https://fef.td.com/about-us/.

TYPES OF SECURITIES

LO 16.2 List the various types of securities.

When businesses and governments borrow funds from savers, they provide different types of guarantees for repayment. **Securities**, also called financial instruments, represent the obligations of the issuers—businesses and governments—to provide the purchasers with the expected or stated returns on the funds invested or loaned. Securities can be grouped into three categories: money market instruments, bonds, and shares (also known as stock). Money market instruments and bonds are debt securities. Shares are units of ownership in public corporations, such as Sun Life Financial, Hudson's Bay, and Bell Canada Enterprises.

securities financial instruments that represent the obligations of the issuers to provide the purchasers with the expected stated returns on the funds invested or loaned.

Money Market Instruments

Money market instruments are short-term debt securities issued by governments, financial institutions, and corporations. All money market instruments mature within one year from the date of issue. The issuer pays interest to the investors for the use of their funds. Money market instruments are generally low-risk securities and are purchased by investors when they have surplus cash. Examples of money market instruments include Canadian Treasury bills, commercial paper, and bank certificates of deposit.

Treasury bills are short-term securities issued by the Canadian Treasury and backed by the full faith and credit of the Canadian government. Treasury bills are sold with a maturity date of 30, 90, 180, or 360 days and must be a minimum of $1,000. They are virtually risk free and are easy to resell. Commercial paper refers to securities sold by corporations, such as TELUS. These securities mature in 1 to 270 days from the date of issue. Although commercial paper is slightly riskier than Treasury bills, it is generally considered to be a very low-risk security.

A certificate of deposit (CD) is a time deposit at a financial institution, such as a commercial bank, a savings bank, or a credit union. The sizes and maturity dates of CDs vary and can often be tailored to meet the needs of purchasers. CDs of $100,000 or less per depositor are insured by the Canada Deposit Insurance Corporation (CDIC). CDs in larger denominations are not federally insured but can be sold more easily before they mature.

Bonds

Bondholders are creditors of a corporation or government body. A firm may sell bonds to obtain long-term debt capital. Federal, provincial, and municipal governments also acquire funds through bonds. Bonds are issued in various denominations, or face values, usually between $1,000 and $25,000. Each issue indicates the rate of interest and the maturity date. The rate of interest to be paid to the bondholder is stated as a percentage of the bond's face value. The maturity date is the date when the bondholder will be paid the bond's full face value. Bondholders are creditors. That means their claim on the firm's assets must be satisfied before any claims of shareholders if the firm enters into bankruptcy, reorganization, or liquidation.

Types of Bonds

A prospective bond investor can choose among several types of bonds. The major types of bonds are summarized in **Table 16.1**. *Government bonds*, such as Canada Savings Bonds, are bonds sold by the Canadian government. Government bonds are backed by the full faith and credit of the Canadian government, which means they are the least risky of all bonds. The Treasury sells bonds that mature in 2, 5, 10, and 30 years from the date of issue.

Municipal bonds are bonds issued by municipal governments. Two types of municipal bonds are available: corporate bonds and mortgage-backed corporate bonds. Corporate bonds include a diverse group of bonds. They often vary depending on the collateral—the property pledged by the borrower—that backs the bond. For example, a *secured bond* is backed by a specific pledge of company assets. These assets are the collateral, just like a home is collateral for a house mortgage. However, many businesses also issue unsecured bonds, called *debentures*. These bonds are backed only by the financial reputation of the issuing corporation.

Table 16.1 Types of Bonds

ISSUER	TYPES OF SECURITIES	RISK	SPECIAL FEATURES
Government of Canada (government bonds)	Canada Savings Bonds: Mature in 10 years, but can be cashed at any time.	Government bonds carry virtually no risk.	Affordable: can be purchased for as little as $100
Provincial and local governments (municipal bonds)	General obligation: Issued by provincial or local governmental units with taxing authority; backed by the full faith and credit of the province or municipality where the bonds are issued.	Risk varies, depending on the financial health of the issuer. Risk is generally very low.	
Corporations	Secured bonds: Bonds that are backed by specific assets.	Risk varies depending on the financial health of the issuer.	A few corporate bonds are convertible into common shares of the issuing company.
	Unsecured bonds (debentures): Bonds that are backed by the financial health and reputation of the issuer.	Most corporate bond issues are rated in terms of credit risk (AAA or Aaa is the highest rating).	
Financial institutions	Mortgage-backed securities	Generally very low risk.	They pay monthly income consisting of both interest and principal.

The second type of bonds are mortgage-backed corporate bonds, also called *mortgage-backed securities (MBSs)*. These bonds are backed by a pool, or group, of mortgage loans purchased from lenders, such as chartered banks. As borrowers make their mortgage payments, these payments are "passed through" to the holders of the securities. MBSs are very safe because all mortgages in the pool, or group, are insured by CMHC. In the United States, during the period of approximately 2004 to 2008, similar securities were issued. But these securities consisted of so-called *subprime mortgages*, loans made to borrowers with poor credit ratings. Many of these securities turned out to be risky and, in part, triggered what became known as the *credit crisis* that began in 2008. The extent of the crisis forced the U.S. government to undertake a massive bailout of the financial system. The Office of Financial Stability—part of the U.S. Treasury department—was created to purchase poor-quality mortgage-backed securities from financial institutions.

Quality Ratings for Bonds

Two factors affect the price of a bond: its risk and its interest rate. Bonds vary in terms of their risk. Bond investors use a tool called a *bond rating* to assess the risk of a bond. Several investment firms rate corporate and municipal bonds. In Canada, the Dominion Bond Rating Service (DBRS) provides bond ratings. The best-known bond rating organizations are Standard & Poor's (S&P), Moody's, and Fitch. **Table 16.2** lists the S&P bond ratings. Moody's and Fitch use similar rating systems. Bonds with the lowest level of risk are rated AAA. As ratings descend, risk increases. Bonds with ratings of BBB and above are classified as *investment-grade bonds*. Bonds with ratings of BB and below are classified as *speculative bonds* or *junk bonds*. Junk bonds attract investors because they offer high interest rates in exchange for greater risk. Today, junk bonds pay about 50 percent more in interest than investment-grade corporate bonds. The recent credit crisis generated a great deal of criticism toward the ratings companies. This criticism centred on the conflict of interest from ratings companies also advising companies on how to structure their bond offerings.

The second factor affecting the price of a bond is its interest rate. All other things being equal, the higher the interest rate, the higher the price of a bond. But often everything else is *not*

Table 16.2 Standard & Poor's Bond Ratings

Investment Grade	Highest	AAA	Extremely strong capacity to meet financial commitments; highest rating
		AA	Very strong capacity to meet financial commitments
		A	Strong capacity to meet financial commitments, but somewhat susceptible to adverse economic conditions and changes in circumstances
		BBB	Adequate capacity to meet financial commitments, but more subject to risk during poor economic conditions
		BBB–	Considered lowest investment grade by market participants
Speculative Grade		BB+	Considered highest speculative grade by market participants
		BB	Less vulnerable in the near term but faces major ongoing uncertainties to adverse business, financial, and economic conditions
		B	More vulnerable to risks from poor business, financial, and economic conditions but currently has the capacity to meet financial commitments
		CCC	Currently vulnerable and dependent on favourable business, financial, and economic conditions to meet financial commitments
		CC	Currently highly vulnerable
		C	A bankruptcy petition has been filed or similar action taken, but payments of financial commitments are continued
	Lowest	D	Payment default on financial commitments

Note: Standard & Poor's occasionally assigns a plus or minus following the letter rating. For instance, AA+ means that the bond is higher quality than most AA bonds but hasn't quite met AAA standards. Ratings below C indicate that the bond is currently not paying interest.

Source: Standard & Poor's Rating Services, "Credit Ratings Definitions and FAQs," accessed February 22, 2012, www.standardandpoors.com/ratings/definitions-and-faqs/en/us#def_1; Standard & Poor's, accessed August 13, 2014, http://img.en25.com/Web/StandardandPoors/SP_CreditRatingsGuide.pdf.

equal: The bonds may not be equally risky, or one bond may have a longer maturity date. Investors must evaluate the individual characteristics of each bond.

Another important influence on bond prices is the *market interest rate*. Bonds pay fixed rates of interest. That means that as market interest rates rise, bond prices fall. The opposite is also true: As market interest rates fall, bond prices rise. For example, the price of a 10-year bond that pays 5 percent per year would fall by about 8 percent if market interest rates rose from 5 percent to 6 percent.

Most corporate and municipal bonds are callable, as are some government bonds. A *call provision* allows the issuer to redeem, or cash, the bond before its maturity at a specified price. Not surprisingly, issuers tend to call bonds when market interest rates are declining. For example, suppose the City of Toronto had $50 million in bonds outstanding with a 5 percent annual interest rate. It would pay $2.5 million annually in interest. Now, suppose interest rates fall to 3 percent. The city may decide to call the 5 percent bonds by repaying the principal from the proceeds, or funds, from the newly issued 3 percent bonds. Calling the 5 percent bonds and issuing 3 percent bonds will save the city $1 million a year in interest payments. The savings in annual interest expense should be greater than the cost of retiring the old bonds and issuing new bonds.

Shares

common shares the basic form of corporate ownership

The basic form of corporate ownership is **common shares**. Purchasers of common shares are the true owners of a corporation. Holders of common shares vote on major company decisions, such as purchasing another company or electing a board of directors. In return for the money they invest, holders of common shares expect to receive some sort of return.

This return can be cash dividend payments, expected increases in the value of the shares, or both. Dividends vary widely from firm to firm. As a general rule, faster-growing companies pay less in dividends because they need more funds to finance their growth. As a result, investors expect shares that pay little or no cash dividends to show a greater increase in value compared with shares paying larger cash dividends.

Sometimes unexpected events can have a major effect on dividends and share prices. On March 8, 2014, Malaysian Airlines flight MH370 disappeared with 259 passengers and crew aboard. Later that year, on July 17, 2014, Malaysian Airlines flight MH17 was shot down over Ukraine. These events have led to a decrease in the share price of Malaysian Airlines of over 35 percent, the virtual elimination of the likelihood of dividends, along with the privatization of the airline.[2]

Investors who hold common shares benefit from a company's success. But they also risk losing their investments if the company fails. If a firm dissolves, claims of the creditors must be satisfied before shareholders receive anything. Because creditors have the first (or senior) claim to assets, holders of common shares are said to have a residual claim on company assets.

The market value of a share is the price that shares are currently selling for. For example, Apple's share price varied between $64 and $99 per share in the 12-month period ending August 13, 2014.[3] What leads to a share's market value? The answer is complicated. Many factors can cause share prices to move up or down. In the long run, share prices tend to follow a company's profits.

Preferred Shares

In addition to common shares, a few companies also issue preferred shares. Holders of preferred shares receive preference in the payment of dividends. TransCanada and Bombardier are examples of firms that have issued preferred shares. Also, if a company is dissolved, holders of preferred shares have claims on the firm's assets that are ahead of the claims of holders of common shares. On the other hand, holders of preferred shares rarely have voting rights. Also, they are paid fixed dividends, regardless of how profitable the firm becomes. Preferred shares are legally classified as equity, but many investors consider preferred shares to be more like a bond than common shares.

Convertible Securities

Companies may issue bonds or preferred shares that include a conversion feature. Such bonds or shares are called *convertible securities*. This feature gives the bondholder or holder of preferred shares the right to exchange the bond or preferred shares for a fixed number of common shares. Convertible bonds pay lower interest rates than bonds without conversion features, which helps to reduce the issuing firm's interest expenses. Investors are willing to accept lower interest rates because they value the possibility of additional gains if the price of the firm's shares increase. For example, at a price of $61 per share, Peabody Energy's convertible bond would have a common share value of at least $1,043 ($61 × 17.1). If the price of Peabody's common shares increases by $10 per share, the value of the convertible bond will increase by at least $171.

ASSESSMENT CHECK

16.2.1 What are the major types of securities?

16.2.2 What areas of the government issue bonds?

16.2.3 Why do investors purchase common shares?

FINANCIAL MARKETS

Securities are issued and traded in **financial markets**. There are many different types of financial markets. One of the most important differences is between primary and secondary markets. In the **primary markets**, firms and governments issue securities and sell them initially to the general public. A company may sell a bond or issue shares to the investing public when it needs capital to purchase inventory, expand a plant, make major investments, acquire another firm, or pursue other business goals. For example, RUSNANO planned to sell $1.7 billion in bonds to pay for expansion and new projects.[4]

In a share offering, investors are offered the opportunity to purchase ownership shares in a firm and to participate in a firm's future growth, in exchange for providing the firm's current capital.

LO 16.3 Define *financial market* and distinguish between primary and secondary financial markets.

financial markets markets where securities are issued and traded.

primary markets a financial market where firms and governments issue securities and sell them initially to the general public.

452 PART 6 Managing Financial Resources

At the Toronto Stock Exchange, current share prices are displayed.

When a company offers shares for sale to the general public for the first time, it is called an *initial public offering (IPO)*. Many of these offerings were from Asian companies.[5] The "Hit & Miss" feature describes an American company's IPO.

Both for-profit corporations and government agencies also rely on primary markets to raise funds by issuing bonds. For example, the federal government sells Treasury bonds to finance some of the federal expenses, such as interest payments on outstanding federal debt. Provincial and local governments sell bonds to finance capital projects, such as the construction of sewer systems, streets, and fire stations.

Announcements of new bond and share offerings appear daily in business publications such as *The Globe and Mail* and the *Financial Post*. These announcements are often in the form of a simple black-and-white ad called a *tombstone*.

Securities are sold to the investing public in two ways: in open auctions and through investment bankers. Almost all securities sold through open auctions are Government of Canada securities. Sales of most corporate and municipal securities are made through financial institutions like TD Securities. These

HIT & MISS

A Major Spinoff for Citigroup

Not long ago, the U.S. banking company Citigroup was involved in not just banking but also other interests, including insurance. Following the financial crisis, Citigroup's CEO, Vikram Pandit, began to dispose of some of these holdings. He wanted to slim the company down to its original core banking business by focusing on large institutions and wealthy individuals. The trend in Canada has been the opposite: Major Canadian banks are now entering the insurance sector and adding to their core banking business.

Primerica Inc. was one of the Citigroup holdings to go. Based in Duluth, Georgia, Primerica sells life insurance, mutual funds, and other financial products door to door. Its middle-class customers earn from $30,000 to $100,000 a year. Primerica never fit well with the rest of Citigroup—and Primerica's 100,000 fiercely independent salespeople liked it that way. As the financial crisis worsened, some of Primerica employees suggested cutting ties with Citigroup.

Citigroup tried to sell Primerica but could not find a buyer willing to pay the asking price. So Citigroup announced that it would spin off Primerica. Primerica would issue an IPO and sell shares in the company for the first time. Primerica planned to sell 18 million shares at $12 to $14 a share. Under the terms of the IPO, Citigroup would take all the profits and keep Primerica's existing accounts. Primerica would be a smaller company but it would keep any new policies. John Addison and Rick Williams, the co-CEOs of Primerica, said, "We're going to be a smaller, faster-growing company going forward."

The IPO went better than expected. Primerica sold more than 21 million shares at almost $20 each. Addison and Williams feel that the company's focus has contributed to its success. "No one else has our business model," said Williams. "No one else focuses on the middle-income, middle market like we do." Analysts took the IPO's success as a sign that both the life insurance industry and the market were recovering from the recession.

Questions for Critical Thinking

1. Visit the websites of Citigroup and Primerica. Why do you think these two companies did not work well together?

2. Although Citigroup failed to find a buyer for Primerica, the IPO was very successful. Why do you think it was so successful?

3. Can you see a similar sale in one of Canada's larger financial institutions, such as RBC Financial Group or TD Bank Financial Group? If so, which line of business can you see being spun off?

Sources: Primerica, accessed June 21, 2010, www.primerica.com; Citigroup, accessed June 21, 2010, www.citigroup.com; Kerri Shannon, "Citigroup Spin-Off Primerica Boasts Strong Stock Debut in Hot IPO Market," *Money Morning*, April 4, 2010, http://moneymorning.com; "Primerica IPO a Success as Shares Jump," *CNBC*, April 1, 2010, www.cnbc.com; Maria Aspan and Clare Baldwin, "Citi Spinoff Primerica Soars on Hopes for Economy," Reuters, April 1, 2010, www.reuters.com; David Enrich, "An IPO of Primerica Will End a Citi Era," *Wall Street Journal*, November 6, 2009, www.online.wsj.com.

institutions purchase the issue from the firm or government and then resell the issue to investors. This process is known as *underwriting*.

Financial institutions underwrite shares and bond issues at a discount. That means they pay the issuing firm or government less than the price that financial institutions charge investors. This discount is compensation for the financial institution's services, including the risk financial institutions take on when they underwrite a new security issue. The discount is often negotiable, but usually averages about 5 percent for all types of securities. The size of the underwriting discount is generally higher for share issues than for bond issues. For example, underwriting discounts for IPOs are generally between 7 and 10 percent.

Corporations and governments are willing to pay for the services provided by financial institutions because they are financial market experts. The underwriter typically locates buyers for the issue and advises the issuer on several details: the general characteristics of the issue, its pricing, and the timing of the offering. Several financial institutions commonly perform the underwriting process. The issuer selects a lead, or primary, financial institution, which forms a syndicate consisting of other financial institutions. Each member of the syndicate purchases a portion of the security issue and resells it to investors.

Media reports of share and bond trading are most likely to refer to trading in the **secondary market**, a collection of financial markets where previously issued securities are traded among investors. The corporations or governments that originally issued the securities being traded are not directly involved in the secondary market. The issuers do not make payments when securities are sold, and they do not receive any proceeds when securities are purchased. For example, the Toronto Stock Exchange (TSX) is a secondary market. The secondary market handles four to five times the dollar value of securities than are handled in the primary market. Each day, millions of shares worth billions of dollars are traded on the TSX.[6] The characteristics of the world's major stock exchanges are discussed in the next section.

secondary market a collection of financial markets where previously issued securities are traded among investors.

ASSESSMENT CHECK

16.3.1 What is a financial market?

16.3.2 Distinguish between a primary and a secondary financial market.

16.3.3 Briefly explain the role of financial institutions in the sale of securities.

UNDERSTANDING STOCK MARKETS

LO 16.4 Describe the characteristics of the major stock exchanges.

Stock markets, or **exchanges**, are probably the best-known of the world's financial markets. In these markets, shares of stock are bought and sold by investors.

stock markets (exchanges) markets where shares of stock are bought and sold by investors.

The Toronto Stock Exchange

The Toronto Stock Exchange, or TSX, is Canada's largest stock exchange. For a company's shares to be traded on the TSX, the firm must apply for a listing and meet certain listing requirements. The firm must continue to meet requirements each year to remain listed on the TSX. Corporate bonds are also traded on the TSX, but bond trading is less than 1 percent of the total value of securities traded on the TSX during a typical year.

Foreign Stock Markets

The *New York Stock Exchange (NYSE)* is sometimes referred to as the "Big Board." The NYSE is the most famous stock market and one of the oldest stock markets in the world. Shares traded on this exchange represent most of the largest, best-known companies in the United States and have a total market value of more than $16 trillion. The NYSE is the world's largest stock market.

The *NASDAQ Stock Market* is the world's second-largest stock market. It is very different from the NYSE. NASDAQ stands for National Association of Securities Dealers Automated Quotation System. It is actually a computerized communications network that links member investment firms. It is the world's largest intranet. All trading on NASDAQ takes place through its intranet, not on a trading floor.

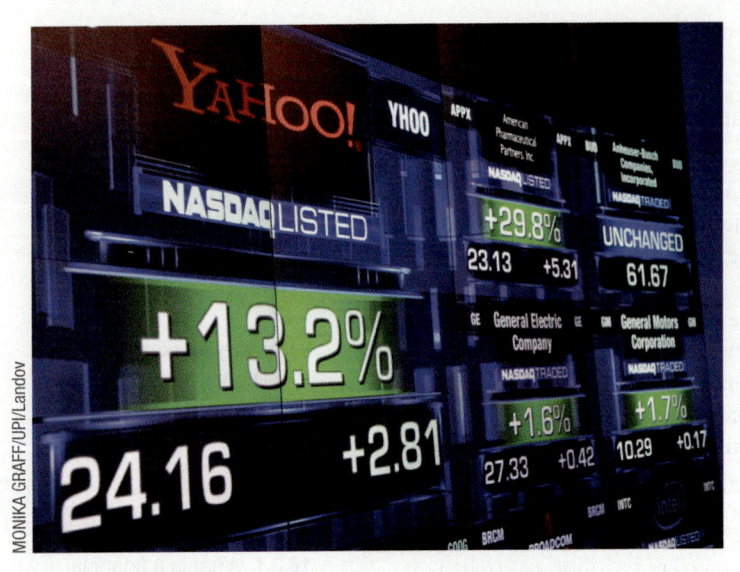

All trading on NASDAQ takes place through its intranet, not on a trading floor.

Stock markets can be found throughout the world. Almost all developed countries and many developing countries have stock exchanges. For example, stock exchanges are located in Mumbai, Helsinki, Hong Kong, Mexico City, and Paris. One of the largest stock exchanges outside the United States is the London Stock Exchange. The London Stock Exchange was founded in the early seventeenth century. It lists over 2,600 stock and bond issues from more than 60 countries around the world. Trading on the London Stock Exchange takes place using a NASDAQ-type computerized communications network.

The London Stock Exchange is the most international of all stock markets. It handles about two-thirds of all cross-border trading in the world, such as the trading of shares of Canadian companies outside of Canada. Institutional investors in Canada may trade TSX-listed shares or NASDAQ-listed shares in London.

Stock markets around the world are closely interconnected. As a result, changes in one country's economy can affect other countries, as explained in the "Hit & Miss" feature.

HIT & MISS

How News Lifts—or Sinks—Shares around the World

The growth of computerized trading has closely connected all the developed nations and many developing nations. A snapshot of the world markets shows how events in one country can affect stock markets everywhere.

Canada was not hit very hard by the global recession of 2008 to 2012. But this recession was the worst in U.S. history since the Great Depression. The Canadian recession was not as damaging as the recessions in the early 1980s or the early 1990s. Still, former Finance Minister Jim Flaherty decided to set up an economic action plan.

In the spring of 2010, Americans grew hopeful that their country was starting to climb out of the recession. The U.S. Federal Reserve announced that although American households were not spending as much as before the recession, the U.S. economy was slowly improving. Some companies were making a profit because of rising consumer demand. Earlier in the recovery, some companies had made money by cutting their costs. The share prices increased in some U.S. companies, like Apple. The computer company Hewlett-Packard announced that it was buying the smartphone maker Palm.

America seemed to be emerging from the credit crisis. But the credit crisis hit Greece, which has had major challenges paying off its debts. As a member of the European Union, Greece had adopted the euro as its currency. Other euro countries, such as Spain and Portugal, also faced financial troubles. Standard & Poor's reduced the bond rating of all three countries.

As Greece tried to recover amid violence and political turmoil, it adopted drastic measures: Government spending was reduced on social programs even though the public protested. Prime Minister George Papandreou said that the public sector was "overly grown, overly expensive." He told Greeks that he hoped the austerity program would "give us a cushion" that will "give us quite a bit of money."

Questions for Critical Thinking

1. Why would a financial crisis on the other side of the world affect the Canadian economy? Why was the Canadian economy less affected by the global financial crisis than the United States?

2. What has happened in Greece, Spain, and Portugal? Have they recovered from their economic crises? Why was Germany expected to help bail out other Eurozone countries from the debt crisis?

3. When Standard & Poor's downgraded the U.S. debt, what was the effect on the Canadian economy in 2011?

Sources: Mark Rohner, "Greece Ahead of Targets, Will Not Default, Papandreou Says," *Bloomberg Businessweek*, February 22, 2012, www.businessweek.com; European Union, accessed February 22, 2012, http://europa.eu; Will Swarts, "Stocks Surge as Earnings Stay Robust," *SmartMoney*, April 29, 2010, www.smartmoney.com; Christine Hauser, "Stocks Higher as Earnings Lift Sentiment," *New York Times*, April 28, 2010, www.nytimes.com; Reuters, "Earnings Lift World Stocks, Greece Stays in Focus," *Economic Times*, April 21, 2010, http://economictimes.indiatimes.com; Spyros Economides, "Viewpoint: The Politics of Greece's Economic Crisis," *BBC News*, June 17, 2011, accessed July 6, 2011, www.bbc.co.uk/news/world-europe-13805391; Department of Finance Canada, "Budget 2009: Canada's Action Plan," January 27, 2009, accessed July 6, 2011, www.fin.gc.ca/n08/09-011-eng.asp; Tavia Grant, "Was Canada's Recession 'Average'?" *Globe and Mail*, May 6, 2010, accessed July 6, 2011, www.theglobeandmail.com/report-on-business/economy/was-canadas-recession-average/article1535179/.

ECNs and the Future of Stock Markets

For years a so-called *fourth market* has existed. The fourth market is the direct trading of exchange-listed stocks off the floor of the exchange. Until recently, trading in the fourth market was limited to institutional investors who were buying or selling large blocks of shares.

The fourth market has begun to open up to smaller, individual investors through markets called *electronic communications networks* (ECNs). In ECNs, buyers and sellers meet in a virtual stock market and trade directly with one another. ECNs have become a significant force in the stock market in recent years. The TSX now uses the services of Savvis to facilitate its ECN.[7]

Investor Participation in the Stock Markets

Most investors aren't members of the TSX or any other stock market; they need to use the services of a brokerage firm to buy or sell shares. Two examples of brokerage firms are Edward Jones and TD Waterhouse. Investors establish an account with the brokerage firm and then enter orders to trade shares. The brokerage firm handles the trade for the investor and charges the investor a fee for the service. Some investors phone in their orders or visit the brokerage firm in person. But today, most investors use their computers to trade stocks online. The requirements for setting up an account vary from broker to broker. Selecting the right brokerage firm is one of the most important decisions investors make.

The most common type of order is a *market order*. This order instructs the broker to obtain the best possible price—the highest price when selling and the lowest price when buying. If the stock market is open, market orders are filled within seconds. Another popular type of order is called a *limit order*. It sets a price ceiling when buying or a price floor when selling. If the order cannot be filled when it is placed, the order is left with the exchange's market maker, a firm who is always ready to buy or sell a specific share at a publicly quoted price. It may be filled later if the price limits are met.

ASSESSMENT CHECK

16.4.1 What are the world's two largest stock markets?

16.4.2 What makes the London Stock Exchange unique?

16.4.3 Explain the difference between a market order and a limit order.

FINANCIAL INSTITUTIONS

LO 16.5 Discuss how financial institutions are organized and how they function.

One of the most important parts of the financial system is its **financial institutions**. They are an intermediary between savers and borrowers. They collect funds from savers and then lend the funds to individuals, businesses, and governments. Financial institutions improve the transfer of funds from savers to users by increasing the efficiency and effectiveness of the process. Financial institutions make it easier for savers to earn more and for users of funds to pay less. It is difficult to imagine how any modern economy could function without well-developed financial institutions. Think about how difficult it would be for a business to obtain financing or for an individual to purchase a new home without using a financial institution. Borrowers would need to identify and negotiate terms with each saver individually.

Traditionally, financial institutions have been classified into depository institutions and nondepository institutions. Depository institutions accept deposits that customers can withdraw on demand. Examples of depository institutions include commercial banks, such as CIBC, RBC, TD Canada Trust, and Scotiabank. Nondepository institutions include life insurance companies, such as Manulife Financial; pension funds, such as the Ontario Teachers' Pension Plan; and mutual funds. Together, Canadian financial institutions have trillions of dollars in assets. **Figure 16.2** illustrates the number and types of major financial institutions in Canada.

financial institutions intermediaries between savers and borrowers that collect funds from savers then lend the funds to individuals, businesses, and governments.

Commercial Banks

Commercial banks are the largest and probably the most important financial institutions in Canada and in most other countries. In Canada, the 28 domestic banks and other foreign-based financial institutions manage assets of more than $4.0 trillion. Commercial banks offer the most services of any financial institution. These services include a wide range of chequing and savings

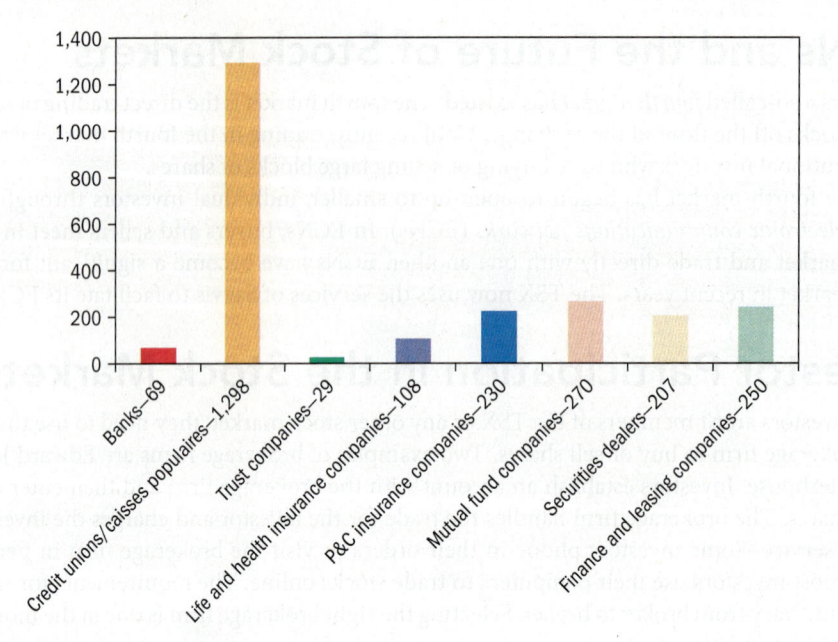

FIGURE 16.2 Financial Institutions in Canada

Note: P&C insurance companies refer to profit and casualty insurance companies.

Source: Department of Finance Canada, "The Canadian Financial Services Sector," accessed July 6, 2011, www.fin.gc.ca/toc/2002/fact-cfss_-eng.asp.

Bar chart data:
- Banks—69
- Credit unions/caisses populaires—1,298
- Trust companies—29
- Life and health insurance companies—108
- P&C insurance companies—230
- Mutual fund companies—270
- Securities dealers—207
- Finance and leasing companies—250

The Royal Bank of Canada (RBC) is Canada's largest financial institution.

deposit accounts, consumer loans, credit cards, home mortgage loans, business loans, and trust services. Commercial banks also sell other financial products, including securities and insurance.[8] Within the past few years, the number of domestic banks increased significantly from 14 to 23.

How Banks Operate

Banks raise funds by offering customers a variety of chequing and savings deposits. The banks then pool, or combine, these deposits and lend most of them out in the form of consumer and business loans. At the end of a recent year, banks held several billion dollars in deposits and outstanding loans.[9] Banks lend a great deal of money to households and businesses for a variety of purposes. Banks currently hold approximately 75 percent of residential mortgages and more than $900 billion in commercial loans.[10] Commercial banks are an especially important source of funds for small businesses. When banks evaluate loan applications, they look at the borrower's ability and willingness to repay the loan. Occasionally, banks reject loan applications.

Banks make money mostly because the interest rate they charge borrowers is higher than the rate of interest they pay depositors. Banks also make money from other sources, such as fees they charge customers for using chequing accounts and ATMs.

After the recent credit crisis, many small business owners have suffered because banks have begun pulling their lines of credit; the "Career Kickstart" feature offers some suggestions if this happens to you.

Electronic Banking

Each year, more and more funds move through electronic funds transfer systems (EFTSs). EFTSs are computerized systems for conducting financial transactions over electronic links. Millions of businesses and consumers now pay bills and receive payments electronically. For example, most

CAREER KICKSTART

What to Do When Your Credit Gets Pulled

For years banks have issued business credit cards to small business owners. The cards come with a line of credit of usually several thousand dollars or more. The line of credit gives these businesses a safety net in case of a late payment from a client or some other emergency. After the credit crisis hit, banks began to either call those loans in or limit the credit lines to the amount currently outstanding. As a result, millions of small business owners lost that safety net. The Canadian Federation of Independent Businesses (CFIB) reported that 20 percent of small and medium-sized business owners had their applications for credit rejected. In some cases, their credit lines had been decreased or their requests to extend their loans had been denied. Here are some steps to consider if this situation happens to you:

1. Be careful not to use all credit you have left; doing so could have a negative impact on your credit score.

2. Make your current monthly payment as quickly as possible, either online or by phone.

3. Obtain debt counselling to learn how to better manage your debt. Use a trusted organization like Credit Canada (www.creditcanada.com).

4. If possible, pay down your existing credit card debt. But if you know you'll need money in the short term, weigh that need against your credit score before you write the cheque.

5. Keep careful track of your credit score. Equifax Canada and TransUnion Canada provide free credit reports.

Sources: Federal Trade Commission, "Credit and Your Consumer Rights," accessed June 21, 2010, www.ftc.gov; Sam Thacker, "Steps to Take When Your Credit Line Is Pulled," *All-Business*, accessed June 21, 2010, www.allbusiness.com; Jeffrey Weber, "What to Do When Your Credit Limit Is Decreased," SmartBalanceTransfers.com, March 4, 2010, www.smartbalancetransfers.com; Julie Bennett, "What to Do When the Bank Pulls Your Line of Credit," *Entrepreneur*, February 2010, www.entrepreneur.com; Industry Canada, *Supporting Small Business Innovation: Review of the Business Development Bank of Canada*, accessed July 28, 2011, www.ic.gc.ca/eic/site/ic1.nsf/vwapj/E-BDC.pdf/$file/E-BDC.pdf; Equifax, accessed July 28, 2011, www.econsumer.equifax.ca/index_en.html?transaction_id5100aca537487668e726bba5aaf22a4; TransUnion, accessed July 28, 2011, www.transunion.ca/.

---

employers directly deposit employees' paycheques into their bank accounts instead of issuing paper cheques. Today, nearly all social assistance payments and other federal payments are sent as electronic data, not as paper documents.

One of the original forms of electronic banking, the automated teller machine (ATM), continues to grow in popularity. ATMs allow customers to make bank transactions at any time by inserting a bank issued electronic card into the machine and entering a personal identification number (PIN). Networked systems enable ATM users to access their bank accounts all across Canada and throughout the world. Customers can use a debit card to pay for purchases directly from their chequing or savings account. All major retailers and even smaller sized merchants offer customers the option to pay by debit card, and some even go further and offer additional cash withdrawals, known as cash back, from the customer's bank account. Consumers enjoy the convenience of debit cards, while at the same time it eliminates the problem of bad cheques for retailers. There were approximately 4.9 billion debit card transactions in Canada in 2014 alone.[11]

Online Banking

Today, many consumers do some or all of their banking online. Data shows that Canadians were the highest users of Internet banking (see **Figure 16.3**). Canadians can choose from two types of online banks: Internet-only banks, such as PC Financial, and traditional bricks-and-mortar banks that also have websites, such as RBC and CIBC. The main reason people use online banking is for convenience. Customers can transfer money, check their account balances, and pay bills, and even deposit cheques via their smartphones.

Deposit Insurance

Most commercial bank deposits are insured by the **Canada Deposit Insurance Corporation (CDIC)**, a federal agency. If a CDIC-insured bank fails, its depositors are paid in full by the CDIC up to $100,000. The CDIC was formed in 1967 to build public confidence in the banking system.

Canada Deposit Insurance Corporation (CDIC) the federal agency that insures deposits at commercial and savings banks.

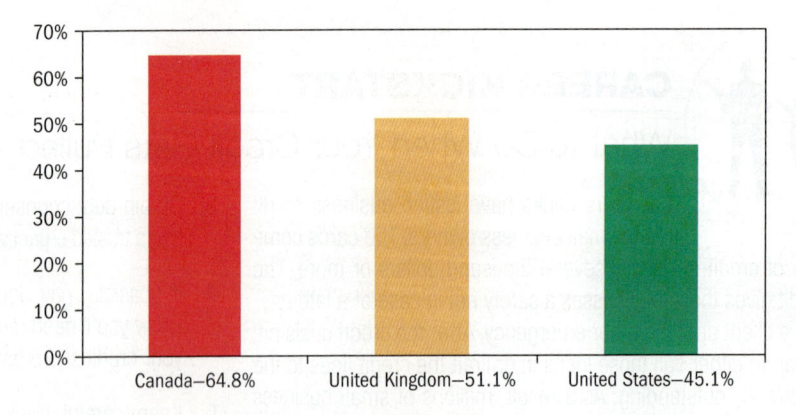

FIGURE 16.3 Online Banking Usages

Source: Comscore, "Top 10 Countries by Online Banking Penetration," accessed August 14, 2014, www.comscore.com/Insights/Data-Mine/Top-10-Countries-by-Online-Banking-Penetration.

Before deposit insurance, banks often experienced so-called *runs*, where people rushed to withdraw their money, often because of a rumour about the bank's unstable financial condition. As banks experienced more and more withdrawals in a short period, they would reach a point where they were unable to meet all the demands for cash and closed their doors. The remaining depositors who could not get to the bank on time often lost most of their money. Deposit insurance shifts the risk of bank failures from individual depositors to the CDIC. Banks can still fail today, but no insured depositor has ever lost any money within the insurable limit.

Credit unions are growing in popularity. The Credit Union Central of Canada is a good place to start when looking for a credit union in your area.

Credit Unions

Commercial banks are the largest depository financial institution in Canada, but credit unions also serve a significant segment of the financial community. Today credit unions offer many of the same services as commercial banks, so despite the strength of the "big banks," many consumers opt to do their banking with smaller financial institutions that offer more personal service.[12]

Credit unions are cooperative financial institutions that are owned by their depositors, all of whom are members. More than 5 million Canadians belong to one of the nation's approximately 320 credit unions. Combined, credit unions have more than $162 billion in assets.[13] The number of credit unions in Canada has decreased in recent years because of their efforts to merge to gain economies of scale.[14] Edmonton-based Servus Credit Union partnered with 20 credit unions across Alberta to launch province-wide inter-credit union banking services.[15]

Credit unions are designed to serve consumers, not businesses. Credit unions raise funds by offering members several different chequing and saving accounts. Credit unions then lend these funds to members. Because credit unions are not-for-profit institutions, consumers often prefer them over commercial banks and other financial institutions: Credit unions often pay higher rates of interest on deposits, charge lower rates of interest on loans, and charge fewer fees. Deposits at credit unions are insured at the provincial level. The Prince Edward Island Credit Union Deposit Insurance Corporation insures deposits at credit unions in the province of Prince Edward Island. It works essentially the same way that the CDIC does.

Nondepository Financial Institutions

Nondepository financial institutions accept funds from businesses and households, and then invest most of these funds. Generally, these institutions do not offer chequing accounts (demand deposits). Three examples of nondepository financial institutions are insurance companies, pension funds, and finance companies.

Insurance Companies

Households and businesses buy insurance to transfer risk from themselves to the insurance company. The insurance company accepts the risk in return for a series of payments, called *premiums*. Underwriting is the process insurance companies use to determine whom to insure and how much to charge. During a typical year, insurance companies collect more in premiums than they pay in claims. After they pay their operating expenses, they invest the difference. Insurance companies are a major source of short- and long-term financing for businesses. Life insurance companies have total assets of more than $615 billion. They invest their funds in everything from bonds and stocks to real estate.[16] Examples of life insurers include Canada Life and Manulife Financial.

Pension Funds

Pension funds provide retirement benefits to workers and their families. They are set up by employers and are funded by regular contributions from employers and employees. Because pension funds have predictable long-term cash inflows and very predictable cash outflows, they invest heavily in assets, such as common stocks and real estate. The Canada Pension Plan (CPP) fund has assets of more than $219 billion. The recovery of global markets led to total investment income of $31.7 billion after the financial crisis era. The fund's current asset mix consists of 31 percent in Canadian assets and 69 percent in foreign investment assets with only 28.4 percent of total assets in less risky bonds. Since the financial crisis, the asset mix has shifted to include more foreign investment and fewer Canadian assets.[17]

Finance Companies

Consumer and commercial finance companies offer short-term loans to borrowers. Two examples are Ford Credit and John Deere Capital Corporation. A commercial finance company supplies short-term funds to businesses that use their tangible assets as collateral for the loan. These tangible assets can include inventory, accounts receivable, machinery, or property. A consumer finance company plays a similar role for consumers. Finance companies raise funds by selling securities or by borrowing funds from commercial banks. Many finance companies, such as Toyota Financial Services, are actually subsidiaries of a manufacturer. Toyota Financial Services finances dealer inventories of new cars and trucks. It also provides loans to consumers and other buyers of Toyota products.

Mutual Funds

One of the most significant types of financial institutions today is the mutual fund. *Mutual funds* are financial intermediaries that raise money from investors by selling shares. They then use the money to invest in securities that meet the mutual fund's objectives. For example, a share-based mutual fund invests mainly in common shares. Mutual funds have become extremely popular over the last few decades. Canada's almost 3,000 mutual funds have over a trillion dollars in assets, up from $125 billion in the early 1990s. One reason for this growth is the increased popularity of registered retirement savings plans (RRSPs) and similar types of retirement plans. In a recent poll, 49 percent of Canadians chose to invest their RRSP assets in mutual fund shares. This amount has increased in recent years as the economy recovers from the financial crisis.[18]

Mutual fund investors are indirect owners of a portfolio of securities. As the value of the securities owned by the mutual fund changes, the value of the mutual fund's shares will also change. Investment income, such as bond interest and stock dividends, is passed through to mutual fund shareholders.

Just less than half of mutual fund assets are invested in company shares. Money market mutual funds are also popular. These funds invest in money market instruments like commercial paper. Money market funds have total assets of just over $2.6 trillion.[19]

✓ ASSESSMENT CHECK

16.5.1 What are the two main types of financial institutions?

16.5.2 What are the primary differences between commercial banks and credit unions?

16.5.3 What is a mutual fund?

LO 16.6 Explain the functions of the Bank of Canada and the tools it uses to carry out these functions.

THE ROLE OF THE BANK OF CANADA

Bank of Canada (the Bank) the central bank of Canada.

Created in 1935, the **Bank of Canada (the Bank)** is the central bank of Canada and an important part of the nation's financial system. The Bank, once privately owned, became a government-owned Crown corporation in 1938. The Bank of Canada has four basic responsibilities: regulating monetary policy, designing and issuing bank notes, regulating the financial system, and managing funds for the federal government and other clients.

Monetary Policy

The Bank's most important function is regulating monetary policy, which means controlling the supply of money and credit. The Bank's job is to make sure that the money supply grows at a suitable rate, allowing the economy to expand and inflation to remain in check. If the money supply grows too slowly, economic growth will slow, unemployment will increase, and the risk of a recession will increase. If the money supply grows too rapidly, inflationary pressures will build. The Bank uses its policy tools to push interest rates up or down. If the Bank pushes interest rates up, the growth rate in the money supply will slow, economic growth will slow, and inflationary pressures will ease. If the Bank pushes interest rates down, the growth rate in the money supply will increase, economic growth will pick up, and unemployment will fall.

The two common measures of the money supply are called M1 and M2. M1 consists of currency in circulation and the balances in bank chequing accounts. M2 equals M1 plus balances in some savings accounts and money market mutual funds. **Figure 16.4** shows the approximate composition of the M2 money supply.

The Bank has two major policy tools for controlling the growth in the supply of money and credit: the discount rate and open market operations. The *discount rate* is the interest rate at which the Bank makes short-term loans to member banks. The discount rate is often referred to as the bank rate. A bank might need a short-term loan if transactions leave it short of reserves. If the Bank wants to slow the growth rate in the money supply, it increases the bank rate. This increase makes it more expensive for banks to borrow funds. Banks, in turn, raise the interest rates they charge on loans to consumers and businesses. The end result is a slowdown in economic activity. Lowering the bank rate has the opposite effect.

The second policy tool, and the one used more often, is *open market operations*, the technique of controlling the money supply growth rate by buying or selling Canadian government securities. If the Bank buys government securities, the money it pays enters circulation, where it increases the money supply and lowers interest rates. When the Bank sells government securities, money is taken out of circulation and interest rates rise. When the Bank uses open market operations it uses as its benchmark, or guideline, the so-called *overnight rate*—the rate at which banks lend money to each other overnight. **Table 16.3** shows how the tools used by the Bank can either stimulate or slow the economy.

The Bank has the authority to use selective credit controls when the economy is growing too rapidly or too slowly. These credit controls include the power to set margin requirements—the percentage of the purchase price of a security that an investor must pay in cash when making credit purchases of shares or bonds.

The Bank can also inject capital into the financial system in response to a financial crisis. For example, during the credit crisis in the United States, which began in 2008, the U.S. Federal Reserve (the American equivalent to the Bank of Canada) pumped hundreds of billions of dollars into the financial system. The Federal Reserve even came to the rescue of AIG, a major U.S. insurance company, by purchasing some of the firm's shares. In Canada, the Bank kept interest rates at historical lows during the global financial crisis.

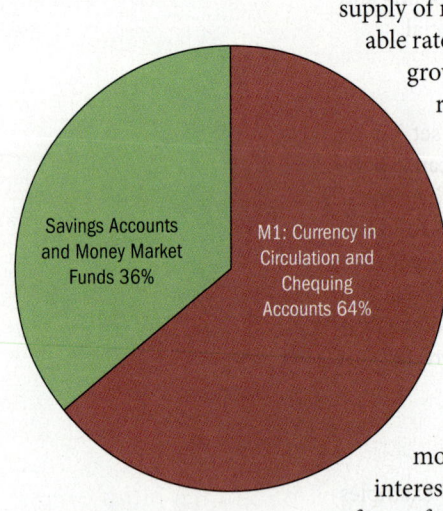

FIGURE 16.4 Total M2 Money Supply

- Savings Accounts and Money Market Funds 36%
- M1: Currency in Circulation and Chequing Accounts 64%

Source: Statistics Canada, "Exchange Rates, Interest Rates, Money Supply and Stock Prices, 2007–2011," accessed August 21, 2014, www.statcan.gc.ca/tables-tableaux/sum-som/l01/cst01/econ07-eng.htm.

Table 16.3 Tools Used by the Bank of Canada to Regulate the Growth in the Money Supply

TOOL	BRIEF DESCRIPTION	IMPACT ON THE GROWTH RATE OF THE MONEY SUPPLY	IMPACT ON INTEREST RATES AND THE ECONOMY	FREQUENCY OF USE
1. Bank rate	The interest rate that the Bank of Canada charges banks for loans.	An increase in the bank rate slows the growth rate in the money supply.	An increase in the bank rate pushes interest rates up and slows economic growth.	Used only with open market operations.
2. Open market operations	The buying and selling of government securities to increase or decrease bank reserves.	Selling government securities reduces bank reserves and slows the growth rate in the money supply.	Selling government securities pushes interest rates up and slows economic growth.	Used frequently.

Transactions in the foreign exchange markets also affect the Canadian money supply and interest rates. The Bank can lower the exchange value of the dollar by selling dollars and buying foreign currencies. It can also raise the dollar's exchange value by doing the opposite—buying dollars and selling foreign currencies. When the Bank buys foreign currencies, the effect is the same as buying securities: the purchase of foreign currencies or securities increases the reserves in Canada's banking system. In contrast, selling foreign currencies is like selling securities: It reduces bank reserves.

Historically, the Bank also influenced the money supply by controlling the *reserve requirement*. The reserve requirement was the percentage of cash that banks were required to maintain for immediate withdrawal by customers. The lower the reserve requirement, the more the money supply could increase. For example, if you deposited $10,000 at your local bank and the reserve requirement was 3 percent, the bank would then likely lend out $9,700 to someone else (perhaps to purchase a car). The purchaser (the borrower) would then give the $9,700 to the seller of the car who would deposit it in the bank. At this point, the money supply related to the initial deposit is $19,700 (the initial $10,000 plus the $9,700 also in the bank). This process would continue, increasing the money supply further. The original deposit of $10,000 would have a potential impact on the money supply of $333,333 ($10,000/3%). In 1992, the Bank of Canada removed the reserve requirement. Banks now decide themselves the proportion of deposits to keep on hand.

✓ **ASSESSMENT CHECK**

16.6.1 What is the Bank of Canada?

16.6.2 List the two main tools the Bank uses to control the supply of money and credit.

REGULATION OF THE FINANCIAL SYSTEM

LO 16.7 Describe the regulation of the financial system.

It is probably not surprising that many parts of the financial system must comply with government regulation and are supervised by government agencies. After all, the financial system is very important to how our economy works.

Bank Regulation

Banks are among the nation's most heavily regulated businesses. The main purpose of bank regulation is to ensure public confidence in the safety and security of the banking system. Banks are critical to the overall functioning of the economy. For example, a collapse of the banking system can have disastrous results. Under the Bank Act, the federal government is responsible for regulating the banking sector. Several regulatory bodies are involved in regulating Canadian banks, including the Department of Finance, the Bank of Canada, the Office of the Superintendent of Financial Institutions (OSFI), and the CDIC. Some regulation is also at the provincial level because of the many lines of business that a commercial bank or credit union may be involved in.[20]

Government Regulation of the Financial Markets

At the provincial level, regulation of Canadian financial markets is primarily administered by organizations such as the Manitoba Securities Commission or the Ontario Securities Commission. These provincial organizations are in turn coordinated by the Canadian Securities Administrators (CSA) to reduce duplication of efforts and provide consistency. But, in the end, responsibility is in the hands of the various provincial bodies.

One area that provincial regulators pay particular attention to is insider trading. **Insider trading** is defined as the use of material, nonpublic information about a company to make investment profits. Examples of material, nonpublic information include a pending merger or a major oil discovery. Releasing information on these activities before they occur could affect the firm's share price. The definition of insider trading goes beyond corporate insiders—people such as the company's officers and directors. It includes lawyers, accountants, investment bankers, and even reporters—anyone who uses nonpublic information to profit in the stock market at the expense of ordinary investors. Although some actions or communications are clearly insider trading, other activities are more difficult to pin down. As a result, all employees of public companies must keep in mind what is and is not permitted.

insider trading use of material, nonpublic information about a company to make investment profits.

Industry Self-Regulation

The securities markets are also heavily self-regulated by professional associations and the major financial markets. The securities industry understands that rules and regulations are designed to ensure fair and orderly markets. The rules and regulations also promote investor confidence and benefit all participants. Two examples of self-regulation are the rules of conduct established by professional organizations and the market surveillance techniques used by the major securities markets.

Market Surveillance

All securities markets use a variety of methods to spot possible violations of trading rules or securities laws. In Canada, the Toronto Stock Exchange (TSX) wants to promote integrity and fairness in all trading across equity marketplaces. The TSX outsources market surveillance to an independent third party—the Investment Industry Regulatory Organization of Canada (IIROC). IIROC's surveillance functions include real-time monitoring of trading activity: A team of experts watch all equity trades as they occur to ensure compliance with the securities trading rules. IIROC is equipped with an experienced team and a dedicated surveillance facility with advanced technology. It monitors company news, stock charts, and chat room activity to detect volume and price anomalies. IIROC also monitors timely disclosure of material information by publicly traded businesses to ensure they comply with Universal Market Integrity Rules (UMIR). State-of-the-art technology and monitoring systems allow IIROC to track trading behaviour in real time and collect evidence needed to pursue cases relating to violations, such as insider trading and manipulative activity.[21] Self-regulation by the financial industry has been an important part of securities market regulation. But some argue that the industry can never truly regulate itself effectively in today's market environment. The "Solving an Ethical Controversy" feature debates the pros and cons of industry self-regulation.

✓ **ASSESSMENT CHECK**

16.7.1 Who regulates banks?

16.7.2 Define *insider trading*.

SOLVING AN **ETHICAL** CONTROVERSY

Can the Securities Market Regulate Itself?

"Those of us who have looked to the self-interest of lending institutions to protect shareholders' equity, myself included, are in a state of shocked disbelief."

That's what was said by Alan Greenspan, former chair of the Federal Reserve Board in the United States, in his testimony before Congress after the credit crisis. He had long supported the idea that the market could always be trusted to regulate itself and should be left free to do so. But with his words, he rejected that policy. The crisis brought an end to a Wall Street bubble that had done well, partly due to unlimited, unregulated speculation. Stricter government regulation of the financial industry seems very likely.

Can the securities market be trusted to regulate itself?

PRO

1. Regulation of the securities market will give the government too much power over private industry.
2. The mere idea of regulation has made some institutions change their behaviour voluntarily. For example, some banks have announced that they will eliminate overdraft fees for consumer accounts.
3. Self-regulation can lead to greater investor confidence.

CON

1. Some analysts feel that existing government regulation is too lax. They believe that the government, which is supposed to regulate the financial industry, was too lenient with some large financial institutions.
2. The TSX has one body that both approves company listings and enforces the rules. Most other exchanges, such as the NYSE and London Stock Exchange, have two separate bodies, one for each purpose.
3. Self-regulation leads to a loss of independence.

Summary

Public disapproval of the securities market is likely to continue as long as people continue to feel the effects of the financial crisis in their everyday lives, especially in the United States. The government has considered new, stricter regulations on financial institutions. Some argue that those regulations are unnecessary and could even be harmful.

Sources: Bill Singer, "Analyzing a Troubling Wall Street Double Standard," *Corporate Compliance Insights*, May 4, 2010, www.corporatecomplianceinsights.com; Felix Salmon, "How the SEC Cracks Down on Unethical Behavior," Reuters, April 20, 2010, http://blogs.reuters.com; Peter Hamby, "DNC Ad: Wall Street Lobbyists Trying to Block Reform," *CNN*, April 20, 2010, http://politicalticker.blogs.cnn.com; Roger Lowenstein, "*The End of Wall Street* by Roger Lowenstein: Book Excerpt," *Bloomberg Businessweek*, April 8, 2010, www.businessweek.com; Andrew Ross Sorkin, "Extreme Makeover, Wall Street Edition," *New York Times*, April 1, 2010, http://dealbook.blogs.nytimes.com; Charles H. Green, "Fixing What Ails Wall Street: Ethics, or Incentives?" Trusted Advisor Associates, September 21, 2009, http://trustedadvisor.com; Tim Kiladze, "TSX Regulation a Conflict of Interest: Report," *Globe and Mail*, July 29, 2010, accessed July 28, 2011, www.theglobeandmail.com/globe-investor/tsx-regulation-a-conflict-of-interest-report/article1653215.

THE FINANCIAL SYSTEM: A GLOBAL PERSPECTIVE

LO 16.8 Describe the global financial system.

Not surprisingly, the global financial system is becoming more and more integrated each year. As we've noted, financial markets exist throughout the world. Shares of Canadian firms trade in other countries, and shares of international companies trade in Canada. Financial institutions have also become a global industry. Major Canadian banks—such as CIBC, RBC, and Scotiabank—have extensive international operations. They have offices, lend money, and accept deposits from customers throughout the world.

Of the 50 largest banks in the world (measured by total assets), only three are Canadian: RBC, TD Bank, and the Bank of Nova Scotia. The largest of the three, RBC, ranks thirty-seventh. Besides the three Canadian banks on the list, the other 47 are based in Belgium, China, France, Germany, Italy, Japan, the Netherlands, Switzerland, the United Kingdom, and other parts of the world. The world's largest bank, the Industrial & Commercial Bank of China, has over $3.2 trillion in assets. Many of these international banks also operate worldwide, including in Canada.[22]

The effects of financial globalization are evident in Canada. Canada's growing cultural diversity has led to an increase in other banking models. Many other financial models exist around the world, including the interest-free Islamic system of banking. Special banks are needed to address the financial needs of devout Muslims who cannot be involved in interest-based transactions, including home mortgages. Islamic finance companies such as Guidance Financial, Hakim Wealth Management, the Islamic Credit Union of Canada, and Ijara Canada provide financial products to the previously underserved niche market of Islamic finance. Globally, financial institutions, including HBSC, Citigroup, and Lloyds Bank, have seen their assets grow at an annual rate of more than 20 percent in this emerging market. Currently their assets total more than $4 trillion worldwide. In recent years, many new initiatives were created because of this rapidly growing market. For example, Standard & Poor's has launched the S&P/TSX 60 Shariah Index, which is a version of the S&P/TSX 60 that complies with Islamic law.[23]

Almost all nations have some sort of a central bank, similar to the Bank of Canada. Examples include the U.S. Federal Reserve (the Fed), the Bank of England, the Bank of Japan, and the European Central Bank. These central banks have a similar role to that of the Bank of Canada—controlling the money supply and regulating banks. Policymakers at the

In Frankfurt, Germany, a sculpture of the euro—the symbol for the European Union's currency—stands outside the headquarters of Europe's central bank. The 12 gold stars represent all the peoples of Europe.

HSBC Amanah was set up to serve the unique financial needs of the Muslim community.

Bank of Canada often respond to changes in the U.S. financial system by making similar changes to the Canadian system. For example, if the Fed pushes U.S. interest rates lower, central banks in Canada, Japan, and Europe may also push their interest rates lower. These changes can influence events in countries around the world. When Canadian and European interest rates are low, they decrease the cost of borrowing for Canadian and European firms but increase the amount of money available for loans to borrowers in other countries, such as Chile and India.

✓ **ASSESSMENT CHECK**

16.8.1 Where do Canadian banks rank compared with international banks?

16.8.2 Do other countries have organizations that play roles similar to those played by the Bank of Canada?

WHAT'S AHEAD

This chapter explored the financial system, a key part of the Canadian economy and a process that affects many aspects of contemporary business. The financial system is the process by which funds are transferred between savers and borrowers. It includes securities, financial markets, and financial institutions. The chapter also described the role of the Bank of Canada and discussed the global financial system. In the next chapter, we discuss the finance functions of a business, including the role of financial managers, financial planning, asset management, and sources of short- and long-term funds.

RETURN TO INSIDE BUSINESS

Canada Weathers the Credit Crisis

The financial crisis has had a significant impact on global financial markets. Countries significantly affected include the United States, Greece, Italy, Australia, Brazil, Russia, and many more.

QUESTIONS FOR CRITICAL THINKING

1. How can financial institutions and countries prevent another major financial crisis?
2. Why was Africa not as affected by the financial crisis as most of the rest of the world?

SUMMARY OF LEARNING OBJECTIVES

LO 16.1 Outline the structure and importance of the financial system.

The financial system is the process by which funds are transferred between those who have excess funds (savers) and those who need additional funds (users). Savers and users are individuals, businesses, and governments. Savers expect to earn a rate of return in exchange for the use of their funds. Financial markets, financial institutions, and financial instruments (securities) make up the financial system. Although direct transfers are possible, most funds flow from savers to users through the financial markets or financial institutions, such as commercial banks. A well-functioning financial system is vital to the overall health of a nation's economy.

✓ **ASSESSMENT CHECK ANSWERS**

16.1.1 What is the financial system? The financial system is the mechanism by which funds are transferred between those who have excess funds (savers) and those who need additional funds (users).

16.1.2 In the financial system, who are the borrowers and who are the savers? Savers and borrowers are individuals, businesses, and governments. Generally, individuals are net savers, meaning they spend less than they make. Businesses and governments tend to be net borrowers.

16.1.3 List the two most common ways that funds are transferred between borrowers and savers. The two most common ways funds are transferred are through the financial markets and through financial institutions.

LO 16.2 List the various types of securities.

Securities, also called *financial instruments*, represent the obligations of the issuers—businesses and governments—to provide purchasers with the expected or stated returns on the funds invested or loaned. Securities can be classified into three categories: money market instruments, bonds, and shares. Money market instruments and bonds are debt instruments. Money market instruments are short-term debt securities and tend to be low-risk securities. Bonds are longer-term debt securities and pay a fixed amount of interest each year. Bonds are sold by the Canadian government (Canada Savings Bonds), provincial and local governments (municipal bonds), and corporations. Mortgage-backed securities are bonds backed by a pool, or group, of mortgage loans. Most municipal and corporate bonds have risk ratings. Common shares represent ownership in corporations. Investors who hold common shares have voting rights and a residual claim on the firm's assets.

✓ ASSESSMENT CHECK ANSWERS

16.2.1 What are the major types of securities? The major types of securities are money market instruments, bonds, and shares.

16.2.2 What areas of the government issue bonds? Bonds are issued by the federal, provincial, and municipal governments.

16.2.3 Why do investors purchase common shares? Investors purchase common shares for two reasons. One reason is to receive dividends, which are cash payments made to shareholders by the firm. The other reason is the potential price increase of the shares.

LO 16.3 Define *financial market* and distinguish between primary and secondary financial markets.

A financial market is a market where securities are bought and sold. The primary market for securities serves businesses and governments that want to sell new security issues to raise funds. Securities are sold in the primary market either through an open auction or through a process called *underwriting*. The secondary market handles transactions of previously issued securities between investors. One example of a secondary market is the Toronto Stock Exchange. The business or government that issued the security is not directly involved in secondary market transactions. The secondary market handles about four to five times the dollar value of securities than are handled in the primary market.

✓ ASSESSMENT CHECK ANSWERS

16.3.1 What is a financial market? A financial market is a market where securities are bought and sold.

16.3.2 Distinguish between a primary and a secondary financial market. The primary market for securities serves businesses and governments that want to sell new security issues to raise funds. The secondary market handles transactions of previously issued securities between investors.

16.3.3 Briefly explain the role of financial institutions in the sale of securities. Financial institutions purchase new securities issues from corporations or provincial and municipal governments, and then resell the securities to investors. The institutions charge a fee for their services.

LO 16.4 Describe the characteristics of the major stock exchanges.

The best-known financial markets are the stock exchanges. Stock exchanges can be found throughout the world. Canada's largest stock exchange is the Toronto Stock Exchange, or TSX. The world's two largest stock exchanges are the New York Stock Exchange and NASDAQ. Both are located in the United States. The NYSE is bigger when measured in terms of the total value of shares traded. Larger and better-known companies dominate the NYSE. The NASDAQ stock market is an electronic market where buy and sell orders are entered into a computerized communication system. Most of the world's major stock markets today use similar electronic trading systems. Electronic trading may be the future for stock markets.

✓ ASSESSMENT CHECK ANSWERS

16.4.1 What are the world's two largest stock markets? The world's two largest stock markets are the New York Stock Exchange and the NASDAQ Stock Market.

16.4.2 What makes the London Stock Exchange unique? The London Stock Exchange is the most international of the world's stock markets. A large percentage of the shares traded there are not from British firms.

16.4.3 Explain the difference between a market order and a limit order. A market order instructs the investor's broker to obtain the best possible price when buying or selling securities. A limit order sets a maximum price (if the investor wants to buy) or a minimum price (if the investor wants to sell).

LO 16.5 Discuss how financial institutions are organized and how they function.

Financial institutions act as intermediaries between savers and users of funds. Depository institutions accept deposits from customers that can be exchanged for cash on demand. Examples of depository institutions are commercial banks, savings banks, and credit unions. Commercial banks are the largest and most important of the depository institutions. They offer the widest range of services. Savings banks are a major source of home mortgage loans. Credit unions are not-for-profit institutions that offer financial services to consumers. The Canada Deposit Insurance Corporation is a government agency that insures deposits at these financial institutions. Nondepository institutions include pension funds and insurance companies. Nondepository institutions invest a large portion of their funds in stocks, bonds, and real estate. Mutual funds are another important financial institution. These companies sell shares to investors and, in turn, invest the proceeds in securities. Many individuals today invest a large portion of their retirement savings in mutual fund shares.

✓ ASSESSMENT CHECK ANSWERS

16.5.1 What are the two main types of financial institutions? The two major types of financial institutions are depository institutions (those that accept chequing and similar accounts) and nondepository institutions.

16.5.2 What are the primary differences between commercial banks and credit unions? Today, commercial banks and credit unions offer many of the same services. Commercial banks lend money to businesses and to individuals. Credit unions lend money mostly to individuals, usually in the form of home mortgage loans.

16.5.3 What is a mutual fund? A mutual fund is an intermediary that raises money by selling shares to investors. It then pools, or combines, investor funds and purchases securities that meet the mutual fund's objectives.

LO 16.6 Explain the functions of the Bank of Canada and the tools it uses to carry out these functions.

The Bank of Canada (the Bank) is the central bank of Canada. The Bank regulates monetary policy, designs and issues bank notes, regulates the financial system, and manages funds for the federal government and other clients. It controls the supply of credit and money in the economy to promote growth and control inflation. The Bank's main tools include the bank rate and open market operations. Selective credit controls and purchases and sales of foreign currencies also help the Bank manage the economy.

✓ ASSESSMENT CHECK ANSWERS

16.6.1 What is the Bank of Canada? The Bank of Canada is Canada's central bank. It is responsible for regulating the financial system, providing banking-related services for the federal government, acting as the banker's bank, designing and issuing bank notes, and setting monetary policy.

16.6.2 List the two main tools the Bank uses to control the supply of money and credit. The two main tools are the bank rate and open market operations.

LO 16.7 Describe the regulation of the financial system.

Commercial banks, savings banks, and credit unions in Canada are heavily regulated by federal banking authorities. Banking regulators require institutions to follow sound banking practices. They have the power to close noncompliant banks. In Canada, financial markets are regulated primarily at the provincial level. Markets are also heavily self-regulated by the financial markets and professional organizations. Provincial regulatory bodies set the requirements for both primary and secondary market activity. They ban a number of practices, including insider trading. They also require public companies to disclose financial information regularly. Professional organizations and the securities markets also have rules and procedures that all members must follow.

✓ ASSESSMENT CHECK ANSWERS

16.7.1 Who regulates banks? All banks are regulated by the federal government.

16.7.2 Define *insider trading*. Insider trading is defined as the use of material, nonpublic information to make an investment profit.

LO 16.8 Describe the global financial system.

Financial markets exist throughout the world and are increasingly interconnected. Investors in other countries purchase Canadian securities, and Canadian investors purchase foreign securities. Large Canadian banks and other financial institutions have a global presence. They accept deposits, make loans, and have branches throughout the world. Foreign banks also operate worldwide. The average European or Japanese bank is much larger than the average Canadian bank. Almost all nations have a central bank that performs the same roles as the Bank of Canada. Central bankers often act together, raising and lowering interest rates to control economic conditions.

✓ ASSESSMENT CHECK ANSWERS

16.8.1 Where do Canadian banks rank compared with international banks? Banks in Asia and Europe are generally much larger than Canadian banks. Only three of the world's 50 largest banks are based in Canada.

16.8.2 Do other countries have organizations that play roles similar to those played by the Bank of Canada? Yes, almost all nations have central banks that perform many of the same functions as the Bank of Canada.

BUSINESS TERMS YOU NEED TO KNOW

Bank of Canada (the Bank) 460
Canada Deposit Insurance Corporation (CDIC) 457
common shares 450
financial institutions 455
financial markets 451
financial system 446
insider trading 462
primary markets 451
secondary market 453
securities 448
stock markets (exchanges) 453

REVIEW QUESTIONS

1. What is the financial system? Why is it rare for funds to be directly transferred from savers to users?
2. What is a security? Give several examples.
3. List the major types of bonds. What is a mortgage-backed security?
4. What are the differences between common shares and preferred shares?
5. Explain the difference between a primary financial market and a secondary financial market.
6. Why are commercial banks and credit unions classified as depository financial institutions? How do commercial banks differ from credit unions?
7. Why are life insurance companies, pension funds, and mutual funds considered financial institutions?
8. Briefly explain the role of the Bank of Canada. List the tools it uses to control the supply of money and credit.
9. What methods are used to regulate banks? Why are Canadian chartered banks also regulated by the CDIC?
10. Explain how the Bank of Canada works with other central banks to affect exchange rates.

PROJECTS AND TEAMWORK APPLICATIONS

1. Collect current interest rates on the following types of bonds: Canada Savings Bonds, AAA-rated municipal bonds, AAA-rated corporate bonds, and BBB-rated corporate bonds. Arrange the interest rates from lowest to highest. Explain the reasons for the ranking.
2. You've probably heard of Canada Savings Bonds. You may even have received some bonds as a gift. What you may not know is that there are *two* different types of Canada Savings Bonds. Do some research and compare the two types of bonds. What are their features? What are their pros and cons? Which of the two bonds do you prefer?
3. Working with a partner, assume you are considering buying shares of RONA or the Home Depot. Describe how you would analyze the two companies' shares to decide which you would buy.
4. Working in a small team, identify a large bank. Visit that bank's website and look up its most recent financial statements. Compare the bank's financial statements to those of a nonfinancial company, such as a manufacturer or retailer. Report on your findings.
5. Assume you're investing money for retirement. What investment criteria are the most important to you? Go to the MSN Money website (http://money.msn.com). Click the "Tools" tab, and select "Fund Picks". Then use the filter on the right side of your screen to find funds that meets your criteria. Identify at least three mutual funds that most closely meet your criteria. Choose one of the funds and research it. Answer the following questions:
    a. What was the fund's average annual return for the past five years?
    b. How well did the fund perform relative to its peer group and relative to an index such as the S&P 500?
    c. What are the fund's 10 largest holdings?

WEB ASSIGNMENTS

1. **Online stock trading.** To learn more about online trading, visit the website of a brokerage firm that offers online trading, such as BMO InvestorLine (www.bmoinvestorline.com) or Scotia iTRADE (www.scotiaitrade.com). Most electronic brokerage firms also offer a trading demonstration. Use the demonstration to see how to obtain price information or company news, place buy or sell orders, and check account balances. Make some notes about your experience and bring them to class to participate in a class discussion.

2. **Banking statistics.** Visit the Bank of Canada web page listed below. Access the most recent year you can find and answer the following questions:

    a. How many commercial banks were operating at the end of the year? How many credit unions were operating?

    b. What were the total assets of commercial banks and credit unions at the end of the year?

    c. How many commercial banks had assets greater than $2 billion at the end of the year? How many commercial banks had assets of less than $300 million at the end of the year? www.bankofcanada.ca/publications/bfs/?page_moved=1.

3. **The Bank of Canada.** Go to the website of the Bank of Canada (www.bankofcanada.ca). Locate information on the Bank of Canada's board of directors. Prepare a short report on the 14-member board. Who are the current members? What are their backgrounds? When were they appointed? When do their terms expire?

Note: Internet Web addresses change frequently. If you don't find the exact sites listed, you may need to access the organization's home page and search from there or use a search engine such as Bing or Google.

17 | FINANCIAL MANAGEMENT

LEARNING OBJECTIVES

LO 17.1 Explain the role of financial managers.

LO 17.2 Describe the parts of a financial plan and the financial planning process.

LO 17.3 Outline how organizations manage their assets.

LO 17.4 Discuss the two major sources of funds for a business and capital structure.

LO 17.5 Identify sources of short-term financing for businesses.

LO 17.6 Discuss long-term financing options.

LO 17.7 Describe mergers, acquisitions, buyouts, and divestitures.

INSIDE BUSINESS

The Wooing of Ratiopharm

Nearly all Canadians know that it is cheaper to buy a generic drug—an over-the-counter drug such as ibuprofen—than the brand-name version, such as Aleve or Advil. Pharmaceutical companies know this, too. Canadian patents on brand-name drugs expire after 20 years. After a patent runs out, a drug company loses its exclusive right to manufacture the brand-name version of the product it has spent time, research, and money to develop. As patents have expired, generic-drug companies have opened all over the world, from Germany to India. The result has been a huge growth in the pharmaceutical industry. Apotex Inc. is Canada's largest generic-drug manufacturer. Every year it produces more than 300 generic pharmaceuticals for more than 85 million individual prescriptions.

Many big pharmaceutical companies have expanded by buying manufacturers of generic drugs. The decision to buy another firm can be difficult. Financial managers need to carefully forecast the expected increase in profits and then weigh that benefit against the costs of acquisition. But these forecasts are not certain, and success is never guaranteed.

In one recent case, several companies wanted to buy a generic-drug maker. They were like gentlemen suitors presenting themselves to an attractive potential bride. In a modern, electronic twist, their courtship was concluded in less than three months. Ratiopharm, based in Ulm, Germany, is one of the world's five largest producers of generic drugs. It specializes in drugs that treat cardiovascular and respiratory disorders, diseases of the central nervous system, and other illnesses. It also deals with medicines that prevent infections. When the family that owned Ratiopharm announced the company was up for sale, several big pharmaceutical firms were interested. That list was then narrowed down to three: Pfizer Inc., based in New York City; Teva Pharmaceutical Industries of Israel; and Actavis of Iceland.

Ratiopharm was especially attractive because Germans buy more generic drugs than other Europeans, and Ratiopharm was the second-biggest seller of generics in Germany. The companies sent their executives to Ulm to explain why Ratiopharm should accept their offer. Some analysts thought that Ratiopharm's decision would depend on which company promised to keep the greatest number of jobs at Ratiopharm.

Pfizer or its subsidiaries manufacture over-the-counter brands from Advil and ChapStick to Centrum vitamins and Robitussin; prescription drugs for women's health, cardiovascular disease, and cancer; and veterinary medicines. One analyst suggested that buying Ratiopharm would help Pfizer move its brand-name products into the worldwide generic market when their patents expire. It would also allow Pfizer to expand into developing markets. Pfizer's bid for Ratiopharm was €3 billion (almost $4 billion). After Pfizer's presentation, Ratiopharm's management wrote a letter to the company's employees, saying "The bidder emphasized the high efficiency of Ratiopharm's domestic and foreign production sites and told the meeting it was ready to make investments in Ulm."

Teva was already the world's largest producer of generic pharmaceuticals. Acquiring Ratiopharm would make Teva the leading generic-drug maker in Europe and the second-biggest in Germany. According to one analyst, Teva aimed to preserve both Ratiopharm's workforce and its locations in Germany. Teva offered €3.63 billion ($4.7 billion).

The Icelandic company Actavis had about 10,000 employees in 40 countries, making it about the same size as Ratiopharm. It also had about the same sales figures as Ratiopharm. Despite being heavily in debt, Actavis made an offer of about €3.32 billion ($4.37 billion).

Analysts had predicted that Ratiopharm would not make a decision quickly, but Teva soon made an announcement. It would acquire Ratiopharm for €3.63 billion. Shlomo Yani, Teva's president and CEO, announced that Ratiopharm would strengthen Teva's presence "in key European markets, most notably in Germany, as well as rapidly growing generic markets such as Spain, Italy and France."[1]

CHAPTER 17 OVERVIEW

Previous chapters discussed two basic functions that a business must perform. First, the company must produce a good or service or contract with suppliers to produce a good or service. Second, the firm must market its good or service to prospective customers. This chapter introduces a third, equally important function: A company's managers must ensure that the company has enough money to perform its other tasks successfully, in both the present and the future, and that these funds are invested properly. The company must have enough funds to buy materials, equipment, and other assets; pay bills; and compensate employees. This third business function is **finance**—planning, obtaining, and managing the company's funds to accomplish its objectives as effectively and efficiently as possible.

An organization's financial objectives include meeting expenses, investing in assets, and maximizing its overall worth, which is often measured by the value of the firm's common shares. Financial managers are responsible for meeting expenses, investing in assets, and increasing profits to shareholders. Solid financial management is critical to the success of a business. You can look at the news any day and find examples of firms that may have offered good products to the marketplace but failed because funds were improperly managed.

This chapter focuses on the finance function of organizations. It begins by describing the role of financial managers, their place in the organizational hierarchy, and the increasing importance of finance. Next, we outline the financial planning process and the parts of a financial plan. Then the discussion focuses on how organizations manage assets as efficiently and effectively as possible. We compare the two major sources of funds: debt and equity. Next, we introduce the concept of leverage. The major sources of short-term and long-term funding are described in the following sections. A description of mergers, acquisitions, buyouts, and divestitures concludes the chapter.

finance the business function of planning, obtaining, and managing the company's funds to accomplish its objectives as effectively and efficiently as possible.

LO 17.1 Explain the role of financial managers.

THE ROLE OF THE FINANCIAL MANAGER

Organizations face intense pressures today. As a result, organizations need to measure and reduce the costs of their business operations. They also need to maximize their revenues and profits. **Financial managers** are the executives who develop and carry out their firm's financial plan and decide on the most appropriate sources and uses of funds. They are among the most vital people on the corporate payroll.

Figure 17.1 shows the finance function of a typical company. At the top is the chief executive officer (CEO). The chief financial officer (CFO) usually reports directly to the company's CEO or chief operating officer (COO). In some companies, the CFO is also a member of the board of directors. In the case of the software maker Oracle, both the current CFO and the former CFO serve on that company's board; the former CFO chairs the board. Moreover, CFOs often serve as independent directors on other firms' boards, such as TELUS, Tim Hortons, or Microsoft. As noted in Chapter 15, the CFO and the firm's CEO must both certify the accuracy of the firm's financial statements.

Three senior managers often report directly to the CFO. The titles can vary, but these three executives are commonly called the *vice-president of financial management* (or *planning*), the *treasurer*, and the *controller*. The vice-president of financial management or planning is responsible for preparing financial forecasts and analyzing major investment decisions related to new

financial managers the executives who develop and carry out their firm's financial plan and decide on the most appropriate sources and uses of funds.

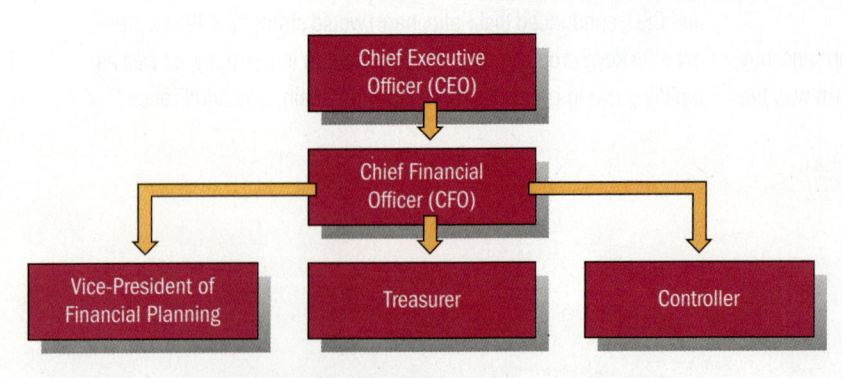

FIGURE 17.1 The Finance Organization at a Typical Firm

```
            Chief Executive
             Officer (CEO)
                   |
            Chief Financial
             Officer (CFO)
          /        |        \
Vice-President of  Treasurer  Controller
Financial Planning
```

products, new production facilities, and acquisitions. The treasurer is responsible for all of the company's financing activities, including cash management, tax planning and preparation, and shareholder relations. The treasurer also works on the sale of new security issues to investors. The controller is the chief accounting manager. The controller's functions include keeping the company's books, preparing financial statements, and conducting internal audits. The "Hit & Miss" feature explains the increasing importance of financially sound IT management.

The growing importance of financial professionals is reflected in the number of CEOs who have been promoted from financial positions. For example, Indra Nooyi, CEO of PepsiCo, and Jim Marsh, CEO of the British telecommunications company Cable and Wireless, both served as their firm's CFO prior to assuming the top job. The importance of finance professionals is also reflected in CFOs' salaries. A survey by the executive compensation consulting firm Equilar found the median annual salary for CFOs of *Fortune* 500 companies to be around $3.76 million.[2] The CFO of the investment firm Berkshire Hathaway is actually paid more than the company's famous chairperson, Warren Buffett.[3]

In their jobs, financial professionals continually balance risks with expected financial returns. *Risk* is the uncertainty of gain or loss; *return* is the gain or loss that results from an investment over a specified period of time. Financial managers try to maximize the wealth of their firm's shareholders by striking the right balance between risk and return. This balance is called the

The importance of financial professionals is reflected in the growing number of CEOs who have been promoted from financial positions. Indra Nooyi, CEO of PepsiCo, served as CFO prior to assuming the top job.

HIT & MISS

Apptio Calculates the Cost of Information Technology

Software as a service (SaaS) is growing. Many companies are making the change to cloud computing to save money and increase efficiency. But is cloud computing always more economical and efficient? Until recently, there was no reliable way to find out.

Apptio provides hosted Internet technology solutions, including its Technology Business Management package. Recently, Apptio introduced its new Cost Transparency Template. This template generates formulas a company can use to calculate how much more—or less—it would cost to invest in cloud computing compared with other options, including traditional in-house hardware and storage. Among Apptio's clients are BNP Paribas, Starbucks, Hallmark, and Expedia. Jeff Day, Apptio's director of marketing, says "We see that cloud computing is going to change the way IT leaders think about how they manage IT."

Saint Luke's Health System has 1,200 doctors among its 9,000 employees in 11 hospitals. The chief information officer, Debe Gash, wanted to get rid of all nonessential IT-related costs. A spending-analytics tool from Apptio helped Gash and her team save millions of dollars. The tool works by highlighting unnecessary or duplicate spending. For example, Saint Luke's had too many desktop software licences, two full-time employees who dealt only with spam management, and large expenses related to electronic storage. Those expenses were reduced or eliminated, and funds are now redirected to pay for needed programs, such as electronic health records. "We were surprised at the efficiencies we were able to derive from getting those insights," Gash said.

In the future, IT managers will need to understand how the cloud works and whether it will be more cost effective than other in-house or external systems. Day says, "The greatest inhibitor of the cloud is a lack of understanding. IT leaders need better systems and tools to perform accurate analysis."

Questions for Critical Thinking

1. Why have companies recently become so concerned with cost management?
2. Why might it be difficult for very large companies to keep accurate account of spending on such items as computer hardware and software licences?

Sources: Apptio, accessed June 24, 2010, www.apptio.com; Denise Dubie, "IT Cost Management and the Cloud," *Network World*, April 13, 2010, www.networkworld.com; Bob Evans, "Global CIO: St. Luke's CIO Saves Millions with Apptio's Help," *InformationWeek*, April 6, 2010, www.informationweek.com; Brian Carlson, "Top 5 Financial Management Predictions for 2010," *CIO*, February 2, 2010, www.cio.com.

risk–return tradeoff the process of maximizing the wealth of the firm's shareholders by striking the right balance between risk and return.

risk–return tradeoff. For example, a firm that relies heavily on borrowed funds may increase the return (in the form of cash) to shareholders. But the more money a firm borrows, the greater the risks to shareholders. An increase in a firm's cash on hand reduces the risk of being unable to meet unexpected cash needs. But cash alone does not earn much, if any, return. Firms that fail to invest their surplus funds in an income-earning asset—such as in securities—reduce their potential return or profitability. This chapter provides many examples of the risk–return tradeoff.

Every financial manager must balance risks and returns. For example, in the late 1990s Airbus had to make a major decision: whether to begin development and production of the giant A380 jetliner, the world's largest jetliner. The development costs for the aircraft were first estimated at more than $10 billion. But before committing to such a huge investment, financial managers weighed the potential profits of the A380 against the risks of investing in the aircraft's development. Airbus's future was on the line. It decided to go ahead with the development of the A380. The company spent more than $15 billion on research and development. The A380 entered commercial service a few years ago. Airbus currently has orders for approximately 318 A380 jetliners at a list price of more than $359 million each. The Airbus A380 has been a success thus far with more than 151,000 revenue flights and an average daily utilization greater than 13 hours.[4]

Financial managers must also adapt to changes in the financial system. The recent credit crisis has made it more difficult for some companies to borrow money from traditional lenders like banks. As a result, many firms have scaled back their expansion plans or are looking for funding from other sources, such as commercial financing companies. Financial managers must also adapt to internal changes.

✓ ASSESSMENT CHECK

17.1.1 What is the structure of the finance function at the typical firm?

17.1.2 Explain the risk–return tradeoff.

LO 17.2 Describe the parts of a financial plan and the financial planning process.

FINANCIAL PLANNING

Financial managers develop their organization's **financial plan**, a document that specifies the funds needed by a firm for a given period of time, the timing of cash inflows and outflows, and the most appropriate sources and uses of funds. *Operating plans* are short-term financial plans that focus on no more than a year or two in the future. *Strategic plans* are financial plans that have a much longer time horizon, up to five or ten years.

A financial plan is based on forecasts of several items: production costs, purchasing needs, plant and equipment expenses, and sales activities for the period covered. Financial managers use forecasts to decide on the specific amounts needed and the timing of expenses and receipts. They build a financial plan based on the answers to three questions:

1. What funds will the firm require during the planning period?
2. When will the firm need additional funds?
3. Where will the firm obtain the necessary funds?

financial plan a document that specifies the funds needed by a firm for a period of time, the timing of cash inflows and outflows, and the most appropriate sources and uses of funds.

Some funds flow into the firm when it sells its goods or services, but funding needs vary. The financial plan must reflect both the amounts and timing of inflows and outflows of funds. Even a profitable firm may face financial difficulties when it needs funds but sales are slow, when the volume of its credit sales increases, or when customers are slow in making payments.

In general, preparing a financial plan consists of three steps. The first step is a forecast of sales or revenue over some future time period. This projection is the key variable in any financial plan: without an accurate sales forecast, the firm will have difficulty accurately estimating other variables, such as production costs and purchasing needs. The best way to forecast sales depends on the type of business. For example, a retailer's CFO might begin by looking at the current sales per store. The CFO would look at the near future, including expected sales growth and any planned store openings or closings. This information can provide a forecast of sales for the next period.

If the company sells merchandise through other channels, such as online, the forecast is adjusted to include those additional channels.

Next, the CFO uses the sales forecast to decide on the expected level of profits for future periods. This longer-term projection involves estimating expenses such as purchases, employee compensation, and taxes. Many expenses are the result of sales. For example, the more a firm sells, generally the more it purchases. The CFO should also decide what portion of these profits will likely be paid to shareholders in the form of cash dividends.

After coming up with the sales and profit forecast, the CFO then needs to estimate how many additional assets the firm will need to support the projected sales. For example, an increase in sales might mean the company needs additional inventory, faster collection of accounts receivable, or even a new plant and equipment. Depending on the type of industry, some businesses need more assets than other businesses to support the same amount of sales. The technical term for this greater requirement is *asset intensity*. For example, the chemical manufacturer DuPont has approximately $4.98 in assets for every dollar in sales. In other words, for every $100 increase in sales, the firm needs about $498 of additional assets. The warehouse retailer Costco is less asset intensive. It needs only about $0.29 in assets for every dollar in sales. In other words, Costco would need an additional $29 of assets for every $100 of additional sales. This difference is not surprising; manufacturing is a more asset-intensive business than retailing.

Costco's *asset intensity* is lower than that of a typical manufacturing business.

A simplified financial plan illustrates these steps. Assume a growing company is forecasting that sales next year will increase by $40 million to $140 million. After estimating the company's expenses, the CFO believes that after-tax profits next year will be $12 million, and the firm will pay nothing in dividends. The projected increase in next year's sales will require the firm to invest another $20 million in assets. Because increases in assets represent a use of funds, the company will need an additional $20 million in funds. The company's after-tax earnings will contribute $12 million, and the remaining $8 million must come from outside sources. The financial plan tells the CFO how much money will be needed and when it will be needed. Using this knowledge, and knowing that the firm has decided to borrow the needed funds, the CFO can then begin negotiations with banks and other lenders.

The cash inflows and outflows of a business are similar to the cash inflows and outflows of a household. The members of a household depend on weekly or monthly paycheques for funds, but their expenses may vary greatly from one pay period to the next. The financial plan should indicate the amount and timing of funds flowing into and out of the organization. One of the largest business expenses is employee compensation.

A good financial plan also includes financial control. Financial control is a process of comparing actual revenues, costs, and expenses with the forecasted amounts. This comparison may show differences between projected and actual figures. It is important to discover any differences early so quick action can be taken.

Bill Morrison is the CFO of GENCO Marketplace, a business that liquidates, or sells off, other companies' excess inventory. GENCO buys inventory that is not selling well, then resells the inventory to wholesalers. In turn, the wholesalers sell the inventory to discount retailers. GENCO is

> **ASSESSMENT CHECK**
>
> 17.2.1 What three questions does a financial plan address?
>
> 17.2.2 Explain the steps involved in preparing a financial plan.

always careful about the cost of freight, including fuel, because GENCO pays the transportation costs of taking the goods from their current location to where they will be liquidated. Some excess inventory is seasonal. For example, when a retailer has winter coats left over in June, GENCO will buy those coats, hold them in inventory, and sell them to a wholesaler in the fall when demand for winter coats increases. But the longer a product remains unsold, the harder it is to liquidate, even at a deep discount. In all cases, Morrison or members of his team need to prepare a financial plan that takes into account both the benefits and risks of buying the merchandise.[5]

> **LO 17.3** Outline how organizations manage their assets.

MANAGING ASSETS

As noted in Chapter 15, assets consist of what a firm owns. But assets also represent uses of funds. To grow and prosper, companies need to obtain additional assets. Sound financial management requires assets to be acquired and managed as effectively and efficiently as possible. The "Career Kickstart" feature offers tips for managing assets.

Short-Term Assets

Short-term assets are also called current assets. These assets consist of cash and assets that can be or are expected to be converted into cash within a year. The major current assets are cash, marketable securities, accounts receivable, and inventory.

Cash and Marketable Securities

The major purpose of cash is to pay for day-to-day expenses. It is similar to individuals who keep a balance in their chequing accounts to pay bills or buy food and clothing. Most organizations try to keep a minimum cash balance so they have funds available for unexpected expenses. As noted earlier, cash earns little if any return; most firms invest their excess cash in *marketable securities*. These are low-risk securities that either have short maturities or can be easily sold in secondary

---

CAREER KICKSTART

Tips for Managing Assets

These are challenging times for all businesses, whether one-person startups or large corporations. One of the most difficult problems is controlling costs. Here are some tips for managing assets—physical, financial, and human—while focusing on both short-term demands and long-term planning:

1. *Define your goals and objectives.* Be realistic when working out the resources you will need to meet both your immediate needs and your long-term plans. If you need to borrow money, be aware that credit is currently very tight and can be difficult to access.

2. *Examine your expenses.* You may find some areas where you can reduce or eliminate unnecessary expenditures, such as travel or discretionary spending. Which makes more financial sense for your company—cloud computing or traditional hardware and storage?

3. *Communicate with all your associates.* Be sure that your employees, suppliers, and clients know what is happening with your business. When people hear nothing, especially during difficult times, they often assume the worst has happened.

4. *Cultivate your human assets.* Identify your valued employees and let them know that they are important to the business. In difficult times, companies often try to hire talented personnel from their competitors. Again, communication is important. If your best employees hear nothing from you, they may also assume the worst has happened—and they may be more willing to leave for what may seem to be better opportunities elsewhere.

5. *Have at least one backup plan.* Your goals and objectives may not work out the way you expected them to. You may plan for a certain amount of receivables, but they may suddenly decrease. If possible, keep sufficient financial reserves available to see the company through the unexpected. That way, you may be able to turn disaster to your advantage.

Sources: "Managing Assets in Volatile Times: Nine Ways CFOs Can Adapt to Changing Financial Markets," Deloitte, accessed June 24, 2010, www.deloitte.com; Fred Jennings and R. W. Beck, "Leveraging Enterprise Value with Asset Management," *Utility Products*, January 14, 2010, www.elp.com; Daniel Solin, "Seven Shocking Tips to Boost Your Returns by 400% (or More)," *DailyFinance*, January 1, 2010, www.dailyfinance.com.

markets. Money market instruments (described in Chapter 16) are popular choices for firms that have excess cash. The cash budget, which we discussed and illustrated in Chapter 15, is one tool for managing cash and marketable securities. The cash budget shows expected cash inflows and outflows for a period of time. The cash budget shows which months the firm will have surplus cash and will be able to invest in marketable securities and which months it will need additional cash.

Critics of some companies' budgeting practices argue that some firms hoard cash. Recently, Cisco Systems had more than $35 billion in cash and marketable securities. But firms may have good reasons for holding large amounts of cash and marketable securities. For example, they may be planning to use these funds soon to make a large investment, pay dividends to shareholders, or repurchase outstanding bonds.

Accounts Receivable

Accounts receivable are uncollected credit sales. They can represent a significant asset. The financial manager's job is to collect the funds owed to the firm as quickly as possible while still offering sufficient credit to customers to attract and generate increased sales. In general, a more liberal credit policy means higher sales but also increased collection expenses, higher levels of bad debt, and a higher investment in accounts receivable.

Management of accounts receivable is composed of two functions: deciding on an overall credit policy and deciding which customers will be offered credit. Formulating a credit policy involves deciding whether the firm will offer credit and, if so, what terms of credit to offer. For example, will a discount be offered to customers who pay in cash? The overall credit policy is often the result of competitive pressures or general industry practices. If all your competitors offer their customers credit, your firm will likely also need to offer credit. The second aspect of a credit policy is deciding which customers will be offered credit. Managers must consider the importance of the customer and the customer's financial health and repayment history.

One simple tool for assessing how well receivables are being managed is to calculate the accounts receivable turnover over two or more time periods in a row. We showed how this ratio is calculated in Chapter 15. If the receivables turnover shows signs of slowing, it means that, on average, credit customers are paying later. This trend may need further investigation.

Inventory Management

For many firms, like retailers, inventory represents the largest single asset. For example, at the home furnishings retailer Bed Bath & Beyond, inventory makes up about 49 percent of total assets. Even for nonretailers inventory is an important asset. At the heavy-equipment manufacturer

At Bed Bath & Beyond, inventory is the most valuable asset. Managing inventory can be a costly and highly complicated task, especially for retailers.

Caterpillar, inventory is almost 12 percent of total assets. On the other hand, some types of firms, such as electric utilities and transportation companies, have no inventory. Most firms carry inventory, and their proper management of inventory is vital to the business's success.

Managing inventory can be complicated. The cost of inventory includes more than just the cost of acquiring goods. It also includes the costs of ordering, storing, insuring, and financing inventory. In addition, businesses take on the costs of stockouts and the costs of lost sales due to insufficient inventory. Financial managers try to minimize the cost of inventory. But production, marketing, and logistics also play important roles in determining proper inventory levels. The production considerations of inventory management were discussed in Chapter 10. In Chapter 12, we outlined the marketing and logistics issues surrounding inventory.

Trends in the inventory turnover ratio (described in Chapter 15) can be early warning signs of difficulties ahead. For example, when inventory turnover has been slowing for several quarters in a row, inventory is rising faster than sales. This situation may suggest that customer demand is slowing. The firm may need to take action, such as reducing production or increasing promotional efforts.

Capital Investment Analysis

In addition to current assets, firms also invest in long-lived assets. Unlike current assets, long-lived assets are expected to produce economic benefits for more than one year. These investments often involve large amounts of money. For example, as noted earlier in the chapter, Airbus invested more than $15 billion in development of the A380. In another example, Target Corporation commenced its expansion into Canada, buying out the store leases of 220 Zellers stores for $1.83 billion. Target invested over $10 million per store in long-lived assets to support the opening of the 133 stores that it opened.[6]

Capital investment analysis is the process financial managers use when deciding whether to invest in long-lived assets. Firms make two basic types of capital investment decisions: expansion and replacement. The A380 and Target investments are examples of expansion decisions. Replacement decisions involve upgrading assets by substituting new assets for older assets. A retailer like Walmart might decide to replace an old store with a new Supercentre, as it did in Concord, Ontario. Walmart Canada also plans to increase to 395 stores in the near future, spending some $500 million on remodelling, expansion, moving, and adding additional locations.[7]

Financial managers must estimate all the costs and benefits of a proposed investment. This task can be very difficult, especially for extremely long-lived investments. Companies should only pursue those investments that offer an acceptable return—measured by the difference between benefits and costs. Target's financial managers believed that the benefits of expanding into Canada outweighed the high cost. The expansion would allow Target to begin an international strategic expansion project. When deciding whether to expand into Canada, Target's financial managers would have considered the expected profit and the strategic benefits from the expansion. Despite aggressive attempts to win customers, Target's Canadian operations resulted in a loss of $941 million before interest and taxes, likely leading to the replacement of its Canadian president Tony Fisher in the same year that Target's CEO Gregg Steinhafel was replaced by the board after a devastating data breach. However, despite Target's aggressive capital expenditures it was still forced to discontinue operations less than two years after entering the Canadian market as it overestimated the expected profits that its Canadian operations would generate.[8]

Managing International Assets

Today, firms often have assets worldwide. Air Canada generates more than half of its annual sales outside of Canada.[9] Most sales for Unilever and Nestlé occur outside their home countries (the Netherlands and Switzerland, respectively). Managing international assets creates several challenges for financial managers. One of the most important challenges is dealing with exchange rates.

As we discussed in several other chapters, an exchange rate is the rate at which one currency can be exchanged for another currency. Exchange rates can vary widely from year to year, which creates a problem for any company that has international assets. For example, assume a Canadian firm has a major subsidiary in the United Kingdom. Assume that the U.K. subsidiary earns an annual profit of £750 million. Over the past five years, the exchange rate between the Canadian dollar and the British pound has varied between 2.061 (dollars per pound) and 1.5353.[10] This means the dollar value of the U.K. profits ranged from $1.55 billion to $1.15 billion.

Many global firms are involved in activities that reduce the risks associated with exchange rate ups and downs. Some of these activities are complicated, but if done correctly they can reduce or even eliminate the risks associated with changes in the value of foreign currencies. Reducing the risks of exchange rate fluctuations will improve the financial performance of the firm, which can have a positive impact on its share price.

ASSESSMENT CHECK

17.3.1 Why do firms often choose to invest excess cash in marketable securities?

17.3.2 What are the two aspects of accounts receivable management?

17.3.3 Explain the difference between an expansion decision and a replacement decision.

SOURCES OF FUNDS AND CAPITAL STRUCTURE

LO 17.4 Discuss the two major sources of funds for a business and capital structure.

The use of debt for financing can increase both the potential for return and the potential for loss. Recall the accounting equation introduced in Chapter 15:

$$\text{Assets} = \text{Liabilities} + \text{Owners' Equity}$$

When this equation is viewed from a financial management perspective, it shows that there are only two types of funding: debt and equity. *Debt capital* consists of funds obtained through borrowing. *Equity capital* consists of funds provided by the firm's owners when they reinvest their earnings, make additional contributions, liquidate assets, issue shares to the general public, or raise capital from outside investors. The mix of a firm's debt and equity capital is known as its **capital structure**.

capital structure the mix of a firm's debt and equity capital.

Companies often take very different approaches to choosing a capital structure. As the company uses more debt, the risk to the company increases: The firm needs to make the interest payments on the money borrowed, regardless of the amount of cash flow coming into the company. Choosing more debt increases the fixed costs a company must pay, which makes a company more sensitive to any change in sales revenues. Debt is frequently the least costly method of raising additional financing dollars, which is why it is so frequently used.

Different industries choose varying amounts of debt and equity to use when financing. Information provided by Datamonitor shows the automotive industry has debt ratios (the ratio of liabilities to assets) of more than 60 percent for both Toyota and Honda and more than 85 percent for Ford. These companies are primarily using debt to finance their asset expenses. Companies such as McDonald's and Starbucks use only 57 percent debt and 61 percent debt, respectively. The mixture of debt and equity a company uses is a major management decision.[11]

Leverage and Capital Structure Decisions

Raising needed cash by borrowing allows a firm to benefit from the principle of **leverage**, increasing the rate of return on funds invested by borrowing funds. The key to managing leverage is to ensure that a company's earnings remain larger than its interest payments, which increases the leverage on the rate of return on shareholders' investment. Of course, if the company earns less than its interest payments, shareholders lose money on their original investments.

Figure 17.2 shows the relationship between earnings and shareholder returns for two identical imaginary firms that choose to raise funds in different ways. Leverage Company obtains 50 percent of its funds from lenders who purchase company bonds. Leverage Company pays 10 percent interest on its bonds. Equity Company raises all of its funds through sales of company stock.

leverage increasing the rate of return on funds invested by borrowing funds.

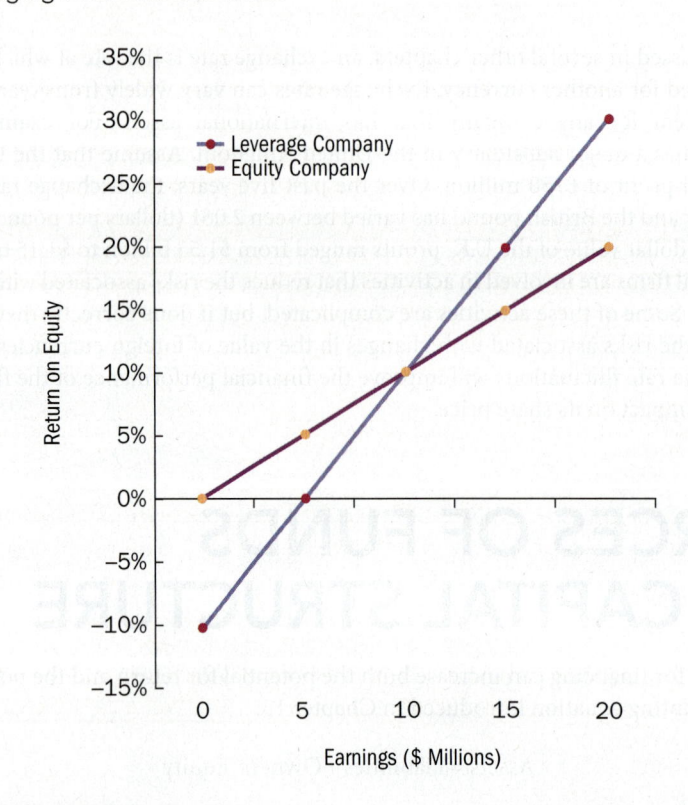

FIGURE 17.2 How Leverage Works

Note: The example assumes that both companies have $100 million in capital. Leverage Company consists of $50 million in equity and $50 million in bonds (with an interest rate of 10 percent). Equity Company consists of $100 million in equity and no bonds. This example also assumes no corporate taxes.

Notice that if earnings double, from $10 million to $20 million, the returns to the shareholders of Equity Company also double—from 10 percent to 20 percent. But returns to shareholders of Leverage Company more than double—from 10 percent to 30 percent. But leverage can also work in the opposite direction. If earnings fall from $10 million to $5 million (a decline of 50 percent), returns to shareholders of Equity Company also fall by 50 percent—from 10 percent to 5 percent. By contrast, returns to shareholders of Leverage Company fall from 10 percent to zero. Thus, leverage increases potential returns to shareholders but also increases risk.

Another problem with borrowing money is that relying too much on borrowed funds may reduce management's flexibility in future financing decisions. If a company raises equity capital this year and needs to raise funds next year, it will probably be able to raise either debt or equity capital. But if it raises debt capital this year, it may be forced to raise equity capital next year.

Equity capital also has downsides. Because shareholders are owners of the company, they usually elect the board of directors and vote on major company issues. But when new equity is sold, the control of the existing shareholders is weakened and the outcome of these votes could potentially change. One sensitive subject today between companies and shareholders is whether shareholders should be able to vote on executive pay packages. The "Solving an Ethical Controversy" feature discusses this issue.

Another downside of equity capital is that it is more expensive than debt capital. First, creditors have a senior claim to the assets of a firm before the shareholders' claims. Because of this advantage, creditors will accept a lower rate of return than shareholders will. Second, the firm can deduct interest payments on debt, reducing its taxable income and its tax bill. In contrast, dividends paid to shareholders are not tax deductible. A key part of the financial manager's job is to weigh the upsides and downsides of debt capital and equity capital, and then create the most suitable capital structure for the firm.

SOLVING AN ETHICAL CONTROVERSY

Executive Pay: Should Shareholders Decide the Salaries of CEOs?

While the world was suffering through the recent financial crisis and its aftermath, the news media were reporting on the huge salaries of CEOs and other top executives at large corporations.

At a Royal Dutch Shell annual meeting, shareholders voted down a proposed executive compensation package. In response, the company announced it would freeze executive pay and base its bonuses on performance. The new CEO received a salary 20 percent lower than that of the previous CEO. The company said that the changes would "demonstrate appropriate restraint in the current economic environment." "Say-on-pay" voting by shareholders has become increasingly common—and controversial.

Should company shareholders help decide how much top executives are paid?

PRO

1. Publicly held corporations are owned by their shareholders, who should have the opportunity to vote on compensation for top executives. Robert E. Denham and Rajiv L. Gupta, co-chairs of the Conference Board's Task Force on Executive Compensation, said "Shareholders . . . and the public deserve to see executive compensation programs that serve shareholders' interests and are explained to shareholders."
2. Some analysts believe that lopsided pay structures played a role in the financial crisis in the United States. Federal Reserve Chair Ben Bernanke said "Compensation practices at some banking organizations have led to misaligned incentives and excessive risk-taking."

CON

1. Shareholders may not necessarily know what appropriate pay is. Many do not have the time or resources to do their own analysis and to judge whether a pay program is suitable or whether it promotes a risk-taking, get-rich-quick mentality in executives.
2. Shareholders recently turned down the chance to vote on executive pay at companies such as Johnson & Johnson and Dow Chemical. Many shareholders prefer to discuss pay structures with management and board members before voting.

Summary

The Ontario Securities Commission has long been considering making it a requirement for companies to give shareholders a say on executive compensation. This approach would begin to position Canada in line with many European countries and in the direction of the United States, where "say-on-pay" regulations are either currently in place or are in the planning stage.

Sources: Alix Stuart, "Reform Bill Mandates Say on Pay," CFO.com, June 29, 2010, www.cfo.com; Jim Kuhnhenn and Alan Fram, "Congress Agrees on Financial Oversight," *Philadelphia Inquirer*, June 26, 2010, www.philly.com; Ann Yerger, "Red Flags for Say-on-Pay Voting," Harvard Law School Forum on Corporate Governance and Financial Regulation, May 18, 2010, http://blogs.law.harvard.edu; A. G. Laffey, "Executive Pay: Time for CEOs to Take a Stand," Harvard Business Review, May 2010, http://hbr.org; Bryant Ruiz Switzky, "CEO Compensation Down in 2009," Washington Business Journal, May 7, 2010, http://washingtonbizjournals.com; "Shell Shareholder 'Rebellion' Leads to New Limits on Executive Pay, Bonuses," *Huffington Post*, February 26, 2010, www.huffingtonpost.com; Helen Coster, "The State of the CEO in 2010," *Forbes*, January 21, 2010, www.forbes.com; David R. Butcher, "Cracking Down on Excessive Executive Pay," IMT Industry Market Trends, October 29, 2009, http://news.thomasnet.com; Danielle Arbuckle, "Should Shareholders Have a Say on Executive Pay?" Wallet Pop, accessed August 2, 2011, www.walletpop.ca/blog/2011/01/19/should-shareholders-have-a-say-on-executive-pay/; Lexpert, "Executive Compensation: High Risk for the Status Quo," accessed August 21, 2014, www.lexpert.ca/magazine/article/executive-compensation-high-risk-for-the-status-quo-2567/.

Mixing Short-Term and Long-Term Funds

Financial managers face another decision: deciding on the suitable mix of short-term and long-term funds. Short-term funds consist of current liabilities; and long-term funds consist of long-term debt and equity. Short-term funds are generally less expensive than long-term funds, but they expose the firm to more risk. This risk occurs because short-term funds need to be renewed, or rolled over, frequently. Short-term interest rates can be unstable. For example, during a recent 12-month period, rates on commercial paper, a popular short-term financing option, ranged from a high of 4 percent to a low of less than 1 percent.[12]

Because short-term rates move up and down frequently, the interest expense on short-term funds can vary greatly from year to year. For example, if a firm borrows $50 million for 10 years at 5 percent interest, its annual interest expense is fixed at $2.5 million for the entire 10 years. On the other hand, if the firm borrows $50 million for one year at a rate of 4 percent, its annual interest expense of $2 million is fixed for only that year. If interest rates increase the following year to 6 percent, then $1 million will be added to the interest expense bill. Another potential risk of relying on short-term funds is availability. Even financially healthy firms can occasionally find it difficult to borrow money.

Because of the added risk of short-term funding, most firms choose to finance all of their long-term assets, and even a portion of their short-term assets, by using long-term funds. Johnson & Johnson is typical of this choice. **Figure 17.3** shows 2013 balance sheet data from the company that divides out the short-term and long-term assets, and the short-term and long-term funds.

Dividend Policy

In addition to decisions regarding capital structure and the mix of short-term and long-term funds, financial managers also make decisions regarding a firm's dividend policy. *Dividends* are periodic cash payments to shareholders. The most common type of dividend is paid quarterly and is often called a *regular dividend*. Occasionally, firms make one-time special dividend payments or extra dividend payments, as Microsoft did some years ago. Earnings that are paid in dividends are not reinvested in the firm and don't contribute additional equity capital.

Firms are under no legal obligation to pay dividends to shareholders. Although some companies pay generous dividends, others pay nothing. Until 2010, Starbucks never paid a dividend to its shareholders. In contrast, 3M has paid dividends for 30-plus consecutive years; during that time, the amount of the dividends has more than quadrupled. Companies that pay dividends try to increase the amount of dividends paid or, at the very least, hold the amount of the dividends steady from year to year. But in rare cases firms must cut or eliminate dividends. After the major oil spill in the Gulf of Mexico in 2010, BP announced it was cancelling dividend payments for the first quarter and suspending those payments to shareholders for the second and third quarters of their fiscal year.[13]

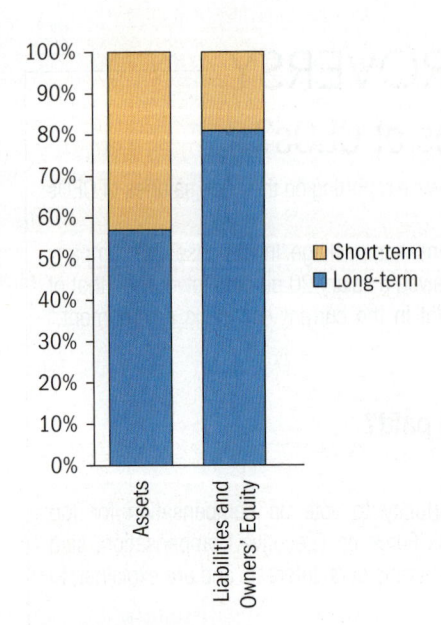

FIGURE 17.3 Johnson & Johnson's Mix of Short-Term and Long-Term Funds

Source: Data from Johnson & Johnson balance sheet, Yahoo! Finance, accessed August 15, 2014, http://finance.yahoo.com/q/bs?s=JNJ+Balance+Sheet&annual.

Attendees arrive for BP's 2011 annual general meeting—its first after the oil spill in the Gulf of Mexico in 2010. As a result of the oil spill, BP announced it was cancelling dividend payments for the first quarter and suspending them for the second and third quarters of its year.

Many factors are considered when deciding on a company's dividend policy. One factor is the firm's investment opportunities. Suppose a firm has numerous investment opportunities and wants to finance some or all of them through equity funding. It will likely pay little, if any, of its earnings in dividends. Shareholders may actually want the company to retain earnings, because if they are reinvested the firm's future profits, and the value of its shares, will increase faster. By contrast, a firm with more limited investment opportunities generally pays more of its earnings in dividends.

In addition to dividends, some firms buy back a portion of their outstanding shares. The Home Depot, for example, has repurchased more than $1 billion worth of shares over the past few years. Generally, shares are purchased on the secondary markets. The main purpose of share buybacks is to raise the market value of the remaining shares, which benefits the shareholders.

> **ASSESSMENT CHECK**
>
> 17.4.1 Explain the concept of leverage.
>
> 17.4.2 Why do firms generally rely more on long-term funds than short-term funds?
>
> 17.4.3 What is an important factor in deciding on a firm's dividend policy?

SHORT-TERM FUNDING OPTIONS

LO 17.5 Identify sources of short-term financing for businesses.

An organization may discover that its cash needs are greater than its available funds. Retailers generate surplus cash for most of the year, but they need to build up inventory during the late summer and fall to get ready for the holiday shopping season. They often need funds to pay for this merchandise until the holiday sales generate revenue. They can then use the incoming funds to repay the amount they borrowed. In this kind of situation, financial managers often look to short-term sources of funds. Short-term sources of funds are repaid within one year. The three major sources of short-term funds are trade credit, short-term loans, and commercial paper. Large firms often rely on a combination of all three sources of short-term financing.

Trade Credit

Trade credit is extended by suppliers when a firm receives goods or services and agrees to pay for them at a later date. Trade credit is common in many industries such as retailing and manufacturing. Suppliers ship billions of dollars of merchandise to retailers each day and are paid at a later date. Without trade credit, the retailing sector would probably look much different—with fewer selections. To record trade credit, the supplier enters the transactions as an account receivable, and the retailer enters it as an account payable. Canadian Tire Corporation currently has more than $1.8 billion of accounts payable on its books.[14] The main upside of trade credit is its easy availability. The main downside to trade credit is that the amount a company can borrow is limited to the amount it purchases.

What is the cost of trade credit? If suppliers do not offer a cash discount, trade credit is effectively free. For example, assume a supplier offers trade credit under the terms net 30. These terms mean that the buyer has 30 days to pay. In other words, companies are borrowing $100 and repaying $100 in 30 days. The effective rate of interest is zero. But some suppliers offer a discount if they are paid in cash. If a discount is offered, trade credit can get expensive. Assume that a 2 percent discount is offered to cash buyers. If buyers do not take the discount, they have 30 days to pay. If the buyer does not pay cash, the terms are the same as borrowing $98 today and repaying $100 in 30 days. The annual interest rate on such a loan is more than 24 percent.

Short-Term Loans

Loans from commercial banks are a significant source of short-term financing for businesses. Businesses often use these loans to finance inventory and accounts receivable. For example, a small manufacturer of ski equipment has its highest sales in late fall and early winter. To meet this demand, it begins building inventory during the summer. The manufacturer also needs to finance accounts receivable (credit sales to customers) during the fall and winter. It takes out a bank loan during the summer. As the inventory is sold and as accounts receivable are collected, the firm repays the loan.

Borrowers can choose from two types of short-term bank loans: lines of credit and revolving credit agreements. A line of credit specifies the maximum amount the firm can borrow over a period of time, usually a year. The bank is under no obligation to actually lend the money. It will lend the money, but only if funds are available. Most lines of credit require the borrower to repay the original amount, plus interest, within one year. In contrast, a revolving credit agreement is basically a guaranteed line of credit—the bank guarantees that the funds will be available when needed. Banks typically charge a fee on top of interest for revolving credit agreements.

The cash budget is an important tool when deciding on the size of a line of credit. The cash budget shows the months when additional financing will be needed or when borrowed funds can be repaid. For example, assume the ski manufacturer's cash budget indicates that it will need $2.5 million from June through November. The financial manager might set up a line of credit with the bank for $2.8 million. The extra $300,000 is added to cover any unexpected cash outflows.

Commercial finance companies also make short-term loans to businesses. Most bank loans are unsecured, which means that no specific assets are pledged as collateral, or security. Loans from commercial finance companies are often secured by using accounts receivable or inventory as collateral.

Factoring is another form of short-term financing that uses accounts receivable. The business sells its accounts receivable at a discount to either a bank or a finance company—which is called a *factor*. The cost of the transaction depends on the size of the discount. Factoring allows the firm to convert its receivables into cash quickly without worrying about collections.

The cost of short-term loans depends on the interest rate and the fees charged by the lender. Some lenders also require the borrower to keep *compensating balances*—5 to 20 percent of the outstanding loan amount—in a chequing account. Compensating balances increase the effective cost of a loan because the borrower does not have full use of the amount borrowed.

For example, suppose a firm borrows $100,000 for one year at 5 percent interest. The borrower will pay $5,000 in interest (5 percent × $100,000). If the lender requires that 10 percent of the loan amount be kept as compensating balance, the firm has use of only $90,000. But because the firm will still pay $5,000 in interest, the effective rate on the loan is actually 5.56 percent ($5,000/$90,000).

Commercial Paper

Commercial paper is a short-term IOU sold by a company; it was briefly described in Chapter 16. Commercial paper is usually sold in multiples of $100,000 to $1 million and has a maturity date that ranges from 1 to 270 days. Most commercial paper is unsecured. It is an attractive source of financing because large amounts of money can be raised at interest rates that are usually 1 to 2 percent less than the interest rates charged by banks. At the end of a recent year, almost $1.15 trillion in commercial paper was outstanding.[15] Although commercial paper is an attractive short-term financing option, only a small percentage of businesses can issue it. Access to the commercial paper market has traditionally been limited to large, financially strong corporations.

ASSESSMENT CHECK

17.5.1 What are the three sources of short-term funding?

17.5.2 Explain trade credit.

17.5.3 Why is commercial paper an attractive short-term financing option?

LO 17.6 Discuss long-term financing options.

SOURCES OF LONG-TERM FINANCING

Funds from short-term sources can help a firm meet its current needs for cash or inventory. But a larger project or plan, such as buying another company or investing in real estate or equipment, usually requires funds for a much longer period of time. Unlike short-term financing, long-term financing is repaid over many years.

Organizations acquire long-term financing from three sources. The first source is long-term loans from financial institutions such as commercial banks, life insurance companies, and pension funds. A second source is bonds—certificates of indebtedness—sold to investors. A third source is equity financing acquired by selling shares in the firm or reinvesting company profits. The "Going Green" feature describes how new investment vehicles are being created to reflect some investors' interests in corporate sustainability.

Going Green: A KNIGHT IN SHINING CAPITALISM

The words *clean* and *capitalism* are not often used together in the same sentence. Many think of capitalism in a negative sense. But can large corporate companies operate under the concept of "clean capitalism"?

Corporate Knights (CK) is a Toronto-based company that understands that many investors have changing objectives. CK publishes an annual "clean capitalism" report. It uses objective measures to assess the environmental, social, and governance (ESG) practices of some of Canada's largest companies. Executives, regulators, investors, and other stakeholders consult this $2,495 report to assess the sustainability practices of these companies. CK also publishes a list of the top 100 companies in the "Global 100 Most Sustainable Corporations in the World." Canadian companies that made the list for 2014 include Tim Hortons (#22), Bombardier Inc. (#24), Teck Resources Limited (#44), and Bank of Montreal (#49). Westpac Banking Corporation of Australia was ranked number one.

CK is currently developing a global collection of clean capitalism passive investments to help investors who want to invest in companies that practise clean capitalism.

CK is responding to investors who want to evaluate companies both on their financial performance and on their "extra-financial" performance, including activities that support the environment, labour, and human rights. The measurement of ESG practices by a single organization allows investors to compare various companies. Many believe that these extra-financial measures can significantly influence a company's long-term performance and affect its true overall value.

Questions for Critical Thinking

1. Why does "going green" make good business sense for large corporations?
2. How do ESG practices affect a company's market value and long-term financial potential?

Sources: Corporate Knights, "Clean Capitalism," accessed August 15, 2014, www.corporateknights.com/report/united-states-clean-capitalism-report-2012; "2012 Global 100 Most Sustainable Companies: The Full List," accessed March 6, 2012, www.global100.org/; Corporate Knights, "Toronto-Based Clean Capitalism Media Company Closes Investment Round to Launch Capital Markets Division," press release, November 16, 2011, accessed March 6, 2012, http://huffstrategy.com/MediaManager/release/Corporate-Knights/31-12-69/Toronto-based-clean-capitalism-media-company-closes-investment-ro/2386.html.

Public Sale of Shares and Bonds

Public sales of securities, such as shares and bonds, are a major source of funds for corporations. These sales provide cash inflows for the issuing firm and either a share in its ownership (for a share purchaser) or a specified rate of interest and repayment at a stated time (for a bond purchaser). Because many shares and bonds are traded in the secondary markets, shareholders and bondholders can easily sell these securities. During the recent European debt crisis there was a massive slowdown in European bond sales. During this time, foreigners flocked to Canadian bonds which had an AAA rating. This led to foreign sales of Canadian bonds reaching a record $16.7 billion in May 2012.[16] Public sales of securities can vary quite a bit from year to year depending on conditions in the financial markets. For example, bond sales tend to be higher when interest rates are low.

In Chapter 16, we discussed how most companies sell securities publicly through investment bankers using a process called *underwriting*. Investment bankers purchase the securities from the issuer and then resell them to investors. The issuer pays a fee to the investment banker, called an *underwriting discount*.

Private Placements

Some new share or bond issues are not sold publicly but are offered instead to a small group of major investors such as pension funds and insurance companies. These sales are referred to as *private placements*. Most private placements involve corporate debt issues. More than $120 billion in corporate bonds were sold privately in a recent year in the United States.[17]

It is often cheaper for a company to sell a security privately than publicly. Private placements are subject to fewer government regulations because registration with the Canadian Securities Administrators is not required. Institutional investors such as insurance companies and pension funds buy private placements because they typically carry slightly higher interest rates than publicly issued bonds. In addition, the terms of the issue can be designed to meet the specific needs of both the issuer and the institutional investors. Of course, the institutional investor gives up liquidity, or ease of cashability, because privately placed securities do not trade in secondary markets.

Venture Capitalists

Venture capitalists business firms or groups of individuals that invest in new and growing firms in exchange for an ownership share.

Venture capitalists are an important source of long-term financing, especially for new companies. **Venture capitalists** are business firms or groups of individuals that invest in new and growing firms in exchange for an ownership share. They typically raise money from wealthy individuals and institutional investors and invest these funds in promising firms. Venture capitalists also provide management consulting advice and funds. In exchange for their investment, venture capitalists become part owners of the business. If the business succeeds, venture capitalists can earn large profits.

One of Canada's largest venture capital firms is Covington Funds. Covington was established in 1994. It has invested in several sectors, including technology and health care. One of the many companies that Covington has invested in is Golf Town. Covington currently manages more than $300 million in assets.[18]

Private Equity Funds

Private equity funds are similar to venture capitalists. They are investment companies that raise funds from wealthy individuals and institutional investors. They then invest those funds in both public and privately held companies. Unlike venture capital funds, which tend to focus on small startup companies, private equity funds invest in all types of businesses, including mature companies. For example, Onex Corporation, a private equity fund, recently bought three of Boeing's parts manufacturing plants for $1.5 billion.[19] Often, private equity funds invest in transactions that take public companies private, also known as leveraged buyouts (LBOs). In these transactions, discussed in more detail in the next section, a public company reverts to private status. The "Hit & Miss" feature profiles another large private equity fund, Harvest Partners.

A variation of the private equity fund is the so-called *sovereign wealth fund*. Sovereign wealth funds are owned by governments. They invest in a variety of financial and real assets, such as real

HIT & MISS

Harvest Partners Grows Its Investments

Is it possible to have too much money to spend in too little time? Harvest Partners and other private equity firms had just a few years to invest about $500 billion.

Harvest Partners is a private equity firm that specializes in leveraged buyouts and growth financing. It focuses on companies in North America and Western Europe. The firm manages funds emphasizing private equity and debt investments. Harvest Partners makes equity investments of $50 million to $200 million in companies with revenues of between $100 million and $750 million. It prefers to be a control investor by becoming a partner in the companies it finances. Those companies tend to be middle-market firms that need investment to adapt to changing times and markets.

Private equity firms usually have three to six years to reinvest the funds they have raised from client investors. If they cannot or do not reinvest during that time, they must return the money. During the boom years, Harvest Partners raised $815 million from client investors. They had reinvested about $293 million. The firm then faced a deadline to reinvest the remaining $522 million.

Not all private equity investments are successful. Harvest Partners had owned the equity of the Natural Products Group (NPG), a manufacturer of organic shampoos and soaps. When NPG went bankrupt, Harvest Partners lost its entire investment.

Recently Harvest Partners joined MTP Energy Management to invest $80 million in Regency Energy Partners, a middle-market natural gas company. Michael DeFlorio is a senior managing director of Harvest Partners. He said that Regency "embodies our investment strategy focused on exceptionally managed . . . midstream service providers participating in the most promising resource plays in the industry."

Questions for Critical Thinking

1. Describe some of the risks faced by a firm like Harvest Partners.

2. Why do you think Harvest Partners and other equity firms are required to invest their clients' funds within a limited time?

Sources: Harvest Partners, accessed June 24, 2010, www.harvpart.com; "Harvest Partners," profile from *Bloomberg Businessweek*, accessed June 24, 2010, http://investing.businessweek.com; Julie Cresswell, "On Wall Street, So Much Cash, So Little Time," *New York Times*, June 23, 2010, www.nytimes.com; Emily Thornton, "LBO Firms Can't Spend $503 Billion as Deadlines Loom (Update 1)," Bloomberg.com, March 10, 2010, www.bloomberg.com; Brian Baxter, "The Bankruptcy Files: Curtain Drops on Movie Gallery, Air America Loses Frequency," *AM Law Daily*, February 4, 2010, http://amlawdailytypepad.com; "Harvest Partners, MTP Energy Invest in Regency Energy Partners," iStockAnalyst, September 7, 2009, www.istockanalyst.com; Find the Best, "Harvest Partners," accessed August 15, 2014, http://private-equity.findthebest.com/l/781/Harvest-Partners.

The television series *Dragons' Den* popularizes entrepreneurs and their search for long-term financing.

estate. Sovereign wealth funds generally make investments that are based on the best risk–return tradeoff. But their investment decisions are also influenced by political, social, and strategic considerations.

Chinese sovereign wealth funds have recently made several purchases in Canada. The China Investment Corporation made several large investments in major Canadian resource companies and the Alberta oil sands. PetroChina Company paid $5.44 billion for a 50 percent stake in Encana Corporation's natural gas assets in Western Canada. China Petrochemical Corporation paid $4.65 billion recently to buy a part of Syncrude Canada Ltd., a company that produces bitumen from Alberta oil sands projects.[20] The assets of the 10 largest sovereign wealth funds are shown in **Figure 17.4**. Together, these 10 funds have more than $5 trillion in assets.

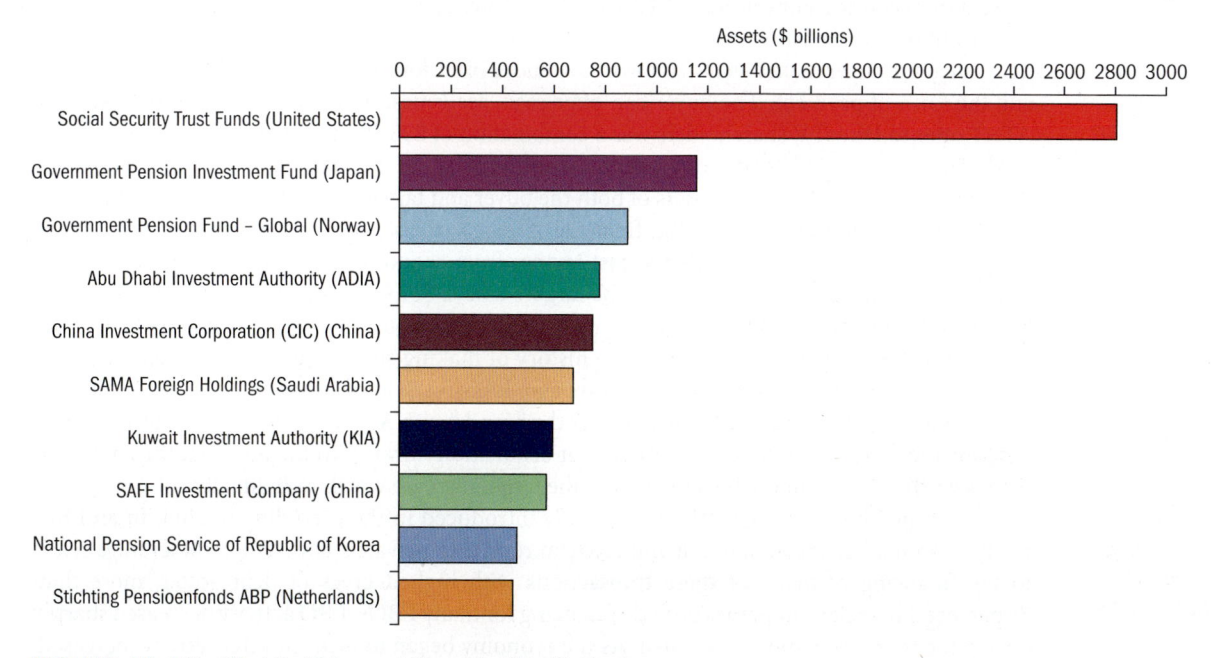

FIGURE 17.4 The World's 10 Largest Sovereign Wealth Funds

Source: Data from Sovereign Wealth Fund Institute, "Sovereign Wealth Fund Rankings," June 2015. Accessed August 20, 2015, www.swfinstitute.org/fund-rankings/.

Hedge Funds

Hedge funds are private investment companies that are available only to qualified large investors. In recent years, hedge funds have become a significant presence in Canadian financial markets, though they have the same relative representation in the United Kingdom and the United States. Before the recent recession, some analysts estimated that Canadian hedge funds and hedge fund–related products totalled more than $30 billion. More recently, hedge fund providers have begun selling these funds, in the form of mutual funds, to smaller investors for as little as $1,000.[21] Hedge funds also make large investments in noninvestment-grade bonds, also known as junk bonds. Globally, hedge funds are estimated to have total assets of more than $2.7 trillion.[22] Traditionally, hedge funds, unlike venture capitalists and private equity funds, did not make direct investments in companies; instead, they usually preferred to purchase existing shares and bond issues.

ASSESSMENT CHECK

17.6.1 What is the most common type of security sold privately?

17.6.2 Explain venture capital.

17.6.3 What is a sovereign wealth fund?

LO 17.7 Describe mergers, acquisitions, buyouts, and divestitures.

MERGERS, ACQUISITIONS, BUYOUTS, AND DIVESTITURES

Chapter 5 briefly described mergers and acquisitions. A *merger* is a transaction where two or more firms combine into one company. In an *acquisition*, one firm buys the assets of another firm and assumes that firm's obligations. Chapter 5 listed the classifications of mergers and acquisitions: vertical, horizontal, and conglomerate. It also noted that many of these transactions involve large sums of money. A recent example is AT&T's $49 billion acquisition of DirecTV. In this section, we focus on the financial implications of mergers and acquisitions, buyouts, and divestitures.

A merger includes a buyer and a seller. The seller is often referred to as the *target*. Financial managers evaluate a proposed merger or acquisition in much the same way they evaluate any large investment—by comparing the costs and benefits. To acquire another company, the buying firm typically needs to offer a premium for the target's shares—in other words, a price higher than the current market price. For example, AT&T paid $95 for each share of DirecTV, a premium of almost 30 percent over the existing price.[23]

tender offer a proposal made by a firm to the target firm's shareholders specifying a price and the form of payment.

When the buyer makes what is known as a **tender offer** for the target's shares, it specifies a price and the form of payment. The buyer can offer cash, securities, or a combination of the two. The AT&T offer to DirecTV shareholders was a combination of $28.50 in cash and AT&T stock valued at $66.50 per share. The tender offer can be friendly, meaning it is backed by the target's board of directors, or unfriendly. Shareholders of both the buyer and target must vote to approve a merger.

Setting a premium requires the financial manager to estimate the benefits of a proposed merger. These benefits can include the cost savings from economies of scale, reduced workforces, or the buyer getting a bargain price for the target's assets. Sometimes a buyer finds that the most cost-effective method of entering a new market is simply to buy an existing company that serves the market. Johnson & Johnson has a long history of making such acquisitions. When it decided to enter the contact lens market several years ago, Johnson & Johnson bought Vistakon, the firm that invented disposable contact lenses under the brand name Acuvue. *Synergy* is the term used to describe the benefits produced by a merger or acquisition. It refers to the idea that the combined firm is worth more than the buyer firm and the target firm are worth individually.

Leveraged buyouts, or LBOs transactions where public shareholders are bought out and the firm reverts to private status.

Leveraged buyouts, or LBOs, were briefly introduced in the preceding section. In an LBO, public shareholders are bought out and the firm reverts to private status. The term *leverage* refers to the financing of many of these transactions with high degrees of debt—often more than 75 percent. Financial companies provide financing for many LBOs. LBO activity decreased sharply during the recent economic downturn. As the economy began to recover, LBO activity increased. According to Standard & Poor's, LBO financing recently grew to $13.6 billion, about 15 times the amount from the same time a year before.[24]

Why do so many LBOs occur? One reason is that private companies enjoy benefits that public companies do not. Private companies are not required to publish financial results, are subject to less regulatory supervision, and are not pressured to produce short-term profits. Some argue that LBOs, because of the high degree of debt, require management to use more discipline to control costs. Although LBOs do have advantages, history has shown that many companies that go private appear as public companies several years later.

In a sense, a **divestiture** is the reverse of a merger. That is, in a divestiture, a company sells its assets, such as subsidiaries, product lines, or production facilities. Two types of divestitures exist: selloffs and spinoffs. In a *selloff,* assets are sold by one firm to another. For example, when Shell Canada decided to focus its resources on "other options," it sold its stake in the Mackenzie Valley Pipeline project in the Northwest Territories and other assets in the region. When asked for a statement, the chairperson of the Aboriginal Pipeline Group said, "We're sure that there's . . . a lot of companies out there that would love to step up to the plate and take over." Similarly, Calgary-based Suncor Energy sold its natural gas assets, located in Trinidad and Tobago, for $396 million. Centrica Plc took ownership of all the assets, allowing Suncor to focus on other aspects of its core business.[25]

divestiture the sale of assets by a firm.

The other type of divestiture is a *spinoff*. In this transaction, the assets sold form a new firm. For example, Motorola announced that it was splitting into two publicly traded firms. The parent company will handle its core business of mobile converged devices, digital home entertainment devices, and video voice and data solutions. The spinoff firm will handle heavy-duty two-way radios, mobile computers, public security systems, wireless network infrastructure, and other business-oriented goods and services. Both organizations will continue to use the Motorola brand name, with the parent company now named Motorola Mobile Devices and Home. Motorola shareholders will receive shares of the new company, Motorola Enterprise Mobility and Networks. Bell Canada also recently spun off its regional small-business operations and rural portions of its residential wire line business to Aliant.

Firms divest assets for several reasons. Sometimes divestitures result from previous acquisitions that didn't work out as well as expected. In early 2001, America Online and Time Warner merged to create AOL Time Warner, Inc. Nine years later, Time Warner announced it was spinning off AOL. The merger is now considered one of the worst mistakes in corporate history. It had failed to generate the expected synergies between the two companies. Shortly after the merger, AOL had 27 million subscribers; more recently, that number had shrunk to about 6.3 million.

In other cases, a firm makes a strategic decision to focus on its core businesses. It then decides to divest any assets that fall outside this core. That was the explanation that Motorola gave when criticized that the company had become too large and after its mobile-device business was taken over first by Nokia, then Samsung, and then Apple. A similar explanation was given by Bell Aliant CEO Karen Sheriff. She explained that the company had sold xwave to Bell to "focus on our core priorities such as fibre-to-the home, improve our balance sheet and ensure long-term value to our investors."

✓ ASSESSMENT CHECK

17.7.1 Define *synergy*.

17.7.2 What is an LBO?

17.7.3 What are the two types of divestitures?

WHAT'S AHEAD

Contemporary Business concludes with several appendices. Appendix A contains additional case studies. Appendix B outlines the main legal issues concerning business. It reviews the types of laws, the regulatory environment of business, and the core of business law, including discussions of contract law and property law. Appendix C examines risk management and insurance. It describes the concept of risk, alternative ways of dealing with risk, and the various kinds of insurance available to businesses and individuals. Appendix D discusses some of the important areas of personal financial planning, such as budgeting, credit, and retirement planning, and Appendix E describes how to write an effective business plan. An additional appendix, Appendix F, features video case studies with accompanying videos. This appendix is available in WileyPLUS Learning Space. Appendix G, which discusses career searches and options to help you prepare for your future in business, is available on the textbook's companion website at www.wiley.com/go/boonecanada.

RETURN TO INSIDE BUSINESS

The Wooing of Ratiopharm

Financial managers make key decisions related to a company's most liquid asset—cash.

QUESTIONS FOR CRITICAL THINKING

1. When making a key investment decision, what projections do management need to prepare?
2. What key external factors can affect the reliability of a manager's financial forecasts?

SUMMARY OF LEARNING OBJECTIVES

LO 17.1 Explain the role of financial managers.

Finance deals with planning, obtaining, and managing a company's funds to accomplish its objectives efficiently and effectively. The major responsibilities of financial managers are developing and carrying out financial plans and deciding on the most appropriate sources and uses of funds. The chief financial officer (CFO) heads a firm's finance organization. Three senior executives reporting to the CFO are the vice-president of financial management, the treasurer, and the controller. When making decisions, financial professionals continually balance risks with expected financial returns.

✓ ASSESSMENT CHECK ANSWERS

17.1.1 What is the structure of the finance function at the typical firm? The head of the finance function of a firm usually has the title of chief financial officer (CFO) and generally reports directly to the firm's chief executive officer. Reporting to the CFO are the treasurer, the controller, and the vice-president of financial management.

17.1.2 Explain the risk–return tradeoff. Financial managers try to maximize the wealth of their firm's shareholders by striking the right balance between risk and return. Often, the decisions that involve the highest potential returns expose the firm to the greatest risks.

LO 17.2 Describe the parts of a financial plan and the financial planning process.

A financial plan is a document that specifies the funds needed by a firm for a given period of time, the timing of cash inflows and outflows, and the most appropriate sources and uses of funds. The financial plan addresses three questions: What funds will be required during the planning period? When will funds be needed? Where will funds be obtained? Three steps are involved in the financial planning process: forecasting sales over a future period of time, estimating the expected level of profits over the planning period, and deciding on the additional assets needed to support the additional sales.

✓ ASSESSMENT CHECK ANSWERS

17.2.1 What three questions does a financial plan address? The financial plan addresses three questions: What funds will be required during the planning period? When will funds be needed? Where will funds be obtained?

17.2.2 Explain the steps involved in preparing a financial plan. The first step is to forecast sales over a future period of time. Second, the financial manager must estimate the expected level of profits over the planning period. The final step is to decide on the additional assets needed to support the additional sales.

LO 17.3 Outline how organizations manage their assets.

Assets consist of what a firm owns. They also represent the uses of its funds. Sound financial management requires assets to be acquired and managed as effectively and efficiently as possible. The major current assets are cash, marketable securities, accounts receivable, and inventory. The goal of cash management is to have enough funds to meet day-to-day transactions and pay for any unexpected expenses. Excess cash should be invested in marketable securities, which are low-risk securities with short maturity dates. Accounts receivable are uncollected credit sales. Managing accounts receivable involves collecting funds owed to the firm as quickly as possible while also offering enough credit to customers to attract and generate increased sales. The main goal of inventory management is to minimize the overall cost of inventory. Production, marketing, and logistics also play roles in determining proper inventory levels. Capital investment analysis is the process financial managers use when deciding whether to invest in long-lived assets. This process involves comparing the benefits and costs of a proposed investment. Managing international assets poses additional challenges for the financial manager, including the problem of fluctuating exchange rates.

✓ ASSESSMENT CHECK ANSWERS

17.3.1 Why do firms often choose to invest excess cash in marketable securities? Cash in hand earns no rate of return. Excess cash should be invested in marketable securities. Marketable securities are low-risk securities that have short maturity dates and can be easily sold in the secondary markets. As a result, they are easily converted into cash when needed.

17.3.2 What are the two aspects of accounts receivable management? The two aspects of accounts receivable management are deciding on an overall credit policy (whether to offer credit and, if so, what terms of credit to offer) and deciding which customers will be offered credit.

17.3.3 Explain the difference between an expansion decision and a replacement decision. An expansion decision involves decisions about offering new products or building or acquiring new production facilities. A replacement decision considers whether to replace an existing asset with a new asset.

LO 17.4 Discuss the two major sources of funds for a business and capital structure.

Businesses have two sources of funds: debt capital and equity capital. Debt capital refers to funds obtained through borrowing, and equity capital consists of funds provided by the firm's owners. The mix of debt and equity capital is known as the firm's capital structure, and the financial manager's job is to find the proper mix. Leverage is a technique of increasing the rate of return on funds invested by borrowing. But leverage also increases risk. Also, relying too much on borrowed funds may reduce management's flexibility in future financing decisions. Equity capital also has its downsides. When additional equity capital is sold, the control of existing shareholders is weakened. In addition, equity capital is more expensive than debt capital. Financial managers also face decisions concerning the suitable mix of short-term and long-term funds. Short-term funds are generally less expensive than long-term funds but expose firms to more risk. Financial managers are also involved in deciding the firm's dividend policy.

✓ ASSESSMENT CHECK ANSWERS

17.4.1 Explain the concept of leverage. Leverage is a technique of increasing the rate of return by borrowing funds. But leverage also increases risk.

17.4.2 Why do firms generally rely more on long-term funds than short-term funds? Although short-term funds are generally less expensive than long-term funds, short-term funds expose the firm to additional risks. The cost of short-term funds can vary greatly from year to year. In addition, short-term funds can sometimes be difficult to obtain.

17.4.3 What is an important factor in deciding on a firm's dividend policy? The main factor in deciding on a firm's dividend policy is its investment opportunities. Firms with more profitable investment opportunities often pay less in dividends than firms that have fewer such opportunities.

LO 17.5 Identify sources of short-term financing for businesses.

The three major short-term funding options are trade credit, short-term loans from banks and other financial institutions, and commercial paper. Trade credit is extended by suppliers when a firm receives goods or services and agrees to pay for them at a later date. Trade credit is relatively easy to obtain and costs nothing unless a supplier offers a cash discount. Loans from commercial banks are a significant source of short-term financing and are often used to finance accounts receivable and inventory. Loans can be either unsecured or secured. In unsecured loans, no assets are pledged as collateral, or security. In secured loans, accounts receivable or inventory are pledged as collateral. Commercial paper is a short-term IOU sold by a company. Large amounts of money can be raised through the sale of commercial paper, usually at interest rates lower than those charged by banks. Access to the commercial paper market is limited to large, financially strong corporations.

✓ ASSESSMENT CHECK ANSWERS

17.5.1 What are the three sources of short-term funding? The three sources of short-term funding are trade credit, short-term loans from banks and other financial institutions, and commercial paper.

17.5.2 Explain trade credit. Trade credit is extended by suppliers when a buyer agrees to pay for goods and services at a later date. Trade credit is relatively easy to obtain and costs nothing unless a cash discount is offered.

17.5.3 Why is commercial paper an attractive short-term financing option? Commercial paper is an attractive financing option because large amounts of money can be raised at interest rates that are usually lower than the interest rates charged by banks.

LO 17.6 Discuss long-term financing options.

Long-term financing is repaid over many years. Organizations acquire long-term financing from three sources: long-term loans from financial institutions, bonds sold to investors, and equity financing. Public sales of securities, such as shares and bonds, are a major source of funds for corporations. These securities can generally be traded in secondary markets. Public sales can vary quite a bit from year to year depending on the conditions in the financial markets. Private placements are securities—new share or bond issues—sold to a small number of institutional investors. Most private placements involve debt securities. Venture capitalists are an important source of long-term financing for new companies. If the business succeeds, venture capitalists can earn large profits. Private equity funds are investment companies that raise funds from wealthy individuals and institutional investors. They then invest the funds in both public and private companies. Unlike venture capitalists, private equity funds invest in all types of businesses. Sovereign wealth funds are investment companies owned by governments.

✓ ASSESSMENT CHECK ANSWERS

17.6.1 What is the most common type of security sold privately? Corporate debt securities are the most common type of security sold privately.

17.6.2 Explain venture capital. Venture capitalists are important sources of funding, especially for new companies. Venture capitalists invest in new companies by taking an ownership position. If the business succeeds, venture capitalists can earn large profits.

17.6.3 What is a sovereign wealth fund? A sovereign wealth fund is a government-owned investment company. These companies invest in a variety of financial and real assets, such as real estate. Although most investments are based on the best risk–return tradeoff, investment decisions are also influenced by political, social, and strategic considerations.

LO 17.7 Describe mergers, acquisitions, buyouts, and divestitures.

A merger is a transaction where two or more firms combine into one company. An acquisition is a transaction where one company buys another. A merger includes a buyer and a seller (called the *target*). The buyer offers cash, securities, or a combination of the two in return for the target's shares. Mergers and acquisitions should be evaluated the same way any large investment is evaluated—by comparing the costs with the benefits. *Synergy* is the term used to describe the benefits a merger or acquisition is expected to produce. A leveraged buyout (LBO) is a transaction where shares are purchased from public shareholders and the company reverts to private status. LBOs are usually financed with large amounts of borrowed funds. Private equity companies are often major financers of LBOs. Divestitures are the opposite of mergers—companies sell their assets such as subsidiaries, product lines, or production facilities. A selloff is a divestiture where assets are sold to another firm. In a spinoff, a new firm is created from the assets divested. Shareholders of the divesting firm become shareholders of the new firm.

✓ ASSESSMENT CHECK ANSWERS

17.7.1 Define *synergy*. *Synergy* is the term used to describe the benefits produced by a merger or acquisition. It refers to the idea that the combined firm is worth more than the buyer firm and the target firm are worth individually.

17.7.2 What is an LBO? An LBO—a leveraged buyout—is where public shareholders are bought out and the firm reverts to private status. LBOs are usually financed with large amounts of borrowed money.

17.7.3 What are the two types of divestitures? The two types of divestitures are selloffs and spinoffs. In a selloff, assets are sold by one firm to another firm. In a spinoff, a new firm is created from the assets divested. Shareholders of the divesting firm become shareholders of the new firm.

BUSINESS TERMS YOU NEED TO KNOW

capital structure 479	financial managers 472	leveraged buyouts (LBOs) 488	venture capitalists 486
divestiture 489	financial plan 474	risk–return tradeoff 474	
finance 472	leverage 479	tender offer 488	

REVIEW QUESTIONS

1. Explain the risk–return tradeoff and give two examples.
2. Describe the financial planning process. How does asset intensity affect a financial plan?
3. What are the main considerations when deciding on an overall credit policy? How do the actions of competitors affect a firm's credit policy?
4. Why do exchange rates pose a challenge for financial managers at companies that operate internationally?
5. Discuss the idea of leverage. Use a numerical example to illustrate the effect of leverage.
6. What are the advantages and disadvantages of debt financing and equity financing?
7. Compare and contrast the three sources of short-term financing.
8. Define *venture capitalist*, *private equity fund*, *sovereign wealth fund*, and *hedge fund*. Which of the four invests the most money in startup companies?
9. Briefly describe the mechanics of a merger or acquisition.
10. Why do firms divest assets?

PROJECTS AND TEAMWORK APPLICATIONS

1. Assume you would like to start a business. Create a rough financial plan that addresses the three financial planning questions listed in the text.

2. Working with a partner, assume that a firm needs $10 million in additional long-term capital. It currently has no debt and $40 million in equity. The firm's options are issuing a 10-year bond (with an interest rate of 7 percent) or selling $10 million in new equity. You expect next year's earnings will be $5 million before interest and taxes. (The firm's tax rate is 35 percent.) Prepare a memo outlining the advantages and disadvantages of debt financing and equity financing. Using the numbers provided, prepare a numerical illustration of leverage similar to Figure 17.2.

3. Your new small business has grown, but it now needs a large amount of capital. A venture capital firm has agreed to provide the money you need. In return, the venture capital firm will own 75 percent of the business, and you will be replaced as CEO by someone chosen by the venture capitalist. You will be considered the founder of the company and the chairperson of the board. Are you willing to take the money in return for losing control over your business? Why or why not?

4. Working in a small team, select three publicly traded companies. Visit each firm's website. Find the part of the website that includes information for investors. Review each firm's dividend policy. Does the company pay dividends? If so, when did it begin paying dividends? Have dividends increased each year, or have they had ups and downs from year to year? Is the company currently repurchasing shares? Has it repurchased shares in the past? Prepare a report to summarize your findings.

5. As noted in the chapter, one of the most unfortunate mergers in corporate history involved Time Warner and America Online. Research this merger. Why did analysts expect it to be successful? Why did it fail? What has happened to AOL since then? What are some examples of failed Canadian mergers?

WEB ASSIGNMENTS

1. **Jobs in financial management.** Visit the website listed below to explore careers in finance. How many people currently work as financial managers? What is the projected increase in employment over the next 10 to 20 years? What is the average level of compensation? www.servicecanada.gc.ca/eng/qc/job_futures/statistics/0111.shtml

2. **Capital structure.** Go to the website listed below to access recent financial statements for Canadian Tire. Access the most recent annual report and locate the balance sheet. What is the firm's current capital structure (the relationship between debt and equity)? Has it changed over the past five years? Why would Canadian Tire choose this capital structure? http://corp.canadiantire.ca/EN/Investors/FinancialReports/Pages/AnnualReports.aspx

3. **Mergers and acquisitions.** Using a news source such as the CBC (www.cbc.ca) or *The Globe and Mail* (www.theglobeandmail.com), search for an announcement of a recent merger or acquisition. An example would be Whitecap Resources Inc.'s recent acquisition of Western Canadian oil and gas properties from Imperial Oil Ltd. (a link is shown below). Print out the articles and bring them to class.

   www.theglobeandmail.com/report-on-business/industry-news/energy-and-resources/imperial-oil-sells-some-western-canada-assets-to-whitecap-for-855-million/article17515518/

Note: Internet Web addresses change frequently. If you don't find the exact sites listed, you may need to access the organization's home page and search from there or use a search engine such as Bing or Google.

PART 6: CASE STUDY Beau's All Natural Brewing Company

Financing Growth

Finances are at the heart of understanding a business and the decisions that managers make to start and then grow their business. Entrepreneurs need to calculate a starting budget that will allocate sufficient spending of funds for the company to establish itself. Inadequate financing to get the business started properly is a primary reason why many new businesses fail to launch. Once operational, the budget should then reflect the generation of cash flow that will eventually pay for all operating costs and provide profits to finance expansion of the business.

Steve and Tim Beauchesne began Beau's All Natural Brewing Company with a loan and Tim's capital totalling $300,000. The loan was tied to the leather finishing plant and land he owned—the primary assets guaranteeing repayment. Until Beau's showed sufficient positive cash flow from actual operations, the amount of bank debt would be limited to the value of the collateral they had—the plant. Any other sources of debt financing could come from those willing to lend without any guarantees of security, such as good friends and family.

On the equity side, Steve and Tim wanted to keep ownership of the company to themselves and the decision-making control that comes with 100 percent ownership. Rather than accept new investors willing to provide cash in exchange for shares in the now well-established brewery, Steve and Tim are maintaining their ability to manage the firm the way they have from the start—guided by the principles discussed in Part 3 of this case study.

In their first year of operation Beau's produced and sold 30,000 litres of beer; eight years later the company is selling 3.5 million litres—a 100 times increase. Steve believes that on average Beau's operating numbers are competitive with the industry. He estimates that Beau's net profit runs about 7 to 10 percent of sales. Production costs are the major expense, running between 40 to 50 percent of sales. Marketing, distribution, and selling expenses each run about 12 percent.

Growth in sales has averaged 40 to 50 percent in each of the last few years, and Beau's has used the profits generated to expand plant facilities to scale up beer production as the company prepares for increasing sales in the Quebec and Northeastern U.S. markets. Financing the costs of expanding into these new markets as well as the growth in the Ontario market has come from internally generated profits and more bank debt. As Steve explains,

> It's pretty simple and keeps us under control as well. Each year we go to our bank with our financial statements, show them our profits for the past year, and they lend us about twice whatever those profits are. We can plan our growth based on what we know our profits are going to be. So those new tanks we installed were bought with some borrowed money along with some of our internally generated profits. And next year the sales from those additional tanks will help us finance future expansion. But to do that we have to hire new salespeople and cover their expenses as they introduce our beer to retail customers. That costs! There's lots of people who haven't discovered our beer yet and we are working our way to them as fast as we can.

Questions for Critical Thinking

1. Should Beau's consider growing faster by taking in equity funding from investors?
2. How else could Beau's finance growth without giving up equity?

6 LAUNCHING YOUR . . .

ACCOUNTING OR FINANCE CAREER

Part 6, "Managing Financial Resources," describes the finance function in organizations. Finance deals with planning, obtaining, and managing an organization's funds to accomplish its objectives in the most effective way possible. In Chapter 15, you read about accounting firms and the variety of large and small public and private organizations that generate and use accounting data. In Chapter 16 we discussed the financial system, including the various types of securities, financial markets and institutions, the Bank of Canada, financial regulators, and global financial markets. In Chapter 17 we examined the role that financial managers play in an organization; financial planning; short-term and long-term financing options; and mergers, acquisitions, buyouts, and divestitures. In both Chapters 16 and 17 we described the finance functions of a variety of businesses, governments, and not-for-profit organizations. As Part 6 illustrates, finance is a diverse profession and includes many different occupations. According to Human Resources and Skills Development Canada (which is now known as Employment and Social Development Canada), over the next decade most finance-related occupations are expected to experience slightly better-than-average employment growth. And employment in several finance occupations is expected to grow much faster than average. Employment in the financial investment industry should be strong for two reasons: the globalization of securities markets and the large number of baby boomers in their peak earning years who have funds to invest.[1]

In most business schools, accounting and finance are popular majors among undergraduates. Many accounting graduates start their careers working for a public accounting firm. At first, their job duties may include auditing or tax services, usually working with more senior accountants. As their careers progress, accounting graduates may take on more supervisory responsibilities. Some may move from public accounting firms to take accounting positions at other organizations. Many accounting graduates spend their entire careers in these fields, while others move into other areas. Let's look briefly at some of the specific jobs you might find after earning a degree in accounting.

Public accountants perform a broad range of accounting, auditing, tax, and consulting services for their clients, which include businesses, governments, not-for-profit organizations, and individuals. Auditing is one of the most important services offered by public accountants, and many accounting graduates begin their careers in this field. Auditors examine a client's financial statements and accounting policies to make sure they conform to all applicable standards and regulations. Public accountants either own their own businesses or work for public accounting firms. Many public accountants are Chartered Professional Accountants (CPAs). To become a CPA, you must meet educational and experience requirements and pass a number of examinations.

Many accountants work for an organization other than a public accounting firm. They record and analyze financial information and financial statements for their organizations. Management accountants are also involved in budgeting, tax preparation, cost management, and asset management. Internal auditors verify the accuracy of their organization's internal controls and check for irregularities, waste, and fraud.

Combining finance with accounting is a common choice for a double major. Individuals who have degrees in finance also enjoy relatively high starting salaries. A recent survey found that the average starting salary for a person with an undergraduate degree in finance was nearly $40,000 per year and could be as high as $94,391 per year.[2]

All organizations need to obtain and manage funds. They employ finance professionals to handle these tasks. Financial institutions and other financial services firms employ a large percentage of all finance graduates. These businesses provide important finance-related services to businesses, governments, and not-for-profit organizations. Some graduates with finance degrees take jobs with financial services firms such as Royal Bank Financial Group and Scotia Capital. Others begin their careers working in the finance departments of businesses in other industries, such as Canadian Tire, Bell Canada, governments, or not-for-profit organizations. You may begin your career by evaluating commercial loan applications for a bank, analyzing capital investments for a business, or helping a not-for-profit organization decide how to invest its endowed funds. Finance professionals often work as members of a team that advises top management. Some individuals spend their entire careers working in finance-related occupations; others use their finance experience to move into other areas of the firm. The chief financial officer—the most senior finance executive—holds one of the most important jobs in any organization. Today, an increasing number of CEOs began their careers in finance.

Finance is a diverse, exciting profession. Here are a few of the specific occupations you might find after earning a degree in finance.

Financial managers prepare financial reports, direct investment activities, raise funds, and carry out cash management strategies. Computer technology has reduced the time needed to produce financial reports. Many financial managers spend less time preparing reports and more time analyzing financial data. All organizations employ financial managers. About 30 percent of all financial managers work for financial services firms such as commercial banks and insurance companies.[3] Specific responsibilities vary depending on the job title. For example, credit managers supervise the firm's issuing of credit, establish credit standards, and monitor the collection of accounts receivable. Cash managers control the flow of cash receipts and disbursements to meet the needs of the organization.

Most *loan officers* work for commercial banks and other financial institutions. They find potential clients and help them apply for loans. Loan officers usually specialize in commercial, consumer, or mortgage loans. Loan officers often act in a sales role by contacting individuals and organizations about their need for funds and trying to persuade them to borrow the funds from the loan officer's institution. As a result, loan officers often need marketing skills in addition to their finance skills.

Security analysts generally work for financial services firms such as Sunlife Financial or Manulife Financial. Security analysts review economic data, financial statements, and other information to predict the outcome for securities such as common shares and bonds. They recommend investment strategies to individual investors and institutional investors. Many senior security analysts hold a chartered financial analyst (CFA) designation. Obtaining a CFA requires a specific educational background, several years of related experience, and a passing grade on a thorough, three-stage examination.

Portfolio managers manage money for an individual client or an institutional client. Many portfolio managers work for pension funds or mutual funds; they make investment decisions to benefit the funds' beneficiaries. Portfolio managers generally have extensive experience as financial managers or security analysts, and many are CFAs.

Personal financial planners help individuals make decisions related to insurance, investments, and retirement planning. Personal financial planners meet with their clients, assess their needs and goals, and make recommendations. Approximately 30 percent of personal financial planners are self-employed. Many hold certified financial planner (CFP) designations. Obtaining a CFP requires a specific educational background, related experience, and passing a thorough examination.

CAREER ASSESSMENT EXERCISES IN ACCOUNTING AND FINANCE

1. CPA Canada is a professional organization for the public accounting profession. Visit the organization's website (www.cpacanada.ca). Review the information on CPA Canada standards and examinations. Write a brief summary on what you learned about how to become a CPA.

2. Suppose you are interested in a career as a security analyst. You've heard that the CFA is an important designation and can help enhance your career. Visit the CFA's website (www.cfainstitute.org) to learn more about the designation. What are the requirements to obtain a CFA designation? What are the professional benefits of having a CFA designation?

3. Arrange for an interview with a commercial loan officer at a local bank. Ask the loan officer about his or her educational background, what a typical day is like, and what the loan officer likes and does not like about the job.

4. TD Waterhouse offers financial planning services to individuals and organizations. Visit the firm's careers website (www.td.com/careers). Review the material and write a brief summary of what you learned about being a personal financial planner. Are you interested in a career as a financial planner? Why or why not?

APPENDIX A
ADDITIONAL CASES

Part 1 Business in a Global Environment

Case Study 1 Vancity: On Top of Its Game

What makes a great organization? Well, if winning multiple national awards is a positive signal, Vancity Credit Union is definitely on the right path! Vancity was on Mediacorp Canada Inc.'s list of Canada's Top 100 Employers for 2013, Canada's top family-friendly employers, and British Columbia's top employers for 2013, and it was one of Canada's Top 30 Greenest Employers. In 2012, Vancity was also ranked number two on the Corporate Knights Best 50 Corporate Citizens in Canada. What does Vancity do right to deserve all this external recognition?

Keeping Employees Happy and Healthy

This Vancouver-based cooperative was founded in 1946; it began with only $22 in total assets, aiming to lend money to those the banks ignored. Today it is Canada's largest credit union, with over 2,565 employees and more than $17.1 billion in assets. As a member-owned credit union, it provides a complete range of financial services to its 492,000 members. Vancity continues to be committed to its original purpose and values: working with people and communities to help them thrive and prosper, all the while operating with integrity, innovation, and responsibility.

Vancity acknowledges that a healthy and committed workforce is the reason it is able to sustain productivity and financial success within a competitive industry. Vancity provides its employees with the opportunity to help set corporate policies and procedures that impact both their work and home life. At work, employees enjoy business casual dress, listening to music while they work, participating on Vancity sports teams, and attending a host of social events.

Vancity has other family-friendly programs as well. For example, the cooperative understands that if an employee has a young child, it may be necessary to build a workday that allows for flexibility. This positive approach recognizes the challenges of balancing work and life commitments and empowers employees to create the right environment to thrive at both.

The organization offers several alternative work options, including telecommuting, flexible hours, shortened workweeks (fewer hours with less pay), and compressed workweeks. Employees are given full pay for working 35 hours a week.

Over the years and primarily driven by the employees' desire for personal development, Vancity has initiated a number of programs to help employees adopt a plan for a healthier life. Programs have included opportunities to work with employee assistance program (EAP) providers for developing personal plans for health and wellness.

Vancity offers a competitive pay and benefits program that includes dental and life insurance, three to six weeks of annual vacation, maternity and paternity leave top-ups, and care days that can be used for personal and family illness or injury. Other rewards include tuition reimbursement, retirement planning, and reduced rates on personal financial services such as mortgages and loans. Employees also have a chance to attend Vancity's cooperative studies program in Italy, where co-ops are well established.

Vancity has a young corporate culture—the average age of its employees is 40, and 94 percent of its new recruits are under 40. Even its CEO, Tamara Vrooman, was only 39 when she took the helm in 2007. The cooperative once threw a party for 2,200 employees and guests, and hip-hop dancers and a slam poet entertained the crowd until 3 a.m. Young employees organized the event for their peers. "We're interested in creating energy, we're interested in having people connect," Vrooman says. "And young people tell us that's an important part of the entire employee experience that they come to Vancity to enjoy."

There are some challenges in human resources, too. Every year the cooperative surveys employees, and it did not meet its targets for employee engagement for three years in a row, which it blamed partly on workforce and budgetary reductions. The employee engagement target is set at 75 percent, but in those years it did not reach beyond 64 percent. "The Executive Leadership Team's compensation is tied to achieving this significant stretch target, reflecting how important it is we improve employee engagement and their pivotal role and responsibility in making this happen," Vancity said in its annual accountability report to members.

In response to the first disappointing employee survey, the cooperative held focus groups with 120 employees, who said they were concerned, among other things, that individual goals were not aligned with those of the organization; that work processes, tools, and resources were not streamlined to improve efficiency; and that managers lacked support to manage performance effectively. To reengage employees, Vrooman said Vancity would increase investment in training and development, renew the organization's IT infrastructure, and provide employees with growth opportunities by focusing on new areas. Among other things, the organization examined its process for conducting employee performance reviews; as a result, it clarified the process, told managers to focus on ongoing employee coaching, and provided employees with online training and support materials to help them improve in areas identified during their performance reviews. It then planned on examining its monetary and nonmonetary compensation strategies.

Keeping the Organization Healthy

Vancity uses a triple bottom line business model; it is driven to achieve financial success but also focuses on environmental and social sustainability. Vancity is in a healthy financial position with rising membership because it takes an innovative approach in serving the financial needs of its members. It was the first Canadian financial institution to offer mortgages to women, the first to use traditional media to market directly to the gay and lesbian community, the first North American credit union to receive an R1 rating from the Dominion Bond Rating Service, and the first financial institution to offer its own socially responsible mutual fund.

Vancity's vision to achieve positive social change has succeeded through a number of programs, such as one called Shared Success. Through this program, Vancity gives back each year a significant portion of net profits (generally 30 percent) to members and to communities. Since the program was introduced, a total of $221 million has been shared with members and redistributed as community grants and other funding initiatives. Among the grant recipients was Just Beginnings Flowers, a not-for-profit florist that provides jobs to people with barriers to employment, which was selected to provide victory ceremony bouquets for the 2010 Winter Olympics in Vancouver. Other successful Vancity programs include its Pigeon Park Savings program, which provides banking services to the poor, and Each One, Teach One, which trains selected employees to teach basic financial literacy skills to newcomers to Canada.

A focus on giving back to the community makes decision making in a credit union more challenging, since maximizing shareholder profit is not the only goal. Vancity managers take leadership training in values-based decision making. An employee survey found that 95 percent said they feel great about the organization's corporate social responsibility approach.

"What makes a credit union is that we are community-based," Vrooman says. "We make decisions locally, we get to know our members, we live and work where they live and work, and when you start to expand beyond that we need to make sure that we keep the key thing that differentiates us from a large bank, which is the local decision-making. That's the biggest challenge: how to keep the credit union niche while you grow."

Starting in 1995, before doing so was popular, Vancity focused on its own environmental performance. Vancity achieved its target of being the first carbon-neutral North American–based financial institution. Through its climate change strategy, Vancity has supported innovative partnerships involving public transportation and green building projects. It also invests in organizations doing climate change work.

The organization is also a strong supporter of women. For example, among its recent board of directors, five of nine directors, including the chair, were women.

Banking on the unbankable is one of the cornerstones of the Vancity story, and today this financial institution continues to look for ways to improve. Vrooman, who was given an accolade herself by being named by the *Vancouver Sun* as one of British Columbia's most influential women in business, says, "We're owned by our members, who have a say in the way our organization is run and a vested interest in how we do things, and we're accountable to them to deliver positive financial, social and environmental returns." And deliver they do—that and win awards!

Questions for Critical Thinking

1. What is Vancity's competitive advantage over other types of financial institutions?
2. Who are Vancity's stakeholders and what value does the organization create for them?
3. Vancity's financial position allows it to take innovative approaches to meeting the needs of its members. If you were a competitor, would you try to emulate Vancity's innovative approach? Why or why not?
4. What new initiatives is Vancity Credit Union undertaking right now for its employees and members?

Sources: Vancity website, www.vancity.com; "Vancity Recognized as One of Canada's Top 100 Employers," news release, October 15, 2010; Nick Rockel, "Luring Young Talent Sets Stage for the Future," *The Globe and Mail*, June 1, 2010; *Vancity 2008–2009 Accountability Report*; Brian Morton, "Vancity's Net Income Near Record Level," *Vancouver Sun*, July 12, 2010, p. B6; Frances Bula, "The Queen of Vancity," *News and Features Vancouver*, September 1, 2009; Regan Ray, "Q&A: Vancity's Tamara Vrooman," *Canadian Business*, November 19, 2007; "B.C.'s Top 100 Influential Women," *Vancouver Sun*, October 29, 2010; "Vancity Believes We Can All Be Wealthy; New Accountability Report from One of Canada's Top Three Corporate Citizens," news release, July 8, 2010; Jobs at Vancouver City Savings Credit Union, eluta.ca; Canada's Top 100 Employers, "BC's Top Employers 2013" and "Canada's Greenest Employers 2013," www.canadastop100.com; Ingenious Awards 2013 website, https://ingeniousawards.ca/panel; The 2012 Best 50 Corporate Citizens of Canada website, www.corporateknights.com/node/1559.

Case Study 2 Patagonia: Leading a Green Revolution

How has Patagonia managed to stay both green and profitable at a time when the economy is tough, consumers are tight for cash, and "doing the profitable thing" is not necessarily doing the right thing? Are Patagonia's business practices good for outdoor enthusiasts, good for the environment, or just good for Patagonia?

Twelve hundred Walmart buyers, a group legendary for their tough-as-nails negotiating tactics, sit in rapt attention in the company's Bentonville, Arkansas, headquarters. They're listening to a small man in a mustard-yellow corduroy sportcoat lecture them on the environmental impact of Walmart's purchasing choices. He's not criticizing the company, per se—*he's criticizing them*. Yet when he finishes speaking, the buyers leap to their feet and applaud enthusiastically.

Such is the authenticity of Yvon Chouinard. Since founding Patagonia in 1972, he's built it into one of the most successful outdoor clothing companies, and one that is steadfastly committed to environmental sustainability.

It's hard to discuss Patagonia without constantly referencing Chouinard, because for all practical purposes the two are one. Where Chouinard ends, Patagonia begins. Chouinard breathes life into the company, espousing the outdoorsy athleticism of Patagonia's customers. In turn, Patagonia's business practices reflect Chouinard's insistence on minimizing environmental impact, even at the expense of the bottom line.

Taking Risks to Succeed

For decades Patagonia has been at the forefront of a cozy niche: high-quality, performance-oriented outdoor clothes and gear sold at top price points. Derided as *Pradagonia* or *Patagucci* by critics, the brand is aligned with top-shelf labels like North Face and Royal Robbins. Patagonia clothes are designed for fly fishermen, rock climbers, and surfers. They are durable, comfortable, and sustainably produced. And they are not cheap.

It seems counterintuitive—almost dangerous—to market a $400 raincoat in a tough economy. But the first thing you learn about Yvon Chouinard is that he's a risk taker. The second thing you learn is that he's usually right.

"Corporations are real weenies," he says. "They are scared to death of everything. My company exists, basically, to take those risks and prove that it's a good business."

And it is a good business. With estimated 2011 revenues of $400 million, up from $333 million the previous year, Patagonia succeeds by staying true to Chouinard's vision. "They've become the Rolls-Royce of their product category," says Marshal Cohen, chief industry analyst with market research firm NPD Group. "When people were stepping back, and the industry became copycat, Chouinard didn't sell out, lower prices, and dilute the brand. Sometimes, the less you do, the more provocative and true of a leader you are."

Chouinard concurs. "I think the key to surviving a conservative economy is quality," he says. "The number one reason is that in a recession, consumers stop being silly. Instead of buying fashion, they'll pay more for a multifunctional product that will last a long time."

Ideal Corporate Behaviour

Chouinard is not shy about espousing the environmentalist ideals intertwined with Patagonia's business model. "It's good business to make a great product, and do it with the least amount of damage to the planet," he says. "If Patagonia wasn't profitable or successful, we'd be an environmental organization."

In many ways, Patagonia is an environmental organization. The company publishes online a library of working documents, *The Footprint Chronicles*, that guides employees in making sustainable decisions in even the most mundane office scenarios. Its mission statement: "Build the best product, cause no unnecessary harm, use business to inspire and implement solutions to the environmental crisis." Patagonia revamped *Footprints* in 2012 and included a world map that shows where all of Patagonia's products are made, profiles of the social and environmental practices of key suppliers and mills, and profiles of key independent partners.

Patagonia's solutions extend well beyond the lip service typically given by profitable corporations. The company itself holds an annual environmental campaign, a recent one being *Our Common Waters*.

Chouinard has co-founded a number of external environmental organizations, including 1% For the Planet, which secures pledges from companies to donate 1 percent of annual sales to a worldwide network of nearly 2,400 environmental causes. To date, almost 1,480 companies participate, raising more than $50 million since 2002.

The name comes from Patagonia's 30-year practice of contributing 10 percent of pre-tax profits or 1 percent of sales—whichever is *greater*—to environmental groups each year. Whatever you do, don't call it a handout. "It's not a charity," Chouinard flatly states. "It's a cost of doing business. We use it to support civil democracy."

Another core value at Patagonia is providing opportunities for motivated volunteers to devote themselves to sustainable causes. Employees can leave their jobs for up to two months to volunteer full time for the environmental cause of their choice, while continuing to receive full pay and benefits from Patagonia. And every 18 months, the company hosts the Tools for Grassroots Activists Conference, where it invites a handful of participants to engage in leadership training, much of it derived from the advocacy experiences of Patagonia management. Patagonia of Japan team members also contributed to cleanup efforts following the devastating March 2011 earthquake and subsequent tsunami.

Growing Green

Patagonia has demonstrated a remarkable ability to thrive despite the unplanned obsolescence of several of its key products. What makes this even more notable is that Chouinard is often the force driving his own bestsellers out of the marketplace.

Chouinard Equipment, Ltd., Patagonia's precursor, was a successful vendor in the nascent rock climbing community. Chouinard himself was well known on the circuit, having made the first successful climbs of several previously unconquered Californian peaks. For more than a decade Chouinard had been hand forging his own steel pitons (pegs driven into rock or ice to support climbers) that were far more durable than the soft iron pitons coming from Europe. Because his pitons could be used again and again, climbing was suddenly more affordable and less of a fringe activity.

But during a 1970 ascent of El Capitan in California, Chouinard saw that the very invention that brought his company success was also irreparably damaging the wilderness he so loved. Though Chouinard Equipment's pitons brought more climbers into the sport, the climbers tended to follow the same routes. And the constant hammering and removal of steel pitons was scarring the delicate rock face of these peaks.

Ignoring the fact that pitons were a mainstay of their success, Chouinard and partner Tom Frost decided to phase themselves out of the piton business. Two years later, the company coupled a new product—aluminum chocks that could be inserted or removed by hand—with a 14-page essay in their catalogue on the virtues of *clean climbing*. A few months later, demand for pitons had withered and orders for chocks outstripped supplies.

Fast forward nearly 20 years. Chouinard Equipment spinoff Patagonia is a booming manufacturer of outdoor clothing. And though it had seen success with products woven with synthetic threads, the majority of its items were still spun with natural fibres like cotton and wool. Patagonia commissioned an external audit of the environmental impact of its four major fibres, anticipating bad news about petroleum-derived nylon and polyester.

Instead, the company was shocked to learn that the production of cotton, a mainstay of the American textile market for hundreds of years, had a more negative impact on the environment than any of its other fibres. The evidence was clear: destructive soil and water pollution, unproven but apparent health consequences for fieldworkers, and the astounding statistic that 25 percent of all toxic pesticides used in agriculture are spent in the cultivation of cotton.

To Chouinard and Patagonia, the appropriate response was equally clear: Source organic fibres for all 66 of their cotton clothing products. They gave themselves until 1996 to complete the transition, which was a manageable lead time of 18 months. But due to the advanced nature of fashion production, they had only four months to lock in fabric suppliers. Worse, at the time there wasn't enough organic cotton being commercially produced to fill their anticipated fabric needs.

Taking a page from their own teaching on grassroots advocacy, Patagonia representatives went directly to organic cotton farmers, ginners, and spinners, seeking pledges from them to increase production, dust off dormant processing equipment, and do whatever it would take to line up enough raw materials to fulfill the company's promise to its customers and the environment.

Not surprisingly, Patagonia met its goal, and every cotton garment made since 1996 has been spun from organic cotton.

Sustaining Momentum

At 74, Chouinard can't helm Patagonia forever. But that's not to say he isn't continuing to find better ways for Patagonia to do business.

"I think entrepreneurs are like juvenile delinquents who say, 'This sucks. I'll do it my own way,'" he says. "I'm an innovator because I see things and think I can make it better. So I try it. That's what entrepreneurs do."

Patagonia's current major project is its Common Threads initiative. To demonstrate that it's possible to minimize the number of Patagonia clothes that wind up in landfills, the company is committing to making clothes built to last, fixing wear-and-tear items for consumers that can be repaired, and collecting and recycling worn-out fashions as efficiently and responsibly as possible.

"It'll be in the front of the catalog—our promise that none of our stuff ever ends up in a landfill," Chouinard says. "We'll make sure of it with a liberal repair policy and by accepting old clothing for recycling. People will talk about it, and we'll gain business like crazy."

It's doubtful that Chouinard will ever stop thinking about how Patagonia can responsibly innovate and improve. "Right now, we're trying to convince zipper companies to make teeth out of polyester or nylon synths, which can be recycled infinitely," he says. "Then we can take a jacket and melt the whole thing down back to its original polymer to make more jackets."

Despite his boundless enthusiasm for all things green, Chouinard admits that no process is truly sustainable. "I avoid using that word as much as I can," he says. He pauses for a moment and adds: "I keep at it, because it's the right thing to do."

Questions for Critical Thinking

1. Patagonia has a history of putting sustainability ahead of profits. Based on what you learned about Patagonia's ideals, how do you think the company determines what possible ventures will be both business practical and environmentally friendly?

2. What could Patagonia do today to make sure that Yvon Chouinard's ideals become a permanent part of the company's culture after he leaves the company?

3. It seems Yvon Chouinard is never satisfied. He comes to you and asks for a proposal on a new—"forward looking"— sustainability agenda for the firm. What would you include in this agenda to stretch the firm beyond what it is already doing, and why?

4. Business decisions can be a compromise between ethics and profitability. Could ethics lose out to greed even in a company with the idealism of Patagonia? See if you can find a decision that appeared to or could put profits ahead of the company's publicly stated environmental goals. Explain why you think that company made this decision and the competing factors you believe were involved.

Sources: Patagonia website, www.patagonia.com, "The Footprint Chronicles," "Environmentalism: Our Common Waters," "Environmental Internships," "Tools for Grassroots Activists Conference," and "Our History," "Introducing the Common Threads Initiative"; Monte Burke, "Wal-Mart, Patagonia Team to Green Business," *Forbes*, May 6, 2010; Kent Garber, "Yvon Chouinard: Patagonia Founder Fights for the Environment," *U.S. News*, October 22, 2009; Diana Random, "Finding Success by Putting Company Culture First," *Entrepreneur*, April 19, 2011; Jennifer Wang, "Patagonia, from the Ground up," *Entrepreneur*, May 11, 2010; 1% For the Planet, www.onepercentfortheplanet.org/en; Kristall Lutz, "What Makes Patagonia 'The Coolest Company on the Planet': Insights from Founder Yvon Chouinard," Opportunity Green, January 27, 2011; Takayuki Tsujii, "A Look Back: Following the Devastation of Tohoku Region Pacific Coast Earthquake," The Cleanest Line, March 11, 2012.

Case Study 3 Canarm Ltd.: Creating Innovation within by Always Looking Outward

Where can you find a wholesaler; an agricultural equipment manufacturer; and a heating, ventilation, and air conditioner manufacturer all in one company? Visit Canarm Ltd., located in Brockville, Ontario.

From humble beginnings, Canarm Ltd. developed into a global marketer and manufacturer of lighting, air moving, and related products, supplying residential, agricultural, and industrial markets. Its customers include wholesalers, retailers, and distributors. The privately owned and operated company has five satellite manufacturing plants in Ontario and one in Illinois, as well as a distribution centre in Montreal. Canarm has over 300 full-time employees.

History

The company started in 1934 as Danor Manufacturing Co. Ltd., a small sheet metal shop in Gorrie, Ontario, making agricultural metal products such as hog troughs and turkey feeders. In 1963, the operation moved to a new 275-square-metre (3,000-square-foot) factory in Brockville, Ontario, the site of the company's current corporate offices.

In the late 1950s and early 1960s, instead of running loose in the fields, pigs and chickens were confined to large barns. This created a need for farmers to remove gases, odours, and heat from the barns, which created an opportunity for Danor to add barn exhaust fans to its product line.

During one of its down cycles, Danor decided to diversify its fan market to include commercial and industrial customers. During the process of trying to break into this new market, a supplier suggested the company consider acquiring a long-established Montreal business whose electrical products ranged from fans and heaters to compact kitchens and hose dryers. A deal was struck, and shortly after the Montreal and Brockville facilities were combined. Truckloads of machinery were transferred from Montreal to Brockville, with several product lines discontinued so everything could squeeze into one location.

In the 1970s, Danor's fan business branched out into the residential market and saw success for several reasons. First, energy conservation and efficiency became a high priority, and many customers asked for slow-moving ceiling fans to push the hot air gathered at the ceiling back to floor level. The company found manufacturers in Hong Kong and started importing industrial ceiling fans for a growing market throughout the 1970s. Second, the 1980s saw a spike in prime interest rates to 22 percent, resulting in commercial buyers making far fewer purchases. The Hong Kong manufacturers now had an excess capacity and were desperate to sell product. Third, by replacing metal blades with wooden ones and painting the fan brown, a more decorative look opened up new markets for ceiling fans with restaurants and homeowners.

The need to develop retail chains and ceiling fan and lighting showrooms to sell these products led to the creation of Canarm Ltd. in 1980 through the merger of Danor and Canadian Armature Works. In 1986, Canarm purchased a Montreal ceiling fan company, which became its main distribution centre for imported products and also provided a Quebec sales office and showroom. In 1990, Canarm entered the retail lighting market, and now has one of the most extensive lighting lines in North America.

Always Putting the Customer First Makes the Company Number One!

The secret to Canarm's success has and continues to be its innovative and nimble nature, which is reflected throughout the company—its front-line employees and its leaders, its products, and its strategic approach to growth. At the core of this innovative nature is the company's unrelenting focus on its customers' needs. "Everything starts and ends with the customer here at Canarm," says company president James Cooper. "We always listen to our customers and look for ways to make it easier for them to use our products," says Cooper, who himself recently invented Easy Connect, a mounting bracket that makes changing a light fixture easy. As further evidence of just how nimble Canarm is, within three days of Cooper sharing the idea with his team, they provided him with a prototype.

Cooper has more than 25 years of experience at Canarm and has been in the president's role since 2007. Under his leadership, Canarm was named one of Canada's Best Managed companies in 2012. However, he is quick to deflect credit to the company's employees. "I will start by saying Canarm is extremely fortunate to have the best people," says Cooper. "Our business model is very unique. Our strategy was to build the perfect three-legged stool. Our acquisition trail over the past 10 years was to strengthen the legs of the stool." Canarm's growth strategy, and an investment of $85 million, resulted in a series of mergers and acquisitions since 2003 in fluorescent lighting products, axial fans, blowers, heat exchangers, roof exhausters, and other equipment servicing the HVAC (heating, ventilating, and air conditioning) and livestock confinement equipment markets. This has strengthened Canarm's strategic position and provided additional manufacturing resources to support growing customer demand in North America and abroad for its consumer, commercial, and agricultural markets. Canarm has also built solid business relationships in China over the past 25 years. The company's operations, centred in Zhongshan, China, include 14 manufacturing sites and a showroom. From there, the company manages engineering, quality, and logistics, to ensure consistent quality and on-time delivery. Canarm imports parts and motors from China that arrive in Vancouver and are shipped cross-country by rail for assembly as fans, lights, and heating and ventilation systems at the company's plants in Brockville; Laval, Quebec; and Arthur, Ontario.

In 2013, Canarm increased its efforts to create growth through cross-pollination of its business units, with all three coming together for strategic planning, which has been "vital to our past success and is critical to our future," says Cooper. "Our retail lighting guys have a lot of expertise and capabilities related to lighting. Well, guess what? It gets dark every day in the hog industry or the HVAC industry," says Cooper. "So they're working together on new ideas. It's the people who make it happen. Once they get excited, you just stand back and watch it grow." The company has successfully balanced the need for organizational structure with the ability to remain agile and innovative to adapt to this ever-changing marketplace.

Questions for Critical Thinking

1. What drives the development of new products at Canarm?

2. How important were the mergers with other companies in the evolution of the company?

3. How might Canarm develop yet another category of products either through a merger or cooperation with another firm?

4. Research other business activities and markets that might fit the current organization well.

Sources: Canarm Ltd. Website, www.canarm.com; Inside View–Business Directory, "Canarm" Alexandra Lopez-Pacheco, "Canarm Ltd.: Unique Business Model Glows with Innovation, Nimbleness," *Financial Post*; "James A. Cooper: Will the Company Spend to Expand?" *Financial Post*, March 11, 2013; Leeds-Grenville website, www.leedsgrenville.com/en/invest/profile/majoremployers.asp; Doreen Barnes, "Brockville Chamber Honours Best in Business for 2012," *St. Lawrence EMC News*, November 15, 2012; Nick Gardiner, "Layoffs Averted at Canarm," *Brockville Recorder*, May 31, 2012.

Case Study 4 McCain Foods: Global Fries—Good in Any Language

What do you get when you mix the lowly potato with a passion for growth? The answer is as close as your freezer! McCain Foods Limited, maker of frozen fries, pizzas, appetizers, and entrees, is one of Canada's most famous world brands. The maker of Canada's favourite French fries was started in 1957 in Florenceville, New Brunswick, by brothers Wallace and Harrison McCain, with one plant, 30 employees, and sales of just over $157,000. Over 50 years later, McCain employs over 20,000 people at 57 facilities worldwide generating over $6 billion in sales. Currently producing nearly one-third of the world's French fries for fast-food giants McDonald's and KFC, McCain also supplies frozen products for restaurants and grocery stores in over 166 countries.

How did a homegrown Canadian company become an international success story? Co-owner Harrison McCain had always been interested in emerging markets as a way to grow and expand the business. McCain embraces multicultural experiences and traditions, which translate into new ways of thinking and doing business. Based on this principle, McCain pursued global expansion with passion; he focused on entering new markets through a variety of strategies, including direct selling, joint ventures, acquisitions of existing local businesses, and greenfield developments by building new production facilities. Currently, McCain has 57 manufacturing facilities on six continents, 45 of which are outside Canada.

One major advantage McCain had was the success of its largest client, McDonald's. Harvard's James L. Watson, author of *Golden Arches East: McDonald's in East Asia*, states that the secret to McDonald's global popularity has almost certainly been its French fries, which he writes are "consumed with great gusto by Muslims, Jews, Christians, Buddhists, Hindus, vegetarians, communists, Tories, marathoners, and armchair athletes." McDonald's fries made from McCain products have resonated with local tastes across the globe.

Globalization: Successes and Challenges

Like many in the North American food industry, McCain has struggled over the past few years with a slowed U.S. economy, the high Canadian dollar, the increased cost of fuel, and low-priced competition from Europe. While most of the company's revenue is generated in the United States, Canada, the United Kingdom, and Australia, emerging countries such as China and India are becoming increasingly important to McCain's future profitability. To compensate for decreasing demand in North America, where fast-food suppliers are increasingly under scrutiny for rising obesity rates, McCain is focusing on strengthening its share in foreign markets, especially Asia.

With a population of over 1.3 billion people China is an attractive market, but success was not guaranteed for McCain. China, the world's largest potato producer, often uses potatoes in traditional dishes, but the average annual per capita consumption of fries is less than 100 grams. Compare that with the 13 kilograms that the average Canadian consumes per year and McCain had one tough market to crack. Back in 1988, McCain was hesitant to get into China; the Chinese market, while exciting, wasn't strong enough to warrant setting up operations. McCain's clients KFC and McDonald's were just breaking into China, but neither was doing well enough to warrant McCain's investment in on-the-ground operations.

Yet by 1995 McCain became interested again as China's economy started to emerge. Practising a "beachhead" strategy, McCain began in 1997 by developing a salesforce in Shanghai to start building relationships with fast-food chains such as McDonald's and KFC, as well as hotel chains and grocery stores, to further expand its sales base and introduce a range of products to Chinese consumers. By 2005 McCain had built its own processing plant surrounded by land on which Chinese farmers had been growing potatoes for centuries. McCain employs mostly local workers at its processing plant in Harbin. Facility managers and line workers are largely hired from within the local community and are sent abroad to be educated in the McCain culture. Joining other production facilities on six continents, McCain's investment in China responded to rising demand from its restaurant and retail markets and helped solidify the company's position as a major supplier to the Chinese market.

In September 2012, McCain Foods announced plans to double capacity in its Harbin, China, potato processing plant, and in early 2013 the company announced that it plans to invest an additional $69 million to double capacity of its potato processing plant at Mehsana in Gujarat, India. It appears McCain's strategic bet on global expansion is paying off. Based on 2012 sales, McCain Foods is the thirtieth-largest private company in Canada.

Questions for Critical Thinking

1. Identify the potential risks in the global business environment that McCain Foods would have to be aware of and manage in regard to its international expansion.

2. What challenges might Canadian managers at McCain face when interacting with their Chinese business colleagues?

3. Much of McCain's global success seems to be closely tied to the success and efforts of its clients, McDonald's and KFC. Describe another globalization strategy that McCain Foods might have used to expand into China using only its own brand name.

4. Identify, through research, the specific cultural differences between China, India, and Canada that could impact how McCain Foods carries out operations.

Sources: McCain Foods Limited website, www.mccain.com, "Our Company," "History," "Worldwide," and "McCain Food's Global Corporate Social Responsibility Report Fiscal 2009"; Grant Catton, "Repeat Issuer McCain Gets Funds via HSBC & BNP," *Private Placement Letter, 27*, no. 35 (August 31, 2009): 3; Rebecca Penty, "McCain's Passion for China; Growth: French Fry Producer Is After a Lion's Share of the Asian Country's Fast Food Market," *The Telegraph-Journal*, Saint John, February 6, 2010, C1; Rebecca Penty, "McCain to Cut Potato Sourcing by 20 Per Cent; Food: Low Demand, High Loonie, Leftover Crop and Competition behind Cutbacks," *The Telegraph-Journal*, Saint John, March 16, 2010, B1; John Greenwood, "McCain Hopes Busy Chinese Like Fries; Asian Expansion," *National Post*, February 26, 2008, FP1; Danielle Flavelle, "McCain to Build Fry Plant in China; Wants to Solidify Its Market There. Joins Influx of Foreign Firms," *Toronto Star*, June 24, 2004, D1; Ben Shingler, "McCain's New Plant Has Latest Bells and Whistles; French Fries Company Looking to Strengthen Its Share of Foreign Markets," *The Telegraph-Journal*, Saint John, September 5, 2008, B1; "McCain Foods Limited Announces the Expansion of its Harbin, China Potato Processing Plant," Reuters, September 19, 2012; "McCain Foods to Invest 350 Crore in Gujarat Unit," *The Economic Times*, January 14, 2013; "2012 Rankings of Canada's 350 Biggest Private Companies," *Report on Business Magazine*, June 28, 2012.

Part 2 Starting and Growing Your Business

Case Study 5 Lululemon Athletica: Successful Yogis Want to Make the World a Better Place

Who would base a business on selling $100 yoga pants? Dennis "Chip" Wilson did just that in 1998, when he founded Lululemon Athletica Inc., a Vancouver-based yoga-inspired athletic clothing company. Lululemon sought employees who had an entrepreneurial spirit and are innovative, risk takers, open to learning new things, and comfortable taking responsibility. And it has worked!

Where Ideas Come From

As a student, Wilson was a top swimmer and solid football player, and found that athletic clothing was generally poorly made with lots of bad seams and not enough stretch. He got involved in designing technical athletic fabrics by founding Westbeach, a surf, skate, and snowboard clothing company. Later, discovering yoga in Vancouver, he became an enthusiastic practitioner, leading to the founding of Lululemon Athletica Inc. The trendy brand—a household name in Canada and growing in popularity in the United States and Australia—has been described as one of Canada's most successful companies. Chip's wife, Shannon Wilson, a competitive athlete, is the lead clothing designer and has been a key player in the company's growth.

Building the Business

The first Lululemon store opened in Vancouver in 2000 with the Wilsons teaching yoga courses and selling their own designed yoga pants. Taking the lessons learned as founder of Westbeach, Chip Wilson realized that to maximize his vision for Lululemon, he needed complete control of the brand—from pricing to quality of product. So instead of selling through wholesalers, right from the start Lululemon designed, manufactured (or managed that process through partners), then sold products in its own retail locations. After starting out as a privately owned venture, the company became publicly traded in 2007 to raise funds to fuel its expansion. Within a few short years, the company has grown to over 200 stores, including expanding heavily in the United States, with revenue now over $1 billion.

Entrepreneurs must successfully deal with control and management issues when their firms grow. Initially, Wilson, a University of Calgary economics graduate, ran every facet of the company as it grew rapidly into an international retailer. However, he recognized his own limitations. When Lululemon reached revenue of $100 million in the mid-2000s, Wilson hired people with more expertise than he had in certain areas of managing a company of that size.

Then, in January 2012, he relinquished his role as chief innovation and brand officer, handing the leadership reins to Christine Day, who had been Lululemon's CEO since 2008. Wilson remained as the company's chairman but was no longer involved in the company's daily operations. He said, "I could have my ego around being the CEO or the head guy, but I knew that wouldn't serve me. So really a big part of success is sometimes just getting out of the way once the base has been set." Wilson's decision proved to be a wise one—from March 2009 to May 2012, Lululemon shares rose an incredible 3,637 percent in value! In 2012, Christine Day was named *Report on Business* magazine's CEO of the year. Even during the economic downturn, when other specialty clothing retailers were struggling in the challenging economy, Lululemon's revenues and profits consistently rose. The only struggle for Lululemon was keeping up with the demand for its fashionable and form-fitting athletic wear and accessories. Lululemon truly appeared unstoppable.

It's About More Than Just Money

Lululemon is dedicated to promoting a healthy lifestyle, and the company's culture is described as laid-back, community-oriented, and self-motivational. Lululemon's Manifesto, found on the company website, offers 31 tips on improving health and life, including "If (Lululemon) can produce products to keep people active and stress-free, we believe the world will become a much better place."

In keeping with tip number 12 on the Lululemon Manifesto—"friends are more important than money"—Wilson personally supports many charitable causes. Among these is the charity he and his wife, Shannon, started called Imagine1Day, with a goal of bringing primary education to 80 percent of children in Ethiopia by 2020. In December 2012, Chip and Sharon committed a donation of $8 million to help fund a new design school with a focus on high-tech clothing at Kwantlen Polytechnic University in Vancouver. Lululemon also allots $2,700 per store to give to charities or events in their community, with store employees getting to decide where the money goes.

Chip Wilson's passion to make better-quality and more comfortable athletic clothes enabled him to create a successful and highly profitable company. As a tip on Lululemon's Manifesto states, "If your passion is not there, your brain won't work at it 24/7." Passion has also enabled Wilson to achieve tremendous personal financial success at age 56. With a net worth of $2.9 billion, he was listed number 10 in Canada on the *Forbes* billionaires list. As well, it has allowed the Wilsons to make significant contributions to society through their charitable work.

Handling Setbacks

One of the tips on Lululemon's Manifesto states, "Life is full of setbacks. Success is determined by how you handle setbacks."

In March 2013, Lululemon encountered a major setback. Product quality issues resulted in the recall of about 17 percent of its popular women's black yoga pants, made with its proprietary "luon" fabric, due to unacceptable sheerness. The product's failure to meet Lululemon's technical specifications was not caught during internal quality testing, but was noticed only after the product was stocked in its retail stores. Consumers—or "guests," as the company calls them—who bought these yoga pants after March 1, 2013, could return the product to stores for a full refund or exchange. However, it was estimated that the recall would cost Lululemon $12 million to $17 million in revenue in the first quarter of 2013, and $45 million to $50 million for the rest of the year. On a conference call with investors, Lululemon CEO Christine Day said, "This has been a challenging time for all of us. Disappointing our guests and shareholders and falling short of our own expectations is not something we take lightly and we deeply regret."

As companies grow and expand their manufacturing capacity, it can be a challenge for its management to continue to keep tight control on all aspects of the product's production. When Lululemon Athletica Inc. opened its first store in the Kitsilano neighbourhood of Vancouver in 1998, Lululemon's factory was just a 20-minute bike ride from the store. However, as the company grew, it formed global manufacturing partnerships to support its need for both capacity and technical capability, and collaborated with other brands in the industry on issues such as environmental responsibility and factory auditing standards, and sharing global best practices for supporting its factory partners. Today Lululemon has a global supply chain, with production outsourced to factories in Canada, the United States, Peru, China, Taiwan, South Korea, Israel, India, Bangladesh, Indonesia, Malaysia, Cambodia, Sri Lanka, Vietnam, and Switzerland.

The material involved in the March 2013 recall, luon, a combination of nylon and Lycra spandex fibres, is manufactured in factories in Vietnam and Taiwan. Immediately after the discovery of the quality problem, Lululemon began an investigation into the cause of the sheerness of the product, reporting that it was not the result of having changed manufacturers or the quality of ingredients. Lululemon also added more stringent quality controls and began diversifying its supplier base. As well as impacting revenue, the quality issue also affected Lululemon's inventory, resulting in a shortage of some styles available to its customers. However, the issue also has the potential to jeopardize the reputation of the company known for its high-quality products, as the luon pants weren't the only product involved: Lululemon also encountered unacceptable sheerness with swimsuits and light-coloured pants. This setback opens an avenue for the company's competitors to cut into Lululemon's market share.

Soon after the yoga pant recall, Day announced she was stepping down as CEO, though didn't give reasons why. Lululemon's future success will be partially determined by how well it handles these kinds of setbacks.

Questions for Critical Thinking

1. What entrepreneurial traits and personal characteristics does Dennis "Chip" Wilson display?
2. What are some of the reasons Lululemon Athletica Inc. did not succumb to the statistically high failure rate of businesses within the first five years of operation?
3. How would you ensure future success of Lululemon?
4. What new challenges does Lululemon face today?

Sources: Lululemon website, , www.lululemon.co; Lululemon, "Black Luon Pants Shortage Expected," news release, March 18, 2013; Michael Mink, "Chip Wilson's Design Made Lululemon a Winner," Investors.com, June 8, 2012; Sunny Freeman, "Lululemon Founder Chip Wilson Steps Down from Management, Will Stay on Board," *Toronto Star*, January 6, 2012; "Lululemon Tries IPO on for Size," *National Post*, March 21, 2007; Mae Anderson, "Lululemon Says No Need for 'Downward Dog' Demo for Yoga Pants Refund," *Financial Post*, March 2, 2013; Colleen Leahey, "Lululemon CEO: How to Build Trust Inside Your Company," *Fortune*, March 16, 2012; "#847: Chip Wilson," *Forbes*; Kim Peterson, "Why Gap Wins in Lululemon's Pants Crisis," *MSN Money*, March 27, 2013; "Lululemon: Yoga Pants Recall Will Hurt 2013 Results," *CBS Money Watch*, March 21, 2013; Richard Blackwell, "'I Am Not the Culture of Lululemon,' Outgoing CEO Christine Day Says," *Globe and Mail*, June 13, 2013.

Case Study 6 G Adventures Canada: The Path Less Travelled

Organizations have cultures, but do they have personalities? If so, do businesses take on the personalities of their founders? Some would say Apple's innovativeness and tremendous success was a reflection of Steve Jobs's incredible imagination, fearlessness, and perfectionist nature. G Adventures Canada founder Bruce Poon Tip walks to the beat of a different drum, and so does the adventure travel company he founded.

Seemingly born to be an entrepreneur, at age 14 Bruce Poon Tip won a gold medal in the prestigious Junior Achievement youth business program. At age 16, he was fired from Denny's restaurant after two weeks and dismissed from McDonald's before his training was complete because of his maverick style that didn't fit with the corporate culture of those organizations. Donning a backpack and setting out to explore the world, his business acumen and personal drive fuelled a visionary, high-growth company and a new travel category: small-group tours to off-the-beaten-path destinations.

In 1990, at age 23, Poon Tip founded G Adventures (formerly Gap Adventures) with a passion to deliver authentic travelling experiences for those who craved a vacation that went beyond coach tours, cruise ships, and all-inclusive resorts. When the banks weren't willing to provide a loan, Poon Tip maxed out his two credit cards. G Adventures is now a leader in adventure travel, with offices around the world, offering small-group experiences in over 100 countries. It has grown to become the world's largest eco-tour operator.

Twenty years after founding the company, Poon Tip's belief in its core values are as strong as ever. The company culture is driven by five core values: We love changing people's lives, lead with service, embrace the bizarre, create happiness and community, and do the right thing.

Poon Tip is passionate about changing the lives of the more than 100,000 customers who travel with G Adventures annually. His belief that change is the key to innovation, and people are the key to change, has him encouraging his customers and 1,500 employees worldwide to explore the road less travelled. His company has led the travel industry in customer service by developing unprecedented benefits such as no single-traveller supplements and 24/7 service.

Poon Tip was determined to build a business that could change the world by doing the right thing every time—including hiring locals to have a positive impact on the local economy. And instead of a traditional human resources department, Poon Tip created the Culture Club, where people with the job title "Karma Chameleons" focus on raising company morale worldwide, and the Talent Agency, where staff are dedicated to recruiting and talent management. Poon Tip believes that the company's culture is its brand—and that culture begins with employees. In the last stage of hiring, G Adventures puts candidates through a "culture fit" interview, asking them, for example, "If you were to be stuck on a desert island for five years, what three things would you not bring?" Once hired, staffers at the Basecamp (company headquarters in Toronto) can run a campaign to be elected by co-workers as "mayor" of the company, get involved in the company's charitable projects, and attend an annual weekend retreat, during which Poon Tip once spoke to employees for seven hours about his vision for the company. Annual staff turnover is 5 percent, whereas it is typically around 35 percent in the travel industry. Poon Tip's constant focus on respect and unbridled enthusiasm keeps G Adventures focused on what matters most—community, people, and cultural exchange.

Poon Tip is also passionate about sustainability and philanthropy. Calling his business a social enterprise, he is committed to a "quadruple bottom line" instead of a "triple bottom line"—that is, corporate social responsibility, environmental responsibility, leading with service, and innovation. In 2003, Poon Tip founded the not-for-profit Planeterra Foundation to make a positive difference around the world and to demonstrate his determination to lead his industry in sustainable tourism and community development. The Planeterra Foundation has close to 40 projects worldwide, supporting communities in education, healthcare, environment, and social development—where travellers have the opportunity to visit.

In 2013, G Adventures entered into a $1.3 million partnership with the Multilateral Investment Fund—the leading source of development funding for Latin America and the Caribbean. G Adventures is the only privately owned travel company to receive such a grant. It will build five new long-term, sustainable tourism projects over three years in Latin America.

Poon Tip has demonstrated how travelling with a conscience can fulfill one's purpose while being a highly profitable endeavour. He believes that tourism travel will double in the next decade and therefore that "tourism as usual" is not enough. He believes business models need to adapt to changing societal concerns to create "tourism as a force for good." Poon Tip believes that responsible travel is about personal integrity: people have changed the way they live at home—from recycling to eating more locally grown foods—and they shouldn't suspend their beliefs when they go on vacation.

The list of Poon Tip's awards for leadership and entrepreneurship is impressive. He was the recipient of the Ethics In Action Award, World Savers Award by the prestigious *Condé Nast Traveler* magazine, and the Travel and Leisure Global Vision Leadership Award for "voluntourism." He has also received the Global Traders Leadership award for his groundbreaking ideas in exporting and international business. Poon Tip has also been honoured twice as the Ernst & Young Entrepreneur of the Year. G Adventures has been named one of Canada's 50 Best Managed Companies for six consecutive years, and a Top 100 Employer.

Poon Tip is a sought-after speaker, making over two dozen public appearances a year. He has shared his views on sustainability and tourism at the TED Whistler and TED Bangkok events, as well as at several United Nations forums.

Poon Tip's passion, authenticity, and maverick personality is strongly reflected in his company. He has proven that you can live your values and be profitable too!

Questions for Critical Thinking

1. How would you describe Bruce Poon Tip's personality? How does his personality influence the company's culture and its core values?

2. Describe how Poon Tip's personality has had an influence on his company's success.

3. In what specific ways does G Adventures's low staff turnover directly impact the organization's revenue and profits?

4. What type of customer does G Adventures most appeal to? Do you think this focus would have an effect on its potential to broaden and diversify its user base?

5. How might another company—one that is having difficulty retaining its employees—draw from G Adventures's approach to develop a company "personality" that is as equally engaging?

6. Research news reports on how recent economic conditions have affected the travel industry. Does G Adventures have special strengths that help it deal better than other travel companies with challenges such as those posed by a declining economy? If so, describe these strengths.

Sources: World Green Tourism website; "Travel Style: Bruce Poon Tip," *Johnny Jet*, March 22, 2012; Todd Henneman, "Is HR at Its Breaking Point?" *Workforce*, April 5, 2013; Joanna Pachner, "The Gospel According to Bruce," ProfitGuide.com, October 7, 2011; Elisa Birnbaum "In Conversation with Bruce Poon Tip," *SeeChange Magazine*, December 4, 2012; "Bruce Poon Tip Founder Gap Adventures," TEDx Toronto [video], 2012; Sean Stanleigh, "Tourism Program for Latin America," *The Globe and Mail*, April 4, 2013.

Part 3 Management: Empowering People to Achieve Business Goals

Case Study 7 Electronic Arts: Inside Fantasy Sports

Electronic Arts (EA) is one of the largest and most profitable video game makers. Exclusive contracts with professional sports teams have enabled it to dominate the sports gaming market. But as gaming has shifted from consoles to laptops, phones, and tablets, it is struggling to stay relevant. The question is: Can EA regain the pole position in a crowded and contentious market?

Founded in 1982 by William "Trip" Hawkins, who once worked at Apple Computer, EA quickly gained merit for its detail-oriented sports titles that worked on Nintendo and Sega platforms. Although EA also received good reviews for its strategy and fighting games, its focus (and heart) was on the gridiron, diamond, court, or any other playing surface. According to former EA Sports marketing chief Jeffrey Karp, EA wanted to be "a sports company that makes games."

Ad Revenue In, Ad Revenue Out

Word of mouth may still be the most trusted form of advertising, and EA has always depended on fans to spread its gaming gospel. But in a highly competitive—and often lucrative—gaming market, EA knows better than to skimp on brand building: It spends over two to three times as much when marketing and advertising a title as it does developing it. EA knows its audience; it promotes heavily to readers of both gaming and sports magazines.

The realism of EA's graphics sets it apart from competitors. However, the energy and talent used to depict that realism would be wasted if EA games didn't include the one element fans most want to see: likenesses of their favourite players. Top athletes aren't cheap. Players such as Sidney Crosby, Tiger Woods, and Jarome Iginla expect a tidy sum to promote any product, including video games that use their likenesses. EA spends $100 million annually—three times its ad budget—to license athletes, players' associations, and teams. Anything but cheap, though you'll likely not hear EA complaining about the 15 million digital and physical copies of *FIFA Soccer 2011* it sold in one year, netting $150 million in revenue in the first week alone.

Losing Ground in a Crowded Market

Until recently, EA's devotion to sports games was a winning asset—it dominated the market as the world's largest video game publisher. But over a few short years, the gaming market radically changed. Now EA finds itself in third place behind two strong competitors whose successes represent areas in which EA needs a powerplay to stay in the game.

Blame the Wii. Or *Guitar Hero*, the iPad, and Facebook. All of these new platforms led popular interest in gaming away from complex sports games played with standard controllers to new types of games and new ways of interacting with consoles that sense movement or are portable. Nintendo's Wii has been tremendously popular, and although EA has several successful titles for the platform, many of the top games are produced by Nintendo itself.

Emerging nearly parallel with the Wii was the popularity of *Guitar Hero* and *Rock Band*. It didn't take long for casual gamers to take up plastic guitars and drum sets, leaving their traditional controllers to gather dust. Small gaming shop Harmonix pulled double duty in this market, first publishing *Guitar Hero*, then selling it to EA adversary Activision only to follow up with the arguably better *Rock Band* series. EA came to the party late; sensing the market for rock-along music games was sufficiently saturated, it resorted to striking a deal with Harmonix to help distribute *Rock Band*.

And then there's Apple. Not long after the iOS App Store debuted in the summer of 2008, specifications improved in iOS devices to make them serious mobile gaming machines. At the same time, Facebook was coming into its own as a destination for simple but time-swallowing games. Together these platforms heralded a new way of acquiring and playing games in which EA had little to no experience: digital distribution. Quick on the draw was Zynga, an upstart publisher that quickly dominated Facebook games with Farmville and Frontierville, among others.

As of press time, EA was the third-place games publisher behind Activision and Zynga. EA knows that the road to riches is paved with recurring sales. And though it has released annual versions of many of the popular sports titles for some time, it hadn't done so for the growing market of massive multiplayer online games (MMOG), which Activision has been lucratively exploiting for years with *Call of Duty* and *World of Warcraft*. EA's entry into the MMOG fray was *Star Wars: The Old Republic*.

There are some bright spots for EA. It has been remarkably successful in creating new franchises, which has historically been difficult in the sequel-heavy video game market. EA's successes include *Mass Effect*, a sci-fi action series that has sold over 7 million units, and *Dead Space*, a survival horror series that sold over 4 million units. The company has also seen continued success with older franchises: *Battlefield 3* has shipped over 12 million units. EA has also launched *The Sims Social*, a popular Facebook game that has performed well against titles from Zynga.

And the company is showing signs that it's shifting gears to compete successfully in the new social gaming landscape. It recently spent $300 million to snatch up social gaming developer Playfish, and it also brought *Madden NFL Superstars* to Facebook, where it has been intensely popular. Origin, EA's digital distribution business, offers profile management, the ability to connect with friends via chat, and integration of scores and game stats to social media and online gaming sites. As of last count, 9.3 million users installed Origin, earning EA more than $100 million and helping it to do battle with rival online platform Steam.

Playing for Keeps

In March 2013, EA's chief executive officer, John Riccitiello, resigned after having overseen a near-two-thirds loss in the company's market value since he became CEO in 2007, saying he held himself accountable for missed operational targets. Under Riccitiello's watch, EA grew its digital and mobile games businesses, but as well as experiencing financial losses, the company had high-profile product launch glitches when its servers were unable to handle user demand for a new title, preventing gamers from accessing the game for days.

Some analysts feel that Riccitiello's tenure is a textbook case of how not to run a company in an innovation-driven sector. Video games depend on in-house innovation. However, rather than create new experiences, many felt that EA merely chased trends.

The company's financial health has significant repercussions for Electronic Arts (Canada) Inc., which employs more than 2,000 people at four locations. In April 2013, EA laid off 170 people in its Montreal development unit and announced the closure of two of its Vancouver studios as part of the company's worldwide restructuring around priorities in new technologies and mobile. In total, the global layoffs affected approximately 10 percent of EA's workforce.

Despite its wild success in the video game market, Electronic Arts faces substantial challenges to its power by competing game companies, the cost of doing business, and even dissatisfied gamers. Can EA overcome these threats and continue producing the sports franchises that brought the company considerable success?

Questions for Critical Thinking

1. How much of the blame lies with the leadership of the company, and why?
2. How should EA change its strategic plan to regain lost business?

3. How should EA be reorganized to deal with its new plan?

4. Should EA include partnerships with other firms or organizations in its new plan?

5. Describe the characteristics of the ideal leader you would hire for the firm.

6. What is the latest in Electronic Arts's quest to regain its former glory as the top gaming publisher? How well is EA positioned for future competitive advantage? Overall, is EA's executive team "on top of its game?"

Sources: Electronic Arts website, www.ea.com, "FIFA 12 for iPad and iPhone"; Electronic Arts Investor Relations, "Investor Presentation"; "EA's Chief Creative Officer Describes Game Industry's Re-Engineering," *Venture Beat*, August 26, 2009; Eric Fisher, "EA Sports to North America: Even If You Don't Necessarily Love Soccer, You'll Still Love New 'FIFA 12' Game," *Sports Business Journal Daily*, September 26, 2011; Ben Fritz, "Viacom Sold Harmonix for $50, Saved $50 Million on Taxes," *Los Angeles Times*, January 4, 2011; Christopher Grant, "Jobs: 1/3 of iPhone App Store Launch Apps Are Games," *Joystiq*, July 10, 2008; Dean Takahashi, "Zynga Confirms It Hired EA's Jeff Karp as Marketing and Sales Chief," *Venture Beat*, August 21, 2011; Chris Morris, "Video Game Faceoff: EA vs. Activision," *CNBC*, February 11, 2010; Matt W., "Mass Effect Sales Top 7 Million," *The Sixth Axis*, April 22, 2011; "Electronic Arts F1Q11 Earnings Call Transcript," *Seeking Alpha*, August 4, 2010; Jake Denton, "News: Battlefield 3 Ships 12 Million Copies," *Computer and Video Games*, November 30, 2011; Alex Pham, "The Sims Social Bests Farmville as Second-Largest Facebook Game," *Los Angeles Times*, September 9, 2011; Tom Senior, "Origin Is Doing Quite Well: 9.3 Million Registered Users, $100 Million Revenue since Launch," *PC Gamer*, February 2, 2012; Malathi Nayak, "Electronic Arts CEO Quits as Stumbling Game Maker Misses Targets," *Globe and Mail*, March 19, 2013; Peter Nowak, "5 Reasons Electronic Arts Is in Big Trouble (Which Is Bad News for Canada)," *Canadian Business*, March 20, 2013; Gillian Shaw, "Electronic Arts Closing PopCap and Quicklime in Latest Layoffs to Hit Vancouver's Gaming Sector," *Vancouver Sun*, April 25, 2013.

Case Study 8 The Ottawa Hospital: Employee Engagement during Times of Organizational Change

The origins of The Ottawa Hospital, a not-for-profit, publicly funded, university teaching hospital, date back to 1845 when a building was purchased for $240 to house the Ottawa General Hospital. In 1922 and 1924, respectively, the Grace Hospital and Ottawa Civic Hospital opened, and the Riverside Hospital opened in 1967. In 1998, an amalgamation of the services of the Ottawa Civic, General, Grace, and Riverside hospitals formed The Ottawa Hospital. Today, The Ottawa Hospital is recognized as one of the largest and most important research and teaching hospitals in Canada, with 1,300 physicians and 12,085 staff at its three sites.

Engaged Employees Are Key to Quality Patient Care

There are few sectors where having engaged and satisfied employees matters more than in healthcare, where the need for skilled and empathic workers can be a matter of life and death. In Canada, 70 percent of healthcare costs go to employee salaries. As healthcare costs continue to rise, hospitals across the country are looking for ways to do more with less, and are finding that paying attention to employee engagement could be one way to do that.

Consider the example of The Ottawa Hospital. In 2009, hospital leadership grew concerned with lower patient satisfaction ratings and decided to take a hard look at its vision. The hospital restated its vision: "To provide each patient with the world-class care, exceptional service and compassion we would want for our loved ones." "We learned quickly that in order to even think about success in our goals we needed a very active and engaged workforce that included all 12,000 employees and 1,300 physicians," says Ottawa Hospital president and CEO Dr. Jack Kitts.

Taking a cue from its patient surveys, the hospital undertook its first employee and physician engagement survey. That survey had a response rate of 75 percent—a good indication that employees had something to say. Staff said they wanted the hospital to improve performance management, to make employee wellness a priority, and to provide further career opportunities. The hospital set up committees to consider these concerns. The efforts seem to be working. Dr. Kitts says the hospital has seen significant improvement in these areas since 2009, but more remains to be done. "If we can improve employee engagement," Dr. Kitts says, "we have no doubt that our patient satisfaction scores will go up, our quality and safety indicators will go up, and we'll become one of the top performing hospitals."

High employee engagement is driven by leadership quality, effective rewards, and strong workplace culture and values, enabling productivity and the support of performance and development.

Engaged employees are committed to their employer, satisfied with their work, and willing to give extra effort to achieve the organization's goals. The Ottawa Hospital has a strong leader in Dr. Kitts, who is known for his inclusive, team-oriented strategic leadership, his passion to ensure delivery of quality patient-centred care, and the development and mentoring of physician leaders.

Adopting Evidence-Based HR Practices

A decade ago, hospitals put the focus on creating healthier workplaces, linking the physical and emotional health of workers to high-quality patient care. Now, taking a more comprehensive, strategically focused approach, hospitals recognize the need to move beyond workplace health promotion programs and also focus on the work environment to improve both performance and quality of care. An Ontario Hospital Association–NRC Picker Employee Experience Survey, involving over 10,000 employees in 16 Ontario hospitals, examined how job, work environment, management, and organizational factors influence levels of engagement among healthcare employees. The findings confirmed that a high level of employee engagement is related to retention, patient-centred care, patient safety, culture, and employees' positive assessments of the quality of care or services provided by their team. Echoing private sector research that shows strong correlations between employee engagement scores and customer experiences, hospitals now recognize the positive relationship between staff satisfaction and patient satisfaction. To support this new direction in evidence-based human resource practices, the Ontario Hospital Association created the Quality Healthcare Workplace Model that integrates a healthy workplace, human resources, quality, and patient safety goals within a performance-focused framework.

Facing Changes and Fiscal Challenges

As hospitals strive to improve employee engagement, the Ontario government, as part of its goal to eliminate the deficit, has looked at ways to reduce public spending on healthcare. Shifting from 7 percent average annual growth of healthcare funding during 2006 to 2010, healthcare funding growth was reduced to 2 percent per year for three years beginning in 2012. In addition, as part of the Ontario government's healthcare reform program, the funding model for hospitals was changed, and more funding for patient care has shifted to community-based facilities, such as medical clinics, home care services, long-term care facilities, and not-for-profit organizations. Most impacted by this reform are hospitals, which saw a reduction to 0 percent growth in their base funding.

To respond, The Ottawa Hospital began looking at the makeup of its workforce, aiming to better match the skills of various health professionals—from registered nurses to social workers—with the needs of patients. Dr. Kitts stated that the projected budget shortfall was "the catalyst to move this forward at an accelerated rate . . . We don't believe that the way we provide service today is achieving the best in quality or the least in cost," Dr. Kitts says. "So we are going to change the way we deliver service." It determined the skills and scope of practice for all healthcare workers. It then went through each unit of the hospital to identify the needs of the typical patient and match staff skills to needs. As an example, changes in technology make it possible for lower-paid technicians to provide dialysis to kidney patients under certain circumstances, a treatment that has traditionally been done by registered nurses. In another cost-cutting move, the hospital was considering moving some diagnostic services to community clinics, where they can be done more cheaply.

As a result of the funding cuts, The Ottawa Hospital had to reduce its annual operational costs by $31 million to balance its $1.04 billion budget for the year. To do so, the hospital announced in January 2013 that it was cutting 290 full-time jobs, including 90 nurses, 100 administrative staff, and 100 people categorized as other health professionals, such as physiotherapists, psychologists, and social workers. The planned staff cuts will save nearly $22 million, with the other $9 million in savings expected to come from increased revenue and reduced supply costs. Aiming to show good "bedside manners" with staff, Dr. Kitts and other administrators spent a morning informing the affected unions of the cuts and held open forums with all hospital staff to notify them about the pending layoffs. Administrators were hopeful that very few people would lose their jobs, promising to move as many of the affected employees as possible into the 600 full-time positions that were vacant at that time, and would also offer early retirement to some staff. Dr. Kitts also stressed that patient care wouldn't suffer as a result of the cuts, and he didn't expect hospital wait times to rise. "(The goal) is to achieve quality care at the least cost," said Dr. Kitts.

Questions for Critical Thinking

1. The Ottawa Hospital is working on processes to better "engage" employees for improved job satisfaction, which leads to greater patient satisfaction in the delivery of quality patient care, while at the same time being forced to execute a workforce reduction plan to reduce costs to balance its annual operational budget. In what ways can strong employee engagement help with the layoff situation? Conversely, how might the layoffs affect employee engagement?

2. Describe and discuss how Dr. Kitts and his management team are practising the major responsibilities of human resource management by undertaking the initiative of examining its staff mix to better match the skills of various health professionals with the needs of patients.

3. In what ways will employee layoffs at The Ottawa Hospital affect the culture of the organization? Discuss ways that hospital management has and can further avoid or minimize negative effects on its culture during this time.

4. Research the reaction of CUPE, the public sector union representing healthcare workers, to layoffs in healthcare facilities across Canada. Discuss some of the issues your research revealed that HR managers and hospital CEOs have to work through with employees and unions when circumstances beyond their control require a reduction and realignment of its workforce.

Sources: "Canada's 50 Best Employers: The Top Perks, Programs and Initiatives Inside Our Best Workplaces," *Maclean's*, October 18, 2012; The Ottawa Hospital website, www.ottawahospital.on.ca, "Our Vision" and "Our Leadership Team"; Graham Lowe, "How Employee Engagement Matters for Hospital Performance," *Healthcare Quarterly* 15, no. 2 (2012): 29–39; "Ontario Nurses Association Submission on 2013 Pre-Budget Consultations to the Standing Committee on Finance and Economic Affairs," March 22, 2013; "Ottawa Hospital to Cut 290 Jobs," *CTV News*, January 30, 2013; Chris Hofley, "Ottawa Hospital Cuts 290 Full-Time Jobs to Trim $31 Million," *Ottawa Sun*, January 30, 2013; Don Butler, "Job Cuts Won't Harm Patient Care, Says Ottawa Hospital CEO," *Ottawa Citizen*, January 30, 2013.

Case Study 9 Canada's Team of the Century: 1972 Summit Series

Team Canada 1972 was voted the Canadian "team of the century." When talking about the iconic hockey series in which Canada beat the Russians, many people remember the all-important goal in the final seconds of the last game. Yet Team Canada's story is really about the greatest comeback in hockey history by a team that just would not give up. What lessons can managers learn from this incredible success story?

The Summit Series was the first competition between the Soviet national team and a Canadian team of professional NHL players. The Soviets had recently become the dominant force in international competitions, overtaking Canada. With this hockey rivalry and with the Summit Series being played at the height of the Cold War, it aroused intense feelings of nationalism in both countries.

With the first seven games resulting in a series draw (the third game ended in a tie), it was only during the last 34 seconds of the eighth and final game that the outcome was finally decided. While the winning goal was an important one for all of Canada, if the players hadn't worked together as a team in the other games, they wouldn't have been positioned to win.

Recruiting the Team

Harry Sinden, who had been head coach of the Boston Bruins, was named Team Canada coach and general manager in the summer of 1972, leaving him only a few weeks to organize the team for the September series. Selecting the best players was the easiest part; convincing them to interrupt their off-season proved more challenging. "I don't think anyone in Canada, including the players, realized the significance of the series at the time," said Sinden. "Also, the players felt they had proven they were the top in their field during past NHL seasons; they had little motivation to play against the Soviets."

Sinden's first job was to convince those selected of the importance of the series and the impact it could have on their careers. He played to their sense of national pride. Coining the name "Team Canada" helped, as did showing players film footage of world championships in which he had played. It also helped that the media had started to focus on the series. When the 1972 Team Canada players were announced, the entire hockey world was certain of Canadian victory, and an eight-game sweep was predicted.

Team Canada and most of the sports media were therefore shocked when the Soviet team won the opening game, 7–3. The Soviet team had proven superior in their conditioning, discipline, and game plan. According to Pat Stapleton, Team Canada defenceman, there had been another major difference between the two teams: "The Soviets had long been practising and playing together as a team; whereas, as members of various NHL teams, we had been playing against each other as competitors," Stapleton said. "We needed time to get to know each other's strengths and get to the point where we began to trust each other as teammates rather than as competitors."

Canada won the second game 4–1, with the third game ending in a tie (4–4). When the Soviets won game four (5–3) in Vancouver, taking a two-to-one game lead, the fans booed Team Canada as they left the ice. The captain, Phil Esposito, passionately scolded the fans on post-game national television. The Vancouver episode left Team Canada disheartened. However, Esposito's outburst fired up his teammates (and the nation), and the experience helped galvanize the team. Stapleton said, "Much of what makes a team successful is the players developing instinct and intuition for the game. We were up against a team that played a different style than we were used to, so it was taking a little time for us to develop the intuition and instinct we needed to make risky split-second decisions." He added, "Hockey is played *on the ice*—and you should never underestimate the competition!"

Creating a High-Performance Team

According to Stapleton, one of Team Canada's biggest challenges was building the trusting relationships that are key to a cohesive team. When they trained in Toronto, many of the players were local and went home after practice. It was only when the team headed overseas for the last four games in the USSR and they spent all their time together that they started to bond. They first stopped in Sweden, spending 10 days together training hard; there the players began to understand each other's strengths and trust each other on the ice.

But when the series resumed in Moscow, the Soviets won game five, leaving Team Canada with the daunting task of having to win all three remaining games. As the exhausted and dejected Team Canada players skated off the ice, the few thousand Canadian fans who had made the trip to Moscow stood up and sang "O Canada" at the top of their lungs.

Coach Sinden had chosen 35 star players for Team Canada with the intent that they would each play at least one game. Now, with the series on the line in every game, Sinden knew he had to choose the best 19 to continue. "We had to pick our team, and if somebody hadn't yet played, we were just going to have to break our promise," he recounted. "People who weren't playing were upset about it." But leaders emerged, Sinden said, who helped the group work through this conflict, convincing the disgruntled players that "this series is bigger than all of us" and that they had to pull together, whether they got ice time or not, and win the series for Canada.

The Canadians then started to develop a team mindset, recognizing which of their skills they could deploy to make the whole team stronger, and how they could best serve the team and accomplish the collective goal. "Each player was prepared to do whatever was required, even if it meant working in obscurity, for the good of the team," said Stapleton. Most of the players on Team Canada who played very little or not at all cheered on their teammates in their street clothes from the stands and behind the bench.

The team developed in other ways. For example, the Soviets' game was becoming very predictable. Sinden and Assistant Coach John Ferguson created an environment conducive to the Canadians adapting their playing style to neutralize the Soviets' strengths. Of Sinden, Stapleton said, "As the leader, Harry left the 'on-the-ice' decisions up to us players; he never passed judgement, he empowered us to figure out how to complement each other, to get the job done." The Canadians also began to draw on emotion, heart, and the will to win.

Team Canada won games six and seven. On the day of the eighth and final game, things almost came to a stop across Canada as people watched the game at home, at school, or at work. Until the men's hockey gold medal game of the 2010 Winter Olympics, the 1972 Summit Series was the most-watched sporting event in the history of Canadian television. In dramatic fashion, Canada won the final game, overcoming a two-goal Soviet lead after two periods by scoring three in the third. As the country sat on edge, the final goal was scored by Paul Henderson, with only 34 seconds left in the game!

"After the game, the entire team gathered in the locker room—those who had played and those who had not, everyone feeling equally part of the team. Emotions were running very high! Their burden was lifted; they would return to Canada as the world's best," Sinden said. Back in Canada, Team Canada was greeted by the prime minister in Montreal, then went on to Toronto, where fans lined the highway from the airport, in a rainstorm, to welcome them home.

Over the decades, the legacy of the Summit Series has grown, making it not just an important hockey moment, but also one of the most significant cultural events in Canadian history. Team Canada 1972 holds the rare distinction of being the only sports team inducted into Canada's Sports Hall of Fame, and it was named the greatest team of the twentieth century in a poll by the Canadian Press.

Questions for Critical Thinking

1. From the information provided in the case, identify aspects of Team Canada's development in each of the five phases of the team's life cycle: forming, storming, norming, performing, and adjourning.

2. Referencing the textbook material, describe the actions by Head Coach Harry Sinden that contributed to team cohesiveness.

3. Although Team Canada was led and managed by both a head and an assistant coach, in what way could it be described as a *self-managed team*? Can you provide examples of *distributed leadership* as described in the case?

4. When the 1972 Team Canada players were announced, the entire hockey world was certain of Canadian victory. However, as Pat Stapleton said, "Hockey is played *on the ice*—and you should never underestimate the competition!" Discuss how this "perception" and "action" understanding also relates to business organizations and highlight a business example. How do you ensure that perceptions (either negative or positive) do not overshadow the importance of the underlying actions that need to be done?

5. Which characteristics of high-performing teams were reflected in Team Canada 1972 and also in the gold medal men's and women's hockey teams at the 2010 Olympics in Vancouver and the 2014 Olympics in Sochi?

Sources: Interview with Team Canada 1972 Head Coach and General Manager Harry Sinden, August 8, 2013, and Pat Stapleton, defenceman, Team Canada 1972, July 30, 2013; Andrew Podnieks, *Team Canada 1972: The Official 40th Anniversary Celebration* (Toronto: Fenn/McClelland & Stewart, 2012); 1972 Summit Series website, www.1972summitseries.com; Ted Blackman, "Esposito Booed, Raps Ungrateful Fans," *Montreal Gazette*, September 9, 1972, 25; "The Canada-Russia Summit Series: 40th Anniversary Special: Dispatches from Montreal Hockey Legends Red Fisher and Ted Blackman," *Montreal Gazette* (2012); Mary Janigan, "Hockey Sidetracked City for Three Hours as Fans All Over Stayed Riveted to Screens," *Montreal Gazette*, September 29, 1972, 1.

Case Study 10 Toyota: Looking Far into the Future

By borrowing the best ideas from North American brands and innovating the rest itself, Toyota has become a paragon of auto manufacturing efficiency. Its vehicles have been widely known for their quality and longevity—and Toyota's sales numbers are once again the envy of the North American Big Three, as it recently regained the global sales crown. Toyota had slipped as low as third following the natural disasters in Japan and Thailand that hurt production and demand. Here is how Toyota became so efficient at producing high-quality automobiles, and yet it is still facing challenges.

Buy Domestic?

There used to be a sentiment encouraging Canadian and U.S. car buyers to purchase domestic models built and assembled in North America. Those who still tout the movement to buy domestic have likely done a good bit of head-scratching over how to classify Toyota—a Japanese company operating in Ontario that employs Canadian workers and that uses Canadian- and American-made parts to produce vehicles sold across North America. What to think when this Japanese brand achieves a product quality superior to long-known North American brands and surges ahead of General Motors and Ford to rank number one in global auto sales? Yet Toyota, the model automotive manufacturing company, is still facing its own quality challenges.

Quality by Design

Toyota's success and growth in the North American auto market have been based on strategies honed since the 1950s to earn and retain customer satisfaction by producing superior vehicles within a highly efficient production environment. From the home office to factories to showrooms, two core philosophies guide Toyota's business: (1) creating fair, balanced, mutually beneficial relationships with both suppliers and employees; and (2) strictly adhering to a just-in-time (JIT) manufacturing principle.

Over the decades, other North American auto manufacturers developed relationships with their suppliers that emphasized tense competition, price cutting, and the modification of suppliers' production capacities with the changing needs of the domestic market. Year after year, parts suppliers had to bid to renew contracts in a process that valued year-to-year price savings over long-term relationships. Domestic manufacturers, notorious for changing production demands mid-season to comply with late-breaking market dynamics or customer feedback, forced suppliers to turn to double or triple shifts to keep up with capacity and thus avoid the problems—quality slips, recalls, line shutdowns, layoffs—that ultimately slow the final assembly of vehicles. When a carmaker doesn't know what it wants, suppliers have little chance of keeping up. This system of industry dynamics proved susceptible to new approaches from Japanese competitors.

Toyota's model of supply chain management displayed an exclusive commitment to parts suppliers, well-forecast parts orders that were not subject to sways in the market, and genuine concern for the success of suppliers. Supply chain relationships among Asian manufacturers are based on a complex system of cooperation and equity interests.

Visiting other North American auto plants and seeing months' worth of excess parts waiting to be installed taught Toyota the benefit of having only enough supplies on hand to fulfill a given production batch. Toyota plans its production schedules months in advance, dictating regularly scheduled parts shipments from its suppliers. Suppliers benefit by being able to predict long-range demand for products so they can schedule production accordingly. This builds mutual loyalty between suppliers and the carmaker—almost as if suppliers are part of Toyota. The fit and finish in Toyota vehicles is precise because its suppliers can afford to focus on the quality of their parts. And consumers notice: Toyota vehicles consistently earned high marks for customer satisfaction and retained their resale value better than almost any other brand.

Keep It Lean

Early Toyota presidents Toyoda Kiichiro and Ohno Taiichi are considered the fathers of the Toyota Production System (TPS), known widely by the JIT moniker or as "lean production." Emphasizing quality and efficiency at all levels, it drives nearly all aspects of decision making at Toyota.

Simply put, TPS is "all about producing only what's needed and transferring only what's needed," said Teruyuki Minoura, senior managing director at Toyota. "The answer is a flexible system that allows the line to produce what's necessary when it's necessary. If it takes six people to make a certain quantity of an item and there is a drop in the quantity required, then your system should let one or two of them drop out and get on with something else."

To achieve maximum efficiency, workers at Toyota plants must be exceptionally knowledgeable about all facets of a vehicle's production so they are able to change responsibilities as needed. "An environment where people have to think brings with it wisdom, and this wisdom brings with it *kaizen* [the notion of continuous improvement]," noted Minoura. "If asked to produce only one unit at a time, to produce according to the flow, a typical line worker is likely to be flummoxed. It's a basic characteristic of human beings that they develop wisdom from being put under pressure." However, kaizen also has to compete with the pressure of Mother Nature. The earthquake and subsequent tsunami that occurred in 2011 in Japan took a heavy toll on Toyota's supply chain and hurt its overall production of vehicles.

Keeping Up with the Times

No vehicle represents Toyota's focus on continuous improvement and innovation better than the wildly successful hybrid, the Prius. A niche car when introduced in Japan in 1997, Prius is now the world's third-bestselling car, recently topping the 3 million mark. Toyota now offers 18 hybrid passenger models in over 80 countries, accounting for 15 percent of total Toyota sales.

On the other hand, no Toyota vehicle has come to represent the challenges of adapting to a changing sales landscape more than its Tundra pickup truck. Toyota built a Tundra plant in Texas to prove that its trucks were as North American as those made by the Big Three. But truck sales began to decline as the price of oil rose. Contractors and builders began to think twice about new pickup purchases; the Tundra plants began to run well under capacity. To try to turn things around, Toyota was betting heavily on its 2014 Tundra model. Based on feedback from focus groups, designers and production paid more attention to power and capacity and less to style and comfort.

Yet quality, and in turn Toyota's reputation, has suffered in the past. Toyota is still dealing with the fallout from negative publicity when it recalled 7.6 million vehicles because of acceleration problems, which led to dozens of accidents and some deaths in the United States. Toyota's reputation for quality took another hit when influential magazine *Consumer Reports* pulled its recommendation on Toyota's popular flagship Camry sedan, plus the RAV4 and Prius v due to poor front crash test results. Toyota's number 2 safety technology officer says, "From a production point of view, it requires a drastic change. So it requires time." As in all things in the fast and flexible world of operations management, time is the essence of success.

Questions for Critical Thinking

1. How could Toyota's competitors draw from kaizen to gain efficiencies in their supply chain management?

2. What problems might a manufacturing firm face when trying to implement and use the just-in-time systems successfully used at Toyota?

3. How must employees' concerns fit in with production tinkering at Toyota?

4. Given the bad news from *Consumer Reports*, what customer relationship management initiatives would you suggest Toyota undertake?

5. Toyota has had to face the same quality challenges that its North American competitors (GM, Chrysler, and Ford) have been facing. Do some investigation on how automobile manufacturers are incorporating quality into their cars and into their image. Who now is doing the best job on both questions?

Sources: Toyota website, www.toyota.com; "Toyota Outsells GM, Ford Posts Eye-Popping Loss," *U.S. News & World Report*, July 24, 2008; M. Reza Vaghefi, "Creating Sustainable Competitive Advantage: The Toyota Philosophy and Its Effects," Mastering Management Online (October 2001), accessed at www.ftmastering.com; "Top 10 SUVs, Pickups and Minivans with the Best Residual Value for 2005," Edmunds.com; Toyota Motor Corporation, "Making Things: The Essence and Evolution of the Toyota Production System," and "The 'Thinking' Production System: TPS as a Winning Strategy for Developing People in the Global Manufacturing Environment"; Alex Taylor III, "The Birth of the Prius," *CNN Money*, February 24, 2006; Rick Newman, "Toyota's Next Turn," *U.S. News & World Report*, June 16, 2008; Greg Keenan, "Trigger-Happy Toyota Recalls 1 Million Corolla, Matrix Vehicles," *The Globe and Mail*, August 26, 2010; Robert E. Cole, "No Big Quality Problems at Toyota?" *Harvard Business Review* blog, March 9, 2010; http://blogs.hbr.org; Yoko Kubota, "Toyota Keeps Top Spot in Global Auto Sales Rankings, Outselling GM, VW," *The Globe and Mail*, October 28, 2013; Deepa Seetharaman, "Toyota Redesigns 2014 Tundra to Appeal to Truck Buyers," Reuters, February 7, 2013; Brad Tuttle, "Toyota Prius: Niche Car No More," *Time*, May 29, 2012; Tiffany Kaiser, "Toyota's Prius Hybrid Crosses 3 Million Unit Threshold in Worldwide Sales," *DailyTech*, July 5, 2013, www.dailytech.com; Jeremy Cato, "Toyota Stumbles on One Crash Test; Still Rated 'Reliable,'" *The Globe and Mail*, October 31, 2013.

Part 4 Marketing Management

Case Study 11 Zara International: Fashion at the Speed of Light

At the announcement of her engagement to Spain's Crown Prince Felipe, Letizia Ortiz Rocasolano wore a chic white trouser suit; within a few weeks, hundreds of European women sported the same look. Welcome to fast fashion, a trend that sees clothing retailers frequently purchasing small quantities of merchandise to stay on top of emerging trends. In this world of "hot today, gauche tomorrow," no company does fast fashion better than Zara International. Shoppers in 78 countries, including Canada, have taken to Zara's knack for bringing the latest styles from sketchbook to clothing rack at lightning speed and reasonable prices.

In Fast Fashion, Moments Matter

Because style-savvy customers expect shorter and shorter delays from runway to store, Zara International employs a stable of more than 200 professionals to help it keep up with the latest fashions. It takes just two weeks for the company to update existing garments and get them into its stores; new pieces hit the market twice a week.

Defying the recession with its cheap-and-chic Zara clothing chain, Zara's parent company Inditex posted strong sales gains. Low prices and a rapid response to fashion trends are enabling it to challenge Gap, Inc., for top ranking among global clothing vendors. The improved results highlight how Zara's formula continued to work even in the downturn. The chain specializes in lightning-quick turnarounds of the latest designer trends at prices tailored to the young—about $27 an item. Louis Vuitton fashion director Daniel Piette described Zara as "possibly the most innovative and devastating retailer in the world."

Inditex Group shortens the time from order to arrival by using a complex system of just-in-time production and inventory reporting that keeps Zara ahead. Their distribution centres can have items in European stores within 24 hours of receiving an order, and in American and Asian stores in under 48 hours. "They're a fantastic case study in terms of how they manage to get product to their stores so quick," said Stacey Cartwright, executive vice-president and CFO of Burberry Group PLC. "We are mindful of their techniques."

Inditex's history in fabrics manufacturing made it good business sense to internalize as many points in the supply chain as possible. Inditex controls design, production, distribution, and retail sales to optimize the flow of goods without having to share profits with wholesalers or intermediary partners. Customers win by having access to new fashions while they're still fresh off the runway. During a Madonna concert tour in Spain, Zara's quick turnaround let young fans at the last show wear Madonna's outfit from the first one.

Twice a week Zara's finished garments are shipped to logistical centres that simultaneously distribute products to stores worldwide. These small production batches help the company avoid the risk of oversupply. Because batches always contain new products, Zara's stores perpetually energize their inventories. Most clothing lines are not replenished. Instead they are replaced with new designs to create scarcity value—shoppers cannot be sure that designs in stores one day will be available the next.

Store managers track sales data with handheld computers. They can reorder hot items in less than an hour. This lets Zara know what's selling and what's not; when a look doesn't pan out, designers promptly put together new products. According to Dilip Patel, managing director for Inditex, new arrivals are rushed to store sales floors still on the black plastic hangers used in shipping. Shoppers who are in the know recognize these designs as the newest of the new; soon after, any items left over are rotated to Zara's standard wood hangers.

Inside and out, Zara's stores are specially dressed to strengthen the brand. Inditex considers this to be of the greatest importance because that is where shoppers ultimately decide which fashions make the cut. In a faux shopping street in the basement of the company's headquarters, stylists craft and photograph eye-catching layouts that are emailed every two weeks to store managers for replication.

Zara stores sit on some of the world's glitziest shopping streets—including New York's Fifth Avenue, near the flagship stores of leading international fashion brands—which make its reasonable prices stand out. "Inditex gives people the most up-to-date fashion at accessible prices, so it is a real alternative to high-end fashion lines," said Luca Solca, senior research analyst with Sanford C. Bernstein in London. That is good news for Zara, as many shoppers trade down from higher-priced chains.

Catfights on the Catwalk

Zara is not the only player in fast fashion. Competition is fierce, but Zara's overwhelming success (sales were US$13.6 billion in 2012) has the competition scrambling to keep up. San Francisco–based Gap, Inc., which had been the largest independent clothing retailer by revenue until Zara bumped them to second place in 2009, posted a 21 percent decline in the first half of 2011 and had plans to close 700 stores by the end of 2013. Only time will tell if super-chic Topshop's entry into the American market will make a wrinkle in Zara's success.

Some fashion analysts are referring to this as the democratization of fashion: bringing high(er) fashion to low(er)-income shoppers. According to James Hurley, managing director and senior research analyst with New York–based Telsey Advisory Group LLC, big-box discount stores such as Target and Walmart are emulating Zara's ability to study emerging fashions and knock out look-alikes in a matter of weeks. "In general," Hurley said, "the fashion cycle is becoming sharper and more immediately accessible."

But making fashion more accessible can have its costs: Zara faced some controversy last year when Brazilian authorities discovered and shut down a São Paulo sweatshop run by AHA, one of Zara's contractors. Inditex denied knowledge of the working conditions, but it acknowledged that the conditions in the sweatshop ran counter to its code of conduct and compensated the affected workers.

A Single Fashion Culture

With a network of over 1,600 stores around the world, Zara International is Inditex's largest and most profitable brand, bringing home 77 percent of international sales and nearly 67 percent of revenues. The first Zara outlet opened shop in 1975 in La Coruña. It remained solely a Spanish chain until opening a store in Oporto, Portugal, in 1988. The brand reached the United States and France in 1989 and 1990 with outlets in New York and Paris, respectively. Zara went into mainland China in 2001, India in 2009, and Australia in 2011.

Essential to Zara's growth and success are Inditex's 100-plus textile design, manufacturing, and distribution companies that employ more than 92,000 workers. The Inditex group began in 1963 when Amancio Ortega Gaona, chairman and founder of Inditex, got his start in textile manufacturing. After a period of growth, he assimilated Zara into a new holding company, Industria de Diseño Textil. Inditex has a tried-and-true strategy for entering new markets: start with a handful of stores and gain a critical mass of customers. Generally, Zara is the first Inditex chain to break ground in new countries, paving the way for the group's other brands, including Pull and Bear, Massimo Dutti, and Bershka.

Inditex farms out much of its garment production to specialist companies, located on the Iberian Peninsula, which it often supplies with its own fabrics. Although some pieces and fabrics are purchased in Asia—many of them not dyed or only partly finished—the company manufactures about half of its clothing in its hometown of La Coruña, Spain. H&M, one of Zara's top competitors, uses a slightly different strategy. Around one-quarter of its stock is made up of fast-fashion items that are designed in-house and farmed out to independent factories. As at Zara, these items move quickly through the stores and are replaced often by fresh designs. But H&M also keeps a large inventory of basic, everyday items sourced from cheap Asian factories.

Inditex CEO Pablo Isla believes in cutting expenses wherever and whenever possible. Zara spends just 0.3 percent of sales on ads, making the 3 to 4 percent typically spent by rivals seem excessive in comparison. Isla disdains markdowns and sales, as well.

Few can criticize the results of Isla's frugality. Inditex opened 358 new stores by the end of Q3 2011 and was simultaneously named Retailer of the Year during the World Retailer Congress meeting. Perhaps most important in an industry predicated on image, Inditex secured bragging rights as Europe's largest fashion retailer by overtaking H&M. According to José Castellano, former deputy chairman of Inditex, the group plans to double in size in the coming years while making sales of more than US$15 billion. He envisioned most of this growth taking place in Europe—especially in trend-savvy Italy.

Fashion of the Moment

Although Inditex's dominance of fast fashion seems virtually complete, it isn't without its challenges. For instance, keeping production so close to home becomes difficult when an increasing number of Zara stores are far-flung across the globe. "The efficiency of the supply chain is coming under more pressure the farther abroad they go," notes Nirmalya Kumar, a professor at London Business School.

Inditex launched its Zara online store in the United States in the fall of 2011, offering free two- to three-day shipping and free returns in the model of uber-successful eretailer Zappos. A Zara application for the iPhone has been downloaded by more prospective clients in the United States than in any other market, according to chief executive Pablo Isla—more than a million iPhone users in just three months. Beginning in 2010, Zara rolled out its online store in 16 European countries and plans to progressively add the remaining countries where Zara operates. Analysts worry that Inditex's rapid expansion may bring undue pressure to its business. The rising number of overseas stores, they warn, adds cost and complexity and is straining its operations. Inditex may no longer be able to manage everything from Spain. But Inditex wasn't worried. By closely managing costs, Inditex said its current logistics system could handle its growth for several more years.

José Luis Nueno of IESE, a business school in Barcelona, says that Zara is here to stay. Consumers have become more demanding and more arbitrary, he says—and fast fashion is better suited to these changes. But is Zara International trying to expand too quickly? Do you think it will be able to introduce a new logistics system able to carry it into another decade of intense growth?

Questions for Critical Thinking

1. What do all Zara customers want?

2. What does the Zara brand mean to customers around the world?

3. How are Zara's customers different than other fashion-oriented shoppers?

4. How can Zara control unwanted inventories?

5. Gather the latest information on competitive trends in the apparel industry and the latest actions and innovations of Zara. Is the firm continuing to do well? Is it adapting in ways needed to stay abreast of both its major competition and the pressures of a changing global economy?

Sources: Inditex website, www.inditex.com, "Inditex: Who We Are: Concepts: Zara," Inditex press kit, "Inditex FY2010 Results," "Our Group," "Who We Are," "Inditex: Our Team," and Inditext 2012 Annual Report; "Inditex Recognized as International Retailer of the Year at the World Retail Congress," news release, March 10, 2011; "The Future of Fast Fashion," *The Economist*, June 16, 2005; "Zara Grows as Retail Rivals Struggle," *Wall Street Journal*, March 26, 2009; "Zara, a Spanish Success Story," *CNN*, June 15, 2001; Cecile Rohwedder and Keith Johnson, "Pace-Setting Zara Seeks More Speed to Fight Its Rising Cheap-Chic Rivals," *Wall Street Journal*, February 20, 2008, B1; "Zara: Taking the Lead in Fast-Fashion," *BusinessWeek*, April 4, 2006; Dana Mattioli and Kris Hudson, "Gap to Slash Its Store Count," *Wall Street Journal*, October 14, 2011; Diana Middleton, "Fashion for the Frugal," *Florida Times-Union*, October 1, 2006; Stephen Burgen and Tom Phillips, "Zara Accused in Brazil Sweatshop Inquiry," *The Guardian*, August 18, 2011; Zara España, S.A. "Hoover's Company Records," February 14, 2012; "Shining Examples," *The Economist*, June 17, 2006; "Ortega's Empire Showed Rivals New Style of Retailing," *The Times*, June 14, 2007; "Zara Launches Online Shopping in the USA," *College Fashion*, September 7, 2011; Christopher Bjork, "Zara Has Online Focus for US Expansion Inditex Says," *Dow Jones Newswires*, March 17, 2010; "Zara Arrived in Australia with a Flagship Store on Sydney's Most Prominent Shopping Street," Inditex news release, April 19, 2011; Walter Loeb, "Zara's Secret to Success: The New Science of Retailing," *Forbes*, October 14, 2013.

Case Study 12 Hudson's Bay Company: From Fur to Fendi

After 300 years, Canada's oldest retailer knows a thing or two about change. Older than the country it serves, Hudson's Bay Company (HBC) has remained a landmark institution in Canada, navigating its way from rural outposts to over 600 locations and nearly 60,000 associates located in every province. Known best for its flagship department store Hudson's Bay (formerly The Bay), HBC also operates Home Outfitters in Canada and U.S. retail chain Lord & Taylor.

Despite its long and glorious past, all is not well at Canada's historic company. Leadership changes, increased competition, a fragmenting retail market, and plummeting sales have plagued HBC well into the new millennium. Will HBC be able to successfully weather the seas of change, or will it sink into history?

History

Two centuries before Confederation, a pair of European explorers discovered a wealth of fur in the interior of Canada accessible by an inland sea, Hudson's Bay. In 1670, with permission from the King of England, trading began, and HBC traded goods and furs in a few forts and posts around James Bay and Hudson Bay throughout the first century. Later, competition forced HBC to expand into Canada's interior, and a string of outposts grew up along river networks that would eventually become the modern cities of Winnipeg, Calgary, and Edmonton.

By the end of the nineteenth century, changing tastes caused the fur trade to lose importance, while western settlements and the gold rush introduced new clientele to HBC—ones who paid in cash, not fur. Trading posts gave way to sales shops with a greater selection of goods, transforming HBC into a modern retail organization. During this time, HBC also started selling homesteads to newly arrived settlers, eventually diversifying into a full-scale commercial property holding and development organization. Shipping and natural resources, particularly oil and gas, were important sidelines.

Challenges

Fast forward to the 1980s. The pace of HBC's retail acquisition and the economic downturn left the company with major debt and caused it to rethink its priorities. Like many other firms at the time, HBC decided to return to its core business. Nonstrategic assets were sold, as were the company's last natural resource holdings. Strategic expansion followed to strengthen its share of the market with the acquisition of other retailers, such as Kmart Canada.

Since the 1980s, the company has continued to navigate its way through the wake of a weakened economy, changing consumer tastes, and intense competition. The popularity of big-box stores, such as Walmart, Old Navy, and Future Shop, changed consumer behaviour away from department store shopping, forcing retailers like The Bay and Zellers to compete on selection of merchandise and price.

With its reputation for unfocused collections of merchandise, shabby stores, and unhelpful sales staff, HBC tried a number of strategies to entice customers back. Some strategies, such as the HBC Rewards program and online shopping, have been successful; however, other strategies haven't fared as well. Early in 2001, it tried to reinvent itself with a more fashionable image for The Bay and reduced the focus on steep discounts. The economy, and frustrated customers, forced it to abandon the move and return to its value-based focus. To try to remain competitive with other low-cost retailers, HBC diversified, although unsuccessfully, through Designer Depot/Style Depot, which operated from 2004 to 2008.

After remaining a Canadian company for over 330 years, HBC was bought in 2006 by U.S. financier Jerry Zucker. He sought to revive the firm by focusing on improving operations and customer satisfaction. In 2008, after Zucker's death, HBC was bought by U.S. private equity firm NRDC Equity Partners, which also owned the U.S. department store chain Lord & Taylor. NRDC's strategy was once again to revitalize HBC with better brands and better service.

Under NRDC's leadership, The Bay quickly focused on reattracting customers by dropping over 60 percent of its former brands and relaunching "The Room," a plush VIP suite at one of its

Toronto locations, with high-end designers such as Armani, Ungaro, and Chanel. Despite the economic downturn in 2008 and while other organizations were laying off workers, The Bay was in the black.

Another coup for HBC was becoming the official clothing outfitter for the Canadian Olympic Team. The $100 million deal made HBC the clothing provider for the 2006, 2008, 2010, and 2012 games. The HBC apparel for the 2010 Winter Olympics in Vancouver was extremely popular, and new customers and those who hadn't shopped at The Bay in years flocked back to snap up hoodies, coats, hats, and the iconic red mittens as fast as the merchandise could be put on the shelves. HBC's Olympic sponsorship has been renewed through 2020.

HBC continued its revitalization strategy by redesigning and renovating stores; offering a higher-end assortment of fashionable brands such as Juicy Couture, Theory, and Hugo Boss; and expanding ecommerce. The company also hoped to capitalize on its history with a redesigned Signature Line, adding a modern twist to HBC classics such as its striped "point" blankets, sweaters, coats, canoes, trapper hats, and maple syrup, reminiscent of its early trading days.

Moving Forward

As HBC continued its reinvention, former CEO Richard Baker spearheaded a number of initiatives to make the retailer the country's top seller of women's shoes, along with introducing more British-based "cheap-chic" Topshop store-within-stores, and by 2014 its downtown Toronto flagship store was to feature New York–based Kleinfeld Bridal salon of *Say Yes to the Dress* reality-show fame.

However, the company faces increased competition from U.S. retailers. "Cheap-chic" retailer Target, which opened 124 stores across Canada in 2013, many in locations formerly occupied by the Zellers retail chain, was one example. It's interesting to note that Target Corporation bought about 220 of the struggling Zellers Inc. chain from HBC in 2011, intending to convert 100 to 150 of them to its Target banner, and eventually planned to have more than 200 Target outlets in Canada within 10 years. Target failed to catch on with Canadian consumers and closed operation in 2015. HBC will also face further competition from Seattle-based upscale department store chain Nordstrom Inc., which planned to expand into the Canadian market between 2014 and 2016. Nordstrom's first Canadian stores opened at Chinook Centre in Calgary and Rideau Centre in Ottawa in 2015 with more scheduled to open soon after.

Undaunted, the iconic Hudson's Bay Company continues its evolution after many years of change and innovation in the Canadian retail landscape. In spring 2013, the company celebrated its past, present, and anticipated future by unveiling a rebranding of its company and store logos, replacing "The Bay" with its classic full name. "We're very proud to say that Hudson's Bay is continuing to advance in 2013, not only with our new business ventures, but with our updated look," says Tony Smith, creative director at HBC. "We've taken what is a very meaningful two-pronged approach to the redesign: maintaining our heritage while modernizing the new Hudson's Bay Company. It's a throwback to our remarkable history and an image for the direction we're heading in."

Based on its recent successes, HBC seems to be on the right track, but will it be enough to make it once again a premier Canadian shopping destination, or is it too late to revive the historic department store?

In July 2013, HBC "rolled the dice" and bought upscale department chain Saks Inc. for US$2.9 billion. While some observers called it risky, there is agreement that this bold move will help HBC defend its turf in Canada against the arrival of big foreign players.

Questions for Critical Thinking

1. Describe the competitive retail landscape HBC faces in Canada today.
2. What strategic moves would you suggest to HBC as it tries to find a place in the retail environment?
3. What are Hudson's Bay Company's current major strengths that provide it with a competitive advantage? What are its current major weaknesses?

4. What types of things should HBC's top management be doing with respect to the company's employees to ensure successful strategy implementation?

5. Are there other successful chains in the world that Hudson's Bay could learn from by examining their innovative strategic path? If so, which ones, and why?

Sources: Hudson's Bay Company website, www.hbc.com, "About" and "History"; Marina Strauss, "HBC Tries to Build on Olympic Momentum," *The Globe and Mail*, August 23, 2012; Kristin Laird, "The Bay, RBC Renew Olympic Sponsorship," *Marketing*, October 28, 2011; Marina Strauss, "New-Look Hudson's Bay Pushes Retail Growth Plan," *The Globe and Mail*, April 7, 2013; Marina Strauss and Jacquie McNish, "With Target, Canada's Retail Landscape Set for Massive Makeover," *The Globe and Mail*, August 24, 2012; "Nordstrom Expands Canadian Footprint to Yorkdale Mall," CBC News, April 8, 2013; "Hudson's Bay Celebrates Its Past, Present and Future with Modern New Logo," news release, March 6, 2013; Mark Anderson, Keith Howlett, Richard Talbot, and Lindsay Meredith, "Subject: Hudson's Bay Co.: Venerable Department Store and Discount Retailer. Problem: More Dynamic Competitors Are Eating Its Market. Question: Can CEO George Heller Beat Off the Big-box Innovators?" *National Post*, July 2002, 29; Rachel Giese, "The Bay's Cinderella Moment," *Canadian Business*, November 23, 2009, 42; "New Owner of The Bay Says No Major Layoffs Planned," *Canada AM*, January 27, 2006; David George-Cash, "Hudson's Bay Co. Owner Dies, Wife Takes Key Role," *Canwest News*, April 13, 2008; David Moin, "Brooks on The Bay Watch," *WWD*, October 19, 2009, 5; David Moin, "Hudson's Bay Scores with Olympics," *WWD*, March 2, 2010, 19; Marina Strauss, "HBC's Wares Get Hot with the 'Coolness' Factor," *The Globe and Mail*, February 27, 2010, B.4.

Case Study 13 Luxury Brands Market to Millennials

Chanel. Armani. BMW. Cartier. These long-established, high-end brands are interested in Generation Y, also known as the Millennials—those born during the 1980s to the mid-2000s. The newest challenge these once-exclusive brands face is marketing to this age group.

According to a recent American marketing survey, which also applies to Canada, Millennials are the "largest consumer group in U.S. history," even bigger than the baby-boom generation, the previous record holders. The 70 million to 85 million Millennials make up 25 percent of the American population. They are the most ethnically diverse population group ever and the age group that is the least limited by gender stereotypes. They spend more than $200 billion a year on purchases. As they enter the workforce and set up their own households, their spending power will overtake the soon-to-retire baby boomers.

Even more important is how Millennials receive information and communicate. Unlike any previous generation, they have grown up with digital technology. They take for granted such things as cellphones, video games, and other high-speed electronic devices and media. They are used to having instantly available information and communication. A survey by the Pew Research Center notes that 75 percent of Generation Y use social media, compared to 50 percent of Generation X (those born between 1961 and 1981) and 30 percent of baby boomers (those born between 1946 and 1964).

Millennials are very aware of the value of what they buy. The marketing survey found that 65 percent of female Millennials and 61 percent of male Millennials describe themselves as brand conscious. But the marketing tools of heritage and exclusivity, which have traditionally been used to promote prestige brands, mean little to Millennials. Instead, they value quality, authenticity, and image. They shun anything that resembles self-promotion in either brands or people, including prominently displayed corporate logos.

Burberry, a maker of high-end clothing and accessories established in 1836, recently began an ambitious multimedia effort to reach Millennials. One of the company's first moves was to hire Emma Watson, an actress famous for playing the role of Hermione Granger in the Harry Potter movies. Watson, a Millennial born in 1990, was the new face of Burberry's spring–summer campaign. In addition to promoting its business through traditional print advertising and its website, Burberry has also used live streaming and 3D filming of its fashion shows. Burberry also hired the photo blogger Scott Schuman, known as the Sartorialist, to launch a special website, Art of the Trench, to promote its classic trench coat. Burberry's Facebook page calls Art of the Trench "a living celebration of the trench coat and the people who wear it." The website, essentially a social networking blog, invites owners to submit photos of themselves wearing their trench coats—and to submit videos to its YouTube channel. Links allow visitors to "view details," "like," "share," and "leave comments" on the photos. They can also sort the photos by popularity, gender, styling, trench colour, and weather. The site features music by the Maccabees, White Lies, and other groups, with links to their websites. Burberry's chief executive officer, Angela Ahrendts, said, "Attracting the Millennial customer to luxury started two years ago—I said that we can either get crushed or ride the greatest wave of our life."

Scott Galloway of New York University's School of Business says, "Gen Y goodwill is arguably the closest thing to a crystal ball for predicting a brand's long-term prospects. Just as Boomers drove the luxury sector for the last 20 years, brands that resonate with Gen Y, whose purchasing power will surpass that of Boomers by 2017, will be the new icons of prestige."

Questions for Critical Thinking

1. Millennials are brand conscious but generally dislike conspicuous, flashy brand logos. How might these likes and dislikes affect a company's brand equity?

2. Burberry is basing its product strategy on how Millennials use the Internet and social media, not on the preferences of their parents. Will this difference in strategy continue as the Millennials mature? If so, how might Burberry change its product strategy?

Sources: Burberry website, http://us.burberry.com; Art of the Trench, http://artofthetrench.com; Sharalyn Hartwell, "Millennials Love Brands, Not Branding," Examiner.com, May 6, 2010; Scott Galloway, "Gen Y Prestige Brand Ranking," May 3, 2010; http://l2thinktank.com/Gen_Y_Report.pdf; Pew Research Center, "The Millennials: Confident. Connected. Open to Change," February 24, 2010; Jessica Bumpus, "Millennial Burberry," *Vogue*, March 3, 2010; Suzy Menkes, "Marketing to the Millennials," *New York Times*, March 2, 2010.

Part 5 Managing Technology and Information

Case Study 14 Technology Drives Zipcar's Success

As a member of Zipcar, the world's largest car-sharing service, consumers avoid the costs associated with car ownership: gasoline, insurance, maintenance, and parking. Based in Cambridge, Massachusetts, Zipcar was founded by two moms who met when their children were in the same kindergarten class. Prior to its launch, Zipcar raised $75,000, most of which was spent to develop technology. Today, Zipcar is owned by Avis Budget and offers self-service, on-demand cars by the hour or day. The company provides automobile reservations to its 850,000 members and offers more than 10,000 cars in urban areas, on college campuses, and at airports worldwide.

With a seamless user experience, it may be difficult for Zipsters (the company's name for its members) to realize the complex technology that goes into making the car-sharing service so user friendly. Zipcar relies on a number of different technologies, including mobile, web, telematics, radio-frequency identification (RFID), operational information administration systems, and phone and interactive voice response systems for support and customer service. In addition, there are teams responsible for the company's security infrastructure, mobile app development, and auto maintenance to make sure its fleet of vehicles is ready for members.

At the heart of Zipcar's technologies is an operational administration system. As a data-driven company, Zipcar relies heavily on information to make company decisions and manage assets. The system enables the company to manage its physical assets—its vehicles—in many locations worldwide. The system provides data about car utilization, when and how people are driving, specific locations, hours used, and miles driven. Using the data, analytics are performed that allow the company to optimize utilization levels. This type of information is valuable for making strategic decisions about supply and demand, including when and where to place cars, the models and types to use, and when to change them.

The technology in the cars provides information that allows the company to understand how its cars are being used. Zipcar has created a telematics board for each vehicle with GPS and RFID, which supplies geographic, customer, and utilization information. Using transponders, the RFID technology works with a card reader physically placed on the car's windshield. After the customer makes a reservation either on the web or via a mobile device, the RFID card is used to enter and exit any Zipcar. This technology identifies the user and his or her car reservation. Once the car is unlocked, the key is in the car attached to a tether on the steering column. The user will also find a toll pass (members pay for tolls) and a gas card (price of gas is included in the rental fee).

Because of Zipcar's technology, the keys can be left in the car without concern of theft. When a user enters or exits a car, hours, usage, and mileage are uploaded to a central computer via a wireless data link. However, for privacy purposes, the location of the vehicle is not tracked. In addition, all cars are equipped with a "kill" function, which allows the company to prevent theft. For security purposes, the car opens only to the designated user. With a mobile device, a user is able to unlock and lock the car and honk its horn, which helps determine a car's location.

Because 98 percent of Zipcar users have smartphones, mobile and web applications are integral to interfacing with customers. At the heart of the Zipcar's car sharing is a self-serve transaction that allows a user to find, reserve, and access a specific car at a specific location at a specific time. The information is then sent wirelessly to the car, and Zipcar members use their Zipcard to open the car door. Once the car is returned and locked, billing is finalized and information is made available to the member.

Although it is rare that Zipsters interact directly with someone from the company because reservations happen via mobile device or online, providing superior service when something goes wrong requires technology. Dedicated phone systems and customer support systems are crucial for things like on-the-road issues. The Zipcar phone system identifies users who are calling, their reservations, and the cars they are driving, so that timely support and problem solving can happen quickly. Technology also supplies information about the vehicle's service history, which helps with troubleshooting and service.

As transportation needs continue to change, Zipcar is working to improve its technology base. The company remains committed to assessing consumer transportation and parking needs for business and personal use. Zipcar is focused on understanding and assessing trip-type needs, whether it is an errand for a few hours, an afternoon at the beach, or a business meeting. Using various technologies, the company has created a seamless experience for consumers who desire alternatives to car ownership. So, the next time you decide to reserve a Zipcar and drive to the beach for the day, you will have a strong support system at the ready thanks to the company's focus on technology.

Questions for Critical Thinking

1. What type of data does Zipcar use to make decisions on behalf of its customers? Its operations? How does the data used to make customer decisions differ from the data used to make decisions related to operations? Discuss.

2. Discuss how Zipcar manages and deals with information security. What are some of the issues the company faces with regard to security?

3. What information does Zipcar use to manage its fleet? What information is used to decide which types of cars to purchase, how they will be used, and where they will be located? How might weather patterns or seasonality impact the types and number of cars the company purchases?

4. Discuss how Zipcar leverages technology to acquire new members. Based on its segmentation of consumers, businesses, and college students, discuss the various technologies used to identify the relevant target audiences and the types of messages conveyed to each of them.

Sources: Zipcar website www.zipcar.com, "Zipcar Overview" and "How to Zip"; Chris Ready, "Zipcar Rolls Out One-Way Service with Guaranteed Parking," *Boston Globe*, May 2, 2014; Mark Rogowsky, "Zipcar, Uber, and the Beginning of Trouble for the Auto Industry," *Forbes*, February 8, 2014; Carol Hymowitz, "Zipcar Founder Robin Chase on Starting Buzzcar and a Portugal Venture," *Bloomberg Businessweek*, August 8, 2013.

Part 6 Managing Financial Resources

Case Study 15 Canadian Pacific: All Dedicated, Hard-Working Railroaders Aboard!

Canadian Pacific (CP), one of Canada's oldest and most iconic companies, is headquartered in Calgary. The railway company has over 15,000 employees and owns approximately 22,500 kilometres (14,000 miles) of track all across Canada and into the United States, stretching from Montreal to Vancouver. Its freight rail network also serves major cities in the United States, such as Minneapolis, Detroit, Chicago, and New York City. CP recently underwent a downsizing that required creative ways to keep employees motivated in a competitive industry.

A Prestigious Past

Canadian Pacific (CP) was incorporated on February 16, 1881. Less than five years later, Canada was united when the rail line to the Pacific coast was completed with the driving of the "last spike" at Craigellachie, British Columbia, on November 7, 1885. Canadian Pacific became Canada's first transcontinental railway. Primarily a freight railway, however, CP was for decades the only practical means of long-distance passenger transport in many regions of Canada. It was instrumental in the settlement and development of Western Canada and has become one of the largest and most powerful companies in Canada.

Over the years, as Canada's rail industry expanded because of immigration, settlement of the west, and our burgeoning natural resources, the CP workforce became heavily unionized and the company became more bureaucratic. The workplace culture meant there were few incentives for employees to excel. That all changed when business developments and the new economy resulted in a leaner CP that was able to better compete in the challenging transportation industry. And key to this transformation was employee motivation.

A New Hill to Climb

In the spring of 2012, the railway's largest shareholder, Pershing Square Capital Management, pushed for leadership change at CP, feeling that the company was underperforming. Pershing Square Capital launched a successful proxy battle, resulting in several board members and the CEO being replaced. The new CEO, industry veteran Hunter Harrison, is an American and the retired CEO of the other company that dominates Canadian rail traffic—Canadian National Railway Company.

Harrison took over in June 2012 and began a major restructuring plan to make the company more streamlined and efficient. In the fall of 2012, CP began to reduce its rail network. Among other things, the company increased the length of its trains, resulting in the need for 195 fewer locomotives and 3,200 fewer leased freight cars. Leaner operations also require fewer employees, so in December 2012 Canadian Pacific announced it was cutting almost a quarter of its workforce over four years, as Harrison aggressively cut costs to create a more competitive railway. Approximately 1,700 jobs were eliminated by the end of 2012 through layoffs, attrition, and the use of fewer contract positions, with up to a total of 4,500 jobs to be cut by 2016—representing about 23 percent of CP's 19,500 employees and contractors. "This is clearly, initially, a cost-takeout story," he told financial investors at a presentation in New York. "We were clearly, in my view, top heavy," he added, noting that three in ten employees were in non-union management positions. "That's far too much."

The company also reviewed its property costs and real estate holdings and decided to move its headquarters out of leased, downtown Calgary office space and relocate by 2014 to a building it already owned in a rail yard on the outskirts of town.

Getting Back on Track

Motivating employees is challenging in any environment, but especially so in a company that is downsizing. Remaining employees often have to work harder, and they may wonder if they'll be the next one to lose their job. How did CP handle this common problem?

Throughout the restructuring, management let employees know there was a place for them if they were willing to move into different positions. The company also made a commitment to training and to focusing on the opportunities for learning new skills. But first, CP had to get over the common hurdle of a company culture that stressed the status quo. "There's some degree of it being a cultural issue. There was lack of a sense of real urgency. You know, headquarters and the top sort of sets the tone for the rest of the organization," Harrison said. "But we have said we're not going to lose good people if they want to work. If where they are now doesn't fit necessarily, we've said, 'If you're willing to be cross-trained, trained in another discipline, and you're mobile and able to move, you've got a job.' If you're stuck in some area, and you won't move, and you don't want to do anything but what you're doing and you don't want to be trained, you're probably going to have look somewhere else to work."

The company also went to work to motivate employees to improve customer service. Instead of focusing on customer service agents, CP encourages and empowers staff in the field to solve problems for customers. "We have had a huge customer service department of about 650 people. You show me a group that has a customer service department of 650 and I'll show somebody who's got bad service," Harrison said. "So, what we said is those aren't the important people. The people we need to get impassioned about service is the people on the ground who are providing the service. So rather than have this huge bureaucracy where if something goes wrong in Toronto and the person is next door to the operating personnel, rather than have the customer call Winnipeg to create a lot of bureaucracy and take a week to get back to the customer, what we're doing is trying to produce a passion about service with everybody on the ground and recognize the commitments we have to do and that's where our customer service department is going to be—on the ground. If those people don't provide the kind of customer service we say we're going to do, then we're going to have somebody else do it."

CP's decision to move its headquarters from downtown Calgary to a suburban location was partly intended to improve morale. "I think it helps the culture and it saves us money. It's going to save us about $17 million or $18 million annually, and I think over time it's a better environment for the employees," Harrison said. "It's going to be much more functional and nicer for the employees to work in. Workout centres and an outdoor track. It's a way to take those people out of headquarters and kind of let them be out there and see what the business is all about. It's not about downtown bank buildings and glass towers. It's about railroading, and they can look out and see track and interface with the people who run the railroad."

Some of the employees who were let go didn't meet company expectations. Harrison said, "75 to 80 percent-plus" of CP was "dedicated, hard-working railroaders," but "some people weren't doing [their jobs] appropriately." He added, "Our culture is a culture of holding people accountable and applying consequences, both good and bad."

By spring 2013, Harrison was facing criticism for his hard-driving approach to running Canadian Pacific. But his numbers spoke for themselves. Harrison delivered a record first-quarter result in April, and said CP was en route to a record year of earnings for its shareholders. By June 2013, the value of CP shares had more than tripled since Pershing Square Capital Management had taken its initial shareholdings in the railway in September 2011. In its 2013 first-quarter earnings announcement, CP listed "controlling and removing unnecessary costs from the organization, eliminating bureaucracy and continuing to identify productivity enhancements" as keys to its success.

Questions for Critical Thinking

1. What accounting information would help management make decisions about what and where to make cuts to operating costs?

2. What accounting information should be used to measure the success of the transition?

3. What impact on employee engagement could result from Harrison's approach to reduce bureaucracy and "produce a passion about service with everybody on the ground and recognize the commitments we have to do"? Likewise, what might be the impact on employee engagement of his plan to move headquarters from downtown to the rail yard in order to "take those people out of headquarters and kind of let them be out there and see what the business is all about"?

4. Harrison used a cost-cutting strategy that focused heavily on employee accountability. What management systems would you need in place before you could initiate a performance-based program such as the one Harrison used?

5. Find out how Canadian Pacific is doing now. Have Harrison's restructuring plans continued to achieve the desired improved results for CP's shareholders? Have there been any negative aspects to his aggressive approach to cut costs and improve efficiency at CP?

Sources: Canadian Pacific Railway website, www.cpr.ca, "Our Past, Present, and Future"; Library and Archives Canada, "Ties That Bind: A Brief History of Railways in Canada"; Ian Austen, "Ackman Wins Proxy Fight at Canadian Pacific," *New York Times*, May 17, 2012; Guy Dixon, "CP Cuts Deep as Hunter Harrison Makes His Mark," *Globe and Mail*, December 4, 2012; Scott Deveau, "Straight-Talking CP Rail CEO Opens Up about Company Overhaul, Job Cuts," *Financial Post*, December 5, 2012; Brady Yauch, "CP Rail CEO Harrison Fixing 'Permissive' Culture," *Business News Network*, May 27, 2013; Scott Deveau, "Share Sale Could Signal CP Rail Shift," *Financial Post*, June 4, 2013; RolandBerger Strategy Consultants, "The Optimal Setup of a Rail System—Lessons Learned from Outside Europe," Munich (August 31, 2012).

Case Study 16 Globalive Communications Corp.: Winds of Change in the Telecom Industry

Founded in 1998, Globalive Communications' mission was to introduce superior telecommunications products and services. Since then, the company has introduced a suite of telecom services including long-distance telephone, high-speed Internet, and VoIP (voice over Internet protocol) services. It is probably best known for its WIND Mobile cellphone service. Globalive has become a leading provider in Canada and abroad to over 1 million consumer and corporate clients. Globalive takes a long-term view and disciplined approach, and its success has stemmed largely from a willingness to take calculated risks, be innovative, and engage consumers in discussing what type of services they want. Globalive has been recognized through numerous awards, including Canada's 50 Best Managed Companies for nine consecutive years, Canada's Fastest Growing Company in 2004, *Canadian Business*'s Top 30 Best Workplaces in Canada, Canadian Technology 50 Hottest Startups, and Canada's Fastest Growing Wireless Carrier. Globalive's founder, Anthony Lacavera, has been recognized as one of Canada's Top 40 under 40.

Setting Sail

In 1998, using money he made developing company websites while a student at the University of Toronto along with $25,000 from Royal Bank's small-business loan program, Anthony Lacavera started Globalive Communications Corp. "I didn't know anything about telecommunications," he laughed, but someone who worked at Bell told his father, who in turn told Lacavera, there was going to be a deregulation of Canada's telecom market. "That's when I got the idea to start Globalive."

Toronto-based Globalive's approach has been to break down the market into smaller segments and identify growth opportunities. The company looks at unique and niche markets and explores what technologies are not currently offered by the competition that it can develop. The company started as a long-distance reseller focused on the hotel sector—an underserviced niche business. With a new and unknown company, Lacavera drove across Canada, visiting hotels and pitching the business. Starting with Canadian Pacific Hotels in 2000, he soon had 2,500 hotels as clients.

However, when the telecommunications industry imploded in the early 2000s, Globalive nearly went out of business. Lacavera realized he had to diversify the company, and so Globalive went into the home phone, teleconference, and Internet businesses by identifying service gaps and offering those services to customers. The company did very well, boasting sales of $160 million in 2007, but telecommunications infrastructure was getting more difficult to access. Lacavera was faced with a decision: either sell the company or find a major investor and go into the wireless business. He decided on the latter, and within six months he had secured $700 million in financing from Egypt-based Orascom Telecom Holding. Lacavera said, "I flew to Cairo for a 15-minute meeting that turned into dinner."

Tacking into the Wind

Financing secured, Globalive was ready to enter the mobile phone market. In 2008, Industry Canada held an auction to sell some of the advanced wireless spectrum—public radio frequencies needed for cellular communication—to open up competition in the wireless market. Lacavera bought a significant amount of spectrum. However, when Globalive set out in 2009 to launch its new cellphone startup called WIND Mobile, the Canadian Radio-television and Telecommunications Commission (CTRC), which regulates the telecommunications industry, determined that the company failed to meet Canadian ownership rules. Under CRTC rules, a telecom carrier is eligible to operate in Canada as long as it is a Canadian-owned and controlled corporation. Globalive Communications and WIND Mobile were mostly funded from outside. Therefore, from the CRTC's perspective, Globalive was owned and controlled by a foreign company—Globalive's investor, Egyptian Orascom Telecom Holding. Stunned by the CRTC ruling, Globalive had no choice but to delay WIND Mobile's launch. Later that year, the Government of Canada, which had indicated two years earlier its intention to allow greater foreign competition in Canada's telecom sector, overruled the CRTC decision. The Canadian government declared that Globalive Communications Corp. satisfied conditions as a Canadian-owned and controlled company, allowing WIND Mobile to launch its service.

With the regulatory issues behind him, Lacavera decided to approach the wireless sector in a unique way by asking Canadians, through a website called WirelessSoapbox.com, what they would like to see in the next wireless company in Canada, and promised to develop WIND's services based on this feedback. Lacavera says this collaborative initiative was "a first in Canada" and that by opening itself up to all comments, including negative ones, Globalive had a head start in determining what consumers wanted. "We knew there was widespread consumer frustration, so we created WirelessSoapbox.com and invited Canadians to share their ideas, thoughts and opinions on all things wireless. And they did—in huge numbers," Lacavera said.

Working with an extraordinary amount of consumer feedback, Globalive launched WIND Mobile in December 2009—Canada's first new national wireless carrier in over a decade. Lacavera said, "We have no contracts with our customers and no early cancellation penalties. We have to earn their business every day." With WIND's customer-focused service and products, the company has been growing at about 10 percent every three months. WIND Mobile is now Canada's fourth-largest wireless carrier, with services in Ontario, Alberta, and British Columbia, and serves over 600,000 subscribers.

Plotting an Upwind Course

In March 2012, the Canadian government stated that it would change foreign ownership rules to encourage the type of foreign investment that was made in WIND Mobile, lifting the stringent conditions it imposes on telecom companies as long as each one makes up less than 10 percent of Canada's overall market. The government felt that lifting the conditions would result in greater competition, which would benefit consumers through enhanced service, further innovations, and lower costs. "I feel really good about approaching our investors and new potential investors that can back us now with confidence that all of our regulatory and legal issues are fully and finally behind us," said Lacavera.

However, one of the biggest challenges for WIND Mobile continues to be a market dominated by three large phone and cable companies—Rogers Communications Inc., TELUS Corp., and BCE Inc.'s Bell Canada—which together control 95 percent of the market. Lacavera also knows that a significant portion of Globalive's market is due to consumer discretionary spending, and when the economy is in a downturn, consumers spend less on items such as mobile phone services.

Lacavera said that WIND was going "on the offense" after its regulatory and legal problems related from its foreign ownership structure were settled. "It's never been more clear that new entrants have to work together. We can't get enough spectrum in the next auction, so we have to find ways to partner," Lacavera said. He stressed that WIND was taking other steps to position itself for growth. In June 2012, WIND began looking at developing strategic partnerships with regional telecommunications and cable companies to grow distribution and coverage on its network and share costs on network infrastructure. Lacavera says, "There's no easy way to start and grow a company. All those clichés about hard work and focus are true. Despite daily disappointments and mistakes, I always kept my eye on the big goal."

Today, Globalive companies include Yak Communications, One Connect, Canopco, and Globalive Carrier Services. In 2013, Globalive announced that Orascom Telecom Holding would indirectly acquire a 99.3 percent stake in WIND Mobile and that Lacavera would step down as WIND's CEO. True to his entrepreneurial roots, Lacavera planned to launch another division, Globalive Capital. "Now that I am confident WIND Mobile Canada is on a course for long-term success, I can focus on launching Globalive Capital to make targeted investments in companies that share my entrepreneurial vision and continue to support innovation through new and emerging entrepreneurs," he said.

Lacavera attributes Globalive's success to its consistent strategy. "Our biggest advantage is that we are prepared to grow in a profitable, sustainable way. Our strength has been low management turnover and a strong, cohesive and consistent strategy. We believe that the drivers of our success have been the right team and a consistent and disciplined approach. We are very focused on continuing to build and enhance our corporate culture and ensuring our people have a similar attitude and approach to problems and are willing to learn from others," he said.

Questions for Critical Thinking

1. Describe the key financial decisions that Anthony Lacavera faced in the startup of Globalive and later in the creation and divestiture of WIND Mobile.

2. Do you think Orascom's early investment in WIND Mobile was a good one, given the legal and regulatory environment at the time?

3. Globalive operates in a risky environment. What action did Lacavera undertake to increase the probability of making good decisions under risky conditions when launching WIND Mobile?

4. WIND's competitors are also making decisions that will impact the success of the company. How would you gather information from the environment so that you have good data from which to make good decisions?

5. What are the latest changes occurring in the telecommunications industry? How is Globalive responding to these changes? Where is WIND Mobile today? What new initiatives is Lacavera undertaking? How is Globalive stacking up in relation to the company's competitors?

Sources: View from the Top: Arcus Innovation Leaders Series, "How Business Leaders Use Innovative Approaches to Shape Their Strategies," www.arcusgroup.ca/innovation_globalive.html; Globalive website, http://globalive.com, "Globalive Named One of Canada's Best Managed Companies Nine Years in a Row"; "Globalive CEO Harnesses WIND Power," *Ontario Business Report*; Grant Robertson, "Globalive Fails Ownership Test: CRTC," *Globe and Mail*, October 29, 2009; "Government of Canada Varies CRTC Decision on Globalive," Canada News Centre news release, December 11, 2009; Globalive, "Orascom Telecom to Acquire AAL Corporation Interest in WIND Mobile Canada; Anthony Lacavera to Step Down as CEO of WIND Mobile Canada, Plans to Launch Globalive Capital in 2013," news release, January 18, 2013; "Globalive Wins Wireless Fight with Public Mobile," *CBC News*, April 26, 2012; Rita Trichur, "Wind 'on Offense,' Globalive Considers Partnerships," *Globe and Mail*, June 6, 2012.

Case Study 17 SunOpta Divests to Grow

SunOpta Inc. focuses on integrated business models in the natural and organic foods and natural health products markets. SunOpta Inc. is based in Brampton, Ontario, and has three business units, including the well-known SunOpta Food Group. This division specializes in sourcing, processing, and packaging natural and organic food products.

On June 14, 2010, SunOpta Inc. announced that it had completed the divestiture of the company's Canadian food distribution assets to United Natural Foods Inc. (UNFI) and UNFI Canada Inc. The food distribution assets included in the divestiture were part of the SunOpta Distribution Group (SDG), but SunOpta did not give up all of its operations. SunOpta ensured that it retained the natural health products distribution and manufacturing assets—which represent the balance of the assets in SDG.

SunOpta was pleased that this divestiture resulted in no jobs lost. All employees involved in the Canadian food distribution operations were offered employment with UNFI (the leading distributor of natural, organic, and specialty foods in the United States).

But the question remains—why the divestiture? This divestiture was done purely for growth. SDG explains that for fiscal 2009, SDG brought in revenues of US$237.3 million. In the same period, its Canadian food distribution operations alone generated revenues of US$169.6 million and raised positive operating earnings. But the natural health products operation was a different story. Despite its revenues of US$67.7 million, this sector had negative operating earnings because of the cost of relaunching some of its natural health product brands. SunOpta could not continue without divesting.

Steve Bromley, the president and CEO of SunOpta, was not discouraged. Instead, he was optimistic about the growth opportunities the divestiture could bring. "Completing this divestiture is an important step in our strategy to focus on our core food manufacturing platform, strengthening our balance sheet and positioning the company for the future," he commented. Again, Bromley showed his employee-focused mindset: "Once again we want to express our sincere appreciation to our dedicated employees for their years of hard work and dedication and wish them continued success under UNFI's leadership."

It appeared that everyone involved in the deal was pleased with the outcome, which is unusual in these types of divestitures. Steve Spinner, the president and CEO of UNFI, was more than pleased about the divestiture. He commented, "We are very happy to have closed this acquisition as it represents the latest step in our strategy to grow our business in the Canadian market and we look forward to working closely with our new UNFI Canada associates." United Natural Foods Inc. carries and distributes more than 60,000 products to more than 17,000 customer locations across North America.

SunOpta continued with its divestures well after the sale to UNFI. In May 2011, SunOpta sold some of its equipment for processing frozen fruit to Cal Pacific Specialty Foods for $1.8 million. "This divestiture is another step in simplifying our frozen fruit business model to focus on value-added private label frozen fruit products for the retail and food service channels and improve long-term profitability," said Bromley. Similar to earlier divestitures, SunOpta plans to reinvest the funds from the divestiture in growth projects.

Questions for Critical Thinking

1. What are some of the reasons that companies divest their assets?

2. How can SunOpta's divestitures assist the company in meeting its growth prospects?

Sources: SunOpta website www.sunopta.com, "SunOpta Completes Divestiture of Canadian Food Distribution Assets," press release, June 14, 2010, www.newsfilecorp.com/release.aspx?id=540; SunOpta website; UNFI, "About Us."

APPENDIX B
BUSINESS LAW

Apple's iPhone: Don't Touch the Patents!

Smartphone users knew right away they really liked the iPhone. And the iPhone quickly grabbed a big chunk of the cellphone market. The innovative device also led to a long line of imitators. The iPhone has many groundbreaking features. Apple either already has the patents to protect those features or is in the process of filing those patents. A patent gives an inventor exclusive rights to an invention for a period of time.

Several years ago, Apple applied for a patent for the iPhone's multi-function touchscreen. The United States Patent and Trademark Office recently granted Apple patent number 7,479,949. This patent covers the touchscreen and the technology behind the phone's hardware and some of its software, including its operating system and some of its phone and camera functions. But patent protection doesn't mean that Apple is protected from lawsuits. Since the iPhone was launched, Apple has been the target of patent infringement lawsuits by other firms. The lawsuits include claims that Apple copied multi-touch technology, visual-voice technology, and digital-camera and imaging technology. The biggest suit so far has come from Nokia, the world's largest manufacturer of mobile phones. Nokia says that Apple has infringed on 10 of its patents related to wireless handsets. But Apple has countersued Nokia, claiming that Nokia is infringing upon 13 of Apple's patents.

Do these lawsuits sound childish to the average consumer? Maybe. But the technology industry is very complex. Innovations happen so fast that it can be hard to know who came up with an idea first—and at what stage of development an idea should be considered proprietary, or under the ownership of its inventor. Patents take a long time to process, and patent infringement cases can take even longer. Many firms are turning to the U.S. International Trade Commission (ITC) instead of other courts and agencies because the ITC can move these cases along more quickly. But because these cases often involve more than two companies, they can become a tangled web of suits and countersuits.

Apple recently sued the Taiwanese mobile phone manufacturer HTC for infringement of 20 Apple patents relating to the iPhone, mostly patents related to iPhone's graphical user interface. Apple was seeking a permanent injunction that would ban HTC from selling its phones in the United States. "We can sit by and watch competitors steal our patented inventions, or we can do something about it," said Steve Jobs, Apple's co-founder and CEO at the time. "We think competition is healthy, but competitors should create their own original technology, not steal ours."

HTC claimed that it was completely surprised by Apple's lawsuit. "HTC is a mobile-technology innovator and patent holder that has been very focused over the past 13 years on creating many of the most innovative smartphones," said a company spokesperson in response to the suit. "HTC values patent rights and their enforcement, but is also committed to defending its own technology innovations."

Some business law experts find it interesting that Apple did not name software makers Google or Microsoft in its legal action against HTC, which makes such popular phones as the Nexus One. The Nexus One is sold by Google, and several other phones named in the suit use Microsoft's Windows Mobile software.

And in case you thought that things are different in Canada, consider the lawsuit BlackBerry (formerly known as Research In Motion or RIM) filed against Ted Livingston and his company, Kik Interactive Inc. Livingston was accused of using proprietary software knowledge gained while he was a student at the University of Waterloo and while he was employed at RIM. Livingston's comment on his blog speaks volumes about the hurt feelings and assumptions made at one's own risk:

> **RIM sued us yesterday. A courier came to drop off a package. I opened up the letter to see a stack of papers with a big gold seal on the first page. Plaintiff: Research In Motion Inc. The company I worked for as a co-op student. The company I loved. The company I thought could benefit from Kik's vision of a mobile community. The company that placed Kik on BlackBerry App World without issue. The company I shared our entire plan with every step of the way, is suing us. I'm not afraid. I'm not surprised. But I am disappointed.**

These cases highlight the importance of every businessperson understanding the basics of business law. It doesn't matter whether you plan to market high-tech devices such as smartphones or sell a simple pair of shoes online—as a businessperson, you will need to know the laws that govern your business activities.[1]

APPENDIX B OVERVIEW

Legal issues affect every part of business. Despite the best efforts of most businesspeople, legal cases are filed against businesses. A disagreement may happen over a contract, an employee may protest being passed over for a promotion, or a town may challenge the environmental impact of a new gas station. Unfortunately, the United States is known as the world's most litigious society because of what seems like an unreasonable fondness for filing lawsuits. Canadian businesses are often participants because of their involvement in the American economy. In the United States, lawsuits are as common as business deals. Consider Walmart, which is involved in as many as 7,000 legal cases at any one time. Even if you are never personally involved in a lawsuit, the cost of these legal actions will still affect you. It is estimated that the average U.S. family pays a hidden "litigation tax" of 5 percent each year because the costs of lawsuits force businesses to increase their prices. Small businesses, such as dentists' offices, doctors' offices, and daycare providers, are often the hardest hit. They may cut back on their services or be forced to close. These problems are as much a Canadian concern as they are American because of the high level of business exchange that takes place across our common border. A Canadian businessperson needs to appreciate both the legal similarities and differences between Canada and the United States.[2]

Legislation that specifically affects business functions is analyzed in each chapter of this book. Chapter 2 presents an overview of the legal environment. Legislation affecting international operations is covered in Chapter 4. Chapter 5 discusses laws related to small businesses. Laws regarding human resource management and labour unions are examined in Chapter 8. Laws affecting other business operations, such as environmental regulations and product safety, are discussed in Chapter 12. Marketing-related legislation is examined in Chapter 13. Finally, legislation relating to banking and the securities markets is discussed in Chapters 16 and 17.

In this appendix, we provide a general overview of legislation at the federal, provincial, and local levels. We point out that, although business executives may not be legal experts, they do need to be knowledgeable in their specific area of responsibility. Some common sense also helps to avoid potential legal problems. This appendix looks at the general nature of business law, the court system, basic legal concepts, and the changing regulatory environment for business. Let's start with some initial definitions and related examples.

LEGAL SYSTEM AND ADMINISTRATIVE AGENCIES

The **judiciary**, or court system, is the branch of government responsible for applying laws to settle disagreements between two or more parties. This court system consists of several types and levels of courts, each with a specific jurisdiction, or area of responsibility. Court systems are organized at the federal, provincial, and local levels. Administrative agencies, such as the Canadian Radio-television and Telecommunications Commission (CRTC), also perform some limited judicial functions, but administrative agencies are more properly viewed as regulatory branches of government.

Canada's court system is divided between the federal and provincial legislatures. Generally, the federal government has exclusive powers over areas that concern the entire country, including criminal law, defence, currency, and telecommunications. The provinces rule mainly on civil matters such as property law. The provinces may empower municipal governments to pass local laws. Both the federal and provincial courts hear civil and criminal cases.

The Supreme Court of Canada will hear only lower-level appeal court cases that they select. These cases are chosen on the basis of their perceived importance to the entire country. Generally speaking, each province has a similar court structure with a *provincial court* level and a *superior court* level. Provincial courts deal with minor criminal and civil cases. The superior courts, which include trial and appeal courts, will generally deal with more serious matters, including murder. There are also several specialized courts, such as *tax court*.

> **judiciary** the branch of government that is responsible for applying laws to settle disagreements; also known as the court system.

TYPES OF LAW

Law consists of the standards set by government and society in the form of either legislation or custom. This broad set of principles, regulations, rules, and customs govern the actions of all members of society, including businesspeople. Our laws come from several sources. **Common law** refers to laws that result from judicial decisions, some of which can be traced to early England. For example, in many countries and provinces, an unmarried couple who has lived together for a certain period of time is said to be legally married by common law.

Statutory law is written law and includes provincial and federal constitutions; legislative enactments; treaties of the federal government; and ordinances of local governments. Statutes must be drawn precisely and reasonably to be constitutional, and thus enforceable. Still, courts must frequently interpret the intentions and meanings of statutes.

As the global economy grows, knowledge of international law becomes more crucial. **International law** refers to the numerous regulations that govern international trade. Companies must be aware of the domestic laws of their trading partners, trade agreements such as the North American Free Trade Agreement (NAFTA), and the rulings by such groups as the World Trade Organization. International law affects trade in all kinds of industries. Recently, defective or tainted products manufactured in China—but sold in North America—were recalled. Although the goods came from China, the companies that imported and sold these products in Canada and United States were liable, or legally responsible, for the products' defects. Tainted or defective toothpaste, pet food, toys, tires, and shrimp were dealt with by the various government regulatory bodies and agencies that hold manufacturers and distributors responsible for the quality of their foreign-made products. Recent cases involve lawsuits against Chinese manufacturers of construction drywall. Evidence suggests that the drywall contains high levels of corrosive gases that have led to health problems among people who live in homes built with the drywall. In the end, billions of dollars in damages may be awarded to affected homeowners.[3]

> **law** the standards set by government and society in the form of either legislation or custom.
>
> **common law** laws that result from judicial decisions, some of which can be traced to early England.
>
> **statutory law** written law that includes provincial and federal constitutions; legislative enactments; treaties of the federal government; and ordinances of local governments.
>
> **international law** the numerous regulations that govern international trade.

business law those parts of law that most directly influence and regulate the management of business activity.

In a broad sense, all law is business law because all firms are subject to all laws, the entire body of law, just as individuals are. But, in a narrower sense, **business law** consists of those parts of law that most directly influence and regulate the management of various types of business activity. Specific laws vary widely in their intent from business to business and from industry to industry. The legal interests of airlines, for example, differ from the legal interests of oil companies.

Provincial and local statutes also differ in how widely their laws apply. Some laws affect all businesses that operate in a province. One example is the workers' compensation laws, which cover payments to workers for workplace injuries. Other provincial laws apply to only certain firms or business activities. Provinces have specific licensing requirements for businesses such as law firms, funeral directors, and hair salons. Many local ordinances deal with specific business activities. Local regulations often guide the sizes and types of business signs allowed. Some communities even restrict the sizes of stores, including height and square footage.

A Toronto PetSmart store collects recalled pet food in a bin. Although the tainted food was manufactured in China, the North American companies that outsourced its production were held liable for damages to consumers.

REGULATORY ENVIRONMENT FOR BUSINESS

Government regulation of business in North America has changed over time. Depending on public opinion, the economy, and the political climate, governments swing between increased regulation and deregulation. But the goal of both types of legislation is the protection of healthy competition.

The federal Competition Act guards against monopolies, price-fixing, and other limitations on competition. The act protects consumers by ensuring that they have a choice in the marketplace. The same act protects businesses by ensuring that they are free to compete. The objectives of the Competition Act are to encourage competition and to prevent monopolies. The act specifically prohibits any contract or agreement for the purpose of limiting trade. *Price-fixing* is an agreement between two or more businesses to set a price for the goods they sell in the marketplace. A *market allocation* is an agreement to divide the market among potential competitors. A *boycott in restraint of trade* is an agreement between businesses not to sell or buy from a particular entity.

THE CORE OF BUSINESS LAW

Business law includes contract law and the law of agency; sales law and negotiable instruments law; property law and the law of bailment; trademark, patent, and copyright law; tort law; bankruptcy law; and tax law. The following sections set out the key provisions of each of these legal concepts.

Contract Law and Law of Agency

contract a legally enforceable agreement between two or more parties regarding a specified act or thing.

Contract law is the legal foundation on which business dealings are conducted. A **contract** is a legally enforceable agreement between two or more parties regarding a specified act or thing.

Contract Requirements

As **Figure B.1** shows, the four elements of an enforceable contract are agreement, consideration, legal and serious purpose, and capacity. The parties must reach agreement about the act or thing specified. For such an agreement, or contract, to be valid and legally enforceable, each party must supply consideration—the value or benefit that each party provides to the others with whom the contract is made. For example, assume that a builder hires an electrician to install electrical wiring in a new house. The wiring job and the resulting payment are the considerations. In addition to consideration, an enforceable contract must involve a legal and serious purpose. Agreements made as a joke or involving the commission of crimes are not enforceable as legal contracts. An agreement between two competitors to fix the prices for their products is not enforceable as a contract because the subject matter is illegal.

The last element of a legally enforceable contract is capacity, the legal ability of a party to enter into agreements. The law does not permit legally enforceable contracts by certain people, such as those judged to be insane. Contracts govern almost all types of business activities. For example, you might sign a contract to lease an apartment or to purchase a car or cellphone service.

Breach of Contract

A violation of a valid contract is called a *breach of contract*. The injured party can go to court to enforce the contract provisions and, in some cases, collect *damages*—financial payments to compensate for a loss and related suffering.

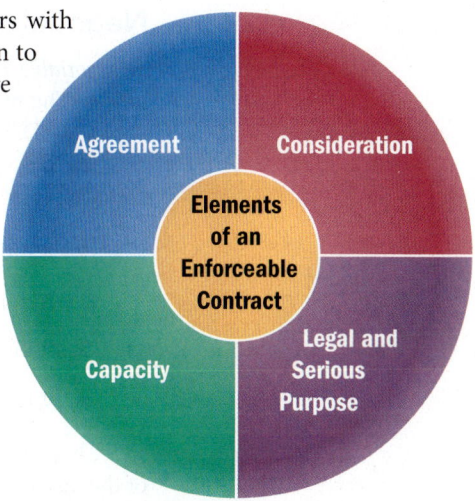

FIGURE B.1 Four Elements of an Enforceable Contract

Law of Agency

All types of firms conduct business affairs through a variety of agents, such as partners, directors, corporate officers, and sales personnel. An agency relationship exists when one party, called the principal, appoints another party, called the agent, to enter into contracts with third parties on the principal's behalf.

The law of agency is based on common-law principles and case law decisions of provincial and federal courts. Relatively little agency law has been enacted into statute. The law of agency is important because the principal is generally limited by the actions of the agent.

The legal basis for holding the principal liable for acts of the agent is the Latin maxim *respondeat superior* ("let the master answer"). In a case involving agency law, the court must decide the rights and obligations of the various parties. Generally, the principal is held liable if an agency relationship exists and the agent has some type of authority to do the wrongful act. In such cases, the agent is liable to the principal for any damages.

Sales law governs the sales of goods or services for money or on credit. Such agreements are based on the conduct of the parties. The law generally requires written agreements for enforceable sales contracts, but the form of a sales contract is quite flexible: if a written contract is missing certain terms or includes unclear terms, the contract can still be legally enforced. A court will look at past dealings, commercial customs, and other standards of reasonableness to evaluate whether a legal contract exists.

sales law the law governing the sale of goods or services for money or on credit.

Courts also consider these variables when the buyer or the seller tries to enforce his or her rights as a result of the other party (either the seller or buyer) failing to meet the terms of the contract, meeting the terms only partially, or meeting the terms in a defective or unsatisfactory way. The legal solutions usually involve the award of monetary damages to the injured parties. The law defines the rights of the parties to have the terms of the contract met, to have the contract terminated, and to reclaim the goods or place a lien—a legal claim—against them.

Warranties

Products carry two basic types of warranties: an express warranty and an implied warranty. An express warranty is a specific representation made by the seller regarding the product. An implied warranty is only legally imposed on the seller. Generally, unless implied warranties are disclaimed by the seller in writing, they are automatically in effect. Other provisions govern the rights of the buyer to inspect, accept, and reject products; the rights of both parties during the manufacture, shipment, delivery, and passing of title to products; the legal significance of sales documents; and the placement of the risk of loss if products are destroyed or damaged during manufacture, shipment, or delivery.

Negotiable Instruments

A *negotiable instrument* is commercial paper that is transferable among individuals and businesses. The most common example of a negotiable instrument is a cheque. Drafts, certificates of deposit (CDs), and notes are also sometimes considered negotiable instruments.

The law specifies that a negotiable instrument must be written and must meet the following conditions:

1. It must be signed by the maker or drawer.
2. It must contain an unconditional promise or an order to pay a certain sum of money.
3. It must be payable on demand or at a definite time.
4. It must be payable to order or to the bearer.

Cheques and other forms of commercial paper are transferred when the payee signs the back of the instrument, a process known as endorsement.

Property Law and Law of Bailment

Property law is a key feature of the private enterprise system. *Property* is something for which a person or firm has the unrestricted right of possession or use. Property rights are guaranteed and protected by law.

As **Figure B.2** shows, property can be divided into three basic categories: tangible personal property, intangible personal property, and real property. Tangible personal property consists of physical items such as equipment, supplies, and delivery vehicles. Intangible personal property is nonphysical property such as mortgages, shares, and cheques. This type of property is most often represented by a document or other written instrument, but it may also be a computer entry. You are probably familiar with certain types of intangible personal property such as cheques and money orders. Other examples include bonds, notes, letters of credit, and receipts.

A third category of property is real property, or real estate. Most firms have some interaction with real estate law because of the need to buy or lease the space where they operate. Some companies are created to serve these real estate needs. Various aspects of real property law are dealt with by real estate developers, builders, contractors, brokers, appraisers, mortgage companies, escrow companies, title companies, and architects.

The law of bailment deals with the surrender of personal property by one person to another when the property is to be returned at a later date. The person delivering the property is known as the bailor, and the person receiving the property is the bailee. Some bailments benefit bailees, others benefit bailors, and still others provide benefits to both. Most courts now require that all parties practise reasonable care in all bailment situations. The degree of benefit received from the bailment can be a factor in court decisions when deciding whether the parties have met the reasonable-care standards.

Bailment disagreements are most likely to arise in business setting such as hotels, restaurants, banks, and parking lots. A series of rules are used to govern the settlement of these disagreements. The law focuses on actual delivery of an item. For example, a restaurant owner is not liable if a customer's coat or purse is stolen from the back of his or her chair. This is because the customer has not given the item to the restaurant for safekeeping. But, if the customer delivers the coat or purse to the restaurant checkroom, receives a claim check, and the item is stolen, then the restaurant is liable.

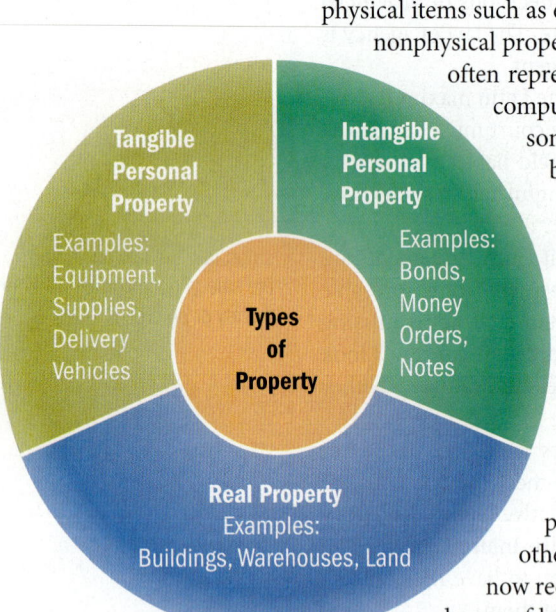

FIGURE B.2 Three Basic Types of Property

TRADEMARKS, PATENTS, AND COPYRIGHTS

Trademarks, patents, and copyrights provide legal protection by giving a firm the exclusive right to use its key business assets. A **trademark** is a brand that has been given legal protection. It consists of words, symbols, or other designations used by firms to identify their products. Trademarks are a valuable commercial property. Coca-Cola and McDonald's are two of the world's most widely recognized trademarks, so they are very valuable to the companies that own them.

If a product becomes too well known, its fame can create problems. After a trademark becomes a part of everyday language, it loses its protection as a legal trademark. Consider the words *aspirin*, *cola*, *nylon*, *kerosene*, and *linoleum*. All these product names were once the exclusive property of their manufacturers, but they have passed into common language, and now anyone can use them. More recent examples are *Xerox*, *Kleenex*, and *Velcro*. Although these names are legally trademarked, people often use them in everyday language instead of the correct generic terms of *photocopy*, *facial tissue*, and *hook-and-loop*.

Companies understand the value of their trademarks. That's why they fight hard to protect them. Louis Vuitton sued Google for allowing other companies to bid for and use the firm's trademarked brand names as keywords to trigger ads on Google's site. Louis Vuitton lost the lawsuit, but a European court ruled that companies borrowing such keywords must be clearer about who they are and what they are actually selling.[4]

By law, a **patent** guarantees an inventor exclusive rights to an invention for 20 years.

A **copyright** protects written or printed material such as books, designs, cartoon illustrations, photos, computer software, music, and videos. This class of business property is referred to as *intellectual property*. Unsurprisingly, the Internet has opened up a whole new world of copyright infringement, ranging from downloading music files to illegally sharing video footage.

Google faces a challenge both in North America and abroad as it compiles a massive digital library in an effort to create the world's largest online library. Google has given consumers online access to nearly 10 million books from around the world. Google has been challenged by authors and publishers on potential copyright infringement. The U.S. Department of Justice is trying to reach a settlement that benefits all parties. Meanwhile, France and Germany oppose any kind of settlement; these countries are supporting a European book-scanning project that complies with their own laws—which includes requiring permission from copyright holders before the books are scanned.[5]

Despite publicity about Internet copyright infringement, many people break copyright laws unknowingly. Some schools are now trying to educate students about the practice so they can make better and more informed choices about downloading material from the Internet.

trademark a brand that has been given legal protection; words, symbols, or other designations used by firms to identify their products.

patent legal protection that guarantees an inventor exclusive rights to an invention for 20 years.

copyright legal protection of written or printed material such as books, designs, cartoons, photos, computer software, music, and videos.

Law of Torts

A **tort** (French for "wrong") refers to a civil wrong inflicted on another person or on another person's property. The law of torts is closely related to the law of agency because a business entity, or principal, can be held liable for torts committed by its agents in the course of business dealings. Tort law differs from both criminal and contract law. While criminal law is concerned with crimes against the state or society, tort law deals with compensation for injured people who are the victims of noncriminal wrongs.

tort a civil wrong inflicted by one person on another person or on another person's property.

Types of Torts

A tort may be intentional, or it may be caused by negligence, or carelessness. Examples of intentional torts include assault, slander, libel, and fraud. Businesses can become involved in tort cases through the actions of both owners and employees. A security guard who uses excessive force to capture a suspected shoplifter may have committed a tort. Under agency law, the guard's employers, such as a shopping mall or retailer, can be also held liable for any damages or injury caused by the security guard.

The other major group of torts results from negligence. This type of tort is based on carelessness, not on intentional behaviour that causes injury to another person. Under agency law, businesses can also be held liable for the negligence of their employees or agents. A delivery truck driver who injures a pedestrian while transporting goods creates a tort liability for his or her employer if the accident results from negligence, such as failure to keep the vehicle's side-view mirrors clean.

Product Liability

An area of tort law known as *product liability* has been developed by both statutory and case law. These laws hold businesses liable for negligence in the design, manufacture, sale, or use of products. Some jurisdictions have extended the theory of tort law to cover injuries caused by products, regardless of whether the manufacturer is proven negligent. This legal concept is known as strict product liability.

The business response to product liability has been mixed. To avoid lawsuits and fines, some businesses recall defective products voluntarily; others decide to fight recall mandates if they believe the recall is not justified. Auto manufacturers and toy makers typically issue voluntary recalls, as do drug manufacturers.

BANKRUPTCY LAW

bankruptcy the legal non-payment of financial obligations.

Bankruptcy, legal nonpayment of financial obligations, is a common occurrence in contemporary society. Bankruptcy has two purposes. One is to protect creditors by providing a way to obtain compensation through debtors' assets. The second goal is to also protect debtors, allowing them to get a fresh financial start.

The law recognizes two types of bankruptcy: voluntary bankruptcy and involuntary bankruptcy. Under voluntary bankruptcy, a person or firm asks to be judged bankrupt because of the inability to repay creditors. Under involuntary bankruptcy, creditors may request that a party be judged bankrupt. Businesses can go bankrupt for a variety of reasons—mismanagement, plunging sales, or an inability to keep up with changes in the marketplace.

TAX LAW

tax an assessment by a governmental unit.

A branch of law that affects every business, employee, and consumer in the country is tax law. A **tax** is an assessment by a governmental unit. Federal, provincial, and local governments and special taxing authorities all levy, or charge, taxes. Appendix D, "Personal Financial Planning," also covers tax law.

Some taxes are paid by individuals, and some taxes are paid by businesses. Both types of taxes have an impact on contemporary business. Business taxes reduce profits, and personal taxes decrease individuals' disposable incomes that they spend on the products of industry. Governments spend the revenue from taxes to buy goods and services produced by businesses. Governments also act as transfer agents: they move tax revenue to other consumers and transfer funds from the working population to retired or disabled people.

Governments can charge taxes on the basis of several different terms: income, sales, business receipts, property, and assets. The type of tax varies from one taxing authority to the other. Individual income tax is the biggest source of revenue for the federal government. The provinces rely heavily on income taxes and on sales taxes. Cities and towns may collect property taxes, which are then used to provide police and security services. So-called *luxury* taxes are charged on items such as yachts and expensive sports cars; so-called sin taxes are charged on items such as cigarettes and alcohol.

BUSINESS TERMS YOU NEED TO KNOW

bankruptcy 540
business law 536
common law 535
contract 536
copyright 539
international law 535
judiciary 535
law 535
patent 539
sales law 537
statutory law 535
tax 540
tort 539
trademark 539

PROJECTS AND TEAMWORK APPLICATIONS

1. Consumer protection is an idea that started in the early 1900s and continues today. Choose an industry that you think should—or will—be the next area of concern for consumer protection law. For example, you could choose travel, organic foods, health care, or any area that interests you. Research the consumer protections that may already be in place in this industry. Outline a plan for future protections.

2. To be effective, laws must be practical and enforceable; they must also be updated periodically to reflect changes in societal views and values. Go online and research your home community. Can you find any outdated, unenforceable, or strange laws that affect businesses? Present these laws in class and discuss how they could be revised so that they actually work.

3. The business world is filled with tort cases, and many involve product liability. One of the most famous cases is the customer who sued McDonald's because she spilled a cup of hot McDonald's coffee in her lap, suffering burns and scalding. A jury awarded her $2.7 million damages, an amount that a judge later reduced to less than $500,000. On your own or with a classmate, go online to research other famous product liability cases. Choose a case and learn as much as you can about it, including the effect of the case's outcome on the firm or firms involved. Present your findings in class.

APPENDIX C
INSURANCE AND RISK MANAGEMENT

Residents under Water without Insurance

The risk from flooding is common for people who live near rivers throughout North America. Some communities, like those along the Red River in Manitoba, are at greater risk because of the geography of where they live. What happened in Nashville, Tennessee, is the story of communities where the risk was often considered low and where insurance was often not purchased.

Nashville looked like a set for a disaster movie: muddy water lapped at the stage of the Grand Ole Opry, the nearby Opryland resort was drowned and deserted, cars were sitting in water up to their windows, and tired citizens waded through the streets. But the disaster was real. In one spring weekend, a record 35 centimetres of rain fell on the city and surrounding areas, causing the Cumberland River to crest nearly 8.5 metres above flood level, resulting in major flood damage. More than 11,000 properties sustained a total of $2 billion in direct damage from the floods; Nashville alone had $1 billion in damage. But those numbers don't include the costs of lost businesses, lost jobs, and lost possessions. And they also don't include the estimated cost to clean up and repair the public infrastructure, buildings, and overtime for city workers—which ultimately could run more than $250 million.

As the waters receded, Tennessee residents were grateful to be alive and uninjured. They located relatives and pets. And they began the grim task of mopping up what was left of their homes and possessions. But most soon discovered that rebuilding was going to be a huge task, if not impossible—they didn't have flood insurance. In fact, only 1.5 percent of all homes in the counties surrounding Nashville were covered by flood insurance. Most homeowners who had purchased it did so because their mortgage lenders required it. Many of those who didn't have it had once asked lenders, real estate agents, and builders about flood insurance—but all had been reassured that they didn't need it, despite living close to a major river. "They all said, 'You're not in a flood plain, so you don't need it,'" recalled one homeowner who left her house in a rescue boat with her dog. The lack

Flood insurance is a gamble for both the homeowner and the insurer.

of flood insurance meant that the Federal Emergency Management Agency (FEMA) and personal savings—if any—would pay the repair bills for these homeowners. For the homeowners who were covered by flood insurance, their insurance companies would be paying out large claims.

How can something like this happen? If flood insurance is not required by a lender, it's an added expense to homeowners. Insurance rates can vary greatly, and flood insurance doesn't cover everything. For example, personal belongings in a flooded basement aren't generally covered by flood insurance. And any water entering the home must be from the flood itself (not from rainwater or a burst pipe). Flood insurance is a gamble both for the homeowner and the insurer. It's also a gamble for the mortgage holder. Still, FEMA points out that having flood insurance is better than not having it. "Anyone who has flood insurance is way ahead of the game," says Eugene Brezany, public affairs officer for FEMA. "FEMA's assistance is designed to get people back on their feet, not to bring people to their pre-disaster conditions." For example, if a homeowner has a $150,000 flood insurance policy and the house sustains $120,000 in damage, it can be restored. But without the policy, the homeowner is out of pocket $120,000 minus the $5,000 or $10,000 FEMA might contribute.

It comes down to a calculated risk: Will there be a flood? If so, how bad will it be? How much will it cost to repair the damage? Insurance companies use complex formulas to calculate the risks associated with natural disasters. Homeowners must decide whether it's worth paying expensive premiums for coverage if a flood never occurs. After the Nashville flood, both sides—homeowners and insurance companies—would be re-examining their position. Meanwhile, residents who could return to their homes would try to recover what they could. "You have to laugh to keep from crying," said one homeowner. That outlook might well apply to the insurance companies, too.[1]

APPENDIX C OVERVIEW

Risk is a daily fact of life for both individuals and businesses. Sometimes, risk appears in the form of a serious illness or injury. Other times, it takes the form of property loss, such as the damage to Nashville homes and businesses due to flooding. Risk can also occur as the result of the actions of others—such as a driver who is busy texting and runs a stop sign. In still other cases, risk may occur as a result of our own actions—we might go out in a boat during a thunderstorm or fail to listen to warnings about high blood pressure.

Businesspeople must understand the types of risk they face and develop ways to deal with risk. One approach to risk is to shift it to the specialized expertise of insurance companies. This appendix discusses the concept of insurance in a business setting. It begins with a definition of risk. We then describe the various ways that a business can manage risk. Next, we list some of the major insurance concepts, such as the definition of an insurable risk. The appendix concludes with an overview of the major types of insurance.

THE CONCEPT OF RISK

risk uncertainty about loss or injury.

Risk is uncertainty about loss or injury. Think about the risks faced by a typical business. A factory or warehouse faces the risk of fire and smoke, burglary, and storm damage. Others risks faced by businesses include data loss, injuries to workers, and loss of facilities. Risks can be divided into two major categories: speculative risk and pure risk.

Speculative risk gives the firm or individual the chance of a profit or a loss. A firm that expands operations into a new market may experience higher profits or the loss of invested funds. A contractor who builds a house without a specific buyer may sell the house at a profit or lose money if the house sits unsold.

Pure risk, in contrast, involves only the chance of loss. Motorists, for example, always face the risk of accidents. If an accident occurs, the result may be both financial and physical losses. But if an accident doesn't occur, drivers do not profit. Insurance often helps individuals and businesses protect themselves against financial loss resulting from some types of pure risk.

RISK MANAGEMENT

Because risk is an unavoidable part of business, managers must find ways to deal with it. The first step in any **risk management** plan is to recognize what is at risk and why it is at risk. The manager must then decide how to handle the risk. In general, businesses have four alternatives in handling risk: avoid it, minimize it, assume it, or transfer it.

Executives must consider many factors when evaluating risks, both at home and abroad. These factors include a nation's economic stability; social and cultural factors, such as language; available technologies; distribution systems; and government regulations. International businesses are typically exposed to less risk in countries that have stable economic, social and cultural, and political and legal environments.

risk management calculations and actions a firm takes to recognize and deal with real or potential risks to its survival.

Avoiding Risk

Some of the pure risks facing people can be avoided by living a healthful life. Not smoking and not swimming alone are two ways of avoiding personal risk. Businesses can also avoid some of the pure risks they face. For example, a manufacturer can locate a new production facility away from an area that is at risk of hurricanes or tornadoes.

Reducing Risk

Managers can reduce or even eliminate many types of risk by removing hazards or by taking preventive measures. Many companies develop safety programs to educate employees about potential hazards and the proper methods of performing certain dangerous tasks. Any employee who works at a hazardous waste site is required to have training and medical monitoring that meet government standards. The training and monitoring reduce risk and can help increase the bottom line. In addition to the human tragedy of accidents, accidents cost companies time and money.

Many actions can reduce the risk involved in business operations, but they cannot do away with risk entirely. Most major insurers help their clients avoid or minimize risk by offering the services of loss-prevention experts, who conduct thorough reviews of the clients' operations. These health and safety professionals evaluate customers' work environments and recommend procedures and equipment to help firms minimize worker injuries and property losses.

Individuals can also take actions to reduce risk. For example, obeying the rules of the road and doing regular maintenance on a car can reduce the risks associated with driving. Boarding up windows in preparation for a hurricane can reduce the risk of wind damage. But taking these actions can't entirely eliminate risk.

Self-Insuring against Risk

Instead of purchasing insurance against certain types of pure risk, some companies accumulate funds to cover potential losses. These self-insurance funds are special funds created by periodically setting aside cash reserves that the firm can draw on in the event of a financial loss resulting from a pure risk. A firm makes regular payments to the fund, and it charges losses to the fund. Such a fund typically works side by side with a risk-reduction program aimed at minimizing losses.

Shifting Risk to an Insurance Company

Although organizations and individuals can take steps to avoid or reduce risk, the most common method of dealing with risk is to shift it to others in the form of **insurance**—a contract in which an insurer, for a fee, agrees to reimburse an insured firm or individual a sum of money if a loss occurs. A *premium* is the insured party's fee to the insurance company for coverage against losses. Insurance substitutes a small, known loss—the insurance premium—for a larger, unknown loss that may or may not occur. In the case of life insurance, the loss—death—is a certainty; the main uncertainty is the date when it will occur.

insurance a contract in which the insurer, for a fee, agrees to reimburse an insured firm or individual a sum of money if a loss occurs.

It is important for the insurer to understand the customer's business, risk exposure, and insurance needs. Firms that operate in several countries usually do business with insurance companies that maintain global networks of offices.

BASIC INSURANCE CONCEPTS

Figure C.1 shows how an insurance company operates. The insurer (the insurance company) collects premiums from policyholders (consumers or businesses) in exchange for insurance coverage. The insurance company uses some of these funds to pay current claims and operating expenses. The remaining funds are held in the form of reserves, which are invested. Reserves can be used to pay for unexpected losses. The returns from insurance company reserves may allow the insurer to reduce premiums, generate profits, or both. By investing reserves, the insurance industry represents a major source of long-term financing for other businesses.

An insurance company is a professional risk taker. For a fee, it accepts risks of loss or damage to businesses and individuals. Four basic principles underlie insurance: the concept of insurable interest, the concept of insurable risk, the rule of indemnity, and the law of large numbers.

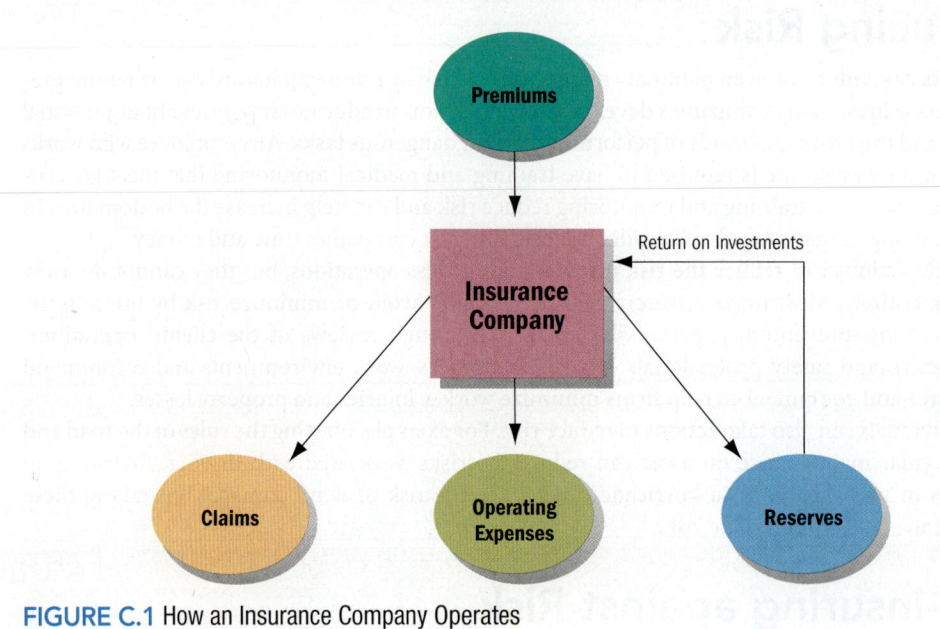

FIGURE C.1 How an Insurance Company Operates

Insurable Interest

To purchase insurance, an applicant must show an *insurable interest* in the property or life of the insured. In other words, the policyholder must stand to suffer a loss, financial or otherwise, due to fire, storm damage, accident, theft, illness, death, or lawsuit. Homeowners have an insurable interest in their home and its contents. When life insurance coverage is purchased for a family's main income provider, the policyholder's spouse and children have a clear insurable interest.

A firm can purchase property and liability insurance on physical assets—such as an office or warehouse—to cover losses due to fire and theft because the company has an obvious insurable interest. Because top executives are important assets to a company, a business often purchases key-person life insurance, which compensates the business should an important individual die.

Insurable Risk

Insurable risk refers to the requirements that a risk must meet for the insurer to provide protection. Only some pure risks are insurable. No speculative risks are insurable. A pure risk must meet four requirements to be considered an insurable risk:

1. The likelihood of loss should be reasonably predictable. If an insurance company cannot reasonably predict losses, it has no basis for setting affordable premiums.

2. The loss should be financially measurable.

3. The loss should be accidental, or fortuitous, the result of chance.

4. The risk should be spread over a certain geographic area.

The insurance company has the right to set standards for accepting risk. This process of setting these standards, and deciding what to charge, is known as *underwriting*.

Rule of Indemnity

The **rule of indemnity** states that the insured individual or firm cannot collect more than the amount of the loss. The insured cannot collect for a loss more than once. Assume that a florist's delivery van is damaged in an accident. If the damage totals $2,500, then that is the most the business can collect from the insurance company.

Occasionally, a loss may be covered by more than one policy. For example, assume that a $5,000 loss is covered by two different policies. The rule of indemnity means that the insured individual or business can collect a total of $5,000 from both insurance companies. The insurers decide how much each pays based on each policy's details.

rule of indemnity the requirement that the insured cannot collect more than the amount of the loss and cannot collect for the same loss more than once.

The Law of Large Numbers

Insurance is based on the law of averages, or statistical probability. Insurance companies cannot afford to sell insurance policies unless they can reasonably predict losses. As a result, insurance companies have studied the chances of occurrences of deaths, injuries, property damage, lawsuits, and other types of hazards. **Table C.1** is an example of the kind of data insurance companies examine. It shows the automobile accident rate, by the age of the driver, for a recent year. From their investigations, insurance companies develop *actuarial tables*. These tables predict the number of fires, automobile accidents, or deaths that will occur in a given year. Premiums charged for insurance coverage are based on these tables. Actuarial tables are based on the law of large numbers. In essence, the **law of large numbers** states that seemingly random events will follow a predictable pattern if enough events are observed.

Let's look at an example to show how insurers use the law of large numbers to calculate premiums. Previously collected statistical data on a city with 50,000 homes indicates that the city will experience an average of 500 fires a year, with damages averaging $30,000 per occurrence. What is the minimum annual premium an insurance company would charge to insure one residence?

To simplify the calculations, assume that the premiums would not produce profits or cover any of the insurance company's operating expenses—they would just produce enough income to pay policyholders for their losses. In total, fires in the city would generate claims of $15 million (500 homes damaged × $30,000). If the cost of these losses was spread over all 50,000 homes, each homeowner would be charged an annual premium of $300 ($15 million ÷ 50,000 homes). In reality, though, the insurer would likely set the premium at a higher figure to cover operating expenses, build reserves, and earn a reasonable profit. For example, during a recent year, the purchase of individual life insurance policies totalled $10 trillion in premiums, but the payout of claims was less.[2]

law of large numbers the idea that seemingly random events will follow predictable patterns if enough events are observed.

Some losses are easier for insurance companies to predict than others. Life insurance companies can predict with high accuracy the number of policyholders who will die within a specified period of time. But losses from such hazards as automobile accidents and weather events are much

Table C.1 Relationship between the Age of the Driver and the Number of Motor Vehicle Accidents

AGE GROUP	ACCIDENT RATE (PER 100 DRIVERS)
19 years old and under	21
16 years old	28
17 years old	23
18 years old	22
19 years old	18
20 to 24 years old	15
20 years old	21
21 years old	16
22 years old	14
23 years old	13
24 years old	12
25 to 34 years old	10
35 to 44 years old	8
45 to 54 years old	7
55 to 64 years old	7
65 to 74 years old	5
75 years old and over	4

Source: "2010 Statistical Abstract," *The National Data Book*, from *Injury Facts*, National Safety Council, Itasca, IL, accessed May 9, 2010, www.nsc.org.

more difficult to predict. For example, the number of damage claims on homeowners' policies due to lightning has increased dramatically. During one recent year, more than 185,000 claims were made, costing insurers nearly $800 million.[3]

SOURCES OF INSURANCE COVERAGE

The insurance industry includes both for-profit companies—such as The Co-operators, Empire Life, and Manulife Financial—and public agencies that provide insurance coverage for business firms, not-for-profit organizations, and individuals.

Public Insurance Agencies

A *public insurance agency* is a government unit established to provide specialized insurance protection for individuals and organizations. It provides protection in such areas as job loss (employment insurance) and work-related injuries (workers' compensation). Public insurance agencies also sponsor specialized programs, such as deposit, flood, and crop insurance. The biggest public insurance program in every province is the health insurance that provides health services.

Private Insurance Companies

Most insurance is provided by private firms. These companies provide protection in exchange for the payment of premiums. Some private insurers are owned by shareholders and must be run like any other business. Other insurers are so-called mutual associations. Most but not all mutual insurance companies specialize in life insurance. Technically, mutual insurance companies are owned by their policyholders, who may receive premium rebates in the form of dividends. But there is no evidence that an insurance policy from a mutual company costs any less than a similar policy from a shareholder-owned insurer. In recent years, some mutual insurance companies have reorganized as shareholder-owned companies, including Prudential, one of the world's largest insurers.

TYPES OF INSURANCE

Individuals and businesses spend hundreds of billions of dollars each year on insurance coverage. **Figure C.2** shows the annual premiums that insurance companies collected for selected types of insurance in a recent year. Unfortunately, both business firms and consumers make poor decisions when buying insurance. Here are four basic tips to remember when buying insurance:

1. Buy insurance against large losses, not small ones. It is usually much more cost effective to self-insure against small losses.

2. Buy insurance with broad coverage, not narrow coverage. For example, it is usually much less expensive to buy a homeowners[1] policy that protects from multiple events (perils such as fire and theft) than to buy several policies that cover individual events.

3. Shop around. Premiums for similar policies can vary widely from company to company.

4. Buy insurance only from financially strong companies. Insurance companies occasionally go bankrupt. If that happens, the insured have no coverage and little hope of getting their premiums back.

Although insurers offer hundreds of different policies, they all fall into three broad categories: property and liability insurance, health and disability insurance, and life insurance.

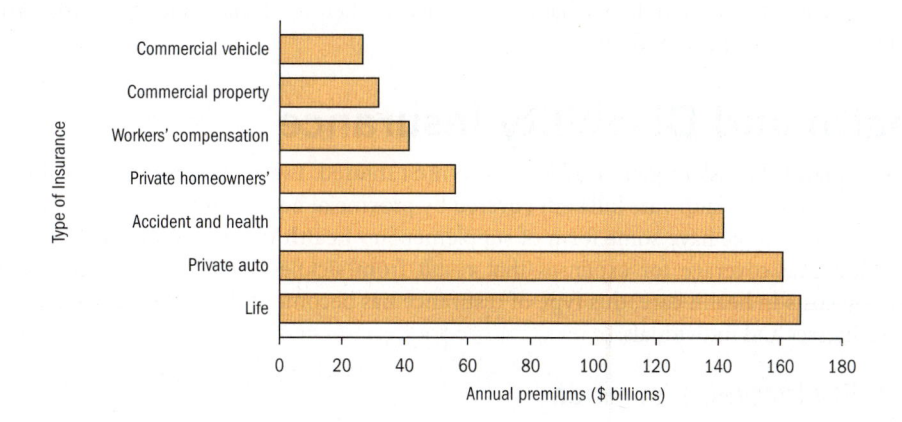

FIGURE C.2 Premiums Collected by Insurance Companies for Selected Types of Insurance

Note: Accident and health includes long-term care and disability insurance.

Source: Insurance Information Institute, *Insurance Fact Book,* www.iii.org.

Property and Liability Insurance

Insurance that protects against fire, accident, theft, or other destructive events, or perils, is called **property and liability insurance**. Examples of this insurance category include homeowners' insurance, auto insurance, business or commercial insurance, and liability insurance. Most property and liability policies are subject to deductibles. A deductible is the amount of the loss the insured pays out of pocket.

property and liability insurance a general category of insurance that protects against losses due to a number of perils, such as fire, accident, and theft.

Homeowners' Insurance

Homeowners' insurance protects homeowners from damage to their residences due to various perils. For example, if a home is destroyed by fire, the homeowners' policy will pay to replace the home and its contents. Nearly all homeowners carry this type of insurance.

Homeowners' insurance premiums have risen sharply in recent years. Homeowners in coastal areas are finding it increasingly difficult to obtain insurance because of the growing number of claims related to erosion, hurricanes, and floods. If homeowners can obtain private coverage, those plans may be very expensive.

Although standard policies cover a wide range of perils, most policies do not cover damage from widespread catastrophes such as floods and earthquakes. Homeowners must purchase separate policies to protect against damage caused by these perils.

Auto Insurance

At more than $150 billion in total annual premiums, automobile insurance is North America's largest category of property and liability insurance. Automobile insurance policies cover losses due to automobile accidents or theft, including personal and property claims.

Commercial and Business Insurance

Commercial and business insurance protects firms from financial losses resulting from the suspension of business operations (*business interruption insurance*) or physical damage to property as a result of destructive events. These policies may also protect employers from employee dishonesty or losses resulting from the nonperformance of contracts.

Liability Insurance

Liability insurance protects an individual or business against financial losses to others that the individual or business was responsible for. For example, if a business sells a defective product, the firm's liability insurance will pay for financial losses sustained by customers. A standard amount of liability coverage is usually attached to auto, homeowners', and commercial insurance policies. Additional amounts of liability insurance can be purchased if needed. Adequate liability insurance is critically important today for both businesses and individuals. For example, Walmart requires its suppliers to have at least $2 million in liability coverage for their products; some "high-risk" products require a minimum of $10 million.[4]

Health and Disability Insurance

Each of us faces the risk of getting sick or becoming injured. Even a relatively minor illness can result in substantial health care bills not covered by provincial health care plans. To guard against this risk, many people have some form of supplementary **health insurance**—insurance that provides additional coverage for expenses that result from sickness or accidents. Because of the increasing costs in health care, this type of insurance has become an important consideration for both businesses and individuals.

health insurance insurance that pays for losses due to illness or injury.

Disability Income Insurance

Disability income insurance is one of the most overlooked forms of insurance. And many workers don't have enough coverage. The odds of a person developing a disability are considerably higher than most people think. Take a group of five randomly selected 45-year-olds. There is approximately a 95 percent chance that one of the five will develop some form of a disability during the next 20 years. Disability income insurance is designed to replace lost income when a wage earner cannot work because of an accident or illness.

Private disability insurance is available on either an individual or a group basis. Similar to health insurance, a group policy is much cheaper than an individual policy. Many employers provide some disability coverage as an employee benefit. Employees often have the option of obtaining additional coverage by paying more.

Insurance and Risk Management   551

Life Insurance

Life insurance protects people against the financial losses that occur with premature death. Three of every four North Americans have some form of life insurance. The main reason people buy life insurance is to provide financial security for their families in the event of their death. The life insurance industry has assets of more than $4 trillion, making it one of North America's largest businesses.

life insurance a type of insurance that protects people against the financial losses that occur with premature death.

Types of Life Insurance

As with health and disability insurance, both individual and group life insurance policies are available. Many employers offer life insurance to employees as part of the firm's benefit program. But, unlike health and disability insurance, an individual life insurance policy is usually cheaper than a group policy for younger people.

The different types of life insurance fall neatly into two categories: term policies and cash value policies. Term policies provide a death benefit if the policyholder dies within a specified period of time. It has no value at the end of that period. Cash value policies—sometimes called whole life and universal life—combine life insurance protection with a savings or investment feature. The cash value represents the amount of the savings or the investment portion of the policy. Although some people prefer cash value policies, many experts believe that term life insurance is a better choice for most consumers. For one thing, a term policy is much cheaper than a cash value policy.

How Much Life Insurance Should You Have?

Life insurance policies can be purchased for almost any amount. The value of the policy is limited only by the amount of premiums people can afford and their ability to meet medical qualifications. But the amount of life insurance a person needs is a very personal decision. The general rule of thumb is that life insurance is needed when family members are financially dependent on an individual's earnings. For example, a young parent with three small children could easily need $500,000 or more in life insurance. A single person with no dependents would reasonably see little or no need for a life insurance policy.

Businesses also buy life insurance. The death of a partner or a key executive is likely to result in a financial loss to an organization. Key person insurance reimburses the organization for the loss of an essential senior executive and to cover the expenses of an executive search to find a

Many businesses offer life insurance as part of their employee benefits. Although groups usually get a better deal on insurance than individuals, it may be cheaper for young employees to purchase an individual insurance policy.

Monkey Business Images/Shutterstock/Getty Images

replacement. Life insurance policies may also be purchased for each member of a partnership. These policies will repay the deceased partner's survivors for his or her share of the firm and permit the business to continue.

BUSINESS TERMS YOU NEED TO KNOW

health insurance 550
Insurance 545
law of large numbers 547
life insurance 551
property and liability insurance 549
risk 544
risk management insurance 545
rule of indemnity 547

PROJECTS AND TEAMWORK APPLICATIONS

1. Choose one of the following companies or select another one that interests you. Research the company online. Learn what you can about the firm's goods and services, work processes, and facilities. Create a chart to identify risks that you believe the company faces—and show ways the firm can avoid or reduce its risks.

   a. VIA Rail
   b. Toronto Maple Leafs
   c. MEGA Brands Inc.
   d. Laura Secord

2. Assess your own personal insurance needs. What types of coverage do you currently have? How do you see your insurance needs changing in the next five to 10 years?

3. Go online and research one of these man-made disasters: the BP oil spill in the Gulf of Mexico or the Westray Mine disaster in Nova Scotia. Learn what you can about the role of insurance companies. Did they meet or exceed their obligations, or did they fall short? Report your findings in class.

4. Table C.1 shows the relationship between the age of a driver and the number of motor vehicle accidents. The greatest number of accidents occurs between the ages of 16 and 19 and the fewest occur starting at age 65. Research the causes of these accidents. Note the similarities and differences. Create a report that outlines your research. Suggest steps you think the younger group of drivers might take to reduce their risks.

# APPENDIX D
PERSONAL FINANCIAL PLANNING

The Credit CARD Trick: Will It Work?

North American college and university students are similar in many ways. What we know about students on one side of the Canada–U.S. border is probably true for students on the other side. In one recent student-loan survey of American college graduates, nearly half said they wished they had learned more in college about managing their finances—specifically, their credit cards. The average college student has 4.6 credit cards and a balance of more than $3,000—and that's on top of any student loans. Only 17 percent of college students pay off their credit card balances in full each month. That means most of them are racking up debt, interest charges, and fees. Critics of the credit card industry point to the credit card issuers that advertise on campus, literally handing out credit cards along with free promotional items, such as backpacks, T-shirts, and water bottles. The water bottles and T-shirts don't build up debt, the credit cards do.

The American government has decided that this situation represents a financial crisis. Students are graduating from college with large debt in addition to their student loans—some have debts of $10,000 or more. The Credit CARD Act (Credit Card Accountability, Responsibility, and Disclosure Act) was signed into law in 2010. This act includes reforms aimed at limiting both the access credit card companies have to students and the amount of credit students are given. Under the new law, credit card issuers cannot offer free incentives such as T-shirts and teddy bears. Also, firms cannot market their cards at a college-sponsored event or within 1,000 feet (300 m) of a college campus. The firms must also have clearer communications with students and with colleges, such as disclosing the terms of their agreements. Students will also have a tougher time actually obtaining credit cards; those under age 21 must have adult co-signers or prove they earn enough income to make payments. Many of these controls, such as the need for co-signing of applications, are already in place under Canadian law.

Some welcome the restrictions in the new law, while others find them too restrictive. "It's my safety line," says one student who happens to have a good summer job and can handle the card. "I use my credit card for everything, from gas to my books to my food and clothes." Another college student thinks that the credit limit should be matched to a student's income and age. "I agree there should be new standards in place. Freshman shouldn't get credit limits of $5,000. However, I don't agree that it should be difficult for them to get credit at all." Others point out the difficulty of finding a co-signer willing to put his or her credit score on the line.

But many adults and students agree that, in general, the steps taken by the Credit CARD Act are positive. "I think it's going to keep a lot of students from getting into trouble," says Irene Leach, associate professor in consumer studies at Virginia Tech University. "I hope it means we'll have more responsible lending and parents don't get surprised that a young person has taken out this debt." And there are options other than the traditional credit card. College students can piggyback on their parents' cards simply by having parents add their name to the card account—that way, parents can monitor their children's credit card spending. Or students can apply for prepaid cards, which are similar to bank debit cards but can have high fees. Visa and other companies file regular reports with credit bureaus, a practice that can help students build a good credit standing without getting into debt.

Students themselves may make the best argument for credit card reform. One student got her first credit card while in college. She built up more than $7,500 in debt and says she has "regretted it ever since."[1]

APPENDIX D OVERVIEW

You are studying business, but much of what you learn in this course also applies to your personal life. For example, you learn about each of the important functions of a business—from accounting to marketing, from finance to management. Learning about each business function will help you choose a career. A career choice is one of the most important personal financial decisions you will make. You will learn why firms prepare budgets and financial statements. But budgets and financial statements are also important tools for individuals and households.

All of us—young or old, rich or poor—can improve how we manage our finances. As a group, North Americans are much better at making money than managing money. This appendix introduces you to personal financial management. **Personal financial management** is the study of economic factors and personal decisions that affect a person's financial well-being. It includes basic money management, credit, tax planning, major consumer purchases, insurance, investing, and retirement planning.

This appendix will draw from many of the topics you will learn while studying business. But it will also introduce you to some new concepts. After you complete this appendix, we hope you will be a better-informed financial consumer and personal money manager. We also hope you will be motivated to learn more about personal finance. The rewards, both financially and otherwise, can be huge.

personal financial management the study of the economic factors and personal decisions that affect a person's financial well-being.

THE MEANING AND IMPORTANCE OF PERSONAL FINANCE

Personal finance is the study of the economic factors and personal decisions that affect a person's financial well-being. Personal finance affects, and is affected by, many things we do and many decisions we make.

On one level, personal finance involves money know-how. Everyone needs to know how to earn money. But we also need to know how to save, spend, invest, and control it so we can achieve goals. The reward of good money management is an improved standard of living. **Standard of living** consists of the necessities, comforts, and luxuries a person wants to achieve or maintain.

On another level, personal finance affects our lifestyles—the way we live our daily lives. Our choice of careers, friends, hobbies, communities, and possessions is shaped by our personal finances—and our personal finances can also be shaped by our lifestyles. If you're a university student living on a tight budget, you may have to make serious financial decisions to achieve your educational goals. Where you live depends on what school you attend and how much you can pay for room and board. Your vacation is set by your academic schedule and your savings account. Your clothing depends on the climate and your budget. All these lifestyle decisions are largely affected by your personal finances.

standard of living the necessities, comforts, and luxuries a person wants to achieve or maintain.

The Importance of Personal Finance Today

Good money management has always been important. But major changes in the economic environment over the past few years have made personal finance even more important today. And this is true whether you're a 20-year-old college student with big tuition bills, a 40-year-old parent with a mortgage to pay, or a 60 year old thinking about retirement. Let's look at three reasons personal financial planning is so important in today's environment.

Slow Growth in Personal Income

Personal income in North America has grown very slowly in recent years. The economy is now moving forward, but most analysts predict that, in the coming years, annual increases in wages and salaries will barely keep pace with the rate of inflation.

The slow growth in personal income makes sound money management very important. You cannot count on rising personal income to improve your standard of living. Instead, you need to save and invest more money, stick to a budget, and make major purchases wisely.

Your lifestyle affects your finances. Skiing at expensive resorts won't leave much money in your savings account.

Changes in the Labour Market

Job security and how we think about work have changed in recent years. The traditional model of working for the same company for one's entire career is very rare today. The average length of employment in one job is five years.[2]

You and your classmates will likely change jobs and employers several times during your careers. Some of you will work part-time or on a contract basis, with little job security and fewer benefits. Others will take time off to care for small children or elderly parents. And many of you will want to start your own business and work for yourselves.

An estimated one in four workers today will be unemployed sometime during their working lives. Your employer may "downsize" and take your job with it, or "outsource" your job to someone else. Take a look at today's headlines. You'll see that big companies are downsizing, and outsourcing is common.

These changes make sound personal financial management even more important. You need to keep your career skills up to date. You also need to build up sufficient financial resources to get you through any unexpected crisis.

More Options

The number of choices today in banking, credit, investments, and retirement planning can be confusing. Today, you can do most of your banking with a brokerage firm and then buy mutual fund shares at a bank. Even the simple chequing account has become more complicated. Most banks offer several different types of chequing accounts, each with its own features and fees. Choosing the wrong account could cost you $100 or more in unnecessary fees each year.

Twenty years ago, few students carried credit cards, and those who did had cards that were tied to their parents' accounts. Banks and other credit card issuers didn't think college and university students represented good risks. Then the situation changed. Now we have a credit card debt crisis among students, as described at the beginning of this appendix. One of the first things you'll do when you start a full-time job is make decisions about employee benefits. Many employers offer lots of choices in such areas as health insurance, disability insurance, group life insurance, and retirement plans. Selecting the right insurance plans can save you thousands of dollars each year. And choosing the right retirement plan can improve your financial security many years from now.

Personal Financial Planning— A Lifelong Activity

Personal financial planning is an important activity whether you're 20, 40, or 60; whether you're single or married with children; or whether your annual income is $20,000 or $200,000. Many experts say that if you can't stick to a budget and control your spending when you're making $25,000 a year, you'll find it difficult to live within your means even if your income doubles or triples.

Good financial planning is a lifelong activity. But that doesn't mean your financial goals and plans will remain the same throughout your life—they won't. The major goal when you're young may be to buy your first home or pay off your student loans. For older people, the major goal is to pay off their home mortgage and save as much as possible for retirement.

A PERSONAL FINANCIAL MANAGEMENT MODEL

personal financial plan a guide to help a person reach his or her desired financial goals.

A **personal financial plan** is a guide to help you reach your targeted goals in the future. It helps you to close the gap between where you are right now and where you'd like to be in the future. Your goals might include buying a home, starting your own business, travelling extensively, sending your children to university, or retiring early. Developing a personal financial plan consists of several steps, as illustrated in **Figure D.1**.

The first step is to create a clear picture of where you currently stand financially. Next, develop a series of short-term and long-term goals. These goals will be influenced by your values and by your assessment of your current financial situation. The next step is to decide on a set of financial strategies—in each of the personal planning areas. These strategies will help you to close the gap between where you are now and where you want to be in the future. Next, put your plan into action and closely track its performance. Every few months, evaluate how effective your financial plan has been and make adjustments when necessary.

Financial plans cannot be developed in isolation. Your financial plan should reflect your available resources—especially your salary and your employment benefits, such as health insurance and retirement plans. For example, your goals and financial strategies should be based on a realistic estimate of your future income. If you cannot reach your financial goals through your present career path, you will need to scale back your goals or think about switching careers.

External factors—such as economic conditions and employment prospects—will affect your financial plan and decisions. For example, assume you currently rent an apartment but want to buy a home. Maybe you can afford to buy a home right now, but you think you might be offered a much better job in a new city in the next year. A wise financial move might be to *not* buy a home now but to wait until your employment future is clearer.

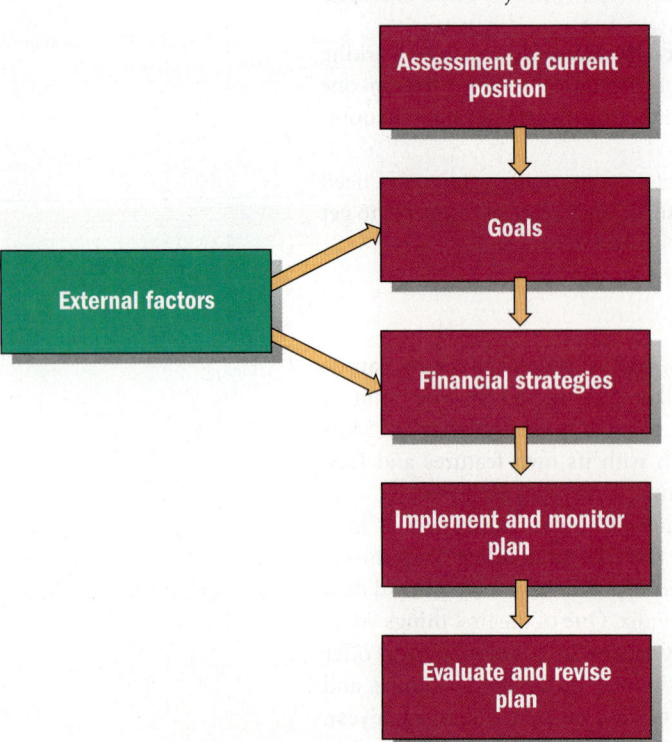

General Themes Common to All Financial Plans

All financial plans revolve around three general themes: (1) maximizing income and wealth, (2) using money more effectively, and (3) monitoring expenditures.

FIGURE D.1 A Model of Personal Finandicial Management

Maximizing Income and Wealth

Maximizing your income and wealth means making more money. For example, you can decide to work smarter; look for retraining so you can get a better, higher-paying job; take career risks that may pay off in the long run; and make sound investment decisions. The amount of money you earn is a big part of any financial plan. It is up to you to make the most of your opportunities.

Using Money More Effectively

Money has two basic uses: consumption and savings. Even if you are a regular saver, you'll still spend most of your income, probably more than 90 percent. You must try to spend every dollar wisely and make every major buying decision part of your overall financial plan. Avoid impulsive spending or giving in to a fast-talking salesperson.

It's not just major purchases that you need to watch. When you cut back your spending on small items, you can make a difference. Little purchases add up. For example, packing your own lunch a few times a week instead of always buying your lunch can save you about $15 a week. Invest that savings at 3 percent interest (per year) and you'll have almost $38,000 in 30 years.

Small expenses add up. Over time, taking your own lunch to the office instead of eating out can add to your bank account.

Monitoring Expenditures

Budgeting is the key to controlling expenditures. A budget focuses on where the money is going and whether a person's goals are being met. It also suggests when it's time to re-evaluate your priorities. If your budget doesn't match what you want from life both now and in the future, change it.

Information also helps you to keep your expenditures under control. The more you know about real estate, consumer loans, credit card rates and laws, insurance, taxes, and major purchases, the more likely you are to spend the least money to purchase products with the greatest value.

The Pitfalls of Poor Financial Planning

Unfortunately, too many people fail to plan effectively for their financial future. Many people find it difficult to improve their standard of living. And others find themselves with growing debts and a general inability to make ends meet.

We have some laws that try to help consumers who run into difficulty, and credit counselling services can help people organize and pay their debt. But foreclosure and bankruptcy are actions of last resort that you want to avoid.

SETTING PERSONAL GOALS

Whatever your personal financial goals, they should work with your values. Values are a set of basic beliefs about what is important, desirable, and worthwhile in your life. Your values will influence how you spend your money. That's why values should be the foundation of your financial plan. Each person's financial goals will be shaped by the individual's values because every individual thinks of some things as more desirable or important than others. Start by asking yourself some questions about your values, the things that are most important to you, and what you would like to do in your life.

net worth the difference between an individual's or a household's assets and liabilities.

Your goals are also influenced by your current financial situation. Prepare a set of current financial statements for yourself and update them at least once a year. Just like a business, a personal income statement shows your income and expenditures during a year. A balance sheet is a statement of what you own (your assets) and what you owe (your liabilities) at a specific point in time. For an individual or household, the difference between assets and liabilities is called **net worth**. As you build assets over your life, your net worth increases.

After reviewing your current financial statements, prepare a budget. A budget is an excellent tool for tracking your spending and cash flow. It helps you to track past and current spending and plan future spending. Budgets are usually prepared on a monthly basis, but make a weekly budget if that works better. Most budgets divide spending into fixed expenses (those that don't change much from month to month) and variable expenses (those that vary). Your monthly apartment rent or your meal plan at school is probably a fixed expense, but the amount you spend on gas for your car or on entertainment is a variable expense. One key to effective budgeting is to make sure that the budgeted amounts are realistic.

Next, set up a series of financial goals based on your values and your current financial situation. Separate your goals into short-term goals (those you want to achieve within the next six months or year) and long-term goals (those you plan to achieve over the next five or 10 years). A short-term goal might be to pay off your credit card balances by the end of this year, or to save enough money to take a vacation next summer. A long-term goal might be to buy a house by age 30. Your goals are reinforced if they support each other. For example, if you pay off your credit cards, you might have enough money saved to take that vacation or to help toward the down payment for a house. Some goals are monetary—such as paying off the credit card. Others are nonmonetary, such as planning to retire by age 55.

Whether your financial goals are short term or long term, monetary or nonmonetary, the best goals are defined specifically and are focused on results. Goals also need to be realistic. You might not be able to pay off all of your credit cards by the end of this year, but you might be able to pay off one credit card. You might not buy the house by age 30, but maybe by age 35. Be sure to set goals that you can actually attain. Keep in mind also that your financial goals will change over your lifetime. It's a good idea to review them every few months and adjust them when necessary, such as when you lose or get a job, relocate to another area of the country, or have children.

YOUR PERSONAL FINANCIAL DECISIONS

You can use financial strategies to help chart your economic future in such areas as career choice, credit management, and tax planning. These strategies should work with your goals. They should be designed to close the gap between where you are and where you want to be.

Career Choice

No factor has a stronger influence on your personal finances than your career choice. Nearly all of your income, especially when you're just starting out, will come from wages and salaries. Through working, we acquire the income we need to build a lifestyle; to buy goods and services, including insurance protection; to save and invest; and to plan for retirement. Your job is also the source of many important fringe benefits that are important to your financial future, such as health insurance and retirement savings plans. Throughout *Contemporary Business*, we've discussed how you can select a career that fits your skills and interests, find a job, and perform in that job.

Basic Money Management

Basic money management includes managing chequing and savings accounts. Properly managing these fairly simple financial assets is an important first step toward proper management of more complicated financial assets such as investment and retirement accounts. You must choose a bank

Table D.1 Some Commonsense Tips for Choosing and Managing a Chequing Account

- Shop around. Most financial institutions offer chequing accounts. Fees and services can vary widely.
- Choose the right account for the way you bank. Think about how many cheques you write each month, how often you use ATMs, and your average monthly balance.
- Keep good records and regularly balance your chequing account.
- Use your personal computer to pay bills electronically, balance your chequebook, and do other banking tasks.
- Watch how you use your ATM card. Know which ATMs are owned by your bank and how much you're charged to use another bank's ATM. When using an ATM, check your current balance.
- Notify your bank immediately if your ATM card is lost or stolen.
- Sign up for overdraft protection.
- Understand how your bank calculates your minimum monthly balance.
- Read the fine print in your monthly statement.

or another financial institution and then select the right chequing account. Financial institutions offer several different types of chequing accounts, each with its own features and fees.

Table D.1 lists several tips for selecting and managing a chequing account. Managing a savings account involves understanding the importance of savings, setting savings goals, and picking the best savings option.

Credit Management

Of all areas of personal finance, credit is the area that gets the most people into financial difficulties.

Credit allows a person to purchase goods and services by borrowing the necessary funds from a lender, such as a bank. The borrower agrees to repay the loan over a specified period of time, paying a specified rate of interest. The **finance charge** is the difference between the amount borrowed and the amount repaid. Credit is available from many sources, but rates vary, so it pays to shop around.

Consumers can choose from two broad types of consumer credit: revolving (or open-end) credit and instalment credit. Revolving credit is a credit arrangement where consumers can make a number of different purchases up to a credit limit, specified by the lender. The consumer has the option of repaying some or all of the outstanding balance each month. If the consumer carries a balance from month to month, finance charges (interest) are added to the account. An example of revolving credit is a credit card, such as Visa or MasterCard.

An instalment loan is a credit arrangement in which the borrower takes out a loan for a specified amount and agrees to repay the loan in regular instalments over a specified period of time. Part of each payment goes toward interest and part goes to repay principal (the amount borrowed). Generally, instalment loan payments are made monthly and are for the same amount. Examples of instalment loans are most student loans, car loans, and home mortgage loans.

People have good reasons for borrowing money. For example, people borrow money to purchase high-priced goods and services (cars, homes, or a postsecondary education), to deal with financial emergencies, to take advantage of opportunities, and to establish or improve their credit rating. These reasons are suitable uses of credit if you can repay the loans in a timely manner.

A wrong reason for borrowing money is to use credit to live beyond your means. For example, you may want to go to Cancun for a vacation but really cannot afford the cost, so you charge the trip to your credit card. Using credit to live beyond your means can lead to financial problems. Watch for these warning signs of potential credit problems:

- You use credit to meet your basic living expenses.
- You use credit to make impulse purchases.
- You take a cash advance on one credit card to repay another.
- The unpaid balance on your credit cards increases every month.

credit receiving money, goods, or services on the basis of an agreement between the lender and the borrower that the loan is for a specified period of time with a specified rate of interest.

finance charge the difference between the amount borrowed and the amount repaid on a loan.

Consumers who think of credit purchases as a series of small monthly payments are fooling themselves. How long would it take to become debt free if you had $2,200 on your credit card and you paid only the minimum payment each month? The answer is nearly 11 years—and you would have paid more than $2,000 in interest.

If you feel you might have a problem with credit, or may be developing a problem, get help as soon as possible. Your college or university may offer credit counselling services. According to the experts, one of the keys to the wise use of credit is education. By learning about the pros and cons of borrowing money and by learning about responsible spending, you can avoid many problems with credit.

Tax Planning

Everyone pays a variety of taxes to federal, provincial, and local governments. The major taxes paid by individuals are federal and provincial income taxes, local real estate taxes, and sales taxes. Think about your own situation and the taxes you pay. Federal and provincial income taxes are withheld from each paycheque. If you rent an apartment, part of your monthly rent goes to pay the landlord's real estate tax bill. Every time you buy something, you pay sales tax to various governments.

By law, you must pay your taxes. You can use some of the popular computer software to calculate your federal and provincial income taxes, or you can pay a professional to handle them. These two options will likely find the legal deductions you can take. If you do the tax return yourself—even with the help of software—you will learn more about your personal finances.

Major Purchases

Even if you follow a strict budget and manage to save money regularly, you will still spend most of your income each year. Effective buying is an important part of your financial plan. Within personal budget limits, an individual uses his or her rights as a consumer to select or reject from a wide range of goods and services. As you purchase an automobile, a home, or any other major item, you need to carefully evaluate your options, separate needs from wants, and decide how you are going to finance the purchase. Your goal is to make every dollar you spend count.

North Americans spend more than $900 billion annually on transportation. Most of that expense goes to purchasing and maintaining automobiles. New vehicles average more than $20,000 today, and even good used cars can cost more than $15,000. Buying an automobile is a major purchase. On top of that, most car purchases are financed. Buying a car involves weighing many factors, including whether you want a new or used car, what makes and models appeal to you, and how much you can afford to pay. Many consumers today choose not to buy a new car but to lease one. Leasing has advantages, but it also has drawbacks. Overall, leasing is often more expensive than buying.

For most people, housing takes up a large share of their monthly budgets, whether in rent or mortgage payments. Home ownership is a goal of most people. Owning a home has advantages, both financial and nonfinancial. The financial benefits include the potential increase in the home's value and, usually, no taxes on those gains. Nonfinancial benefits include pride of ownership and the freedom to improve or change the home as you want. The major barriers to home ownership are the money required for a down payment and the income required to obtain a mortgage loan.

The other major housing option is renting. Renting offers many advantages, including cost savings (the landlord takes care of maintenance and repairs) and mobility. It is much easier to move when you rent than when you own a home. People who plan on staying in an area for a short period of time are usually better off renting even if they can afford to buy a home. The choice between buying and renting is a major financial decision that needs to be approached rationally, not emotionally.

Insurance

Another important personal planning area is insurance. Insurance is an expensive but necessary purchase. North Americans spend about $150 billion each year on car insurance. Some of the basic principles and the various types of insurance are described in Appendix C. Although the focus of that appendix is business insurance, much of the discussion also applies to your personal insurance needs.

Your goal is to have adequate and appropriate coverage in each of the major insurance types—life, health, disability, and property and liability. Insurance needs can vary from individual to individual. As noted earlier in *Contemporary Business*, some types of insurance are provided to employees as fringe benefits. Employer-provided insurance typically includes supplementary health insurance, disability insurance, and life insurance. In the standard arrangement, employers pay a portion of the premium. A few employers contract with insurance companies to offer employees car and homeowners' insurance at discounts.

Investment Planning

Investing is a process by which money acquired through work, inheritance, or other sources is preserved and increased. Sound investment management is an important part of the financial plan and can make it easier to reach other personal goals, such as buying a home, financing children's education, starting a business, or retiring comfortably. It is very difficult today to increase your wealth significantly without investing. Because of the changes in the external environment—such as employer-sponsored retirement plans—you will likely need to make investment decisions at some point during your life.

Leasing a car has some advantages, but over the long run it may cost more than buying the same car.

The investment process consists of four steps. The first step is to complete some preliminary tasks, such as setting overall personal goals, contributing to a regular savings program, and managing credit properly. The second step is to establish a set of investment goals—why you want to invest, what you want to accomplish, and your time frame. Your investment goals should be closely related to your overall personal goals. Next, you need to assess risk and return. You invest because you expect to earn some future rate of return. But all investing will expose you to a variety of risks. You need to find the proper balance between risk and return; investments that offer the highest potential returns also expose you to more risk. Your age, income, and your short-term or long-term investment time frames all have an impact on the risk–return tradeoff.

The final step is to select the appropriate investments. As discussed in Chapter 16 of *Contemporary Business*, you can choose from three general types of investments: money market instruments, bonds, and common shares. The proper mix of these three investments depends on several factors, including your investment goals and your investment time horizon. For example, a 25 year old who is investing for retirement should have almost 100 percent of his or her funds invested in common shares because growth in capital is the main investment objective. Even with the recent turmoil in the stock market, common shares generally outperform all other investment alternatives over longer periods of time. On the other hand, if the 25 year old is investing to have sufficient funds for a down payment on a house within the next couple of years, the investor should have a portion of his or her funds invested in money market instruments or bonds because of the short time horizon. Even after selecting the appropriate investments, the investor must monitor the investments' performance and be prepared to make changes when necessary.

Financial Planning for Tomorrow

The last major personal planning area deals with future financial issues, such as paying for children's college or university education and retirement and estate planning. As you know, postsecondary education is expensive. The costs are rising at a rate greater than the overall rate of inflation. By beginning an education savings program early, parents will have a better chance of offering their children more choices when the time comes. While parents might not have enough savings to cover tuition entirely, they (and their children) can likely borrow less and will add less debt if an education savings program is in place. A variety of educational savings programs exist, including some that offer tax benefits. You can learn more about Canada's educational savings plans at the CanLearn website www.canlearn.ca/eng/savings/resp.shtml.

Most people want to retire with sufficient funds to ensure their financial security. Canadian government pensions will provide only a fraction of what you will need; you will be responsible for the rest. Depending on the standard of living you hope to have, you will probably need savings of at least $1.5 million by the time you retire. Four important principles apply when it comes to saving for retirement: start early, save as much as you can each month, take advantage of all tax-deferred retirement savings plans you can, and invest your retirement savings appropriately.

Consumers can choose from two major sources of retirement income: employer-sponsored retirement plans and individual retirement plans. Most employers offer their workers a retirement plan; some offer more than one plan. For most people, employer-sponsored retirement plans will likely provide most of their retirement income. Two types of employer-sponsored retirement plans exist. A defined benefit plan guarantees a worker a certain retirement benefit each year. The size depends on many factors, including the worker's income and the length of time he or she worked for the employer. Pension plans are classified as defined benefit plans.

The other type of employer-sponsored retirement plan is the defined contribution plan. In this type of retirement plan, you contribute to your retirement account and so does your employer. You are given some choice of where your retirement funds can be invested. For example, you may be given a list of mutual funds where you can invest your money. Defined contribution plans are widely used. They are now often replacing defined benefit plans.

Millions of North Americans have some sort of individual retirement plan that is not tied to any employer. These workers may be self-employed or may want to add to their employer-sponsored retirement savings. Examples of individual retirement plans include regular RRSPs (Registered Retirement Savings Plans) and TFSAs (Tax-Free Savings Accounts). Although the TFSA can be thought of as a general savings plan, most people think of it as part of their retirement planning. To set up one of these retirement plans, you must meet certain eligibility requirements.

Another element of financial planning for tomorrow is estate planning. Of all the personal planning areas, estate planning is probably the least meaningful for you today, although your parents and grandparents probably face some estate-planning issues. All adults, regardless of age, need to have two documents: a valid will (naming a guardian if you have any minor children) and a durable power of attorney (a document that gives someone else the power to make financial and medical decisions if you cannot).

This appendix has just scratched the surface of personal financial planning. We hope it has encouraged you to learn more. Consider taking a class in personal financial planning if your college or university offers one. It may be one of the most helpful classes you take while you're in school.

BUSINESS TERMS YOU NEED TO KNOW

credit 559

finance charge 560

net worth 558

personal financial management 554

personal financial plan 556

standard of living 554

PROJECTS AND TEAMWORK APPLICATIONS

1. Prepare a chart outlining your current standard of living, the standard of living you had while growing up, and the standard of living you expect or hope to achieve after you complete your education.

2. Create a chart detailing how you think you could use your money most effectively. What are your pitfalls? In what areas do you already use your money well?

3. Create a weekly budget and a monthly budget. Keep a daily journal of your expenses for the next month to see how well you stick to the budget. Compare your results in class. In what areas did you do well? In what areas do you need improvement? For help creating a budget, go to www.fcac-acfc.gc.ca/Eng/forConsumers/lifeEvents/payingPostSecEd/Pages/StudentB-Grillepo.aspx.

4. Even though you are still in school, you face many important financial issues, from paying college or university expenses to dealing with credit cards. Visit the website www.youth.gc.ca/eng/topics/money/manage_finances.shtml. Look at other websites for more suggestions on managing your money while in school.

5. Analyze your current credit situation. What are your existing debts? How much are you paying each month? Did you borrow for the right reasons? List some steps you could take to improve your management of credit. For advice on managing credit, visit www.fcac-acfc.gc.ca/Eng/forConsumers/topics/creditLoans/Pages/home-accueil.aspx

APPENDIX E
DEVELOPING A BUSINESS PLAN

What's Next? A New Business Model for Restaurants

You're probably familiar with buying airline tickets and concert tickets in advance—but what about a restaurant meal? We're not talking about a fast-food chain; we're talking about a fine dining restaurant. Usually, restaurant customers walk in the door and hope to find a vacant table; if they plan ahead, they might call for a reservation. But the idea of purchasing advance tickets for a restaurant is new to most of us.

Grant Achatz is a well-known chef and restaurant owner. He has a new restaurant called Next—based on a new kind of business plan. Instead of taking reservations, the restaurant sells tickets. The plan makes sense. Next will probably be as popular as Achatz's other restaurant, Alina, which is sold out many weeks in advance. "We now pay three or four reservationists all day long to basically tell people they can't come to the restaurant," explains Achatz. When customers purchase tickets in advance, they are assured of a ready table just as they would with a reservation. Achatz and his partner, Nick Kokonas, will be able to save the costs of the full-time reservation staff. They plan to pass along savings like this to their diners. Selling tickets "allows us to give an experience that is actually a great value," notes Achatz.

Diners who want a meal at Next simply visit the restaurant's website. They can look at the menu, which changes four times a year, and then lock into the fixed price for the entire six-course meal. They can also choose to dine at peak or off-peak hours, which will be reflected in the ticket price. For example, a table at 9:30 on a Tuesday night will cost less than a table at 8:00 on Saturday night. Meals range from $45 to $75, with wine and other beverages costing extra. A service charge—instead of a traditional tip—is included in the ticket price. This way, Achatz and Kokonas can distribute the gratuities among the staff as they see fit.

Achatz is known to offer unique dining experiences that many customers are willing to pay for. Next offers patrons a total experience in the cuisine of a specific place and time. It isn't just a theme; it's an experience that re-creates an era, with everything researched by Achatz and his team. The first offering was based on Paris in 1912, with Escoffier-era cuisine prepared, cooked, and served down to the last detail. When the menu changes, every three months, the chef may choose recipes that take diners to postwar Sicily or a fantasy of Chinese cuisine in the year 2020.

In the same way that sports fans buy season tickets, customers of Next can purchase a year's subscription to Next. That way they lock in the price and are guaranteed a reserved table for each of the seasonal menus. Achatz believes that once people get used to the idea of a prepaid meal, they will enjoy the experience. The dinner is paid for, and there's no fumbling for the wallet. "There's no transaction in the restaurant at all," Achatz points out. "So you can literally come in, sit down, start your experience, and when you're done, you just get up and leave."[1]

APPENDIX E OVERVIEW

Many entrepreneurs and small-business owners write business plans to help them organize their businesses, get them up and running, and raise money for expansion. In this appendix, we cover the basics of business planning: what business plans are, why they're important, and who needs them. We also explain the steps involved in writing a good plan and the major elements it should include. Finally, we cover additional resources to get you started with your own business plan—to help you bring your unique ideas to reality with a business of your own.

WHAT IS A BUSINESS PLAN?

You may wonder how the millions of different businesses operating throughout the world today got their start. Many of them got started with a formal business plan. A *business plan* is a written document that defines what a company's objectives are, how these objectives will be achieved, how the business will be financed, and how much money the company expects to bring in. In short, it describes where a company is, where it wants to go, and how it intends to get there.

Why a Business Plan Is So Important

A well-written business plan serves two key functions:

1. It organizes the business and validates (or gives justification for) its central idea.
2. It summarizes the business and its strategy to obtain funding from lenders and investors.

First, a business plan gives a business formal direction, whether it is just starting, going through a phase of growth, or struggling. The business plan forces the principals—the owners—to do some thorough planning, to think through the realities of running and financing a business. In their planning, they consider many details. How will inventory be stored, shipped, and stocked? Where should the business be located? How will the business use the Internet? And most important, how will the business make enough money to make it all worthwhile?

A business plan also gives the owners a well-thought-out blueprint, or plan, to refer to when daily challenges come up. It also acts as a benchmark by which successes and disappointments can be measured. A solid business plan will sell the potential owner on the real possibilities of the idea. In some cases, the by-product of developing the plan is demonstrating to a dreamy person that he or she is trying to start a business that won't work. In other words, the process of writing a plan benefits a would-be businessperson as much as the final plan benefits potential investors.

Finally, a business plan communicates the business's strategy to financiers who may fund the business. A business plan is usually required to obtain a bank loan. Lenders and venture capitalists need to see that the business owner has thought through the critical issues and has presented a promising idea before they will consider investing. After all, they're really interested in whether investing in the business will bring them significant returns.

Who Needs a Business Plan?

Every business owner who expects to be successful needs a business plan. Some people mistakenly believe that they need a business plan only if it will land on the desk of a venture capitalist or the loan committee of a bank. Others think that writing a plan is unnecessary if their bank or lending institution doesn't need it. But these people miss the point of planning. A business plan acts as a map to guide the way through the often tangled roads of running a business. Every small-business owner should develop a business plan because it empowers that person to take control.

HOW DO I WRITE A BUSINESS PLAN?

Developing a business plan should mean something different to everyone. Think of a business plan as a clear statement of a business's identity. A construction company has a different identity from a newly launched magazine, which has yet a different identity from a restaurant hoping to expand its share of the market. Each business has unique objectives and processes, and each faces different obstacles.

At the same time, good business plans contain some similar elements no matter who the business owner is, what he or she sells, or how far the owner is into the venture. A smart business owner shapes the elements of a business plan into a professional and personal representation of the firm's needs and goals. The plan should also be realistic in its assessment of the risks and obstacles specific to the business, and then present solutions for overcoming them.

Because the document is important, it takes time to collect needed information and organize it. Don't be misled into believing that you will simply sit down and begin writing. Before any writing begins, the business owner must become an expert in his or her field. Gathering important information about the company and the market will make the writing easier and faster. The following items are some critical pieces of information that you should have on hand:

- The company's name, legal form of organization, location, financial highlights, and owners or shareholders (if any).
- Organization charts, list of top managers, consultants or directors, and employee agreements.
- Marketing research, customer surveys, and information about the company's major competitors.
- Product information, including goods and services offered; brochures; patents, licences, and trademarks; and research and development plans.
- Marketing plans and materials.
- Financial statements (both current and forecasted).

The business owner also must do a lot of soul searching and brainstorming to answer important questions necessary to build a healthy business. **Figure E.1** lists some critical questions to ask yourself.

Once you have answered these questions, you can begin writing the document. It can be between 10 and 50 pages long. The length of the plan depends on the complexity of the company, whether the company is a startup (established companies have longer histories to detail), and how the plan will be used. Regardless of size, the document should be well organized and easy to use, especially if the business plan is intended for external uses, such as to secure financing. Number all pages, include a table of contents, and make sure the format is attractive and professional. Include two or three charts or graphs, and highlight the sections and important points with headings and bulleted lists. **Figure E.2** outlines the major sections of a business plan.

The following paragraphs discuss the most common elements of an effective business plan. When you need additional instruction or information, refer to the "Resources" section at the end of the appendix.

Executive Summary

The primary purpose of an executive summary is to interest readers so that they want to learn more about the business. An *executive summary* is a one- to two-page snapshot of what the overall business plan explains in detail. Consider it a business plan within a business plan. By expressing enthusiasm and energy, the summary should capture the reader's imagination. Describe your strategy for succeeding in a positive, intriguing, and realistic way. Briefly yet thoroughly answer the first questions anyone would have about your business: who, what, why, when, where, and how. Financiers always turn to the executive summary first. If it isn't well presented or is missing the

> **Take a few minutes to read and answer these questions.
> Don't worry about answering in too much detail at this point.
> The questions are preliminary and
> intended to help you think through your venture.**
>
> 1. In general terms, how would you explain your idea to a friend?
> 2. What is the purpose or objective of your venture?
> 3. What service are you going to provide, or what goods are you going to manufacture?
> 4. Is there any significant difference between what you are planning and what already exists?
> 5. How will the quality of your product compare with competitive offerings?
> 6. What is the overview of the industry or service sector you are going to enter? Write it out.
> 7. What is the history, current status, and future of the industry?
> 8. Who is your customer or client base?
> 9. Where and by whom will your good or service be marketed?
> 10. How much will you charge for the product you are planning?
> 11. Where is the financing going to come from to initiate your venture?
> 12. What training and experience do you have that qualifies you for this venture?
> 13. Does such training or experience give you a significant edge?
> 14. If you lack specific experience, how do you plan to gain it?

FIGURE E.1 Self-Evaluation Questions

proper information, they will quickly move on to the next business plan in the stack. The executive summary is also important to people funding the business with their own resources. The business plan channels their motivations into a clear, well-written mission statement. It is a good idea to write the executive summary last because it will almost always be revised again, when the business plan takes its final shape.

To write an effective executive summary, focus on the issues that are most important to your business's success, and save the supporting information for the body of the business plan. The executive summary should describe the firm's strategy and goals, the good or service it is selling, and the advantages it has over the competition. It should also give a quick overview of how much money will be required to launch the business, how the money will be used, and how the lenders or investors will recoup their funds.

Introduction

The introduction follows the executive summary. After the executive summary has offered an attractive overview, the introduction should begin to discuss the fine details of the business. It should include any material the upcoming marketing and financing sections do not cover. The introduction should describe the company, the management team, and the product in detail. If one

THE BUSINESS PLAN
I. Executive Summary
- Who, what, when, where, why, and how?

II. Table of Contents

III. Introduction
- The concept and the company
- The management team
- The product

IV. Marketing Strategy
- Demographics
- Trends
- Market penetration
- Potential sales revenue

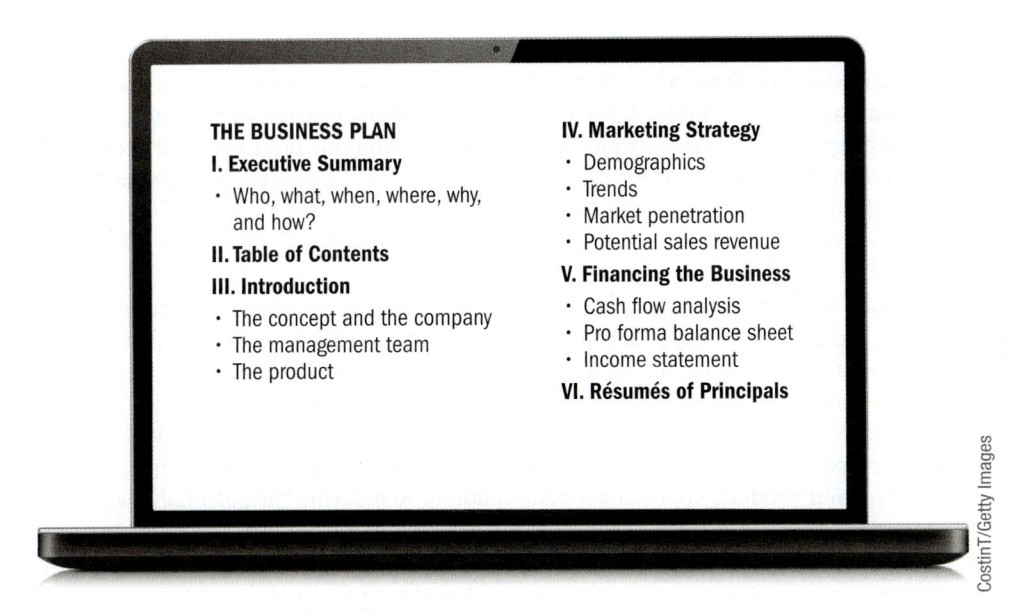

V. Financing the Business
- Cash flow analysis
- Pro forma balance sheet
- Income statement

VI. Résumés of Principals

FIGURE E.2 Outline of a Business Plan

of these topics is particularly noteworthy for your business, you may want to present that topic as its own section. Listen to what you write and respond as the plan takes shape.

Include basic information about the company—its past, present, and future. What are the company's roots, what is its current status, and what actions does it need to take to achieve its goals? If you are starting a company, include a description of the evolution of the concept. Be sure to tie all of the business's goals and plans to the industry it will operate in, and describe the industry itself.

A business doesn't run itself, of course. People are the heart of a business, so write an interesting profile of the business's management team. Who are the key players and how does their experience support the company's goals? Describe their—or your, if you are a sole proprietor (an owner–operator)—education, training, and experience, and highlight and refer to résumés included later in the plan. Be honest—not all businesses are started by experts. If you lack demonstrated experience in a certain area, explain how you plan to gain experience.

Also describe the product, which is the driving force behind the venture. What are you offering, and why is it special? What are the costs of the service or the price tag on the good? Analyze the features of the offering and the effect these features have on the overall cost.

Marketing Strategy

Next comes the marketing strategy section. The *marketing strategy* describes the market's need for the item and the way the business will fulfill it. Marketing strategies are not based on informal projections or observations. They are the result of a careful market analysis. Putting together a marketing strategy allows the business owner to become familiar with every aspect of the particular market. If done properly, it will allow you to define your target market and position your business within that sector to get its share of sales.

The marketing strategy will include discussing the size of the customer base that will want to purchase your good or service and the projected rate of growth for the product or category. Highlight information on the demographics of your customers. *Demographics* are statistical characteristics of the segment of the market, such as income, gender, and age. What types of people will purchase your product? How old are they, and where do they live? What is their lifestyle like? For example, someone starting an interior design business will want to report how many homeowners live within a certain distance from the firm and their median income. Of course, this section of the marketing analysis will be quite different for a company that does all of its business online. You will want to know the types of people who will shop at your website, but your discussion won't be limited to one geographic area. It is also a good idea to describe the trends in your product category. Trends are consumer and business tendencies or patterns that business owners can use to gain market share.

The marketing strategy should also detail your distribution, pricing, and promotional goals. Discuss the average price of your offering and the reasons behind the price you have chosen. How do you intend to let your potential customers know that you have a product to sell? How will you sell it—through a catalogue, in a retail location, online, or maybe a combination of all three? The effectiveness of your distribution, pricing, and promotional goals will determine the extent to which you will be able to gain market share.

Competitors are another important part of your marketing strategy. What companies are already selling products similar to yours? Include a list of your competitors to show that you know exactly who they are and what you are up against. Describe what you think are their major strengths and weaknesses and how successful they have been within your market.

Also include the *market penetration*, which is the percentage of total customers who have purchased a company's product. For example, if there are 10,000 people in your market, and 5,000 have purchased your product, your market penetration is 50 percent. The *potential sales revenue*, also an important figure to include, is the total revenue of a company if it captured 100 percent market penetration. In other words, this figure represents the total dollar value of sales you would bring in if everyone who is a potential customer purchased your product.

Financing the Business

The goal of a business is to make money. Everything in the business plan lays the foundation for the *financing section*. Business owners should not skip this section even if they are not seeking outside money. It is crucial to have an accurate financial analysis to get financing, but it also is a necessary exercise for business owners funding the venture themselves. The financing section shows the cost of the product, operating expenses, expected sales revenue and profit, and the amount of the business owner's personal funds that will be invested to get the business up and running. The financial projections should be encouraging but also accurate and based on realistic assumptions. The owner should be able to defend the numbers projected.

Any assumptions made in the body of the business plan should be tied into the financial section. For example, if you think you will need a staff of five, your cash flow analysis should explain how you are going to pay them. A cash flow analysis, a required section of a financial analysis, shows how much money will flow through your business throughout the year. It helps you plan for staggered purchasing, high-volume months, and slow periods. Your business may be cyclical or seasonal; the cash flow projection lets you know whether you need to arrange a line of credit to cover periodic shortfalls. An income statement is another critical document. The income statement is a statement of income and expenses your company has taken on over a period of time.

Remember that leaving out important details can reduce your credibility, so be thorough. The plan must include your assumptions about the conditions under which your business will operate. It should cover details such as market strength; date of startup; sales buildup; gross profit margin; equipment, furniture, and fixtures required; and payroll and other key expenses that will affect the financial plan. In addition, a banker will want a pro forma balance sheet, which provides an estimate of what the business owns (its assets), what it owes (its liabilities), and what it is worth (the owner's equity). Refer to chapters 15, 16, and 17 of *Contemporary Business* for additional details on accounting, financial statements, and financial management.

Résumés of Principals

The final element of the business plan is the inclusion of the résumés of the principals behind the business: the management team. Each résumé should include detailed employment information and accomplishments. Consider expanding on the traditional résumé by including business affiliations, professional memberships, hobbies, and leisure activities, but only if this information applies to your business.

Whichever method you choose to develop a business plan, make sure that *you* develop the plan. It should sound as though it was written by the entrepreneur, not by some outside "expert."

RESOURCES

Whether a person has been in business for decades or is just starting out, many resources are available. A tremendous amount of material can help business owners write effective business plans. The biggest task is narrowing down the resources to the ones that are right for you. The Internet offers many sound business-planning tools and advice, much of which are free. You can look up different examples and opinions, which is important. Remember that no one source will match your situation exactly. Your library and career centre also offer many resources. Following are some helpful resources for business planning.

Books

Dozens of books describe how to write a business plan. Examples include the following:

- Edward Blackwell, *How to Prepare a Business Plan*, 5th ed. (London: Kogan Page Ltd., 2011).
- Michael Gerber, *The E-Myth Enterprise: How to Turn a Great Idea into a Thriving Business* (New York: Harper Collins, 2010).
- Mike McKeever, *How to Write a Business Plan*, 11th ed. (Berkeley, CA: Nolo Press, 2012).
- John W. Mullins, *The New Business Road Test: What Entrepreneurs and Executives Should Do Before Writing a Business Plan*, 3rd ed. (Financial Times/Prentice Hall, 2012).
- Steven D. Peterson, Peter E. Jaret, and Barbara Findlay Schenck, *Business Plans Kit for Dummies*, 4th ed. (Wiley, 2013).
- Hal Shelton, *The Secrets to Writing a Successful Business Plan: A Pro Shares a Step-by-Step Guide to Creating a Plan That Gets Results* (Rockville, MD: Summit Valley Press, 2014).
- Paul Tiffany, Steven D. Peterson, and Nada Wagner, *Business Plans for Canadians for Dummies*, 2nd ed. (Wiley, 2012).

Websites

- *Entrepreneur, Inc.* and *BusinessWeek* magazines offer knowledgeable guides to writing a business plan. *Entrepreneur*'s website also contains sample business plans.

    www.entrepreneur.com

    www.inc.com

    www.bloomberg.com

- If you are hoping to obtain funding with your business plan, it is a good idea to become familiar with what investors are looking for. The following are professional associations for the venture capital industry:

    www.cvca.ca/ (Canadian Venture Capital & Private Equity Association)

    www.nvca.org (National Venture Capital Association)

    www.sbia.org (Small Business Investor Alliance)

    www.bdc.ca/EN/bdc-capital/venture-capital/Pages/venture-capital.aspx (Business Development Bank of Canada - BDC Capital)

Software

Business-planning software can help to give an initial shape to your business plan. But a word of caution if you write a business plan using a software template—bankers and potential investors, such as venture capitalists, read so many business plans that the plans that are based on templates may sink to the bottom of the pile. Also, if you aren't looking for funding, using software can undercut a chief purpose of writing a plan—learning about your unique idea. Think twice before you deprive yourself of that experience. Remember, software is a tool. It can help you get started, stay organized, and build a professional-looking business plan, but it can't actually write the plan for you.

Associations and Organizations

Many government and professional organizations provide assistance to would-be business owners. Here is a partial list:

- The Business Development Bank of Canada (BDC) is Canada's business development bank providing Canadian businesses with flexible financing, venture capital, and consulting services.

    www.bdc.ca/Pages/SplashPage.aspx

- The U.S. Small Business Administration offers planning materials, along with other resources.

    www.sba.gov/category/navigation-structure/starting-managing-business

- The SBA also has a centre specifically designed for female entrepreneurs.

    www.sba.gov/content/women-owned-businesses

PROJECTS AND TEAMWORK APPLICATIONS

1. Visit the website for Next Restaurant at www.nextrestaurant.com to learn more about the restaurant's innovative method of selling tickets in advance. Think of another business that doesn't usually sell tickets in advance—yet. Write a brief plan for converting that business to the pre-selling business model. Why do you think this business would be successful? What might be the drawbacks?

2. Do you dream of starting your own business? Take your idea and answer as many of the self-evaluation questions in **Figure E.1** as you can. Share your answers with the class. Then file your answers away to read at a future date—either when you have graduated from college or university or when you think you are ready to pursue your own business.

3. Write the executive summary portion of the business plan for your potential business. You may use the answers to the questions in **Figure E.1** to help you get started.

GLOSSARY

accounting the process of measuring, interpreting, and communicating financial information to support internal and external business decision making.

accounting cycle the set of activities involved in converting information and individual transactions into financial statements.

accounting equation the relationship that should reflect a firm's financial position at any time: assets should always equal the sum of liabilities and owners' equity.

Accounting Standards Board (AcSB) the organization that interprets and modifies GAAP in Canada for private and not-for-profit businesses.

accrual accounting an accounting method that records revenues and expenses when they occur, not when cash actually changes hands.

acquisition an agreement in which one firm purchases another.

advertising paid nonpersonal communication usually targeted at large numbers of potential buyers.

affective conflict a disagreement that focuses on individuals or personal issues.

affinity program a marketing effort sponsored by an organization that targets people who share common interests and activities.

angel investors wealthy individuals who invest directly in a new venture in exchange for an equity stake.

application service provider (ASP) an outside supplier that provides both the computers and the application support for managing an information system.

asset anything with future benefit owned or controlled by a firm.

balance of payments the overall money flows into and out of a country.

balance of trade the difference between a nation's exports and imports.

balance sheet a statement of a firm's financial position—what it owns and claims against its assets—at a particular point in time.

balanced budget a situation where total revenues raised by taxes and fees equal the total proposed government spending for the year.

Bank of Canada (the Bank) the central bank of Canada.

bankruptcy the legal nonpayment of financial obligations.

benchmarking the process of looking at how well other companies perform business functions or tasks and using their performance as a standard for measuring another company's performance.

board of directors the governing body of a corporation.

botnet a network of PCs that have been infected with one or more data-stealing viruses.

brand a name, term, sign, symbol, design, or some combination that identifies the products of one firm and shows how they differ from competitors' offerings.

brand equity the added value that a respected and successful name gives to a product.

brand name the part of a brand that is made up of words or letters that form a name. It is used to identify a firm's products and show how they differ from the products of competitors.

branding the process of creating in consumers' minds an identity for a good, service, or company; a major marketing tool in contemporary business.

breakeven analysis the pricing-related technique used to calculate the minimum sales volume a product must generate at a certain price level to cover all costs.

budget an organization's plan for how it will raise and spend money during a specific period of time.

budget deficit a situation where the government spends more than it raises through taxes.

budget surplus the excess funding when government spends less than it raises through taxes and fees.

business all profit-seeking activities and enterprises that provide goods and services necessary to an economic system.

Business Development Bank of Canada (BDC) a governmental agency that assists, counsels, and protects the interests of small businesses in Canada.

business ethics standards of conduct and moral values regarding right and wrong actions in the business environment.

business incubator a local program designed to provide low-cost, shared business facilities to small startup companies.

business intelligence a field of research that uses activities and technologies for gathering, storing, and analyzing data to make better competitive decisions.

business law those parts of law that most directly influence and regulate the management of business activity.

business plan a formal document that details a company's goals, methods, and standards.

business product or business-to-business (B2B) product a good or service purchased to be used, either directly or indirectly, in the production of other goods for resale.

Canada Deposit Insurance Corporation (CDIC) the federal agency that insures deposits at commercial and savings banks.

capital production inputs consisting of technology, tools, information, and physical facilities.

capital structure the mix of a firm's debt and equity capital.

capitalism an economic system that rewards firms for their ability to perceive and serve the needs and demands of consumers; also called the private enterprise system.

category advisor the individual that the business customer assigns as the major supplier to deal with all the other suppliers for a project. The category advisor also presents the entire package to the business buyer.

cause advertising a form of institutional advertising that promotes a specific viewpoint on a public issue as a way to influence public opinion and the political process.

cause marketing marketing that promotes a cause or social issue, such as preventing child abuse, anti-littering efforts, and stop-smoking campaigns.

Central America–Dominican Republic Free Trade Agreement (CAFTA-DR) an agreement among the United States, Costa Rica, the Dominican Republic, El Salvador, Guatemala, Honduras, and Nicaragua to reduce tariffs and trade restrictions.

chief information officer (CIO) the executive responsible for managing a firm's information systems and related computer technologies.

classic entrepreneur a person who sees a business opportunity and sets aside resources to gain access to that market.

cloud computing the use of powerful servers that store applications software and databases that users access by using any Internet-connected device, such as a PC or a smartphone.

co-branding a cooperative arrangement where two or more businesses team up to closely link their names on a single product.

code of conduct a formal statement that defines how an organization expects its employees to resolve ethical issues.

cognitive conflict a disagreement that focuses on problem- and issue-related differences of opinion.

collective bargaining the process of negotiation between management and union representatives.

co-marketing a cooperative arrangement where two businesses jointly market each other's products.

common law laws that result from judicial decisions, some of which can be traced to early England.

common shares the basic form of company ownership; shares that give owners voting rights but only residual claims to the firm's assets and income distributions.

communication a meaningful exchange of information through messages.

communism an economic system where all property is shared equally by the people in a community under the direction of a strong central government.

compensation the amount employees are paid in money and benefits.

competition the battle among businesses for consumer acceptance.

competitive differentiation the unique combination of organizational abilities, products, and approaches that sets one company apart from its competitors in the minds of customers.

competitive pricing a strategy that tries to reduce the emphasis on price competition by matching other firms' prices and by focusing their own marketing efforts on the product, distribution, and promotional elements of the marketing mix.

computer-aided design (CAD) a process used by engineers to design parts and entire products on the computer. Engineers who use CAD can work faster and with fewer mistakes than those who use traditional drafting systems.

computer-aided manufacturing (CAM) a computer tool that a manufacturer uses to analyze CAD output and the steps that a machine must take to produce a needed product or part.

computer-based information systems information systems that use computer and related technologies to store information electronically in an organized, accessible manner.

computer-integrated manufacturing (CIM) an integrated production system that uses computers to help workers design products, control machines, handle materials, and control the production function.

conflict the outcome when one person's, or one group's, needs do not match those of another, and one side may try to block the other side's intentions or goals.

conflict of interest a situation in which an employee must choose between a business's welfare and personal gain.

conglomerate merger a merger that combines unrelated firms, usually with the goal of diversification, increasing sales, or spending a cash surplus to avoid a takeover attempt.

consumer behaviour end consumers' activities that are directly involved in obtaining, consuming, and disposing of products, and the decision processes before and after these activities.

consumer orientation a business philosophy that focuses first on consumers' unmet wants and needs, and then designs products to meet those needs.

Consumer Price Index (CPI) a measurement of the monthly average change in prices of goods and services.

consumer product or business-to-consumer (B2C) product a good or service that is purchased by end users.

consumerism public demand that a business consider the wants and needs of its customers when making decisions.

contract a legally enforceable agreement between two or more parties regarding a specified act or thing.

controlling the function of assessing an organization's performance against its goals.

cooperative advertising allowances that marketers provide to share with channel partners the cost of local advertising of their firm's product or product line.

copyright legal protection of written or printed material such as books, designs, cartoons, photos, computer software, music, and videos.

core inflation rate the inflation rate after energy prices and food prices are removed.

corporate culture an organization's collection of principles, beliefs, and values.

corporate philanthropy an organization's contribution to the communities where it earns profits.

corporation a legal organization with assets and liabilities separate from the assets and liabilities of its owners.

Corruption of Foreign Public Officials Act a federal law that prohibits Canadian citizens and companies from bribing foreign officials to win or continue business.

cost-based pricing calculating total costs per unit and then adding markups to cover overhead costs and generate profits.

countertrade a barter agreement whereby trade between two or more nations involves payment made in the form of local products instead of currency.

creative selling a persuasive type of promotional presentation.

creativity the capacity to develop novel solutions to perceived organizational problems.

credit receiving money, goods, or services on the basis of an agreement between the lender and the borrower that the loan is for a specified period of time with a specified rate of interest.

critical thinking the ability to analyze and assess information to pinpoint problems or opportunities.

cross-functional team a team made up of members from different functions, such as production, marketing, and finance.

cyclical unemployment the joblessness of people who are out of work because of a cyclical contraction in the economy.

data raw facts and figures that may or may not be meaningful to a business decision.

data mining the use of computer searches of customer data to detect patterns and relationships.

data warehouse a customer database that allows managers to combine data from several different organizational functions.

database a centralized integrated collection of data resources.

debt financing borrowed funds that entrepreneurs must repay.

decision making the process of seeing a problem or opportunity, assessing possible solutions, selecting and carrying out the best-suited plan, and assessing the results.

decision support system (DSS) an information system that gives direct support to businesspeople during the decision-making process.

deflation the opposite of inflation, occurs when prices continue to fall.

delegation the managerial process of assigning work to employees.

demand the willingness and ability of buyers to purchase goods and services.

demand curve a graph of the amount of a product that buyers will purchase at different prices.

demographic segmentation dividing markets on the basis of various demographic or socioeconomic characteristics, such as gender, age, income, occupation, household size, stage in family life cycle, education, or ethnic group.

departmentalization the process of dividing work activities into units within the organization.

devaluation a reduction in a currency's value in terms of other currencies or in terms of a fixed standard.

directing guiding and motivating employees to accomplish organizational goals.

discrimination biased treatment toward a job candidate or employee.

distribution channels the paths that products—and their legal ownership—follow from producer to consumers or business users.

distribution strategy a plan that deals with the marketing activities and institutions that get the right good or service to the firm's customers.

diversity the blending of individuals of different genders, ethnic backgrounds, cultures, religions, ages, and physical and mental abilities to enhance a firm's chances of success.

divestiture the sale of assets by a firm.

double-entry bookkeeping the process used to record accounting transactions; each individual transaction is always balanced by another transaction.

downsizing the process of reducing the number of employees within a firm by eliminating jobs.

dumping selling products in other countries at prices below production costs or below typical prices in the home market to capture market share from domestic competitors.

economics the social science that studies the choices people and governments make when dividing up their scarce resources.

embargo a total ban on importing specific products or a total stop to trading with a particular country.

employee benefits additional compensation—such as vacation time, retirement savings plans, profit-sharing, health insurance, gym memberships, child and elder care, and tuition reimbursement—paid entirely or in part by the company.

employee separation a broad term for the loss of an employee for any reason, voluntary or involuntary.

Employment Equity Act (EEA) an act created (1) to increase job opportunities for women and members of minority groups and (2) to help end discrimination based on race, colour, religion, disability, gender, or national origin.

empowerment giving employees shared authority, responsibility, and decision making with their managers.

end-use segmentation a marketing strategy that focuses on the precise way a B2B purchaser will use a product.

entrepreneur a person who seeks a profitable opportunity and takes the necessary risks to set up and operate a business.

entrepreneurship the willingness to take risks to create and operate a business.

equilibrium price the current market price for an item.

equity financing funds invested in new ventures in exchange for part ownership.

equity theory an individual's perception of fair and equitable treatment.

European Union (EU) a 28-nation European economic alliance.

event marketing marketing or sponsoring of short-term events such as athletic competitions and cultural and charitable performances.

everyday low pricing (EDLP) a strategy of maintaining continuous low prices instead of using short-term price cuts such as cents-off coupons, rebates, and special sales.

exchange control a restriction on importing certain products or a restriction against certain companies to reduce trade and the spending of foreign currency.

exchange process an activity in which two or more parties trade something of value (such as goods, services, or cash) that satisfies each other's needs.

exchange rate the value of one country's currency in terms of the currencies of other countries.

executive support system (ESS) an information system that lets senior executives access the firm's primary databases, often by touching the computer screen, pointing and clicking a mouse, or using voice recognition.

expansionary monetary policy a plan to increase the money supply to try to decrease the cost of borrowing. Lower interest rates encourage businesses to make new investments, which leads to employment and economic growth.

expectancy theory the process people use to evaluate the likelihood that their efforts will lead to the results they want and the degree to which they want those results.

expert system a computer program that imitates human thinking through complicated sets of "if-then" rules.

exports domestically produced goods and services sold in other countries.

external communication a meaningful exchange of information through messages sent between an organization and its major audiences.

factors of production four basic inputs for effective operation: natural resources, capital, human resources, and entrepreneurship.

fair trade a market-based approach of paying higher prices to producers for goods exported from developing countries to developed countries in an effort to promote sustainability and to ensure the people in developing countries receive better trading conditions.

finance the business function of planning, obtaining, and managing the company's funds to accomplish its objectives as effectively and efficiently as possible.

finance charge the difference between the amount borrowed and the amount repaid on a loan.

Financial Accounting Standards Board (FASB) the organization that interprets and modifies GAAP in the United States.

financial institutions intermediaries between savers and borrowers that collect funds from savers and then lend the funds to individuals, businesses, and governments.

financial managers the executives who develop and carry out their firm's financial plan and decide on the most appropriate sources and uses of funds.

financial markets markets where securities are issued and traded.

financial plan a document that specifies the funds needed by a firm for a period of time, the timing of cash inflows and outflows, and the most appropriate sources and uses of funds.

financial system the process by which money flows from savers to users.

firewall a type of security system for computers that limits data transfers to certain locations; it also tracks system use so that managers can identify threats to the system's security, including attempts to log on with invalid passwords.

fiscal policy a plan of government spending and taxation decisions designed to control inflation, reduce unemployment, improve the general welfare of citizens, and encourage economic growth.

flexible manufacturing system (FMS) a production facility that workers can quickly change to manufacture different products.

foreign licensing agreement an international agreement in which one firm allows another firm to produce or sell its product, or use its trademark, patent, or manufacturing processes, in a specific geographical area, in return for royalties or other compensation.

franchise a contract-based agreement in which a franchisee can produce and/or sell the franchisor's products under that company's brand name if the franchisee agrees to the operating terms and requirements.

franchisee the individual or business firm purchasing a franchise.

franchising a contract-based business arrangement between a manufacturer or other supplier, and a dealer, such as a restaurant operator or retailer.

franchisor the firm whose products are sold to customers by the franchisee.

frequency marketing a marketing initiative that rewards frequent purchases with cash, rebates, merchandise, or other premiums.

frictional unemployment the joblessness of people in the workforce who are temporarily not working but are looking for jobs.

General Agreement on Tariffs and Trade (GATT) an international trade accord that has greatly reduced worldwide tariffs and other trade barriers.

generally accepted accounting principles (GAAP) principles that outline the conventions, rules, and procedures for deciding on the acceptable accounting practices at a particular time.

geographical segmentation dividing an overall market into similar groups on the basis of their locations.

global business strategy the offering of a standardized, worldwide product and the selling of it in basically the same way throughout a firm's domestic and foreign markets.

goal-setting theory the idea that people will be motivated to the extent to which they accept specific, challenging goals and receive feedback that shows their progress toward goal achievement.

grapevine an internal information channel that passes information from unofficial sources.

green marketing a marketing strategy that promotes environmentally safe products and production methods.

grid computing a network of smaller computers that run special software.

gross domestic product (GDP) the sum of all goods and services produced within a country during a specific time period, such as a year.

guerrilla marketing innovative, low-cost marketing efforts designed to get consumers' attention in unusual ways.

hardware all tangible, or physical, elements of a computer system.

health insurance insurance that pays for losses due to illness or injury.

home-based businesses firms operated from the residence of the business owner.

horizontal merger a merger that joins firms in the same industry for the purpose of diversification, increasing customer bases, cutting costs, or expanding product lines.

human resource management the function of attracting, developing, and retaining employees who can perform the activities needed to meet organizational objectives.

human resources production inputs consisting of anyone who works, including both the physical labour and the intellectual inputs contributed by workers.

hyperinflation an economic situation marked by soaring prices.

imports foreign goods and services purchased by domestic customers.

income statement a financial record of a company's revenues, expenses, and profits over a specific period of time.

inflation rising prices caused by a combination of excess consumer demand and higher costs of raw materials, component parts, human resources, and other factors of production.

infomercials a form of broadcast direct marketing; 30-minute programs resemble regular TV programs, but sell goods or services.

information knowledge gained from processing data.

information system an organized method for collecting, storing, and communicating past, present, and projected information on internal operations and external intelligence.

infrastructure the basic systems of a country's communication, transportation, and energy facilities.

insider trading use of material nonpublic information about a company to make investment profits.

institutional advertising messages that promote concepts, ideas, or philosophies. It can also promote goodwill toward industries, companies, organizations, or government entities.

insurance a contract in which the insurer, for a fee, agrees to reimburse an insured firm or individual a sum of money if a loss occurs.

integrated marketing communications (IMC) the coordination of all promotional activities—media advertising, direct mail, personal selling, sales promotion, and public relations—to produce a unified customer-focused message.

integrity behaving according to one's deeply felt ethical principles in business situations.

International Accounting Standards Board (IASB) the organization that promotes worldwide consistency in financial reporting practices.

International Financial Reporting Standards (IFRS) the standards and interpretations adopted by the IASB.

international law the numerous regulations that govern international trade.

International Monetary Fund (IMF) an organization created to promote trade, eliminate barriers, and make short-term loans to member-nations that are unable to meet their budgets.

International Organization for Standardization (ISO) an international organization whose mission is to develop and promote international standards for business, government, and society. The aim is to improve and encourage global trade and cooperation.

intranet a computer network that is similar to the Internet but limits access to authorized users.

intrapreneurship the process of promoting innovation within the structure of an existing organization.

inventory control a function that balances the costs of storing inventory with the need to have stock on hand to meet demand.

joint venture a partnership between companies for a specific activity.

judiciary the branch of government that is responsible for applying laws to settle disagreements; also known as the court system.

just-in-time (JIT) system a broad management philosophy that reaches beyond the narrow activity of inventory control to affect the entire system of production and operations management.

labour union a group of workers who organize themselves to work toward common goals in the areas of wages, hours, and working conditions.

law the standards set by government and society in the form of either legislation or custom.

law of large numbers the idea that seemingly random events will follow predictable patterns if enough events are observed.

leadership the ability to direct or inspire people to reach goals.

LEED (Leadership in Energy and Environmental Design) a voluntary certification program administered by the Canada Green Building Council, aimed at promoting the most sustainable construction processes available.

Glossary

leverage increasing the rate of return on funds invested by borrowing funds.

leveraged buyouts (LBOs) transactions where public shareholders are bought out and the firm reverts to private status.

liability a claim against a firm's assets by creditors.

life insurance a type of insurance that protects people against the financial losses that occur with premature death.

lifestyle entrepreneur a person who starts a business to reduce work hours and create a more relaxed lifestyle.

lifetime value of a customer the revenues and intangible benefits (such as referrals and customer feedback) from a customer over the life of the relationship, minus the amount the company must spend to acquire and serve that customer.

listening receiving a message and interpreting its intended meaning by grasping the facts and feelings the message conveys.

local area networks (LANs) computer networks that connect machines within limited areas, such as a building or several nearby buildings.

logistics the process of coordinating flow of goods, services, and information among members of the supply chain.

macroeconomics the study of a nation's overall economic issues, such as how an economy maintains and divides up resources and how a government's policies affect its citizens' standards of living.

make, buy, or lease decision choosing whether to manufacture a needed product or part in-house, buy it from an outside supplier, or lease it.

malware any malicious software program designed to infect computer systems.

management the process of achieving organizational goals through people and other resources.

management by objectives (MBO) a structured approach that helps managers to focus on reachable goals and to achieve the best results based on the organization's resources.

management information system (MIS) an information system designed to produce reports for managers and other professionals.

management support systems information systems that are designed to provide support for effective decision making.

market segmentation the process of dividing a total market into several relatively similar groups.

marketing an organizational function and set of processes for creating, communicating, and delivering value to customers and for managing customer relationships in ways that benefit the organization and its stakeholders.

marketing concept a companywide consumer focus on promoting long-term success.

marketing mix a blending the four elements of marketing strategy—product, distribution, promotion, and pricing—to satisfy chosen customer segments.

marketing research the process of collecting and evaluating information to support marketing decision making.

Maslow's hierarchy of needs a theory of motivation proposed by Abraham Maslow. According to the theory, people have five levels of needs that they try to satisfy: physiological, safety, social, esteem, and self-actualization.

mass production a system for manufacturing products in large quantities by using effective combinations of employees with specialized skills, mechanization, and standardization.

materials requirement planning (MRP) a computer-based production planning system that ensures a firm has all the parts and materials it needs to produce its output at the right time and place and in the right amounts.

merger an agreement in which two or more firms combine to form one company.

microeconomics the study of small economic units, such as individual consumers, families, and businesses.

mission statement a written description of an organization's overall business purpose and aims.

missionary selling an indirect form of selling where the representative promotes goodwill for a company or provides technical or operational assistance to the customer.

mixed market economy an economic system that draws from both private enterprise economies and planned economies, to different degrees.

monetary policy a government plan to increase or decrease the money supply and to change banking requirements and interest rates to affect bankers' willingness to make loans.

monopolistic competition a market structure where large numbers of buyers and sellers exchange distinct and differentiated (dissimilar) products so each participant has some control over price.

monopoly a market situation where a single seller controls trade in a good or service, and buyers can find no close substitutes.

multidomestic business strategy a plan to develop and market products to serve different needs and tastes in separate national markets.

multinational corporation (MNC) a firm with many operations and marketing activities outside its home country.

national debt the money owed by government to individuals, businesses, and government agencies who purchase Treasury bills, Treasury notes, and Treasury bonds.

natural resources all production inputs that are useful in their natural states, including agricultural land, building sites, forests, and mineral deposits.

nearshoring the outsourcing of production or services to locations near a firm's home base.

net worth the difference between an individual's or a household's assets and liabilities.

nonpersonal selling forms of selling such as advertising, sales promotion, direct marketing, and public relations.

North American Free Trade Agreement (NAFTA) an agreement among the United States, Canada, and Mexico to break down tariffs and trade restrictions.

not-for-profit corporations organizations whose goals do not include pursuing a profit.

not-for-profit organizations organizations whose primary aims are public service, not returning a profit to their owners.

objectives guideposts by which managers define the organization's desired performance in such areas as new-product development, sales, customer service, growth, environmental and social responsibility, and employee satisfaction.

odd pricing a pricing method that uses uneven amounts to make prices appear to be less than they really are.

offshoring the relocation of business processes to lower-cost locations overseas.

oligopoly a market situation where relatively few sellers compete and high startup costs act as barriers to keep out new competitors.

on-demand computing the use of software time from application providers; firms pay only for their usage of the software, not for purchasing or maintaining the software.

operational support systems information systems designed to produce a variety of information on an organization's activities for both internal and external users.

order processing a form of selling used mostly at the wholesale and retail levels; involves identifying customer needs, pointing out products that meet those needs, and completing orders.

organization a structured group of people working together to achieve common goals.

organization marketing a marketing strategy that influences consumers to accept the goals of and organization, receive the services of an organization, or contribute in some way to an organization.

organizing the process of blending human and material resources through a formal structure of tasks and authority: arranging work, dividing tasks among employees, and coordinating them to ensure plans are carried out and goals are met.

outsourcing using outside vendors to produce goods or fulfill services and functions that were previously handled in-house or in-country.

owners' equity the funds that owners invest in the business plus any profits not paid to owners in the form of cash dividends.

partnership an association of two or more persons who operate a business as co-owners by voluntary legal agreement.

patent legal protection that guarantees an inventor exclusive rights to an invention for 20 years.

penetration pricing a strategy that sets a low price as a major marketing tactic.

performance appraisal evaluation of and feedback on an employee's job performance.

person marketing efforts that are designed to attract the attention, interest, and preference of a target market toward a person.

personal financial management the study of the economic factors and personal decisions that affect a person's financial well-being.

personal financial plan a guide to help a person reach his or her desired financial goals.

personal selling the most basic form of promotion: a direct person-to-person promotional presentation to a potential buyer.

physical distribution the actual movement of products from producer to consumers or business users.

place marketing an attempt to attract people to a particular area, such as a city, state, or country.

planned economy an economic system where business ownership, profits, and resource allocation are shaped by a plan to meet government goals, not goals set by individual firms.

planning the process of looking forward to future events and conditions and deciding on the courses of action for achieving organizational goals.

point-of-purchase (POP) advertising displays or demonstrations that promote products when and where consumers buy them, such as in retail stores.

positioning a concept whereby marketers try to establish their products in the minds of customers by communicating to buyers the meaningful differences about the attributes, price, quality, or use of a good or service.

preferred shares shares that give owners limited voting rights and the right to receive dividends or assets before owners of common shares.

prestige pricing setting a relatively high price to develop and maintain an image of quality and exclusiveness.

price the exchange value of a good or service.

primary markets financial markets where firms and governments issue securities and sell them initially to the general public.

private enterprise system an economic system that rewards firms for their ability to identify and serve the needs and demands of customers.

private property the most basic freedom under the private enterprise system; the right to own, use, buy, sell, and hand down land, buildings, machinery, equipment, patents, individual possessions, and various intangible kinds of property.

privatization the conversion of government-owned and -operated companies to privately held businesses.

problem-solving team a temporary combination of workers who gather to solve a specific problem and then disband.

process control systems operational support systems that monitor and control physical processes.

product a bundle of physical, service, and symbolic attributes designed to satisfy buyers' wants.

product advertising messages designed to sell a particular good or service.

product liability the responsibility of manufacturers for injuries and damages caused by their products.

product life cycle the four basic stages in the development of a successful product—introduction, growth, maturity, and decline.

product line a group of related products that share physical similarities or are targeted toward a similar market.

product mix the assortment of product lines and individual goods and services that a firm offers to consumers and business users.

product placement a form of promotion where marketers pay placement fees to have their products featured in various media, from newspapers and magazines to television and movies.

production the use of resources, such as workers and machinery, to convert materials into finished goods and services.

production and operations management the process of overseeing the production process by managing the people and machinery that convert materials and resources into finished goods and services.

production control creating well-defined procedures for coordinating people, materials, and machinery to provide the greatest production efficiency.

productivity the relationship between the number of units produced and the number of human and other production inputs needed to produce them.

product-related segmentation dividing consumer markets into groups that are based on benefits sought by buyers, usage rates, and loyalty levels.

profitability objectives common goals that are included in the strategic plans of most firms.

profits rewards for businesspeople who take the risks involved to offer goods and services to customers.

promotion the function of informing, persuading, and influencing a purchase decision.

promotional mix the combination of personal and nonpersonal selling that marketers use to meet the needs of a firm's target customers and to effectively and efficiently communicate its message to them.

property and liability insurance a general category of insurance that protects against losses due to a number of perils, such as fire, accident, and theft.

psychographic segmentation dividing consumer markets into groups with similar attitudes, values, and lifestyles.

public accountant an accountant who provides accounting services to other organizations.

public relations an organization's communications and relationships with its various public audiences.

publicity the nonpersonal stimulation of demand for a good, service, place, idea, event, person, or organization by unpaid placement of information in print or broadcast media.

pulling strategy promotion of a product by generating consumer demand for it, mainly through advertising and sales promotion appeals.

pure competition a market structure where large numbers of buyers and sellers exchange similar products, and no single participant has a large influence on price.

pushing strategy personal selling to market an item to wholesalers and retailers in a company's distribution channels.

quality the state of being free of deficiencies or imperfections.

quality control measuring output against quality standards.

quota a limit set on the amounts of particular products that can be imported.

recession a cycle of economic contraction that lasts for six months or longer.

recycling reprocessing of used materials for reuse.

regulated monopoly a firm that is granted exclusive rights in a specific market by a local, provincial, or federal government.

relationship era the business era where firms seek to actively promote customer loyalty by carefully managing every interaction.

relationship management the collection of activities that build and maintain ongoing, mutually beneficial ties with customers and others.

relationship marketing developing and maintaining long-term, cost-effective exchange relationships with partners.

restrictive monetary policy a plan to reduce the money supply to control rising prices, overexpansion, and concerns about overly rapid economic growth.

retailers distribution channel members that sell goods and services to individuals for their own use, not for resale.

risk uncertainty about loss or injury.

risk management calculations and actions a firm takes to recognize and deal with real or potential risks to its survival.

risk–return tradeoff the process of maximizing the wealth of the firm's shareholders by striking the right balance between risk and return.

rule of indemnity the requirement that the insured cannot collect more than the amount of the loss and cannot collect for the same loss more than once.

salary pay calculated on a periodic basis, such as weekly or monthly.

sales law the law governing the sale of goods or services for money or on credit.

sales promotion forms of promotion such as coupons, product samples, and rebates that support advertising and personal selling.

Sarbanes-Oxley Act of 2002 U.S. federal legislation designed to deter and punish corporate and accounting fraud and corruption. It is also designed to protect the interests of workers and shareholders by requiring enhanced financial disclosures, criminal penalties for CEOs and CFOs who defraud investors, and safeguards for whistle-blowers. The act also established a new regulatory body for public accounting firms.

seasonal unemployment the joblessness of workers in a seasonal industry.

secondary market a collection of financial markets where previously issued securities are traded among investors.

securities financial instruments that represent the obligations of the issuers to provide the purchasers with the expected stated returns on the funds invested or loaned.

seed capital the initial funding needed to launch a new venture.

self-managed team a work team that has the authority to decide how its members complete their daily tasks.

serial entrepreneur a person who starts one business, runs it, and then starts and runs more businesses, one after another.

server the heart of a midrange computer network.

sexism discrimination against members of either sex, but usually against women.

sexual harassment unwelcome and inappropriate actions of a sexual nature.

shareholders owners of a corporation as a result of their purchase of shares in the corporation.

skimming pricing a strategy that sets an intentionally high price relative to the prices of competing products.

small business an independent business with fewer than 100 employees and revenues less than $2 million, not dominant in its market.

social audits formal procedures that identify and evaluate all company activities that relate to social issues, such as conservation, employment practices, environmental protection, and philanthropy.

social entrepreneur a person who sees societal problems and uses business principles to develop new solutions.

social era the business era in which firms seek ways to connect and interact with customers using technology.

social responsibility business's consideration of society's well-being and consumer satisfaction, in addition to profits.

socialism an economic system where the government owns and operates the major industries, such as communications.

software all the programs, routines, and computer languages that control a computer and tell it how to operate.

sole proprietorship a business ownership in which the sole proprietor's status as an individual is not legally separate from his or her status as a business owner.

specialty advertising promotional items that prominently display a firm's name, logo, or business slogan.

sponsorship providing funds for a sporting or cultural event in exchange for a direct association with the event.

spyware software that gathers user information through the user's Internet connection without his or her knowledge, usually for advertising purposes.

stakeholders customers, investors, employees, and public affected by or with an interest in a company.

standard of living the necessities, comforts, and luxuries a person wants to achieve or maintain.

statement of cash flows a record of the sources and uses of cash during a period of time.

statement of changes in equity a record of the change in equity from the end of one fiscal period to the end of the next fiscal period.

statutory law written law that includes provincial and federal constitutions; legislative enactments; treaties of the federal government; and ordinances of local governments.

stock markets (exchanges) markets where shares of stock are bought and sold by investors.

strategic alliance a partnership formed to create a competitive advantage for the businesses involved; in international business, the business strategy of one company partnering with another company in the country where it wants to do business.

structural unemployment the joblessness of people who remain unemployed for long periods of time, often with little hope of finding a job.

subcontracting an agreement that involves hiring other companies to produce, distribute, or sell goods or services; in international subcontracting, local companies in a specific country or geographical region are hired to produce, distribute, or sell goods or services.

supply the willingness and ability of sellers to provide goods and services.

supply chain the complete sequence of suppliers that help to create a good or service and deliver it to business users and final consumers.

supply curve a graph that shows the relationship between different prices and the amount of goods that sellers will offer for sale, regardless of demand.

sustainable the capacity to endure in ecology.

SWOT analysis SWOT is a short form for *strengths, weaknesses, opportunities,* and *threats*. By assessing all four factors one by one, a firm can then develop the best strategies for gaining a competitive advantage.

target market a group of people that an organization markets its goods, services, or ideas toward, using a strategy designed to satisfy this group's specific needs and preferences.

tariffs taxes imposed on imported goods.

tax an assessment by a governmental unit.

team a group of people with certain skills who share a common purpose, approach, and performance goals.

team cohesiveness the extent to which team members feel attracted to the team and motivated to remain part of it.

team diversity the team's differences in ability, experience, personality, or any other factor.

team level the team's average level of ability, experience, personality, or any other factor.

team norm a standard of conduct shared by team members that guides their behaviour.

technology the business application of knowledge based on scientific discoveries, inventions, and innovations.

telemarketing personal selling by telephone, which provides marketers with a high return on their expenses, an immediate response, and an opportunity for a personalized two-way conversation.

tender offer a proposal made by a firm to the target firm's shareholders specifying a price and the form of payment.

test marketing the introduction of a new product and a complete marketing campaign to a selected city or TV coverage area.

tort a civil wrong inflicted by one person on another person or on another person's property.

trade promotion sales promotion geared to marketing intermediaries, not to final consumers.

trademark a brand that has been given legal protection; words, symbols, or other designations used by firms to identify their products.

transaction management building and promoting products in the hope that enough customers will buy them to cover costs and earn profits.

transaction processing systems operational support systems that record and process data from business transactions.

Trojan horse a program that claims to do one thing but in reality does something else, usually something malicious.

unemployment rate the percentage of the total workforce actively seeking work but currently unemployed.

utility the power of a good or service to satisfy a want or need.

vendor-managed inventory the process in which the producer and the retailer agree that the producer (or the wholesaler) will decide how much of a product a buyer needs and automatically ship new supplies when needed.

venture capital money invested in a business by another business firm or group of individuals in exchange for an ownership share.

venture capitalists business firms or groups of individuals that invest in new and growing firms in exchange for an ownership share.

vertical merger a merger that combines firms operating at different levels in the production and marketing process.

virtual private networks (VPNs) secure connections between two points on the Internet.

virtual teams groups of geographically or organizationally separated co-workers who use a combination of telecommunications and information technologies to accomplish an organizational task.

viruses malicious software programs that secretly attach themselves to other programs (called *hosts*) and change them or destroy data.

vision the ability to perceive marketplace needs and what an organization must do to satisfy them.

VoIP an alternative to traditional telecommunication services provided by companies such as Bell Canada and Telus; uses the Internet instead of telephone lines to transmit messages.

volume objectives pricing decisions that are based on market share, the percentage of a market controlled by a certain company or product.

wage pay based on an hourly rate or the amount of work accomplished.

whistle-blowing disclosure to company officials, government authorities, or the media of illegal, immoral, or unethical practices committed by an organization.

wholesaler a distribution channel member that sells primarily to retailers, other wholesalers, or business users.

wide area networks (WANs) computer networks that tie larger geographical regions together by using telephone lines and microwave and satellite transmission.

WiFi a wireless network that connects various devices and allows them to communicate with one another through radio waves.

work teams relatively permanent groups of employees with complementary skills who perform the day-to-day work of organizations.

World Bank an organization established by industrialized nations to lend money to less developed countries.

World Trade Organization (WTO) a 157-member international institution that monitors GATT agreements and mediates international trade disputes.

worm a small piece of software that uses a security hole in a network to replicate itself.

NOTES

Chapter 1

1. Official Website for Justin Bieber, accessed March 20, 2015, www.justinbiebermusic.com; Justin Bieber Facebook, accessed March 20, 2015, www.facebook.com/JustinBieber; Justin Bieber Twitter, accessed March 20, 2015, http://twitter.com/justinbieber; Justin Bieber Zone, accessed March 20, 2015, www.justinbieberzone.com; Caitlin Dewey, "From Startup to Pop Culture Conqueror," *Montreal Gazette*, February 18, 2015, C8; Marcus Hondro, "Bieber Hits 16 Million Twitter Followers on New Year's Day," *Digital Journal*, January 3, 2012, accessed January 3, 2012, www.digitaljournal.com/article/317183#ixzz1iP4EpfDS; Michael Paterniti, "How to Drake It in America," GQ, June 2013, accessed June 11, 2015, www.gq.com/entertainment/celebrities/201307/rapper-drake-in-america-july-2013?currentPage=1; YouTube video, "Drake before He Got famous!!" produced 2004, posted July 23, 2013, accessed June 11, 2015, www.youtube.com/watch?v=DKqmXJtDh7Y.

2. "Summary of the Findings of the National Survey of Nonprofit and Voluntary Organizations (NSNVO)," Statistics Canada, accessed January 23, 2011, www.statcan.gc.ca/pub/61-533-s/61-533-s2005001-eng.htm#5.

3. "Facts, Figures and Funding," Hospital for Sick Children (SickKids), accessed January 25, 2011, www.sickkids.ca/Research/AbouttheInstitute/Facts-Figures-and-Funding/Fact-Figures-and-Funding.html.

4. Doctors Without Borders, "Nepal," accessed May 23, 2015, www.doctorswithoutborders.org/country-region/nepal; "Powerful Earthquake Hits Nepal," CNN, May 3, 2015, accessed May 23, 2015, www.cnn.com/2015/04/25/world/gallery/nepal-earthquake; World Health Organization, "Nepal Earthquake 2015," accessed May 23, 2015, www.searo.who.int/entity/emergencies/nepal-earthquake-2015/en.

5. "SickKids Book Series," Hospital for Sick Children, accessed January 25, 2011, www.sickkids.ca/Learning/PatientsandFamilies/SickKids-book-series/index.html.

6. Livestrong Foundation, www.livestrong.org.

7. Netflix, "Company Overview," accessed January 10, 2014, https://pr.netflix.com/WebClient/loginPageSalesNetWorksAction.do?contentGroupId=10476&contentGroup=Company+Facts.

8. Beyond the Rack, accessed January 25, 2011, www.beyondtherack.com.

9. "Tech's Top Ten," *Financial Post*, December 29, 2011, FP12; Iain Marlow, "Small ISPs Lament CRTC Fee Change, Look to Invest in Own Infrastructure," *Globe and Mail*, January 13, 2011, accessed January 27, 2011, www.theglobeandmail.com/news/technology/tech-news/small-isps-lament-crtc-fee-change-look-to-invest-in-own-infrastructure/article1868429.

10. "Small Business Forum 2010," *Canadian Business Journal*, November 10, 2010, accessed January 27, 2011, www.canadianbusinessjournal.ca/business_in_action/november_10/small_business_forum_2010.html.

11. Industry Canada, *Key Small Business Statistics: July 2010*, Small Business and Tourism Branch, accessed January 27, 2011, www.ic.gc.ca/eic/site/061.nsf/vwapj/KSBS-PSRPE_July-Juillet2010_eng.pdf/$FILE/KSBS-PSRPE_July-Juillet2010_eng.pdf.

12. Ciara, "Vibe by Ciara," accessed February 18, 2015, www.ciaravibe.com/index-en.html; Jason Magder, "Homegrown Tablet, the Vibe, Takes on iPad," *Montreal Gazette*, January 27, 2011, accessed February 18, 2011, www.montrealgazette.com/technology/Homegrown+tablet+Vibe+takes+iPad/4175127/story.html; ExoPC, accessed February 18, 2011, www.exopc.com/en/index.php; TMC, "At Dumoulin Électronique First! The CIARA VIBE Tablet, Powered by ExoPC, Now Available to the Public," *TMCnet*, January 26, 2011, accessed February 18, 2011, www.tmcnet.com/usubmit/ 2011/01/26/5269403.htm.

13. Patrick May, "So Many Apps, So Little Time," *San Jose Mercury News*, February 7, 2010, www.mercurynews.com.

14. Home Depot, accessed February 4, 2010, http://ir.homedepot.com.

15. Andreas Kaplan and Michael Haenlein, "Users of the World, Unite! The Challenges and Opportunities of Social Media," *Business Horizons* 53 (2010): 59–68.

16. Jennifer Van Grove, "Why Facebook Is Giving Out Free Wi-Fi for Check-In," CNET, October 2, 2013, accessed January 10, 2014, www.cnet.com/news/why-facebook-is-giving-out-free-wi-fi-for-check-ins.

17. Overstock.com, accessed February 9, 2010, www.overstock.com.

18. Canada Newswire, "Endura Energy Begins Construction of Inaugural Rooftop Solar Power System," March 4, 2011, accessed

January 2, 2012, http://cnw.ca/UO3x; Endura Energy, accessed January 2, 2012, www.enduraenergy.ca.

19. John Teresko, "Ford's Light Idea," *Industry Week*, November 1, 2007, www.industryweek.com.

20. Endura Energy, accessed January 2, 2012, www.enduraenergy.ca.

21. "A Change in Climate," *Economist*, January 17, 2008, www.economist.com.

22. "The Diversity Inc. Top 50 Companies for Diversity," Diversity Inc., accessed February 4, 2010, www.diversityinc.com.

23. "Survey: Workplace Discrimination Still Prevalent," *Inc.*, March 1, 2007, accessed March 2, 2010, www.inc.com/news/briefs/200703/0301survey.html.

24. James Cameron Online: The Home of James Cameron Fans, accessed February 18, 2011, www.jamescamerononline.com.

25. Michael Wilson, "Flight 1549 Pilot Tells of Terror and Intense Focus," *New York Times*, February 8, 2009, accessed May 8, 2015, www.nytimes.com/2009/02/09/nyregion/09interview.html?_r=0.

26. "World's Most Admired Companies 2014," *Fortune*, accessed April 11, 2014, http://fortune.com/worlds-most-admired-companies.

Chapter 2

1. Best of Vegas, "O—Cirque du Soleil," accessed February 15, 2011, www.bestofvegas.com/Shows-Tickets/O/; Cirque du Soleil, accessed February 15, 2011, www.cirquedusoleil.com/en/home.aspx#/en/home/about/details/cirque-du-soleil-at-a-glance.aspx; One Drop Foundation, "Who We Are," accessed February 15, 2011, www.onedrop.org/en/DiscoverOneDrop_Canada/WhoWeAre.aspx; One Drop Foundation, "Project Haiti: Water, a Source for Rebuilding," accessed August 14, 2014, www.onedrop.org/en/projects/projects-overview/haiti.aspx; BSR, accessed February 15, 2011, www.bsr.org; Ellen Barry, "What a Dump!," *Metropolis Magazine*, April 1998, accessed February 15, 2011, www.metropolismag.com/html/content_0498/ap98dump.htm; "Global Warming Fast Facts," *National Geographic News*, June 14, 2007, accessed February 15, 2011, http://news.nationalgeographic.com/news/2004/12/1206_041206_global_warming.html; Couvre Planchers Labrosse Inc., "Cirque du Soleil," accessed August 14, 2014, http://cplsolutions.ca/en/goods-and-service/achievements/cirque-du-soleil/.

2. Industry Canada, "New Standard on Social Responsibility Launched," accessed February 17, 2011, www.ic.gc.ca/eic/site/csr-rse.nsf/eng/rs00583.html.

3. "The List," *Maclean's*, accessed August 11, 2014, www.macleans.ca/general/266237/.

4. Johnson & Johnson, "Our Credo," accessed August 11, 2014, www.jnj.com/sites/default/files/pdf/jnj_ourcredo_english_us_8.5x11_cmyk.pdf; "Most Admired 2015," *Fortune*, accessed July 29, 2014, http://fortune.com/worlds-most-admired-companies/apple-1/.

5. Walmart Canada, "2013 Corporate Responsibility Leadership Council," accessed July 29, 2014, www.walmartcanada.ca/Pages/Corporate%20Responsibility%20Leadership%20Council/224/254/254.

6. Cliff Kuang, "The GOOD 100: Wal-Mart's Sustainability Push," *Good*, October 7, 2009; Michael Garry, "Wal-Mart Cites Progress on Sustainability Index," *Supermarket News*, November 23, 2009; SEIA, "Solar Means Business 2013: Top U.S. Commercial Solar Users," accessed July 29, 2014, www.seia.org/research-resources/solar-means-business-2013-top-us-commercial-solar-users.

7. National Business Ethics Survey, "About the National Business Ethics Survey of the U.S. Workforce 2013," accessed July 29, 2014, www.ethics.org/nbes/about.

8. Daniel Franklin, "Just Good Business," *Economist*, January 17, 2008.

9. Ethics Resource Center, "2009 National Business Ethics Survey," November 2009.

10. Tom Kemp, "Despite Privacy Concerns, It's Time to Kill the Password," *Forbes*, accessed August 18, 2014, www.forbes.com/sites/frontline/2014/07/18/despite-privacy-concerns-its-time-to-kill-the-password; Symantec, "2013 Cost of Data Breach Study: United States," accessed July 30, 2014, www.symantec.com/content/en/us/about/media/pdfs/b-cost-of-a-data-breach-us-report-2013.en-us.pdf?om_ext_cid=biz_socmed_twitter_facebook_marketwire_linkedin_2013Jun_worldwide_CostofaDataBreach.

11. Jim Dwyer, "H&M Says It Will Stop Destroying Unworn Clothing," *New York Times*, January 6, 2010; Jim Dwyer, "A Clothing Clearance Where More Than Just the Prices Have Been Slashed," *New York Times*, January 5, 2010.

12. "Obama Renews Ban on Ruby, Jade from Myanmar," *National Jeweler*, July 30, 2009, www.nationaljewelernetwork.com.

13. Jessica Murphy, "One in Five Job Seekers Lie on Resume: Poll," *Toronto Sun*, October 27, 2010, accessed January 15, 2011, www.torontosun.com/news/canada/2010/10/27/15855051.html; Dale Brazao, "Osgoode Hall Law School Vows to Weed out Fakes," *Toronto Star*, December 30, 2008, accessed February 12, 2011, www.thestar.com/news/gta/article/559484.

14. Heather Tooley, "Personal Internet Usage in the Workplace—A Serious Epidemic," *Associated Content*, January 17, 2010, www.associatedcontent.com; Jeffrey R. Smith, "No 'LOL' over Misuse of Email and Internet at Work," *Canadian HR Reporter*, September 28, 2009, http://chrremploymentlaw.wordpress.com.

15. Canadian Press, "University of Saskatchewan Dean Fired, Banned for Life from Campus after Speaking out about Cuts," *National Post*, May 14, 2014, accessed August 11, 2014, http://news.nationalpost.com/2014/05/14/dean-who-spoke-out-about-university-of-saskatchewan-cuts-fired-banned-for-life-from-campus; Canadian Press, "'We Want to See the Current Leadership . . . Gone': Protest Calls for University of Saskatchewan Resignations over Firing," *National Post*, May 21, 2014, accessed August 11, 2014, http://news.nationalpost.com/2014/05/21/we-want-to-see-the-current-leadershipgone-protest-calls-for-university-of-saskatchewan-resignations-over-firing; Josh Visser, "University of Saskatchewan 'Reconsiders' Decision on Fired Prof, Will Offer Him a New Position," *National Post*, May 15, 2014, accessed August 11, 2014, http://news.nationalpost.com/2014/05/15/university-of-saskatchewan-reconsiders-lifetime-ban-of-fired-prof-will-offer-him-a-new-position; Canadian Press, "University of Saskatchewan Provost Resigns Amid Controversy over Firing of Outspoken Professor," *National Post*, May 19, 2014, accessed August 11, 2011, http://news.nationalpost.com/2014/05/19/university-of-saskatchewan-provost-resigns-amid-controversy-over-firing-of-outspoken-

professor; Canadian Press, "University of Saskatchewan Fires President Ilene Busch-Vishniac Amid Controversy over Professor's Dismissal," *National Post*, May 22, 2014, accessed August 11, 2014, http://news.nationalpost.com/2014/05/22/university-of-saskatchewan-fires-president-ilene-busch-vishniac-amid-controversy-over-professors-dismissal.

16. "Whistleblower Legislation Bill C-25, Disclosure Protection," *CBC News*, April 28, 2004, accessed February 23, 2011, www.cbc.ca/news/background/whistleblower.

17. "Alberta Whistleblower Faces $10M Lawsuit from Gaming Company," *CBC News*, October 27, 2006, accessed February 23, 2011, www.cbc.ca/news/canada/edmonton/story/2006/10/27/alberta-gaming.html.

18. Air Canada, "Corporate Policy and Guidelines on Business Conduct," accessed February 27, 2011, www.aircanada.com/en/about/media/codeofconduct.pdf.

19. The Skald Group, "Ethical Awareness and Leadership," accessed February 17, 2011, www.skaldgroup.com.

20. SAI Global, "Compliance and Rish," accessed March 20, 2012, www.saiglobal.com/compliance.

21. Umaimah Mendhro and Abhinav Sinha, "Three Keys to Staying Ethical in the Age of Madoff," *Forbes*, February 6, 2009.

22. Pricewaterhouse Coopers Canada, "PricewaterhouseCoopers Canada Foundation," accessed August 11, 2014, www.pwc.com/ca/en/foundation/index.jhtml.

23. Tim Horton Children's Foundation, "One Dream Transforming Many Lives," accessed February 17, 2011, www.timhortons.com/ca/en/difference/childrens_about.html.

24. Brendan Kennedy, "Smoking Ban Sparks Drop in Hospitalization, Study Finds," *Toronto Star*, accessed February 23, 2011, www.thestar.com/life/health_wellness/2010/04/13/smoking_ban_sparks_drop_in_hospitalization_study_finds.html.

25. Childhood Obesity Foundation, www.childhoodobesityfoundation.ca, accessed February 17, 2011.

26. Coca-Cola Company, "New Program Puts Veterans to Work Teaching Physical Fitness to Youths and Families," April 23, 2015, www.coca-colacompany.com/press-center/press-releases/new-program-puts-veterans-to-work-teaching-physical-fitness-to-youths-and-families; Boys & Girls Clubs of America, "Triple Play: A Game Plan for Mind, Body and Soul," www.bgca.org/whatwedo/SportsFitnessRecreation/Pages/TriplePlayResources.aspx.

27. "Ben Johnson: Canada's Shame," *CBC Digital Archives*, September 26, 1988, accessed February 17, 2011, http://archives.cbc.ca/sports/drugs_sports/clips/8702; "1988: Johnson Stripped of Olympic Gold," *BBC on This Day*, accessed February 17, 2011, http://news.bbc.co.uk/onthisday/hi/dates/stories/september/27/newsid_2539000/2539525.stm.

28. "Mount Polley Mine Tailings Spill: Imperial Metals Could Face $1M Fine," *CBC News*, accessed August 18, 2014, www.cbc.ca/news/canada/british-columbia/mount-polley-mine-tailings-spill-imperial-metals-could-face-1m-fine-1.2728832.

29. US Environmental Protection Agency, "Where Can I Donate or Recycle My Old Computer and Other Electronic Products?" accessed February 4, 2010, www.epa.gov; Best Buy, "We Now Offer Electronics Recycling at All Best Buy Stores Nationwide," accessed February 4, 2010, www.bestbuy.com.

30. Recycling Council of Ontario, "Take Back the Light," accessed February 17, 2011, www.takebackthelight.ca.

31. William J. Watkins, Jr., "Rethinking Patent Enforcement: Tesla Did What?" *Forbes*, accessed August 12, 2014, www.forbes.com/sites/realspin/2014/07/17/rethinking-patent-enforcement-tesla-did-what.

32. Statistics Canada, "Waste Management Industry: Business and Government Sectors," *The Daily*, December 22, 2010, accessed February 17, 2011, www.statcan.gc.ca/daily-quotidien/101222/dq101222b-eng.htm.

33. Ontario Ministry of Finance, "Ontario Electronic Stewardship Fees," accessed February 17, 2011, www.rev.gov.on.ca/en/notices/rst/74.html.

34. Competition Bureau, *Environmental Claims: A Guide for Industry and Advisors*, June 2008, accessed February 18, 2011, www.competitionbureau.gc.ca/eic/site/cb-bc.nsf/eng/02701.html.

35. Martin LaMonica, "Bill Gates Investing in Vinod Khosla Green-Tech Fund," *CNET News*, January 25, 2010.

36. Natural Resources Canada, "ecoACTION," accessed August 12, 2014, www.nrcan.gc.ca/ecoaction.

37. Tim Hortons, "Tim Hortons Coffee Partnership," accessed February 18, 2011, www.timhortons.com/ca/en/difference/coffee-partnership.html.

38. Tim Hortons, "Our Scholarship Program," accessed February 18, 2011, www.timhortons.com/ca/en/join/scholarship.html.

39. COSTI Immigrant Services, "Programs and Services," accessed February 18, 2011, www.costi.org/programs/service_details.php?stype_id=53.

40. Coca-Cola, "Diversity," accessed February 12, 2010, www.thecocacolacompany.com.

41. Canadian Breast Cancer Foundation CIBC Run for the Cure, accessed February 22, 2011, www.runforthecure.com/site/PageServer?pagename=about_the_run.

42. Marlene Rego, "Tickled Pink: Top Breast Cancer Products," *Chatelaine*, accessed February 22, 2011, www.chatelaine.com/en/article/3972--tickled-pink-top-breast-cancer-products; Cook for the Cure, accessed August 12, 2014, www.cookforthecure.ca/about.html.

43. "UPS Pilots Volunteer to Help Haiti Relief Effort," *Forbes*, January 14, 2010.

44. Consumers' Association of Canada, "About Us," accessed February 18, 2011, www.consumer.ca/1480.

45. "15th Listeria Death Linked to Maple Leaf Foods," *CBC News*, September 10, 2008, accessed February 18, 2011, www.cbc.ca/consumer/story/2008/09/10/listeria-ontario.html; "How Maple Leaf Foods Is Handling the Listeria Outbreak," *CBC News*, accessed February 18, 2011, www.cbc.ca/money/story/2008/08/27/f-crisisresponse.html; "Maple Leaf Settles Class Action Listeriosis Lawsuits for $27M," *CBC News*, accessed August 12, 2014, www.cbc.ca/news/canada/maple-leaf-settles-class-action-listeriosis-lawsuits-for-27m-1.696972.

46. Sharon Oosthoek, "Rogers Faces $10M Fine over Dropped-Call Ads," *CBC News*, November 19, 2010, accessed February 21, 2011,

www.cbc.ca/news/business/story/2010/11/19/consumer-chatr-rogers-competition-bureau.html; Canadian Press, "Ontario Court Fines Rogers $500,000 over Chatr Ads," *CBC*, accessed August 12, 2014, www.cbc.ca/news/technology/ontario-court-fines-rogers-500-000-over-chatr-ads-1.2550590.

47. Department of Justice, Food and Drugs Act, accessed February 21, 2011, http://laws.justice.gc.ca/en/f-27/.
48. "Ontario Seeks Appeal of Private-Label Drug Ruling," *CBC News*, February 19, 2011, accessed February 21, 2011, www.cbc.ca/news/health/story/2011/02/19/ontario-drug-ruling-appeal.html.
49. eBay, "eBay Rules and Policies Overview," accessed February 14, 2010, http://pages.ebay.com/help/policies/overview.html.
50. Human Resources and Skills Development Canada, "Work—Work-Related Injuries," accessed February 21, 2011, http://www4.hrsdc.gc.ca/.3ndic.1t.4r@-eng.jsp?iid=20.
51. "Canada's Top 100 Employers," accessed August 12, 2014, www.canadastop100.com/national/.
52. Robert Smithson, "Is Unlimited Vacation Time a Recipe for Business Success?" *Kelowna Capital News*, February 16, 2010.
53. Research In Motion, "Search Full Time Opportunities: Explore the World of RIM," accessed January 31, 2012, www.rim.com/careers/search/index.shtml; WestJet, "Great Jobs," accessed January 3, 2012, www.westjet.com/guest/en/jobs.shtml.
54. Canadian Charter of Rights and Freedoms, accessed February 22, 2011, http://laws.justice.gc.ca/en/charter/1.html#anchorbo-ga:l_I-gb:s_15.
55. "Exotic Dancer Files Age Discrimination Complaint," *CBC News*, accessed February 22, 2011, www.cbc.ca/news/canada/story/2008/11/03/dancer-ohrt-complaint.html.
56. Liz Wolgemuth, "20 Ways Older Workers Can Sell Themselves," *U.S. News & World Report*, November 26, 2008.
57. "Baby Boomers Swell Ranks of Retirement-Aged Canadians," *CBC News*, July 17, 2007, accessed February 21, 2011, www.cbc.ca/news/canada/story/2007/07/17/census-canada.html; Jamie Sturgeon, "Retiring Boomers Could Cost Economy $11,500 a Head in Lost Growth," *Global News*, accessed August 12, 2014, http://globalnews.ca/news/1240976/the-number-of-working-age-canadians-is-plummeting-report/.
58. Pay Equity Commission, "Gender Wage Gap," accessed August 12, 2014, www.payequity.gov.on.ca/en/about/pubs/genderwage/wagegap.php.
59. Gail Zoppo, "Why Are Women Still Earning Less than Men?" *Diversity Inc.*, April 28, 2009.
60. "Livent Co-founders Drabinsky, Gottlieb Convicted of Fraud and Forgery," *CBC News*, March 25, 2009, accessed February 23, 2011, www.cbc.ca/news/business/story/2009/03/25/livent-decision-fraud.html.

Chapter 3

1. Kent Spencer, "Signs of Life in Olympic Village," *The Province*, December 28, 2011, www.theprovince.com/technology/Signs+life+Olympic+Village/5917801/story.html; Kent Spencer, "Vancouver Drops Prices on Olympic Condo Units," *National Post*, February 11, 2011, p. A6; Canada Mortgage and Housing Corporation (CMHC), "Housing Market Information, Housing Market Outlook—Fourth Quarter 2010," accessed February 15, 2011, www.cmhc-schl.gc.ca/odpub/esub/61500/61500_2010_Q04.pdf?fr=1297379904219; CMHC, "Housing Market Information, Housing Market Outlook—Fall 2010," accessed February 15, 2011, www.cmhc-schl.gc.ca/odpub/esub/64363/64363_2010_B02.pdf?lang=en; CMHC, "Housing Market Information, Housing Market Outlook—Vancouver and Abbotsford CMAs, Date Released: Fourth Quarter 2007," accessed February 15, 2011, http://dsp-psd.pwgsc.gc.ca/collection_2007/cmhc-schl/nh12-56/NH12-56-2007-2E.pdf; CMHC, "Canadian Housing at a Glance 2010," accessed February 15, 2011, www.cmhc-schl.gc.ca/en/corp/about/cahoob/upload/dashboard_en.pdf.
2. Nathan Eddy, "Video Game Sales Down 8 Percent in 2009," *TechWeek Europe*, January 18, 2010, accessed May 14, 2015, www.techweekeurope.co.uk/cloud/datacenter/computer-games-sales-down-8-percent-3053.
3. Jeff Bercovici, "Soon, You'll Have to Pay for Hulu," *Daily Finance*, June 3, 2009, accessed May 14, 2015, www.dailyfinance.com/2009/06/03/soon-youll-have-to-pay-for-hulu; Dawn C. Chmielewski and Alex Pham, "At Hulu, 'Free' May Turn to 'Fee,'" *Los Angeles Times*, January 21, 2010, accessed May 14, 2015, http://articles.latimes.com/2010/jan/21/business/la-fi-ct-newhulu21-2010jan21.
4. Jad Mouawad, "Demand for Oil Set to Rise Anew," *New York Times*, February 15, 2010, accessed May 14, 2015, www.nytimes.com/2010/02/15/business/energy-environment/15renoil.html?_r=0.
5. David P. Schulz, "Top 100 Retailers," *Stores*, NRF Stores, accessed February 4, 2010, www.stores.org.
6. Pascal Fletcher, "Freeze Mauls Florida Citrus, Significant Damage Seen," Reuters, January 11, 2010, accessed May 14, 2015, http://mobile.reuters.com/article/idUSTRE60913020100111.
7. Sustainable Produce Urban Delivery, accessed March 26, 2012, www.spud.ca,; Eat Local, accessed March 26, 2012, www.eatlocal.org.
8. Bettina Wassener, "Fed's Move Prompts Drop in Asian Stocks, Oil and Gold, but Dollar Rises," *New York Times*, February 20, 2010, www.nytimes.com; Lewa Pardomuan, "Gold Slips 1 Percent after Fed Raises Discount Rate," Reuters, February 18, 2010, accessed March 26, 2012, www.reuters.com/article/2010/02/19/markets-precious-idUSSGE61I04C20100219.
9. Gold Price, "10 Year Gold Price in CAD/oz," accessed March 21, 2015, http://goldprice.org/charts/history/gold_10_year_o_cad.png.
10. William Spain, "Fast-Food Outlook: Intense Competition, Margin Pressures," *MarketWatch*, January 14, 2010, accessed May 14, 2015, www.marketwatch.com/story/fast-food-2010-stiff-competition-margin-pressure-2010-01-14.
11. Larissa MacFarquhar, "When Giants Fall," *The New Yorker*, May 14, 2012, accessed January 18, 2014, www.newyorker.com/magazine/2012/05/14/when-giants-fail.
12. "CRTC Issues Video-on-Demand Licence Conditions," *The Wire Report*, January 31, 2011, accessed February 11, 2011, www.thewirereport.ca/reports/content/11903-crtc_issues_video_on_demand_licence_conditions.

13. Air Canada, accessed February 4, 2010, www.aircanada.com.
14. Central Intelligence Agency, *World Factbook*, accessed January 24, 2014, www.cia.gov.
15. Alexis Leondis, "U.S. Millionaires' Ranks Rose 16% in 2009, Study Says," *BusinessWeek*, March 9, 2010, www.businessweek.com.
16. Statistics Canada, *Canada Year Book 2010*, p. 278, Table 21.7, "Employment, by Industry, 1995 to 2009," CANSIM table 282-0008, accessed February 3, 2011, www.statcan.gc.ca/pub/11-402-x/2010000/pdf/labour-travail-eng.pdf.
17. World Bank, accessed February 4, 2010, http://web.worldbank.org; "Disaster Experts Share Lessons for Haiti," http://web.worldbank.org; Jack Ewing, "Emerging Economies Gain a Voice at Davos," *New York Times*, January 26, 2010, accessed May 14, 2015, www.nytimes.com/2010/01/27/business/global/27global.html.
18. DaveManuel.com, "Canadian Debt Clock March 2015," accessed March 25, 2015, www.davemanuel.com/canada-debt-clock.php; Brillig.com, "U.S. National Debt Clock," accessed March 25, 2015, www.brillig.com/debt_clock.
19. U.S. and World Population Clocks, U.S. Census Bureau, accessed February 4, 2010, www.census.gov.
20. Justin Pritchard, "U.S. Agency Goes after Cadmium in Children's Jewelry," *ABC News*, January 11, 2010, http://abcnews.go.com.

Chapter 4

1. PotashCorp, accessed March 25, 2015, www.potashcorp.com; Yahoo Finance Canada, "PotashCorp," accessed March 25, 2015, https://ca.finance.yahoo.com/q/ks?s=POT.TO; "Reaction to Conference Board Report on Potash," Business News Network, October 4, 2010, accessed February 18, 2011, http://watch.bnn.ca/the-close/october-2010/the-close-october-4-2010/#clip356483; Brenda Bouw and Boyd Erman, "PotashCorp Value Tops $170/share: CEO," *Globe and Mail*, October 7, 2010, accessed February 11, 2011, www.bnn.ca/News/2010/10/7/PotashCorp-value-tops-170-share-CEO.aspx; Brenda Bouw, "Potash Corp. Doubles Profit, Vows to Avoid Dramatic Price Spike," *Globe and Mail*, January 28, 2011, accessed February 11, 2011, www.theglobeandmail.com/globe-investor/potash-corp-doubles-profit-vows-to-avoid-dramatic-price-spike/article1884428/.
2. Statistics Canada, "Imports, Exports and Trade Balance of Goods on a Balance-of-Payments Basis, by Country or Country Grouping," accessed March 25, 2015, www.statcan.gc.ca/tables-tableaux/sum-som/l01/cst01/gblec02a-eng.htm; Statistics Canada, "Exports of Goods on a Balance-of-Payments Basis, by Product," accessed February 27, 2011, www40.statcan.ca/l01/cst01/gblec04.htm; Central Intelligence Agency, "Canada," *World Factbook*, accessed February 27, 2011, www.cia.gov; Statistics Canada, "International Trade," *Canada Year Book*, pp. 255–266, accessed February 27 2011, www.statcan.gc.ca/pub/11-402-x/2010000/pdf/international-eng.pdf.
3. U.S. Census Bureau, "International Database," accessed January 6, 2014, www.census.gov; "You Think! But Do You Know?" World Bank, accessed January 6, 2014, http://youthink.worldbank.org.
4. World Bank, accessed January 6, 2014, http//worldbank.org.
5. Walmart, "International," accessed January 6, 2014, http://corporate.walmart.com.
6. Sahar Saffron, accessed March 8, 2010, http://safarsaffron.com; Spice Advice, accessed March 8, 2010, www.spiceadvice.com.
7. Steve Hamm, "Big Blue's Global Lab," *Businessweek*, August 27, 2009, www.bloomberg.com/bw/magazine/content/09_36/b4145040683083.htm.
8. Statistics Canada, "Imports, Exports and Trade Balance of Goods on a Balance-of-Payments Basis, by Country or Country Grouping," accessed March 25, 2015, www.statcan.gc.ca/tables-tableaux/sum-som/l01/cst01/gblec02a-eng.htm.
9. CIA, "Canada," *World Factbook*, accessed March 2, 2011, www.cia.gov/library/publications/the-world-factbook/geos/ca.html.
10. Illinois Oil and Gas Association, "History of Illinois Basin Posted Crude Oil Prices," accessed March 2, 2011, www.ioga.com/Special/crudeoil_Hist.htm.
11. Statistics Canada, "Table 380-00701, Exports and Imports of Goods and Services," accessed March 27, 2015, www5.statcan.gc.ca/cansim/pick-choisir?lang=eng&p2=33&id=3800070.
12. U.S. Census Bureau, "Annual Trade in Goods and Services, 1960–2012," accessed January 30, 2014, www.cencus.gov; U.S. Bureau of Economic Analysis, "U.S. International Trade in Goods and Services," press release, accessed January 30, 2014, www.bea.gov.
13. Bank for International Settlements, accessed March 26, 2015, www.bis.org.
14. Vivian Wai-yin Kwok, "How Kraft Won in China," *Forbes*, December 8, 2009, accessed March 26, 2015, www.forbes.com/2009/12/08/china-oreo-tang-cmo-network-kraft.html.
15. Tanya Mohn, "Going Global, Stateside," *New York Times*, March 8, 2010, accessed March 26, 2015, www.nytimes.com/2010/03/09/business/global/09training.html?_r=0.
16. "India Needs 400 Airports to Cater to People's Needs," LiveMint, March 3, 2010, www.livemint.com; Samar Halarnkar, "Delhi Airport's T3: Bags Packed, Ready to Go," LiveMint, February 28, 2010, www.livemint.com.
17. Transparency International, "Foreign Bribery and OECD Countries: A Hollow Commitment? Progress Report 2009," www.transparency.org, June 22, 2009.
18. Joe Ayling "'Made in Italy' Thrives without EU Label Law," *Just Style*, accessed January 6, 2014, www.just-style.com.
19. Canada Border Services Agency, "Fact Sheet," accessed March 2, 2011, www.cbsa-asfc.gc.ca/media/facts-faits/060-eng.html.
20. Louis Uchitelle, "Glassmaking Thrives Offshore, but Is Declining in U.S.," *New York Times*, January 19, 2010, accessed May 28, 2015, www.nytimes.com/2010/01/19/business/19glass.html.
21. World Trade Organization, "Lamy Calls for March Stocktaking to 'Inject Political Energy and Momentum' in the Negotiations," February 22 and 23, 2010, www.wto.org.
22. "G7 to Forgive Haiti Foreign Debt," *ABC News*, February 7, 2010; World Bank, "World Bank Statement on Haiti Debt," press release, January 21, 2010, www.worldbank.org.
23. CIA, "North America," *World Factbook*, accessed February 8, 2014, www.cia.gov; Office of the United States Trade Representative,

"North American Free Trade Agreement," accessed January 6, 2014, www.ustr.gov.

24. Ibid.

25. Ibid.

26. U.S. Census Bureau, "2013: Trade in Good with CAFTA-DR," accessed January 6, 2014, www.census.gov.

27. European Union, "Countries," accessed January 6, 2014, http://europa.eu/about-eu/countries/index_en.htm; CIA, "European Union," *World Factbook*, accessed January 6, 2014, www.cia.gov.

28. Pete Evans, "Tim Hortons, Burger King Agree to Merger Deal," *CBC News*, August 26, 2014, accessed March 25, 2015, www.cbc.ca/news/business/tim-hortons-burger-king-agree-to-merger-deal-1.2746948; "The Story of Tim Hortons," Tim Hortons, accessed January 14, 2012, www.timhortons.com/ca/en/about/index.html.

29. Morinaga & Company, accessed March 9, 2010, www.morinagamilk.co.jp.

30. Kate O'Sullivan, "Best Buys in Offshore Manufacturing," CFO.com, February 18, 2010, accessed May 28, 2015, http://ww2.cfo.com/technology/2010/02/best-buys-in-offshore-manufacturing.

31. "Target Buys Zellers Leases for $1.8B," *CBC News*, January 13, 2011, accessed March 3, 2011, www.cbc.ca/news/business/story/2011/01/13/target-zelles-takeover.html; Hollie Shaw, "Target Corp to Exit Canada after Racking up Billions in Losses," *Financial Post*, January 15, 2015, accessed March 27, 2015, http://business.financialpost.com/2015/01/15/target-corp-calls-it-quits-in-canada-plans-fair-and-orderly-exit.

32. Alcoa, accessed March 17, 2010, www.alcoa.com.

Part 1 Case Study: Beau's All Natural Brewing Company: Building a Craft Brewery in a Competitive Canadian Industry

Based on interviews with Steve Beauchesne at Beau's All Natural Brewery Company offices, Vankleek Hill, Ontario, on March 30, 2015; Beau's All Natural Brewery Company, accessed April 3, 2015, www.beaus.ca; Beau's Beer Blog, "How to Start a Brewery in 1 Million Easy Steps," January 9, 2007, accessed April 3, 2015, http://beausbeer.blogspot.ca/2007/01/brewery-measurements.html; Small Business Accelerator, "Industry Overview: Craft Breweries & Microbreweries," accessed April 3, 2015, www.sba-bc.ca/blog/industry-overview-craft-breweries-microbreweries; Glen Hodgson, "From Farm to Glass: The Value of Beer in Canada," November 5, 2013, accessed April 3, 2015, www.beercanada.com/sites/default/files/13-11-03-from_farm_to_glass.pdf; IBISWorld, "Breweries in Canada: Market Research Report," January 2015, accessed April 3, 2015, www.ibisworld.ca/industry/default.aspx?indid=288; Statistics Canada, Agriculture and Agri-Food Canada, "The Canadian Brewing Industry," accessed April 3, 2015, www.agr.gc.ca/eng/industry-markets-and-trade/statistics-and-market-information/by-product-sector/processed-food-and-beverages/the-canadian-brewery-industry/?id=1171560813521#s1; Beer Canada, "Industry Statistics," accessed April 3, 2015, www.beercanada.com/industry-statistics; Tracey Lindeman, "The Entrepreneurs: Beau's Beers to Flow in Quebec," *Montreal Gazette*, August 10, 2014, accessed April 3, 2015, www.montrealgazette.com/life/Entrepreneurs+Beau+beers+flow+Quebec/10109168/story.html.

Part 1: Launching Your Global Business and Economics Career

1. U.S. Department of Labor, "Tomorrow's Jobs," *Occupational Outlook Handbook*, 2010–2011 edition, U.S. Bureau of Labor Statistics, www.bls.gov.

2. U.S. Department of Labor, "Economists," *Occupational Outlook Handbook*, 2010–2011 edition, U.S. Bureau of Labor Statistics, www.bls.gov.

3. Adapted from Michael R. Czinkota, Ilkka A. Ronkainen, and Michael H. Moffett, "Criteria for Selecting Managers for Overseas Assignments," in *International Business*, 7th ed. (Mason, OH: SouthWestern, 2005), Table 19.2, p. 634.

4. Ursula Milton, "MBA Still Packs a Punch," *Financial Times*, January 28, 2008, accessed March 17, 2010, www.ft.com/intl/cms/s/0/0b99d4de-cd42-11dc-9b2b-000077b07658.html#axzz3bXYEJ9H9.

5. Sattar Bawany, "Transition Coaching Helps Ensure Success for Global Assignments," *Today's Manager*, January 2008, accessed March 17, 2010, entrepreneur.com.

Chapter 5

1. Pi Athlete Management Inc., accessed April 4, 2015, www.piathlete.com; interviews with Martin Bindman and Daniel Smajovits of Pi Athlete Management Inc., January 2012; "Pro Baseball Player Marc Bourgeois Visits Home Base in Granby," *CTV Montreal*, Pi Athlete Management Inc., accessed January 6, 2012, http://vimeo.com/31769085; National Collegiate Athletic Association, accessed January 6, 2012, http://ncaa.org; Ron Sirak, "The Golf Digest 50: Golf's Top Earners," *Golf Digest*, February 2012, accessed January 13, 2012, www.golfdigest.com/golf-tours-news/2012-02/top-earners#intro; Kurt Badenhausen, "Sports' First Billion-Dollar Man," Forbes, September 29, 2009, accessed January 13, 2012, www.forbes.com/2009/09/29/tiger-woods-billion-business-sports-tiger.html; "The Average NFL Player," *Businessweek*, January 27, 2011, accessed January 13, 2012, www.businessweek.com/magazine/content/11_06/b4214058615722.htm; Steve Aschburner, NBA.com, "NBA's 'Average' Salary—$5.15M—A Trendy, Touchy Subject," August 11, 2011, accessed January 13, 2012, www.nba.com/2011/news/features/steve_aschburner/08/19/average-salary/index.html; National Hockey League Players' Association, "NHL Player Compensation," accessed January 13, 2012, www.nhlpa.com/Players/compensation; "MLB Salaries," *CBS Sports*, accessed January 13, 2012, www.cbssports.com/mlb/salaries/avgsalaries.

2. Statistics Canada, "Self-Employment, Historical Summary," accessed April 4, 2015, www.statcan.gc.ca/tables-tableaux/sum-som/l01/cst01/labor64-eng.htm.

Notes 587

3. Industry Canada, Small Business Branch, "Key Small Business Statistics," July 2011, accessed March 21, 2012, www.ic.gc.ca/eic/site/sbrp-rppe.nsf/vwapj/KSBS-PSRPE_July-Juillet2011_eng.pdf/$FILE/KSBS-PSRPE_July-Juillet2011_eng.pdf.

4. Paul Delean, "Riding the Health Wave," *Montreal Gazette*, February 28, 2011, p. A16; Nutrisoya, accessed April 4, 2015, www.nutrisoya,ca.

5. Mary Teresa Bitti, "Running on the Fitness Regimen," *Financial Post*, Canada's 50 Best Special Report, February 22, 2011, p. SR 28; Running Room, accessed April 4, 2015, www.runningroom.com.

6. Industry Canada, "Small Business Research and Statistics: Key Small Business Statistics—August 2013," accessed April 4, 2015, www.ic.gc.ca/eic/site/061.nsf/eng/h_02800.html.

7. Statistics Canada, "The Financial Picture of Farms in Canada," *2006 Census of Agriculture*, accessed March 9, 2011, www.statcan.gc.ca/ca-ra2006/articles/finpicture-portrait-eng.htm#A1.

8. Industry Canada, "Small Business Research and Statistics: Key Small Business Statistics—August 2013: What Is the Contribution of Small Businesses to Canada Gross Domestic Product?" accessed April 5, 2015, www.ic.gc.ca/eic/site/061.nsf/eng/02812.html.

9. Industry Canada, "Small Business Research and Statistics: Key Small Business Statistics—August 2013: What Is the Contribution of Small Businesses to Canada's Exports?" accessed April 5, 2015, www.ic.gc.ca/eic/site/061.nsf/eng/02811.html.

10. Industry Canada, "Small Business Research and Statistics: Key Small Business Statistics—August 2013: How Many Jobs Do Small Businesses Create?" accessed April 6, 2015, www.ic.gc.ca/eic/site/061.nsf/eng/02806.html.

11. Facebook, accessed April 6, 2015, www.facebook.com/press.

12. John Tozzi, Stacy Perman, and Nick Leiber, "2009 Finalists: America's Best Young Entrepreneurs," *Businessweek*, October 12, 2009, accessed April 6, 2015, www.bloomberg.com/sSs/09/10/1009_entrepreneurs_25_and_under/21.htm.

13. Industry Canada, "Small Business Research and Statistics: Key Small Business Statistics—August 2013: How Many Jobs Do Small Businesses Innovate?" accessed April 6, 2015, www.ic.gc.ca/eic/site/061.nsf/eng/02810.html.

14. "Advocacy Small Business Statistics and Research," U.S. Small Business Administration, accessed April 2, 2010, http://web.sba.gov/faqs.

15. Industry Canada, "Small Business Research and Statistics: Key Small Business Statistics—July 2010: How Many Businesses Appear and Disappear Each Year?" accessed March 9, 2011, www.ic.gc.ca/eic/site/sbrp-rppe.nsf/eng/rd02494.html.

16. Carol Kopp, "The Tragedy of Krispy Kreme," *Yahoo! Finance*, October 13, 2009, http://finance.yahoo.news.

17. Patricia Schaefer, "The Seven Pitfalls of Business Failure and How to Avoid Them," BusinessKnowHow.com, accessed April 2, 2010, www.businessknowhow.com/Startup/business-failure.htm.

18. Ibid.

19. "Advocacy Small Business Statistics and Research."

20. Leona Liu, "Meet the Celebrity Gardener," *Businessweek*, October 13, 2009, accessed April 2, 2010, www.bloomberg.com/bw/stories/2009-10-13/meet-the-celebrity-gardenerbusinessweek-business-news-stock-market-and-financial-advice.

21. Statistics Canada, "Survey of Regulatory Compliance Costs, 2008," *The Daily*, July 9, 2010, accessed March 10, 2011, www.statcan.gc.ca/daily-quotidien/100709/dq100709c-eng.htm.

22. Canada Business Network, "Small Business Investor Tax Credit," accessed March 21, 2012, www.canadabusiness.ca/eng/summary/6038.

23. TOMS Shoes, "One for One," accessed April 2, 2010, www.tomsshoes.com/Our-Movement.

24. "Top 10 Tips for Writing Your Business Plan," *AllBusiness*, accessed April 2, 2010, www.allbusiness.com/business-planning-structures.

25. Business Development Bank of Canada (BDC), accessed March 10, 2011, www.bdc.ca/EN/Pages/home.aspx.

26. Industry Canada, "Canada Small Business Financing Program," accessed March 10, 2011, www.ic.gc.ca/eic/site/csbfp-pfpec.nsf/eng/home.

27. Robert Joseph, Michael Bordt, and Daood Hamdani, "Characteristics of Business Incubation in Canada, 2005," Statistics Canada, accessed March 10, 2011, http://dsp-psd.pwgsc.gc.ca/Collection/Statcan/88F0006X/88F0006XIE2006007.pdf.

28. Canada's Venture Capital and Private Equity Association, "2014 Canadian Venture Market Capital Overview," accessed April 6, 2015, www.cvca.ca/wp-content/uploads/2014/07/2014-CDN-VC-market-activity-infographic-FINAL.pdf; John Tozzi, "Venture Capital's Favorite Startups," *Businessweek*, December 19, 2008, www.bloomberg.com/bw/stories/2008-12-19/venture-capitals-favorite-startupsbusinessweek-business-news-stock-market-and-financial-advice.

29. Arlene Dickinson, accessed January 15, 2012, http://arlenedickinson.com; CBC, "The Dragons: Arlene Dickinson," accessed January 15, 2012, www.cbc.ca/dragonsden/dragons_arlene.html.

30. Industry Canada, "Small Business Research and Statistics: Sustaining the Momentum: An Economic Forum on Women Entrepreneurs—Summary Report," accessed March 9, 2011, www.ic.gc.ca/eic/site/sbrp-rppe.nsf/eng/rd01309.html.

31. Franchiselink.com, "Canadian Franchise Statistics & Info," accessed April 8, 2015, www.franchiselink.ca/canadian-franchise-faqs/canadian-franchise-statistics-info/.

32. International Franchise Association, "The Economic Impact of Franchised Businesses," accessed February 10, 2014, www.franchise.org; IHS Global Insight, *Franchise Business Economic Outlook 2014*, January 13, 2014, accessed February 10, 2014, http://franchiseeconomy.com/wp-content/uploads/2014/01/Franchise_Business_Outlook_January_2014-1-13-13.pdf.

33. Marina Strauss, "Tim Hortons Borrows Burger King's Global Expansion Plan," *Business News Network*, March 27, 2015, accessed April 8, 2015, www.bnn.ca/News/2015/3/27/Tim-Hortons-borrows-Burger-Kings-global-expansion-plan.aspx.

34. Subway Restaurants, "Franchising FAQs," accessed April 8, 2015, www.subway.com/subwayroot/Own_a_Franchise/FranchiseFAQs.aspx.

35. Edward N. Levitt, "What's so Great about Franchising?" *Franchise Know How*, accessed April 2, 2010, www.franchiseknowhow.com/articles/franchising-benefits.htm.

36. Ibid.
37. "Why People Are Drawn to Franchising," FranChoice, accessed April 2, 2010, www.franchoice.com/resources/Why_People_Are_Drawn_To_Franchising.
38. Levitt, "What's so Great about Franchising?"
39. "How Much Does a Franchise Cost?" AllBusiness.com, accessed April 2, 2010, www.allbusiness.com.
40. Levitt, "What's so Great about Franchising?"
41. Ashley M. Heher, "Food Fight: Burger King Franchisees Sue Chain," USA Today, November 12, 2009, accessed April 2, 1010, http://usatoday30.usatoday.com/money/industries/food/2009-11-12-burger-king-franchises-lawsuit_N.htm.
42. Laura Northrup, "Recent Class Action Lawsuits: Are You Eligible?" Consumerist, May 22, 2009, accessed April 2, 2010, http://consumerist.com/2009/05/22/recent-class-action-lawsuits-are-you-eligible.
43. Sun Youth Organization, accessed March 13, 2011, http://sunyouthorg.com.
44. The Electricity Forum, "Canadian Electricity Generation, Transmission and Distribution Company Sites," accessed March 13, 2011, www.electricityforum.com/links/cdautil.html.
45. VIA Rail Canada, accessed March 13, 2011, www.viarail.ca.
46. "Cooperatives around the World," accessed February 3, 2014, http://usa2012.coop.
47. Government of Canada, Co-operatives Secretariat, "About Co-ops in Canada," accessed March 13, 2011, www.coop.gc.ca/COOP/display-afficher.do?id=1232131333489&lang=eng.
48. Peter Koven and Kim Covert, "Canada Leads in Mining M&As, China Well Back," Calgary Herald, March 4, 2011, accessed March 13, 2011, www.calgaryherald.com/business/Canada+leads+mining+China+well+back/4382198/story.html.
49. Canadian Breast Cancer Foundation, "CIBC Run for the Cure," accessed May 23, 2015, www.cbcf.org/ontario/GetInvolved/Events/Pages/CIBC-Run-for-the-Cure.aspx, accessed May 23, 2015.
50. Barbara Quinn, "Partnering on Sustainability," Pollution Engineering, January 2009, p. 17.

Chapter 6

1. N.R. Kleinfield, "Airbnb Host Welcomes Travelers from All Over," The New York Times, accessed April 28, 2014, www.nytimes; company website, "About Us," www.airbnb.com, accessed April 28, 2014; company website, "How FlightCar Works," https://flightcar.com, accessed April 28, 2014; Ryan Lawler, "Airport Car Rental Startup FlightCar Launches at LAX, Unveils Mobile App," Tech Crunch, accessed February 4, 2014, http://techcrunch.com; Tamara Warren, "Peer-to-Peer Car Sharing at the Airport," The New York Times, accessed February 4, 2014, www.nytimes.com; Tomio Geron, "Airbnb and the Unstoppable Rise of the Share Economy," Forbes, accessed February 4, 2014, www.forbes.com; Alan Farnham, "Rental Car Co. Run by Teenagers Undercuts Hertz, Avis," ABC News, accessed February 4, 2014, http://abcnews.go.com.
2. The Jim Pattison Group, "About Us," accessed April 8, 2015, www.jimpattison.com/about/our-story.
3. Stella & Dot, accessed January 19, 2014, http://stelladot.com; Jefferson Graham, "Stella and Dot Brings Tech to At-Home Jewellery Parties," USA Today, accessed January 19, 2014, www.usatoday.com/story/tech/columnist/talkingtech/2013/11/03/stella-dot-bring-tech-women-parties/3004733/; Vikram Alexei Kansara, "Jessica Herrin of Stella & Dot on Remaking Direct Sales to the Digital Age," Business of Fashion, accessed January 19, 2014, www.businessoffashion.com/articles/founder-stories/jessica-herrin-stella-dot-sequoia-capital.
4. Navkirat Sodhi, "Meet India's Leading Ladies," Women Entrepreneur, September 22, 2009, www.womenentrpreneur.com.
5. Industry Canada, "Small Business Research and Statistics: Key Small Business Statistics—August 2013," accessed April 8, 2015, www.ic.gc.ca/eic/site/061.nsf/eng/h_02800.html; "Kauffman Index of Entrepreneurial Activity," accessed January 19, 2014, www.kauffman.org.
6. Monster Gym, accessed April 8, 2015, www.monstergym.net.
7. Coramark Inc., "Our History," accessed April 8, 2015, www.chezcora.com/our-company/history.
8. Industry Canada, "Small Business Research and Statistics: Key Small Business Statistics—August 2013," accessed April 8, 2015, www.ic.gc.ca/eic/site/061.nsf/eng/h_02800.html; Office of Advocacy, U.S. Small Business Administration, "The Facts about Small Businesses," accessed January 19, 2014, www.sba.gov/content/small-business-facts.
9. Hannah Seligson, "Nine Young Chinese Entrepreneurs to Watch," Forbes, February 28, 2010, www.forbes.com/2010/02/26/young-chinese-entrepreneurs-to-watch-entrepreneurs-technology-china.html.
10. Eve Gumpel, "Gypsy Tea Steeped in Health and Fun," Women Entrepreneur, January 24, 2010, www.womenentrepreneur.com.
11. TronSports.ca, accessed October 28, 2015, http://tronsports.ca.
12. Niels Bosma, Kent Jones, Erkko Autio, and Jonathan Levie, "Global Entrepreneurial Monitor: Executive Report," accessed March 11, 2010, www.gemconsortium.org.
13. Sodhi, "Meet India's Leading Ladies."
14. Simon Fraser University, "Beedie School of Business News: Beedie Looks Back at Extraordinary Year at Surrey," accessed January 18, 2012, http://beedie.sfu.ca/blog/tag/sfu-student-entrepreneur-of-the-year.
15. Students in Free Enterprise, "Leadership and Career Connections," accessed March 11, 2010, www.sife.org.
16. Mark Henricks, "Honor Roll," Entrepreneur, accessed March 11, 2010, www.entrepreneur.com.
17. "Cool College Startups 2010," Inc., accessed March 10, 2010, www.inc.com/ss/cool-college-start-ups-2010.
18. Tamara Schweitzer, "Study: Inc. 500 CEOs Aggressively Use Social Media for Business," Inc., November 25, 2009, www.inc.com/news/articles/2009/11/inc500-social-media-usage.html.
19. "Kauffman Index of Entrepreneurial Activity," accessed January 20, 2014.
20. Newswire, "23-Year-Old Donates US$1 Million to Support University of Waterloo Student Entrepreneurs," accessed March 29, 2011, www.newswire.ca/en/releases/archive/March2011/29/c7314.html.

21. Play It Again, accessed April 8, 2015, www.playitagainsports.com.
22. Eve Gumpel, "The Accidental Inventor," *Women Entrepreneur*, August 18, 2009, www.womenentrepreneur.com.
23. "A Day in the Life of an Entrepreneur," *Princeton Review*, accessed March 14, 2010, www.princetonreview.com.
24. "Oprah Winfrey—About.com Readers' Most Admired Entrepreneur," accessed March 14, 2010, www.entrepreneurs.about.com.
25. Dan Moren, "Forget Oprah: Jobs Is Teens' Most Admired Entrepreneur," About.com, October 13, 2009, http://pcworld.about.com.
26. Sodhi, "Meet India's Leading Ladies."
27. Bobbi Brown, accessed January 20, 2014, www.bobbibrowncosmetics.co.uk; "How Bobbi Brown Put a New Face on the Makeup Industry," *CBS News*, accessed January 20, 2014, www.cbsnews.com/news/how-bobbi-brown-put-a-new-face-on-the-makeup-industry; Bobbi Brown and Athena Schindelheim, "How I Did It," *Inc.*, accessed January 20, 2014, www.inc.com/magazine/20071101/how-i-did-it-bobbi-brown-founder-and-ceo-bobbi-brown_pagen_2.html.
28. Donna Fenn, "The Kid Behind a $170 Million Website," *Inc.*, accessed March 15, 2010, www.inc.com/articles/2009/09/mint-qa.html.
29. Amy S. Choi, "Entrepreneurs Who Thrive on Risky Business," *Businessweek*, December 4, 2009, www.bloomberg.com/bw/magazine/content/09_72/s0912056528669.htm.
30. Kasey Wehrum, "How I Did It: Ralph Braun of BraunAbility," *Inc.*, December 1, 2009, www.inc.com/magazine/20091201/how-i-did-it-ralph-braun-of-braunability.html.
31. "Entrepreneurial America: A Comprehensive Look at Today's Fastest-Growing Private Companies," *Inc.: The Handbook of the American Entrepreneur*, accessed April 9, 2010, www.inc.com.
32. Darren Dahl, "How to Read a Term Sheet," *Inc.*, accessed March 1, 2010, www.inc.com/magazine/20100301/how-to-read-a-term-sheet.html.
33. Alexandra Paul, "City's First Urban Reserve Open," *Winnipeg Free Press*, January 10, 2012, accessed on January 20, 2012, www.winnipegfreepress.com/breakingnews/136997393.html.
34. Michael Goldman Inc., accessed March 16, 2010, www.michaelgoldman.com.
35. 3M, "A Culture of Innovation," accessed March 16, 2010, www.3M.com; Michael Goldman Inc., www.michaelgoldman.com.
36. 3M, "A Culture of Innovation."

Part 2 Case Study Beau's All Natural Brewing Company: Getting Started: Choosing a Location, Building the Plant and Hiring Employees

Based on interviews with Steve Beauchesne at Beau's All Natural Brewery Company offices, Vankleek Hill, Ontario, on March 30, 2015; Beau's All Natural Brewery Company, accessed April 3, 2015, www.beaus.ca; Beau's Beer Blog, "How to Start a Brewery in 1 Million Easy Steps," January 9, 2007, accessed April 3, 2015, http://beausbeer.blogspot.ca/2007/01/brewery-measurements.html.

Part 2: Launching Your Entrepreneurial Career

1. Michael Ames, cited in "Is Entrepreneurship for You?" Small Business Administration, accessed April 9, 2010, www.sba.gov.
2. Business Development Bank of Canada, "A Quick Refresher on Patents and Trademarks for Business Services," accessed May 1, 2012, www.bdc.ca/EN/advice_centre/articles/Pages/a_quick_refresher_on_patents_trademarks_for_business_services.aspx.

Chapter 7

1. Based on information from BlackBerry, accessed April 10, 2015, http://ca.blackberry.com/company.html; "Research In Motion Names Thorsten Heins President and CEO," press release, January 22, 2012, accessed January 23, 2012, www.rim.com/investors/documents/pdf/financial/2012/Research_In_Motion_Names_Thorsten_Heins_President_and_CEO.pdf; RIM stock chart, *Globe and Mail*, accessed January 23, 2012, www.theglobeandmail.com/globe-mvestor/markets/stocks/chart/?q=RIM-T; Tim Kiladze and Iain Marlow, "RIM Shakeup Brings Muted Market Response," *Globe and Mail*, January 23, 2012, accessed January 23, 2012, www.theglobeandmail.com/globe-investor/rim-shakeup-brings-muted-market-response/article2311427.
2. Loblaw, accessed April 10, 2015, www.loblaw.ca.
3. TD Bank, "Meet Our President & CEO," accessed April 10, 2015, www.td.com/about-tdbfg/corporate-information/executive-profiles/president.jsp; John Greenwood, "Canada's Outstanding CEO of the Year," *Financial Post*, January 14, 2011, accessed April 5, 2011, www.financialpost.com/executive/ceo/Canadas+Outstanding+Year+Clark/4110716/story.html.
4. "*Businessweek* Names Customer Service Champs," Customers 1st Blogspot, February 23, 2010, www.customers1stblogspot.com.
5. Cold Stone Creamery, accessed March 28, 2010, www.coldstonecreamery.com.
6. "Zappos.com Power by Service," accessed March 28, 2010, http://about.zappos.com.
7. Helen Coster, "The State of the CEO in 2010," Forbes, January 21, 2010, www.forbes.com/2010/01/21/state-of-ceo-leadership-governance-boards.html.
8. John Shmuel and Scott Deveau, "Stronach Resigns as Chairman of Magna," *Financial Post*, March 31, 2011, accessed April 5, 2011, www.canada.com/business/Frank+Stronach+step+down+Magna+chair man/4536966/story.html.
9. Christopher Steiner, "Go Green and Stay in the Black," *Forbes*, March 8, 2010, www.forbes.com/2010/03/08/green-small-business-entrepreneurs-technology-small-biz-toolkit-green-tips.html.

10. Facebook, accessed April 5, 2011, www.facebook.com/facebook.
11. Coster, "The State of the CEO in 2010."
12. Mattel, "Mattel Named One of the World's Most Ethical Companies Again in 2010," press release, March 22, 2010, http://news.mattel.com/news/mattel-named-one-of-the-world-s-most-ethical-companies-again-in-2010.
13. Reid Hoffman, as told to Mark Lacter, "How I Did It: Reid Hoffman of LinkedIn," *Inc.*, May 1, 2009, www.inc.com/author/reid-hoffman,-as-told-to-mark-lacter.
14. Geoff Colvin, "Housing Is Back—and so Is Home Depot," *Fortune*, September 19, 2013, accessed January 22, 2014, http://fortune.com/2013/09/19/housing-is-back-and-so-is-home-depot.
15. Brent Robinson, "Omnichannel Retailing and the Mobile Solution to Showroom Shoppers," *Bazaar Voice*, accessed January 23, 2014, http://blog.bazaarvoice.com/2013/10/23/omnichannel-retailing-and-the-mobile-solution-to-showroom-shoppers.
16. Sylvia Hui, "British Airways Cabin Crews Strike for 2nd Day," *Businessweek*, March 21, 2010, www.businessweek.com/ap/financialnews/D9EJ49700.htm.
17. Starbucks, accessed January 25, 2014, www.starbucks.com; Candice Choi, "Starbucks Hit by Migration to Online Shopping," *Yahoo Finance*, accessed January 25, 2014, http://finance.yahoo.com/news/starbucks-hit-migration-online-shopping-180105714.html;_ylt=AwrBT83vi3dVhC8A.UtXNyoA;_ylu=X3oDMTEyYzc5ams3BGNvbG8gDYmYxBHBvcwMxBHZ0aWQDQjAwMjd-fMQRzZWMDc3I-; Annie Gasparo, "Green Mountain to Change Name to Include Keurig Brand," *Wall Street Journal*, accessed January 20, 2014, www.wsj.com/articles/SB10001424052702303754404579312940698163828; Stephanie Strom, "Starbucks Aims to Move Beyond Beans," *New York Times*, accessed January 20, 2014, www.nytimes.com/2013/10/09/business/a-juice-and-croissant-with-that-starbucks-latte.html.
18. Ibid.
19. Brooks Barnes, "But It Doesn't Look Like a Marriott," *New York Times*, accessed January 25, 2014, www.nytimes.com/2014/01/05/business/marriott-international-aims-to-draw-a-younger-crowd.html.
20. Becel, accessed April 5, 2011, www.loveyourheart.ca/en_ca/about_becel/default.aspx.
21. "How Companies Manage the Front Line Today," McKinsey & Company, pp. 1–2.
22. Jena McGregor, Alli McConnon, and David Kiley, "Customer Service in a Shrinking Economy," *Businessweek*, March 9, 2010, www.bloomberg.com/bw/stories/2009-02-18/customer-service-in-a-shrinking-economy.
23. Apple, accessed April 1, 2010, www.apple.com.
24. "Best 50 Corporate Citizens 2014," *Corporate Knights Magazine*, accessed April 10, 2015, www.corporateknights.com/reports/2014-best-50/2014-best-50-results-14020615/; "CR's 100 Best Corporate Citizens 2013," *Corporate Responsibility Magazine*, accessed January 25, 2014, www.thecro.org.
25. Bruce Horovitz, "CEO Profile: Campbell Exec Nears 'Extraordinary' Goal," *USA Today*, January 26, 2009, http://usatoday30.usatoday.com/money/companies/management/profile/2009-01-25-campbell-ceo-conant-profile_N.htm.
26. Scott D. Anthony, "Google's Management Style Grows Up," *Businessweek*, March 9, 2010, www.businessweek.com/managing/content/jun2009/ca20090623_918721.htm.
27. Dean Foust, "US Airways: After the 'Miracle on the Hudson,'" *Businessweek*, March 9, 2010, www.bloomberg.com/bw/stories/2009-02-18/us-airways-after-the-miracle-on-the-hudson.
28. Google, "Corporate Information," accessed March 30, 2010, www.google.com/corporate/culture.html.
29. Walt Disney Company, "Culture," accessed March 30, 2010, http://corporate.disney.go.com/careers/culture.html.
30. Ben Fritz, "Company Town," *Los Angeles Times*, March 30, 2010, http://latimesblogs.latimes.com.
31. Enterprise Rent-A-Car, "Enterprise Facts," accessed March 30, 2010, www.erac.com.
32. 3M, "Products and Services," accessed April 5, 2010, www.3M.com.
33. Brandon Gutman, "Zappos' Marketing Chief: 'Customer Service Is the New Marketing!'" *Fast Company*, March 15, 2010, www.fastcompany.com/1583321/zappos-marketing-chief-customer-service-new-marketing.
34. Mike Gordon, Chris Musso, Eric Rebentisch, and Nisheeth Gupta, "The Path to Successful New Products," *Forbes*, January 7, 2010, www.forbes.com/2010/01/07/new-products-innovation-leadership-managing-mckinsey.html.
35. Jason Del Rey, "How I Did It: Omniture's Josh James," *Inc.*, March 1, 2010, www.inc.com/magazine/20100301/how-i-did-it-omnitures-josh-james.html.

Chapter 8

1. Charles Duhigg and Keith Bradsher, "Iron Law of Economics," *New York Times*, published in *National Post*, January 23, 2012, p. FP3; Allan Swift, "Stretching with the Times," *Montreal Gazette*, November 20, 2006, pp. B1–B2; Industry Canada, "Canadian Apparel Profile," accessed January 29, 2012, www.ic.gc.ca/eic/site/026.nsf/eng/h_00070.html#statistical; Industry Canada, "Clothing Manufacturing," accessed January 29, 2012, www.ic.gc.ca/cis-sic/cis-sic.nsf/IDE/cis-sic315empe.html; Apparel Human Resources Council, "Pressing Ahead: Canada's Transforming Apparel Industry, 2011 Labour Market Information Study," March 31, 2011, accessed January 29, 2012, www.apparelconnexion.com/apparel/tools/files/b891ecaf-4376-7b1f.pdf; The Conference Board of Canada, "Canada's Textiles and Apparel Industry," Spring 2011.
2. Brandresume.com, "Predicting the Top 5 In Demand Skills for 2014," accessed January 25, 2014, https://brandredresume.com/2013/12/24/top-5-in-demand-skills-for-2014-prediction/.
3. Jobs in Pods, accessed January 25, 2014, www.jobsinpods.com.
4. Peter M. LaSorsa, "UPS Settles EEOC Lawsuit for $46,000," *Illinois Sexual Harassment Attorney Blog*, February 20, 2010, http://eeoc.gov/eeoc/newsroom/release/2-17-10.cfm.
5. "Executive Recruiting Advice—Don't Underestimate the Cost of a Mis-Hire," *Fortune 100 Best Companies to Work For*, accessed April 13, 2010, www.focussearchpartners.com/articles.html?item=executive-recruiting-advice-dont-underestimate-the-cost-of-a-mis-hire.

6. "McDonald's Puts Apprenticeships on the Menu," accessed April 15, 2010, https://people1st.wordpress.com/2009/01/08/mcdonalds-put-apprenticeships-on-the-menu/; McDonald's UK, "Apprentice," accessed April 11, 2015, www.mcdonalds.co.uk/ukhome/People/Join-the-team/Pick-your-role/Apprentice.html.

7. "Welcome to EYU," accessed January 25, 2015, www.ey.com.

8. "Systems Integration Consulting Training," accessed April 13, 2010, https://microsite.accenture.com.

9. The Conference Board of Canada, "Education and Learning," accessed April 11, 2015, www.conferenceboard.ca/topics/education/default.aspx.

10. Samuel A. Culbert, "Yes, Everyone Really Does Hate Performance Reviews," *Wall Street Journal*, April 19, 2010, http://finance.yahoo.com.

11. "Turn Your Performance Review System into One That Works," *Quality Digest Magazine*, accessed January 29, 2014, www.qualitydigest.com/inside/twitter-ed/turn-your-performance-review-system-one-works.html.

12. "Gather and Analyze 360 Degree Feedback More Quickly and Easily," Halogen Software, accessed April 11, 2015, www.halogensoftware.com/uploads/pdf/product-sheet/360-degree-feedback-datasheet.pdf.

13. Bureau of Labor Statistics, "Employer Costs for Employee Compensation, September 2013" press release, accessed January 25, 2014, www.bls.gov/news.release/archives/ecec_12112013.pdf.

14. Qualcomm, accessed January 25, 2014, www.qualcomm.com; "100 Best Companies to Work For 2013: Best Benefits," *Fortune*, accessed January 26, 2014, http://money.cnn.com/search/index.html?sortBy=date&primaryType=mixed&search=Search&query=100+Best+Companies+to+Work+For+2013%3A+Best+Benefits&symb=BEYSQ%20BBY%20FTEG%20ANNO%20BEST%20XSJDX%20XSCOX%20MUAB%20KRFDX%20BSJD.

15. "Advantages and Disadvantages of Paid Time Off," *The Thriving Small Business*, March 19, 2010, www.thethrivingsmallbusiness.com.

16. Eugene Eteris, "European Social Market Economy: Flexibility Issues," *The Baltic Course*, March 16, 2010, www.baltic-course.com.

17. "Things You Should Know about BidShift" San Angelo Community Medical Center, accessed April 14, 2010, www.sacmc.com.

18. Dan Schawbel, "Why a Flexible Workplace Makes Sense," accessed January 26, 2014, http://ehotelier.com; Richard Eisenberg, "It's High Time for a Four-Day Workweek," *Next Avenue*, accessed January 26, 2014, www.nextavenue.org.

19. Curt Finch, "The Rise of Telecommuting and What It Means for Your Business," *Small Business Trends*, accessed January 26, 2014, http://smallbiztrends.com/2013/05/telecommuting-business-benefits.html.

20. Millennial Branding, "The GenY Workplace Expectations Study," *Millennial Branding*, accessed January 28, 2014, http://millennialbranding.com.

21. Marshall Goldsmith, "How to Keep Good Employees in a Bad Economy," February 26, 2010, https://hbr.org/2010/02/how-to-keep-good-employees-in.

22. Dustin Ensinger, "Why Layoffs Are Not Beneficial to Companies," *Economy in Crisis*, February 8, 2010, http://economyincrisis.org/content/why-layoffs-are-not-beneficial-companies; Laura Hemphill, "Amid Layoffs—A Financial Analyst's Survivor Guilt," *Bloomberg Businessweek*, accessed January 27, 2014, www.businessweek.com; Ken Eisold, "The American Way of Unemployment," *Psychology Today*, accessed January 28, 2014, www.psychologytoday.com/blog/hidden-motives/201108/the-american-way-unemployment.

23. Ibid.

24. Christopher D. Zatzik, Mitchell L. Marks, Roderick D. Iverson, "Downsizing Case Studies," *MIT Sloan Management Review*, January 7, 2010, www.nationalpost.com.

25. "Maslow's Hierarchy of Needs," Accel-Team.com, accessed April 14, 2010, www.accel-team.com.

26. Mediacorp Canada Inc., "Canada's Top Employers for Young People," accessed January 30, 2012, www.canadastop100.com/young_people/.

27. Canadian Labour Congress, accessed April 11, 2015, www.canadianlabour.ca/home; Human Resources and Skills Development Canada, "Union Membership in Canada 2010," accessed January 30, 2012, www.hrsdc.gc.ca/eng/labour/labour_relations/info_analysis/union_membership/2010/unionmembership2010.shtml#results.

28. Jim Balsillie, *An Investigation into the Collective Bargaining Relationship between the NHL and the NHLPA 1994–2005* (Kingston, ON: Queens University Industrial Relations Centre, 2005), accessed January 30, 2012, http://irc.queensu.ca/gallery/1/dps-nhl-lockout.pdf.

29. Jamie Doward, "BA Strike: Airline and Union Swap Barbs on Second Weekend of Walkouts," *Guardian*, March 27, 2010, www.theguardian.com/business/2010/mar/27/british-airways-strike-heathrow-gatwick.

30. Ibid.

31. Human Resources and Skills Development Canada, "Union Membership in Canada 2010."

Chapter 9

1. Interview with Pam Cooley, March 16, 2012; Pam Cooley, accessed April 11, 2015, www.pamcooley.ca; CarShareHFX, accessed April 11, 2015, http://carsharehfx.ca; "CarShareHFX Welcomes a New Mobility Option at Dalhousie University," *CNW CanadaWire*, March 11, 2011, accessed online March 16, 2012, www.newswire.ca/en/story/753625/carsharehfx-welcomes-a-new-mobility-option-at-dalhousie-university.

2. Anderson & Associates, accessed April 11, 2015, www.andassoc.com.

3. Chris Atchison, "Pride of Ownership," *Globe and Mail*, October 7, 2011, accessed February 1, 2012, www.theglobeandmail.com/report-on-business/careers/top-employers/top-employers-2012/pride-of-ownership-works-both-ways/article2193177.

4. The ESOP Association Canada (Employee Share Ownership Plan), accessed April 11, 2015, www.esop-canada.com; ESOP Association, "Corporate Performance," accessed February 1, 2014, www.esopassociation.org.

592 Notes

5. National Center for Employee Ownership, "Employee Ownership as a Retirement Plan," accessed February 1, 2014, www.nceo.org.
6. "Employee Stock Options Fact Sheet," The National Center for Employee Ownership, accessed February 1, 2014, www.nceo.org/articles/employee-stock-options-factsheet.
7. Ibid.
8. Toyota, accessed May 10, 2010, www.toyota.com/recall.
9. "Whole Foods Market's Core Values," accessed February 1, 2014, www.wholefoodsmarket.com/site_search/Whole%20Foods%20Market%E2%80%99s%20Core%20Values.
10. "Harley-Davidson: The Sound of a Legend," accessed April 19, 2010, www.lmsintl.com.
11. BBC, accessed May 10, 2010, www.bbc.co.uk; Lynda Gratton, Andreas Voigt, and Tamara Erickson, "Bridging Faultlines in Diverse Teams," *MIT Sloan Management Review*, summer 2007, pp. 22–29.
12. Kate Rogers, "Commitment to Standards, Mission, Clients and Fun," *Nonprofit Times*, April 1, 2010, www.thenonprofittimes.com/news-articles/commitment-to-standards-mission-clients-and-fun.
13. Robert Grice, "How to Build a Unified Team," *Helium*, accessed April 19, 2010, www.helium.com.
14. Nick Grabbe, "Experts: Don't Fear Workplace Conflict," *Gazettenet.com*, March 1, 2010, www.gazettenet.com.
15. Ken Thomas and Larry Margasak, "Toyota Waited Months to Tell U.S. about Sticking Accelerator Fixes It Gave to Dealers in Europe," *Associated Press*, April 6, 2010, www.cleveland.com/business/index.ssf/2010/04/toyota_waited_months_to_tell_u.html.
16. Ibid.
17. David Woods, "i-level Redesigns Its Employee Reward Communication Strategy," *HR Magazine*, March 8, 2010, www.hrmagazine.co.uk/hro/news/1017558/-level-redesigns-employee-reward-communication-strategy-reflect-innovative-image.
18. Norma Chew, "Are You a Good Listener?" Associated Content, accessed April 19, 2010, www.associatedcontent.com.
19. Open Text Corporation, accessed February 1, 2012, www.opentext.com/2/global.htm.
20. "Expand Trust in Your Organization," *Peter Stark.com*, accessed April 19, 2010, www.peterstark.com.
21. Joni F. Johnston, "How to Deal with Office Gossip," *Ezine Articles*, accessed April 19, 2010, http://ezinearticles.com.
22. John Boe, "How to Read Your Prospect Like a Book!" *John Boe International*, accessed April 19, 2010, http://johnboe.com.
23. Amar Toor, "Nestlé's Palm Oil PR Crisis Pervades Facebook," *Switched*, March 22, 2010, www.switched.com.
24. "Nestlé's Social Media PR Crisis: How Would You Handle It?" *Pierce Mattie Public Relations*, accessed April 19, 2010, www.piercemattiepublicrelations.com.
25. Emily Steel, "Nestlé Takes a Beating on Social-Media Sites," *Wall Street Journal*, March 29, 2010, www.wsj.com/articles/SB10001424052702304434404575149883850508158.

Chapter 10

1. GE, "Additive Manufacturing Is Reinventing the Way We Work," accessed February 22, 2014, www.ge.com/stories/advanced-manufacturing; Tim Catts, "GE Printing Engine Fuel Nozzles Propels $6 Billion Market," *Bloomberg News*, accessed February 22, 2014, www.bloomberg.com/news/articles/2013-11-12/ge-printing-engine-fuel-nozzles-propels-6-billion-market; Chelsey Levingston, "3-D Manufacturing Next Industrial Revolution?" *Dayton Daily News*, accessed February 22, 2014, www.daytondailynews.com/news/news/3-d-manufacturing-seen-to-be-next-industrial-revol/nbdcb; Rich Benvin, "3D Printing—The Future of Manufacturing," Association of 3D Printing, accessed February 22, 2014, http://associationof3dprinting.com.
2. Honda, "Operations Facilities," accessed February 5, 2014, http://corporate.honda.com; "Honda Builds Record 84% of 2009 U.S. Auto Sales in North America," *Auto Channel*, accessed April 26, 2010, www.theautochannel.com/news/2010/01/08/461055.html.
3. Shibui Designs, accessed February 5, 2014, www.custommade.com; Lydia Dishman, "Retire? Forget about It," *Entrepreneur*, January 11, 2010, www.entrepreneur.com/article/204568.
4. Barbara Quinn, "Carving a Roadway to Sustainability," *Pollution Engineering*, May 2010, p. 17.
5. Canada Green Building Council (CaGBC), accessed April 14, 2011, www.cagbc.org; "LEED," U.S. Green Building Council, accessed May 27, 2010, www.usgbc.org.
6. Consolidated Technologies, accessed April 14, 2011, http://consolidatedtechnologies.ca.
7. Clara Maria Cabrera, "CAD/CAM Dental Technology," Associated Content, accessed April 26, 2010, www.associatedcontent.com.
8. Roger Schreffler, "Nissan's Flexible Manufacturing Moves to India, Other JVs," Wards Auto.com, February 3, 2010, http://wardsauto.com/ar/nissan_flexible_manufacturing_100203.
9. Vince Lapinski, "We Are Print," Manroland, www.manroland.us.com.
10. Anupam Govil, "Shifting of the Global Sourcing Axis," *Near Shore Americas*, April 6, 2010, www.nearshoreamericas.com/nearshoring-shift-of-the-global-sourcing-axis.
11. Mike Pare, "VW Prototypes on Local Horizon," *Chattanooga Times Free Press*, January 11, 2010, www.gaccsouth.com/en/news/single-view/artikel/vw-prototypes-on-local-horizon/?cHash=03a5e0fcfa650ffc17108a0241002afb.
12. "Holland Car's Assembly Line to Evolve," *Fortune*, April 18, 2010, www.addisfortune.com/Vol%2010%20No%20507%20Archive/Holland%20Car%E2%80%99s%20Assembly%20Line%20to%20Evolve.htm.
13. "Advantages and Disadvantages of Outsourcing," The Thriving Small Business, February 8, 2010, www.thethrivingsmallbusiness.com.
14. "Supplier Management," Ariba, accessed April 26, 2010, www.ariba.com/solutions/buy/supplier-management.
15. Shruti Date Singh, "Deere Shortage Prompts Kansas Farmer to Buy Dragotec," *Bloomberg Businessweek*, April 26, 2010,

16. SAP, "Loblaw Selects SAP to Strengthen Its Business Processes in Canada," November 10, 2008, accessed April 14, 2011, www.sap.com/press.epx?pressid=10365.

17. "Seattle Children's Hospital Saves $2.5 Million in First Year with Streamlined Inventory Distribution," accessed April 26, 2010, www.seattlechildrens.org/news/2010/seattle-children%E2%80%99s-hospital-saves-_2-5-million-in-first-year-with-streamlined-inventory-distribution.

18. "Allan Candy Company," *Microsoft Case Studies*, April 19, 2010, www.microsoft.com.

19. Judy Miller, "Still Made in America: The Super Bowl Footballs from Ada, Ohio," *Encyclopedia Britannica Blog*, February 1, 2010, http://blogs.britannica.com/2010/02/still-made-in-america-the-super-bowl-footballs-from-ada-ohio.

20. "Success Stories: Sleepmaster, LTD," *Usersolutions.com*, accessed April 26, 2010, www.usersolutions.com.

21. "Contrite Facebook CEO Promises new Privacy Controls," *Yahoo! News*, May 24, 2010, http://news.yahoo.com.

22. Jamie Liddell, "Top Ten Tips for Better Benchmarking," *SSON Network*, accessed April 26, 2010, www.ssonetwork.com/articleiframe.cfm?id=10707.

23. Six Sigma Inc. Canada, accessed February 3, 2012, www.sixsigmacanada.net/; Vic Nanda, "Preempting Problems," *Six Sigma Forum Magazine*, February 2010, pp. 9–18.

24. "Maintaining the Benefits and Continual Improvement," International Organization for Standardization, accessed April 26, 2010, www.iso.org.

Part 3 Case Study Beau's All Natural Brewing Company: Managing the Pains of Early Growth

Based on interviews with Steve Beauchesne at Beau's All Natural Brewery Company offices, Vankleek Hill, Ontario, on March 30, 2015; Beau's All Natural Brewery Company, accessed April 3, 2015, www.beaus.ca; Beau's Beer Blog, "How to Start a Brewery in 1 Million Easy Steps," January 9, 2007, accessed April 3, 2015, http://beausbeer.blogspot.ca/2007/01/brewery-measurements.html.

Part 3: Launching Your Management Career

1. Living in Canada, "Canadian Salary Survey," accessed May 1, 2012, www.livingin-canada.com/wages-for-management-jobs-canada.html.

Chapter 11

1. Etsy for Lisa Lutz, accessed April 17, 2015, www.etsy.com/shop/beadcrazed; Etsy, accessed April 17, 2015, www.etsy.com; Hiroko Tabuchi, "Etsy I.P.O. Tests Pledge to Balance Social Mission and Profit," *New York Times*, April 16, 2015, accessed April 17, 2015, www.nytimes.com/2015/04/17/business/dealbook/etsy-ipo-tests-pledge-to-emphasize-social-mission-over-profit.html?_r=0; Artfire, accessed April 17, 2015, www.artfire.com; 1000 Markets, accessed April 17, 2015, www.1000markets.com; Janell Mooney, accessed April 17, 2015, www.etsy.com/shop/dancingmooney; Janell Mooney, "What You Should Know about Etsy.com," Associated Content, accessed March 25, 2010, http://associatedcontent.com; Cyndia Zwahlen, "Independent Artisans Are Crowding onto the Web," *Los Angeles Times*, March 1, 2010, http://articles.latimes.com/2010/mar/01/business/la-fi-smallbiz-crafts1-2010mar01; Alex Williams, "That Hobby Looks Like a Lot of Work," *New York Times*, December 17, 2009, www.nytimes.com/2009/12/17/fashion/17etsy.html?_r=0.

2. American Marketing Association, "AMA Adopts New Definition of Marketing," *Marketing-Power*, accessed February 24, 2014, www.danavan.net.

3. Target, accessed February 10, 2014, www.target.com; Brad Gilligan, "Target Starts Mobile Coupon Program," *All Tech Considered*, accessed February 10, 2014, www.npr.org/sections/alltechconsidered/2010/03/target_starts_mobile_coupon_pr.html; "Target Launches First-Ever Scannable Mobile Coupon Program," *Business Wire*, accessed February 10, 2014, www.businesswire.com/news/home/20100310005092/en/Target-Launches-First-Ever-Scannable-Mobile-Coupon-Program#.VZvoORtViko; Marguerite Reardon, "Attention Shoppers: Target Offers Mobile Coupons," *CNET News*, accessed February 10, 2014, www.cnet.com/news/attention-shoppers-target-offers-mobile-coupons.

4. Apple, www.apple.com, accessed April 17, 2015; "Apple IPAD: Get to Know the Apple iPad," *NY Breaking News*, n.d., www.nybreakingnews.com; Arik Hesseldahl, "Apple's Hard iPad Sell," *Businessweek*, February 5, 2010, www.bloomberg.com/bw/technology/content/feb2010/tc2010024_830227.htm; Erica Ogg, "Who Will Buy the iPad?" *CNET News*, January 28, 2010, www.cnet.com/news/who-will-buy-the-ipad.

5. Michael Hall, David Lasby, Steven Ayer, and William David Gibbons, *Caring Canadians, Involved Canadians: Highlights from the Canada Survey of Giving, Volunteering and Participating*, Catalogue no. 71-542-XWE, Chapter 2, Volunteering (Ottawa: Statistics Canada, 2007), accessed May 8, 2012, www.statcan.gc.ca/pub/71-542-x/2009001/chap/ch2-eng.htm; *Summary of the Findings of the National Survey of Nonprofit and Voluntary Organizations* (NSNVO), Statistics Canada, accessed January 23, 2011, www.statcan.gc.ca/pub/61-533-s/61-533-s2005001-eng.htm#5; "Facts and Figures about Charitable Organizations," *Independent Sector*, October 30, 2009, www.independentsector.org.

6. Lester M. Salamon, Megan A. Haddock, S. Wojciech Sokolowski, and Helen S. Tice, *Measuring Civil Society and Volunteering: Initial Findings from Implementation of the UN Handbook on Nonprofit Institutions*, Working Paper No. 23 (Baltimore: Johns Hopkins Center for Civil Society Studies, 2007), www.jhu.edu.

7. Scotiabank Rat Race for United Way, accessed October 28, 2015, www.unitedwaytyr.com/ratrace.

8. Avon Foundation, accessed April 25, 2015, www.avoncompany.com; "Avon Foundation for Woman Grants $500,000 to the U.S. Department of State Secretary's Fund for Global Women's Leadership," press release, April 25, 2015, www.newswire.ca/en/story/570469/avon-foundation-for-women-grants-500-000-to-the-u-s-department-of-state-secretary-s-fund-for-global-womens-leadership.

9. "The Adventures of Quatchi, Miga, and Sumi Begin in Earnest," Vancouver 2010, accessed April 25, 2015, www.vancouver2010.com.

10. The Canadian Diabetes Association, accessed April 25, 2015, www.diabetes.ca.

11. The University of Western Ontario's Alternative Spring Break, accessed April 25, 2015, www.asb.uwo.ca.

12. Seventh Generation, accessed April 25, 2015, www.seventhgeneration.com.

13. Oprah's Angel Network, accessed April 2015, http://oprahsangelnetwork.org and www.oprah.com/pressroom/About-Oprahs-Angel-Network.

14. McDonald's, "Our Story," accessed February 11, 2014, www.mcdonalds.com/us/en/our_story.html; SUBWAY, "Restaurant Locator," accessed February 11, 2014, http://world.subway.com; SUBWAY Restaurants International, accessed February 11, 2014, http://world.subway.com; Marco Lui, "Subway Plans to Open 500 Stores across China in Next Five Years," *Bloomberg News*, accessed February 11, 2014, www.bloomberg.com/apps/news?pid=newsarchive&sid=acUIqNJjyUPQ; Farah Master, "Subway Eyes Matching McDonalds in China in 10 Years," *Reuters*, accessed February 11, 2014, www.reuters.com/article/2010/03/08/us-subway-china-idUSTRE62723220100308; Ben Yue, "Subway Eyes Further China Expansion," *China Daily USA*, accessed February 11, 2014, www.chinadaily.com.cn/business/2011-07/04/content_12827599.htm.

15. Blank Label, accessed April 25, 2015, www.blanklabel.com; Spreadshirt, accessed April 25, 2015, www.spreadshirt.com.

16. "Procter & Gamble Readies Online Market-Research Push," *InformationWeek*, accessed February 10, 2014, www.informationweek.com/procter-and-gamble-readies-online-market-research-push/d/d-id/1012232?; Hal Gregersen, "A.G. Lafley's Innovation Skills Will Weather P&G's Storm," *Knowledge.com*, accessed February 10, 2014, http://knowledge.insead.edu.

17. TRU-Insight, accessed April 25, 2015, www.tru-insight.com.

18. Stephanie Rosenbloom, "In Bid to Sway Sales, Cameras Track Shoppers," *New York Times*, March 20, 2010, www.nytimes.com/2010/03/20/business/20surveillance.html?_r=0.

19. Mark Clothier, "P&G's McDonald Pins Growth on Closer Shave than Mumbai Barber," *Bloomberg*, accessed February 11, 2014, www.bloomberg.com/apps/news?pid=newsarchive&sid=aK6vXFvwPUXA.

20. Andrew McMains, "CEO Pushes Soup Giant to Move Faster, 'Think Outside the Can,'" *AdWeek*, accessed February 11, 2014, www.adweek.com.

21. Unilever, "Challenges and Wants," accessed February 10, 2014, www.unilever.com/about/innovation/open-innovation/challenges-and-wants/; "5 Examples of Companies Innovating with Crowdsourcing," *Innocentive.com*, accessed February 10, 2014, www.innocentive.com/blog/2013/10/18/5-examples-of-companies-innovating-with-crowdsourcing.

22. Leah Betancourt, "How Companies Are Using Your Social Media Data," *Mashable*, accessed February 12, 2014, http://mashable.com/2010/03/02/data-mining-social-media; Jim Cooper, "Yahoo's Carol Bartz Touts Data," *Mediaweek*, accessed February 12, 2014, www.mediaweek.com; Jared Newman, "Google Buzz Bites the Dust," *PCWorld*, accessed February 12, 2014, www.pcworld.com/article/241965/google_buzz_bites_the_dust.html; Declan McCullagh, "Why No One Cares about Privacy Anymore," *CNETNews*, accessed February 12, 2014, www.cnet.com/news/why-no-one-cares-about-privacy-anymore.

23. Playnomics, accessed February 12, 2014, www.playnomics.com; "Playnomics Releases a Free Player Scoring Dashboard for Game Platforms and Publishers," PR Newswire, accessed February 12, 2014, www.prnewswire.com/news-releases/playnomics-releases-a-free-player-scoring-dashboard-for-game-platforms-and-publishers-141580613.html.

24. Pew Research Center, "Social Media User Demographics," accessed February 12, 2014, www.pewinternet.org/data-trend/social-media/social-media-user-demographics.

25. Craig Smith, "21 Interesting Pandora Statistics," *Expanded Ramblings*, accessed July 13, 2014, http://expandedramblings.com; Pandora, accessed February 12, 2014, www.pandora.com; Marcello Ballve, "Silicon Valley and Detroit Are Battling Over the Future of the Internet-Connected Car," *Business Insider*, accessed February 12, 2014, www.businessinsider.com/the-future-of-internet-connected-cars-2013-10; Peter High, "Gartner: Top 10 Strategic Technology Trends for 2014," *Forbes*, accessed February 12, 2014, www.forbes.com/sites/peterhigh/2013/10/14/gartner-top-10-strategic-technology-trends-for-2014; Farhad Manjoo, "Smart Cars: Fill 'Er with Apps," *Fast Company*, accessed February 12, 2014, www.fastcompany.com/3012499/tech-edge/why-cars-should-be-more-like-smartphones.

26. Ford, "Now on Duty," accessed February 12, 2014, www.ford.com; "Ford e-News—July 24, 2013," P R Newswire, accessed February 12, 2014, www.prnewswire.com/news-releases/ford-enews---july-24-2013-216800001.html; Brandon Turkus, "Ford's Explorer-based Police Interceptor to Get 365-hp EcoBoost Option," *Auto Blog*, accessed February 12, 2014, www.autoblog.com/2013/08/20/fords-explorer-based-police-interceptor-365-hp-ecoboost/; Brent Snavely, "Ford to Unveil Police Interceptor," *Detroit Free Press*, accessed February 12, 2014, www.managemylife.com; Chris Woodyard, "Ford Unveils Next-Generation, V-6-Only Taurus Police Car," *USA Today*, accessed February 12, 2014, http://content.usatoday.com/communities/driveon/post/2010/03/ford-unveils-next-generation-v-6-only-taurus-police-car/1#.VZ6awF9Viko; Fran Spielman, "Chicago Police Department to Buy 500 Police Cars from South Side Ford Plant," *Chicago Sun Times*, accessed February 12, 2014, www.suntimes.com; Owen Ray, "San Francisco Police: Ford Police Interceptor to Replace Crown Victoria," *Examiner*, accessed February 12, 2014, www.examiner.com/article/san-francisco-police-ford-police-interceptor-to-replace-crown-victoria.

27. Joseph Yi, "Male Shopping Habits vs. Female Shopping Habits," *E-Commerce Rules*, accessed February 12, 2014, http://

ecommercerules.com/male-shopping-gabits-versus-female-shopping-habits.

28. Nielsen, "Women Control the Purse Strings," accessed February 12, 2014, www.nielsen.com/ca/en/insights/news/2013/u-s--women-control-the-purse-strings.html.

29. Amazon, "Join Amazon Mom and Enjoy," accessed February 12, 2014, http://join-amazon-mom-and-enjoy-today.blogspot.ca/2014/01/learn-more-about-amazon-mom.html.

30. U.S. Census Bureau, "2012 Statistical Abstract, Resident Population Projections by Sex and Age: 2010 to 2050," accessed February 10, 2014, www.census.gov.

31. Emily Brandon, "The Recession's Impact on Baby Boomer Retirement," *US News Money*, accessed February 13, 2014, http://money.usnews.com/money/retirement/articles/2011/10/31/the-recessions-impact-on-baby-boomer-retirement.

32. Jeanine Poggi, "Nickelodeon Targets 'Post-Millennials' in Upfront," *Advertising Age*, accessed February 13, 2014, http://adage.com/article/special-report-tv-upfront/nickelodeon-targets-post-millennials-upfront/240045/.

33. General Motors, "Social Hub," accessed April 17, 2015, www.gm.com/company/social_hub.html.

34. "Research Shows $15.39 Billion Spent on Video Game Content in US in 2013, a One Percent Increase over 2012," *NPD Group*, accessed February 25, 2014, www.npd.com/wps/portal/npd/us/news/press-releases/research-shows-15.39-billion-dollars-spent-on-video-game-content-in-the-us-in-2013-a-1-percent-increase-over-2012/; Toy Industry Association, "Annual Sales Data for Traditional Toy Categories," accessed February 25, 2014, www.toyassociation.org/tia/industry_facts/salesdata/industryfacts/sales_data/sales_data.aspx?hkey=6381a73a-ce46-4caf-8bc1-72b99567df1e#.VZ6ejl9Viko.

35. Crate & Barrel, accessed April 17, 2015, www.crateandbarrel.com.

36. Sodexo, accessed February 10, 2014, www.sodexousa.com; "Sodexo Introduces Food Truck at Assumption College," *Food Service Director*, January 30, 2014, www.foodservicedirector.com/industry-news-opinion/news/articles/sodexo-introduces-food-truck-assumption-college.

37. McDonald's, "About Us," accessed April 25, 2015, www.aboutmcdonalds.com/mcd.html; Katherine Glover, "More Bad News for Starbucks as McCafé Moves in for the Kill," *CBS Money Watch*, April 20, 2009, www.cbsnews.com/news/more-bad-news-for-starbucks-as-mccafe-moves-in-for-the-kill.

38. Resources for Entrepreneurs staff, "Consumer Habits Could Be Permanently Changed by Recession," *Resources for Entrepreneurs*, accessed February 13, 2014, www.gaebler.com/News/Small-Business-Marketing/Consumer-habits-could-be-permanently-changed-by-recession-19690314.htm; Joshua Brustein, "Walgreen's Beth Stiller on Customer Behavior and the Recession," *Bloomberg Businessweek*, accessed February 13, 2014, www.bloomberg.com/bw/articles/2013-10-03/walgreens-beth-stiller-on-retail-customer-behavior-since-the-recession.

39. Timberland, accessed April 17, 2015, www.timberland.com.

40. Marriott, accessed April 17, 2015, www.marriott.com.

41. Apple, accessed April 17, 2015, www.apple.com/ipod/nike.

42. Netcall, accessed April 17, 2015, www.netcall.com.

Chapter 12

1. Monster Gym, accessed April 24, 2015, www.monstergym.net; Cielo Studios, accessed April 24, 2015, www.cielostudios.ca; Grant Brothers Boxing & MMA Gym, accessed April 24 16, 2015, http://grantbrothersmma.com; interviews with Carmine Petrillo and Howard Grant.

2. "Research and Markets: Global Retail Touch Screen Display Market 2014–2018: One of the Main Drivers Contributing to Market's Growth Is the Use of Hi-Tech Touchscreen Display," Reuters, January 24, 2014, accessed February 16, 2014, www.reuters.com/article/2014/01/24/research-and-markets-idUSnBw245379a+100+BSW20140124.

3. "Pepsi to Sign Rock Star to Distribution Deal," *AdWeek*, February 19, 2009, accessed February 15, 2014, www.adweek.com/news/advertising-branding/pepsico-signs-rockstar-distribution-deal-105310.

4. Natalie Jarvey, "Tablet Company Fuhu Launches Original Animated Series on BabyFirst TV," *The Hollywood Reporter*, March 10, 2014, www.hollywoodreporter.com/news/tablet-company-fuhu-launches-original-687204; Nabi, accessed February 15, 2014, http://nabitablet.com; Burt Helm, "Kid You Not: The Very Serious Business of Building the Fastest Growing Company in America," *Inc.*, accessed February 15, 2014, www.inc.com/magazine/201309/burt-helm/inc.500-2013-number-one-company-fuhu.html.

5. "A Strong Holiday Quarter for the Worldwide Tablet Market, But Signs of Slower Growth Are Clear," *IDC*, January 29, 2014, accessed February 16, 2014, www.idc.com/getdoc.jsp?containerId=prUS24650614; Michael Endler, "iPad Dominates Enterprise Tablet Market," *InformationWeek*, February 12, 2014, accessed February 15, 2014, www.informationweek.com/mobile/mobile-devices/ipad-dominates-enterprise-tablet-market/d/d-id/1113813; "Kindle vs. Nook vs. iPad2 Video Comparison," *Deaf Tech News*, February 20, 2012, accessed February 15, 2014, www.deafhh.net/wp/2012/02/20/kindle-vs-nook-vs-ipad-2-video-comparison.

6. Raymond Soneira, "From Tablets to TVs: What's Next for Display Tech in 2014," *Gizmodo.com*, February 4, 2014, accessed February 15, 2014, http://gizmodo.com/from-tablets-to-tvs-whats-next-for-display-tech-in-20-1515670567; Ken Werner, "HDTV Expert—What Do You Do after You Realize LCD's Glory Days Are Gone?" *HDTV Magazine*, accessed February 15, 2014, www.hdtvmagazine.com/forum/viewtopic.php?t=16944; Alfred Poor, "HDTV Almanac—LED Backlight Prices Falling," *HDTV Magazine*, accessed February 15, 2014, www.hdtvmagazine.com/forum/viewtopic.php?t=13366.

7. "A Gadget's Life: From Gee-Whiz to Junk," *Washington Post*, accessed February 15, 2014, www.washingtonpost.com/wp-srv/special/business/a-gadgets-life; Adam Griff, "Retail after Disruption: DVD Rental," accessed February 15, 2014, www.adamgriff.com.

8. Adam Tschorn, "Old Spice Talks to the Ladies, Man," *Los Angeles Times*, March 6, 2010, http://articles.latimes.com/2010/mar/06/image/la-ig-oldspice-20100306; Drew Grant, "Old Spice's Spicy Ad Campaign," *Mediaite*, February 20, 2010, www.mediaite.com; Liz Shannon Miller, "The Viral Genius of Wieden+Kennedy's New Old Spice Campaign," *Gigaom*, February 19, 2010, https://

gigaom.com/2010/02/19/the-viral-genius-of-wiedenkennedys-new-old-spice-campaign.

9. Mattel, accessed April 26, 2015, www.mattel.com; Amy Graff, "Are Today's Girls Abandoning Their Dolls Too Soon?" *SF Gate*, April 6, 2010, http://blog.sfgate.com/sfmoms/2010/04/06/are-todays-girls-abandoning-their-dolls-too-soon; Andrea Chang, "Toy Fair 2010: After Strong Holiday Sales, Barbie Flaunts New Jobs and Fashions," *Los Angeles Times*, February 14, 2010, http://latimesblogs.latimes.com/money_co/2010/02/toy-fair-2010-mattel-strong-holiday-sales-barbie-flaunts-new-jobs-and-fashions.html; The White House Project, "Barbie Celebrates 125th Career with Global Initiative to Inspire Girls," press release, January 21, 2010, http://thewhitehouseproject.org.

10. Febreze, accessed April 26, 2015, www.febreze.com; PR Newswire, "P&G Leads 2010 Edison Best New Product Award Finalists with Five Nods," press release, February 11, 2010, http://ca.sys-con.com/node/1282608.

11. Electronic Arts, accessed April 26, 2015, www.ea.com; Ben Gilbert, "Report: EA Planning Premium, Pre-Launch DLC for Retail Games at $10-$15," *Engadget*, March 22, 2010, www.engadget.com/2010/03/22/report-ea-planning-premium-pre-launch-dlc-for-retail-games-at-10-15.

12. Tom Merritt, "Top 10 Worst Products," *CNET*, accessed April 30, 2010, www.cnet.com; John Biggs, "Ten Years: The Biggest Product Flops of the Decade," *TechCrunch*, December 31, 2009, http://techcrunch.com/2009/12/31/tenyears-the-biggest-product-flops-of-the-decade.

13. IKEA, accessed February 15, 2014, www.ikea.com.

14. Quiznos, accessed April 26, 2015, www.quiznos.com; Quiznos, "Quiznos Rolls Out Green Packaging," press release, February 23, 2010, www.chainleader.com.

15. Fedex, accessed April 26, 2015, www.fedex.com.

16. Industry Canada, "Canadian Industry Statistics: Wholesale Trade (NAICS 41): Establishments," accessed April 20, 2015; www.ic.gc.ca/app/scr/sbms/sbb/cis/establishments.html?code=41&lang=eng; Statistics Canada, "Annual Wholesale Trade Survey — 2009," March 29, 2011, accessed April 20, 2015, www.statcan.gc.ca/cgibin/imdb/p2SV.pl?Function=getSurvey&SDDS=2445&lang=en&db=imdb&adm=8&dis=2; Bureau of Labor Statistics, "Occupational Outlook Handbook, 2013–2014 Edition," accessed February 15, 2014, www.bls.gov; U.S. Census Bureau, "County Business Patterns," accessed February 15, 2014, www.census.gov.

17. Federated Co-operatives Limited, accessed April 26, 2015, www.coopconnection.ca.

18. U.S. Census Bureau, "Quarterly Retail E-Commerce Sales, 3rd Quarter 2013," accessed February 16, 2014, www.census.gov.

19. Herb Weisbaum, "The Future of Banking: Putting Human Tellers in ATMs," *CNBC*, August 3, 2013, accessed February 15, 2014, www.cnbc.com/id/100925605.

20. Seventh Generation, accessed April 25, 2015, www.seventhgeneration.com; Romy Ribitzky, "Talking about an Ad Generation," *Upstart Business Journal*, February 11, 2010, http://upstart.bizjournals.com/companies/rebel-brands/2010/02/11/seventh-generation-embarks-on-first-ever-national-ad-campaign.html?page=all; Romy Ribitzky, "7 Facts about Seventh Generation," *Upstart Business Journal*, February 11, 2010, http://upstart.biz journals.com/industry-news/advertising-marketing/2010/02/11/seven-facts-about-seventh-generation.html?page=all; Elaine Wong, "How Seventh Generation Is Going Mainstream," *Adweek*, January 26, 2010, www.adweek.com/news/advertising-branding/how-seventh-generation-going-mainstream-106986.

21. Under Armour, accessed February 16, 2014, www.underarmour.com.

22. Mondou, accessed April 25, 2015, www.mondou.com.

23. Starbucks Coffee Twitter feed, accessed June 16, 2014, http://twitter.com/starbucks; Starbucks Facebook page, accessed June 16, 2014, http://facebook.com/starbucks; Starbucks, accessed February 16, 2014, http://mystarbucksideas.com; Robert Gembarski, "How Starbucks Built an Engaging Brand on Social Media," *Branding Personality*, accessed February 16, 2014, www.brandingpersonality.com/how-starbucks-built-an-engagin-brand-on-social-media; "Happy Third Anniversary My Starbucks Idea," accessed February 16, 2014, http://blogs.starbucks.com/blogs/customer/archive/2011/03/18/happy-anniversary-my-starbucks-idea.aspx.

24. James Kanter, "Luxury Goods May Pick and Choose Venues for Sales," *New York Times*, April 20, 2010, www.nytimes.com/2010/04/21/technology/21goods.html?_r=0.

25. easyGroup, "About Us," accessed April 25, 2015, www.easy.com.

26. Samuel Axon, "How Small Businesses Are Using Social Media for Real Results," *Mashable*, March 22, 2010, http://mashable.com/2010/03/22/small-business-social-media-results.

27. Brooke Crothers, "iPad Sold Out at Best Buy Nationwide," *CNET News*, April 7, 2010, www.cnet.com/news/ipad-sold-out-at-best-buy-nationwide; Mary Ellen Lloyd, "Best Buy Shares Benefit from Apple iPad Launch," *Dow Jones Newswires*, April 5, 2010, www.advfn.com/nyse/StockNews.asp?stocknews=BBY&article=42253421; Michael Grothaus, "Best Buy to Carry iPad on April 3 at ASC-Stores Only," *Engadget*, March 26, 2010, www.engadget.com/2010/03/26/best-buy-to-carry-ipad-on-april-3-at-asc-stores-only.

28. Beyond the Rack, accessed April 25, 2015, www.beyondtherack.com.

29. "Nano-Based RFID Tags Could Replace Bar Codes," *Science Daily*, March 19, 2010, www.sciencedaily.com/releases/2010/03/100318113300.htm; "Verayo Launches Next Generation of Unclonable RFID Chips," *BusinessWire*, March 2, 2010, www.businesswire.com/news/home/20100302005719/en/Verayo-Launches-Generation-Unclonable-RFID-Chips#.Va1AgaRViko.

30. Gord Baldwin, "Too Many Trucks on the Road?" Statistics Canada, November 12, 2009, accessed April 20, 2015, www.statcan.gc.ca/pub/11-621-m/11-621-m2005028-eng.htm; American Trucking Associations, "Reports, Trends & Statistics," accessed March 12, 2014, www.trucking.org.

31. Association of American Railroads, "Class I Railroad Statistics," accessed March 12, 2014, www.aar.org.

Chapter 13

1. Wasserman & Partners Advertising Inc., interview with Alvin Wasserman, May 13, 2011; Wasserman & Partners Advertising Inc., accessed May 18, 2011, www.wasserman-partners.com; WorkSafeBC, accessed April 20, 2015, www.worksafebc.com; WorkSafeBC, "WorkSafeBC Statistics 2009 Report," accessed

May 19, 2011, www.worksafebc.com/publications/reports/statistics_reports/assets/pdf/stats2009.pdf.

2. "Monster.com Launches New Integrated Marketing Campaign to Help Job Seekers and Employers 'Get a Monster Advantage,'" press release, January 25, 2010, www.bloomberg.com/apps/news?pid=newsarchive&sid=asDGv_DSrOjA.

3. Alexandra Sifferlin "Why We're Spending $1 Trillion on Health Medications," *Time*, accessed February 21, 2014, http://healthland.time.com/2013/11/19/why-were-spending-1-trillion-on-health-medications; "Persuading the Prescribers: Pharmaceutical Industry Marketing and Its Influence on Physicians and Patients," *Pew Charitable Trusts*, accessed February 19, 2014, www.pewtrusts.org/en/research-and-analysis/fact-sheets/2013/11/11/persuading-the-prescribers-pharmaceutical-industry-marketing-and-its-influence-on-physicians-and-patients.

4. Michelle Krebs, "For Upcoming Chevrolet Cruze, GM Bets Safety Will (Up) Sell," *Edmunds Auto Observer*, April 19, 2010, www.edmunds.com/autoobserver-archive/2010/04/for-upcoming-chevrolet-cruze-gm-bets-safety-will-up-sell.html.

5. Edward Owen, "10 Incredibly Shameless Product Placements in Well-Loved TV Shows," *WhatCulture.com*, accessed February 20, 2014, http://whatculture.com/tv/10-incredibly-shameless-product-placements-well-loved-tv-shows.php; Anthony Crupi, "Ford, Coca-Cola Return for Season 13 of American Idol," *AdWeek*, accessed February 20, 2014, www.adweek.com/news/television/ford-coca-cola-return-season-13-american-idol-155001; Brad Tuttle, "Superman the Sellout? Man of Steel Has over 100 Promotional Partners," *Time*, accessed February 20, 2014, http://business.time.com/2013/06/04/superman-the-sell-out-man-of-steel-has-over-100-promotional-partners.

6. "Cathay Pacific Staff Surprise Travelers with Festive Flash Mob," *HR Grapevine*, accessed February 20, 2014, www.hrgrapevine.com/markets/hr/article/2013-12-12-cathay-pacific-staff-surprise-travellers-with-festive-flash-mob.

7. Lorraine Carter, "Guerrilla Marketing: Targeting One to Reach Many with Your Brand," *Persona Design*, accessed February 20, 2014, www.personadesign.ie/blog/guerrilla_marketing_targeting_one_to_reach_many_with_your_brand; Calum McGuigan, "Red Bull: Masterminds of New Age Marketing," *Creative Guerrilla Marketing*, accessed February 20, 2014, www.creativeguerrillamarketing.com/viral-marketing/red-bull-masterminds-of-new-age-marketing.

8. Jim Tierney, "Live from NEMOA: Why Your Brand Should Be Like Elvis," *Multichannel Merchant*, March 11, 2010, http://multichannelmerchant.com/news/live-from-nemoa-why-your-brand-should-be-like-elvis-11032010.

9. Bradley Johnson, "10 Things You Should Know About the Global Ad Market," *Advertising Age*, accessed February 22, 2014, http://adage.com/article/global-news/10-things-global-ad-market/245572.

10. Research and Management, "WSI Internet Marketing Trends Report, 2010 Executive Summary," accessed February 4, 2012, www.wsisme.com/files/Articles/TrendsReport10_Canada.pdf; Statistics Canada, "Advertising and Related Services—2012" accessed April 20, 2015, www.statcan.gc.ca/pub/63-257-x/63-257-x2014001-eng.htm.

11. "Kantar Media Reports U.S. Advertising Expenditures Increased 3.5% in the Second Quarter of 2013," *Kantar Media*, accessed February 21, 2014, www.kantarmedia.com; "Top 10 Advertisers January–September 2013," *Kantar Media*, accessed February 21, 2014, http://content.kantarmedia.com.

12. Avon company, "Corporate Responsibility," accessed June 14, 2010, http://responsibility.avoncompany.com.

13. Johnson, "10 Things You Should Know About the Global Ad Market."

14. James Bradshaw, "More Canadians Cutting the Cord? TV Subscriber Numbers Fall for First Time," *Globe and Mail*, May 15, 2014, accessed April 20, 2015, www.theglobeandmail.com/report-on-business/more-canadians-cutting-the-cord-tv-subscriber-numbers-fall-for-first-time/article18685129; CRTC, "How Many Canadians Subscribe to Cable TV or Satellite TV?" August 2006, accessed May 11, 2011, www.crtc.gc.ca/eng/publications/reports/radio/cmri.htm; Erick Schonfeld, "Estimate: 800,000 U.S. Households Abandoned Their TVs for the Web," *TechCrunch*, April 13, 2010, http://techcrunch.com/2010/04/13/800000-households-abandoned-tvs-web; John Latchem, "More U.S. Homes Have Game Consoles than Cable Boxes," *Home Media Magazine*, March 3, 2010, www.homemediamagazine.com; Bill Carter, "DVR, Once TV's Mortal Enemy, Helps Ratings," *New York Times*, November 1, 2009, www.nytimes.com/2009/11/02/business/media/02ratings.html?pagewanted=all&_r=0; Jim Edwards, "TV Is Dying and Here Are the Stats That Prove It," *Business Insider*, accessed February 23, 2014, www.businessinsider.com/cord-cutters-and-the-death-of-tv-2013-11.

15. Small Business Big Game, accessed February 20, 2014, www.smallbusinessbiggame.com.

16. Jane Sasseen, Kenny Olmstead, and Amy Mitchell, "The State of the News Media 2013," *State of the Media*, accessed February 23, 2014, www.stateofthemedia.org/2013; "Most Digital Ad Growth Now Goes Mobile, Desktop Growth Falters," *eMarketer*, accessed February 23, 2014, www.emarketer.com/Article/Most-Digital-Ad-Growth-Now-Goes-Mobile-Desktop-Growth-Falters/1010458; Jane Sasseen, Kenny Olmstead, and Amy Mitchell, "Digital: As Mobile Grows Rapidly, the Pressure on News Intensifies," *State of the Media*, accessed February 23, 2014, www.stateofthemedia.org/2013/digital-as-mobile-grows-rapidly-the-pressures-on-news-intensify.

17. Laura Stampler, "How Dove's 'Real Beauty Sketches' Became the Most Viral Video Ad of All Time," *BusinessInsider*, accessed February 20, 2014, www.businessinsider.com/how-doves-real-beauty-sketches-became-the-most-viral-ad-video-of-all-time-2013-5; "Dove's Sketches of Real Women Hit 30 Million Views, Tops Viral Chart," *Advertising Age*, accessed February 20, 2014, http://adage.com/article/the-viral-video-chart/dove-s-sketches-real-women-top-viral-chart/241055.

18. "Newspapers: By the Numbers," *StateoftheMedia*, accessed February 23, 2014, http://stateofthemedia.org; Amy Mitchell, Mark Jurkowitz, and Emily Guskin, "The Newspaper Industry Overall," *Pew Research Journalism Project*, accessed February 23, 2014, www.journalism.org/2013/08/07/the-newspaper-industry-overall.

19. Levi Shapiro, "State of the Digital Music Industry 2014: An Insider's View," *The Jerusalem Post*, accessed February 21, 2014, www.jpost.com/Blogs/Unleavened-Media/State-of-the-Digital-Music-Industry-2014-An-Insiders-View-364175; "Online Radio

Consumption Growing," *Marketing Charts*, accessed February 19, 2014, www.marketingcharts.com/online/online-radio-consumption-growing-36978; "Despite Small Audience, Internet Radio Ads Have a Special Appeal to Marketers," *eMarketer*, accessed February 19, 2014, www.emarketer.com.

20. Outdoor Advertising Association of America, "Out of Home Advertising Second Quarter Revenue up 5%," accessed February 19, 2014, www.oaaa.org/NewsEvents/News/PressReleases/tabid/327/id/3915/Default.aspx.

21. E.J. Schultz, "Forecast: Sponsorship Spending Will Slow in 2014," *Advertising Age*, accessed February 20, 2014, http://adage.com/article/news/forecast-sponsorship-spending-slow-2014/290961.

22. Jennifer Wood, "10 Best Selling Infomercial Products," *Mental Floss*, accessed February 21, 2014, http://mentalfloss.com/article/50246/10-best-selling-infomercial-products.

23. "Local Biz Spending on Promotion Easily Trumps Ad Dollars," *Marketing Charts*, accessed February 21, 2014, www.marketingcharts.com/uncategorized/local-biz-spending-on-promotions-easily-trumps-ad-dollars-28011.

24. Motorola, "Motorola Trade Up," accessed February 21, 2014, www.motorolatradeup.com; "Inmar Releases Coupon Trends for 2013," *Inmar*, accessed February 21, 2014, www.inmar.com/Pages/InmarArticle/Press-Release-01152014.aspx.

25. Herb Weisbaum, "Fewer Rebates Offered, but Deals Are Getting Better," *Today News*, accessed February 21, 2014, www.today.com/news/fewer-rebates-offered-deals-are-getting-better-1C6749597; Wirespring, accessed February 21, 2014, www.wirespring.com; Josh Constine, "Facebook Reveals 78% of Its Users Are Mobile as It Starts Sharing User Counts by Country," *TechCrunch*, accessed February 21, 2014, http://techcrunch.com/2013/08/13/facebook-mobile-user-count.

26. Wirespring, accessed February 21, 2014, www.wirespring.com; Josh Constine, "Facebook Reveals 78% of Its Users Are Mobile as It Starts Sharing User Counts by Country," *TechCrunch*, accessed February 21, 2014, http://techcrunch.com/2013/08/13/facebook-mobile-user-count.

27. Steve Crowe, "CES 2014 Attendance Tops 150,000," *CEPro*, accessed February 21, 2014, www.cepro.com/article/ces_2014_attendance_tops_150000; "U.S. Trade Shows Certified by U.S. Department of Commerce," *International Trade Administration*, accessed February 21, 2014, http://export.gov.

28. U.S. Department of Labor, Economic News Release, "Table 5. Occupations with the Most Job Growth, 2012 and Projected 2022," Bureau of Labor Statistics, accessed February 21, 2014, www.bls.gov/news.release/ecopro.t05.htm.

29. Mark Huber, "Life of a Salesman," *Air & Space Magazine*, February-March 2007, www.airspacemag.com/flight-today/life-of-a-salesman-15987478/?no-ist.

30. Matthew Hathaway, "Recession-Weary Consumers Find Haggling Can Cut Costs," *Chicago Tribune*, March 14, 2010, http://articles.chicagotribune.com/2010-03-14/business/sc-ym-0314-haggling-20100311-2_1_lower-prices-consumers-hagglers; Michael S. Rosenwald, "In Tough Economic Times, Shoppers Take Haggling to New Heights," *Washington Post*, January 31, 2010, www.washingtonpost.com/wp-dyn/content/article/2010/01/28/AR2010012803512.html.

31. Lee Howard, "Pfizer Ups Its Commitment to E-Marketing," *The Day*, January 21, 2010, www.theday.com/article/20100121/BIZ02/301219500.

32. Canadian Radio-television and Telecommunications Commission, "Canadian Radio-television and Telecommunications Commission Unsolicited Telecommunication Rules," accessed May 21, 2012, www.crtc.gc.ca/eng/trules-reglest.htm.

33. Bruce Wilson, "Generating B2B Sales Leads Using Social Media," *Many Doors Marketing*, February 24, 2010, http://manydoors.net.

34. Nat Robinson, "SlideRocket Presentation Tip—4 Ways For Using MultiMedia Strategically," *SlideRocket*, April 1, 2010, www.sliderocket.com/blog/2010/04/sliderocket-presentation-tip-4-ways-for-using-multimedia-strategically.

35. David Parker Brown, "Spirit Airlines Installs 'Pre-Reclined' Seats on New Airbus A320's," *Airline Reporter*, April 21, 2010, www.airlinereporter.com/2010/04/spirit-airlines-installs-pre-reclined-seats-on-new-airbus-a320s.

36. Jennifer Campbell, "Social Notes," *Montreal Gazette*, May 14, 2011, accessed May 15, 2011, www.montrealgazette.com/sports/Social+Notes/4783511/story.html#ixzz1MRJHiWPy.

37. Elaine Wong, "Dove Super Bowl Spot Scores Initial Points with Men," *Adweek*, February 9, 2010, www.adweek.com/news/advertising-branding/dove-super-bowl-spot-scores-initial-points-men-107033; Jack Neff and Rupal Parekh, "Dove Takes Its New Men's Line to the Super Bowl," *Advertising Age*, January 5, 2010, http://adage.com/article/special-report-super-bowl-2010/dove-takes-men-s-line-super-bowl/141312.

38. Justin Scheck, "Windows 7 Fails to Boost Profits of PC Makers," *Wall Street Journal*, January 31, 2010, www.wsj.com/articles/SB10001424052748704343104575034233214601248.

39. Sean Poulter, "The High Price of Fashion: Sales of Luxury It Bags Soar by 60%," *Mail Online*, March 12, 2010, www.dailymail.co.uk/femail/article-1257208/The-high-price-fashion-Sales-luxury-It-bags-soar-60.html.

40. Meg Sullivan, "For California Vintners, It's Not Easy Being Green," *UCLA Newsroom*, March 4, 2010, http://newsroom.ucla.edu/releases/for-california-vintners-it-isn-154669.

Part 4 Case Study Beau's All Natural Brewing Company: Building Brand Awareness

Based on interviews with Steve Beauchesne at Beau's All Natural Brewery Company offices, Vankleek Hill, Ontario, on March 30, 2015; Beau's All Natural Brewery Company, accessed April 3, 2015, www.beaus.ca; Beau's Beer Blog, "How to Start a Brewery in 1 Million Easy Steps," January 9, 2007, accessed April 3, 2015, http://beausbeer.blogspot.ca/2007/01/brewery-measurements.html; Mojo Junction, "Beau's All Natural Brewing: Crafting Beer. Inspiring Community," accessed April 12, 2015, http://mojojunction.com/articles/beaus; Mirella Amato, "Who Really Came First . . ." Beerology.ca, Fall 2009, accessed February 1, 2015, http://beerology.ca/articles/who-really-came-first . . .; Howe Sound Brewing, accessed February 1, 2015, www.howesound.com/aboutus/history.aspx.

Chapter 14

1. Stock-Trak, "Academic Solutions," accessed April 23, 2015, www.stocktrak.com/public/products/Stock-Trak.aspx; Stock-Trak, "Stock-Trak Group Partners with Scottrade to Provide Stock and Option Simulation Training Tools," press release, October 29, 2008, accessed May 23, 2012, www.stocktrak.com/pdf/Scottrade_102908.pdf.

2. Ernest Von Simpson, "The New Role of the CIO," *Bloomberg Businessweek*, May 22, 2013, accessed February 24, 2014, www.bloomberg.com/bw/articles/2013-05-22/the-new-role-of-the-cio; David Moschella, Doug Neal, John Taylor, and Piet Opperman, "Consumerization of Information Technology," *Leading Edge Forum*, November 18, 2004, accessed February 24, 2014, https://leadingedgeforum.com/publication/the-consumerization-of-information-technology-1701.

3. Rhea Wessel, "Airbus Signs Contract for High-Memory RFID Tags," *RFID Journal*, January 19, 2010, www.rfidjournal.com/articles/view?7323.

4. TradeInsight, accessed April 24, 2015, www.tradeinsight.com.

5. IEEE Computer Society, "History of Computing Timeline," www.computer.org/cms/Computer.org/Publications/timeline.pdf; Computer History Museum, accessed May 24, 2010, www.computerhistory.org; Roy Schestowitz, "Computer History Development Timeline: Microsoft Perspective," *Techrights*, February 4, 2010, http://techrights.org/2010/02/04/microsoft-perspective.

6. Stephen Vaughan-Nichols, "A Third of American Adults Now Own Tablet Computers," *ZDNet*, June 16, 2013, accessed February 25, 2014, www.zdnet.com/article/a-third-of-american-adults-now-own-tablet-computers.

7. Nicole Kobie, "Tablet Sales to Overtake PCs This Quarter," *PC Pro*, September 12, 2013, accessed February 21, 2014, www.alphr.com/news/384172/tablet-sales-to-overtake-pcs-this-quarter.

8. "'Come Together'—Intranets Are Re-emerging as a Way to Connect Dislocated Employees," *HR Monthly*, April 12, 2010, www.intranetdashboard.com/blog/2010/latest-news/lesson-learned-jetstar-mr-monthly.

9. Elliott Drucker, "Tech Insights—The Future of Voice," *Wireless Week*, March 7, 2010, www.wirelessweek.com/articles/2010/03/tech-insights-future-voice; "Future of VoIP in 2010, a New Beginning?" *Cheapest VoIP Calls.net*, January 2010, http://cheapestvoipcalls.net.

10. Diane Bartz, "Apple Users Lose Some Immunity to Cybercrime," *Reuters*, April 20, 2010, www.reuters.com/article/2010/04/20/us-cybersecurity-symantec-idUSTRE63J0K420100420; Jeremy Kirk, "E-Crime Reporting Format Draws Closer to a Standard," *CIO*, March 23, 2010, www.cio.com/article/2419561/security0/e-crime-reporting-format-draws-closer-to-a-standard.html; Sue Marquette Poremba, "Report: Dangers of Cyber Crime on the Rise," *IT Business Edge*, January 27, 2010, www.itbusinessedge.com/cm/blogs/poremba/report-dangers-of-cyber-crime-on-the-rise/?cs=39029.

11. Gillian Mahoney, "Hackers Steal Credit Card Data from Neiman Marcus Customers," *ABC News*, January 11, 2014, accessed February 25, 2014, http://abcnews.go.com/Business/hackers-steal-credit-card-data-neiman-marcus-customers/story?id=21499430.

12. Abby Simmons, "Lawmakers Take on Smart Phone Theft," *Star Tribune*, January 5, 2014, accessed February 26, 2014, http://www.startribune.com/lawmakers-take-on-smartphone-theft/238736851.

13. Gautum Prabhu, "Protect Your iPhone Against Theft with Activation Lock in iOS 7," iPhone Hacks, September 27, 2013, accessed February 26, 2014, www.iphonehacks.com/2013/09/ios-7-protect-iphone-against-theft-with-activation-lock.html.

14. Dan Steiner, "Staggering Cost of Malware Is Now over $100 Billion a Year," Yahoo Small Business, accessed February 26, 2014, https://smallbusiness.yahoo.com/advisor/staggering-cost-malware-now-over-100-billion-023014986.html.

15. Elinor Mills, "Malware Delivered by Yahoo, Fox, Google Ads," *CNET News*, March 22, 2010, www.cnet.com/news/malware-delivered-by-yahoo-fox-google-ads; Joseph R. Perone, "Expect New, Evolving Computer Viruses in 2010," *Star-Ledger*, December 31, 2009, www.nj.com/business/index.ssf/2009/12/expect_new_evolving_computer_v.html.

16. Tony Bradley, "McAfee Debacle Shows Why Malware Defense Must Evolve," *PCWorld*, April 27, 2010, www.pcworld.com/article/195093/mcafee_debacle_shows_why_malware_defense_must_evolve.html.

17. Associated Press, "Mastermind of World's Worst Computer Virus Still at Large," *Fox News*, March 4, 2010, www.foxnews.com/tech/2010/03/04/mastermind-worlds-worst-virus-large/.

18. "New Security Threat Against 'Smart Phone' Users, Researchers Show," *Science Daily*, February 22, 2010, www.sciencedaily.com/releases/2010/02/100222121624.htm.

19. Joshua Levinson, "Watchout—There's a New Android Trojan Horse About," Cult of Android, June 10, 2013, accessed February 26, 2014, www.cultofandroid.com/29156/watch-out-theres-a-new-android-trojan-horse-in-the-wild.

20. "Data Loss Statistics," *Boston Computing Network*, accessed May 24, 2010, www.bostoncomputing.net/consultation/databackup/statistics.

21. Bureau of Labor Statistics, "Work-at-Home Patterns by Occupation," *Issues in Labor Statistics*, March 2009, www.bls.gov/opub/btn/archive/work-at-home-patterns-by-occupation-pdf.pdf.

22. Infosys, accessed February 27, 2014, www.infosys.com.

Part 5: Case Study: Beau's All Natural Brewing Company: Using Technology to Manage Communications and Information

Based on interviews with Steve Beauchesne at Beau's All Natural Brewery Company offices, Vankleek Hill, Ontario, on March 30, 2015; Beau's All Natural Brewery Company, accessed April 3, 2015, www.beaus.ca; Beau's Beer Blog, "How to Start a Brewery in 1 Million Easy Steps," January 9, 2007, accessed April 3, 2015, http://beausbeer.blogspot.ca/2007/01/brewery-measurements.html; Mojo Junction, "Beau's All Natural Brewing: Crafting Beer. Inspiring Community," accessed April 12, 2015, http://mojojunction.com/articles/beaus.

Part 5: Launching Your Information Technology Career

1. U.S. Department of Labor, "Tomorrow's Jobs," *Occupational Outlook Handbook, 2010–2011*, Bureau of Labor Statistics, accessed June 28, 2010, www.bls.gov.

Chapter 15

1. "SEC Charges Four More Former Nortel Execs with Fraud," *CBC News*, September 12, 2007, accessed June 2, 2011, www.cbc.ca/news/business/story/2007/09/12/sec-nortel.html; "Toronto's Longest-Running Musical Returns," Broadway World, accessed June 2, 2011, http://toronto.broadwayworld.com/article/TORONTOS_LONGESTRUNNING_MUSICAL_RETURNS_20061017; "Livent Co-founders Drabinsky, Gottlieb Convicted of Fraud and Forgery," *CBC News*, March 25, 2009, accessed June 2, 2011, www.cbc.ca/news/business/story/2009/03/25/livent-decision-fraud.html; Dave Itzkoff, "Convicted Producers Suggest Lecture Tour Instead of Prison," *Arts Beat* (*New York Times* blog), July 8, 2009, accessed June 2, 2011, http://artsbeat.blogs.nytimes.com/2009/07/08/convicted-producers-suggest-lecture-tour-instead-of-prison/; Allison Jones, "Drabinsky, Gottlieb, Found Guilty of Livent Fraud, Take Case to Appeal Court," *City News*, April 30, 2011, accessed June 2, 2011, http://www.citynews.ca/2011/04/30/drabinsky-gottlieb-found-guilty-of-livent-fraud-take-case-to-appeal-court/; Anders Ross, "22 Largest Bankruptcies in World History," Instant Shift, February 3, 2010, accessed June 2, 2011, www.instantshift.com/2010/02/03/22-largest-bankruptcies-in-world-history/; Ronald Fink, "Beyond Enron: The Fate of Andrew Fastow and Company Casts a Harsh Light on Off-Balance-Sheet Financing," *CFO Magazine*, February 1, 2002, accessed June 2, 2011, www.cfo.com/article.cfm/3003186/c_3036065; "How to Hide $3.8 Billion in Expenses," *Bloomberg Business*, July 7, 2002, accessed June 2, 2011, www.businessweek.com/magazine/content/02_27/b3790022.htm.

2. Statistics Canada, "2011 National Household Survey: Data Tables," accessed August 13, 2014, www12.statcan.gc.ca/nhs-enm/2011/dp-pd/dt-td/Rp-eng.cfm?LANG=E&APATH=3&DETAIL=0&DIM=0&FL=A&FREE=0&GC=0&GID=0&GK=0&GRP=0&PID=105897&PRID=0&PTYPE=105277&S=0&SHOWALL=1&SUB=0&Temporal=2013&THEME=96&VID=0&VNAMEE=&VNAMEF.

3. Robert Colapinto, "Yes, We'll Show You the Money," *CPA Magazine*, January 1, 2014, accessed August 13, 2014, http://cpacanada.ca/en/CPA-magazine/Articles/yes-well-show-you-the-money.

4. Imran Ahmed, "CEO Talk: Brian Hill, Chief Executive Officer, Aritzia," Business of Fashion, August 25, 2009, accessed June 3, 2011, www.businessoffashion.com/2009/08/ceo-talk-brian-hill-chief-executive-officer-aritzia.html#more-5968.

5. Bottom Line News, *Canada's Accounting Top 30*, accessed August 13, 2014, www.thebottomlinenews.ca/documents/Canadas_Accounting_Top_30.pdf.

6. "IFRS FAQs," IFRS.com, accessed May 27, 2011, www.ifrs.com/ifrs_faqs.html#q3.

7. Johnson & Johnson, *Annual Report 2013*, accessed August 13, 2014, http://files.shareholder.com/downloads/JNJ/3357129072x0x733042/DDD2ABD5-2CC6-41D2-8ACB-EC2A967727E4/ar2013_JNJ.pdf.

8. "Sage 300 ERP: Extending Enterprise Suite—Industry Examples," Business Solutions Inc., accessed May 27, 2011, www.caplus.com/articles.aspx?aid=150.

9. Quicken, accessed February 20, 2012, http://quicken.intuit.ca/personal-finance-software/index.jsp.

10. Air Canada, *Annual Report 2013*, accessed August 13, 2014, www.aircanada.com/en/about/investor/documents/2013_ar.pdf.

11. Thomas Black, "Weak Dollar Is 'Welcome Change' for McDonald's, PPG Profits," Bloomberg.com, October 29, 2009.

Chapter 16

1. *CTV News*, "U.S.-Style Meltdown Won't Happen Here: Harper," September 24, 2008, accessed May 25, 2012, www.ctv.ca/CTVNews/TopStories/20080924/mortgage_meltdown_080924; Keith B. Richburg, "Worldwide Financial Crisis Largely Bypasses Canada," *Washington Post*, October 16, 2008, accessed July 14, 2011, www.washingtonpost.com/wp-dyn/content/article/2008/10/15/AR2008101503321.html; Anthony Haddad, "Ever-Growing Yields from Post-Crisis Winners," Street Authority, October 13, 2009, accessed July 14, 2011, www.streetauthority.com/a/ever-growing-yields-post-crisis-winners-909; Anup Shah, "Global Financial Crisis," Global Issues, December 11, 2010, accessed July 14, 2011, www.globalissues.org/article/768/global-financial-crisis.

2. Gaurav Raghuvanshi, Jason Ng, and P.R. Venkat, "Government Fund with Majority Malaysia Airlines Stake Considers Taking It

Private—Sources," *Wall Street Journal*, July 20, 2014, www.wsj.com/articles/government-fund-with-major-stake-in-malaysia-airlines-considers-taking-company-private-1405869189#.

3. Yahoo Finance, accessed August 13, 2014, https://ca.finance.yahoo.com.

4. Catarina Saraiva, William Selway, and Brendan A. McGrail, "California Markets Second-Biggest Taxable Bond Sale of 2010," Bloomberg.com, March 25, 2010, www.bloomberg.com; Katrina Nicholas, "Russian Nanotechnology Corporation Considers $1.7 Billion Bond Sale," *Nanowerk*, March 11, 2010, www.nanowerk.com.

5. "Strong Global IPO Market in Q1 Sets Tone for 2010," Ernst & Young, news release, April 8, 2010, www.ey.com; Eric Fox, "The Worst IPOs of 2009," *Investopedia*, December 16, 2009.

6. "NYSE Euronext Announces First Quarter 2010 Financial Results," news release, May 4, 2010, www.nyse.com; "New York Stock Exchange," *Money-Zine*, accessed June 21, 2010, www.money-zine.com.

7. Savvis, "Financial Services: Toronto Stock Exchange Connectivity," accessed July 6, 2011, www.savvis.com/en-US/Info_Center/Documents/FIN-US-TorontoStockExchangeConnectivity.pdf.

8. Office of the Superintendent of Financial Institutions, "Federally Regulated Financial Institutions," accessed August 13, 2014, www.osfi-bsif.gc.ca/Eng/wt-ow/Pages/wwr-er.aspx?sc=1&gc=1#WWRLink11; Relbanks, "Top Banks in Canada," accessed August 13, 2014, www.relbanks.com/rankings/top-banks-in-canada.

9. Federal Deposit Insurance Corporation, "Statistics on Depository Institutions Report," accessed June 21, 2010, www2.fdic.gov.

10. Allan Crawford, "The Residential Mortgage Market in Canada: A Primer," Bank of Canada, accessed August 18, 2014, www.bankofcanada.ca/wp-content/uploads/2013/12/fsr-december13-crawford.pdf; Canadian Bankers Association, "Bank Lending to Businesses," accessed August 21, 2014, www.cba.ca/en/media-room/50-backgrounders-on-banking-issues/128-business-credit-availability.

11. Interac, "Research and Statistics: Interac Debit Transactions," accessed April 22, 2015, www.interac.ca/en/total-transactions.

12. Department of Finance Canada, "Canada's Banks," accessed July 6, 2011, www.fin.gc.ca/toc/2002/bank_eng.asp.

13. Credit Union Central of Canada, "Facts & Figures," accessed August 14, 2014, www.cucentral.ca/SitePages/Publications/FactsAndFigures.aspx.

14. Credit Union Central of Canada, accessed June 14, 2011, www.cucentral.com/ Q1Results14JUN11.

15. Dave Cooper, "Credit Union Connect Launches across Alberta," *Edmonton Journal*, May 2, 2011, accessed July 6, 2011, www.edmontonjournal.com/business/Credit+Unions+Connect+launches+across+Alberta/4710413/story.html?cid=megadrop_story.

16. Canadian Life and Health Insurance Association, "About the Canadian Life and Health Insurance Industry," accessed August 14, 2014, www.clhia.ca/domino/html/clhia/clhia_lp4w_lnd_webstation.nsf/page/CBCBAF89BB17D8488525793B0063A1C9.

17. CPP Investment Board, accessed August 14, 2014, www.cppib.com/en/home.html.

18. The Investment Funds Institute of Canada, "Our Industry," accessed August 14, 2014, www.ific.ca/en/articles/who-we-are-our-industry/, LuAnn LaSalle, "Two-thirds Canada Contributed to RRSPs with 49% Choosing Mutual Funds, 12% ETFs," *Financial Post*, accessed August 8, 2014, http://business.financialpost.com/personal-finance/retirement/rrsp/two-thirds-canada-contributed-to-rrsps-with-49-choosing-mutual-funds-12-etfs.

19. Investment Company Institute, "Money Market Fund Assets: August 14, 2014," accessed August 14, 2014, www.ici.org/research/stats/mmf.

20. Bank of Canada, "Regulation of the Canadian Financial System," accessed May 18, 2012, www.bankofcanada.ca/wp-content/uploads/2010/11/regulation_canadian_financial.pdf.

21. Investment Industry Regulator Organization of Canada, accessed July 28, 2011, www.iiroc.ca/English/Pages/home.aspx.

22. Accuity, "Bank Rankings—Top Banks in the World," accessed August 14, 2014, www.accuity.com/useful-links/bank-rankings.

23. Emily Mathieu, "No-Interest MasterCard Aims at Devout Muslims," *Toronto Star*, April 12, 2010, accessed July 12, 2011, www.thestar.com/business/article/794124--operating-financies-in-good-faith?bn=1; Toronto Financial Services Alliance, "Islamic Financial Working Group," accessed August 21, 2014, www.tfsa.ca/resources/pdf/TFSA_IFWG_Prelim_Report_May14_2010_final_2.pdf.

Chapter 17

1. Ratiopharm GmbH, accessed June 24, 2010, www1.ratiopharm.com; Pfizer Inc., accessed June 24, 2010, www.pfizer.com; Teva Pharmaceutical Industries Ltd., accessed June 24, 2010, www.tevapharm.com; Actavis, accessed June 24, 2010, www.actavis.com; Yoram Gabison, "Teva Snubs Israelis: Ratiopharm Purchase Being Financed Abroad," *Haaretz*, May 14, 2010, www.haaretz.com; Robert Daniel and Polya Lesova, "Teva to Acquire Ratiopharm in Deal Valued Near $5 Billion," *MarketWatch*, March 18, 2010, www.marketwatch.com; Frank Siebelt, Ludwig Burger, and Lewis Krauskopf, "Pfizer to Make Bid for Ratiopharm: Source," Reuters, March 16, 2010, www.reuters.com; Andrew Ross Sorkin, ed., "Bidding War Pits Pfizer against Teva," *New York Times DealBook*, March 9, 2010, http://dealbook.blogs.nytimes.com; Frank Siebelt, "Pfizer Woos Ratiopharm with Ramp-Up Pledge—Sources," Reuters, March 7, 2010, www.reuters.com; Aaron Kirchfeld, "Pfizer Chief Said to Make Case for Ratiopharm Deal (Update 2)," Bloomberg.com, March 5, 2010, www.bloomberg.com; Cyrus Sanati, "Pfizer Said to Set Sights on German Drug Maker," *New York Times DealBook*, March 2, 2010, http://dealbook.blogs.nytimes.com; Ludwig Burger, "Pfizer, Teva Set to Tussle for Ratiopharm: Report," Reuters, January 18, 2010, www.reuters.com; Apotex Inc., "About Apotex," accessed August 1, 2011, www.apotex.com/global/about/default.asp, Industry Canada, "Canadian Pharmaceutical Industry Profile," accessed August 14, 2014, www.ic.gc.ca/eic/site/lsg-pdsv.nsf/eng/h_hn01703.html.

2. Equilar, "2010 CEO Pay Analysis & Strategies for Mid-Caps," May 2010, www.equilar.com.

3. Josh Funk, "Warren Buffet Still Gets $100K Salary at Berkshire Hathaway, but Security Costs Grow to $345K," *Business News*, March 10, 2010, http://blog.taragana.com.

4. Aude Lagorce, "Emirates in Record Airbus A380 Order," *MarketWatch*, June 8, 2010, www.marketwatch.com; Andrea Rothman, "Airbus A380 Order Dearth Risks Double-Decker-Dud Fate (Update 1)," *Bloomberg Businessweek*, May 13, 2010, www.businessweek.com; David Kaminski-Morrow, "A380 to Remain a Financial Burden for Years: Airbus Chief," *Flightglobal*, January 12, 2010, www.flightglobal.com.

5. Sarah Johnson, "CFO: Stop Treating Your Inventories Like Fine Wine," CFO.com, September 10, 2009, http://cfo.com.

6. Lauren Coleman-Lochner, "Target Sets Canada for First Expansion Outside U.S.," *Businessweek*, January 13, 2011, accessed August 8, 2011, www.businessweek.com/news/2011-01-13/target-sets-canada-for-first-expansion-outside-u-s-.html; Target, press release, accessed August 15, 2014, http://pressroom.target.ca/news/target-confirms-store-locations-236413.

7. Stefania Moretti, "Walmart Canada to Open 40 Supercenters," *CNews*, accessed August 2, 2011, http://cnews.canoe.ca/CNEWS/Canada/2011/01/26/17039171.html; *CBC News*, "Wal-Mart Planning $500M Expansion in Canada," accessed August 15, 2014, www.cbc.ca/news/business/wal-mart-planning-500m-expansion-in-canada-1.2522424.

8. Lochner, "Target Sets Canada for First Expansion Outside U.S."; Bloomberg, "Target Replaces Canada President after Troubled Expansion," accessed August 15, 2014, www.bloomberg.com/news/2014-05-20/target-replaces-canadian-president-after-troubled-expansion.html; Marina Straus, "How Target Botched a $7-Billion Rollout," *Globe and Mail*, January 15, 2015, accessed August 20, 2015, www.theglobeandmail.com/report-on-business/international-business/us-business/target-killing-canadian-operations/article22458161.

9. Air Canada, *Annual Report 2013*, accessed August 13, 2014, www.aircanada.com/en/about/investor/documents/2013_ar.pdf.

10. Historical Exchange Rates, OANDA website, accessed September 21, 2015, www.oanda.com/currency/historical-rates.

11. Yahoo Finance, accessed August 28, 2014, https://finance.yahoo.com.

12. Barchart, "Commercial Paper Interest Rates," accessed August 15, 2014, www.barchart.com/economy/commercialpaper.php.

13. "BP Suspends Dividend after Deepwater Horizon Spill," *MarketWatch*, June 16, 2010, www.marketwatch.com; "The Case for (and against) BP Cutting Its Dividend," *U.S. News & World Report*, June 14, 2010, www.usnews.com; Jeff Plungis and Christopher Condon, "U.S. Lawmakers Say BP Should Suspend Dividends, Ads (Update 2)," *Bloomberg Businessweek*, June 9, 2010, www.businessweek.com; Whitney Kisling, "Dividend Slump Ending as Record Profits Lift Payouts for S&P 500," *China Post*, April 29, 2010, www.chinapost.com.tw.

14. Canadian Tire, *2013 Annual Report*, accessed August 15, 2014, http://corp.canadiantire.ca/EN/Investors/Documents/2013%20Annual%20Report.pdf.

15. Federal Reserve Board, "Commercial Paper Outstanding," Federal Reserve Release, May 12, 2010, http://federalreserve.gov.

16. Jonathan Ratner, "Bondholders Find Safety in Canada," *Financial Post*, October 10, 2012, accessed August 15, 2014, http://business.financialpost.com/2012/10/10/bondholders-find-safety-in-canada-2/.

17. Board of Governors of the Federal Reserve System, "Federal Reserve Statistical Release, Z.1, Flow of Funds Accounts of the United States," March 12, 2009, www.federalreserve.gov.

18. Covington, accessed August 3, 2011, www.covingtonfunds.com.

19. *CBC News*, "Onex Buys Boeing Parts Plant for $1.5 Billion," February 22, 2005, accessed August 2, 2011, www.cbc.ca/news/business/story/2005/02/22/onex-050222.html.

20. Andy Hoffman and Tara Perkins, "China's Sovereign Wealth Fund Sets up Shop in Toronto," *Globe and Mail*, January 17, 2011, accessed August 3, 2011, www.theglobeandmail.com/report-on-business/chinas-sovereign-wealth-fund-sets-up-shop-in-toronto/article1867917/; Jeremy van Loon and Jim Polson, "Albert to Win Chinese Oil-Sands Investment, Minister Says." *Bloomberg*, May 17, 2011, accessed August 3, 2011, www.bloomberg.com/news/2011-05-17/alberta-to-win-chinese-oil-sands-investment-minister-says-1-.html.

21. Alastair Sharp, "Canadian Hedge Funds' Growth Dreams Face Tough Reality," *Globe and Mail*, January 31, 2013, accessed August 18, 2014, www.theglobeandmail.com/globe-investor/canadian-hedge-funds-growth-dreams-face-tough-reality/article8058888/.

22. Hedge Fund Association, "About Us," accessed August 18, 2014, http://thehfa.org/aboutus.

23. Cecilia Kang, "AT&T, DirecTV Announce $49 Billion Merger," *Washington Post*, May 18, 2014, accessed August 18, 2014, www.washingtonpost.com/business/technology/atandt-directv-announce-48-billion-merger/2014/05/18/62ffc980-dec1-11e3-810f-764fe508b82d_story.html; Alex Sherman and Scott Moritz, "AT&T Joins U.S. TV Revamp with $48.5 Billion DirecTV Deal," Bloomberg, accessed August 21, 2014, www.bloomberg.com/news/2014-05-18/at-t-agrees-to-buy-directv-for-48-5-billion-to-add-video-users.html.

24. Emre Peker, "Cerberus Taps Banks for LBO as Leveraged Loan Rally Spurs M&As," *Bloomberg Businessweek*, May 14, 2010, www.businessweek.com; David Russell, "LBOs Loom as Credit Market Recovers," *NASDAQ*, March 19, 2010, www.nasdaq.com.

25. Oilweek, accessed August 5, 2011, www.oilweek.com/news.asp?ID=34515; "Canadian Company Sells Natural Gas Assets in T&T," Caribbean 360, March 4, 2010, accessed August 5, 2011, www.caribbean360.com/business/canadian_company_sells_natural_gas_assets_in_t_t.rss#axzz1Tzqz6XRf.

Launching Your Career

1. Human Resources and Skills Development Canada, "Looking Ahead: A 10-Year Outlook for the Canadian Labour Market" (2006–2015), accessed May 20, 2012, www.hrsdc.gc.ca/eng/publications_resources/research/categories/labour_market_e/sp_615_10_06/supply.shtml.

2. Payscale, "Bachelor's Degree, Finance Average Salary," accessed August 28, 2014, www.payscale.com/research/CA/Degree=Bachelor's_Degree,_Finance/Salary.

3. U.S. Department of Labor, "Financial Managers," *Occupational Outlook Handbook 2010–2014*, Bureau of Labor Statistics, accessed July 8, 2010, www.bls.gov.

Appendix B

1. Arik Hesseldahl, "Apple's Smartphone Battle Plan," *Bloomberg Business*, March 2, 2010, www.bloomberg.com/bw/technology/content/mar2010/tc2010032_755256.htm; Philip Elmer-DeWitt, "Apple Talks Tough to Handset Makers," *Fortune*, March 9, 2010, http://fortune.com/2010/03/09/apple-talks-tough-to-handset-makers/; "Will Apple's Patents Banish HTC Phones?" *TechHive*, March 3, 2010, www.techhive.com/article/190746/will_apples_patents_banish_htc_phones.html; Marguerite Reardon, "Apple Sues HTC Over iPhone Patents," *CNET News*, March 2, 2010, www.cnet.com/news/apple-sues-htc-over-iphone-patents/; Brad Stone, "Apple Sues Nexus One Maker HTC," *New York Times*, March 2, 2010, www.nytimes.com/2010/03/03/technology/03patent.html?_r=0; Ted Livingston, "A Sad Day in Waterloo," Kik Interactive Blog, December 1, 2010, accessed March 30, 2011, www.kik.com/blog/2010/12/a-sad-day-inwaterloo.

2. "Frivolous Lawsuits," *NFIB*, accessed May 7, 2010, www.nfib.com.

3. Peter J. Brown, "US Lawsuit May Flood China Drywalls," *Asia Times*, April 10, 2010, www.atimes.com/atimes/Global_Economy/LD10Dj01.html.

4. Mark Sweney, "Google Wins Louis Vuitton Trademark Case," *The Guardian*, March 23, 2010, www.theguardian.com/media/2010/mar/23/google-louis-vuitton-search-ads.

5. B. Smith, "Google Digital Library Faces Major Public Outcry at NYC Hearing," *Daily News*, February 18, 2010, www.nydailynews.com/news/money/google-digital-library-faces-major-public-outcry-nyc-hearing-article-1.197867.

Appendix C

1. Joey Garrison, "Private Flood Damage Estimate Climbs to $1.9 Billion," *The City Paper*, May 19, 2010, http://nashvillecitypaper.com/content/city-news/private-flood-damage-estimate-climbs-19-billion; Tom Weir, "In Nashville, a Way of Life Washed Away," *USA Today*, May 7, 2010, http://usatoday30.usatoday.com/weather/floods/2010-05-06-nashville-flood_N.htm; Melinda Hudgins, "Few Take Advantage of Flood Insurance," *DNJ.com*, May 9, 2010, www.dnj.com; "Stories of Tragedy, Survival Surface as Tennessee Flood Waters Recede," CNN.com, May 5, 2010, www.cnn.com/2010/US/weather/05/05/tennessee.flooding; Emily Holbrook, "Few in Tennessee Covered by Flood Insurance," *Risk Management Monitor*, May 6, 2010, www.riskmanagementmonitor.com/few-in-tennessee-covered-by-flood-insurance; Geert de Lombaerde, "Less Than 4,000 Davidson Homes Insured against Floods," *The City Paper*, May 4, 2010, http://nashvillecitypaper.com/content/2010-flood/less-4000-davidson-homes-insured-against-floods.

2. *ACLI Life Insurers Fact Book 2009*, accessed May 9, 2010, www.acli.com/Tools/Industry%20Facts/Life%20Insurers%20Fact%20Book/Pages/GR09-%20215.aspx.

3. "Lightning Sparks Concern for Insurance Industry; Homeowners Claims Rise Sharply over Last Five Years," Insurance Information Institute, March 31, 2010, www.iii.org/press-release/lightning-sparks-concern-for-insurance-industry-homeowners-claims-rise-sharply-over-last-five-years-033110.

4. Walmart, "Insurance Requirements," accessed May 9, 2010, http://walmartstores.com.

Appendix D

1. Patrick Lohmann, "Campus Debtors," *Alibi*, May 6–12, 2010, http://alibi.com/news/32025/Campus-Debtors.html; David Ellis, "Credit Card Relief Is Here, But Watch Out for New Traps," *CNN Money.com*, February 22, 2010, http://money.cnn.com/2010/02/17/news/companies/credit_card_rules; Jennifer Liberto, "Under 21? Getting a Credit Card Just Got Tougher," CNN Money.com, February 22, 2010, http://money.cnn.com/2010/02/19/news/economy/student_credit_cards; George Gombossy, "New Credit Card Rules Go into Effect Monday," *Connecticut Watchdog*, February 20, 2010, http://ctwatchdog.com; David K. Randall, "New Credit Card Choices for College Students," *Forbes*, February 4, 2010, www.forbes.com/2010/02/04/college-credit-cards-personal-finance-credit-card-rules.html.

2. "Employee Tenure, 2008, and Retiree Health Benefit Trends among the Medicare-Eligible Population," *Employee Benefit Research Institute*, 31, no. 1 (January 2010), www.ebri.org/publications/notes/index.cfm?fa=notesDisp&content_id=4447.

Appendix E

1. Next, accessed May 9, 2010, http://nextrestaurant.com; Pete Wells, "In Chicago, the Chef Grant Achatz Is Selling Tickets to His New Restaurant," *New York Times*, May 4, 2010, www.nytimes.com/2010/05/05/dining/05achatz.html; "'US' Next Hot Restaurant Will Require Prepaid Tickets," *AOL News*, May 5, 2010, www.aolnews.com; Chuck Sudo, "Achatz's Next Two Projects: Time Travel, Cocktails," *Chicagoist*, May 4, 2010, http://chicagoist.com/2010/05/04/achatzs_next_two_projects_cocktails.php; Paul Frumkin, "Grant Achatz to Open New Restaurant and Bar," *Nation's Restaurant News*, May 4, 2010, http://nrn.com/archive/grant-achatz-open-new-restaurant-and-bar-0.

NAME INDEX

A

A Bis Gourmet, 377
Abercrombie & Fitch, 361
Aboriginal Pipeline Group, 489
About.com, 163
Accenture, 212, 214
Actavis, 471
Activision Blizzard Inc., 198
Adidas, 339*t*
ADP, 35
Advertising Age, 361
African Barrick Gold, 7
Agency3, 161
Agilent Technologies, 404
Agropur, 338
AHA, 520
AIG, 460
Airbnb, 153, 154
Air Canada, 37–38, 70, 140, 278, 437, 478
Airbus, 393, 474, 478
Alberta Health Services, 417
Alberta Securities Commission, 53
Alberta Society for the Prevention of Cruelty to Animals, 198, 296
Aliant, 489
Alibaba Group, 17
Allan Candy Company, 275
Amazon, 15, 17, 127, 182, 315, 326, 338, 344, 373, 395
Amazon.ca, 340, 361
American Express, 330, 361
American Federation of Labour and Congress of Industrial Organizations (AFL–CIO), 226
American Management Association, 403
American Marketing Association, 292
American National Standards Institute, 279
Angel Network, 299
Anheuser-Busch InBev, 117
AOL, 218, 219, 360, 489
AOL Time Warner, Inc., 489

Apotex Inc., 471
Apple Computer, Inc., 11, 23, 68, 111, 125, 163, 179, 190, 191, 202, 295, 305, 314, 324, 326, 344, 358, 360, 374, 395, 396, 401, 454, 489, 510, 511, 533–534
Apptio, 473
Aritzia, 417
Arizona Diamondbacks, 123
Arm & Hammer, 327, 330
Army & Navy, 339*t*
Art Gallery of Ontario, 417
Art Meets Commerce, 344
ArtFire, 291
Associated Press, 81
Association of Collegiate Entrepreneurs, 160
AT&T, 18, 193, 488
Avon Foundation for Women, 296, 359
Avon Products, 50, 296, 359
Ayurvedic, 160

B

Bank of Montreal (BMO), 30, 292, 485
Bank of Nova Scotia. *See* ScotiaBank
Barnes & Noble, 326, 373
Barrick Gold Corporation, 6
Barron's, 181
Bass Pro Shops, 339*t*
The Bay, 522
   see also Hudson's Bay Company
BC Hydro, 417
BCE Inc. *See* Bell Canada Enterprises
Beau's All Natural Brewing Company, 117, 174, 284–285, 383, 410–411
Becel, 190
Bed Bath & Beyond, 477
Beedie School of Business, 160
Bell Aliant, 10, 489
Bell Canada Enterprises, 4, 124, 292, 530
Bell Canada Inc., 10, 12, 62, 392, 398, 400, 489, 494

Berkshire Hathaway, 192
Berkshire Partners, 417
Best Buy, 44, 326, 338, 344
Better Business Bureau, 138
Beyond the Rack, 7, 345
Biodegradable Products Institute, 333
BlackBerry Ltd., 4, 50, 179, 202, 330, 358, 534
Blank Label, 302
Bloomberg, 108*t*
BMO. *See* Bank of Montreal (BMO)
BMW, 44, 268, 345
BNP Paribas, 473
Bobbi Brown, 163
The Body Shop, 159
Boeing, 404
Bombardier Inc., 90, 109, 193, 451, 485
Bon Appetit, 301
Boni Soir, 339*t*
Boston Bruins, 514
Bottleworks, 410
BraunAbility, 165
Brisco, 95
Bristol-Myers Squibb, 193
British Airways, 187, 228
British Broadcasting Corporation (BBC), 241
Budweiser, 360
Burberry, 344, 524
Burberry Group PLC, 519
Burger King, 110, 135, 138, 364
Business Development Bank of Canada, 174, 569, 570
Business for Social Responsibility (BSR), 29
BusinessWeek, 569
Buy.ca, 340

C

Cable and Wireless, 473
Cal Pacific Specialty Foods, 532
Campbell Soup Company, 193–194, 303, 336
Canada Business, 154*f*

Name Index

Canada Deposit Insurance Corporation (CDIC), 448, 457–458, 462
Canada Green Building Council (CaGBC), 264
Canada Industrial Relations Board, 226
Canada Life, 459
Canada Mortgage and Housing Corporation (CMHC), 445, 449
Canada Post, 7, 362, 392
Canada Revenue Agency (CRA), 139, 417, 419
Canada's Gateways, 108t
Canada's Top 100 Employers, 50
Canadian Airlines International, 70
Canadian Apparel Federation, 209
Canadian Armature Works, 503
Canadian Association of Business Incubation (CABI), 133
Canadian Breast Cancer Foundation, 47, 146, 363
Canadian Business, 529
Canadian Business for Social Responsibility (CBSR), 41
Canadian Cancer Society, 292, 299
Canadian Centre for Occupational Health and Safety (CCOHS), 49
Canadian Chamber of Commerce, 154f
Canadian Diabetes Association, 292, 298
Canadian Federation of Independent Businesses (CFIB), 154, 457
Canadian Franchise Association (CFA), 138
Canadian Human Rights Commission, 52, 53
Canadian Intellectual Property Office (CIPO), 166
Canadian Labour Congress (CLC), 226
Canadian Marketing Association, 362
Canadian Medical Association, 296
Canadian National Railway Company, 527
Canadian Olympic Committee, 296
Canadian Olympic Team, 523
Canadian Pacific, 45, 526–528
Canadian Pacific Hotels, 529
Canadian Radio-television and Telecommunications Commission (CRTC), 10, 69, 529, 535
Canadian Red Cross, 5, 47
Canadian Securities Administrators (CSA), 462, 485
Canadian Security Intelligence Service (CSIS), 419–420
Canadian Society for the Prevention of Cruelty to Animals, 5
Canadian Society of Immigration Consultants, 76
Canadian Tire Corporation, 326, 327, 483, 494
Canadian Trade Commissioner Service, 108, 108t

Canadian Trade Data Online, 108t
Canadian Treasury, 448
Canadian Union of Public Employees (CUPE), 228
Canadian Venture Capital & Private Equity Association, 569
Canarm Ltd., 502–504
Canon, 263
Canon Canada, 297
Canopco, 530
Canpar, 146
Capital and Private Equity Association, 134
Capital One, 358
CARE, 312
Carling, 383
CarShare Atlantic Limited, 235
CarShareHFX, 235, 253
Cartier, 35
Cathay Pacific, 357
CBC, 134, 160, 167, 169
Cenovus Energy, 193
Centrica Plc, 489
China Investment Corporation, 487
China Petrochemical Corporation, 487
Choices Markets, 339t
Chouinard Equipment Ltd., 501
Chrysler, 268
CIBC, 30, 47, 50, 146, 455, 457, 463
Cielos Studios, 321
Cirque du Soleil, 29
Cisco Systems, 331, 405, 406, 477
Citigroup, 452, 464
City of St. John's, 420
City of Toronto, 450
City Year, 312
Citytv.com, 62
Clean Air–Cool Planet, 312
Clean Nova Scotia, 235
Clearasil, 361
Clinique, 364
Clorox, 251, 252
Co-operative Retailing System (CRS), 338
The Co-operators, 548
Co-operators Group, 193
Coca-Cola Company, 18, 46, 69, 325, 330, 345, 357, 360, 539
Coca-Cola Enterprises, 193
Coca-Cola Foundation, 42
Cold Stone Creamery, 182
Columbia University, 389
Competition Bureau, 45, 48
Conference Board of Canada, 214, 481
Consolidated Technologies Inc., 264
Consumer Reports, 194, 518
Consumers' Association of Canada (CAC), 48
Cooper–Hewitt Smithsonian Design Museum, 98
Corporate Knights, 485, 497

Corporate Knights Magazine, 193
Costco Wholesale, 50, 63, 72, 190, 339, 339t, 340, 343
COSTI Immigrant Services, 46
Covington Funds, 486
CPS, 424
Crate & Barrel, 309

D

Danor Manufacturing Co. Ltd., 502
Datamonitor, 479
Dell Computer, 182, 273
Deloitte, 418, 424–425
Dennison's Brewing, 174
Department of Finance, 462
Designer Depot/Style Depot, 522
Deutsche Bank, 161
DigiScent, 329
Direct Marketing Association, 362
DirectBuy, 339t
DirecTV, 488
Doctors Without Borders, 5
Dollar Store, 340
Dominion Bond Rating Service (DBRS), 449
Dove, 360, 372
Dow Chemical, 202, 481
DP Image Consulting, 82
Dragons' Den, 134, 160, 167, 169
Dropbox, 391
Dunkin' Donuts, 135, 331
DuPont, 475

E

East Side Mario's, 146
easyGroup, 344
Eat Local, 64
Eaton, 193
eBay, 17, 49, 291, 338, 344, 367, 374
Economic Development Corporation, 363
Ecosphere, 163
Ecosphere Technologies Inc., 163, 264
Edition, 190
Edward Jones, 455
Egg Farmers of Ontario, 354
Egyptian Orascom Telecom Holding, 529
Electronic Arts (EA), 329, 510–512
Elle, 356
Empire Life, 548
Employment and Social Development Canada, 494
Enbridge, 412
Encana Corporation, 6, 487
Endura Energy, 15
Enron Corporation, 415
Enterprise Rent-A-Car, 198
Entrepreneur, 154, 569
Environmental Defense Fund, 146
Environmental Technologies Ltd., 264
ePolicy Institute, 403

Equifax, 300
Ernst & Young, 18, 213, 241, 418
Estée Lauder, 163
Etelesolv, 392
Ethisphere Institute, 184
Etsy.com, 291, 292
Europages, 108*t*
European Alliance, 344
Evernote, 391
ExoPC, 10
Expedia, 367, 473
Experian, 300

F
Facebook, 15, 68, 127, 129, 156, 161, 183, 245, 252, 278, 295, 303, 304, 333, 342, 343, 344, 353, 355, 360, 366, 403
Fast Company, 154, 355
Federal Emergency Management Agency (FEMA), 544
Federal Reserve Board, 463, 481
Federal Reserve System, 78
Federated Co-operatives Limited (FCL), 338
FedEx, 335, 396
FIFA, 100, 241
Financial Post, 452
Financial Times, 17
Fitch, 449
Fitness City, 321, 322
Five Guys and a Burger, 66
FlightCar, 153
Forbes, 154, 361, 507
Ford Credit, 459
Ford Motor Company, 15, 98, 106, 145, 261, 268, 305, 306
Foreign Affairs, Trade and Development Canada, 108, 108*t*
Forest Stewardship Council, 30
Fortune, 23, 31, 189, 215, 361
Forzani Group, 327
Fox, 62
Frito-Lay, 332, 333
Front Row Marketing Services, 363
Fruits & Passion, 158, 159
Fuhu, 325–326
Fujitsu, 368
Fund for Global Women's Leadership, 296
Future Shop, 522

G
G Adventures Canada, 508–509
The Gap, 193, 520
GazMet, 392
GENCO Marketplace, 475–476
General Electric, 17, 118, 145, 259, 279, 426
General Mills, 50
General Motors, 44, 49, 91, 193, 194, 268, 306, 308, 356
Giant Tiger, 339*t*

Globalive Carrier Services, 530
Globalive Communications Corp., 529–531
Globe and Mail, 308, 452
GNC, 376
GoldieBlox, 360
Golf Town, 339*t*, 486
Goodwill Industries, 260
Goodyear, 362
Google, 62, 68, 127, 179, 184–185, 195, 196, 219, 238, 330, 360, 395, 397, 400, 402, 534, 539
Gourmet Chips and Sauces, 334, 335
Grant Brothers Boxing, 321
Grant Thornton, 418
Green Grid, 397
Green Mama, 128
Green Mountain Roasters, 190
GreenLawn, 263
Greenpeace, 251–252, 397
Gucci, 344
Guidance Financial, 464

H
Haagen-Dazs, 296, 297
Habitat for Humanity, 47, 296, 299
Hachette Book Group, 373
Hakim Wealth Management, 464
Hallmark, 473
Halogen Software, 214
Hamilton Tire & Garage Ltd., 327
Hanns R. Neumann Stiftung Foundation, 46
Harley-Davidson, 38, 239, 272
Harvard Business School, 39
Harvest Partners, 486
Hasbro, 193
Hay Group, 23
HBSC, 464
Health Canada, 48
Heinz, 279, 394
Hewlett-Packard, 44, 330, 454
H&M, 34–35, 520, 521
Holland Car PLC, 271
Holt Renfrew, 63, 340, 343
Holy Crap, 167
Home Depot, 13, 125, 182, 186, 238, 361, 483
Home Outfitters, 522
Honda, 262, 268, 479
Hospital for Sick Children (SickKids), 5–6, 260
H&R Block, 263
HR Executive, 355
HTC, 533–534
Hudson's Bay Company, 339*t*, 522–524
Hulu.com, 62, 326, 360
Human Resources and Skills Development Canada, 494
Humane Society, 47
Husky Energy, 193

I
Iberdrola Renewables, 72
IBM, 18, 50, 101, 102, 211, 331, 394, 412
IESE, 521
IHOP, 357
Ijara Canada, 464
IKEA, 91, 331
iLEVEL, 245
Inc., 154, 161, 569
Indiana Pacers, 363
Indigo, 125
Inditex Group, 519, 520, 521
Industry Canada, 30, 138, 166
Instagram, 15
Intel, 193, 211, 331
International Business School, 158
International Consumer Electronics Show, 366
International Franchise Association, 135
International Organization for Standardization, 279
Internet and American Life Project, 395
Internet Engineering Task Force (IETF), 401
Intuit, 164, 360, 436
Investment Industry Regulatory Organization of Canada (IIROC), 462
Islamic Credit Union of Canada, 464

J
J.D. Power, 196
JetBlue, 404
Jewish General Hospital, 371
Jiffy Lube, 357
Jim Pattison Group, 154
John Deere Capital Corporation, 459
Johnson & Johnson, 18, 31, 32*f,* 188, 330, 422, 481, 488
JP Morgan Chase, 363
Junior Achievement, 508
Juvenile Diabetes Research Foundation, 359

K
Kauffman Center for Entrepreneurial Leadership, 160
Kauffman Foundation, 154*f*
Kellogg, 91, 394
Kelly Services, 324
Keurig, 190
Keystone XL Pipeline, 99
KFC, 504, 505
Kik Interactive Inc., 161–162, 534
Killam Properties, 235
King Diesel, 45
King's Wharf, 235
KitchenAid, 330
KitchenAid Canada, 47
Kleinfeld Bridal, 523

Name Index

The Knot, 156
KPMG, 418
Kraft, 96, 330, 332
Krispy Kreme, 130
Kwantlen Polytechnic University, 507

L

La Boulange Café and Bakery, 189
Labatt, 383
Lance Armstrong Foundation, 6
LCBO, 174, 410
Le Bistro Fit, 321
Lijjat Papad, 156
LinkedIn, 15, 129, 161, 185, 295, 343
LinkExchange, 182
Live Nation Entertainment, 8, 9
Livent Inc., 54, 415
Livestrong Foundation, 6
Lloyds Bank, 464
Loblaw, 68, 180, 273, 330, 339t, 341, 365
London Business School, 521
London Stock Exchange, 454
Long Plain First Nation, 169
Lord & Taylor, 522
L'Oréal, 331, 358, 394
Lotus Development, 50
Lotus Software, 50
Louis Vuitton Moët Hennessey (LVMH), 344, 519, 539
Lululemon Athletica Inc., 90, 308, 330, 506–508

M

Maclean's, 30
Mac's, 339t
Magna International, 182–183, 436
Make-a-Wish Foundation, 292
Malaysian Airlines, 451
Mall of America, 341
Manitoba Hydro, 50, 140
Manitoba Securities Commission, 462
Manroland, 266
Manulife Financial, 455, 459, 495, 548
Maple Leaf Foods, 48
Marie Claire, 356
MarketWatch, 389
Mark's Work Wearhouse, 327
Marriott Corporation, 190, 314
Marriott International, 18
Marvel Entertainment, 307
Matsushita, 111
Mattel, 50, 184, 193
Mazda, 268
MBNA Canada Bank, 314
McAfee, 402
McAuslan Brewing, 174
McCain Foods Limited, 504–505

McDonald's, 66, 69, 110, 135, 136, 138, 146, 213, 263, 292, 302, 311, 330, 364, 479, 504, 505, 508, 539
McGill University, 249, 250, 371, 389
MCI, 39
Médecins Sans Frontières (MSF), 5
Mediacorp Canada Inc., 497
MEI Computer Technology Group, 394
Merck, 68
Metro Group, 346
MGM Studios, 62
Miami Heat, 363
Microsoft, 10, 145, 162, 182, 202, 238, 308, 329, 356, 360, 391, 396, 402, 405, 472, 534
Millennium Development Corporation, 59
Minnesota Twins, 123
Mint.com, 164
Mitnick Security Company, 165
MMA Gyms, 321
Molson Coors, 117, 383
Mondou, 341
Monster.com, 354–355
Monster Gym, 156, 321
Moody's, 449
Morinaga, 110
MOSAIC, 76
Motor Trend Magazine, 194
Motorola, 489
Motorola Enterprise Mobility and Networks, 489
Motorola Mobile Devices and Home, 489
Mount Polley Mining Corporation, 43
Mountain Equipment Co-op, 193
Mouvement des caisses Desjardins (The Desjardins Group), 193
Mr. Lube, 263
MTP Energy Management, 486
Mulberry, 374
Multilateral Investment Fund, 509
MyStarbucksIdea.com, 342

N

Nabisco, 359
NASDAQ Stock Market, 453
National Collegiate Athletic Association (NCAA), 123
National Franchise Association, 138
National Hockey League, 227
National Hockey League Players' Association, 227
National Union of Public and General Employees (NUPGE), 228
National Venture Capital Association, 134, 569
Natura Foods Inc., 124
Natural Products Group, 486
Natural Resources Canada, 45, 79
Naturalizer, 356

NBA, 362
NBC, 62
NCR Corporation, 338
Neiman Marcus, 401
Nestlé, 251–252, 253, 437, 478
Netflix, 7, 326, 360
New Balance, 146
New Brunswick Power, 140
New Locomotion, 52
New York City Clothing Bank, 34
New York Knicks, 363
New York Stock Exchange (NYSE), 453
New York Times, 34
New York University, 389
New York University's School of Business, 525
Next, 563
Nickelodeon, 326
Nielsen Company, 360
Nike, 111, 314, 315, 330, 426
Nipissing University, 389
Nissan Motor Company, 266, 268
Nokia, 118, 489, 533
Nordstrom Inc., 523
Nortel Networks, 419
Norton, 402
NPD Group, 500
NRDC Equity Partners, 522
Nuance Spa, 321

O

Odeo, 16
Office Depot, 340
Office of Energy Efficiency, 79
Office of Financial Stability, 449
Office of the Superintendent of Financial Institutions (OSFI), 462
Offshore Odysseys, 117f
Oil & Gas Journal, 361
O'Keefe, 383
Old Navy, 522
Olympic Games, 241, 297
One Connect, 530
1000 Markets, 291
Onex Corporation, 486
Ontario Craft Brewers Association, 174
Ontario Energy Board, 68
Ontario Hospital Association, 513
Ontario Human Rights Commission, 52
Ontario Lottery and Gaming Corporation, 279
Ontario Securities Commission, 53, 462
Ontario Teachers' Pension Plan, 455
OpenText Corporation, 248
Operation Come Home, 410
Operative Plasterers' and Cement Masons' International Association (OPCMIA), 228, 229
Opryland, 543

Oracle, 368, 424
Orascom Telecom Holding, 529
Orbitz, 367
Origin, 511
Osgoode Hall, 36
The Ottawa Hospital, 512–514
OvernightPetTags.com, 161
Overstock, 15, 367

P
Pacific Biodiesel, 45
PacSun, 361
Pampered Chef, 339
Panasonic Automotive Systems Asia Pacific, 111
Pandora Internet Radio, 305
Paralympic Winter Games, 297
Patagonia, 499–502
Patent Office, 166
PayPal, 17, 68, 155
Peabody Energy, 451
PepsiAmericas, 325
Pepsi Bottling Group, 325
Pepsi Bottling Ventures, 325
PepsiCo, 325, 329, 473
Pershing Square Capital Management, 527
PetroChina Company, 487
PetSmart, 340, 341
Pew Research Center, 395, 524
Pfizer, 68, 368, 471
Pharmaprix, 327
Pi Athlete Management Inc., 123, 124, 147
Pillsbury, 95
Pinkerton, 324
Piper Cub, 367
Pizza Hut, 136
Planeterra Foundation, 509
Play It Again, 162
Playnomics, 304
Popular Science, 301
Population Reference Bureau, 307
PotashCorp, 89, 113
Pottery Barn, 339*t*
Priceline, 367
PricewaterhouseCoopers (PwC), 418, 437
PricewaterhouseCoopers Canada, 41
Primerica Inc., 452
Prince Edward Island Credit Union Deposit Insurance Corporation, 458
Procter & Gamble, 202, 303, 328, 330, 332, 358
Province of Manitoba, 420
Public Service Alliance (PSA), 228

Q
Qualcomm, 217
QueueBuster, 315
Quiznos, 175, 332

R
Ralph Lauren, 339*t*
Rapleaf Inc., 304
Ratiopharm, 471
RBC Financial Group, 392, 436, 455, 457, 463, 464, 494
RE/MAX, 337
Reader's Digest, 361
Real Canadian Superstore, 339*t*
Red Bull, 358
Red Cross. *See* Canadian Red Cross
Red Cross/Red Crescent, 296
Regency Energy Partners, 486
Research In Motion Ltd., 179
    see also BlackBerry Ltd.
Restaurant Brands International Inc., 135
Revlon, 146
Rexall, 49
Rockstar Energy Drink, 325
Rogers Communications Inc., 4, 48, 62, 124, 279, 392, 398, 436, 530
RONA, 392
Rotman School of Management, 445
Royal Bank of Canada, 4, 118, 124, 298, 529
Royal Dutch Shell, 481
Running Room, 125, 146
RUSNANO, 451

S
Safeway, 339*t*
SAI Global, 38
Saint Luke's Health System, 473
Salesforce.com, 391
Salvation Army, 198
Samsung, 363, 395, 489
SAP, 273, 424
Scotiabank, 292, 337, 447, 455, 463, 464
Scotia Capital, 494
ScotiaMcLeod, 337
Scottrade Inc., 389
Seagate, 278
Sears, 279, 330, 357
Selfridges, 374
ServiceMaster, 324, 331
Services Canada, 212
Servus Credit Union, 458
7-Eleven, 339*t*, 340, 357
Seventh Generation, 263, 299, 340
Shell Canada, 489
Shibui Designs, 262
Shoppers Drug Mart, 49, 327
Sierra Club, 163, 252
Silpada, 339
Simon Fraser University, 5, 160
The Skald Group, 38
Skype, 276, 400
Sleeman Breweries, 174
Sleepmaster, 276
Small Business Administration (SBA), 133, 154*f*

Small Business Investor Alliance, 569
Society for Human Resource Management (SHRM), 212, 221
Sodexho Marriott Services, 310
Solar City, 155
Sony, 62, 395
Southwest Properties, 235
SpaceX, 155
Sports Illustrated, 361
Spreadshirt, 302
Spud.ca, 64
Square, 16
STA, 315
Standard & Poor's (S&P), 449, 464, 488
Standards Council of Canada (SCC), 279
Stanford University, 219
Staples, 44
Starbucks, 40, 189, 331, 342, 404, 426, 473, 479
STAT-USA, 108*t*
Statistics Canada, 10, 44, 77, 127, 131, 133, 209, 306, 336, 358, 392
Stella & Dot, 156
Stock-Trak Global Portfolio Simulations, 389, 406
Stouffer, 311
SUBWAY, 136, 137, 302
Success, 154
Suncor Energy, 489
Sunlife Financial, 392, 495
Sun Microsystems, 45, 404
SunOpta, 531–532
SunOpta Distribution Group (SDG), 531
SunOpta Food Group, 531
Sun Youth Organization, 140
Super 8, 136
Sustainalytics, 30
Symantec, 402
Syncrude Canada Ltd., 487
Sysco, 336

T
T-Mobile, 360
Take Our Daughters and Sons to Work Foundation, 327
Target Corporation, 33, 111, 294, 326, 340, 346, 478, 520
Tata Motors, 97, 98, 145
TD Ameritrade, 90
TD Bank, 4, 90, 181, 193, 447, 464
TD Canada Trust, 354, 447, 455
TD Friends of the Environment Foundation, 447
TD Securities, 452
TD Waterhouse, 455
Team Canada 1972, 514–516
Teavana, 189
Technomic, 66
Teck Resources Limited, 193, 485

Teen Vogue, 361
Teenage Research Unlimited, 303
Telfer School of Management, 31, 32*f*
Telsey Advisory Group LLC, 520
TELUS Corp., 30, 48, 392, 398, 400, 448, 472, 530
Tesla Motors, 44, 155
Teva Pharmaceutical Industries, 471
Texas Instruments, 39
3G Capital, 136
3M, 169, 170, 198, 279
Ticketmaster Entertainment, 9
Tiffany & Co., 35
Tim Horton Children's Foundation, 41
Tim Hortons Coffee Partnership, 46
Tim Hortons Inc., 30, 110, 135, 136, 175, 238, 293, 331, 472, 485
Timberland, 299, 312, 313
Time, 361
Time Warner, 219, 489
Tommy Hilfiger, 339*t*
TOMS Shoes, 131, 132
Topshop, 520, 523
Toronto Raptors, 363
Toronto Stock Exchange (TSX), 238, 419, 438, 453, 462
Toronto Transit Commission, 141
Toyota, 118, 239, 244, 262, 479, 516–518
Toyota Financial Services, 459
TradeInsight, 394
TransCanada Corporation, 99, 451
Transparency International, 100
TransUnion, 300
TronSports.ca, 155, 159
TRU-Insight, 303
The Trunk Club, 128
Tumblr, 15
Twitter, 15, 16, 129, 161, 245, 295, 303, 304, 342, 343, 344, 353, 360
Tylenol, 359

U
Uber, 153, 154
Under Armour, 341
UNFI Canada Inc., 531
Unilever, 303, 358, 478
United Nations, 509

United Natural Foods Inc., 531
University of British Columbia, 76
University of Idaho, 45
University of Ottawa, 31
University of Saskatchewan, 36
University of Toronto, 5, 50, 52, 314, 389, 445, 529
University of Waterloo, 162
University of Western Ontario, 298
Unsynced, 162
UnusualThreads.com, 161
Upper Canada Brewing, 174
UPS, 396
UPS Freight, 211–212
U.S. Census Bureau, 306, 394
U.S. Chamber of Commerce, 154*f*
U.S. Department of Commerce, 108
U.S. Department of Justice, 539
U.S. Federal Trade Commission, 138
U.S. International Trade Commission, 533
U.S. Patent and Trademark Office, 166
U.S. Securities and Exchange Commission (SEC), 22, 183
U.S. Small Business Administration, 570
U.S. Treasury, 449
US Airways, 21, 195

V
Vancity. *See* Vancouver City Savings Credit Union
Vancouver 2010 Olympic Games, 59
Vancouver City Savings Credit Union, 76, 193, 497–499
VeloCity, 162
VIA Rail Canada, 141
Vice, 9
Videotron, 400
Vistakon, 488
Volkswagen, 43, 145, 268

W
Wall Street Journal, 154*f,* 355
Wall Street Survivor, 389
Walmart, 63, 72, 92, 111, 190, 263, 326, 327, 338, 339*t,* 341, 346, 365, 376, 499, 520, 522, 534, 550
Walmart Canada, 31, 32, 478

Walmart International, 92
Walt Disney Company, 16, 50, 62, 195, 307, 326
Walt Disney World, 267
Wasserman & Partners Advertising Inc., 353
WeddingChannel.com, 155
Wendy's, 66
West Edmonton Mall, 341
WestJet Airlines, 50, 190, 196
Westpac Banking Corporation, 485
The Westwood, 235
White House Project, 327
Whole Foods Market, 127, 239, 292, 339*t*
Wildeboer Dellelce, LLP, 36
Williams-Sonoma, 339*t*
Wilson Sporting Goods Company, 275
WIND Mobile, 529–530
Wired, 355
Workers' Compensation Board of Alberta, 49
Workers' Compensation Board of Nova Scotia, 49
Workplace Safety and Insurance Board (Ontario), 49
WorkSafeBC, 353, 379
World Economic Forum, 445

X
Xerox, 331
Xilinx Inc., 219

Y
Yahoo, 360, 402
Yak Communications, 530
Yale University, 389
Yellow Pages, 364
Yellowquill College, 169
YMCA, 180
YouTube, 7, 15, 62, 344, 353, 358, 360

Z
Zappos, 182, 199, 307
Zara International, 519–521
Zellers Inc., 111, 522, 523
Zhena's Gypsy Tea, 50, 158
Zipcar, 525–526

SUBJECT INDEX

A
absolute advantage, 92–93
accessory equipment, 324
accountants, 415, 418–420, 494
accounting, 415
   accounting cycle, 422–424, 422f
   accounting equation, 422–424
   accounting professionals, 418–420
   accounting software programs, 424
   accrual accounting, 430
   business activities involving accounting, 417
   career, 494–495
   computers, impact of, 424
   cooking the books, 415, 438
   financial statements, 425–431
   foundation of the accounting system, 420–421
   generally accepted accounting principles (GAAP), 420
   international accounting, 437–438
   Internet, impact of, 424
   users of accounting information, 416–417, 416f
accounting cycle, 422–424, 422f
accounting equation, 422–424, 479
accounting identity, 423
accounting professionals, 418–420
accounting standards, 420
Accounting Standards Board (AcSB), 420
Accounting Standards for Private Enterprises (ASPE), 420, 421
accounts receivable, 477
accrual accounting, 430
acid-test ratio, 432t, 433
acquisition, 111, 145, 488
active listening, 247
activity ratios, 432t, 433–434
actuarial tables, 547
adaptation strategy, 112–113, 301–302

adapting strategic plans, 190–191
Addison, John, 452
address lists, 361–362
adjourning stage, 242
administrative agencies, 535
administrative barriers, 102, 104
administrative services managers, 286
admired companies, 22–23
advertising, 355t, 358
   advertising media, 359–364, 359f
   advocacy advertising, 359
   cause advertising, 359
   comparative advertising, 359
   cooperative advertising, 371
   deceptive advertising and packaging, 10
   floor ads, 363
   informative advertising, 359
   institutional advertising, 358–359
   outdoor advertising, 362
   persuasive advertising, 359
   point-of-purchase (POP) advertising, 366
   product advertising, 358
   and product life cycle, 359
   reminder-oriented advertising, 359
   specialty advertising, 366
   truthfulness in, 48
   types of advertising, 358–359
   viral advertising, 360
advertising media, 359–364, 359f
   direct mail, 361–362
   Internet advertising, 360
   magazines, 361
   newspapers, 361
   other media options, 363–364
   outdoor advertising, 362
   radio, 361
   sponsorship, 363
   television, 359–360
advertising specialties, 366
advocacy advertising, 359

affective conflict, 243
affinity programs, 314
after-tax profits, 9
age, 307
age discrimination, 52
age of industrial entrepreneurs, 12
agency, 537
agents, 337
aggressive competitive practices, 10
aging population, 18, 81t
agriculture, 45, 64
AIO statements, 308
alliances, 314
alternative energy development, 72
ambiguity, 165
analysts, 332
analytic production system, 263
angel investors, 169
angry customers, 313
Anti-Bribery Convention, 100
apparel manufacturing, 209
Appleton, Frank, 383
application service provider (ASP), 405
application software, 396
approach, 369
arbitration, 226
Armstrong, Tim, 219
articles of incorporation, 142f
ASEAN, 105
asking for a raise, 215
assembly line, 261, 271
assessment of competitive position, 188–190
asset, 422, 476–477
asset management, 476–479
Association of Southeast Asian Nations (ASEAN), 105
audience feedback, 245
Australia, 105
auto insurance, 550
auto manufacturing, 268

612 Subject Index

autocratic leadership, 194
automated teller machines (ATMs), 338–339, 364, 447, 457, 457
automatic merchandising, 338

B
baby boomers, 199, 304, 524–525
backup, 404
bailment, 538
balance of payments, 93
balance-of-payments deficit, 93
balance-of-payments surplus, 93
balance of trade, 93
balance sheet, 426–427, 428f
balanced budget, 80, 105
Balsillie, Jim, 179
Bank Act, 461–462
bank loan, 168, 483–484
Bank of Canada (the Bank), 78, 175, 460–461, 462, 465
Bank of England, 464
Bank of Japan, 464
bank regulation, 461–462
bankruptcy, 430, 540
banks, 168, 436, 455–458
Barberini, Marco, 161
Barra, Mary, 194, 194f
barriers to international trade, 96–103
    administrative barriers, 102, 103
    cultural differences, 96–97
    economic differences, 97–99
    legal differences, 99–101
    nontariff barriers, 102, 103
    political differences, 99–101
    reducing barriers to international trade, 104–107
    religious attitudes, 97
    social differences, 96–97
    tariffs, 102
    trade restrictions, 102–103
    values, 97
Beatty, Douglas, 419
Beauchesne, Steve and Tim, 117, 174, 284–285, 383, 410–411
being your own boss, 156–157
belongingness needs, 222
benchmarking, 278
benefits sought, 309
Bernanke, Ben, 481
"The Best Corporate Citizens," 193
Beyoncé, 294
Bieber, Justin, 3, 4, 10, 23
Bill 198, 33, 54, 421, 426
Billes, John W. and Alfred J., 327
Bindman, Marty, 123
biodiesel fuel, 45
blogs, 308
board of directors, 144
bond rating, 449–450, 450t

bonds, 448–450, 449t, 485
botnet, 402
Bourgeois, Marc, 123
boycott, 228
boycott in restraint of trade, 536
brand, 13, 329, 332f
brand awareness, 331
brand categories, 330
brand equity, 331–332
branding, 13
brand insistence, 331
brand loyalty, 310, 331
brand manager, 331
brand name, 330
brand preference, 331
brand recognition, 331
Braun, Scooter, 3
breach of contract, 537
breakeven analysis, 375–376, 375f
breakeven point, 375–376
bribes, 100
brokers, 337
Brooke, Beth, 241
Brookshire, Mark, 389
Brown, Bobbi, 163f
Brunei, 105
budget, 79–80, 435–437, 558
budget deficit, 80
budget surplus, 80
Buffett, Warren, 192
business, 4
business analysis, 328
business buying behaviour, 311
business cycle, 71–73
Business Development Bank of Canada (BDC), 133, 154f, 175
business ethics, 23, 30
    see also ethical controversies
    avoiding ethical dilemmas at work, 34
    Bill 198, 33
    concern for ethical and societal issues, 30–31
    conflict of interest, 35
    contemporary ethical environment, 31–37
    creating a good ethical foundation, 34
    development of individual ethics, 34
    ethical action, 39
    ethical awareness, 37–38
    ethical education, 38–39
    ethical leadership, 39–40
    ethical tone of business, 184
    ethics compliance officers, 33
    ethics training programs, 38–39
    honesty, 35–36
    individuals making a difference, 33
    information system, 403
    integrity, 35–36
    loyalty vs. truth, 36
    on-the-job ethical dilemmas, 34–37

    Sarbanes-Oxley Act of 2002, 33
    shaping ethical conduct, 37–40
    whistle-blowing, 36–37
business goods, 323–324
business history eras, 12–14
business incubator, 133
business intelligence, 303
business intelligence software, 392
business interruption insurance, 550
business law, 536
    bailment, 538
    bankruptcy, 540
    contract law, 536–538
    core of, 536
    law of agency, 537
    legal system and administrative agencies, 535
    negotiable instruments, 538
    product liability, 540
    property law, 538
    regulatory environment, 536
    tax law, 540
    torts, 539–540
    trademarks, patents, and copyrights, 539
    types of law, 535–536
    warranties, 537
business markets, 310
business meetings, 273
business ownership. See forms of business ownership
business plan, 131–132, 167, 167t, 564–570
    executive summary, 565–566
    financing section, 568
    introduction, 566–567
    marketing strategy, 567–568
    outline, 567
    resources, 569–570
    résumés of principals, 568
business products, 323
business-to-business (B2B), 301, 305
business-to-consumer (B2C), 299–301, 305
buyer's market, 295
buying an existing business, 166
buying offices, 337–338

C
C-SOX. See Bill 198
cable television, 360
cafeteria plans, 217
CAFTA-DR. See Central America-Dominican Republic Free Trade Agreement
callable bonds, 450
call provision, 450
calming the angry customer, 313
Cameron, James, 20f
Canada, 97
    Anti-Bribery Convention, 100
    balance of trade, 93

and credit crisis, 445
financial institutions, 456f
GDP per capita, 74, 91t
hedge funds, 488
and IFRS, 420
low-context culture, 245
major exports and imports, 93–94, 94t
NAFTA, 105, 310
national debt, 80
political stability, 99
population, 80, 91t
railroads, 347
tariffs, 102
top trading partners, 92
trade with U.S., 92
Trans-Pacific Partnership (TPP), 105
treaties, 100–101
unions in, 228
vacation time, 97
venture capital, 134
Canada Pension Plan (CPP), 459
Canada Savings Bonds, 448
Canada Small Business Financing Program (CSBFP), 133
Canadian apparel manufacturing, 209
Canadian Census of Population, 392–393
Canadian Charter of Rights and Freedoms, 51
Canadian Disability Vocational Rehabilitation Program, 51t
Canadian Human Rights Act (CHRA), 51t, 52, 53
Cantin, Murielle, 29
capital, 7
capital investment analysis, 478
capitalism, 8, 67–69, 70–71t
capital structure, 479–483
Carbone, Michael, 123
career choice, 558
careers
accounting or finance career, 494–495
entrepreneurial careers, 175–176
global business and economics career, 118–119
information technology career, 412
management career, 286–287
case study, 117, 174, 284–285, 410
cases, 497–532
cash, 476–477
cash budget, 436–437, 436f, 484
cash flow, 430
cash flow statement, 429–430, 431f
category advisor, 332
category manager, 332
cause advertising, 359
cause marketing, 298–299
cause-related marketing, 47
Central America-Dominican Republic Free Trade Agreement (CAFTA-DR), 106–107

central banks, 103
centralization, 200
CEO compensation, 144, 481
certificate of deposit (CD), 448
Certified Fraud Examiner (CFE), 418, 419
Certified Internal Auditor (CIA), 418
chain of command, 200
Chan, Sherman, 76
change. *See* organizational change
Chartered Professional Accountants (CPAs), 418
Chelios, Chris, 123
Chen, John S., 179, 202
chief executive officer (CEO), 30, 43, 144, 145, 180, 183, 286, 421, 472, 473
chief financial officer (CFO), 144, 145, 180, 183, 286, 421, 472
chief information officer (CIO), 144, 286, 390
chief operating officer (COO), 144, 286, 472
Chile, 105
China, 17, 19, 69, 72, 73, 74, 81, 81t, 89, 91t, 93, 96, 97, 100, 101, 104, 110, 111, 112, 160, 184–185, 244, 278, 279, 437, 487
choice, 49
Choquette, Éric, 29
CHRA. *See* Canadian Human Rights Act (CHRA)
CIA *World Factbook*, 108, 108t
classic entrepreneurs, 155
classification of goods and services, 322–324
business goods, 323–324
consumer goods and services, 322–323, 323f
marketing strategy implications, 324–325
services, 324
classroom training, 213–214
"clean capitalism" report, 485
closed corporation, 143
closely held corporation, 143
closing, 370
cloud computing, 397f, 405, 406
co-branding, 314
code of conduct, 37–38
cognitive conflict, 243
cohesive groups, 242–243
collaboration, 19
collective bargaining, 226
collective ownership of business, 140–142
colonial period, 12
colony collapse disorder (CCD), 297
co-marketing, 314–315
commerce treaties, 100–101
commercial and business insurance, 550
commercial banks, 455–458
commercial paper, 484
committee organizations, 201
commodity prices, 81t

common law, 535
common market, 105
common shares, 144, 450
communication, 244
communication process, 244–245, 244f
context, 245
crisis management, 251–253
downward communication, 248
external communication, 251–253
formal communication channels, 246t, 248, 249f
forms of, 246–251, 246t
informal communication channels, 246t, 249, 249f
integrated marketing communications. *See* integrated marketing communications (IMC)
noise, 245
nonverbal communication, 246t, 249–251
open communication, 248
oral communication, 246–247, 246t
sender, 244–245
upward communication, 248
via mobile devices, 396
written communication, 246t, 247–248
communication barriers, 96–97
communication process, 244–245, 244f
communism, 69, 70–71t
company responsibilities
to consumers, 47–49
to employees, 49–53
to investors and financial community, 53–54
comparability, 420
comparative advantage, 93
comparative advertising, 359
compensation, 215–218
employee benefits, 216–217
executive compensation, 144, 481
flexible benefit plans, 217
flexible work plans, 217–218
incentive compensation, 216, 216f, 236–238
competition, 8, 67–69
see also market structures
Competition Act, 48, 68, 536
Competition Bureau, 46t, 48
competitive differentiation, 8, 190
competitiveness, 67
competitive performance, 344
competitive pricing, 377–378
competitive tactics of unions and management, 227–228
complaints, 347
component parts and materials, 324
compressed workweek, 217
computer-aided design (CAD), 259, 265
computer-aided manufacturing (CAM), 265

614 Subject Index

computer-based information system, 391
computer-based training, 213–214
computer hardware, 391, 394–396
computer-integrated manufacturing (CIM), 266
computer networks, 398–400
computer security specialists, 412
computer software, 396, 397t, 424
computerized trading, 454
Conant, Doug, 193f
concept development, 328
concept testing, 328
conceptual skills, 182
confidentiality, 304
conflict, 243–244, 248
conflict of interest, 35
conglomerate merger, 145
Connor, Michael, 164
consistency, 420
construction industry, 228
construction managers, 286
consumer behaviour, 311–312, 312f
Consumer Bill of Rights, 48
consumer complaints, 347
consumer desire, 354
consumer goods and services, 322–323, 323f
consumerism, 47–49
consumer markets, 305–310
consumer orientation, 13
consumer-oriented promotions, 364–366, 364f
consumer perceptions of price, 378
Consumer Price Index (CPI), 75
consumer's rights, 47–49
contests, 366
context, 245
contingency planning, 186–187
continuous production process, 263
contract, 536
contract-based agreements, 109–110
contract law, 536–538
contract requirements, 536–537
controller, 472
controlling, 183
convenience products, 322
convenience store, 339t
convertible securities, 451
Cook, Gary, 397
cooking the books, 415, 437, 438
Cool, Tracy, 192
Cooley, Pam, 235, 253
Cool IT Challenge, 397
cooperative advertising, 371
cooperatives, 140–142, 337–338
copyrights, 539
core inflation rate, 74
corporate charter, 142–143
corporate culture, 195–196
corporate insiders, 462

corporate management, 143–145, 143f
corporate philanthropy, 42, 46–47
corporate social responsibility (CSR), 30, 425
corporation, 140
   articles of incorporation, 142f
   board of directors, 144
   closed corporation, 143
   closely held corporation, 143
   corporate charter, 142–143
   corporate officers and managers, 144–145
   how to incorporate, 142–143
   incorporation, 142–143
   management, 143–145, 143f
   open corporation, 144
   organizing a corporation, 142–145
   publicly held corporation, 144
   shareholder rights, 143–144
   stock ownership, 143–144
   where to incorporate, 142
corruption, 100, 101f
Corruption of Foreign Public Officials Act (CFPOA), 100, 421
Corruption Perceptions Index, 100
cost-based pricing, 374
cost-push inflation, 74
costs, 375
countertrade, 109
coupons, 365
CPI market basket, 75, 76f
creative leadership, 21
creative selling, 368
creativity, 21, 164, 169
credit, 559
The Credit CARD Act, 553
credit cards, 130, 401, 457, 553–554
credit crisis, 445, 449, 454, 460, 465
credit management, 559–560
Credit Reporting Act, 300
credit reports, 300
credit unions, 458
crisis management, 251–253
critical path, 276
critical thinking, 20–21
Crosby, Sidney, 123
cross-functional team, 239
cultural differences, 96–97
currency blocs, 95
currency conversion and shifts, 98–99
currency devaluation, 95
current assets, 476
current ratio, 432t, 433
customer-based segmentation, 310
customer departmentalization, 198
customer-driven production, 262
customer-oriented layout, 270f, 271
customer relationship management (CRM), 315
customer service standards, 347
customer service strategy, 341

customs union, 105
cyberattacks, 402
cybercrime, 400–401
cyclical unemployment, 77
cynical listening, 247

D

damages, 537
data, 390
database, 392–393
database programs, 397f
data mining, 304
data warehouse, 304
Davis, Jeffrey T., 137
debenture, 448
debt capital, 479, 480
debt financing, 168
debt forgiveness, 79
debt ratio, 432t, 435
decentralization, 200, 249
deceptive advertising and packaging, 10
deceptive marketing, 48
decision making, 191
   how managers make decisions, 192
   make, buy, or lease decision, 271
   nonprogrammed decision, 191
   programmed decision, 191
decision-making authority, 236
decision support system (DSS), 393–394
decline stage, 326
defensive listening, 247
deflation, 75
DeFlorio, Michael, 486
delegation, 198–199
demand, 61
   changes in quantity demanded, 62–63
   factors driving demand, 61–63
   interaction of demand and supply, 64–66
   primary demand, 354
   selective demand, 354
demand curve, 62–63, 63f, 63t
demand-pull inflation, 74
democratic leadership, 194–195
demographics, 567
demographic segmentation, 306–307, 306f, 310
demographic trends, and the entrepreneur, 161–162
demonstration, 369
Denham, Robert E., 481
department store, 339t
departmentalization, 198, 199f
deposit insurance, 457–458
depository institutions, 455
deregulation, 68–69
desktop publishing, 397f
detailers, 368
devaluation, 95, 99
developing countries, 92, 105
development banks, 104–105

Subject Index

diabetes, 42
Dickinson, Arlene, 134f
digital ad market, 360
direct distribution channel, 334, 335–336
direct exporting, 109
directing, 183
direct mail, 361–362
direct reports, 200
direct-response retailing, 338
direct-response television (DRTV), 364
direct selling, 339
disability income insurance, 550
disaster recovery planning, 404
discount pricing, 376
discount rate, 460
discount store, 339t
discrimination, 51, 52
dispatching, 277
distributed workforce, 404–405
distribution channel decisions, 343–345
distribution channels, 334–336, 334f, 344
distribution intensity, 345
distribution strategy, 301, 334
    logistics, 345–346
    physical distribution, 334, 345–346, 346f
    retailing, 338–343
    wholesaling, 336–338
diverse workforce, 18–19
diversity, 18–19, 240–241
divestiture, 489
dividend policy, 482–483
dividends, 450–451, 482
Dorsey, Jack, 16
double-entry bookkeeping, 423
downsizing, 127, 218–220, 219
downward communication, 248
Drabinsky, Garth, 415
Drake, *See* Graham, Aubrey Drake
drop shipper, 337
Drucker, Peter, 224
drug testing, 212
dumping, 103
Dungan, Peter, 445
Dunn, Frank, 419

E

ebusiness, 15
economic differences, 97–99
economic performance, 71–77
    employment levels, 77
    flattening the business cycle, 71–73
    gross domestic product (GDP), 73–74, 74f
    inflation, 74
    management of economy's performance, 78–80
    price level changes, 74–77
    productivity, 73–74, 75
economics, 60
    budget, 79–80
    evaluation of economic performance, 71–77
    fiscal policy, 78–79
    global business and economics career, 118–119
    global economic challenges, 80–82, 81t
    macroeconomics, 60, 66–71
    market structures, 67–71
    microeconomics, 60–66
    monetary policy, 78, 460–461
economic systems, 60
    capitalism, 8, 67–69, 70–71t
    communism, 69, 70–71t
    comparison of alternative economic systems, 70–71t
    mixed market economy, 70–71t
    planned economy, 69
    socialism, 69, 70–71t
economic trends, and the entrepreneur, 161–162
economic union, 105
education, 46, 160
Edwards, Mickey, 185
EEA. *See* Employment Equities Act (EEA)
80/20 principle, 310, 314
electronic banking, 456–457
electronic communications, 157
electronic communications networks (ECNs), 455
electronic funds transfer systems (EFTSs), 456–457
email, 157, 248
embargo, 103
employee benefits, 216–217
employee motivation, 220–225
    equity theory, 223
    expectancy theory, 223, 223f
    goal-setting theory, 224, 224f
    Herzberg's two-factor model of motivation, 222–223
    job design, 224–225
    management by objectives (MBO), 224
    managers' attitudes, 225
    Maslow's hierarchy of needs, 221–222
    process of motivation, 220f
    Theory X, 225
    Theory Y, 225
    Theory Z, 225
employee separation, 218–220
employee stock ownership plans (ESOPs), 236–238, 237t
employee theft, 36
employees
    age discrimination, 52
    drug testing, 212
    empowerment. *See* empowerment
    equal opportunity, 51–52
    flexible work schedules, 50
    high employee morale, 220
    input of, 248
    Internet use, 403
    intrapreneurship, 169–170
    monitoring employees' social media activities, 221
    overseas assignments, 118
    quality-of-life issues, 50–51
    recruitment and selection, 211–213, 211f
    responsibilities to, 49–53
    sexism, 53
    sexual harassment, 53
    workplace safety, 49
employer businesses by firm size, 126t
Employment Equity Act (EEA), 52
employment levels, 77
Employment Standards Act, 97
empowerment, 195, 236
    decision-making authority, 236
    ethical controversies, 237
    information sharing, 236
    linking rewards to company performance, 236–238
end-use segmentation, 310
EnerGuide, 79
Energy Efficiency Act, 79
energy level, 163
ENERGY STAR symbol, 79
English, 96
enterprise resource planning, 397f
enterprise zones, 169
entrepreneur, 10, 154–156
    categories of, 155–156
    characteristics of, 162–165
    classic entrepreneurs, 155
    creativity, 164
    demographic trends, 161–162
    economic trends, 161–162
    education, 160
    environment for, 159–162
    and ethics, 164
    and globalization, 159–160
    high energy level, 163
    homepreneurs, 161
    information technology (IT), 160–161
    internal locus of control, 165
    need to achieve, 163
    optimism, 163
    self-confidence, 163
    serial entrepreneurs, 155
    social entrepreneur, 156
    starting a new venture, 165–169
    tolerance for ambiguity, 165
    tolerance for failure, 163–164
    vision, 162
entrepreneurship, 7, 10–11
    being your own boss, 156–157
    financial success, 158
    job security, 158
    lifestyle entrepreneurship, 158
    quality of life, 158
    reasons for choosing, 156–159, 156f

environmental concerns, 15
environmental impact study, 267
environmentally friendly packages, 332
environmental protection, 43–46
equal opportunity, 51–52, 51t
equal pay for equal work, 51t
equal rights, 51t
equilibrium price, 65
equity capital, 479, 480
equity financing, 168–169
equity theory, 223
esteem needs, 222
e-readers, 395
ethical action, 39
ethical awareness, 37–38
ethical controversies
   alternative energy development, 72
   CEO compensation, 144
   CEO responsibility, 43
   China, and quality controls, 279
   employee empowerment, 237
   entrepreneurs and ethics, 164
   executive compensation, 481
   free credit reports, 300
   free e-books, 373
   Google, and Chinese market, 184–185
   Keystone XL Pipeline, 99
   monitoring employees' Internet use, 403
   monitoring employees' social media activities, 221
   securities fraud, 22
   securities market self-regulation, 462
   teens at the mall, 342
   whistle-blowers, 426
ethical education, 38–39
ethical leadership, 39–40
ethics. *See* business ethics
ethics compliance officers, 33
ethics training programs, 38–39
EU. *See* European Union (EU)
euro, 95, 107, 454
European Central Bank, 464
European Commission, 344
European Union (EU), 95, 97, 104, 107, 107f, 228, 420, 445, 454
evaluation, 214
event marketing, 298
everyday low pricing (EDLP), 376
exchange control, 103
exchange process, 293
exchange rates, 95–96, 438
exclusive distribution, 345
executive compensation, 144, 481
executive summary, 131
executive support system (ESS), 394
executive vice-president, 180, 286
expansionary monetary policy, 78
expectancy theory, 223, 223f
expert system, 394

exporters, 109
export management company, 109
exports, 90, 93–94
external communication, 251–253
external data, 303

F
facility layout, 269–271, 270f
factor, 484
factoring, 484
factor payments, 6t
factors of production, 6–7, 6t, 64, 90–91
factory outlet, 339t
failed products, 329t
failure, 163–164
Fair Credit Reporting Act (FCRA), 300
fair trade, 50
False Claims Act, 426
family brand, 330
family medical leave, 51t
fast-food chains, 66
federal budget, 79–80
Feed-in Tariff Program, 15, 16
feedback, 214, 224, 245, 248
Ferrari, Michael and Mary, 161
field robots, 265
field selling, 367
finance, 472
   asset management, 476–479
   capital structure, 479–483
   career, 494–495
   dividend policy, 482–483
   finance organization of typical firm, 472f
   long-term financing, 484–488
   mixing short-term and long-term funds, 481–482
   short-term funding options, 483–484
   sources of funds, 479–483
finance charge, 559
finance companies, 459, 484
Financial Accounting Standards Board, 421
financial assistance, 133
financial community, 53–54
financial crisis, 445, 449, 454, 460, 465
financial institutions, 455–459
   in Canada, 456f
   commercial banks, 455–458
   credit unions, 458
   depository institutions, 455
   finance companies, 459
   as financial market experts, 453
   insurance companies, 459
   mutual funds, 459
   nondepository institutions, 455, 459
   pension funds, 459
   and small business, 133
financial manager, 472–474, 495
financial markets, 451–453, 462
financial plan, 474–476

financial planning, 474–476
financial ratio analysis, 432–435, 432t
financial records, 302
financial section, 131
financial software, 397f
financial statements, 425–431
financial success, 158
financial system, 98, 446
   Bank of Canada, 460–461
   bank regulation, 461–462
   financial institutions, 455–459
   financial markets, 451–453, 462
   global perspective, 463–465
   overview, 446f
   regulation, 461–463
   securities, 448–451
   stock markets, 453–455
   understanding the financial system, 446–447
financing
   debt financing, 168
   equity financing, 168–169
   finding financing, 168–169
   inadequate financing, and small businesses, 130–131
   seed capital, 168
   for small businesses, 132–134
financing activities, 417
firewall, 399
fiscal policy, 78–79
fishing, 67f
fixed costs, 375
fixed-position layout, 270f, 271
flag colours, 333
flattening the business cycle, 71–73
flexibility, 19
flexible benefit plans, 217
flexible manufacturing system (FMS), 265–266
flexible production, 262
flexible work plans, 217–218
flexible work schedules, 50
flextime, 217
floating exchange rates, 95
floor ads, 363
focus group, 303, 328
follow-up, 277, 370
Food and Drugs Act, 48
food service managers, 286
Ford, Henry, 13, 261
Foreign Corrupt Practices Act, 100, 426
foreign exchange rates, 95–96, 438
foreign licensing agreement, 110
foreign stock markets, 453–454
forensic accountants, 418, 419
form utility, 293
formal communication channels, 246t, 248, 249f
forming stage, 242

forms of business ownership
  corporation, 140
  partnership, 139
  sole proprietorship, 138–139
fourth market, 455
franchise, 109–110
franchisee, 136
franchising, 135
  benefits of, 136–138
  buying a franchise, 166
  franchise fee, 135
  franchising agreements, 136
  franchising sector, 135–136
  problems of, 136–138
franchisor, 136
Frankel, Stuart, 137
fraud, 10, 22, 415, 419, 426
free credit reports, 300
free e-books, 373
free-rein leadership, 195
free trade, 106
free-trade area, 105
freedom of choice, 9–10
frequency marketing, 314
frequency of use, 326
frictional unemployment, 77
friendship treaties, 100–101
full-function merchant wholesalers, 337
functional departmentalization, 198
Furman, Don, 72

G

G7 countries, 105
gain sharing, 216
games, 366
Gantt chart, 276, 277f
gasoline prices, 62, 63f, 64f
GATT. See General Agreement on Tariffs and Trade (GATT)
GDP. See gross domestic product (GDP)
GDP per capita, 74
Gelinas, Johanne, 425
gender, 306, 307–308
General Agreement on Tariffs and Trade (GATT), 104
general public, responsibilities to, 42–47
generally accepted accounting principles (GAAP), 420
Generation X, 18, 199, 524
Generation Y, 18, 199, 218, 307, 524–525
geographical departmentalization, 198
geographical segmentation, 305–306, 310
gift-giving traditions, 97
Gillespie, Manda Aufochs, 128
Gillis, Derek, 235
global business. See international business
global business and economics career, 118–119
global business strategy, 112

global economic challenges, 80–82, 81t
global economy, 80–82, 93
global financial system, 463–465
global information economy, 81t
globalization, 73, 159–160, 464
goal acceptance, 224
goal difficulty, 224
goal-setting theory, 224, 224f
goal specificity, 224
going global. See international business
gold, 65, 65f
Gollogly, Michael, 419
Goodman, Jodi, 9
Gorsky, Alex, 188
gossip, 249
Gottlieb, Myron, 415
government accountants, 419–420
government agencies, 124–125
government bonds, 448
government regulation, 131, 462
government support for new ventures, 169
Graham, Aubrey Drake, 3, 23
Grant brothers, 321
grapevine, 249
Graziano, Fred, 447
Great Depression, 73, 454
green initiatives, 17
green manufacturing processes, 263–264
green marketing, 45, 46t
green packaging, 332–333
Greenspan, Alan, 462, 463
grid computing, 405
grievance, 226–227, 227f
gross domestic product (GDP), 73–74, 74f, 92
gross profit margin, 432t, 434–435
growth stage, 326
guerilla marketing, 357–358
Gupta, Rajiv, 481

H

hackers, 401
hand-held devices, 395, 401
handling objections, 369–370
hard currencies, 95–96
hardware, 394–396
health insurance, 550
heart disease, 42
hedge funds, 488
Heins, Thorsten, 179
Herzberg, Frederick, 222
Herzberg's two-factor model of motivation, 222–223
hierarchy of needs, 221–222
high-context cultures, 245
home-based businesses, 125, 161
home-based work programs, 218
homeowners' insurance, 550
homepreneurs, 161
honesty, 35–36

honey bee research, 297
Hong Kong, 437
horizontal merger, 145
hosts, 402
households, 446
Howe, Gordie, 123
human factors, and location decision, 266t, 267
human resource management, 210
  compensation, 215–218
  downsizing, 218–220
  drug testing, 212
  employee separation, 218–220
  evaluation, 214
  finding qualified candidates, 211
  hiring restrictions, 212
  human resource plans, 211
  laws, understanding of, 212
  management development, 214
  orientation, 213–214
  outsourcing, 220
  performance appraisal, 214
  recruitment and selection, 211–213, 211f
  responsibilities, 210f
  selecting and hiring employees, 211–213
  training programs, 213–214
  turnover, 218
human resource managers, 286
human resource plans, 211
human resources, 7
human skills, 182
Hurteau, Guy and Jean, 159
hydraulic fracturing, 264
hygiene factors, 222
hyperinflation, 74

I

illegal payoffs, 100
IMC. See integrated marketing communications (IMC)
immigration, 18, 18f
implementation of strategy, 190
importers, 109
imports, 90, 93–94
inbound telemarketing, 368
incentive compensation, 216, 216f, 236–238
income, changes in, 63
income statement, 427, 429f
incorporation, 142–143
independent wholesaling intermediaries, 337
India, 73, 81t, 91t, 93, 97, 98, 110, 112, 160, 244, 245, 420
indirect exporting, 109
individual branding, 330
individuals, and ethics, 33–34
Industrial Revolution, 12, 14
industry creation, 127–128
industry self-regulation, 462
inflation, 74
infomercials, 363–364

informal communication channels, 246t, 249, 249f
information, 356, 390
information overload, 392
information sharing, 236
information system, 390
   administration, 401
   application service provider (ASP), 405
   backup, 404
   cloud computing, 405
   components of, 391–394
   computer-based information system, 391
   computer hardware, 394–396
   computer software, 396, 397t
   cybercrime, 400–401
   database, 392–393
   decision support system (DSS), 393–394
   design of, 391
   disaster recovery planning, 404
   distributed workforce, 404–405
   and ethics, 403
   executive support system (ESS), 394
   expert system, 394
   grid computing, 405
   malware, 401–402
   management information system (MIS), 393
   management support systems, 393–394
   on-demand computing, 405
   operational support systems, 393
   process control systems, 393
   security issues, 400–402
   transaction processing systems, 393
   trends, 404–406
   types of, 393–394
information technology (IT), 160–161, 220, 404, 473
information technology career, 412
informative advertising, 359
infrastructure, 98
initial public offering (IPO), 452
innovation, 19, 128–129
insider trading, 462
installations, 324
institutional advertising, 358–359
insurable interest, 546
insurable risk, 547
insurance, 545–552, 560–561
insurance companies, 459
intangible assets, 422
intangible property, 538
integrated marketing communications (IMC), 354
   objectives of promotional strategy, 356–357, 356f
   promotional mix, 355, 355t
   promotional planning, 357–358
integrity, 35–36
intellectual property, 539

intensive distribution, 345
interconnection, 80
intermittent production process, 263
internal locus of control, 165
international accounting, 437–438
International Accounting Standards Board (IASB), 420
international assets, 478–479
international barter, 109
international business
   see also international trade
   adaptation strategy, 112–113
   contract-based agreements, 109–110
   countertrade, 109
   expanding into overseas market, 107–111
   exporters, 109
   foreign licensing agreement, 110
   franchise, 109–110
   global business and economics career, 118–119
   global business strategy, 112
   importers, 109
   international direct investment, 110–111
   levels of involvement, 108–111
   multidomestic business strategy, 112–113
   multinational corporation (MNC), 111
   offshoring, 110
   packaging, 332–333
   reshoring, 111
   standardization strategy, 112
   strategy development, 112–113
   subcontracting, 110
international direct investment, 110–111
international economic communities, 105–107
International Financial Reporting Standards (IFRS), 420, 426, 427
international fiscal policy, 79
international law, 535
International Monetary Fund (IMF), 105
International Organization for Standardization, 279
international regulations, 100–101
international terrorism, 81t
international trade
   see also international business
   absolute advantage, 92–93
   balance of payments, 93
   balance of trade, 93
   barriers to international trade, 96–103
   comparative advantage, 93
   exchange rates, 95–96
   exports, 90, 93–94
   importance of, 90
   imports, 90, 93–94
   international economic communities, 105–107
   international sources of factors of production, 90–91

   Internet research resources, 108
   major Canadian exports and imports, 93–94, 94t
   measurement of, 93–96
   organizations promoting international trade, 104–105
   reasons for trade, 90–93
   reducing barriers to international trade, 104–107
   risks of, 81
   size of international marketplace, 91–92
   trade restrictions, 102–103
international travel, 82
international union, 226
Internet
   accounting, impact on, 424
   advertising, 360
   China, and censorship, 184–185
   cultural sensitivity, 97
   and globalization, 73
   international trade research resources, 108
   monitoring employees' Internet use, 403
   and music industry, 3
   online banking, 457, 458f
   social networking, 14
   supplier selection, 272–273
Internet retailing, 338
interpersonal skills, 182
intimate zone, 250–251, 251t
intranets, 399
intrapreneurship, 169–170
introduction (business plan), 131
introduction stage, 325–326
inventors, 12, 166
inventory control, 273, 346
inventory management, 477–478
inventory turnover, 432t, 433
investing activities, 417
investment-grade bonds, 449
investment planning, 561
investors, 53–54, 133–134, 169, 455
invisible hand, 8
involuntary turnover, 218
Islam, 97, 464
ISO standards, 279–280

J
Japan, 105
Japanese management style, 225
job applications, 35–36
job creation, 127
job design, 224–225
job enlargement, 224
job enrichment, 225
job rotation, 225
job search, 129
job security, 158
job sharing program, 217–218
Jobs, Steve, 163, 179

joint venture, 111, 145–146
judiciary, 535
junk bonds, 449
junk mail, 362
just-in-time (JIT) system, 274

K
Kelsay, Will, 167
King, Robert, 45

L
labels, 332–333
labour-management relations
    arbitration, 227
    collective bargaining, 226
    grievance, 226–227, 227f
    labour relations board, 226
    labour unions, 225–226, 228–229
    management tactics, 228
    mediation, 226–227
    settling labour-management disputes, 226–227
    union tactics, 227–228
labour market, 555
labour productivity, 73
labour relations board, 226
labour unions, 104, 225–226, 228–229
Labuda, Stephen, 161
Laliberté, Guy, 29
language differences, 96
Latin America, 97, 106–107, 112, 245, 251
law, 535–536
law of agency, 537
law of large numbers, 547–548
layoffs, 219
Lazaridis, Mike, 179
leadership, 193
    autocratic leadership, 194
    creative leadership, 21
    democratic leadership, 194–195
    ethical leadership, 39–40
    free-rein leadership, 195
    leadership styles, 194–195
    managers as leaders, 193–195
leadership styles, 194–195
LEED (Leadership in Energy and Environmental Design), 188, 235, 264, 425, 447
legal differences, 99–101
legal environment, 100
legal system, 535
leverage, 479–480, 480f
leverage ratios, 432t, 435
leveraged buyout (LBOs), 488–489
liability, 423
liability insurance, 550
life insurance, 551–552
lifestyle centres, 342
lifestyle entrepreneurship, 158

lifetime value of a customer, 313
lights out facilities, 263
limit order, 455
limited-function merchant wholesalers, 337
line-and-staff organizations, 200–201, 200f
line managers, 200
line of credit, 168
line organizations, 200
liquidity ratios, 432t, 433
listening, 246–247
loan officers, 495
local area networks (LANs), 398, 398f
local union, 226
location decision, 266–268, 266t, 341–342
lockout, 228
locus of control, 165
lodging managers, 287
logistics, 345–346
long-term debt to equity ratio, 432t, 435
long-term financing, 484–488
long-term funds, 481–482
low-context cultures, 245
loyalty, 36
Lui, Tim, 437
lump-sum bonuses, 216
Lutz, Lisa, 291
luxury taxes, 540

M
M1, 460
M2, 460
Ma, Jack, 17
MacDonald, Chris, 164
macroeconomics, 60, 66–71
Madoff, Bernard, 22
magazines, 361
major purchases, 560
make, buy, or lease decision, 271
Malaysia, 105
Mallette, Patricia, 3
malware, 401–402
management, 180
    see also managers
    career, 286–287
    conceptual skills, 182
    controlling, 183
    corporate management, 143–145, 143f
    directing, 183
    human skills, 182
    interpersonal skills, 182
    Japanese management style, 225
    management hierarchy, 180–181, 180f
    managerial functions, 182–183
    middle management, 181, 187t
    organizing, 183
    planning, 182–183, 185–187
    production and operations management. *See* production and operations management

    shortcomings, in small business, 129–130
    skills needed for managerial success, 182
    supervisory management, 181, 187t
    tactics, in labour-management relations, 228
    technical skills, 182
    top management, 180–181, 184, 187t
management accountant, 418–419
management by objectives (MBO), 224
management development program, 214
management information system (MIS), 393
management support systems, 393–394
managerial functions, 182–183
managers, 144–145
    see also management
    ability to lead change, 21
    administrative services managers, 286
    attitudes of, and motivation, 225
    brand manager, 331
    category manager, 332
    construction managers, 286
    creativity, 21
    critical thinking, 20–21
    as decision makers, 191–193
    employee motivation, 220–225
    financial manager, 472–474, 495
    food service managers, 286
    human resource managers, 286
    as leaders, 193–195
    line managers, 200
    lodging managers, 287
    marketing managers, 354
    medical and health services managers, 287
    multigenerational workforce, 199
    product manager, 331
    production and operations managers, 269–275
    production managers, 287
    purchasing managers, 287
    staff managers, 200
    team conflict, management of, 243–244
    twenty-first-century manager, 20–21
    vision, importance of, 20
Mandarin Chinese, 96
manufacturer-owned wholesaling intermediaries, 337
manufacturers' agents, 337
manufacturer's brand, 330
manufacturers' reps, 337
manufacturing, 260
market allocation, 536
market basket, 75, 76f
market economy, 67–69
market interest rate, 450
market order, 455
market penetration, 568

Subject Index

market segmentation, 304–310, 305f
  by benefits sought, 309
  by brand loyalty, 310
  business markets, 310
  consumer markets, 305–310
  criteria, 304t
  customer-based segmentation, 310
  demographic segmentation, 306–307, 306f, 310
  end-use segmentation, 310
  geographical segmentation, 305–306, 310
  how it works, 305
  product-related segmentation, 308–310
  by product usage rate, 310
  psychographic segmentation, 308
market structures
  monopolistic competition, 67–68, 67t
  monopoly, 67t, 68–69
  oligopoly, 67t, 68
  pure competition, 67, 67t
market surveillance, 462
marketable securities, 476–477
marketing, 292
  affinity programs, 314
  cause marketing, 298–299
  cause-related marketing, 47
  co-marketing, 314–315
  consumer behaviour, 311–312, 312f
  deceptive marketing, 48
  event marketing, 298
  evolution of the marketing concept, 294–295, 295f
  frequency marketing, 314
  green marketing, 45, 46t
  guerilla marketing, 357–358
  marketing research, 302–304
  marketing strategy, 299–302
  market segmentation, 304–310
  nontraditional marketing, 296–299, 296f
  not-for-profit marketing, 296
  one-on-one marketing, 315
  organization marketing, 299
  person marketing, 297
  place marketing, 297
  relationship marketing, 312–315
  utility, creation of, 293–294, 336
marketing concept, 294–295
marketing era, 13–14, 294
marketing intermediary, 334, 336, 336f
marketing managers, 354
marketing mix, 301–302, 323
marketing research, 302–304
  application of data, 303
  data mining, 304
  obtaining marketing research data, 302–303
marketing section, 131
marketing strategy, 299–302
  classification of goods and services, 324–325

marketing mix for international markets, 301–302
  product life cycle, 326–327
  target market, 299–301
Markopolos, Harry, 22
Marx, Karl, 69
Maslow, Abraham H., 221–222, 225
Maslow's hierarchy of needs, 221–222
mass customization, 302
mass production, 261–262
material inputs, 275
materials handling, 346
materials requirement planning (MRP), 274–275
matrix structure, 201–202, 201f
maturity stage, 326
McClung, Gavin, 168f
McElroy, Mark W., 425
McGregor, Douglas, 225
McMillon, Doug, 435f
mechanization, 261
mediation, 226–227
medical and health services managers, 287
Menard, France, 159
mental disabilities, 51t
merchant wholesalers, 337
Mercosur, 105
merger, 145, 488
Mexico, 97, 105, 106, 110, 244, 245, 268, 310, 347
Meyer, Stephanie, 373
microeconomics, 60–66
  demand, 61
  demand curve, 62, 63f, 63t
  factors driving demand, 61–63
  factors driving supply, 63–64
  interaction of demand and supply, 64–66
  supply, 61
  supply curve, 63–64, 64f, 64t
Middle East, 100, 112
middle management, 181, 187t
middleman, 334
millennials. See Generation Y
Mintzberg, Henry, 249, 250
misleading representations, 48
mission, 131
missionary selling, 368
mission statement, 188
Mitchell, John, 383
mixed market economy, 70–71t
mobile devices, 395, 396, 401
mobility, 19
modified breakeven analysis, 376
monetary policy, 78, 460–461
money management, 558–559
money market instruments, 448, 477
money supply, 460
monitoring
  employees' Internet use, 403

  employees' social media activities, 221
  strategic plans, 190–191
monopolistic competition, 67–68, 67t
monopoly, 67t, 68–69, 69
Moody, Jeff, 137
mortgage-backed securities (MBSs), 449
mortgages, 445
motivation. See employee motivation
motivator factors, 222
MRO (maintenance, repair, and operating supplies), 324
Mullins, Corin and Brian, 166f, 167
multidomestic business strategy, 112–113
multigenerational workforce, 199
multinational corporation (MNC), 111
multivitamins, 279
municipal bonds, 448
Murrell, Jerry, 66
Muslim. See Islam
mutual funds, 459
Muzyka, Zhena, 50

N

NAFTA. See North American Free Trade Agreement (NAFTA)
national brand, 330
national debt, 80
National Do Not Call List, 339
national union, 226
national unity, 97
natural gas, 264
natural resources, 6–7
navigation treaties, 100–101
nearshoring, 19
need to achieve, 163
negative balance of payments, 93
negotiable instruments, 538
net profit margin, 432t, 434–435
net savers, 446–447
net users, 446
net worth, 447, 558
network administrators, 412
new industries, 127–128
new-product development, 328–329, 328f
newspapers, 361
new ventures. See starting a new venture
New Zealand, 105
noise, 245
nondepository institutions, 455, 459
nonpersonal selling, 355
nonprogrammed decision, 191
nonstore retailers, 338–339, 338f
nontariff barriers, 103
nontraditional marketing, 296–299, 296f
nonverbal communication, 246t, 249–251
Nooyi, Indra, 473f
norming stage, 242
North America, 97, 251

North American Free Trade Agreement (NAFTA), 105–106, 310, 420, 535
North American Industry Classification System (NAICS), 310
not-for-profit accountants, 419–420
not-for-profit corporations, 140
not-for-profit marketing, 296
not-for-profit organizations, 5–6, 76, 296

O

obesity, 42
objections, 369–370
objectives, 190
observational studies, 303
odd pricing, 378
offensive listening, 247
officers, 144–145
offset agreement, 109
offshoring, 19, 110
O'Hara, Matthew, 174, 285
oligopoly, 67t, 68
on-demand computing, 405
one-on-one marketing, 315
on-the-job ethical dilemmas, 34–37
    conflict of interest, 35
    honesty, 35–36
    integrity, 35–36
    loyalty *vs.* truth, 36
    whistle-blowing, 36–37
on-the-job training, 213
online banking, 457, 458f
open communication, 248
open corporation, 144
open market operations, 460
operating activities, 417
operating plans, 474
operating system, 396
operational planning, 186
operational support systems, 393
optimism, 163
oral communication, 246–247, 246t
order processing, 368
Organisation for Economic Co-operation and Development, 100
organization, 196
organizational change, 21
organizational structures, 196–202
    centralization, 200
    committee organizations, 201
    decentralization, 200
    delegation, 198–199
    departmentalization, 198, 199f
    line-and-staff organizations, 200–201, 200f
    line organizations, 200
    matrix structure, 201–202, 201f
    span of management, 200
    types of, 200–202
organization chart, 197, 197f
organizing, 183, 197f

organization marketing, 299
orientation, 213–214
Ouchi, William, 225
outbound telemarketing, 368
outdoor advertising, 362
output per labour-hour, 73
outsourcing, 19, 220
over-the-counter selling, 367
overnight rate, 460
overseas business. *See* international business
overseas division, 111
owners' equity, 423
ownership utility, 293

P

pacing programs, 170
packages, 332–333
paid time off (PTO), 217
Pandit, Vikram, 452
Papandreou, George, 454
parental leave, 51t
partnership, 139
passwords, 401
patent, 533–534, 539
Pattison, Jim, 155f
Pavlovsky, Kathryn, 424
pay for knowledge, 216
penetration pricing, 376
pension funds, 459
People's Republic of China. *See* China
performance appraisal, 214
performance feedback, 224
performing stage, 242
perpetual inventory, 273
Persia, Dana, 82
personal finance, 554–562
personal financial goals, 557–558
personal financial management, 554
personal financial management model, 556
personal financial plan, 556–557
personal financial planners, 495
personal information managers, 397f
Personal Information Protection Act (PIPA), 300
Personal information Protection and Electronic Document Act (PIPEDA), 300
personal selling, 355, 355t, 367–371
    approach, 369
    closing, 370
    creative selling, 368
    demonstration, 369
    field selling, 367
    follow-up, 370
    handling objections, 369–370
    missionary selling, 368
    order processing, 368
    over-the-counter selling, 367
    presentation, 369
    prospecting, 369

    qualifying, 369
    sales process, 369–370
    sales tasks, 368–369
    telemarketing, 367, 368–369
personal space, 250–251, 251f
personal zone, 250–251, 251t
person marketing, 297
persuasive advertising, 359
PERT (program evaluation and review technique), 276, 277f
Peru, 105
Petrillo, Carmine, 268f
Pfeffer, Jeffrey, 219
pharmaceutical industry, 471
physical disabilities, 51t
physical distribution, 334, 345–346, 346f
physical factors, and location decision, 266t, 267
physiological needs, 222
picketing, 227–228
P&L statement, 427
place marketing, 297
place utility, 293
planned economy, 69
planned shopping centre, 341
planning, 182–183, 187t
    contingency planning, 186–187
    at different organizational levels, 187
    importance of, 185–187
    operational planning, 186
    production planning, 275
    promotional planning, 357–358
    strategic planning, 186
    strategic planning process, 187–191, 187f
    tactical planning, 186
    types of, 185–187
plastic shopping bags, 365
point-of-purchase (POP) advertising, 366
polite listening, 247
political climate, 99–100
political differences, 99–101
Poloz, Stephen S., 78
Ponzi scheme, 22
Pope, Carl, 252
population projections, 18f
portfolio managers, 495
positioning, 356
positive balance of payments, 93
potential sales revenue, 568
The Practice of Management (Drucker), 224
preferred shares, 144, 451
pregnancy leave, 51t
premiums, 364–365, 459, 545
presentation, 369
presentation software, 397f
prestige objectives, 373–374
price, 372
price discrimination, 10
price-fixing, 536

622 Subject Index

price level changes, 74–77
price-quality relationships, 378
price war, 373
pricing objectives, 372–374
pricing strategy, 301
   alternative pricing strategies, 376–378
   breakeven analysis, 375–376, 375f
   competitive pricing, 377–378
   consumer perceptions of price, 378
   cost-based pricing, 374
   discount pricing, 376
   everyday low pricing (EDLP), 376
   odd pricing, 378
   penetration pricing, 376
   price determination in practice, 374–375
   price-quality relationships, 378
   in retailing, 341
   skimming pricing, 376
primary data, 303
primary demand, 354
primary markets, 451
privacy norms, 304
private brand, 330
private enterprise system, 7, 8–11, 67–69
   basic rights, 8–10, 8f
   entrepreneurship alternative, 10–11
private equity funds, 486–487
private insurance company, 548–549
private placements, 485
private property, 9
private sector employees, 11f
privatization, 70
problem-solving team, 239
process control systems, 393
process departmentalization, 198
process layout, 270f, 271
product, 322
product advertising, 358
product departmentalization, 198
product differentiation, 356
product identification, 329–333
product layout, 270f, 271
product liability, 48, 540
product life cycle, 325–327
   and advertising, 359
   decline stage, 326
   growth stage, 326
   introduction stage, 325–326
   marketing strategy implications, 326–327
   maturity stage, 326
   stages of, 325–326
product lines, 324–325
product manager, 331
product mix, 324–325
product placement, 357
product-related segmentation, 308–310
product strategy, 301, 322–325
   labels, 332–333
   packages, 332–333

product identification, 329–333
   in retailing, 341
product usage rate, 310
product value, 357
production, 260
   see also production and operations management
   analytic production system, 263
   continuous production process, 263
   customer-driven production, 262
   flexible production, 262
   intermittent production process, 263
   mass production, 261–262
   production process, 260, 260f, 262–263
   strategic importance of, 260–262
   synthetic production system, 263
   technology, 263–266
   typical production systems, 261f
   vs. manufacturing, 260
production and operations management, 260
   dispatching, 277
   follow-up, 277
   inventory control, 273
   just-in-time (JIT) system, 274
   location decision, 266–268, 266t
   make, buy, or lease decision, 271
   materials requirement planning (MRP), 274–275
   planning the production process, 269
   production. See production
   production and operations managers, 269–275
   production control, 275–277
   production management tasks, 269f
   production plan, 271–275
   production planning, 275
   quality, 278–280
   routing, 276
   scheduling, 276, 277f
   selection of facility layout, 269–271, 270f
   suppliers, selection of, 272–273
production and operations managers, 269–275
production control, 275–277
   dispatching, 277
   follow-up, 277
   production planning, 275
   routing, 276
   scheduling, 276, 277f
production era, 13, 294
production managers, 287
production plan, 271–275
production planning, 275
production process, 260, 260f, 262–263
productivity, 73–74, 75
productivity ratios, 73
profit-and-loss statement, 427
profit sharing, 216
profitability objectives, 372, 372f

profitability ratios, 432t, 434–435
profits, 4–5
   after-tax profits, 9
   quest for profits, 5
programmed decision, 191
promotion, 354
promotional mix, 355, 355t
   advertising. See advertising
   personal selling, 367–371
   public relations, 370–371
   sales promotion. See sales promotion
promotional planning, 357–358
promotional strategy, 301, 356–357, 356f
   pulling strategy, 372
   pushing strategy, 371
   in retailing, 342
property, 538
property and liability insurance, 549–550
property law, 538
prospecting, 369
protectionist policies, 95
protective tariffs, 102
provincial court, 535
provincial employment standards acts, 51t
provincial human rights codes, 51t
provincial labour ministries, 51t
provincial vocational rehabilitation acts, 51t
psychographic segmentation, 308
public accountant, 418, 494
Public Company Accounting Oversight Board, 421
public health issues, 42
public insurance agency, 548
public ownership of business, 140–142
public relations, 355t, 370–371
public relations crisis, 251–253
public sales of securities, 485
Public Sector Accounting Board (PSAB), 420
Public Servants Disclosure Protection Act, 426
public zone, 250–251, 251t
publicity, 371
publicly held corporation, 144
pulling strategy, 372
purchasing managers, 287
purchasing power, 306–307
purchasing power parity (PPP), 73–74
pure competition, 67, 67t
pure risk, 544
pushing strategy, 371

Q

qualifying, 369
quality, 278
   benchmarking, 278
   importance of, 278–280
   ISO standards, 279–280
   price-quality relationships, 378
   quality control, 278–279

quality control, 278–279
quality of life, 158
quality-of-life issues, 50–51
quick ratio, 432t, 433
quotas, 103

R
rack jobber, 337
radio, 361
radio-frequency identification (RFID) technology, 333, 346
raises, 215
Rapino, Michael, 9
ratio analysis, 432–435, 432t
raw materials, 324
real property, 538
rebates, 365
receivables turnover, 432t, 434
recession, 72, 454
recovery, 73
recruitment, 211–213, 211f
recycling, 44
Reece, Daryl, 45
regional differences, 97
regional malls, 341–342
registered retirement savings plans (RRSPs), 459
regular dividend, 482
regulated monopoly, 68
relationship era, 14–15, 294
relationship management, 15
relationship marketing, 312–315
relevance, 420
religious attitudes, 97
reminder-oriented advertising, 359
renewable electricity standard (RES), 72
representational faithfulness, 420
reserve requirement, 461
reservists, 51t
reshoring, 111
responsibilities of companies. *See* company responsibilities
restaurants, 563–564
restrictive monetary policy, 78
résumés, 35–36
résumés of principals, 131
retailer-owned cooperatives or buying offices, 337–338
retailers, 336, 338
retailing, 338–343
    automatic merchandising, 338
    competition, 340–343
    customer service strategy, 341
    direct-response retailing, 338
    direct selling, 339
    Internet retailing, 338
    "last three feet," 338
    location, 341–342
    nonstore retailers, 338–339, 338f
    pricing strategy, 341
    product strategy, 341
    promotional strategy, 342
    store retailers, 339, 339t
    target market, 340
    wheel of retailing, 340, 340f
Reti, Tom, 389
return, 473
return on equity, 432t, 434
revenue tariffs, 102
right to be heard, 49
right to be informed, 48
right to be safe, 48
right to choose, 49
rights
    of consumers, 47–49
    equal rights, 51t
    in private enterprise system, 8–10, 8f
    shareholder rights, 143–144
risk, 473, 544–546
risk management insurance, 545
risk-return tradeoff, 474
robots, 264–265
Rosen, Al, 419
Ross, Rich, 308
routing, 276
Rubinfeld, Arthur, 40
rule of indemnity, 547
runs, 458

S
safety issues, 48
safety needs, 222
saffron, 92f
salary, 215, 287, 423
sales branches, 337
sales era, 294
sales increase, 356
sales law, 537
sales office, 337
sales process, 369–370
sales promotion, 355t, 364
    consumer-oriented promotions, 364–366, 364f
    trade-oriented promotions, 366–367
sales stabilization, 356–357
sales tasks, 368–369
samples, 365–366
sandwich generation, 50
Sarbanes-Oxley Act of 2002, 33, 54, 183, 415, 421, 426
savers, 446–447
Sawhney, Robert, 437
scarcity, 374
scheduling, 276, 277f
seasonal unemployment, 77
secondary data, 303
secondary market, 453
secured bond, 448
securities, 448–451, 476–477
securities fraud, 22
security analysts, 495
seed capital, 168
selection, 211–213, 211f
selective demand, 354
selective distribution, 345
self-actualization needs, 222
self-confidence, 163
self-managed team, 239
self-regulation, 462
seller's market, 295
selloff, 489
sender, 244–245
serial entrepreneurs, 155
server, 395
services, 324
sexism, 53
sexual harassment, 53
shaping ethical conduct, 37–40
share offering, 451–452
shareholder rights, 143–144
shareholders, 143–144
shares, 144, 450–451, 485
shopping malls, 341
shopping products, 323
short-term assets, 476
short-term funding options, 483–484
short-term funds, 481–482
short-term loans, 483–484
shrinking labour pool, 18
Singapore, 105
Silver, Adam, 363
Six Sigma, 279
skimming pricing, 376
skunkworks, 170
Smajovits, Daniel, 123, 147
small business, 124
    assistance for, 132–135
    business plan, 131–132
    contributions to economy, 127–129
    failure, 129–131
    government regulation, 131
    inadequate financing, 130–131
    industry creation, 127–128
    innovation, 128–129
    job creation, 127
    management shortcomings, 129–130
    social media, 343
    typical small-business ventures, 125
    women and, 134–135
smartphones, 395, 396
Smith, Adam, 8
social audits, 41
social differences, 96–97
social entrepreneur, 156
social era, 15–17, 294–295
social media, 3, 15, 221, 343
social needs, 222

social networking, 14, 129, 157, 161, 304
social responsibility, 23, 40–47, 41f
    corporate philanthropy, 46–47
    environmental protection, 43–46
    general public, responsibilities to, 42–47
    public health issues, 42
    social audits, 41
social zone, 250–251, 251t
socialism, 69, 70–71t
software, 396, 397t, 424
software as a service (SaaS), 405, 406, 473
sole proprietorship, 138–139
sovereign wealth funds, 487, 487f
S&P/TSX 60 Shariah Index, 464
spam, 362
span of control, 200
span of management, 200
specialized skills, 261
specialty advertising, 366
specialty products, 323
specialty store, 339t
speculative bonds, 449
speculative risk, 544
Spierkel, Yannick, 29
"spinning" bad news, 248
spinoff, 489
sponsorship, 355t, 363
spreadsheets, 397f
spyware, 402
staff managers, 200
stakeholders, 39–40
standard of living, 554
standardization, 261
standardization strategy, 112, 301
Stanton, John, 125f
starting a new venture, 165–169
    business plan, 167, 167t
    buying an existing business, 166
    finding financing, 168–169
    government support, 169
    selecting a business idea, 165–166
statement of cash flows, 429–430, 431f
statement of changes in equity, 429, 430f
statement of comprehensive position, 427
statement of financial position, 426
statistics, 307
statutory law, 535
stock. See shares
stock exchanges, 453–455
stock markets, 453–455
stock options, 216, 237t, 238
stock ownership, 143–144
store brand, 330
store retailers, 339, 339t
storming stage, 242
strategic alliance, 15
strategic planning, 186
strategic planning process, 187–191, 187f

assessment of competitive position, 188–190
defining the organization's mission, 188
implementation of strategy, 190
monitoring and adapting strategic plans, 190–191
objectives, 190
strategies for competitive differentiation, 190
strategic plans, 474
strategy
    adaptation strategy, 112–113, 301–302
    customer service strategy, 341
    distribution strategy. See distribution strategy
    implementation of strategy, 190
    marketing strategy. See marketing strategy
    pricing strategy. See pricing strategy
    product strategy, 301, 322–325
    promotional strategy, 301, 342, 356–357
    pulling strategy, 372
    pushing strategy, 371
    standardization strategy, 112, 301
    strategies for competitive differentiation, 190
strengths, weaknesses, opportunities, and threats. See SWOT analysis
strike, 227
structural unemployment, 77
subcontracting, 110
subprime mortgages, 445, 449
substance abuse, 42
supercentre, 339t
supercomputers, 395
superior court, 535
supermarket, 339t
supervisory management, 181, 187t
suppliers, 272–273
supplies, 324
supply, 61
    factors driving supply, 63–64
    interaction of demand and supply, 64–66
    money supply, 460
supply chain, 345
supply curve, 63–64, 64f, 64t
Supreme Court of Canada, 535
sustainability, 424–425
sustainable, 45
sustainable agriculture, 45
sweepstakes, 366
SWOT analysis, 188–190, 189f
symbolism, 97
synthetic production system, 263

T
tablets, 395
tactical planning, 186
tangible assets, 422
tangible property, 538

target market, 299–301, 340
tariffs, 101, 102
tax, 540
tax court, 535
taxes, 80, 131
tax planning, 560
team, 238
    characteristics of, 240–241
    conflict, 243–244
    cross-functional team, 239
    problem-solving team, 239
    self-managed team, 239
    stages of team development, 242, 242f
    team cohesiveness, 242–243
    team diversity, 240–241
    team level, 240
    team norm, 243
    team size, 240
    types of, 239, 239f
    virtual team, 239
    work teams, 239
team cohesiveness, 242–243
team development stages, 242, 242f
team diversity, 240–241
team level, 240
team norm, 243
technical skills, 182
technical support specialists, 412
technology, 7, 18
    computer-aided design (CAD), 265
    computer-aided manufacturing (CAM), 265
    computer-integrated manufacturing (CIM), 266
    flexible manufacturing system (FMS), 265–266
    green manufacturing processes, 263–264
    information technology (IT), 160–161, 220, 404
    and production process, 263–266
    radio-frequency identification (RFID) technology, 333
    robots, 264–265
teen market, 307
telecommuters, 218
telemarketing, 367, 368–369
television, 359–360
tender offer, 488
terrorism, 81t
test marketing, 328
texting, 157
Theory X, 225
Theory Y, 225
Theory Z, 225
Thierry, Christopher, 392
360-degree performance review, 214
time utility, 293
timeliness, 420
tolerance for ambiguity, 165

tolerance for failure, 163–164
tombstone, 452
top management, 180–181, 184, 187t
torts, 539–540
total asset turnover, 432t, 434
total cost, 375
total productivity, 73
total revenue, 375
trade. *See* international trade
trade credit, 483
trade deficit, 93
trademark, 330, 539
trade promotion, 366–367
trade restrictions, 102–103
trade shows, 366
trade surplus, 93
trade unions. *See* labour unions
training programs, 213–214
transaction management, 14
transaction processing systems, 393
Trans-Pacific Partnership (TPP), 105
transportation, 266t, 346, 346f
travel etiquette, 82
treasurer, 472
Treasury bills, 80, 448
Treaty of Lisbon, 107
Trojan horse, 402
Trottier, Marie, 29
trust, 248
truth, 36
Tsouflidou, Cora, 158f
Turley, James S., 241
turnover, 218
twenty-first-century manager, 20–21
two-factor model of motivation, 222–223

U

understandability, 420
underwriting, 453, 485
underwriting discount, 485
unemployment, 73, 77
unemployment rate, 77
union tactics, 227–228
unions. *See* labour unions
United States, 33, 54, 72, 74, 78, 80, 91t, 92, 93, 94, 97, 100, 101, 105, 106, 134, 183, 228, 245, 300, 310, 347, 415, 421, 426, 445, 449, 454, 460, 488
Universal Market Integrity Rules (UMIR), 462
universal product code (UPC), 333
upset customers, 313
upward communication, 248
urban reserve, 169
U.S. Federal Reserve, 65, 454, 460, 462, 464
usage-based billing, 10
users, 446–447
users of accounting information, 416–417, 416f
Usher, 3
utility, 260, 293–294, 336, 372
utility computing, 405

V

vacation time, 97
values, 97
variable costs, 375
vendor-managed inventory, 273, 346
venture capital, 133–134
venture capitalists, 168–169, 486
verifiability, 420
vertical merger, 145
vice-president of financial management, 472
Vietnam, 105
viral advertising, 360
virtual offices, 404
virtual private networks (VPNs), 400
virtual team, 239
viruses, 402
vision, 20, 131, 162, 183–184
VoIP, 400
volume objectives, 372
voluntary turnover, 218
volunteerism, 47
Vroom, Victor, 223

W

wage, 215, 423
warehouse club, 339t
warehousing, 346
warranties, 347, 537
The Wealth of Nations (Smith), 8
wheel of retailing, 340, 340f
whistle-blowing, 36–37, 426
wholesalers, 336
wholesaling, 336–338
wide area networks (WANs), 398
Wi-Fi, 398
Williams, Rick, 452
Wi-Max, 398
Winfrey, Oprah, 163, 299
Winterkorn, Martin, 43
wireless fidelity, 398
wireless local networks, 398
women
    as entrepreneurs, 160
    GM's first female CEO, 194
    purchasing power, 306
    and small business, 134–135
Woods, Tiger, 123
word processing software, 397f
work teams, 239
workers' compensation, 49
workforce
    changes in, 18–19
    and changing nature of work, 19
    distributed workforce, 404–405
    diverse workforce, 18–19
    enhancement of competitiveness of, 81t
    multigenerational workforce, 199
    quality of the workforce, 46
    today's business workforce, 17–19
workplace safety, 49
World Bank, 79, 104–105
world's top 10 nations, 91t
World Trade Organization (WTO), 104, 108t, 209, 535
World War II, 13
worm, 402
written communication, 246t, 247–248

Y

Yakadawela, Dharmasena, 76
Yamashita, Asafumi, 130f
Yani, Shlomo, 471
Yellen, Janet, 78
Young, David, 373

Z

Zuckerberg, Mark, 184f